CASES AND MATERIALS ON

GRATUITOUS TRANSFERS

WILLS, INTESTATE SUCCESSION, TRUSTS, GIFTS, FUTURE INTERESTS AND ESTATE AND GIFT TAXATION

Sixth Edition

■ ■ ■

By

Mark L. Ascher
Joseph D. Jamail Centennial Chair in Law
University of Texas

Elias Clark
Late Lafayette S. Foster Professor of Law
Yale University

Grayson M.P. McCouch
Professor of Law, University of San Diego
Visiting Professor of Law, University of Florida

Arthur W. Murphy
Joseph Solomon Professor Emeritus in Wills, Trusts, and Estates
Columbia University

AMERICAN CASEBOOK SERIES®

WEST.
A Thomson Reuters business

Mat #41245779

American Casebook Series is a trademark registered in the U.S. Patent and Trademark Office.

COPYRIGHT © 1967, 1977, 1985 WEST PUBLISHING CO.
© West, a Thomson business, 1999, 2007
© 2013 Thomson Reuters

610 Opperman Drive
St. Paul, MN 55123
1–800–313–9378

Printed in the United States of America

ISBN: 978–0–314–28027–5

Who owns the watch? See Chapter 6, Section B.

PREFACE TO THE SIXTH EDITION

Every casebook is constructed primarily to meet the teaching needs of its editors, and this one is no exception. The book has two main objectives. It is designed, first, to equip the general practitioner for practice in the estates field—more specifically, for planning, drafting, and administration in estates of medium size which do not involve major tax problems. The second purpose is to provide a broad base of general information from which the prospective specialist may proceed to more detailed study.

The opening chapter asks the student to consider the role of wealth transmission in contemporary society and to appraise various theories concerning testamentary freedom and its limitations. The next six chapters (2 through 7) deal with the law of intestate succession; protection of the family; wills, including grounds for contest and formalities of execution and revocation; gifts; and trusts. The chapter on trusts covers methods of creation and termination, and considers special problems involving, inter alia, spendthrift, discretionary, self-settled, constructive, resulting, and charitable trusts. These chapters include a substantial amount of note and text material to expedite consideration of essential but relatively uncomplicated points.

The final three chapters (8 through 10) are intended to be introductory rather than definitive. The primary purpose is to introduce the student to fiduciary administration, future interests, and wealth transfer taxation, without precluding more detailed study of the subject matter in more advanced courses.

Chapter 8 on fiduciary administration explains the procedures for probating a will, appointing a fiduciary, and processing claims of the decedent's creditors. It also surveys several important aspects of fiduciary responsibility, with particular reference to management of trust funds. These materials touch on the significant doctrines but do not attempt to explore their application in all possible situations.

Chapter 9 on future interests opens with an introduction to classification and terminology, then proceeds directly to coverage of the Rule against Perpetuities, and concludes with a section on powers of appointment. Relatively little attention is given to problems of construction or to the historical development of future interests, which could easily form the subject matter of a full separate course. Instead, the focus here is on aspects of planning and drafting which a general practitioner is likely to encounter in the trusts and estates field. Substantial economy of time and space has been achieved by dealing with various topics such as class gifts in the context of the perpetuities materials rather than under separate headings.

Chapter 10 provides an overview of the federal wealth transfer taxes, which affect almost all substantial gratuitous transfers of property. Here, as in the chapter on future interests, the materials have been selected with an eye to the needs of the generalist rather than the expert. Accordingly, the primary emphasis is on the structure of the estate and gift taxes and their relationship to each other and to the generation-skipping transfer tax.

The book has considerable flexibility as a teaching tool. It is possible, for example, to cover substantially the entire book in a single comprehensive course, or to cover only the first seven chapters in a basic survey course and leave the last three chapters for a more advanced course.

This book began as a set of mimeographed teaching materials prepared by Professor Gulliver for use in his courses on the law of wills and trusts at Yale in the 1930s. In 1965 Professor Clark of the Yale faculty joined with his colleagues at Columbia, Professors Lusky and Murphy, to revise the book and broaden its coverage. In 1997, at their invitation, Professors Ascher and McCouch assumed primary responsibility for updating the book to reflect recent judicial decisions, statutory amendments, scholarly commentary, and reform proposals. From its inception the book has evolved considerably, but its basic structure and approach continue to reflect the original editors' contributions.

In the text and notes, we have used the words "testator," "executor," and "administrator" to include both males and females. In editing the cases and other materials, we have freely omitted footnotes and renumbered those that remain. Furthermore, we have conformed punctuation and citation form to standard usage, and have corrected obvious typographical errors.

We are grateful to the authors and publishers who have consented to our use of excerpts from their copyrighted works. In addition, we wish to express our gratitude to the many students who served as research and editorial assistants in the preparation of successive editions of this book, to colleagues from other schools for their helpful suggestions, and to support staff at our respective institutions for their invaluable assistance in preparing the manuscript for publication.

We are deeply saddened by the loss of our senior co-author, Elias Clark, who passed away in June 2011. Professor Clark inspired many generations of colleagues and students with his good judgment, generous spirit, and fine sense of humor.

MARK L. ASCHER
GRAYSON M.P. McCOUCH

December 2012

ACKNOWLEDGMENTS

The editors wish to acknowledge permission to reproduce from the following copyrighted material:

Alford, Collecting a Decedent's Assets without Ancillary Administration, 18 Sw. L.J. 329 (1964). Originally appearing in Vol. 18 *SMU Law Review 331–332*. Reprinted with permission from the *SMU Law Review* and the Southern Methodist University Dedman School of Law.

American Law Institute, Restatement (Second) of Conflict of Laws; Restatement (Second) of Property (Donative Transfers); Restatement (Third) of Property: Wills and Other Donative Transfers; Restatement (Second) of Restitution; Restatement (Third) of Restitution and Unjust Enrichment; Restatement (Second) of Trusts; Restatement (Third) of Trusts. Reprinted with permission of the American Law Institute.

American Law of Property (A. James Casner ed.) (Little, Brown & Co., 1952 & Supp.). Reprinted with permission.

Bittker, The *Church* and *Spiegel* Cases: Section 811(c) Gets a New Lease on Life, 58 Yale L.J. 825 (1949). Reprinted by permission of The Yale Law Journal Company and Fred B. Rothman & Company from *The Yale Law Journal*, Vol. 58, pages 825-870.

Cartoon by Dedini. © The New Yorker Collection 1962 Eldon Dedini from cartoonbank.com. All rights reserved. Reprinted with permission.

Chart of Relationships and Table of Consanguinity from Section 7.82 of *California Decedent Estate Practice* (1986-1997) copyright by the Regents of the University of California. Reproduced with the permission of Continuing Education of the Bar—California.

Dukeminier, Perpetuities Law in Action (1962). Copyright © 1962, from PERPETUITIES LAW IN ACTION, by Jesse Dukeminier. Reprinted with permission of The University Press of Kentucky.

Dukeminier, The Uniform Statutory Rule Against Perpetuities: Ninety Years in Limbo, 34 UCLA L. Rev. 1023 (1987). Originally published in 34 UCLA L. Rev. 1023. Copyright 1987, The Regents of the University of California. All Rights Reserved. Reprinted with permission.

Friedman, The Law of Succession in Social Perspective, in Death, Taxes and Family Property 9 (Halbach ed.) (West Publishing Co. 1977). Reprinted with permission of Thomson Reuters.

Friedrich, The Economics of Inheritance, in 1 Social Meaning of Legal Concepts 27 (Cahn ed., 1948). Reprinted with permission of New York University School of Law.

Gray, The Rule Against Perpetuities (4th ed.) (Little, Brown & Co. 1942). Reprinted with permission.

Gulliver & Tilson, Classification of Gratuitous Transfers, 51 Yale L.J. 1 (1941). Reprinted by permission of The Yale Law Journal Company and Fred B. Rothman & Company from *The Yale Law Journal*, Vol. 51, pages 1-39.

Halbach, An Introduction to Chapters 1–4, in Death, Taxes and Family Property 3 (Halbach ed.) (West Publishing Co. 1977). Reprinted with permission of Thomson Reuters.

Langbein, Excusing Harmless Errors in the Execution of Wills: A Report on Australia's Tranquil Revolution in Probate Law, 87 Colum. L. Rev. 1 (1987) This article originally appeared at 87 Colum. L. Rev. 1 (1987). Reprinted by permission.

Langbein, Mandatory Rules in the Law of Trusts, 98 Nw. U. L. Rev. 1105 (2004). Reprinted by special permission of Northwestern University School of Law, *Northwestern University Law Review*.

Langbein, The Nonprobate Revolution and the Future of the Law of Succession, 97 Harv. L. Rev. 1108 (1984). Reprinted with permission.

Langbein, Questioning the Trust Law Duty of Loyalty: Sole Interest or Best Interest?, 114 Yale L.J. 929 (2005). Reprinted by permission of The Yale Law Journal Company and William S. Hein & Company from *The Yale Law Journal*, Vol. 114, pages 929–990.

Langbein, Substantial Compliance With the Wills Act, 88 Harv. L. Rev. 489 (1975). Reprinted with permission.

Langbein, The Twentieth-Century Revolution in Family Wealth Transmission, 86 Mich. L. Rev. 722 (1988). Originally published by the Michigan Law Review. Reprinted with permission.

Langbein, The Uniform Prudent Investor Act and the Future of Trust Investing, 81 Iowa L. Rev. 641 (1996). Reprinted with permission.

Langbein & Posner, Social Investing and the Law of Trusts, 79 Mich. L. Rev. 72 (1980). Originally published by the Michigan Law Review. Reprinted with permission.

Leslie, Trusting Trustees: Fiduciary Duties and the Limits of Default Rules, 94 Geo. L.J. 67 (2005). Reprinted with permission of the publisher, Georgetown Law Journal © 2005.

Lynn, The Modern Rule Against Perpetuities (Bobbs-Merrill Co. 1966). Reprinted from *The Modern Rule Against Perpetuities* with permission. Copyright 1966 Matthew Bender & Company, Inc., a part of LexisNexis. All rights reserved.

National Conference of Commissioners on Uniform State Laws, Uniform Disclaimer of Property Interests Act; Uniform Health Care Decisions Act; Uniform Marital Property Act; Uniform Parentage Act; Uniform Principal and Income Act; Uniform Probate Code; Uniform Prudent Investor Act; Uniform Simultaneous Death Act; Uniform Statutory Rule Against Perpetuities; Uniform Testamentary Additions to Trusts Act; Uniform Transfers to Minors Act; Uniform Trust Code. Reprinted with permission.

Niles, A Contemporary View of Liability for Breach of Trust, 114 Trusts & Estates 12, 82 (1975). Reprinted courtesy of Intertec Publishing Corp. © TRUSTS & ESTATES, 1975, Overland Park, KS 66212. All rights reserved.

Scott & Ascher, Scott and Ascher on Trusts (5th ed., Aspen Publishers, 2006 & Supp.). Reprinted with permission.

Simes, Public Policy and the Dead Hand (1955). Reprinted with permission.

Simes & Smith, The Law of Future Interests (West Publishing Co. 1956). Reprinted with permission.

Sussman, Cates & Smith, The Family and Inheritance (1970). Reprinted with permission.

Wedgwood, The Economics of Inheritance (1929). Reprinted with permission.

Wellman, Recent Developments in the Struggle for Probate Reform, 79 Mich. L. Rev. 501 (1981). Originally published by the Michigan Law Review. Reprinted with permission.

TABLE OF ABBREVIATIONS USED IN REFERRING TO TEXTS

Am. L. Prop.: American Law of Property (1952), written by various authors and edited by A.J. Casner.

Atkinson: Atkinson, The Law of Wills (2d ed. 1953).

Gray: Gray, The Rule Against Perpetuities (Gray ed.) (4th ed. 1942).

Holds.: Holdsworth, History of English Law (1922-38).

Mait. Eq.: Maitland, Equity (1909).

Page: Bowe & Parker, Page on the Law of Wills (rev. ed. 1960).

P. & M.: Pollock & Maitland, History of English Law (2d ed. 1923).

Scott and Ascher on Trusts: Scott and Ascher on Trusts (5th ed. 2006 & Supp.).

Simes & Smith: Simes & Smith, Law of Future Interests (2d ed. 1956).

SUMMARY OF CONTENTS

TABLE OF CONTENTS

TABLE OF CASES

The principal cases are in bold type. Cases cited or discussed in the text are in roman type. References are to pages.

CASES AND MATERIALS ON

GRATUITOUS TRANSFERS

WILLS, INTESTATE SUCCESSION, TRUSTS, GIFTS, FUTURE INTERESTS AND ESTATE AND GIFT TAXATION

Sixth Edition

CHAPTER 1

INTRODUCTION

■ ■ ■

A. INHERITANCE AND PUBLIC POLICY

These materials provide an introduction to the law of gratuitous transfers of wealth, including transfers by will, gift, trust, and intestate succession. The field of estates and trusts holds considerable practical importance for lawyers. Planning, drafting and administering estates and trusts is a major activity of individual practitioners and requires a separate department in law firms of substantial size. Even a specialist whose professional interests are far removed from the field may be compelled to pay attention to these matters at the request of family members, friends or clients. Estates lawyers look at problems from the point of view of the individual property owner whom they represent. Their objective, in general terms, is to ensure that their client's intent is carried out reliably and efficiently, with minimal administrative complications and tax burdens. They know that contact with the law is direct, frequent, and unavoidable. Estate, inheritance, gift and income taxes are an ever-present consideration, and failure to observe formal requirements or carelessness in drafting documents of transfer may lead to disputes between rival claimants. But judicial intervention is not limited to matters in controversy. Indeed, there is a longstanding tradition in this country of administering estates and testamentary trusts—including those which are not contested—under court supervision. Thus, in addition to a large body of substantive law in the field there is also a separate set of elaborate procedural rules regulating the process of estate and trust administration.

With few exceptions, this structure of substantive and procedural rules rests on one basic premise. In a capitalistic system based on the institution of private property, individual owners enjoy remarkably broad freedom to dispose of their property in accordance with their own wishes, no matter how wise or foolish. For the most part, statutes and cases in the field aim to discover the true intent of the property owner, not to thwart it, but to give it effect.

The process of wealth transmission has significance not only for individual property owners and practicing lawyers but also for society as a whole. No systematic attempt has been made to estimate the magnitude of the continuous flow of wealth by gratuitous transfers or to evaluate its impact on the structure of American society. More than 2 million people die each year in the United States. Most of these deaths bring about transfers of wealth—items of tangible personal property, bank accounts, life insurance proceeds, real property, and perhaps substantial business or investment assets. The cumulative value of these deathtime transfers plus the value of inter vivos gifts and of shifting interests in trusts has not been accurately established. We do have a few isolated statistics, however. By the end of 2010, the total amount of life insurance in force was more than $18 trillion. In 2009, some 33,000 estate tax returns were filed, showing gross estates with a combined value of nearly $195 billion (including some $58 billion in corporate stock, $35 billion in real estate, $25 billion in bonds, $21 billion in cash, and $4 billion in life insurance), and deductions of around $93 billion. After taking tax credits into account, nearly 15,000 taxable estates owed total estate taxes of around $21 billion. The significance of these figures can best be appreciated by emphasizing that the estates of around 1 percent of all decedents, admittedly the wealthiest, are required to file estate tax returns, with less than half that number actually owing any tax. Based on those statistics it seems reasonable to suppose that the total wealth passing at death each year may amount to $400 billion or more.

The economics of the process are not the only basis on which to judge its impact on society. Wealth is an important factor affecting family stability. The opportunities for power, position and prestige available to the recipients of hereditary fortunes are obvious. In less well-endowed families, failure to anticipate and provide for a family member's death may lead to a severe retrenchment in living standards. Wealth may be used to ensure a secure and united family. Conversely, a disposition that is perceived as unfair may ignite some of the most bitter and destructive disputes known to the law. Expectations of inheritance or fears of disinheritance frequently control the behavior of family members and their relationships with each other. Love, hate, jealousy, avarice—the whole range of human emotions—come into play.

Inevitably, the ethical, economic, sociological and psychological aspects of the process have prompted challenges from many quarters to the principle of unfettered dispositive freedom for property owners. A voluminous body of literature, frequently more speculative than scientific, concerning the process of inheritance has developed over the years. Most critics of the process agree that individuals should be permitted relatively unrestricted enjoyment of wealth which they have earned and that such enjoyment should include the power to give it away during life. The criticism is directed at the proposition that people should also be permitted to perpetuate the accumulation of dynastic wealth and to control its use and enjoyment long after death. As might be expected, there is wide variation in the solutions proposed by those who have considered the problem. Some favor a mild death tax levied at rates graduated in accordance with the amount of wealth transferred or received. Others go much further and advocate the abolition of inheritance with some exceptions for spouses, minor children and disabled or dependent family members. Franklin D. Roosevelt recommended a supplemental inheritance tax "in respect to all very large amounts received by any one legatee or beneficiary," in his message to Congress of June 19, 1935, reprinted at 1939–1 (pt. 2) C.B. 642, 643:

> . . . The transmission from generation to generation of vast fortunes by will, inheritance, or gift is not consistent with the ideals and sentiments of the American people.
>
> The desire to provide security for one's self and one's family is natural and wholesome, but it is adequately served by a reasonable inheritance. Great accumulations of wealth cannot be justified on the basis of personal and family security. In the last analysis such accumulations amount to the perpetuation of great and undesirable concentration of control in a relatively few individuals over the employment and welfare of many, many others.
>
> Such inherited economic power is as inconsistent with the ideals of this generation as inherited political power was inconsistent with the ideals of the generation which established our Government.
>
> Creative enterprise is not stimulated by vast inheritances. They bless neither those who bequeath nor those who receive. . . .
>
> Those who argue for the benefits secured to society by great fortunes invested in great businesses should note that such a tax does not affect the essential benefits that remain after the death of the creator of such a business. The mechanism of production that he created remains. The benefits of corporate organization remain. . . . All that is gone is the initiative, energy, and genius of the creator— and death has taken these away.

Despite the theorizing about the inequities of inheritance, there has never been significant popular demand in this country for its abolition. Federal and state death taxes impose some restrictions on the transfer from generation to generation of large concentrations of wealth, but beyond this few are willing to go. In reading the following materials, consider the standards and policies that are invoked, explicitly or implicitly, to support or criticize the institution of inheritance.

JOSIAH WEDGWOOD, THE ECONOMICS OF INHERITANCE
200–04 (1929).

The usual economic defence of Inheritance rests on the advantages of the right of bequest rather than on the right of inheritance. It is that, unless men have the right to dispose of their property after their death as they please, they will not take the trouble either to preserve or to increase their capital, and to provide in this way for the needs of the coming generation. It is said that, without the secure ability of private persons to provide after death for those whom they love, the material equipment of society will diminish, and, however much the gain in greater equality of distribution, it will not compensate for the loss in productivity. . . .

The argument is frequently accepted as based on self-evident propositions and beyond the reach of critical analysis. In fact, it is no more water-tight than most hasty generalisations. Let us agree that the desire to provide for children is a most important incentive to industry and saving among parents, and that the fact that property can be disposed of after the death of its owner in accordance with his wishes makes property more desirable, and therefore acts as an additional stimulant to its acquisition and preservation. But it does not follow that inheritance is therefore essential to the maintenance and increase of capital; still less may one infer that *unlimited* inheritances are necessary for that purpose. . . .

We may conclude, then, . . . that the right of bequest and inheritance is *not essential* as a stimulus to private saving. For, as regards those saving from other motives than the provision for dependants, there seems no reason why the abolition of the right of bequest should greatly affect their actions. And, in the case of those who save with the object of handing on property to their family, they can achieve their object as well by gift during life as by bequest at death. . . .

Thus, in general, the chief effect of the abolition of inheritance by itself would be—not to diminish the incentive to save and to encourage the dissipation of capital . . . —but to stimulate gifts between the living, as the obvious alternative to bequests at death. . . .

––––––––––––––

A. ANTON FRIEDRICH, THE ECONOMICS OF INHERITANCE, IN 1 SOCIAL MEANING OF LEGAL CONCEPTS
27, 33–37 (1948).

A social-economic appraisal of the institution of inheritance is concerned also with the effect of inheritance upon the distribution of wealth. An economy based upon private property will result in an unequal distribution of wealth and income. Differences in talent, energy, endurance, drive, personality, and also luck will result in unequal earnings and in windfall acquisitions. And this will happen even under the most favorable circumstances where, as nearly as possible, opportunities are equal to all.

So long as the individual family persists, opportunities cannot be wholly equalized although educational facilities available at general public expense may lessen the inequalities greatly. The children of the families with higher incomes will have superior advantages over the children of the very poor,—in part of a material sort such as training and social contacts, in part of a more subtle psychological kind. Attitudes and habits, ambition, determination, expectations, a sense of self-assurance are communicated in the milieu of family life. . . .

Moreover, so long as the economy is dependent upon private savings to an appreciable extent for new capital, the conditions which facilitate accumulation have some measure of social justification. Inequality of income can offer a defense on grounds that the higher incomes are the major source of savings. The lower incomes are required wholly or primarily for the daily necessities of life. It is only when there is some excess that savings can accumulate in any considerable amount.

But this is true only within limits. If the inequality of income is greater than is necessary to inspire the superior to excel and the poor to emulate, then inequality loses its claims to social merit and becomes merely the expression of acquisitive license and unrestrained greed. If the inequality which is conducive to accumulation by the few imposes undue hardship upon the many, its beneficence may justly be questioned.

Equality is also a positive good. According to Jeremy Bentham the maximum happiness of society can best be realized, assuming that productivity would not be impaired, when income is equally distributed. This conclusion follows from the premises that happiness consists of a total of pleasures and pains, that pleasures and pains of all individuals are commensurable, and that the pleasure one derives from goods and services varies inversely with the quantity available. Thus the poor lose more by having less than the rich gain by having more.

We do not need to rest our case for equality upon the hedonistic premises of Bentham and the marginal utility school of economics. There are the ethical grounds; in addition there are social and political reasons for presuming that a society in which wealth, income, and opportunity are more or less evenly distributed is likely to be more stable and peaceable than one in which there are great extremes between the rich and the poor. . . .

The institution of inheritance is not the sole cause of inequality of wealth and opportunity. But the inheritance of property is of equal and perhaps even of greater importance than inherited abilities, environment, and opportunity in accounting for economic inequality. "Its influence," asserts F.W. Taussig, . . . "is enormous. It is this which explains the perpetuation of the incomes derived from capital, land, income-yielding property of all sorts, and so explains the great continuing gulf between the haves and have-nots. It serves also to strengthen all the lines of social stratification and reenforce the influences of custom and habit. Persons who inherit property also inherit opportunity. They have a better start, a more stimulating environment, a higher ambition. They are likely to secure higher incomes and preserve a higher standard of living. . . ." [1]

A hereditary-wealth class and the social stratification which it supports are sharply at variance with ideas of fair competition and equal opportunity. In competition on the athletic field, all contestants start from the same position, and if there are handicaps they are placed upon those who have superior ability. Competition for economic prizes works on opposite principles. Those who have inherited great wealth may win the coveted prizes without competing at all, and if they choose to compete they may extend their advantages even more and by inheritance bequeath them to their successors. In economic competition, the contestants are distributed over the course with the largest number farthest back. There are handicaps but they are placed not on the strong but on the weak. . . .

In summary the social-economic interest in inheritance may be expressed as follows: (1) The institution of inheritance distributes wealth not in accord with productive performance and competence but according to family relationships and the interest and caprice of the testator. Wealth so distributed may in some cases, perhaps in many cases, and under some circumstances be generally at variance with the capital requirements of an expanding economy. (2) But in a society based on private property, the institution of inheritance may be the better, or if you will, the least bad alternative for disposing of property upon the death of the owners. (3) And the expectations of founding a family fortune and the right of bequest may offset, or outweigh, the disadvantages of inheritance by strengthening incentives for the accumulation of capital. (4) Yet the "continuing gulf between the haves and have-nots" not only violates the norms of social ethics but may exaggerate the divisive tendencies within society, thus leading to social discord and political instability, and, it should be added, may also weaken the incentives to produce on the part of the discontented many.

---

[1]F.W. Taussig, Principles of Economics vol. II, 298 (1939).

The relative importance which economists and social philosophers generally will attach to the above opposing considerations will depend upon their basic premises and ultimate values. Those who attach supreme importance to the ideal of economic and social equality will relegate the bearing of inheritance upon the formation of capital to a secondary position or will disregard it altogether. Those who regard private property as the more workable pattern of economic organization will stress the importance of inheritance as a factor in the accumulation of capital. . . .

EDWARD C. HALBACH, JR., AN INTRODUCTION TO CHAPTERS 1–4, IN DEATH, TAXES AND FAMILY PROPERTY

3, 4–6 (Halbach ed., 1977).

No society recognizes private ownership without some limitations, but all respect and protect some form of individual property. It does not necessarily follow from the existence of private property, however, that the individual's family or selected successors must have a right to assets after the owner's death. Nor, according to the prevailing view in this country, is the right to pass wealth at death a natural or constitutional right. Despite all this, some form of inheritance is virtually a universal institution of ancient and modern societies, including the socialist world.

There is no such universal acceptance, however, of a right to select successors and to dispose of property by will. If, as some argue, succession is justified as a source of a happier life and family unity and as an encouragement to industry and thrift, the right of testation may be viewed as a means of making succession more meaningful, valuable and responsive to the owner's wishes, permitting it to be adapted to the needs and circumstances of a particular family. Yet, it does not follow even from this that trusts and other forms of post-death control should be accepted with the extraordinary freedom found in the Anglo–American world.

Even admitting that a system of inheritance responds to an apparently basic human urge and is supported by a variety of societal values, powerful arguments can be made against it. These are most often expressed in terms of perpetuating significant inequalities based on unearned wealth and on the possession of power that has ceased to reflect merit. The inheritance of modest amounts of property for use does not create serious social issues, even if a slight degree of privilege, status and opportunity accompany it. But a system allowing inherited wealth that can significantly affect the lives of others requires explanation. So does a system that is charged, only partially inconsistently, both with impairing equality of opportunity and encouraging a class of idle rich. Thus, the questions: What justifications are there for the private transmission of wealth from generation to generation? And how do we rationalize allowing only some individuals, selected by accident of birth, to enjoy significant comforts and power they have not earned? . . .

Many arguments are offered in support of the institution of inheritance. One is simply that, in a society based on private property, it may be the least objectionable arrangement for dealing with property on the owner's death.

Another is that inheritance is natural and proper as both an expression and a reinforcement of family ties, which in turn are important to a healthy society and a good life. After all, a society should be concerned with the total amount of happiness it can offer, and to many of its members it is a great comfort and satisfaction to know during life that, even after death, those whom one cares about can be provided for and may be able to enjoy better lives because of the inheritance that can be left to them. Furthermore, it is argued, giving and bequeathing not only express but beget affection, or at least responsibility. Thus, society is seen as offering a better and happier life by responding to the understandable desire of an individual to provide for his or her family after death.

Just as individuals may be rewarded through this desire, it can also be used by society, via inheritance rights, to serve as an incentive to bring forth creativity, hard work, initiative and ultimately productivity that benefits others, as well as encouraging individual responsibility— encouraging those who can to make provision that society would otherwise have to make for those who are or may be dependents. Of course, some doubt the need for such incentives, at least beyond modest levels of achievement and wealth accumulation, relying on the quest for power (or for recognition) and other motivations—not to mention habit. Long after these forces have taken over to stimulate the industry of such individuals, however, society may continue to find it important to offer property inducements to the irrepressibly productive to save rather than to consume, and to go on saving long after their own lifelong future needs are provided for. And what harm is there if individuals, through socially approved channels, pursue immortality and psychological satisfactions? The direct and indirect (e.g., through life insurance and through corporate accumulations) savings of individuals are vital to the economy's capital base and thus to its level of employment and to the productivity of other individuals.

Consequently, it is concluded, inheritance may grant wealth to *donees* without regard to their competence and performance, but the economic reasons for allowing inheritance are viewed in terms of proper rewards and socially valuable incentives to the *donor*. In fact, some philosophers would insist, these rewards are required by ideals of social justice as the fruits of one's labors.

Still another argument is made to justify inheritance, at least inheritance by immediate family members, and even to justify (at the risk of a two-edged sword) a certain amount of freedom of testation. This is the idea that other individuals will normally have contributed to the wealth accumulated and held by the property owner or owners within the family unit. Support at home and help on the job, reinforced by a happy life in union with an understanding and loving family (and maybe other relatives and even friends), are the essence of this argument. In combination with other rationales for inheritance and testation, this argument is not seriously undermined by the difficulty—and, in fact, the undesirability (at least for others than a spouse)—of attempting to sort out the contributions and thus alleged entitlements of various individuals.

Ultimately, it is not at all easy to weigh against these and other claimed justifications the charges of unjustified inequalities of means and power, and of associated societal divisiveness and conflict. The charges extend to include economic inefficiencies that may result from allowing wealth to be allocated by the chance and caprice of inheritance, especially where testamentary freedom permits broad, long-term and potentially intrusive use of trusts.

LAWRENCE M. FRIEDMAN, THE LAW OF SUCCESSION IN SOCIAL PERSPECTIVE, IN DEATH, TAXES AND FAMILY PROPERTY

9, 11–14 (Halbach ed., 1977).

How do societies deal with rights when the man or woman who held these rights dies or is killed?

1. One response is to destroy the property, allow it to decay, or bury it with the dead. Many societies have believed in an afterworld; many have thought that food, drink, jewelry, and clothing can be useful to the soul in its trip to the place of the dead. . . .

2. Another way to treat the assets of the dead is to turn them loose, so to speak, so that anybody who finds them, or takes them, may keep them. This technique, if we can call it that, is the fate of small and unimportant possessions in our society—the pencils, or cheap costume jewelry we leave behind. Family and friends take these without further ado, along with some letters and keepsakes. Usually custom defines who has the moral right to these goods—family or friends. . . .

3. The government, state, or collective can *confiscate* property at death and redistribute it. Some rights may pass back into the bosom of the collective, from whom the holder of the right, during his lifetime, merely "borrowed" or rented it. "Common" rights are often of this nature. The right to pasture one's animals in a public pasture, or the right to share in a collective garden, often go back to the source, for redistribution (although many societies do recognize some sort of inheritance). The more modern form of confiscation is heavy death taxation, often treated . . . as an important aspect of a general policy aiming to reduce inequality of wealth. Death taxes can be quite high; consequently confiscation (by a more polite term) is an important part of the law of succession in modern nations.

4. The principle of *freedom of testation* stands in sharp contrast to confiscation. This is the idea that a person has the right to choose who will succeed to things of value left behind at death. This principle is characteristically modern—it was and is rare in simpler societies; but it is a leading principle in the United States and most western countries. Even in these, . . . it is not absolute and unrestricted.

5. What we might call inheritance by *rule* is probably the leading principle or technique of inheritance, if we consider all societies and all periods. By inheritance by *rule* we mean simply that the society has definite rules, laws or customs to designate who shall inherit and when. Property is not confiscated, does not rot or follow the deceased to the grave, does not return to the market, and cannot be handed on by will. It passes automatically to those who become entitled at death. Almost invariably, these are close living relatives, by blood or marriage; but societies differ greatly in details. . . .

Even countries which recognize, as a general principle, freedom of testation, give much play to inheritance by *rule*. And there will be rules to determine how property should pass at death, if the deceased did not designate his wishes, or if he or she did not use the proper forms. Each of the 50 states has its own *intestacy* laws. These set out rules of inheritance for people who die without a will. Modern intestacy laws favor the surviving spouse and the children, that is, members of the nuclear family of the deceased. If a person dies without a wife and children, his parents will take; if they are dead, his brothers and sisters; if they are dead, his nieces and nephews, and so on. The closest living blood relatives will inherit the estate. Inheritance by *rule* is a rigid scheme; the rules follow bloodlines and ignore the life-situation of the particular person who died. The property of a woman whose deepest affection was for a neighbor and friend, but who died without a will, may pass to a cousin the dead woman never saw. . . .

Laws of inheritance reflect . . . the social background and the social structure. They are the product of society. But they also perform a function *for* society. These laws and rules help define, maintain and strengthen the social and economic structure. They act as a kind of pattern or template through which the society reproduces itself each generation. . . . Any radical change in the rules, if carried out, will radically change the society.

For general discussions of the philosophical and historical bases of inheritance, as well as its social and economic implications, see Inheritance and Wealth in America (Miller & McNamee eds., 1998); Ascher, Curtailing Inherited Wealth, 89 Mich. L. Rev. 69 (1990); Chester, Inheritance, Wealth, and Society (1982); Brittain, Inheritance and the Inequality of Material Wealth (1978); Friedman, The Law of the Living, the Law of the Dead: Property, Succession, and Society, 1966 Wis. L. Rev. 340.

B. THE PROBATE SYSTEM AND THE WEALTH TRANSMISSION PROCESS

Any discussion of the process by which property passes at death from a decedent to his or her successors requires some understanding of the probate system and the terminology of decedents' estates. Technically, the term *probate* (derived from the Latin word for proof) refers to a judicial proceeding to determine the validity of one or more instruments as the decedent's will. The proceeding is commenced in a court with jurisdiction over the administration of decedents' estates, generally known as the *probate court* (or, in some jurisdictions, the surrogate's court or orphans' court). The term "probate" is often used more broadly to refer to the process of judicially-supervised estate administration. The person charged with administering a decedent's estate is generally known as the *personal representative*. (More specifically, an *executor* is a personal representative who is named in the will; an *administrator* is a personal representative who is not so named, as in the case of an intestate estate.)

A person who dies without a will is called an *intestate*. In that case, the decedent's successors are determined under the applicable intestacy laws; if there are no intestate successors, the estate goes to the state by *escheat*. Traditionally, the *statutes of descent and distribution* specified separate (and often different) patterns of succession for an intestate's real and personal property. Land "descended" to the decedent's *heirs*, while personalty was "distributed" to the *distributees* or *next of kin*. In modern practice, such distinctions have largely disappeared, and the term "heirs" is often used to refer generally to intestate successors. Chapter 2 examines patterns of intestate succession and eligibility of particular successors to participate in an intestate's estate.

A person who makes a will is called a *testator*. The will, if admitted to probate, controls the disposition of the testator's estate. In traditional usage, a testamentary gift of land is called a *devise*; a testamentary gift of personalty is called a *bequest* (or a *legacy*, in the case of a sum of money). Here again, such technical distinctions have faded in importance, and the term "devise" is often used today to refer to a testamentary gift of either real or personal property. A will remains *ambulatory* during the testator's life, meaning that it does not take effect until the testator's death. Moreover, a will is not self-executing, but must be admitted to probate in order to operate in favor of the testator's beneficiaries. Thus, if a will is in existence but is never offered for probate, the estate passes by intestacy. The same is true if probate is denied—for example, because the will was not properly executed or the testator lacked testamentary capacity. Chapters 4 and 5 address various aspects of the law of wills, including grounds for contest, formalities of execution and revocation, and problems of interpretation.

Each of the fifty states has its own separate probate statutes governing matters of intestate succession, wills, and administration of decedents' estates. The statutes vary substantially from state to state, especially in the area of estate administration. Administration of a decedent's estate generally involves three basic functions: (1) collecting assets of the estate; (2) paying expenses, creditors' claims, taxes, and other charges; and (3) distributing the remaining assets to the decedent's successors. Traditionally these functions have been carried out by a personal representative under the supervision of the probate court, with elaborate procedural safeguards to protect the interests of creditors and other third parties. Chapter 8 addresses the process of estate administration as well as various matters involving the relationship between fiduciaries and beneficiaries.

The Uniform Probate Code (UPC) has played a central role in efforts to reform and simplify the probate process in recent years. Since its original promulgation in 1969, the UPC has been adopted in around one-third of the states. Subsequent amendments, including a comprehensive 1990 overhaul of the provisions concerning intestacy, wills and donative transfers, have been adopted in whole or in part in several states as well. Comparing the original and revised versions of the UPC with non-uniform state probate codes offers valuable opportunities for evaluating divergent statutory approaches and assessing prospects for further reform.

For purposes of probate administration, the *estate* comprises all property owned by the decedent at death which is capable of being transferred by will. The net estate remaining after payment of expenses, creditors' claims, taxes, and other charges passes either by will or by intestacy to the decedent's successors. The converse is also true. Property that the decedent transferred during life does not pass by will and generally is not subject to administration. For many years property owners have used various techniques to transfer property outside the probate system while retaining substantial beneficial rights over the property until death. An outstanding modern example of such a "will substitute" is a revocable trust, in which a *settlor* transfers property to a *trustee* who agrees to hold it in trust for the benefit of one or more *beneficiaries* (e.g., income to the settlor for life, with remainder at the settlor's death to other designated takers, subject to the settlor's reserved right to revoke or amend the trust). As a practical matter, the revocable trust achieves much the same effect as a will, but it does so outside the probate system. In this sense, will substitutes challenge the notion that "probate is the sole means by which our legal system permits a transferor to pass his property on death." Langbein, The Nonprobate Revolution and the Future of the Law of Succession, 97 Harv. L. Rev. 1108, 1129 (1984). Further discussion of lifetime gifts and trusts appears in Chapters 6 and 7, respectively.

JOHN H. LANGBEIN, THE NONPROBATE REVOLUTION AND THE FUTURE OF THE LAW OF SUCCESSION
97 Harv. L. Rev. 1108, 1109–25 (1984).

I. THE WILL SUBSTITUTES

Four main will substitutes constitute the core of the nonprobate system: life insurance, pension accounts, joint accounts, and revocable trusts. When properly created, each is functionally indistinguishable from a will—each reserves to the owner complete lifetime dominion, including the power to name and change beneficiaries until death. . . . [These four] will substitutes may also be described as mass will substitutes: they are marketed by financial intermediaries using standard form instruments with fill-in-the-blank beneficiary designations. . . .

II. THE HIDDEN CAUSES OF THE NONPROBATE REVOLUTION

The typical propertied decedent in modern America leaves a will and many will substitutes. The will substitutes differ from the ordinary "last will and testament" in three main ways. First, most will substitutes—but not all—are asset-specific: each deals with a single type of property, be it life insurance proceeds, a bank balance, mutual fund shares, or whatever. Second, property that passes through a will substitute avoids probate. A financial intermediary ordinarily takes the place of the probate court in effecting the transfer. Third, the formal requirements of the Wills Act—

attestation and so forth—do not govern will substitutes and are not complied with. Of these differences, only probate avoidance is a significant advantage that transferors might consciously seek.

. . . The probate system has earned a lamentable reputation for expense, delay, clumsiness, makework, and worse. In various jurisdictions, especially the dozen-odd that have adopted or imitated the simplified procedures of the Uniform Probate Code of 1969 ("UPC"), the intensity of hostility to probate may have abated a little. There are, however, intrinsic limits to the potential of probate reform. . . . Because the Anglo–American procedural tradition is preoccupied with adversarial and litigational values, the decision to organize any function as a judicial proceeding is inconsistent with the interests that ordinary people regard as paramount when they think about the transmission of their property at death: dispatch, simplicity, inexpensiveness, privacy. As long as probate reform still calls for probate, it will not go far enough for the tastes of many transferors, who view probate as little more than a tax imposed for the benefit of court functionaries and lawyers.

The puzzle in the story of the nonprobate revolution is not that transferors should have sought to avoid probate, but rather that other persons whose interests probate was meant to serve—above all, creditors—should have allowed the protections of the probate system to slip away from them. Probate performs three essential functions: (1) making property owned at death marketable again (title-clearing); (2) paying off the decedent's debts (creditor protection); and (3) implementing the decedent's donative intent respecting the property that remains once the claims of creditors have been discharged (distribution). It is in the sphere of distribution or gratuitous transfer that the will substitutes have proved themselves to be such formidable competitors of the probate system. Although the will substitutes are not well suited to clearing title and protecting creditors, a series of changes in the nature of wealth and in the business practices of creditors has diminished the importance of these functions.

A. Title–Clearing

The probate court is empowered to transfer title to a decedent's real property and thereby to restore it to marketability under the recording system. . . . In theory, the probate court should exercise a similar title-clearing function for all personalty, down to the sugar bowl and the pajamas, because only a court decree can perfect a successor's title in any item of personalty. Of course, ordinary practice quite belies the theory. Beyond the realm of vehicles and registered securities, which are covered by recording systems and thus resemble realty in some of the mechanics of transfer, formal evidence of title is not required to render personalty usable and marketable.

If a decedent's survivors can agree among themselves on a division of his personalty, they can distribute it without court decree. . . . The reason most deaths do not lead to probate is not that the decedents are property-less, but simply that they do not own real property (at least not in single tenancy). The survivors can therefore divide up the personalty in a fashion that satisfies those who are entitled to institute probate either under a will or under intestacy. . . .

. . . The bulk of modern wealth takes the form of contract rights rather than rights in rem—promises rather than things. . . . Promissory instruments—stocks, bonds, mutual funds, bank deposits, and pension and insurance rights—are the dominant component of today's private wealth. Together with public promises (that is, government transfer payments) these instruments of financial intermediation eclipse realty and tangible personalty.

The instruments of financial intermediation depend upon an underlying administrative capacity that is without counterpart in the realm of realty and tangible personalty. Financial intermediation is, as the term signifies, intrinsically administrative. Administrators intermediate between savers and borrowers, between passive owners and active users of capital. Pooling wealth and servicing the resulting liabilities involves recurrent transactions and communications. Once a bureaucracy appropriate to such tasks is in operation, only a scant adaptation is necessary to extend its functions and procedures to include the transfer of account balances on death.

The probate system nonetheless backstops the practice of financial intermediaries in important ways. The standard form instruments of the nonprobate system all but invariably name the transferor's probate estate as the ultimate contingent beneficiary. If, therefore, the named beneficiaries predecease the transferor or cannot be identified, the financial intermediary remits the fund to probate distribution. Messy heirship determinations are foisted off onto the courts. Likewise, if the proper course of distribution is for some reason doubtful, or if contest threatens, financial intermediaries can force the probate (or other) courts to decide the matter. . . . In this way the nonprobate system rides "piggyback" on the probate system. Financial intermediaries execute easy transfers and shunt the hard ones over to probate. But because virtually all transfers are easy, this attribute of the nonprobate system is a major source of its efficiency and comparative advantage. In the nonprobate system, genuine disputes still reach the courts, but routine administration does not.

B. Creditor Protection

The other set of changes that underlie the nonprobate revolution concerns another great mission of probate: discharging the decedent's debts.

Many of the details of American probate procedure, as well as much of its larger structure, would not exist but for the need to identify and pay off creditors. These procedures are indispensable, but—and here I am asserting a proposition that has not been adequately understood—only for the most exceptional cases. In general, *creditors do not need or use probate,* . . .

[Nevertheless,] when survivors will not acknowledge or pay decedents' debts without court coercion, when survivors cannot pay, or when a decedent's estate is insolvent and apportionment of assets is necessary, creditors still elect their probate remedies if outstanding debts are large enough to justify the expense of the court proceedings. Furthermore, creditors may benefit from the probate system without actually employing it. A creditor's access to the coercive powers of the probate system has a deterrent influence that aids the creditor in his attempts to obtain out-of-court satisfaction from survivors (and from probate representatives—executors and administrators). . . .

In the late twentieth century, creditor protection and probate have largely parted company. Had this development been otherwise, the rise of the will substitutes could not have occurred. If creditors had continued to rely significantly upon probate for the payment of decedents' debts, creditors' interests would have constituted an impossible obstacle to the nonprobate revolution. For—make no mistake about it—the will substitutes do impair the mechanism by which probate protects creditors. Even though the substantive law governing most of the major will substitutes usually recognizes the priority of creditors' claims over the claims of gratuitous transferees (life insurance is sometimes an exception), the decentralized procedures of the nonprobate system materially disadvantage creditors. Whereas probate directs all assets and all claimants to a common pot, the nonprobate system disperses assets widely and facilitates transfer without creditors' knowledge. If modern creditors had needed to use probate very much, they would have applied their considerable political muscle to suppress the nonprobate system. Instead, they have acquiesced without struggle. . . .

JOHN H. LANGBEIN, THE TWENTIETH–CENTURY REVOLUTION IN FAMILY WEALTH TRANSMISSION
86 Mich. L. Rev. 722, 732–46 (1988).

[I]n striking contrast to the patterns of the last century and before, in modern times the business of educating children has become the main occasion for intergenerational wealth transfer. Of old, parents were mainly concerned to transmit the patrimony—prototypically the farm or the firm, but more generally, that "provision in life" that rescued children from the harsh fate of being a mere laborer. In today's economic order, it is education more than property, the new human capital rather than the old physical capital, that similarly advantages a child. . . .

From the proposition that the main parental wealth transfer to children now takes place inter vivos, there follows a corollary: Children of propertied parents are much less likely to expect an inheritance. Whereas of old, children did expect the transfer of the farm or firm, today's children expect help with educational expenses, but they do not depend upon parental wealth transfer at death. Lengthened life expectancies mean that the life-spans of the parents overlap the life-spans of their adult children for much longer than used to be. Parents now live to see their children reaching peak earnings potential, and those earnings often exceed what the parents were able to earn. Today, children are typically middle-aged when the survivor of their two parents dies, and middle-aged children are far less likely to be financially needy. It is still the common practice within middle- and upper-middle-class families for parents to leave to their children (or grandchildren) most or all of any property that happens to remain when the parents die, but there is no longer a widespread sense of parental responsibility to abstain from consumption in order to transmit an inheritance. . . .

. . . Not only have the demographics altered so that the elders are routinely surviving for long intervals beyond their years of employment, but in consequence of the transformation in the nature of wealth, their property has taken on a radically altered character. That family farm or family firm that was the source of intrafamilial support in former times has become ever more exceptional. Most parental wealth (apart from the parents' own human capital) now takes the form of financial assets, which embody claims upon those large-scale enterprises that have replaced family enterprise. . . .

In propertied families, today's elderly no longer expect much financial support from their children. The shared patrimony in farm or firm that underlay that reverse transfer system in olden times has now largely vanished. Instead, people of means are expected to foresee the need for retirement income while they are still in the workforce, and to conduct a program of saving for their retirement. Typically, these people have already undertaken one great cycle of saving and dissaving in their lives—that program by which they effected the investment in human capital for their children. Just as that former program of saving was oriented toward a distinctively modern form of wealth, human capital, so this second program centers on the other characteristic form of twentieth-century wealth, financial assets. . . .

[W]hat is especially important about the pension system is that it has been deliberately designed to promote lifetime exhaustion of the accumulated capital. . . .

The mechanism by which pension wealth is consumed is annuitization. Just as life insurance is insurance against dying too soon, annuitization insures against living too long. . . . Annuitization is wonderfully effective in allowing a person to consume capital without fear of outliving his capital, but the corollary is also manifest: Accounts that have been annuitized disappear on the deaths of the annuitants. Not so much as a farthing remains for the heirs.

. . . Using their human capital to create lifetime income streams, modern parents now undertake two cycles of saving and dissaving, one for the children's education, the other for retirement. The investment in the children necessarily occurs in the parents' lifetimes. And especially when the retirement saving program is channelled through the enticing format of the qualified pension plan, the pressures for annuitization cause this enormous component of modern family wealth to be largely exhausted upon the parents' deaths. Transfer on death, the fundamental pattern of former times, is, therefore, ceasing to characterize the dominant wealth transmission practices of the broad middle classes.

C. TESTAMENTARY FREEDOM AND ITS LIMITATIONS

JOHN LOCKE, TWO TREATISES OF GOVERNMENT
Book 1, Chapter IX, § 88, at 76–77 (1728).

It might reasonably be asked here, how come Children by this Right of possessing, before any other, the Properties of their Parents upon their Decease? For it being personally the Parents, when they die, without actually transferring their Right to another, why does it not return again to the common Stock of Mankind? 'Twill perhaps be answered, that common Consent hath disposed of it to their Children. Common Practice, we see indeed, does so dispose of it, but we cannot say, that it is the common Consent of Mankind; for that hath never been asked, nor actually given; and if common tacit Consent hath establish'd it, it would make but a positive, and not a natural Right of Children to inherit the Goods of their Parents: But where the Practice is universal,'tis reasonable to think the Cause is natural. The ground then, I think to be this: The first and strongest Desire God Planted in Men, and wrought into the very Principles of their Nature, being that of Self-preservation, that is the Foundation of a Right to the Creatures for the particular Support, and Use of each individual Person himself. But next to this, God Planted in Men a strong Desire also of propagating their Kind, and continuing themselves in their Posterity; and this gives Children a Title to share in the *Property* of their Parents, and a Right to inherit their Possessions. Men are not Proprietors of what they have merely for themselves, their Children have a Title to part of it, and have their kind of Right join'd with their Parents, in the Possession; which comes to be wholly theirs, when Death, having put an end to their Parents Use of it, hath taken them from their Possessions; and this we call Inheritance . . . .

WILLIAM BLACKSTONE, 2 COMMENTARIES ON THE LAWS OF ENGLAND
*2, *9–13 (1765–69).

    . . . For, naturally speaking, the instant a man ceases to be, he ceases to have any dominion: else, if he had a right to dispose of his acquisitions one moment beyond his life, he would also have a right to direct their disposal for a million of ages after him: which would be highly absurd and inconvenient. All property must therefore cease upon death, considering men as absolute individuals, and unconnected with civil society: for, then, by the principles before established, the next immediate occupant would acquire a right in all that the deceased possessed. But as, under civilized governments, which are calculated for the peace of mankind, such a constitution would be productive of endless disturbances, the universal law of almost every nation (which is a kind of secondary law of nature) has either given the dying person a power of continuing his property, by disposing of his possessions by will; or, in case he neglects to dispose of it, or is not permitted to make any disposition at all, the municipal law of the country then steps in, and declares who shall be the successor, representative, or heir of the deceased; that is, who alone shall have a right to enter upon this vacant possession, in order to avoid that confusion which its becoming again common would occasion. And further, in case no testament be permitted by the law, or none be made, and no heir can be found so qualified as the law requires, still, to prevent the robust title of occupancy from again taking place, the doctrine of escheats is adopted in almost every country; whereby the sovereign of the state, and those who claim under his authority, are the ultimate heirs, and succeed to those inheritances to which no other title can be formed.

    The right of inheritance, or descent to the children and relations of the deceased, seems to have been allowed much earlier than the right of devising by testament. We are apt to conceive at first view that it has nature on its side; yet we often mistake for nature what we find established by long and inveterate custom. It is certainly a wise and effectual, but clearly a political, establishment; since the permanent right of property, vested in the ancestor himself, was no *natural*, but merely a *civil*, right. It is true, that the transmission of one's possessions to posterity has an evident tendency to make a man a good citizen and a useful member of society; it sets the passions on the side of duty, and prompts a man to deserve well of the public, when he is sure that the reward of his services will not die with himself, but be transmitted to those with whom he is connected by the dearest and most tender affections. Yet, reasonable as this foundation of the right of inheritance may seem, it is probable that its immediate original arose not from speculations altogether so delicate and refined, and, if not from fortuitous circumstances, at least from a plainer and more simple principle. A man's children or nearest relations are usually about him on his death-bed, and are the earliest witnesses of his decease. They become therefore generally the next immediate occupants, till at length in process of time this frequent usage ripened into general law. . . .

While property continued only for life, testaments were useless and unknown: and, when it became inheritable, the inheritance was long indefeasible, and the children or heirs at law were incapable of exclusion by will; till at length it was found, that so strict a rule of inheritance made heirs disobedient and headstrong, defrauded creditors of their just debts, and prevented many provident fathers from dividing or charging their estates as the exigencies of their families required. This introduced pretty generally the right of disposing of one's property, or a part of it, by *testament*; that is, by written or oral instructions properly *witnessed* and authenticated, according to the *pleasure* of the deceased, which we therefore emphatically style his *will*. This was established in some countries much later than in others. With us in England, till modern times, a man could only dispose of one-third of his movables from his wife and children; and, in general, no will was permitted of lands till the reign of Henry the Eighth; and then only of a certain portion: for it was not until after the restoration that the power of devising real property became so universal as at present.

Wills therefore and testaments, rights of inheritance and successions, are all of them creatures of the civil or municipal laws, and accordingly are in all respects regulated by them; every distinct country having different ceremonies and requisites to make a testament completely valid: neither does any thing vary more than the right of inheritance under different national establishments. . . .

1. CONSTITUTIONAL LIMITATIONS

Under the prevailing view in this country since colonial times, the ability to transmit property at death is conceived as a creature of positive law rather than an inalienable natural right. This view suggests that the legislature has plenary power to define and restrict inheritance and testation, subject only to general constitutional limitations on arbitrary or oppressive legislation. As the Supreme Court stated in early decisions rejecting constitutional challenges to inheritance taxes, "The right to take property by devise or descent is the creature of the law, and not a natural right—a privilege; and therefore the authority which confers it may impose conditions upon it." Magoun v. Illinois Trust & Savings Bank, 170 U.S. 283, 288 (1898); Knowlton v. Moore, 178 U.S. 41, 55 (1900). Subsequently, the Court put the matter in even stronger terms in Irving Trust Co. v. Day, 314 U.S. 556 (1942), upholding a widow's right to elect against her deceased husband's will:

> Rights of succession to the property of a deceased, whether by will or by intestacy, are of statutory creation, and the dead hand rules succession only by sufferance. Nothing in the Federal Constitution forbids the legislature of a state to limit, condition, or even abolish the power of testamentary disposition over property within its jurisdiction. [314 U.S. at 562.]

Nevertheless, courts occasionally invoke the language of natural rights in reviewing the constitutional validity of restrictions on rights of inheritance or testation. See, e.g., Shriners Hospitals for Crippled Children v. Zrillic, 563 So.2d 64 (Fla.1990) (striking down statutory restriction on charitable bequests); Estate of Eisenberg, 280 N.W.2d 359 (Wis.App. 1979) (upholding surviving spouse's elective share). In Nunnemacher v. State, 108 N.W. 627 (Wis.1906), the Wisconsin Supreme Court considered the validity of a progressive inheritance tax under the state constitution. The court accepted the proposition that "the right to take property by inheritance or by will is a natural right protected by the Constitution, which cannot be wholly taken away or substantially impaired by the Legislature," as follows:

> . . . We are fully aware that the contrary proposition has been stated by the great majority of the courts of this country, including the Supreme Court of the United States. The unanimity with which it is stated is perhaps only equaled by the paucity of reasoning by which it is supported. In its simplest form it is thus stated: "The right to take property by devise or descent is the creature of the law and not a natural right." Magoun v. Bank, 170 U.S. 283, 18 Sup.Ct. 594, 42 L.Ed. 1037. In Eyre v. Jacob, 14 Grat. (Va.) 422, 73 Am. Dec. 367, it is stated more sweepingly thus: "It [the Legislature] may tomorrow, if it pleases, absolutely repeal the statute of wills, and that of descents and distributions, and declare that, upon the death of a party, his property shall be applied to the payment of his debts and the residue appropriated to public uses." . . .

> That there are inherent rights existing in the people prior to the making of any of our Constitutions is a fact recognized and declared by the Declaration of Independence, and by substantially every state Constitution. Our own Constitution says in its very first article: "All

men are born equally free and independent and have certain inherent rights; among these are life, liberty and the pursuit of happiness; to secure these rights governments are instituted among men deriving their just powers from the consent of the governed." Notice the language, "to secure these (inherent) rights governments are instituted"; not to manufacture new rights or to confer them on its citizens, but to conserve and secure to its citizens the exercise of pre-existing rights. It is true that the inherent rights here referred to are not defined but are included under the very general terms of "life, liberty and the pursuit of happiness." It is relatively easy to define "life and liberty," but it is apparent that the term "pursuit of happiness" is a very comprehensive expression which covers a broad field. Unquestionably this expression covers the idea of the acquisition of private property; not that the possession of property is the supreme good, but that there is planted in the breast of every person the desire to possess something useful or something pleasing which will serve to render life enjoyable, which shall be his very own, and which he may dispose of as he chooses, or leave to his children or his dependents at his decease. To deny that there is such universal desire, or to deny that the fulfillment of this desire contributes in a large degree to the attainment of human happiness is to deny a fact as patent as the shining of the sun at noonday. And so we find that, however far we penetrate into the history of the remote past, this idea of the acquisition and undisturbed possession of private property has been the controlling idea of the race, the supposed goal of earthly happiness. From this idea has sprung every industry, to preserve it governments have been formed, and its development has been coincident with the development of civilization. And so we also find that, from the very earliest times, men have been acquiring property, protecting it by their own strong arm if necessary, and leaving it for the enjoyment of their descendants; and we find also that the right of the descendants, or some of them, to succeed to the ownership has been recognized from the dawn of human history. The birthright of the firstborn existed long before Esau sold his right to the wily Jacob, and the Mosaic law fairly bristles with provisions recognizing the right of inheritance as then long existing, and regulating its details. The most ancient known codes recognize it as a right already existing and Justice Brown was clearly right when he said, in U.S. v. Perkins, 163 U.S. 625, 16 Sup.Ct. 1073, 41 L.Ed. 287: "The general consent of the most enlightened nations has from the earliest historical period recognized a natural right in children to inherit the property of their parents."[2]

---

[2]The quoted passage is taken from the following sentence in Justice Brown's opinion for the Court in United States v. Perkins, 163 U.S. 625, 628 (1896):

    Though the general consent of the most enlightened nations has, from the earliest historical period, recognized a natural right in children to inherit the property of their parents, we

. . . So clear does it seem to us from the historical point of view that the right to take property by inheritance or will has existed in some form among civilized nations from the time when the memory of man runneth not to the contrary, and so conclusive seems the argument that these rights are a part of the inherent rights which governments, under our conception, are established to conserve, that we feel entirely justified in rejecting the dictum so frequently asserted by such a vast array of courts that these rights are purely statutory and may be wholly taken away by the Legislature. It is true that these rights are subject to reasonable regulation by the Legislature, lines of descent may be prescribed, the persons who can take as heirs or devisees may be limited, collateral relatives may doubtless be included or cut off, the manner of the execution of wills may be prescribed, and there may be much room for legislative action in determining how much property shall be exempted entirely from the power to will so that dependents may not be entirely cut off. These are all matters within the field of regulation. The fact that these powers exist and have been universally exercised affords no ground for claiming that the Legislature may abolish both inheritances and wills, turn every fee-simple title into a mere estate for life, and thus, in effect, confiscate the property of the people once every generation. [108 N.W. at 628–30.]

The Wisconsin court ultimately concluded that "the general principle of inheritance taxation may be justified under the power of reasonable regulation and taxation of transfers of property," and sustained the validity of the inheritance tax.

HODEL V. IRVING

Supreme Court of the United States, 1987.
481 U.S. 704, 107 S.Ct. 2076, 95 L.Ed.2d 668.

JUSTICE O'CONNOR delivered the opinion of the Court.

The question presented is whether the original version of the "escheat" provision of the Indian Land Consolidation Act of 1983, Pub. L. 97–459, Tit. II, 96 Stat. 2519, effected a "taking" of appellees' decedents' property without just compensation.

---

know of no legal principle to prevent the legislature from taking away or limiting the right of testamentary disposition or imposing such conditions upon its exercise as it may deem conducive to public good.

The *Perkins* decision upheld New York's inheritance tax against a federal constitutional challenge.—EDS.

I

Towards the end of the 19th century, Congress enacted a series of land Acts which divided the communal reservations of Indian tribes into individual allotments for Indians and unallotted lands for non-Indian settlement. This legislation seems to have been in part animated by a desire to force Indians to abandon their nomadic ways in order to "speed the Indians' assimilation into American society," Solem v. Bartlett, 465 U.S. 463, 466 (1984), and in part a result of pressure to free new lands for further white settlement. Ibid. Two years after the enactment of the General Allotment Act of 1887, ch. 119, 24 Stat. 388, Congress adopted a specific statute authorizing the division of the Great Reservation of the Sioux Nation into separate reservations and the allotment of specific tracts of reservation land to individual Indians, conditioned on the consent of three-fourths of the adult male Sioux. Act of Mar. 2, 1889, ch. 405, 25 Stat. 888. Under the Act, each male Sioux head of household took 320 acres of land and most other individuals 160 acres. 25 Stat. 890. In order to protect the allottees from the improvident disposition of their lands to white settlers, the Sioux allotment statute provided that the allotted lands were to be held in trust by the United States. Id., at 891. Until 1910, the lands of deceased allottees passed to their heirs "according to the laws of the State or Territory" where the land was located, ibid., and after 1910, allottees were permitted to dispose of their interests by will in accordance with regulations promulgated by the Secretary of the Interior. 36 Stat. 856, 25 U.S.C. § 373. Those regulations generally served to protect Indian ownership of the allotted lands.

The policy of allotment of Indian lands quickly proved disastrous for the Indians. Cash generated by land sales to whites was quickly dissipated, and the Indians, rather than farming the land themselves, evolved into petty landlords, leasing their allotted lands to white ranchers and farmers and living off the meager rentals. . . . The failure of the allotment program became even clearer as successive generations came to hold the allotted lands. Thus 40–, 80–, and 160–acre parcels became splintered into multiple undivided interests in land, with some parcels having hundreds, and many parcels having dozens, of owners. Because the land was held in trust and often could not be alienated or partitioned, the fractionation problem grew and grew over time.

A 1928 report commissioned by the Congress found the situation administratively unworkable and economically wasteful. . . . Good, potentially productive, land was allowed to lie fallow, amidst great poverty, because of the difficulties of managing property held in this manner. . . . In discussing the Indian Reorganization Act of 1934, Representative Howard said:

It is in the case of the inherited allotments, however, that the administrative costs become incredible. . . . On allotted reservations, numerous cases exist where the shares of each individual heir from lease money may be 1 cent a month. Or one heir may own minute fractional shares in 30 or 40 different allotments. The cost of leasing, bookkeeping, and distributing the proceeds in many cases far exceeds the total income. The Indians and the Indian Service personnel are thus trapped in a meaningless system of minute partition in which all thought of the possible use of land to satisfy human needs is lost in a mathematical haze of bookkeeping.

78 Cong. Rec. 11728 (1934). In 1934, in response to arguments such as these, the Congress acknowledged the failure of its policy and ended further allotment of Indian lands. Indian Reorganization Act of 1934, ch. 576, 48 Stat. 984, 25 U.S.C. § 461 et seq.

But the end of future allotment by itself could not prevent the further compounding of the existing problem caused by the passage of time. Ownership continued to fragment as succeeding generations came to hold the property, since, in the order of things, each property owner was apt to have more than one heir. In 1960, both the House and the Senate undertook comprehensive studies of the problem. . . . These studies indicated that one-half of the approximately 12 million acres of allotted trust lands were held in fractionated ownership, with over 3 million acres held by more than six heirs to a parcel. . . . Further hearings were held in 1966, . . . but not until the Indian Land Consolidation Act of 1983 did the Congress take action to ameliorate the problem of fractionated ownership of Indian lands.

Section 207 of the Indian Land Consolidation Act—the escheat provision at issue in this case—provided:

No undivided fractional interest in any tract of trust or restricted land within a tribe's reservation or otherwise subjected to a tribe's jurisdiction shall descedent [sic] by intestacy or devise but shall escheat to that tribe if such interest represents 2 per centum or less of the total acreage in such tract and has earned to its owner less than $100 in the preceding year before it is due to escheat.

96 Stat. 2519. Congress made no provision for the payment of compensation to the owners of the interests covered by § 207. The statute was signed into law on January 12, 1983, and became effective immediately.

The three appellees—Mary Irving, Patrick Pumpkin Seed, and Eileen Bissonette—are enrolled members of the Oglala Sioux Tribe. They are, or represent, heirs or devisees of members of the Tribe who died in March, April, and June 1983. Eileen Bissonette's decedent, Mary Poor Bear–

Little Hoop Cross, purported to will all her property, including property subject to § 207, to her five minor children in whose name Bissonette claims the property. Chester Irving, Charles Leroy Pumpkin Seed, and Edgar Pumpkin Seed all died intestate. At the time of their deaths, the four decedents owned 41 fractional interests subject to the provisions of § 207. . . . The Irving estate lost two interests whose value together was approximately $100; the Bureau of Indian Affairs placed total values of approximately $2,700 on the 26 escheatable interests in the Cross estate and $1,816 on the 13 escheatable interests in the Pumpkin Seed estates. But for § 207, this property would have passed, in the ordinary course, to appellees or those they represent.

Appellees filed suit in the United States District Court for the District of South Dakota, claiming that § 207 resulted in a taking of property without just compensation in violation of the Fifth Amendment. The District Court concluded that the statute was constitutional. It held that appellees had no vested interest in the property of the decedents prior to their deaths and that Congress had plenary authority to abolish the power of testamentary disposition of Indian property and to alter the rules of intestate succession. . . .

The Court of Appeals for the Eighth Circuit reversed. Irving v. Clark, 758 F.2d 1260 (1985). Although it agreed that appellees had no vested rights in the decedents' property, it concluded that their decedents had a right, derived from the original Sioux allotment statute, to control disposition of their property at death. The Court of Appeals held that appellees had standing to invoke that right and that the taking of that right without compensation to decedents' estates violated the Fifth Amendment.[3]

II

[In an omitted portion of the opinion, the Court held that appellees had standing to assert the deceased owners' Fifth Amendment rights, noting that the Secretary of the Interior, who normally would act as the decedents' executor or administrator, could not be expected to challenge the constitutionality of a statute that he was responsible for administering.]

III

The Congress, acting pursuant to its broad authority to regulate the descent and devise of Indian trust lands, Jefferson v. Fink, 247 U.S. 288,

---

[3]The Court of Appeals, without explanation, went on to "declare" that not only the original version of § 207, but also the amended version not before it, 25 U.S.C. § 2206 (1982 ed., Supp. III), unconstitutionally took property without compensation. Since none of the property which escheated in this case did so pursuant to the amended version of the statute, this "declaration" is, at best, dicta. We express no opinion on the constitutionality of § 207 as amended.

294 (1918), enacted § 207 as a means of ameliorating, over time, the problem of extreme fractionation of certain Indian lands. By forbidding the passing on at death of small, undivided interests in Indian lands, Congress hoped that future generations of Indians would be able to make more productive use of the Indians' ancestral lands. We agree with the Government that encouraging the consolidation of Indian lands is a public purpose of high order. The fractionation problem on Indian reservations is extraordinary and may call for dramatic action to encourage consolidation. The Sisseton–Wahpeton Sioux Tribe, appearing as amicus curiae in support of the Secretary of the Interior, is a quintessential victim of fractionation. Forty-acre tracts on the Sisseton–Wahpeton Lake Traverse Reservation, leasing for about $1,000 annually, are commonly subdivided into hundreds of undivided interests, many of which generate only pennies a year in rent. The average tract has 196 owners and the average owner undivided interests in 14 tracts. The administrative headache this represents can be fathomed by examining Tract 1305, dubbed "one of the most fractionated parcels of land in the world." Lawson, Heirship: The Indian Amoeba, reprinted in Hearing on S. 2480 and S. 2663 before the Senate Select Committee on Indian Affairs, 98th Cong., 2d Sess., 85 (1984). Tract 1305 is 40 acres and produces $1,080 in income annually. It is valued at $8,000. It has 439 owners, one-third of whom receive less than $.05 in annual rent and two-thirds of whom receive less than $1. The largest interest holder receives $82.85 annually. The common denominator used to compute fractional interests in the property is 3,394,923,840,000. The smallest heir receives $.01 every 177 years. If the tract were sold (assuming the 439 owners could agree) for its estimated $8,000 value, he would be entitled to $.000418. The administrative costs of handling this tract are estimated by the Bureau of Indian Affairs at $17,560 annually. Id., at 86, 87. . . .

This Court has held that the Government has considerable latitude in regulating property rights in ways that may adversely affect the owners. See Keystone Bituminous Coal Assn. v. DeBenedictis, 480 U.S. 470, 491–492 (1987); Penn Central Transportation Co. v. New York City, 438 U.S. 104, 125–127 (1978); Goldblatt v. Hempstead, 369 U.S. 590, 592–593 (1962). The framework for examining the question whether a regulation of property amounts to a taking requiring just compensation is firmly established and has been regularly and recently reaffirmed. See, e.g., Keystone Bituminous Coal Assn. v. DeBenedictis, supra, at 485; Ruckelshaus v. Monsanto Co., 467 U.S. 986, 1004–1005 (1984); Hodel v. Virginia Surface Mining and Reclamation Assn., Inc., 452 U.S. 264, 295 (1981); Agins v. Tiburon, 447 U.S. 255, 260–261 (1980); Kaiser Aetna v. United States, 444 U.S. 164, 174–175 (1979); Penn Central Transportation Co. v. New York City, supra, at 124. As the Chief Justice has written:

[T]his Court has generally "been unable to develop any 'set formula' for determining when 'justice and fairness' require that economic injuries caused by public action be compensated by the government, rather than remain disproportionately concentrated on a few persons." [Penn Central Transportation Co. v. New York City, 438 U.S.], at 124. Rather, it has examined the "taking" question by engaging in essentially ad hoc, factual inquiries that have identified several factors—such as the economic impact of the regulation, its interference with reasonable investment backed expectations, and the character of the governmental action—that have particular significance. Ibid. [Kaiser Aetna v. United States, supra, at 175.]

There is no question that the relative economic impact of § 207 upon the owners of these property rights can be substantial. Section 207 provides for the escheat of small undivided property interests that are unproductive during the year preceding the owner's death. Even if we accept the Government's assertion that the income generated by such parcels may be properly thought of as de minimis, their value may not be. While the Irving estate lost two interests whose value together was only approximately $100, the Bureau of Indian Affairs placed total values of approximately $2,700 and $1,816 on the escheatable interests in the Cross and Pumpkin Seed estates. . . . These are not trivial sums. . . . Of course, the whole of appellees' decedents' property interests were not taken by § 207. Appellees' decedents retained full beneficial use of the property during their lifetimes as well as the right to convey it inter vivos. There is no question, however, that the right to pass on valuable property to one's heirs is itself a valuable right. Depending on the age of the owner, much or most of the value of the parcel may inhere in this "remainder" interest. See 26 CFR § 20.2031–7(f) (Table A) (1986) (value of remainder interest when life tenant is age 65 is approximately 32% of the whole).

The extent to which any of appellees' decedents had "investment-backed expectations" in passing on the property is dubious. Though it is conceivable that some of these interests were purchased with the expectation that the owners might pass on the remainder to their heirs at death, the property has been held in trust for the Indians for 100 years and is overwhelmingly acquired by gift, descent, or devise. Because of the highly fractionated ownership, the property is generally held for lease rather than improved and used by the owners. None of the appellees here can point to any specific investment-backed expectations beyond the fact that their ancestors agreed to accept allotment only after ceding to the United States large parts of the original Great Sioux Reservation.

Also weighing weakly in favor of the statute is the fact that there is something of an "average reciprocity of advantage," Pennsylvania Coal Co. v. Mahon, 260 U.S. 393, 415 (1922), to the extent that owners of escheatable interests maintain a nexus to the Tribe. Consolidation of Indian lands in the Tribe benefits the members of the Tribe. All members do not own escheatable interests, nor do all owners belong to the Tribe. Nevertheless, there is substantial overlap between the two groups. The owners of escheatable interests often benefit from the escheat of others' fractional interests. Moreover, the whole benefit gained is greater than the sum of the burdens imposed since consolidated lands are more productive than fractionated lands.

If we were to stop our analysis at this point, we might well find § 207 constitutional. But the character of the Government regulation here is extraordinary. In Kaiser Aetna v. United States, 444 U.S., at 176, we emphasized that the regulation destroyed "one of the most essential sticks in the bundle of rights that are commonly characterized as property—the right to exclude others." Similarly, the regulation here amounts to virtually the abrogation of the right to pass on a certain type of property— the small undivided interest—to one's heirs. In one form or another, the right to pass on property—to one's family in particular—has been part of the Anglo–American legal system since feudal times. See United States v. Perkins, 163 U.S. 625, 627–628 (1896). The fact that it may be possible for the owners of these interests to effectively control disposition upon death through complex inter vivos transactions such as revocable trusts is simply not an adequate substitute for the rights taken, given the nature of the property. Even the United States concedes that total abrogation of the right to pass property is unprecedented and likely unconstitutional. . . . Moreover, this statute effectively abolishes both descent and devise of these property interests even when the passing of the property to the heir might result in consolidation of property—as for instance when the heir already owns another undivided interest in the property. Cf. 25 U.S.C. § 2206(b) (1982 ed., Supp. III). Since the escheatable interests are not, as the United States argues, necessarily de minimis, nor, as it also argues, does the availability of inter vivos transfer obviate the need for descent and devise, a *total* abrogation of these rights cannot be upheld. But cf. Andrus v. Allard, 444 U.S. 51 (1979) (upholding abrogation of the right to sell endangered eagles' parts as necessary to environmental protection regulatory scheme).

In holding that complete abolition of both the descent and devise of a particular class of property may be a taking, we reaffirm the continuing vitality of the long line of cases recognizing the States', and where appropriate, the United States', broad authority to adjust the rules governing the descent and devise of property without implicating the guarantees of the Just Compensation Clause. See, e.g., Irving Trust Co. v. Day, 314 U.S. 556, 562 (1942); Jefferson v. Fink, 247 U.S., at 294. The difference in this case is the fact that both descent and devise are completely abolished; indeed they are abolished even in circumstances when the governmental purpose sought to be advanced, consolidation of ownership of Indian lands, does not conflict with the further descent of the property.

There is little doubt that the extreme fractionation of Indian lands is a serious public problem. It may well be appropriate for the United States to ameliorate fractionation by means of regulating the descent and devise of Indian lands. Surely it is permissible for the United States to prevent the owners of such interests from further subdividing them among future heirs on pain of escheat. See Texaco, Inc. v. Short, 454 U.S. 516, 542 (1982) (Brennan, J., dissenting). It may be appropriate to minimize further compounding of the problem by abolishing the descent of such interests by rules of intestacy, thereby forcing the owners to formally designate an heir to prevent escheat to the Tribe. What is certainly not appropriate is to take the extraordinary step of abolishing both descent and devise of these property interests even when the passing of the property to the heir might result in consolidation of property. Accordingly, we find that this regulation, in the words of Justice Holmes, "goes too far." Pennsylvania Coal Co. v. Mahon, 260 U.S., at 415. The judgment of the Court of Appeals is

Affirmed.

[Justice O'Connor's opinion was joined by Chief Justice Rehnquist and Justices Brennan, Marshall, Blackmun, Powell, and Scalia. The separate concurring opinions of Justices Brennan (joined by Justices Marshall and Blackmun), Scalia (joined by Chief Justice Rehnquist and Justice Powell), and Stevens (joined by Justice White) are omitted.]

NOTES

1. *Constitutional restrictions.* In Hodel v. Irving, the Supreme Court struck down the original version of the tribal escheat provision of the Indian Land Consolidation Act as an unconstitutional taking of property. Precisely which property rights were abrogated? Presumably Congress could seek to avoid the constitutional problem by offering to pay compensation to the property owners whose rights were abrogated. If Congress chose this course, who would be entitled to receive compensation, and how should the amount of compensation be measured? What is the fair market value of the right to dispose of specific property at death by will or intestacy? Why is an inter vivos arrangement such as a revocable trust "simply not an adequate substitute for the rights taken"?

The Court insists that it "reaffirm[s] the continuing vitality of the long line of cases recognizing [the legislature's] broad authority to adjust the rules governing the descent and devise of property." Do you agree? In Andrus v. Allard, 444 U.S. 51 (1979), the Court upheld a federal statute prohibiting the sale of feathers and other parts taken from eagles, in furtherance of a regulatory scheme aimed at protecting the environment. For purposes of constitutional analysis, what is the difference between a statute prohibiting the sale of eagle parts and one prohibiting the deathtime transfer of small undivided fractional interests in land? Compare the concurring opinions in *Irving* of Justice Scalia (finding the statute in *Irving* "indistinguishable" from the statute in *Allard* "insofar as concerns the balance between rights taken and rights left untouched," and concluding that *Irving* "effectively limits *Allard* to its facts") and Justice Brennan (finding "nothing in [*Irving*] that would limit [*Allard*] to its facts").

2. *Subsequent developments.* In 1984, while the *Irving* case was pending before the Eighth Circuit, Congress amended § 207 of the Indian Land Consolidation Act to require escheat of an undivided fractional interest in land only if "such interest represents 2 per centum or less of the total acreage in such tract and is incapable of earning $100 in any one of the five years from the date of decedent's death." The amended statute raised a rebuttable presumption that an interest which had earned less than $100 in any one of the five years before the decedent's death was incapable of earning $100 after death. The amended statute also contained an exception which permitted the devise of an otherwise escheatable interest "to any other owner of an undivided fractional interest" in the same parcel or tract. In Babbitt v. Youpee, 519 U.S. 234 (1997), the Supreme Court held that the 1984 amendments did not cure the constitutional defect of the original statute. In *Youpee* the owner of several undivided fractional interests in land devised each of them to a single descendant, thereby perpetuating (but neither ameliorating nor exacerbating) the existing degree of fractionation. Noting that the "very limited group" of permissible devisees was unlikely to include any of the owner's descendants, the Supreme Court concluded that the statute "severely restrict[ed] the right of an individual to direct the descent of his property" even where the attempted disposition did not undermine the governmental purpose of consolidation.

Section 207 has been amended several times following the decisions in *Irving* and *Youpee*. The current version of the statute, codified at 25 U.S.C. § 2206, generally allows the owner of any interest in trust or restricted land to devise it by will to specified beneficiaries, including the testator's lineal descendants, holders of undivided interests in the same parcel, and individual Indians. A devise to two or more persons is presumed to create a joint tenancy with right of survivorship. In the absence of a will, the land passes by intestacy to the decedent's surviving spouse for life, with remainder to the decedent's lineal descendants, parents, or siblings. If the decedent's interest amounts to less than 5 percent of the entire parcel, a special "single heir" rule further limits intestate succession (after the surviving spouse's life estate) to the decedent's oldest surviving child, grandchild or great-grandchild. The statute further directs the Secretary of the Interior to provide "estate planning assistance" to Indian landowners in order to "increase the use of wills and other methods of devise" and "reduce the quantity and complexity of Indian estates that pass intestate through the probate process." Does § 207 in its current form satisfy the constitutional test announced in *Irving* and *Youpee*?

Does the statute effectively address the problem of fractionated Indian land ownership?

2. PUBLIC POLICY AND THE DEAD HAND

Some testators, motivated perhaps by thoughts of immortality, go to great lengths to control the use and enjoyment of property for many years after death. Trust instruments often include detailed conditions and restrictions reflecting the settlor's whims and preferences which may remain in force for several generations. The principle of testamentary freedom allows great latitude in such dispositions, regardless of their wisdom, fairness, or social utility. Nevertheless, over many years the law has developed several constraints on the duration and extent of "dead hand" control.

a. Duration

One important limitation on the testator's power to control property after death is the Rule Against Perpetuities, which evolved through centuries of struggle. The classic statement of the common law Rule was formulated by John Chipman Gray in a single sentence: "No interest is good unless it must vest, if at all, not later than twenty-one years after some life in being at the creation of the interest." Gray § 201. Roughly speaking, the Rule permits a testator to tie up property for up to twenty-one years after the death of persons living at the time of his or her death—a period which can easily extend for 100 years or more. Behind this simple idea lurks a formidable tangle of conflicting interpretations, opinions and exceptions. No attempt is made here to explore the operation of the Rule; detailed discussion is reserved for Chapter 9.

Most modern commentators agree that the traditional common law Rule leaves much to be desired, but there is a sharp divergence of opinion concerning how to give effect to the Rule's underlying policies. Indeed, identifying and articulating a coherent policy justification for the Rule is by no means an easy task. The Rule is sometimes viewed as promoting free alienability of property by preventing the creation of contingent future interests that might vest remotely. In modern life, however, this explanation is hardly convincing, since most future interests are equitable interests held by trust beneficiaries which do not impair the trustee's power to sell the trust property. Furthermore, while the Rule is sometimes defended as a measure to combat undue concentrations of wealth, it does not seem to have been especially effective in this regard. Writing in 1952, W. Barton Leach suggested that in the absence of a Rule against Perpetuities "it seems unlikely that there would be a clamor for such a rule either in the legislatures or in the courts." Although he saw no harm in continuing the Rule to restrain the occasional excesses of testators with dynastic aspirations, he urged that the Rule should be limited so as not to disrupt the "prudent dispositions of reasonable men." Leach, Perpetuities in Perspective: Ending the Rule's Reign of Terror, 65 Harv. L. Rev. 721, 727 (1952).

In a series of lectures delivered in 1955, Lewis M. Simes offered two contemporary policy justifications for the Rule:

> First, the Rule against Perpetuities strikes a fair balance between the desires of members of the present generation, and similar desires of succeeding generations, to do what they wish with the property which they enjoy. . . . [O]ne of the most common human wants is the desire to distribute one's property at death without restriction in whatever manner he desires. Indeed, we can go farther, and say that there is a policy in favor of permitting people to create future interests by will, as well as present interests, because that also accords with human desires. The difficulty here is that, if we give free rein to the desires of one generation to create future interests, the members of succeeding generations will receive the property in a restricted state. They will thus be unable to create all the future interests they wish. Perhaps, they may not even be able to devise it at all. Hence, to come most nearly to satisfying the desires of peoples of all generations, we must strike a fair balance between unrestricted testamentary disposition of property by the present generation and unrestricted disposition by future generations. In a sense this is a policy of alienability, but it is not alienability for productivity. It is alienability to enable people to do what they please at death with the property which they enjoy in life. As Kohler says in his treatise on the Philosophy of Law: "The far-reaching hand of a testator who would enforce his will in distant future generations destroys the liberty of other individuals, and presumes to make rules for distant times."
>
> But, in my opinion, a second and even more important reason for the Rule is this. It is socially desirable that the wealth of the world be controlled by its living members and not by the dead. I know of no better statement of that doctrine than the language of Thomas Jefferson, contained in a letter to James Madison, when he said: "The earth belongs always to the living generation. They may manage it then, and what proceeds from it, as they please during their usufruct." Sidgwick, in his *Elements of Politics*, also discusses the problem in the following words: " . . . it rather follows from the fundamental assumption of individualism, that any such posthumous restraint on the use of bequeathed wealth will tend to make it less useful to the living, as it will interfere with their freedom in dealing with it. Individualism, in short, is in a dilemma. . . . Of this difficulty, there

is, I think, no general theoretical solution: it can only be reduced by some practical compromise."

Simes, Public Policy and the Dead Hand 58–60 (1955). On the historical development of the Rule, see Haskins, Extending the Grasp of the Dead Hand: Reflections on the Origins of the Rule Against Perpetuities, 126 U. Pa. L. Rev. 19 (1977) (arguing that the Rule represented a "clear victory for the 'dead hand,' not for free alienability"); Haskins, "Inconvenience" and the Rule for Perpetuities, 48 Mo. L. Rev. 451 (1983).

More recently, the underlying policy justifications and continued viability of the Rule have increasingly come into question, and many states have enacted statutes repealing or significantly curtailing the Rule. See Hirsch & Wang, A Qualitative Theory of the Dead Hand, 68 Ind. L.J. 1 (1992) (discussing different types of restrictions on use, investment, and distribution, and arguing that "[a]s a matter of public policy, lawmakers should consider not only for how long but also in what ways a testator proposes to control property after her death"); Dobris, The Death of the Rule Against Perpetuities, or the RAP Has No Friends—An Essay, 35 Real Prop. Prob. & Tr. J. 601 (2000) (discussing popular attitudes toward wealth, inheritance and long-term trusts); Gallanis, The Rule Against Perpetuities and the Law Commission's Flawed Philosophy, 59 Camb. L.J. 284 (2000) (concluding that "the Rule cannot be supported by abstract concepts, such as liberty, equality, or property rights, because the Rule embodies a compromise among these abstractions").

NOTE

Political accountability. Reconciling the rights of successive generations also raises fundamental questions of political accountability and fiscal responsibility. For example, running up annual deficits to finance current spending may be popular with today's voters and their elected representatives, but the burden of paying the accumulated debt, with interest, will ultimately fall on future taxpayers. In a letter to James Madison dated September 6, 1789, Thomas Jefferson argued that no generation should be obligated to repay debts incurred by previous generations:

> I set out on this ground, which I suppose to be self evident, *"that the earth belongs in usufruct to the living"*: that the dead have neither powers nor rights over it. The portion occupied by an individual ceases to be his when himself ceases to be, and reverts to the society. If the society has formed no rules for the appropriation of it's lands in severalty, it will be taken by the first occupants. These will generally be the wife and children of the decedent. If they have formed rules of appropriation, those rules may give it to the wife and children, or to some one of them, or to the legatee of the deceased. So they may give it to his creditor. But the child, the legatee, or creditor takes it, not by any natural right, but

by a law of the society of which they are members, and to which they are subject. Then no man can, by *natural right*, oblige the lands he occupied, or the persons who succeed him in that occupation, to the paiment of debts contracted by him. For if he could, he might, during his own life, eat up the usufruct of the lands for several generations to come, and then the lands would belong to the dead, and not to the living, which would be the reverse of our principle. [15 Papers of Thomas Jefferson 392–93 (Boyd ed., 1958).]

Thomas Paine went even further. In The Rights of Man, published in 1791, he argued that no government or generation has "the right or the power of binding and controlling posterity to the '*end of time*,' or of commanding forever how the world shall be governed, or who shall govern it":

> Every age and generation must be as free to act for itself, *in all cases*, as the ages and generation which preceded it. The vanity and presumption of governing beyond the grave, is the most ridiculous and insolent of all tyrannies. . . .

> Every generation is, and must be, competent to all the purposes which its occasions require. It is the living, and not the dead, that are to be accommodated. When man ceases to be, his power and his wants cease with him; and having no longer any participation in the concerns of this world, he has no longer any authority in directing who shall be its governors, or how its government shall be organized, or how administered. [1 Complete Writings of Thomas Paine 243, 251 (Foner ed., Citadel Press 1945).]

b. Conditions

In general, courts uphold testamentary conditions and limitations which are designed to induce a beneficiary to engage in (or refrain from) specified behavior. For example, a testator may leave a bequest to a child on condition that the child attend college, get married, or refrain from smoking and drinking. Although such conditions may strike the child as burdensome and intrusive, the testator has considerable freedom to attach strings to his or her bounty or to withhold it altogether. Accordingly, the child faces a choice between accepting the bequest with strings attached and forgoing the bequest. Nevertheless, courts are not required to enforce a condition that violates some rule of law or public policy.

UNITED STATES NATIONAL BANK OF PORTLAND V. SNODGRASS

Supreme Court of Oregon, 1954.
202 Or. 530, 275 P.2d 860.

WARNER, JUSTICE.

The United States National Bank of Portland (Oregon) in its capacity as trustee under the last will and testament of C.A. Rinehart, deceased, brings this suit against Merle Rinehart Snodgrass, the decedent's married daughter and sole heir, and 17 other defendants who are relatives and contingent beneficiaries of C.A. Rinehart. Plaintiff prays for a declaratory judgment establishing the validity and correct interpretation of the trusts set up by the testament and the rights, if any, of the defendants as beneficiaries thereunder.

On May 31, 1929, at a time when his daughter Merle was about 10 years old, Mr. Rinehart executed the instrument now before us for construction. [Paragraph 7 of the will established a fund to be held in trust for the benefit of the testator's daughter, who was to receive distributions from net income as follows: $50 each month until she reached age 18, then $75 each month until she reached age 25, then the entire net income until she reached age 32. The remaining funds held in trust were to be distributed to the daughter at age 32, "provided she shall have proved conclusively to my trustee and to its entire satisfaction that she has not embraced, nor become a member of, the Catholic faith nor ever married to a man of such faith." If before reaching age 32 the daughter died or became ineligible to receive the trust fund, the will named several other relatives of the testator as contingent beneficiaries.]

The testator died in January 1932. It was stipulated that his daughter Merle became 32 years old on May 18, 1951; that sometime in 1944 she married a man who was a member of the Catholic faith; and that at the time she knew of the provisions of the foregoing paragraph 7 of her father's will.

The lower court concluded that the conditions of the bequest to the defendant Merle Rinehart Snodgrass, declaring a forfeiture of her rights in the corpus of the trust if she married a Catholic before her 32nd birthday, were valid and binding upon her and so decreed. The court then proceeded to declare and determine the respective interests of the various defendants who were contingent beneficiaries, succeeding by reason of the forfeiture of Mrs. Snodgrass' gift in her father's estate. From this decree the defendant daughter alone appeals.

The appellant asserts that the court erred in holding as valid that provision of the will which disinherited her because of her marriage to a member of the Catholic faith before she was 32 years old. She leans heavily upon the proposition that such a provision violates public policy.

Mrs. Snodgrass did not join the Catholic church and therefore the clause restraining membership in that faith is not before us. Her loss, if any, accrues by reason of the restriction on her marriage to a Catholic within the time limitation. If the provision is valid, then the defendants-respondents take the entire corpus of the trust set up in the contested paragraph 7, and testator's daughter takes nothing.

The problem here is one of the validity of testamentary restraints upon marriage. While there is an abundance of law on the subject from other jurisdictions, the question and its solution are one of first impression in this court.

The briefs of both parties and some of their citations unavoidably employ various words and phrases which bring into focus the presence of religious prejudice which apparently dictated the contents of the paragraph occasioning this appeal. There we find, among other significant phrases, references to "religious tolerance," "religious freedom" and the "bigotry reflected by the will." No one will venture to gainsay that the father and his daughter in adulthood had entertained antipodal beliefs in the area of religious thought and faith. Indeed, it was the militant hostility of the father to the religion of Mrs. Snodgrass' husband that kindled the flames of the controversy from which this appeal arises.

Litigation springing from religious differences, tincturing, as here, every part and parcel of this appeal, tenders to any court problems of an extremely delicate nature. This very delicacy, together with the novelty of the legal questions in this jurisdiction, warrants pausing before proceeding further and re-orienting our thinking in terms of the real legal problem which we must resolve. As a first step we rid ourselves of some erroneous definitions and the smug acceptance of conclusions arising from the too-frequent and inept employment of such terms as "religious freedom," "religious intolerance" and "religious bigotry." We also disassociate ourselves from the erstwhile disposition of many persons to treat any opposition to a religious faith as a prima facie manifestation of religious bigotry, requiring legal condemnation.

The testamentary pattern of Mr. Rinehart may offend the sense of fair play of some in what appears as an ungracious and determined effort to bend the will of another to an acceptance of the testator's concept of the superiority of his own viewpoint.

In terms of common parlance, "bigotry" and its concomitant "intolerance" are ordinarily odious and socially distasteful. They usually connote some intrusion upon or a variance with our traditional thoughts on religious liberty and religious tolerance; but we find nothing in the law declaring religious bigotry or intolerance to be mala in se. It is not until actions motivated by the intolerant extremes of bigotry contravene the positive law or invade the boundaries of established public policy that the law is quickened to repress such illegal excesses and in proper cases levy toll upon the offenders as reparation to those who have been damaged thereby. It is the quality of the act or expression of the bigot—not one's bigotry—which determines the necessity, if any, for legal interposition.

The appellation "bigot" is therefore a word of social opprobrium, not one of legal condemnation. It can be, and often is, applied with equal force and propriety both to the proponents and opponents of a given thesis of public or religious interest, depending on the degree of their respective uncompromising and dogmatic assertions in the espousal of their several divergent views.

While one may personally and loudly condemn a species of "intolerance" as socially outrageous, a court on the other hand must guard against being judicially intolerant of such an "intolerance," unless the court can say the act of intolerance is in a form not sanctioned by the law. We are mindful that there are many places where a bigot may safely express himself and manifest his intolerance of the viewpoint of others without fear of legal restraint or punishment. With certain limitations, one of those areas with a wide latitude of sufferance is found in the construction of the pattern of one's last will and testament. It is a field wherein neither this court nor any other court will question the correctness of a testator's religious views or prejudices. . . .

Our exalted religious freedom is buttressed by another freedom of coordinate importance. In condemning what may appear to one as words of offensive religious intolerance, we must not forget that the offending expression may enjoy the protection of another public policy—the freedom of speech.

The right to espouse any religious faith or any political cause short of one dedicated to the overthrow of the government by force carries with it the cognate right to engage as its champion in the proselytization of followers or converts to the favored cause or faith. To that end its disciples are free to emphasize and teach what is believed by them to be its superior and self-evident truths and to point out and warn others against what its votaries deem to be the inferior, fallacious or dangerous philosophical content of opposing faiths or doctrines. No matter how specious, how intolerant, how narrow and no matter how prejudiced or how dogmatic the arguments of the devotees of one belief may appear to others of different persuasion, the right of either to so express himself is so emphatically a part and parcel of our public policy that it will be defended and protected by the courts of the land to the uttermost, unless it is found that the fanatical and unrestrained enthusiasm of its followers results in acts offensive to the positive law.

It is this unique right to freedom of expression, whether manifested in the political forum, the church chancel or other arenas of thought and action, that has not only contributed so much to the greatness of our country and has given it such a distinctive and distinguished place in the world family of nations but has given additional vitality and substance to our valued religious freedom.

If we will take heed of these findings, we can better appreciate and more readily understand why the great majority of the courts have sustained rather than repudiated gifts limited by conditions such as Mr. Rinehart attached to his bequest to his daughter.

We therefore have no intention or disposition to disturb the provisions of Mr. Rinehart's will unless it can be demonstrated that they do violence to some legal rule or precept. Two general and cardinal propositions give direction and limitation to our consideration. One is the traditionally great freedom that the law confers on the individual with respect to the disposition of his property, both before and after death. The other is that greater freedom, the freedom of opinion and right to expression in political and religious matters, together with the incidental and corollary right to implement the attainment of the ultimate and favored objectives of the religious teaching and social or political philosophy to which an individual subscribes. We do not intend to imply hereby that the right to devise or bequeath property is in any way dependent upon or related to the constitutional guarantees of freedom of speech.

We will first give attention to appellant's claim that the provision for Mrs. Snodgrass is at odds with the public policy of both the state and national governments. . . .

As we shall soon discover, there is nothing in our organic or statutory law or in prior decisions of this court which would strike down or limit a testamentary expression in the form that Mr. Rinehart elected to use in providing for his daughter.

Although the appellant rests her appeal primarily upon the premise that paragraph 7 of the will violates public policy, she brings to us no precise statute or judicial pronouncement in support of this contention; but before examining and demonstrating that the authorities cited by appellant are inapplicable, we think it is proper to observe here that it has long been a firmly-established policy in Oregon to give great latitude to a testator in the final disposition of his estate, notwithstanding that the right to make a testamentary disposition is not an inherent, natural or constitutional right but is purely a creation of statute and within legislative control. Leet v. Barr, 104 Or. 32, 39, 202 P. 414, 206 P. 548. This is supported by both statutory and judicial expression and points the way as an over-all direction to our own inquiry here.

As early as 1853 our legislature conferred upon every person of qualified age and sound mind the right to devise and bequeath all his estate, real and personal, saving such as is specially reserved by law to the decedent's spouse. ORS 114.020. This generous latitude in testamentary disposition conferred by statute is emphasized and expanded in the often-repeated statement of Mr. Justice Wolverton in Holman's Will, 1902, 42 Or. 345, 356, 70 P. 908, 913:

> The right of one's absolute domination over his property is sacred and inviolable, so that he may do what he will with his own, if it is not to the injury of another. He may bestow it whithersoever he will and upon whomsoever he pleases, and this without regard to natural or legitimate claims upon his bounty; and if there exists no defect of donative capacity, whereby his individual will or judgment does not have intelligent and conscious play in the bestowal, or undue influence or fraud, whereby an unconscionable advantage may be taken of him through the wicked designs of another, the law will give effect to the disposition; and the right to dispose of one's property by will, and bestow it upon whomsoever he likes, is a most valuable incident to ownership, and does not depend upon its judicious use. . . . And this court has held, in effect, that "while it seems harsh and cruel that a parent should disinherit one of his children and devise his property to others, or cut them all off and devise it to strangers, from some unworthy motive, *yet so long as that motive, whether from pride or aversion or spite or prejudice, is not resolvable into mental perversion, no court can interfere.*" . . . (Italics ours.)

Also see In re Estate of Hill, 198 Or. 307, 317, 256 P.2d 735, 739, and cases cited, where it is said that our previous holdings teach us that a "testator is invested by law with substantially all the rights he enjoyed in life to make unfettered disposition of his property."

No one has had the temerity to suggest that Mr. Rinehart in his lifetime could not have accomplished the equivalent of what he sought to accomplish by his will. It was within his power, with or without assigning any reason therefor, to have completely disinherited his daughter and left her in a state of impecunious circumstances. He could have gone even further and given all his fortune to some institution or persons with directions to propagandize his views adverse to any certain religion or creed for which he harbored antipathies.

In Magee v. O'Neill, 19 S.C. 170, 45 Am. Rep. 765, the bequest was on the condition that the beneficiary granddaughter be educated in the Roman Catholic faith. There the court said, 45 Am. Rep. 776:

> The power of disposition is general. The power to give includes the right to withhold or to fix the terms of gift, no matter how whimsical or capricious they may be, only provided they do not in any way violate the law. Mr. Magee, in his life-time, could have given money to educate his granddaughter at a particular school, or he could have

withheld it at his pleasure. Suppose he had entered into a covenant with Elizabeth or her mother, that if she was educated at a particular school named and under certain religious influences, he would, upon her attaining twenty-one years, pay to her five thousand dollars, we suppose that if she were not so educated, she could not go into the court and recover the money. Suppose, further, that before the time for payment arrived John Magee had died, would that strengthen her claim to recover the money against her [his] personal representatives? We are unable to see any material difference in regard to the necessity of complying with the terms imposed, between this supposed case and that of a voluntary gift by will.

While neither ORS 114.020 nor the *Holman* case affords a complete answer to the contentions of the plaintiff here, yet we submit that taken together they reveal a long-accepted pattern of public attitude and public policy in this state respecting an almost unrestricted right to dispose of one's property on death. In view of this liberality of testamentary power, we find no occasion to narrow the freedom of a testator's right to dispose of his accumulations unless we are compelled to bend before some other public law or policy establishing limitations not presently apparent.

To sustain the contention that the contested provision of the will is against the public policy of the United States, appellant depends upon the First and Fourteenth Amendments to the United States Constitution; 42 U.S.C.A. §§ 1981–1983, relating to civil rights (formerly, and as cited by appellant, 8 U.S.C.A. Ch. 3, §§ 41–43); and Shelley v. Kraemer, 334 U.S. 1, 68 S. Ct. 836, 92 L. Ed. 1161, 3 A.L.R.2d 441.

The First Amendment prohibits Congress from making any law respecting the establishment of a religion. Everson v. Board of Education, 330 U.S. 1, 15, 67 S. Ct. 504, 91 L. Ed. 711, 168 A.L.R. 1392. That amendment is a limitation upon the power of Congress. It has no effect upon the transactions of individual citizens and has been so interpreted. McIntire v. Wm. Penn Broadcasting Co. of Philadelphia, 151 F.2d 597, 601, certiorari denied 327 U.S. 779, 66 S. Ct. 530, 90 L. Ed. 1007; In re Kempf's Will, 252 App. Div. 28, 297 N.Y.S. 307, 312, affirmed 278 N.Y. 613, 16 N.E.2d 123. Neither does the Fourteenth Amendment relate to individual conduct. The strictures there found circumscribe state action in the particulars mentioned and in no way bear on a transaction of the character now before us. In re Civil Rights Cases, 1883, 109 U.S. 3, 3 S. Ct. 18, 27 L. Ed. 835.

Appellant presses upon our attention 42 U.S.C.A. § 1983 as embodying a statement of federal public policy controlling here. It reads:

Every person who, under color of any statute, ordinance, regulation, custom, or usage, of any State or Territory, subjects, or causes to be subjected, any citizen of the United States or other person within the jurisdiction thereof to the deprivation of any rights, privileges, or immunities secured by the Constitution and laws, shall be liable to the party injured in an action at law, suit in equity, or other proper proceeding for redress.

The inapplicability of this argument is demonstrated by Robeson v. Fanelli, D.C., 94 F. Supp. 62. . . . The court in the *Robeson* case said, at page 66: "In general, civil liberties are beyond the constitutional power of Congress to protect from encroachment by individuals unassociated with state action, inasmuch as the prohibitions of the Fourteenth Amendment with regard to due process, and equal protection are directed against the states exclusively. . . ."

Shelley v. Kraemer, supra, is authority only for the proposition that the enforcement by state courts of a covenant in a deed restricting the use and occupancy of real property to persons of the Caucasian race falls within the purview of the Fourteenth Amendment as a violation of the equal protection clause, but, said the court, "That Amendment [Fourteenth] erects no shield against merely private conduct, however discriminatory or wrongful." 334 U.S. 1, 68 S.Ct. 842, 3 A.L.R.2d 460. . . .

It is not clear to us from appellant's argument whether she reads the offending provision of the will as an invasion of her constitutional right to religious freedom or views it as an unconstitutional act of discrimination; but whether one or the other, we are content that it does no violence to public policy arising from either category. If the contested portion is to fall, it must be by force of some precept of public policy resting upon different grounds from those here urged by appellant.

We are not unmindful that even though no positive law can be found in Oregon limiting a testator as appellant would have us do here, we should, nevertheless, look into the decisions of the courts of other states to discover, if we can, the prevailing rule applied elsewhere when a testator attempts to limit or restrain the marriage of a beneficiary in the manner that the late C.A. Rinehart attempted to do.

The general rule seems to be well settled that conditions and limitations in partial restraint of marriage will be upheld if they do not unreasonably restrict the freedom of the beneficiary's choice. In 35 Am. Jur. 357–358, Marriage, § 256, we find:

> . . . where the restraint is not general, but is merely partial or temporary, or otherwise limited in effect, then the condition may or may not be void, according to whether it is considered reasonable or otherwise, and does not operate merely in terrorem. . . .

> Among the restrictions which have been held reasonable are: Conditions to marry or not to marry . . . a person of a particular . . . religion. . . .

Of the same tenor is 1 Restatement, Trusts, 194, § 62(g), reading, so far as pertinent:

> . . . such a provision is not invalid if it does not impose an undue restraint on marriage. Thus, a provision divesting the interest of the beneficiary if he or she should marry . . . a person of a particular religious faith or one of a different faith from that of the beneficiary, is not ordinarily invalid. . . .

We turn to an examination of the controverted provision and note that the condition is not one of complete restraint, in which character it might well be abhorrent to the law. It is merely partial and temporary. . . . Mr. Rinehart's daughter is not thereby restrained from ever marrying a Catholic. This inhibition as a condition to taking under the will at the age of 32 lasts only 11 years, that is, from the legal marriageable age without parental consent (in this state, 21 years). After the age of 32 she is free to marry a Catholic or become a Catholic if she so pleases and have her estate, too. Moreover, the condition imposed does not restrict the beneficiary from enjoying marital status either before or after attaining the age of 32. Here, unfortunately, appellant would eat her cake and have it, too. . . .

In In re Kempf's Will, supra, 297 N.Y.S. 307, 309, the testator made substantial gifts to his grandchildren payable when they became 21 years of age but made upon the condition that said children " 'shall be brought up and educated in the faith of and according to the Roman Catholic Religion,' " otherwise the provision to be void. In response to the argument seeking to invalidate the condition, the court says, 297 N.Y.S. at page 312:

> It is said that the condition violates the provisions of the Federal Constitution (First Amendment) and the State Constitution (article 1, § 3) which guarantee religious freedom. With this argument we do not agree. The purpose of the constitutional provisions which petitioner invokes was to protect all denominations by prohibiting the establishment under state sanction of any single form of religion which would deprive nonadherents to a church thus established of the right to worship according to the dictates of their own conscience. These constitutional guarantees of religious freedom are limitations upon the power of government, not upon the right of an individual to make such testamentary disposition of his property as he may desire provided always that positive law or public policy is not contravened. We find nothing in the condition here in question which deprives the pe-

titioner of freedom of conscience as to his religion; nor is it against public policy. Such an inducement by the testator, if it be so considered, to further the interests of his chosen religion and to perpetuate it within the circle of his family, can hardly be said to be a denial of religious freedom to those affected thereby. True it is that terms were annexed to the bequest which some might have found onerous, but they could have been declined from motives of conscience or for any other reason. If the petitioner could not in conscience accept the faith of his grandfather, knowing its demands, he could have renounced the legacy thus conditioned. Having chosen to make the petitioner an object of his bounty, the testator had the right to burden his gift with conditions. If those conditions are legal the petitioner cannot disregard the burden and successfully demand the bounty.

In Delaware Trust Co. v. Fitzmaurice, [27 Del. Ch. 101, 31 A.2d 383 (1943)], we find a will wherein the receipt of income from a testamentary trust created by decedent was made payable to Ruth M. Ogle " 'so long as she lives up to and observes and follows the teachings and faith of the Roman Catholic Church, and no longer.' " Here the court in upholding the provision . . . meets the contention of the beneficiary Ogle as follows, 31 A.2d 389:

> Ruth M. Ogle contends that such a condition, attached to a material gift, tends to induce fraud and hypocrisy, and tends to replace the real religious beliefs of a legatee by a mere pretended belief in other doctrines, with which she may have no real sympathy, and is, therefore, contrary to the moral wellbeing of the State, and an invalid restriction on her rights. Maddox v. Maddox's Adm'r, 11 Grat., Va., 804; 2 Page on Wills, 2nd Ed., 1920. Few courts have adopted that broad contention. . . .

The court held that Ruth M. Ogle was not entitled to the gift in question.

It will be observed that the condition of restraint imposed by the will construed in Delaware Trust Co. v. Fitzmaurice, supra, above quoted and in that case declared valid, is far more inclusive than the one in the will now before us in that the condition was operative during the entire life of the donee. In the instant matter, the restraint on free choice of religion became inoperative after the legatee became 32 years old.

So far as we are able to ascertain, only two states—Pennsylvania and Virginia—have invalidated testamentary provisions committing the beneficiary to adhere to the doctrines of a particular religion. This departure from the majority rule is reflected by Drace v. Klinedinst, 1922, 275 Pa. 266, 118 A. 907, 25 A.L.R. 1520; and Maddox v. Maddox's Adm'r, 1854, 11 Grat., Va., 804.

The appellant can garner no comfort from the Pennsylvania case wherein the testamentary provision is declared invalid on the basis of an entirely different theory from the one here present. It rests upon a state of facts wholly unlike those apparent in the instant matter. In the *Maddox* case the condition was that the testator's daughter should marry a member of the Society of Friends. There were only five or six marriageable males of that faith within the circle of her acquaintances, and under the circumstances peculiar to that case the court held that the condition was an unreasonable restraint on marriage. . . .

We conclude with a statement from Magee v. O'Neill, supra, 19 S.C. 170, 45 Am. Rep. 765, 776–777, substituting the name of the beneficiary here for the one named in the Magee will:

> We cannot say that the terms of this will so far exceed the license which is allowed the citizen in the disposition of his own property, as to render it void as against public policy. We do not understand that there was anything in this bequest which can be properly called coercion, or that [Merle Rinehart Snodgrass] was "deprived" of the liberty of conscience. Terms were attached to the bequest which may seem to us exacting, unkind and unnecessary, but we cannot say they were unlawful or that they were complied with. If they were declined from conscientious motives, far be it from us to say that such conduct was wrong; but from our view of the law, we are constrained to hold that the legacy . . . must go to those to whom, in the event which has happened, it was given by the will.

Affirmed. Neither party will recover costs.

Brand, J., dissents.

NOTES

1. *Conditions relating to marriage or religion.* A condition designed to induce a legatee to marry (or not marry) a person of a particular religious faith is ordinarily valid unless it imposes an unreasonable restriction on the legatee's opportunity to marry. See Shapira v. Union Nat'l Bank, 315 N.E.2d 825 (Ohio C.P. 1974) (bequest to son on condition that he marry "a Jewish girl whose both parents were Jewish" within seven years after testator's death); Restatement (Second) of Property (Donative Transfers) § 6.2 (1983). However, a condition designed to disrupt an existing family relationship may contravene public policy. See Estate of Romero, 847 P.2d 319 (N.M.App.1993) (gift of house in trust for two sons, on condition that their mother, testator's former wife, not live with them); Girard Trust Co. v. Schmitz, 20 A.2d 21 (N.J.Ch.1941) (bequest to testator's four siblings on condition that they have no contact with two other siblings); Restatement (Second) of Property (Donative Transfers) § 7.2 (1983).

In *Snodgrass*, suppose that at the time of the testator's death his daughter Merle is already engaged to marry a Catholic. Should the court strike down the condition on the ground that it is designed to induce the daughter to break off her impending marriage? See Turner v. Evans, 106 A. 617 (Md. 1919); In re Will of Seaman, 112 N.E. 576 (N.Y.1916). Alternatively, suppose that Merle defies her father's wishes by marrying a Catholic during her father's lifetime, and the father responds by leaving property in trust for Merle on condition that she marry a non-Catholic following the termination of her first marriage by death or divorce. Should the court uphold the condition? See Estate of Keffalas, 233 A.2d 248 (Pa. 1967). Note that the problem of dead hand control usually does not arise if a condition has already been satisfied (or broken) during a testator's lifetime and therefore cannot influence a beneficiary's future behavior. Thus, if Merle violated the condition in her father's will by marrying a Catholic before her father's death, presumably there would be no violation of public policy. See Estate of Feinberg, 919 N.E.2d 888 (Ill. 2009), cert. denied, 130 S.Ct. 3354 (2010) (settlor's widow appointed trust property at her death outright to descendants, excluding those who had married outside Jewish faith).

Suppose a testator leaves property in trust for his daughter on condition that she not marry without obtaining the consent of her cousin; if the daughter breaches the condition, her share of the trust property passes to the cousin. The daughter proposes to marry and seeks her cousin's consent but the cousin refuses, claiming that the marriage is unsuitable. If the daughter goes ahead and marries without her cousin's consent, should she lose her share of the trust property? See In re Liberman, 18 N.E.2d 658 (N.Y.1939) (holding condition void as unreasonable restraint on marriage; if enforced, its "natural tendency might be to induce the beneficiary to live in either celibacy or adultery").

Why should courts enforce testamentary conditions aimed at influencing a beneficiary's choice of spouse, career, or religious affiliation? Do such conditions really promote stable and harmonious family relationships, or do they represent an unwarranted exercise of dead hand control? The Restatement (Third) of Trusts observes that "society's interest in a property owner's freedom of disposition must be weighed against the risk of excessive influence on a personal decision significantly affecting the life of the beneficiary," and suggests that a testamentary condition may be invalid if it is "unreasonably intrusive into significant personal decisions or interests" or imposes "an unreasonable restraint on personal associations." Restatement (Third) of Trusts, § 29 cmt. *l* (2003). Might a court applying this standard find that the testator's disposition in *Snodgrass* unreasonably interfered with his daughter's freedom to marry by limiting her choice of a spouse? See id. cmt. j. Should a court enforce a condition that tends to restrain a beneficiary's religious freedom by offering a financial inducement to embrace or reject a particular religion? See id. cmt. k.

The enforceability of testamentary conditions concerning a beneficiary's choice of marital partner or religious observance remains controversial. One commentator describes such conditions as "posthumous meddling" and argues that they should not be enforced. See Sherman, Posthumous Meddling: An Instrumentalist Theory of Testamentary Restraints on Conjugal and Religious Choices, 1999 U. Ill. L.Rev. 1273. Other commentators find testamentary conditions less objectionable. See Scalise, Public Policy and Antisocial Testators, 32 Cardozo L.Rev. 1315 (2011) (endorsing presumption of enforceability based on a "robust theory of testation"); see also Hirsch, Freedom of Testation/Freedom of Contract, 95 Minn. L.Rev. 2180 (2011) (suggesting that only "conditions that involve irreversible choices or that entail tangible spillover effects" should be subject to challenge on public policy grounds).

2. *Racial restrictions.* Dr. Jesse Coggins died in January 1963. During his professional career, Dr. Coggins was closely associated with Keswick Home, a private nonprofit hospital in Baltimore. In his will, executed one month before his death, Dr. Coggins left his residuary estate, worth some $30 million, in trust for his wife and three other individual beneficiaries; at the death of the last beneficiary, the trust property was to go to Keswick Home to provide housing for "white patients" in need of physical rehabilitation, with a gift over to the University of Maryland in the event the bequest proved "not acceptable" to Keswick Home. By the time Mrs. Coggins died in 1998, it was clear that the racial restriction was unenforceable. (In fact, for many years after Dr. Coggins' death, Keswick Home had operated on a racially nondiscriminatory basis, as required by federal and state civil rights laws.) Keswick Home argued that it was entitled to receive the trust property free of the racial restriction—in other words, that the illegal restriction should simply be ignored. Not surprisingly, the University contended that Dr. Coggins' will required that the trust property be paid to the University if the gift to Keswick Home failed for any reason (including the illegality of the racial restriction). What result? See Home For Incurables v. University of Maryland Medical System Corp., 797 A.2d 746 (Md. 2002).

In *Snodgrass*, suppose that the testator left a bequest to his daughter on condition that she not marry a person of a different race. In the absence of state involvement sufficient to invalidate the condition on constitutional grounds, how might the daughter attack the racial restriction? See Restatement (Second) of Property (Donative Transfers), § 5.1 cmt. c (1983). For a discussion of racial restrictions, see Roisman, The Impact of the Civil Rights Act of 1866 on Racially Discriminatory Donative Transfers, 53 Ala. L. Rev. 463 (2002).

3. *Capricious conditions.* During life a property owner is free to dispose of property in ways that might strike others as capricious, wasteful, or antisocial. Does the owner have the same freedom in disposing of property by will? In Eyerman v. Mercantile Trust Co., 524 S.W.2d 210 (Mo.App.1975), the testator owned a house in a picturesque planned subdivision in St. Louis. In her will she directed her executor to raze the house, sell the land and distri-

bute the proceeds to named beneficiaries. Although razing the house would produce a substantial net loss to the estate, none of the beneficiaries complained. The neighbors, however, sought an injunction, claiming that destruction of the house would impair the subdivision's aesthetic integrity and depress property values. A divided court concluded that the testator's direction should not be carried out:

> It becomes apparent that no individual, group of individuals nor the community generally benefits from the senseless destruction of the house; instead, all are harmed and only the caprice of the dead testatrix is served. . . . No reason, good or bad, is suggested by the will or record for the eccentric condition. This is not a living person who seeks to exercise a right to reshape or dispose of her property; instead, it is an attempt by will to confer the power to destroy upon an executor who is given no other interest in the property. To allow an executor to exercise such power stemming from apparent whim and caprice of the testatrix contravenes public policy. [524 S.W.2d at 214.]

Compare Estate of Beck, 676 N.Y.S.2d 838 (Sur. 1998) (upholding testator's direction to demolish her house and offer the property to the city for $100 pursuant to an agreement entered into during testator's life).

4. *Other public policy constraints.* Consider the following facts which are taken from the N.Y. Times, March 5, 1982, p. B3. Fred L. Sparks, who worked for many years as a journalist and won a Pulitzer Prize in 1951 for his reporting from post-war Europe, died in 1981. In his will he left $30,000 to the Palestine Liberation Organization. There was no suggestion that the will was tainted by fraud, undue influence, or lack of testamentary capacity. According to friends, Mr. Sparks was deeply impressed by his experiences while covering the plight of Palestinian refugees after the Israeli war of independence in 1948.

The American Jewish Congress and the Anti–Defamation League of the B'nai B'rith challenged the bequest, characterizing the P.L.O. as a "terrorist organization" and arguing that the probate system should not be used "to funnel money to an organization engaged in violent crime." In response, the P.L.O.'s permanent observer to the United Nations said: "This is a violation of Mr. Sparks' rights to dispose of his funds according to his wishes. If this man were alive who could prevent him from giving whatever he wants to whomever he wants?" The New York Civil Liberties Union filed an amicus brief in support of the bequest; its executive director expressed "grave misgivings about the process being established by the Manhattan Surrogate of allowing an intrusive and ill-defined inquiry into a political organization under the broad rubric of 'public policy.'"

The issue never came to trial. Under a compromise settlement, the $30,000 was turned over to the International Committee of the Red Cross "for the betterment of the living conditions of the Palestinian people," to be used solely to provide "aid to civilian hospital facilities in the form of medicines, medical care, food and new or improved housing." See N.Y. Times, Feb. 7, 1984, p. B3.

3. PROTECTION OF THE FAMILY

MARVIN B. SUSSMAN, JUDITH N. CATES & DAVID T. SMITH, THE FAMILY AND INHERITANCE
4–7 (1970).

Edmund Burke once said, "The power of perpetuating our property in families is one of the most valuable and interesting circumstances belonging to it, and that which tends the most to the perpetuation of society itself."[4] The likelihood of perpetuating property within family systems is potentially diminished by the presence of testamentary freedom, which allows the testator to will property away from the family in favor of outsiders. The exercise of this freedom without considering the context in which it occurs appears to be in sharp contradiction with the major intent of inheritance: to provide continuity to family systems and to maintain the social structure. Yet testamentary freedom is an accommodation mechanism in American society. It functions to meet multiple demands: those of continuity; a multilineal descent system; values that espouse freedom, democracy, and rationality; and a complex and highly differentiated modern industrial society. . . .

Succession law reveals an uneasy compromise among the interests of the individual, the family, and the community. Because man cannot live alone and determine for himself exactly what he wants to do in a given situation, such a compromise puts controls over the exercise of testamentary freedom. To understand the resulting limitations, it is necessary to consider a series of related questions: What kinds of property are not subject to testation? Is it likely that the needs of the community will be considered before the needs of the family? How much property is subject to the will of the testator? Namely, what kinds of property does he have control over that are judged not vital to the survival of the community or the family? Lastly, can the testator include or exclude any person he desires?

Assets garnered through forced savings—for example, some company and union insurance and benefit programs and programs sponsored by the government under social security legislation—are not available to be freely distributed by the testator. These valuable rights in job-related death or survivorship benefits specify recipients; and in almost all instances, these assets are allocated to surviving spouses and children. There is a marked increase in such benefit programs in modern societies, whereby the decedent's successors are predetermined by statutes, and the

---

[4]Edmund Burke, Reflections on the French Revolution and Other Essays (New York: E.P. Dutton & Co., Inc., 1910), p. 49.

implementation of the transfer of such assets is done automatically and impersonally by a bureaucratic public or quasi-public agency.

The testator of a small estate is effectively restricted in his freedom to distribute because the estate can be consumed entirely in payment of debts or by the exemption, year's allowance, and other provisions awarded to the widow, widower, or children. Limited assets induce forced succession even though the testator might have had other things in mind.

The more wealthy testator can to some degree choose his successors and distribute his estate in a manner in keeping with his desires; he has the greatest opportunity to express testamentary freedom. But even in this instance, state and federal estate taxes prevent him from freely disposing of all his assets. The progressive tax on estates forces the testator to leave an increasingly larger proportion of his estate to the public. All he can do is to determine the manner in which he serves the public, either through progressively increasing estate taxes (depending upon the size of his estate) or through tax-free gifts to charity. . . .

The current societal posture toward testamentary freedom is predicated on values which assure that caring for one's own kin and orderly social relationships among family members are highly desirable. Testamentary freedom is highly correlated with the condition of sufficient assets. A person has to have equity in order to be able to dispense it. Individuals who are well-to-do usually have sufficient assets to take care of the natural objects of their bounty and also to give to others. Frequently, their spouses and children are not in great need of their beneficence. In many instances, wives will have legacies from their own side of the family, and children may in part have been taken care of by grandparents. Well-to-do individuals are in the best position to meet their familial responsibilities and to a large degree fulfill community expectations, based on an assessment of the financial and status needs of their potential descendants. If spouses and children are amply provided for from other sources, such as legacies and trusts, or are potential inheritors from grandparents and members of their own familial line and will thus be enabled to maintain sufficiently their position and status within the community, then testators have an alternative for distribution of their assets and are more likely to exercise testamentary freedom. The allocations that they would make to institutions and nonrelated individuals would meet with no disapproval because they would have fulfilled community expectations of taking care of their next of kin.

For most individuals, will making is related to the desire to exercise testamentary freedom under conditions that warrant its use. It is possible to say that the making of a will is tantamount to testamentary freedom. In an ideological sense, it is. In practice, however, will makers conform, by and large, to cultural prescriptions of familial responsibility over generational time. The will provides a mechanism for exercising preferred choices if conditions and circumstances are appropriate.

———————

The materials in Chapters 2 and 3 illustrate how the law of estates responds, either directly or indirectly, to the goal of promoting family security and stability.

4. TAXATION

Although many states enacted inheritance taxes during the nineteenth century, only later did these taxes—together with the federal estate tax, enacted in 1916—become important tools of public policy in attempting to limit concentrations of inherited wealth. The federal estate, gift and generation-skipping transfer taxes are examined in more detail in Chapter 10. But in an introduction to the process of wealth transmission the role of these taxes deserves mention.

1. *Federal income tax.* This tax enters the field in two obvious ways: first, it impedes to some extent the initial accumulation of large fortunes; and, second, it diverts a portion of the income stream flowing from such fortunes. But the influence of the income tax is infinitely more subtle and pervasive than this. Indeed, income tax considerations affect almost every decision concerning property—whether to give away, sell or retain particular property; how to structure gifts made outright or in trust; whether to conduct a business in corporate, partnership or other form; when and how to make charitable contributions, to mention but a few examples.

2. *State death taxes.* Many states have enacted some sort of tax on transfers of property at death. Today the most common form of death tax is an *estate tax*, although several states continue to use an *inheritance tax*. Conceptually, an estate tax is levied on the privilege of transmitting property at death, while an inheritance tax is levied on the privilege of receiving property from the dead. More specifically, "the difference is between [an estate] tax graduated according to the size of the decedent's entire estate and [an inheritance tax] that is graduated for each beneficiary according to the size of his or her share and relationship to the decedent." Bittker, Clark & McCouch, Federal Estate and Gift Taxation 9 (10th ed. 2011). A number of states borrow their definitions of the "gross estate" and the deductions allowable in arriving at the "taxable estate" directly from the federal estate tax statute. This approach has the practical advantage of allowing the state tax authorities to ride piggyback on the federal reporting and collection process.

Compared with the federal estate tax, the state death taxes touch a much greater number of estates because they set a considerably lower taxable threshold. But they raise far less revenue due to their relatively low rates. In addition, until recently the federal estate tax allowed a percentage credit for state death taxes, resulting in a shift of revenue from the federal government to the states. By 2001 most states had come to rely exclusively on a "sponge" or "pick-up" tax which was designed to collect only the amount covered by the federal credit. Beginning in 2005, however, the federal credit was replaced by a deduction for state death taxes, with the result that state pick-up taxes have in effect been abolished. A number of states have responded by decoupling their death taxes from federal law, at least on a temporary basis. It remains to be seen whether the repeal of the federal credit will be made permanent, and if so whether a substantial number of states will continue to maintain free-standing death taxes in the future.

3. *Federal estate, gift and generation-skipping transfer taxes.* The federal wealth transfer taxes are particularly noteworthy in this context for two reasons: they have the most immediate and dramatic impact on large estates, and they have long been justified primarily in social policy terms as a means of limiting concentrations of inherited wealth. "Justification for the federal estate tax must be sought in its social significance. It is aimed directly at the destruction of large accumulations of property. . . . [T]he federal estate tax is part of a deliberate plan to redistribute both the capital and income of the nation." Lowndes, Tax Avoidance and the Federal Estate Tax, 7 Law & Contemp. Probs. 328 (1940). These taxes are not important sources of government revenue. Today they raise on average only around one percent of total federal tax revenues—their yield is infinitesimal in comparison with the federal income tax, and meager even in comparison with federal excise taxes on alcohol and tobacco. Nor can these taxes be justified as devices to combat fluctuations in the business cycle. Thus, it appears that "the case for today's gift and estate taxes rests squarely on equalitarian foundations, to which those other theories are little more than decorative buttresses." Bittker, Clark & McCouch, supra, at 5. In recent years, the policy justification of these taxes has become increasingly controversial.

The federal estate tax is imposed on the transfer of a decedent's taxable estate. In computing the tax, the starting point is the gross estate, which includes all property owned by the decedent at death (e.g., tangible personalty, real property, and intangibles such as cash, stocks, and bonds), along with some less obvious types of property controlled by the decedent and also the value of certain transfers made by the decedent during life which are treated as substitutes for testamentary transfers. The gross estate may have a value far in excess of the property actually owned by the decedent at death. From the gross estate are subtracted allowable deductions (e.g., for administration expenses and debts, gifts to charity or a surviving spouse, and state death taxes) to arrive at the taxable estate, on which the tax is imposed at graduated rates. Certain credits (e.g., for foreign death taxes and taxes on prior transfers) are allowable against the estate tax.

The federal gift tax was enacted in 1932 as a backstop for the federal income and estate taxes, which had already been in force for several years. The gift tax is imposed on all taxable gifts made by a living donor in each calendar year. For gift tax purposes, a completed gift occurs when a donor relinquishes dominion and control of property without receiving "adequate and full consideration" in return. In calculating taxable gifts, deductions are allowed for certain gifts to charity or a spouse. In addition, by virtue of the "annual exclusion," a donor may make tax-free gifts to any number of donees each year, up to a specified amount per donee. The annual exclusion is indexed for inflation; in 2012, the excludable amount was $13,000 per donee.

The estate and gift taxes are imposed on a cumulative basis under a "unified" schedule of graduated rates which applies to transfers made during life and at death. In effect, as explained more fully in Chapter 10, each year's taxable gifts are "stacked" on top of the taxable gifts made by the donor in prior years and are taxed at increasing marginal rates. At death, the taxable estate is stacked on top of the decedent's cumulative lifetime taxable gifts and is taxed under the same rate schedule. The "unified credit" automatically eliminates the gift and estate taxes that would otherwise be payable on cumulative taxable transfers up to a specified amount. Under legislation enacted in 2010, the exempt amount was set at $5 million for both gift and estate tax purposes. Thus, in effect, the first $5 million of taxable transfers made during life or at death are exempt from tax, and subsequent taxable transfers are subject to a marginal rate of 35 percent.

The third component of the federal wealth transfer tax system is the generation-skipping transfer (GST) tax, enacted in substantially its present form in 1986. In general, the GST tax is imposed on gratuitous transfers made during life or at death to beneficiaries who are at least two generations younger than the transferor (e.g., a gift from a grandparent to a grandchild, or a trust to pay income to the settlor's child for life with remainder to the child's descendants). The GST tax is imposed at a flat rate equal to the maximum estate tax rate, but its impact is mitigated by a lifetime exemption which is allowed to each transferor in an amount equal to the estate tax exemption. The GST tax supplements the estate and gift taxes, and has significant implications for the use of long-term trusts established for successive generations of beneficiaries.

The overall impact of these taxes on transfers of accumulated wealth from generation to generation remains a topic of concern for lawyers, economists, and legislators. If a decedent leaves a multi-million-dollar estate without having taken steps during life to minimize the impact of the wealth transfer taxes, the size of the tax bite may come as an unpleasant surprise to surviving family members. On the other hand, even without resort to sophisticated estate planning it is possible to transfer substantial wealth at negligible tax cost. At the least, it may be concluded that although these taxes undoubtedly influence patterns of wealth disposition, their social and economic effects have not been nearly as dramatic as was widely predicted at one time. In recent years, popular anti-tax sentiment has prompted renewed scrutiny of the wealth transfer taxes. In 2001 and 2010, Congress enacted legislation which drove the top marginal rate down to its lowest level in 70 years while increasing the exemption from $1 million to $5 million. These changes, however, are not permanent. In the absence of further Congressional action, the statutory changes enacted in 2001 and 2010 will automatically expire at the end of 2012, leaving prior law in effect for 2013 and subsequent years.[5] Admittedly, in today's political climate it seems unlikely that Congress will allow rates and exemptions to return to pre–2001 levels. Nevertheless, in a time of mounting budget deficits and increasing economic inequality, the political backlash against the estate tax may be overshadowed by more pressing national concerns such as meeting the retirement and health care needs of an aging population and guarding against threats to national security.

There is an extensive literature concerning the role of wealth transfer taxation and prospects for reform. See, e.g., Rethinking Estate and Gift Taxation (William G. Gale et al. eds., 2001); Graetz, To Praise the Estate Tax, Not to Bury It, 93 Yale L.J. 259 (1983). For an extended debate over the rationale and justification for taxing wealth transfers, see McCaffery, The Uneasy Case for Wealth Transfer Taxation, 104 Yale L.J. 283 (1994), and the responses by Professors Alstott, Holtz–Eakin, and Rakowski in 51 Tax L. Rev. 363, 495, and 419 (1996). See also the follow-

---

[5]In their book, Death by a Thousand Cuts (2005), Professors Michael Graetz and Ian Shapiro recount the story of how anti-tax activists worked to shape public opinion and mobilize political support for estate tax repeal, culminating in the 2001 legislation. By the late 1990s, polls revealed an apparent groundswell of public support for estate tax repeal. What accounts for the widespread unpopularity of a tax that reaches only the wealthiest 1 or 2 percent of decedents' estates and imposes no burden on the vast majority of taxpayers? Graetz and Shapiro point to several contributing factors. Most Americans routinely overestimate their own relative wealth and upward mobility. According to some polls, 20 percent of the population believe themselves to be in the wealthiest 1 percent and another 20 percent expect that they will soon join that select group. In addition, many people are misinformed about the reach of the estate tax and believe that it affects decedents at all levels of wealth. Most importantly, in a deft twist on its populist origins, opponents of the estate tax (which they invariably call the "death tax") have invoked the mythology of the "American dream" in challenging the morality and fairness of the tax.

ing essays collected in Death, Taxes and Family Property (Halbach ed., 1977): Boskin, An Economist's Perspective on Estate Taxation; Jantscher, The Aims of Death Taxation; and McNulty, Fundamental Alternatives to Present Transfer Tax Systems.

CHAPTER 2

INTESTATE SUCCESSION

■ ■ ■

A. INTRODUCTION

Intestacy occurs when an individual dies owning property which is not effectively disposed of by will. Intestacy may arise in various ways: some individuals deliberately choose to avoid the trouble and expense of making a will, believing that the intestacy laws provide a satisfactory disposition; others procrastinate until the opportunity to make a will is lost through incapacity or death; others execute a valid will which is deemed revoked by loss or destruction; others execute an instrument which is ultimately denied probate due to some defect in execution; still others simply fail to consider the advisability of making a will. Studies suggest that a substantial majority of Americans die intestate (or at least without a will that is admitted to probate).

Obviously, some system of prescribed rules is necessary to identify the takers of an intestate decedent's property and to determine their respective shares. In this country, all fifty states have adopted their own separate intestacy laws, which exhibit countless variations of detail but share several essential structural features. In general, American intestacy laws identify members of the decedent's family as intestate successors, with first priority accorded to the decedent's surviving spouse and issue, if any; in the absence of a spouse or issue, other relatives share in the estate based on their relationship to the decedent. If no takers are found within the circle of eligible family members, the decedent's property escheats to the state. This general pattern of intestate succession is so familiar and widespread that it is often taken for granted, but its underlying premises should not pass unnoticed.

One outstanding feature of American intestacy laws is the prevalence of fixed shares based on family status. Ordinarily, the individual successors can be identified and their respective shares determined solely by reference to their relationship to the decedent. Admittedly, such a scheme does not produce the most equitable result in every case. In terms of fairness, merit or need, not every spouse or child has an equally strong claim;

indeed, in many cases a close friend may have a stronger moral claim than any of the decedent's relatives. But proof of such claims would be difficult, costly and time-consuming, and courts are not especially well equipped to make such determinations. Furthermore, as long as the option of making a will is readily available, the fairness of the intestacy scheme may seem less important than the efficiency of its administration. From a practical standpoint, the paramount concerns are that the intestacy scheme be clear and definite (so that property owners can decide whether to make a will) and that its operation be quick and inexpensive (so that judicial resources are not wasted). Judged by these criteria, a system of fixed shares based on readily ascertainable family status may be preferable to a more flexible discretionary system framed to meet the equities of particular cases.

Assuming that some system of fixed intestate shares is acceptable, the question remains how those shares should be determined. In this country, succession law is firmly rooted in a system of private property which affords individual owners a large measure of freedom to choose their successors. Accordingly, it is sometimes suggested that the intestacy scheme should reflect the probable wishes of the typical or average decedent—in other words, the law should approximate the result such a decedent would have preferred if he or she had made a will. Studies indicate that will making is positively correlated with age, education, income and wealth, and that individuals who make wills customarily leave the bulk of their estates to their spouses, children or other close family members. Public opinion polls suggest similar dispositive preferences on the part of living individuals who do not have wills. But these findings offer only a rough guess as to the probable intent of a hypothetical intestate decedent. A scheme of intestate succession involves the formulation of fixed rules for millions of different individuals, without the benefit of express statements of intent and without considering the widely varying personal, social and economic circumstances of the individuals involved. Any attempt to rationalize a particular pattern of intestate succession based on probable intent is of necessity a highly speculative undertaking.

A family-centered intestacy scheme may be justified instead in terms of public policy. Presumably, the family members who are designated as intestate successors are likely to have had the closest social and economic connections with the decedent. Apart from considerations of personal affection, such connections may justify receiving an inheritance in two ways: first, as a return to those who are likely to have assisted in building up the decedent's estate (e.g., in the case of inheritance by one spouse from the other or by a parent from a child); second, as continuing the support of those who are likely to have been supported by the decedent during his or her lifetime, and perhaps as preventing them from becoming public charges (e.g., in the case of inheritance by one spouse from the other or by a minor or dependent child from a parent). Of course, these factors may also be expressed in terms of probable intent if it is presumed that intestate decedents would wish to reward those who contributed to the estate, or to continue support for those who depended on them during life.

Given the widespread acceptance of a family-centered system of intestate succession, it becomes necessary to define the group of potential successors and to determine which of them take priority of inheritance. In general, with the important exception of a surviving spouse, family members must be related to the decedent by blood to qualify as intestate successors. Blood relatives are classified as lineal descendants, lineal ascendants, or collaterals. Lineal descendants, or "issue," include children, grandchildren, great-grandchildren, and so on; lineal ascendants, or ancestors, include parents, grandparents, great-grandparents, and so on. By definition, a person stands in a direct line of descent between all of his or her ancestors and all of his or her issue. Collaterals are blood relatives who are neither issue nor ancestors; they include brothers and sisters, uncles and aunts, nephews and nieces, cousins, and so on. By definition, a person and each one of his or her collateral relatives are lineal descendants of some common ancestor.

In general, an intestate decedent's nearer blood relatives succeed to the estate, excluding more remote relatives, although, as will appear in the following materials, this generalization requires several qualifications. Priority of succession may be determined either by lines of descent (a "parentelic" system) or by degrees of consanguinity (a "gradual" system). In a parentelic system, priority is given to nearer ancestors and their descendants over more remote ancestors and their descendants, without regard to degrees of consanguinity. In such a system, which shaped the descent of real property at common law, the decedent's own issue take first priority, followed by the decedent's parents and their other issue, then by the decedent's grandparents and their other issue, and so on. For example, consider a decedent whose only surviving relatives are an aunt (related in the third degree) and a grandniece (related in the fourth degree). In a parentelic system, the grandniece would take priority over the aunt because the former is descended from the decedent's parents (she is a member of their parentela), while the latter is descended from the decedent's grandparents (a more remote parentela).

By contrast, in a gradual system, priority is given to relatives who are nearest in degree of consanguinity—the decedent's next of kin. (Such a system can be traced back to the original English Statute of Distributions (1670), governing intestate succession to personal property.) In computing degrees of consanguinity between an ancestor and a lineal descendant, each generation counts as a degree. For example, a parent and child are related to each other in the first degree, a grandparent and grandchild in the second degree, and so on. Between a decedent and a collateral relative, the degree of consanguinity is computed by counting the total number of generations from the decedent up to the nearest common ancestor and then down to the collateral relative.[1] For example, siblings are related to each other in the second degree, uncles and aunts to their nieces and nephews in the third degree, and first cousins to each other in the fourth degree.

The following diagrams[2] illustrate graphically the relationships between blood relatives and the computation of degrees of consanguinity.

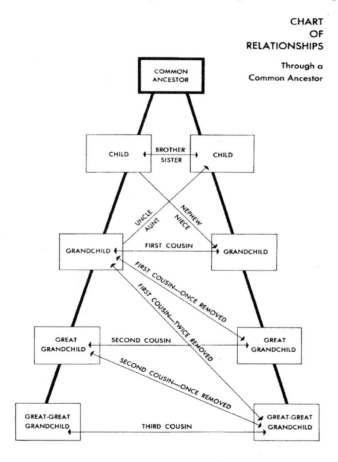

_____

[1] This is the "civil law" method of computation generally used for purposes of succession law in this country and in England. Under the "canon law" method formerly used by ecclesiastical courts in England to determine the permissibility of marriages between relatives, the degree of consanguinity was the largest number of generations between either prospective spouse and the nearest common ancestor.

[2] This material is reproduced from Section 7.82 of *California Decedent Estate Practice* (1986–1997), copyright by the Regents of the University of California. Reproduced with the permission of Continuing Education of the Bar—California.

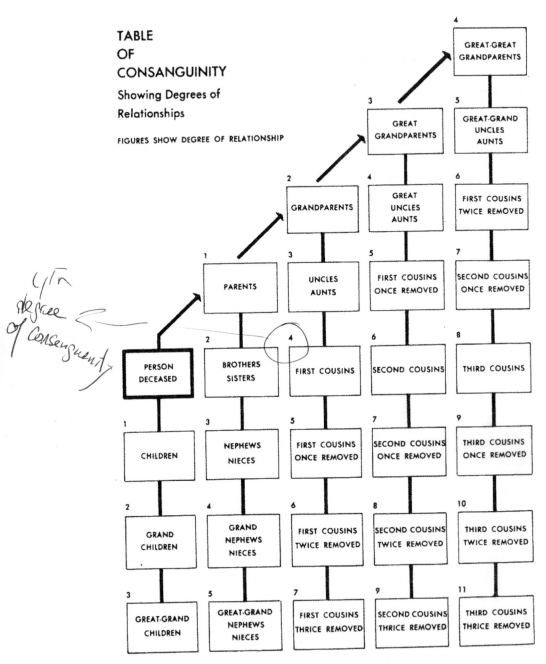

TABLE OF CONSANGUINITY

Showing Degrees of Relationships

FIGURES SHOW DEGREE OF RELATIONSHIP

(handwritten margin note: 4th degree of consanguinity)

The principle of *representation*, where applicable, permits the living descendants of a predeceased relative to "represent" (i.e., take the place of) their ancestor for purposes of inheritance. For example, consider a decedent whose only surviving relatives are an aunt and two first cousins. If the cousins, children of the decedent's predeceased uncle, are permitted to represent him, they will take the one-half share of the estate that would have passed to the uncle had he survived, and the other half will pass to the aunt. Note that the cousins inherit directly from the decedent; their shares do not pass through the predeceased uncle's estate and are not subject to his will or claims of his creditors.

Since the class of potential intestate successors has traditionally included all blood relatives, no matter how remote, there is at least a theoretical possibility that the entire estate might pass to a "laughing heir"— a distant and unknown relative who feels no grief at the decedent's death but only joy at receiving an unexpected inheritance. In many states, however, the spectre of the laughing heir has faded from the scene with the enactment of statutes which cut off inheritance beyond some specified line of descent or degree of relationship. Although the primary purpose of such statutes is to avoid cumbersome and expensive intestacy proceedings, they also tend to increase the number of estates which escheat for lack of an eligible intestate successor. In any event, escheat remains a relatively rare event, since it occurs only if there are no eligible intestate successors *and* there is property in the estate which is not effectively disposed of by will.

For further perspectives on the theory and structure of intestate succession, see DiRusso, Testacy and Intestacy: The Dynamics of Wills and Demographic Status, 23 Quinnipiac Prob. L.J. 36 (2009) (discussing impact of age, sex, race, marital status, education and income on will making and intestacy); Foster, The Family Paradigm of Inheritance Law, 80 N.C. L. Rev. 199 (2001) (noting the "inflexibility, obsolescence, and cultural bias" of rigid inheritance rules based on family status); Glendon, Fixed Rules and Discretion in Contemporary Family Law and Succession Law, 60 Tul. L. Rev. 1165 (1986) (warning of "the futility of attempting to achieve perfect, individualized justice by reposing discretion in a judge or other third party"); Hirsch, Default Rules in Inheritance Law: A Problem in Search of Its Context, 73 Fordham L. Rev. 1031 (2004) (discussing problems of "armchair empiricism" in attempting to ascertain probable intent of intestate decedents); see also Beckstrom, Sociobiology and Intestate Wealth Transfers, 76 Nw. U. L. Rev. 216 (1981). For the historical background and development of intestacy laws, see Shammas, Salmon & Dahlin, Inheritance in America From Colonial Times to the Present (1987); Cates & Sussman, Family Systems and Inheritance Patterns (1982); Symposium on Succession to Property by Operation of Law, 20 Iowa L. Rev. 181 (1935).

B. INTESTACY STATUTES

In this country, intestate succession is based entirely on statute. Despite myriad local variations, the intestacy statutes exhibit substantial similarities in their broad outlines. Typically, a share is set aside for the decedent's surviving spouse, if any, and the balance of the estate is then allocated to the decedent's issue or other blood relatives in a specified order of priority. Vestiges of the traditional differentiation between real and personal property can still be found in a few states, especially in connection with the surviving spouse's share. For the most part, however, modern intestacy statutes afford identical treatment to real and personal property. The Uniform Probate Code provisions are illustrative.

Uniform Probate Code (2011)

Section 2–101. Intestate Estate.

(a) Any part of a decedent's estate not effectively disposed of by will passes by intestate succession to the decedent's heirs as prescribed in this [code], except as modified by the decedent's will. . . .

Section 2–102. Share of Spouse.[3]

The intestate share of a decedent's surviving spouse is:

(1) the entire intestate estate if:

(A) no descendant or parent of the decedent survives the decedent; or

(B) all of the decedent's surviving descendants are also descendants of the surviving spouse and there is no other descendant of the surviving spouse who survives the decedent;

(2) the first [$300,000], plus three-fourths of any balance of the intestate estate, if no descendant of the decedent survives the decedent, but a parent of the decedent survives the decedent;

(3) the first [$225,000], plus one-half of any balance of the intestate estate, if all of the decedent's surviving descendants are also descendants of the surviving spouse and the surviving spouse has one or more surviving descendants who are not descendants of the decedent;

(4) the first [$150,000], plus one-half of any balance of the intestate estate, if one or more of the decedent's surviving descendants are not descendants of the surviving spouse.

Section 2–103. Share of Heirs Other than Surviving Spouse.

(a) Any part of the intestate estate not passing to the decedent's surviving spouse under Section 2–102, or the entire intestate estate if there is no

---

[3] Under UPC § 2–102A, an alternative provision for community property states, the surviving spouse takes all of the decedent's share of the community property, in addition to the share of separate property set forth in § 2–102.—EDS.

surviving spouse, passes in the following order to the individuals who survive the decedent:

(1) to the decedent's descendants by representation;

(2) if there is no surviving descendant, to the decedent's parents equally if both survive, or to the surviving parent if only one survives;

(3) if there is no surviving descendant or parent, to the descendants of the decedent's parents or either of them by representation;

(4) if there is no surviving descendant, parent, or descendant of a parent, but the decedent is survived on both the paternal and maternal sides by one or more grandparents or descendants of grandparents:

(A) half to the decedent's paternal grandparents equally if both survive, to the surviving paternal grandparent if only one survives, or to the descendants of the decedent's paternal grandparents or either of them if both are deceased, the descendants taking by representation; and

(B) half to the decedent's maternal grandparents equally if both survive, to the surviving maternal grandparent if only one survives, or to the descendants of the decedent's maternal grandparents or either of them if both are deceased, the descendants taking by representation;

(5) if there is no surviving descendant, parent, or descendant of a parent, but the decedent is survived by one or more grandparents or descendants of grandparents on the paternal but not the maternal side, or on the maternal but not the paternal side, to the decedent's relatives on the side with one or more surviving members in the manner described in paragraph (4).

(b) If there is no taker under subsection (a), but the decedent has:

(1) one deceased spouse who has one or more descendants who survive the decedent, the estate or part thereof passes to that spouse's descendants by representation; or

(2) more than one deceased spouse who has one or more descendants who survive the decedent, an equal share of the estate or part thereof passes to each set of descendants by representation.

Section 2–104. Requirement of Survival by 120 Hours; Individual in Gestation.

(a) [Requirement of Survival by 120 Hours; Individual in Gestation.] For purposes of intestate succession, homestead allowance, and exempt property, and except as otherwise provided in subsection (b), the following rules apply:

(1) An individual born before a decedent's death who fails to survive the decedent by 120 hours is deemed to have predeceased the decedent. If it is not established by clear and convincing evidence that an individual born before a decedent's death survived the decedent by 120 hours, it is deemed that the individual failed to survive for the required period.

(2) An individual in gestation at a decedent's death is deemed to be living at the decedent's death if the individual lives 120 hours after birth. If it is not established by clear and convincing evidence that an individual in gestation at the decedent's death lived 120 hours after birth, it is deemed that the individual failed to survive for the required period.

(b) [Section Inapplicable If Estate Would Pass to State.] This section does not apply if its application would cause the estate to pass to the state under Section 2–105.

Section 2–105. No Taker.

If there is no taker under the provisions of this [article], the intestate estate passes to the state.

Section 2–106. Representation.

(a) [Definitions.] In this section:

(1) "Deceased descendant," "deceased parent," or "deceased grandparent" means a descendant, parent, or grandparent who either predeceased the decedent or is deemed to have predeceased the decedent under Section 2–104.

(2) "Surviving descendant" means a descendant who neither predeceased the decedent nor is deemed to have predeceased the decedent under Section 2–104.

(b) [Decedent's Descendants.] If, under Section 2–103(a)(1), a decedent's intestate estate or a part thereof passes "by representation" to the decedent's descendants, the estate or part thereof is divided into as many equal shares as there are (i) surviving descendants in the generation nearest to the decedent which contains one or more surviving descendants and (ii) deceased descendants in the same generation who left surviving descendants, if any. Each surviving descendant in the nearest generation is allocated one share. The remaining shares, if any, are combined and then divided in the same manner among the surviving descendants of the deceased descendants as if the surviving descendants who were allocated a share and their surviving descendants had predeceased the decedent.

(c) [Descendants of Parents or Grandparents.] If, under Section 2–103(a)(3) or (4), a decedent's intestate estate or a part thereof passes "by representation" to the descendants of the decedent's deceased parents or either of them or to the descendants of the decedent's deceased paternal or maternal grandparents or either of them, the estate or part thereof is divided into as many equal shares as there are (i) surviving descendants in the generation nearest the deceased parents or either of them, or the deceased grandparents or either of them, that contains one or more surviving descendants and (ii) deceased descendants in the same generation who left surviving descendants, if any. Each surviving descendant in the nearest generation is allocated one share. The remaining shares, if any, are combined and then divided in the same manner among the surviving descendants of the deceased descendants as if the surviving descendants who were allocated a share and their surviving descendants had predeceased the decedent.

1. SURVIVING SPOUSE

When the Uniform Probate Code was originally promulgated in 1969, it provided a more generous intestate share for the surviving spouse than most state statutes in force at the time. Under those statutes, a spouse typically took a share ranging from one-third to one-half of the estate, depending on whether the decedent left surviving issue. A similar scheme can be traced back to the original English Statute of Distributions (1670), which governed intestate succession to personal property.[4]

UPC § 2–102, reproduced supra, substantially improves the spouse's position by allowing the spouse in many cases to take the entire intestate estate to the exclusion of the decedent's blood relatives. Even in cases where the spouse is not the sole intestate successor, UPC § 2–102 gives the spouse a priority share of the intestate estate up to a specified dollar amount, plus a fractional share—in no event less than one-half—of the balance. The specified dollar amount is sufficiently large that in all but exceptional cases the spouse receives the entire intestate estate. For a discussion of the rationale and operation of UPC § 2–102, see Fried, The Uniform Probate Code: Intestate Succession and Related Matters, 55 Alb. L. Rev. 927 (1992); Waggoner, The Multiple–Marriage Society and Spousal Rights Under the Revised Uniform Probate Code, 76 Iowa L. Rev. 223 (1991).

Several studies have attempted to gauge how closely the statutory intestacy scheme conforms to popular preferences, through analysis of probated wills and through public opinion polls. The reported findings suggest that in a substantial majority of cases the preferred plan is to leave everything to the surviving spouse, omitting the children altogether. This preference apparently does not stem from any lack of regard for the dece-

---

[4] The Statute of Distributions specified a spouse's intestate share only for the "wife" of a decedent; a surviving husband would already have become the owner of his wife's personal property upon marriage. Under the common law rules governing intestate succession to land, a surviving spouse was never an heir but took only a life estate in the form of dower or curtesy at the decedent's death. Dower and curtesy are discussed infra at p. 158.

dent's children but rather reflects confidence that the spouse will take care of the children and provide for them at his or her death. See Contemporary Studies Project, A Comparison of Iowans' Dispositive Preferences with Selected Provisions of the Iowa and Uniform Probate Codes, 63 Iowa L. Rev. 1041 (1978); Fellows, Simon & Rau, Public Attitudes About Property Distribution at Death and Intestate Succession Laws in the United States, 1978 Am. B. Found. Res. J. 321; Fellows, Simon, Snapp & Snapp, An Empirical Study of the Illinois Statutory Estate Plan, 1976 U. Ill. L.F. 717; Sussman, Cates & Smith, The Family and Inheritance 83–120 (1970); and earlier studies cited therein; see also Fellows et al., An Empirical Assessment of the Potential for Will Substitutes to Improve State Intestacy Statutes, 85 Ind. L.J. 409 (2010).

NOTES

1. *Surviving spouse's minimum share.* Under the Uniform Probate Code, a surviving spouse is likely to be the sole intestate successor of a small or moderate estate. Two possible rationales for this approach come to mind: first, the entire estate may be needed for the support of the decedent's spouse and minor children, if any; second, the couple's issue may ultimately inherit any property remaining in the spouse's hands at death. To test these rationales, consider the operation of the Uniform Probate Code in the following situation: *H* dies intestate, survived by his wife *W*, their minor child *A*, and also by *B*, *W*'s adult child from a previous marriage. *H*'s net probate estate, after statutory allowances and administration expenses, amounts to $200,000. Now consider some additional facts: *W* has property of her own worth $400,000; *W* receives $400,000 of life insurance proceeds as beneficiary of a policy on *H*'s life; a few years after *H*'s death *W* remarries and eventually dies intestate, survived by her new husband and by *A* and *B*. What problems might arise if the spouse's intestate share were defined as a fixed fraction of the estate, with no minimum share?

2. *Marital status.* Usually there is little doubt about whether an individual qualifies as a decedent's spouse for purposes of intestate succession. As divorce, remarriage, and unmarried cohabitation become more common, however, the question of marital status is likely to arise more and more frequently. Consider the following possibilities:

a. *Common law marriage.* Several jurisdictions recognize the validity of marriages contracted by the parties without a formal ceremony. In general, a "common law" marriage requires that the parties live together and hold themselves out as husband and wife; in some jurisdictions they must also specifically agree or consent to be married. See Estate of Antonopoulos, 993 P.2d 637 (Kan. 1999); Estate of Hunsaker, 968 P.2d 281 (Mont. 1998); Adams v. Boan, 559 So.2d 1084 (Ala.1990). Even states which do not recognize informal marriages contracted within their borders may respect common law marriages validly contracted elsewhere, absent countervailing considerations of public policy. Suppose *A* and *B*, residents of Kentucky (which does not recognize common law marriage), agree to marry during an overnight stay in Ohio (which does recognize common law marriage). On returning to Kentucky, *A* and *B* live together and hold themselves out as husband and wife but never participate in a formal marriage ceremony. At *A*'s death, does *B* qualify as a surviving spouse? See Vaughn v. Hufnagel, 473 S.W.2d 124 (Ky.1971), cert. denied, 405 U.S. 1041 (1972) (no; "it takes more than riding across the Ohio River to make [a common law marriage] legal"). See generally Lovas, When Is A Family Not a Family? Inheritance and the Taxation of Inheritance Within the Non-traditional Family, 24 Idaho L. Rev. 353 (1987).

b. *Putative spouse.* In some jurisdictions, an individual who believes in good faith that he or she is validly married may be entitled to marital property rights as a "putative spouse," even though the marriage turns out to be invalid. For example, suppose that *H*, divorced from his first wife *W*, goes through a marriage ceremony with *Z* in Mexico. *H* subsequently dies without a will, and *Z* learns that their marriage was technically invalid because it was not recorded as required by Mexican law. As a putative spouse, *Z* may be entitled to an intestate share of *H*'s estate. See Estate of Leslie, 689 P.2d 133 (Cal.1984). Suppose instead that *H* was separated, but not divorced, from *W* at the time of his "marriage" to *Z*; though duly recorded, the Mexican marriage was invalid for bigamy, as *Z* discovers to her surprise when *W* claims a surviving spouse's intestate share of *H*'s estate. What result? See Estate of Hafner, 229 Cal.Rptr. 676 (App. 1986); Estate of Vargas, 111 Cal.Rptr. 779 (App. 1974). Suppose that *H*, separated but not divorced from his first wife *W*, contracts a bigamous second marriage with *Z*. If *H* survives *W*, is he entitled to a surviving spouse's share of *W*'s estate? See Estate of Anderson, 70 Cal.Rptr.2d 266 (App. 1997) (discussing estoppel).

c. *Same-sex marriage.* The traditional view of marriage as a union of husband and wife implicitly excludes same-sex couples, who are barred in most states from contracting a legally valid marriage. Recently, however, a more expansive view of marriage as a "voluntary union of two persons as spouses, to the exclusion of all others" has gained ground, and several courts have held that same-sex couples have a constitutionally protected right to marry. Goodridge v. Department of Public Health, 798 N.E.2d 941 (Mass. 2003) (finding no "constitutionally adequate reason for denying civil marriage to same-sex couples"); see also Baker v. State, 744 A.2d 864 (Vt. 1999) ("the State is constitutionally required to extend to same-sex couples the common benefits and protections that flow from marriage under Vermont law"); Lewis v. Harris, 908 A.2d 196 (N.J. 2006) (committed same-sex couples entitled to same rights and benefits as married couples under state constitution). As a result, by judicial decision or statute, at least nine states now recognize same-sex marriage. Moreover, several other states recognize a separate status (e.g., a civil union or domestic partnership) substantially equivalent to civil marriage; in these states, same-sex couples who comply with registration and other statutory requirements are treated for most purposes, including intestate succession, employee benefits, and health care decisionmaking, as if they were married.

In 1996, Congress codified the traditional view of marriage in the Defense of Marriage Act (DOMA), 1 U.S.C. § 7, which defines marriage as "a legal union between one man and one woman as husband and wife" for purposes of federal law. Consequently, same-sex couples are not entitled to marital allowances for purposes of federal income, estate or gift taxation or for purposes of Social Security benefits. The DOMA also provides that no state is required to recognize "a relationship between persons of the same sex that is treated as a marriage under the laws of [another state] . . . or a right or claim arising from such relationship." Several states have enacted similar legislation, and more than half the states have specifically amended their constitutions to preclude recognition of same-sex marriage. A few lower federal courts have held the DOMA invalid on federal constitutional grounds, setting the stage for review by the Supreme Court. See Massachusetts v. Dep't of Health & Human Services, 682 F.3d 1 (1st Cir. 2012); Windsor v. United States, 699 F.3d 169 (2d Cir. 2012), cert. granted, 81 U.S.L.W. 3116 (2012).

Christopher, who was born 25 years ago as a male, undergoes sex reassignment surgery, changes his name to Christine, and obtains a revised birth certificate confirming a new female identity. Christine then marries Mike. If Mike subsequently dies intestate, should Christine be treated as his surviving spouse for purposes of intestate succession? See Estate of Gardiner, 42 P.3d 120 (Kan. 2002), cert. denied, 537 U.S. 825 (2002) (no; male-to-female transsexual remained male as a matter of law; purported marriage was void, and intestate decedent's estate passed to his estranged son); Littleton v. Prange, 9 S.W.3d 223 (Tex. App. 1999), cert. denied, 531 U.S. 872 (2000) (court asked, "can a physician change the gender of a person with a scalpel, drugs and counseling, or is a person's gender immutably fixed by our Creator at birth?" and answered, "once a man, always a man"); but cf. M.T. v. J.T., 355 A.2d 204 (N.J.App. 1976) (recognizing marriage of transsexual as giving rise to support obligation on dissolution).

d. *Unmarried cohabitants.* Frequently, two individuals decide to live together, pooling earnings and assets, sharing expenses, and generally holding themselves out as a married couple, even though they are not legally married to each other. Except in jurisdictions that still recognize common law marriage, such informal arrangements are not treated as marriages for purposes of succession law. Thus, at the death of one party the survivor is not entitled to claim a spouse's intestate share of the decedent's estate. See Peffley–Warner v. Bowen, 778 P.2d 1022 (Wash.1989). Nevertheless, subject to public policy limitations, a pooling agreement between nonmarital partners may be enforceable on a theory of express or implied contract. See Marvin v. Marvin, 557 P.2d 106 (Cal.1976) (express or implied contract enforceable except to extent explicitly founded on consideration of meretricious sexual services); Morone v. Morone, 413 N.E.2d 1154 (N.Y.1980) (express contract is enforceable, but implied contract is not); but cf. Hewitt v. Hewitt, 394 N.E.2d 1204 (Ill.1979) (denying relief on ground that such contracts undermine legal marriage). In theory, the same analysis applies whether the parties are of the same or opposite sex. Does it matter that the option of formal marriage may be legally unavailable in the former but not the latter case? See generally Blumberg, Cohabitation Without Marriage: A Different Perspective, 28 UCLA L. Rev. 1125 (1981).

Some commentators have urged that the law should provide an intestate share for a decedent's surviving "committed partner" who "shar[ed] a common household with the decedent in a marriage-like relationship," even if the relationship was not formally registered as a domestic partnership or civil union. Do two people share a "common household" if they spend weekends together but live separately during the rest of the week? What if their relationship is intermittent or they are living apart at the first partner's death? Should two roommates be treated as committed partners if they share common living quarters and pool their financial resources? What additional factors might a court consider in determining whether their relationship is "marriage-like"? See Waggoner, Marital Property Rights in Transition, 59 Mo. L. Rev. 21 (1994); Fellows et al., Committed Partners and Inheritance: An Empirical Study, 16 L. & Ineq. 1 (1998); Gallanis, Inheritance Rights for Domestic Partners, 79 Tul. L. Rev. 55 (2004); Spitko, An Accrual/Multi–Factor Approach to Intestate Inheritance Rights for Unmarried Committed Partners, 81 Or. L. Rev. 255 (2002).

2. SIMULTANEOUS DEATH

Succession to an intestate decedent's estate occurs at death, when ownership passes from the decedent to his or her heirs. As long as the decedent was alive, potential intestate successors had no legally recognized interest in his or her property but only an inchoate expectancy of inheritance. Moreover, the intestacy statutes require that an heir must *survive* the decedent in order to participate in the estate. It is therefore axiomatic that no rights of inheritance can be claimed by or on behalf of any person who predeceased the intestate decedent. (This is fully consistent with the doctrine of representation, which allows a surviving heir to take all or part of the intestate share that his or her predeceased ancestor would have taken had the ancestor survived the intestate. In such a case, the heir inherits directly from the intestate decedent; no interest passes through the hands of the predeceased ancestor.)

If the intestate and a potential successor die in a common disaster such as an automobile accident, airplane crash, or natural disaster, obvious difficulties arise in establishing the precise order of deaths. To clarify the devolution of property in such cases, the vast majority of states have adopted some version of the Uniform Simultaneous Death Act. In its original version, the Act provides generally that if there is "no sufficient evidence that the persons have died otherwise than simultaneously, the property of each person shall be disposed of as if he had survived." Uniform Simultaneous Death Act § 1 (1940). In effect, the statute raises a presumption of nonsurvival which can be rebutted by "sufficient evidence" that the successor survived for even an instant. Thus, if *H* and *W* die in circumstances such that the order of deaths cannot be determined, *H*'s property passes as if *W* predeceased him and *W*'s property passes as if *H* predeceased her. The presumption of nonsurvival applies equally to testate and intestate succession, and similar rules apply to joint tenancies with right of survivorship and to life insurance proceeds.

In numerous cases, representatives of deceased claimants have sought to rebut this rather flimsy presumption with circumstantial evidence and highly speculative accounts concerning the order of deaths. Consider whether there is sufficient evidence to establish the order of deaths in the following situations:

(a) *H* and *W* drowned when their boat capsized in the middle of a lake. No witnesses were present. The evidence showed that *W* was mildly obese but generally in better physical condition than *H*, who had endured a heart attack a few years earlier and was suffering from emphysema. There was also some evidence that *W* was a better swimmer than *H*, and that unlike *H* she died after a violent struggle. See Estate of Campbell, 641 P.2d 610 (Or.App.1982).

(b) *S* and his mother *M* died of carbon monoxide poisoning, apparently in a joint suicide. Their bodies were discovered strapped into the front seats of a parked car which was locked in an enclosed garage with the engine running. At the time of death, *S* was 41 years old and *M* was 79. Both were in relatively good health, but based on age, sex, and physical condition it could be inferred that *M* might well have succumbed before See Estate of Moran, 395 N.E.2d 579 (Ill.1979).

(c) *H* and *W*, newly married, returned from their honeymoon to attend a family gathering. Suffering from headaches, both spouses swallowed Tylenol capsules, unaware that the capsules had been laced with cyanide. *H* collapsed immediately, and within minutes *W* began having seizures. *H* was still breathing when the ambulance arrived but was pronounced dead shortly after arriving at the hospital emergency room; *W* was kept on artificial life support for two days before she too was pronounced dead. See Janus v. Tarasewicz, 482 N.E.2d 418 (Ill.App.1985).

(d) *H* and *W* were killed in a head-on automobile collision. Witnesses testified that *W* appeared to have survived *H* by a few minutes because she continued to make gurgling sounds after *H* stopped breathing. However, no one checked *H*'s pulse after his breathing ceased, and the witness who thought he detected *W*'s pulse after she stopped breathing conceded that he might have been feeling his own pulse instead. See Estates of Perry, 40 P.3d 492 (Okla.App. 2001).

Even if the order of deaths can be established, practical problems arise when the deaths occur in quick succession. For example, in a state that follows the original Uniform Simultaneous Death Act, if a husband dies intestate and his wife survives him by even an instant, most or all of the husband's estate will pass through the wife's probate estate and be distributed, along with her own estate, to the wife's testate or intestate successors. This outcome may be undesirable both because the husband's property must pass through a second probate administration and because the ultimate disposition may be at odds with both spouses' expectations— due to the brief interval between the two deaths, the wife probably had no realistic opportunity to enjoy her inheritance or to update her estate plan by making a new will or modifying an existing one. To alleviate these problems, the Uniform Probate Code imposes an enhanced survival requirement. Under UPC § 2–104(a)(1), reproduced supra, "[a]n individual . . . who fails to survive the decedent by 120 hours is deemed to have predeceased the decedent" for purposes of intestate succession, and the presumption applies unless it is established by "clear and convincing evidence" that the 120–hour survival requirement was met. See also UPC § 2–702 (similar requirement for beneficiary under will or other governing instrument). By requiring clear and convincing evidence of survival, the UPC drafters hope to stem the flow of unproductive litigation that arose under the "sufficient evidence" standard of the original Uniform Simultaneous Death Act. The Uniform Simultaneous Death Act has also been revised to conform to the UPC's enhanced survival requirement. For a discussion of the operation and rationale of the UPC provisions, see Halbach & Waggoner, The UPC's New Survivorship and Antilapse Provisions, 55 Alb. L. Rev. 1091 (1992).

In cases involving simultaneous (or nearly simultaneous) deaths, it is especially important to establish the time of each death as accurately as possible. Although traditionally death is defined as the "irreversible cessation of circulatory and respiratory functions," modern technology makes it possible to maintain those functions long after a person's brain has ceased to operate. To reflect evolving medical standards, the Uniform Determination of Death Act (1980) provides that death occurs when an individual "has sustained either (1) irreversible cessation of circulatory and respiratory functions, or (2) irreversible cessation of all functions of the entire brain, including the brain stem." Under this provision, a person may be declared legally dead even though circulatory and respiratory functions are being artificially maintained (for example, to preserve organs for transplantation). The same provision concerning determination of death appears in the Uniform Probate Code, which also provides that an official death certificate is prima facie evidence of the fact, place, date and time of death. See UPC § 1–107.

3. REPRESENTATION AMONG DESCENDANTS

Modern intestacy statutes invariably provide that, after the surviving spouse's share has been set aside, the balance of the estate passes to the decedent's surviving descendants, if any, excluding all other blood relatives.[5] Moreover, the rule is well established that the particular descendants entitled to share in the estate are those within each line of descent who are nearest to the decedent in degree of consanguinity. Thus, a surviving descendant who has issue of his or her own always takes to the exclusion of such issue. For example, if a decedent is survived by a daughter A, by A's children, and by the children of a predeceased son B, A takes half the estate and B's children take the other half. This result is implicit in the principle of representation, which ensures both that no line of descendants is excluded and that descendants in lower generations do not compete with their living ancestors who are also descendants of the decedent.

In every state, if all of an intestate decedent's children are living at the decedent's death, they share equally in the estate. If there are surviving descendants of one or more predeceased children, however, the computation of the descendants' respective shares becomes more complicated. Although the general principle of representation is universally recognized for purposes of intestate succession among a decedent's lineal descendants, the specific form of representation varies substantially from state to state. Traditionally, most states followed one of two alternative systems of representation, sometimes referred to as "per stirpes" (by the stocks or roots) and "per capita" (by the head). These terms are used so indiscriminately in the cases and statutes, however, that they more often confuse than clarify matters.

In a strict *per stirpes* system, the estate is divided into equal shares, with one share allocated to each living child of the decedent and one to each predeceased child who has descendants living at the decedent's death. Each predeceased child's share is then redivided among the child's descendants in the same manner until the entire share has been allocated to living takers. This method governed the distribution of personal property to an intestate's descendants under the Statute of Distributions, which called for an equal division among the decedent's children "and such persons as legally represent such children, in case any of the said children be then dead." Statute of Distributions, 22 & 23 Car. II, c. 10, § 5 (1670). In this country, intestacy statutes in a substantial number of

---

[5] Under the system of primogeniture which prevailed in England until 1925, an intestate decedent's land descended to the eldest son to the exclusion of the other children. Among its other functions, this feudal relic served to perpetuate concentrations of landed wealth and avoid the sort of fragmentation that occurs when all children share equally. In this country, primogeniture was rejected at an early date in favor of a representational division among surviving descendants.

states call for a per stirpes distribution, both among a decedent's own descendants and among the descendants of predeceased parents, siblings or other relatives. See, e.g., Del. Code tit. 12, § 503; Fla. Stat. § 732.104; Ill. Comp. Stat. ch. 755, § 5/2–1. The distinctive feature of a strict per stirpes system is that the initial division into shares occurs at the level of the decedent's children, regardless of whether any of them survive the decedent.

→ Modern Persepves

By contrast, in a traditional *per capita* system (also known as per capita with representation), the initial division into equal shares occurs at the nearest generation of descendants which has a member living at the decedent's death. One share is allocated to each living member of that generation, and one to each predeceased member who has living descendants. Each predeceased member's share is then distributed among his or her living descendants according to the traditional (per stirpes) form of representation. The hallmark of a per capita system is that the surviving descendants in the closest degree of relationship to the decedent take equal shares in their own right and not as representatives of a predeceased ancestor. A substantial number of states have adopted a traditional per capita system, by statute or judicial decision, for purposes of intestate succession. See, e.g., Balch v. Stone, 20 N.E. 322 (Mass. 1889); Martin's Estate, 120 A. 862 (Vt.1923); Kraemer v. Hook, 152 N.E.2d 430 (Ohio 1958).

In the usual case where the decedent is survived by at least one child, the per stirpes and traditional per capita systems produce identical results. For example, suppose that *X* dies intestate, survived by a child *A*, by two children of a predeceased child *B*, and by three children of a predeceased child *C* (predeceased relatives are shown in brackets, those who survived in bold type):

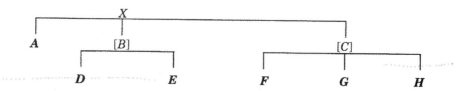

In each system, the estate is initially divided into three equal shares at the children's level, with one share allocated to *A*, one share divided among *B*'s children, and one share divided among *C*'s children. Thus, *A* takes one-third of the estate, *B*'s children each take one-sixth, and *C*'s children each take one-ninth.

To illustrate the difference between the two systems, assume the same facts as above except that *A* is predeceased with no descendants. In a strict per stirpes system, the initial division is still made at the children's level, and *B*'s children share one-half of the estate (taking one-fourth each) while *C*'s children share the other half (taking one-sixth each). By contrast, in a traditional per capita system, the initial division is now made at the grandchildren's level, with each grandchild taking an equal one-fifth share of the estate.

The Uniform Probate Code has introduced two further variations on the traditional per capita system. Under UPC § 2–106, as originally promulgated in 1969, when representation is called for,

> the estate is divided into as many shares as there are surviving heirs in the nearest degree of kinship and deceased persons in the same degree who left issue who survive the decedent, each surviving heir in the nearest degree receiving one share and the share of each deceased person in the same degree being divided among his issue in the same manner.

As in a traditional per capita system, the original Uniform Probate Code begins by dividing the estate into equal shares at the nearest generation of descendants which has a member living at the decedent's death and allocating one share to each living member and one share to each predeceased member who has living descendants. In disposing of a predeceased member's share, however, the original Uniform Probate Code departs from the traditional per capita system. Instead of allocating the deceased member's share among his or her living descendants according to the traditional (per stirpes) form of representation, the original Uniform Probate Code requires that the deceased member's share be divided among those descendants "in the same manner" as the initial division—i.e., in equal shares at the next generation which has a living member.

To illustrate the difference between a traditional per capita system and the original Uniform Probate Code, consider a variation on the above example, in which *X* dies intestate, survived by a child *A*, by three grandchildren of a predeceased child *B*, and by three children of a predeceased child *C* (predeceased relatives are shown in brackets, those who survived in bold type):

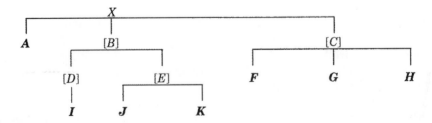

The estate is divided into three equal shares at *A*'s generation, with one share allocated to *A*, one share allocated to *B*'s grandchildren, and one share allocated to *C*'s children. In a traditional per capita system, *I* takes one-half of *B*'s one-third share and *J* and *K* share the other half equally. By contrast, the original Uniform Probate Code requires that *B*'s one-third share be divided equally among *I*, *J*, and *K*. A substantial number of states have adopted the original Uniform Probate Code's variant of a per capita system by statute for purposes of intestate succession.

The revised version of UPC § 2–106, promulgated in 1990 and reproduced supra, introduces yet another variant of a per capita system, often referred to as *per capita at each generation*, which has been adopted in a substantial number of states. The revised version of UPC § 2–106, like its predecessor, calls for an initial division into equal shares at the nearest generation of descendants which has a member living at the decedent's death and allocates one share to each living member and one share to each predeceased member who has living descendants. However, instead of allocating the share of each deceased member among his or her living descendants, the revised Uniform Probate Code combines the shares of all deceased members and allocates them among their respective living descendants "in the same manner"—i.e., in equal shares at the next generation which has a living member. This provision is premised on the notion that within each generation successors who are related to the decedent in equal degree should receive equal intestate shares.

To illustrate the operation of the per capita at each generation system, consider another variation on the above example, in which *X* dies intestate, survived by a child *A* and by descendants of predeceased children *B* and *C* (predeceased relatives are shown in brackets, those who survived in bold type):

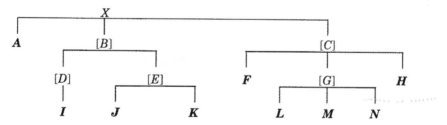

The estate is divided into three equal shares at *A*'s generation, with one share allocated to *A*. The two shares initially allocated to *B* and *C* are recombined and divided into five equal shares at the next generation, with one share allocated to *F* and one to *H*. The balance of the estate is divided into six equal shares at the next generation. In sum, the estate is divided as follows: *A* takes one-third of the estate; *F* and *H* each take two-fifteenths ($2/3 \times 1/5$); and *I*, *J*, *K*, *L*, *M* and *N* each take one-fifteenth ($2/3 \times 3/5 \times 1/6$).

NOTES

1. *Methods of representation.* Note that the identities of the takers remain the same under all of the methods of representation described above; the choice of one method or the other affects only the size of the respective shares. In terms of the decedent's probable intent, what might be said for each method? Is it significant that a high proportion of professionally drafted wills specify a per stirpes distribution? See Young, Meaning of "Issue" and "Descendants," 13 Prob. Notes 225 (1988). For discussions of different systems of representation, see Page, Descent Per Stirpes and Per Capita, 1946 Wis. L. Rev. 3; Waggoner, A Proposed Alternative to the Uniform Probate Code's System for Intestate Distribution Among Descendants, 66 Nw. U. L. Rev. 626 (1971).

2. *Representation among collaterals.* Our discussion so far has focused primarily on methods of representation among a decedent's own descendants, but the same principles apply to representation among collaterals. Indeed, questions concerning representation arise most frequently with respect to descendants of a decedent's predeceased siblings or aunts and uncles. In the last example given in text, suppose that A, having outlived X, dies intestate survived by F, H, and the children of D, E and G. How should A's estate be distributed under (a) a per stirpes system, (b) a traditional per capita system, (c) the original Uniform Probate Code, or (d) the revised Uniform Probate Code?

D dies intestate. Her closest surviving relatives are three first cousins and the children of six deceased first cousins, the offspring of several deceased aunts and uncles. The applicable intestacy statute directs that the estate shall pass "to the grandfather, grandmother, uncles, aunts and their descendants, the descendants taking collectively the share of their immediate ancestors in equal parts." Should D's estate be distributed (a) per stirpes, using the aunts and uncles as the stocks, (b) per stirpes, using grandparents, aunts and uncles as the stocks, (c) per stirpes, using the nearest generation with living members (i.e., the first cousins) as the stocks, or (d) per capita with equal shares to each surviving heir? See Estate of Fosler, 13 P.3d 686 (Wyo. 2000). What if one grandparent and one aunt also survive? See Thatcher v. Thatcher, 29 P. 800 (Colo. 1892).

3. *Relatives by affinity.* Except for a surviving spouse or adopted children, intestate succession is generally limited to the decedent's blood relatives. Relatives by affinity—spouses of blood relatives and blood relatives of spouses—are excluded. Thus, a son-in-law or daughter-in-law does not inherit from his or her deceased spouse's parents. See Dunaway v. McEachern, 37 So.2d 767 (Miss.1948). The same is true, of course, in the case of a brother-in-law or sister-in-law. See In re Will of Meyer, 152 A.2d 160 (N.J.App. 1959). Similarly, unadopted stepchildren do not inherit from their stepparents. See Estate of McLaughlin, 523 P.2d 437 (Wash.App.1974); In re Wall's Will, 5 S.E.2d 837 (N.C.1939). The Uniform Probate Code, however, permits inheritance by

stepchildren as a last resort to avoid escheat, and several states have enacted similar provisions. See UPC § 2–103(b), reproduced supra; Conn. Gen. Stat. § 45a–439(a)(4); Ohio Rev. Code § 2105.06(J).

4. *Offsetting debts.* A died owing his brother B $5,000, which remained unpaid when B died one month later survived by A's children and by a sister. Assuming that A's children take an intestate share of B's estate as representatives of A, is their share subject to reduction by the amount of A's unpaid debt? By the weight of authority, it is not; even though the children represent their deceased parent, they are treated as taking their share directly from B, not from A. See Estate of Berk, 16 Cal.Rptr. 492 (App. 1961). The same result is codified in UPC § 2–110, which states: "A debt owed to a decedent is not charged against the intestate share of any individual except the debtor. If the debtor fails to survive the decedent, the debt is not taken into account in computing the intestate share of the debtor's descendants."

5. *Testamentary gifts.* A decedent's will that calls for a distribution by representation raises questions analogous to those already discussed in connection with intestate succession. In the case of a testamentary gift, the problem is one of interpretation: Even if the will specifies a "per stirpes" or "per capita" distribution, the testator's intent may be unclear. For example, consider the confusion created by a testamentary gift "in equal shares to my nieces and nephews per stirpes." Do the nieces and nephews take per capita in their own right or as representatives of their deceased parents? What if a predeceased niece or nephew has living descendants? See Wachovia Bank & Trust Co. v. Livengood, 294 S.E.2d 319 (N.C.1982); In re Will of Griffin, 411 So.2d 766 (Miss.1982). Suppose instead that the gift is to "the issue of my nephews A, B and C, share and share alike." If the three nephews have 60 living descendants, should the property be divided into 60 equal shares or should the descendants take by representation? See Warren v. First New Haven Nat'l Bank, 186 A.2d 794 (Conn.1962); B.M.C. Durfee Trust Co. v. Borden, 109 N.E.2d 129 (Mass.1952).

4. ANCESTORS AND COLLATERALS

If a decedent leaves no surviving spouse or descendants, modern intestacy statutes generally provide for inheritance by ancestors and collaterals, with nearer relatives taking priority over more remote relatives. In broad outline, leaving aside numerous variations in detail, intestacy laws tend to follow either a parentelic system based on lines of descent, a gradual system based on degrees of consanguinity, or a hybrid combining aspects of both systems. A few states have a full-fledged parentelic system with unlimited representation, in which nearer ancestors and their descendants take categorical priority over more remote ancestors and their descendants. See, e.g., Va. Code § 64.2–200. Others adhere to the pattern established in the English Statute of Distributions, giving priority to the decedent's next of kin based on degree of consanguinity and permitting representation only among a limited group of takers (e.g., children of predeceased siblings). Most states permit unlimited representation at least among descendants of the intestate's parents and grandparents. In practical effect such a system is ordinarily indistinguishable from a parentelic system, since it is rarely necessary to look further than grandparents and their descendants to find an eligible successor. This is the approach taken by UPC § 2–103, reproduced supra. A substantial number of states follow the Uniform Probate Code in cutting off inheritance beyond grandparents and their descendants, but in many states the group of potential successors includes all blood relatives, no matter how remote.

IN RE WENDEL'S WILL

Surrogate's Court, 1932.
143 Misc. 480, 257 N.Y.S. 87.

FOLEY, S.

This is a proceeding for the probate of the purported last will and testament of the decedent, Miss Wendel. The supplemental citation directed to numerous alleged heirs and next of kin, who were specifically named therein, was recently returnable before me. Service was also directed by publication generally to all those claiming to be heirs and next of kin of the decedent. Over sixteen hundred claimants through their attorneys or personally have appeared and contend that they are within the class of legal distributees. Application has also been made by the proponents of the will to procure the filing of a bill of particulars by these various claimants. The proponents seek to obtain a verified statement of the degree of relationship claimed and the particulars of the ancestry of the claimants and of their collateral relationship to Miss Wendel. Upon the return of the order to show cause for the bill of particulars and the return of the supplemental citation, the scope of the immediate application was widened by the various attorneys representing the opposing parties. They seek the advice and direction of the court as to a method of simplifying the issues, of expediting the disposal of certain preliminary questions which have been raised, and of reaching an ultimate determination of the validity or invalidity of the propounded will. Over one hundred and sixty attorneys or firms of attorneys have appeared in the proceeding.

The Surrogate stated upon the hearing that respect for justice and for our system of probate practice required that an orderly and expeditious mode of procedure, consistent with the rights of all the parties, should be established. The Surrogate also stressed the necessity for the co-operation of all the attorneys who have appeared, in order that undue delay, burdensome expense, or other injustice should be avoided. The proceeding is only extraordinary in the number of claimants who have appeared. The magnitude of the estate is relatively unimportant, for in other large estates similar difficulties have not arisen.

1. In accordance with the suggestion of the attorneys and the pronounced policy of the Surrogate, the order of procedure for the trial and the disposal of the successive issues, preliminary and final, will be as follows:

(A) The jurisdiction of the Surrogate's Court of New York County over the probate proceeding will be first brought on and determined. That question involves an adjudication as to whether Miss Wendel died a legal resident of New York county or Westchester county. If it be found that this court has no jurisdiction, the entire proceeding will be remitted to Westchester County for further action there.

(B) If jurisdiction be found in this court, there will be taken up next the trial of the relationship of the claimants to the decedent. Those claiming to be of the nearest degree will be tried first. When the standing of one person of the nearest degree is established, the status of only those claiming to be within that degree will be heard.

(C) Every other person beyond that degree has no legal interest in this estate and all appearances for such distantly related persons will be stricken out on motion.

(D) If Rosa Dew Stansbury is proven to be of the nearest degree, the validity of the waiver executed by her and filed in this proceeding will be next tried.

(E) Finally, if there are any persons found to be next of kin and heirs at law of Miss Wendel, and legally entitled to contest the will, the trial of their objections to the validity of the will shall be brought on and determined.

2. The application for a bill of particulars is granted. The mere assertion of a claim of relationship to the decedent does not entitle a person to appear and contest the will. The fact that a claimant bears the name "Wendel," without any supporting proof of relationship, is worthless. The legal standing of a claimant as one of the next of kin and heirs at law of the maker of the alleged will must first be established before a contest will be permitted. Matter of Cook's Will, 244 N.Y. 63, 154 N.E. 823, 55 A.L.R. 806. Furthermore, only those within the nearest degree of kinship are entitled to contest the will. It appears to be conceded in the present proceeding that Miss Wendel left no descendants, no brothers or sisters, or nephews or nieces. The claimants rely upon their contention that they are first cousins or of a more remote collateral relationship.

The attention of counsel is called to the fact that our recent revision of the inheritance laws made by chapter 229 of the Laws of 1929 fundamentally changed the classes of persons entitled to inherit the property of a person dying without a will, or the classes of persons entitled to contest a will. Reports of the Commission to Investigate Defects in the Laws of Estates, Legislative Document No. 69 of 1930. The rules for the inheritance of property of every nature, real and personal, were made uniform. The inheritance of property was concentrated, instead of being scattered to the more distant relations. The former antiquated method of computing the degree of consanguinity and the canons of descent formerly relating to real property were abolished, Decedent Estate Law, § 81, as added by Laws 1929, c. 229, § 6, as amended by Laws 1930, c. 174, § 2. In their place there was substituted the modern method of computing degrees, and the rules of inheritance applicable formerly to personal property. . . .

An important change was made as to the inheritance of real estate in the abolition of the former rule which permitted representation in collateral lines to the remotest degree. Representation is now permitted only as far as brothers and sisters and their descendants. Beyond brothers and sisters and their descendants, only persons within the nearest degree of relationship to the decedent are entitled to inherit intestate real or personal property. In other words, where there is a group of first cousins, as the nearest relatives, they alone are entitled to inherit. In such case if there are children or grandchildren of deceased first cousins, they are not entitled to inherit. The same rule applies to the ascertainment of the class of next of kin or heirs where there are second cousins or third cousins or more distant classes of relatives. When persons of the nearest degree of relationship establish that standing, those more remote are excluded.

These changes in the Decedent Estate Law took effect on September 1, 1930. Miss Wendel died thereafter on the 13th day of March, 1931. The new statutes, therefore, regulate and affect the property left by her and the determination of her heirs and next of kin.

For the benefit of the attorneys who have appeared in this proceeding, the statutory method of computing the degree of relationship to Miss Wendel may be shown by example. The statutory rule of computation requires the exclusion of the decedent and the counting of each person in the chain of ascent to and including the common ancestor, and then the counting downward of each subsequent descendant from the common ancestor to the claimant. . . . Thus, Rosa Dew Stansbury is alleged in the petition to be the sole next of kin of Miss Wendel. The method of computing the degree of her relationship, starting from the decedent and excluding her from the count, is as follows:

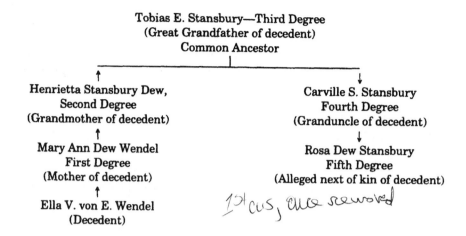

Tobias E. Stansbury—Third Degree
(Great Grandfather of decedent)
Common Ancestor

Henrietta Stansbury Dew,
Second Degree
(Grandmother of decedent)

Mary Ann Dew Wendel
First Degree
(Mother of decedent)

Ella V. von E. Wendel
(Decedent)

Carville S. Stansbury
Fourth Degree
(Granduncle of decedent)

Rosa Dew Stansbury
Fifth Degree
(Alleged next of kin of decedent)

1st cus, ance removed

There are certain claimants who contend they are first cousins. They would be of the fourth degree. If such status be ultimately established by them, Rosa Dew Stansbury, and every person claiming to be within the fifth degree, and those of every other more remote degree, are not proper parties to this proceeding. Similarly, if next of kin of the fifth degree establish their status, all persons beyond that degree must be eliminated and their appearances stricken out. Similar procedure must be adopted as to each widened circle of kinship beyond the established status of the nearest group of legal next of kin. In order to simplify the issues, the Surrogate has provided in the order of procedure set forth above that the claims of those persons contending that they are of the nearest degree to Miss Wendel should be tried first.

3. A suggestion has been made for the convenience of counsel that the proponents file genealogical charts of the ancestors and collaterals of Miss Wendel to a reasonable degree. That suggestion will be adopted by the Surrogate. It would appear that such procedure will assist attorneys in identifying the relationship of their clients, and the probability or improbability of their being next of kin of the decedent. Such charts, with the available dates of birth, death, and marriage of the ancestors of Miss Wendel to a reasonable degree, and of her collaterals to a reasonable degree, are directed to be filed by the proponents with the probate clerk of this court on or before April 25, 1932. These instructions and reasonable inquiry by the attorneys for the various claimants should disclose to them the possibility of a near relationship of their clients to the decedent. Where such relationship to Miss Wendel is revealed as too remote, or where no relationship at all is disclosed, it will be the duty of the attorney, as an officer of the court, to inform his client of the fact and the law, and promptly to withdraw, by written notice, his appearance in the proceeding.

4. The bill of particulars by the various claimants will be directed to be served upon the proponents' attorneys and filed in this court on or before May 21, 1932. The most important item of such bill is a definite statement of the numerical degree of the relationship of the specific claimant to Miss Wendel, with the further information as to the specific names in the chain from the decedent to the claimant, of the ancestors and descendants from the common ancestor.

The proposed form of the bill of particulars submitted by the proponents is approved as modified by the Surrogate. For the convenience of the attorneys for the various claimants and the Surrogate, the proponents are directed to print and supply copies of such form of a bill of particulars. The expense thereof may be charged out of the estate. . . .

NOTES

1. *Proof of relationship.* The administrative procedures adopted by court in *Wendel* have served as prototypes in other cases involving complex or uncertain claims of heirship. Consider the types of evidence a claimant might offer in attempting to establish an alleged family relationship—photographs, correspondence written by or addressed to the decedent, recollections of family and friends, probate and family court records, perhaps even forensic analysis of genetic material. What sort of evidence should be admissible in a proceeding to identify a decedent's heirs?

In her will, Ella Wendel left the bulk of her $40 million fortune to charity. The litigation over her estate ultimately produced over 2,000 claimants, the most dramatic of whom was one Thomas Patrick Morris, who claimed to be Miss Wendel's nephew on the theory that he was the child of a secret marriage of her brother, John Gottlieb Wendel; his claim proved spurious, however, and he was convicted of conspiracy to defraud. The will contest was finally dropped after payment of a substantial sum to the nearest proved relatives. For an account of the probate litigation, see Laporte, John M. Harlan Saves the Ella Wendel Estate, 59 A.B.A.J. 868 (1973).

Fortunately, cases of this kind are extremely rare. One of the most sensational involved the estate of Henrietta E. Garrett, who died intestate in 1930 leaving a fortune of over $17 million. During the next 20 years nearly 26,000 claims were filed by persons claiming the estate as next of kin; some 2,000 hearings took place; over 1,100 witnesses were heard; the record totalled 390 volumes covering over 115,000 pages. In 1950 a special Master submitted a 900–page report finding that three first cousins were entitled to distribution. The distribution was approved by the Orphans' Court in 1952 and ultimately affirmed by the Supreme Court of Pennsylvania in 1953. See Garrett Estate, 94 A.2d 357 (Pa.1953).

2. *Standing to contest a will.* As the *Wendel* case indicates, intestacy statutes have ramifications beyond the distribution of intestate estates. The per-

sons designated by statute as intestate successors are entitled to notice of probate proceedings and have standing to contest the decedent's will. See Kerin v. Goldfarb, 280 A.2d 143 (Conn.1971) (cousins, related to intestate in fourth degree, lacked standing to appeal probate decree awarding entire estate to aunt, related in third degree). The theory of the contestants in the *Wendel* case was that Miss Wendel lacked testamentary capacity. If that case had arisen under the Uniform Probate Code, who would have had standing to raise this claim?

Miss Wendel apparently left only one will. Suppose instead that she executed two wills, one in 1915 and the other in 1925, each disposing of her entire estate, and that a successful contest of the later will would leave the earlier one in force. Who would have standing to challenge the 1925 will? A devisee under the earlier will? See Estate of Glennie, 265 P.3d 654 (Mont. 2011). An intestate successor who was disinherited in the earlier will? See Jolley v. Henderson, 154 S.W.3d 538 (Tenn.App. 2004); Newman v. Newman, 766 So.2d 1091 (Fla.App. 2000); Stephens v. Brady, 73 S.E.2d 182 (Ga.1952). An executor named in the earlier will? See Agee v. Brown, 73 So.3d 882 (Fla.App. 2011). The trustee of a testamentary trust created in the earlier will? See Melican v. Parker, 657 S.E.2d 234 (Ga. 2008).

3. *Inheritance by remote relatives.* In many states, if there are no eligible takers within a specified class of close relatives, the estate passes by intestacy to the "next of kin"—the living blood relative nearest to the decedent in degree of consanguinity. If there are two or more takers related in the same degree, they share the estate equally. Representation is usually not allowed among remote relatives. A typical example is Conn. Gen. Stat. § 45a–439(a)(3), which provides that, in the absence of spouse, descendants, parents, siblings or their representatives, "the estate shall be distributed equally to the next of kin in equal degree. No representatives shall be admitted among collaterals after the representatives of brothers and sisters." Under this expansive formula any blood relative, no matter how remote, may succeed to the estate unless preempted by a nearer relative.

To foreclose the possibility of succession by a "laughing heir," many statutes cut off inheritance by relatives beyond the decedent's grandparents and their descendants. See UPC §§ 2–103 and 2–105, reproduced supra. One incidental effect of such provisions is to increase the percentage of estates—still minute, to be sure—that pass to the state by escheat. See, e.g., Newlin v. Gill, 237 S.E.2d 819 (N.C. 1977). This limitation on inheritance has been sustained against an equal protection challenge. See Estate of Jurek, 428 N.W.2d 774 (Mich.App.1988).

4. *Division between maternal and paternal kindred.* In a system of intestate succession which identifies "next of kin" solely by degree of consanguinity there is no distinction between maternal and paternal kindred; relatives nearest to the decedent in degree take to the exclusion of those more remote in degree. See Dahood v. Frankovich, 746 P.2d 115 (Mont.1987) (maternal

uncles and aunts related in third degree took priority over paternal first cousins related in fourth degree). In a number of jurisdictions, however, the traditional system is modified by statute to give half of the estate to kindred on the maternal side and half to kindred on the paternal side; in the absence of kindred on one side, the entire estate goes to the kindred on the other side. See, e.g., Tex. Prob. Code § 38(a)(4); cf. UPC § 2–103(a)(4) and (a)(5) (similar division between parentelae of maternal and paternal grandparents, with no inheritance by more remote relatives), reproduced supra. Under such a statute, half of the estate could pass to a maternal first cousin (related to decedent in the fourth degree), while the other half could be divided among several paternal aunts and uncles (related in the third degree). See State ex rel. Swift v. Tullar, 462 P.2d 409 (Ariz.App.1969); Golden v. York, 407 S.W.2d 293 (Tex. App. 1966).

5. *Parentelic tie-breakers.* In discussing succession by collateral relatives, it is customary to speak of a "common ancestor." This is legal shorthand since, except for half-bloods (see infra Note 6), collaterals generally have at least two common ancestors: siblings have the same parents; first cousins have the same maternal or paternal grandparents; and so on. Where there are two or more collateral kindred of equal degree who claim through different common ancestors, a number of statutes give priority to those claiming through the nearest common ancestor. See, e.g., Cal. Prob. Code § 6402(f); Mass. Gen. L. ch. 190B, § 2–103(4). For example, suppose that a decedent's closest surviving relatives are a first cousin once removed (a grandchild of the decedent's great-grandparents) and a great-grand-aunt (a daughter of the decedent's great-great-grandparents), both relatives of the fifth degree. Instead of dividing the estate equally between them, these tie-breaking statutes invoke the parentelic principle and give the entire estate to the first cousin once removed.

6. *Half-bloods.* A half-blood relationship arises when a collateral relative has one, but not two, ancestors in common with the decedent. For example, if a parent has one child from a first marriage and another child from a second marriage, each child is the other's half-blood sibling; and each is likewise a half-blood relative of the other's descendants. Half-blood relationships can occur only between collaterals, never between ancestors and descendants. In this country, the overwhelming majority of states give half-blood relatives exactly the same share that they would take if they were of the whole blood. See, e.g., UPC § 2–107; Dahood v. Frankovich, 746 P.2d 115 (Mont.1987) (half-blood uncles and aunts took priority over more remote whole-blood relatives). In a few states, however, a half-blood relative takes only half the share of a whole blood relative of the same degree. See, e.g., Fla. Stat. § 732.105; Va. Code § 64.2–202. A Mississippi statute permits half-bloods to inherit only if there are no whole blood relatives of the same degree. See Miss. Code § 91–1–5; Jones v. Stubbs, 434 So.2d 1362 (Miss.1983) (children of decedent's deceased whole-blood brothers took entire estate, excluding a living half-blood sister). For more on inheritance by half-blood collaterals, see Brashier, Consanguinity, Sibling Relationships, and the Default Rules of Inheritance Law:

Reshaping Half–Blood Statutes to Reflect the Evolving Family, 58 SMU L. Rev. 137 (2005).

Decedent owned land which she inherited from her paternal grandfather. She is survived only by a maternal brother of the half-blood and by a paternal cousin of the whole blood. An applicable statute provides: "Kindred of the half-blood inherit equally with those of the whole blood in the same degree, unless the inheritance come to the intestate by descent, devise or gift of some one of his ancestors, in which case all those who are not of the blood of such ancestors must be excluded from such inheritance." Okla. Stat. tit. 84, § 222. Does the statute prevent the half-blood brother from inheriting the land, even though he is closer to the decedent in degree than the whole-blood cousin? See Estate of Robbs, 504 P.2d 1228 (Okla.1972) (overruling prior decisions and holding that statute applies only if half-blood and whole-blood kindred are related to decedent in same degree).

C. CHILDREN

1. ADOPTED CHILDREN

Although adoption is found in many societies, ancient and modern, and is recognized by the civil law, it was unknown at common law. Accordingly, in this country, adoption is entirely a creature of statute, and its impact on intestate succession is essentially a matter of statutory construction. Beginning in the latter half of the 19th century, the states enacted general adoption statutes which authorized the creation of a legal parent-child relationship through formal judicial proceedings. The early statutes, which seem to have been drafted primarily with humanitarian ends in mind, contained only the most elementary provisions concerning intestate succession. For the most part, the statutes simply declared that an adopted child could inherit from the adoptive parents (and vice versa), and remained silent as to whether the child could also inherit from the natural parents. This question was resolved in the affirmative by the courts, which reasoned that in the absence of a contrary provision in the adoption statute the child remained entitled to inherit from the natural parents under the general intestacy statutes.

The modern statutes, while far from uniform, are considerably more comprehensive in scope. In the overwhelming majority of states, for purposes of intestate succession, an adopted child is generally treated as a child of the adopting parents and not of the natural parents. In effect, an adopted child is "transplanted" from the natural family to the adoptive one, severing all ties (including reciprocal rights of inheritance) with the former. What is the justification for this approach: probable intent of the average intestate decedent? welfare of the child? administrative convenience?

The general rule terminating the adopted child's right to inherit from or through the natural parents and their kindred (and vice versa) operates relatively smoothly in an "out-of-family" adoption where the adoptive parents are unrelated to either natural parent. In recent years, however, it has become increasingly common for children to be adopted by a spouse or blood relative of one natural parent, often after the death or divorce of the natural parents. Modern statutes often make no special provision for such "in-family" adoptions, except in the limited circumstance where the child is adopted by a stepparent (i.e., the spouse of a natural parent). In the case of a stepparent adoption, many intestacy statutes preserve the child's right to inherit from one or both of the natural parents. Some statutes provide similar protection where the child is adopted by a close relative. The Uniform Probate Code goes even further and preserves the child's right to inherit from both natural parents (referred to as "genetic" parents) if the adoption occurs after the death of both parents:

Uniform Probate Code (2011)

Section 2–118. Adoptee and Adoptee's Adoptive Parent or Parents.

(a) [Parent–Child Relationship Between Adoptee and Adoptive Parent or Parents.] A parent-child relationship exists between an adoptee and the adoptee's adoptive parent or parents. . . .

Section 2–119. Adoptee and Adoptee's Genetic Parents.

(a) [Parent–Child Relationship Between Adoptee and Genetic Parents.] Except as otherwise provided in subsections (b) through (e), a parent-child relationship does not exist between an adoptee and the adoptee's genetic parents.

(b) [Stepchild Adopted by Stepparent.] A parent-child relationship exists between an individual who is adopted by the spouse of either genetic parent and:

(1) the genetic parent whose spouse adopted the individual; and

(2) the other genetic parent, but only for the purpose of the right of the adoptee or a descendant of the adoptee to inherit from or through the other genetic parent.

(c) [Individual Adopted by Relative of Genetic Parent.] A parent-child relationship exists between both genetic parents and an individual who is adopted by a relative of a genetic parent, or by the spouse or surviving spouse of a relative of a genetic parent, but only for the purpose of the right of the adoptee or a descendant of the adoptee to inherit from or through either genetic parent.

(d) [Individual Adopted After Death of Both Genetic Parents.] A parent-child relationship exists between both genetic parents and an individual who is adopted after the death of both genetic parents, but only for the purpose of the right of the adoptee or a descendant of the adoptee to inherit through either genetic parent. . . .

Note that in the case of a stepparent adoption, UPC § 2–119(b) preserves the child's right to inherit from both natural parents and their kindred, but the reverse is not necessarily true. The natural parent who is married to the adopting stepparent is permitted to inherit from or through the child, but the other natural parent is not. What is the rationale for this distinction? For discussion of the UPC provision, see Gary, We Are Family: The Definition of Parent and Child for Succession Purposes, 34 AC-TEC L.J. 171 (2008); Tritt, Technical Correction or Tectonic Shift: Competing Default Rule Theories Under the New Uniform Probate Code, 61 Ala. L.Rev. 273 (2010); see also Roberts, Adopted and Nonmarital Children—Exploring the 1990 Uniform Probate Code's Intestacy and Class Gift Provisions, 32 Real Prop. Prob. & Tr. J. 539 (1998).

As the following materials indicate, the modern statutes resolve many, but by no means all, of the problems concerning the impact of adoption on intestate succession.

IN RE ESTATES OF DONNELLY

Supreme Court of Washington, 1972.
81 Wash.2d 430, 502 P.2d 1163.

NEILL, ASSOCIATE JUSTICE.

May an adopted child inherit from her natural grandparents? Both the trial court and the Court of Appeals (5 Wash. App. 158, 486 P.2d 1158 (1971)), answered "yes." We granted review (79 Wash. 2d 1010 (1971)), and disagree. In speaking of heirs and inheritance, we refer to the devolution of property by law in intestacy and not by testamentary or other voluntary disposition.

John J. and Lily Donnelly, husband and wife, had two children, a daughter, Kathleen M., now Kathleen M. Kelly, and a son, John J., Jr. The son had one child, Jean Louise Donnelly, born October 28, 1945. Jean Louise's father, John J. Donnelly, Jr., died on July 9, 1946, less than a year after her birth. Her mother, Faith Louise Donnelly, married Richard Roger Hansen on April 22, 1948. By a decree entered August 11, 1948, Jean Louise was adopted by her step-father with the written consent of her natural mother. She lived with her mother and adoptive father as their child and kept the name Hansen until her marriage to Donald J. Iverson. Thus she is a party to this action as Jean Louise Iverson.

Lily Donnelly, the grandmother, died October 7, 1964, leaving a will in which she named but left nothing to her two children. All of her property she left to her husband, John J. Donnelly, Sr., Jean Louise Iverson's grandfather.

John J. Donnelly, Sr., the grandfather, died September 15, 1970, leaving a will dated October 16, 1932, in which he left his entire estate to his wife, Lily, who had predeceased him. He, too, named but left nothing to his two children, and made no provision for disposition of his property in event his wife predeceased him. His daughter, Kathleen M. Kelly, as administratrix with wills annexed of the estates of her parents, brought this petition to determine heirship and for a declaration that Jean Louise Iverson, the granddaughter, take nothing and that she, Kathleen M. Kelly, the daughter, be adjudged the sole heir of her mother and father, Lily and John J. Donnelly, Sr., to the exclusion of Jean Louise Iverson, her niece and their granddaughter.

The trial court decided that each was an heir. It concluded that Jean Louise Iverson, daughter of John J. Donnelly, Jr., and granddaughter of his father, John J. Donnelly, Sr., should inherit one-half of the latter's estate and that Kathleen M. Kelly, daughter of John J. Donnelly, Sr., should inherit the other half of the estate.

Kathleen M. Kelly, the daughter of decedent, appealed to the Court of Appeals which affirmed, and now to this court. . . .

[A] statutory right to inherit one-half of the grandfather's estate is vested in Jean Louise Iverson, the granddaughter, unless that right is divested by operation of RCW 11.04.085, which declares that an adopted child is not to be considered an heir of his natural parents:

> A lawfully adopted child shall not be considered an "heir" of his natural parents for purposes of this title.

When the question of the right of an adopted child to inherit from his natural parents came before us, the intent of the legislature was clear from the literal language of the statute. We held that RCW 11.04.085 prevents an adopted child from taking a share of the natural parent's estate by intestate succession. In re Estate of Wiltermood, 78 Wash. 2d 238, 242–243, 472 P.2d 536 (1970). However, reference to the literal language of RCW 11.04.085 does not answer the instant question, i.e., whether, by declaring that an adopted child shall not take from his natural parent, the legislature also intended to remove the adopted child's capacity to represent the natural parent and thereby take from the natural grandparent. . . .

The legislature has addressed itself to the inheritance rights of adopted children in both the probate and domestic relations titles of RCW (RCW Titles 11 and 26). For example, RCW 26.32.140 also directly affects the inheritance rights of an adopted child:

> By a decree of adoption the natural parents shall be divested of all legal rights and obligations in respect to the child, and *the child* shall be free from all legal obligations of obedience and maintenance in respect to them, and *shall be* to all intents and purposes, and for all legal incidents, *the child, legal heir, and lawful issue of his or her adopter or adopters, entitled to all rights and privileges, including the right of inheritance* and the right to take under testamentary disposition, and subject to all the obligations of a child of the adopter or adopters begotten in lawful wedlock. (Italics ours.) . . .

It is clear that: (1) the adopted child cannot take from his natural parent because he is no longer an "heir" (RCW 11.04.085); and, (2) the adopted child enjoys complete inheritance rights from the adoptive parent, as if he were the natural child of the adoptive parent (RCW 26.32.140). Both statutes are in harmony with the fundamental spirit of our adoption laws—i.e., that for all purposes the adopted child shall be treated as a "child of the adopter . . . begotten in lawful wedlock." . . .

The question at bench should, therefore, be decided in the context of the broad legislative objective of giving the adopted child a "fresh start" by treating him as the natural child of the adoptive parent, and severing all ties with the past. We believe it clearly follows that the legislature intended to remove an adopted child from his natural bloodline for purposes of intestate succession.

The trial court and Court of Appeals, however, held that although an adopted child may not take *from* a natural parent dying intestate, the same child may take *through* the natural parent, by representation, if the natural parent dies before the natural grandparent. Little supportive reasoning is offered for this inconsistent result. In reaching its conclusion, the Court of Appeals reasoned that consanguineal ties are so fundamental that an explicit expression of legislative intent is required to deprive an adopted child of the bounty which would normally be his by reason of the "intuitive impulses" generated by the blood relationship. In re Estates of Donnelly, 5 Wash. App. 158, 164, 486 P.2d 1158 (1971). The Court of Appeals reasoned that had the legislature desired to remove an adopted child from its natural bloodline, it could have used the word "kin" in place of the word "parents" in RCW 11.04.085. Thus, since RCW 11.04.085 does not specify that an adopted child may not take from an intestate natural grandparent, this capacity is not lost.

However, . . . the legislature did *not* consider consanguinity to be of controlling importance where the blood relationship must be presumed to be strongest—the natural parent. Moreover, RCW 26.32.140 provides that an adopter and his kin shall inherit from an adopted child to the exclusion of the child's natural parents or kin. Thus if respondent here had predeceased her natural grandfather, he would not have been permitted to inherit from his natural grandchild, any "intuitive impulses" of kinship notwithstanding. And, if consanguinity had *in fact* moved the grandparent to provide for respondent here, he could easily have done so by will.

The legislative policy of providing a "clean slate" to the adopted child permeates our scheme of adoption. The natural grandparents are not entitled to notice of any hearing on the matter of adoption. RCW 26.32.080. RCW 26.32.150 provides that, unless otherwise requested by the adopted, all records of the adoption proceeding shall be sealed and not open to inspection. Pursuant to RCW 26.32.120, a decree for adoption shall provide: (1) for the issuance of a certificate of birth for the adopted child, containing such information as the court may deem proper; and (2) that the records of the registrar shall be secret. RCW 70.58.210 declares that the new birth certificate shall bear the new name of the child and the names of the adoptive parents of the child, but shall make no reference to the adoption of the child. Thus, the natural grandparents have no assurance that they will know the new name or residence of the adopted child. Indeed, in the usual "out of family" adoption situation the administrator of a deceased natural grandparent's estate will be unable to locate—much less to identify—the post-adoption grandchild.

The consistent theme of the relevant legislation is that the new family of the adopted child is to be treated as his natural family. The only conclusion consistent with the spirit of our overlapping adoption and inheritance statutes is that RCW 11.04.085 was intended to transfer all rights of inheritance out of the natural family upon adoption and place them entirely within the adopted family.

Respondent suggests it is most probable that the legislature never considered the problem of inheritance by adopted persons from their remote natural kin when it passed RCW 11.04.085. Thus, respondent contends that the word "parents" should be strictly construed. We disagree. . . .

The broad legislative purpose underlying our statutes relating to adopted children is consistent only with the inference that RCW 11.04.085 was intended to remove respondent, an adopted child, from her natural bloodline for inheritance purposes. If the adopted child cannot take from her natural father, she should not represent him and take from his father.

The chain of inheritance was broken by respondent's adoption. Reversed.

HAMILTON, C.J., and STAFFORD, WRIGHT and UTTER, JJ., concur.

HALE, Associate Justice (dissenting).

I dissent. This court asks whether an adoptive child may inherit from her natural grandparents. Both the trial court and the Court of Appeals, 5 Wash. App. 158, 486 P.2d 1158 (1971), answered yes, and I agree. I would, therefore, adopt the opinion of the Court of Appeals verbatim as declaring the law of the state in this case.

But there are other reasons, I think, why the granddaughter is entitled to an inheritance and why the statute, RCW 11.04.085, declaring that an adopted child shall not be *considered* an heir of his natural parents, does not operate to disinherit the granddaughter from her grandfather's estate. As the Court of Appeals so clearly delineated, the statute applies to a parent and child; it does not, except by the most strained analysis and construction, apply to grandparent and grandchild—particularly where the adoption arose from the marriage of the grandchild's widowed natural mother. The grandchild's adoption by her widowed mother's second husband should not be held to affect the lineal relationship between granddaughter and grandfather.

One should note the absence of the simple declarative in RCW 11.04.085. The statute does not say that the adopted child shall not inherit, but instead employs the less categorical terminology that an adopted child shall not be *considered* an "heir of his natural parents" for the purpose of the title. In reaching the result obtained, the court has had to follow what appears to me to be a labyrinthine maze of statutory interpretation, which I find both unnecessary and inapplicable. If the legislature had intended that the grandchild be disinherited, it could readily have said so. This would, of course, have raised the constitutional question of whether the legislature can lawfully provide that some grandchildren may inherit from their grandparents and greatgrandparents and other grandchildren in the same degrees of propinquity shall not, and whether there exists sufficient basis under the constitution to sustain the creation of two distinct classes of grandchildren under the descent and distribution statutes.

If the circumstances of this case are changed slightly, the flaw in the court's opinion becomes apparent. Had the plaintiff granddaughter, Jean Louise Iverson, in this case been the sole surviving descendant of her grandfather, John J. Donnelly, Sr., then under the court's opinion, all of the estate of her grandfather, John J. Donnelly, Sr., would escheat to the state. Such a forfeiture of estate, I think, was neither intended by the legislature nor reasonably contemplated by the language it employed in RCW 11.04.085.

One can readily agree with the court's proposition that the legislature has designed the adoption and inheritance code so as to make an adopted child the full equal in law with a natural child and, so far as the law can do so, to establish a relationship between adopted parents and adopted children identical to that of natural parents and children. To that end it expressly enacted that the *natural parents* are divested of all legal rights and obligations; that the adopted child becomes "to all legal intents and purposes and for all legal incidents" the child, legal heir and lawful issue of her adopters, RCW 26.32.140, and that all adoption papers shall be sealed, and remain unopened except upon order of the superior court for good cause shown, and, if so opened, to be sealed again as before. RCW 26.32.150.

But nothing in the Court of Appeals opinion militates against the integrity and totality of an adoption. To the contrary, that opinion augments this legislatively declared public policy of upholding and preserving the adoption, where this court's opinion will operate against it. Here, the grandfather's son died; his widowed daughter-in-law eventually remarried, and she consented that her new husband adopt her daughter. The new family relationship created by the marriage and adoption presented none of the circumstances of an adoption designed in law to cut off all familial and legal relationships with the adopted child's natural mother nor her grandparents either. The grandchild continued to live with her natural mother and adoptive father presumably with the full knowledge of her grandfather, whose lineal descendant she remained. None of the factors upon which the legislature legislated to seal the records of adoption against the grandfather existed here. And, although the adoption statute makes this granddaughter no less an adopted daughter of her mother's husband, it ought not to be read to make her less a granddaughter of her natural grandfather either. The statute which the court now says disinherits the granddaughter cannot, as the court now says, serve to give the natural granddaughter a "fresh start" or a "clean slate" in the relationship created by the adoption. One is hard put to find where a statute which operates to cut off the plaintiff grandchild from her grandfather's estate gives her a fresh start or a clean slate. The statute could not, and thus did not, sever all ties with the past. While it might have severed whatever legal ties existed between her and her dead father, whose heir she had *already* been, the adoption could not be reasonably said to do the same with respect to her natural grandfather. . . .

Thus, as earlier observed, I would affirm the Court of Appeals and thereby affirm the trial court.

Finley, Hunter, and Rosellini, JJ., concur.

Notes

1. *Adoption by stepparent.* How, if at all, would the Uniform Probate Code affect the analysis or the outcome in a case like *Donnelly*? See UPC § 2–119(b), reproduced supra; Estate of Ryan, 928 P.2d 735 (Ariz.App.1996); see also Hall v. Vallandingham, 540 A.2d 1162 (Md.App.1988); Estate of Holt, 622 P.2d 1032 (N.M.1981).

Suppose that a child is adopted by a stepfather, the second husband of the child's natural mother. Some statutes permit the child to inherit from the natural father's kindred only if the mother's remarriage occurred after the natural father's death. See Fla. Stat. § 732.108(1)(b) (preserving reciprocal inheritance rights where child is adopted by stepparent "who married the natural parent after the death of the other natural parent"). What is the rationale for such a restriction? What if the natural father died after the mother's remarriage but before the adoption? See First Nat'l Bank of East Liverpool v. Collar, 272 N.E.2d 916 (Ohio C.P. 1971).

2. *In-family adoption.* In most states, the legal adoption of a child severs all inheritance rights between the child and the natural parents and their kindred, except where the adopting parent is married to one of the natural parents. What is the justification for this limitation? Suppose that a child's natural parents are killed in an accident and the child is subsequently adopted by the natural mother's parents. Should the adoption extinguish the child's right to inherit from the natural father's relatives? See Pyles v. Russell, 36 S.W.3d 365 (Ky. 2000); Ellis v. West, 971 So.2d 20 (Ala. 2007). If a child is adopted by an aunt by marriage (the wife of the natural mother's deceased brother), should the adoption extinguish the right of the child and her descendants to inherit from her natural siblings? See Kummer v. Donak, 715 S.E.2d 7 (Va. 2011); cf. UPC § 2–119(c), reproduced supra.

Suppose that a household consists of a child C, his natural mother M, and the mother's same-sex domestic partner P. In a jurisdiction that does not recognize same-sex marriage, is it possible for the P to adopt C without extinguishing the reciprocal inheritance rights between C and M? See In re Jacob, 660 N.E.2d 397 (N.Y.1995) (approving adoption by natural parent's partner); Adoption of Tammy, 619 N.E.2d 315 (Mass.1993) (approving joint adoption); cf. UPC § 2–119, reproduced supra. See Polikoff, This Child Does Have Two Mothers: Redefining Parenthood to Meet the Needs of Children in Lesbian–Mother and Other Nontraditional Families, 78 Geo. L.J. 459 (1990).

3. *Dual inheritance.* If the applicable statute permits an adopted child to inherit from or through the adoptive parents and does not preclude inheritance from or through the natural parents, the question arises whether the child is permitted to take a dual intestate share. For example, suppose that a child whose natural parents are dead is adopted by a grandparent who subsequently dies intestate. Is the child entitled to two intestate shares—one as

an adopted child and another as a natural grandchild? If so, the child would fare better than either a natural child or an unadopted natural grandchild. See In re Benner's Estate, 166 P.2d 257 (Utah 1946) (permitting dual inheritance); cf. Estate of Cregar, 333 N.E.2d 540 (Ill.App.1975) (child of decedent's sister, adopted by another sister, entitled to inherit from decedent in two capacities, despite statute prohibiting dual inheritance "from the estate of the adopting parent").

In the case of an adopted child, the question of dual inheritance arises only to the extent that the child is permitted to inherit from or through the natural parents (or vice versa). If the adoption is treated as severing all links with the natural parents, the child takes only from or through the adoptive parents. See Crego v. Monfiletto, 250 A.2d 161 (N.J. Super. 1969). Under UPC § 2–113, an individual who is related to an intestate decedent through two lines of relationship takes only a single intestate share "based on the relationship that would entitle the individual to the larger share." In what circumstances is this provision likely to apply?

4. *Inheritance from or through adopted child.* In general, the modern statutes treat adopted children and their lineal descendants as integral members of the adoptive family, fully entitled to inherit from and through the adoptive parents. Similarly, the adoptive parents and their kindred inherit from and through the adopted child. See UPC §§ 2–116 and 2–118(a). This represents a significant shift away from earlier statutes which focused more narrowly on reciprocal rights of inheritance between the adopted child and the adoptive parents. See Estate of Edwards, 273 N.W.2d 118 (S.D.1978) (property inherited by child from adoptive parents passed by intestacy to child's natural half sister, not to adoptive mother's niece); Black v. Washam, 421 S.W.2d 647 (Tenn.App.1967) (adoptive parents' collateral relatives not entitled to inherit, resulting in escheat); cf. Estate of Smith, 326 P.2d 400 (Utah 1958) (adopted child not entitled to inherit from adoptive parents' kindred). The adopted child's enhanced ties with members of the adoptive family come at the expense of members of the natural family, who are generally precluded from participating in the estate of a child who has been "adopted out." See Estate of Kirkpatrick, 77 P.3d 404 (Wyo. 2003) (out-of-family adoption extinguished right of unadopted natural siblings and their descendants to inherit from adopted child); Estate of Mills, 374 N.W.2d 675 (Iowa 1985) (natural siblings not entitled to inherit from decedent, who had been adopted by their mother's half-brother; estate passed instead to adoptive parent's descendants).

5. *Successive adoptions.* Occasionally a child is adopted more than once, raising the question whether the initial adoptive parents stand in the shoes of the natural parents for purposes of intestate succession. Suppose that Mr. and Mrs. Smith adopted a child, but Mrs. Smith died soon afterward and Mr. Smith gave the child up for adoption to Mr. and Mrs. Jones. Mr. Smith then dies intestate. Is the child entitled to inherit from Mr. Smith? Statutes cutting off an adopted child's right to inherit from or through the natural par-

ents have been interpreted to have the same effect with respect to the initial adoptive parents. See Estate of Luckey, 291 N.W.2d 235 (Neb.1980); In re Adolphson Estate, 271 N.W.2d 511 (Mich.1978).

6. *Equitable adoption.* Often a child is brought up in the home of a foster parent—typically, a friend or relative of a natural parent—pursuant to an informal agreement, without any official adoption proceedings. If the foster parent dies intestate, the child may be able to participate in the estate under the doctrine of equitable adoption. In general, an equitable adoption requires (1) an agreement between the natural parents and the foster parent for adoption of the child, (2) performance on the part of the natural parents in giving up custody, (3) performance on the part of the child in living in the foster parent's home, and (4) partial performance by the foster parent in treating the child as an adopted child. If these elements are shown by clear and convincing evidence, there is ample authority for awarding an intestate share of the foster parent's estate to the child. See Lankford v. Wright, 489 S.E.2d 604 (N.C.1997); Estate of Ford, 82 P.3d 747 (Cal. 2004) (requiring "some direct expression, on the decedent's part, of an intent to adopt" as well as "objective conduct indicating mutual recognition of an adoptive parent and child relationship"). In cases refusing to apply the doctrine, the most common stumbling block involves insufficient proof of an agreement to adopt the child. See Urick v. McFarland, 625 So.2d 1253 (Fla.App.1993) (child not entitled to inherit from stepfather in absence of agreement). In this setting, how realistic is it to expect proof of such an agreement? See Welch v. Welch, 453 S.E.2d 445 (Ga.), cert. denied, 515 U.S. 1162 (1995) (no equitable adoption in absence of enforceable agreement; court order authorizing child's legal custodian to commence adoption proceedings not sufficient); O'Neal v. Wilkes, 439 S.E.2d 490 (Ga.1994) (same result where child's aunt lacked legal authority to enter into purported agreement). One court has explicitly abandoned the requirement of an agreement for adoption, emphasizing that the child's status must be "identical to that of a formally adopted child, except only for the absence of a formal order of adoption." Wheeling Dollar Savings & Trust Co. v. Singer, 250 S.E.2d 369 (W.Va.1978).

The doctrine of equitable adoption is usually explained either in terms of specific performance (i.e., enforcing the foster parent's agreement to adopt the child) or in terms of estoppel (i.e., precluding the foster parent's successors from relying on the lack of a formal adoption). Under either theory, it is generally held that the doctrine affords equitable relief exclusively to the child in the form of an intestate share of the intestate foster parent's estate. Thus, the child is not entitled to inherit from the foster parent's relatives, and neither the foster parents nor their relatives inherit from the child. See Board of Educ. v. Browning, 635 A.2d 373 (Md.1994); Estate of Furia, 126 Cal.Rptr.2d 384 (App. 2002); but cf. First Nat'l Bank v. Phillips, 344 S.E.2d 201 (W.Va.1985) (allowing child to inherit from foster parent's other child). If equity recognizes a right on the part of the child to inherit from a foster parent, why does the doctrine not also operate in favor of the parent? For a discussion of the rationale and operation of equitable adoption, see Rein, Relatives by Blood, Adoption, and Association: Who Should Get What and Why, 37 Vand. L. Rev. 711 (1984).

7. *De facto families.* As divorce, remarriage and cohabitation without marriage become more widespread, there has been a corresponding surge in the number and variety of blended and nontraditional families. In many cases a child is placed at an early age in the care of relatives, stepparents, or foster parents who provide support and treat the child as their own without ever formalizing the relationship through legal adoption proceedings. Several commentators have argued that the intestacy statutes should recognize such de facto parent-child relationships, and at least one state has taken a step in this direction. In California, a child may inherit from or through a foster parent or stepparent if (1) "[t]he relationship began during the [child's] minority and continued throughout the joint lifetimes" of the child and the foster parent or stepparent, and (2) it is established by clear and convincing evidence that "the foster parent or stepparent would have adopted the [child] but for a legal barrier." Cal. Prob. Code § 6454. Suppose that decedent and his wife took *A* into their home at age three and raised her as their daughter. They supported *A* throughout her minority, financed her college education, and stood in as *A*'s parents at her wedding. On several occasions during *A*'s minority, decedent and his wife sought permission to adopt her, but *A*'s natural parents refused. Decedent survived his wife and eventually died intestate when *A* was around 40 years old. Under the California statute, is *A* entitled to a child's intestate share of decedent's estate? See Estate of Joseph, 949 P.2d 472 (Cal.1998). Alternatively, if *A* dies intestate, with no spouse or issue, and her foster father survives her, does the foster father inherit from *A*?

For commentary and reform proposals, see Brashier, Inheritance Law and the Evolving Family (2004); Gary, The Parent–Child Relationship Under Intestacy Statutes, 32 U. Mem. L. Rev. 643 (2002); Gary, Adapting Intestacy Laws to Changing Families, 18 L. & Ineq. 1 (2000); Brashier, Children and Inheritance in the Nontraditional Family, 51 Utah L. Rev. 93 (1996); Mahoney, Stepfamilies in the Law of Intestate Succession and Wills, 22 U.C. Davis L. Rev. 917 (1989).

8. *Adoption of adult.* Although an adopted child is usually a minor at the time of adoption, most jurisdictions also authorize the adoption of one adult by another. One major purpose of an adult adoption may be to ensure exclusive inheritance rights for the adoptee and thereby deprive other relatives of standing to contest the adoptive parent's will. In one early case the court characterized this as a "perfectly proper" motive on the part of a 70–year-old man who adopted two adult nieces and a nephew. Collamore v. Learned, 50 N.E. 518 (Mass.1898) (Holmes, J.); see also Tinney v. Tinney, 799 A.2d 235 (R.I. 2002) (84–year-old woman adopted 38–year-old man five years before death; adoptive son entitled to intestate share); but cf. In re Jones, 411 A.2d 910 (R.I. 1980) (denying 30–year-old married man's petition to adopt 20–year-old paramour as "a perversion of the adoption process"). Is a parent-

child relationship a condition precedent to an adoption or a legal consequence thereof?

In an effort to forestall potential will contests, same-sex couples occasionally resort to adult adoption, with mixed results. Compare Adoption of Swanson, 623 A.2d 1095 (Del. 1993) (approving 66–year-old man's adoption of 51–year-old partner to "formalize [their] close emotional relationship" and "facilitate their estate planning"; no implied requirement of "pre-existing parent-child relationship") with Adoption of Robert Paul P., 471 N.E.2d 424 (N.Y.1984) (denying 57–year-old man's petition to adopt 50–year-old partner; it would be "unreasonable" to permit "one lover, homosexual or heterosexual, to adopt the other and enjoy the sanction of the law on their feigned union as parent and child"). Today same-sex couples may accomplish the desired result more directly and reliably by marriage or by entering into a civil union, domestic partnership or similar arrangement in a jurisdiction that recognizes the resulting relationship. Note that in some states an individual may be prohibited from adopting his or her spouse. See Uniform Adoption Act § 5–101 (1994).

An adult adoption may be vulnerable to collateral attack after one party's death on grounds of fraud or undue influence. See Estate of Reid, 825 So.2d 1 (Miss. 2002) (85–year-old widow adopted 31–year-old man); Adoption of Sewall, 51 Cal.Rptr. 367 (App. 1966) (72–year-old man adopted 45–year-old widow); Adoption of Russell, 73 A.2d 794 (Pa.Super.1950) (elderly woman adopted 33–year-old man); Greene v. Fitzpatrick, 295 S.W. 896 (Ky.1927) (attorney adopted his stenographer, who allegedly lived with him in "a state of concubinage").

9. *Testamentary gifts.* Questions concerning the status of adopted children arise frequently in connection with class gifts to "children," "issue," "descendants," or "heirs" in wills and trusts. Consider a testamentary trust that pays income to A for life with remainder to A's "children." Is a child adopted by A eligible to take a share of the remainder at A's death? The question requires an interpretation of the will rather than a mechanical application of the local intestacy statute, though courts often look to such statutes as indicia of public policy which may serve as a guide to will construction. At one time courts generally presumed that children adopted by a person other than the testator were excluded from class gifts unless the testator knew and approved of the adoption and viewed the adopted child as a member of the family. However, this "stranger-to-the-adoption" rule has been widely repudiated by statute or judicial decision. See Haley v. Regions Bank, 586 S.E.2d 633 (Ga. 2003); Elliott v. Hiddleson, 303 N.W.2d 140 (Iowa 1981); Estate of Fortney, 611 P.2d 599 (Kan.App.1980). See generally Halbach, The Rights of Adopted Children Under Class Gifts, 50 Iowa L. Rev. 971 (1965).

The prevailing modern rule of construction presumes that a class gift includes not only the testator's own adopted children but also children adopted by other persons, at least where the child's relationship with the adoptive parent began during the child's minority. See UPC § 2–705; Restatement (Third) of Property: Wills and Other Donative Transfers § 14.5 (2011) (class gift includes child adopted by third person if adoption occurred before child reached age of majority, adoptive parent "functioned as a parent of the child" before child reached age of majority, or adoptive parent was child's stepparent or foster parent). Not surprisingly, courts remain skeptical of adult adoptions undertaken for the purpose of affecting the operation of class gifts. For example, in one case a settlor created a trust to pay income to her daughter for life with remainder to the daughter's descendants. A few years after her mother's death, the daughter adopted her same-sex partner with a view to securing a share of the trust property for the partner. Although by its terms the class gift included a "legally adopted child," the court rejected the partner's claim, stating that "an adopted adult will not ordinarily be included in a class gift from a stranger to the adoption as a 'child' or 'legally adopted child' unless the adult was taken into the adoptive home as a minor and reared as a member of the adopting parent's family." First Nat'l Bank of Dubuque v. Mackey, 338 N.W.2d 361 (Iowa 1983); see also Minary v. Citizens Fidelity Bank & Trust Co., 419 S.W.2d 340 (Ky.1967) (spousal adoption; same result); Davis v. Neilson, 871 S.W.2d 35 (Mo. App. 1993) (class gift included only "individuals with familial ties to the adopting parent"); Estate of Bovey, 132 P.3d 510 (Mont. 2006) (stepdaughter, adopted as adult by stepfather, was not a "regular member of [stepfather's] household" although she lived with her mother and stepfather for two years during minority before being placed in foster care); Chichester v. Wilmington Trust Co., 377 A.2d 11 (Del. 1977) (stepchildren adopted as adults by stepfather were entitled to share in gift to his "issue"; the court distinguished cases involving the use of adult adoption "to perpetrate a fraud or to prevent the operation of a gift over"). On the status of children who are "adopted out," see Restatement (Third) of Property: Wills and Other Donative Transfers § 14.6 (2011); In re Accounting by Fleet Bank, 884 N.E.2d 1040 (N.Y. 2008); Miller v. Walker, 514 S.E.2d 22 (Ga. 1999); Newman v. Wells Fargo Bank, 926 P.2d 969 (Cal. 1996); Crumpton v. Mitchell, 281 S.E.2d 1 (N.C.1981).

2. NONMARITAL CHILDREN

An increasing number of children in this country are born out of wedlock. It is estimated that more than one out of every three children born today has parents who are not married to each other. Apart from the obvious difficulties relating to custody and child support, the legal status of children born out of wedlock also raises special problems in the area of intestate succession. The evolving state of the law is reflected in the terminology used by legislatures, courts and commentators. The traditional term "illegitimate child," with its overtones of moral reproach concerning the child's provenance, has been rejected by some reformers in favor of less value-laden terms such as "out-of-wedlock child" or "nonmarital child." The term "bastard," in its technically exact sense, has fallen into almost complete disuse.

At common law, a child born out of wedlock was deemed to be "filius nullius"—the child of no one—and treated with unremitting severity for purposes of inheritance. Such children were isolated from their forebears; their only relatives were their own issue. Accordingly, they could not inherit from any lineal ancestors or collateral relatives, nor could the ancestors or relatives inherit from them. A child who was born while the parents were lawfully married was deemed legitimate, even if conceived before marriage, but a child born before the marriage of the parents was not legitimated by that marriage. Although the common law rule is sometimes said to reflect a desire to discourage extramarital sexual relations, it seems naive to suppose that it had a significant deterrent effect, and, at least to modern eyes, the unfairness of visiting retribution on children for their parents' transgressions is evident.

From the outset, the American statutes ameliorated in some measure the harshness of the common law with respect to children born out of wedlock. Even today, however, distinctions based on the parents' marital status have by no means been eradicated. In general, the statutes recognize reciprocal rights of inheritance between nonmarital children on the one hand and their mothers and maternal kindred on the other. With respect to fathers and paternal kindred, however, the situation is more complicated. Until the late 1970s, statutes routinely permitted inheritance between a nonmarital child and the father and paternal kindred only if the child had been legitimated by the subsequent marriage of the father and mother. The usual justifications offered for such statutory restrictions were that they strengthened family ties and facilitated prompt administration of decedents' estates.

In a series of cases beginning with Levy v. Louisiana, 391 U.S. 68 (1968), the Supreme Court considered the constitutionality of discrimination based on illegitimacy. Three of these cases involved statutory restrictions on inheritance. In Labine v. Vincent, 401 U.S. 532 (1971), the Court upheld a Louisiana intestacy statute which barred an illegitimate child from sharing equally with legitimate children in the estate of their father, even though the father had publicly acknowledged the child during life. In rejecting the child's equal protection challenge, the Court commented:

> Of course, it may be said that the rules adopted by the Louisiana Legislature "discriminate" against illegitimates. But the rules also discriminate against collateral relations, as opposed to ascendants, and against ascendants, as opposed to descendants. Other rules determining property rights based on family status also "discriminate" in favor of wives and against "concubines." The dissent attempts to distinguish these other "discriminations" on the ground that they have a biological or social basis. There is no biological difference between a wife and a concubine, nor does the Constitution require that

there be such a difference before the State may assert its power to protect the wife and her children against the claims of a concubine and her children. The social difference between a wife and a concubine is analogous to the difference between a legitimate and an illegitimate child. One set of relationships is socially sanctioned, legally recognized, and gives rise to various rights and duties. The other set of relationships is illicit and beyond the recognition of the law. [401 U.S. at 537–38.]

The 5–4 decision in Trimble v. Gordon, 430 U.S. 762 (1977), went a long way toward recognizing a constitutional basis for permitting illegitimate children to share equally with legitimate children in the estate of an intestate father whose identity was not in dispute. *Trimble* involved an Illinois intestacy statute which permitted an illegitimate child to inherit only from or through the mother, and declared the child legitimate if the parents married and the child was acknowledged by the father. The decedent in *Trimble* had been established before death as the father of an illegitimate child in state court proceedings, and had openly acknowledged and supported the child. Because the father and mother had not married, however, the child was ineligible to inherit from the father. According to a majority of the Court, difficulties in proving paternity "might justify a more demanding standard for illegitimate children claiming under their fathers' estates than that required either for illegitimate children claiming under their mothers' estates or for legitimate children generally" but such difficulties did not justify "total statutory disinheritance of illegitimate children whose fathers die intestate." The court held that the child was entitled to inherit from the father, pointing out that in view of the prior judicial determination of paternity the state's interest in "accurate and efficient disposition of property at death" would not be compromised in any way.

One year later, the Court retreated from the implications of *Trimble* in Lalli v. Lalli, 439 U.S. 259 (1978), another 5–4 decision. *Lalli* involved a New York intestacy statute which permitted an illegitimate child to inherit from the father only if a court made an "order of filiation" declaring paternity during the father's life in proceedings instituted no later than two years after the child's birth. This requirement was not met because, although the decedent had openly acknowledged and supported his illegitimate children, no judicial declaration of paternity was obtained during his life. The Court distinguished *Trimble*, noting that the New York statute required only a judicial determination of paternity during the father's life, not marriage of the parents. The majority found that this "evidentiary" requirement was substantially related to the state's interest in providing for the "just and orderly disposition of property at death," as follows:

The administration of an estate will be facilitated, and the possibility of delay and uncertainty minimized, where the entitlement of an illegitimate child to notice and participation is a matter of judicial record before the administration commences. Fraudulent assertions of paternity will be much less likely to succeed, or even to arise, where the proof is put before a court of law at a time when the putative father is available to respond, rather than first brought to light when the distribution of the assets of an estate is in the offing. [439 U.S. at 272–73.]

The four dissenters saw matters differently:

[I]t is difficult to imagine an instance in which an illegitimate child, acknowledged and voluntarily supported by his father, would ever inherit intestate under the New York scheme. Social welfare agencies, busy as they are with errant fathers, are unlikely to bring paternity proceedings against fathers who support their children. Similarly, children who are acknowledged and supported by their fathers are unlikely to bring paternity proceedings against them. First, they are unlikely to see the need for such adversary proceedings. Second, even if aware of the rule requiring judicial filiation orders, they are likely to fear provoking disharmony by suing their fathers. For the same reasons, mothers of such illegitimates are unlikely to bring proceedings against the fathers. Finally, fathers who do not even bother to make out wills (and thus die intestate) are unlikely to take the time to bring formal filiation proceedings. Thus, as a practical matter, by requiring judicial filiation orders entered during the lifetime of the fathers, the New York statute makes it virtually impossible for acknowledged and freely supported illegitimate children to inherit intestate. [439 U.S. at 278 (Brennan, J., dissenting).]

The decisions in *Labine*, *Trimble*, and *Lalli* left the states with considerable latitude to regulate inheritance by nonmarital children from their fathers. Nevertheless, the constitutional tug-of-war documented in this trilogy of cases prompted a widespread reexamination of existing statutory restrictions. Most statutes (including the New York statute upheld in *Lalli*, as well as the Illinois statute struck down in *Trimble*) were revised to permit alternative methods of proving paternity which avoided the risk of renewed constitutional scrutiny.

Today most intestacy statutes avoid any explicit distinction between marital and nonmarital children. For example, the Uniform Probate Code generally recognizes the existence of a parent-child relationship between a child and its "genetic parents" for purposes of intestate succession, "regardless of the parents' marital status," but provides no specific guidelines for identifying the child's father in cases of doubtful or disputed paternity. UPC § 2–117; cf. UPC § 2–115(5) (referring to presumption of paternity under "applicable state law"). Of course, such statutes do not achieve complete functional parity between marital and nonmarital children, but they do make clear that any obstacles to inheritance by nonmarital children stem from the difficulty of proving paternity and not from any special discrimination in the intestacy scheme.

When doubts arise concerning the parentage of a child, whether born in or out of wedlock, it is usually the father whose identity is uncertain; ordinarily there is no difficulty identifying the mother. To assist in establishing paternity, the Uniform Parentage Act raises several presumptions. A man is presumed to be the child's father if he is married to the child's mother and the child is born during the marriage (or within 300 days after its termination). Even if the man is not married to the mother, he is presumed to be the father if "for the first two years of the child's life, he resided in the same household with the child and openly held out the child as his own." Uniform Parentage Act § 204. Paternity may also be established by a voluntary acknowledgment in writing, signed by both parents and filed with the agency that maintains birth records. Id. §§ 301, 302 and 305. If there is a presumed father, a proceeding to establish another man's paternity ordinarily must be commenced within two years after the child's birth, but if there is no presumed father—e.g., where an alleged father refuses to acknowledge a nonmarital child as his own—the child may bring a proceeding to establish paternity "at any time." Id. §§ 606 and 607. The Act authorizes a court to order genetic testing of the child, the alleged father, and other relatives if necessary. Id. §§ 501–511. Indeed, upon a showing of "good cause," a court may order genetic testing of a deceased individual. Id. § 509.

NOTES

1. *Lingering constitutional questions.* Today most states, but by no means all, allow a nonmarital child an opportunity to prove paternity in a judicial proceeding after the alleged father's death. Some states still require that paternity be established during the father's lifetime by marriage, judicial decree, or a formal acknowledgment in writing. In these states, the nonmarital child may be barred from sharing in the father's estate if the statutory requirements are not met during the father's lifetime, even though paternity is undisputed. See Phillips v. Ledford, 590 S.E.2d 280 (N.C. App. 2004) (father acknowledged paternity to family, friends, and public, but failed to sign written acknowledgment or obtain court order); Pinckney v. Warren, 544 S.E.2d 620 (S.C. 2001).

The statute upheld in *Lalli* required that paternity be established during the alleged father's lifetime as a condition of inheritance by a nonmarital child. Nevertheless, in cases involving claims for support of nonmarital children, the Supreme Court has applied the equal protection clause to strike down statutes which impose unreasonably short limitation periods on actions to establish paternity. See Mills v. Habluetzel, 456 U.S. 91 (1982) (one year from child's birth); Clark v. Jeter, 486 U.S. 456 (1988) (six years from child's birth). Similar considerations may be relevant in the context of intestate succession. One court has held that a requirement that paternity proceedings be maintained during the alleged father's lifetime is unconstitutional "as applied to illegitimates whose fathers have died within one year after their birth, and who would thereby effectively be barred from receiving child's benefits under [an intestacy statute] because of legal inability to prove paternity." Handley v. Schweiker, 697 F.2d 999 (11th Cir.1983) (father was in coma for four months before child's birth and subsequently died without regaining consciousness).

State constitutions may provide independent grounds for attacking restrictions on inheritance by nonmarital children. For example, in Lowell v. Kowalski, 405 N.E.2d 135 (Mass.1980), the court struck down a Massachusetts statute which permitted a nonmarital child to inherit from the father only if the child's parents married each other and the father's paternity was established by acknowledgment or adjudication. No such restrictions were imposed on inheritance from the mother. While recognizing that the "absolute requirement that the child's parents have intermarried" would fail to pass muster under the federal equal protection clause, the court invoked strict scrutiny under the state constitution. On the question of whether the statute was "as narrow in its impact as is possible, consistent with the purpose of avoiding fraudulent claims against the estate of a man who died intestate," the court stated:

> We accept a judicial adjudication of paternity as one appropriate method of establishing inheritance rights. If, however, judicial classification were the only permitted means of establishing those rights, the classification would be unconstitutionally restrictive because it would unnecessarily foreclose the rights of illegitimates who could convincingly establish their parentage. An option limited to an adjudication of paternity would deny, for example, rights to a child whose natural father publicly and consistently acknowledged his child and did so in writing, perhaps even under oath. [405 N.E.2d at 141.]

Compare the Supreme Court's analysis in *Lalli*, supra.

A nonmarital child died intestate, survived by no spouse, issue, or maternal kindred; the child's only surviving relatives were children of the alleged father's brother. The Virginia intestacy statute then in force (but subsequently replaced) permitted inheritance by maternal but not paternal kindred. In King v. Commonwealth, 269 S.E.2d 793 (Va.1980), the court rejected the alleged cousins' equal protection challenge, resulting in an escheat of the child's estate. The court distinguished *Trimble* and *Lalli* on the grounds that no disability was being visited upon an innocent child and that the father had never acknowledged or supported the child. Compare Estate of Hicks, 675

N.E.2d 89 (Ill.1996) (statute permitting mother but not father to inherit from nonmarital child violated equal rights provision of state constitution).

2. *Proving (or disproving) paternity.* If a child is born to a married woman, the common law presumes that the woman's husband is the child's father. The presumption can be rebutted by showing that the husband was sterile, impotent or physically absent during the relevant time period. On the type and weight of evidence admissible to prove the paternity of a man other than the husband, see Estate of Willis, 574 N.E.2d 172 (Ill.App.1991) (birth certificate, life insurance beneficiary designations, photographs and cards); Estate of Calloway, 502 A.2d 1169 (N.J.App.1986) (nonmarital child permitted to inherit from alleged father who openly acknowledged her as his child and provided support).

While an alleged father is alive the methods of proving paternity are relatively straightforward. After the alleged father's death, however, proof is often more complicated. May a person claiming to be the nonmarital child of an intestate decedent compel the decedent's surviving relatives to submit to blood tests? See Estate of Gaynor, 818 N.Y.S.2d 747 (Sur. 2006); Estate of Sanders, 3 Cal.Rptr.2d 536 (App. 1992). May the claimant obtain a judicial order that the decedent be disinterred so that paternity can be established by genetic testing? See Estate of Kingsbury, 946 A.2d 389 (Me. 2008); Batcheldor v. Boyd, 423 S.E.2d 810 (N.C. App. 1992); Estate of Janis, 620 N.Y.S.2d 342 (App. Div. 1994).

3. *Parent's right to inherit from child.* Even if paternity is established, many statutes prohibit the father or his kindred from inheriting from a nonmarital child unless the father has openly treated the child as his own and has not refused to support the child. See Estate of Ford, 552 So.2d 1065 (Miss.1989) (father never openly recognized child, who was raised by mother and maternal grandparents; held, father's kindred not entitled to inherit from child); Estate of McCoy, 988 So.2d 929 (Miss. 2008) (father, incarcerated throughout child's two-year life, barred from inheriting due to nonsupport). The Uniform Probate Code extends these requirements to both parents of any child, regardless of their marital status. See UPC § 2–114 (parent ineligible to inherit if parental rights are subject to termination for "nonsupport, abandonment, abuse, neglect, or other actions or inactions of the parent toward the child"). If a father dies before his child is born, how can he acknowledge the child as his own? See Estate of Evjen, 448 N.W.2d 23 (Iowa 1989) (father who died seven months before child's birth "recognized" child by oral declarations).

A mother gave up her infant son to a charitable organization for adoption, and the mother's parental rights were terminated by court order. The son was never adopted, however, and fifty years later he died intestate, unmarried and without issue. If his mother survives him, is she entitled to an intestate share of his estate? See Estate of Fleming, 21 P.3d 281 (Wash. 2001) (son had "no legal parent," resulting in escheat); UPC § 2–114 (termination of parental rights bars parent from inheriting from or through child).

A parent who neglects or abuses a child or is determined to be "unfit" on other grounds may have his or her parental rights involuntarily terminated. In some states, the termination of parental rights automatically divests both the unfit parent and the child of all legal rights and obligations, including rights of inheritance. As a result, unless and until the child is adopted into a new family, the child may be barred—through no fault on the child's part— from inheriting from the parent. See Estate of Braa, 452 N.W.2d 686 (Minn. 1990) (termination of adoptive mother's parental rights). Should the status of such "legal orphans" be subject to constitutional scrutiny similar to that of nonmarital children? See Brown, Disinheriting the "Legal Orphan": Inheritance Rights of Children After Termination of Parental Rights, 70 Mo. L. Rev. 125 (2005) (concluding that "[e]xtinguishing the inheritance rights of children of terminated parents is unwarranted").

4. *Testamentary gifts.* Nonmarital children, like adopted children, have traditionally been excluded from class gifts to "children," "issue," "descendants" and the like in wills and trusts, in the absence of language or circumstances supporting a contrary intent on the part of the testator or settlor. Today, however, most courts have abandoned the "archaic" traditional rule in favor of a rule of construction that "the word 'issue,' absent clear expressions of a contrary intent, must be construed to include all biological descendants." Powers v. Wilkinson, 506 N.E.2d 842 (Mass.1987). The inclusive rule extends not only to the testator's own children, but also to children of other persons, at least where the functional parent-child relationship began during the child's minority. See UPC § 2–705; Restatement (Third) of Property: Wills and Other Donative Transfers § 14.7 (2011) (class gift includes child of third person if the parent or the parent's spouse or close relative "functioned as a parent of the child" before child reached age of majority). If the new rule of construction applies only to instruments executed after the statute's effective date, does the application of the traditional rule to older instruments constitute a denial of equal protection? See Estate of Dulles, 431 A.2d 208 (Pa.1981).

3.　CHILDREN OF ASSISTED REPRODUCTION

Modern medicine offers an ever-expanding array of techniques for conceiving children by artificial means. One relatively simple and inexpensive method is artificial insemination—a woman is impregnated with a (usually anonymous) male donor's sperm, and the woman then carries the resulting child to term and gives birth in the usual manner. Even if a woman is unable to conceive or give birth, it is possible to extract an egg from her body, fertilize it, and then implant it in the uterus of a woman (who may be the same individual or a surrogate) who bears the resulting child; this process is known as in vitro fertilization.

The evolving technology of "assisted reproduction" raises questions about who should be legally recognized as a child's parents. No longer can it be assumed that every child has one pair of natural parents who can be identified conclusively based on a genetic tie. Instead, depending on the circumstances of a particular case, at least two candidates might plausibly vie for recognition as a child's mother, including the "birth mother" who gave birth to the child and the "genetic mother" whose egg was fertilized to conceive the child. Similarly, the child's father might be identified either as the husband of the woman who gave birth to the child or the "genetic father" whose sperm was used to conceive the child. In addition, a man or woman who intended to raise the child as his or her own pursuant to a surrogacy agreement might qualify as an "intended parent." To complicate matters further, the criteria for determining parentage in enforcing custodial rights or support obligations during the parties' joint lifetime may differ from those for determining inheritance rights at the death of the parent or the child.

The Uniform Probate Code provides extensive and detailed rules governing the existence and effect of a parent-child relationship for purposes of intestate succession. The rules are intricate and detailed; we can offer only an abbreviated summary here. In the case of a child conceived by assisted reproduction (other than pursuant to a surrogacy agreement, discussed infra), the birth mother is recognized as the child's mother. If the birth mother is married and uses her husband's sperm to conceive the child during the husband's lifetime, the husband is recognized as the child's father. A third-party sperm or egg donor is not recognized as the child's parent. UPC § 2–120(b)–(d). A person (other than the birth mother) who is identified on the birth certificate as the child's other parent is presumptively recognized as such. UPC § 2–120(e). Moreover, a person "who consented to assisted reproduction by the birth mother with intent to be treated as the other parent of the child" may qualify as a parent, if that person either signed a record evidencing consent or functioned as a parent within two years after the child's birth. UPC § 2–120(f). If the birth mother is married and no divorce proceeding is pending, her spouse is presumed to have the requisite intent to function as the child's other parent. UPC § 2–120(h). In this context, functioning as a parent means "behaving toward a child in a manner consistent with being the child's parent and performing functions that are customarily performed by a parent, including fulfilling parental responsibilities toward the child, recognizing or holding out the child as the individual's child, materially participating in the child's upbringing, and residing with the child in the same household as a regular member of that household." UPC § 2–115(4). To illustrate the operation of these provisions, consider the following examples:

(a) *W*, a married woman, conceives a child *C* by artificial insemination, using the sperm of her husband *H*. *W* and *H* are recognized as *C*'s parents under UPC § 2–120(c) and (d).

(b) *W*, a married woman, conceives a child *C* by artificial insemination, using the sperm of an anonymous donor *D*, with the written consent of her (presumably infertile) husband *H*. *W* and *H* are recognized as *C*'s parents under UPC § 2–120(c) and (f).

(c) *W*, an unmarried woman, gives birth to a child *C*, who was conceived in vitro, using an egg donated by *W*'s sister *S* and sperm donated by *W*'s friend *F*. *F* is identified as *C*'s father on the birth certificate. *W* and *F* are recognized as *C*'s parents under UPC § 2–120(c) and (e).

(d) *W*, an unmarried woman, conceives a child *C* by artificial insemination, using sperm donated by an anonymous donor *D*, with the consent of *W*'s same-sex domestic partner *P* who functions as *C*'s parent from the time of *C*'s birth. *W* and *P* are treated as *C*'s parents under UPC § 2–120(c) and (f).

Among the most difficult questions are those involving surrogacy agreements—personal service contracts under which a woman (who may or may not be the genetic mother) is hired to bear a child on behalf of an "intended" parent. Several courts have upheld "gestational" surrogacy arrangements in which the intended parents (or third-party donors) furnish the sperm and egg and the gestational mother is not genetically related to the resulting child. See Johnson v. Calvert, 851 P.2d 776 (Cal.), cert. denied, 510 U.S. 874 (1993); Culliton v. Beth Israel Deaconess Medical Center, 756 N.E.2d 1133 (Mass.2001). In contrast, courts have repeatedly refused to enforce "traditional" surrogacy arrangements in which a woman conceives a child through artificial insemination and agrees to surrender the resulting child to the intended parents. See In re Baby M., 537 A.2d 1227 (N.J.1988); Marriage of Moschetta, 30 Cal.Rptr.2d 893 (App. 1994); R.R. v. M.H., 689 N.E.2d 790 (Mass. 1998); see also N.Y. Dom. Rel. L. § 122 (declaring surrogacy agreements void and unenforceable).

The Uniform Probate Code does not distinguish between surrogacy agreements of the gestational or traditional variety, nor does it expressly authorize or prohibit such agreements. Instead, it provides that the parentage of a child born pursuant to such an agreement is "conclusively established by a court order designating the [child's] parent or parents." UPC § 2–121(b). In the absence of a court order, an intended parent who entered into the surrogacy agreement is recognized as the child's parent if he or she functioned as a parent within two years after the child's birth. UPC § 2–121(d). The intended parent need not have any genetic link to the child. The woman who gave birth to the child (the "gestational carrier") is generally not recognized as a parent. UPC § 2–121(c).

The Uniform Probate Code provisions concerning children of assisted reproduction are discussed in Gary, We Are Family: The Definition of Parent and Child for Succession Purposes, 34 ACTEC J. 171 (2008); Kurtz & Waggoner, The UPC Addresses the Class-Gift and Intestacy Rights of Children of Assisted Reproduction Technologies, 35 ACTEC L.J. 30 (2009); and Tritt, Sperms and Estates: An Unadulterated Functionally Based Approach to Parent-Child Property Succession, 62 SMU L. Rev. 367 (2009). For general discussions of assisted reproduction technology and inheritance law, see Brashier, Children and Inheritance in the Nontraditional Family, 1996 Utah L. Rev. 93; Guzman, Property, Progeny, Body Part: Assisted Reproduction and the Transfer of Wealth, 31 U.C. Davis L. Rev. 193 (1997); McAllister, Defining the Parent–Child Relationship in an Age of Reproductive Technology: Implications for Inheritance, 29 Real Prop. Prob. & Tr. J. 55 (1994); Shapo, Matters of Life and Death: Inheritance Consequences of Reproductive Technologies, 25 Hofstra L. Rev. 1091 (1997).

4. POSTHUMOUS CHILDREN

To qualify as an intestate successor, a person generally must be in existence at the time of the decedent's death. If a child is "en ventre sa mère" (i.e., in gestation) at the decedent's death and is subsequently born alive, the child is treated as a life in being at the decedent's death for purposes of inheritance. This rule is an application of a more general principle of property law which treats a child who is ultimately born alive as a life in being from the time of conception whenever this is beneficial to the child. In some states, however, the rule applies only to children and other descendants of the intestate, with the result that collaterals must actually be born before the intestate's death in order to inherit. At common law, the presumed period of gestation is 280 days; accordingly, a child born within 280 days after the intestate's death is presumed to have been in existence at the time of death, while a child born later is not. The presumption is rebuttable. See Byerly v. Tolbert, 108 S.E.2d 29 (N.C. 1959) (child born 323 days after intestate's death).

Technology for storing human genetic material (sperm and eggs) has developed to the point where a child can be conceived long after the death of one or both parents. For example, a husband may deposit samples of his sperm in a sperm bank with the understanding that his wife can use them to conceive a child through artificial insemination after his death. Should the resulting child be eligible to inherit from the deceased husband? Alternatively, suppose that an egg is extracted from the wife's body, fertilized with the husband's sperm, and the resulting embryo is then frozen. Both spouses are subsequently killed in an automobile accident. Is the frozen embryo a life in being for purposes of inheritance? If the embryo is subsequently implanted in the body of a surrogate mother who carries it to term and gives birth, should the resulting child inherit from or through the genetic parents?

WOODWARD V. COMMISSIONER

Supreme Judicial Court of Massachusetts, 2002.
435 Mass. 536, 760 N.E.2d 257.

MARSHALL, C.J.

The United States District Court for the District of Massachusetts has certified the following question to this court. . . .

> If a married man and woman arrange for sperm to be withdrawn from the husband for the purpose of artificially impregnating the wife, and the woman is impregnated with that sperm after the man, her husband, has died, will children resulting from such pregnancy enjoy the inheritance rights of natural children under Massachusetts' law of intestate succession?

We answer the certified question as follows: In certain limited circumstances, a child resulting from posthumous reproduction may enjoy the inheritance rights of "issue" under the Massachusetts intestacy statute. These limited circumstances exist where, as a threshold matter, the surviving parent or the child's other legal representative demonstrates a genetic relationship between the child and the decedent. The survivor or representative must then establish both that the decedent affirmatively consented to posthumous conception and to the support of any resulting child. Even where such circumstances exist, time limitations may preclude commencing a claim for succession rights on behalf of a posthumously conceived child. Because the government has conceded that the timeliness of the wife's paternity action under our intestacy law is irrelevant to her Federal appeal, we do not address that question today.

The United States District Court judge has not asked us to determine whether the circumstances giving rise to succession rights for posthumously conceived children apply here. . . .

I

The undisputed facts and relevant procedural history are as follows. In January, 1993, about three and one-half years after they were married, Lauren Woodward and Warren Woodward were informed that the husband had leukemia. At the time, the couple was childless. Advised that the husband's leukemia treatment might leave him sterile, the Woodwards arranged for a quantity of the husband's semen to be medically withdrawn and preserved, in a process commonly known as "sperm banking." The husband then underwent a bone marrow transplant. The treatment was not successful. The husband died in October, 1993, and the wife was appointed administratrix of his estate.

In October, 1995, the wife gave birth to twin girls. The children were conceived through artificial insemination using the husband's preserved semen. In January, 1996, the wife applied for two forms of Social Security survivor benefits: "child's" benefits . . . , and "mother's" benefits. . . .[6]

The Social Security Administration (SSA) rejected the wife's claims on the ground that she had not established that the twins were the husband's "children" within the meaning of the Act.[7] . . . The wife appealed to the United States District Court for the District of Massachusetts, seeking a declaratory judgment to reverse the commissioner's ruling.

The United States District Court judge certified the above question to this court because "the parties agree that a determination of these children's rights under the law of Massachusetts is dispositive of the case and . . . no directly applicable Massachusetts precedent exists."

II

A

We have been asked to determine the inheritance rights under Massachusetts law of children conceived from the gametes of a deceased individual and his or her surviving spouse. We have not previously been asked to consider whether our intestacy statute accords inheritance rights to posthumously conceived genetic children. Nor has any American court of last resort considered, in a published opinion, the question of posthumously conceived genetic children's inheritance rights under other States' intestacy laws.

This case presents a narrow set of circumstances, yet the issues it raises are far reaching. . . . Moreover, the parties have articulated extreme positions. The wife's principal argument is that, by virtue of their genetic connection with the decedent, posthumously conceived children

---

[6] In the case of a fully insured decedent (such as the husband here), the Social Security Act provides "child's" benefits for the decedent's children as well as "mother's" benefits for the decedent's widow who has care of such children, under conditions set forth in the statute. See 42 U.S.C. § 402(d), (g).—EDS.

[7] In the present case, the twins would be eligible for child's benefits if they were treated as the husband's children in disposing of his personal estate under the Massachusetts law of intestate succession, 42 U.S.C. §§ 402(d) and 416(h)(2). An administrative law judge concluded that the twins were not entitled to inherit from the husband under Massachusetts intestacy law because they were neither born nor conceived before the husband's death. This conclusion was affirmed by the appeals council and thus became the Social Security commissioner's final decision for purposes of judicial review.—EDS.

must *always* be permitted to enjoy the inheritance rights of the deceased parent's children under our law of intestate succession. The government's principal argument is that, because posthumously conceived children are not "in being" as of the date of the parent's death, they are *always* barred from enjoying such inheritance rights.

Neither party's position is tenable. In this developing and relatively uncharted area of human relations, bright-line rules are not favored unless the applicable statute requires them. The Massachusetts intestacy statute does not. Neither the statute's "posthumous children" provision, see G.L. c. 190, § 8, nor any other provision of our intestacy law limits the class of posthumous children to those in utero at the time of the decedent's death. . . . On the other hand, with the act of procreation now separated from coitus, posthumous reproduction can occur under a variety of conditions that may conflict with the purposes of the intestacy law and implicate other firmly established State and individual interests. We look to our intestacy law to resolve these tensions.

B

. . . Section 1 of the intestacy statute directs that, if a decedent "leaves issue," such "issue" will inherit a fixed portion of his real and personal property, subject to debts and expenses, the rights of the surviving spouse, and other statutory payments not relevant here. See G.L. c. 190, § 1. To answer the certified question, then, we must first determine whether the twins are the "issue" of the husband.

The intestacy statute does not define "issue." However, in the context of intestacy the term "issue" means all lineal (genetic) descendants, and now includes both marital and nonmarital descendants. . . . The term " 'descendants' . . . has long been held to mean persons 'who by consanguinity trace their lineage to the designated ancestor.' " . . .

Turning to "issue" who are the nonmarital children of an intestate, the intestacy statute treats different classes of nonmarital children differently based on the presumed ease of establishing their consanguinity with the deceased parent. A nonmarital child is presumptively the child of his or her mother and is entitled by virtue of this presumption to enjoy inheritance rights as her issue. G.L. c. 190, § 5. However, to enjoy inheritance rights as the issue of a deceased father, a nonmarital child, in the absence of the father's acknowledgment of paternity or marriage to the mother, must obtain a judicial determination that he or she is the father's child. G.L. c. 190, § 7. The general purpose of such a specific adjudication requirement is to ensure that wealth passes from and to the actual family. . . . We held, at a time when the means for establishing the paternity of a child were less certain than they are today, that such disparate treatment between the mother and the father of a child advanced the Legislature's interests in preventing fraudulent claims against the estate and in administering estates in an orderly fashion. See *Lowell v. Kowalski,* 380 Mass. 663, 668, 405 N.E.2d 135 (1980) ("distinction between rights to inherit from a natural father and rights to inherit from a natural mother may properly be based on the greater difficulty of proving paternity than of proving maternity").

The "posthumous children" provision of the intestacy statute, G.L. c. 190, § 8, is yet another expression of the Legislature's intent to preserve wealth for consanguineous descendants. That section provides that "posthumous children shall be considered as living at the death of their parent." The Legislature, however, has left the term "posthumous children" undefined. . . .

The Massachusetts intestacy statute thus does not contain an express, affirmative requirement that posthumous children must "be in existence" as of the date of the decedent's death. The Legislature could surely have enacted such a provision had it desired to do so. . . . We must therefore determine whether, under our intestacy law, there is any reason that children conceived after the decedent's death who are the decedent's direct genetic descendants—that is, children who "by consanguinity trace their lineage to the designated ancestor"—may not enjoy the same succession rights as children conceived before the decedent's death who are the decedent's direct genetic descendants. . . .

To answer that question we consider whether and to what extent such children may take as intestate heirs of the deceased genetic parent consistent with the purposes of the intestacy law, and not by any assumptions of the common law. . . . In the absence of express legislative directives, we construe the Legislature's purposes from statutory indicia and judicial decisions in a manner that advances the purposes of the intestacy law. . . .

The question whether posthumously conceived genetic children may enjoy inheritance rights under the intestacy statute implicates three powerful State interests: the best interests of children, the State's interest in the orderly administration of estates, and the reproductive rights of the genetic parent. Our task is to balance and harmonize these interests to effect the Legislature's over-all purposes.

1. First and foremost we consider the overriding legislative concern to promote the best interests of children. "The protection of minor children, most especially those who may be stigmatized by their 'illegitimate' status . . . has been a hallmark of legislative action and of the jurisprudence of this court." . . . Repeatedly, forcefully, and unequivocally, the Legislature has expressed its will that all children be "entitled to the same rights and protections of the law" regardless of the accidents of their

birth. G.L. c. 209C, § 1. . . . Among the many rights and protections vouchsafed to all children are rights to financial support from their parents and their parents' estates. . . .

We also consider that some of the assistive reproductive technologies that make posthumous reproduction possible have been widely known and practiced for several decades. See generally Banks, Traditional Concepts and Nontraditional Conceptions: Social Security Survivor's Benefits for Posthumously Conceived Children, 32 Loy. L.A. L. Rev. 251, 267–273 (1999). In that time, the Legislature has not acted to narrow the broad statutory class of posthumous children to restrict posthumously conceived children from taking in intestacy. Moreover, the Legislature has in great measure affirmatively supported the assistive reproductive technologies that are the only means by which these children can come into being. See G.L. c. 46, § 4B (artificial insemination of married woman). . . . We do not impute to the Legislature the inherently irrational conclusion that assistive reproductive technologies are to be encouraged while a class of children who are the fruit of that technology are to have fewer rights and protections than other children.

In short, we cannot, absent express legislative directive, accept the commissioner's position that the historical context of G.L. c. 190, § 8, dictates as a matter of law that all posthumously conceived children are automatically barred from taking under their deceased donor parent's intestate estate. We have consistently construed statutes to effectuate the Legislature's overriding purpose to promote the welfare of all children, notwithstanding restrictive common-law rules to the contrary. . . . Posthumously conceived children may not come into the world the way the majority of children do. But they are children nonetheless. We may assume that the Legislature intended that such children be "entitled," in so far as possible, "to the same rights and protections of the law" as children conceived before death. See G.L. c. 209C, § 1.

2. However, in the context of our intestacy laws, the best interests of the posthumously conceived child, while of great importance, are not in themselves conclusive. They must be balanced against other important State interests, not the least of which is the protection of children who are alive or conceived before the intestate parent's death. In an era in which serial marriages, serial families, and blended families are not uncommon, according succession rights under our intestacy laws to posthumously conceived children may, in a given case, have the potential to pit child against child and family against family. Any inheritance rights of posthumously conceived children will reduce the intestate share available to children born prior to the decedent's death. See G.L. c. 190, § 3 (1). Such considerations, among others, lead us to examine a second important leg-

islative purpose: to provide certainty to heirs and creditors by effecting the orderly, prompt, and accurate administration of intestate estates. . . .

The intestacy statute furthers the Legislature's administrative goals in two principal ways: (1) by requiring certainty of filiation between the decedent and his issue, and (2) by establishing limitations periods for the commencement of claims against the intestate estate. In answering the certified question, we must consider each of these requirements of the intestacy statute in turn.

First, as we have discussed, our intestacy law mandates that, absent the father's acknowledgment of paternity or marriage to the mother, a nonmarital child must obtain a judicial determination of paternity as a prerequisite to succeeding to a portion of the father's intestate estate. Both the United States Supreme Court and this court have long recognized that the State's strong interest in preventing fraudulent claims justifies certain disparate classifications among nonmarital children based on the relative difficulty of accurately determining a child's direct lineal ancestor. See Lowell v. Kowalski, 380 Mass. 663, 668–669, 405 N.E.2d 135 (1980). See also Trimble v. Gordon, 430 U.S. 762, 771, 52 L. Ed. 2d 31, 97 S. Ct. 1459 (1977).

Because death ends a marriage, . . . posthumously conceived children are always nonmarital children. And because the parentage of such children can be neither acknowledged nor adjudicated prior to the decedent's death, it follows that, under the intestacy statute, posthumously conceived children must obtain a judgment of paternity as a necessary prerequisite to enjoying inheritance rights in the estate of the deceased genetic father. Although modern reproductive technologies will increase the possibility of disputed paternity claims, sophisticated modern testing techniques now make the determination of genetic paternity accurate and reliable. . . .

We now turn to the second way in which the Legislature has met its administrative goals: the establishment of a limitations period for bringing paternity claims against the intestate estate. Our discussion of this important goal, however, is necessarily circumscribed by the procedural posture of this case and by the terms of the certified question. [The paternity action in this case was filed more than two years after the husband's death, well beyond the one-year limitation period set forth in the state intestacy statute, but the court noted that the commissioner had in effect conceded that the timeliness of the paternity action was "not relevant to the Federal law question whether the wife's children will be considered the husband's 'natural children' for Social Security benefits purposes."]

Nevertheless, the limitations question is inextricably tied to consideration of the intestacy statute's administrative goals. In the case of posthumously conceived children, the application of the one-year limitations period of G.L. c. 190, § 7 is not clear; it may pose significant burdens on the surviving parent, and consequently on the child. It requires, in effect, that the survivor make a decision to bear children while in the freshness of grieving. It also requires that attempts at conception succeed quickly. Cf. Commentary, Modern Reproductive Technologies: Legal Issues Concerning Cryopreservation and Posthumous Conception, 17 J. Legal Med. 547, 549 (1996) ("It takes an average of seven insemination attempts over 4.4 menstrual cycles to establish pregnancy"). Because the resolution of the time constraints question is not required here, it must await the appropriate case, should one arise.

3. Finally, the question certified to us implicates a third important State interest: to honor the reproductive choices of individuals. We need not address the wife's argument that her reproductive rights would be infringed by denying succession rights to her children under our intestacy law. Nothing in the record even remotely suggests that she was prevented by the State from choosing to conceive children using her deceased husband's semen. The husband's reproductive rights are a more complicated matter.

In A.Z. v. B.Z., 431 Mass. 150, 725 N.E.2d 1051 (2000), we considered certain issues surrounding the disposition of frozen preembryos. A woman sought to enforce written agreements between herself and her former husband. The wife argued that these agreements permitted her to implant frozen preembryos created with the couple's gametes during the marriage, even in the event of their divorce. We declined to enforce the agreements. Persuasive to us, among other factors, was the lack of credible evidence of the husband's "true intention" regarding the disposition of the frozen preembryos, and the changed family circumstance resulting from the couple's divorce. See id. at 158–159. Recognizing that our laws strongly affirm the value of bodily and reproductive integrity, we held that "forced procreation is not an area amenable to judicial enforcement." Id. at 160. In short, A.Z. v. B.Z., supra, recognized that individuals have a protected right to control the use of their gametes.

Consonant with the principles identified in A.Z. v. B.Z., supra, a decedent's silence, or his equivocal indications of a desire to parent posthumously, "ought not to be construed as consent." See Schiff, Arising from the Dead: Challenges of Posthumous Procreation, 75 N.C. L. Rev. 901, 951 (1997). The prospective donor parent must clearly and unequivocally consent not only to posthumous reproduction but also to the support of any resulting child. . . . After the donor-parent's death, the burden rests with the surviving parent, or the posthumously conceived child's other legal representative, to prove the deceased genetic parent's affirmative consent to both requirements for posthumous parentage: posthumous reproduction and the support of any resulting child.

This two-fold consent requirement arises from the nature of alternative reproduction itself. It will not always be the case that a person elects to have his or her gametes medically preserved to create "issue" posthumously. A man, for example, may preserve his semen for myriad reasons, including, among others: to reproduce after recovery from medical treatment, to reproduce after an event that leaves him sterile, or to reproduce when his spouse has a genetic disorder or otherwise cannot have or safely bear children. That a man has medically preserved his gametes for use by his spouse thus may indicate only that he wished to reproduce after some contingency while he was alive, and not that he consented to the different circumstance of creating a child after his death. Uncertainty as to consent may be compounded by the fact that medically preserved semen can remain viable for up to ten years after it was first extracted, long after the original decision to preserve the semen has passed and when such changed circumstances as divorce, remarriage, and a second family may have intervened. . . .

Such circumstances demonstrate the inadequacy of a rule that would make the mere genetic tie of the decedent to any posthumously conceived child, or the decedent's mere election to preserve gametes, sufficient to bind his intestate estate for the benefit of any posthumously conceived child. Without evidence that the deceased intestate parent affirmatively consented (1) to the posthumous reproduction and (2) to support any resulting child, a court cannot be assured that the intestacy statute's goal of fraud prevention is satisfied.

As expressed in our intestacy and paternity laws, sound public policy dictates the requirements we have outlined above. Legal parentage imposes substantial obligations on adults for the welfare of children. Where two adults engage in the act of sexual intercourse, it is a matter of common sense and logic, expressed in well-established law, to charge them with parental responsibilities for the child who is the natural, even if unintended, consequence of their actions. Where conception results from a third-party medical procedure using a deceased person's gametes, it is entirely consistent with our laws on children, parentage, and reproductive freedom to place the burden on the surviving parent (or the posthumously conceived child's other legal representative) to demonstrate the genetic relationship of the child to the decedent and that the intestate consented both to reproduce posthumously and to support any resulting child.

C

The certified question does not require us to specify what proof would be sufficient to establish a successful claim under our intestacy law on behalf of a posthumously conceived child. Nor have we been asked to determine whether the wife has met her burden of proof. . . .

It is undisputed in this case that the husband is the genetic father of the wife's children. However, for the reasons stated above, that fact, in itself, cannot be sufficient to establish that the husband is the children's legal father for purposes of the devolution and distribution of his intestate property. In the United States District Court, the wife may come forward with other evidence as to her husband's consent to posthumously conceive children. She may come forward with evidence of his consent to support such children. We do not speculate as to the sufficiency of evidence she may submit at trial. . . .

III

[W]e have been confronted with novel questions involving the rights of children born from assistive reproductive technologies. . . . As these technologies advance, the number of children they produce will continue to multiply. So, too, will the complex moral, legal, social, and ethical questions that surround their birth. The questions present in this case cry out for lengthy, careful examination outside the adversary process, which can only address the specific circumstances of each controversy that presents itself. They demand a comprehensive response reflecting the considered will of the people.

In the absence of statutory directives, we have answered the certified question by identifying and harmonizing the important State interests implicated therein in a manner that advances the Legislature's over-all purposes. In so doing, we conclude that limited circumstances may exist, consistent with the mandates of our Legislature, in which posthumously conceived children may enjoy the inheritance rights of "issue" under our intestacy law. These limited circumstances exist where, as a threshold matter, the surviving parent or the child's other legal representative demonstrates a genetic relationship between the child and the decedent. The survivor or representative must then establish both that the decedent affirmatively consented to posthumous conception and to the support of any resulting child. Even where such circumstances exist, time limitations may preclude commencing a claim for succession rights on behalf of a posthumously conceived child. In any action brought to establish such inheritance rights, notice must be given to all interested parties. . . .

NOTES

1. *Social security benefits and intestate succession.* The status of posthumous children under state law has ramifications far beyond the administration of decedents' estates. For instance, at the death of an individual who was fully insured under the Social Security system, the decedent's minor or

dependent child may be eligible to receive survivor benefits. For this purpose, the Social Security Act relies primarily on state intestacy law to identify the decedent's eligible children. 42 U.S.C. §§ 402(d), 402(e) and 416(h)(2). See Astrue v. Capato, 132 S.Ct. 2021 (2012) (discussing statutory definition of "child"). Thus, to establish eligibility for Social Security benefits, a posthumous child may have to seek a judicial determination that he or she qualifies as an intestate successor of the decedent, even if there is no probate estate to be administered. Several courts have obliged. In addition to the principal case, see Estate of Kolacy, 753 A.2d 1257 (N.J. Super. 2000) (New Jersey law). In many states, however, the intestacy law tacitly or expressly denies inheritance rights to posthumous children. In Khabbaz v. Commissioner, 930 A.2d 1180 (N.H. 2007), the court held that a posthumous child did not qualify as the decedent's "surviving issue" within the meaning of the intestacy statute:

> [T]he plain meaning of the word "surviving" is "remaining alive or in existence." . . . In order to remain alive or in existence after her father passed away, [the child] would necessarily have to have been "alive" or "in existence" at the time of his death. She was not. She was conceived more than a year after his death. It follows, therefore, that neither she nor any posthumously conceived child is a "surviving issue" within the plain meaning of the statute. [930 A.2d at 1183–84.]

See also Finley v. Astrue, 270 S.W.3d 849 (Ark. 2008) (statutory requirement that child be "conceived" before decedent's death not satisfied where embryo created by in vitro fertilization during decedent's lifetime was not implanted in widow's uterus until after death); Schafer v. Astrue, 641 F.3d 49 (4th Cir. 2011), cert. denied, 132 S.Ct. 2680 (2012) (child not born within statutory 10–month period after decedent's death).

What exactly did the court decide in *Woodward*? Do the twins that Lauren Woodward conceived using her deceased husband's sperm qualify as her husband's children for purposes of intestate succession? Are they eligible for survivor benefits under the Social Security Act? Note that in the case of nonmarital children, the Massachusetts intestacy statute requires that a determination of the decedent's paternity be made within one year after the decedent's death. If this requirement is not met, would the twins be eligible to claim an intestate share of their father's estate? Would they be eligible to inherit through their predeceased father from his relatives?

2. *Intestacy statutes and posthumous children.* Several states have enacted legislation concerning inheritance by children conceived after the parent's death. A few states have adopted § 707 of the Uniform Parentage Act (2000), which provides that an individual who "dies before placement of eggs, sperm, or embryos" is not a parent of the resulting child unless the decedent "consented in a record that if assisted reproduction were to occur after death, the deceased individual would be a parent of the child." In addition to the decedent's written consent, some states also require that the child be in utero or be born alive within a specified time after the decedent's death. See, e.g., Cal.

Prob. Code § 249.5 (child must be in utero within two years after official determination of parent's death); Va. Code § 20–164 (child must be born within ten months after parent's death). In Florida, a posthumous child is not eligible to share in the decedent's estate "unless the child has been provided for by the decedent's will." Fla. Stat. § 742.17. For a discussion of existing statutes and alternative proposals, see Knaplund, Equal Protection, Postmortem Conception, and Intestacy, 53 Kan. L. Rev. 627 (2005).

In the context of assisted reproduction, the Uniform Probate Code defines the parent-child relationship primarily on the basis of intent and behavior rather than consanguinity. Recall that UPC § 2–120(f)(1) generally treats a person as a child's parent if he or she consents in writing to assisted reproduction by the birth mother with the intent to be treated as the child's "other parent." Note that this provision applies with equal force regardless of whether the child is conceived before or after the consenting parent's death. Thus, for example, if a married woman's husband, or an unmarried woman's male partner, signs a written consent for her to use his banked sperm to conceive a child after his death by artificial insemination or in vitro fertilization, he is treated as the father of the resulting child. Likewise, in the case of a same-sex couple, if the woman's spouse or domestic partner signs a written consent for posthumous assisted reproduction (using the sperm of a third-party donor), the consenting spouse or partner is treated as the other parent of the resulting child. Even in the absence of written consent, a spouse or partner is treated as the child's other parent if it is established by clear and convincing evidence that he or she "intended to be treated as the other parent of a posthumously conceived child." UPC § 2–120(f)(2)(C). A child who is in gestation at the parent's death is deemed to be in existence for purposes of intestate succession if the child lives for at least 120 hours after birth. UPC § 2–104(a)(2). A posthumously conceived child is treated as being in gestation at the parent's death "if the child is: (1) in utero not later than 36 months after the [parent's] death; or (2) born not later than 45 months after the [parent's] death." UPC § 2–120(k).

The Uniform Probate Code also addresses the parentage of a child conceived posthumously pursuant to a surrogacy agreement. See UPC § 2–121. For an incisive commentary on the differential impact of the Uniform Probate Code's presumptions concerning spousal consent to posthumous conception, see Knaplund, The New Uniform Probate Code's Surprising Gender Inequities, 18 Duke J. of Gender Law & Policy 335 (2011) (noting the "delicious irony" of provisions that allow "a woman, especially a married woman, to alter the property distribution of a man's estate by having a [posthumous] child (even a child without his genetic material), but accord very few men the same power").

Who should decide whether a decedent's sperm or eggs may be used for posthumous conception—the surviving spouse? a surviving domestic partner? the personal representative? See Kane v. Superior Court, 44 Cal.Rptr.2d 578 (App. 1995) (banked sperm released to decedent's girlfriend, in accordance with decedent's express wishes). Suppose that the decedent directed that his banked sperm be discarded at his death, but his widow wishes to use the sperm to conceive a posthumous child. What result? See Estate of Kievernagel, 83 Cal.Rptr.3d 311 (App. 2008). Should a decedent's surviving spouse, domestic partner, or parent be allowed to harvest the decedent's sperm for posthumous conception? See Fuselier, Preembryos in Probate: Property, Person, or Something Else?, Prob. & Prop. 31 (Sept./Oct. 2010).

3. *Testamentary gifts.* Suppose that a settlor creates a trust for the benefit of himself, his two sons and their "descendants." One of the sons, diagnosed with terminal cancer, deposits his sperm at a laboratory and gives written consent for his wife to use the sperm to conceive a child. Three years after the son's death, his widow uses his sperm to conceive a child. Should the posthumous child be entitled to share in the class gift to descendants under the terms of the trust? See Matter of Martin B., 841 N.Y.S.2d 207 (Sur. 2007) (yes; "where a governing instrument is silent, children born of this new biotechnology with the consent of their parent are entitled to the same rights 'for all purposes as those of a natural child' "). See Knaplund, Postmortem Conception and a Father's Last Will, 46 Ariz. L. Rev.91 (2004).

4. *References.* For further discussion of legal, ethical, and moral issues raised by posthumous conception, see Robertson, Posthumous Reproduction, 69 Ind. L.J. 1027 (1994); Schiff, Arising From the Dead: Challenges of Posthumous Procreation, 75 N.C. L. Rev. 901 (1997).

D. DISQUALIFICATION FOR MISCONDUCT

In general, conduct toward the decedent which might, by conventional community standards, seem morally reprehensible does not bar a person from participating in the estate of a testate or intestate decedent. Nevertheless, certain types of misconduct constitute grounds for disqualification by statute in a number of jurisdictions.

1. BREACH OF PARENTAL OBLIGATIONS

Under UPC § 2–114(a), a parent is barred from inheriting from or through a deceased child if his or her parental rights were terminated (and not judicially reestablished) or if "the child died before reaching [18] years of age and there is clear and convincing evidence that immediately before the child's death the parental rights of the parent could have been terminated . . . on the basis of nonsupport, abandonment, abuse, neglect, or other actions or inactions of the parent toward the child." This is a modified version of an earlier, widely adopted provision barring inheritance from or through a nonmarital child by the father or his kindred "unless the father has openly treated the child as his, and has not refused to support the child." UPC § 2–109 (1969). By statute in a few states, a parent who abandoned a child during the child's minority is barred from inheriting from the child. See, e.g., N.Y. EPTL § 4–1.4; N.C. Gen. Stat. ch.

31A, § 2; Ohio Rev. Code tit. 21, § 2105.10. A couple divorced when their daughter was two years old; the court awarded custody of the child to the mother but did not order the father to pay any child support. In subsequent years the father had sporadic contact with the daughter, and occasionally offered to contribute small amounts toward her support, but the mother refused to accept any money from the father. The child died intestate in a motor vehicle accident at age 18. Should the father be allowed to inherit from the daughter? See Estate of Lunsford, 610 S.E.2d 366 (N.C. 2005); see also White v. Gosiene, 420 S.E.2d 567 (W.Va. 1992); Hotarek v. Benson, 557 A.2d 1259 (Conn.1989). In the absence of a statutory bar, a father who abused his child and failed to provide support during minority has been allowed to inherit an intestate share of the child's estate. Blackstone v. Blackstone, 639 S.E.2d 369 (Ga.App. 2006); see also Estate of Shellenbarger, 86 Cal.Rptr.3d 862 (App. 2008); Crosby v. Corley, 528 So.2d 1141 (Ala.1988).

In some legal systems, courts have broad discretion to adjust intestate shares based on an heir's behavior and individual circumstances. For a comparative account of this aspect of Chinese inheritance law, see Foster, Towards a Behavior–Based Model of Inheritance? The Chinese Experiment, 32 U.C. Davis L. Rev. 77 (1998); Foster, Linking Support and Inheritance: A New Model From China, 1999 Wis. L. Rev. 1199. See also Rhodes, Consequences of Heirs' Misconduct: Moving From Rules to Discretion, 33 Ohio N.U. L. Rev. 975 (2007). What advantages or disadvantages do you see in such an approach?

2. BREACH OF MARITAL OBLIGATIONS

By statute in several states, a surviving spouse who abandoned or refused to support the decedent is barred from inheriting from the decedent. See, e.g., N.Y. EPTL § 5–1.2; 20 Pa. Cons. Stat. § 2106; Va. Code § 64.2–308. In a few others, adultery is also a ground of disqualification. See, e.g., Ind. Code § 29–1–2–14. The Uniform Probate Code does not provide for forfeiture on any of these grounds.

With the rise of "no-fault" divorce, it has become increasingly common for troubled marriages to end in divorce. A final divorce decree, of course, dissolves the marital relationship and terminates the spouses' rights to inherit from each other. By contrast, spouses who merely live apart, whether pursuant to a decree of separation or an informal arrangement, remain legally married for purposes of inheritance. Suppose that a wife, separated but not divorced from her husband, moves in with another man with whom she establishes a common law marriage. In the absence of a statutory bar, is the wife entitled to inherit from her original husband? See Estate of Allen, 738 P.2d 142 (Okla.1987) (discussing doctrine of estoppel); Estate of Montanez, 687 So.2d 943 (Fla.App.1997).

The effect of a valid decree of divorce on the right of each former spouse to inherit from the other is reasonably clear. A more difficult problem arises where a divorce decree turns out to be defective (e.g., for lack of jurisdiction). While the Uniform Probate Code does not define precisely who qualifies as a surviving spouse, it expressly negates a person's status as a surviving spouse in a few specific situations.

Uniform Probate Code (2011)

Section 2–802. Effect of Divorce, Annulment, and Decree of Separation.

(a) An individual who is divorced from the decedent or whose marriage to the decedent has been annulled is not a surviving spouse unless, by virtue of a subsequent marriage, he [or she] is married to the decedent at the time of death. A decree of separation that does not terminate the status of husband and wife is not a divorce for purposes of this section.

(b) For purposes of [Parts] 1 [intestate succession], 2 [elective share], 3 [pretermitted spouse and children] and 4 [statutory allowances] of this [article], and of Section 3–203 [priority among persons seeking appointment as personal representative], a surviving spouse does not include:

(1) an individual who obtains or consents to a final decree or judgment of divorce from the decedent or an annulment of their marriage, which decree or judgment is not recognized as valid in this state, unless subsequently they participate in a marriage ceremony purporting to marry each to the other or live together as husband and wife;

(2) an individual who, following an invalid decree or judgment of divorce or annulment obtained by the decedent, participates in a marriage ceremony with a third individual; or

(3) an individual who was a party to a valid proceeding concluded by an order purporting to terminate all marital property rights.

3. HOMICIDE

Today nearly every state has a "slayer statute" which bars a killer from taking the deceased victim's property by will or intestacy. Prior to the enactment of these statutes, the weight of early judicial authority refused to disturb the ordinary course of succession on the grounds that to do so would represent an unwarranted departure from the literal terms of the statutes governing testate and intestate succession and would amount to an additional punishment for the killer's crime. See Wall v. Pfanschmidt, 106 N.E. 785 (Ill.1914); McAllister v. Fair, 84 P. 112 (Kan.1906); Carpenter's Estate, 32 A. 637 (Pa.1895). A passage from *Carpenter's Estate* illustrates the tenor of these decisions:

The intestate law in the plainest words designates the persons who shall succeed to the estates of deceased intestates. It is impossible for the courts to designate any different persons to take such estates without violating the law. We have no possible warrant for doing so. . . . It is argued that the son who murders his own father has forfeited all right to his father's estate, because it is his own wrongful act that has terminated his father's life. The logical foundation of this argument is, and must be, that it is a punishment for the son's wrongful act. But the law must fix punishments, the courts can only enforce them. In this state no such punishment as this is fixed by any law, and therefore the courts cannot impose it. It is argued however that it would be contrary to public policy to allow a parricide to inherit his father's estate. Where is the authority for such a contention? How can such a proposition be maintained when there is a positive statute which disposes of the whole subject? How can there be a public policy leading to one conclusion when there is a positive statute directing a precisely opposite conclusion? In other words when the imperative language of a statute prescribes that upon the death of a person his estate shall vest in his children in the absence of a will, how can any doctrine, or principle, or other thing called public policy, take away the estate of a child and give it to some other person. The intestate law casts the estate upon certain designated persons, and this is absolute and peremptory, and the estate cannot be diverted from those persons and given to other persons without violating the statute. There can be no public policy which contravenes the positive language of a statute. 32 A. at 637.]

The early authority was not unanimous, however. In the leading case of Riggs v. Palmer, 22 N.E. 188 (N.Y.1889), the decedent was murdered by his 16–year-old grandson Elmer Palmer, who was named as residuary beneficiary in the decedent's will. The court held that the grandson took nothing by will or by intestacy:

> What could be more unreasonable than to suppose that it was the legislative intention in the general laws passed for the orderly, peaceable and just devolution of property, that they should have operation in favor of one who murdered his ancestor that he might speedily come into the possession of his estate? Such an intention is inconceivable. We need not, therefore, be much troubled by the general language contained in the laws.

> Besides, all laws as well as all contracts may be controlled in their operation and effect by general, fundamental maxims of the common law. No one shall be permitted to profit by his own fraud, or to take advantage of his own wrong, or to found any claim upon his own iniquity, or to acquire property by his own crime. . . .

Here there was no certainty that this murderer would survive the testator, or that the testator would not change his will, and there was no certainty that he would get this property if nature was allowed to take its course. He, therefore, murdered the testator expressly to vest himself with an estate. . . . If he had met the testator and taken his property by force, he would have had no title to it. Shall he acquire title by murdering him? If he had gone to the testator's house and by force compelled him, or by fraud or undue influence had induced him to will him his property, the law would not allow him to hold it. But can he give effect and operation to a will by murder, and yet take the property? To answer these questions in the affirmative, it seems to me, would be a reproach to the jurisprudence of our state, and an offense against public policy. . . .

For the same reasons the defendant Palmer cannot take any of this property as heir. Just before the murder he was not an heir, and it was not certain that he ever would be. He might have died before his grandfather, or might have been disinherited by him. He made himself an heir by the murder, and he seeks to take property as the fruit of his crime. What has before been said as to him as legatee applies to him with equal force as an heir. He cannot vest himself with title by crime.

My view of this case does not inflict upon Elmer any greater or other punishment for his crime than the law specifies. It takes from him no property, but simply holds that he shall not acquire property by his crime, and thus be rewarded for its commission. [22 N.E. at 190.]

Accord, Perry v. Strawbridge, 108 S.W. 641 (Mo.1908); Price v. Hitaffer, 165 A. 470 (Md.1933).

In the absence of an applicable slayer statute, several courts have invoked the equitable device of a constructive trust to deprive the killer of beneficial enjoyment while preserving logical consistency with the statutes governing testate and intestate succession. See Estate of Mahoney, 220 A.2d 475 (Vt.1966); Will of Wilson, 92 N.W.2d 282 (Wis.1958); Garner v. Phillips, 47 S.E.2d 845 (N.C.1948); see also Ellerson v. Westcott, 42 N.E. 540 (N.Y.1896). In effect, the constructive trust functions as an equitable remedy to prevent unjust enrichment. The killer is treated as receiving bare legal title to the victim's property by will or by intestacy, subject to an obligation, enforceable in equity, to turn the property over to the rightful beneficiaries. Of course the killer has not actually agreed to act as a trustee pursuant to an express trust, but the killer's position is nevertheless analogous to that of a trustee who has misappropriated trust property, and the remedy is framed accordingly. In the words of Justice

Cardozo, "A constructive trust is nothing but 'the formula through which the conscience of equity finds expression.' Property is acquired in such circumstances that the holder of legal title may not in good conscience retain the beneficial interest. Equity, to express its disapproval of his conduct, converts him into a trustee." Cardozo, The Nature of the Judicial Process 42 (1921). See generally Restatement (Third) of Restitution and Unjust Enrichment § 55 (2011).

Slayer statutes vary considerably in detail. Some early statutes, enacted directly in response to judicial decisions upholding inheritance by convicted murderers, provided simply that a person who stands "convicted" (or "adjudged guilty") of a felonious and intentional killing forfeits all beneficial rights in the victim's property. In *Tarlo's Estate*, reproduced infra, the court wrestles with the question of whether, in the absence of a criminal conviction, such a statute leaves open the possibility of establishing grounds for forfeiture in a separate civil proceeding. More recently, many states have enacted comprehensive slayer statutes which address the disposition of the victim's property and the treatment of third parties in cases of felonious and intentional killing. The Uniform Probate Code provision is illustrative:

Uniform Probate Code (2011)

Section 2–803. Effect of Homicide on Intestate Succession, Wills, Trusts, Joint Assets, Life Insurance, and Beneficiary Designations.

(a) [Definitions.] In this section:

(1) "Disposition or appointment of property" includes a transfer of an item of property or any other benefit to a beneficiary designated in a governing instrument.

(2) "Governing instrument" means a governing instrument executed by the decedent.

(3) "Revocable," with respect to a disposition, appointment, provision, or nomination, means one under which the decedent, at the time of or immediately before death, was alone empowered, by law or under the governing instrument, to cancel the designation in favor of the killer, whether or not the decedent was then empowered to designate himself [or herself] in place of his [or her] killer and whether or not the decedent then had capacity to exercise the power.

(b) [Forfeiture of Statutory Benefits.] An individual who feloniously and intentionally kills the decedent forfeits all benefits under this [article] with respect to the decedent's estate, including an intestate share, an elective share, an omitted spouse's or child's share, a homestead allowance, exempt property, and a family allowance. If the decedent died intestate, the decedent's intestate estate passes as if the killer disclaimed his [or her] intestate share.

(c) [Revocation of Benefits Under Governing Instruments.] The felonious and intentional killing of the decedent:

(1) revokes any revocable (i) disposition or appointment of property made by the decedent to the killer in a governing instrument, (ii) provision in a governing instrument conferring a general or nongeneral power of appointment on the killer, and (iii) nomination of the killer in a governing instrument, nominating or appointing the killer to serve in any fiduciary or representative capacity, including a personal representative, executor, trustee, or agent; and

(2) severs the interests of the decedent and killer in property held by them at the time of the killing as joint tenants with the right of survivorship [or as community property with the right of survivorship], transforming the interests of the decedent and killer into equal tenancies in common.

(d) [Effect of Severance.] A severance under subsection (c)(2) does not affect any third-party interest in property acquired for value and in good faith reliance on an apparent title by survivorship in the killer unless a writing declaring the severance has been noted, registered, filed, or recorded in records appropriate to the kind and location of the property which are relied upon, in the ordinary course of transactions involving such property, as evidence of ownership.

(e) [Effect of Revocation.] Provisions of a governing instrument are given effect as if the killer disclaimed all provisions revoked by this section or, in the case of a revoked nomination in a fiduciary or representative capacity, as if the killer predeceased the decedent.

(f) [Wrongful Acquisition of Property.] A wrongful acquisition of property or interest by a killer not covered by this section must be treated in accordance with the principle that a killer cannot profit from his [or her] wrong.

(g) [Felonious and Intentional Killing; How Determined.] After all right to appeal has been exhausted, a judgment of conviction establishing criminal accountability for the felonious and intentional killing of the decedent conclusively establishes the convicted individual as the decedent's killer for purposes of this section. In the absence of a conviction, the court, upon the petition of an interested person, must determine whether, under the preponderance of evidence standard, the individual would be found criminally accountable for the felonious and intentional killing of the decedent. If the court determines that, under that standard, the individual would be found criminally accountable for the felonious and intentional killing of the decedent, the determination conclusively establishes that individual as the decedent's killer for purposes of this section.

(h) [Protection of Payors and Other Third Parties.]

(1) A payor or other third party is not liable for having made a payment or transferred an item of property or any other benefit to a beneficiary designated in a governing instrument affected by an intentional and felonious killing, or for having taken any other action in good faith reliance on the validity of the governing instrument, upon request and satisfactory proof of the decedent's death, before the payor or other third party received written notice of a claimed forfeiture or revocation under this section. A payor or other third party is liable for a payment made or other action taken after the payor or other third party received written notice of a claimed forfeiture or revocation under this section.

(2) Written notice of a claimed forfeiture or revocation under paragraph (1) must be mailed to the payor's or other third party's main office or home by registered or certified mail, return receipt requested, or served upon the payor or other third party in the same manner as a summons in a civil action. Upon receipt of written notice of a claimed forfeiture or revocation under this section, a payor or other third party may pay any amount owed or transfer or deposit any item of property held by it to or with the court having jurisdiction of the probate proceedings relating to the decedent's estate, or if no proceedings have been commenced, to or with the court having jurisdiction of probate proceedings relating to decedents' estates located in the county of the decedent's residence. The court shall hold the funds or item of property and, upon its determination under this section, shall order disbursement in accordance with the determination. Payments, transfers, or deposits made to or with the court discharge the payor or other third party from all claims for the value of amounts paid to or items of property transferred to or deposited with the court.

(i) [Protection of Bona Fide Purchasers; Personal Liability of Recipient.]

(1) A person who purchases property for value and without notice, or who receives a payment or other item of property in partial or full satisfaction of a legally enforceable obligation, is neither obligated under this section to return the payment, item of property, or benefit nor is liable under this section for the amount of the payment or the value of the item of property or benefit. But a person who, not for value, receives a payment, item of property, or any other benefit to which the person is not entitled under this section is obligated to return the payment, item of property, or benefit, or is personally liable for the amount of the payment or the value of the item of property or benefit, to the person who is entitled to it under this section.

(2) If this section or any part of this section is preempted by federal law with respect to a payment, an item of property, or any other benefit covered by this section, a person who, not for value, receives the payment, item of property, or any other benefit to which the person is not entitled under this

section is obligated to return the payment, item of property, or benefit, or is personally liable for the amount of the payment or the value of the item of property or benefit, to the person who would have been entitled to it were this section or part of this section not preempted.

IN RE TARLO'S ESTATE

Supreme Court of Pennsylvania, 1934.
315 Pa. 321, 172 A. 139.

Argued before FRAZER, C.J., and SIMPSON, KEPHART, SCHAFFER, MAXEY, DREW, and LINN, JJ.

SCHAFFER, JUSTICE.

Albert Tarlo arose early on the morning of November 27, 1930, fired one shot into the brain of his wife, who was asleep in the same room, proceeded to the bedroom of his sleeping daughter, and shot her in the same way, and then turned the pistol on his own head. The wife and daughter died instantly in their sleep. He survived for a few hours. The daughter left no will. The question before us is whether her estate shall be distributed to the administrator of her father, or to her maternal grandfather, Louis Koch, who is her next of kin if the inheritance may not pass through her father. The orphans' court awarded the property to the administrator of the father. Louis Koch has appealed.

Full and most complete briefs have been submitted to us in which the general policy of the law and decisions from many jurisdictions have been discussed and analyzed. As we see it, however, the question to be decided lies in a very narrow field, that embraced by the language of section 23 of the Intestate Act approved June 7, 1917, P.L. 429, 20 P.S. § 136, which reads as follows: "No person who shall be finally adjudged guilty, either as principal or accessory, of murder of the first or second degree, shall be entitled to inherit or take any part of the real or personal estate of the person killed, as surviving spouse, heir, or next of kin to such person under the provisions of this act." With the section in view, it is quite apparent that the field of inquiry is further limited to the meaning of but one of its words, "adjudged." Does it connote final conviction in the court of oyer and terminer? If it does, then of course there can be no blocking of the usual course of descent, as the killer was not tried and convicted. His suicide prevented this.

We are of the opinion that the language used in the section is that of the criminal law, and that the expression "shall be finally adjudged guilty" means the judgment of a court of competent jurisdiction to pass on the question of guilt in murder, the court of oyer and terminer; that the word "adjudged" as used in the statute is the equivalent of "convicted and sentenced." . . . There must be not only a conviction, but judgment of the court and the judgment in criminal cases is the sentence. "Finally adjudged" means convicted and sentenced, and the sentence not appealed, or, if appealed, that the judgment of sentence has been affirmed.

While it is true that the views expressed by those who draft or enact laws are not a safe guide when the courts are called upon to determine the meaning of the words employed therein . . . , yet in order to get at the old law, the mischief and the remedy, and properly to understand and construe a statute embodying the latter, the history of the enactment in question may always be considered. . . .

. . . The act which we are considering was the result of the study and recommendation of an able commission appointed by the governor of the commonwealth. Section 23 is in the exact language of their recommendation. In their report (p. 47) they say:

> This is a new section framed to meet the situation presented in Carpenter's Est., 170 Pa. 203 [32 A. 637, 29 L.R.A. 145, 50 Am. St. Rep. 765]. In that case, a son killed his father, was convicted of murder and was executed therefor. His mother, the widow of the intestate, was convicted as an accessory after the fact and duly sentenced. The motive of the crime was to get possession of the estate of the decedent, and the Supreme Court was constrained to hold that the criminals had not forfeited their rights under the intestate law. . . . The Commissioners are of opinion however that the guilt of the party charged with the crime should be determined by his conviction in the proper forum.

It is impossible to conclude that the legislature in approving the language of the section as the commission had drafted it did not do so with the intent that it should have the effect which the commission designed and pointed out to the law makers. To give it a wider effect by our saying that in using the words "adjudged guilty" the Legislature meant more than the commission intended and meant "adjudged guilty" by the orphans' court, as appellant contends, would be to close our eyes to the obvious when everything points the other way. If the law is to be changed so as to cover the situation before us, it is for the Legislature to make the change, not for us.

The decree is affirmed at appellant's cost.

DREW, JUSTICE (concurring).

I feel compelled, rather unwillingly, to arrive at the conclusion that the decree of the court below is right and must be affirmed. I think it impossible, on legal grounds, to reach any other conclusion. The language of section 23 of the Intestate Act of 1917 (20 P.S. § 136) is too plain. When considered in the light of the law as declared by us in Carpenter's Est., 170 Pa. 203, 32 A. 637, 29 L.R.A. 145, 50 Am. St. Rep. 765, which has been changed only to the extent expressed clearly and unequivocally in the act, the conclusion is inevitable that, except in the case of one "finally adjudged guilty, either as principal or accessory, of murder of the first or second degree," our statute regulating descent and distribution is adamant, and we are powerless to change the course of descent from that expressed therein. As we said in that case: "The intestate law in the plainest words designates the persons who shall succeed to the estates of deceased intestates. It is impossible for the courts to designate any different persons to take such estates without violating the law. We have no possible warrant for doing so." That case has never been overruled, and is the law of the commonwealth to-day, except in the one respect changed by the act. As we have seen, that change affects only inheritance by one "finally adjudged guilty . . . of murder," which certainly means after trial, conviction, and final judgment in a court of oyer and terminer; and, by the same token, it certainly does not affect the inheritance of one not so adjudged guilty of murder. We have not the power to set aside the plain mandate of the statute of descent, and we would do that if, for any reason, we wrote into it a course of descent other than that provided therein. Without overruling the principle expressed in *Carpenter's Estate*, which I have quoted above, and doing violence to the statute of descent, the device of a constructive trust cannot be employed.

For these reasons I agree with the majority that the decree of the court below should be affirmed, hoping that the Legislature in its wisdom will so change the law that on facts such as those which have caused our division the question of guilt will be submitted to, and determined by, a jury.

KEPHART, JUSTICE (dissenting).

The record shows an unlawful killing, and the majority opinion fully sets forth the facts, which raise but one question: Can a murderer profit from the estate of his victim? The majority opinion decides that he can. I do not agree with that conclusion.

The question is not new in this or other states; many conflicting decisions have answered it. One group, to stop such a flagrant injustice as to permit an atrocious criminal to enrich himself by his crime, adhere to the fundamental principle of equity that no one shall be permitted to profit by his own fraud, to take advantage of his own wrong, or to enjoy the fruits of his inequity, and holds that the enjoyment of property, whether by will, or under the statutes of descent, or through contracts such as life insurance policies, procured through crime, must be subjected to the scrutiny of this universally recognized principle of morality, equity and justice. As a matter of public policy, equity will interpose to prevent such unconscionable modes of acquiring property. . . .

The opposite view of a few states is that the force of this principle has been terminated and denied further effect by the Legislature which created a new and different public policy in the enactment of statutes determining the descent and distribution of property at death; but no statute anywhere has ever expressed such a thought. The conclusion in every instance is but an inference of the particular court reached because the statute under review has not expressed the opposite conclusion. . . .

The court below and the majority must rely on Carpenter's Est., 170 Pa. 203, 32 A. 637, 29 L.R.A. 145, 50 Am. St. Rep. 765, as the Intestate Act, hereinafter discussed, does not help. In that case a son, motivated by the desire to acquire his father's property, and conniving with his mother, murdered his father. The son was convicted of murder and hanged. The mother was convicted as an accessory before the fact. The collateral kinsmen of the father claimed the son had forfeited any interest he had in his father's estate, and that they were therefore entitled to inherit. This court held on two grounds (Justice Williams dissenting) that the son had not forfeited his right to inherit, regardless of the means by which he inherited, because: (1) Under article 1, §§ 18, 19, of the Declaration of Rights, it is provided that "no person shall be attainted of treason or felony by the legislature," and that "no attainder shall work corruption of blood, nor, except during the life of the offender, forfeiture of estate to the commonwealth." It is apparent that the court erred in using this reason as a basis for its opinion, since there can be no forfeiture of an estate of which one has not yet come into possession, nor was there in that case, nor is there in this, any question of "forfeiture of estate to the Commonwealth." Moreover, such provisions indubitably apply to the estate in the possession of the one guilty of the treason or felony at the time he commits the act, and do not govern the question of the transmission to or through him of other interests or estates thereafter. Price v. Hitaffer (1933) 164 Md. 505, 165 A. 470.

The second reason given was that "the intestate law in the plainest words designates the persons who shall succeed to the estates of deceased intestates. It is impossible for the courts to designate any different persons to take such estates without violating the law." Justice Green, in meeting the argument that it was against public policy to permit a murderer to profit by his crime, stated that there could be no public policy directly in opposition to a positive statute on the subject. There was, however, no "positive statute on the subject," but only an inference by the court. Upon such legalistic reasoning as that stated, without regard to the fundamental principles and concepts of equity which this court had prior thereto often announced and applied to prevent the consummation of fraud, duress, undue influence, and other analogous situations, the decision was reached. . . .

The natural result of the unjust and inequitable decision in *Carpenter's Est.*, supra, was section 23 of the Intestate Act of June 7, 1917, P.L. 429, which provided: "No person who shall be finally adjudged guilty, either as principal or accessory, of murder of the first or second degree, shall be entitled to inherit or take any part of the real or personal estate of the person killed, as surviving spouse, heir, or next of kin to such person under the provisions of this act." The title to the estate would not pass to the murderer as an heir, spouse, or next of kin. The act dealt with descent only.

The Legislature, however, enacted this section with *Carpenter's Est.*, supra, in mind. It was advisedly overruling the reasoning of that decision; it wiped out and completely destroyed its effect, and declared as the policy of the commonwealth the principle that those found guilty of murder shall not profit by their wrong and inherit from their victims. This policy is the reverse of that stated in the court's opinion in *Carpenter's Est.*, supra.

We need not discuss the intention of the Legislature in using the word "adjudged," and we may accept for our present purpose the conclusion of the lower court and the majority as to that intention, but such determination wholly neglects the substance of the problem before us. While it was, of course, the function of the Legislature to declare the public policy as it related to inheritance resulting from murder, the mere fact that the Legislature set aside the public policy announced in *Carpenter's Estate* and declared a new policy as to inheritance by those "adjudged guilty" of murder does not prevent us in those cases which may fall outside the statute from considering, under the principles of equity and common law, the legal effect of murder on the transmission of title to the property of the deceased. The Legislature did not declare that murderers who were not "adjudged guilty" should profit by the crime.

The function of courts is to execute the policy enunciated by the Legislature within the specific spheres covered by the act, but such legislative expressions, unless intended to do so, do not preclude this court from considering the entire subject-matter not covered by the act, and we may review anew under equitable and common-law principles the question involved, unfettered by precedent or statute.

In considering the various situations involving the procurement and enjoyment of property as the result of murder, the court must envisage not merely the commands of the common and statutory law, but must hearken to the dictates of conscience where fraud, force, or crime appear, and, depending on the strong arm of equity acting in personam, compel the perpetrator of the crime to surrender that to which at law, whether statutory or unwritten, he has acquired title. The Legislature has expressed the public policy in section 23 of the Intestate Act, supra, and as it relates to wills in the Act of June 7, 1917, P.L. 403, section 22 (20 P.S. § 244). It has there pointed the way for our action in the cases not coming within the statutory terms.

It is not the province of equity to administer the criminal law but to secure restitution to a person wronged by compelling the wrongdoer to give up the fruits of his misconduct to the extent to which he was benefited by such misconduct or to the closest approximation to complete justice. On principle, it is apparent that a court of conscience must, if possible, intervene to prevent a murderer from enjoying the property of his victim, a result so sordid and so abhorrent to all principles of fairness and right. This may be done by the application of the well-established and frequently employed equitable doctrine or principle that no person shall be permitted to profit or be unjustly enriched as the result of unlawful acts committed by him. All laws as well as contracts may be controlled in their operation and effect by the general fundamental concepts of equity and the common law. . . . It is uniformly stated that no one shall be permitted to profit by his own fraud, to take advantage of his own wrong, to found any claim upon his own iniquity, or to acquire property by his own crime. These are not new, novel, or untried principles, but are constantly applied by this court under its great equity powers. No interference with the operation of the law of intestacy, descent, and wills is involved. The title under the law passes to the wrongdoer, but, to prevent him from being unjustly enriched as a result of his crime, chancery compels him to hold the property he has thus received as constructive trustee for the benefit, use, and enjoyment of those whom by his act he has attempted to cheat, and there being no legal or equitable reason for continuing such a trust, may decree it ended and give the estate to those beneficially interested. . . .

SIMPSON, J. concurs in this dissent.

FRAZER, CHIEF JUSTICE (dissenting).

. . . In my opinion, *Carpenter's Estate* is the law to-day and should be followed except to the extent changed as indicated in the act of 1917. While the language of the act of 1917 is somewhat uncertain, the intention of its framers should be ascertained by "rational interpretation" of its provisions; applying this rule to the situation before us, it seems to me that under the legislation in question, in adjudicating estates of murdered persons, the killer should be "finally adjudged guilty [of the killing], either as principal or accessory," by the tribunal having jurisdiction in such cases, before his next of kin can be barred from participating in the distribution of the estate of his victim. As I read the act, its provisions do not require that the killer be convicted of murder in the court of oyer and terminer, as this would be impossible in many cases, especially the one now before us, as here the offender died by his own hand within a few hours following the killing. We should assume the Legislature did not intend the act of 1917 to be of little or no effect or its provisions to be applicable only in cases where conviction is had in the court of oyer and terminer; what it undoubtedly intended was that the circumstances of each particular case should be "adjudged"; that is, decided and determined in a competent tribunal, either civil or criminal, as the situation demands. In this case, in my opinion, the orphans' court, in adjudicating distribution of the deceased's estate is the proper tribunal to determine the parties entitled to participate in the distribution. If the killer had survived and been convicted and sentenced in the court of oyer and terminer for murder of the first or second degree or accessory, that conviction would be conclusive in determining the right of those entitled to participate in the distribution. Here, the offender's suicide immediately following the killing precludes a trial in the court of oyer and terminer, and, if the legislation is to have any bearing on cases of this character, its provisions require the right of those claiming to participate in the distribution of the decedent's estate to be passed upon by a proper tribunal. That he took the life of his daughter is not disputed. Do the circumstances surrounding the unfortunate occurrence establish the elements necessary to sustain murder of either first or second degree or accessory? If they do, and the father is, after hearing testimony, adjudged to have been sane at the time of committing the deed, his next of kin is not entitled to inherit; if, on the contrary, he was insane, and as a result of that condition or because of some other legal reason not chargeable for his act, the next of kin should participate in the distribution under the intestate laws. The question of the killer's responsibility should under the situation here before us be determined by the orphans' court and distribution made in accordance with the finding supported by the testimony after full hearing. . . .

NOTES

1. *Criminal conviction.* After the decision in the principal case, the Pennsylvania slayer statute was amended to eliminate the requirement that the killer be "adjudged guilty." The statute now makes a criminal conviction "admissible in evidence" in a separate civil proceeding to determine succession rights. See Pa. Cons. Stat. tit. 20, § 8814. Under the amended statute, a wife convicted of her husband's murder was held to be automatically disqualified from taking under or against her husband's will. See Kravitz Estate, 211 A.2d 443 (Pa.1965). In the absence of a criminal conviction, the amended Pennsylvania statute, like the Uniform Probate Code, leaves the question of intentional and felonious killing to be determined in a separate civil proceeding. Thus, for example, a killer may be disqualified from inheriting from the victim despite an acquittal in a prior criminal proceeding. Cf. Estate of Congdon, 309 N.W.2d 261 (Minn.1981) (rejecting daughter's argument, based on

double jeopardy, res judicata and collateral estoppel, that acquittal of mother's murder in criminal proceeding precluded determination in subsequent civil proceeding that killing was felonious and intentional). What if the killer pleads guilty to a charge of deliberate homicide? See Estates of Swanson, 187 P.3d 631 (Mont. 2008).

The divergent opinions in *Tarlo's Estate* are echoed in subsequent cases arising under similar statutes. Some courts hold that a statute requiring a criminal conviction preempts the common law and represents the exclusive means of preventing the killer from inheriting. See Holliday v. McMullen, 756 P.2d 1179 (Nev.1988) (son acquitted of mother's murder, entitled to inherit). Others hold that cases falling outside the scope of the statute are governed by the common law rule which bars the killer from inheriting. See Plumley v. Bledsoe, 613 S.E.2d 102 (W.Va. 2005); State Mutual Life Assur. Co. v. Hampton, 696 P.2d 1027 (Okla.1985); Harper v. Prudential Ins. Co., 662 P.2d 1264 (Kan.1983) (overruling contrary precedent).

2. *Felonious and intentional killing.* Most modern slayer statutes reach not only murder—the quintessential example of "felonious and intentional" killing—but also voluntary manslaughter. See Estate of Mahoney, 220 A.2d 475 (Vt.1966) (wife convicted of manslaughter; remanded pending determination whether killing was voluntary or involuntary). Not every unlawful killing triggers a forfeiture under the statute, however. For example, a person who kills another by accident may be guilty of involuntary manslaughter and nonetheless eligible to inherit. See Estate of Klein, 378 A.2d 1182 (Pa.1977) (wife killed in automobile accident caused by husband's drunken driving). May a son convicted of causing his mother's death by "reckless conduct" inherit from her? See Estate of Safran, 306 N.W.2d 27 (Wis.1981). What if the decedent's death was hastened by the heir's "grossly negligent" conduct? See Cheatle v. Cheatle, 662 A.2d 1362 (D.C. App. 1995).

In the absence of a criminal conviction, it may seem anomalous to determine in a civil proceeding that a killing is "felonious." Suppose that a minor child kills his parents. The child is adjudicated as delinquent in juvenile court; under state law this does not constitute a criminal conviction. The child argues that he should inherit from his parents because he cannot legally be tried or convicted on a felony charge. What result? See Estates of Josephsons, 297 N.W.2d 444 (N.D.1980) (defining killing as felonious if done without excuse or justification).

May a killer who has been found not guilty in a criminal proceeding by reason of insanity inherit from the victim? Compare Ford v. Ford, 512 A.2d 389 (Md.1986) (yes; "if a killer is 'insane' at the time he killed, the killing is not felonious in the contemplation of the slayer's rule") with Estate of Kissinger, 206 P.3d 665 (Wash. 2009) (statutory bar applicable if killer acted "intentionally and designedly and therefore willfully"; nevertheless, "[n]ot every homicide committed by the criminally insane is willful and deliberate"—a killer might be "so delusional that he did not intend or even know that he was killing a human being").

Occasionally problems arise in determining the extent of an alleged killer's involvement in bringing about the decedent's death. See Estate of Eliasen, 668 P.2d 110 (Idaho 1983) (decedent was shot in the stomach by his wife, interrupting his chemotherapy treatment and hastening his death; held, wife barred from inheriting); Estate of Sargent v. Benton State Bank, 652 S.W.2d 10 (Ark.1983) (reversing trial court's finding that son participated as accomplice of his mother and brothers in murdering his father); Dill v. Southern Farm Bureau Life Ins. Co., 797 So.2d 858 (Miss. 2001) (wife murdered by husband's friends at his instigation).

The slayer rule may operate even where the killer does not inherit directly from the victim. Suppose that X murders his grandmother, and her entire estate passes to her daughter, X's mother. A few months later, the daughter dies intestate, leaving X as her sole heir. Should X inherit his mother's estate, including the property she inherited from her mother? See Vallerius v. White, 629 N.E.2d 1185 (Ill. App. 1994); see also Estate of Mueller, 655 N.E.2d 1040 (Ill. App. 1995); Estate of Macaro, 699 N.Y.S.2d 634 (Sur. 1999).

What is the legal or moral foundation of the rule barring a felonious and intentional killer from inheriting from a victim? The slayer rule is widely viewed as an application of the equitable maxim that a person should not profit from his or her own wrongful conduct. See UPC § 2–803(f), reproduced supra. On that account, even an unintentional killing (for example, a fatal automobile accident caused by drunk driving) should be subject to the rule. Alternatively, the rule might be seen as a protective measure which prevents the killer from interfering with the victim's testamentary freedom and effectuates the victim's probable intent. See Fellows, The Slayer Rule: Not Solely a Matter of Equity, 71 Iowa L. Rev. 489 (1986). Suppose that D, afflicted with a painful and incurable disease, decides to take her own life and asks her brother X for assistance. X reluctantly agrees. At D's request, X aims a shotgun at D's head and pulls the trigger, killing her instantly. If X is named as the beneficiary of D's life insurance policy, should he be barred from receiving the proceeds? What if X helps to arrange the shotgun and D kills herself by pulling a string attached to the trigger? See Fister v. Allstate Life Ins. Co., 783 A.2d 194 (Md. 2001); cf. Estate of Schunk, 760 N.W.2d 446 (Wis.App. 2008). For a thoughtful discussion of mercy killing and assisted suicide, see Sherman, Mercy Killing and the Right to Inherit, 61 U. Cin. L. Rev. 803 (1993).

3. *Disposition of forfeited share.* If a killer forfeits the right to inherit from the victim, most slayer statutes provide that the victim's property passes as if the killer were predeceased; the devolution of the killer's own property is unaffected. See Luecke v. Mercantile Bank of Jonesboro, 691 S.W.2d 843 (Ark.1985). The Uniform Probate Code reaches essentially the

same result by treating the killer as disclaiming any interest that would otherwise pass from the victim to the killer. See UPC §§ 2–803 and 2–1106. Suppose that *D* died intestate, survived by her son *X*, her daughter *Y*, and *X*'s child. *X*, who has been convicted of *D*'s murder, forfeits the right to inherit from her. Does *Y* inherit *D*'s entire estate, or does *X*'s child take *X*'s forfeited one-half share? See Estate of Van Der Veen, 935 P.2d 1042 (Kan.1997) (slayer's nonmarital, adopted-out child entitled to inherit slayer's forfeited share); Estates of Covert, 761 N.E.2d 571 (N.Y. 2001) (slayer's relatives allowed to inherit); but see Cook v. Grierson, 845 A.2d 1231 (Md. 2004) (slayer's children not entitled to slayer's forfeited intestate share). If a second child is born to *X* one year after *D*'s death, is that child entitled to an intestate share of *D*'s estate? See Wright v. Wright, 449 S.W.2d 952 (Ark.1970). What if *D* left a will which created a trust to pay income to *X* for life with remainder at *X*'s death to *X*'s issue then living? See Estate of Safran, 306 N.W.2d 27 (Wis.1981).

4. *Survivorship rights.* Most slayer statutes bar the killer not only from participating in the victim's estate by will or intestacy but also from enjoying survivorship rights in property held by the killer and the victim as joint tenants or tenants by the entirety. The disposition of such property raises special problems. For example, suppose that *H* and *W* hold Blackacre as tenants by the entirety. *H* murders *W*, who dies intestate leaving a child *C* as her heir. Under UPC § 2–803(c)(2), the murder severs the tenancy by the entirety, leaving *H* and *C* with equal undivided interests as tenants in common. This outcome, while supported by judicial authority (see Grose v. Holland, 211 S.W.2d 464 (Mo. 1948)), is not the only conceivable one. Consider the following possibilities: (1) *H* forfeits his entire beneficial interest and holds Blackacre as constructive trustee for *C* (see Van Alstyne v. Tuffy, 169 N.Y.S. 173 (Sup. 1918)); (2) *H* holds Blackacre as constructive trustee for *C*, subject to a lien for the commuted value of *H*'s outstanding life estate in half the property (see Neiman v. Hurff, 93 A.2d 345 (N.J.1952); Estate of Mathew, 706 N.Y.S.2d 432 (App. Div. 2000)); (3) *H* takes the entire property (see Beddingfield v. Estill & Newman, 100 S.W. 108 (Tenn.1907)). Which of these alternative approaches best reflects the principle that the killer should not profit from his own wrongdoing? See Gallimore v. Washington, 666 A.2d 1200 (D.C. 1995); Restatement (Third) of Restitution and Unjust Enrichment § 45 cmt. h (2011).

5. *Life insurance.* Even in the absence of a slayer statute, it is well established that the beneficiary of a life insurance policy who kills the insured is not entitled to the resulting life insurance proceeds. See New York Mutual Life Ins. Co. v. Armstrong, 117 U.S. 591 (1886). In the case of a policy owned by the insured, most courts treat the killer as predeceased and award the proceeds to the person named as contingent beneficiary, if there is one, or to the insured's estate. See Beck v. West Coast Life Ins. Co., 241 P.2d 544 (Cal.1952); Lee v. Aylward, 790 S.W.2d 462 (Mo. 1990). If the contingent beneficiary is closely related to the killer, should the proceeds be paid to the victim's estate, in order to prevent an indirect benefit to the killer? See Diep v. Rivas, 745 A.2d 1098 (Md. 2000) (proceeds payable to killer's "completely

blameless" siblings); Beck v. Downey, 191 F.2d 150 (9th Cir. 1951) (proceeds payable to victim's estate, not to killer's mother). An even more difficult question arises in the case of a policy owned by the killer. Should the proceeds be paid to the person named (by the killer) as contingent beneficiary or to the insured's estate? See Seidlitz v. Eames, 753 P.2d 775 (Colo.App.1987) (proceeds payable to contingent beneficiary); Estate of Draper v. Commissioner, 536 F.2d 944 (1st Cir.1976) (for federal estate tax purposes, proceeds deemed payable to insured's estate).

6. *Pension benefits.* Most private employee benefit plans are subject to federal regulation under the Employee Retirement Income Security Act of 1974 (ERISA). By its terms, the federal statute preempts "any and all State laws" to the extent they "relate to" any employee benefit plan governed by ERISA. 29 U.S.C. § 1144(a). Does ERISA preclude application of a state slayer statute to a death benefit payable under such a plan? If so, is a killer who is a designated beneficiary entitled to claim the death benefit? See Ahmed v. Ahmed, 817 N.E.2d 424 (Ohio App. 2004) (holding state statute preempted but adopting slayer rule as federal common law); Connecticut Gen. Life Ins. Co. v. Riner, 351 F.Supp.2d 492 (W.D. Va.), aff'd, 142 Fed. Appx. 690 (4th Cir. 2005) ("Congress could not have intended ERISA to allow one spouse to recover benefits after intentionally killing the other spouse"); Atwater v. Nortel Networks, Inc., 388 F.Supp.2d 610 (M.D.N.C. 2005); cf. Mendez–Bellido v. Board of Trustees, 709 F.Supp. 329 (E.D.N.Y.1989) (no preemption). Cf. UPC § 2–803(i)(2) (creating right of recovery in "person who would have been entitled" to benefit in absence of preemption).

7. *References.* See generally Maki & Kaplan, Elmer's Case Revisited: The Problem of the Murdering Heir, 41 Ohio St. L.J. 905 (1980); D'Amato, Elmer's Rule: A Jurisprudential Dialogue, 60 Iowa L. Rev. 1129 (1975); McGovern, Homicide and Succession to Property, 68 Mich. L. Rev. 65 (1969); Wade, Acquisition of Property by Wilfully Killing Another—A Statutory Solution, 49 Harv. L. Rev. 715 (1936).

E. ADVANCEMENT, RELEASE, AND ASSIGNMENT

1. ADVANCEMENT

An "advancement" is traditionally defined as a gift of property made by a parent to a child during life in anticipation of the child's intestate share of the parent's estate. Accordingly, if the parent dies intestate, the amount of the advancement is charged against the child's share. Where the parent has given different amounts to several children during life, the doctrine of advancement produces a rough equality of benefit among the children regardless of whether they receive their shares during life or at death. Some intestacy statutes follow the original English Statute of Distributions (1670) and speak only of advancements to the decedent's "children"; others use more comprehensive words such as "heirs" or "descendants." See UPC § 2–109, reproduced infra.

A simple example illustrates the operation of the doctrine. During her lifetime D, a widow, advanced $30,000 to her child A, $20,000 to her child B and nothing to her child C. Later D dies intestate, leaving an estate of $130,000 to be distributed to the three children. To compute the children's intestate shares, the value of D's distributable estate ($130,000) is notionally increased by the total amount of the gifts she made to the children by way of advancement ($50,000); this is referred to as bringing the advancements into "hotchpot." The resulting tentative base ($180,000) is divided equally among the three children, and each child's tentative share ($60,000) is reduced by the amount previously advanced to that child. Thus, A ends up with an intestate share of $30,000, B with $40,000, and C with $60,000. These shares add up to precisely $130,000, the amount of D's distributable estate. Note that no child is required to return any amount received as an advancement; the sole function of the hotchpot computation is to equalize the amounts received by the children from their parent.

Even a child who receives more than his or her tentative share by way of advancement is not required to return any part of the advancement. Thus, in the preceding example, suppose that A received an advancement of $90,000 (rather than $30,000). Bringing $110,000 of advancements into hotchpot would increase the tentative base to $240,000, resulting in a tentative share of $80,000 for each child. A is entitled to retain the full $90,000 given to her by D during life, but as a consequence of doing so she receives nothing further from D's estate. Moreover, A drops out of the hotchpot computation, leaving a tentative base of $150,000 and tentative shares of $75,000 for B and C. After the reduction for advancements, B ends up with $55,000 and C with $75,000.

Although there is much to be said for equalizing children's intestate shares as an abstract proposition, the doctrine of advancement has proved troublesome in application. The main problem stems from the difficulty of distinguishing a transfer that was intended as a downpayment on a child's inheritance from one that was intended as an absolute gift (or perhaps as a loan or sale). The distinction depends on the parent's intent at the time of the transfer. Evidence of that intent, often compiled long afterward in contemplation of litigation, may be fragmentary and inconclusive. See Estate of Martinez, 633 P.2d 727 (N.M.App.1981). In addition to the parent's written and oral declarations, courts have looked at the size and nature of the transfer, the recipient's use of the transferred property, and other surrounding circumstances. Traditionally courts recognized a presumption in favor of treating substantial transfers made by a parent to a child as advancements. See Cravens v. Cravens, 410 S.W.2d 424 (Tenn.App.1966).

To avoid speculation about the unexpressed intent of intestate decedents, many modern statutes recognize advancements only if the requisite intent is shown by a written declaration of the intestate or the advancee. As a practical matter, these statutes go a long way toward abolishing the doctrine of advancement, since the transfers in question are usually made with minimal formalities. The Uniform Probate Code provision is typical:

Uniform Probate Code (2011)

Section 2–109. Advancements.

(a) If an individual dies intestate as to all or a portion of his [or her] estate, property the decedent gave during the decedent's lifetime to an individual who, at the decedent's death, is an heir is treated as an advancement against the heir's intestate share only if (i) the decedent declared in a contemporaneous writing or the heir acknowledged in writing that the gift is an advancement, or (ii) the decedent's contemporaneous writing or the heir's written acknowledgment otherwise indicates that the gift is to be taken into account in computing the division and distribution of the decedent's intestate estate.

(b) For purposes of subsection (a), property advanced is valued as of the time the heir came into possession or enjoyment of the property or as of the time of the decedent's death, whichever first occurs.

(c) If the recipient of the property fails to survive the decedent, the property is not taken into account in computing the division and distribution of the decedent's intestate estate, unless the decedent's contemporaneous writing provides otherwise.

For background and commentary on this provision, see Fellows, Concealing Legislative Reform in the Common–Law Tradition: The Advancements Doctrine and the Uniform Probate Code, 37 Vand. L. Rev. 671 (1984).

NOTES

1. *Partial intestacy.* The doctrine of advancements has no application if the decedent leaves a will which disposes of the entire estate. The doctrine is traditionally also held inapplicable in cases of partial intestacy (i.e., where part, but not all, of the estate is disposed of by will), presumably on the theory that any desired equalization of shares is expressed in the will. UPC § 2–109, reproduced supra, extends the doctrine to apply to cases of partial intestacy.

2. *Valuation.* In general, an advancement is valued at the time of the transfer, without regard to subsequent fluctuations in value. For this purpose, the transfer is deemed to occur when the recipient obtains possession or enjoyment of the property. Thus, for example, if a parent conveys land to a child subject to a reserved life estate by way of advancement, the land is valued at the parent's death for purposes of adjusting the child's intestate share. Suppose that a parent takes out a life insurance policy on her own life and assigns it to her child as an advancement when the policy is worth $20,000; at the parent's death four years later the child receives proceeds of $1,000,000. At what value should the advancement be taken into account? Does it matter whether the insurance premiums are paid by the parent or the child?

3. *Predeceased advancee.* At common law, if a child who had received an advancement from a parent died before the parent, leaving issue who represented the child in the distribution of the parent's intestate estate, the child's advancement was generally charged against the share of his or her issue. Apparently, the issue were presumed to have benefited indirectly from the advancement received by the child. This rule has been widely repudiated by statute. See UPC § 2–109(c).

4. *Written declaration or acknowledgment.* D made a gift to his son A of $50,000 which A used to purchase Blackacre. After D's death, his daughter B claimed that the gift to A was intended as an advancement which should be offset against A's intestate share of D's estate. In the absence of a written declaration by D, should evidence of an oral understanding be admissible to show that the gift was intended as an advancement? If B can prove such an intent, does she have an equitable remedy against A for unjust enrichment? See Stewart v. Walters, 602 S.E.2d 642 (Ga. 2004).

5. *References.* For a succinct treatment of the common law doctrine of advancements, see Atkinson § 129; for an exhaustive discussion, see Elbert, Advancements, 51 Mich. L. Rev. 665 (1953), 52 Mich. L. Rev. 231 (1953), and 52 Mich. L. Rev. 535 (1954). The related doctrine of "satisfaction" in the law of wills is discussed infra at p. 479.

2. RELEASE OR ASSIGNMENT OF EXPECTANCY

A living person has no heirs; not until death does it become possible to identify the decedent's intestate successors and reckon their respective shares. By the same token, a potential heir has no legally recognized interest in a living person's property, but only an expectancy—a prospect of succession which may vanish if the potential heir dies or is disinherited by will. Only at the property owner's death can it be said that there are heirs with legally protected interests in the decedent's estate. These distinctions, while admittedly formalistic, may have significant implications where a potential heir purports to release or assign an expectancy prior to the decedent's death.

Although a gratuitous transfer of an expectancy is unenforceable, a release (to the living owner) or an assignment (to a third party) is generally held to be enforceable in equity if made for fair and adequate consideration. For example, suppose that *D*, the widowed mother of three children, conveys Blackacre to her child *C* in exchange for *C*'s release of all rights to inherit from *D*; *D* then dies intestate survived by all three children. Assuming that Blackacre constitutes fair and adequate consideration, *C*'s release is enforceable and *D*'s estate is divided between the other two children. Similarly, if *C* assigned his expectancy to a third party for fair and adequate consideration, the assignee would be entitled to compel *C* to turn over any interest ultimately inherited from *D*. See Rector v. Tatham, 196 P.3d 364 (Kan. 2008). What if *C* predeceased *D*, leaving a child who claimed *C*'s intestate share by right of representation? See Donough v. Garland, 109 N.E. 1015 (Ill.1915) (assignor's child inherits in own right, assignee takes nothing). For a discussion of the differences between a release and an assignment, see Guzman, Releasing the Expectancy, 34 Ariz. St. L.J. 775 (2002).

F. DISCLAIMER

A disclaimer (sometimes called a renunciation) is an affirmative refusal to accept a gratuitous transfer of an interest in property. The doctrine of disclaimer has its roots in the common law, which presumed acceptance by the donee in the usual case of a beneficial gift but permitted the donee to disclaim within a reasonable time after learning of the gift. The common law doctrine of disclaimer applied equally to inter vivos and testamentary gifts, but not to intestate succession. Upon the death of an intestate, title to the decedent's property was deemed to vest immediately in the heir by operation of law, with or without the heir's consent. An heir who attempted to disclaim was treated as constructively receiving the intestate share and retransferring it to the ultimate recipient. See Coomes v. Finegan, 7 N.W.2d 729 (Iowa 1943); Lauritzen, Only God Can Make an Heir, 48 Nw. U. L. Rev. 568 (1953).

In general, a disclaimer "relates back" to the time of the gift, and causes the gift either to fail entirely or to take effect as if the disclaimant had died immediately before the time of the gift. In the case of a testamentary gift, the disclaimed interest is treated as passing directly from the decedent to the ultimate recipient without ever passing through the disclaimant's hands. Evidently, the disclaimant could accept the gift and then turn it over to the ultimate recipient, but a disclaimer offers two significant advantages: it keeps the disclaimed interest out of reach of the disclaimant's creditors, and it avoids the gift tax that might otherwise be imposed on a transfer by the disclaimant.

Almost all of the states have enacted disclaimer statutes which authorize disclaimers of a wide variety of interests in property, including inter vivos and testamentary gifts, intestate shares, survivorship interests, and benefits under contractual arrangements such as life insurance policies. The statutes, which vary greatly in detail, specify formalities for making a valid disclaimer. The Uniform Disclaimer of Property Interests Act (1999), which is now incorporated in the Uniform Probate Code, provides in relevant part as follows:

Uniform Disclaimer of Property Interests Act (2010)

§ 2. Definitions.

In this [Act]:

(1) "Disclaimant" means the person to whom a disclaimed interest or power would have passed had the disclaimer not been made.

(2) "Disclaimed interest" means the interest that would have passed to the disclaimant had the disclaimer not been made.

(3) "Disclaimer" means the refusal to accept an interest in or power over property.

(4) "Fiduciary" means a personal representative, trustee, agent acting under a power of attorney, or other person authorized to act as a fiduciary with respect to the property of another person.

(5) "Jointly held property" means property held in the name of two or more persons under an arrangement in which all holders have concurrent interests and under which the last surviving holder is entitled to the whole of the property. . . .

§ 5. Power to Disclaim; General Requirements; When Irrevocable.

(a) A person may disclaim, in whole or part, any interest in or power over property, including a power of appointment. A person may disclaim the interest or power even if its creator imposed a spendthrift provision or similar restriction on transfer or a restriction or limitation on the right to disclaim.

(b) Except to the extent a fiduciary's right to disclaim is expressly restricted or limited by another statute of this State or by the instrument creating the fiduciary relationship, a fiduciary may disclaim, in whole or part, any interest in or power over property, including a power of appointment, whether acting in a personal or representative capacity. A fiduciary may disclaim the interest or power even if its creator imposed a spendthrift provision or similar restriction on transfer or a restriction or limitation on the right to disclaim, or an instrument other than the instrument that created the fiduciary relationship imposed a restriction or limitation on the right to disclaim.

(c) To be effective, a disclaimer must be in a writing or other record, declare the disclaimer, describe the interest or power disclaimed, be signed by the person making the disclaimer, and be delivered or filed in the manner provided in Section 12. . . .

(d) A partial disclaimer may be expressed as a fraction, percentage, monetary amount, term of years, limitation of a power, or any other interest or estate in the property.

(e) A disclaimer becomes irrevocable when it is delivered or filed pursuant to Section 12 or when it becomes effective as provided in Sections 6 through 11, whichever occurs later.

(f) A disclaimer made under this [Act] is not a transfer, assignment, or release.

§ 6. Disclaimer of Interest in Property.

(a) In this section:

(1) "Future interest" means an interest that takes effect in possession or enjoyment, if at all, later than the time of its creation.

(2) "Time of distribution" means the time when a disclaimed interest would have taken effect in possession or enjoyment.

(b) Except for a disclaimer governed by Section 7 or 8, the following rules apply to a disclaimer of an interest in property:

(1) The disclaimer takes effect as of the time the instrument creating the interest becomes irrevocable, or, if the interest arose under the law of intestate succession, as of the time of the intestate's death.

(2) The disclaimed interest passes according to any provision in the instrument creating the interest providing for the disposition of the interest, should it be disclaimed, or of disclaimed interests in general.

(3) If the instrument does not contain a provision described in paragraph (2), the following rules apply:

(A) If the disclaimant is not an individual, the disclaimed interest passes as if the disclaimant did not exist.

(B) If the disclaimant is an individual, except as otherwise provided in subparagraphs (C) and (D), the disclaimed interest passes as if the disclaimant had died immediately before the time of distribution.

(C) If by law or under the instrument, the descendants of the disclaimant would share in the disclaimed interest by any method of representation had the disclaimant died before the time of distribution, the disclaimed interest passes only to the descendants of the disclaimant who survive the time of distribution.

(D) If the disclaimed interest would pass to the disclaimant's estate had the disclaimant died before the time of distribution, the disclaimed interest instead passes by representation to the descendants of the disclaimant who survive the time of distribution. If no descendant of the disclaimant survives the time of distribution, the disclaimed interest passes to those persons, including the state but excluding the disclaimant, and in such shares as would succeed to the transferor's intestate estate under the intestate succession law of the transferor's domicile had the transferor died at the time of distribution. However, if the transferor's surviving spouse is living but is remarried at the time of distribution, the transferor is deemed to have died unmarried at the time of distribution.

(4) Upon the disclaimer of a preceding interest, a future interest held by a person other than the disclaimant takes effect as if the disclaimant had died or ceased to exist immediately before the time of distribution, but a future interest held by the disclaimant is not accelerated in possession or enjoyment.

§ 7. Disclaimer of Rights of Survivorship in Jointly Held Property.

(a) Upon the death of a holder of jointly held property, a surviving holder may disclaim, in whole or part, the greater of:

(1) a fractional share of the property determined by dividing the number one by the number of joint holders alive immediately before the death of the holder to whose death the disclaimer relates; or

(2) all of the property except that part of the value of the entire interest attributable to the contribution furnished by the disclaimant.

(b) A disclaimer under subsection (a) takes effect as of the death of the holder of jointly held property to whose death the disclaimer relates.

(c) An interest in jointly held property disclaimed by a surviving holder of the property passes as if the disclaimant predeceased the holder to whose death the disclaimer relates.

§ 8. Disclaimer of Interest by Trustee.

If a trustee disclaims an interest in property that otherwise would have become trust property, the interest does not become trust property.

§ 12. Delivery or Filing. . . .

(c) In the case of an interest created under the law of intestate succession or an interest created by will, other than an interest in a testamentary trust:

(1) a disclaimer must be delivered to the personal representative of the decedent's estate; or

(2) if no personal representative is then serving, it must be filed with a court having jurisdiction to appoint the personal representative.

(d) In the case of an interest in a testamentary trust:

(1) a disclaimer must be delivered to the trustee then serving, or if no trustee is then serving, to the personal representative of the decedent's estate; or

(2) if no personal representative is then serving, it must be filed with a court having jurisdiction to enforce the trust.

(e) In the case of an interest in an inter vivos trust:

(1) a disclaimer must be delivered to the trustee then serving;

(2) if no trustee is then serving, it must be filed with a court having jurisdiction to enforce the trust; or

(3) if the disclaimer is made before the time the instrument creating the trust becomes irrevocable, it must be delivered to the settlor of a revocable trust or the transferor of the interest.

(f) In the case of an interest created by a beneficiary designation which is disclaimed before the designation becomes irrevocable, the disclaimer must be delivered to the person making the beneficiary designation.

(g) In the case of an interest created by a beneficiary designation which is disclaimed after the designation becomes irrevocable:

(1) the disclaimer of an interest in personal property must be delivered to the person obligated to distribute the interest; and

(2) the disclaimer of an interest in real property must be recorded in [the office of the county recorder of deeds] of the [county] where the real property that is the subject of the disclaimer is located.

(h) In the case of a disclaimer by a surviving holder of jointly held property, the disclaimer must be delivered to the person to whom the disclaimed interest passes. . . .

§ 13. When Disclaimer Barred or Limited.

(a) A disclaimer is barred by a written waiver of the right to disclaim.

(b) A disclaimer of an interest in property is barred if any of the following events occur before the disclaimer becomes effective:

(1) the disclaimant accepts the interest sought to be disclaimed;

(2) the disclaimant voluntarily assigns, conveys, encumbers, pledges, or transfers the interest sought to be disclaimed or contracts to do so; or

(3) a judicial sale of the interest sought to be disclaimed occurs. . . .

(f) A disclaimer of a power over property which is barred by this section is ineffective. A disclaimer of an interest in property which is barred by this section takes effect as a transfer of the interest disclaimed to the persons who would have taken the interest under this [Act] had the disclaimer not been barred.

The provisions of the uniform act are discussed in La Piana, Some Property Law Issues in the Law of Disclaimers, 38 Real Prop. Prob. & Tr. J. 207 (2003); Hirsch, The Code Breakers: How States Are Modifying the Uniform Disclaimer of Property Interests Act, 46 Real Prop. Tr. & Est. L.J. 325 (2011).

NOTES

1. *Creditors' rights.* By statute in virtually every state, a transfer that is made by an insolvent person without fair consideration may be set aside by the transferor's creditors. See Uniform Fraudulent Transfer Act § 5 (1984). Suppose that *A* wins a large personal injury judgment against *B*. *B* has no significant assets, and the judgment remains unsatisfied. Subsequently *B*'s aunt dies intestate, leaving *B* as her sole heir. *A* attempts to reach the estate assets to satisfy the judgment, but *B* promptly files a disclaimer which causes the estate to pass to *B*'s children as if *B* were predeceased. Can *A* attack the disclaimer as a fraudulent transfer of *B*'s interest in the aunt's estate? Most courts answer in the negative, noting that the disclaimer prevents *B* from acquiring or transferring any interest in the estate. See Essen v. Gilmore, 607 N.W.2d 829 (Neb. 2000); Tompkins State Bank v. Niles, 537 N.E.2d 274 (Ill.1989); but see Pennington v. Bigham, 512 So.2d 1344 (Ala.1987) (treating disclaimer as transfer); Stein v. Brown, 480 N.E.2d 1121 (Ohio 1985) (same). On similar reasoning, most courts conclude that *A*'s judgment lien does not constitute an "encumbrance" that bars *B* from disclaiming. See Estate of Opatz, 554 N.W.2d 813 (N.D.1996); Parks v. Parker, 957 S.W.2d 666 (Tex.App.1997); but see Estate of Abesy, 470 N.W.2d 713 (Minn.App.1991) (post-judgment garnishee summons bars disclaimer).

In the preceding example, suppose that shortly after the entry of *A*'s judgment *B* declares bankruptcy. One week later *B*'s aunt dies and *B* files the disclaimer. In the bankruptcy proceeding, *B*'s disclaimed interest in the aunt's estate may be reachable on behalf of *B*'s creditors (including *A*) if the disclaimer is treated as a transfer. See 11 U.S.C. §§ 541 and 549; In re Chenoweth, 3 F.3d 1111 (7th Cir.1993) (treating disclaimer as voidable post-petition transfer); cf. In re Atchison, 925 F.2d 209 (7th Cir.), cert. denied, 502 U.S. 860 (1991) (different result for pre-petition disclaimer); In re Costas, 555 F.3d 790 (9th Cir. 2009). Can *B* shield the inheritance from creditors' claims by making an anticipatory disclaimer during the aunt's lifetime? See Estate of Baird, 933 P.2d 1031 (Wash.1997) (disallowing attempted disclaimer of expectancy). See generally Hirsch, Inheritance and Bankruptcy: The Meaning of "Fresh Start," 45 Hastings L.J. 175 (1994).

A few statutes expressly bar an insolvent person from making a valid disclaimer. See, e.g., Fla. Stat. § 739.402(2)(d); Mass. Gen. L. ch. 191B, § 2–801(h)(2). Should a disclaimer by an insolvent heir be effective against voluntary creditors even if it is ineffective against involuntary creditors? See Hirsch, The Problem of the Insolvent Heir, 74 Cornell L. Rev. 587 (1989).

Even if a disclaimer is valid under state law, certain creditors of the disclaimant may have an overriding statutory right to reach the disclaimed property. In one case, a son disclaimed his interest in his deceased mother's estate, causing the disclaimed interest to pass directly to his own daughter under state law. Nevertheless, as a matter of federal law, the Supreme Court held that the disclaimer did not defeat a federal tax lien which attached to all "property and rights to property" belonging to the son. Noting that a disclaimant "inevitably exercises dominion" over an inheritance by choosing to accept it or to channel it to another beneficiary, the Court concluded that the disclaimed interest remained subject to the federal tax lien. Drye v. United States, 528 U.S. 49 (1999).

2. *Eligibility for public assistance.* Apart from the question of creditors' rights, a disclaimer may affect the disclaimant's eligibility for means-tested public assistance programs such as Medicaid. In general, a person whose "available resources" exceed a specified amount (e.g., $2,000) is ineligible for Medicaid. Suppose that *D*, a Medicaid recipient who lives in a nursing home, learns that her brother has just died leaving his entire $50,000 estate to her. If *D* accepts her inheritance she will lose her Medicaid eligibility until she exhausts her available resources. Can *D* preserve her eligibility by disclaiming the inheritance? The answer is likely to be negative. As one court noted in similar circumstances, "the petitioner's renunciation of a potentially available asset was the functional equivalent of a transfer of an asset since by refusing to accept it herself, she effectively funnelled it to other familial distributees." Molloy v. Bane, 631 N.Y.S.2d 910 (App. Div. 1995); see also Opp v. Ward County Social Services Board, 640 N.W.2d 704 (N.D. 2002); Hoesly v. State of Nebraska, Dep't of Social Services, 498 N.W.2d 571 (Neb.1993). See generally

Dobris, Medicaid Asset Planning by the Elderly: A Policy View of Expectations, Entitlement and Inheritance, 24 Real Prop. Prob. & Tr. J. 1 (1989).

3. *Time and manner of disclaimer.* Many disclaimer statutes require that a disclaimer be filed within a specified period of time (e.g., nine months after the decedent's death). The Uniform Disclaimer of Property Interests Act imposes no specific time limit. Under the Act, how long can an heir or beneficiary wait before deciding whether to accept or disclaim an inheritance?

Many disclaimer statutes authorize a guardian or conservator, with advance judicial approval, to make a disclaimer on behalf of a minor or incompetent beneficiary. UDPIA § 5, reproduced supra, goes further and permits a personal representative to disclaim on behalf of a decedent. The authority to disclaim on behalf of a decedent may produce substantial tax savings, especially where two spouses die within a short time of each other. See Estate of Rolin v. Commissioner, 588 F.2d 368 (2d Cir.1978) (revocable trust); Estate of Lamson, 662 A.2d 287 (N.H.1995) (joint property). The federal estate and gift tax consequences of disclaimers are discussed infra at p. 1000.

4. *Disposition of disclaimed interest.* In specifying the effect of a disclaimer, many statutes provide that the disclaimed interest passes "as if the disclaimant had predeceased the decedent." Consider how such a statute would apply in the following circumstances. *D*, a widow, dies intestate, survived by her son *A* and by her granddaughter *B* (the only child of *D*'s predeceased daughter). *A*, who has two children, disclaims his intestate share. Should *A*'s disclaimed one-half share be divided equally between his two children, leaving the other half of the estate for *B*? See Welder v. Hitchcock, 617 S.W.2d 294 (Tex.App. 1981); Estate of Fienga, 347 N.Y.S.2d 150 (Sur. 1973). Or should the entire estate be split equally among the three grandchildren, leaving *B* with one-third of the estate? UDPIA § 6(b)(3)(C), reproduced supra, is intended to ensure the former result.

Decedent left a will leaving her entire estate to her daughter or, if the daughter predeceased her, to charity. The daughter disclaims, causing the estate to pass to charity. Does the disclaimer operate to give decedent's sibling, who would take the estate if the will were invalid, standing to contest the will? See Estate of Estes, 718 P.2d 298 (Kan.1986).

5. *Family settlement agreements.* The Uniform Probate Code authorizes successors to "agree among themselves to alter the interests, shares, or amounts to which they are entitled under the will of the decedent, or under the laws of intestacy," subject to the rights of creditors and taxing authorities. The agreement is binding on the personal representative. UPC § 3–912. A family settlement agreement may prove useful where the successors are all competent adults and there is no disagreement over the proposed distribution. However, such an agreement does not necessarily offer the tax advantages of a disclaimer, since the parties may be treated for tax purposes as

having exchanged the interests to which they were originally entitled for the interests they ultimately received.

CHAPTER 3

PROTECTION OF THE FAMILY

∎ ∎ ∎

A. INTRODUCTION

From a policy perspective, the law of gratuitous transfers has profound implications for the structure of the family and the well-being of its members. Wealth may serve to reinforce family loyalties and relationships, open access to opportunities, and provide care and security for members who are disabled by reason of youth, old age, or other circumstances. Wealth may also give rise to conflicts of unmatched intensity and bitterness when disappointed expectations of inheritance pit family members against each other. Inevitably, the law regulating the transmission of wealth must take into account the role of wealth in shaping the family.

In the vast majority of cases wealth devolves to members of the decedent's immediate family. This happens automatically if the decedent dies intestate. Furthermore, although testators are free to leave the bulk of their property by will to other beneficiaries, they do not necessarily choose to do so. Indeed, according to one commentator, "it is probable that through the centuries freedom of testation has been used more as an instrument of family protection than as a weapon of disinheritance." Macdonald, Fraud on the Widow's Share 40 (1960). Contemporary studies also indicate that testators who depart from the scheme of intestate succession most frequently do so by augmenting the surviving spouse's share. As noted earlier, the fact that an increase in the spouse's share generally comes at the expense of the children may not indicate any lack of affection for the children but rather an expectation that the surviving spouse will take care of the children and ultimately leave them any property remaining at the spouse's death. Nevertheless, the law does not leave the protection of surviving family members to the testator's unfettered discretion. Various statutes compel, or at least encourage, testators to make provision for the surviving spouse and children, if any.

Protection of Surviving Spouse

By statute in almost every state, a decedent's surviving spouse enjoys some measure of protection against disinheritance. Although the statutes vary considerably from state to state, reflecting differing historical roots and underlying policy concerns, the most fundamental distinction is between the community property model followed in nine or ten states[1] and the common law model followed in the rest of the country. Broadly speaking, the community property model reflects a conception of marriage as an "economic partnership" which gives both spouses equal concurrent interests in all property earned during the marriage. When one spouse dies, one half of the community property is subject to the decedent's power of testation; the other half belongs to the survivor and does not pass as part of the decedent's probate estate. By contrast, the common law model generally treats each spouse as owning whatever property is titled in his or her individual name, with full power of testation. To protect a surviving spouse against complete disinheritance, all but one[2] of the common law states have statutes which permit the spouse to claim dower or an elective share in a specified portion of the decedent's property, notwithstanding any contrary provisions of the decedent's will. The modern statutes concerning marital property rights are formally sex-neutral, in that they prescribe uniform treatment for widows and widowers. Nevertheless, in view of the statistical fact that widows outnumber widowers by more than four to one, discussion of these statutes often focuses on the rights of a surviving wife at the death of her husband. Of course, the roles may be reversed.

The traditional policy analysis takes as its starting point a traditional family in which the husband acts as breadwinner and the wife as homemaker. The concern is that the wife, having forgone her own economic opportunities in order to work in the home and enable the husband to accumulate substantial wealth in his own name, may find herself without adequate means of support if the husband dies leaving his estate to other beneficiaries. Here, the spouse's right to dower or an elective share may be rationalized as a guarantee of support after the decedent's death—a continuation of the support that the decedent was legally obligated to provide during life. But this rationale fits less comfortably in other, increasingly common situations involving two-earner couples, second marriages entered into late in life, short-lived marriages, and unmarried cohabitants. Moreover, even in a traditional family, the notion of marriage as an economic partnership has achieved widespread acceptance as the animating principle of statutes, now enacted in nearly all of the states, which authorize "equitable distribution" upon divorce of property accumulated during the marriage, regardless of the form in which the property is

---

[1] The eight traditional community property states are Arizona, California, Idaho, Louisiana, Nevada, New Mexico, Texas, and Washington. Wisconsin, the first (and only) state to adopt the Uniform Marital Property Act, became a community property state for all practical purposes as of 1986. The tenth state is Alaska, which enacted an opt-in version of community property for married residents in 1998.

[2] The exception is Georgia, which has no statutory form of dower or elective share.

held. To many observers it seems anomalous that the spouses' respective property rights may vary dramatically depending on whether the marriage terminates by death or by divorce. Nevertheless, as one court observed, "Death is not divorce, and the problems posed by each of those two life-altering events are profoundly different. It should not surprise us . . . that the Legislature has adopted quite differing rules governing the disposition of property following those two events." Bongaards v. Millen, 793 N.E.2d 335, 345 (Mass. 2003). What policy considerations might explain the differing allocation of spousal property rights at death and divorce? See Rosenbury, Two Ways to End a Marriage: Divorce or Death, 2005 Utah L. Rev. 1227 (noting that "the women who benefit most from the partnership theory of marriage are those who forego market work and are married to wealthy men").

One recurring problem involves the extent to which one spouse may disinherit the other by means of inter vivos transfers outright or in trust. This problem is especially acute in common law states where the surviving spouse is entitled to receive a specified portion of property owned by the decedent at death. Some courts hew strictly to the literal terms of the statute, leaving the surviving spouse with no real protection against disinheritance. Others take a more flexible view of the statute, invoking any of several tests to determine whether a particular transfer is effective as against the surviving spouse. A number of states, following the lead of the Uniform Probate Code, define the spouse's elective share by reference to an "augmented estate" which includes not only property owned by the decedent at death but also various enumerated types of inter vivos transfers. Analogous issues arise in community property states when one spouse makes a gift of community property without the other spouse's knowledge or consent.

Another problem involves the method of satisfying the surviving spouse's rights. The problem is exacerbated where the spouse is required to renounce all benefits under the decedent's will in order to claim a statutory share. In some states, the statutory share is satisfied in much the same manner as claims of the decedent's creditors from assets subject to administration, by analogy to the doctrine of abatement. In other states, some version of equitable apportionment is adopted, so that each transferee's interest abates ratably.

Protection of Children

The materials in Section E of this Chapter present two contrasting policy perspectives concerning the fate of a child following the death of the parents. One pictures the typical child as an orphan and a pauper; the other sees the child as being middle-aged and, by upbringing and education in a family with property, well established in his or her own right. In a given situation either one of these views might be accurate, and therein lies the major deficiency in legislation that establishes a forced share for a surviving child. It might appear preferable to have legislation which is selective and capable of allocating the decedent's resources to meet the specific, real needs of close family members. This approach has been rejected in this country, however, on the ground that it would set off an uncontrollable avalanche of lawsuits. Although the states have enacted various statutes protecting a decedent's surviving spouse, they have not provided similar protection for children, and in all states (except Louisiana, which retains from its civil law background a limited form of the continental *légitime*), children may be completely disinherited by their parents. The law is content either to remain totally silent on the point, or to make sure that if a parent disinherits a child it is done intentionally and not by mistake or inadvertence.

B. STATUTORY ALLOWANCES AND SOCIAL SECURITY

1. STATUTORY ALLOWANCES

By statute in many states, surviving family members are entitled to allowances from the decedent's estate for homestead, exempt property, and family support. These statutory allowances generally take priority over creditors' claims and thus provide a measure of security for family members even in the case of an insolvent estate. Moreover, to the extent that the statutory allowances cannot be defeated by will, they operate as a safeguard against disinheritance and, correspondingly, as a restriction on testamentary disposition.

The primary function of homestead is to guarantee the continuance of a home for the family of a debtor by exempting it from the claims of creditors. In some states real property automatically becomes a homestead when it is used as the family home, without any special formalities. In other states, the owner must record a formal declaration of homestead to qualify the property for the statutory exemption. Many modern statutes not only exempt the property from creditors' claims but also give the family some indestructible interests in it. Some statutes authorize the owner's spouse to claim the exemption from creditors if the owner refuses to do so. Some permit the owner to make an effective inter vivos conveyance only with the spouse's consent. After the owner's death, the property generally passes free of creditors' claims to the surviving spouse or minor children, and continues to qualify as homestead in their hands.

The allowances for exempt property and family support set aside a limited amount of personal property (e.g., household furniture, clothing, and personal effects) as well as temporary support from the estate for surviving family members during the period of administration. The persons entitled to family support usually include the surviving spouse and any minor children. These allowances are generally exempt from claims of the decedent's creditors.

The cumulative value of the statutory allowances set forth in the Uniform Probate Code may be substantial. Indeed, in an estate of small or moderate size, after payment of statutory allowances and creditors' claims there may be little or no property upon which the decedent's will can operate.

Uniform Probate Code (2011)

Section 2–402. Homestead Allowance.

A decedent's surviving spouse is entitled to a homestead allowance of [$22,500]. If there is no surviving spouse, each minor child and each dependent child of the decedent is entitled to a homestead allowance amounting to [$22,500] divided by the number of minor and dependent children of the decedent. The homestead allowance is exempt from and has priority over all claims against the estate. Homestead allowance is in addition to any share passing to the surviving spouse or minor or dependent child by the will of the decedent, unless otherwise provided, by intestate succession, or by way of elective share.

Section 2–403. Exempt Property.

In addition to the homestead allowance, the decedent's surviving spouse is entitled from the estate to a value, not exceeding $15,000 in excess of any security interests therein, in household furniture, automobiles, furnishings, appliances, and personal effects. If there is no surviving spouse, the decedent's children are entitled jointly to the same value. If encumbered chattels are selected and the value in excess of security interests, plus that of other exempt property, is less than $15,000, or if there is not $15,000 worth of exempt property in the estate, the spouse or children are entitled to other assets of the estate, if any, to the extent necessary to make up the $15,000 value. Rights to exempt property and assets needed to make up a deficiency of exempt property have priority over all claims against the estate, but the right to any assets to make up a deficiency of exempt property abates as necessary to permit earlier payment of homestead allowance and family allowance. These rights are in addition to any benefit or share passing to the surviving spouse or children by the decedent's will, unless otherwise provided, by intestate succession, or by way of elective share.

Section 2–404. Family Allowance.

(a) In addition to the right to homestead allowance and exempt property, the decedent's surviving spouse and minor children whom the decedent was obligated to support and children who were in fact being supported by the decedent are entitled to a reasonable allowance in money out of the estate for their maintenance during the period of administration, which allowance may not continue for longer than one year if the estate is inadequate to discharge allowed claims. The allowance may be paid as a lump sum or in periodic installments. It is payable to the surviving spouse, if living, for the use of the surviving spouse and minor and dependent children; otherwise to the children, or persons having their care and custody. If a minor child or dependent child is not living with the surviving spouse, the allowance may be made partially to the child or his [or her] guardian or other person having the child's care and custody, and partially to the spouse, as their needs may appear. The family allowance is exempt from and has priority over all claims except the homestead allowance.

(b) The family allowance is not chargeable against any benefit or share passing to the surviving spouse or children by the will of the decedent, unless otherwise provided, by intestate succession, or by way of elective share. The death of any person entitled to family allowance terminates the right to allowances not yet paid.

Section 2–405. Source, Determination, and Documentation.

(a) If the estate is otherwise sufficient, property specifically devised may not be used to satisfy rights to homestead allowance or exempt property. Subject to this restriction, the surviving spouse, guardians of minor children, or children who are adults may select property of the estate as homestead allowance and exempt property. The personal representative may make those selections if the surviving spouse, the children, or the guardians of the minor children are unable or fail to do so within a reasonable time or there is no guardian of a minor child. The personal representative may execute an instrument or deed of distribution to establish the ownership of property taken as homestead allowance or exempt property. The personal representative may determine the family allowance in a lump sum not exceeding $27,000 or periodic installments not exceeding $2,250 per month for one year, and may disburse funds of the estate in payment of the family allowance and any part of the homestead allowance payable in cash. The personal representative or an interested person aggrieved by any selection, determination, payment, proposed payment, or failure to act under this section may petition the court for appropriate relief, which may include a family allowance other than that which the personal representative determined or could have determined. . . .

2. SOCIAL SECURITY

Although the law of succession focuses primarily on transfers of privately owned wealth, many families have little or no accumulated wealth. For them, protection in the form of statutory allowances and other restrictions on testamentary disposition are largely irrelevant. Indeed, the federal Social Security program (officially known as Old Age, Survivors and Disability Insurance) often proves to be the single most significant source of financial protection for a decedent's surviving spouse and minor children. Today virtually all workers in the United States (except for certain government employees) are covered by Social Security, which is funded by a payroll tax imposed at a flat rate on wages up to a specified dollar amount.[3] Most of the amounts collected each year are paid out currently in the form of old age and survivors benefits to retired workers and their families.

Upon retirement at full retirement age, a worker becomes entitled to a basic retirement benefit known as the "primary insurance amount" (PIA) which is payable in the form of a monthly annuity for life.[4] The PIA reflects the worker's lifetime earnings history and is calculated by applying a progressive benefit formula to the worker's "average indexed monthly earnings" (AIME). For example, upon retirement at age 66 in 2012, a worker with maximum covered AIME would be eligible for a PIA of $2,513 per month, or $30,156 per year; for the vast majority of workers, the basic retirement benefit would be considerably smaller. In addition to the retired worker's own benefit, a spouse or child may be eligible for separate Social Security benefits based on the worker's PIA both before and after the worker's death. During the worker's life, the benefit for an eligible spouse is generally equal to one-half of the worker's PIA; after the worker's death, the spouse is entitled to a survivors benefit equal to the deceased worker's full PIA. By statute, the amount of Social Security benefits is subject to annual cost-of-living adjustments. Moreover, benefits cannot be assigned or diverted to alternative beneficiaries. For an overview of the program, see Myers, Social Security (4th ed. 1993); Social Security Administration, Social Security Handbook (updated annually).

For many years, widows were eligible for survivors benefits but widowers were not. After the Supreme Court held this feature of the statute unconstitutional, the statute was amended to extend similar benefits to widowers. See Weinberger v. Wiesenfeld, 420 U.S. 636 (1975) (rejecting "archaic" notion that "male workers' earnings are vital to the support of their families, while the earnings of female wage-earners do not significantly contribute to their families' support"); see also Califano v. Goldfarb, 430 U.S. 199 (1977) (striking down dependency requirement applicable only to widowers). The system of spousal and survivors benefits, and especially its impact on women, remain controversial. Several reform

---

[3] The payroll tax rate is currently 12.4 percent, of which half is withheld from the worker's wages and half is collected from the employer. In 2012 the maximum amount of wages subject to the payroll tax was $110,100.

[4] Full retirement age, originally set at 65 years for workers born before 1938, is scheduled to rise gradually to 67 years for workers born after 1959. The amount of the benefit is subject to downward adjustment in the case of early retirement or upward adjustment in the case of delayed retirement.

proposals recommend an "earnings sharing" model, which would allocate the combined earnings of a married couple equally between the spouses for purposes of calculating benefits, by analogy to community property. See A Challenge to Social Security: The Changing Roles of Women and Men in American Society (Burkhauser & Holden eds., 1982); see also Burke & McCouch, Women, Fairness, and Social Security, 82 Iowa L. Rev. 1209 (1997); Blumberg, Adult Derivative Benefits in Social Security, 32 Stan. L. Rev. 233 (1980); Martin, Social Security Benefits for Spouses, 63 Cornell L. Rev. 789 (1978).

While some observers question whether Social Security provides adequate protection for retired workers and their families, others question whether the existing program is financially sustainable. Proposed solutions range from incremental reform of the existing system to full-fledged privatization. See Report of the 1994–1996 Advisory Council on Social Security (1997); President's Commission to Strengthen Social Security, Final Report (2001); Steuerle & Bakija, Retooling Social Security for the 21st Century: Right and Wrong Approaches to Reform (1994); Social Security: Beyond the Rhetoric of Crisis (Marmor & Mashaw eds., 1988); Boskin, Too Many Promises: The Uncertain Future of Social Security (1986).

C. SURVIVING SPOUSE: DOWER AND ELECTIVE SHARE

1. DOWER

The common law estate of *dower* entitled a widow to a life estate in one-third of all land owned by her deceased husband at any time during the marriage. Technically, dower attached by operation of law at the moment the husband became seised of an inheritable freehold estate in land, either at the time of the marriage or thereafter; but it remained "inchoate" during the husband's life and became "consummate" (i.e., possessory) only if the wife survived the husband. If the wife died first, her dower was extinguished. Dower operated as an encumbrance on the husband's land, which he could not defeat by unilateral action. If he conveyed or mortgaged the land during life, his transferee took subject to the wife's dower; if the land passed by will or intestacy at his death, the devisee or heir likewise took subject to the wife's dower. By similar reasoning, dower took priority over claims of creditors. At the husband's death, the widow could demand that her dower be assigned to her in kind, i.e., that one-third of each parcel of land be set aside by metes and bounds for her lifetime possession, if this was feasible; otherwise, she could claim a life interest in one-third of the income from each parcel of land.

The husband took a somewhat similar estate of *curtesy* in the wife's land, the major differences being that curtesy arose only upon the birth of issue of the marriage and entitled the husband to a life estate in all of the wife's lands. (The practical importance of curtesy was limited to the period after the wife's death, since upon marriage the husband received an estate by the *marital right* which entitled him to all the rents and profits from the wife's land even before the birth of issue.) For a historical perspective on the development and characteristics of common law dower and curtesy, see George L. Haskins' contribution in 1 Am. L. Prop., pt. 5 (Casner ed. 1952).

Today common law dower and curtesy have been abolished throughout the United States. Several states have adopted statutory versions of dower, applicable equally to widows and widowers, which give the surviving spouse the right to claim a life estate in a specified portion of all land owned by the decedent at any time during the marriage. Statutory dower often includes an outright share of any personal property owned by the decedent at death, and usually conditions the spouse's dower rights on a renunciation of any provisions for the spouse in the decedent's will. See Ark. Stat. §§ 28–11–301 et seq.; Ky. Rev. Stat. §§ 392.020 et seq.

Although dower provides effective protection for the surviving spouse against complete disinheritance where the decedent owned land, it has three major disadvantages. First, a life estate in one-third (or even one-half) of the decedent's property may be woefully inadequate to support a surviving spouse, especially if the estate is small and the spouse has little property of his or her own. Second, since dower traditionally attaches only to land owned by the decedent, it offers no protection to the extent the decedent's accumulated wealth takes the form of intangible personal property. Even with respect to land, dower can be circumvented fairly easily by acquiring the land indirectly through a real estate holding company. Third, dower makes it necessary for a prospective purchaser of land to ascertain the seller's marital status. This creates additional expense and uncertainty in title searches, and ultimately impairs the value and marketability of land. In response to these disadvantages, most states have abolished dower and instead allow the surviving spouse to claim a statutory elective share in the decedent's property.

NOTES

1. *Elective share compared to dower.* In one respect the statutory elective share is more comprehensive than common law dower because it applies not only to land but to all of the decedent's property, real and personal, tangible and intangible. In another respect, the elective share is narrower than common law dower because it typically reaches only property that was owned by the decedent and transferred at death. (Even the Uniform Probate Code, which includes certain lifetime transfers in the elective share, does not reach

property that the decedent gave away with no strings attached more than two years before death.) Although in theory a property owner can avoid the elective share by making substantial irrevocable lifetime gifts, as a practical matter most owners are unwilling to go to such lengths.

2. *Constitutional limitations.* A statutory scheme that treats widows differently from widowers is open to constitutional challenge on equal protection grounds. Can a statute that provides dower for widows but no comparable rights for widowers survive such a challenge on the the ground that widows as a group tend to have less property of their own than widowers and therefore stand in greater need of support? In Hall v. McBride, 416 So.2d 986, 989–90 (Ala.1982), the court stated:

> The purpose of enacting § 43–1–15 [permitting a wife to dissent from her deceased husband's will and claim statutory dower rights] is to protect the wife from a husband who would cut her from his will, leaving her with few or no assets for her support. . . .

> In order to withstand scrutiny under the Equal Protection Clause, this gender-based classification must serve "important governmental objectives and must be substantially related to achievement of those objectives." Orr v. Orr, [440 U.S. 268, 279, 99 S.Ct. 1102, 59 L.Ed.2d 306 (1979)]. Our next step is to examine the governmental objectives of the statutory scheme.

> One obvious objective of the statute has its roots in romantic paternalism—protection of women because it is assumed that their role as wives and mothers leaves them financially helpless. The statute "effectively announce[s] the State's preference for an allocation of family responsibilities under which the wife plays a dependent role, and as seeking for [its] objective the reinforcement of that model among the State's citizens." Orr v. Orr, 440 U.S. 279, 99 S. Ct. 1111. The United States Supreme Court has stated repeatedly that such an objective which is part of the baggage of sexual stereotypes presuming certain roles of males and females in the home and the working world cannot sustain the constitutionality of statutes. . . . The statute, if it is to survive constitutional attack, must be validated on some other basis.

> It may be asserted that . . . § 43–1–15, giving only a widow the right to dissent from the spouse's will, serves to reduce the economic disparity between men and women which is the result of our long history of discrimination against women. Furthermore, it may be asserted that § 43–1–15 serves the purpose of assisting needy spouses. The United States Supreme Court has recognized that these are both important governmental objectives. See Orr v. Orr, 440 U.S. at 280, 99 S. Ct. at 1112; Califano v. Webster, 430 U.S. 313, 97 S.Ct. 1192, 51 L.Ed.2d 360 (1977); Kahn v. Shevin, 416 U.S. 351, 94 S.Ct. 1734, 40 L.Ed.2d 189 (1974).

The final step in our analysis under the Equal Protection Clause is to determine whether the classification contained in the statute is substantially related to the aforementioned important governmental objectives. We hold that it is not.

In general, gender is not "a reliable proxy for need." Orr v. Orr, 440 U.S. at 281, 99 S. Ct. at 1112. The statute provides aid to women who are excluded from their husbands' wills, but no aid to men who are destitute and who are inequitably excluded from their wives' wills. The statute also gives aid to widows who are not needy, to the exclusion of other needy devisees. Thus, the alleged purpose of the statute, to help needy spouses, could be fulfilled by a gender-neutral statute. "Where, as here, the State's compensatory and ameliorative purposes are as well served by a gender-neutral classification as one that gender classifies and therefore carries with it the baggage of sexual stereotypes, the State cannot be permitted to classify on the basis of sex." Orr v. Orr, 440 U.S. at 283, 99 S. Ct. at 1113.

The court considered the possibility of expanding the coverage of the statute to provide identical benefits to widowers, but instead held the statute totally invalid. Noting that the "statutes on decedents' estates are so complex and interwoven," the court found itself "ill-equipped to tinker with the various parts" and therefore left the issue to the legislature. Subsequently, Alabama adopted a statutory elective share modeled on the Uniform Probate Code. Courts in other jurisdictions have reached similar results. See Estate of Reed, 354 So.2d 864 (Fla.1978) (family allowance payable only to widow); Stokes v. Stokes, 613 S.W.2d 372 (Ark.1981) (special dower and statutory allowances for widow); but see Estate of Miltenberger, 737 N.W.2d 513 (Mich. App. 2007), app. den., 753 N.W.2d 219 (Mich. 2008) (upholding statutory dower available only to widow as "reasonably designed to further the state policy of cushioning the financial impact of spousal loss upon the sex for which that loss imposes a disproportionately heavy burden").

2. TRADITIONAL ELECTIVE SHARE

Most states have replaced common law dower and curtesy with a statutory elective share which gives the surviving spouse a right to claim a share of property owned by the decedent at death, often on condition that the spouse renounce the decedent's will. The Illinois statute is typical:

Illinois Compiled Statutes, ch. 755

Sec. 5/2–8. Renunciation of will by spouse. (a) If a will is renounced by the testator's surviving spouse, whether or not the will contains any provision for the benefit of the surviving spouse, the surviving spouse is entitled to the following share of the testator's estate after payment of all just claims: $1/3$ of the entire estate if the testator leaves a descendant or $1/2$ of the entire estate if the testator leaves no descendant.

(b) In order to renounce a will, the testator's surviving spouse must file in the court in which the will was admitted to probate [within a specified time] a written instrument signed by the surviving spouse and declaring the renunciation. . . . The filing of the instrument is a complete bar to any claim of the surviving spouse under the will. . . .

(c) If a will is renounced in the manner provided by this Section, any future interest which is to take effect in possession or enjoyment at or after the termination of an estate or other interest given by the will to the surviving spouse takes effect as though the surviving spouse had predeceased the testator, unless the will expressly provides that in case of renunciation the future interest shall not be accelerated.

(d) If a surviving spouse of the testator renounces the will and the legacies to other persons are thereby diminished or increased in value, the court, upon settlement of the estate, shall abate from or add to the legacies in such a manner as to apportion the loss or advantage among the legatees in proportion to the amount and value of their legacies.

A recurring issue under this type of statute involves the extent to which the surviving spouse can reach property transferred by the decedent during life or otherwise outside the will.

NEWMAN V. DORE

Court of Appeals of New York, 1937.
275 N.Y. 371, 9 N.E.2d 966.

LEHMAN, JUDGE. . . .

Ferdinand Straus died on July 1, 1934, leaving a last will and testament dated May 5, 1934, which contained a provision for a trust for his wife for her life of one-third of the decedent's property both real and personal. In such case the statute did not give the wife a right of election to take her share of the estate as in intestacy.[5] She receives the income for life from a trust fund of the amount of the intestate share, but does not take the share. That share [under section 83 of the Decedent Estate Law] is one-third of the decedent's estate. It includes no property which does not form part of the estate at the decedent's death. The testator on June 28, 1934, three days before his death, executed trust agreements by which, in form at least, he transferred to trustees all his real and personal property. If the agreements effectively divested the settlor of title to his

---

[5] Section 18, subdivision 1 of the Decedent Estate Law, effective September 1, 1930, provided a personal right of election for the surviving spouse to take an intestate share of the estate subject to enumerated limitations and exceptions. These limitations and exceptions included a case where "the testator has devised or bequeathed in trust an amount equal to or greater than the intestate share, with income thereof payable to the surviving spouse for life." Thus, by leaving one-third of his estate in trust to pay income to his wife for life, Mr. Straus prevented his wife from claiming an outright one-third elective share. The New York statute retained this limitation on the elective share, with minor changes, until 1994. See N.Y. EPTL § 5–1.1–A(a)(5).—EDS.

property, then the decedent left no estate and the widow takes nothing. The widow has challenged the validity of the transfer to the trustees. The beneficiary named in the trust agreement has brought this action to compel the trustees to carry out its terms. The trial court has found that the "trust agreements were made, executed and delivered by said Ferdinand Straus for the purpose of evading and circumventing the laws of the State of New York, and particularly sections 18 and 83 of the Decedent Estate Law." Undoubtedly the settlor's purpose was to provide that at his death his property should pass to beneficiaries named in the trust agreement to the exclusion of his wife. Under the provisions of the Decedent Estate Law the decedent could not effect the desired purpose by testamentary disposition of his property. The problem in this case is whether he has accomplished that result by creating a trust during his lifetime.

The validity of the attempted transfer depends upon whether "the laws of the State of New York and particularly sections 18 and 83 of the Decedent Estate Law" prohibit or permit such transfer. If the statute, in express language or by clear implication, prohibits the transfer, it is illegal; if the laws of the state do not prohibit it, the transfer is legal. In strict accuracy, it cannot be said that a "purpose of evading and circumventing" the law can carry any legal consequences. "We do not speak of evasion, because, when the law draws a line, a case is on one side of it or the other, and if on the safe side is none the worse legally that a party has availed himself to the full of what the law permits. When an act is condemned as an evasion what is meant is that it is on the wrong side of the line indicated by the policy if not by the mere letter of the law." Bullen v. Wisconsin, 240 U.S. 625, 630, 36 S. Ct. 473, 474, 60 L. Ed. 830. In a subsequent case it was said of a defendant: "The fact that it desired to evade the law, as it is called, is immaterial, because the very meaning of a line in the law is that you intentionally may go as close to it as you can if you do not pass it." Superior Oil Co. v. State of Mississippi, 280 U.S. 390, 395, 50 S. Ct. 169, 170, 74 L. Ed. 504, both opinions by Mr. Justice Holmes. Under the laws of the State of New York, and particularly sections 18 and 83 of the Decedent Estate Law, neither spouse has any immediate interest in the property of the other. The "enlarged property right" which the Legislature intended to confer is only an expectant interest dependent upon the contingency that the property to which the interest attaches becomes a part of a decedent's estate. The contingency does not occur, and the expectant property right does not ripen into a property right in possession, if the owner sells or gives away the property. Herrmann v. Jorgenson, 263 N.Y. 348, 189 N.E. 449; Matter of McCulloch's Will, 263 N.Y. 408, 189 N.E. 473, 91 A.L.R. 1440. Defeat of a contingent expectant interest by means available under the law cannot be regarded as an unlawful "evasion" of the law. A duty imperfectly defined by law may at times be evaded or a right imperfectly protected by law may be violated with impunity, but to say that an act, lawful under common-law rules and not prohibited by any express or implied statutory provision, is in itself a "fraud" on the law or an "evasion" of the law, involves a contradiction in terms.

That does not mean, of course, that the law may not place its ban upon an intended result even though the means to effect that result may be lawful. The statute gives to a spouse a property right. The question is, how far the statute protects that right even while it remains only expectant and contingent. A right created by law may be protected by law against invasion through acts otherwise lawful. A wrong does not cease to be a wrong because it is cloaked in form of law. The test of legality, then, is whether the result is lawful and the means used to achieve that result are lawful. Here, we should point out that the courts below have not based their decision primarily upon the finding that the trust agreements were executed for the purpose of evading and circumventing the law of the state of New York. The courts have also found, and the evidence conclusively establishes, that the trust agreements were made for the purpose of depriving the decedent's widow of any rights in and to his property upon his death. Upon the trust agreements executed a few days before the death of the settlor, he reserved the enjoyment of the entire income as long as he should live, and a right to revoke the trust at his will, and in general the powers granted to the trustees were in terms made "subject to the settlor's control during his life," and could be exercised "in such manner only as the settlor shall from time to time direct in writing." Thus, by the trust agreement which transferred to the trustees the settlor's entire property, the settlor reserved substantially the same rights to enjoy and control the disposition of the property as he previously had possessed, and the inference is inescapable that the trust agreements were executed by the settlor, as the court has found, "with the intention and for the purpose of diminishing his estate and thereby to reduce in amount the share" of his wife in his estate upon his death and as a "contrivance to deprive . . . his widow of any rights in and to his property upon his death." They had no other purpose and substantially they had no other effect. Does the statute intend that such a transfer shall be available as a means of defeating the contingent expectant estate of a spouse?

In a few states where a wife has a similar contingent expectant interest or estate in the property of her husband, it has been held that her rights may not be defeated by any transfer made during life with intent to deprive the wife of property, which under the law would otherwise pass to her. Thayer v. Thayer, 14 Vt. 107, 39 Am. Dec. 211; Evans v. Evans, 78 N.H. 352, 100 A. 671; Dyer v. Smith, 62 Mo. App. 606; Payne v. Tatem, 236 Ky. 306, 33 S.W.2d 2. In those states it is the intent to defeat the wife's contingent rights which creates the invalidity and it seems that an absolute transfer of all his property by a married man during his life, if made with other purpose and intent than to cut off an unloved wife, is valid even though its effect is to deprive the wife of any share in the property of her husband at his death. Dunnett v. Shields & Conant, 97 Vt. 419, 123 A. 626; Patch v. Squires, 105 Vt. 405, 165 A. 919. The rule has been stated that "while the wife cannot complain of reasonable gifts or advancements by a husband to his children by a former marriage, yet, if the gifts constitute the principal part of the husband's estate and be made without the wife's knowledge, a presumption of fraud arises, and it rests upon the beneficiaries to explain away that presumption." Payne v. Tatem, supra, 236 Ky. 306, at page 308, 33 S.W.2d 2, 3.

Motive or intent is an unsatisfactory test of the validity of a transfer of property. In most jurisdictions it has been rejected, sometimes for the reason that it would cast doubt upon the validity of all transfers made by a married man, outside of the regular course of business; sometimes because it is difficult to find a satisfactory logical foundation for it. Intent may, at times, be relevant in determining whether an act is fraudulent, but there can be no fraud where no right of any person is invaded. "The great weight of authority is that the intent to defeat a claim which otherwise a wife might have is not enough to defeat the deed." Leonard v. Leonard, 181 Mass. 458, 462, 63 N.E. 1068, 1069, 92 Am. St. Rep. 426, and cases there cited. Since the law gives the wife only an expectant interest in the property of her husband which becomes part of his estate, and since the law does not restrict transfers of property by the husband during his life, it would seem that the only sound test of the validity of a challenged transfer is whether it is real or illusory. That is the test applied in Leonard v. Leonard, supra. The test has been formulated in different ways, but in most jurisdictions the test applied is essentially the test of whether the husband has in good faith divested himself of ownership of his property or has made an illusory transfer. "The 'good faith' required of the donor or settlor in making a valid disposition of his property during life does not refer to the purpose to affect his wife but to the intent to divest himself of the ownership of the property. It is, therefore, apparent that the fraudulent intent which will defeat a gift inter vivos cannot be predicated of the husband's intent to deprive the wife of her distributive . . . share as widow." Benkart v. Commonwealth Trust Co. of Pittsburgh, 269 Pa. 257, 259, 112 A. 62, 63. In Pennsylvania the courts have sustained the validity of the trusts even where a husband reserved to himself the income for life, power of revocation, and a considerable measure of control. Cf. Lines v. Lines, 142 Pa. 149, 21 A. 809, 24 Am. St. Rep. 487; Potter Title & Trust Co. v. Braum, 294 Pa. 482, 144 A. 401, 64 A.L.R. 463; Beirne v. Continental–Equitable Trust Co., 307 Pa. 570, 161 A. 721. In other jurisdictions transfers in trust have been upheld regardless of their purpose where a husband retained a right to enjoy the income during his life. Rabbitt v. Gaither, 67 Md. 94, 8 A. 744; Cameron v. Cameron, 10 Smedes & M. (Miss.) 394, 48 Am. Dec. 759; Gentry v. Bailey, 6 Gratt. (47 Va.) 594; Hall v. Hall, 109 Va. 117, 63 S.E. 420, 21 L.R.A. (N.S.) 533; Stewart v. Stewart, 5 Conn. 317; Osborn v. Osborn, 102 Kan. 890, 172 P.

23. In some of these cases the settlor retained, also, a power of revocation. In no jurisdiction has a transfer in trust been upheld where the conveyance is intended only to cover up the fact that the husband is retaining full control of the property though in form he has parted with it. Though a person may use means lawfully available to him to keep outside of the scope of a statute, a false appearance of legality, however attained, will not avail him. Reality, not appearance, should determine legal rights. Cf. Jenkins v. Moyse, 254 N.Y. 319, 172 N.E. 521, 74 A.L.R. 205.

In this case the decedent, as we have said, retained not only the income for life and power to revoke the trust, but also the right to control the trustees. We need not now determine whether such a trust is, for any purpose, a valid present trust. It has been said that, "where the settlor transfers property in trust and reserves not only . . . a power to revoke and modify the trust but also such power to control the trustee as to the details of the administration of the trust that the trustee is the agent of the settlor, the disposition so far as it is intended to take effect after his death is testamentary. . . ." American Law Institute, Restatement of the Law of Trusts, § 57, subd. 2. We do not now consider whether the rule so stated is in accord with the law of this state or whether in this case the reserved power of control is so great that the trustee is in fact "the agent of the settlor." We assume, without deciding, that except for the provisions of section 18 of the Decedent Estate Law the trust would be valid. Cf. Robb v. Washington & Jefferson College, 185 N.Y. 485, 78 N.E. 359; Von Hesse v. Mackaye, 136 N.Y. 114, 32 N.E. 615. Perhaps "from the technical point of view such a conveyance does not quite take back all that it gives, but practically it does." That is enough to render it an unlawful invasion of the expectant interest of the wife. Leonard v. Leonard, supra; Brownell v. Briggs, 173 Mass. 529, 54 N.E. 251.

Judged by the substance, not by the form, the testator's conveyance is illusory, intended only as a mask for the effective retention by the settlor of the property which in form he had conveyed. We do not attempt now to formulate any general test of how far a settlor must divest himself of his interest in the trust property to render the conveyance more than illusory. Question of whether reservation of the income or of a power of revocation, or both, might even without reservation of the power of control be sufficient to show that the transfer was not intended in good faith to divest the settlor of his property must await decision until such question arises. In this case it is clear that the settlor never intended to divest himself of his property. He was unwilling to do so even when death was near.

The judgment should be affirmed, with costs. . . .

NOTES

1. *Background of the Newman case.* The marriage in Newman v. Dore was not a model of domestic tranquillity. Mr. Straus was a widower, eighty years old, while his wife was in her thirties and the mother of two children whom he adopted as part of the arrangement. At his death four years after the marriage, there was pending an action brought by his wife for separation with alimony on the grounds that his perverted sexual habits made it impossible for her to live with him. (The record does not make clear the nature of his alleged perversions, although it does include a newspaper account in which he is described as having received a transplant of monkey glands by surgical operation.) Highly indignant over these charges, Mr. Straus brought an action, which was also pending at his death, to annul the marriage and instructed his lawyer to see to it that that his wife (whom he characterized as a "whore" and "son of a bitch") would not receive any of his estate at death. The lawyer told him that in 1930 New York had enacted Section 18 of the Decedent Estate Law which made it impossible to disinherit his wife by will. A first step was to restrict her to the minimum provision required by the statute, and in May of 1934 he executed a will under which the wife was given a life income interest in a trust consisting of one-third of his estate. Prodded by the testator to show more ingenuity, the lawyer consulted a few friends (including a law professor) and came up with the idea of creating an inter vivos trust of all Mr. Straus' property, which would leave no probate estate upon which the provisions of the will could operate. On June 28, 1934 Mr. Straus executed a trust agreement naming Dore and another as trustees. At his death the trust property was to be distributed to Emma Newman, the niece of his first wife, for whom he showed all the affection of a natural father. Three days later he died. Emma Newman subsequently brought an action against the trustees to enforce the inter vivos trust. The widow appeared as the real party defendant to challenge the validity of the trust by which she was disinherited.

These seamy details of an unhappy second marriage suggest a slightly different perspective on this type of litigation from the one set forth in the usual policy statements on the subject.

2. *Illusory transfer doctrine.* Although the ruling in Newman v. Dore has been superseded by statute in New York (see N.Y. EPTL § 5–1.1–A), the decision represents the starting point for judicial analysis of the illusory transfer doctrine, and is widely followed in other jurisdictions. See Dreher v. Dreher, 634 S.E.2d 646 (S.C. 2006); Pezza v. Pezza, 690 A.2d 345 (R.I.1997); Johnson v. Farmers & Merchants Bank, 379 S.E.2d 752 (W.Va. 1989); Staples v. King, 433 A.2d 407 (Me.1981). What factors made the trust in *Newman* "illusory": The amount of property transferred? The timing of the transfer? The degree of control retained by Mr. Straus? His intent to disinherit his wife? Lack of donative intent?

Several courts refuse to follow the New York lead and hold that a surviving spouse cannot reach any property transferred by the decedent during life or by a will substitute such as a revocable trust. See Estate of George, 265 P.3d 222 (Wyo. 2011); Russell v. Russell, 758 So.2d 533 (Ala. 1999); Dumas v. Estate of Dumas, 627 N.E.2d 978 (Ohio 1994); Dalia v. Lawrence, 627 A.2d 392 (Conn.1993) (Totten trusts and joint bank account).

3. *Transfers in fraud of marital rights.* Some courts focus on the decedent's intent and other circumstances surrounding a transfer to determine whether it amounts to a "fraud" on the surviving spouse's marital rights. See Hanke v. Hanke, 459 A.2d 246 (N.H.1983); Merz v. Tower Grove Bank & Trust Co., 130 S.W.2d 611 (Mo.1939). Among the factors that courts consider in determining whether a transfer is in fraud of marital rights are: motive of the transferor; presence or absence of consideration; whether the amount of the transfer was disproportionate compared to the value of the decedent's total estate; the degree of control retained over the transferred property; whether the transfer was made openly and with frank disclosure or surreptitiously; proximity in time between the transfer and death; identity of the transferee as a natural object of the transferor's bounty; and the extent to which the surviving spouse is left without means of support. See Nelson v. Nelson, 512 S.W.2d 455 (Mo.App.1974) (joint bank account with decedent's sister, included in widow's elective share); cf. Finley v. Finley, 726 S.W.2d 923 (Tenn.App.1986) (joint bank account with decedent's children from prior marriage, not included in widow's elective share). See also Karsenty v. Schoukroun, 959 A.2d 1147 (Md. 2008) (discussing factors bearing on nature of nonprobate transfer and decedent's intent; extensive review of case law).

A few states have codified the fraudulent transfer test. See Mo. Rev. Stat. § 474.150 (at surviving spouse's election, gifts made "in fraud of the marital rights" may be recovered and applied to elective share; conveyance made during marriage without spouse's express assent presumed in fraud of marital rights); Tenn. Code § 31–1–105 (at spouse's election, conveyances voidable if made "fraudulently" with intent to defeat spouse's elective share). These statutes allow considerable leeway for interpretation, as demonstrated by the contrasting results in Sherrill v. Mallicote, 417 S.W.2d 798 (Tenn.App.1967) (irrevocable trust for benefit of decedent's brothers and sisters held voidable by widow) and Warren v. Compton, 626 S.W.2d 12 (Tenn.App.1981) (decedent's gift of $40,000 to "girl friend" not recoverable by widow).

4. *Retained control.* Some courts refuse to inquire whether a transfer is "colorable," "fraudulent," or "illusory," and focus instead on the objective nature and extent of the decedent's retained control. In Sullivan v. Burkin, 460 N.E.2d 572 (Mass.1984), the court prospectively overruled its prior decisions shielding a revocable inter vivos trust from the surviving spouse's claims, and announced that:

> the estate of a decedent, for the purposes of [the elective share statute], shall include the value of assets held in an inter vivos trust created by

the deceased spouse as to which the deceased spouse alone retained the power during his or her life to direct the disposition of those trust assets for his or her benefit, as, for example, by the exercise of a power of appointment or by revocation of the trust. [460 N.E.2d at 574–75.]

Under this standard, would a surviving spouse be able to reach trust property that was subject to a power of revocation held jointly by the decedent and a third-party trustee? Property held by the decedent and another person as joint tenants with right of survivorship? Life insurance proceeds payable to a beneficiary designated by the decedent? What if the decedent had a power to amend or terminate a trust created by a third party? See Bongaards v. Millen, 793 N.E.2d 335 (Mass. 2003) (surviving spouse not entitled to reach trust created by third party, even though decedent had life estate, power to withdraw property during life, and power to appoint remainder).

Suppose that *H*, while married to *W*, conveys real property to his child *A* from a previous marriage. On its face the deed is absolute and irrevocable; *H* retains no legally protected interest in the property. Nevertheless, with *A*'s consent, *H* continues to occupy and manage the property, collect rent and pay property taxes until his death more than ten years later. *W* claims that the property is subject to her elective share. What result? See Estate of Fries, 782 N.W.2d 596 (Neb. 2010). Does it matter if the transfer occurred before *H* and *W* were married? See Estate of Chrisp, 759 N.W.2d 87 (Neb. 2009); cf. UPC § 2–205.

DAVIS V. KB & T CO.

Supreme Court of Appeals of West Virginia, 1983.
172 W.Va. 546, 309 S.E.2d 45.

McGRAW, CHIEF JUSTICE.

This is an appeal by Dorothy Evelyn Davis on behalf of her incompetent sister, Pennsy Davis Farley, from a decision of the Circuit Court of Kanawha County which upheld an inter vivos trust created by Mrs. Farley's husband in 1976, effectively depriving Mrs. Farley of property she would have received under a will executed by her husband in 1973.

Pennsy Davis and David T. Farley were married in 1918 when they were, respectively, twenty-five and twenty-three years of age. Both Mr. and Mrs. Farley worked hard. David operated a hardware store and Pennsy engaged in the securities business. Mr. and Mrs. Farley had no children, and they maintained a relatively frugal lifestyle. Consequently, they accumulated substantial assets.

On or about May 23, 1973, Mr. Farley executed a will prepared by his attorney, wherein he devised his entire estate to his wife. Several months later, Mr. Farley typed an identical will for his wife, which devised her entire estate to him. Mrs. Farley executed this will on or about October 1, 1973.

In March 1976, Mrs. Farley suffered a mental collapse. She has remained hospitalized since that time. Immediately following his wife's mental collapse, Mr. Farley suffered several heart attacks requiring his temporary hospitalization. On May 14, 1976, after his release from the hospital, Mr. Farley established an inter vivos trust and executed a new will. On July 8, 1976, less than two months later, David T. Farley died.

The inter vivos trust established by Mr. Farley named Kanawha Banking & Trust Company, N.A., (KB & T) as trustee. The trust provides that the net income should be paid to Mr. Farley during his lifetime, and that should Mrs. Farley survive him, the net income should be paid to Mrs. Farley, "if the income of said Pennsy D. Farley from other sources known to said trustee is for any reason insufficient to provide unto her comfortable support and maintenance and medical and hospital care. . . ." Upon the death of Mr. Farley and his wife, the trust terminates and the principal and accumulated income is directed to be distributed to certain named beneficiaries. Finally, the trust reserved to Mr. Farley the right to amend or revoke the trust during his lifetime.

Simultaneously with the execution of the trust instrument, Mr. Farley executed a new will in which he bequeathed to his widow all his tangible personal property. The residue of his estate, consisting solely of personalty, was bequeathed to KB & T as trustee under the inter vivos trust. The will further provided that should Mr. Farley survive his wife, and thereby acquire her property, valued at approximately $700,000, said property, after payment of all debts, taxes, and costs of administration, was to be distributed to certain named heirs of his wife.

Upon execution of the trust instrument and will, Mr. Farley transferred and delivered to KB & T personal property consisting of stocks, bonds, certificates of deposit, and cash, all valued at approximately $145,000. He also executed change of beneficiary forms naming KB & T, as trustee, the beneficiary under certain life insurance policies valued at approximately $27,000.

Upon Mr. Farley's death, his new will was probated by the Kanawha County Commission. The appraisal of the decedent's estate disclosed probate assets valued at approximately $12,000.

On February 23, 1977, the appellant was qualified as committee for Mrs. Farley. Thereafter, she commenced this action seeking to renounce Mr. Farley's 1976 will, alleging . . . that Mrs. Farley was entitled to a dower interest in all the property in the control of her husband at the

time of his death, including the property placed in the inter vivos trust.
. . .

By order entered January 15, 1982, the Circuit Court of Kanawha
County dismissed the appellant's action, ruling that . . . Mr. Farley's estate did not include the assets transferred to the inter vivos trust, and,
therefore, it would not be in Mrs. Farley's best interest to renounce the
1976 will and take her statutory share. . . .

On appeal, the appellant contends that the lower court erred in determining . . . that the property transferred to the inter vivos trust is not
a part of the probate estate to which Mrs. Farley's dower interest would
attach. We affirm the decision of the lower court. . . .

We now reach the question of the validity of the inter vivos trust established by Mr. Farley in 1976. The appellant alleges that the trust was
a scheme designed to permit Mr. Farley to retain ownership and control
of the trust assets during his lifetime, and upon his death, to deprive his
wife of the share in his estate to which she is entitled by statute. Accordingly, the appellant argues that the trust is illusory and operates as a
fraud upon Mrs. Farley's statutory entitlement in her husband's estate.
The lower court ruled that the trust was a valid inter vivos conveyance
which effectively removed the trust assets from Mr. Farley's estate, and
that it did not constitute a fraud upon Mrs. Farley's interests.

The question of the validity of an inter vivos trust which impairs the
statutory right of the surviving spouse to share in the settlor's estate is
an issue which has been addressed in numerous jurisdictions. See Annot.,
39 A.L.R. 3d 14 (1971 & Supp. 1982). Generally, in resolving the issue,
courts have taken one of two approaches. The first approach involves a
determination of whether the transfer of property is real and bona fide, or
whether the settlor has reserved such powers of ownership and control
over the trust property as to make the transfer illusory or testamentary
in character. See cases collected at 39 A.L.R. 3d 23–24, 29. The second
approach involves examination of the question whether the transfer of
property in trust constituted a fraud upon the rights of the spouse. See
cases collected at 39 A.L.R. 3d 25–26. The appellant has incorporated
both of these approaches in her argument.

To support her argument that the trust established by Mr. Farley is
illusory or testamentary in character, the appellant relies primarily upon
the fact that the trust instrument reserves to Mr. Farley the right to
amend or revoke the trust during his lifetime. It is well established, however, that the retention by the settlor of the power to revoke or modify a
trust is insufficient, standing alone, to render the trust illusory or testamentary. See, e.g., I A. Scott, The Law of Trusts § 57.1 (3d. ed. 1967) and

cases cited therein. As is stated in Restatement (Second) of Trusts § 57 (1959):

> Where an interest in the trust property is created in a beneficiary other than the settlor, the disposition is not testamentary and invalid for failure to comply with the requirements of the Statute of Wills merely because the settlor reserves a beneficial life interest or because he reserves in addition a power to revoke the trust in whole or in part, and a power to modify the trust, and a power to control the trustee as to the administration of the trust. . . .

The appellant further argues that Mr. Farley established the trust with the intent to deprive his wife of her statutory share in his estate, and therefore, it is, per se, a fraudulent conveyance and void as to Mrs. Farley's interests. The appellant relies upon our recent decision Wallace v. Wallace, W.Va., 291 S.E.2d 386 (1982), as support for this proposition. *Wallace* is a divorce case in which the wife sought to set aside a stock conveyance made by her husband. The wife alleged the conveyance was fraudulent and void because it was made in contemplation of divorce. In *Wallace* there was testimonial evidence which indicated that the conveyance was made with the express intent to deprive the wife of any claim to the stock assets. We recognized in the syllabus of *Wallace* that "[s]pouses are protected from acts before, during or after marriage that are intended to deprive them of part of their marital partners' estates upon which to base claims for support." In holding that the conveyance in question was fraudulent, we further stated that "[i]ntent to deprive is per se fraud; and proof of such intent establishes a fraudulent conveyance. Whether intent to deprive existed is determined from the specific facts of each case." 291 S.E.2d at 388 (citation omitted).

Wallace did not involve an inter vivos trust nor the claim that the spouse was being deprived of her statutory share of the estate under W. Va. § 42–3–1. It involved fraudulent transfer of property in contemplation of ordering a divorce. Courts from other jurisdictions which have considered the validity of an inter vivos trust, attacked as a fraud upon the rights of a spouse, have generally recognized "that the settlor's intention or purpose to deprive his or her spouse of a distributive share or other statutory right in the property transferred is not, in and of itself, sufficient to establish a fraudulent intent on the settlor's part. . . ." Annot., 39 A.L.R.3d 14, 19 (1971).

An examination of cases from other jurisdictions reveals no single standard which can be applied to test the validity of an inter vivos trust attacked by the settlor's spouse as a fraud upon his or her marital rights. Rather, the majority of courts which have addressed the question appear to decide the issue in a case by case basis, in light of the particular facts and circumstances. See, e.g., Johnson v. La Grange State Bank, [73 Ill. 2d 342, 383 N.E.2d 185 (1978)]; Gianakos v. Magiros, 234 Md. 14, 197 A.2d 897 (1964); Merz v. Tower Grove Bank & Trust Co., 344 Mo. 1150, 130 S.W.2d 611 (1939); Sherrill v. Mallicote, 57 Tenn. App. 241, 417 S.W.2d 798 (1967). Cf. Newman v. Dore, 275 N.Y. 371, 9 N.E.2d 966 (1937); Land v. Marshall, 426 S.W.2d 841 (Tex. 1968). This approach is understandable, given the myriad factual situations in which the issue may arise. Accordingly, we believe the better course is to adopt a flexible standard which takes into account all of the circumstances and weighs the equities on each side.

In this case, the facts do not support a conclusion that the inter vivos trust established by Mr. Farley was illusory, testamentary, or created with an intent to deprive his wife of her statutory share in his estate. This is not a case involving a sham trust wherein the settlor names himself as trustee and sole beneficiary, thus retaining both legal and equitable title to the trust property with the right to control the disposition of the trust assets. On the contrary, the trust established by Mr. Farley is a bona fide trust. In this regard we note that the trust agreement names a trustee other than the settlor who is given sole discretion to manage the trust property. Further, the property placed in trust was transferred and physically delivered to the named trustee. Moreover, the trust agreement grants discretion to the trustee during the settlor's lifetime to use all or any of the income and principal for the support and maintenance of both Mr. and Mrs. Farley if either of them became incapacitated by illness, age, or other cause. Upon the death of the settlor, the trustee is further directed to distribute to Mrs. Farley all or part of the net income of the trust necessary to provide for "her comfortable support and maintenance and medical and hospital care." The fact that Mr. Farley retained a right to amend or revoke the trust is insufficient to render the trust illusory or testamentary. Indeed, it appears from the testimony that the trust was made revocable upon the recommendation of the attorney who prepared the trust document, and not by the design of the settlor.

Mr. Farley's apparent purpose in creating the trust was to provide for himself and his wife in the event of incapacity. It is relevant to note that at the time the trust was established Mrs. Farley was hospitalized for a complete mental breakdown, and that Mr. Farley himself was in poor health, having suffered several heart attacks following his wife's hospitalization. The Farleys had no children, and Mr. Farley was concerned with who would manage their affairs should he become further incapacitated. Thus, it appears the trust was established not with an intent to deprive Mrs. Farley of her marital rights, but to provide for both Mr. and Mrs. Farley in the event of further misfortune.

It is clear from the record that Mrs. Farley is a wealthy woman in her own right with an estate valued at approximately $700,000, which does not include the family residence owned outright by Mrs. Farley. Thus, Mrs. Farley will not be left destitute should the appellant fail in her attempt to increase her elderly aunt's estate. Moreover, the appellee asserts, and the appellant does not dispute, that Mr. Farley's business acumen played a substantial role in the acquisition of his wife's sizable estate.

The ultimate effect of the circuit court's ruling is consistent with Mr. Farley's intent, apparent on the face of the 1976 trust agreement and will, that his estate should go to his side of the family and his wife's estate should go to her side of the family. This intent, not being contrary to any positive rule of law, is entitled to great weight. . . .

We believe the intended distribution of property pursuant to the 1976 trust agreement and will is an equitable result under the facts and circumstances of this case. Mr. Farley's estate will pass to his side of the family upon termination of the trust. Because Mr. Farley predeceased her, Mrs. Farley's devise contained in her 1973 will lapsed, and her property will go to her heirs. . . .

For the foregoing reasons, the decision of the Circuit Court of Kanawha County . . . that the property transferred by David T. Farley to the inter vivos trust is not a part of his probate estate, is affirmed. . . .

NOTES

1. *Illusory and fraudulent transfers.* The court in *Davis* cites the *Newman* decision with apparent approval. Are the rationales and results of the two decisions consistent with each other? For a comprehensive survey of problems arising from illusory or fraudulent transfers in relation to a surviving spouse's elective share, see Macdonald, Fraud on the Widow's Share (1960).

2. *Totten trusts.* A Totten trust is a deposit in a savings bank in the depositor's name "as trustee" for a named beneficiary and is freely revocable by the depositor on presentation of the pass book at any time. On Totten trusts generally, see infra p. 585.

The experience with Totten trusts in New York is instructive. In its first case on the issue after Newman v. Dore, the New York Court of Appeals held that a decedent's Totten trust in favor of his daughter who lived in Germany was illusory and subject to his widow's elective share, thereby making a reality of the *Newman* court's dictum to the effect that a transfer could be valid as a matter of property law but invalid as to the surviving spouse. See Krause v. Krause, 32 N.E.2d 779 (N.Y. 1941). A year later the same court upheld a joint savings account with right of survivorship against the wife's challenge on the ground that the section of the Banking Law authorizing such accounts vested title in the surviving tenant. See Inda v. Inda, 43 N.E.2d 59 (N.Y. 1942). (In this context, there is no significant difference between a Totten trust and a joint savings account; the depositor who retains the bank book has complete control over the funds in both instances.) In the last case coming to the Court of Appeals involving Totten trusts, the court refused to follow its recent precedent and held four Totten trusts, created by the decedent for the benefit of his granddaughter, not subject to his widow's elective share because the decedent had an affirmative intent to benefit the granddaughter. See In re Halpern's Estate, 100 N.E.2d 120 (N.Y.1951). Is an "intent to benefit" test any easier to administer than an "intent to disinherit" test? The *Halpern* decision attracted sharp criticism and left the New York law in a such a confused state that legislative intervention became inevitable.

In Montgomery v. Michaels, 301 N.E.2d 465 (Ill. 1973), the court indicated that the surviving spouse was entitled to invalidate the Totten trusts only to the extent necessary to make up his elective share, leaving the balance of the accounts to pass to the decedent's designated beneficiaries. In *Halpern's Estate*, supra, the New York Court of Appeals reached a different conclusion. There the decedent executed a will leaving his entire estate to his second wife. A few years later, as disaffection set in, he put all his available cash (approximately $14,000) into four Totten trusts naming his granddaughter as beneficiary. The Appellate Division held the Totten trusts illusory but voided them only to the extent necessary to make up the widow's elective share. Thus, assuming there was $4,000 in the probate estate, the widow's share was $6,000 of which $2,000 would come from the Totten trusts. In re Halpern's Estate, 100 N.Y.S.2d 894 (App. Div. 1950), aff'd, 100 N.E.2d 120 (N.Y.1951). The Court of Appeals, though affirming because the issue had not been preserved on appeal, said:

> We see no power in the courts to divide up such a Totten trust and call part of it illusory and the other part good. The only test is that quoted above, from Newman v. Dore, supra, and Krause v. Krause, supra, and the results of its application would necessarily be either total validity or total invalidity, as to any one transfer. [100 N.E.2d at 123.]

3. *Impact on will provisions.* Quite apart from the disposition of recaptured property, the surviving spouse's exercise of a right of election may have a dramatic impact on the provisions of the decedent's will. Suppose, for example, that the will leaves $60,000 outright to the decedent's child A, $30,000 in trust to pay income to the decedent's spouse for life with remainder at the spouse's death to the decedent's issue then living, and the residue (worth $90,000) to charity C. If the spouse renounces the provisions of the will and claims an elective share of $60,000 (one-third of the net estate), should the elective share be charged entirely against the residuary estate or equitably apportioned among the several bequests? Should the trust property be distributed immediately to the decedent's surviving issue (as if the spouse were predeceased), or should it be held in trust until the spouse's death, with in-

come payable to the beneficiaries whose shares were diminished by the spouse's election? See Sellick v. Sellick, 173 N.W. 609 (Mich.1919) (no acceleration); Atkinson § 33.

4. *Death or incapacity of surviving spouse.* In many states the right to claim an elective share is personal to the surviving spouse. The election must be made during the spouse's lifetime; it cannot be made by a personal representative after the spouse's death. See UPC § 2–212(a); Burch v. Griffe, 29 S.W.3d 722 (Ark. 2000). What if the spouse files written notice of the election but dies before the election is confirmed by the probate court? See In re Will of Sayre, 415 S.E.2d 263 (W.Va.1992); Wilson v. Wilson, 197 P.3d 1141 (Or. App. 2008).

If the surviving spouse is alive but incapacitated, does a conservator—or an agent acting under a durable power of attorney—have discretion to make (or not make) an election on behalf of the spouse? What considerations should guide the conservator or agent in exercising such discretion: Securing the largest possible pecuniary benefit for the spouse? Preserving the maximum amount for the spouse's heirs? Deferring taxes or minimizing overall tax liability? Giving effect to the spouse's probable intent? See Kinnett v. Hood, 185 N.E.2d 888 (Ill.1962); Estate of Clarkson, 226 N.W.2d 334 (Neb.1975); Estate of Cross, 664 N.E.2d 905 (Ohio 1996).

When an election is made on behalf of an incapacitated surviving spouse, the Uniform Probate Code requires that any portion of the elective share recovered from the decedent's probate estate or from nonprobate beneficiaries "must be placed in a custodial trust for the benefit of the surviving spouse." The custodial trust provides discretionary distributions during the surviving spouse's life to the spouse and his or her dependents; at the spouse's death, the trust property reverts to the first spouse's residuary devisees or heirs. See UPC § 2–212(b).

5. *Separation or divorce.* When a marriage terminates by the death of one spouse, the surviving spouse's elective share may be substantially greater or less than what the spouse would have received by way of a negotiated property settlement or equitable distribution award if the marriage had terminated by divorce. Suppose that *H* and *W*, realizing that their marriage has deteriorated beyond repair, decide to separate and file for divorce. While divorce proceedings are pending, *H* dies; in his will he disinherits *W* and leaves all his property to his siblings. Is *W* entitled to claim an elective share of *H*'s estate? See Estate of Peck, 497 N.W.2d 889 (Iowa 1993); Hamilton v. Hamilton, 879 S.W.2d 416 (Ark. 1994); Estate of Pfeiffer, 658 N.W.2d 14 (Neb. 2003).

6. *Professional responsibility.* At the time of their marriage, *H* and *W* each had substantial wealth and each had children from prior marriages. In separate wills prepared by their lawyer, *H* and *W* disinherited each other and left all their property to their respective children. Unfortunately, the lawyer

failed to mention the spousal elective share. After *H*'s death, *W* elects against *H*'s will and claims a one-half share of his estate, much to the surprise and chagrin of *H*'s children. What advice should the lawyer have given *H* and *W*? Is the lawyer potentially liable for malpractice? See Estate of Gaspar v. Vogt, Brown & Merry, 670 N.W.2d 918 (S.D. 2003).

3. AUGMENTED ESTATE

Dissatisfaction with the narrow scope of traditional elective share statutes, and with the vagueness of doctrinal subterfuges invoked by courts in applying them, eventually led to further statutory reform, beginning with a landmark 1966 revision of the New York elective share statute. The distinctive feature of the New York legislation is its enumeration of various "testamentary substitutes" (including, for example, revocable trusts, Totten trusts, and joint bank accounts) which are counted, along with property passing by will or intestacy, as part of the decedent's "net estate" in determining the surviving spouse's elective share. N.Y. EPTL § 5–1.1–A. As a result, the enumerated testamentary substitutes are no longer effective to defeat the spouse's elective share rights, although they remain valid for other purposes. By replacing the unpredictable "illusory transfer" test with objective rules based on the nature and extent of the decedent's retained interest in and control of property transferred outside the will, the New York statute affords a measure of certainty to married testators and to their spouses and other beneficiaries.

Following the lead of the New York statute, the Uniform Probate Code introduced the concept of the "augmented estate," which serves as a point of reference both for measuring the amount of the elective share and for identifying the sources from which it is payable. In general, the augmented estate includes the decedent's net probate estate as well as specified types of property transferred by the decedent outside the will. Under the original 1969 version of the Code, property transferred by the decedent during the marriage to a beneficiary other than the surviving spouse is included in the augmented estate if the decedent (1) retained possession or enjoyment of the property or its income, (2) retained a power to revoke the transfer, (3) held the property jointly with a right of survivorship, or (4) made gifts of more than $3,000 to a beneficiary during either of the two years before death. UPC § 2–202(1) (1969). The purpose of including these nonprobate transfers is "to prevent the [decedent] from making arrangements which transmit his property to others by means other than probate deliberately to defeat the right of the surviving spouse to a share." The limitation to transfers made during the marriage "makes it possible for a person to provide for children by a prior marriage, as by a revocable living trust, without concern that such provisions will be upset by later marriage." Id. cmt. Under the original 1969 Code, the augmented estate also includes property owned by the surviving spouse (or transferred by the spouse in a manner that would give rise to inclusion in the spouse's augmented estate) to the extent the spouse received the property from the decedent by gift. UPC § 2–202(2) (1969). This provision is intended "to prevent the surviving spouse from electing a share of the probate estate when the spouse has received a fair share of the total wealth of the decedent either during the lifetime of the decedent or at death by life insurance, joint tenancy assets and other nonprobate arrangements." Id. cmt. Note that under the original 1969 Code, life insurance is included in the augmented estate only to the extent the proceeds are payable to the surviving spouse. Life insurance payable to other beneficiaries is excluded because, according to the UPC drafters, "it is not ordinarily purchased as a way of depleting the probate estate and avoiding the elective share of the spouse." Id.

Once the components of the augmented estate are identified and valued, the remaining computations are relatively straightforward. Under the original 1969 Code, the amount of the elective share is equal to one third of the augmented estate. UPC § 2–201 (1969). To minimize disruption of the decedent's dispositive scheme, the Code does not require any renunciation by a surviving spouse who claims an elective share. Instead, the Code leaves undisturbed any transfers to the spouse of property included in the augmented estate and charges the value of those transfers dollar for dollar against the elective share. UPC § 2–207(a) (1969). As a result, the amount taken from other beneficiaries to satisfy the elective share is limited to the amount, if any, by which the provisions in favor of the spouse fall short of the elective share amount. If such a shortfall occurs, it is apportioned among other beneficiaries of the augmented estate in proportion to the value of their respective interests. UPC § 2–207(b) (1969).

To illustrate the operation of the elective share under the original 1969 Code, suppose that H died with a net probate estate of $120,000. In his will, H left $20,000 to his wife W and the rest of the estate (worth $100,000) to charity C. In addition, H named W as pay-on-death beneficiary of a $30,000 bank account and a nephew N as beneficiary of a $300,000 revocable trust. These assets, totalling $450,000, comprise H's augmented estate. See UPC § 2–202 (1969).[6] W's elective share is one third of the augmented estate, or $150,000. See UPC § 2–201 (1969). The elective share is satisfied first from the $20,000 bequest and the $30,000 bank account passing to W; the balance of the elective share ($100,000) is recoverable from C (who received a bequest of $100,000) and N (who re-

---

[6] Under the original 1969 Code, property owned or transferred by a surviving spouse is includible in the augmented estate only "to the extent the owned or transferred property is derived from the decedent by any means other than testate or intestate succession without a full consideration in money or money's worth." UPC § 2–202(2) (1969). In the example given in text it is assumed that none of W's property was derived from H.

ceived a trust share of $300,000) in proportion to their respective interests in the augmented estate. Therefore, $25,000 (one fourth of $100,000) comes from *C* and $75,000 (three fourths of $100,000) from *N*. See UPC § 2–207 (1969).

The Uniform Probate Code's elective share provisions were substantially revised in 1990 and in 2008 to achieve an approximately equal division of the couple's combined marital property at the death of the first spouse. To accomplish this goal, the revised Code treats a portion of the property included in the augmented estate as marital property (the "marital-property portion"), based on the number of years the decedent and the surviving spouse were married to each other, and awards the surviving spouse one half of that amount as an elective share. If the spouse's own assets and amounts credited as part of the elective share fall short of $75,000 (indexed for inflation), the Code allows the spouse a "supplemental" amount to make up the balance.

Uniform Probate Code (2011)

Section 2–202. Elective Share.

(a) [Elective–Share Amount.] The surviving spouse of a decedent who dies domiciled in this state has a right of election, under the limitations and conditions stated in this [part], to take an elective-share amount equal to 50 percent of the value of the marital-property portion of the augmented estate.
. . .

Section 2–203. Composition of the Augmented Estate; Marital–Property Portion.

(a) . . . [T]he value of the augmented estate, to the extent provided in Sections 2–204, 2–205, 2–206, and 2–207, consists of the sum of the values of all property, whether real or personal, movable or immovable, tangible or intangible, wherever situated, that constitute:

(1) the decedent's net probate estate [§ 2–204];

(2) the decedent's nonprobate transfers to others [§ 2–205];

(3) the decedent's nonprobate transfers to the surviving spouse [§ 2–206]; and

(4) the surviving spouse's property and nonprobate transfers to others [§ 2–207].

(b) The value of the marital-property portion of the augmented estate consists of the sum of the values of the four components of the augmented estate as determined under subsection (a) multiplied by the following percentage:

If the decedent and the spouse were married   The percentage is:
to each other:

Less than 1 year	3%
1 year but less than 2 years	6%
2 years but less than 3 years	12%
3 years but less than 4 years	18%
4 years but less than 5 years	24%
5 years but less than 6 years	30%
6 years but less than 7 years	36%
7 years but less than 8 years	42%
8 years but less than 9 years	48%
9 years but less than 10 years	54%
10 years but less than 11 years	60%
11 years but less than 12 years	68%
12 years but less than 13 years	76%
13 years but less than 14 years	84%
14 years but less than 15 years	92%
15 years or more	100%

The four categories of property included in the augmented estate may be summarized as follows:

1. *Decedent's net probate estate (§ 2–204)*: the decedent's probate estate, net of funeral and administration expenses, statutory allowances, and creditors' claims;

2. *Decedent's nonprobate transfers to others (§ 2–205)*: property of the following types passing to beneficiaries other than the surviving spouse:

(a) property owned or "owned in substance" by the decedent which passed outside probate at death, including: (1) property subject to a general power of appointment; (2) property held in joint tenancy with right of survivorship, to the extent of the decedent's fractional interest; (3) property held in pay-on-death form; and (4) proceeds of life insurance policies on the decedent;

(b) property transferred by the decedent during the marriage in which the decedent retained lifetime possession, enjoyment, income rights, or a general power of appointment; and

(c) certain property transferred by the decedent during the marriage and within two years before death, including property subject to a retained interest or power, life insurance policies, and gifts exceeding $12,000 per year to any donee;

3. *Decedent's nonprobate transfers to surviving spouse (§ 2–206)*: property passing to the surviving spouse in the forms described in 2(a) and (b) above; and

4. *Surviving spouse's property and nonprobate transfers to others (§ 2–207)*:

(a) property which was owned by the surviving spouse at the decedent's death, or which passed to the spouse by reason of the decedent's death; and

(b) property which would have been included in the spouse's augmented estate as "nonprobate transfers to others" (described in 2 above) if the spouse had died at the same time as the decedent.

In general, the elective share is payable from property included in the augmented estate, in the following order of priority: (1) from property passing from the decedent to the surviving spouse, either as part of the net probate estate or outside probate, to the extent of the value thereof; (2) from the surviving spouse's own property and nonprobate transfers to others, to the extent of the value of the marital-property portion thereof; and (3) from property passing from the decedent to beneficiaries other than the surviving spouse, either as part of the probate estate or outside probate, to the extent of the value thereof, with liability apportioned among such beneficiaries in proportion to the value of their respective interests. UPC § 2–209.

To illustrate the operation of the elective share provisions, suppose that *H* died with a net probate estate of $120,000. In his will, *H*'s left $20,000 to his wife *W* and the rest of the estate (worth $100,000) to charity *C*. In addition, *H* named *W* as pay-on-death beneficiary of a $30,000 bank account and a nephew *N* as beneficiary of a $300,000 revocable trust. *W* owns other property worth $150,000. All of these assets, totalling $600,000, are included in *H*'s augmented estate. Assuming that *H* and *W* had been married for 15 years at *H*'s death, the marital-property portion is 100 percent, and *W*'s elective share amount is $300,000. This amount is satisfied first from *W*'s $20,000 bequest and the $30,000 bank account; next from *W*'s own property worth $150,000; finally, the balance of the elective share ($100,000) is recoverable from *C* and *N* in proportion to their respective interests in the augmented estate—$25,000 (one quarter of $100,000) from *C*, and $75,000 (three quarters of $100,000) from *N*. What result if *H* and *W* had been married for only 10 years? 5 years? What if *W* died first?

H dies and leaves his residuary estate in trust to pay income to his surviving wife *W* for life with remainder at her death to *H*'s issue from a previous marriage. *W* claims her elective share. How should *W*'s income interest be valued in determining her elective share? See UPC § 2–208(b)(2); Estate of Myers, 594 N.W.2d 563 (Neb. 1999); Estate of Karnen, 607 N.W.2d 32 (S.D. 2000). Suppose that *W*, who has a comfortable income of her own and prefers to receive an outright share of *H*'s property, renounces the income interest. What effect does *W*'s renunciation of the income interest have on the computation of her elective share? See UPC § 2–209 & cmt.

The Uniform Probate Code's "accrual-type" elective share is intended "to bring elective-share law into line with the contemporary view of marriage as an economic partnership." UPC art. 2, pt. 2 cmt. From this perspective, the marital-property portion of the augmented estate represents the portion of the couple's combined assets that is subject to equal division at the first spouse's death. Depending on the duration of the marriage, the surviving spouse's 50-percent elective share may apply to between 3 percent and 100 percent of the couple's combined assets. Thus, the Code uses the duration of the marriage as a proxy for measuring the portion of the couple's combined assets which is treated as "partnership" assets. For further discussion of the accrual-type elective share and its rationale, see Langbein & Waggoner, Redesigning the Spouse's Forced Share, 22 Real Prop. Prob. & Trust J. 303 (1987); Waggoner, Spousal Rights in Our Multiple–Marriage Society: The Revised Uniform Probate Code, 26 Real Prop. Prob. & Trust J. 683 (1992); Newman, Incorporating the Partnership Theory of Marriage into Elective–Share Law: The Approximation System of the Uniform Probate Code and the Deferred–Community–Property Alternative, 49 Emory L.J. 487 (2000).

NOTES

1. *Community property analogy.* The Uniform Probate Code drafters explain that the economic partnership theory of marriage is already implemented under the equitable distribution system which governs division of marital property upon divorce in both community property and separate property states. When the marriage ends by the death of one spouse, the partnership theory also applies in community property states, but in common law states "elective-share law has not caught up to the partnership theory of marriage." UPC art. 2, pt. 2 cmt. In a community property system, each spouse has an equal, present, vested interest in all property acquired during the marriage (other than by gift, devise or inheritance). Property acquired by either spouse before the marriage (or during the marriage by gift, devise or inheritance) is separate property which can be freely disposed of during life or at death. See the discussion of community property infra at p. 193. The Uniform Probate Code seeks to approximate the results of an equal marital partnership at the first spouse's death while avoiding the need to determine

when or how specific property was acquired. To what extent do the Code's elective share provisions mimic the results of a community property model? In what respects are they different? Consider how the order of deaths affects the spouses' respective property rights. If most of their combined assets are titled in the name of the spouse who dies first, the Code allows the survivor to claim an elective share of the decedent's property. What if the order of deaths is reversed?

2. *Estate tax analogy.* The Uniform Probate Code's augmented estate provisions differ in language and policy objectives from the federal estate tax provisions that draw certain lifetime transfers into the gross estate (I.R.C. §§ 2035–2038). Common to both provisions, however, is the problem of defining the degree of retained enjoyment or control which will justify recapturing transfers that were formally made during life. Experience in the tax field demonstrates the difficulties of drafting a statute that nails down the mercurial concept of quasi-testamentary transfers. See Del. Code, tit. 12, §§ 901, 902 (defining elective share as one-third of amount equal to federal gross estate). For further discussion of the estate tax analogy, see Kwestel & Seplowitz, Testamentary Substitutes: Retained Interests, Custodial Accounts and Contractual Transactions—A New Approach, 38 Am. U. L. Rev. 1 (1988); Gary, Marital Partnership Theory and the Elective Share: Federal Estate Tax Law Provides a Solution, 49 U. Miami L. Rev. 567 (1995).

3. *Pension benefits.* The Employee Retirement Income Security Act of 1974 (ERISA), which applies to most private pension plans, mandates specified benefits for the surviving spouse of a deceased participant. In the case of a vested participant who dies after reaching retirement age, the plan must provide benefits in the form of a "qualified joint and survivor annuity" (QJSA) for the lives of the participant and the surviving spouse. The surviving spouse's benefit must be not less than 50 percent nor more than 100 percent of the benefit payable while both spouses are living (e.g., annual payments of $7,500 to the participant for life and then the same amount to the surviving spouse for life; or $10,000 to the participant and then $5,000 to the surviving spouse). The spouses' combined benefits must have at least the same actuarial value as a single life annuity for the participant's life. In the case of a vested participant who dies before retirement age, the plan must provide benefits in the form of a "qualified preretirement survivor annuity" (QPSA) consisting of an annuity for the life of the surviving spouse computed in a manner analogous to the survivor component of a QJSA. The plan must provide benefits in the form of a QJSA or QPSA, but the participant may elect a different form of benefits (including a "qualified optional survivor annuity") with the spouse's written consent, subject to specified formal requirements. Note that the spouse's benefit is contingent on surviving the participant; if the spouse dies first, the entire benefit is payable to the participant. In effect, ERISA provides an elective share for undistributed pension plan assets as a matter of federal law. Does ERISA preempt the application of the UPC's elective share to such assets? Cf. Boggs v. Boggs, 520 U.S. 833 (1997) (preemp-

tion of nonparticipant spouse's community property interest in pension benefits where spouse died before participant).

4. *Sex-distinct mortality tables.* As a class, women live longer than men. Insurance companies have traditionally taken this statistical fact into account in pricing annuities issued to employee benefit plans. In City of Los Angeles, Dep't of Water & Power v. Manhart, 435 U.S. 702 (1978), the Supreme Court held that Title VII of the Civil Rights Act of 1964 prohibited a municipal employer from requiring that female employees make larger contributions than male employees to a pension fund. While the *Manhart* case involved a municipal employer, Title VII applies with equal force to private employers. A few years later, in Arizona Governing Comm. for Tax Deferred Annuity and Deferred Compensation Plans v. Norris, 463 U.S. 1073 (1983), the Court held that differential retirement benefits based on sex violated Title VII. See also Spirt v. Teachers Ins. & Annuity Ass'n, 691 F.2d 1054 (2d Cir.1982), vacated and remanded, 463 U.S. 1223 (1983), on remand, 735 F.2d 23 (2d Cir.), cert. denied, 469 U.S. 881 (1984) (use of sex-distinct mortality tables to calculate TIAA–CREF benefits violated Title VII). For a full examination of the issues presented in these cases, see Brilmayer, Hokeler, Laycock & Sullivan, Sex Discrimination in Employer–Sponsored Insurance Plans: A Legal and Demographic Analysis, 47 U. Chi. L. Rev. 505 (1980) (arguing that constitution requires unisex actuarial tables in employer-sponsored insurance plans); Benston, The Economics of Gender Discrimination in Employee Fringe Benefits: Manhart Revisited, 49 U. Chi. L. Rev. 489 (1982) (defending use of sex-distinct actuarial tables in this context); Brilmayer, Laycock & Sullivan, The Efficient Use of Group Averages as Nondiscrimination: A Rejoinder to Professor Benston, 50 U. Chi. L. Rev. 222 (1983); Benston, Discrimination and Economic Efficiency in Employee Fringe Benefits: A Clarification of Issues and a Response to Professors Brilmayer, Laycock, and Sullivan, 50 U. Chi. L. Rev. 250 (1983).

Prior to December 1, 1983, the Treasury Department promulgated separate sets of actuarial tables, one for men and one for women, to establish the value of life estates, terms for years, remainders, reversions, and annuities for federal estate and gift tax purposes. Effective on that date, the Treasury adopted unisex tables. See Treas. Reg. §§ 20.2031–7, 25.2512–5. How accurately do the unisex tables measure the actuarial life expectancy of any particular individual?

4. WAIVER

With divorce and remarriage rates at historically high levels, it has become increasingly common for spouses to attempt to regulate their marital property rights through a contract or agreement. Typically the agreement is entered before marriage—a so-called antenuptial or prenuptial agreement—and specifies in advance how property will be allocated between the parties upon divorce or at the death of either spouse. Antenuptial agreements were traditionally disfavored by courts on the ground that such agreements facilitated divorce and violated public policy, and such agreements are still scrutinized with special care because of the potential for overreaching, fraud, and duress. Nevertheless, antenuptial agreements have achieved widespread acceptance since the advent of no-fault divorce. Many states have enacted statutes which expressly authorize the prospective waiver by one spouse of property rights that would ordinarily accrue at the other spouse's death. The Uniform Probate Code provision is typical:

Uniform Probate Code (2011)

Section 2–213. Waiver of Right to Elect and of Other Rights.

(a) The right of election of a surviving spouse and the rights of the surviving spouse to homestead allowance, exempt property, and family allowance, or any of them, may be waived, wholly or partially, before or after marriage, by a written contract, agreement, or waiver signed by the surviving spouse.

(b) A surviving spouse's waiver is not enforceable if the surviving spouse proves that:

(1) he [or she] did not execute the waiver voluntarily; or

(2) the waiver was unconscionable when it was executed and, before execution of the waiver, he [or she]:

(i) was not provided a fair and reasonable disclosure of the property or financial obligations of the decedent;

(ii) did not voluntarily and expressly waive, in writing, any right to disclosure of the property or financial obligations of the decedent beyond the disclosure provided; and

(iii) did not have, or reasonably could not have had, an adequate knowledge of the property or financial obligations of the decedent.

(c) An issue of unconscionability of a waiver is for decision by the court as a matter of law.

(d) Unless it provides to the contrary, a waiver of "all rights," or equivalent language, in the property or estate of a present or prospective spouse or a complete property settlement entered into after or in anticipation of separation or divorce is a waiver of all rights of elective share, homestead allowance, exempt property, and family allowance by each spouse in the property of the other and a renunciation by each of all benefits that would otherwise pass to him [or her] from the other by intestate succession or by virtue of any will executed before the waiver or property settlement.

HOOK V. HOOK

Supreme Court of Ohio, 1982.
69 Ohio St.2d 234, 431 N.E.2d 667, 23 Ohio Op.3d 239.

Agnes Bates Hook (plaintiff-appellee herein) and Donal D. Hook were married in Cuyahoga County on December 23, 1970. Two days prior to their marriage, the couple met with Mr. Hook's attorney, Raymond Cookston, at which time information was obtained in order to prepare an antenuptial agreement and wills for both parties. On the morning of their wedding, the couple again went to Cookston's office and signed an antenuptial "agreement," which divested each of any legal claims to the other's estate, and executed identical wills, each leaving the other all his property, "if he [or she] survives me and is my husband [or wife]."

In August 1974, Donal Hook filed for divorce from Agnes Hook in DuPage County, Illinois. The action was subsequently dismissed, but another suit for divorce was filed in Cuyahoga County by Donal Hook in June 1977. The action was still pending at the time of his death on October 28, 1977. Under the terms of his will, executed May 6, 1977, Donal Hook left Agnes Hook no share of his estate.[7] Following Donal Hook's death, Agnes Hook brought this action to set aside the antenuptial agreement, naming as defendants the executor of her husband's estate, and the beneficiaries under his will (appellants herein). The Probate Court entered judgment for plaintiff, finding Donal Hook failed to materially disclose the nature, amount, and value of his property to plaintiff prior to the execution of the agreement. On appeal to the Court of Appeals, that court affirmed, finding both that the agreement was not entered into in good faith and inadequate disclosure. The lower courts held the agreement null and void, restoring to plaintiff her legal rights as surviving spouse of Donal Hook.

The case is before this court upon the allowance of a motion to certify the record.

PER CURIAM.

In Ohio, there is no public policy, statute or case law which prevents parties to antenuptial agreements from cutting one another off entirely from any participation in the estate of the other upon the death of either. Troha v. Sneller (1959), 169 Ohio St. 397, 402. The agreement, however, must meet certain minimum levels of good faith, and will be set aside as invalid as a matter of law if the agreement is not fair and reasonable un-

---

[7] The will reads, in relevant part, as follows:

Item I.

I am married to Agnes Bates Hook, but having entered into an antenuptial agreement with my wife, Agnes Bates Hook, on the 23rd of December, 1970, I intentionally make no provision herein for her under this will since she has a substantial estate in her own right.

der the circumstances. This court announced the relevant considerations in its syllabus to Juhasz v. Juhasz (1938), 134 Ohio St. 257, as follows:

> 1. An agreement to marry gives rise to a confidential relation between the contracting parties.
>
> 2. An antenuptial contract voluntarily entered into during the period of engagement is valid when the provision for the wife is fair and reasonable under all the surrounding facts and circumstances.
>
> 3. When the amount provided for the wife in an antenuptial contract entered during the existence of the confidential relation arising from an engagement is wholly disproportionate to the property of the prospective husband in the light of all surrounding circumstances and to the amount she would take under the law, the burden is on those claiming the validity of the contract to show that before it was entered into he made full disclosure to her of the nature, extent and value of his property or that she then had full knowledge thereof without such disclosure.
>
> 4. Although the provision made for the intended wife in an antenuptial contract is wholly disproportionate, she will be bound by voluntarily entering into the contract after full disclosure or with full knowledge. . . .

The law in Ohio, as announced in *Juhasz*, requires the decedent to have fully apprised his prospective spouse of the character and extent of his property prior to entering into an antenuptial agreement which disproportionately limits her share of his estate. The trial court, faced with an attack on the agreement, must consider all facts and circumstances bearing upon the validity of that agreement, and determine whether it is binding and valid.

The threshold consideration when applying the *Juhasz* test is whether the agreement provided the prospective spouse a disproportionate share of the property. In this case, plaintiff-appellee renounced any claims to Donal Hook's property. Absent the agreement, she was entitled to receive one-half the net estate under R.C. 2107.39, as the surviving spouse. It appears that share would be substantial. We conclude, therefore, that the amount of property to be received by the appellee under the terms of the agreement is wholly disproportionate to the value of the decedent's property and to the amount she would take under the law. Accordingly, the agreement will be upheld only if it appears appellee voluntarily entered into the agreement with full knowledge of the nature, extent and value of her prospective husband's property.

Two witnesses, appellee and Raymond Cookston, testified concerning the circumstances surrounding the drafting and execution of the antenuptial agreement. Cookston testified that on December 21, he obtained a figure from Donal Hook approximating the monetary value of his property and from appellee, the approximate monetary value of her property. No itemization of Donal's property was given to appellee. On the 23rd, Cookston recalls meeting with both Donal Hook and appellee, and telling both the effect this agreement would have on their rights in each other's property:

> My observation and understanding as far as not only Donal, but Agnes, was that each party could keep their own property, do whatever they wanted with it, they could leave it by Will to whomever they wanted to. Each of them had no rights in the other's property.

Appellee testified that she and Donal went to Cookston's office on December 21 solely to make out a will. She recalled Cookston asking her what her property was worth, and stated that Donal supplied the figure for the value of her property, $80,000. Appellee testified she had no idea the information was for an antenuptial agreement, believing the information was needed for "inheritance tax" purposes.

Appellee testified that on the morning of her wedding, she again went with Donal to Cookston's office, believing it to be for the sole purpose of signing wills. When the antenuptial agreement was placed before her to sign, appellee testified she asked what it was, and Donal Hook responded: " 'Never mind, just sign it. It just means what is mine is mine and what is yours is yours.' "

Appellee further testified that she did not read the document because she "trusted Don and Mr. Cookston and I just signed it. I didn't read it. I didn't have time to read it. I was too nervous."

The antenuptial agreement states, in pertinent part, that "Donal D. Hook is the owner of real and personal property the value of which (after deducting the amount of all encumbrances thereon and the amount of his other indebtedness and liabilities) is in excess of Sixty Thousand ($60,000) Dollars, at the date hereof. . . ." In fact, Donal Hook then owned real property valued at $30,000, five savings accounts totalling $28,037.32, six life insurance policies with cash surrender value of $8,443.19—totalling $66,480.51. He also had vested pension death benefits of $20,172.02, which makes the total of the assets $86,652.53, less any indebtedness or liabilities. Prior to the execution of the antenuptial agreement Donal had made appellee the beneficiary of his life insurance policies.

Nowhere does it appear appellee was misled concerning the extent of Donal Hook's assets. Rather, appellee asserts she did not know the significance of what she was signing. However, appellee testified that she was told that the document assured that what was her husband's property before the marriage would remain his, and what was her property would remain hers. This is an accurate statement of the import of the document.

Appellee's assertions that she signed an instrument which she did not comprehend have little force. "Ordinarily, one of full age in the possession of his faculties and able to read and write, who signs an instrument and remains acquiescent to its operative effect for some time, may not thereafter escape the consequences by urging that he did not read it or that he relied upon the representations of another as to its contents or significance." Kroeger v. Brody (1936), 130 Ohio St. 559, 566.[8]

In the light of all surrounding circumstances, we conclude that appellants, who are claiming the validity of the agreement, demonstrated an adequate disclosure by Donal Hook of the extent of his assets. We find no requirement that the parties to such an agreement itemize their various assets and their worth. In this case, the statement that Donal Hook owned property "in excess of . . . $60,000," together with appellee's knowledge of his insurance policies, satisfies the requirement of full disclosure. Excluding the pension's value, which Donal Hook conceivably could have omitted as "property," the total assets held by him approximated the stated figure. Furthermore, we conclude that the agreement was entered into voluntarily by the parties and that it was fair and reasonable.

Accordingly, the antenuptial agreement at issue here is valid and binding on appellee. The judgment of the Court of Appeals is reversed.

FRANK D. CELEBREZZE, C.J., SWEENEY, LOCHER, HOLMES, CLIFFORD F. BROWN and STEPHENSON, JJ., concur.

WILLIAM B. BROWN, JUSTICE, dissenting.

Being ever mindful of the long-established rule that "[j]udgments supported by some competent, credible evidence going to all the essential elements of the case will not be reversed by a reviewing court as being against the manifest weight of the evidence," C.E. Morris Co. v. Foley Construction Co. (1978), 54 Ohio St. 2d 279, I must dissent. It is my view that sufficient evidence was presented at trial to allow reasonable minds

---

[8] In her answer to the complaint for divorce filed by Donal Hook in Illinois, appellee admitted the existence of the antenuptial agreement at issue here. Her failure to raise the question of its validity at the earlier date infers a past willingness to abide by the agreement and a tacit admission that it was fair and reasonable. Also appellee has an extensive background in legal matters, acting as administratrix of her second husband's estate (Bates), and having dealings in real estate, and rental property. This circumstance indicates appellee fully understands the significance of legal documents.

to conclude that the antenuptial agreement was not entered into in good faith and with full knowledge of the assets involved therein.

The testimony of appellee fully supports such a conclusion. Appellee testified that she thought the purpose of the meetings with decedent's attorney, Mr. Cookston, was for will preparation and that there had been no discussion of an antenuptial agreement previously. As to the events of the day upon which the agreement was actually signed, appellee testified that she and the decedent had an appointment to see attorney Cookston 40 minutes before their wedding, that she did not read the papers because she was too nervous and afraid of being late for their wedding, that she thought the agreement dealt with inheritance taxes and that there had never been any discussion as to the nature of the decedent's assets.

Furthermore, appellee gave the following account of the conversation which occurred in Mr. Cookston's office after he gave her some papers to sign:

> . . . I said to Mr. Cookston, "Are these our Wills?" because he just said, "Sign here."
>
> He said, "No."
>
> I said, "What is it?"
>
> He looked at Don. Don said, "Never mind, just sign it. It just means what is mine is mine and what is yours is yours."

The only other witness to testify as to the events surrounding the signing of the agreement was attorney Cookston. Attorney Cookston's testimony, however, did not relate to the events which actually took place on the date of the signing of the antenuptial agreement, for he testified that he had no independent recollection of this specific transaction. Rather, Cookston's testimony related only to his "usual and customary practice."

In essence, the trial court was presented with testimony that depicted two completely different views of the facts of this case. In finding for the appellee, the trial court necessarily found appellee's testimony to be the most credible. It is well established that a reviewing court cannot and should not disturb the findings of a trial judge respecting the credibility of witnesses. (See, e.g., C.E. Morris Co. v. Foley Construction Co., supra.)

Moreover, the record is void of any evidence that appellee had any independent knowledge of decedent's net worth, that the attorney questioned the parties as to their knowledge of the property interests of each other, or that there was any discussion whatsoever as to property interests.

Thus, in my opinion, sufficient evidence was presented to support the determination by the trier of fact that the antenuptial agreement was invalid, for there was credible evidence that the antenuptial agreement was not entered into in good faith and that the appellee did not voluntarily sign the agreement with knowledge of the nature, extent and value of her husband's assets as is required. (See Juhasz v. Juhasz [1938], 134 Ohio St. 257.)

For the foregoing reasons, I respectfully dissent.

NOTES

1. *Waiver in antenuptial agreement.* Antenuptial agreements often include mutual waivers by each party of all rights in the other party's property arising by reason of the marriage. Where one or both parties were previously married, waivers may serve "to insure that property derived from the prior spouse passes at death to the joint children (or descendants) of the prior marriage instead of to the later spouse." UPC § 2–213 cmt. Suppose that *H* and *W* execute a valid antenuptial agreement providing that all property held or acquired by either party shall remain that party's separate property and that "their respective rights to each other's property acquired by operation of law shall be solely determined and fixed by this agreement." Upon the death of one spouse, is the survivor barred from claiming an elective share? See Pysell v. Keck, 559 S.E.2d 677 (Va. 2002); Dowling v. Rowan, 621 S.E.2d 397 (Va. 2005).

In general, a waiver of marital property rights by either spouse is enforceable if the waiving spouse executed the waiver voluntarily and with adequate disclosure or knowledge of the other spouse's property. See UPC § 2–213. Is an antenuptial agreement entered into voluntarily if it is drafted by one spouse's lawyer and the other spouse lacks independent counsel? See, in addition to the principal case, Estate of Kinney, 733 N.W.2d 118 (Minn. 2007) (opportunity to consult with independent counsel is relevant factor but not necessary to make antenuptial agreement enforceable); Estate of Lutz, 620 N.W.2d 589 (N.D. 2000). Although a well-drafted agreement should include a specific and detailed list of assets and values for each party, courts routinely accept general and approximate disclosure. In addition to the principal case, see Estate of Lopata, 641 P.2d 952 (Colo.1982). May a decedent's surviving spouse attack the validity of a waiver on grounds of nondisclosure despite a recital of full disclosure in the written agreement? See Thies v. Lowe, 903 P.2d 186 (Mont.1995); Estate of Grassman, 158 N.W.2d 673 (Neb.1968). See generally Haskell, The Premarital Estate Contract and Social Policy, 57 N.C. L. Rev. 415 (1979).

2. *Burden of proof.* Under UPC § 2–213, a surviving spouse who attacks an antenuptial agreement has the burden of proving that the agreement is invalid. In contrast, some courts hold that if an antenuptial agreement makes a provision for one party which is "wholly disproportionate" to the other party's property, the party seeking to enforce the agreement has the burden of proving its validity. See, in addition to the principal case, Hartz v. Hartz, 234 A.2d 865 (Md.1967); Estate of Cassidy, 356 S.W.3d 339 (Mo. App. 2011) (waiver not enforceable where antenuptial agreement drafted by husband's lawyer was presented to wife six hours before wedding with no opportunity for investigation, disclosure of husband's assets was grossly inadequate, and wife was not represented by independent counsel).

3. *Waiver in separation or divorce agreement.* Under UPC § 2–213, a waiver of marital property rights in a separation or divorce agreement is tested under the same standards as a waiver in an antenuptial agreement. Suppose that *H* and *W* enter into a valid separation agreement, releasing each other from "all claims and demands arising by reason of the marriage" and agreeing that henceforth each shall "require nothing whatsoever of the other, as though the marriage relation had never existed between them." *W* dies one year later, still married to (but separated from) *H*. Her will, executed before the separation agreement, leaves her entire estate to *H*. Does the estate pass to *H* under the will notwithstanding the separation agreement? See Blunt v. Lentz, 404 S.E.2d 62 (Va.1991); cf. UPC § 2–213.

4. *Pension benefits.* ERISA mandates specified benefits for the surviving spouse of a deceased participant in a covered pension plan. See Note 3, supra p. 183. Although a married participant may elect a different beneficiary or form of benefits, such an election ordinarily is valid only if:

> (i) the spouse of the participant consents in writing to such election, (ii) such election designates a beneficiary (or a form of benefits) which may not be changed without spousal consent (or the consent of the spouse expressly permits designations by the participant without any requirement of further consent by the spouse), and (iii) the spouse's consent acknowledges the effect of such election and is witnessed by a plan representative or a notary public. [29 U.S.C. § 1055(c)(2)(A).]

Suppose that *H*, a participant in an employee benefit plan covered by ERISA, and his prospective wife *W* enter into an antenuptial agreement which provides that "each party hereby waives and releases to the other party all rights which may arise from the marriage with respect to all property now owned or hereafter acquired by the other party, as fully as though the parties had never married." Assuming the agreement satisfies the requirements of UPC § 2–213, is *H* free to designate a different beneficiary (e.g., a child from a prior marriage) without any further consent on *W*'s part? See Hurwitz v. Sher, 982 F.2d 778 (2d Cir.1992), cert. denied, 508 U.S. 912 (1993); Hagwood v. Newton, 282 F.3d 285 (4th Cir. 2002).

D. SURVIVING SPOUSE: COMMUNITY PROPERTY

1. TRADITIONAL COMMUNITY PROPERTY

Community property in one form or another has existed for centuries in civil law jurisdictions. In this country, eight states—Arizona, California, Idaho, Louisiana, Nevada, New Mexico, Texas, and Washington—have traditional community property systems based on Spanish or French law. In addition, Wisconsin has joined the ranks of the community property states by adopting the Uniform Marital Property Act, and Alaska has enacted its own opt-in version of community property for married residents. Despite myriad local variations in implementation, the community property system in these states exhibits fundamentally similar traits which provide an illuminating comparison with the common law model.

In general, all property acquired during marriage, other than by gift, devise, or inheritance, is classified as community property in which both spouses have equal, concurrent interests. On the other hand, property owned by either spouse before the marriage, or acquired during the marriage by gift, devise, or inheritance, is separate property which belongs exclusively to the spouse who acquired it. Upon a sale, exchange, or other disposition of community or separate property, the character of the original property carries over to any new property acquired in the transaction. In the absence of evidence concerning the time or method of acquisition, property acquired or possessed during the marriage is generally presumed to be community property, even if title is held in the name of one spouse alone. The spouses may, by mutual agreement, "transmute" community property into separate property and vice versa. The basic definition of community property reflects the notion of marriage as an economic partnership in which the spouses pool all property earned by their combined labor, industry, and skill.

In theory, each spouse has an equal, present, vested interest in community property, which arises at the moment of acquisition and cannot be defeated by the unilateral act of the other spouse. Under the modern statutes, either spouse acting alone generally has the right to manage and control community property, though the consent of both spouses may be required for transactions such as conveyances of community real property or gifts to third persons. Moreover, the spouses may be held to fiduciary standards of loyalty, good faith, and fair dealing in managing community property. As a practical matter, the system of equal management rights is likely to work relatively well in a stable marriage, but if one spouse dissipates community funds or absconds, the aggrieved spouse may be left without a fully effective remedy.

When one spouse dies, one half of the community property passes by will or intestacy to the decedent's successors; the other half belongs absolutely to the surviving spouse. Accordingly, there is no need for dower or an elective share in a community property system, since each spouse automatically takes an equal one-half share of the community property. Nevertheless, a problem arises where one spouse makes unauthorized inter vivos gifts of community property to third persons. If a gift is challenged while both spouses are still alive, the usual remedy is to avoid the gift entirely and thereby restore the status quo ante. On the other hand, if the surviving spouse challenges a gift after the donor's death, courts generally permit the surviving spouse to recover half the amount of the gift from the donee, leaving the donee with the other half; in some states, the entire gift is recoverable. In fashioning a remedy for unauthorized gifts, most courts follow the "item" theory, which holds that each spouse is entitled to an equal one-half interest in each particular item of community property and cannot be forced to accept other assets of equivalent value.

ESTATE OF BRAY

California Court of Appeal, 1964.
230 Cal.App.2d 136, 40 Cal.Rptr. 750.

SALSMAN, JUSTICE. This is an appeal by Belle Bray, as co-executrix of the will of her late husband, Walter G. Bray, from an order of the probate court. . . .

Appellant and decedent Walter G. Bray were married in 1919, and their marriage continued until decedent's death in 1960. At the time of marriage neither party had any substantial amount of property. It is undisputed that all property involved in the present controversy is community property.

In 1929 decedent started a food brokerage business. For a short time he had a partner, but this relationship was terminated and the business continued and was solely owned by decedent until the time of his death.

In 1938 the decedent requested his son by a former marriage, who is the respondent here, to come and work in the business. Respondent accepted the offer of employment, and from 1938 until decedent's death continued his employment in the business as a salaried employee.

In 1944, without the knowledge or consent of his wife, decedent opened a joint tenancy savings account with respondent, and each year thereafter deposited in the account funds withdrawn from his business bank account. No withdrawals were ever made from the joint account. At date of death the balance in the account, including interest additions, amounted to $74,385.88. Although respondent knew of the existence of this bank account, because he signed a form card for the bank when the account was opened, he did not know when deposits were made in the account, or in what amount, nor did he at any time before his father's death know the balance in the account. The bank book was at all times kept by the decedent.

The decedent also purchased U.S. Savings Bonds with community funds. These too were registered in the joint names of decedent and respondent, without the knowledge or consent of appellant. The value of these bonds at date of death was $10,701.94. The respondent did not know when the bonds were purchased, but he did know of their existence, because his father once asked him to make a list of the bonds, and respondent had them in his possession briefly for this purpose. After the list was prepared, respondent returned the bonds to his father, who retained possession of them until his death.

In proceedings for distribution of the decedent's estate, respondent claimed the bank account and bonds as surviving joint tenant. Appellant claimed the joint tenancies had been created by the use of community funds, without her consent and without valuable consideration, and therefore respondent should restore to the estate one-half the value of such joint tenancies. (Civil Code, § 172; Estate of McNutt, 36 Cal.App.2d 542, 553 [98 P.2d 253].)

The probate court found that respondent had rendered valuable consideration to the decedent in return for the creation of the joint tenancies in the bank account and bonds and that no part of such joint tenancy property belonged to the estate of the decedent. The valuable consideration relied upon by the court consisted of services rendered by respondent to the decedent in the conduct of his business during decedent's lifetime. We have concluded that this finding is not supported by substantial evidence and that the order from which this appeal is taken must be reversed.

Respondent presented various witnesses in support of his contention that he rendered valuable consideration in return for the creation of the joint tenancies. He offered his own testimony thus:

Q. . . . the fact is that you paid nothing to your father for any of those deposits that went into this joint tenancy account?

A. That is debateable [sic].

Q. Did you pay any money to him at all for that?

A. I did not hand my father money out of my pocket for him to make a deposit, but the services that I rendered, and the consideration for that, to bring money into that business for my services, my father set that aside for me for my reward for the services rendered over the period of time when my salary was not exhorbitant [sic] and the fact that I worked Saturdays and Sundays and did not take vacations was considered. . . .

Appellant testified that her husband had once told her that respondent "was a fine son and a fine boy and was doing a good job."

Grace Lillon, a niece of the decedent, testified that decedent had told her "God never blessed a man with a finer son than Dick. I could not run the business without him."

The testimony of Calvin Rossi, an employee of the bank where the joint account was maintained, was to the effect that the decedent had told him that his son had earned the money; that he did not want his son to know about the money but he "wanted him to have it at the end." Mr. Solinsky, decedent's attorney, testified that the decedent had told him "Dick was always on the job, was there, and was doing excellent work, and that he was taking care of Dick in view of all of his services."

Appellant objected to most of this testimony on the ground that it was hearsay and self-serving. . . . The trial court overruled these objections. Respondent asserts the testimony was properly admitted because it tended to show decedent's state of mind and his intentions regarding compensation for his son at the time the joint tenancies were created and as they were increased from time to time by the addition of deposits and the purchase of bonds. We think the evidence was properly admitted . . . , but that it falls far short of substantial evidence to show that a valuable consideration was received sufficient to support the transfer of community funds.

At the time the decedent opened the joint bank account with respondent there was no promise on his part to deposit any money in it in exchange for any promise, act or service on the part of respondent. There was evidence that once or twice the decedent had said to respondent that there was too much cash in the bank account—presumably the business checking account—and that some should be transferred to savings. But there was no evidence that such excess was deposited in the joint account because of any act or promise on the part of respondent. During the entire 15–year period, respondent never knew of any amounts deposited by decedent or when the deposits were made.

In 1944, when the account was opened, respondent's salary was $225 per month and he received no bonus. His compensation was at the same rate for the year 1945. Thereafter, respondent's basic salary increased from $250 in 1946 to $375 in 1959. In all years following 1945 save one respondent received a substantial annual bonus varying from $1,800 in 1946 to $5,000 for each of the four years prior to his father's death. There is evidence that in later years respondent had greater responsibilities than he had at first, but there is no evidence to show that these duties were assumed because of any promise by his father to deposit any money in the joint bank account.

Thus, we find no substantial evidence in the record to show that respondent rendered any valuable consideration to the decedent or gave any consideration at all for the creation of the joint tenancies in either the bank account or the bonds.

Consideration may be either (1) a benefit conferred or agreed to be conferred upon the promisor or some other person; or (2) a detriment suffered or agreed to be suffered by the promisee or some other person. (Civil Code, § 1605.) It must be an act or a return promise, bargained for and given in exchange for a promise. (Simmons v. California Institute of Technology, 34 Cal. 2d 264, 272 [209 P.2d 581], and cases cited; Rest., Contracts, § 75, com. b.) Here there is no evidence of any promise on the part of the decedent to make deposits in the joint bank account, or to buy bonds registered jointly in the names of decedent and respondent, in return for any promise on the part of respondent, or any act on respondent's part. After the joint account was opened in 1944, respondent continued to render services to decedent's business as a salaried employee, with no knowledge of what money, if any, was actually being deposited in the joint account, or how many bonds were being purchased, if any. Respondent was duty-bound to render faithful service to the decedent in return for his salary and a bonus. Under the definition of consideration in Civil Code section 1605, doing what one is already legally bound to do cannot be consideration. (Pacific Finance Corp. v. First Nat. Bank, 4 Cal.2d 47, 49 [47 P.2d 460])....

It is undoubtedly true that, as one witness testified, decedent wished to keep the joint account secret from respondent as well as his wife and that he intended respondent should have it "at the end," that is, upon decedent's death. It is undisputed also that all deposits to the account were made from community funds. This evidence discloses only a gift, unsupported by a valuable consideration, and hence voidable in part by appellant, pursuant to Civil Code, section 172.

There was some evidence received, over objection of appellant, that decedent had established joint tenancies with appellant during his lifetime, and that upon decedent's death appellant had received at least one-half of all property in which decedent had an interest at the time of his death. This evidence was immaterial to a resolution of the issue of whether a valuable consideration had been given for the creation of the joint tenancy bank account and the joint tenancies in the bonds. A wife has a vested interest in all of the community property and her interest extends to every part and parcel of the community property estate. The husband during the lifetime of the parties may not give away any portion of it. In Dargie v. Patterson, 176 Cal. 714, 721 [169 P. 360], the court said:

> . . . upon the death of a husband who has attempted to convey community property contrary to the provisions of section 172, his nonconsenting wife may recover an undivided one-half of such property in an action brought against the grantee, and this without regard to the amount or condition of the estate remaining in his hands at the time of his death. . . .

Respondent further claims that Belle Bray ratified and confirmed the creation of the joint tenancies in the bank account and the bonds. This assertion derives from the fact that she signed the inventory and appraisement and the federal estate tax return and that both the inventory and the tax return showed the joint tenancy character of the bank account and the bonds. It does not appear however that the widow understood the significance or the legal meaning of the term "joint tenancy," or that the term was explained to her by counsel. Moreover, there is substantial evidence that she was ill at the time the documents were presented to her for signature and that she did not read them. Although the issue of ratification was raised in the trial court, the respondent requested no finding on it, and the probate court made none. From our examination of the record we conclude that the claim is without merit.

The order is reversed, with directions to the probate court to require respondent to account to the estate for one-half of the joint tenancy bank account and for one-half of the U.S. Savings Bonds, and upon the basis of such accounting, to fix and determine the fees of the executors and their attorneys as provided by law. . . .

NOTES

1. *Classification.* Determining the spouses' respective interests in property may present thorny questions of classification and valuation, especially when property is acquired on credit or the purchase price is paid in installments with a combination of community and separate funds. For example, consider how the following assets might be classified:

> (a) Before marriage, *W* purchased a house in her own name for $200,000, paying $20,000 in cash and taking out a $180,000 mortgage loan to finance the balance of the purchase price. At the time of her marriage to *H*, *W* had paid down $20,000 of the mortgage principal from her separate funds. During the marriage, she paid down another $40,000 from community funds. At *W*'s death, the outstanding mortgage princip-

al is $120,000 and the value of the house is $300,000. See Marriage of Moore, 618 P.2d 208 (Cal. 1980); Marriage of Marsden, 181 Cal.Rptr. 910 (Cal. App. 1982); Pringle v. Pringle, 712 P.2d 727 (Idaho App.1985).

(b) Before marriage, W took out an ordinary whole-life insurance policy on her own life in the face amount of $100,000 and designated her child C as beneficiary. W paid the annual premiums from her own separate funds until her marriage to H, and then paid subsequent premiums from community funds during marriage until her death. Of the total premiums paid before W's death, $4,000 came from W's separate funds and $6,000 came from community funds. See Modern Woodmen of America v. Gray, 299 P. 754 (Cal. App. 1931); McCurdy v. McCurdy, 372 S.W.2d 381 (Tex.App. 1963).

(c) Before marriage, H started a property management business with minimal capital. At the time of his marriage to W, the business was worth $100,000. During the marriage, H continued to manage the business and drew a reasonable salary for his services. At H's death, the business is worth $500,000. See Pereira v. Pereira, 103 P. 488 (Cal. 1909); Van Camp v. Van Camp, 199 P. 885 (Cal. App. 1921); Hamlin v. Merlino, 272 P.2d 125 (Wash. 1954); Jensen v. Jensen, 665 S.W.2d 107 (Tex. 1984).

(d) W takes care of her ailing cousin C, who agrees to leave her a bequest of $10,000. At C's death, W receives the promised bequest. Alternatively, C dies intestate and W recovers $10,000 from the estate.

2. *Community property "widow's election."* If one spouse purports to dispose of both halves of the community property by will, the attempted disposition is ordinarily enforceable only as to the decedent's half of the property. Suppose that H's will leaves his separate property as well as both halves of the community property in trust to pay income to W for life with remainder to their surviving issue. The will goes on to specify that if W elects to claim her half of the community property free of trust, she will forfeit all provisions made for her in the will. (Assume that there is a valid gift over to other beneficiaries in the event W elects against the will.) H has put W to a "forced election," meaning that W must choose between (1) a life income interest in the trust funded with H's separate property and both halves of the community property, and (2) absolute ownership of half the community property; she cannot take both. What considerations might H have in mind in making such a will? Even assuming that the pecuniary value of W's half of the community property exceeds the value of her interests under the will, why might she nevertheless accept the terms of the will? Is it proper for an attorney who represents both spouses to draft such a will? See ABA Special Committee on Professional Responsibility, Comments and Recommendations on the Lawyer's Duties in Representing Husband and Wife, 28 Real Prop. Prob. & Tr. J. 765 (1994); Link et al., Developments Regarding the Professional Responsi-

bility of the Estate Planning Lawyer: The Effect of the Model Rules of Professional Conduct, 22 Real Prop. Prob. & Tr. J. 1 (1987).

Similar issues can also arise in common law jurisdictions. Suppose *T*'s will devises Blackacre to *A* and Greenacre to *B*. As it happens, Blackacre is subject to *T*'s power of testation but Greenacre actually belongs to *A*. Whether *A* can accept Blackacre and also retain Greenacre depends on *T*'s intent. Should it matter whether *T* knew that Greenacre was actually *A*'s property?

3. *Federal preemption.* In Free v. Bland, 369 U.S. 663 (1962), the Supreme Court held that the federal regulations creating a right of survivorship in federal savings bonds registered in co-ownership form preempted inconsistent provisions of state community property law. However, the court left open the possibility that federal law might permit relief "where the circumstances manifest fraud or a breach of trust tantamount thereto on the part of a husband while acting in his capacity as manager of the general community property." See also Yiatchos v. Yiatchos, 376 U.S. 306 (1964) (federal POD savings bonds). If one spouse uses community funds to purchase a federal savings bond and designates a child from a previous marriage as POD beneficiary, without the other spouse's knowledge or consent, would this constitute the type of "fraud" contemplated by the Court?

The federal Employee Retirement Income Security Act of 1974 (ERISA) requires that qualified pension plans provide benefits to the surviving spouse of a deceased participant in the form of an annuity for life, and imposes restrictions on the assignment or alienation of plan benefits. See Note 3, supra p. 183. In Boggs v. Boggs, 520 U.S. 833 (1997), a married employee participated in a qualified pension plan which was classified as community property under state law. His first wife died, and in her will the wife left her community property interest in the pension plan to the couple's children. Later the husband remarried and died survived by his second wife, who claimed that she was entitled to all distributions from the plan as sole beneficiary. The Supreme Court held that the state community property laws conflicted with ERISA and were preempted to the extent they allowed a nonparticipant spouse to make a testamentary disposition of an interest in a surviving participant spouse's undistributed pension benefits. What difference, if any, would it make if the husband had not remarried, or if he had received a distribution of his entire interest in the pension plan before his first wife's death? Did ERISA prevent a community property interest from arising in the first wife's hands, or merely extinguish her interest when she failed to survive her husband?

Suppose that a husband, without his wife's knowledge or consent, designates his estate as the beneficiary of a community property life insurance policy provided by his employer. The husband's will, executed during the marriage, leaves all his property to his mother. Under state community property law, the husband has committed a constructive fraud on the wife's community property rights and she is entitled to recover half of the life insurance proceeds from the husband's estate. Under ERISA, however, state laws are expressly preempted to the extent they "relate to" an employee benefit plan. Can the wife pursue her remedy against the estate, or is her claim preempted by ERISA? Should it matter that the wife seeks to reach her share of the life insurance proceeds in the hands of the husband's executor, after distribution from the employee benefit plan? See Barnett v. Barnett, 67 S.W.3d 107 (Tex. 2001) (community property rights preempted); Guidry v. Sheet Metal Workers Nat'l Pension Fund, 39 F.3d 1078 (10th Cir. 1994), cert. denied, 514 U.S. 1063 (1995) (ERISA does not protect benefits after distribution). If the wife's remedy is preempted, should she be able to assert her claim as a matter of federal common law?

4. *Choice of law.* A court in a common law jurisdiction may have occasion to apply community property principles when determining ownership of local assets purchased with community property. For example, suppose *H* and *W*, a California couple, plan to move their domicile to New York. *H* precedes *W* and purchases a home, acquires some stock, and opens a bank account, using community property to fund each transaction. He puts title to the various assets in his own name, with the intention of making them joint following *W*'s arrival, but dies before having an opportunity to do so. The situation may be further complicated if they have moved several times. A number of states have adopted the Uniform Disposition of Community Property Rights at Death Act, which basically represents a codification of existing law. The Act provides that assets acquired with or traceable to community property retain their community character unless the spouses indicate a contrary intent. Thus, *W* is entitled to half of the New York realty and assets even though she may have been entitled to less by intestacy or under the terms of *H*'s will. Section 3 of the Act prevents the surviving spouse from claiming an elective share in the deceased spouse's half of the property, and § 6 protects purchasers and creditors who have relied on the title being in one spouse's name.

2. UNIFORM MARITAL PROPERTY ACT

The Uniform Marital Property Act (1983) is intended to facilitate the importation of community property principles into common law states. Although the Act has so far been adopted only in Wisconsin, it commands attention from reformers in community property as well as common law states and provides a useful perspective for comparing the treatment of surviving spouses under both systems.

The Act follows the traditional community property distinction between community and separate property (defined as "marital" and "individual" property, respectively). The character of property carries over to any unrealized appreciation; income earned or accrued during the marriage with respect to any property, whether individual or marital, is classified as marital property. Special rules address issues relating to life insurance, deferred compensation, and commingled individual and marital funds. Each spouse has a present, undivided one-half interest in the marital property.

Although title does not govern beneficial ownership of marital property, it does determine who has rights of management and control. The wife has control over assets held in her name, the husband over assets in his name, and both of them over assets held in their joint names. The Act provides protection for bona fide purchasers for value who rely on title in dealing with marital property. It also contains a number of safeguards against unilateral dissipation of marital assets by either spouse.

A married couple may enter into a marital property agreement that varies most provisions of the Act. In the absence of such an agreement, each spouse has the power to dispose of his or her undivided half by will; to the extent not effectively disposed of by will, his or her half passes by intestacy.

Uniform Marital Property Act (1983)

§ 2. Responsibility Between Spouses

(a) Each spouse shall act in good faith with respect to the other spouse in matters involving marital property or other property of the other spouse. This obligation may not be varied by a marital property agreement.

(b) Management and control by a spouse of that spouse's property that is not marital property in a manner that limits, diminishes, or fails to produce income from that property does not violate subsection (a).

§ 6. Gifts of Marital Property to Third Persons.

(a) A spouse acting alone may give to a third person marital property that the spouse has the right to manage and control only if the value of the marital property given to the third person does not aggregate more than [$500] in a calendar year, or a larger amount if, when made, the gift is reasonable in amount considering the economic position of the spouses. Any other gift of marital property to a third person is subject to subsection (b) unless both spouses act together in making the gift.

(b) If a gift of marital property by a spouse does not comply with subsection (a), the other spouse may bring an action to recover the property or a compensatory judgment in place of the property, to the extent of the noncompliance. The other spouse may bring the action against the donating spouse, the recipient of the gift, or both. The action must be commenced within the earlier of one year after the other spouse has notice of the gift or 3 years after the gift. If the recovery occurs during marriage, it is marital property. If the recovery occurs after a dissolution or the death of either spouse, it is limited to one-half of the value of the gift and is individual property.

§ 15. Interspousal Remedies

(a) A spouse has a claim against the other spouse for breach of the duty of good faith imposed by Section 2 resulting in damage to the claimant spouse's present undivided one-half interest in marital property.

(b) A court may order an accounting of the property and obligations of the spouses and may determine rights of ownership in, beneficial enjoyment of, or access to, marital property and the classification of all property of the spouses.

(c) A court may order that the name of a spouse be added to marital property held in the name of the other spouse alone, except with respect to:

(1) a partnership interest held by the other spouse as a general partner;

(2) an interest in a professional corporation, professional association, or similar entity held by the other spouse as a stockholder or member;

(3) an asset of an unincorporated business if the other spouse is the only spouse involved in operating or managing the business; or

(4) any other property if the addition would adversely affect the rights of a third person.

(d) Except as provided otherwise in Section 6(b), a spouse must commence an action against the other spouse under subsection (a) not later than 3 years after acquiring actual knowledge of the facts giving rise to the claim.

E. OMITTED HEIRS

1. CHILDREN

Compare the following statements:

The Commission has left to be considered by others whether a parent has a moral duty, which should be made a legal duty, to provide for the support and maintenance of children during the period of their dependence. Should the law compel a parent at death to provide for his helpless dependents? The right of a testator to pauperize his helpless dependents now exists under our law. When will the State step in and take away that privilege? When will such public policy be changed? The State is vitally interested in the care of minor children from both a pecuniary and a social viewpoint.

Slater, *Reforms in the New York Law of Property*, in
Report of New York Decedent Estate Commission 293 (1930).

The legal right of the next of kin to inherit a part at any rate of the deceased's property—observed in cases of intestacy in England and in all cases in other Western European countries—is often thought to have some sort of moral justification, particularly where the next of kin are the widows or children of the deceased. They had a moral claim to his support during life, it is argued, and they have a moral claim to the support his property gives after death. One is expected to conjure up a picture of a penniless widow, or of orphans in their teens. Their father's hard-earned savings have rightly been put by for their benefit. Have they not a moral claim to these savings? Certainly no wise State, confronted with such a case, would deny that claim; it would rather hope that the savings were sufficient to pay for the orphans' upkeep, lest the ratepayers have to contribute.

But it is nonsense to suggest that the great bulk of the property bequeathed and inherited goes to sustain indigent widows and young children, who cannot fend for themselves. Most of the widows of rich men have, in fact, some property of their own; and the large majority of penniless widows have practically penniless husbands from whom they will never inherit anything substantial, whatever the law on the subject. Again, the average age of children who survive well-to-do parents is somewhere about forty. The description "children," for inheritors in the direct line of descent, is therefore apt to be misleading. The sons who inherit large estates are usually men rather beyond the prime of life, at the time of their inheritance, whose parents gave them in youth an expensive training, and who were already receiving before their inheritance a considerable income whether from earnings and savings, or from gifts of property made during their parents' lifetime. The advent of a large inheritance in such cases is only likely to deter them from exerting themselves to earn a living.

But even if all children were too young or otherwise unfitted at the time of their parents' death to earn a livelihood by their own exertions, would our sense of justice or of social expediency demand that they should be supported at a scale of living in proportion to their parents' property? Has the child of a man with £100,000 for example, a fair claim to inherit one hundred times as much as the child of the man with £1,000? For the idea that such a claim is fair and reasonable appears to underlie the Continental law of *legitim* and the English law of inheritance in cases of intestacy. The only argument for such a claim, on the grounds of social equity, would appear to be that the parent has accumulated property with the expectation that his children will inherit, that the children have been brought up with the expectation that they will inherit, and that it is unfair and causes unhappiness to disappoint such established expectations. Yet clearly such expectations are entertained because of the laws of inheritance, and if those laws did not exist, neither would the expectations exist. We are still faced with the question of whether or not such expectations are fair and reasonable in themselves, apart from the existing law on the subject.

Personally I agree with John Stuart Mill that children may reasonably claim from their parent that he should "provide, so far as depends on him, such education and such appliances and means, as will enable them to start with a fair chance of achieving by their own exertions a successful life. *To this every child has a claim*; and I cannot admit that as a child he has a claim to more. . . ."

If this view is accepted, it follows that, in the large majority of cases where the sons of well-to-do parents have reached maturity before the latter's death, and have previously received education, appliances and means, which were not insufficient on grounds of expense to give them a fair start, there can be no reasonable claim to any inheritance in addition—except on the score of previously raised expectations, for which the existing law and custom must be chiefly responsible.

Wedgwood, The Economics of Inheritance 189–92 (1929).

Although there continue to be expressions of concern for minor children who have been disinherited by their parents (see, e.g., N.Y. Commission on Estates, Fourth Report 184 (1965); Haskell, Restraints Upon the Disinheritance of Family Members, in Death, Taxes and Family Property 105, 114 (Halbach ed., 1977) (proposing provision for support of minor children)), no state except Louisiana has enacted legislation to provide a forced share for them. The law does intervene for certain children in a roundabout way. On the questionable assumption that a parent who fails to mention or provide for a child by will does so inadvertently, statutes in many states operate in specified circumstances to save an intestate share for the omitted child. These statutes purport to implement the testator's true intent. In effect, they announce that a parent who really intends to disinherit a child should clearly express that intent in his or her will.

The *Goff* case, which follows, illustrates an application of a traditional type of pretermitted heir statute. If Granville Goff could be revived for an interview, might he be expected to express appreciation of the law's solicitude for his true intent? In the *Goff* case, who ultimately receives the testator's property and what moral claims do they have to it?

GOFF v. GOFF

Supreme Court of Missouri, 1944.
352 Mo. 809, 179 S.W.2d 707.

BARRETT, COMMISSIONER.

This is a suit for an accounting of rents and profits, for an injunction and to try and determine title to a tract of land in Worth County. The de-

fendants are the legatees and devisees and the executor of the estate of
Charles Granville Goff who died on September 7, 1942. The plaintiffs,
Marjorie Anne Goff, age twelve, and Dean Joe Goff, age ten, are the children of Joe Goff who died on December 31, 1936. The plaintiffs assert title
to the land as the grandchildren and pretermitted heirs of Charles Granville Goff, neither they nor their father, Joe Goff, being named or provided
for in this will. Mo. R.S.A. § 526.[9]

Charles Granville Goff was a farmer and spent most of his life in
Worth County. About five months before his death, at the age of about
sixty-six years, he went to California and stayed with a nephew, Roy S.
Goff. While there and about five weeks before he died he executed his
will. His will appointed his brother, Silas C. Goff, executor and provided
that his executor should sell all of his property "in a manner which may
seem best to him and in his discretion" and that he should distribute the
proceeds as follows: $5.00 to his brother George L. Goff; $1,000.00 to his
brother Silas, the executor, and the remainder between his nephews, Roy
S. Goff and L. Jay Goff, equally. The second [sic] clause of the will said: "I
am not married and have no children." The fifth clause said: "I hereby
give and bequeath to any person who might contest this will the sum of
$1.00 only, in lieu of any other share or interest in my estate, either un-
der this will or through intestate succession."

The trial court found that Charles Granville Goff was not aware of
the existence of the plaintiffs, Marjorie Anne and Dean Joe, but found
that he had provided for them by item five of the will and, therefore, they
were not pretermitted heirs. The respondents contend that item five
shows the testator's intention but if it does not do so clearly the extrinsic
evidence, including the testator's declarations, makes definitely certain
his intention that these plaintiffs were in his mind and provided for by
this clause of his will. The plaintiffs contend that the language of the will
is plain and unambiguous and, therefore, the court was in error in admitting extrinsic evidence to show the testator's intention to be other than
that expressed in his will. The plaintiffs contend, in any event that the
court erred in holding that the plaintiffs, grandchildren unknown to the
testator, were named or provided for by item five of the will.

The facts with reference to those who are specifically named in the
will are that the testator, Charles Granville Goff, was survived by two

---

[9] The applicable pretermitted-heir statute provided as follows: "If any person make his last
will, and die, leaving a child or children, or descendants of such child or children in case of their
death, not named or provided for in such will, although born after the making of such will, or the
death of the testator, every such testator, so far as shall regard any such child or children, or
their descendants, not provided for, shall be deemed to die intestate; and such child or children,
or their descendants, shall be entitled to such proportion of the estate of the testator, real and
personal, as if he had died intestate, and the same shall be assigned to them, and all the other
heirs, devisees and legatees shall refund their proportional part." Mo. Rev. Stat. § 526 (1939).—
EDS.

brothers, Silas and George. One brother, Edward, predeceased the testator and his son, Roy, is one of the residuary beneficiaries. The other residuary beneficiary is Silas' son, L. Jay Goff. Silas was appointed executor of the will and given a bequest of $1,000. Before Granville went to California he and his brother George quarreled over a tenant George had secured for Granville's farm. Granville experienced some difficulty in getting the tenant off the farm and the controversy between the brothers became so bitter that Granville said to Silas: "I will sure fix it so George . . . will not participate in my property." He told Silas' daughter, Mrs. Akard, that he "didn't want Uncle George to have anything he had." And so, in his will, he gave his brother George five dollars. Having made the son of his deceased brother, Edward, one of his residuary beneficiaries and having given Silas $1,000 and George five dollars, the testator specifically named or provided for every blood relative, as far as this record is concerned, except Joe or these plaintiffs.

The facts with reference to the testator, Joe and Joe's mother and their relationship to one another furnish the background for this litigation and the circumstances which the respondents claim exclude the plaintiffs as pretermitted heirs under this will. In the 1890's the testator, Granville, was a young man living on his father's farm in Worth County. David White and his family were farm neighbors, living a few miles distant. On October 10, 1895, Granville Goff and Cassie M. White procured a marriage license in Worth County and were married in the White home by a minister, Joshua Florea. They immediately went to Granville's home to live with his people. After four or five weeks Cassie left the Goff home or Granville took her back to her home and she instituted an action against him for divorce in the Circuit Court of Worth County. When Cassie and Granville were married Cassie was pregnant and on February 22, 1896, a son, Joe, was born. In her divorce action she was awarded a divorce and custody of the minor child of whom she alleged she was enceinte by Granville at the time of their marriage. Cassie and her child remained on her father's farm, in the vicinity of the Goff's home, eight or ten years. In 1901 Cassie married J.W. McCann, with whom she lived until his death in 1932. At the time of the trial she was living in Wisconsin with her daughters and sons.

Joe Goff was reared in the McCann home. He was married on June 21, 1929 and the plaintiffs are his children. Prior to his death in 1936 he had been cashier of the Swea City and Hawkeye banks in Iowa and at the time of his death was an assistant state bank examiner.

Silas Goff testified that Granville and Cassie were married at the request of Cassie and her father. Silas called it a "shotgun" wedding. He testified that after Granville and Cassie came to their home to live they quarreled continuously. He says that they quarreled violently over whether Granville was the father of the unborn baby—Cassie contending that he was its father and Granville denying it. Silas testified that throughout his life Granville denied Joe's paternity. A neighbor, as well as Silas and Silas' daughter, Mrs. Akard, all testified that Granville was always most reluctant to discuss Joe and the marriage to Cassie. According to this record he mentioned them but two or three times in the forty-seven years, and Ezekiel Goff, a cousin of Granville's, said that when Granville was notified of Joe's death in 1936 he said: "I am not interested." We mention and call attention to the evidence reviewed in this paragraph because it furnishes a background for the plaintiffs' contention, as the court found, that Granville Goff was not even aware of Joe's children and, therefore, could not have had them in mind and did not provide for or mention them in item five, and the defendants' contrasting contention that the testator did know of the children, had them in mind and provided for them in item five.

Silas testified that just prior to the time Granville went to California Granville was telling him about his difficulties with George and the tenant. In that conversation Granville stated that he intended to fix his business before he went to California and he said: "I will sure fix it so George and Joe's children will not participate in my property." Silas says Granville referred to Joe's children three or four times in the course of five or six years. Mrs. Akard, Silas' daughter, said that she once asked Granville whether he had ever been married and he told her he had but he denied Joe's paternity and "he told me he had these two grandchildren. I have never repeated that. He didn't want it repeated." Subsequently he told her about the quarrel with his brother George and said: "I am going to take care of those who would take care of me. I don't know of anyone but you and Jay and Roy." Then Mrs. Akard testified "he said he was going to take care of the ones that would take care of him and he very definitely said he didn't want Uncle George to have anything he had and he didn't want Joe's children to have anything because Joe was not his boy."

Joe's wife, the mother of the plaintiffs, said: "To my knowledge, I don't think he (Granville) knew there were children." There was other evidence from the plaintiffs indicating that Granville did not know of Joe's two children. But, as we have said, the respondents contend that item five was designed to and did mention and provide for these children regardless of whether the testator knew of their existence or not.

Deferring to and accepting, as we do in this instance, the trial court's finding and judgment (based for the most part on the credibility, weight and probative force of the evidence) that Marjorie Anne Goff and Dean Joe Goff are the grandchildren of the testator and the children of his deceased son Joe and that "Charles Granville Goff did not know of the existence of the plaintiffs" we eliminate all questions as to the admissibility of the extrinsic evidence, as to which there may be some doubt. . . . But with this assumption of fact as a starting point the conclusion that they were not provided for by item five of this will within the meaning of Section 526 is inescapable.

In item five of this will Marjorie Anne's and Dean Joe's father, Joe Goff (who to the testator's knowledge predeceased him), is neither "named" nor "provided for" specifically and hence the children are not excluded by reason of their father's being named or provided for, which would clearly and on the face of the will show that the testator remembered his child and intentionally disinherited his descendants whether he knew of their existence or not, as was the fact in Lawnick v. Schultz, 325 Mo. 294, 28 S.W.2d 658, and Miller v. Aven, 327 Mo. 20, 34 S.W.2d 116. The word "child" or "grandchildren" does not appear in item five and so they were not all remembered collectively and excluded as a class or provided for as a class as was the case with McCourtney v. Mathes, 47 Mo. 533, and Ernshaw v. Smith, Mo. Sup., 2 S.W.2d 803.

The respondents say that item five is an exclusion clause and is sufficient to exclude the plaintiffs because "through intestate succession" could only mean an heir. In this respect the instance is comparable to Williamson v. Roberts, Mo. Sup., 187 S.W. 19. There the testator had five children, one of whom was an unmarried, epileptic daughter. He was particularly anxious to provide for her and devised his land to her without mentioning the other children. In a separate item of his will he said: "I desire that all the rest and residue and remainder of my estate be disposed of as the law directs" and it was urged that this language was a sufficient compliance with the statute but the court could not find from this language that the testator had the other children in mind. As was said in Pounds v. Dale, 48 Mo. 270, 272: "He had nine children, and defendant urges that it is unreasonable to suppose that he forgot the seven while naming the two. I certainly would conjecture that all were in his mind, and that he meant to disinherit them. But it is a mere guess. The will must show upon its face that he remembered them; and though they be not directly named, there must be provisions or language that point directly to them." See also Baker v. Grossglauser, Mo. Sup., 250 S.W. 377, 378, and Wyatt v. Stillman Institute, 303 Mo. 94, 103, 260 S.W. 73.

The respondents, relying on the fact that Granville always denied Joe's paternity and the testimony of Silas and his daughter, Mrs. Akard, that Granville said he did not want Joe's children to have anything or that he would fix it so they would not get anything, contend that the testator intended to disinherit the plaintiffs and that the testator's declarations clearly identify the persons to whom he intended the exclusionary clause to apply. Our acceptance of the trial court's finding that Granville was not even aware of the plaintiffs is decisive of that contention as far as these two children are concerned, it seems to us. But, even if the argument might be made as to Joe we do not think it applicable under our statute. . . .

The soundness of the reasons for, the policy of and the practical operation of the statutes with reference to pretermitted heirs are not now open to question. It is sufficient to say that such statutes are a limitation upon and modify one's unlimited and unqualified power and right to disinherit and to dispose of one's property. The policy behind the statutes "[f]undamentally, . . . is a desire to prevent inadvertent disinheritance." 29 Col. L.R., 748, 750. To accomplish the purpose of preventing inadvertent disinheritance, from which there was no relief at common law, two types of statutes have been enacted. One is called the Massachusetts type statute and the other is commonly called the Missouri type statute. 32 Ill. L.R. 1. The Massachusetts type statutes provide that if the testator omits to provide for any of his children or the issue of a deceased child such omitted child or issue shall take as though the testator had died intestate "unless it appears that the omission was intentional and not occasioned by accident or mistake." G.L. (Ter. Ed.) c. 191, § 20. The Missouri type statutes provide that if a person make his last will and die leaving a child or descendants of a child "not named or provided for in such will, . . . every such testator . . . shall be deemed to die intestate" as to the omitted child or descendants. Mo. R.S.A. § 526. The Massachusetts type statutes emphasize intention and "intention is the material factor in determining its applicability." Annotation 65 A.L.R. 472, 473. It is for this reason that many of the respondents' cited cases are inapplicable; they are taken from California where a Massachusetts type statute has been enacted and "The section requires that the omission appear from the will to be intentional," there is "no requirement . . . either that a child be named in the will or that he be provided for therein." In re Estate of Lombard, 16 Cal.App.2d 526, 60 P.2d 1000, 1001; In re Estate of Allmaras, 24 Cal. App. 2d 457, 75 P.2d 557; In re Estate of Kurtz, 190 Cal. 146, 210 P. 959. On the other hand, the Missouri type statutes omit all reference to intention and the statutes, by their terms, arbitrarily apply unless the child or descendant is named or provided for. Annotation 65 A.L.R. 472, 481; 1 Page, Wills, Secs. 526, 528; 16 Am. Jur., Secs. 82, 85. Under these statutes it is immaterial that the testator intended to disinherit a child or descendants of a deceased child unless there is some language or provision in his will indicative of his purpose. Annotation 94 A.L.R. 26, 211; 51 L.R.A., N.S., 646; 1 Page, Wills, Sec. 530; Thomas v. Black, 113 Mo. 66, 20 S.W. 657. Joe, having predeceased Granville, could not have been intended or included in the phrase "or through intestate succession" and, as we have said, the court found that Granville did not know of Joe's children. Furthermore, the first [sic] clause of the will says, "I am not married and have no children," and so, obviously, he could not have had children or their descendants in mind. Even if he knew of these plaintiffs he must have regarded their status as foreclosed by Cassie's divorce or Joe's death, of which he had been informed in 1936. Wadsworth v. Brigham, 125 Or. 428, 259 P. 299, 266 P. 875; In re Parrott's Estate, 45 Nev. 318, 203 P. 258.

Finally, it is argued that the phrase "I hereby give and bequeath to any person who might contest this will the sum of $1.00 only," shows that the testator "meant to exclude someone." And the respondents argue that the will shows that "someone" meant any person not provided for in the will and included these plaintiffs or anyone who would share in his estate by intestate succession. The respondents emphasize the word "contest" and urge that the word was used in a generic sense and not in the restricted sense of a statutory will contest. But there is nothing in this record nor in the context in which the word is used to indicate that it was used with reference to the plaintiffs or anyone else occupying their relationship to the testator and the will. A pretermitted child, under the statute, takes independently of the will and has no remedy by way of attacking the will itself or its probate. Schneider v. Koester, 54 Mo. 500; Cox v. Cox, 101 Mo. 168, 13 S.W. 1055; Story v. Story, 188 Mo. 110, 86 S.W. 225; Campbell v. St. Louis Union Trust Co., 346 Mo. 200, 139 S.W.2d 935, 129 A.L.R. 316; annotation 123 A.L.R. 1073, 1084. It may be that in some uses of the word the plaintiffs "contest" the will but nevertheless the will, though it does not name pretermitted heirs, is valid in all other respects (Gibson v. Johnson, 331 Mo. 1198, 56 S.W.2d 783, 88 A.L.R. 369) and in the absence of other circumstances with reference to the clause other than the testator's general intent, not expressed in his will, it cannot be assumed that the word was used in the sense of applying to these plaintiffs.

It is our view, under the assumed facts, that neither the testator's child, Joe, nor Joe's descendants, Marjorie Anne and Dean Joe, were "named or provided for in" his will and he is "deemed" to have died intestate as to them. Thomas v. Black, supra; Williamson v. Roberts, supra; Barker v. Hayes, 347 Mo. 265, 147 S.W.2d 429.

The judgment is reversed and the cause is remanded for further proceedings consistent with this opinion.

NOTES

1. *Traditional pretermitted heir statutes.* Most states extend some sort of statutory protection to a testator's "pretermitted" ("passed by," "omitted," "not provided for") children or issue against inadvertent disinheritance. The traditional statutes vary considerably in phraseology and construction. Some of them, following the so-called Massachusetts approach, provide an intestate share for a child of the testator, or issue of a deceased child, who is not provided for in the will "unless it appears that the omission was intentional and

not occasioned by accident or mistake." Mass. Gen. L. ch. 191, § 20. These statutes do not require specific language of disinheritance in the will, and most courts are willing to look beyond the four corners of the will if necessary to determine whether the omission was intentional. In contrast, other statutes, such as the Missouri statute in the principal case, award an intestate share to any child of the testator, or issue of a deceased child, who is not "named or provided for" in the will. In applying these statutes, courts confine their inquiry to the language of the will; if the will is silent, extrinsic evidence of the testator's intent cannot be introduced to bar the omitted heir's statutory share.

Although at first glance the underlying policy justifications may seem appealing, in operation the traditional statutes sometimes produce unexpected results, especially in the case of a child who was already in existence when the will was executed. Is it realistic to assume, as these statutes do, that the testator did not know of, or inadvertently overlooked, the omitted child?

Today, pretermitted heir statutes more commonly apply only to the testator's children who are born (or adopted) after the execution of the will, on the theory that failure to provide for such children is more likely to be inadvertent than failure to provide for children who were in existence when the will was executed. Some of the modern statutes permit the omitted child to share in the estate unless "it appears from the will that the omission was intentional," while allowing extrinsic evidence to determine whether a provision for the child outside the will was intended to be in lieu of a testamentary provision. See UPC § 2–302(b), reproduced infra.

2. *Testamentary language.* The principal case raises the question of whether a will which simply denies the existence of children or disinherits any person who "contests" the will precludes application of the pretermitted heir statute. The decisions go both ways. For cases allowing an omitted heir to claim a statutory share, see Estate of Padilla, 641 P.2d 539 (N.M.1982) ("I declare that I have no children whom I have omitted to name or provide for herein."); Estate of Gardner, 580 P.2d 684 (Cal.1978) (disinheritance of "any person not mentioned" in will). On the other hand, a token bequest of $1 to any person claiming to be a child or heir has been held sufficient to bar the omitted heir's claim. See Estate of Hilton, 649 P.2d 488 (N.M. 1982) (will recited "I have only three children" and left $1 to any other claimant); Estate of Hirschi, 170 Cal.Rptr. 186 (App. 1980) (will left $1 to any person claiming "by reason of relationship or otherwise"). In Estate of Hester, 671 P.2d 54 (Okla. 1983), the will recited that the testator had "no children" although in fact he had a son, not otherwise mentioned or provided for, who claimed an pretermitted child's share. The court denied the son's claim and offered the following explanation:

A person can express the intention to omit to provide for his children in many ways. He may expressly state that the named child is to receive nothing. He may provide that a child who claims to be pretermitted shall receive only a nominal amount. . . . He may name the child, but leave nothing to him. . . . He may declare that any child claiming to be a pretermitted heir shall take nothing. . . . In the instant case . . . the testator mentioned his son by class, stating that he had no children. While the statement was false, the intention to exclude "children" from taking any part of his estate was clear. . . . [A] specific denial of the existence of members of a class to which the claimant belongs, coupled with a complete disposition of the estate by will, evinces a definite intent that all members of the named class are intentionally omitted from the provisions of the testator's will. [671 P.2d at 55.]

Disputes often arise over whether particular testamentary language suffices to defeat an omitted heir's statutory share. Assume the statute provides an intestate share for an omitted child of the testator, or issue of a deceased child, who is not "named or referred to" in the will. Does a will which leaves the estate to the testator's sibling and expressly disinherits "any other heir of mine" prevent an omitted child from claiming an intestate share? Compare Estate of Robbins, 756 A.2d 602 (N.H. 2000) ("[A] testator's use of the term 'heirs' is insufficient to preclude application of the pretermitted heir statute. The words 'children' or 'issue' must be used.") with Leatherwood v. Meisch, 759 S.W.2d 559 (Ark. 1988) (omitted child's share barred by contingent bequest to "heirs at law"). Is it sufficient merely to mention a child by name? See Estate of Osgood, 453 A.2d 838 (N.H.1982) (bequest to the "children of my son Neil" prevented Neil from taking intestate share). Suppose a will mentions the testator's daughter by name but leaves her nothing and makes no reference to the daughter's issue. If the daughter predeceases the testator, are her issue who survive the testator entitled to an intestate share of the estate? See Estate of Laura, 690 A.2d 1011 (N.H. 1997) (no, reference to daughter cuts off statutory share of issue). Alternatively, suppose that, after the daughter's death, the testator executes a new will which does not mention the daughter but names her surviving husband as executor. Are the daughter's surviving issue entitled to a statutory share? See Estate of Treloar, 859 A.2d 1162 (N.H. 2004) (yes; new will made no direct or indirect reference to daughter or her issue). Does a reference to the testator's "issue" in a perpetuities saving clause prevent application of the statute? See Alexander v. Estate of Alexander, 93 S.W.3d 688 (Ark. 2002).

The Uniform Probate Code provides some protection for omitted heirs, but the provision generally applies only to children of the testator who were born or adopted after the execution of the will. UPC § 2–302, as originally promulgated in 1969, allowed an after-born or after-adopted child of the testator who was not provided for in the will to claim an intestate share of the estate unless: (1) it appeared from the will that the omission was intentional; (2) when the will was executed the testator had one or more children and left substantially all the estate to the other parent of the omitted child; or (3) the testator provided for the child outside the will and the intent that the transfer be in lieu of a testamentary provision was shown by statements of the testator, the amount of the transfer, or other evidence. UPC § 2–302 (1969). This version of the statute is still in force in a number of states. Other states have adopted a revised version of UPC § 2–302, which currently provides as follows:

Uniform Probate Code (2011)

Section 2–302. Omitted Children.

(a) Except as provided in subsection (b), if a testator fails to provide in his [or her] will for any of his [or her] children born or adopted after the execution of the will, the omitted after-born or after-adopted child receives a share in the estate as follows:

(1) If the testator had no child living when he [or she] executed the will, an omitted after-born or after-adopted child receives a share in the estate equal in value to that which the child would have received had the testator died intestate, unless the will devised all or substantially all the estate to the other parent of the omitted child and that other parent survives the testator and is entitled to take under the will.

(2) If the testator had one or more children living when he [or she] executed the will, and the will devised property or an interest in property to one or more of the then-living children, an omitted after-born or after-adopted child is entitled to share in the testator's estate as follows:

(A) The portion of the testator's estate in which the omitted after-born or after-adopted child is entitled to share is limited to devises made to the testator's then-living children under the will.

(B) The omitted after-born or after-adopted child is entitled to receive the share of the testator's estate, as limited in subparagraph (A), that the child would have received had the testator included all omitted after-born and after-adopted children with the children to whom devises were made under the will and had given an equal share of the estate to each child.

(C) To the extent feasible, the interest granted an omitted after-born or after-adopted child under this section must be of the same character, whether equitable or legal, present or future, as that devised to the testator's then-living children under the will.

(D) In satisfying a share provided by this paragraph, devises to the testator's children who were living when the will was executed abate ratably. In abating the devises of the then-living children, the court shall preserve to the maximum extent possible the character of the testamentary plan adopted by the testator.

(b) Neither subsection (a)(1) nor subsection (a)(2) applies if:

(1) it appears from the will that the omission was intentional; or

(2) the testator provided for the omitted after-born or after-adopted child by transfer outside the will and the intent that the transfer be in lieu of a testamentary provision is shown by the testator's statements or is reasonably inferred from the amount of the transfer or other evidence.

(c) If at the time of execution of the will the testator fails to provide in his [or her] will for a living child solely because he [or she] believes the child to be dead, the child is entitled to share in the estate as if the child were an omitted after-born or after-adopted child.

(d) In satisfying a share provided by subsection (a)(1), devises made by the will abate under Section 3–902.

NOTES

1. *After-born children.* UPC § 2–302 applies only if a child is born or adopted "after the execution" of the will. In Azcunce v. Estate of Azcunce, 586 So.2d 1216 (Fla.App.1991), the testator executed a will leaving his estate in trust for his wife and three living children. The following year a fourth child was born, and the testator subsequently executed a codicil which named a new trustee and republished the remaining provisions of the original will. The testator then died unexpectedly of a heart attack. The fourth child, through a guardian ad litem, claimed an intestate share of the estate, but a divided court held that the pretermitted heir statute, based on the original version of UPC § 2–302, did not apply because the will was republished by codicil after the child's birth. (The doctrine of republication is discussed infra at p. 390.) Cf. Restatement (Third) of Property: Wills and Other Donative Transfers § 9.6 cmt. 3, illus. 3 (2001) (allowing child to take intestate share on similar facts). Should the omitted child be able to bring a malpractice suit against the lawyer who drafted the codicil? See Espinosa v. Sparber, Shevin, Shapo, Rosen & Heilbronner, 612 So.2d 1378 (Fla.1993) (child lacked standing because she could not show that "testator's intent *as expressed in the will* was frustrated by the negligence of the testator's attorney").

UPC § 2–302 specifically treats a child adopted by the testator after the execution of the will the same as an after-born child. Even in the absence of a specific statutory provision, courts generally arrive at the same result. In one case a testator left a $1 bequest "to my step daughter Shirley McGuire Hamilton." The testator formally adopted Shirley four years after executing the will, and subsequently died without updating the will. The court found that the testator referred to Shirley only as a stepdaughter—a status which gave her no legal rights as an heir—and did not intend to exclude her as a child.

Accordingly, Shirley was entitled to a pretermitted child's share. Estate of Hamilton, 441 P.2d 768 (Wash.1968). Accord, Estate of Turkington, 195 Cal.Rptr. 178 (App. 1983); Brown v. Crawford, 699 P.2d 162 (Okla. App. 1984); but see Ozuna v. Wells Fargo Bank, 123 S.W.3d 429 (Tex. App. 2003).

2. *Testator's mistake.* UPC § 2–302 generally applies only to children born or adopted after the execution of the will, but in one special situation it extends protection to a child who was already alive when the will was executed. If failure to provide for a living child results solely from the testator's mistaken belief that the child is dead, the omitted child enjoys the same protection as an after-born child. UPC § 2–302(c). This provision stands out as an exception to the traditional rule denying direct relief for a beneficiary omitted from a will by mistake. How frequently does this particular type of mistake occur, and why should it merit special treatment? What sort of evidence should be admissible concerning the testator's erroneous belief? What if the testator was simply unaware of the child's existence? See In re Gilmore, 925 N.Y.S.2d 567 (App. Div. 2011); cf. Cal. Prob. Code § 21622 (allowing intestate share if testator "believed the child to be dead or was unaware of the birth of the child").

3. *Impact on dispositive plan.* Many statutes allow an inadvertently omitted child to take an intestate share of the estate. This approach may severely distort the testator's dispositive plan. For example, suppose a testator executes a will which leaves $100 to each of her four living children and the rest of her estate to charity. Subsequently a fifth child is born and the testator dies without changing the will. What is the omitted child's intestate share of the estate? Is an award of that amount to the omitted child consistent with the testator's probable intent?

UPC § 2–302 attempts to put after-born children on a par with children who were born before the execution of the will, by reallocating to the former a share of the aggregate gifts made by will to the latter. Suppose, in the preceding example, that the testator left her entire estate to one of her four living children. Under UPC § 2–302(a)(2), reproduced supra, the after-born child would apparently take one-half of the net estate. See Estate of Newman, 451 N.Y.S.2d 637 (Sur. 1982). Is this consistent with the testator's probable intent?

The Wisconsin statute generally follows UPC § 2–302, but also gives the court discretion to adjust the omitted child's statutory share, as follows:

> If . . . the court determines that the share is in a different amount or form from what the testator would have wanted to provide for the omitted child or issue of a deceased child, the court may in its final judgment make such provision for the omitted child or issue out of the estate as it deems would best accord with the intent of the testator. [Wis. Stat. § 853.25(5).]

What difficulties might be expected under this type of statute?

4. *Nonprobate transfers.* Like most pretermitted heir statutes, UPC § 2–302 applies only to probate assets. Although transfers outside the will may be taken into account in determining whether the testator intentionally failed to provide for a child in the will, the omitted child's statutory share cannot be satisfied from nonprobate assets. Thus, for example, a child omitted from the testator's will may claim a statutory share of the estate only to discover that the bulk of the testator's assets were placed in a revocable trust during life and cannot be reached at death. See Robbins v. Johnson, 780 A.2d 1282 (N.H. 2001); Kidwell v. Rhew, 268 S.W.3d 309 (Ark. 2007); Estate of Jackson, 194 P.3d 1269 (Okla. 2008). Should UPC § 2–302 be expanded to reach nonprobate transfers?

5. *Express disinheritance.* None of the pretermitted heir statutes prevents an articulate and determined testator from disinheriting his or her heirs. To be effective, however, an express disinheritance clause must be coupled with an effective, affirmative gift of the estate to other beneficiaries. In most states, any property not effectively disposed of by will passes to the heirs by intestacy, even if this flouts the testator's clearly expressed intent. See Cook v. Estate of Seeman, 858 S.W.2d 114 (Ark.1993); Estate of Cancik, 476 N.E.2d 738 (Ill.1985); but see Estate of Eckart, 348 N.E.2d 905 (N.Y. 1976) (giving effect to clear and unambiguous intent to disinherit). One explanation for the traditional rule is that a testator is authorized by statute to make an affirmative disposition by will but not to alter the scheme of intestate distribution. See In re Brown Estate, 106 N.W.2d 535 (Mich.1960). Does this distinction withstand analysis?

UPC § 2–101(b) reverses the traditional rule and provides:

A decedent by will may expressly exclude or limit the right of an individual or class to succeed to property of the decedent passing by intestate succession. If that individual or a member of that class survives the decedent, the share of the decedent's intestate estate to which that individual or class would have succeeded passes as if that individual or each member of that class had disclaimed his [or her] intestate share.

Suppose testator leaves her entire estate to her child and expressly disinherits "any person not named or provided for in this will." The child predeceases testator, leaving no issue, and consequently the devise lapses. Should the estate escheat or pass by intestacy to testator's heirs? Compare Estate of Walter, 97 P.3d 188 (Colo. App. 2003) (escheat); Estate of Melton, 272 P.3d 668 (Nev. 2012) (same) with Estate of Jetter, 570 N.W.2d 26 (S.D. 1997) (contra). One testator, estranged from his wife, left his estate by will to a friend who predeceased him. The will stated that testator was seeking a divorce, that he had no children, and that all of his heirs not mentioned in the will were intentionally omitted. The court held that the entire estate passed to the wife by intestacy, observing that UPC § 2–101(b) requires "express language, not just uncertainty" and that the will did not expressly disinherit the wife. Estate of Haugen, 794 N.W.2d 448 (N.D. 2011). For further discussion see Heaton, The Intestate Claims of Heirs Excluded by Will: Should "Negative Wills" Be Enforced?, 52 U. Chi. L. Rev. 177 (1985); Hirsch, Incomplete Wills, 111 Mich. L.Rev. (2013).

2. SURVIVING SPOUSE

At common law a will executed before marriage was completely revoked by operation of law upon marriage (in the case of a woman) or upon marriage and the birth of issue (in the case of a man). The common law rule achieved a measure of protection for after-married spouses, but in doing so it obliterated the testator's premarital testamentary plan. Today most states have abandoned the common law rule in favor of a more narrowly targeted, less intrusive statutory approach that protects a surviving spouse against unintentional disinheritance without invalidating a premarital will in its entirety. Many states follow either the original or the revised version of the Uniform Probate Code, which leaves the testator's will in place but awards an overriding intestate share to a surviving spouse who married the testator after the will was executed.

UPC § 2–301, as originally promulgated in 1969, allowed a surviving spouse who married a testator after the execution of the will to claim an intestate share of the estate if the will failed to provide for the spouse, unless: (1) it appeared from the will that the omission was intentional; or (2) the testator provided for the spouse outside the will and the intent that the transfer be in lieu of a testamentary provision was shown by statements of the testator, the amount of the transfer, or other evidence. UPC § 2–301 (1969). Some states have statutes modeled on this provision. Others have adopted a revised version of UPC § 2–301, which currently provides as follows:

Uniform Probate Code (2011)

Section 2–301. Entitlement of Spouse; Premarital Will.

(a) If a testator's surviving spouse married the testator after the testator executed his [or her] will, the surviving spouse is entitled to receive, as an intestate share, no less than the value of the share of the estate he [or she] would have received if the testator had died intestate as to that portion of the testator's estate, if any, that neither is devised to a child of the testator who was born before the testator married the surviving spouse and who is not a child of the surviving spouse nor is devised to a descendant of such a child or passes under Sections 2–603 or 2–604 [relating to lapsed or failed devises] to such a child or to a descendant of such a child, unless:

(1) it appears from the will or other evidence that the will was made in contemplation of the testator's marriage to the surviving spouse;

(2) the will expresses the intention that it is to be effective notwithstanding any subsequent marriage; or

(3) the testator provided for the spouse by transfer outside the will and the intent that the transfer be in lieu of a testamentary provision is shown by the testator's statements or is reasonably inferred from the amount of the transfer or other evidence.

(b) In satisfying the share provided by this section, devises made by the will to the testator's surviving spouse, if any, are applied first, and other devises, other than a devise to a child of the testator who was born before the testator married the surviving spouse and who is not a child of the surviving spouse or a devise or substitute gift under Sections 2–603 or 2–604 to a descendant of such a child, abate as provided in Section 3–902.

NOTES

1. *Omitted spouse.* By analogy to the omitted child provision, the original 1969 version of UPC § 2–301 awards an intestate share of a testator's estate to an after-married spouse if the testator "fails to provide by will" for the spouse. UPC § 2–301 (1969). Suppose an unmarried testator executes a will leaving $10,000 to her "dear friend" A and the rest of the estate to her brother B. Two years later the testator marries A and subsequently dies without changing her will. Is A "provided for" in the will and therefore barred from claiming an intestate share under the original UPC? Should it matter whether the bequest is $1, $10,000, or $1,000,000? Whether the will was executed in contemplation of marriage? Compare Estate of Ganier v. Estate of Ganier, 418 So.2d 256 (Fla.1982) (statutory share not barred where will was not made in contemplation of marriage); Miles v. Miles, 440 S.E.2d 882 (S.C. 1994) (same), with Estate of Christensen, 655 P.2d 646 (Utah 1982) (contra, but suggesting different result if the will made "token gifts to various friends, one of whom married the testator years later"); Estate of Keeven, 716 P.2d 1224 (Idaho 1986) (same); Estate of Herbach, 583 N.W.2d 541 (Mich. App. 1998) (statute "makes no distinction between a devise made to a future spouse in contemplation of marriage and a devise made to a future spouse as a friend" but "simply requires a failure by the testator to provide for a surviving spouse in any capacity"). What if, after marrying A, the testator executes a codicil which republishes the will and subsequently revokes the codicil by tearing it up? See Estate of Ivancovich, 728 P.2d 661 (Ariz.App.1986) (will deemed reexecuted during marriage, negating statutory protection).

Note that the current version of UPC § 2–301 no longer requires that the after-married spouse be omitted from the will, but it expressly denies protection if the will was made in contemplation of marriage. See UPC § 2–301(a), reproduced supra. Under this provision, an after-married spouse's intestate share does not include any portion of the estate that is "devised to a child of the testator who was born before the testator married the surviving spouse and who is not a child of the surviving spouse." Suppose that testator's will, executed a few months before his second marriage, pours over the entire estate to a revocable inter vivos trust for the benefit of testator's two children from his first marriage. (Pour-over wills are discussed infra at p. 400.) Testator dies without having amended his will, survived by the two children and by his second wife. Does the trust provision for the children constitute a "devise" to them which defeats the second wife's intestate share under the current version of UPC § 2–301, reproduced supra? Should it matter whether the trust is amended after the testator's marriage? See Bell v. Estate of Bell, 181 P.3d 708 (N.M. App. 2008).

2. *Provision outside will.* UPC § 2–301 does not allow an after-married spouse to claim a statutory share if the testator provided for the spouse outside the will with the "intent that the transfer be in lieu of a testamentary provision." UPC § 2–302(a)(3). What difficulties do you foresee in applying this provision? See Estate of Shannon, 274 Cal.Rptr. 338 (App. 1990) (no evidence that nonprobate death benefit was intended to be in lieu of testamentary provision).

3. *Relationship to elective share.* UPC § 2–301 protects a surviving spouse from unintentional disinheritance under a testator's premarital will. This provision differs in purpose and operation from the elective share, which seeks to ensure that the surviving spouse receives a fair share of the couple's combined assets regardless of the testator's intent. Unlike the elective share, an omitted spouse's entitlement to an intestate share under § 2–301 is automatic; no election is necessary. Moreover, the intestate share under § 2–301 is computed differently from the elective share and applies only to probate assets. A surviving spouse's eligibility, or lack of eligibility, for an intestate share under § 2–301 has no effect on the spouse's right to claim an elective share. See Mongold v. Mayle, 452 S.E.2d 444 (W.Va. 1994).

3. REFORM PROPOSALS

The American law pertaining to the rights of surviving family members is often criticized as inflexible and inadequate: The surviving spouse's fixed share is fixed and cannot be altered to meet particular needs; surviving dependents may be disinherited entirely. Consider, by way of comparison, the English system of family maintenance established in the Inheritance (Provision for Family and Dependants) Act 1975, c. 63, as amended. Under this statute, certain surviving family members or dependents may apply for a court order "on the ground that the disposition of the deceased's estate effected by his will or the law relating to intestacy, or the combination of his will and that law, is not such as to make reasonable financial provision for the applicant." Among the persons eligible to make such an application are: the decedent's surviving spouse or civil partner, if any; any person who lived in the same household with the decedent as his or her spouse or civil partner for the entire two-year period ending at the decedent's death; any child of the decedent, as well as any other person "who, in the case of any marriage or civil partnership to which the deceased was at any time a party, was treated by the deceased as a child of the family in relation to that marriage or civil partnership"; and any other person "who immediately before the death of the deceased was being maintained, either wholly or partly, by the deceased." Id. § 1.

The court, if satisfied of the need to order reasonable financial provision for the applicant, is authorized to order the payment of specific sums of money (either periodically or in a lump sum) or the distribution of other property from the net estate. The court is specifically authorized to "order any person who holds any property which forms part of the net estate of the deceased to make such payment or transfer such property as may be specified in the order," and to "vary the disposition of the deceased's estate effected by the will or the law relating to intestacy, or by both the will and the law relating to intestacy, in such manner as the court thinks fair and reasonable having regard to the provisions of the order and all the circumstances of the case." In determining whether and in what manner to exercise its powers, the court is to consider several matters, including: the financial resources and needs of the applicant and other beneficiaries of the estate; any obligations and responsibilities of the decedent towards the applicant or other beneficiaries of the estate; the size and nature of the decedent's net estate; any physical or mental disability of the applicant or other beneficiaries of the estate; and "any other matter, including the conduct of the applicant or any other person, which in the circumstances of the case the court may consider relevant." Id. §§ 2 and 3.

To prevent the intentional depletion of the decedent's net estate through lifetime transfers, the statute authorizes the court to order certain transferees to restore money or other property received from the decedent for inadequate consideration within six years before death, if the decedent made the transfer "with the intention of defeating an application for financial provision." In exercising its power to recover such property, the court is to consider "the circumstances in which any disposition was made and any valuable consideration which was given therefor, the relationship, if any, of the donee to the deceased, the conduct and financial resources of the donee and all the other circumstances of the case." See id. § 10.

NOTES

1. *English statute.* The English statute summarized above is a revised version of the Inheritance (Family Provision) Act, 1938 (1 & 2 Geo. VI, c. 45), which permitted the court to deal only with fractional shares of the decedent's estate (determined by reference to the relationship between the decedent and the survivors), and did not grant the court such extensive powers to redistribute the estate. The statute's prototype was first enacted in New Zealand in 1900. Today the six states of Australia and all the common law

provinces of Canada have similar legislation. The experience with the statute in New Zealand does not suggest any large increase in litigation. Over a five-year period, according to one commentator, the average number of wills proved per year was 4,396; the average number of wills contested under the Act per year during the same period was 77. It was pointed out that, had there been no procedure as set forth in the Act, a substantial proportion of the 77 cases would have ended up in contests based on undue influence, lack of capacity, etc. in any event. The courts in Australia and New Zealand have taken a generous view of their powers under these Acts. In England, however, it appears that courts are ready to award costs against unsuccessful petitioners where the application is not well grounded. See Leach, Cases and Text on the Law of Wills 36 (2d ed. 1960) (noting the "obvious deterrent to applications based on spite or the what-can-we-lose theory"). The English experience with the statute is described in Bromley, Family Law, 508–17 (4th ed. 1971); Note, Dependants' Applications under the Inheritance (Provision for Family and Dependants) Act 1975, 96 L.Q. Rev. 534 (1980).

See generally Macdonald, Fraud on the Widow's Share 290–98, 301–27 (1960) (proposing adaptation of original act); Crane, Family Provision on Death in English Law, 35 N.Y.U. L. Rev. 984 (1960); Laufer, Flexible Restraints on Testamentary Freedom—A Report on Decedents' Family Maintenance Legislation, 69 Harv. L. Rev. 277 (1955); Dainow, Limitations on Testamentary Freedom in England, 25 Cornell L.Q. 337 (1940).

2. *New York proposal*. The New York Law Commission considered legislation based on the 1938 English statute in place of the elective-share provisions of section 18 of the Decedent Estate Law (which was ultimately replaced by N.Y. EPTL § 5–1.1–A). Such legislation was in fact introduced in the legislature to protect dependent children of a decedent, but no action was taken on it. N.Y. Temp. Comm'n on Estates, Fourth Report 184–87 (1965). The reasons for rejecting this approach as a means of protecting the spouse appear in N.Y. Temp. Comm'n on Estates, Third Report 211–12 (1964):

> Such legislation would require that the share of the surviving spouse, if any, would be determined by the judge to whom the application was made. That this would promote litigation in most estates of married decedents, where the surviving spouse has not received the entire assets of the decedent or has not acquiesced in the provisions made by the decedent is evident. Aside from the burden that this would place upon the courts, the wisdom of allowing the courts to dispose of the decedent's assets as the particular judge deems just, rather than allowing the decedent to dispose of his property as he sees fit, is open to serious objections. We believe that our tradition of limited restraint upon the disposition of property by will has become part of our public policy. Of course, the law should prevent a person from pauperizing his dependents but it is submitted that at least insofar as the faithful surviving spouse is concerned, a minimal statutory share will not only adequately protect him or her, but will avoid the expense and inconvenience of court pro-

ceedings to obtain maintenance from an estate which he or she probably had a hand in accumulating.

Nor would maintenance legislation be consistent with today's emphasis on the need for estate planning. A trust contemplated by section 18 [providing a life income interest for the surviving spouse] does not necessarily qualify for the marital deduction and thus increases estate taxes, but the testator in creating such a trust balances this against his desired aims. He knows the effects of his disposition with some certainty in advance. Under the maintenance theory, any plan for the future would be at most a guess.

Finally, maintenance legislation is essentially and designedly flexible and uncertain and would inherently breed litigation. While no one can gainsay the rash of litigation which followed the enactment of section 18, who can estimate the amount of litigation which has been avoided by its certain, definite and to some extent arbitrary provisions? It is axiomatic that the law must be certain as well as just, especially the law governing the devolution of property. Perhaps maintenance legislation is in order for what is the rare case where a person disinherits his minor or dependent children as well as their surviving parent and a Commission Staff Report advocates its enactment. The surviving spouse should be treated differently, however, since his or her claim is not based solely on dependency (certainly it is not insofar as the husband is concerned), but also in recognition of the partnership created by marriage.

Nor is it an answer to say that maintenance legislation has worked well in the countries which adopted it. Macdonald and Laufer attribute this to the nature of maintenance legislation and its inherent large discretion which discourages inheritance claims. Except in England, no jurisdiction with as large a population as New York has adopted it. That there is more familial harmony in England than here is reflected in the fact that the divorce rate there, while increasing, is about one-half of ours. Statistics collected by Professor Macdonald from 10 states indicate that in nearly one of every four marriages here one of the parties was married before. While he attributes the increase in what he calls "evasion cases" to, among other things, the frequency of remarriage and the presence of children by the first marriage, and there can be no quarrel with that conclusion, it is submitted that much of the litigation which has arisen over section 18 is caused by the same family situation. Finally, while there are no statistics available on the subject, it is doubtful if there is any country in the world as litigation-minded as the United States. While New York probably has an amount of litigation which is disproportionate even to its large population, this litigation is not restricted to controversies over the right of election. New York has a litigious population and especially where there are second marriages, it is doubtful that making the share of the surviving spouse dependent upon the discretion of a court will alleviate the burden on our courts. For this and many other reasons the maintenance legislation for the surviving spouse should not be adopted here.

3. *Alternative proposals.* Several commentators have advanced alternative proposals to protect surviving family members, especially minor children. Some recommend a flexible system of family maintenance along the lines of the English and Commonwealth systems. See Chester, Disinheritance and the American Child: An Alternative From British Columbia, 1998 Utah L. Rev. 1; Shapo, "A Tale of Two Systems": Anglo–American Problems in the Modernization of Inheritance Legislation, 60 Tenn. L. Rev. 707 (1993). Others favor a posthumous duty of support for minor children as an extension of existing lifetime parental obligations. See Brashier, Disinheritance and the Modern Family, 45 Case W. Res. L. Rev. 83 (1994). Still others propose a modified version of a forced share for a decedent's surviving minor children or dependent parents. See Haskell, The Power of Disinheritance: Proposal for Reform, 52 Geo. L.J. 499 (1964); Batts, I Didn't Ask to Be Born: The American Law of Disinheritance and a Proposal for Change to a System of Protected Inheritance, 41 Hastings L.J. 1197 (1990). For perceptive analysis of the flexible system of rewards for good behavior and punishments for bad behavior in Chinese inheritance law, see Foster, Towards a Behavior–Based Model of Inheritance?: The Chinese Experiment, 32 U.C. Davis L. Rev. 77 (1998); Foster, Linking Support and Inheritance: A New Model From China, 1999 Wis. L.Rev. 1199.

F. RESTRICTIONS ON CHARITABLE GIFTS

Until the 1970s a number of states imposed statutory limitations on testamentary gifts to charity. The so-called "mortmain" (literally, dead hand) statutes were predicated on the assumption that a testator might make improvident or excessive charitable gifts due to frailty or fear of impending death. Another justification frequently offered for such statutes focused on the general legislative policy of protecting the testator's family against disinheritance. The statutes usually operated by invalidating charitable gifts in excess of a specified percentage of the estate, see former N.Y. EPTL § 5–3.3 (gifts exceeding half the estate); by invalidating charitable gifts made in a will executed within a specified time of death, see former Fla. Stat. § 732.803 (will executed within six months of death); or some combination of these two approaches, see former Ohio Code § 2107.06 (charitable gifts exceeding one quarter of the estate in will executed within six months of death).

By the late 1990s the last remaining mortmain statutes in this country disappeared due to legislative repeal (e.g., New York) or to judicial invalidation on constitutional grounds (e.g., Pennsylvania). In striking down the Pennsylvania statute, which made voidable any charitable gift made in a will executed within 30 days of death, the court in Estate of Cavill, 329 A.2d 503 (Pa.1974), stated:

[The statute] divides testators into two classes. One class is composed of those testators whose wills provide for charitable gifts and who die within 30 days of executing their wills. The other class is composed of those testators who either make no charitable gifts or survive the execution of their wills by at least 30 days. The statute renders invalid any charitable gifts made by a testator in the first class if any person "who would benefit by its invalidity" objects. In all other cases, one who wishes to invalidate a testamentary gift must prove lack of testamentary capacity or undue influence.

Clearly, the statutory classification bears only the most tenuous relation to the legislative purpose. The statute strikes down the charitable gifts of one in the best of health at the time of the execution of his will and regardless of age if he chances to die in an accident 29 days later. On the other hand, it leaves untouched the charitable bequests of another, aged and suffering from a terminal disease, who survives the execution of his will by 31 days. Such a combination of results can only be characterized as arbitrary.

Furthermore, while the legislative purpose is to protect the decedent's family, the statute nevertheless seeks to nullify bequests to charity even where, as here, the testator leaves no immediate family. In these circumstances, the statute would operate to "protect" only distant relatives, with whom the testator may have had little or no contact during life, against the carefully selected and clearly identified objects of the testator's bounty. This protection of a nonexistent "family" defeats the testator's expressed intent without any relation to the purpose which is sought to be promoted, further demonstrating the irrationality of the statutory classification.

Because the statute sweeps within its prohibition many testamentary gifts which present no threat of the evils which the statute purports to minimize, it is substantially over-inclusive. Since the statute also leaves unaffected many gifts which do present such a threat, it is also substantially under-inclusive. We are thus compelled to conclude that it lacks "a fair and substantial relation" to the legislative object. Therefore, the Equal Protection Clause forbids us to give it any effect. [329 A.2d at 505–06.]

For other cases reaching similar results, see Estate of French, 365 A.2d 621 (D.C. 1976), cert. denied, 434 U.S. 59 (1977) (statute invalidated any bequest to a clergyman or religious organization in will made within 30 days of death); Estate of Kinyon, 615 P.2d 174 (Mont.1980) (statute invalidated any charitable gift of more than one-third of the estate in will made within 30 days of death); Shriners Hospitals for Crippled Children v. Zrillic, 563 So.2d 64 (Fla.1990) (statute made voidable any charitable gift in will made within six months of death). For a good discussion of the rise and decline of mortmain statutes, see Sherman, Can Religious Influence Ever Be "Undue" Influence?, 73 Brook. L. Rev. 579 (2008).

CHAPTER 4

GROUNDS FOR CONTEST: INCAPACITY, UNDUE INFLUENCE, FRAUD, DURESS, AND MISTAKE

■ ■ ■

The several statutory approaches discussed in the previous chapter illustrate the limitations which legislatures have imposed on individual testamentary freedom in order to protect surviving family members. This chapter and the next one deal with various methods of ascertaining and effectuating donative intent. Courts routinely proclaim that, absent statutory authority, they do not indulge their own notions of fairness or morality in determining the validity and effect of gratuitous wealth transfers. In reading the following cases, consider whether the reality is not something else again and whether sympathy for the family does not affect the outcome.

A. TESTAMENTARY CAPACITY

BARNES V. MARSHALL

Supreme Court of Missouri, 1971.
467 S.W.2d 70.

HOLMAN, JUDGE.

This action was filed to contest a will and two codicils executed by Dr. A.H. Marshall a short time before his death which occurred on July 29, 1968. The plaintiff is a daughter of the testator. The defendants are the beneficiaries of the alleged will. A number are relatives of testator, but many are religious, charitable, and fraternal organizations. A trial resulted in a verdict that the paper writings were not the last will and codicils of Dr. Marshall. A number of the defendants have appealed. We will hereinafter refer to the appellants as defendants. We have appellate jurisdiction because the will devises real estate and also because of the amount in dispute.

One of the "Points Relied On" by defendants is that the verdict is against the greater weight of the credible evidence. Since this court will not weigh the evidence in a case of this nature this point, strictly speaking, would not present anything for review. However, in considering the argument under that point we have concluded that defendants actually intended to present the contention that plaintiff did not make a submissible case and that the trial court erred in not directing a verdict for defendants, and we will so consider the point. The petition charged that testator was not of sound mind and did not have the mental capacity to make a will. The transcript contains more than 1,100 pages and there are a large number of exhibits. We will state the facts as briefly as possible and we think they will clearly support our conclusion that the submission is amply supported by the evidence.

The will, executed April 30, 1968, made specific bequests of testator's home and office furniture and equipment. The remainder of the net estate was devised to trustees, with annual payments to be made from the income to various individuals, churches, charities, and fraternal organizations. Plaintiff, her husband and two children were to receive $5.00 each per year. The estate was appraised in the inventory at $525,400.

The Marshalls had three children: plaintiff who lived in St. Louis, Mary Taylor Myers who lived in Dexter, Missouri, and died in May 1965, and Anetta Ester Vogel who lived near Chicago and who died about a month after her father's death.

In stating the evidence offered by plaintiff we will deal specifically with five witnesses: three lay witnesses because of contentions concerning their testimony, hereinafter discussed, and the two medical witnesses because of the importance we attribute to their testimony. There were many other witnesses whose testimony we will endeavor to summarize in a general way.

Ward Barnes, husband of plaintiff, testified that he visited in the Marshall home frequently from the time of his marriage in 1930 until Dr. Marshall's death; that Mrs. Marshall was a very cultured, refined, patient, and accommodating woman; that he spent a great deal of time with testator and soon learned that testator would dominate the conversation in accordance with a certain pattern; that testator told him that he discontinued his medical practice at the command of the Lord so that he might use his time in saving the nation and the world; that testator had told him "that the Lord had revealed to him the secrets of heaven; that he was the only man on earth to whom the Lord had revealed these secrets; that he had told him that heaven was a glorious place and that when he went to heaven he would have a beautiful crown and a wonderful throne sitting next to Thee Lord. He said that there were three powers in heaven, the Lord, Thee Lord, and God, and he said that this throne that he would have would be on the right hand side of Thee Lord in heaven. He said that heaven was a wonderful place, Thee Lord had revealed to him that whatever pleasures man had on earth he would have in heaven. If it was whiskey, if it was gambling, if it was women, that these would be provided him." He stated that testator had also told him that the Lord had given him a special power of calling upon the Lord to right the wrongs which people had done to him; that many times he related instances of various people whom he had "turned over to the Lord" and the Lord had meted out justice at his instance by taking away the person's wealth, and usually that the person lost his health, had a long period of suffering, and eventually died; that when testator related stories about the men he had turned over to the Lord he would become highly emotional, would pound on the table with his fists, would call these men dirty profane names, his face would become flushed, and the veins in his neck would stand out; that testator had told him that he (testator) had run for Congress on two occasions and had run for President of the United States (although apparently never nominated by any party) on two or three occasions; that he had told him that "if he were made President of the United States he would cancel all public debt, that he would call in all government bonds and discontinue the interest on all of these obligations, and that he would then print money and control the currency, and that he would kill the damn bankers and the crooks and the thieves that were robbing the people in political office and that the world would then be able to settle down and live in peace." He stated that on one occasion testator took him to his office and showed him a number of young women who were mailing out material in the interest of his candidacy; that he had said it was costing him "thousands of dollars to mail this material out, but the Lord had told him to do it and he had no right to go counter to what the Lord had told him to do." He further stated that in one of his campaigns for President testator had purchased a new car and had many biblical quotations and sayings of his own printed all over the automobile; that he had observed him, campaigning from this car, at the corner of Grand and Lindell Boulevard in St. Louis.

Witness Barnes further testified that testator had told him that Mrs. Marshall had inherited a piece of land and that when it was sold he took part of the money and gave her a note for $3,500; that later Mrs. Marshall had pressed him for payment and had conferred with Moore Haw, an attorney, and that because of that testator had locked her out of the house; that Mrs. Marshall then filed a suit and caused him to pay her the $3,500; that eventually the Marshalls were reconciled and resumed their life together; that at the time Mrs. Marshall died he and plaintiff went immediately to Charleston and at testator's request plaintiff made the funeral arrangements; that testator went to his wife's bedroom and searched the room looking for money and called him and plaintiff in to help him; that he found only a few dollars and then became enraged, "his fists clenched ... his hands were shaking, his body was trembling; his face was red and he was—you could see he was in a terrible emotional state as he stood there shaking his fists and shouting. He said, 'I know she had more money than that. . . . Your mother made me pay and that scoundrel Moore Haw, the dirty, low down . . . made me pay that thirty-five hundred dollars,' and he said, 'I want my money back. I want you to give it to me.' " Witness further testified that of the $3,500 testator had paid his wife in 1941 Mrs. Marshall had given plaintiff $1,500; that from the time of his wife's death until his own death testator had frequently demanded that plaintiff send him $3,500 and stated that if she didn't he would cut her out of his will; that it was his opinion that from the time he first became acquainted with him until his death Dr. Marshall was not of sound mind.

Frank Eaves testified that he had known testator for about eight years before his death; that he was Plant Supervisor for Crenshaw Packing Company and that testator would come to the plant about once a week; that he had heard testator talk about having the Lord come down on people, making them suffer, and having them killed; that he said his furnace didn't work and he had the Lord put a curse on it and it had worked good ever since; that he said he "talked directly to God and God told him things"; that when he would discuss subjects of that kind "his face would get real red, his eyes would bug out, the vessels would stand out on his neck, he would slobber and shout, and pound on anything available"; that he would sometimes come in dressed in nothing but his nightgown and his house shoes; that on one occasion he came to the plant with nothing on but a housecoat; that he was talking about a rash on his body and opened his housecoat and exposed his private parts to the female secretary and others present. Mr. Eaves was of the opinion that testator was of unsound mind over the period he had known him.

William West testified that he was a drug clerk in the Myers Drug Store in Dexter; that he had known testator from 1951 until his death; that testator came in the drug store about once a month during that period; that he had heard testator say that he talked directly to the Lord and the Lord told him the things he was to do; that one of these was that he should save the world and should be prime minister of the United States; that he also talked about turning people over to the Lord for punishment and when he did so the Lord would mete out the punishment and the men would die, or lose their wealth or something of that nature; that when he would talk about such things he used loud abusive language, his face would be flushed, and he would pound the table; that at the funeral of testator's daughter, Mrs. Myers, he (the witness) started to assist Mrs. Marshall, who was then about 80 years old, out of her chair and Dr. Marshall "slapped me on the arm and told me to keep my hands off of her"; that he was present when Mrs. Marshall was trying to get out of the car and in so doing exposed a portion of her leg and testator "bawled her out for it." Witness was of the opinion that testator, during the time he had known him, was of unsound mind.

Dr. Charles Rolwing testified that he first saw testator professionally in 1940; that at that time testator complained of heart trouble but he was unable to find any evidence of such; that he was of the opinion that he was then suffering from manic-depressive psychosis for which there is no cure and that it would gradually get worse; that he also attended testator from the first part of May 1968 until his death in July; that at that time he was suffering from a serious heart ailment; that he was at that time still suffering from manic-depressive psychosis; that he was of the opinion that on April 30, May 17, and May 24, 1968, testator was of unsound mind.

Plaintiff also presented the testimony of Dr. Paul Hartman, a specialist in psychiatry and neurology, who testified in response to a hypothetical question. This question hypothesized much of the evidence related by the other witnesses for plaintiff and utilizes ten pages of the transcript. In response thereto Dr. Hartman expressed the opinion that Dr. Marshall was of unsound mind on the dates he executed his will and codicils; that he would classify Dr. Marshall's mental disease as manic-depressive psychosis with paranoid tendencies; that it was his opinion that Dr. Marshall was incapable of generalized logical thinking.

In addition to the foregoing evidence plaintiff testified herself and offered more than a dozen other witnesses, all of whom related unusual conduct and statements of testator. Plaintiff also offered a large number of exhibits in the nature of letters from testator and various publications containing advertisements and statements written by testator. There was evidence that plaintiff had been a dutiful daughter, had been solicitous of testator and her mother, had visited them frequently and often would take prepared food which she knew they liked. A number of these witnesses testified that testator had told them of various men who had wronged him and that he had turned them over to the Lord who meted out punishment in the form of financial loss, illness, death, or all three; that when he would tell of these things he would speak loud, get excited, his face would become red, his eyes bulge out, and he would gesture violently; that testator was unreasonably jealous of his wife and often said that all women who wore short skirts, or smoked, were immoral.

There was testimony that on the Christmas before the death of his daughter, Mary Myers, the Myers and Barnes families ate Christmas dinner with the Marshalls, and after the dinner testator "jumped on" Mary about her skirt being short and continued doing so until Mary became so upset that she and her husband had to leave.

A number of witnesses testified concerning the fact that testator would go to various public establishments dressed in his nightgown and bathrobe. An article written by testator and published in a local newspaper under date of June 4, 1942, under the heading of "DR. MARSHALL SAYS," contained the following: "Providence they say always raises up a great leader in every crisis. . . . I am that great leader. I am that prophet that Moses and all the other prophets have spoken about. I am the Messiah that the people of this world have been talking and praying about and believing and hoping that he would soon show up. I am the inspired prophet."

In contending that plaintiff did not make a submissible case defendants point to the testimony of their witnesses to the effect that testator was of sound mind and was calm, quiet, and collected on the day the will was executed. The difficulty with that argument is that in determining this question "we must disregard the evidence offered by defendants unless it aids plaintiffs' case, accept plaintiffs' evidence as true, and give them the benefit of every inference which may legitimately be drawn from it." Sturm v. Routh, Mo. Sup., 373 S.W.2d 922, 923.

It is also contended that most of plaintiff's evidence dealt with testator's "sickness, peculiarities, eccentricities, miserliness, neglect of person or clothing, forgetfulness, anger, high temper, unusual or peculiar political and religious views, jealousy, mistreatment of family, unusual moral views, and repeating of stories, which are not evidence of testamentary incapacity or of unsound mind."

As we have indicated, we do not agree with defendants' contentions. We have stated a portion of the evidence and it need not be repeated here. It is sufficient to say that we think testator's stated views on government, religion, morals, and finances go beyond the classification of peculiarities and eccentricities and are sufficient evidence from which a jury could reasonably find he was of unsound mind. When we add the strong medical testimony to that of the lay witnesses there would seem to be no doubt that a submissible case was made.

Defendants also point out that there is evidence that a person suffering from manic-depressive psychosis has periods of normalcy between the abnormal periods of elation or depression and that testator was in a normal period at the time the will was executed. The mental condition of testator at the precise time the will was executed was a question for the jury to decide. The jury was obviously persuaded that he was not of sound mind and since there was evidence to support that verdict it is conclusive. . . .

Plaintiff's evidence relating to the mental condition of testator encompassed the period from 1940 until his death in 1968. The next point briefed by defendants is that the court erred in admitting evidence of occurrences years prior to the execution of the will because it was too remote to have any probative value. It is true, as defendants contend, that "[e]vidence, not too remote, of mental unsoundness either before or after the will's execution is admissible, provided it indicates that such unsoundness existed at the time the will was made." Rothwell v. Love, Mo. Sup., 241 S.W.2d 893, 895. There can be no question, however, but that evidence concerning testator's mental condition long prior to the execution of the will is admissible if it tends to show his condition at the time of said execution. Holton v. Cochran, 208 Mo. 314, 106 S.W. 1035, l.c. 1069; Buford v. Gruber, 223 Mo. 231, 122 S.W. 717[4]; Clingenpeel v. Citizens' Trust Co., Mo. Sup., 240 S.W. 177. Dr. Rolwing testified that he treated testator in 1940 and that he was of unsound mind at that time; that he was suffering from manic-depressive psychosis, an incurable mental disease which would gradually get worse. That testimony was certainly admissible as it would have a direct bearing on testator's mental condition at the time the will was executed. And in view of that testimony it was appropriate to admit other evidence concerning testator's statements and conduct tending to support the submission of mental incapacity occurring during the intervening period. This point is accordingly ruled adversely to defendants' contention.

The next point briefed by defendants is that the court erred in permitting lay witnesses Ward Barnes, Frank Eaves, and William L. West to express an opinion that testator was of unsound mind. This for the reason that the facts related by those witnesses were not inconsistent with sanity and hence the necessary foundation was not established. The rule regarding the competency of lay witnesses to express an opinion on the issue as to whether a person is or is not of sound mind is that "a lay witness is not competent to testify that, in the opinion of such witness, a person is of unsound mind or insane, without first relating the facts upon which such opinion is based; and, when the facts have been stated by such lay witness, unless such facts are inconsistent with such person's sanity, the opinion of such lay witness that the person under consideration was insane or of unsound mind, is not admissible in evidence and may not be received. . . . In this connection it has repeatedly been determined that evidence of sickness, old age, peculiarities, eccentricities in dress or oddities of habit, forgetfulness, inability to recognize friends, feebleness resulting from illness, and other facts or circumstances not inconsistent with the ability to understand the ordinary affairs of life, comprehend the nature and extent of one's property and the natural objects of his bounty, and which are not inconsistent with sanity, cannot be used as a basis for the opinion testimony of a lay witness that a person is of unsound mind or insane. . . . 'The rule is well settled that, ordinarily, before a lay witness will be permitted to give his opinion that a person is of unsound mind, he must first detail the facts upon which he bases such opinion, but if he expresses an opinion that such person is of sound mind, he is not required to detail the facts upon which he founds his opinion. The reason for the rule is obvious. An opinion that a person is of unsound mind is based upon abnormal or unnatural acts and conduct of such person, while an opinion of soundness of mind is founded upon the absence of such acts and conduct.'" Lee v. Ullery, 346 Mo. 236, 140 S.W.2d 5, l.c. 9, 10.

Because of this point we have heretofore detailed the testimony of these three witnesses in the factual statement and such need not be repeated here. We think it is obvious that each witness detailed sufficient facts upon which to base the opinion stated. Those facts went far beyond a mere showing of peculiarities and eccentricities. They were clearly inconsistent with the conclusion that testator was of sound mind. . . .

The defendants also contend that the court erred in refusing to permit their witness, Harris D. Rodgers, to express an opinion that testator was of sound mind. This witness operated an abstract business in Benton, Missouri, which is about 20 miles from Charleston. However, he had known testator for about 35 years and had seen and visited with him on an average of from two to four times a year. We have concluded that we need not determine whether or not the court erred in excluding this testimony. This for the reason that it is "well settled that, if in a specific instance the evidence should not have been excluded, the error is harmless if the same evidence is found in the testimony of the same or other witnesses, given before or after the objection was sustained." Steffen v. Southwestern Bell Telephone Co., 331 Mo. 574, 56 S.W.2d 47, 48. In this instance defendants offered ten lay witnesses who were permitted to testify that in their opinion testator was of sound mind. With such an abundance of testimony on that issue it seems apparent to us that the exclusion of the opinion of one additional witness could not have been prejudicial. No reversible error appearing this point is ruled adversely to defendants. . . .

The judgment is affirmed.

All concur.

NOTES

1. *General definition.* The usual definition of testamentary capacity requires that the testator "be capable of knowing and understanding in a general way the nature and extent of his or her property, the natural objects of his or her bounty, and the disposition that he or she is making of that property." In addition, the testator must "be capable of relating these elements to one another and forming an orderly desire regarding the disposition of the property." Restatement (Third) of Property: Wills and Other Donative Transfers § 8.1 (2003).

It is questionable whether a generalized formula of this kind is very helpful in analyzing cases or predicting results. The contestant in Barnes v. Marshall attempts to make out a case of general incapacity rather than trying to show that the will results from a single "insane delusion" (see next case). The evidence is typical in that it describes all of the testator's idiosyncratic behavior and his deteriorating health. The subject of all this attention is by definition dead and unable to defend himself.

Many will contests alleging incapacity, undue influence, or fraud are brought in the hope of extracting a settlement from family members who wish to avoid disclosure of embarrassing or unsavory family secrets. Moreover, since in this country the estate generally bears the costs of defending a will contest, even if the claim lacks merit, it may be less costly for the executor to settle quickly than to defend the validity of the will in protracted litigation. See Langbein, Living Probate: The Conservatorship Model, 77 Mich. L. Rev. 63 (1978) (discussing reasons for volume of capacity litigation and noting that "the odor of the strike suit hangs heavily over this field"); Cahn, Undue Influence and Captation: A Comparative Study, 8 Tul. L. Rev. 507, 517 (1934) (characterizing will contests as "unrestricted fishing expeditions into the life, the inner thoughts and the intimate personal relations of the decedent" which impose heavy costs on decedents' estates).

2. *Threshold for testamentary capacity.* A testator need not possess superior or even average mental capacity to make a will. Even a "modest level of competence," described by one court as "the weakest class of sound minds," is sufficient. Estate of Rosen, 447 A.2d 1220, 1222 (Me.1982) (will valid despite evidence that testator was "ravaged by cancer and dulled by medication"). As one court observed:

> It is not necessary that a testator possess high quality or strength of mind, to make a valid will, nor that he then have as strong mind as he formerly had. The mind may be debilitated, the memory enfeebled, the understanding weak, the character may be peculiar and eccentric, and he may even want capacity to transact many of the business affairs of life; still it is sufficient if he understands the nature of the business in which he is engaged and when making a will, has a recollection of the property he means to dispose of, the object or objects of his bounty, and how he wishes to dispose of his property. [Milhoan v. Koenig, 469 S.E.2d 99 (W.Va. 1996), quoting Stewart v. Lyons, 47 S.E. 442 (W.Va. 1903).]

In making a case of total incapacity, no single factor—e.g., senility, mental disorder, substance abuse, etc.—is enough in the absence of evidence that the testator was under the influence of that condition at the time the will was executed. For example, a testator may suffer from chronic dementia or be a habitual drunkard and yet be capable of executing a will during a lucid interval. The focus is on the testator's state of mind at the time the will was executed. See Wilson v. Lane, 614 S.E.2d 88 (Ga. 2005) (testator afflicted with blindness, senile dementia, and irrational fear of floods and fires, but nevertheless had testamentary capacity); Estate of Dokken, 604 N.W.2d 487 (S.D. 2000) (testator suffered from dementia and schizophrenia but had testamentary capacity); Estate of Kietrys, 432 N.E.2d 930 (Ill.App.1982) (testator, who allegedly drank a quart of whiskey a day, was not intoxicated when he executed will).

The fact that a testator has been judged incapable of managing his or her affairs and has been placed under guardianship or conservatorship is relevant but not conclusive in assessing testamentary capacity. Thus, a testator may be capable of making a will even though a guardian or conservator has been appointed to administer his or her property. See Parish v. Parish, 704 S.E.2d 99 (Va. 2011); Will of Maynard, 307 S.E.2d 416 (N.C. App. 1983).

3. *Evidentiary factors.* Because the legal test of capacity is articulated in terms that are both broad and vague, the outcome in a particular case depends on the facts. One author offers a useful grouping of evidentiary facts into four categories: "(1) symptomatic conduct of the alleged incompetent; (2) opinion testimony of incompetency; (3) organic condition and habits of the alleged incompetent; (4) moral aspects of the transaction and its consequences." Green, Proof of Mental Incompetency and the Unexpressed Major Premise, 53 Yale L.J. 271 (1944). The weight given to the testimony of the witnesses on these points appears to vary with the witness's opportunity to observe and standing in the community.

a. *Attending physician.* A doctor has the best opportunity to observe the testator's "organic condition" and to speak with experience and authority about the testator's capabilities. The cases confirm that the party who has the medical testimony in support of his or her position has a distinct advantage. See Estate of O'Loughlin, 183 N.W.2d 133 (Wis.1971) (will of testator with severe Parkinson's disease upheld on testimony of two doctors); Estate of Bennight, 503 P.2d 203 (Okla.1972) (will invalid on attending physician's testimony, corroborated by nurse, as to testator's inability to remember and understand); but cf. Estate of Kuzma, 408 A.2d 1369 (Pa.1979) (will upheld despite testimony of two attending physicians that testator lacked capacity).

b. *Attorney.* Often the attorney who drafted the will is called as a witness. The attorney is often the best witness on the "moral aspects of the transaction" and can describe the extent to which the testator had independent advice, was free of outside influence, and made a "normal" disposition under the circumstances. See Blackmer v. Blackmer, 525 P.2d 559 (Mont.1974); Estate of Velk, 192 N.W.2d 844 (Wis.1972). The attorney who anticipates the problem may attempt to prepare the case for capacity while the testator is still alive. Of course, an attorney who tactlessly suggests that the client undergo a psychiatric examination before executing a will may lose a client. If the client is willing, however, a medical or psychiatric statement may be useful.

c. *Friends, neighbors, and business associates.* As the principal case illustrates, lay witnesses may be called to testify concerning the testator's "idiosyncratic behavior." The weight of such testimony depends in part on the proximity in time between the events observed by the witness and the execution of the will. See Estate of Berg, 783 N.W.2d 831 (S.D. 2010); Estate of Milligan, 280 N.E.2d 244 (Ill.App.1972). A trial court has been upheld in ruling that proof be limited to facts occurring within two years before or after the execution of the will. See Will of Hall, 113 S.E.2d 1 (N.C.1960). As noted in the principal case, a nonexpert witness who had an opportunity to observe the testator is usually permitted to express an opinion as to capacity, provided there is a sufficient factual foundation.

d. *Attesting witnesses.* The testimony of an attesting witness in support of the will is said to be entitled to great weight. See Estate of Whitteberry, 496 P.2d 240 (Or.App.1972). An attesting witness need not know the testator or have personal knowledge of the testator's mental capacity, but that fact tends to diminish the weight of the witness's testimony on the subject. See Estate of Camin, 323 N.W.2d 827 (Neb.1982). By contrast, the attesting witness who testifies against the will is an object of judicial scorn. See Estate of Wright, 60 P.2d 434 (Cal.1936) ("If it could be said that the testimony of the three persons who participated in the creation of the will and who by their solemn acts gave the stamp of approval and verity to its due execution, and afterwards attempted to repudiate all they had done, had any convincing force or any substantial factual basis, their testimony would nevertheless be subject to the scrutiny and suspicion which courts rightfully exercise in considering the testimony of persons who out of their own mouths admit their guilt of self-stultification."); Warren v. Sidney's Estate, 184 So. 806 (Miss. 1938) ("while the testimony of attesting witnesses denying or impeaching the execution of the will is to be considered and may be sufficient in some cases to prevent probate, it is, nevertheless, to be viewed with caution and suspicion and it is usually entitled to little credence"); Estate of Warren, 4 P.2d 635 (Or.1931) ("The law does not leave a will wholly at the mercy of subscribing witnesses."); but see Estate of Nigro, 52 Cal.Rptr. 128 (App.1966) (witnesses knew testator well and witnessed his will only reluctantly, "to quiet him down").

e. *Psychiatrist.* A distinction must be made between a psychiatrist who has treated the testator and one who has not observed the testator but is called as an expert witness to give an opinion in response to a hypothetical question. Although the opinion of the former might be expected to carry special weight, courts frequently emphasize the differences between the legal and psychiatric definitions of capacity and give no special weight to the psychiatrist's testimony. See Webster v. Larmore, 299 A.2d 814 (Md.1973); Estate of Wagner, 252 P.2d 789 (Ariz.1953) (will upheld on testimony of 22 lay witnesses that testator was competent, despite contrary opinions of two psychiatrists who examined testator). The psychiatric opinion of an expert witness who has not seen the testator is given little weight. See Dorsey v. Dorsey, 156 S.W.3d 442 (Mo. App. 2005).

4. *Terms of will.* Commentators frequently point out that disinheritance of worthy members of the testator's immediate family is the most decisive factor in persuading a court to invalidate a will on the ground of incapacity. See Green, Proof of Mental Incompetency and the Unexpressed Major Premise, 53 Yale L.J. 271 (1944); Note, Testamentary Capacity in a Nutshell: A Psychiatric Reevaluation, 18 Stan. L. Rev. 1119 (1966). Is it realistic to expect that a factfinder will determine the issue of capacity without regard to the terms of the will? The traditional test for capacity requires the testator to be able to identify the natural objects of his or her bounty. The inquiry focuses on "whether the testator has the capacity to know who these objects of his bounty are and to appreciate his relationship to them (i.e., they are my sons) and not whether in fact the testator appreciates his moral obligations and duties toward such heirs in accordance with some standard fixed by society, the courts or psychiatrists." Estate of Weil, 518 P.2d 995 (Ariz.App.1974).

The family does not always win. Upholding a will which disinherited a daughter in favor of a niece and two nephews, one court observed:

> Many a contestant's high hopes, destined to disappointment, spring from a carelessly bandied use of that phrase which refers to them as the "natural objects of the testator's bounty." Too many seem to garner therefrom a rule of law not present nor to be implied. It confers no inferential rights, nor indeed any rights, to take from one dying testate. It compels no duty upon the part of a testator to make any provision for those comprehended by its words. The phrase "natural objects of the testator's bounty" is no more, no less, than a euphemistic way of defining what can be more simply said and with equal meaning, i.e., "next of kin," [or] those who "would take in the absence of a will because they are the persons whom the law has so designated." Moreover, a will is not unnatural because it excludes one's next of kin in preference to those who may have enjoyed a closer and perhaps an affectionate relationship with the testator. [Estate of Hill, 256 P.2d 735, 738–39 (Or.1953).]

5. *Jury trial.* Although there is no constitutional right to trial by jury in a proceeding to probate or contest a will, some form of jury trial is now authorized by statute in most states. There is considerable variation among the statutes as to whether the verdict controls or is advisory only and as to the circumstances under which a jury may be claimed. One party or the other usually sees an advantage in having a jury. See Schoenblum, Will Contests— An Empirical Study, 22 Real Prop. Prob. & Tr. J. 607 (1987) (noting potential advantage to contestants).

The court's allocation of the burden of proof controls the order in which the facts are presented to the jury. The party with the burden has the obligation to go forward in presenting evidence, has the right to open and close the argument, and bears the risk of losing if the jury is not persuaded by a preponderance of the evidence. The cases are about equally split as to whether the burden is on the proponent or the contestant. One theory views capacity as an essential element of the proponent's case and places the risk of nonpersuasion on the proponent. The proponent is aided initially in going forward with the evidence by a presumption of capacity, but, if the contestant produces contrary evidence, the proponent must proceed to prove capacity unaided by the presumption. See Estate of Washburn, 690 A.2d 1024 (N.H.1997); Estate of Hastings, 387 A.2d 865 (Pa. 1978) (burden on proponent where testator executed will after adjudication of incompetency). The other theory holds that the contestant is the moving party and that the burden traditionally falls on the one who initiates the action. See Estate of Wagner, 551 N.W.2d 292 (N.D.1996). Under UPC § 3–407, the proponent has the burden of establishing proof of due execution, but the contestant has the burden of proving lack of testamentary intent or capacity, undue influence, fraud, duress, mistake, or revocation.

6. *Inter vivos gifts*. The threshold of capacity appears to be higher for making an inter vivos gift than for executing a will, perhaps on the theory that the former tends to have a more direct and immediate effect on the donor's welfare than the latter. The courts are divided on whether a person under guardianship or conservatorship, who lacks capacity to enter into contracts, may nevertheless have capacity to make inter vivos gifts. Compare Bryan v. Century Nat'l Bank of Broward, 498 So.2d 868 (Fla.1986) with Bye v. Mattingly, 975 S.W.2d 451 (Ky. 1998); Conservatorship of Spindle, 733 P.2d 388 (Okla.1986); see also Lee v. Lee, 337 So.2d 713 (Miss.1976) (testator had capacity to make will, but lacked contractual capacity to make conveyance of land on same day). See generally Green, The Operative Effect of Mental Incompetency on Agreements and Wills, 21 Tex. L. Rev. 554 (1943); Meicklejohn, Contractual and Donative Capacity, 39 Case W. Res. L. Rev. 307 (1989).

Should the capacity needed to create or modify a will substitute such as a revocable trust or a pay-on-death beneficiary designation be determined under the standard for inter vivos gifts or the more lenient standard for testamentary transfers? See Queen v. Belcher, 888 So.2d 472 (Ala. 2003) (creation of inter vivos trust); Estate of Marquis, 822 A.2d 1153 (Me. 2003) (change of annuity beneficiary); SunTrust Bank v. Harper, 551 S.E.2d 419 (Ga. App. 2001) (change of beneficiary on individual retirement account); see also Restatement (Third) of Property: Wills and Other Donative Transfers § 8.1 (2003).

7. *Professional responsibility*. As a matter of professional responsibility, an attorney should not prepare a will for a client if the attorney reasonably believes that the client lacks testamentary capacity. On the other hand, the attorney may properly draft a will for a client whose mental capacity appears to be borderline, and in such cases the attorney should take steps to preserve available evidence concerning the client's capacity. See American College of Trust & Estate Counsel, Commentaries on the Model Rules of Professional Conduct 132 (4th ed. 2006). If the client's mental capacity is doubtful, does the attorney have an ethical or legal duty to undertake an investigation be-

fore preparing the will? If the attorney goes ahead and supervises the execution of a will which ultimately fails on the ground of incapacity, should the beneficiary named in the will be able to sue the attorney for malpractice? See Boranian v. Clark, 20 Cal.Rptr.3d 405 (App. 2004).

IN RE HONIGMAN'S WILL

Court of Appeals of New York, 1960.
8 N.Y.2d 244, 168 N.E.2d 676.

DYE, JUDGE.

Frank Honigman died May 4, 1956, survived by his wife, Florence. By a purported last will and testament, executed April 3, 1956, just one month before his death, he gave $5,000 to each of three named grandnieces, and cut off his wife with a life use of her minimum statutory share plus $2,500, with direction to pay the principal upon her death to his surviving brothers and sisters and to the descendants of any predeceased brother or sister, per stirpes. The remaining one half of his estate was bequeathed in equal shares to his surviving brothers and sisters and to the descendants of any predeceased brother or sister, per stirpes, some of whom resided in Germany.

When the will was offered for probate in Surrogate's Court, Queens County, the widow Florence filed objections. A trial was had on framed issues, only one of which survived for determination by the jury, namely: "At the time of the execution of the paper offered for probate was the said Frank Honigman of sound and disposing mind and memory?" The jury answered in the negative, and the Surrogate then made a decree denying probate to the will.

Upon an appeal to the Appellate Division, Second Department, the Surrogate's decree was reversed upon the law and the facts, and probate was directed. Inconsistent findings of fact were reversed and new findings substituted.

We read this record as containing more than enough competent proof to warrant submitting to the jury the issue of decedent's testamentary capacity. By the same token the proof amply supports the jury findings, implicit in the verdict, that the testator, at the time he made his will, was suffering from an unwarranted and insane delusion that his wife was unfaithful to him, which condition affected the disposition made in the will. The record is replete with testimony, supplied by a large number of disinterested persons, that for quite some time before his death the testator had publicly and repeatedly told friends and strangers alike that he believed his wife was unfaithful, often using obscene and abusive language. Such manifestations of suspicion were quite unaccountable, coming as they did after nearly 40 years of a childless yet, to all outward appearances, a congenial and harmonious marriage, which had begun in 1916. During the intervening time they had worked together in the successful management, operation and ownership of various restaurants, bars and grills and, by their joint efforts of thrift and industry, had accumulated the substantial fortune now at stake.

The decedent and his wife retired from business in 1945 because of decedent's failing health. In the few years that followed he underwent a number of operations, including a prostatectomy in 1951, and an operation for cancer of the large bowel in 1954, when decedent was approximately 70 years of age.

From about this time, he began volubly to express his belief that Mrs. Honigman was unfaithful to him. This suspicion became an obsession with him, although all of the witnesses agreed that the deceased was normal and rational in other respects. Seemingly aware of his mental state, he once mentioned that he was "sick in the head" ("Mich krank gelassen in den Kopf"), and that "I know there is something wrong with me" in response to a light reference to his mental condition. In December, 1955 he went to Europe, a trip Mrs. Honigman learned of in a letter sent from Idlewild Airport after he had departed, and while there he visited a doctor. Upon his return he went to a psychiatrist who Mr. Honigman said "could not help" him. Finally, he went to a chiropractor with whom he was extremely satisfied.

On March 21, 1956, shortly after his return from Europe, Mr. Honigman instructed his attorney to prepare the will in question. He never again joined Mrs. Honigman in the marital home.

To offset and contradict this showing of irrational obsession the proponents adduced proof which, it is said, furnished a reasonable basis for decedent's belief, and which, when taken with other factors, made his testamentary disposition understandable. Briefly, this proof related to four incidents. One concerned an anniversary card sent by Mr. Krauss, a mutual acquaintance and friend of many years, bearing a printed message of congratulation in sweetly sentimental phraseology. Because it was addressed to the wife alone and not received on the anniversary date, Mr. Honigman viewed it as confirmatory of his suspicion. Then there was the reference to a letter which it is claimed contained prejudicial matter—but just what it was is not before us, because the letter was not produced in evidence and its contents were not established. There was also proof to show that whenever the house telephone rang Mrs. Honigman would answer it. From this Mr. Honigman drew added support for his suspicion that she was having an affair with Mr. Krauss. Mr. Honigman became so upset about it that for the last two years of their marriage he positively forbade her to answer the telephone. Another allegedly significant happening was an occasion when Mrs. Honigman asked the decedent as he was leaving the house what time she might expect him to return. This aroused his suspicion. He secreted himself at a vantage point in a nearby park and watched his home. He saw Mr. Krauss enter and, later, when he confronted his wife with knowledge of this incident, she allegedly asked him for a divorce. This incident was taken entirely from a statement made by Mr. Honigman to one of the witnesses. Mrs. Honigman flatly denied all of it. Their verdict shows that the jury evidently believed the objectant. Under the circumstances, we cannot say that this was wrong. The jury had the right to disregard the proponents' proof, or to go so far as to hold that such trivia afforded even additional grounds for decedent's irrational and unwarranted belief. The issue we must bear in mind is not whether Mrs. Honigman was unfaithful, but whether Mr. Honigman had any reasonable basis for believing that she was.

In a very early case we defined the applicable test as follows:

If a person persistently believes supposed facts, which have no real existence except in his perverted imagination, and against all evidence and probability, and conducts himself, however logically, upon the assumption of their existence, he is, so far as they are concerned, under a morbid delusion; and delusion in that sense is insanity. Such a person is essentially mad or insane on those subjects, though on other subjects he may reason, act and speak like a sensible man. (American Seamen's Friend Soc. v. Hopper, 33 N.Y. 619, 624–625.)

It is true that the burden of proving testamentary incapacity is a difficult one to carry (Dobie v. Armstrong, 160 N.Y. 584, 55 N.E. 302), but when an objectant has gone forward, as Mrs. Honigman surely has, with evidence reflecting the operation of the testator's mind, it is the proponents' duty to provide a basis for the alleged delusion. We cannot conclude that as a matter of law they have performed this duty successfully. When, in the light of all the circumstances surrounding a long and happy marriage such as this, the husband publicly and repeatedly expresses suspicions of his wife's unfaithfulness; of misbehaving herself in a most unseemly fashion, by hiding male callers in the cellar of her own home, in various closets, and under the bed; of hauling men from the street up to her second-story bedroom by use of bed sheets; of making contacts over the household telephone; and of passing a clandestine note through the fence on her brother's property—and when he claims to have heard noises which he believed to be men running about his home, but which he had not investigated, and which he could not verify—the courts should have no hesitation in placing the issue of sanity in the jury's hands. To hold to the contrary would be to take from the jury its traditional function of passing on the facts.

Clapp v. Fullerton, 34 N.Y. 190, is not controlling in the circumstances of this case. There, the decedent had not expressed his suspicion of the infidelity of his first wife, who had died 45 years earlier, until after the making of the will, and even then he did so casually and discreetly. His belief was based on a statement made by the wife during her last illness, while she was in a state of delirium. Here, on the other hand, Mr. Honigman persisted over a long period of time in telling his suspicions to anyone who would listen to him, friends and strangers alike. That such belief was an obsession with him was clearly established by a preponderance of concededly competent evidence and, prima facie, there was presented a question of fact as to whether it affected the will he made shortly before his death.

The proponents argue that, even if decedent was indeed laboring under a delusion, the existence of other reasons for the disposition he chose is enough to support the validity of the instrument as a will. The other reasons are, first, the size of Mrs. Honigman's independent fortune, and, second, the financial need of his residuary legatees. These reasons, as well as his belief in his wife's infidelity, decedent expressed to his own attorney. We dispelled a similar contention in American Seamen's Friend Soc. v. Hopper, supra, 33 N.Y. at page 625, where we held that a will was bad when its "dispository provisions were or *might have been* caused or affected by the delusion" (emphasis supplied). . . .

[The court discussed certain evidentiary rulings made by the Surrogate at trial, and concluded that errors in those rulings necessitated a new trial.]

The order appealed from should be reversed and a new trial granted, with costs to abide the event.

FULD, JUDGE (dissenting).

I am willing to assume that the proof demonstrates that the testator's belief that his wife was unfaithful was completely groundless and unjust. However, that is not enough; it does not follow from this fact that the testator suffered from such a delusion as to stamp him mentally defective or as lacking in capacity to make a will. See, e.g., Matter of Hargrove's Will, 288 N.Y. 604, 42 N.E.2d 608, affirming 262 App. Div. 202, 28 N.Y.S.2d 571; Dobie v. Armstrong, 160 N.Y. 584, 593–594, 55 N.E. 302, 304–305; Matter of White, 121 N.Y. 406, 414, 24 N.E. 935; Clapp v. Fullerton, 34 N.Y. 190, 197. "To sustain the allegation," this court wrote in the *Clapp* case, 34 N. Y. 190, 197,

it is not sufficient to show that his suspicion in this respect was not well founded. It is quite apparent, from the evidence, that his distrust of the fidelity of his wife was really groundless and unjust; but it does not follow that his doubts evince a condition of lunacy. The right of a testator to dispose of his estate, depends neither on the justice of his prejudices nor the soundness of his reasoning. He may do what he will with his own; and if there be no defect of testamentary capacity, and no undue influence or fraud, the law gives effect to his will, though its provisions are unreasonable and unjust.

As a matter of fact, in the case before us, a goodly portion of the widow's testimony bearing on her husband's alleged delusion should have been excluded, as the court itself notes. . . . And, of course, if such testimony had not been received in evidence, a number of items of proof upon which the widow relies would not have been available, with the consequence that the record would have contained even less basis for her claim of delusion.

Moreover, I share the Appellate Division's view that other and sound reasons, quite apart from the alleged [delusion], existed for the disposition made by the testator. Indeed, he himself had declared that his wife had enough money and he wanted to take care of his brothers and sisters living in Europe. See Matter of Nicholas, 216 App. Div. 399, 403, 215 N.Y.S. 292, 296, affirmed 244 N.Y. 531, 155 N.E. 885; Coit v. Patchen, 77 N.Y. 533, 541–542; Matter of White, 121 N.Y. 406, 414, 24 N.E. 935, 937, supra.

In short, the evidence adduced utterly failed to prove that the testator was suffering from an insane delusion or lacked testamentary capacity. The Appellate Division was eminently correct in concluding that there was no issue of fact for the jury's consideration and in directing the entry of a decree admitting the will to probate. Its order should be affirmed.

DESMOND, C.J., and FROESSEL and BURKE, JJ., concur with DYE, J.; FULD, J., dissents in an opinion in which VAN VOORHIS and FOSTER, JJ., concur.

Order reversed, etc.

NOTES

1. *Disposition of estate.* If Mrs. Honigman ultimately prevailed in contesting her husband's will, she would take an outright share of his estate by intestacy. Since Mr. Honigman left a surviving spouse and siblings but no descendants or parents, Mrs. Honigman's intestate share would be $5,000 plus half the residue of the estate, under New York law as it existed in 1956 (former Decedent Estate Law § 83). Under current law, she would be entitled to the entire estate. See N.Y. EPTL § 4–1.1. In a proceeding to contest a decedent's will, should the jury be made aware of how the estate will be distri-

buted if the contestant prevails? How might such information affect the verdict in a case like *Honigman*?

2. *Insane delusions.* Certain types of delusion recur: spouse's infidelity, see, in addition to the principal case, Benjamin v. Woodring, 303 A.2d 779 (Md.1973) (sufficient evidence of delusion to go to jury); belief that testator was not the father of one or more of his wife's children, see Estate of Flaherty, 446 N.W.2d 760 (N.D.1989) (will invalid); belief that testator was married and father of a child, see Estate of Rask, 214 N.W.2d 525 (N.D.1974) (will invalid); fear that a person intends to kill or do bodily harm to testator, see Rizzo v. D'Ambrosio, 310 N.E.2d 925 (Mass.App.1974) (testator believed niece was poisoning him; will invalid); Huffman v. Dawkins, 622 S.W.2d 159 (Ark.1981) (testator believed wife intended to kill him; sufficient factual basis to defeat contestants' claim). More exotic beliefs also arise. See Estate of Killen, 937 P.2d 1368 (Ariz.App.1996) (testator believed her niece and nephews "lived in her attic . . . and sprinkled chemicals and parasites down on her, put her to sleep and then pulled a tooth out and cut her arms and hands with glass, were in the Mafia, and were trying to kill her"); Powell v. Thigpen, 199 S.E.2d 251 (Ga.1973) (delusion that sister "cast a spell" on testator raised issue sufficient to go to jury).

3. *Causation.* In contesting a will on the ground of insane delusion, it is not enough to show that the testator suffered from a delusion; the contestant must also demonstrate a causal connection between the delusion and the disposition made by the will. See Pendarvis v. Gibb, 159 N.E. 353 (Ill. 1927) (testator believed people butchered his oxen and hung them in trees on his farm, but delusion did not affect execution of will); Estate of Marquis, 822 A.2d 1153 (Me. 2003) (decedent believed someone spoke to her through the television, saw visions of her dead brother, feared non-existent Quakers would invade her home at night, and believed she was going to marry Jesus; none of these delusions affected designation of annuity beneficiary, which nevertheless failed because decedent lacked general contractual capacity). In the principal case, the majority finds ample evidence to support a finding that Mr. Honigman's delusion about his wife "affected the disposition made in the will." Is it sufficient for the contestant to show that the provisions of the will "were or might have been caused or affected by the delusion," or should the will be upheld if the testator had "other and sound reasons" apart from the delusion for the challenged disposition? See Estate of Watlack, 945 P.2d 1154 (Wash. App. 1997) (denying probate where testator's insane delusion was "controlling reason" for disinheriting daughter).

4. *Delusion or mistake.* Not every false belief amounts to an insane delusion. Courts often distinguish mistakes of fact from insane delusions on the ground that the former have some basis in fact while the latter do not. See Boney v. Boney, 462 S.E.2d 725 (Ga.1995) (upholding will against challenge by disinherited son, where testator had some factual basis for believing that son had insulted testator's wife; an "erroneous conclusion based upon an illogical deduction drawn from facts as they really exist" does not amount to an

insane delusion); Estate of Raney, 799 P.2d 986 (Kan.1990) (testator had factual basis for believing that his children established conservatorship to preserve his property for themselves). Sometimes it is said that a mistake of fact is susceptible of correction through argument, reason, or proof, while an insane delusion is not. See 1 Page § 12.34 ("A belief that food was poisoned is not an insane delusion if the testator would eat it after other persons had first partaken thereof."). Does this mean that a party alleging insane delusion must show that attempts were made without success to correct the testator's false belief? How else can it be proved that the testator was "incapable of being reasoned out of his false belief"? See Dixon v. Webster, 551 S.W.2d 888 (Mo.App.1977) (reversing finding of insane delusion where no one attempted to dissuade testator from her belief).

DOUGHERTY V. RUBENSTEIN

Court of Special Appeals of Maryland, 2007.
172 Md. App. 269, 914 A.2d 184.

EYLER, J.

The "insane delusion rule" of testamentary capacity came into being almost 200 years ago, as the invention of British jurists in Dew v. Clark, 162 Eng. Rep. 410 (Prerog. 1826). The rule was devised to cover a gap in the existing law, which held that "idiots and persons of non-sane memory" could not make wills, see 34 & 35 Hen. 7, ch. 5 (1534), but accepted as valid the will of a testator "who knew the natural objects of his or her bounty, the nature and extent of his or her property, and could make a 'rational' plan for disposition, but who nonetheless was as crazy as a March hare[.]" Eunice L. Ross & Thomas J. Reed, Will Contests § 6:11 (2d. ed. 1999).

In the Dew case, a father insisted that his grown daughter, who by all accounts was a well-behaved, sweet, and docile person, was the devil incarnate. The father's wife had died in childbirth, and so as a young child the daughter was raised for the most part away from the father, by nannies and in boarding schools. The father's peculiar thinking about her first manifested itself when, in response to a letter reporting that the child was suffering "chilblains" that were "gross," the father went on a tirade, sending letter after letter insisting that the child was "gross" in every way.[1]

By the time his daughter was 8 or 9 years old, the father spoke of her only as wicked, having vices not possible of a girl that young, depraved in spirit, vile, of unequaled depravity, deceitful, and violent in temper. He told others that she was a child of the devil and a "special property of Sa-

---

[1] Chilblains are inflammatory sores on the hands or feet that can develop from contact with water in cold weather.

tan." Id. at 426. When the child came to live with him, he treated her as a servant and physically tortured her.

In 1818, the father made a will that disinherited his daughter. Three years later, he was the subject of a writ "de lunatico inquirendo" and was declared by a court of chancery to be of unsound mind. He died later that year.

In a caveat proceeding by the daughter, the evidence showed that the daughter was known by all for her good disposition and that the father had boasted to others that he lavished his daughter with love and material items, when the exact opposite was true. The probate court found that, although in 1818, when the will was made, the father's behavior was usual in all respects, except toward his daughter, his warped thinking about her was a delusion that "did and could only proceed from, and be founded in, insanity." Dew, supra, 162 Eng. Rep. at 430. The court further found that the father's "partial insanity" or "monomania"—insanity about a particular subject—about the evil nature of his daughter had caused him to disinherit her. On that basis, the court held that the father had been without testamentary capacity when he made his will, and set the will aside.

Within a few years of the decision in Dew v. Clark, the insane delusion rule made its way into will contest cases in the United States, first appearing in the Maryland law of estates and trusts in Townshend v. Townshend, 7 Gill. 10 (1848).[2] . . .

In the case before us, James J. Dougherty, IV ("Jay"), the appellant, invoked the insane delusion rule before the Circuit Court for Harford County, sitting as the Orphans' Court, in an effort to set aside the June 9, 1998 Will of his father, James J. Dougherty, III ("James"), the decedent, which disinherited him. Jay is James's only child. According to Jay, James's Will was the product of an insane delusion that Jay had stolen his money. The Will named James's sister, Janet C. Rubenstein, the appellee, personal representative ("PR") of James's estate and bequeathed virtually all of James's assets to Rubenstein and his two other sisters, Elizabeth J. Hippchen and Dorothy D. Schisler. The estate was comprised mainly of James's house, valued at about $200,000.

---

[2] The *Townshend* case is a startling example of the changes in American society and law in the past 200 years. There, a testator slave-owner made a will in which he freed his slaves and bequeathed all of his property to them. When he died, his relatives brought a caveat proceeding, seeking to have the will set aside. The evidence disclosed, prophetically, that the testator had claimed to have spoken "face to face" with God, who directed him how to dispose of his property "for the safety of his soul." See Townshend, supra, 7 Gill. at 15. The relatives argued that the testator was laboring under an insane delusion that God wanted him to free his slaves and give them his property, and that that delusion produced the will. A jury in the caveat proceeding found in favor of the caveators. The Court of Appeals reversed on evidentiary issues and remanded the matter for further proceedings.

James died on October 29, 2004, at age 59, of congestive heart failure. On December 10, 2004, Jay filed a petition for judicial probate in the Circuit Court for Harford County, sitting as the Orphans' Court, asking that he be named PR of the Estate, in place of Rubenstein, and that the Will not be admitted into probate. He filed a list of interested persons that included his three paternal aunts. On December 14, 2004, Rubenstein delivered a copy of James's Will to the Register of Wills.

On February 17, September 29, and September 30, 2005, the orphans' court held an evidentiary hearing on the issue of whether James had had the requisite testamentary capacity to make his Will. Three witnesses, including Rubenstein, testified so as to establish the existence of the Will. Jay then went forward with his evidence challenging the Will; he testified and called six witnesses. In rebuttal, Rubenstein testified and called six rebuttal witnesses.

The evidence, viewed in a light most favorable to the verdict, showed the following. James and Jay had a rocky father-son relationship over the years. When Jay was a teenager, James divorced Jay's mother. That led to a four-year estrangement between the two, beginning in 1986, when Jay was 18 years old. In 1990, at the urging of a friend, Jay reinitiated contact with his father. The two were close for the next seven years. During that time, Jay talked to James by telephone daily and visited him regularly.

On October 26, 1990, James executed a Last Will and Testament that appointed Rubenstein as PR and left his estate to Jay.

Throughout the 1990's, James's health deteriorated due, in large part, to alcohol abuse.[3] On several occasions, he experienced breathing difficulties that necessitated a trip to the emergency room. Eventually, he developed a dependency on certain prescription narcotics. At one time, he was admitted to an in-patient substance abuse program, but left before completing it.

On March 20, 1996, James executed a Power of Attorney appointing Jay as his attorney-in-fact. . . .

The chain of events most immediately relevant to the issue on appeal began on December 9, 1997, when James suffered a minor stroke and was admitted to Fallston General Hospital. He was diagnosed with congestive heart failure and dilated cardiomyopathy (an enlarged heart caused by alcohol abuse). During the hospitalization, James often was disoriented and confused and had trouble expressing himself and understanding

---

[3] There was testimony that James was in the habit of drinking one to two bottles of gin a day.

what was being said to him. He was rarely oriented to where he was or what day or time it was.

On December 18, 1997, the doctors at Fallston General transferred James to Harford Memorial Hospital's psychiatric unit for evaluation. James's confused state of mind and inability to communicate persisted during his stay at Harford Memorial. His speech was garbled. He was observed to be prone to confabulation and paranoia.

Linda Freilich, M.D., an internist, was in charge of James's medical care during his Harford Memorial admission. She diagnosed him with dementia. Dr. Freilich and a second doctor, Lakshmi P. Baddela, M.D., executed "Physician's Certificate of Disability" affidavits, attesting that James was suffering from dementia, that the condition was "lifelong" or "permanent," and that:

> [D]ue to the present condition of dementia, he is without sufficient capacity to consent to the appointment of a guardian of his person and property and affairs or to consent to the care and confinement of his person or the management of his property and affairs[.]

Dr. Freilich recommended that James be placed in a nursing home. Jay and his wife Christy decided instead to place him in the Cantler's Personal Care Home ("Cantler Home"), which the doctors referred to as a boarding home. James adamantly objected, insisting that he be returned to his own house to live.

On January 5, 1998, James was discharged from Harford Memorial and was transported to the Cantler Home. There, he was assigned a small private bedroom with access to a common area and to a bathroom that he shared with three other residents. The other residents of the Cantler Home were considerably older than James, who was 52.

By all accounts, James was miserable at the Cantler Home. He complained incessantly to his sisters, his mother, his friends, and Jay and Christy about being there. He told his sisters that he did not have access to the telephone because it was located in a locked area of the home. When Richard Hodges, an old friend, visited James at the Cantler Home, the first thing James said was that he wanted help to "get out." James told him that the owners of the home kept the residents locked downstairs, even for meals. James said he had asked Jay and Christy to "get me out of here," but they would not, because they wanted "to keep me here."

James's sisters and his mother visited him at the Cantler Home and were disturbed by the conditions they saw. James was in a small area sitting on a hard chair. The first thing he said when they walked in was,

"Get me out of here before I go crazy like the rest of them." One of the sisters sat on a chair not realizing it was covered with urine from another boarder.

Every other day, Jay tried to visit James at the Cantler Home. James "wanted nothing to do with [him]," however, because James was angry that Jay had placed him in the home instead of letting him move back to his own house. About a week after James moved into the Cantler Home, Jay and Christy left for an annual five-day ski trip with Christy's family. While they were away, Rubenstein removed James from the Cantler Home and returned him to his house.

When Jay and Christy returned from their trip, they learned that James was back at home. They went to see him. Jay had started handling his father's financial affairs when James was admitted to the hospital, and therefore was in possession of all of James's financial records. Jay and Christy brought the financial records with them because James "needed to take [them] back over." James lashed out at Jay, accusing him of stealing his money and saying that, to James, Jay "didn't exist." Jay tried to show James the financial records, to prove that nothing had been stolen, but James would not look at the records or listen to what Jay had to say.

Over the next few weeks, Jay tried to reason with James, but James ignored him. He insisted that Jay had stolen money from him. James told Jay, "As far as I'm concerned, you are dead." That was the last time the two saw each other.

On January 23, 1998, James executed a new Power of Attorney appointing Rubenstein as his attorney-in-fact. A week later, James came under the care of Richard DeSantis, M.D., for whom Rubenstein was working as a secretary. Dr. DeSantis is an internist and endocrinologist. For the next two years, Dr. DeSantis treated James's heart condition. According to Dr. DeSantis, James did not exhibit any symptoms of dementia aside from some minor speech difficulties, which could have been caused by his stroke.

In late spring of 1998, James met with Ed Seibert, a lawyer and long-time friend, and asked him to draft a new will for him. There was no evidence that anyone encouraged or urged James to see a lawyer or assisted him in doing so. James went to Seibert's office by himself.

Seibert testified that, when he and James met, James's demeanor was "just as lucid as you and I." He described his conversation with James as follows:

It seemed to be perfectly normal up to a point. The point I am talking about has to do with the antipathy he generated or seemed to be suffering toward his son.

I told him, Look—he didn't want any part of his son in the Will. At that time I said, [']Look, [James], you should consider this twice. Don't leave him out. Leave him something. Put his name in it. Do something. You can't, because he is your only heir, really.[']

So I did admonish him about that, but he was bound and determined to leave [Jay] out altogether. . . . I wanted to know why, and all he told me was that his son had cleaned out his bank account.

I know nothing about how that was done. I am just saying what he told me. [Jay] also had placed him somewhere where he was virtually in a prison and he couldn't get out, and it was a terrible thing for him, and it affected him badly. So he didn't want [Jay] remotely mentioned, or even indirectly referred to in that Will. So I did what he asked me to do.

On June 9, 1998, James returned to Seibert's office to execute his new Will. Seibert's daughter, Heather, and his daughter-in-law, Susanne Reising, signed as witnesses. Both described James's demeanor that day as normal. According to Seibert, from what he saw, there was no reason to think that James was not competent to make his Will or that anyone had exerted undue influence over him to get him to change his Will.

From 1998 until his death in 2004, James lived alone. There was much conflicting testimony about his mental state during those years. The sisters, a nephew, and several family friends testified that James's mental state improved dramatically once he left the Cantler Home and that, from then on, he essentially cared for himself. Two family friends and Jay's stepfather testified that James was not the same person he had been before the late 1997 hospitalizations, and that he required considerable outside assistance in his daily activities. The evidence showed that, during this time period, James drove a car, wrote his own checks, and dressed and groomed himself. Several witnesses testified that James devoted time to his favorite hobby of flying model airplanes.

James complained to almost all of his friends and family members that Jay had stolen his money. Fred Visnaw, the son of a close friend of James, witnessed many conversations between his own father and James about James's belief that Jay had stolen money from him. On three occasions, Visnaw's father tried to reason with James about these thoughts, but James's mind was made up. On one occasion, Visnaw himself tried to intervene with James on Jay's behalf, to no avail.

Another of James's friends, Hodges, testified that James told him he was going to "cut [Jay] out" because Jay had stolen from him. Two of James's sisters, Rubenstein and Schisler, also testified that they were aware that James thought that Jay had stolen money from him. The parties stipulated, however, that there was absolutely no evidence that Jay had ever actually stolen any money from James.

James also continued to complain to many of his friends and family members that Jay had put him in the Cantler Home against his wishes. He described the Cantler Home as a prison. He believed that Jay had sent him there to live permanently.

James died on October 29, 2004, never having reconciled with his son. Jay was not notified of his father's death. There was no obituary published. Jay learned of his father's death through a friend, in early December of 2004.

[The orphans' court held that when James executed the will on June 9, 1998, he was "lucid" and "coherent" and "understood the extent of his assets and the object of his bounty." On the issue of insane delusion, the court found that James's false belief that Jay stole from him "caused [James] to make a new Will disinheriting Jay, and [he] was also prompted by the fact that he was angry with his son for putting him in the Cantler home, and that was not a false belief." The court rejected Dr. Freilich's opinion that James was suffering from permanent and progressive dementia, finding that diagnosis inconsistent with James's ability to take care of himself for the last six years of his life. Believing that James's false belief was in all likelihood the product of "a rigid personality and a stubborn mind" rather than "a mental disease," the court concluded: "I think [James] made up his mind his son had done something wrong, and he just never was going to change his mind about that. But I don't find that the evidence before me establishes that that delusion or incorrect belief was the product of a mental disease, so I will admit the Will of June 9, 1998, to probate."]

DISCUSSION

The sole issue for decision in this appeal is whether the trial judge erred in concluding that the Will was not the product of an insane delusion on the part of the testator.

Jay argues that the court committed legal error by requiring proof not only that James was suffering from an insane delusion that produced the Will, but also that the delusion was caused by a mental illness. He further argues that the evidence adduced at trial compelled a factual finding that, when James made his Will on June 9, 1998, he was experiencing an insane delusion that he (Jay) had stolen his money; and that the Will was a product of that insane delusion. That being so, the court was obligated to set the Will aside.

Rubenstein counters that the orphans' court properly rejected Dr. Freilich's opinion that James had been suffering from dementia; and the evidence supported the judge's finding that, on June 9, 1998, James was competent to execute the Will. Alternatively, Rubenstein asserts that, even if the orphans' court erred in finding that James's mistaken belief was *not* an insane delusion, that error was harmless, because the court also found that James's decision to disinherit Jay was based in part upon a true belief: that Jay had placed him in the Cantler Home against his wishes.

We review the factual findings of the orphans' court for clear error. . . . Its legal conclusions, however, are reviewed de novo. "The standard, or test of testamentary capacity is a matter of law" while the question of "whether the evidence in the case measures up to that standard is . . . a matter of fact[.]"Johnson v. Johnson, 105 Md. 81, 85, 65 A. 918 (1907).

"A will, although facially valid, cannot stand unless the testator was legally competent." Wall v. Heller, 61 Md. App. 314, 326, 486 A.2d 764 (1985); see also Md. Code (2001 Repl. Vol.), § 4–101 of the Estates and Trusts Article ("ET") (stating "[a]ny person may make a will if he is 18 years of age or older, and legally competent to make a will").

The law presumes that every person is sane and has the mental capacity to make a valid will. Wall, supra, 61 Md. App. at 327; see also Sykes, Contest of Wills, § 63 (1941) . . . . To rebut that presumption, one challenging a will for lack of testamentary capacity must prove either that the testator was suffering from a permanent insanity before he made his will, and therefore would have been insane when he made the will; or, although not permanently insane, he was of unsound mind when he made the will. Wall, supra, 61 Md. App. at 326–27, 486 A.2d 764 . . . . The latter inquiry is to be decided from an assessment of the testator's external acts and appearances at that time:

> It must appear that at the time of making the will, [the testator] had a full understanding of the nature of the business in which he was engaged; a recollection of the property which he intended to dispose and the persons to whom he meant to give it, and the relative claims of the different persons who were or should have been the objects of his bounty. [Ritter v. Ritter, 114 Md. App. 99, 105, 689 A.2d 101 (1997) (quoting Sykes, supra, at § 61).]

A testator's "insane delusion," also called "monomania," is in the law a type of unsoundness of mind that will invalidate his will, for lack of capacity, if the delusion produced the disposition made in the will. The testator's delusion must have been *insane* and his will must have been a consequence of the insane delusion, however. Benjamin v. Woodring, 268 Md. 593, 601, 303 A.2d 779 (1973). . . .

The Court of Appeals has said that an "insane delusion" is "a belief in things impossible, or a belief in things possible, but so improbable under the surrounding circumstances, that no man of sound mind could give them credence." Johnson, supra, 105 Md. at 85–86, 65 A. 918. It also has defined the term to mean "a false belief for which there is no reasonable foundation . . . concerning which [the testator's] mind is not open to permanent correction through argument or evidence." Doyle v. Rody, 180 Md. 471, 479, 25 A.2d 457 (1942). Eccentricity, peculiar beliefs (such as in spiritualism or healing powers), and hostility or aversion to one relative or another are not, standing alone, insane delusions. See Brown v. Ward, 53 Md. 376 (1880) (testatrix who spoke to spirits, believed they could heal diseases, did not believe in the Bible, and despised some of her relatives was not suffering from an insane delusion when she made her will).

"Insane delusion" or "monomania" insanity is not a general defect of the mind. It is an insanity directed to something specific, that is, a particular person or thing. A testator can be laboring under the influence of an insane delusion while otherwise acting and appearing competent. Benjamin, supra, 268 Md. at 601, 303 A.2d 779 (quoting Doyle, supra, 180 Md. at 477–78, 25 A.2d 457) ("It is settled law in this State '. . . that when a [will] is the direct consequence . . . of the testator's delusion . . . the court should hold that he did not possess testamentary capacity, although he may have been rational and sane on other subjects.' "); Doyle, supra, 180 Md. at 478, 25 A.2d 457 (quoting Banks v. Goodfellow, 5 L.R.Q.B. 549, 560 (1870)) ("there often are . . . delusions, which, though the offspring of mental disease and so far constituting insanity, yet leave the individual in all other respects rational, and capable of transacting the ordinary affairs and fulfilling the duties and obligations incidental to the various relations of life"); Johnson, supra, 105 Md. at 86–90, 65 A. 918 (approving the trial court's instruction that the decedent could have been suffering from an insane delusion despite the jury finding that he "conducted his ordinary business with shrewdness and apparent discretion, and did not make any exhibition of insanity to many persons"). . . .

In Johnson v. Johnson, 105 Md. 81, 65 A. 918 (1907), the evidence showed that the testator and his wife married in 1898, and then had two children. The testator already had four children from a prior marriage. Until the wife's second pregnancy, the couple and their child lived happily and the testator showed pride in his family and fondness for them. Suddenly, and for no apparent reason, the husband started abusing the wife and accusing her of being unfaithful. He insisted that their child and the unborn baby were not his. After the second child was born, he denied paternity of both children and treated his wife and the children with such harshness, hostility, and aversion that the wife was forced to leave the home. The evidence showed that there was no rational basis whatsoever for the testator's obsessive belief about his wife and children.

In late 1904, the testator made a will that left nothing to his wife and two youngest children; his entire estate was bequeathed to his four oldest children from his first marriage. The testator died eight months later, in August 1905. The wife challenged the will on the ground that the testator was laboring under the insane delusion that his two youngest children had been fathered by someone else. The parties agreed that the will was the product of this false belief. Their dispute centered upon whether the false belief was an insane delusion.

The Court held that a testator's hostility or aversion toward a particular close family member (or members) is not alone sufficient to prove insanity; however, such an aversion that is without cause and is founded upon a delusion may be. Johnson, supra, 105 Md. at 88, 65 A. 918 (quoting Brown, supra, 53 Md. at 387–88). In deciding that the evidence supported a finding that the testator's delusion was insane, the Court relied upon Bell v. Lee, 28 Grant, Ch. R.U.C. 50 (1883), in which the Chancery Court of Upper Canada held that "a fixed and unalterable conviction on the part of the testator that his child was illegitimate was evidence of an insane delusion, when it appeared that there was not a scintilla of evidence to support such a belief." 105 Md. at 88, 65 A. 918. . . .[4]

Doyle v. Rody, 180 Md. 471, 25 A.2d 457 (1942), concerned a trust bank account established by a grantor shortly before his death. The grantor had a wife, a brother, and nephews and nieces. He had been separated from his wife for two years, during which he lived in a boarding house. In late 1939, at the age of 68, he was briefly hospitalized and was diagnosed with senility and hardening of the arteries. Two days after being discharged from the hospital, he went to Westminster to visit his brother.

A few days later, the grantor walked into a police station in Baltimore City, in a dazed and confused state, claiming that he had been robbed. He was carrying with him some medicines, $26.47 in cash, a

---

[4] In *Bell*, the court, quoting Sir James Hannen in Boughton v. Knight, L.R. 3 Prob. & Div., 64, explained:

It is unfortunately not a thing unknown to parents, and in justice to women I am bound to say that it is more frequently the case with fathers than mothers, that they take unduly harsh views of the character of their children, some especially. That is not unknown. But there is a limit, beyond which one feels that it ceases to be a question of harsh, unreasonable judgment and character, and that the repulsion which a parent exhibits towards one or more of his children must proceed from some mental defect in himself. It is so contrary to the whole current of human nature that a man should not only form a harsh judgment of his children, but that he should put that into practice so as to do them injury, or deprive them of advantages which most men desire above all things to confer upon their children. I say there is a point at which such repulsion and aversion are in themselves evidence of unsoundness in mind.—EDS.

bankbook showing an account with a balance of $11,000, and a piece of paper bearing his niece's address. The police contacted the niece, who with her husband retrieved the grantor from the station house and kept him at their house for the night, giving him food and drink.

The next day, the niece helped the grantor get organized and took him to his boarding house, where he wanted to be. When they arrived, he became insistent that his clothes had been taken away, when they had not. The niece called a doctor for assistance, but before help arrived the grantor ran away. He managed to return to his brother's house in Westminster. There, he insisted that his niece and her husband had "ganged up against [him]" and had held him at their house against his will. Doyle, supra, 180 Md. at 474, 25 A.2d 457. He became obsessed with the thought that his niece and her husband had conspired to injure him and to rob him of his money. There was no basis in fact for this belief; on the contrary, the niece had treated the grantor kindly.

The brother in Westminster took the grantor to the bank and had him transfer his $11,000 into a new trust account, in both of their names, the balance to be paid at the death of either to the survivor. About a month later, the grantor died. The administrator of his estate brought suit, seeking a declaration that the trust account funds belonged to the estate and not to the brother. The chancellor found upon the evidence that, when the grantor established the trust account, he was operating under the insane delusion that his niece had stolen money from him; and the trust account benefitting the brother upon the grantor's death was the product of that delusion.

The Court of Appeals affirmed the decree, remarking:

> Th[is] case falls within the definition of an insane delusion: a false belief, for which there is no reasonable foundation, and which would be incredible under similar circumstances to the same person if he were of sound mind, and concerning which his mind is not open to permanent correction through argument or evidence. [Id. at 479, 25 A.2d 457.]

The Court observed that the grantor's false belief that he had been robbed, which prompted his visit to the police station, became misdirected, for no reason, toward his niece and her husband, the only family members who actually had helped him. The Court drew a distinction between "eccentricities or peculiarities of behavior[,]" which are not sufficient in and of themselves "to constitute mental incapacity[,]" and a "delusion, which was calculated to pervert [a testator's] judgment and control his will in respect to the disposition of his estate." Id. at 477–78, 25 A.2d 457. When the latter is the case, "the court should hold that [the testator] did not possess testamentary capacity, although he may have been rational and sane on other subjects. . . . It has been specifically held by this court that violent dislike for one's near relatives, when founded upon an insane delusion, may be proof of his insanity." Id. at 478, 25 A.2d 457.

In the most recent Maryland case addressing the insane delusion rule, the Court of Appeals reversed a "directed verdict" granted in favor of the caveatee in a will contest case. The Court held that the evidence adduced by the caveator at trial had been legally sufficient to make it a question of fact whether the testator was under the influence of an insane delusion when he made a will disinheriting his wife. In Benjamin v. Woodring, 268 Md. 593, 303 A.2d 779 (1973), the testator made his will about a month before he died from an overdose of prescription medication. In a handwritten note penned about five weeks before he died, the testator ranted about his wife's infidelity during and before their marriage and said that he would leave her nothing after his death, as punishment.

The testator never spoke of this with his wife directly. Instead, his manner toward her suddenly changed; he became withdrawn during the six months prior to his death. There also was evidence that the testator confided in a friend his belief that his wife had been unfaithful. The friend testified that he tried to persuade the testator that there was no truth to his belief, to no avail. There was no evidence whatsoever that the testator's wife ever had been unfaithful to him. The testator's false belief in his wife's infidelity was a preoccupation that seemed to have entered the testator's mind out of the blue, with no basis in fact.

The Court held that the testator's letter, the friend's testimony, and the evidence that there was no truth to the testator's belief about his wife constituted legally sufficient evidence to support a finding that the testator was laboring under an insane delusion that resulted in the disposition in his will; therefore, the issue of testamentary capacity should have been submitted to the trier of fact for decision.

The insane delusions in these three cases share common features. All were negative false beliefs about the character of a particular close relative of the testator that were not connected to any reality or true experience, existing only in the testator's (or grantor's) mind. Even an illogical thought process or generalization could not link the negative false belief to some true fact about the subject of the delusion. Not only was there no evidence in any of the cases that the subject of the delusion had done whatever it was the testator was convinced he or she had done; there also was no evidence that the subject of the delusion had done *anything* negative toward the testator (or any one else) that could account, even irrationally, for the testator's wrath. The delusions did not suggest mistake, unreasonableness, confusion, stubbornness, poor judgment, denial, or willfulness; they only could be explained by a deranged mind.

Mindful of the above, we return to the case at bar. Jay's first argument is strictly legal. He maintains that the trial court erred by adding an element to the insane delusion rule and then basing its finding that there was not an insane delusion upon the absence of proof of that element. Specifically, he complains that the trial court not only required proof that James's delusion was insane and that it resulted in the disinheritance, but also that the delusion was caused by a mental disease. He argues that the controlling cases hold that proof that the testator was suffering from an insane delusion gives rise to a reasonable inference that he was mentally ill; and therefore the existence of a mental disease need not be separately proven. . . .

We do not read the trial judge's references, in his ruling, to a "mental disease" as injecting an additional element of proof into the insane delusion rule. The judge framed the question before him as whether James's "false belief" that Jay had stolen from him was "the product of a mental disease[,]" and ultimately found that the evidence did not show that James's "delusion or incorrect belief was the product of a mental disease[.]" It is clear that the judge was using "mental disease" and "insanity" interchangeably, and that his references showed his understanding that it is not sufficient that the testator have held a false belief or a delusion; it also is necessary that the false belief or delusion was insane, i.e., the product of a mental disease. Indeed, in one state in which the courts have continued to use the somewhat antiquated medical label "monomania" to mean an insane delusion, the supreme court observed: "Monomania is *a mental disease* which leaves the sufferer sane generally but insane on a particular subject or class of subjects." Boney v. Boney, 265 Ga. 839, 839, 462 S.E.2d 725 (1995) (emphasis supplied). The court in the case at bar did not add an element to the insane delusion rule, and therefore did not commit legal error.

Jay next argues that the application of the insane delusion rule to the evidence adduced at trial compelled a finding that James disinherited him due to an insane delusion that Jay had stolen his money. Jay points out that there was no evidence that he had stolen James's money (or that any of James's money had been stolen), as the parties stipulated, and therefore James's belief plainly was false; that no amount of reasoning could get James to change his mind about his false belief, and James's mind was not open to being changed, even by records that would have shown conclusively that no money was missing; that the false belief arose soon after a hospitalization during which James was unable to understand what was being said to him or to communicate and was disoriented; that while James's functional abilities improved over time, after he was discharged from the Cantler Home, he could not overcome the false belief that Jay had stolen his money; and all of the evidence, and especially that of Mr. Siebert, a disinterested person, showed that James left nothing to

Jay in his Will because he was convinced that Jay already had all of his money.

Beginning with the last point, we note that the orphans' court indeed found that James's false belief that Jay had stolen from him had caused James to disinherit Jay. The court observed that James also was angry with Jay for moving him into the Cantler Home but that "that was not a false belief"; and that, if the false belief (about stealing money) was an insane delusion "then it's going to invalidate the Will. If it is not, then the Will stands, given the other findings I made." So, the court in fact found, as Jay argues it was compelled to find, that the delusion about his having stolen money prompted James to disinherit him.

We disagree, however, that the law of insane delusions compelled a finding by the orphans' court that James's delusion that Jay stole his money was an *insane* delusion. To be sure, James's delusion shared many of the characteristics of the insane delusions in the *Johnson*, *Doyle*, and *Benjamin* cases. James and Jay were close relatives, and Jay would be expected to have been the object of James's bounty. James came suddenly to believe that Jay had harmed him by stealing his money, when there was no evidence to support that belief, and he refused to hear the evidence that would refute it. James's false belief did not subside, but became central to his thinking about Jay, causing hostility and aversion.

This case is factually distinguishable from the three cases discussed at length above, however. In those cases, there simply was no explanation, whether or not rational, for the testator's sudden false belief, and therefore the delusion only could have come from within the testator's own mind. In this case, the delusion entered James's mind when he was a resident, not by choice, of the Cantler Home, which for him was a terrible experience that he blamed completely upon Jay. As James saw it, he was confined to a home similar to a nursing home, without privacy or access to a telephone, in the company of residents who were enfeebled by old age, and with no hope of being let out. The witnesses who testified about having visited James in the Cantler Home confirmed that the accommodations were insufficient for him and that he felt like he had been imprisoned—and that he was of the view that Jay had failed him by forcing him in and by not coming to his aid to get out.

From the time he arrived at the Cantler Home forward, James was convinced that Jay had betrayed him by not letting him go home instead. James's delusion that Jay also had betrayed him by stealing his money was a generalization, albeit not a logical one, drawn from his true belief that Jay had been the decision-maker who had kept him in the Cantler Home until his sisters rescued him. In essence, this is what the trial judge found from the evidence: that James's delusion was an outgrowth of a stubborn conviction that Jay had "done something wrong" by "imprisoning" him at the Cantler Home. Although it was false, and it prompted James to disinherit Jay, it was not an inexplicable delusion that only could have come into being as the product of an insane mind.

The facts as found by the orphans' court did not compel a finding that James was suffering from an insane delusion, under the law of testamentary capacity. The court's finding that James was suffering from a delusion that Jay had stolen his money, but that the delusion was not an insane delusion, was a reasonable interpretation of the evidence. Accordingly, we shall not disturb it on appeal.[5]

Judgment affirmed. Costs to be paid by the appellant.

NOTE

Family tensions. The family of a person who is becoming increasingly disabled by physical or mental illness may be compelled to make a series of difficult and painful decisions. Consider the wrench to everyone involved in telling an elderly person that he or she may no longer write checks, conduct business, or drive a car. Legal proceedings such as a petition for commitment or appointment of a conservator, even if commenced with the best intentions, may generate bitter resentments which find expression in a new will disinheriting those family members whom the testator now perceives as enemies. For example, the testator in Estate of Bonjean, 413 N.E.2d 205 (Ill.App. 1980), was a "troubled woman" who suffered from acute depression and attempted several times to take her own life. Testator became increasingly antagonistic toward her siblings, who sought unsuccessfully to have her involuntarily committed to a psychiatric ward "for her own health and safety." Testator eventually died from cyanide poisoning, leaving a will which disinherited her siblings and left her estate to other relatives. Noting that "[t]he act of suicide, or attempted suicide, is not, per se, proof of insanity or insane delusions," the court concluded that while testator may have misinterpreted her siblings' well-intentioned efforts to help her, nevertheless her hostility toward them was not groundless. Instead, their attempt to force her commitment posed a threat to her personal liberty and provided a rational explanation for their disinheritance.

---

[5] In his brief, Jay complains that the orphans' court did not place sufficient weight upon Dr. Freilich's testimony, supported by the hospital records, that James was suffering from dementia. There was opposing testimony, however, from which the court reasonably could find that James's addled state while in the hospital was not permanent dementia but was a temporary condition caused by his minor stroke and substance abuse withdrawal. To the extent that there was any argument by Jay as to whether James's Will should have been invalidated because, prior to executing it, he had become permanently insane due to dementia, the court's factual findings rejected that argument. It was the court's prerogative to make credibility findings; its determination that James did not have dementia was based upon its crediting the expert opinion of Dr. DeSantis, which it was entitled to do. . . .

Whether the testator's beliefs amount to "insane delusions springing from a disordered intellect" or are merely "illogical deductions from actual facts" ordinarily presents a question of fact for the jury. A jury verdict of insane delusion is unlikely to be reversed on appeal. See Johnson v. Dodgen, 260 S.E.2d 332 (Ga.1979) (testator believed nephew wanted to put her in a nursing home so he could steal her possessions); Estate of Koch, 259 N.W.2d 655 (N.D.1977) (paranoid testator believed wife and children were against him and cut himself off, reinforcing his beliefs and prompting children to testify in commitment hearing and divorce proceeding).

B. UNDUE INFLUENCE

Undue influence arises when a testator is induced by another person to make a will that does not reflect the testator's true testamentary wishes. In essence, the problem is one of substituted volition. Undue influence has been described as "pressure brought to bear directly on the testamentary act, sufficient to overcome the testator's free will, amounting in effect to coercion destroying the testator's free agency." Rice v. Clark, 47 P.3d 300 (Cal. 2002). In a more discursive vein, one court commented as follows on the contestant's case:

> [I]t must be shown that the influence exercised amounted to a moral coercion, which restrained independent action and destroyed free agency, or which, by importunity which could not be resisted, constrained the testator to do that which was against his free will and desire, but which he was unable to refuse or too weak to resist. It must not be the promptings of affection; the desire of gratifying the wishes of another; the ties of attachment arising from consanguinity, or the memory of kind acts and friendly offices, but a coercion produced by importunity, or by a silent resistless power which the strong will often exercises over the weak and infirm, and which could not be resisted, so that the motive was tantamount to force or fear. [Children's Aid Society v. Loveridge, 70 N.Y. 387, 394 (1877).]

The testator is inevitably influenced to some extent by myriad relationships and dealings with spouses and other family members, friends and confidants, attorneys, physicians, clergy, and so on. These relationships may for the most part be constructive and supportive, but there is always a possibility of manipulation or exploitation. Given the subtle and secret ways in which influence can be exercised, it is often difficult to establish by direct evidence precisely what was said or done to procure a particular testamentary disposition. Moreover, even if the circumstances surrounding the execution of the will come to light, the words and actions of the testator and other persons may be subject to radically different characterizations, especially with the benefit of hindsight when the will is contested after the testator's death. In reading the following materials, consider what factors are likely to support a finding of undue influence in a particular case as well as what steps might be taken at the time of execution to avert a will contest.

IN RE WILL OF MOSES

Supreme Court of Mississippi, 1969.
227 So.2d 829.

SMITH, JUSTICE:

Mrs. Fannie Traylor Moses died on February 6, 1967. An instrument, dated December 23, 1957 and purporting to be her last will and testament, was duly admitted to probate in common form in the Chancery Court of the First Judicial District of Hinds County. Thereafter, on February 14, 1967, appellant, Clarence H. Holland, an attorney at law, not related to Mrs. Moses, filed a petition in that court tendering for probate in solemn form, as the true last will and testament of Mrs. Moses, a document dated May 26, 1964, under the terms of which he would take virtually her entire estate. This document contained a clause revoking former wills and Holland's petition prayed that the earlier probate of the 1957 will be set aside.

The beneficiaries under the 1957 will (the principal beneficiary was an elder sister of Mrs. Moses) responded to Holland's petition, denied that the document tendered by him was Mrs. Moses' will, and asserted, among other things, that it was (1) the product of Holland's undue influence upon her, (2) that at the time of its signing, Mrs. Moses lacked testamentary capacity, and, (3) that the 1957 will was Mrs. Moses' true last will and testament and its probate should be confirmed. . . .

[The chancellor heard the case without a jury, and ruled (1) that the 1964 document, tendered for probate by Holland, was the product of undue influence and was not entitled to be admitted to probate, and (2) that the earlier probate of the 1957 will should be confirmed.]

A number of grounds are assigned for reversal. However, appellant's chief argument is addressed to the proposition that even if Holland, as Mrs. Moses' attorney, occupied a continuing fiduciary relationship with respect to her on May 26, 1964, the date of the execution of the document under which he claimed her estate, the presumption of undue influence was overcome because, in making the will, Mrs. Moses had the independent advice and counsel of one entirely devoted to her interests. It is argued that, for this reason, a decree should be entered here reversing the chancellor and admitting the 1964 will to probate. . . .

Mrs. Moses died at the age of 57 years, leaving an estate valued at $125,000. She had lost three husbands in less than 20 years. Throughout the latter years of her life her health became seriously impaired. She suffered from serious heart trouble and cancer had required the surgical removal of one of her breasts. For 6 or 7 years preceding her death she was an alcoholic.

On several occasions Mrs. Moses had declared her intention of making an elder sister her testamentary beneficiary. She had once lived with this sister and was grateful for the many kindnesses shown her. Mrs. Moses' will of December 23, 1957 did, in fact, bequeath the bulk of her estate to this sister. . . .

The evidence supports the chancellor's finding that the confidential or fiduciary relationship which existed between Mrs. Moses and Holland, her attorney, was a subsisting and continuing relationship, having begun [several years before the execution of the purported 1964 will] and having ended only with Mrs. Moses' death. Moreover, its effect was enhanced by the fact that throughout this period, Holland was in almost daily attendance upon Mrs. Moses on terms of the utmost intimacy. There was strong evidence that this aging woman, seriously ill, disfigured by surgery, and hopelessly addicted to alcoholic excesses, was completely bemused by the constant and amorous attentions of Holland, a man 15 years her junior. There was testimony too indicating that she entertained the pathetic hope that he might marry her. Although the evidence was not without conflict and was, in some of its aspects, circumstantial, it was sufficient to support the finding that the relationship existed on May 26, 1964, the date of the will tendered for probate by Holland.

The chancellor's factual finding of the existence of this relationship on that date is supported by evidence and is not manifestly wrong. Moreover, he was correct in his conclusion of law that such relationship gave rise to a presumption of undue influence which could be overcome only by evidence that, in making the 1964 will, Mrs. Moses had acted upon the independent advice and counsel of one entirely devoted to her interest.

Appellant takes the position that there was undisputed evidence that Mrs. Moses, in making the 1964 will, did, in fact, have such advice and counsel. He relies upon the testimony of the attorney in whose office that document was prepared to support his assertion.

This attorney was and is a reputable and respected member of the bar, who had no prior connection with Holland and no knowledge of Mrs. Moses' relationship with him. He had never seen nor represented Mrs. Moses previously and never represented her afterward. He was acquainted with Holland and was aware that Holland was a lawyer.

A brief summary of his testimony, with respect to the writing of the will, follows:

Mrs. Moses had telephoned him for an appointment and had come alone to his office on March 31, 1964. She was not intoxicated and in his opinion knew what she was doing. He asked her about her property and "marital background." He did this in order, he said, to advise her as to possible renunciation by a husband. She was also asked if she had children in order to determine whether she wished to "pretermit them." As she had neither husband nor children this subject was pursued no further. He asked as to the values of various items of property in order to consider possible tax problems. He told her it would be better if she had more accurate descriptions of the several items of real and personal property comprising her estate. No further "advice or counsel" was given her.

On some later date, Mrs. Moses sent in (the attorney did not think she came personally and in any event he did not see her), some tax receipts for purposes of supplying property descriptions. He prepared the will and mailed a draft to her. Upon receiving it, she telephoned that he had made a mistake in the devise of certain realty, in that he had provided that a relatively low valued property should go to Holland rather than a substantially more valuable property which she said she wanted Holland to have. He rewrote the will, making this change, and mailed it to her, as revised, on May 21, 1964. On the one occasion when he saw Mrs. Moses, there were no questions and no discussion of any kind as to Holland being preferred to the exclusion of her blood relatives. Nor was there any inquiry or discussion as to a possible client-attorney relationship with Holland. The attorney-draftsman wrote the will according to Mrs. Moses' instructions and said that he had "no interest in" how she disposed of her property. He testified "I try to draw the will to suit their purposes and if she (Mrs. Moses) wanted to leave him (Holland) everything she had, that was her business as far as I was concerned. I was trying to represent her in putting on paper in her will her desires, and it didn't matter to me to whom she left it . . . I couldn't have cared less."

When Mrs. Moses returned to the office to execute the will, the attorney was not there and it was witnessed by two secretaries. . . .

The attorney's testimony supports the chancellor's finding that nowhere in the conversations with Mrs. Moses was there touched upon in any way the proposed testamentary disposition whereby preference was to be given a nonrelative to the exclusion of her blood relatives. There was no discussion of her relationship with Holland, nor as to who her legal heirs might be, nor as to their relationship to her, after it was discovered that she had neither a husband nor children.

It is clear from his own testimony that, in writing the will, the attorney-draftsman, did no more than write down, according to the forms of law, what Mrs. Moses told him. There was no meaningful independent advice or counsel touching upon the area in question and it is manifest that the role of the attorney in writing the will, as it relates to the present issue, was little more than that of scrivener. The chancellor was justified in holding that this did not meet the burden nor overcome the presumption. . . .

The sexual morality of the personal relationship is not an issue. However, the intimate nature of this relationship is relevant to the present inquiry to the extent that its existence, under the circumstances, warranted an inference of undue influence, extending and augmenting that which flowed from the attorney-client relationship. Particularly is this true when viewed in the light of evidence indicating its employment for the personal aggrandizement of Holland. For that purpose, it was properly taken into consideration by the chancellor. . . .

The chancellor was justified in finding that the physical absence of Holland during Mrs. Moses' brief visit to the office of the attorney who wrote the will did not suffice to abate or destroy the presumption of undue influence.

The chancellor was the judge of the credibility of the witnesses and the weight and worth of their testimony. Moreover, as trier of facts, it was for him to resolve conflicts and to interpret evidence where it was susceptible of more than one reasonable interpretation. It was also his prerogative to draw reasonable inferences from facts proved. . . . This Court, in passing upon the sufficiency of the evidence to support the factual findings of the chancellor, must accept as true all that the evidence proved or reasonably tended to prove, together with all reasonable inferences to be drawn from it, supporting such findings.

Viewed in the light of the above rules, it cannot be said that the chancellor was manifestly wrong in finding that Holland occupied a dual fiduciary relationship with respect to Mrs. Moses, both conventional and actual, attended by suspicious circumstances as set forth in his opinion, which gave rise to a presumption of undue influence in the production of the 1964 will, nor that he was manifestly wrong in finding that this presumption was not overcome by "clearest proof" that in making and executing the will Mrs. Moses acted upon her "own volition and upon the fullest deliberation," or upon independent advice and counsel of one wholly devoted to her interest. . . .

. . . [T]he decree of the chancery court will be affirmed. . . .

ETHRIDGE, C.J., and GILLESPIE, RODGERS and JONES, JJ., concur.

ROBERTSON, JUSTICE (dissenting):

I am unable to agree with the majority of the Court that Mrs. Moses should not be allowed to dispose of her property as she so clearly intended. . . .

Mrs. Fannie T. Moses was 54 years of age when she executed her last will and testament on May 26, 1964, leaving most of her considerable estate to Clarence H. Holland, her good friend, but a man fifteen years her junior. She had been married three times, and each of these marriages was dissolved by the death of her husband. Holland's friendship with Mrs. Moses dated back to the days of her second husband, Robert L. Dickson. He was also a friend of her third husband, Walter Moses.

She was the active manager of commercial property in the heart of Jackson, four apartment buildings containing ten rental units, and a 480–acre farm until the day of her death. All of the witnesses conceded that she was a good businesswoman, maintaining and repairing her properties with promptness and dispatch, and paying her bills promptly so that she would get the cash discount. She was a strong personality and pursued her own course, even though her manner of living did at times embarrass her sisters and estranged her from them.

The chancellor found that she was of sound and disposing mind and memory on May 26, 1964, when she executed her last will and testament, and I think he was correct in this finding. . . .

There is no proof in this voluminous record that Holland ever did or said anything to Mrs. Moses about devising her property to anybody, much less him. It is conceded that in the absence of the presumption of undue influence that there is no basis to support a finding that Holland exercised undue influence over Mrs. Moses. This being true, the first question to be decided is whether the presumption of undue influence arises under the circumstances of this case.

It is my opinion that the presumption did not arise. The fact, alone, that a confidential relationship existed between Holland and Mrs. Moses is not sufficient to give rise to the presumption of undue influence in a will case. We said in [Croft v. Alder, 237 Miss. 713, 723–24, 115 So.2d 683, 686 (1959)]:

> [S]uch consequence follows where the beneficiary *"has been actively concerned in some way with the preparation or execution of the will,* or where the relationship is coupled with some suspicious circumstances, *such as mental infirmity of the testator"*; or where *the beneficiary* in the confidential relation *was active directly in preparing the will or procuring its execution*, and obtained under it a substantial benefit. . . . (Emphasis added.)

It was not contended in this case that Holland was in any way actively concerned with the preparation or execution of the will. Appellees rely solely upon the finding of the chancellor that there were suspicious circumstances. However, the suspicious circumstances listed by the chancellor in his opinion had nothing whatsoever to do with the preparation or execution of the will. These were remote antecedent circumstances having to do with the meretricious relationship of the parties, and the fact that at times Mrs. Moses drank to excess and could be termed an alcoholic, but there is no proof in this long record that her use of alcohol affected her will power or her ability to look after her extensive real estate holdings. It is common knowledge that many persons who could be termed alcoholics, own, operate and manage large business enterprises with success. The fact that she chose to leave most of her property to the man she loved in preference to her sisters and brother is not such an unnatural disposition of her property as to render it invalid. . . .

In this case, there were no suspicious circumstances surrounding the preparation or execution of the will, and in my opinion the chancellor was wrong in so holding. However, even if it be conceded that the presumption of undue influence did arise, this presumption was overcome by clear and convincing evidence of good faith, full knowledge and independent consent and advice.

When she got ready to make her will she called Honorable Dan H. Shell for an appointment. Shell did not know her, although he remembered that he had handled a land transaction for her third husband, Walter Moses, some years before. Shell had been in the active practice of law in Jackson since 1945; he was an experienced attorney with a large and varied practice. . . .

The majority was indeed hard put to find fault with his actions on behalf of his client. . . . The question is, did he do all that was reasonably required of him to represent his client in the preparation of her will. He was not required to be perfect, nor was he required to meet a standard of exact precision. He ascertained that Mrs. Moses was competent to make a will; he satisfied himself that she was acting of her own free will and accord, and that she was disposing of her property exactly as she wished and intended. No more is required. . . .

There is not one iota of testimony in this voluminous record that Clarence Holland even knew of this will, much less that he participated in the preparation or execution of it. The evidence is all to the contrary. The evidence is undisputed that she executed her last will after the fullest deliberation, with full knowledge of what she was doing, and with the independent consent and advice of an experienced and competent attorney whose sole purpose was to advise with her and prepare her will exactly as she wanted it.

In January 1967, about one month before her death and some two years and eight months after she had made her will, she called W.R. Patterson, an experienced, reliable and honorable attorney who was a friend of hers, and asked him to come by her home for a few minutes. Patterson testified:

> She said, "Well, the reason I called you out here is that I've got an envelope here with all of my important papers in it, and *that includes my last will and testament*," and says, "I would like to leave them with you if you've got a place to lock them up in your desk somewhere there in your office."

> . . . [A]nd she said, "*Now, Dan Shell drew my will for me two or three years ago,*" and she says, "*It's exactly like I want it,*" and says, "*I had to go to his office two or three times to get it the way I wanted it, but this is the way I want it,* and if anything happens to me I want you to take all these papers and give them to Dan," and she says, "He'll know what to do with them." (Emphasis added.)

What else could she have done? She met all the tests that this Court and other courts have carefully outlined and delineated. The majority opinion says that this still was not enough, that there were "suspicious circumstances" and "antecedent agencies," but even these were not connected in any shape, form or fashion with the preparation or execution of her will. They had to do with her love life and her drinking habits and propensities.

It would appear that the new procedure will be to fine-tooth comb all the events of a person's life and if, in the mind of the judge on the bench at that particular time, there are any "suspicious circumstances" or "antecedent agencies" in that person's life even though they are in nowise connected with the preparation or execution of that person's will, such last will and testament will be set aside and held for naught. With all time-honored tests out the window, the trial judge will be in the dangerous predicament of embarking on an unknown sea, without chart or compass.

If full knowledge, deliberate and voluntary action, and independent consent and advice have not been proved in this case, then they just cannot be proved. We should be bound by the uncontradicted testimony in the record; we should not go completely outside the record and guess, speculate and surmise as to what happened.

I think that the judgment of the lower court should be reversed and the last will and testament of Fannie T. Moses executed on May 26, 1964, admitted to probate in solemn form.

BRADY, PATTERSON and INZER, JJ., join in this dissent.

NOTES

1. *Proving undue influence.* Due to the difficulty of proving undue influence by direct evidence, allegations of undue influence often rely heavily on circumstantial evidence. Relevant considerations include: the testator's mental and physical condition at the time the will was executed; the nature of the relationship between the testator and the beneficiary; the beneficiary's role in procuring the execution of the will; independent advice provided to the testator by a disinterested lawyer or other competent adviser; haste or secrecy in the preparation of the will; the effect of the testator's relationship with the beneficiary on the testator's attitude toward others; discrepancies between the challenged will and earlier wills; continuity of purpose running through earlier wills indicating a settled dispositive plan; and the fairness or naturalness of the disposition in the challenged will. See Estate of Reddaway, 329 P.2d 886 (Or. 1958).

The traditional rule assigns the burden of persuasion to the contestant in cases involving undue influence. See UPC § 3–407. Nevertheless, the contestant is aided by a presumption of undue influence which arises upon proof of a "confidential relationship" between the testator and the beneficiary coupled with active participation by the beneficiary in procuring the will or other "suspicious circumstances" resulting in an undue benefit under the will. See, in addition to the principal case, Will of Rittenhouse, 117 A.2d 401 (N.J. 1955). If not rebutted, the presumption justifies judgment for the contestant as a matter of law. What are the suspicious circumstances surrounding the preparation or execution of the will that support a presumption of undue influence in *Moses*? What additional steps might Attorney Shell have taken in anticipation of a will contest?

Even if a presumption of undue influence does not arise or is rebutted, the contestant may prevail by showing that: (1) the testator was susceptible to undue influence; (2) the beneficiary had an opportunity to exert undue influence; (3) the beneficiary was inclined or disposed to exercise undue influence; and (4) the terms of the will reflect the coveted result. See Estate of Pringle, 751 N.W.2d 277 (S.D. 2008).

In the case of inter vivos gifts, some courts hold that the mere existence of a confidential relationship between the donor and the donee raises a presumption of undue influence, even in the absence of active participation by the donee or other suspicious circumstances. See Wright v. Roberts, 797 So.2d 992 (Miss. 2001).

2. *Confidential relationship.* What relationships have the potential for control that justifies a characterization of "confidential" and the creation of a presumption of undue influence?

a. Testator's *attorney* is the most obvious candidate for suspicion. The attorney who drafts a will containing a bequest in his or her favor has little or no chance of receiving the bequest. Many courts impose a heightened evidentiary standard and require clear and convincing evidence to rebut the presumption of undue influence. See Matlock v. Simpson, 902 S.W.2d 384 (Tenn. 1995); Estate of Auen, 35 Cal.Rptr.2d 557 (App. 1994). The attorney may also be subject to disciplinary proceedings for unethical conduct. See Attorney Grievance Comm'n v. Brooke, 821 A.2d 414 (Md. 2003) (attorney prepared will naming self as executor and sole beneficiary, as favor to testator, a longtime friend about to go into hospital; attorney suspended indefinitely, even though no undue influence); Committee on Professional Ethics v. Randall, 285 N.W.2d 161 (Iowa 1979) (attorney disbarred for drafting business partner's will which named attorney as sole beneficiary).

Upon discovery of the testator's desire to benefit him or her, the attorney is obligated to refer the testator to another attorney for independent advice and assistance in drafting the will. See Franciscan Sisters Health Care Corp. v. Dean, 448 N.E.2d 872 (Ill.1983) (presumption of undue influence rebutted where testator consulted another lawyer before executing will which left half of residuary estate to lawyer-drafter). Merely arranging for another attorney to draft the will does not insulate the will from challenge on grounds of undue influence. See Estate of Smith, 827 So.2d 673 (Miss. 2002). In some cases the attorney may be able to provide a satisfactory explanation and keep the legacy. See Vaupel v. Barr, 460 S.E.2d 431 (W.Va. 1995) (lawyer and longtime family friend who took care of elderly testator and managed her affairs under power of attorney was allowed to take residuary estate to exclusion of testator's son and grandchildren, under will drafted by another lawyer).

b. A *guardian* or *conservator*, appointed to manage the property of a person disabled by illness, injury or age, occupies a sensitive position, and courts examine gifts made by a ward to a guardian with special care. Similarly, an *agent* named in a *durable general power of attorney* has broad authority to manage the affairs of a disabled principal with little or no court supervision. If the agent exercises that authority to make gifts to himself or herself, the gifts are subject to heightened scrutiny. See Estate of Elias, 946 N.E.2d 1015 (Ill. App. 2011); Comeau v. Nash, 233 P.3d 572 (Wyo. 2010); Basham v. Duffer, 238 S.W.3d 304 (Tenn. App. 2007). Sometimes, of course, the guardian or agent may be able to provide a satisfactory explanation and retain the gift. A testator may also be especially susceptible to the influence of a *financial adviser* or *business associate*.

c. A *spouse* may wield enormous influence, but a court is not likely to classify it as "undue." In upholding a will which left the entire estate to testator's second wife against a challenge by the children from testator's first marriage, one court noted that "marriage does not give rise to a presumption of undue influence." Estate of Karmey, 658 N.W.2d 796 (Mich. 2003); see also Will of Rasnick, 186 A.2d 527 (N.J. Co. 1962) (noting "the great latitude which is and should be given to a wife in counseling and persuading her husband with respect to the making of a will"). However, the spouse does not always win. See Estate of Pope, 5 So.3d 427 (Miss.App. 2008) (six months before death, elderly testator married caregiver and executed will naming her as sole beneficiary, disinheriting children from previous marriage; probate denied); Estate of Waters, 629 P.2d 470 (Wyo.1981) (setting aside will which left entire estate to testator's fourth wife and disinherited his children). The wife has been described as "the darling of the probate court," a characterization that suggests a powerful sense of sympathy for widows. By her behavior, however, a widow may forfeit the court's special regard. See Estate of Hamm, 262 N.W.2d 201 (S.D.1978) (widow, described as a prostitute, who at one time had "taken off for other climes with [testator's] car and a portion of his money" and who had been convicted of conspiracy in the murder of testator's son from his first marriage, failed to set aside will which left estate in trust naming attorney as trustee with discretion to make distributions to a nursing home in which the attorney had an interest).

In the principal case, would the court likely have reached a different result if Mrs. Moses had married Clarence Holland?

d. Courts often view with skepticism a will which excludes the testator's blood relatives in favor of a *lover*. The following statement as to the effect of the relationship on the process is representative:

> As we have seen, the evidence indicates that a meretricious relationship existed between P.J. Kelly and Mrs. Northrop. The mere existence of such a relationship does not render invalid a bequest made to the paramour, because one possessed of an estate may settle his bounty upon an immoral person if he chooses; nor does such a relationship create a presumption that the beneficiary exerted undue influence in obtaining the testamentary recognition. But, since the relationship which arises out of illegal amours may provide favorable opportunities for the exertion of undue influence, proof of the relationship is admissible when undue influence is charged. It is frequently said that the relationship casts suspicion upon the will, and cautions the court to examine the evidence with unusual care. Proof that the relationship existed and that the will makes an unnatural disposition of the estate, when accompanied with only a small amount of evidence that undue influence was exerted, may overcome positive denials from the paramour and her witnesses. This is due to a conviction that the usual difficulty of unmasking deceit and wrongful conduct is greatly increased when the alleged wrongdoer has employed as an aid sensual pleasures. [In re Kelly's Estate, 46 P.2d 84, 92 (Or.1935).]

There are, however, many cases in which the relationship did not disqualify the beneficiary. See Estate of Saucier, 908 So.2d 883 (Miss. App. 2005) (upholding will which left entire estate to testator's lover and caregiver; beneficiary rebutted presumption of undue influence by showing her good faith and testator's full knowledge, deliberation, and independent consent); Estate of Schlagel, 89 P.3d 419 (Colo. App. 2003) (upholding residuary devise to testator's lover, who was also his disabled wife's caregiver, against contest by disinherited grandchildren); Ramsey v. Taylor, 999 P.2d 1178 (Or. App. 2000) (upholding will, inter vivos trust and gifts to testator's lover and caregiver, against contest by son).

In the case of a same-sex couple, a will naming the testator's lover as principal beneficiary may invite a contest from members of the testator's family who disapprove of the relationship. See Will of Kaufmann, 247 N.Y.S.2d 664 (App. Div. 1964), aff'd, 205 N.E.2d 864 (N.Y.1965) (setting aside will which named surviving partner of 10–year relationship as principal beneficiary; the majority characterized the testator as "weak-willed, trusting, inexperienced" and the beneficiary's influence as "unnatural" and "insidious," but a vigorous dissent characterized the relationship as one of "love and affection," "mutual esteem and self-respect"). Depending on the circumstances surrounding the relationship, the will may well withstand attack even if it leaves the entire estate to the testator's lover. See Evans v. May, 923 S.W.2d 712 (Tex.App.1996); Estate of Sarabia, 270 Cal.Rptr. 560 (App. 1990). See generally Sherman, Undue Influence and the Homosexual Testator, 42 U. Pitt. L. Rev. 225 (1981).

In the principal case, suppose Clarence Holland was a woman named Clara who established a domestic partnership with Mrs. Moses. Would the court likely have reached a different result?

e. A presumption of undue influence may arise where the testator made a will in favor of a *friend* or *caregiver* if it is shown that the testator was particularly dependent on the beneficiary, that the will was executed under suspicious circumstances, or that the disposition was unnatural or unjust. See Estate of Moretti, 871 N.E.2d 493 (Mass. App. 2007) (undue influence by caregiver who isolated elderly testator from friends, squandered testator's money, and actively procured will naming himself as primary beneficiary); Will of Ferrill, 640 P.2d 489 (N.M.App.1981) (setting aside 82–year old testator's will which left estate to couple who took care of her during last year of her life); cf. Curry v. Sutherland, 614 S.E.2d 756 (Ga. 2005) (upholding will which disinherited daughter and left entire estate to caregiver and two friends; no evidence of undue influence).

Courts cast a suspicious eye on a relationship between an elderly testator and a young friend. See Christensen v. Britton, 784 P.2d 908 (Mont.1989) (setting aside inter vivos gifts by which donor transferred virtually all his property to younger friends, purportedly to avoid a will contest by his children); Estate of Van Aken, 281 So.2d 917 (Fla.App.1973) (setting aside elderly widower's will which disinherited his children and left the entire estate to a nurse-housekeeper-secretary who had been in his employ for only two months); cf. Casper v. McDowell, 205 N.W.2d 753 (Wis.1973) (upholding residuary legacy to nurse-housekeeper who was 50 years younger than testator); Sweeney v. Eaton, 486 S.W.2d 453 (Mo.1972) (will of widow in her seventies leaving estate to a 31–year-old delivery man upheld, despite evidence that he "would like to see every one of his children have a dollar bill in one hand and a candy bar in the other").

f. A *member of the clergy* may be overzealous in presenting the financial needs of his or her religious community to the testator, causing the courts to shift the burden of explanation to the clergy member. See Estate of Maheras, 897 P.2d 268 (Okla. 1995) (setting aside will which left most of elderly testator's estate to church and named pastor as co-executor, on ground of undue influence, even though pastor received no direct personal benefit); In re The Bible Speaks, 869 F.2d 628 (1st Cir. 1989) (series of multi-million-dollar inter vivos gifts to evangelical church). See Sherman, Can Religious Influence Ever Be "Undue" Influence?, 73 Brook. L. Rev. 579 (2008) (arguing that the relationship between testator and religious or spiritual adviser should be treated as "per se confidential" in undue influence inquiry).

g. The *owner or operator of a nursing or foster home* often has the opportunity to influence elderly and vulnerable patients. See Looney v. Estate of Wade, 839 S.W.2d 531 (Ark.1992) (two days after entering residential care center, testator executed will leaving entire estate to owner-administrator); Estate of Brandon, 433 N.E.2d 501 (N.Y.1982) (setting aside inter vivos gifts to owner of "Friendly Acres" nursing home; findings of undue influence by same donee in other cases admissible to show intent); but see Estate of Podgursky, 271 N.W.2d 52 (S.D.1978) (admitting will to probate over dissent that pointed out foster home owners' pattern of manipulating elderly patients for financial advantage).

3. *Testamentary freedom.* In theory, the concept of undue influence serves as a bulwark against imposition or overreaching by other persons who seek to substitute their own testamentary wishes for those of the testator. In application, however, the open-ended nature of the applicable legal standard leaves considerable leeway for a court or jury to bring its own views of morality and propriety to bear in determining whether a will was procured through undue influence. According to one commentator, "courts often evaluate potential beneficiaries from their own perspective, as opposed to that of the testator, thus appearing less concerned with effectuating testamentary intent than in forcing the testator to distribute his or her estate in accordance with prevailing notions of morality." Leslie, The Myth of Testamentary Freedom, 38 Ariz. L. Rev. 235, 246 (1996). Another commentator goes even further and speculates that "rather than furthering freedom of testation, the undue influence doctrine denies freedom of testation for people who deviate from judicially imposed testamentary norms—in particular the norm that people should provide for their families. . . . The doctrine does not act to protect the intent of

the testator, but rather to protect the testator's biological family from disinheritance." Madoff, Unmasking Undue Influence, 81 Minn. L. Rev. 571, 572 (1997). Is it fair to say that the doctrine of undue influence functions "as a form of forced heirship"? Id. at 611.

In Estate of Reid, 825 So.2d 1 (Miss. 2002), Michael Cupit, a 24–year-old law student, befriended Mary Reid, a 78–year-old widow, and began an "intimate relationship" with testator which lasted until her death 18 years later. During that time, Reid made gifts to Cupit of real property, heirlooms, and significant amounts of cash; in addition, she left her remaining property to him by will, granted him a durable power of attorney, and formally adopted him as her son. In a contest brought after her death, the court held that the lifetime and testamentary gifts to Cupit were the product of undue influence. Citing *Moses*, the court noted that the lawyer who drafted the will acted as a "mere scrivener" and that Reid did not receive independent counsel. Under the unusual circumstances of the case, the court also set aside the adoption on the ground that it was obtained by fraud. Did the court give undue weight to "prevailing notions of morality" at the expense of testamentary freedom? See Spivack, Why the Testamentary Doctrine of Undue Influence Should Be Abolished, 58 Kan. L. Rev. 245 (2010) (discussing *Reid* as an example of "courts imposing their ideology-driven views of morality and propriety upon the will of the testator").

4. *Partial or total invalidity of will.* Where specific provisions of a will are the product of undue influence, courts usually ignore the tainted provisions and give effect to the remaining provisions:

> Where a provision in a will which gives a legacy is void because of undue influence, the will itself is not necessarily void nor are other legacies unless such influence directly or impliedly affects them. Undue influence invalidates such part of a will as is affected by it. If the whole will is procured through undue influence, it is entirely void. Where, however, part of the will is caused by undue influence, and the remainder is not affected by it, and the latter can be so separated as to leave it intelligible and complete in itself, such part of the will is valid and enforceable. [Carothers' Estate, 150 A. 585 (Pa.1930).]

See also Williams v. Crickman, 405 N.E.2d 799 (Ill.1980).

If a will is invalid for want of testamentary capacity or undue influence, can the defect be cured by a subsequent codicil which republishes the will?

HAYNES V. FIRST NATIONAL STATE BANK OF NEW JERSEY

Supreme Court of New Jersey, 1981.
87 N.J. 163, 432 A.2d 890.

HANDLER, J.

This is a will contest in which the plaintiffs, two of the decedent's six grandchildren, seek to set aside the probate of their grandmother's will and two related trust agreements. The major issue presented is whether the will is invalid on the grounds of "undue influence" attributable to the fact that the attorney, who advised the testatrix and prepared the testamentary instruments, was also the attorney for the principal beneficiary, the testatrix's daughter, in whom the testatrix had reposed trust, confidence and dependency. A second question concerns the enforceability of a "non-contestability" or *in terrorem* clause in the testamentary documents. . . .

In an unreported opinion upholding the probate of the will and related trusts, the trial court held that the circumstances created a presumption of undue influence but that this presumption had been rebutted by defendants. It ruled further that the *in terrorem* clause was unenforceable. The case was appealed to the Appellate Division, which affirmed the trial court as to the lack of undue influence, sustaining the probate of the will and its judgment upholding the related trust agreements, but disagreed with the trial court's ruling that the *in terrorem* clause was unenforceable. Plaintiffs then filed their petition for certification which was granted. 85 N.J. 99, 425 A.2d 264 (1980).

I

The issues raised by this appeal, particularly whether the contested will was invalid as a result of "undue influence," require a full exposition of the facts.

Mrs. Isabel Dutrow, the testatrix, was the widow of Charles E. Dutrow, an employee of Ralston Purina Co. who had acquired substantial stock in that corporation. Upon his death the stock, aggregating almost eight million dollars, was distributed to his widow and their two daughters, both outright and in trust.

Betty Haynes, one of the daughters of Charles and Isabel Dutrow, came with her two sons to live with her parents in the Dutrow family home in York, Pennsylvania in 1941 while Betty's husband was in military service during World War II. Following Charles Dutrow's death in 1945 and her own divorce, Betty and her sons continued to live with Mrs. Dutrow in York. The relationships between mother and daughter were extremely close, Mrs. Dutrow having deep affection for Betty, as well as her grandsons whom she practically raised. The two boys, however, left the York home sometime around 1968 to the considerable aggravation and disappointment of their grandmother.[6] But Betty remained with her mother until Betty's death in June 1973.

At the time of Betty's death, she had been living with her mother for more than 30 years. Mrs. Dutrow was then 84 years old and suffered from a number of ailments including glaucoma, cataracts and diverticulitis, and had recently broken her hip. Mrs. Dutrow, distraught over the death of her closest daughter and somewhat alienated from the Haynes children, decided to move in with her younger daughter, Dorcas Cotsworth, and Dorcas' husband, John, who had homes in Short Hills and Bay Head, New Jersey. This decision was a reasonable one, freely made by Mrs. Dutrow, who despite her age, physical condition and feelings of despair was and remained an alert, intelligent and commanding personality until the time of her death.

During her lifetime, Mrs. Dutrow executed a great many wills and trust agreements. All of these instruments, as well as those her husband had executed prior to his death, were prepared by the longstanding family attorney, Richard Stevens, of Philadelphia. By June 1967 Stevens had prepared five wills and several codicils for Mrs. Dutrow.

As of the time she moved in with the Cotsworths, Mrs. Dutrow's estate plan reflected a basic disposition to treat the Haynes and the Cotsworth family branches equally. During the last four years of her life, however, while living with daughter Dorcas, Mrs. Dutrow's will went through a series of changes which drastically favored Dorcas and her children while diminishing and excluding the interests of the Haynes brothers. These changes, and their surrounding circumstances, bear most weightily upon the issue of undue influence.

Shortly after moving in with Dorcas, following a conference between her daughter and Stevens, the first of many will and trust changes was made by Mrs. Dutrow on July 25, 1973. Under the new provisions of the will, Mrs. Dutrow's residuary estate was to be divided into two equal trusts, one for Dorcas, the principal of which Dorcas could invade up to certain limits and the other a trust with income to each of the Haynes boys without a power of invasion. A new will and an inter vivos trust with almost identical provisions, including approximately 60,000 shares of Ralston Purina stock, were later executed on November 24, 1973 and December 4, 1973, respectively. Mrs. Dutrow also gave Dorcas 5,000 shares

---

[6] The Haynes children apparently undertook lifestyles which caused both their mother and grandmother great anguish; one son resisted military service and took refuge in Canada during the Vietnam war and both had live-in girlfriends whom they eventually married.

of stock outright to compensate her for the expense of having Mrs. Dutrow live with her.

During the time these instruments were being drawn, Dorcas and her husband, John Cotsworth, began actively to express their views about Mrs. Dutrow's estate plans to Stevens. In a meeting between Stevens, Mrs. Dutrow, and the Cotsworths on November 13, 1973 at the Cotsworth home in Short Hills, John Cotsworth gave Stevens two charts of Mrs. Dutrow's estate which Cotsworth had prepared. According to Stevens' testimony at trial, the import of the charts was to make "substantial outright gifts to the members of the Cotsworth family and similar gifts to [plaintiffs, the Haynes children]." Stevens further testified that Mrs. Dutrow had told him at this meeting that the pressure upon her by the Cotsworths to change her will was enormous. On November 19, 1973, John Cotsworth wrote Stevens a long letter in which he summarized what he, Cotsworth, saw as Mrs. Dutrow's "objectives" with regard to her estate plans and then detailing in over five pages the calculations as to how these "objectives" could be achieved. An important aspect of his proposal was to deplete substantially the estate to simplify Mrs. Dutrow's "money worries." Cotsworth further noted at the beginning of this letter to Stevens that

> [o]ur joint obligation—you and the family—is to accomplish these objectives with minimum tax effects upon the total estate. Obviously you are in a far better position to work out the details than I am, but you appear reluctant to go as fast or as far as I have suggested for reasons that are not clear to us.

Then, on November 26, 1973, Cotsworth proceeded to consult Grant Buttermore, his own lawyer, regarding Mrs. Dutrow's estate plans. Buttermore had been the attorney for the Cotsworth family and the Cotsworth family business, the Berry Steel Corporation, for six to seven years and had provided substantial legal advice concerning the corporation. He had also prepared wills for both Mr. and Mrs. Cotsworth and some of their children. For all intents and purposes, Buttermore can be viewed as having been the family attorney for the Cotsworths.

On November 29, 1973, following the initial contact by her husband, Dorcas Cotsworth went to Buttermore concerning the trust agreement of November 24 that Stevens had prepared for her mother. As a result, Buttermore called Stevens while Dorcas was in his office and discussed the matter of Mrs. Dutrow's domicile. This subject, in addition to a proposal concerning "gifting" by Mrs. Dutrow, had earlier been broached to Buttermore by John Cotsworth. Both lawyers agreed that Mrs. Dutrow's domicile should be changed to New Jersey for tax purposes and Buttermore made the change on the instrument by hand. Later that day Buttermore wrote to Stevens to confirm the results of the call, as well as the fact that the Cotsworths were personally involved in Mrs. Dutrow's estate planning, viz.:

> We are in the process of reviewing Mrs. Dutrow's estate with her and Mr. and Mrs. Cotsworth along the lines suggested by Mr. Cotsworth in his outline heretofore submitted to you.

Buttermore concluded this letter by relaying Mrs. Dutrow's request to Stevens to provide "a complete list of all [her] assets . . . in order that we may make a proper analysis."

Stevens immediately responded, writing separate letters to Buttermore and Mrs. Dutrow on November 30. He gave Buttermore a skeletal list of Mrs. Dutrow's assets with no detail. At the same time he also undertook to make some technical corrections of Mrs. Dutrow's will, which was executed, as noted, on December 4. In the letter accompanying the will, he mentioned his conversation with Buttermore and his "assumption" that Mrs. Dutrow wanted him to give Buttermore the information he was requesting.

The response to this communication was a letter written to Stevens on December 3, 1973 in Dorcas Cotsworth's handwriting on her personal stationary, and signed by Dorcas and Mrs. Dutrow, which contained the following:

> These are my mother's observations as she sits here besides me—and she insists she is *not* being pressured. . . .

> Mother and I have discussed this so often—now she says get it over and let me forget it—as it worries her with everything undone. . . .

> Her desire and intent is to have Dorcas rewarded while alive—to have an Irrevocable Trust set up to let Dorcas have income and right to sprinkle money to Grandchildren when necessary. . . .

> When Dorcas dies then the per stirpes takes over. . . .

> Mother approves of Mr. Grant Buttermore knowing all details and keeping in this estate.

A meeting of Buttermore and John Cotsworth with Stevens was scheduled for December 13, 1973. Prior to this meeting Buttermore met with Mrs. Dutrow alone, as he testified was his customary practice, "so that I could get the intent directly from . . . the testatrix." During this two hour conference, according to Buttermore, he explained various legal and tax aspects of estate planning to Mrs. Dutrow. He also told her "that intent was much more important and controlled over the other two items, meaning taxation and liquidity." Buttermore also reviewed at length Mrs. Dutrow's assets and her present will and trusts. Among other things, Mrs. Dutrow, according to Buttermore's testimony, said that "her first priority was to make sure she had enough to last during her lifetime," for which purpose Mrs. Dutrow said she would need $26,000 per year. Buttermore also explained to Mrs. Dutrow that the practical effect of the per stirpes disposition of the November 24 trust agreement would be to enable the two plaintiffs, the Haynes brothers, ultimately to "receive twice as much as each of the other grandchildren," to which Mrs. Dutrow responded, according to Buttermore, "I didn't realize that."

Buttermore testified that he told Stevens at the December 13 meeting that Mrs. Dutrow "wanted to go to the per capita basis equally among the grandchildren." Stevens, according to Buttermore, was very skeptical that Mrs. Dutrow wanted to do this and asked Buttermore to doublecheck it with her. Buttermore replied that "[i]n my mind she'd already made that decision after our talk on December the eleventh."

On December 17 and 18, a concerned Stevens wrote Buttermore letters confirming the discussion of December 13, and on December 18, specifically adverted to the possibility of "undue influence." There is no indication in the record that Buttermore responded to Stevens on this matter.

Buttermore, in response to a call from Dorcas Cotsworth, again met alone with Mrs. Dutrow in Short Hills on January 11 to discuss a problem concerning some back dividends. While he was with her, Buttermore, at his own initiative, told her what had happened during his December 13 meeting with Stevens and John Cotsworth and reviewed with her Stevens' letter of December 17 concerning her estate plans. Following that exchange, Buttermore related, Mrs. Dutrow instructed *him* to "draw the papers." Although Stevens had previously asked Buttermore to write him in Vermont, where he was vacationing, if there were any further developments concerning Mrs. Dutrow's estate planning, Buttermore did not do so, apparently believing that Mrs. Dutrow, who complained of Stevens' absence, did not desire or need Stevens to be further involved. Thus, Buttermore, still the Cotsworths' attorney, also stepped in, exclusively, as Mrs. Dutrow's attorney for purposes of planning her estate.

Significantly, at this juncture, drastic changes in Mrs. Dutrow's estate planning materialized. According to Buttermore, he and Mrs. Dutrow then proceeded to discuss in detail her wishes for a new will and trust agreements. Mrs. Dutrow assertedly indicated that she wanted "to leave [her estate] equally . . . between the grandchildren," and did not care about the adverse tax consequences which Buttermore claimed he had explained to her. Buttermore also seemed to minimize the effect of the proposed change allegedly requested by Mrs. Dutrow by pointing out to her that altering the particular trust in question would not accomplish her goals; although all six grandchildren would inherit equally under the particular trust in question, the consequence of other trusts already in existence would be that the two Haynes grandchildren would "still be getting greater in the end" than Mrs. Cotsworth's children. During that meeting, Buttermore also apparently showed Stevens' letter of December 18 concerning undue influence to Mrs. Dutrow.

These discussions resulted in the near total severance of the Haynes children from their grandmother's estate. Assertedly, at Mrs. Dutrow's request, Buttermore promptly prepared two new trust agreements, which provided for the payment of income with full right of invasion of principal to Dorcas Cotsworth during her lifetime and that, upon Dorcas' death, "the then remaining balance in said trust shall be divided equally among settlor's grandchildren." In addition, Mrs. Dutrow's new will provided for the bequest of all her tangible personal property to Dorcas Cotsworth, "or if she does not survive me to my grandchildren who survive me, equally." These instruments were executed by Mrs. Dutrow on January 16, 1974.

On January 19 Buttermore sent Stevens copies of the new instruments along with a letter in which he explained that after going over everything "meticulously with Mrs. Dutrow," the new instruments had been prepared "along the lines we have discussed" and that, in Stevens' absence, Mrs. Dutrow had become "quite upset with the Fidelity Bank and decided that she wanted to immediately revoke" the existing trust agreements and will. Stevens testified to astonishment at the proposed distribution. He also expressed surprise about the provision in both trust agreements, which permitted Dorcas Cotsworth to withdraw the principal each year so that, if exercised, there might be nothing left when she died.

In early May 1974 Buttermore again met with Mrs. Dutrow to make some changes in the trust agreements. The most important change allowed the corporate trustee First National Bank of New Jersey to distribute principal, "in its sole discretion," to Dorcas Cotsworth and any of Mrs. Dutrow's grandchildren (i.e., plaintiffs as well as Dorcas' children). This was in contrast to the original terms of this trust agreement, as executed by Mrs. Dutrow in January 1974, which allowed for such discretionary distribution by the bank only to Mrs. Cotsworth and her children, not to plaintiffs. According to Buttermore's testimony, this change was clearly Mrs. Dutrow's idea.

On April 24, 1975, Mrs. Dutrow amended the revocable trust agreement and added a codicil to her will in order to add *in terrorem* clauses to each instrument. Both the amendment and the codicil were prepared by Buttermore. At trial, Buttermore said that Mrs. Dutrow had decided to add the clause after reading that J. Paul Getty had included such a clause in his will to prevent litigation.

Buttermore next met with Mrs. Dutrow to discuss her estate on December 11, 1975. At this meeting, according to Buttermore's testimony, Mrs. Dutrow told him that she had decided to give her estate, other than special bequests or amounts, to Dorcas Cotsworth, to enable Dorcas to enjoy it during Dorcas' lifetime. Buttermore testified that he was "taken by surprise" by this proposal and tried to explain to Mrs. Dutrow that this change would result in additional taxes of between $700,000 and $800,000 when Dorcas died. But, according to Buttermore, Mrs. Dutrow insisted on making the change. The necessary amendments to the revocable trust agreement were prepared by Buttermore and executed by Mrs. Dutrow on January 9, 1976, providing for distribution of the principal to Dorcas upon Mrs. Dutrow's death, or, if Dorcas was not then living, equally among Mrs. Dutrow's grandchildren. A new will executed the same day provided, as had previous wills, that Dorcas would inherit all of Mrs. Dutrow's tangible personal property. The final change made by Mrs. Dutrow in her estate plans before she died in September 1977, was to amend the revocable trust to give $10,000 to each of her grandchildren at her death, apparently realizing that otherwise the Haynes children would likely not inherit anything.

The last testamentary document executed by the testatrix was a will dated April 8, 1976. It contained no further major changes in her dispositions. Mrs. Dutrow died on September 27, 1977 and her final will was admitted to probate by the Surrogate of Ocean County on October 12, 1977, with the First National State Bank of New Jersey as executor.

II

In any attack upon the validity of a will, it is generally presumed that "the testator was of sound mind and competent when he executed the will." Gellert v. Livingston, 5 N.J. 65, 71, 73 A.2d 916 (1950). If a will is tainted by "undue influence," it may be overturned. "Undue influence" has been defined as "mental, moral or physical" exertion which has destroyed the "free agency of a testator" by preventing the testator "from following the dictates of his own mind and will and accepting instead the domination and influence of another." In re Neuman, 133 N.J.Eq. 532, 534, 32 A.2d 826 (E. & A. 1943). When such a contention is made

> the burden of proving undue influence lies upon the contestant unless the will benefits one who stood in a confidential relationship to the testatrix and there are additional circumstances of a suspicious character present which require explanation. In such case the law raises a presumption of undue influence and the burden of proof is

shifted to the proponent. [In re Rittenhouse's Will, 19 N.J. 376, 378–379, 117 A.2d 401 (1955).] . . .

The first element necessary to raise a presumption of undue influence, a "confidential relationship" between the testator and a beneficiary, arises

> where trust is reposed by reason of the testator's weakness or dependence or where the parties occupied relations in which reliance is naturally inspired or in fact exists. . . . [In re Hopper, 9 N.J. 280, 282, 88 A.2d 193 (1952).]

Here, the aged Mrs. Dutrow, afflicted by the debilitations of advanced years, was dependent upon her sole surviving child with whom she lived and upon whom she relied for companionship, care and support. This was a relationship sustained by confidence and trust. The determination of the trial court, in this case, that there was a confidential relationship between the testatrix and the chief beneficiary of her will is unassailable.

The second element necessary to create the presumption of undue influence is the presence of suspicious circumstances which, in combination with such a confidential relationship, will shift the burden of proof to the proponent. Such circumstances need be no more than "slight." . . .

In this case there were suspicious circumstances attendant upon the execution of the will. There was a confidential relationship between the testatrix and her attorney, who was also the attorney for the daughter and the daughter's immediate family. Furthermore, following the establishment of the confidential relationship of the daughter's attorney with the testatrix, there was a drastic change in the testamentary dispositions of the testatrix, which favored the daughter. These factors collectively triggered the presumption that there was undue influence in the execution of the will.

On this record, the trial court correctly posited a presumption of undue influence that shifted the burden of proof on this issue to the proponents of the will. The court concluded ultimately on this issue, however, that the proponents, the defendants, had overcome the presumption of undue influence. The trial judge determined that Mrs. Dutrow was of firm mind and resolve, that the final testamentary disposition, though markedly different from previous plans, was not unnatural or instinctively unsound and it represented her actual intent. Further, the court found the explanation for Mrs. Dutrow's final testamentary disposition to be candid and satisfactory.

The plaintiffs argue vigorously that the trial court's findings of fact and conclusions are not supported by sufficient evidence. They contend that in view of the strength of the presumption of undue influence created by the confidential relationships and the peculiarly suspicious circumstances of this case, there is an unusually heavy burden of proof required to disprove undue influence, which defendants failed to meet.

In this jurisdiction, once a presumption of undue influence has been established the burden of proof shifts to the proponent of the will, who must, under normal circumstances, overcome that presumption by a preponderance of the evidence. In re Weeks' Estate, supra, 29 N.J. Super. at 538–539, 103 A.2d 43. . . .

In re Weeks' Estate, supra, recognized, however, that there were situations calling for a stronger presumption of undue influence and a commensurately heavier burden of proof to rebut the presumption. While in that case the presumption of undue influence was deemed to be rebuttable by a preponderance of evidence, the court acknowledged other

> cases where the presumption of undue influence is so heavily weighted with policy that the courts have demanded a sterner measure of proof than that usually obtaining upon civil issues. That is the situation, for instance, where an attorney benefits by the will of his client and especially where he draws it himself. [29 N.J. Super. at 539, 103 A.2d 43.]

It has been often recognized that a conflict on the part of an attorney in a testimonial situation is fraught with a high potential for undue influence, generating a strong presumption that there was such improper influence and warranting a greater quantum of proof to dispel the presumption. Thus, where the attorney who drew the will was the sole beneficiary, the Court required "substantial and trustworthy evidence of explanatory facts" and "candid and full disclosure" to dispel the presumption of undue influence. In re Blake's Will, 21 N.J. 50, 58–59, 120 A.2d 745 (1956). And, where an attorney-beneficiary, who had a preexisting attorney-client relationship with the testatrix, introduced the testatrix to the lawyer who actually drafted the challenged will, this Court has required evidence that was "convincing or impeccable," In re Rittenhouse's Will, supra, 19 N.J. at 382, 117 A.2d 401, "convincing," In re Hopper, supra, 9 N.J. at 285, 88 A.2d 193, and, "clear and convincing," In re Davis, supra, 14 N.J. at 170, 101 A.2d 521. . . .

In imposing the higher burden of proof in this genre of cases, our courts have continually emphasized the need for a lawyer of independence and undivided loyalty, owing professional allegiance to no one but the testator. In In re Rittenhouse's Will, supra, 19 N.J. at 380–382, 117 A.2d 401, the Court questioned the attorney's independence and loyalty in view of the attorney-beneficiary's role in bringing the draftsman and the testatrix together, noting that the beneficiary had been "unable to give a satisfactory explanation of the relationship" between himself, the draftsman and the testatrix, viz.:

> [I]t would appear the testatrix did not independently choose [the draftsman] as the scrivener of her will. It is fair to assume from the record that she was influenced to do so by [the beneficiary].

Similarly, in In re Davis, supra, 14 N.J. at 171, 101 A.2d 521, the Court observed:

> We wish to reiterate what has been said repeatedly by our courts as to the proprieties of a situation where the testatrix wishes to make her attorney or a member of his immediate family a beneficiary under a will. Ordinary prudence requires that such a will be drawn by some other lawyer of the testatrix' own choosing, so that any suspicion of undue influence is thereby avoided. Such steps are in conformance with the spirit of Canons 6, 11, of the Canons of Professional Ethics promulgated by this court. . . .

It is not difficult to appreciate the policy reasons for creating an especially strong presumption of undue influence in cases of attorney misconduct. Such professional delinquency is encompassed by our official rules governing the professional ethics of attorneys. Our disciplinary rules cover all gradations of professional departures from ethical norms, and, the existence of an ethical conflict exemplified in this case is squarely posited under DR 5–105.[7] This ethical rule prohibits an attorney from engaging in professional relationships that may impair his independent and untrammeled judgment with respect to his client. This disciplinary stricture

> should be practically self-demonstrative to any conscientious attorney. There is nothing novel about the ethical dilemma dealt with by DR 5–105. A lawyer cannot serve two masters in the same subject

---

[7] DR 5–105 Refusing to Accept or Continue Employment if the Interests of Another Client May Impair the Independent Professional Judgment of the Lawyer.

(A) A lawyer shall decline proffered employment if the exercise of his independent professional judgment in behalf of a client will be or is likely to be adversely affected by the acceptance of the proffered employment, except to the extent permitted under DR 5–105(C).

(B) A lawyer shall not continue multiple employment if the exercise of his independent professional judgment in behalf of a client will be or is likely to be adversely affected by his representation of another client, except to the extent permitted under DR 5–105(C).

(C) In situations covered by DR 5–105(A) and (B) except as prohibited by rule, opinion, directive or statute, a lawyer may represent multiple clients if he believes that he can adequately represent the interests of each and if each consents to the representation after full disclosure of the facts and of the possible effect of such representation on the exercise of his independent professional judgment on behalf of each.

(D) If a lawyer is required to decline employment or to withdraw from employment under DR 5–105, no partner or associate of his or his firm may accept or continue such employment.

matter if their interests are or may become actually or potentially in conflict. [In re Chase, 68 N.J. 392, 396, 346 A.2d 89 (1975).] . . .

Accordingly, it is our determination that there must be imposed a significant burden of proof upon the advocates of a will where a presumption of undue influence has arisen because the testator's attorney has placed himself in a conflict of interest and professional loyalty between the testator and the beneficiary. In view of the gravity of the presumption in such cases, the appropriate burden of proof must be heavier than that which normally obtains in civil litigation. . . . The standard in our evidence rules that conforms most comfortably with the level of proofs required by our decisions in this context is the burden of proof by clear and convincing evidence. . . . Hence, the presumption of undue influence created by a professional conflict of interest on the part of an attorney, coupled with confidential relationships between a testator and the beneficiary as well as the attorney, must be rebutted by clear and convincing evidence.

Applying these principles to this case, it is clear that attorney Buttermore was in a position of irreconcilable conflict within the common sense and literal meaning of DR 5–105. In this case, Buttermore was required, at a minimum, to provide full disclosure and complete advice to Mrs. Dutrow, as well as the Cotsworths, as to the existence and nature of the conflict and to secure knowing and intelligent waivers from each in order to continue his professional relationship with Mrs. Dutrow. DR 5–105(C). Even these prophylactic measures, however, might not have overcome the conflict, nor have been sufficient to enable the attorney to render unimpaired "independent professional judgment" on behalf of his client, DR 5–105(B); see Lieberman v. Employers Ins. of Wausau, supra, 84 N.J. at 338–340, 419 A.2d 417. Any conflict, of course, could have been avoided by Buttermore simply refusing to represent Mrs. Dutrow. DR 5–105(A), (B); see In re Davis, supra, at 171, 101 A.2d 521. But, Buttermore was apparently insensitive or impervious to the presence or extent of the professional conflict presented by these circumstances. He undertook none of these measures to eliminate the dual representation or overcome the conflict.[8] Consequently, a strong taint of undue influence was permit-

---

[8] In this case, we recognize that Buttermore believed in good faith that he was taking proper precautions to overcome or avoid the consequences of the improper conflict and did not believe or perceive that his position involved an impermissible conflict of interest in light of these measures. He also expressed the view that frequently estate planning involves members of an entire family and therefore no conflict exists for an attorney who has professional relationships with members of the family, in addition to the testator. This position is, of course, inconsistent with our explicit holding that such conduct, as exemplified by the facts of this case, violates DR 5–105. Since this application of DR 5–105 to such situations has not been generally acknowledged, we do not think it fair that ethical sanctions be pursued retroactively in this case for such conduct, since there are no additional aggravating circumstances. See In re Smock, 86 N.J. 426, 432 A.2d 34 (1981).

ted, presumptively, to be injected into the testamentary disposition of Mrs. Dutrow.

Accordingly, the attorney's conduct here, together with all of the other factors contributing to the likelihood of wrongful influence exerted upon the testatrix, has engendered a heavy presumption of undue influence which the proponents of the will must overcome by clear and convincing evidence.

This determination that clear and convincing evidence must be marshalled to overcome the presumption of undue influence appropriately requires that the matter be remanded to the trial court for new findings of fact and legal conclusions based upon application of this burden of proof. We remand, recognizing that there is considerable evidence in the record as to Mrs. Dutrow's intelligence, independence and persistence, of her alienation, to some extent, from the Haynes children, and as to her natural intent primarily to benefit her children, rather than her grandchildren. Moreover, all of this evidence is based upon the credibility of witnesses, which we cannot independently evaluate. We are also mindful that the trial court found that the explanation for Mrs. Dutrow's testamentary disposition was candid and satisfactory.

Nevertheless, the trial court does not appear to have given full weight to the additional significant factor generating the heightened presumption of undue influence in this case, namely, that occasioned by the conflict of interest on the part of the attorney drafting the will, whose testimony was crucial to the outcome of this case. Most importantly, the court's conclusion was premised upon an application of the conventional standard of proof entailing only a preponderance of the evidence. We therefore cannot with any certitude predict that the trial court's findings of fact and resultant conclusion would be the same were he to reassess the evidence, imposing upon the proponents of the will the burden of proof of lack of undue influence by clear and convincing evidence. Consequently, the fair disposition, which we now direct, is to remand the matter to the trial court for a redetermination of facts and conclusions based upon the record.

III

The second issue involves the enforceability of the *in terrorem* clauses challenged by the plaintiffs. . . .

As noted earlier, on April 24, 1975, Mrs. Dutrow amended the revocable trust agreement and added a codicil to her will in order to add *in terrorem* clauses to each instrument. The clause in the amendment to the revocable trust agreement, almost identical to that in the will, provided:

If any beneficiary under this trust shall contest the validity of, or object to this instrument, or attempt to vacate the same, or to alter or change any of the provisions hereof, such person shall be thereby deprived of all beneficial interest thereunder and of any share in this Trust and the share of such person shall become part of the residue of the trust, and such person shall be excluded from taking any part of such residue and the same shall be divided among the other persons entitled to take such residue.[9]

In 1977 the Legislature enacted N.J.S.A. 3A:2A–32 as part of the new probate code.[10] This statute renders *in terrorem* clauses in wills unenforceable if probable cause for a will contest exists:

A provision in a will purporting to penalize any interested person for contesting the will or instituting other proceedings relating to the estate is unenforceable if probable cause exists for instituting proceedings.

In Alper v. Alper, 2 N.J. 105, 65 A.2d 737 (1949), the Court said that the existence of probable cause to bring the challenge to the will should result in nonenforcement of an *in terrorem* clause "where the contest of the will is waged on the ground of forgery or subsequent revocation by a later will or codicil." However, where typical grounds of challenge were advanced—"fraud, undue influence, improper execution or lack of testamentary capacity"—the clause was deemed to be enforceable, notwithstanding probable cause, as a safeguard against deleterious, acrimonious and wasteful family litigation. Id. at 112–113, 65 A.2d 737. . . .

The new statute, N.J.S.A. 3A:2A–32, however, abolishes the distinction drawn by the Court in *Alper* between cases in which *in terrorem* clauses in wills shall be enforced, and those in which they shall not, stating quite simply that *whenever* there is probable cause to contest a will, the clause should not be enforced. While the statute applies neither to the will in this case, which was probated prior to the statute's effective date, nor to the trust agreement, since the statute applies only to wills, the statute is indicative of a legislative intent to create a policy less inhibitory to the bringing of challenges to testamentary instruments. There does not appear to be any logical reason why the purpose of the statute should not be presently recognized and be applied equally to trust instruments or should not be applied in the circumstances of this case.

There are public policy considerations both favoring and disfavoring the enforcement of *in terrorem* clauses. On the one hand, such provisions

---

[9] If enforced, the result would be to deprive each of the two plaintiffs of $10,000 which they were to receive under this trust agreement as modified by the fourth amendment thereto of April 7, 1976.

[10] N.J.S.A. 3A:2A–32 is identical to Uniform Probate Code (U.L.A.) § 3–905 (1969). . . .

seek to reduce vexatious litigation, avoid expenses that debilitate estates and give effect to a testator's clearly expressed intentions. . . .

On the other hand, a majority of jurisdictions have declined to enforce *in terrorem* clauses where challenges to testamentary instruments are brought in good faith and with probable cause. . . .

Given this relative equipoise of considerations, it is entirely appropriate for the courts to be sensitive and responsive to the Legislature's perception of the public interest and policy in these matters. . . . The assessment, balancing and resolution of these concerns by the Legislature, now reflected in the statute law, is, of course, not binding upon the judiciary's decisional authority in a matter not governed by such enactments. Nevertheless, the legislative handling of the subject is, and should be, strongly influential in the judicial quest for the important societal values which are constituent elements of the common law and find appropriate voice in the decisions of the court expounding the common law. . . .

We therefore decline to enforce an *in terrorem* clause in a will or trust agreement where there is probable cause to challenge the instrument. The trial court concluded that the plaintiffs in this case "proceeded in good faith and on probable cause." That finding is amply supported by evidence of record.

IV

We have determined that *in terrorem* clauses in the will and trust instruments are not enforceable. We have also directed, for reasons set forth in this opinion, that the case be remanded for new findings of fact and legal conclusions with respect to the major issue of undue influence in the execution of the will.

Accordingly, the judgment below is reversed and the matter remanded. Jurisdiction is not retained.

CLIFFORD, J., dissenting in part.

I am in full accord with the majority's meticulous treatment of the "undue influence" issue, but I part company on its decision concerning the *in terrorem* clauses.

On April 24, 1975, when Mrs. Dutrow added the challenged clauses to the testamentary instruments, enforcement of *in terrorem* clauses was perfectly in keeping with the public policy of this state, as it was at the time of the testator's death in 1977. As the Court acknowledges, . . . that policy was to give effect to such clauses where, as here, the instrument was contested on the ground of undue influence.

. . . As *Alper* instructs us, an *in terrorem* clause is

> a reasonable safeguard against attempted overthrow of the testamentary dispositions by a disappointed heir, striving for an undue advantage, and a device to lessen the wastage of the estate in litigation and the chance of increasing family animosities by besmirching the reputation of the testator when he is no longer alive to defend himself and to discourage the contesting of wills as a means of coercing a settlement. [2 N.J. at 112, 65 A.2d 737.]

Mrs. Dutrow's intentions in insisting on such a provision comported entirely with the judicially-declared public policy as of the time she made her testamentary dispositions and as of the time of her death.

Instead of honoring the testator's manifest wishes, however, the court looks for guidance to a statute not effective until a year after her death. . . . The majority bows to this "legislative handling" of the subject as an aid in the "judicial quest for the important societal values that are the constituent elements of the common law. . . ." Quite apart from the tardy surfacing of this newly recognized public policy is the shaky foundation upon which it rests. The Legislature, clearly in error (as forthrightly conceded by plaintiffs), believed that N.J.S.A. 3A:2A–32 codifies existing New Jersey case law on the subject. See Statement of Assembly Comm. on Judiciary, Law, Public Safety and Defense, Assembly Doc. No. 1717, L. 1977, c. 412 (1977). As demonstrated above, the statute does no such thing. It runs directly contrary to the case law.

We may view an *in terrorem* clause in a less charitable fashion than did the *Alper* court, perhaps as a device to wreak revenge on a disgruntled object of one's testamentary disposition. We may see such clauses as representing the most disagreeable impulses of a testator. They may lay bare one's mean, uncharitable, impervious, suspicious, hostile, downright churlish nature—and then some. I do *not* suggest that Mrs. Dutrow manifested any of those characteristics, but I *do* suggest that testators are allowed to exhibit all of them, and worse, without fear that a court will disregard their final wishes.

In keeping with both the testator's unambiguously-declared intent and the public policy of this state at the time of her death, I would give effect to the *in terrorem* clauses.

For reversal—JUSTICES SULLIVAN, PASHMAN, CLIFFORD, SCHREIBER and HANDLER—5.

For affirmance—None.

NOTES

1. *Estate planning considerations.* The opinion makes clear that Mrs. Dutrow was a wealthy woman, but it does not specify the precise amount of her net estate against which the death taxes were assessed. Her husband died in 1945, leaving an estate of approximately $8 million to Mrs. Dutrow and their two daughters. In a family situation of this kind, it is fair to speculate that the widow received the largest share, that her inheritance appreciated substantially between 1945 and 1977, and that she may have owned wealth derived from sources other than her husband. Had Mrs. Dutrow, like her husband, left an $8 million estate at her death in 1977, her estate would have had to pay a federal estate tax of approximately $4,600,000. (There would also have been a substantial state death tax, which would have been wholly or partially offset by a credit against the federal estate tax.) The same estate today would incur a much smaller tax liability due to the substantially higher exemption and lower rates applicable to large estates. On the operation of the federal estate tax, see Chapter 10.

A number of references in the opinion raise points mentioned elsewhere in the book. Mrs. Dutrow changed her domicile from York, Pennsylvania, to Short Hills, New Jersey. To accomplish this, she had to sever completely her settled connections with her original domicile to insure that her estate would not face liability for two sets of domiciliary death taxes, as did the estate of John T. Dorrance. Mr. Dorrance, the chief executive of the Campbell Soup Company, maintained two homes, one in New Jersey and one in Pennsylvania. Following his death, each state claimed that Dorrance was domiciled within its jurisdiction and on that basis assessed full death taxes upon his estate, amounting to more than $14 million in Pennsylvania and $12 million in New Jersey. The United States Supreme Court refused to resolve the conflicting claims of domicile, although in theory a person can possess only one domicile at any given time. For a discussion of the Dorrance rulings and of related cases, see Chapter 8, Section A.

Mrs. Dutrow was urged by her daughter and son-in-law to make inter vivos gifts. At that time, a donor was entitled to give $3,000 to each donee, each year, without incurring any gift tax. Under present law, this amount, known as the annual exclusion, has been increased to $13,000 per donee. Thus, today Mrs. Dutrow would be able to make gifts totaling $91,000 each year to her daughter and six grandchildren without any gift or estate tax. On the federal gift tax and the annual exclusion, see infra p. 997.

In its final form, Mrs. Dutrow's estate plan was set out in two documents: a will that bequeathed to her daughter her tangible personal property (e.g., jewelry and antiques), and a revocable inter vivos trust covering the rest of her property (including her Ralston Purina stock). Because she retained control over the trust, the trust principal was subject to estate tax just as if she continued to own it outright. Attorney Buttermore warned Mrs. Dutrow that an outright disposition of the estate to her daughter (who appears to have been independently wealthy) would add $700,000 or $800,000 to the daughter's estate taxes at the daughter's death. The attorney probably had in mind the creation of a trust which would pay income to the daughter for her life, with the trust property passing free of estate tax to the grandchildren at the daughter's death. On the present status of "generation-skipping" transfers for tax purposes, see infra p. 1048.

2. *Burden of proof.* In the principal case the court finds ample evidence of a confidential relationship between Mrs. Dutrow and Dorcas, coupled with suspicious circumstances attending the execution of the will, to raise a presumption of undue influence. Moreover, due to a conflict of interest on the part of attorney Buttermore, the court characterizes the presumption as a "heavy" one which can be overcome only by "clear and convincing" evidence. How likely is it that the proponents will prevail on remand?

Note that a will which favors one of the testator's children over the others is unlikely to be considered "unnatural" in the absence of other suspicious circumstances. See Estate of Holcomb, 63 P.3d 9 (Okla. 2002) (upholding will which left estate to one daughter and disinherited two other children; daughter successfully rebutted presumption of undue influence); Holland v. Holland, 596 S.E.2d 123 (Ga. 2004) (upholding will which left homestead to one son and property of equal value to be divided among other children and their issue; presumption of undue influence did not arise, even though will was drafted by son's lawyer at son's request, because testator did not have "confidential relationship" with son).

3. *No-contest clauses.* Clients frequently find the inclusion of an in terrorem or no-contest clause reassuring. Is a word of caution from the attorney appropriate? Consider again the competing views on the subject set out in Judge Clifford's separate opinion, supra.

The New Jersey statute described in the majority opinion, enacted in 1977, brought New Jersey into line with the majority of jurisdictions, which treat an in terrorem clause as unenforceable if probable cause exists for initiating the proceedings. The issue of probable cause will arise only if the contest fails to invalidate the will. What is the test of probable cause under such circumstances? See Restatement (Third) of Property: Wills and Other Donative Transfers § 8.5 cmt. c (2003) ("evidence that would lead a reasonable person, properly informed and advised, to conclude that there was a substantial likelihood that the challenge would be successful"). To the extent a no-contest clause is enforceable, secondary questions may arise. Does the clause apply to a person who seeks to ascertain the terms of the will in a judicial construction proceeding? To an infant beneficiary whose guardian joins the contest? To a person who refuses to initiate the contest but is made a party to it? To a surviving spouse who elects against the will and claims an elective share? To a pretermitted child who claims a statutory share? To a person who challenges an executor's qualification or seeks to hold the executor accountable for an alleged breach of fiduciary duty? To a person who asserts a claim as a creditor of the estate rather than as a beneficiary under the will? To a person who claims to be the true owner of property in derogation of the testator's title?

For further discussion of no-contest clauses, see Begleiter, Anti-Contest Clauses: When You Care Enough to Send the Final Threat, 26 Ariz. St. L.J. 629 (1994) (arguing in favor of general enforceability, subject to limited exceptions); see also Hirsch, Freedom of Testation/Freedom of Contract, 95 Minn. L.Rev. 2180 (2011) (comparing testamentary no-contest clause with functionally equivalent unilateral contract offer).

4. *Attorney-drafter as executor.* Often the attorney who drafted a client's will is particularly well situated to serve as executor, by reason of familiarity with the client's personal and financial circumstances. Although there is nothing improper in naming the attorney-drafter as executor, the confidential relationship between attorney and client gives rise to an obligation of "full disclosure and fair dealing" on the attorney's part. See Estate of Weinstock, 351 N.E.2d 647 (N.Y.1976). To avoid even the appearance of impropriety or overreaching, the attorney should take special precautions to ensure that the client understands the implications of naming the attorney or another person as executor. Unfortunately, however, in the absence of vigorous judicial enforcement, the standard of professional conduct has commanded mainly lip service. See, e.g., Will of Cromwell, 552 N.Y.S.2d 480 (Sur. 1989) (permitting attorney-drafter to serve as co-executor, despite lack of disclosure, but awarding costs against attorney and noting that "courts, in the past, have been remiss in overlooking [this] type of conduct"); State v. Gulbankian, 196 N.W.2d 733 (Wis.1972) (dismissing disciplinary proceedings against two attorneys for inserting provisions in wills naming themselves as executors or attorneys for estates, but warning that active solicitation of this kind of business is unethical). In 1995 the New York legislature responded by placing a burden of disclosure on an attorney who prepares a will in which he or she is named as executor. N.Y. SCPA § 2307–a requires that the testator be informed, prior to the execution of the will, of the range of persons eligible to serve as executor, the right of the executor to receive statutory commissions, and the right of the attorney to receive additional compensation if he or she renders legal services in connection with the executor's official duties. A written acknowledgment of disclosure, signed by the testator, must be filed in the proceeding for issuance of letters testamentary. If the written acknowledgment is not filed, the attorney-drafter is entitled to only one-half of the normal statutory executor's commissions.

5. *Professional responsibility.* As illustrated in the principal case, even an attorney who is not named as a beneficiary in the will may have conflicting interests which give rise to a heavy burden of explaining his or her representation of the testator. What steps, if any, might attorney Buttermore have taken to enable him to exercise "independent professional judgment" on behalf of his client?

In 1983 the American Bar Association promulgated Model Rules of Professional Conduct governing the professional behavior of attorneys. The Model Rules, either in their original form or as revised in 2002, have been adopted in most states. Rules 1.7 and 1.8 concerning conflicts of interest have special importance for estate planners. Rule 1.7 generally prohibits a lawyer from representing a client if there is a "significant risk" that the representation of a client will be "materially limited" by the lawyer's responsibilities to other persons or by the lawyer's own personal interest. Notwithstanding such a conflict of interest, the lawyer may nevertheless be permitted to represent the client if the lawyer reasonably believes that he or she will be able to provide "competent and diligent representation" to each affected client and each affected client gives "informed consent, confirmed in writing."

Rule 1.8(c) generally prohibits a lawyer from soliciting any "substantial gift" (including a testamentary gift) from a client or preparing an instrument which effectuates a substantial gift from a client to the lawyer or a person related to the lawyer, "unless the lawyer or other recipient of the gift is related to the client." The Official Comment notes that Rule 1.8(c) does not prevent a lawyer from accepting a simple gift such as a holiday present or a "token of appreciation" from a client if the transaction meets general standards of fairness. M.R.P.C. 1.8 cmt. However, if the gift is substantial and requires the preparation of a legally operative instrument such as a will or a deed, the Comment warns that "the client should have the detached advice that another lawyer can provide." Id. According to the Comment, Rule 1.8(c) does not prevent a lawyer from seeking appointment as executor or trustee of a client's will or trust, but such an appointment may be subject to the general conflict of interest provisions of Rule 1.7. In obtaining the client's informed consent, the lawyer should advise the client about "the nature and extent of the lawyer's financial interest in the appointment, as well as the availability of alternative candidates for the position." Id.

How well do these provisions address the issues raised in *Moses* and *Haynes*? Would the analysis in *Haynes* be different if Mr. Cotsworth were a lawyer who drafted a will for his mother-in-law? See McGovern, Undue Influence and Professional Responsibility, 28 Real Prop. Prob. & Tr. J. 643 (1994); Monopoli, Drafting Attorneys as Fiduciaries: Fashioning an Optimal Ethical Rule for Conflicts of Interest, 66 U. Pitt. L. Rev. 411 (2005).

C. FRAUD, DURESS, AND MISTAKE

LATHAM V. FATHER DIVINE
Court of Appeals of New York, 1949.
299 N.Y. 22, 85 N.E.2d 168.

DESMOND, JUDGE.

The amended complaint herein has, in response to a motion under rule 106 of the Rules of Civil Practice, been dismissed for insufficiency. Its principal allegations are these: plaintiffs are first cousins, but not distributees, of Mary Sheldon Lyon, who died in October, 1946, leaving a will, executed in 1943, which gave almost her whole estate to defendant Father Divine, leader of a religious cult, and to two corporate defendants in some way connected with that cult, and to an individual defendant (Patience Budd) said to be one of Father Divine's active followers; that said will has been, after a contest instituted by distributees, probated under a compromise agreement with the distributees, by the terms of which agreement, to which plaintiffs were not parties, the defendants just above referred to will receive a large sum from the estate; that after the making of said will, decedent on several occasions expressed "a desire and a determination to revoke the said will, and to execute a new will by which the plaintiffs would receive a substantial portion of the estate," "that shortly prior to the death of the deceased she had certain attorneys draft a new will in which the plaintiffs were named as legatees for a very substantial amount, totalling approximately $350,000"; that "by reason of the said false representations, the said undue influence and the said physical force" certain of the defendants "prevented the deceased from executing the said new Will"; that, shortly before decedent's death, decedent again expressed her determination to execute the proposed new will which favored plaintiffs, and that defendants "thereupon conspired to kill, and did kill, the deceased by means of a surgical operation performed by a doctor engaged by the defendants without the consent or knowledge of any of the relatives of the deceased."

Nothing is better settled than that, on such a motion as this, all the averments of the attacked pleading are taken as true. For present purposes, then, we have a case where one possessed of a large property and having already made a will leaving it to certain persons, expressed an intent to make a new testament to contain legacies to other persons, attempted to carry out that intention by having a new will drawn which contained a large legacy to those others, but was, by means of misrepresentations, undue influence, force, and indeed, murder, prevented, by the beneficiaries named in the existing will, from signing the new one. Plaintiffs say that those facts, if proven, would entitle them to a judicial declaration, which their prayer for judgment demands, that defendants, taking under the already probated will, hold what they have so taken as constructive trustees for plaintiffs, whom decedent wished to, tried to, and was kept from, benefiting.

We find in New York no decision directly answering the question as to whether or not the allegations above summarized state a case for relief in equity. But reliable texts, and cases elsewhere, see 98 A.L.R. 474 et seq., answer it in the affirmative. Leading writers, 3 Scott on Trusts, pp. 2371–2376; 3 Bogert on Trusts and Trustees, part 1, §§ 473–474, 498, 499; 1 Perry on Trusts and Trustees [7th ed.], pp. 265, 371, in one form or another, state the law of the subject to be about as it is expressed in comment *i* under section 184 of the Restatement of the Law of Restitution:

> *Preventing revocation of will and making new will.* Where a devisee or legatee under a will already executed prevents the testator by fraud, duress or undue influence from revoking the will and executing a new will in favor of another or from making a codicil, so that the testator dies leaving the original will in force, the devisee or legatee holds the property thus acquired upon a constructive trust for the intended devisee or legatee.

A frequently-cited case is Ransdel v. Moore, 153 Ind. 393, at pages 407–408, 53 N.E. 767, at page 771, 53 L.R.A. 753, where, with listing of many authorities, the rule is given thus:

> when an heir or devisee in a will prevents the testator from providing for one for whom he would have provided but for the interference of the heir or devisee, such heir or devisee will be deemed a trustee, by operation of law, of the property, real or personal, received by him from the testator's estate, to the amount or extent that the defrauded party would have received had not the intention of the deceased been interfered with. This rule applies also when an heir prevents the making of a will or deed in favor of another, and thereby inherits the property that would otherwise have been given such other person.

To the same effect, see 4 Page on Wills [3d ed.], p. 961.

While there is no New York case decreeing a constructive trust on the exact facts alleged here, there are several decisions in this court which, we think, suggest such a result and none which forbids it. Matter of O'Hara's Will, 95 N.Y. 403, 47 Am. Rep. 53; Trustees of Amherst College v. Ritch, 151 N.Y. 282, 45 N.E. 876, 37 L.R.A. 305; Edson v. Bartow, 154 N.Y. 199, 48 N.E. 541, and Ahrens v. Jones, 169 N.Y. 555, 62 N.E. 666, 88 Am. St. Rep. 620, which need not be closely analyzed here as to their facts, all announce, in one form or another, the rule that, where a legatee has taken property under a will, after agreeing outside the will, to devote that property to a purpose intended and declared by the testator, equity will enforce a constructive trust to effectuate that purpose, lest there be a fraud on the testator. In Williams v. Fitch, 18 N.Y. 546, a similar result was achieved in a suit for money had and received. In each of those four cases first above cited in this paragraph, the particular fraud consisted of the legatee's failure or refusal to carry out the testator's designs, after tacitly or expressly promising so to do. But we do not think that a breach of such an engagement is the only kind of fraud which will impel equity to action. A constructive trust will be erected whenever necessary to satisfy the demands of justice. Since a constructive trust is merely "the formula through which the conscience of equity finds expression" Beatty v. Guggenheim Exploration Co., 225 N.Y. 380, 386, 122 N.E. 378, 380 . . . , its applicability is limited only by the inventiveness of men who find new ways to enrich themselves unjustly by grasping what should not belong to them. Nothing short of true and complete justice satisfies equity, and, always assuming these allegations to be true, there seems no way of achieving total justice except by the procedure used here.

The Appellate Division held that Hutchins v. Hutchins [7 Hill 104 (1845)], was a bar to the maintenance of this suit. Hutchins v. Hutchins, supra, was a suit at law, dismissed for insufficiency in the days when law suits and equity causes had to be brought in different tribunals; the law court could give nothing but a judgment for damages, see discussion in 41 Harv. L. Rev. 313, supra. Testator Hutchins' son, named in an earlier will, charged that defendant had, by fraud, caused his father to revoke that will and execute a new one, disinheriting plaintiff. The court sustained a demurrer to the complaint, on the ground that the earlier will gave the son no title, interest or estate in his father's assets and no more than a hope or expectancy, the loss of which was too theoretical and tenuous a deprivation to serve as a basis for the award of damages. See, also, Simar v. Canaday, 53 N.Y. 298, 302, 303, 13 Am. Rep. 523. Plaintiffs' disappointed hopes in the present case, held the Appellate Division, were similarly lacking in substance. But disappointed hopes and unrealized expectations were all that the secretly intended beneficiaries, not named in the wills, had in Matter of O'Hara's Will, supra; Trustees of Amherst College v. Ritch, supra and Edson v. Bartow, supra, but that in itself was not enough to prevent the creation of constructive trusts in their favor. Hutchins v. Hutchins, supra, it seems, holds only this: that in a suit at law there must, as a basis for damages, be an invasion of a common-law right. To use that same standard in a suit for the declaration and enforcement of a constructive trust would be to deny and destroy the whole equitable theory of constructive trusts.

Nor do we agree that anything in the Decedent Estate Law, Consol. Laws, c. 13, § 1 et seq., or the Statute of Frauds stands in the way of recovery herein. This is not a proceeding to probate or establish the will which plaintiffs say testatrix was prevented from signing, nor is it an attempt to accomplish a revocation of the earlier will as were Matter of Evans' Will, 113 App. Div. 373, 98 N.Y.S. 1042 and Matter of McGill's Will, 229 N.Y. 405, 411, 128 N.E. 194, 195, 196. The will Mary Sheldon Lyon did sign has been probated and plaintiffs are not contesting, but proceeding on, that probate, trying to reach property which has effectively passed thereunder. See Ahrens v. Jones, 169 N.Y. 555, 561, 62 N.E. 666, 667, 668, 88 Am. St. Rep. 620, supra. Nor is this a suit to enforce an agreement to make a will or create a trust or any other promise by decedent. . . . This complaint does not say that decedent or defendants promised plaintiffs anything or that defendants made any promise to decedent.

The story is, simply, that defendants, by force and fraud, kept the testatrix from making a will in favor of plaintiffs. We cannot say, as matter of law, that no constructive trust can arise therefrom.

The ultimate determinations in Matter of O'Hara's Will, supra, and Edson v. Bartow, supra, that the estate went to testator's distributees do not help defendants here, since, after the theory of constructive trust had been indorsed by this court in those cases, the distributees won out in the end, but only because the secret trusts intended by the two testators were, in each case, of kinds forbidden by statutes.

We do not agree with appellants that Riggs v. Palmer, 115 N.Y. 506, 22 N.E. 188, 5 L.R.A. 340, 12 Am. St. Rep. 819, completely controls our decision here. That was the famous case where a grandson, overeager to get the remainder interest set up for him in his grandfather's will, murdered his grandsire. After the will had been probated, two daughters of the testator who, under the will, would take if the grandson should predecease testator, sued and got judgment decreeing a constructive trust in their favor. It may be, as respondents assert, that the application of Riggs v. Palmer, supra, here would benefit not plaintiffs, but this testator's distributees. We need not pass on that now. But Riggs v. Palmer, supra, is generally helpful to appellant, since it forbade the grandson profiting by his own wrong in connection with a will; and, despite an already probated will and the Decedent Estate Law, Riggs v. Palmer, supra, used the device or formula of constructive trust to right the attempted wrong, and prevent unjust enrichment.

The reference to a conspiracy in the complaint herein makes it appropriate to mention Keviczky v. Lorber, 290 N.Y. 297, 49 N.E.2d 146, 146 A.L.R. 1410. Keviczky, a real estate broker, got judgment on findings that a conspiracy by defendants had prevented him from earning a commission which he would otherwise have gotten. All sides agreed that he had not in fact performed the engagement which would have entitled him to a commission as such; thus, when the conspiracy intervened to defeat his efforts, he had no contractual right to a commission but only an expectation thereof which was frustrated by the conspirators. Thus again we see, despite the broad language of Hutchins v. Hutchins, supra, that it is not the law that disappointed expectations and unrealized probabilities may never, under any circumstances, be a basis for recovery.

This suit cannot be defeated by any argument that to give plaintiffs judgment would be to annul those provisions of the Statute of Wills requiring due execution by the testator. Such a contention, if valid, would have required the dismissal in a number of the suits herein cited. The answer is in Ahrens v. Jones, 169 N.Y. 555, 561, 62 N.E. 666, 668, 88 Am. St. Rep. 620, supra:

The trust does not act directly upon the will by modifying the gift, for the law requires wills to be wholly in writing; but it acts upon the gift itself as it reaches the possession of the legatee, or as soon as he is entitled to receive it. The theory is that the will has full effect by passing an absolute legacy to the legatee, and that then equity, in order to defeat fraud, raises a trust in favor of those intended to be benefited by the testator, and compels the legatee, as a trustee ex maleficio, to turn over the gift to them.

The judgment of the Appellate Division, insofar as it dismissed the complaint herein, should be reversed, and the order of Special Term affirmed, with costs in this court and in the Appellate Division.

LOUGHRAN, C.J., and CONWAY and FULD, JJ., concur with DESMOND, J.

LEWIS and DYE, JJ., dissent and vote for affirmance upon the grounds stated by VAUGHAN, J., writing for the Appellate Division.

Judgment reversed, etc.

NOTES

1. *Undue influence or fraud.* Although the distinction between fraud and undue influence frequently becomes blurred in cases where a will is challenged as having been wrongfully procured, the two concepts are theoretically distinct. Fraud requires proof that a person has made a false representation, knowing it to be false, with the intention that the testator rely on it, which in fact the testator has done, leading to the conclusion that the will does not truly represent the testator's intent. Fraud may be practiced on an intelligent person who is in no way susceptible to undue influence. See Estate of Ford, 120 N.W.2d 647 (Wis.1963) (brother named as beneficiary in will told testator that disinherited niece and nephew were making claims to his property; no fraud, since statements were not shown to be false); Lowe Foundation v. Northern Trust Co., 96 N.E.2d 831 (Ill.App.1951) (testator, relying on attorney's advice, failed to execute codicil; intended beneficiaries not entitled to relief because attorney's statements were not knowingly false and were not intended to benefit any person under will).

A contestant alleging fraud must prove that the fraud affected the disposition in the will. See Estate of Roblin, 311 P.2d 459 (Or. 1957) (no fraud where sister's comments about brother, while not strictly accurate, merely provided occasion for testator to disinherit brother, which he might have done independently even if sister had said nothing). In Estate of Carson, 194 P. 5 (Cal.1920), testator left a bequest of more than $100,000 to "my husband J. Gamble Carson." In fact, although Carson had fraudulently concealed the fact, his marriage to testator was invalid because he was already married to another woman. The case was remanded to the trial court to determine whether Carson's fraud was causally related to the bequest in testator's will:

> Now, a case can be imagined where, nothing more appearing than that the testatrix had been deceived into a void marriage and had never been undeceived, it might fairly be said that a conclusion that such deceit had affected a bequest to the supposed husband would not be warranted. If, for example, the parties had lived happily together for twenty years, it would be difficult to say that the wife's bequest to her supposed husband was founded on her supposed legal relation with him and not primarily on their long and intimate association. It might well be that if she were undeceived at the end of that time, her feeling would be, not one of resentment at the fraud upon her, but of thankfulness that she had been deceived into so many years of happiness. But, on the other hand, a case can easily be imagined where the reverse would be true. If in this case the will had been made immediately after marriage and the testatrix had then died within a few days, the conclusion would be well-nigh irresistible, in the absence of some peculiar circumstance, that the will was founded on the supposed legal relation into which the testatrix had been deceived into believing she was entering. [194 P. at 8–9.]

A man ingratiated himself with a terminally ill woman and induced her to make a will naming him as sole beneficiary. He then persuaded her to marry him, in the hope of securing his inheritance from challenge, and she died shortly afterward. Assuming the will is void on the ground of fraud or undue influence, is the husband nevertheless entitled to claim statutory allowances and an omitted spouse's share of the wife's estate? Compare Estate of Lint, 957 P.2d 755 (Wash. 1998) (allowing post-mortem challenge to marriage on ground of fraud), with Riddell v. Edwards, 76 P.3d 847 (Alaska 2003) (refusing to allow post-mortem challenge to marriage in absence of gross fraud coupled with mental disability).

Testator, elderly and infirm, became agitated when her son told her that her daughter was "a thief and a burglar" and was planning to have testator declared incompetent and confined to a nursing home. Testator promptly executed a will which disinherited the daughter and left the bulk of her estate to the son. After the testator's death, the daughter challenges the will on the ground of fraud, alleging that the son intentionally made false statements for the purpose of inducing testator to make a new will. What result? See Geduldig v. Posner, 743 A.2d 247 (Md. App. 1999). What if the son believed that his statements about the daughter were true? What if the son made no false representations of fact, but led the testator to doubt the daughter's honesty ("she's driving an expensive new car and she won't say where she found the money to pay for it") and then stood by silently when the testator explained that she had decided to disinherit the daughter because she no longer trusted her? See Harper v. Harper, 554 S.E.2d 454 (Ga. 2001) (no fraud where statements not literally untrue); Rood v. Newberg, 718 N.E.2d 886 (Mass. App. 1999) (silence may constitute fraud in context of confidential relationship giving rise to duty of disclosure); Hagen v. Hickenbottom, 48 Cal.Rptr.2d 197 (App. 1995) (remanding for determination whether beneficiary's truthful statements to testator about disinherited grandson's behavior amounted to undue influence). What if the son merely told the testator that the daughter was devious, untrustworthy, and immoral?

2. *Constructive trust.* Where a wrongdoer obtains a legacy by fraud, duress, or undue influence, the usual remedy is by way of a will contest in the probate court. If, for some reason, no relief is available in the probate proceeding, the equitable remedy of a constructive trust has long been available in courts of general jurisdiction. For example, if the decedent was wrongfully prevented by his or her heirs from executing a will, the probate proceeding provides no recourse against the heirs; there is no procedure for contesting an intestacy. Similarly, if a beneficiary of an existing will wrongfully prevented the testator from revoking the will, there is no ground for contesting the lack of revocation. In such cases, courts generally impose a constructive trust in favor of the intended beneficiaries to prevent unjust enrichment of those who would otherwise profit from the wrongdoer's actions. See, in addition to the principal case, Pope v. Garrett, 211 S.W.2d 559 (Tex. 1948) (heirs forcibly prevented testator from making a will); Morris v. Morris, 642 S.W.2d 448 (Tex.1982) (beneficiary of will fraudulently prevented revocation); Brazil v. Silva, 185 P. 174 (Cal.1919) (beneficiary of will pretended to destroy it in testator's presence but later offered it for probate); White v. Mulvania, 575 S.W.2d 184 (Mo.1978) (testator failed to change will in reliance on attorney's fraudulent promise).

Is the constructive trust remedy available only to recapture property from a wrongdoer or may it also be used to award the property to a person whom the court believes the testator meant to benefit? Recall that in the principal case Mary Sheldon Lyon's heirs had settled their contest of the will before the plaintiffs, her cousins (who were not her heirs), brought their action against Father Divine. Suppose that, instead of settling the will contest, the heirs had obtained a decree invalidating the will and ordering an intestate distribution. Would the plaintiffs then be entitled to recover $350,000 from the heirs on a constructive trust theory? See Pope v. Garrett, supra, imposing a constructive trust on the intestate shares of all the heirs (not merely the wrongdoers) in favor of the decedent's intended beneficiaries. If the rationale for imposing a constructive trust depends on wrongdoing, why is the remedy not limited to depriving the wrongdoer of the fruits of his or her own misconduct?

3. *Tortious interference.* Many courts recognize a cause of action sounding in tort for wrongful interference with an expected gift or inheritance. The interference may involve inducing the decedent to make a new will or change the terms of an existing will; preventing the execution, revocation, or amendment of a will; or draining assets from the probate estate through inter vivos gifts or nonprobate transfers. See Barone v. Barone, 294 S.E.2d 260 (W.Va.1982) (preparation of new will); Cyr v. Cote, 396 A.2d 1013 (Me.1979)

(estate depleted by inter vivos transfers). The elements of the claim have been summarized as follows: (1) the existence of an expectancy; (2) intentional interference with that expectancy; (3) tortious conduct involved with the interference, such as fraud, duress, or undue influence; (4) reasonable certainty that the expectancy would have been realized but for the interference; and (5) damages. See Estate of Ellis, 923 N.E.2d 237 (Ill. 2009); Doughty v. Morris, 871 P.2d 380 (N.M.App.1994); see also Restatement (Second) of Torts § 774B (1979) ("One who by fraud, duress or other tortious means intentionally prevents another from receiving from a third person an inheritance or gift that he would otherwise have received is subject to liability to the other for loss of the inheritance or gift."). Statutes limiting the time within which a probate court order may be contested or appealed are not applicable to actions based on fraud in courts of general jurisdiction. If, however, adequate remedies are available in the probate proceedings, the parties will be required to exhaust those remedies before pursuing a separate action for tortious interference elsewhere. See Jackson v. Kelly, 44 S.W.3d 328 (Ark. 2001) (dismissing tort claim which was in effect a collateral attack on will already admitted to probate); Robinson v. First State Bank of Monticello, 454 N.E.2d 288 (Ill.1983) (same); DeWitt v. Duce, 408 So.2d 216 (Fla.1981) (tort claim recognized only where no adequate remedy available in probate proceeding); cf. Huffey v. Lea, 491 N.W.2d 518 (Iowa 1992) (allowing tort claim following successful will contest).

A person, not an heir, who was named as a beneficiary in an earlier will has standing to bring an action for malicious interference with the expected legacy. See Nemeth v. Banhalmi, 466 N.E.2d 977 (Ill.App.1984) (revocation of will naming testator's stepdaughter as beneficiary); Davison v. Feuerherd, 391 So.2d 799 (Fla.App.1980) (beneficiary of revocable trust). The *Latham* decision is unusual in extending standing to persons who were neither heirs nor beneficiaries of a previously executed will.

See generally Goldberg & Sitkoff, Torts and Estates: Remedying Wrongful Interference With Inheritance, 65 Stan. L. Rev. (2013); Fried, The Disappointed Heir: Going Beyond the Probate Process to Remedy Wrongdoing or Rectify Mistake, 39 Real Prop. Prob. & Tr. J. 357 (2004); Evans, Torts to Expectancies in Decedents' Estates, 93 U. Pa. L. Rev. 187 (1944).

4. *Secret trust.* A "secret trust" arises where a testator leaves property to a legatee in reliance on the latter's promise to hold the property for the benefit of a third person. If the legacy is absolute on its face, the arrangement cannot be enforced as an express testamentary trust because the will does not manifest an intent to benefit the third person. This does not mean, however, that the legatee can repudiate his promise and keep the property for himself. To prevent unjust enrichment, a court will require the legatee to hold the property as constructive trustee for the intended beneficiary. The *Latham* opinion refers to the secret trust doctrine with approval: "where a legatee has taken property under a will, after agreeing outside the will, to devote that property to a purpose intended and declared by the testator, equity will en-

force a constructive trust to effectuate that purpose, lest there be a fraud on the testator." See also Restatement (Third) of Trusts § 18 (2003).

T's son *S* predeceased *T* leaving a widow *W* and minor child *C* from a prior marriage. *T* was very close to *W*, and relied on *W*'s advice and assistance in business matters. *T* died leaving her entire estate to *W* with the oral understanding that *W* would see to *C*'s support and education. *T*'s heirs contest the will on grounds of fraud and undue influence. *W* insists that she is prepared to carry out *T*'s intent, but has had no opportunity to show her good or bad faith. What result? See Wilhoit v. Fite, 341 S.W.2d 806 (Mo.1960).

MATTER OF SNIDE

Court of Appeals of New York, 1981.
52 N.Y.2d 193, 437 N.Y.S.2d 63, 418 N.E.2d 656.

WACHTLER, JUDGE.

This case involves the admissibility of a will to probate. The facts are simply stated and are not in dispute. Harvey Snide, the decedent, and his wife, Rose Snide, intending to execute mutual wills at a common execution ceremony, each executed by mistake the will intended for the other. There are no other issues concerning the required formalities of execution (see EPTL 3–2.1), nor is there any question of the decedent Harvey Snide's testamentary capacity, or his intention and belief that he was signing his last will and testament. Except for the obvious differences in the names of the donors and beneficiaries on the wills, they were in all other respects identical.

The proponent of the will, Rose Snide, offered the instrument Harvey actually signed for probate. The Surrogate, 96 Misc. 2d 513, 409 N.Y.S.2d 204 decreed that it could be admitted, and further that it could be reformed to substitute the name "Harvey" wherever the name "Rose" appeared, and the name "Rose" wherever the name "Harvey" appeared. The Appellate Division, 74 A.D.2d 930, 426 N.Y.S.2d 155, reversed on the law, and held under a line of lower court cases dating back into the 1800's, that such an instrument may not be admitted to probate. We would reverse.

It is clear from the record, and the parties do not dispute the conclusion, that this is a case of a genuine mistake. It occurred through the presentment of the wills to Harvey and Rose in envelopes, with the envelope marked for each containing the will intended for the other. The attorney, the attesting witnesses, and Harvey and Rose, all proceeding with the execution ceremony without anyone taking care to read the front pages, or even the attestation clauses of the wills, either of which would have indicated the error.

Harvey Snide is survived by his widow and three children, two of whom have reached the age of majority. These elder children have executed waivers and have consented to the admission of the instrument to probate. The minor child, however, is represented by a guardian ad litem who refuses to make such a concession. The reason for the guardian's objection is apparent. Because the will of Harvey would pass the entire estate to Rose, the operation of the intestacy statute (EPTL 4–1.1) after a denial of probate is the only way in which the minor child will receive a present share of the estate.

The gist of the objectant's argument is that Harvey Snide lacked the required testamentary intent because he never intended to execute the document he actually signed. This argument is not novel, and in the few American cases on point it has been the basis for the denial of probate (see Nelson v. McDonald, 61 Hun. 406, 16 N.Y.S. 273; Matter of Cutler, Sur., 58 N.Y.S.2d 604; Matter of Bacon, 165 Misc. 259, 300 N.Y.S. 920; see, also, Matter of Pavlinko, 394 Pa. 564, 148 A.2d 528; Matter of Goettel, 184 Misc. 155, 55 N.Y.S.2d 61). However, cases from other common-law jurisdictions have taken a different view of the matter, and we think the view they espouse is more sound (Matter of Brander, 4 Dom. L. Rep. 688 [1952]; Guardian, Trust & Executor's Co. of New Zealand v. Inwood, 65 N.Z. L. Rep. 614 [1946] [New Zealand]; see Wills, 107 U. of Pa. L. Rev. 1237, 1239–1240; Kennedy, Wills—Mistake—Husband and Wife Executing Wills Drawn for Each Other—Probate of Husband's Will With Substitutions, 31 Can. Bar. Rev. 185).

Of course it is essential to the validity of a will that the testator was possessed of testamentary intent (Matter of May, 241 N.Y. 1, 148 N.E. 770; 64 N.Y. Jur., Wills, § 11; see EPTL 1–2.18), however, we decline the formalistic view that this intent attaches irrevocably to the document prepared, rather than the testamentary scheme it reflects. Certainly, had a carbon copy been substituted for the ribbon copy the testator intended to sign, it could not be seriously contended that the testator's intent should be frustrated (Matter of Epstein, Sur., 136 N.Y.S.2d 884, see 81 A.L.R.2d 1112, 1120–1121). Here the situation is similar. Although Harvey mistakenly signed the will prepared for his wife, it is significant that the dispositive provisions in both wills, except for the names, were identical.

Moreover, the significance of the only variance between the two instruments is fully explained by consideration of the documents together, as well as in the undisputed surrounding circumstances. Under such facts it would indeed be ironic—if not perverse—to state that because what has occurred is so obvious, and what was intended so clear, we must act to nullify rather than sustain this testamentary scheme. The instrument in question was undoubtedly genuine, and it was executed in the manner required by the statute. Under these circumstances it was properly admitted to probate (see Matter of Pascal, 309 N.Y. 108, 113–114, 127 N.E.2d 835).

In reaching this conclusion we do not disregard settled principles, nor are we unmindful of the evils which the formalities of will execution are designed to avoid; namely, fraud and mistake. To be sure, full illumination of the nature of Harvey's testamentary scheme is dependent in part on proof outside of the will itself. However, this is a very unusual case, and the nature of the additional proof should not be ignored. Not only did the two instruments constitute reciprocal elements of a unified testamentary plan, they both were executed with statutory formality, including the same attesting witnesses, at a contemporaneous execution ceremony. There is absolutely no danger of fraud, and the refusal to read these wills together would serve merely to unnecessarily expand formalism, without any corresponding benefit. On these narrow facts we decline this unjust course.

Nor can we share the fears of the dissent that our holding will be the first step in the exercise of judicial imagination relating to the reformation of wills. Again, we are dealing here solely with identical mutual wills both simultaneously executed with statutory formality.

For the reasons we have stated, the order of the Appellate Division should be reversed, and the matter remitted to that court for a review of the facts.

JONES, JUDGE (dissenting).

I agree with the Appellate Division that the Surrogate's Court had no authority to reform the decedent's will and am of the conviction that the willingness of the majority in an appealing case to depart from what has been consistent precedent in the courts of the United States and England will prove troublesome in the future. This is indeed an instance of the old adage that hard cases make bad law.

Our analysis must start with the recognition that any statute of wills (now articulated in this State at EPTL 3–2.1) operates frequently to frustrate the identifiable dispositive intentions of the decedent. It is never sufficient under our law that the decedent's wishes be clearly established; our statute, like those of most other common-law jurisdictions, mandates with but a few specific exceptions that the wishes of the decedent be memorialized with prescribed formality. The statutes historically have been designed for the protection of testators, particularly against fraudulent changes in or additions to wills. "[W]hile often it may happen that a will truly expressing the intention of the testator is denied probate for failure of proper execution, it is better that this should happen under a proper construction of the statute than that the individual case should be permitted to weaken those provisions intended to protect testators generally from fraudulent alterations of their wills" (64 N.Y. Jur., Wills, § 198, p. 348).

Next it must be recognized that what is admitted to probate is a paper writing, a single integrated instrument (codicils are considered integral components of the decedent's "will"). We are not concerned on admission to probate with the substantive content of the will; our attention must be focused on the paper writing itself. As to that, there can be no doubt whatsoever that Harvey Snide did not intend as his will the only document that he signed on August 13, 1970.

Until the ruling of the Surrogate of Hamilton County in this case, the application of these principles in the past had uniformly been held in our courts to preclude the admission to probate of a paper writing that the decedent unquestionably intended to execute when he and another were making mutual wills but where, through unmistakable inadvertence, each signed the will drawn for the other. Nor had our courts blinkingly invoked a doctrine of equitable reformation to reach the same end. . . .

On the basis of commendably thorough world-wide research, counsel for appellant has uncovered a total of 17 available reported cases involving mutual wills mistakenly signed by the wrong testator. Six cases arise in New York, two in Pennsylvania, three in England, one in New Zealand and five in Canada. With the exception of the two recent Surrogate's decisions (*Snide* and *Iovino*) relief was denied in the cases from New York, Pennsylvania and England. The courts that have applied the traditional doctrines have not hesitated, however, to express regret at judicial inability to remedy the evident blunder. Relief was granted in the six cases from the British Commonwealth. In these cases it appears that the court has been moved by the transparency of the obvious error and the egregious frustration of undisputed intention which would ensue from failure to correct that error.

Under doctrines both of judicial responsibility not to allow the prospect of unfortunate consequence in an individual case to twist the application of unquestioned substantive legal principle and of *stare decisis*, I perceive no jurisprudential justification to reach out for the disposition adopted by the majority. Not only do I find a lack of rigorous judicial reasoning in this result; more important, I fear an inability to contain the logical consequences of this decision in the near future. Thus, why should the result be any different where, although the two wills are markedly different in content, it is equally clear that there has been an erroneous contemporaneous cross-signing by the two would-be testators, or where the scrivener has prepared several drafts for a single client and it is established beyond all doubt that the wrong draft has been mistakenly signed? Nor need imagination stop there.

For the reasons stated, I would adhere to the precedents, and affirm the order of the Appellate Division.

JASEN, FUCHSBERG and MEYER, JJ., concur with WACHTLER, J.

JONES, J., dissents and votes to affirm in a separate opinion in which COOKE, C.J., and GABRIELLI, J., concur.

NOTES

1. *Remedies for mistake.* The "settled principles" to which the majority opinion refers are embodied in the traditional rule that there is no remedy to reform mistakes of law or fact made by a testator in the drafting or execution of a will. See Gifford v. Dyer, 2 R.I. 99 (1852) (omission from will of testator's only child, who had been absent many years, was not the result of mistake, but court indicated that in any event a mistake can be remedied only if the will shows what testator would have intended if true facts were known); Sadler v. Sadler, 167 N.W.2d 187 (Neb.1969) (wife entitled to elect against will although husband mistakenly believed he had satisfied her claim by inter vivos settlement). The "no-reformation" rule has been applied where the mistake was more on the part of the attorney than of the testator. See Mahoney v. Grainger, infra p. 454; Estate of Pavlinko, 148 A.2d 528 (Pa.1959) (denying relief on facts similar to those of *Snide*; according to the majority, granting reformation for mistake would render the Wills Act a "meaningless . . . scrap of paper" and would open the door to "countless fraudulent claims"); but see UPC § 2–805, infra p. 467 (authorizing judicial reformation to cure mistake of fact or law).

Courts generally refuse to reform wills on the ground that they cannot accept extrinsic statements of testator's intent which have not been formally attested in accordance with the requirements of the Statute of Wills. In interpreting ambiguous language in a will, however, courts may resort to extrinsic evidence; in theory, the process involves discovering the meaning of the terms of the will, not altering or supplementing them. For further discussion of the process of interpretation and the admissibility of extrinsic evidence, see Chapter 5, Section D. See generally Henderson, Mistake and Fraud in Wills, 47 B.U. L. Rev. 303, 461 (1967) (parts 1 & 2).

2. *Ante-mortem probate.* A will may be attacked by a disappointed heir on grounds of lack of testamentary capacity, undue influence, fraud, or mistake. By the time the validity of the will is called into question in a probate proceeding, the testator is necessarily dead and unable to testify. Frequently the contestant attacks the will not in the expectation of prevailing on the merits but rather in the hope of reaching a settlement with the beneficiaries under the will, who are often eager to avoid the expense, delay, and publicity of

a trial. To ward off such strike suits, the attorney may take various precautions at the time the will is executed: preparing for the record an affidavit which recounts the events that occurred during the attestation proceedings and describes the testator's demeanor and conduct; securing supporting affidavits from the witnesses, the testator's physician or psychiatrist, and friends and acquaintances of the testator. Some attorneys go even further and videotape the execution of the will, though this procedure may prove counterproductive. See Geduldig v. Posner, 743 A.2d 247 (Md. App. 1999) (noting that videotape of "orchestrated events" provided strong evidence of capacity but was also consistent with claims of fraud and undue influence); cf. Estate of Lakatosh, 656 A.2d 1378 (Pa. Super. 1995) (audiotape showed testator was "easily distracted," had a "weakened intellect," and was "somewhat out of touch with reality"). See generally Beyer & Buckley, Videotape and the Probate Process: The Nexus Grows, 42 Okla. L. Rev. 43 (1989); Jaworski, Will Contests, 1 Baylor L. Rev. 87 (1958).

Commentators have argued that many of these problems could be avoided by probating the will when the testator is still alive and able to rebut spurious claims. See Cavers, Ante Mortem Probate: An Essay in Preventive Law, 1 U. Chi. L. Rev. 440 (1934). One commentator recommends a declaratory judgment procedure which could be invoked by the testator to determine the validity of the will and the issue of testamentary capacity. See Fink, Ante–Mortem Probate Revisited: Can an Idea Have a Life After Death?, 37 Ohio St. L.J. 264 (1976). See also Leopold & Beyer, Ante–Mortem Probate: A Viable Alternative, 43 Ark. L. Rev. 131 (1990).

A few states have enacted ante-mortem probate statutes. See, e.g., Alaska Stat. §§ 13.12.530 et seq.; Ark. Stat. §§ 28–40–201 et seq.; N.D. Cent. Code §§ 30.1–08.1–01 et seq.; Ohio Rev. Code §§ 2107.081 et seq. In practical effect, these statutes authorize the testator to institute a contest of his or her own will, by giving notice to the persons who would be interested parties (i.e., intestate successors, takers under earlier wills, etc.) if the testator died at the commencement of the suit, and thereby to require them to proceed with the contest in the testator's presence. A number of flaws in the procedure have been cited: the testator's heirs, who cannot be finally determined until the testator actually dies, may not have received notice of the ante-mortem probate and thus may not have had an opportunity to be heard; the contestants have no incentive to participate (or to incur the expense of litigation), since the testator may revoke the will after the proceeding is concluded; the testator may not wish to disclose the contents of the will; and it may be difficult and costly to determine who is entitled to notice. See Fellows, The Case Against Living Probate, 78 Mich. L. Rev. 1066 (1980). Recommendations to remedy these problems have been forthcoming. See Langbein, Living Probate: The Conservatorship Model, 77 Mich. L. Rev. 63 (1978) (recommending the appointment of a conservator to represent all the persons who might be contestants, with the testator paying the conservator's reasonable costs); Alexander, The Conservatorship Model: A Modification, 77 Mich. L. Rev. 86 (1978); Alexander & Pearson, Alternative Models of Ante–Mortem Probate and Procedural Due Process Limitations on Succession, 78 Mich. L. Rev. 89 (1979) (recommending an administrative proceeding to which only the guardian ad litem, representing all interested parties, receives notice and in which the contents of the will are not necessarily made public).

3. *Alternative dispute resolution.* Another alternative to a full-fledged will contest is a mediation proceeding in which the interested parties seek to reach a mutually acceptable resolution with the assistance of a neutral third party. Mediation is voluntary; even in a court-ordered proceeding, no settlement can be imposed on parties without their consent, and a successful resolution depends on the voluntary and active participation of the parties. For discussions of the potential advantages and drawbacks of mediation in the probate context, see Love & Sterk, Leaving More Than Money: Mediation Clauses in Estate Planning Documents, 65 Wash. & Lee L. Rev. 539 (2008) (comparing mediation and no-contest clauses); Madoff, Lurking in the Shadow: The Unseen Hand of Doctrine in Dispute Resolution, 76 So. Cal. L.Rev. 161 (2002) (analyzing doctrinal obstacles to nonjudicial settlement); Gary, Mediation and the Elderly: Using Mediation to Resolve Probate Disputes Over Guardianship and Inheritance, 32 Wake Forest L.Rev. 397 (1997) (evaluating benefits and shortcomings of mediation).

CHAPTER 5

WILLS

■ ■ ■

A. FORMALITIES OF EXECUTION

1. ATTESTED WILLS

Each of the fifty states has its own statute prescribing formalities for the execution of wills. In general, a will must be in writing, signed by the testator, and witnessed by at least two witnesses. Many states require additional formalities, the most common being that the testator sign in the "presence" of the witnesses or that the witnesses sign in the presence of the testator. Furthermore, several states require that the will be "subscribed" or signed "at the end," and a few require the testator to "declare" (or "publish") to the witnesses that the instrument is a will and "request" them to witness it. The statutory formalities for attested wills vary considerably in detail from one state to another, but virtually all of them can be traced back to one or both of the primary English antecedents: the Statute of Frauds (1676), and the Wills Act (1837).

a. Background and Policy

The development of wills law bears traces of the jurisdictional division in English law, dating from the time of the Norman Conquest, between the law courts and the ecclesiastical courts.[1] By the end of the thirteenth century, the law courts had developed a rule prohibiting wills of land in any form. The common law rule, however, was readily circumvented through the system of uses recognized by the chancery courts; by the end of the fourteenth century it was common practice for a landowner to convey land to another (the *feoffee to uses*) for the use of a person (the *cestui que use*) as the landowner might appoint, with the instrument of appointment serving as a will substitute. (For a discussion of this precursor of the trust, see Chapter 7.) Within a few years after the Statute of Uses (1535) curtailed the system of uses, the persistent demands of landowners led to the original Statute of Wills (1540), which authorized wills

---

[1] The jurisdiction of the ecclesiastical courts was finally transferred to the newly-created Court of Probate in 1857.

of land and required that they be "in writing," without any additional formalities.

By contrast, succession to personal property fell within the jurisdiction of the ecclesiastical courts, which drew on Roman law in recognizing testaments of personalty, without imposing any strict formal requirements. Indeed, prior to the Statute of Frauds (1676) it was apparently common for testators in extremis to make oral (or "nuncupative") wills.[2]

The first detailed statutory formalities for the execution of wills of land appeared in the Statute of Frauds, which provided:

> . . . That all Devises and Bequests of any Lands or Tenements . . . shall be in Writing, and signed by the Party so devising the same, or by some other Person in his Presence and by his express Directions, and shall be attested and subscribed in the Presence of the said Devisor by three or four credible Witnesses, or else they shall be utterly void and of none Effect. [29 Car. II, c. 3, § 5 (1676).]

The statutory formalities for execution and revocation of wills of land were modified and made applicable to wills of personalty by the Wills Act (1837).[3] The Wills Act, which continues to form the basis of the English law of wills, provided:

> . . . That no Will shall be valid unless it shall be in Writing and Executed in manner herein-after mentioned; (that is to say,) it shall be signed at the Foot or End thereof by the Testator, or by some other Person in his Presence and by his Direction; and such Signature shall be made or acknowledged by the Testator in the Presence of Two or more Witnesses present at the same Time, and such Witnesses shall attest and shall subscribe the Will in the Presence of the Testator, but no Form of Attestation shall be necessary. [7 Wm. IV & 1 Vict., c. 26, § 9 (1837).]

A will is unique in the number and variety of formalities required for its execution and in the traditional requirement that the witnesses be produced in court before the will is declared operative. Critics of the status quo have observed: (1) the vast majority of wills do not need such ela-

---

[2] The Statute of Frauds imposed a general requirement that testaments of personalty be in writing, without any further requirement of signature or attestation. Nuncupative wills of personalty were still recognized, subject to various restrictions. In the case of a nuncupative will of personalty worth more than £30, the Statute required, inter alia, that the will be made during the testator's "last Sickness" and be witnessed by at least three witnesses at the testator's request. No writing was required, however, for dispositions of personalty worth up to £30 or for dispositions made by soldiers "in actual Military Service" and sailors "at sea." Statute of Frauds, 29 Car. II, c. 3, §§ 19–23 (1676).

[3] The Wills Act continued the special provisions for nuncupative wills made by soldiers and sailors. Several modern American wills acts contain similar provisions. See, e.g., N.Y. EPTL § 3–2.2.

borate safeguards; (2) the more obstacles interposed, the more likely that genuine expressions of a property owner's intent will be upset; and (3) the various formalities and requirements are of doubtful value in protecting the testator from determined crooks and schemers. These criticisms are hardly novel. See Wyndham v. Chetwynd, 96 Eng. Rep. 53 (K.B. 1757) ("I am persuaded many more fair wills have been overturned for want of form, than fraudulent have been prevented by introducing it. I . . . hardly recollect a case of a forged or fraudulent will, where it has not been solemnly attested."). What useful functions are served by the wills formalities?

ASHBEL G. GULLIVER & CATHERINE J. TILSON, CLASSIFICATION OF GRATUITOUS TRANSFERS
51 Yale L.J. 1, 2–10 (1941).

One fundamental proposition is that, under a legal system recognizing the individualistic institution of private property and granting to the owner the power to determine his successors in ownership, the general philosophy of the courts should favor giving effect to an intentional exercise of that power. This is commonplace enough, but it needs constant emphasis, for it may be obscured or neglected in inordinate preoccupation with detail or dialectic. A court absorbed in purely doctrinal arguments may lose sight of the important and desirable objective of sanctioning what the transferor wanted to do, even though it is convinced that he wanted to do it.

If this objective is primary, the requirements of execution, which concern only the form of the transfer—what the transferor or others must do to make it legally effective—seem justifiable only as implements for its accomplishment, and should be so interpreted by the courts in these cases. They surely should not be revered as ends in themselves, enthroning formality over frustrated intent. Why do these requirements exist and what functions may they usefully perform? . . .

In the first place, the court needs to be convinced that the statements of the transferor were deliberately intended to effectuate a transfer. People are often careless in conversation and in informal writings. Even if the witnesses are entirely truthful and accurate, what is the court to conclude from testimony showing only that a father once stated that he wanted to give certain bonds to his son, John? Does this remark indicate finality of intention to transfer, or rambling meditation about some possible future disposition? Perhaps he meant that he would like to give the bonds to John later if John turned out to be a respectable and industrious citizen, or perhaps that he would like to give them to John but could not because of his greater obligations to some other person. Possibly, the remark was inadvertent, or made in jest. Or suppose that the evidence shows, without more, that a writing containing dispositive language was found among the papers of the deceased at the time of his death? Does this demonstrate a deliberate transfer, or was it merely a tentative draft of some contemplated instrument, or perhaps random scribbling? Neither case would amount to an effective transfer, under the generally prevailing law. The court is far removed from the context of the statements, and the situation is so charged with uncertainty that even a judgment of probabilities is hazardous. Casual language, whether oral or written, is not intended to be legally operative, however appropriate its purely verbal content may be for that purpose. Dispositive effect should not be given to statements which were not intended to have that effect. The formalities of transfer therefore generally require the performance of some ceremonial for the purpose of impressing the transferor with the significance of his statements and thus justifying the court in reaching the conclusion, if the ceremonial is performed, that they were deliberately intended to be operative. This purpose of the requirements of transfer may conveniently be termed their ritual function.

Secondly, the requirements of transfer may increase the reliability of the proof presented to the court. The extent to which the quantity and effect of available evidence should be restricted by qualitative standards is, of course, a controversial matter. Perhaps any and all evidence should be freely admitted in reliance on such safeguards as cross-examination, the oath, the proficiency of handwriting experts, and the discriminating judgment of courts and juries. On the other hand, the inaccuracies of oral testimony owing to lapse of memory, misinterpretation of the statements of others, and the more or less unconscious coloring of recollection in the light of the personal interest of the witness or of those with whom he is friendly, are very prevalent; and the possibilities of perjury and forgery cannot be disregarded. These difficulties are entitled to especially serious consideration in prescribing requirements for gratuitous transfers, because the issue of the validity of the transfer is almost always raised after the alleged transferor is dead, and therefore the main actor is usually unavailable to testify, or to clarify or contradict other evidence concerning his all-important intention. At any rate, whatever the ideal resolution may be, it seems quite clear that the existing requirements of transfer emphasize the purpose of supplying satisfactory evidence to the court. This purpose may conveniently be termed their evidentiary function.

Thirdly, some of the requirements of the statutes of wills have the stated prophylactic purpose of safeguarding the testator, at the time of the execution of the will, against undue influence or other forms of imposition. As indicated below, the value of this objective and the extent of its accomplishment are both doubtful. It may conveniently be termed the protective function.

THE FUNCTIONS OF THE STATUTES OF WILLS

Formal Wills

Ritual Function. Compliance with the total combination of requirements for the execution of formal attested wills has a marked ritual value, since the general ceremonial precludes the possibility that the testator was acting in a casual or haphazard fashion. The ritual function is also specifically emphasized in individual requirements. It furnishes one justification for the provision that the will be signed by the testator himself or for him by some other person. Under the English Statute of Wills of 1540, specifying a will "in writing," no signature was expressly required. In construing this statute, the courts gave effect to various informal writings of the testator or others, even though the circumstances furnished no assurance that the testator intended them to be finally operative. These decisions are said to have been influential in the enactment of the provisions of the Statute of Frauds, which were the first to require a signature. The signature tends to show that the instrument was finally adopted by the testator as his will and to militate against the inference that the writing was merely a preliminary draft, an incomplete disposition, or a haphazard scribbling. The requirement existing in some states that the signature of the testator be at the end of the will has also been justified in terms of this function; since it is the ordinary human practice to sign documents at the end, a will not so signed does not give the impression of being finally executed. The occasional provisions that the testator publish the will or that he request the witnesses to sign also seem chiefly attributable to this purpose, since such actions indicate finality of intention.

Evidentiary Function. The absence of any procedure for determining the validity of a will before the death of the testator has two important consequences relevant to this function. First, as has already been stated, the testator will inevitably be dead and therefore unable to testify when the issue is tried. Secondly, an extended lapse of time, during which the recollection of witnesses may fade considerably, may occur between a statement of testamentary intent and the probate proceedings. Both factors tend to make oral testimony even less trustworthy than it is in cases where there is some likelihood of the adverse party being an available witness and where the statute of limitations compels relative promptness in litigation. The statute of wills may therefore reasonably incorporate unusual probative safeguards requiring evidence of testamentary intent to be cast in reliable and permanent form. The requirement that a will be in writing has, of course, great evidentiary value. A written statement of intention may be ambiguous, but, if it is genuine and can be produced, it has the advantage of preserving in permanent form the language chosen by the testator to show his intent. While, for the purpose of preventing frustration of intent through accident or design, the contents of a lost or destroyed will may usually be probated on satisfactory secondary evidence, such cases are relatively infrequent. The requirement of the testator's signature also has evidentiary value in identifying, in most cases, the maker of the document. While the typical statutory authorization of a signature made by another for the testator, and the generally recognized rule that the testator's signature need not be his correct name, both indicate lack of complete adherence to this purpose, such cases are probably quite rare in view of the usual custom in a literate era of signing documents with a complete name. The possibility of a forged signature must be controlled by the abilities of handwriting experts. There is judicial support for the theory that the requirement that the will be signed at the end has an evidentiary purpose of preventing unauthenticated or fraudulent additions to the will made after its execution by either the testator or other parties.

The important requirement that this type of will be attested obviously has great evidentiary significance. It affords some opportunity to secure proof of the facts of execution, which may have occurred long before probate, as contrasted with the difficulties that might otherwise arise if an unattested paper purporting to be a will executed, according to its date, thirty or forty years before, were found among the papers of the testator after his death. Of course, this purpose is not accomplished in every case since all of the attesting witnesses may become unavailable to testify because of death or some other reason, and their unavailability will not defeat probate of a will. The high evidentiary value placed by the courts and legislatures on the testimony of those chosen by the testator as attesting witnesses is shown by the requirement, unusual under the philosophy of the general rules of evidence which leave the calling of witnesses to the initiative of the parties, but regularly accepted for wills, that one or more of the attesting witnesses must be produced at probate if available.

The provision existing in some states that the will be signed or acknowledged by the testator in the presence of the attesting witnesses may be justified as having some evidentiary purpose in requiring a definitive act of the testator to be done before the witnesses, thus enabling them to testify with greater assurance that the will was intended to be operative.

Protective Function. Some of the requirements of the statutes of wills have the objective, according to judicial interpretation, of protecting the testator against imposition at the time of execution. This is difficult to justify under modern conditions. First, it must be reiterated that any requirement of transfer should have a clearly demonstrable affirmative value since it always presents the possibility of invalidating perfectly genuine and equitable transfers that fail to comply with it; there are numerous decisions interpreting these requirements, particularly with reference to the competency of attesting witnesses, wholly or partially invalidating wills that do not seem from the opinions to be in any way improper or suspicious. Secondly, there are appropriate independent remedies for the various forms of imposition, and these prophylactic provisions are therefore not, in the long run, of any essential utility except in instances where the imposition might not be detected. Thirdly, as indicated below, it is extremely doubtful that these provisions effectively accomplish any important purpose. Fourthly, they are atypical; no similar purpose is indicated in the requirements for inter vivos dispositions. Why should there be a differentiation between inter vivos and testamentary transfers in this respect? The purely legal elements of the two categories suggest no justification; in fact, the automatic revocability of a will presents a simpler and more uniformly prevalent means of nullifying the effect of imposition than exists for inter vivos transfers. In spite of the benevolent paternalism expressed in some of the decisions interpreting these requirements, the makers of wills are not a feeble or oppressed group of people needing unusual protection as a class; on the contrary, as the owners of property, earned or inherited, they are likely to be among the more capable and dominant members of our society. It is probable that the distinction originally arose because of a difference in the factual circumstances customarily surrounding the execution of the two types of transfer. The protective provisions first appeared in the Statute of Frauds, from which they have been copied, perhaps sometimes blindly, by American legislatures. While there is little direct evidence, it is a reasonable assumption that, in the period prior to the Statute of Frauds, wills were usually executed on the death bed. A testator in this unfortunate situation may well need special protection against imposition. His powers of normal judgment and of resistance to improper influences may be seriously affected by a decrepit physical condition, a weakened mentality, or a morbid or unbalanced state of mind. Furthermore, in view of the propinquity of death, he would not have as much time or opportunity as would the usual inter vivos transferor to escape from the consequences of undue influence or other forms of imposition. Under modern conditions, however, wills are probably executed by most testators in the prime of life and in the presence of attorneys. If this assumption is correct, the basis for any general distinction disappears. . . .

NOTE

Functional analysis. In addition to the ritual, evidentiary, and protective functions discussed by Gulliver & Tilson, it has been observed that wills formalities serve a "channeling function." By prescribing a standardized, easily recognizable mode of testamentary expression, the formalities tend to reduce the cost of routine probate administration. See Langbein, Substantial Compliance With the Wills Act, 88 Harv. L. Rev. 489, 493–94 (1975). Should courts adopt a functional approach in evaluating compliance with the formalities for execution of wills? For an argument elaborating this approach, see the excerpt from Langbein's article, infra p. 341.

b. Wills Formalities in Operation

Many contemporary American wills statutes are modeled more or less closely on the Statute of Frauds, the Wills Act of 1837, or some combination thereof, and the formalities for attested wills have proved remarkably durable. For example, the Florida statute provides:

Florida Statutes

§ 732.502. Execution of wills.

Every will must be in writing and executed as follows:

(1) (a) Testator's signature.—
     1. The testator must sign the will at the end; or
     2. The testator's name must be subscribed at the end of the will by some other person in the testator's presence and by the testator's direction.
     (b) Witnesses.—The testator's:
     1. Signing, or
     2. Acknowledgment:
          a. That he or she has previously signed the will, or
          b. That another person has subscribed the testator's name to it, must be in the presence of at least two attesting witnesses.
     (c) Witnesses' signatures.—The attesting witnesses must sign the will in the presence of the testator and in the presence of each other. . . .

Compare the Florida statute with the wills statute in your state, as well as with UPC § 2–502, reproduced below.

In recent years several states have followed the lead of the Uniform Probate Code in reforming their wills statutes. As a general matter, UPC § 1–102 announces that "the Code shall be liberally construed and applied to promote its underlying purposes and policies," which include, inter alia, "to discover and make effective the intent of a decedent in distribution of his property." Among the notable features of the Code, as originally promulgated in 1969, was a streamlined set of wills formalities for execution of attested wills. The original version of the Code provided that a will must be (1) in writing, (2) signed by the testator (or signed in the testator's name by another person in the testator's presence and by the testator's direction), and (3) signed by at least two persons who witnessed either the signing of the will or the testator's acknowledgment of his or her signature or of the will. UPC § 2-502 (1969). The Official Comment explained the rationale of this provision as follows:

The formalities for execution of a witnessed will have been reduced to a minimum. Execution under this section normally would be accomplished by signature of the testator and of two witnesses; each of the persons signing as witnesses must "witness" any of the following: the signing of the will by the testator, an acknowledgment by the testator that the signature is his, or an acknowledgment by the testator that the document is his will. Signing by the testator may be by mark under general rules relating to what constitutes a signature; or the will may be signed on behalf of the testator by another person signing the testator's name at his direction and in his presence. There is no requirement that the testator publish the document as his will, or that he request the witnesses to sign, or that the witnesses sign in the presence of the testator or of each other. The testator may sign the will outside the presence of the witnesses if he later acknowledges to the witnesses that the signature is his or that the document is his will, and they sign as witnesses. There is no requirement that the testator's signature be at the end of the will; thus, if he writes his name in the body of the will and intends it to be his signature, this would satisfy the statute. The intent is to validate wills which meet the minimal formalities of the statute. . . .

The UPC drafters reduced the statutory formalities still further by subsequent amendments. The most recent amendment, promulgated in 2008, allows a will to be acknowledged before a notary public as an alternative to the traditional requirement of attestation by witnesses. In its current form, UPC § 2–502 provides as follows:

Uniform Probate Code (2011)

§ 2–502. Execution; Witnessed or Notarized Wills . . . .

(a) [Witnessed or Notarized Wills.] Except as otherwise provided in subsection (b) [concerning holographic wills] . . . , a will must be:

(1) in writing;

(2) signed by the testator or in the testator's name by some other individual in the testator's conscious presence and by the testator's direction; and

(3) either:

(A) signed by at least two individuals, each of whom signed within a reasonable time after the individual witnessed either the signing of the will as described in paragraph (2) or the testator's acknowledgment of that signature or acknowledgement of the will; or

(B) acknowledged by the testator before a notary public or other individual authorized by law to take acknowledgements.

Courts have traditionally required strict compliance with the pre-scribed statutory formalities, frequently leading to denial of probate on highly technical grounds. In the words of one court, "the frustration of decedent's apparent testamentary intent by her own failure to observe the proper formalities may seem at first a harsh result, but it is a result which is required by our Legislature and which this Court may not alter." Estate of Proley, 422 A.2d 136, 138 (Pa.1980) (will invalid where testator signed in the wrong place; denial of probate affirmed by evenly divided court). At the same time, courts readily infer compliance with certain formalities—for example, the testator's declaration or request to the wit-nesses—from circumstances surrounding the execution of a will. See Es-tate of Burk, 468 N.W.2d 407 (S.D.1991); Estate of Bearbower, 426 N.W.2d 392 (Iowa 1988). What factors might lead a court to interpret a particular statutory formality more or less strictly in a particular case?

Virtually all American wills statutes require that a formal will (i.e., one which is not holographic or nuncupative) be attested by at least two witnesses. Probably more wills are challenged for lack of proper attesta-tion than for any other formal defect.

BURNS V. ADAMSON

Supreme Court of Arkansas, 1993.
313 Ark. 281, 854 S.W.2d 723.

HAYS, JUSTICE.

The question in this will contest is whether one of the two attesting witnesses' signatures on a will satisfies the statutory requirements of at-testation.

On February 3, 1992, Nettie Frost signed a will in her hospital room in Memphis, Tennessee. She died the following day. Appellant, Larry Burns, nephew of Ms. Frost, filed a petition for probate of the will as sole beneficiary. Other nephews and a niece contested the will.

A hearing established that around noon February 3, Ms. Frost asked a friend, Jewell Burns, to sign her will, which Ms. Burns did. Ms. Burns signed in the presence of Ms. Frost but at that time Ms. Frost had not yet signed the will, and did not sign it until several hours later, out of the presence of Ms. Burns. Ms. Burns testified unequivocally that Ms. Frost's signature was not on the will at the time she signed as a witness, and that she did not see Ms. Frost again before she died.

At approximately 5:00 p.m. the same day, Ms. Frost was visited by Faye Burns, Larry's wife, and Ethel Pettus, a long time friend of Ms.

Frost. Ms. Frost then signed the will in the presence of both of them and Ms. Pettus signed the will as a witness in the presence of Ms. Frost. Faye Burns did not sign the will as a witness. There is no dispute that Jewell Burns was not there at the time Ms. Frost signed her name to the will, and Ms. Pettus testified that when she signed the will, Jewell Burns's signature was on it.

The trial court entered an order finding the will was not validly executed in the presence of two persons and that the estate of Nettie Frost should be administered according to the laws of descent and distribution. Larry Burns brings this appeal challenging the trial court's holding. We agree with the ruling of the probate judge.

The statute setting out the requirements for proper execution of a will provides:

Ark. Code Ann. § 28–25–103 (1987). Execution generally.

(a) The execution of a will, other than holographic, must be by the signature of the testator and of at least two (2) witnesses.

(b) The testator shall declare to the attesting witnesses that the instrument is his will and either:

(1) Himself sign; or

(2) Acknowledge his signature already made; or

(3) Sign by mark, his name being written near it and witnessed by a person who writes his own name as witness to the signature; or

(4) At his discretion [sic] and in his presence have someone else sign his name for him. The person so signing shall write his own name and state that he signed the testator's name at the request of the testator; and

(5) In any of the above cases, the signature must be at the end of the instrument and the act must be done in the presence of two (2) or more attesting witnesses.

(c) The attesting witnesses must sign at the request and in the presence of the testator.

The provision governing this case is Section (5), which provides that the act of the testator signing *must be done in the presence of two or more attesting witnesses.*

Clearly the statute was not complied with in this case and appellant acknowledges that. He argues that because we have accepted substantial compliance with this procedure in the past, we should do so now.

While we have found substantial compliance in some situations, we have never extended it to allow a witness to attest a will before the testator signs it and who in fact never sees the testator sign. Where substantial compliance has been found, it was on circumstances much less substantive and material than these. We have found substantial compliance with the requirement that a signature be placed at the "end" of the will, Clark v. National Bank of Commerce, 304 Ark. 352, 802 S.W.2d 452 (1991); Weems, Administrator v. Smith, 218 Ark. 554, 237 S.W.2d 880 (1951). And we have applied it to the requirement that the testator declare to the witnesses that this is his will, Faith v. Singleton, 286 Ark. 403, 692 S.W.2d 239 (1985); Green v. Holland, 9 Ark. App. 233, 657 S.W.2d 572 (1983); and to the requirement that the witnesses must sign at the request of the testator, Hanel v. Springle, Adm'r, 237 Ark. 356, 372 S.W.2d 822 (1963).

Appellant cites Anthony v. College of the Ozarks, 207 Ark. 212, 180 S.W.2d 321 (1944), as controlling in this case. In *Anthony*, one of the two witnesses' signatures was in question, that of L.M. Guthrie. The testator had brought the will to Guthrie's office and asked him to sign it as a witness. The two were well acquainted. Guthrie testified as follows:

> I did not read the instrument thus presented to me, but signed same and then asked him if this was his will and he said that it was. He did not sign the instrument in my presence. Nothing was said at the time whether he had signed it, and nothing was said about his signature. The [other witness] was not present when I signed the instrument, and I was not present when he signed it, if he did sign it, and did not see him sign it.

The court noted that Guthrie did not say the testator's signature was *not* on the instrument at the time he signed it and it would presume the testator's name was on the instrument at the time he gave it to Guthrie to sign.

> When [the testator] presented the instrument to the witness, Guthrie, it was for the purpose of securing Guthrie's signature as a witness, not to the will, but as a witness to [the testator's] signature on the will. When Guthrie signed the will as a witness the testator told him the instrument was a will. It could not have been a will without his signature being on it at that time, and while the testator said nothing about his signature, *the presumption is, in the absence of proof to the contrary, that his signature was on the will when he presented it to Guthrie.* [Our emphasis.] [Id. at 216, 180 S.W.2d 321.]

This case is distinguishable from *Anthony*, where we could indulge in the presumption that the testator's signature was on the will, there being no evidence to the contrary. Here there is clear evidence to the contrary and no presumption is permissible. We believe this result is consistent with other authorities on this issue.

It is stated in 2 W. Bowe & D. Parker, Page on The Law of Wills, § 19.138 (1960), that under the great weight of authority if the subscribing witnesses sign their names to the will before the testator signs, the will is not executed in compliance with the statutes. And in In re Brashear's Estate, 54 Ariz. 430, 96 P.2d 747 (1940) it was pointed out there were two lines of authority on the strictness of this rule—one being the English rule holding unanimously the attestation of a will is not valid unless the testator signs before the attesting witnesses and this is followed by a number of American jurisdictions. The other line of cases holds when the execution and attestation of a will occur at the same time and place and form part of the same transaction, it is immaterial that the witnesses subscribe before the testator. The opinion reads:

> *But, we know of no case* which holds the will is valid where one of the necessary witnesses attested the will before the testator signed it and the attestation of the witness and signature of the testator were at different times and places, so that the witness did not see the testator sign or hear him acknowledge his signature after signing. There are a number of cases on the other hand, which expressly hold that under such circumstances the will cannot stand. (Citations omitted). [Our emphasis.]

To the same effect, see the selected cases in Annotation, Validity of Will as Affected by Fact that Witnesses Signed Before Testator, 91 A.L.R.2d 737 (1963).

In sum, where the witness did not see the testatrix sign the will or acknowledge it, there was a failure to follow the requirements of § 28–25–103 and the probate judge was correct in so ruling.

Affirmed.

NOTES

1. *Significance of attestation.* Modern will statutes typically provide that a formal written will must be signed by the testator and by at least two attesting witnesses. See UPC § 2–502, reproduced supra, as well as the Arkansas statute quoted in the principal case. Aside from signing the will, what are the specific responsibilities of attesting witnesses: To authenticate the testator's signature? To identify the instrument as the testator's will? To confirm that the applicable wills formalities are satisfied? To review the provisions of

the will? To observe the testator's state of mind? Courts have described the objective of the process as giving the witnesses an opportunity to observe the testator's execution of the will so that in a probate proceeding after the testator's death the witnesses can "give testimony as to the essential elements of the two statutory issues of due execution and testamentary capacity sufficient, if credited by the jury, to prove both issues." Wheat v. Wheat, 244 A.2d 359 (Conn.1968) (recognizing, however, that because lay witnesses often do not fully understand their function, other competent evidence is admissible). See also Estate of Peters, 526 A.2d 1005 (N.J.1987) (discussing "observatory" and "signatory" functions). The witnesses' understanding of the transaction may be significant. See Estate of Griffith, 30 So.3d 1190 (Miss. 2010) ("an attesting witness must have some knowledge that the document being signed is, in fact, the testator's last will and testament"; witnesses who did not know what they were signing "were not 'attesting' witnesses . . . but merely subscribing witnesses"); cf. Weaver v. Grant, 394 So.2d 15 (Ala.1981) (witness must intend to witness some document, though need not know that it is a will); Slack v. Truitt, 791 A.2d 129 (Md. 2002) (will admitted to probate even though one witness thought she was signing a neighborhood petition and could not recall seeing testator's signature).

2. *Testator's signature.* All the wills statutes permit the testator to execute a will by signing it. A full longhand signature is not necessary; indeed, a mark written by the testator and intended as a signature is sufficient. See Mitchell v. Mitchell, 264 S.E.2d 222 (Ga.1980) ("X" sufficient where semi-literate testator knew how to write a few words, including his name); Phillips v. Najar, 901 S.W.2d 561 (Tex.App.1995) ("X" sufficient where testator's manual dexterity was severely impaired). Furthermore, in all but a handful of states, the statutes permit someone else to sign the will for the testator, subject to various safeguards. See, e.g., UPC § 2–502 (will may be signed "in the testator's name by some other individual in the testator's conscious presence and by the testator's direction"); see also the Arkansas statute quoted in the *Burns* case (person signing for testator must write own name as well). However, a testator's own signature may be invalid if the testator is physically unable to complete the intended act. See Estate of DeThorne, 471 N.W.2d 780 (Wis.App.1991) (will invalid where another person guided testator's hand in signing); Estate of Wait, 306 S.W.2d 345 (Tenn.App.1957) (will invalid where testator was too frail to finish signing in presence of witnesses and completed signature later); cf. Strong v. Holden, 697 S.E.2d 189 (Ga. 2010) (will validly executed where witness "assisted [testator] by moving her hand to the signature line" and testator then "made a mark on the page").

Several statutes expressly require that the testator sign the will "at the end." In other jurisdictions, courts have construed the requirement that the will be "subscribed" to require a signature at the end. The decisions locate this point at the "logical end of the language used by decedent in expressing his testamentary purpose." Estate of Treitinger, 269 A.2d 497 (Pa.1970); see also Estate of Proley, 422 A.2d 136 (Pa.1980) (evenly divided court affirmed denial of probate where testator wrote her name on a printed will form in the portion normally used for identifying the document when properly folded). If significant material (e.g., an additional dispositive provision) appears after the signature, the additional material is usually held ineffective on the ground that it was presumably inserted after the will was executed. This represents a liberalization of the traditional view that held the entire will invalid due to the lack of a signature at the end. A misplaced signature, however, may still render the entire will invalid. See Estate of Zaharis, 457 N.Y.S.2d 995 (App. Div. 1982) (will on single file card invalid where testator signed in margin on front side).

3. *Electronic documents*. Testator prepares his will on a word processor and prints it out with his stylized, cursive, computer-generated signature at the end of the document. Testator acknowledges the document as his will to two attesting witnesses, and at his request they sign their names by hand. Is the will validly executed? See Taylor v. Holt, 134 S.W.3d 830 (Tenn. App. 2003) (yes, computer-generated signature fell within statutory definition; testator "simply used a computer rather than an ink pen as the tool to make his signature"). What if a will is stored in the form of an electronic record rather than a tangible writing? If such an "electronic will" is authorized by statute, what safeguards should be included to ensure authenticity and protect against unauthorized alteration? See Nev. Rev. Stat. § 133.085.

4. *Acknowledgment*. Although it is common for the testator to sign the will in the presence of the attesting witnesses, most statutes permit the testator to sign the will in advance and then to acknowledge the signature or the will to the attesting witnesses. See, e.g., UPC § 2–502. The testator's acknowledgment need not be express, but may be inferred from the testator's conduct and surrounding circumstances. See Norton v. Georgia R.R. Bank & Trust Co., 285 S.E.2d 910 (Ga.1982) (adequate acknowledgment where witness saw testator's signature on will and was asked by attorney in testator's presence to witness it).

5. *Publication and request*. A few statutes require that the testator (1) declare to the witnesses that the document is a will, and (2) request that they witness it. In the absence of any other formal defect, these requirements seldom cause serious problems. Most courts readily accept a declaration (traditionally referred to as "publication") or request made by a person other than the testator; indeed, if the surrounding circumstances indicate that the witnesses "knew why they were there and what they were doing," the will may be upheld without any express declaration or request. Estate of Burke, 613 P.2d 481 (Okla. App. 1979); Jackson v. Patton, 952 S.W.2d 404 (Tenn.1997).

6. *Order and time of witnesses' signing*. Most modern courts attach little importance to the order of signing as long as the testator and witnesses sign in a single transaction. See James v. Haupt, 573 S.W.2d 285 (Tex. App. 1978) ("where the execution and attestation of a will occur at the same time and place and form parts of the same transaction, it is immaterial that the witnesses subscribe before the testator signs"); Hopson v. Ewing, 353 S.W.2d 203

(Ky.1961); Waldrep v. Goodwin, 195 S.E.2d 432 (Ga.1973); but cf. Wheat v. Wheat, 244 A.2d 359 (Conn.1968) (testator must sign before witnesses).

Several statutes modeled on the original version of UPC § 2–502 provide that the witnesses must sign the will, without requiring that the signing take place in the testator's presence or within any specified time period. Suppose that an attesting witness forgets to sign the will at the time of execution, and the omission is not discovered until after the testator's death. If the witness signs the will before it is offered for probate, should the will be admitted? Several courts have held that the witnesses must sign before the testator's death. See Estate of Saueressig, 136 P.3d 201 (Cal. 2006); Estate of Royal, 826 P.2d 1236 (Colo.1992); Pope v. Clark, 551 So.2d 1053 (Ala.1989). Others reach the opposite conclusion. See Estate of Miller, 149 P.3d 840 (Idaho 2006) (witness not required to sign before testator's death; "the legislature has not enacted any requirement as to when the witnesses must sign, and therefore no such requirement can be imposed by the court"). The Uniform Probate Code requires only that the witnesses sign "within a reasonable time" after witnessing the execution or acknowledgment. UPC § 2–502 & cmt. (noting that "[i]n a particular case, the reasonable-time requirement could be satisfied even if the witnesses sign after the testator's death"). Cf. Estate of Peters, 526 A.2d 1005 (N.J.1987) (witnesses must sign within reasonable time after execution or acknowledgment, though not necessarily before testator's death; 18–month delay was not reasonable).

7. *Testamentary intent.* No particular form of words (e.g., "I give, devise, and bequeath") is necessary to manifest testamentary intent. Even a cursory list of property and beneficiaries may be sufficient. In Hopson v. Ewing, 353 S.W.2d 203 (Ky.1961), the following "nondescript" typewritten instrument, signed by the testator and two witnesses, was admitted to probate:

> Sadie Rose, Mary Rose and Joe Ellis 443 South 7th Street 1124 South 8th Street 3208–3210 Southern Avenue (2) Lots—3608–3610 Grand Avenue City Truck—Jewelry—Bank Account—(1) Three Karat Diamond Ring.

> Alonzo Dorsey—524 South Ninth Street

> Mary C. Duncan All contents at 3606 Grand Avenue and 1120 South 36th Street My home and everything.

> She shall take care of George Smith as long as he lives.

> /s/ Preston O. Davis

> /s/ Thomas Manier

> /s/ Ike Weathers

> Nov. 20—1951

The court, finding the instrument ambiguous on its face, held that extrinsic evidence (i.e., testimony of the attesting witnesses) was admissible to show testamentary intent. See also UPC § 2–502(c) ("[i]ntent that a document constitute the testator's will can be established by extrinsic evidence"); compare Edmundson v. Estate of Fountain, 189 S.W.3d 427 (Ark. 2004) (handwritten list of property and beneficiaries, signed by decedent and two witnesses, was "defective on its face" because it set forth "no words of a dispositive nature"; extrinsic evidence not admissible to establish testamentary intent).

8. *Testator under disability.* If the probate court finds that an individual is disabled (other than for reasons of minority) and in need of protection, the court may appoint a conservator to manage the individual's property and business affairs. In many states the conservator is authorized, with express court approval, to make gifts of the disabled individual's property and to take further steps to implement an estate plan (e.g., by creating an inter vivos trust, or by amending or revoking a revocable trust) in accordance with the individual's known or probable wishes. In a few states the conservator is even authorized, with express court approval, to make, amend, or revoke a will on behalf of the disabled person. See UPC § 5–411. See also Brashier, Policy, Perspective, and the Proxy Will, 61 S.C. L. Rev. 63 (2009).

IN RE ESTATE OF WEBER

Supreme Court of Kansas, 1963.
192 Kan. 258, 387 P.2d 165.

WERTZ, JUSTICE.

This was a proceeding to admit a document to probate as the last will and testament of Henry H. Weber. The facts are undisputed and are substantially as follows:

Henry H. Weber, the decedent, died November 21, 1960. At the time of his death he was seventy-three years of age, lawfully married to Rosa Weber, who had been adjudicated an incompetent person, and who, on the above-mentioned date, was, and had been for several years prior thereto, hospitalized at Topeka State Hospital.

Shortly after 12:00 p.m. on November 16, 1960, Henry Weber went to the home of Ben Heer in Riley. Mr. Heer was not at home but his wife was, and Mr. Weber advised Mrs. Heer he was ill and needed help to get into the hospital. He stated he wished to go to the Riley County Hospital in Manhattan. Mrs. Heer telephoned the hospital and made arrangements to have Mr. Weber admitted.

After arrangements were completed Mrs. Heer offered to put Mr. Weber's clothes in a suitcase and otherwise help him prepare to go to the hospital. Next, she called a neighbor who in turn went to where Mr. Heer was working, which was about four miles from Riley, and told Mr. Heer that Henry Weber was at Heer's home and wanted to see him. Heer went immediately to his home. When he arrived Weber advised Heer of his illness and of his desire to make a will leaving one-half of his estate to his wife and one-half to his niece, Lillian Price. Heer and Weber then decided to go to see Harold Holmes, president of the Riley State Bank, to have the will prepared.

The distance from the Heer residence to the bank was three or four blocks. The two men drove to the bank, each in his own automobile. Mr. Weber parked his car at an angle against the curb of the street and beneath a window on the north side of the bank and asked Mr. Heer, who had parked on the east side and had come over to the Weber car, to see if Mr. Holmes would come out to the car and talk to him. Weber remained in his car and Heer went into the bank and talked to Holmes who then came out and got into the front seat of Weber's car. At Weber's request Heer got into the back seat of the automobile. It was a chilly November day and the car windows were kept closed. Weber explained to Holmes how he desired to dispose of his property, one-half to be left to his wife and one-half to his niece, and that he wanted Heer to be his executor. Holmes took notes as Weber talked. After Holmes concluded taking notes he went back into the bank and prepared the purported will on a printed form captioned "Last Will and Testament" by filling in a portion of the blank spaces thereof with the information contained in the notes he had made, except that he failed to mention Weber's wife in the purported will.

The third paragraph of the will reads:

> Third. I give, devise and bequeath to *My Niece, Lillian Price of Junction City, Kansas My share of land situated in the Eureka Valley in Ogden and Manhattan Townships also My share of all Real estate located in Madison Township, Riley County Kansas* and I do devise and bequeath all the rest and residue of my estate both real, personal and mixed to *My Niece Lillian Price, any and all, money, stocks or Bonds, any and all personal property which I may possess at my death, whatsoever.*

The italicized portion of the above quotation was that part typed from Holmes' notes onto the printed will form.

While Holmes was inside the bank he directed three bank employees, Mr. and Mrs. Chamberlain and Mrs. Carlson, to go to and stand in front of a closed window in the bank in order that they could serve as witnesses to the signing of the will. The window was approximately eight to ten feet from where Weber was sitting in his closed automobile.

About fifteen minutes later Holmes returned to Weber's automobile with a clipboard to which the purported will was fastened. Holmes re-entered Weber's automobile and handed the document to him. Weber read the document, Holmes and Heer being in the automobile at this time.

Holmes and Weber having previously discussed the need for witnesses, Holmes directed Weber's attention to the window of the bank where the above-named bank employees were standing. By waving to them, Weber indicated he saw them, and they in turn waved back to him. After looking the purported will over, Weber placed the clipboard on the steering wheel of his automobile where it could be seen through the closed windows by the witnesses, and signed the document.

Holmes then returned to the bank with the document, and there, standing before the bank window as heretofore described, the witnesses signed their names. The table upon which the signing occurred was against the window but the table top was a foot to a foot and a half beneath the window sill. Hence Weber could see the witnesses in the window as they signed but could not see the pen or the purported will on the table at the time of signing. Only that portion of the body of each witness in the window could be seen by him.

After the three witnesses signed the purported will Holmes took it back out to Weber's automobile, showed it to him, Weber looked it over, and at Weber's request Holmes retained the document at the bank.

The record disclosed that all three witnesses were acquainted with Weber prior to November 16, 1960, and knew his signature when they saw it. They recognized Weber's signature on the purported will. However, none of the witnesses could read any of the writing or printing on the document while it was being signed by Weber in his automobile.

It is noted from the record that at no time was there any type of communication between Weber and the witnesses other than their waving to one another; no verbal communication whatsoever. Weber never entered the bank building during this period of time and heard nothing of what was said inside the building; and even more important, the witnesses never left the building, so they couldn't possibly have heard any of the conversation that occurred in Weber's automobile.

The transaction at the bank took approximately one to one and a half hours to complete. Weber then proceeded to drive his automobile, unaccompanied, approximately twenty miles to the Riley County Hospital where the earlier admittance arrangements had been made, and it was there on November 21, 1960, just five days later, he died.

At the conclusion of the evidence the trial court made findings of fact and concluded as a matter of law that the will was duly executed by the decedent and attested by two competent witnesses in conformity with the provisions of G.S. 1949, 59–606; that it was a valid will of the decedent and should be admitted to probate as the last will and testament of Henry H. Weber, deceased; and entered judgment accordingly.

From an order overruling his motion for a new trial, R.R. Bennett, guardian of the person and estate of Rosa Weber, an incompetent person, has appealed.

The determinative question in this case is whether or not the purported will was duly executed and attested in accordance with the provisions of G.S. 1949, 59–606, which reads:

> Every will, except an oral will as provided in section 44 [59–608], shall be in writing, and signed at the end thereof by the party making the same, or by some other person in his presence and by his express direction, and shall be attested and subscribed in the presence of such party by two or more competent witnesses, who saw the testator subscribe or heard him acknowledge the same.

The mentioned statute, insofar as is pertinent to the issues involved, contains the following elements: (1) The will must be attested and subscribed by two competent witnesses in the presence of the testator; (2) the witnesses must have either seen the testator subscribe or have heard him acknowledge the will. It is apparent that the statute clearly requires two essential factors: (1) presence, and (2) sight or hearing. There must be presence and sight or presence and hearing. Presence only, sight only, hearing only, or sight and hearing only are not sufficient. It is quite possible that one could see a testator subscribe to his will, i.e., by television, or one could hear the testator acknowledge his will, i.e., by telephone, but in either instance the witnesses would not be in the presence of the testator as contemplated by our statute. Conversely, one could be in the testator's presence and yet not see him sign or hear him acknowledge his will. The witnessing of a will is a matter of great importance and solemnity, and this is especially so because dispute about it does not arise until the testator's lips are sealed. (Rice v. Monroe, 108 Kan. 526, 527, 196 P. 756.)

In In re Estate of Bond, 159 Kan. 249, 252, 153 P.2d 912, 914, we stated: "The fact is that aside from an oral will, as provided in G.S. 1943 Supp., 59–608, there is only one way to make a will in Kansas and that is by signing in the presence of two witnesses who saw the testator sign or heard him acknowledge it."

In Fuller v. Williams, 125 Kan. 154, 163, 264 P. 77, 81, this court stated:

One who attests and subscribes a will as a witness should do so with the understanding that he is competent to testify on the probate of the will that the testator had mental capacity to make a will and was not under restraint or undue influence. . . . The attesting witnesses to a will must not only witness the signing or publishing of it by the testator, but it is also their duty to satisfy themselves that the testator is of sound and disposing mind and memory and capable of executing a will. . . . This duty necessarily requires that the attesting witnesses to a will should know and understand that the instrument they are signing as witnesses is a will, and they should do so prepared to testify to the testamentary capacity of the testator and that he is free from restraint and undue influence.

We are aware there is a line of authorities to the effect that a witness to a will need not know whether he is witnessing a will or some other instrument, but we do not regard such authorities as being in accord with the duties required by an attesting and subscribing witness to a will under our statute, in accordance with the decision of our court.

In *In re Estate of Bond*, supra, it was stated that we prefer the strict construction of the statute to one which would tend to break down the formalities with which our legislature has seen fit to cloak the passing of property by devise. This strict construction rule was reaffirmed in the case of In re Estate of Davis, 168 Kan. 314, 322, 212 P.2d 343. It is possible that at times an honest attempt to execute a last will and testament is defeated by the failure to include some one or more of the statutory requirements. However, it is far more important that this should happen under a proper construction of the statute than that the individual case should be permitted to weaken the legislative mandate calculated to protect testators generally from fraud, duress, bad faith, overreaching, or undue influence in the making of their wills. The right to make a testamentary disposition of property is wholly statutory and the testator's intent to execute a valid will is not by itself sufficient to give validity to an instrument not executed in accordance with the statutory requirements.

The proponent of the will (the executor) in his brief invites our attention to Kitchell v. Bridgeman, 126 Kan. 145, 267 P. 26. However, in that case the will was executed by the testator in his room before two witnesses who saw him sign the will. In re Estate of Davis, 168 Kan. 314, 212 P.2d 343, is cited to us. In this case the testator signed in the presence of one witness and subsequently the second witness was brought into the room where the testator acknowledged to her and the witness signed in the testator's presence. The proponent also cites Humphrey v. Wallace, 169 Kan. 58, 216 P.2d 781, where the witnesses did not see the testatrix sign but did in their presence hear her acknowledge her signature and that it was her last will and testament. Attention is invited to Moore v. Glover, 196 Okl. 177, 163 P.2d 1003, where the testatrix handed the witnesses the will and stated that it was her will and requested the witnesses to sign as witnesses to her will. The witnesses clearly heard testatrix acknowledge it as her will, and after they signed as witnesses returned it to her. None of these cases supports the very liberal construction which the proponent wishes to place upon the statute under the facts of the instant case.

The statute was designed to require the attestation to be made in the presence of the testator so as to prevent the substitution of a surreptitious will. The testator must be able to see the witnesses attest the will; or, to speak with more precision, their relative position to him at the time they are subscribing their names as witnesses must be such that he may see them, if he thinks it proper to do so, and satisfy himself by actual view that they are witnessing the very paper he signed to be his last will. In the instant case there is evidence that Weber told Mr. Heer and Banker Holmes that he wanted one-half of his property to go to his wife and one-half to his niece. The document, as prepared, failed to mention the wife in any manner. It is further noted that Holmes took some time in preparing the purported will, placed it upon a clipboard and then stationed three of his employees at the window and had them remain there while he took the instrument through the door and into the closed car where the witnesses saw Weber sign a paper, or document, which Holmes advised the witnesses was Weber's will. A statement by the person who supervises the execution of the document that it is the testator's will and the like does not amount to an acknowledgment by testator if he does not hear such statement. (2 Bowe–Parker: Page on Wills, § 19.115, p. 224.) The witnesses testified that there was no communication whatsoever between Weber and themselves. There is nothing in the record to show that the witnesses read the provisions of the purported will but only knew Weber's signature appeared thereon.

Appellee seems to place much stress upon conscious presence and substantial compliance. However, where the execution of a will in testator's presence is at issue, neither words nor intentions suffice. The rule is that the burden of proof rests upon proponent of a will to establish that the will was executed according to the provisions of the statute. To hold that the requirements of the statute were complied with in the instant case would subvert the purpose and intent of the statute and would amount to a disregard of its substance. Failure to halt here under the facts in the instant case would permit substantial compliance and conscious presence to run wild so that if in any given case the intention of the testator is ascertained his will may be sustained. Application of the rule of substantial compliance or conscious presence under the facts in the instant case is to ignore the statute intended to prevent fraud.

While it is unfortunate in this case that Lillian Price must suffer from the lack of legal ability and understanding of a scrivener who sought to perform a legal act of great importance and solemnity, that of drafting a will and purporting to supervise the execution thereof, it is better that she be denied her would-be beneficial interests in the will than to open the door and set a pattern, by those not versed in the law of wills and in utter disregard to the plain provisions of the statute, for the drafting of future wills so as to permit fraud, undue influence, overreaching and bad faith which might in some other instances be practiced upon the weak, aged or infirm testators in the disposition of their worldly goods.

We are of the opinion that the facts of the instant case disclose the proximity between the witnesses and the testator was not sufficient to establish "presence," and, therefore, the will does not meet the necessary requirements of G.S. 1949, 59–606, authorizing its admission to probate as the last will and testament of Henry H. Weber, deceased. The judgment of the trial court is reversed and the case is remanded with instructions to set aside the judgment admitting the will to probate.

It is so ordered.

PARKER, C.J., and PRICE and FATZER, JJ., dissent.

NOTES

1. *Drafting error and due execution.* In the principal case, suppose that Mr. Holmes had drafted the will in accordance with Mr. Weber's instructions, leaving half the residuary estate to Rosa Weber. Might the court have reached a different result?

The niece, Lillian Price, died while the appeal in the principal case was pending, twelve days before the Supreme Court of Kansas rendered its decision. Should Mr. Holmes be liable to her successors for failing to ensure that Henry Weber's will was properly executed? See Price v. Holmes, 422 P.2d 976 (Kan.1967).

2. *Presence requirements.* Three types of "presence" may be required: (1) signature by the testator in the presence of the witnesses; (2) signature by the witnesses in the presence of the testator; and (3) signature by the witnesses in the presence of each other. The first of these three types is not universally required. Frequently, the testator's acknowledgment of his or her signature is sufficient. See UPC § 2–502. A majority of the wills statutes, however, require that the witnesses sign in the testator's presence; a few also require that the witnesses sign in the presence of each other. These "presence" requirements are applied with varying degrees of strictness. What is the purpose of a "presence" requirement? The traditional answer, often repeated without adequate explanation or analysis, is that requiring that the witnesses sign in the testator's presence serves "to prevent a fraud's being

perpetrated . . . by substituting another for the true will." Glenn v. Mann, 214 S.E.2d 911 (Ga.1975). How likely is it that a substitution would be attempted or, if attempted, would successfully escape detection? Consider the following possibilities:

a. The witnesses forge the testator's signature on a spurious will favoring themselves; out of the testator's presence, they attest the spurious will and return it to the testator instead of the genuine will.

b. Some people other than the witnesses forge the testator's signature to a spurious will in favor of themselves, and then bribe the witnesses to attest it and return it to the testator instead of the genuine will.

c. The witnesses (or others who have bribed them) are intestate successors and substitute an inoperative document for the intended will.

Note that if the substitution comes to light while the testator is still alive, the testator can destroy the spurious document and execute a new will.

Statutory "presence" requirements continue to provide a fertile source of litigation. In Stevens v. Casdorph, 508 S.E.2d 610 (W.Va. 1998), an elderly testator, confined to a wheelchair, brought his will to a bank where he signed it in the presence of a bank employee and asked to have it witnessed. The employee took the will across the lobby to two co-workers who signed it as attesting witnesses. The applicable statute required that the will be signed or acknowledged by the testator in the presence of the witnesses and subscribed by the witnesses in the testator's presence. Although the entire transaction took place in the bank lobby and "everyone involved with the will knew what was occurring," the court held that the will was not properly executed because the witnesses did not observe the testator sign or acknowledge the will and the testator did not see the witnesses sign. A vigorous dissent criticized the majority for taking an overly formalistic and technical view of the statute and reaching a "patently absurd" result at odds with the purposes of the statute. See also Chester v. Smith, 677 S.E.2d 128 (Ga. 2009) (testator "could not have seen the witnesses sign the Will inside the bank" from vantage point in parked car outside bank; probate denied); Estate of Fischer, 886 A.2d 996 (N.H. 2005) (bedridden testator acknowledged will in presence of witnesses and asked them to sign; witnesses left bedroom and signed on porch; probate denied). On similar facts, however, another court admitted the will to probate, noting that "[a]n attestation in the same room or close vicinity with the testator is generally considered to be in his/her presence, unless there is a physical obstacle blocking the view." Estate of Ross, 969 S.W.2d 398 (Tenn. App. 1997). See also Conner v. Donahoo, 145 S.W.3d 395 (Ark. App. 2004) (witness observed testator sign will, then moved to adjoining room where he sat down and signed the will as witness; held, witness subscribed will in testator's presence, will admitted to probate).

How might the presence requirement, if strictly applied, aid in the successful prosecution of a dishonest claim? Conversely, how might it be used to defeat an "inequitable" testamentary disposition?

3. *Meaning of "presence."* The test of presence is usually stated in terms of whether the testator could have seen the witnesses sign the will and how much effort would have been required on the testator's part. In application the presence requirement varies widely. Some courts adhere to a "line of sight" rule, requiring that the testator be able to see the witnesses as they sign the will. See McCormick v. Jeffers, 637 S.E.2d 666 (Ga.2006) (testator must "be able to see the witnesses sign the will" without changing position, but need not actually watch them sign); In re Hill's Estate, 84 N.W.2d 457 (Mich.1957) (will invalid where witnesses knew testatrix's signature but signed 40 or 50 feet away from her in another room); In re Palmer's Estate, 122 N.W.2d 920 (Iowa 1963) (will invalid where witnesses signed outside testator's room and out of his sight). Other courts have adopted a more flexible "conscious presence" rule. See In re Tracy's Estate, 182 P.2d 336 (Cal.App.1947) ("the testator need not actually view the act of signing by the witnesses, but . . . these elements must be present: (1) the witnesses must sign within the testator's hearing, (2) the testator must know what is being done, and (3) the signing by the witnesses and the testator must constitute one continuous transaction"); In re Demaris' Estate, 110 P.2d 571 (Or.1941) ("It is unnecessary, we believe, that the attestation and execution occur in the same room. And . . . it is unnecessary that the attesters be within the range of vision of the testator when they sign. If they are so near at hand that they are within the range of any of his senses, so that he knows what is going on, the requirement has been met."). How can "presence" be determined in the case of a blind testator? See Welch v. Kirby, 255 F. 451 (8th Cir.1918), cert. denied, 249 U.S. 612 (1919).

Suppose that one witness signs in the testator's presence and then, at the testator's request, takes the will to be attested by a second witness out of the testator's presence. The second witness telephones the testator, who confirms that the will is genuine, and the second witness signs the will. Does the will comply with the statutory requirement of attestation by both witnesses in the presence of the testator? See Estate of Jefferson, 349 So.2d 1032 (Miss. 1977); Estate of McGurrin, 743 P.2d 994 (Idaho App.1987); Estate of Kirkeby, 970 P.2d 241 (Or. App. 1998).

4. *Self-proved will.* Today, most states permit a will to be "self-proved" by means of a sworn affidavit signed by the testator and the witnesses in the presence of a notary public and attached to or incorporated in the will. See UPC § 2–504. A self-proving affidavit raises a presumption of due execution, with the result that the will can be admitted to probate without live witness testimony in uncontested cases. See UPC § 3–406. In some states the presumption of due execution applies only in the absence of an objection from an interested party. See Estate of Giuliano, 949 A.2d 386 (R.I. 2008). By contrast, the Uniform Probate Code provides that, in the absence of fraud or for-

gery, the presumption is conclusive with respect to the signature requirements for execution, but the will can be contested on other grounds such as
undue influence or lack of capacity. UPC § 3–406. Does this provision preclude a contest on the ground of defective execution where an attesting witness testifies that she signed a self-proving affidavit without having observed
the testator's signature or acknowledgment of the will? See Estate of Zeno,
672 N.W.2d 574 (Minn. App. 2003).

5. *Liability for negligent supervision.* If a will is declared invalid for failure to satisfy all the statutory formalities, the attorney who supervised its
execution may be liable in a suit for damages brought by the disappointed
beneficiaries. Courts have widely discarded the traditional bar of lack of privity, at least with respect to beneficiaries named in the will. See Licata v.
Spector, 225 A.2d 28 (Conn. C.P. 1966) (will invalid for lack of additional witness required by statute; named beneficiaries may sue attorney for negligence); Auric v. Continental Casualty Co., 331 N.W.2d 325 (Wis.1983); cf.
Guy v. Liederbach, 459 A.2d 744 (Pa.1983) (named beneficiary deprived of
legacy under purging statute may sue attorney in assumpsit). Persons other
than attorneys who draft wills or supervise their execution may also be liable
for unauthorized practice of law. See Biakanja v. Irving, 320 P.2d 16
(Cal.1958) (notary public); Persche v. Jones, 387 N.W.2d 32 (S.D.1986) (bank
officer). See generally Johnston, Legal Malpractice in Estate Planning—
Perilous Times Ahead for the Practitioner, 67 Iowa L. Rev. 629 (1982).

Testator, in failing health, instructed his lawyer to prepare a will. The
lawyer drafted the will as requested, but testator suffered a heart attack and
died before he could execute it. The intended beneficiary brings a malpractice
suit against the lawyer, seeking to recover the value of the lost bequest. What
result? See Krawczyk v. Stingle, 543 A.2d 733 (Conn. 1988) (denying relief on
ground that "imposition of liability to third parties for negligent delay in the
execution of estate planning documents would not comport with a lawyer's
duty of undivided loyalty to the client"); Radovich v. Locke–Paddon, 41
Cal.Rptr.2d 573 (App. 1995).

c. Interested Witnesses

The early cases concerning the competency of attesting witnesses
arose at a time when the disqualification of witnesses in ordinary lawsuits was far more extensive than it is today. Well into the nineteenth
century, the common law barred parties to the action and interested persons from testifying; furthermore, under the rule prohibiting one spouse
from testifying in favor of the other, the disqualification also extended to
spouses of parties and interested persons. These disqualifications have
generally been abolished in this country as far as ordinary lawsuits are
concerned; a witness's financial or other interest may be considered in
determining credibility, but it is no longer a ground for excluding testimony.

Traces of the common law disqualification are still discernible in the law of wills. The original Statute of Frauds required that a will be attested "by three or four credible witnesses." In accordance with the usage of the time, interested persons were not competent to testify at common law and therefore could not be "credible" witnesses to a will within the meaning of the Statute. Thus, if one of the necessary witnesses was a devisee, the will failed completely. To ameliorate this harsh result, the original English "purging" statute was enacted in 1752. 25 Geo. II, c. 6. This statute voided any gift made in a will to an attesting witness, thereby removing the witness's disqualification and permitting the remaining provisions of the will to be given effect. The Wills Act (1837) carried forward the provisions of the original purging statute and extended them to cover any gift to the spouse of an attesting witness. 7 Wm. IV & 1 Vict., c. 26, §§ 14–17. In this country, most states have purging statutes. Some are modeled on the original English statute. For example, the Rhode Island statute provides as follows:

Rhode Island General Laws

§ 33–6–1. Gifts to Attesting Witnesses.

> If any person shall attest the execution of any will or codicil to whom any beneficial devise, legacy, estate, interest, gift, or appointment, or affecting any real or personal estate, other than and except charges and direction for the payment of any debt or debts, shall be thereby given or made, the devise, legacy, estate, interest, gift or appointment shall, so far only as concerns that person attesting the execution of the will, or codicil, or any person claiming under that person, be utterly null and void; but the person so attesting shall be admitted as a witness to prove the execution of the will, or codicil, or to prove the validity or invalidity thereof, notwithstanding the devise, legacy, estate, interest, gift, or appointment, mentioned in the will, or codicil.

Many statutes are more limited in scope. Typically, the witness is permitted to keep benefits under the will to the extent they do not exceed any intestate share that the witness would receive if the will were not established. In this respect the Ohio statute is typical:

Ohio Revised Code

§ 2107.15. Witness a devisee or legatee.

> If a devise or bequest is made to a person who is one of only two witnesses to a will, the devise or bequest is void. The witness shall then be competent to testify to the execution of the will, as if the devise or bequest had not been made. If the witness would have been entitled to a share of the testator's estate in case the will was not established, the witness takes so much of that share that does not exceed the bequest or devise to the witness. . . .

See also N.Y. EPTL § 3–3.2.

In practical effect, the purging statutes raise an irrebuttable presumption that a beneficiary of a will who acts as an attesting witness is dishonest. The rule is traditionally defended as a safeguard against perjury and as a means of protecting testators from overreaching or coercion by attesting witnesses. See Dorfman v. Allen, 434 N.E.2d 1012 (Mass.1982) (upholding purging statute against constitutional challenge). How real is the danger? Does the rule barring attesting witnesses from receiving benefits under a will offer significant protection to the testator? Several states, following the Uniform Probate Code, have abrogated the rule entirely.

Uniform Probate Code (2011)

§ 2–505. Who May Witness.

(a) An individual generally competent to be a witness may act as a witness to a will.

(b) The signing of a will by an interested witness does not invalidate the will or any provision of it.

COMMENT

This section . . . simplifies the law relating to interested witnesses. Interest no longer disqualifies a person as a witness, nor does it invalidate or forfeit a gift under the will. Of course, the purpose of this change is not to foster use of interested witnesses, and attorneys will continue to use disinterested witnesses in execution of wills. But the rare and innocent use of a member of the testator's family on a home-drawn will is not penalized.

This approach does not increase appreciably the opportunity for fraud or undue influence. A substantial devise by will to a person who is one of the witnesses to the execution of the will is itself a suspicious circumstance, and the devise might be challenged on grounds of undue influence. The requirement of disinterested witnesses has not succeeded in preventing fraud and undue influence; and in most cases of undue influence, the influencer is careful not to sign as witness but to procure disinterested witnesses. . . .

IN RE ESTATE OF WATTS

Appellate Court of Illinois, 1979.

67 Ill.App.3d 463, 384 N.E.2d 589, 23 Ill.Dec. 795.

CRAVEN, JUSTICE.

Melvin M. Fitzpatrick and Arnold F. Fitzpatrick appeal from an order of the circuit court of Coles County declaring the will of Laura Viola Watts to have been properly admitted to probate and ordering distribution in accordance therewith.

On January 31, 1977, following the death of the decedent, Carl Manhart, Virginia Warren, and Frank Warren petitioned the court for admission of the will to probate and for letters testamentary. The will devised items of personalty and money to named beneficiaries, one of whom was Virginia Warren, and devised the residuary estate to Carl Manhart. Virginia Warren and Frank Warren were named as contingent beneficiaries of the residuary estate. The will was signed by the decedent, attested by Carl Manhart, Virginia Warren, and Frank Warren, and notarized by Virginia Warren. Carl Manhart, Virginia Warren, and Frank Warren were named in the will as co-executors.

The court admitted the will to probate on February 18, 1977, appointed Carl Manhart, Virginia Warren, and Frank Warren as co-executors, and found Melvin and Arnold Fitzpatrick to be the decedent's heirs at law. No appeal was taken from the trial court's order at that time and no suit to contest the validity of the will was instituted within the statutorily prescribed period. . . .

On August 25, 1977, the co-executors filed a complaint for declaration of rights of the beneficiaries and heirs at law. The trial court's order entered on February 15, 1978, upheld the validity of the will and ordered distribution in accordance therewith.

On appeal, Melvin and Arnold Fitzpatrick seek to have the trial court's order admitting the will to probate reversed, or, in the alternative, seek to have the February 15, 1978, order vacated to have all interests of the attesting witnesses declared void.

We conclude that since no appeal was taken from the order admitting the will to probate and no suit to contest the validity of the will was instituted within the six-month period prescribed by statute, the trial court, and, hence, this court, lacked jurisdiction to hear any question regarding the validity of the will. Will contests and probate proceedings are dependent entirely upon statutory authority and none exists for appeal of the question of validity of the will at this point.

Although we will not disturb the trial court's finding that the decedent died testate, ... this court does have jurisdiction to declare the rights of the parties interested in the will. Melvin and Arnold Fitzpatrick have argued that the interests of Carl Manhart, Virginia Warren, and Frank Warren are invalid since they were attesting witnesses to the will and testified at the hearing to admit the will to probate. According to this argument, the interests of all three would pass by intestacy to Melvin and Arnold Fitzpatrick, the decedent's heirs at law.

The relevant statute reads:

If any beneficial devise, legacy, or interest is given in a will to a person attesting its execution or to his spouse, the devise, legacy, or interest is void as to that beneficiary and all persons claiming under him, unless the will is otherwise duly attested by a sufficient number of witnesses as provided by this Article exclusive of that person; . . . . [Ill. Rev. Stat. 1971, ch. 3, par. 44.]

We cannot agree with the argument of the co-executors that the testimony of Frank Warren and Virginia Warren was sufficient to uphold the interest of Carl Manhart, and that the testimony of Carl Manhart and Frank Warren was sufficient to uphold the interest of Virginia Warren. The policies underlying the requirement of two credible witnesses to a will are too strong to permit an interpretation of the statute which would allow attesting witnesses to bootstrap the interests of one another.

We conclude that the statute must be applied such that if the will is duly attested by two credible, disinterested witnesses, then the witnesses who have an interest under the will may take. In this case, the will was not attested by two credible, disinterested witnesses, and as a result, the interests of Virginia Warren and Carl Manhart are void and the contingent interests of Virginia Warren and Frank Warren must likewise be declared void.

Since the attesting witnesses are declared to have no beneficial interests under the will, it is our conclusion that the attestation of the will is sufficient to uphold the validity of the remainder of the bequests.

The specific bequests to Virginia Warren and the bequests of the residuary estate having been declared void that portion of the estate shall pass by intestacy to the decedent's heirs at law.

Accordingly, the order of the trial court is reversed and remanded with directions to order distribution in accordance with this opinion.

Reversed and remanded with directions.

NOTES

1. *Pecuniary interest.* Purging statutes apply where an attesting witness is named as a beneficiary or otherwise stands to receive a direct pecuniary benefit under the will. Even an indirect benefit may bring the statute into play. Suppose that the will directs that all estate taxes, including those attributable to nonprobate assets, shall be paid from the residuary estate without apportionment. (Assume that in the absence of such a provision, the estate tax would be apportioned among the beneficiaries based on the value of their respective shares.) Testator's brother, the designated beneficiary on testator's existing life insurance policy, is one of the attesting witnesses. Does the purging statute deprive the brother of the benefit conferred by the tax clause? See Estate of Wu, 877 N.Y.S.2d 886 (Sur. 2009) (yes; brother receives insurance proceeds net of estate tax, "precisely as if there had been no will or if the will did not include this tax clause"). Does it matter whether the brother was aware of the provisions of the will or the life insurance policy when he signed the will as an attesting witness? What if testator did not name the brother as life insurance beneficiary until two years after executing the will?

Does a gift to a corporation, town or church fail if one of the witnesses to the will is a stockholder, taxpayer or parishioner? See Estate of Tkachuk, 139 Cal.Rptr. 55 (App. 1977) (legacy to church was valid even though minister witnessed will; legacy was not "to a subscribing witness" within meaning of purging statute); Appeal of Cox, 137 A. 771 (Me.1927) (legacy to club was valid even though club member witnessed will; interest too indirect and slight). Even if the purging statute does not defeat such a gift, may the will still be contested on the ground that the gift was procured by undue influence?

Is a person nominated in the will as executor or trustee disqualified from acting as an attesting witness? Courts generally hold that the executor or trustee is a competent witness, on the theory that fiduciary commissions are compensation for services rather than gratuitous benefits; and on similar reasoning, the fees are not treated as a gift for purposes of the purging statutes. See In re Marsloe, 931 N.Y.S.2d 414 (App. 2011); In re Longworth, 222 A.2d 561 (Me.1966); see also In re Koop's Estate, 143 So.2d 693 (Fla.App.1962) (bequest to bank as trustee valid even though employee-stockholders of the bank were witnesses). Nevertheless, the purging statutes have been held applicable where the will specifies a commission exceeding that allowed by statute. See Estate of Small, 346 F.Supp. 600 (D.D.C.1972).

2. *Capacity of witnesses.* As in any other court proceeding, a witness to a will must have the capacity and maturity to observe, recall and narrate the events that took place at the attestation of the will. A few statutes set a minimum age. See, e.g., Ark. Code § 28–25–102 (18 years); Iowa Code § 633.280 (16 years). For an analysis of the age factor, absent a statute, see Dejmal's Estate, 289 N.W.2d 813 (Wis.1980) ("Certainly nineteen is not such a tender age that it would preclude one from testifying in court to the facts relating to execution of a will."). It has been held that a person convicted of an "infam-

ous" crime such as perjury is competent as an attesting witness, because to hold otherwise would create a "needless trap for the unwary testator who, by failing to discover an attesting witness' prior criminal record, risks having his will declared void." McGarvey v. McGarvey, 405 A.2d 250 (Md.1979). See generally Evans, The Competency of Testamentary Witnesses, 25 Mich. L. Rev. 238 (1927).

3. *Beneficiary's spouse as witness.* In a few states, the purging statute covers testamentary gifts not only to an attesting witness but also to the witness's spouse. See, e.g., Conn. Gen. Stat. § 45a–258; N.H. Rev. Stat. § 551:3; N.C. Gen. Stat. § 31–10. In the absence of an express statutory bar, however, modern courts are reluctant to imply such a result. See Estate of Harrison, 738 P.2d 964 (Okla.App.1987) (statutory removal of common law disqualification of beneficiary's spouse to act as attesting witness; purging statute not applicable). Thus, where real property was devised to a married couple in a will witnessed by the wife, it was held that the wife forfeited her share but the husband was entitled to take the entire property. Matter of Flynn, 329 N.Y.S.2d 249 (Sur. 1972). The witness's marital status is determined at the time the will is executed, not when it is offered for probate. See Berndtson v. Heuberger, 173 N.E.2d 460 (Ill.1961) (purging statute not applicable to witness who married beneficiary after execution of the will).

4. *Supernumerary witnesses.* If one of three witnesses is a beneficiary and the applicable wills statute requires only two witnesses, the interested witness, being superfluous, need not forfeit his or her benefit under the will. Rogers v. Helmes, 432 N.E.2d 186 (Ohio 1982). There appears to be no escape from the purging statute where two of three necessary witnesses are beneficiaries. Thus, where witnesses A and B are beneficiaries but witness C is disinterested, it has been held that A and C may not join to validate B's legacy, nor B and C to validate A's legacy. Both A and B must forfeit their legacies. In addition to the principal case, see Estate of Overt, 768 P.2d 378 (Okla. App. 1989) (notary's signature did not save bequest to one of two necessary witnesses).

5. *Application of purging statutes.* Some purging statutes contain a blanket exemption for a witness who is an heir of the testator. See, e.g., Conn. Gen. Stat. § 45a–258. The more common approach is to permit the witness to take the legacy, but only to the extent it does not exceed the value of the intestate share to which the witness would be entitled if there were no will. See, e.g., Ohio Rev. Code § 2107.15, reproduced supra. Suppose that X, an attesting witness, would receive an intestate share of $100,000 if the will were not admitted to probate; probate is granted, however, and the will includes a bequest to X of (a) nothing, (b) $50,000, or (c) $150,000. Under the Ohio purging statute, how much does X receive under the will? Would the result be the same under the Connecticut statute? What difference would it make, under either type of statute, if X had been disinherited under an earlier will which would be controlling if the present will were ineffective? Cf. Es-

tate of Johnson, 359 So.2d 425 (Fla.1978) (allowing witness, who was not an heir, to take a $10,000 legacy where earlier will included an identical legacy).

In a few states the purging statute no longer operates as an automatic bar on testamentary gifts to an attesting witness but instead raises a rebuttable presumption of fraud or undue influence on the witness's part. See, e.g., Cal. Prob. Code § 6112; Mass. Gen. L. ch. 190B, § 2–505. Under this modified form of purging statute, what sort of evidentiary showing must an interested witness make to rebut the presumption?

6. *Disclaimer.* In the principal case, suppose that Virginia Warren and Frank Warren disclaimed their respective bequests. (On the operation and effect of disclaimers, see supra p. 142.) Would the beneficiaries' disclaimers be effective to transform them into disinterested witnesses and thereby salvage the residuary bequest to Carl Manhart? See Estate of Parsons, 163 Cal.Rptr. 70 (App. 1980).

d. Excusing Harmless Errors

JOHN H. LANGBEIN, SUBSTANTIAL COMPLIANCE WITH THE WILLS ACT

88 Harv. L. Rev. 489, 498–99, 513, 524–26 (1975).

What is peculiar about the law of wills is not the prominence of the formalities, but the judicial insistence that any defect in complying with them automatically and inevitably voids the will. In other areas where legislation imposes formal requirements, the courts have taken a purposive approach to formal defects. The common examples are the judicial doctrines which sustain transactions despite noncompliance with the Statute of Frauds—the main purpose and part performance rules. The essential rationale of these rules is that when the purposes of the formal requirements are proved to have been served, literal compliance with the formalities themselves is no longer necessary. The courts have boasted that they do not permit formal safeguards to be turned into instruments of injustice in cases where the purposes of the formalities are independently satisfied.

Why has the Wills Act not been interpreted with a similar purposiveness? There are factors which distinguish Wills Act defects from Statute of Frauds violations, but we submit that none of them really justifies the harsher treatment of Wills Act defects. . . .

The substantial compliance doctrine is a rule neither of maximum nor of minimum formalities, and it is surely not a rule of no formalities. It applies to any Wills Act, governing the consequences of defective compliance with whatever formalities the legislature has prescribed. Our major theme is that substantial compliance fits easily into the existing doctrinal structure and judicial practice of the law of wills.

Proper compliance with the Wills Act, so-called due execution, is the basis in modern law for certain presumptions which shift the burden of proof from the proponents of a will to any contestants. Unless the contestants advance disproof, the proponents need establish no more than due execution. Because there are usually no contestants, the effect of the presumptions is to limit the proofs in the probate proceeding to the question of due execution, and there are further presumptions which allow due execution to be easily inferred from seeming regularity of signature and attestation.

These presumptions are extremely wise and functional. They routinize probate. They transform hard questions into easy ones. Instead of having to ask, "Was this meant to be a will, is it adequately evidenced, and was it sufficiently final and deliberate?," the court need only inquire whether the checklist of Wills Act formalities seems to have been obeyed. In all but exceptional cases, a will is simply whatever complies with the formalities.

The substantial compliance doctrine would permit the proponents in cases of defective execution to prove what they are now entitled to presume from due execution—the existence of testamentary intent and the fulfillment of the Wills Act purposes. . . .

The Wills Acts govern the transmission of "millions of estates and billions of dollars in assets." The substantial compliance doctrine must necessarily impair something of the channeling function, because it permits the proponents of noncomplying instruments to litigate the question of functional compliance, an issue which the rule of literal compliance presently forecloses. If testation were transformed from routine administration into routine adjudication, the social cost and the cost to estates and distributees would be intolerable.

We assert therefore a fundamental point when we say that the substantial compliance doctrine would have no effect whatever upon primary conduct. The incentive for due execution would remain. Precisely because the substantial compliance doctrine is a rule of litigation, it would have no place in professional estate planning. Today lawyers in holograph jurisdictions have their clients' wills executed as attested wills; that is, they opt for maximum formality, in order to be in the best possible position to defend the will against any claim of imposition or want of finality. The counselor's job is to prevent litigation. Only when the lawyer has bungled his supervision of the execution of a will would he have occasion to fall back on substantial compliance.

Hence, the substantial compliance doctrine would apply overwhelmingly to homemade wills. We know from long and sad experience that the rule of literal compliance with the Wills Act does not deter laymen from drafting and executing their own wills without professional advice. The substantial compliance doctrine would not attract the reliance of amateurs, nor increase the number of homemade wills. Anyone who would know enough about the probate process to know that the substantial compliance doctrine existed would know enough not to want to rely upon it.

The substantial compliance doctrine would pertain not to every will, but to that fraction of wills where the testator, acting without counsel or with incompetent counsel, has failed to comply fully with the Wills Act formalities. Two important factors would operate to diminish the incidence and the difficulty of such litigation. First, by no means would every defectively executed instrument result in a contest. On many issues the proponents' burden of proof would be so onerous that they would forego the trouble and expense of hopeless litigation; and on certain other issues the proponents' burden would be so light that potential contestants would not bother to litigate. Evidentiary and cautionary formalities like signature and writing are all but indispensable, whereas omitted protective formalities like competence of witnesses are easily shown to have been needless in the particular case.

Second, the litigation which would occur would for the most part raise familiar issues which the courts have demonstrated their ability to handle well. We have seen that the elements of the substantial compliance doctrine arise in other contexts in current litigation when courts examine whether purported wills evidence testamentary intent and were executed freely and with finality.

The substantial compliance doctrine would not simply add to the existing stock of probate litigation, but would to some extent substitute one type of dispute for another. The rule of literal compliance can produce results so harsh that sympathetic courts incline to squirm. Many of the formalities have produced a vast, contradictory, unpredictable and sometimes dishonest case law in which the courts purport to find literal compliance in cases which in fact instance defective compliance. Is a wave of the testator's hand a publication or an acknowledgement? Was the signature "at the end"? When the attesting witnesses were in the next room, were they in the testator's presence? The courts now purport to ask in these cases: did the particular conduct constitute literal compliance with the formality? The substantial compliance doctrine would replace that awkward, formalistic question with a more manageable question: did the conduct serve the purpose of the formality? By substituting a purposive analysis for a formal one, the substantial compliance doctrine would actually decrease litigation about the formalities. The standard would be more predictable, and contestants would lose their present incentive to prove up harmless defects.

NOTES

1. *Self-proving affidavits and substantial compliance.* A significant procedural innovation introduced by the Uniform Probate Code is the self-proving affidavit, which preserves the sworn testimony of attesting witnesses concerning the due execution of a will and dispenses with the need for live testimony in uncontested probate proceedings. See Note 4, supra p. 333. Technically, a traditional self-proving affidavit is not part of the will but a separate instrument executed by the testator and the witnesses before a notary public. See UPC § 2–504(b). Nevertheless, a self-proving affidavit resembles a standard attestation clause so closely that one can easily be mistaken for the other. All too often, a testator duly signs a will and the attesting witnesses sign the attached self-proving affidavit but fail to sign the will itself. If the mistake is not discovered until after the testator's death, the will may be challenged on the ground of defective execution. Most courts are willing to overlook the technical defect and treat the witnesses' signatures on the self-proving affidavit as if they appeared on the will itself. See In re Will of Carter, 565 A.2d 933 (Del.1989); Gardner v. Balboni, 588 A.2d 634 (Conn.1991); Hampton Roads Seventh-Day Adventist Church v. Stevens, 657 S.E.2d 80 (Va. 2008). Contrary judicial decisions, holding that a will cannot be probated if the witnesses sign only the affidavit and not the will itself, have been overruled by statutes modeled on the Uniform Probate Code. See UPC § 2–504(c) (signature on separate self-proving affidavit deemed part of will if necessary to prove due execution).

A leading case is In re Will of Ranney, 589 A.2d 1339 (N.J. 1991), in which the court framed the issue as follows:

> Self-proving affidavits and attestation clauses, although substantially similar in content, serve different functions. . . . Attestation clauses facilitate probate by providing "prima facie evidence" that the testator voluntarily signed the will in the presence of the witnesses. . . . An attestation clause also permits probate of a will when a witness forgets the circumstances of the will's execution or dies before the testator. . . .

> Self-proving affidavits, by comparison, are sworn statements by eyewitnesses that the will has been duly executed. . . . The affidavit performs virtually all the functions of an attestation clause, and has the further effect of permitting probate without requiring the appearance of either witness. . . . One difference between an attestation clause and a subsequently-signed, self-proving affidavit is that in an attestation clause, the attestant expresses the present intent to act as a witness, but in the affidavit, the affiant swears that the will has already been witnessed. This difference is more apparent than real when, as here, the affiants, with the intent to act as witnesses, sign the self-proving affidavit immediately after witnessing the testator's execution of the will. [589 A.2d at 1342-43.]

Although the court found that the witnesses' signatures on the self-proving affidavit "d[id] not literally comply with the statutory requirements," it concluded that the will should nevertheless be admitted to probate if it "substantially complie[d] with the statutory requirements" and remanded the case to the trial court for proceedings "in solemn form," i.e., with live testimony from the attesting witnesses, thereby ensuring that the self-proving affidavit would not serve "both to validate the execution of the will and to render the will self-proving." (For the procedural difference between probate in solemn form and probate in common form, see Chapter 8.).

To reduce the confusion arising from the standard separate form of self-proving affidavit, the Uniform Probate Code now provides that a will "may be simultaneously executed, attested, and made self-proved" in a single step requiring only one set of signatures. See UPC § 2–504(a) (one-step form).

2. *Limits of substantial compliance.* In embracing the doctrine of substantial compliance, the *Ranney* court offered the following observations:

> Compliance with statutory formalities is important not because of the inherent value that those formalities possess, but because of the purposes they serve. . . . It would be ironic to insist on literal compliance with statutory formalities when that insistence would invalidate a will that is the deliberate and voluntary act of the testator. Such a result would frustrate rather than further the purpose of the formalities. . . .

> The execution of a last will and testament, however, remains a solemn event. A careful practitioner will still observe the formalities surrounding the execution of wills. When formal defects occur, proponents should prove by clear and convincing evidence that the will substantially complies with statutory requirements. . . . Our adoption of the doctrine of substantial compliance should not be construed as an invitation either to carelessness or chicanery. The purpose of the doctrine is to remove procedural peccadillos as a bar to probate. [589 A.2d at 1344-45.]

In *Ranney*, the defect of execution consisted of misplaced signatures of the attesting witnesses; there was no question that Mr. Ranney intended to execute a will and attempted to comply with the statutory requirements. How expansive a view of substantial compliance are other courts likely to take in cases involving more serious defects?

For example, suppose that a will is signed by the testator, by one attesting witness, and by a notary public, each in the presence of the others, as part of a single transaction. Strictly speaking, the notary's function is to authenticate the signatures of the other persons who signed the will, not to attest to the accuracy of the factual recitals in the attestation clause. Should the notary nevertheless be treated as a second attesting witness in order to satisfy the attestation requirement? See Land v. Burkhalter, 656 S.E.2d 834 (Ga. 2008). What if the notary signed a separate self-proving affidavit but not the will itself? See Estate of Friedman, 6 P.3d 473 (Nev. 2000). Cf. UPC § 2–502 (recognizing notarization as valid substitute for attestation).

Now suppose that a testator executes a will in the presence of two witnesses. Both witnesses write their initials on the bottom of each page of the will, and one witness signs his name beneath the attestation clause on the last page, but the second witness inadvertently fails to sign on the last page. After the testator's death, the second witness signs a separate affidavit describing the circumstances of the will's execution. Assume that the applicable statutory formalities require that a will be signed by both witnesses in the presence of the testator and each other. Should a court apply the doctrine of substantial compliance to uphold the will? See Estate of Leavey, 202 P.3d 99 (Kan.App. 2009); Estate of Stringfield, 283 S.W.3d 832 (Tenn. App. 2008).

———————

One advantage of the "substantial compliance" doctrine, as elaborated by Langbein, is that it can be adopted by courts without any change in the statutory wills formalities. The corresponding risk, however, is that courts may be reluctant to break new ground without express legislative approval, or that in doing so they may interpret substantial compliance as requiring something closely approaching literal compliance. See Estate of Peters, 526 A.2d 1005 (N.J. 1987) ("The statutory policy to reduce the required formalities to a minimum should not, in our view, be construed to sanction relaxation of the formalities the statute retained."). In 1987, noting the "snail's pace of progress under a nonstatutory substantial compliance doctrine," Langbein reformulated his proposal in terms of a "dispensing power," i.e., a statute authorizing courts to excuse harmless errors in the execution of wills. Langbein, Excusing Harmless Errors in the Execution of Wills: A Report on Australia's Tranquil Revolution in Probate Law, 87 Colum. L. Rev. 1 (1987). In discussing the operation of a similar statute in South Australia, Langbein observed:

> . . . [T]he South Australian courts have given the dispensing power a purposive interpretation. The larger the departure from the purposes of the Wills Act formality, the harder it is to excuse a defective instrument. Breach of the peripheral presence rule, indeed of any attestation requirement, has been relatively lightly excused. By contrast, the courts have excused the testator's failure to sign his will only in extraordinary circumstances.

> . . . Implicitly, this case law has produced a ranking of the Wills Act formalities. Of the three main formalities—writing, signature, and attestation—writing turns out to be indispensable. Because [the statute] requires a "document," nobody has tried to use the dispensing power to enforce an oral will. Failure to give permanence to the terms of your will is not harmless. Signature ranks next in impor-

tance. If you leave your will unsigned, you raise a grievous doubt about the finality and genuineness of the instrument. An unsigned will is presumptively only a draft, . . . but that presumption is rightly overcome in compelling circumstances such as in the switched-will cases. By contrast, attestation makes a more modest contribution, primarily of a protective character, to the Wills Act policies. But the truth is that most people do not need protecting, and there is usually strong evidence that want of attestation did not result in imposition. . . .

Id. at 52. Langbein's reformulated proposal bore fruit in 1990, when the UPC was amended to include a dispensing power in § 2–503, which follows.

Uniform Probate Code (2011)

§ 2–503. Writings Intended as Wills, etc.

Although a document or writing added upon a document was not executed in compliance with Section 2–502, the document or writing is treated as if it had been executed in compliance with that section if the proponent of the document or writing establishes by clear and convincing evidence that the decedent intended the document or writing to constitute:

(1) the decedent's will,

(2) a partial or complete revocation of the will,

(3) an addition to or an alteration of the will, or

(4) a partial or complete revival of his [or her] formerly revoked will or of a formerly revoked portion of the will.

COMMENT

. . . Consistent with the general trend of the revisions of the UPC, section 2–503 unifies the law of probate and nonprobate transfers, extending to will formalities the harmless error principle that has long been applied to defective compliance with the formal requirements for nonprobate transfers. . . .

Evidence from South Australia suggests that the dispensing power will be applied mainly in two sorts of cases. . . . When the testator misunderstands the attestation requirements of Section 2–502(a) and neglects to obtain one or both witnesses, new Section 2–503 permits the proponents of the will to prove that the defective execution did not result from irresolution or from circumstances suggesting duress or trickery—in other words, that the defect was harmless to the purpose of the formality. . . .

The other recurrent class of case in which the dispensing power has been invoked in South Australia entails alterations to a previously executed will. Sometimes the testator adds a clause, that is, the testator attempts to interpolate a defectively executed codicil. More frequently, the amendment has the character of a revision—the testator crosses out former text and inserts replacement terms. . . .

MATTER OF ESTATE OF EHRLICH

Superior Court of New Jersey, Appellate Division, 2012.
427 N.J. Super. 64, 47 A.3d 12.

The opinion of the court was delivered by PARRILLO, P.J.A.D. . . .

The material facts are not genuinely in dispute. Richard Ehrlich, a trust and estates attorney who practiced in Burlington County for over fifty years, died on September 21, 2009. His only next of kin were his deceased brother's children—Todd and Jonathan Ehrlich and Pamela Venuto. The decedent had not seen or had any contact with Todd or Pamela in over twenty years. He did, however, maintain a relationship with Jonathan, who, he had told his closest friends as late as 2008, was the person to contact if he became ill or died, and to whom he would leave his estate.

Jonathan learned of his uncle's death nearly two months after the passing. An extensive search for a Will followed. As a result, Jonathan located a copy of a purported Will in a drawer near the rear entrance of decedent's home, which, like his office, was full of clutter and a mess. Thereafter, on December 17, 2009, Jonathan filed a verified complaint seeking to have the document admitted to probate. His siblings, Todd and Pamela, filed an answer, objecting. The court appointed a temporary administrator, Dennis P. McInerney, Esquire, who had been previously named as Trustee of decedent's law practice, and by order of June 23, 2010, directed, among other things, an inspection of decedent's home. Pursuant to that order, on July 8, 2010, Jonathan, Todd and Pamela, along with counsel and McInerney, accessed and viewed the contents of decedent's home and law office. No other document purporting to be decedent's Will was ever located.

The document proffered by Jonathan is a copy of a detailed fourteen-page document entitled "Last Will and Testament." It was typed on traditional legal paper with Richard Ehrlich's name and law office address printed in the margin of each page. The document does not contain the signature of decedent or any witnesses. It does, however, include, in decedent's own handwriting, a notation at the right-hand corner of the cover page: "Original mailed to H.W. Van Sciver, 5/20/2000[.]" The document names Harry W. Van Sciver as Executor of the purported Will and Jonathan as contingent Executor. Van Sciver was also named Trustee, along with Jonathan and Michelle Tarter as contingent Trustees. Van Sciver predeceased the decedent and the original of the document was never returned.

In relevant part, the purported Will provides a specific bequest of $50,000 to Pamela and $75,000 to Todd. Twenty-five percent of the residuary estate is to pass to a trust for the benefit of a friend, Kathryn Harris, who is to receive periodic payments therefrom. Seventy-five percent of the residuary estate is to pass to Jonathan.

It is undisputed that the document was prepared by decedent and just before he was to undergo life-threatening surgery. On the same day this purported Will was drafted—May 20, 2000—decedent also executed a Power of Attorney and Living Will, both witnessed by the same individual, who was the Burlington County Surrogate. As with the purported Will, these other documents were typed on traditional legal paper with Richard Ehrlich's name and law office address printed in the margin of each page.

Years after drafting these documents, decedent acknowledged to others that he had a Will and wished to delete the bequest to his former friend, Kathryn Harris, with whom he apparently had a falling out. Despite his stated intention, decedent never effectuated any change or modification to his Will as no such document ever surfaced, even after the extensive search conducted of his home and law office after his death.

The contested probate matter proceeded on cross-motions for summary judgment following completion of discovery. After hearing argument, the General Equity Judge granted Jonathan's motion and admitted the copy entitled "Last Will and Testament" of Richard Ehrlich to probate. The court reasoned:

> First, since Mr. [Richard] Ehrlich prepared the document, there can be no doubt that he viewed it. Secondly, while he did not formally execute the copy, his hand written notations at the top of the first page, effectively demonstrating that the original was mailed to his executor on the same day that he executed his power of attorney and his health directive is clear and convincing evidence of his "final assent" that he intended the original document to constitute his last will and testament as required both by N.J.S.A. 3B:3–3 and [In re Probate of Will and Codicil of Macool, 416 N.J.Super. 298, 310, 3 A.3d 1258 (App.Div.2010)].

The judge later denied Jonathan's motion for sanctions for frivolous litigation.

This appeal and cross-appeal follow.

I

At issue is whether the unexecuted copy of a purportedly executed original document sufficiently represents decedent's final testamentary intent to be admitted into probate under N.J.S.A. 3B:3–3. Since, as the parties agree, there is no genuine issue of material fact, the matter was ripe for summary judgment as involving only a question of law, . . . to which we owe the motion court no special deference. . . .

N.J.S.A. 3B:3–2 contains the technical requirements for writings intended as wills:

a. Except as provided in subsection b. and in N.J.S.[A.] 3B:3–3, a will shall be:

(1) in writing;

(2) signed by the testator or in the testator's name by some other individual in the testator's conscious presence and at the testator's direction; and

(3) signed by at least two individuals, each of whom signed within a reasonable time after each witnessed either the signing of the will as described in paragraph (2) or the testator's acknowledgment of that signature or acknowledgment of the will.

b. A will that does not comply with subsection a. is valid as a writing intended as a will, whether or not witnessed, if the signature and material portions of the document are in the testator's handwriting.

c. Intent that the document constitutes the testator's will can be established by extrinsic evidence, including for writings intended as wills, portions of the document that are not in the testator's handwriting.

A document that does not comply with the requirements of N.J.S.A. 3B:3–2a or b is nevertheless valid as a document intended as a Will and may be admitted into probate upon satisfaction of N.J.S.A. 3B:3–3, which provides:

Although a document or writing added upon a document was not executed in compliance with N.J.S.[A.] 3B:3–2, the document or writing is treated as if it had been executed in compliance with N.J.S.[A.] 3B:3–2 if the proponent of the document or writing establishes by clear and convincing evidence that the decedent intended the document or writing to constitute: (1) the decedent's will. . . .

The Legislature enacted N.J.S.A. 3B:3–3 in 2004, as an amendment to the New Jersey Probate Code. . . . It is virtually identical to Section 2–503 of the Uniform Probate Code (UPC), upon which it was modeled. . . . The comments to that Section by the National Conference of Commissioners on Uniform State Laws express its clear purpose: "[s]ection 2–503 means to retain the intent-serving benefits of Section 2–502 formality without inflicting intent-defeating outcomes in cases of harmless error." Unif. Probate Code, cmt. on § 2–503. Of particular note, the Commissioners' comments state that Section 2–503 "is supported by the Restatement (Third) of Property: Wills and Other Donative Transfers § 3.3 (1999)." Recognizing that strict compliance with the statutory formalities has led to harsh results in many cases, the comments to the Restatement explain,

> . . . the purpose of the statutory formalities is to determine whether the decedent adopted the document as his or her will. Modern authority is moving away from insistence on strict compliance with statutory formalities, recognizing that the statutory formalities are not ends in themselves but rather the means of determining whether their underlying purpose has been met. A will that fails to comply with one or another of the statutory formalities, and hence would be invalid if held to a standard of strict compliance with the formalities, may constitute just as reliable an expression of intention as a will executed in strict compliance. . . .

> The trend toward excusing harmless errors is based on a growing acceptance of the broader principle that mistake, whether in execution or in expression, should not be allowed to defeat intention nor to work unjust enrichment. [Restatement (Third) of Property, § 3.3 cmt. b (1999).]

We recently had occasion to interpret N.J.S.A. 3B:3–3 in a case wherein we held that under New Jersey's codification of the "harmless error" doctrine, a writing need not be signed by the testator in order to be admitted to probate. In re Probate of Will and Codicil of Macool, 416 N.J.Super. 298, 311, 3 A.3d 1258 (App.Div.2010).

> [T]hat for a writing to be admitted into probate as a will under N.J.S.A. 3B:3–3, the proponent of the writing intended to constitute such a will must prove, by clear and convincing evidence, that: (1) the decedent actually reviewed the document in question; and (2) thereafter gave his or her final assent to it. Absent either one of these two elements, a trier of fact can only speculate as to whether the proposed writing accurately reflects the decedent's final testamentary wishes. [Id. at 310, 3 A.3d 1258.]

Thus, N.J.S.A. 3B:3–3, in addressing a form of testamentary document not executed in compliance with N.J.S.A. 3B:3–2, represents a relaxation of the rules regarding formal execution of Wills so as to effectuate the intent of the testator. This legislative leeway happens to be consonant with "a court's duty in probate matters . . . 'to ascertain and give effect to the probable intention of the testator.' " Macool, supra, 416 N.J.Super. at 307, 3 A.3d 1258 (quoting Fidelity Union Trust v. Robert, 36 N.J. 561, 564, 178 A.2d 185 (1962)) (internal citations and quotation marks omitted in original). As such, Section 3 dispenses with the requirement that the proposed document be executed or otherwise signed in some fashion by the testator. Macool, supra, 416 N.J.Super. at 311, 3 A.3d 1258.

Our dissenting colleague, who participated in *Macool,* retreats from its holding and now discerns a specific requirement in Section 3 that the document be signed and acknowledged before a court may even move to the next step and decide whether there is clear and convincing evidence that the decedent intended the document to be his Will, and therefore excuse any deficiencies therein. We find no basis for such a constrictive construction in the plain language of the provision, which in clear contrast to Section 2, expressly contemplates an unexecuted Will within its scope. Otherwise what is the point of the exception?

Because N.J.S.A. 3B:3–3 is remedial in nature, it should be liberally construed. See Singleton v. Consolidated Freightways Corp., 64 N.J. 357, 362, 316 A.2d 436 (1974). Indeed, if the Legislature intended a signed and acknowledged document as a condition precedent to its validation under Section 3, it would have, we submit, declared so expressly . . . . The fact that the Legislature chose not to qualify its remedial measure as the dissent suggests is also consistent with the Commissioners' commentary expressly citing those foreign jurisdictions that excuse non-compliance with the signature requirement, although "reluctant[ly]" so. Unif. Probate Code, cmt. on § 2–503. And like the Commissioners' discussion, the comments to the Restatement also acknowledge that the absence of a signature is excusable, albeit the "hardest" deficiency to justify as it "raises serious, *but not insuperable* doubt." Restatement (Third) of Property, § 3.3 cmt. b (1999) (emphasis added).

To be sure, as a general proposition, the greater the departure from Section 2's formal requirement, the more difficult it will be to satisfy Section 3's mandate that the instrument reflect the testator's final testamentary intent. And while the dissent's concern over the lack of a signature and attestation is obviously understandable, their absence in this instance, as recognized by both sets of commentators and the express wording of Section 3, does not present an insurmountable obstacle.

Instead, to overcome the deficiencies in formality, Section 3 places on the proponent of the defective instrument the burden of proving by clear and convincing evidence that the document was in fact reviewed by the testator, expresses his or her testamentary intent, and was thereafter assented to by the testator. In other words, in dispensing with technical conformity, Section 3 imposes evidential standards and safeguards appropriate to satisfy the fundamental mandate that the disputed instrument correctly expresses the testator's intent.

Here, as noted, decedent undeniably prepared and reviewed the challenged document. In disposing of his entire estate and making specific bequests, the purported Will both contains a level of formality and expresses sufficient testamentary intent. As the motion judge noted, in its form, the document "is clearly a professionally prepared Will and complete in every respect except for a date and its execution." Moreover, as the only living relative with whom decedent had any meaningful relationship, Jonathan, who is to receive the bulk of his uncle's estate under the purported Will, was the natural object of decedent's bounty.

The remaining question then is whether, under the undisputed facts of record, decedent gave his final assent to the document. Clearly, decedent's handwritten notation on its cover page evidencing that the original was sent to the executor and trustee named in that very document demonstrates an intent that the document serve as its title indicates—the "Last Will and Testament" of Richard Ehrlich. In fact, the very same day he sent the original of his Will to his executor, decedent executed a power of attorney and health care directive, both witnessed by the same individual. As the General Equity judge noted, "[e]ven if the original for some reason was not signed by him, through some oversight or negligence his dated notation that he mailed the original to his executor is clearly his written assent of his intention that the document was his Last Will and Testament."

Lest there be any doubt, in the years following the drafting of this document, and as late as 2008, decedent repeatedly orally acknowledged and confirmed the dispositionary contents therein to those closest to him in life. The unrefuted proof is that decedent intended Jonathan to be the primary, if not exclusive, beneficiary of his estate, an objective the purported Will effectively accomplishes. Indeed, the evidence strongly suggests that this remained decedent's testamentary intent throughout the remainder of his life.

Moreover, decedent acknowledged the existence of the Will to others to whom he expressed an intention to change one or more of the testamentary dispositions therein. As the wife of decedent's closest friend recounted: "And [Richard] has to change [the Will] because there is another person that he gave, I don't know how you say it, annuities every month . . . in case he passed away, and he wants to take her off the [W]ill. And by that time Richard could barely write or sign, so I'm not surprised he didn't sign his [W]ill." Although there is no evidence whatsoever that decedent ever pursued this intention, the very fact that he admitted to such a document is compelling proof not only of its existence but of decedent's belief that it was valid and of his intention that it serve as his final testamentary disposition.

Given these circumstances, we are satisfied there is clear and convincing evidence that the unexecuted document challenged by appellants was reviewed and assented to by decedent and accurately reflects his final testamentary wishes. As such, it was properly admitted to probate as his Last Will and Testament.

The fact that the document is only a copy of the original sent to decedent's executor is not fatal to its admissibility to probate. Although not lightly excused, there is no requirement in Section 3 that the document sought to be admitted to probate be an original. Moreover, there is no evidence or challenge presented that the copy of the Will has in any way been altered or forged.

As with the case of admitting a copy of a Last Will to probate where the proof is clear, satisfactory, and convincing to rebut the presumption of the original's revocation or destruction, . . . here, as noted, the evidence is compelling as to the testamentary sufficiency of the document, its preparation and reflection of decedent's intent. As has been stressed, a court's duty in probate matters is "to ascertain and give effect to the probable intent of the testator." Fidelity Union Trust, supra, 36 N.J. at 564, 178 A.2d 185 (internal citations and quotation marks omitted). In our view, the challenged document was properly admitted to probate because it meets all the intent-serving benefits of Section 2's formality and we discern no need to inflict the intent-defeating outcome requested by appellants and advocated by the dissent.

II

That said, we also find the court properly exercised its discretion in not imposing sanctions under the Frivolous Litigation statute . . . . [The court found that "there was nothing in the record to suggest appellants' objection was filed to harass, delay or cause malicious injury." Indeed, since the document was not witnessed, notarized or dated, and was only a copy of a purported original, "it was neither unreasonable nor unfair for appellants to hold respondent to his rather exacting statutory burden" under N.J.S.A. 3B:3–3.]

Affirmed.

SKILLMAN, J.A.D. (retired and temporarily assigned on recall), dissenting.

I do not believe that N.J.S.A. 3B:3–3 can be reasonably construed to authorize the admission to probate of an unexecuted will. Therefore, I dissent.

By its plain terms, N.J.S.A. 3B:3–3 only allows the admission to probate of a defectively executed will, not an unexecuted will. N.J.S.A. 3B:3–3 provides that if "a document . . . was not executed in compliance with N.J.S.A. 3B:3–2," it may nonetheless be "treated as if it had been executed in compliance with N.J.S.A. 3B:3–2 if the proponent . . . establishes by clear and convincing evidence that the decedent intended the document or writing to constitute [his or her] will." Thus, N.J.S.A. 3B:3–3 may be invoked only in a circumstance where the document "was not executed in compliance with N.J.S.A. 3B:3–2"; it does not apply if the document was not executed at all.

The conclusion that N.J.S.A. 3B:3–3 was only intended to authorize the admission to probate of a defectively executed will, and not an unexecuted will, is confirmed by its legislative history. . . .

[B]oth the comments to section 2–503 of the 1990 version of the Uniform Probate Code, from which N.J.S.A. 3B:3–3 was derived, and the comments to the Third Restatement of Property, which are cited with approval in the comments to the Uniform Probate Code, indicate that N.J.S.A. 3B:3–3 only authorizes probate of a defectively executed will, and not a document such as the one the trial court admitted to probate, which does not contain either the signature of the decedent or any form of attestation. This view of the intent of section 2–503 of the 1990 Uniform Probate Code is also reflected in In re Will of Ranney, 124 N.J. 1, 10, 589 A.2d 1339 (1991), decided before our Legislature's enactment of N.J.S.A. 3B:3–3, in which the Court described section 2–503 as adopting "the doctrine of substantial compliance."

The majority's decision relies heavily upon this court's interpretation of N.J.S.A. 3B:3–3 in In re Will of Macool, 416 N.J.Super. 298, 310, 3 A.3d 1258 (App.Div.2010), which concluded that for a will to be admitted to probate under this section, it must be established "by clear and convincing evidence, that: (1) the decedent actually reviewed the document in question; and (2) thereafter gave his or her final assent to it." Although I was on the panel that decided *Macool,* upon further reflection I have concluded that that opinion gives too expansive an interpretation to N.J.S.A. 3B:3–3; specifically, I disagree with the dictum that seems to indicate a draft will that has not been either signed by the decedent or attested to by any witnesses can be admitted to probate, provided the putative testator gave his or her "final assent" to the proposed will. See id. at 310–12, 3 A.3d 1258.

The comments to section 2–503 of the 1990 Uniform Probate Code and section 3.3 of the Restatement (Third) of Property both indicate that N.J.S.A. 3B:3–3 may be invoked only if there has been "harmless error" in the execution of a will, or what the Court in *Ranney* characterized as "substantial compliance" with the requirements for execution of a will. Under this view of N.J.S.A. 3B:3–3, a will could be admitted to probate if, as described in the comments to both the Code and Restatement, a husband and wife mistakenly signed each other's wills, or as described in illustration two in the comments to section 3.3 of the Restatement, a testator began signing his or her will but suddenly died before completing the signature. However, a mere verbal "assent" to the terms of a will that was not formalized by any signature on the document would not satisfy the prerequisites of N.J.S.A. 3B:3–3.

Moreover, even if it were appropriate to give N.J.S.A. 3B:3–3 a more expansive interpretation than is supported by the comments to the 1990 Uniform Probate Code and Third Restatement of Property, it still would not be appropriate to admit the unexecuted copy of the decedent's will to probate. The decedent was a trusts and estates attorney, who certainly would have known that a draft will had to be properly executed to become effective. Consequently, he could not have "intended the [unexecuted copy of the document] to constitute [his] will."

The majority states, quoting Fidelity Union Trust Co. v. Robert, 36 N.J. 561, 564, 178 A.2d 185 (1962), that "a court's duty in probate matters is 'to ascertain and give effect to the probable intent of the testator.' " Ante at 76, 47 A.3d at 19. However, "the doctrine of probable intent is available only to interpret, but not to validate, a will." In re Will of Smith, 108 N.J. 257, 265, 528 A.2d 918 (1987). "Probable intent comes into play only after a will is found to be valid." Ibid. Therefore, even if the probate of the decedent's unexecuted will would be more likely to effectuate his testamentary intent than intestacy, a draft will that was not executed in conformity with N.J.S.A. 3B:3–2 and does not satisfy the prerequisites of N.J.S.A. 3B:3–3 may not be admitted to probate.

Although N.J.S.A. 3B:3–3 does not authorize the admission to probate of the unexecuted copy of the decedent's purported will, there is a common law doctrine under which a copy of a lost will may be admitted to probate if the party seeking probate can present satisfactory evidence of the original will's contents and execution and that the will was not revoked before the testator's death. See generally 3 Bowe–Parker, Page on Wills, §§ 27.1 to .15; 29.156 to .166 (3rd ed.2004). The term "lost will" includes a will "which may be in existence but which cannot be found so as to be produced for probate." Page on Wills, supra, § 27.1, p. 433. . . .

Despite Jonathan Ehrlich's reliance upon N.J.S.A. 3B:3–3 in seeking to probate the unexecuted copy of the decedent's will found after his death, Jonathan does not appear to claim that the decedent actually intended that document to be his will, as required for probate under N.J.S.A. 3B:3–3. Instead, Jonathan's claim appears to be that the will found in the decedent's home was an unexecuted copy of an original executed will, which the decedent sent to his executor Van Sciver, and that the original was lost by Van Sciver or Van Sciver's estate after his death. For the reasons previously discussed, N.J.S.A. 3B:3–3 does not address such a claim.

In my view, Jonathan is entitled to prevail only if he can show, in conformity with the common law authority dealing with lost wills, that the unexecuted will found in the decedent's home is a copy of an original executed will sent to Van Sciver, which was lost and not revoked by the decedent. However, because this case was presented solely under N.J.S.A. 3B:3–3, the trial court did not make any findings of fact regarding these issues. Indeed, the trial court concluded that the copy of the will found in the decedent's home could be admitted to probate under N.J.S.A. 3B:3–3 "[e]ven if the original . . . was not signed by [the decedent]." Therefore, I would remand to the trial court to make such findings. I would not preclude the parties from moving to supplement the record to present additional evidence on the question whether the unexecuted copy of the will found in the decedent's home may be admitted to probate as a copy of the alleged executed original sent to Van Sciver.

For these reasons, I dissent from the part of the majority opinion affirming the judgment admitting the decedent's unexecuted will to probate. . . .

NOTES

1. *Harmless error.* What sort of defects in executing a will constitute "harmless error" under UPC § 2–503? According to the *Ehrlich* majority, a document should be admitted to probate if the proponent establishes by clear and convincing evidence that it "was in fact reviewed by the testator, expresses his or her testamentary intent, and was thereafter assented to by the testator." Is this a fair reading of UPC § 2–503? Note the dissenting judge's view that the statutory dispensing power "does not apply if the document was not executed at all."

Does UPC § 2–503 require that the very document that is offered for probate was intended by the decedent to operate as a will, even though it was not executed in compliance with the wills formalities? What if that document is an identical copy of a document that the decedent actually executed or attempted to execute? Note the statement in the majority opinion that the statutory dispensing power does not require "that the document sought to be admitted to probate be an original." What if the document offered for probate is a transcript of the decedent's orally expressed testamentary wishes?

If the decedent duly executed a will but the original document cannot be found, does UPC § 2–503 allow an unexecuted copy of the will to be admitted to probate? For more on lost wills, see Harrison v. Bird, infra p. 423, and Note 3, infra p. 426.

2. *Scope of the dispensing power.* UPC § 2–503 has been adopted in several states, but the case law interpreting it remains relatively sparse in this country. Experience with similar provisions in other countries, however, offers some indication of how a statutory dispensing power may apply in particular situations. Consider the following cases:

(a) Attorney prepares a formal will for testator, who is ill in hospital. Testator reads the will and approves its contents, but asks the attorney to correct the spelling of one beneficiary's name. Attorney takes the will back and returns later the same day with a retyped will for testator to sign, only to discover that testator has died. The unsigned will is offered for probate. See Baumanis v. Praulin, 25 S.A.S.R. 423 (1980); Will of Macool, 3 A.3d 1258 (N.J. App. 2010).

(b) Attorney prepares "mirror wills" for husband and wife. At a joint execution ceremony in the attorney's office, each spouse mistakenly signs the will prepared for the other. The mistake comes to light after husband's death, when his will is offered for probate. See Estate of Blakely, 32 S.A.S.R. 473 (1983); Matter of Snide, supra p. 302.

(c) Testator prepares a typewritten will and signs it, but fails to have it witnessed. After testator's death, the signed but unwitnessed will is offered for probate. See Estate of Kelly, 32 S.A.S.R. 413, aff'd, 34 S.A.S.R. 370 (1983); Estate of Hall, 51 P.3d 1134 (Mont. 2002); Estate of Palmer, 744 N.W.2d 550 (S.D. 2007).

(d) Husband and wife write out their respective wills by hand, and invite some neighbors over to witness the wills. Husband signs his will but wife fails to sign hers. The omission goes unnoticed, and the neighbors sign both wills as attesting witnesses. After wife's death her witnessed but unsigned will is offered for probate. See Estate of Williams, 36 S.A.S.R. 423 (1984); Allen v. Dalk, 826 So.2d 245 (Fla. 2002).

For a survey of case law from Australia involving statutory dispensing powers, see Lester, Admitting Defective Wills to Probate, Twenty Years Later: New Evidence for the Adoption of the Harmless Error Rule, 42 Real Prop. Prob. & Tr. J. 577 (2007).

3. *Sliding scale of formalities.* The Official Comment to UPC § 2–503 indicates that "[t]he larger the departure from Section 2–502 formality, the harder it will be to satisfy the court that the instrument reflects the testator's intent." Does the statutory language reflect an implicit "ranking" of wills formalities? Recall that the Uniform Probate Code makes attesting witnesses unnecessary if the will is acknowledged by the testator before a notary. See UPC § 2–502, reproduced supra. If attestation is no longer viewed as an essential formality, should it be made completely optional? For an elaboration of this argument, see Lindgren, Abolishing the Attestation Requirement for Wills, 68 N.C. L. Rev. 541 (1990).

For critical discussions of UPC § 2–503, see Orth, Wills Act Formalities: How Much Compliance Is Enough?, 43 Real Prop. Tr. & Est. L.J. 73 (2008); Miller, Will Formality, Judicial Formalism, and Legislative Reform: An Examination of the New Uniform Probate Code "Harmless Error" Rule and the Movement Toward Amorphism, 43 Fla. L. Rev. 167, 599 (1991) (parts 1 & 2); Sherwin, Clear and Convincing Evidence of Testamentary Intent: The Search for a Compromise Between Formality and Adjudicative Justice, 34 Conn. L. Rev. 453 (2002).

4. *Distinguishing alternative approaches.* Substantial compliance is a common law doctrine, while the dispensing power is embodied in statutory form. Moreover, under substantial compliance, a court asks whether the formalities actually observed come sufficiently close to meeting the statutory requirements, while under UPC § 2–503 the court asks whether the instrument was intended as a will. What is the substantive difference between the two approaches to excusing harmless errors in the execution of wills?

e. Illustrative Form of Attested Will

The following will form is included here to give students a sense of the format, organization, and content of a hypothetical testator's testamentary instructions. The form is by no means a model of impeccable drafting, nor should it be taken as a guide for preparing a will for a flesh-and-blood testator. Instead, by providing an example of provisions typically found in a will, the form is intended to draw attention to recurring issues and problems confronting the drafter of even a relatively simple will.

LAST WILL AND TESTAMENT

I, Henry A. Wagner, of Springfield in the County of Midway and State of New Caledonia, make this my last will and testament, hereby revoking all wills and codicils at any time heretofore made by me.

FIRST: I bequeath all my tangible personal property to my wife, Ruth S. Wagner, if she survives me, or if she does not survive me to those of my children who survive me, in equal shares. If I leave a signed memorandum concerning the disposition of any articles of such property, I hope that my wife or my children will carry out my wishes as expressed therein, but I impose no legal obligation on them to do so.

SECOND: I devise all my right, title and interest in and to any real property used by us for residential purposes to my wife, Ruth S. Wagner, if she survives me, or if she does not survive me any such real property shall be part of my residuary estate.

THIRD: I bequeath to each of my sisters, Judith N. Hall and Chloe E. Moore, who survives me, the sum of five thousand dollars ($5,000), and I bequeath to the Alma Mater Foundation the sum of ten thousand dollars ($10,000), to be used to provide scholarships for needy students.

FOURTH: All the rest, residue and remainder of my property, both real and personal, of whatever kind, nature and description and wherever situated (hereinafter referred to as my residuary estate), I give, devise and bequeath to those of my descendants who survive me, by right of representation; provided, that if any such descendant is under the age of twenty-one (21) years, my executor is authorized, in my executor's discretion, (a) to deliver such descendant's share directly to such descendant or to a parent or guardian of or a custodian for such descendant, or to deposit the same in a savings account in such descendant's name, and the receipt of such descendant or other payee shall be a full and complete discharge for and with respect to such share, or (b) to hold such descendant's share in trust, to manage, invest and reinvest the same, and to distribute or apply so much of the net income and so much of the principal thereof to or for the benefit of such descendant as may be deemed advisable until such descendant reaches the age of twenty-one (21) years, at which time all accumulated income and any remaining principal shall be distributed to such descendant free of trust.

FIFTH: I appoint as executor of this will, and as trustee of any trust created hereunder, my wife, Ruth S. Wagner, or if she fails to qualify or ceases to act for any reason, I appoint Reliable Trust Co., of Springfield, New Caledonia, to be executor and trustee in her place. No executor or trustee shall be required to furnish bond or, if a bond shall be required by law, no surety shall be furnished thereon. I request that representation by a guardian ad litem of the interests of any person with respect to the allowance of accounts or any other matters under this will be dispensed with.

SIXTH: In administering my estate and any trust created hereunder, my executor shall have the following powers which may be exercised by my executor in my executor's discretion, without the license or approval of any court, and which shall be in addition to the powers conferred by law:

(1) to retain any property of any kind received hereunder, without regard to diversification and without being restricted to property authorized by law for trust investment;

(2) to sell, exchange, or otherwise dispose of any property, real or personal, at any time held hereunder, on such terms for cash or credit, secured or unsecured, and in such manner as may be deemed advisable;

(3) to invest and reinvest in such securities or other property, real or personal (including, without limitation, bonds, notes, mortgages and other obligations, preferred and common stocks, investment trusts or companies and common trust funds), as may be deemed advisable, whether or not such securities or other property be of the character authorized by law for trust investment and without regard to diversification;

(4) to operate, maintain, alter, improve, mortgage and lease for any term (whether or not longer than the period of administration of my estate or any trust hereunder), any real property held hereunder;

(5) to borrow money, if deemed necessary or advisable, and to secure any such loan by mortgage or pledge of any property held hereunder;

(6) to exercise all option, conversion, subscription, voting and other rights pertaining to any property held hereunder, in person or by proxy;

(7) to employ and pay the compensation of such attorneys, accountants, agents, custodians and investment counsel as may be deemed advisable;

(8) to delegate to third parties any discretionary or nondiscretionary powers and duties; and

(9) to make any required division or distribution, in whole or in part, in cash or in other property, real or personal, or undivided interests in property, whether or not the same kind of property is allocated to others.

SEVENTH: I direct that all estate, inheritance and similar taxes imposed by reason of my death with respect to any property which passes or has passed from me under this will or otherwise than under this will (including, without limitation, proceeds of insurance on my life and property held in joint tenancy or tenancy by the entirety) shall be paid from my residuary estate, without apportionment.

EIGHTH: Except to the extent to which I have included them in the provisions of this will, I have intentionally, and not as the result of any accident or mistake, omitted to provide in this will for any of my children or the descendants of a deceased child, whether born before or after my death.

IN WITNESS WHEREOF, I, Henry A. Wagner, have hereunto set my hand this ___ day of _____ , 2013.

_____

Henry A. Wagner

Signed, published and declared by the above-named testator, Henry A. Wagner, as and for his last will and testament in the presence of us who, at his request, in his presence and in the presence of one another, have hereunto subscribed our names as witnesses this ___ day of _____ , 2013.

_____ , residing at _____

_____ , residing at _____

State of New Caledonia

County of Midway

We, Henry A. Wagner, _____ , and _____ , the testator and the witnesses, respectively, whose names are signed to the attached or foregoing instrument, being first duly sworn, do hereby declare to the undersigned authority that the testator signed and executed the instrument as the testator's will and that he signed it willingly (or willingly directed another to sign it for him), and that he executed it as his free and voluntary act for the purposes therein expressed, and that each of the witnesses, in the presence and hearing of the testator, signed the will as witness and that to the best of his knowledge the testator was at that time eighteen years of age or older, of sound mind, and under no constraint or undue influence.

_____

Henry A. Wagner

_____

Witness

_____

Witness

Subscribed, sworn to and acknowledged before me by Henry A. Wagner, the testator, and subscribed to and sworn before me by _____ and _____ , the witnesses, this ___ day of _____ , 2013.

_____

Notary Public

NOTES

1. *Execution ceremony.* Given the variations in statutes prescribing formalities for the execution of wills, combined with the possibility that a testator may move from one state to another or own property in more than one state, it is often recommended that wills be executed in a manner that ensures maximum acceptability. One suggested form of execution ceremony is as follows:

1. The testator should examine the will in its entirety and the lawyer should make certain that the testator understands the terms of the will.

2. The testator and three persons who are to be witnesses to the will and who have no interest vested or contingent in the property disposed of by the testator's will or in the testator's estate in the event of an intestacy, along with the lawyer supervising the execution of the will, should be in a room from which everyone else is excluded. No one should enter or leave this room until the execution of the will is completed.

3. The lawyer supervising the execution of the will should ask the testator the following question: "Do you declare in the presence of [witness 1], [witness 2], and [witness 3] that the document before you is your will, that its terms have been explained to you, and that the document expresses your desires as to the disposition of the property referred to therein on your death?" The testator should answer "yes," and the answer should be audible to the three witnesses.

4. The lawyer supervising the execution of the will should then ask the testator the following question: "Do you request [witness 1], [witness 2], and [witness 3] to witness your signing of your will?" Again, the testator should answer "yes," and the answer should be audible to the three witnesses.

5. The three witnesses should then be so placed that each can see the testator sign, and the testator should then sign in the place provided for the testator's signature at the end of the will. The testator should also sign on the bottom of each page of the will.

6. One of the witnesses should then read aloud the attestation clause, which should provide in substance that the foregoing instrument was signed on such a date by the testator (giving the testator's name); that the testator requested each of the witnesses to witness his signing of the document; that each of the witnesses did witness the signing of the document; that each witness in the presence of the testator and in the presence of the other witnesses does sign as witness, and that each witness does declare the testator to be of sound mind and memory.

7. Each witness should declare that the attestation clause is a correct statement.

8. Each witness should then sign in the place provided for the signatures of the witnesses following the attestation clause. As each witness signs, the testator and the other two witnesses should be so placed that each one can see the witness sign. Each witness should give an address opposite his or her signature.

If under controlling local law the observance of certain formalities will make the will self-proving, and additional formalities to those listed above are required to make it self-proving, such additional formalities should be adopted.

Restatement (Second) of Property (Donative Transfers) § 33.1 cmt. c (1992).

2. *Attestation clause.* Note the attestation clause following the testimonium clause in the illustrative will form. Such a clause is commonly included for two reasons. First, it provides a convenient summary of the execution ceremony, and thus serves as a prompting device to ensure that all the required steps are actually followed. In addition, the attestation clause raises a presumption of due execution, which may play a decisive role if the attesting witnesses are unavailable or unable to testify in the probate proceeding. As one court remarked:

> The probate of a will cannot be made to depend upon the recollection or veracity of subscribing witnesses, for if it were necessary for them to remember and testify to the fact that all the prescribed formalities were in fact complied with very few wills could be upheld. The law wisely requires such instruments to be executed and attested with precautions which will usually guard against fraud, and if the attestation clause shows on its face that all the forms required by law have been met, and the signatures on the instrument are admittedly genuine, the presumption of due execution must prevail unless clear and affirmative proof shows the contrary. If it is merely doubtful from the evidence whether the requirements have been complied with, the presumption arising from the attestation clause is not overcome.

Conway v. Conway, 153 N.E.2d 11, 14 (Ill.1958). See also Gardner v. Balboni, 588 A.2d 634 (Conn.1991) (attestation clause raises presumption of due execution); Young v. Young, 313 N.E.2d 593 (Ill.App.1974) (no presumption of due execution in absence of attestation clause, despite appearance of regularity); but cf. Patten v. Patten, 558 P.2d 659 (Mont.1976) (attestation clause on separate page not sufficient where witness could not remember seeing testator sign or acknowledge will). Indeed, wills are often admitted to probate based on the recitals in the attestation clause, despite contrary live testimony offered by a subscribing witness. See Estate of Thomas, 284 N.E.2d 513 (Ill.App.1972) (attestation clause not rebutted by testimony of subscribing witness); Morris v. Estate of West, 602 S.W.2d 122 (Tex.App. 1980) (attestation clause sufficient to prevent summary judgment based on testimony of subscribing witnesses); cf. Estate of Johnson, 780 P.2d 692 (Okla.1989) (attestation clause rebutted by testimony of subscribing witness).

3. *Proof of due execution.* The wills statutes typically require that a will be attested by two witnesses at the time of execution or acknowledgment by the testator. Between the time the will was signed and the time it is probated, one or more witnesses may become unavailable due to death, absence from the jurisdiction, or other cause. Accordingly, probate statutes commonly permit the will to be admitted to probate based on the live testimony of a single attesting witness or, if none is available, on proof of the signatures of the testator and witnesses.

Furthermore, in most states a will may be made "self-proved" by a notarized affidavit in prescribed form reciting the essential facts of execution and attestation. (See the form of self-proving affidavit appended to the illustrative will form, supra.) The effect of a self-proving affidavit is discussed in Note 4, supra p. 333.

4. *Governing law.* A substantial majority of states have statutes providing that a will is valid if executed in compliance with the law either of the testator's domicile or of the place where the will was executed. See UPC § 2–506. Nevertheless, a careful attorney routinely follows standard procedures designed to satisfy the most exacting wills formalities in any state. See supra Note 1.

5. *Statutory will forms.* A few states have enacted statutes setting out forms of simple wills and instructions for their use. The forms include pre-printed dispositive and administrative provisions, with blanks for the names of the executor and beneficiaries. See, e.g., Cal. Prob. Code §§ 6240–6243; Mich. Comp. L. § 700.2519. Although these forms make it easy for a testator to execute a will without the assistance of an attorney, they are by no means foolproof. Statutory wills are subject to the same formal requirements as other attested wills, and there is no guarantee that testators will understand or follow instructions for executing a will. See Beyer, Statutory Fill–In Will Forms—The First Decade: Theoretical Constructs and Empirical Findings, 72 Or. L. Rev. 769 (1993).

6. *Military wills.* Certain members of the armed forces and their dependents are eligible for legal assistance in making a will. Under federal law, an eligible testator is authorized to execute a will in the presence of a "military legal assistance counsel" acting as presiding attorney and in the presence of two disinterested witnesses who attest the will by signing it. If these requirements are met, the will "has the same legal effect as a testamentary instrument prepared and executed in accordance with the laws of the State in which it is presented for probate." 10 U.S.C. § 1044d.

7. *International wills act.* In 1977, the National Conference of Commissioners on Uniform State Laws recommended that all of the states enact the Uniform International Wills Act, either as part of the Uniform Probate Code or as separate legislation. The purpose of the Act is to provide testators with a method of executing wills which will be valid as to form in all countries joining the Washington Convention of 1973. As stated in a Prefatory Note, "the objective would be achieved through uniform local rules of form, rather than through local or international law that makes recognition of foreign wills turn on choice of law rules involving possible application of foreign law." The Act, which appears as UPC §§ 2–1001 through 2–1010, sets out requirements of writing, signature or acknowledgment, publication, attestation, and the like. States adopting the Act are encouraged to make additional provisions for the registration and safekeeping of international wills. For a discussion of the origins and purposes of the Act, see UPC Article 2, Part 10, Prefatory Note.

NOTE ON POWERS OF ATTORNEY AND HEALTH CARE DIRECTIVES

For many persons, advances in modern medicine bring not only dramatically increased longevity but also a heightened risk of incapacity in the final years of life. Attorneys involved in drafting testamentary instruments should be aware of the need to plan for potentially extended periods of incapacity. For this purpose, a power of attorney, by which one person (the principal) authorizes another (the agent or attorney-in-fact) to do certain actions on his or her behalf, may prove especially useful.

An ordinary power of attorney is freely revocable by the principal at any time, and automatically terminates upon the death or incapacity of the principal. To overcome the obstacle of premature termination during the principal's lifetime, almost all states have enacted statutes authorizing a *durable power of attorney.* See Uniform Power of Attorney Act (2006). The distinguishing feature of a durable power of attorney is that it remains effective even if the principal becomes incapacitated; unless otherwise terminated, the authority of an agent under a durable power continues until the principal's death. See UPAA § 110(a) and (b).[4]

A durable power of attorney can be created by a writing which specifically expresses the intent of the principal that the authority conferred shall be exercisable notwithstanding the principal's subsequent disability or incapacity. Cf. UPAA § 104 (providing that a written power of attorney is durable "unless it expressly provides that it is terminated by the incapacity of the principal"). In some states the written instrument must be witnessed or notarized. The power may be a "springing" power, i.e., one which takes effect at some future time. For example, a power which by its terms will become effective if certain persons (e.g., the principal's regular physician and attorney) determine that the principal is no longer capable of managing his or her affairs may help to avoid uncomfortable and costly conservatorship proceedings.

An agent acting under a durable power may be authorized not only to handle the principal's business affairs but also, if the terms of the power are sufficiently clear, to make gifts to family members or to charity and to establish inter vivos trusts. (Even a durable power, however, cannot authorize the agent to make or revoke a will on behalf of the principal.) As a practical matter, financial institutions and other third parties may be reluctant to rely on a durable power where large amounts of property are concerned. In such cases, it may be more appropriate to use a revocable trust (see Chapters 6 and 7). For comprehensive discussions of durable powers of attorney and alternative arrangements for managing the property of an incompetent person, see McGovern, Trusts, Custodianships, and Durable Powers of Attorney, 27 Real Prop. Prob. & Tr. J. 1 (1992); Boxx, The Durable Power of Attorney's Place in the Family of Fiduciary Relationships, 36 Ga. L. Rev. 1 (2001); Dessin, Acting as Agent Under a Financial Durable Power of Attorney: An Unscripted Role, 75 Neb.L.Rev. 574 (1996).

Powers of attorney also find application in the area of health care. A competent person is entitled to make his or her own health care decisions, including the decision to refuse medical treatment. The problem of making health care decisions for incompetent persons gives rise to medical, legal, ethical, moral and financial dilemmas, which become more pressing as medical technology makes it possible to prolong the lives of patients who are terminally ill or in a persistent vegetative state. Many people contemplating incapacity due to advanced age, illness or accident seek to direct the course of future medical treatment through an advance directive. At the same time, doctors and hospitals seek to insulate themselves

---

[4] Indeed, the uniform act goes even further and validates actions taken under a written power of attorney by an agent who acts in good faith and without actual knowledge of the principal's death. See UPAA § 110(d).

from liability in making life-and-death decisions for incompetent patients. See In re Quinlan, 355 A.2d 647 (N.J.), cert. denied, 429 U.S. 922 (1976) (patient's father sought appointment as guardian for purpose of disconnecting respirator).

Beginning with the California Natural Death Act in 1976, all but a handful of states have enacted statutes authorizing some form of "living will."[5] This is a special form of "instruction directive" which contains specific instructions concerning medical treatment to be administered or withheld in the event the declarant is unable to make contemporaneous health care decisions. Typically, a living will takes effect if the declarant is terminally ill or in a persistent vegetative state (as determined by doctors), and authorizes measures for pain relief (and, in some cases, artificial nutrition and hydration) while refusing any other measures which would serve merely to prolong the process of dying. The Supreme Court has held that "a State may apply a clear and convincing evidence standard in proceedings where a guardian seeks to discontinue nutrition and hydration of a person diagnosed to be in a persistent vegetative state." Cruzan v. Director, 497 U.S. 261 (1990) (5–4 decision).

In the wake of the *Cruzan* decision, almost every state has enacted a statute authorizing a "durable power of attorney for health care." This is a "proxy directive" which authorizes a designated agent to make health care decisions on behalf of an incompetent principal; the power ordinarily takes effect only if the declarant becomes incapacitated.[6] Unlike a living will, a durable power of attorney for health care authorizes a third party to make contemporaneous health care decisions in light of existing circumstances, based on the declarant's expressed or presumed wishes.

In 1990 Congress enacted the Patient Self–Determination Act, codified at 42 U.S.C. § 1395cc(f), which requires that facilities receiving Medicare funds provide information to patients at the time of admission concerning the right to make advance directives under state law. For statutes authorizing advance directives, see Choice in Dying, Right-to-Die Law Digest (1995) (listing specific state statutes). There is a burgeoning literature on advance directives. See generally King, Making Sense of Advance Directives 108–83 (1996); Hastings Center, Guidelines on the Termination of Life–Sustaining Treatment and the Care of the Dying (1987); President's Commission for the Study of Ethical Problems in Medicine and Biomedical and Behavioral Research, Deciding to Forego Life–

---

[5] The use of the term "will" in this context is something of a misnomer. Although a living will is usually executed and attested in much the same manner as a testamentary instrument, there are several important differences: a living will makes no disposition of property; it takes effect, if at all, while the declarant is still alive; and it is ordinarily implemented without any court involvement.

[6] The power is said to be "durable" because it remains effective despite the principal's incapacity, much like the traditional durable power of attorney relating to property transactions.

Sustaining Treatment: A Report on the Ethical, Medical, and Legal Issues in Treatment Decisions 136–53 (1983).

NOTES

1. *Power of attorney for health care.* The Uniform Health–Care Decisions Act (1993) provides that a power of attorney for health care must be in writing and signed by the principal. Unless otherwise specified, the agent's authority "becomes effective only upon a determination that the principal lacks capacity, and ceases to be effective upon a determination that the principal has recovered capacity." In making health care decisions on behalf of the principal, the agent is required to act in accordance with the principal's instructions, if any, and "other wishes" known to the agent; otherwise, the agent is to act in accordance with the principal's "best interest" as determined by the agent (with due regard for the principal's "personal values" to the extent known to the agent). Id. § 2. The principal can revoke the designation of an agent by a signed writing or by personally informing the supervising health care provider; other portions of a power of attorney for health care can be revoked "at any time and in any manner that communicates an intent to revoke." Id. § 3. Health care providers are generally required to comply with health care decisions made by the agent on behalf of the principal, but may decline to do so for "reasons of conscience" or if the agent's decision would require "medically ineffective health care or health care contrary to generally accepted health-care standards." Id. § 7. The statute provides immunity from civil and criminal liability for a health care provider who, acting "in good faith and in accordance with generally accepted health-care standards," complies with health care decisions made by "a person apparently having authority" or declines to comply "based on a belief that the person then lacked authority." An agent enjoys similar immunity for health care decisions made "in good faith." Id. § 9.

2. *Right to die.* Although a competent person is free to refuse life-saving medical treatment, in most states it is a criminal offense to assist another in taking his or her own life. In two cases brought by physicians and their terminally ill patients, the Supreme Court rejected constitutional challenges to state laws banning physician-assisted suicide. See Washington v. Glucksberg, 521 U.S. 702 (1997) (due process); Vacco v. Quill, 521 U.S. 793 (1997) (equal protection). As a practical matter, the ban on assisted suicide does not prevent a physician from withdrawing artificial life support or prescribing pain-killing drugs which may hasten the patient's death. While acknowledging that "in some cases, the line between [refusing unwanted medical treatment and assisted suicide] may not be clear," the Court found a rational basis for the distinction in "[l]ogic and contemporary practice." The Court also found that a general ban on assisted suicide was rationally related to legitimate government interests: preserving human life; promoting public health; protecting "the integrity and ethics of the medical profession"; protecting vulnerable groups, including poor, elderly and disabled persons; and blocking "the path to voluntary and perhaps even involuntary euthanasia." The Court con-

cluded that "Americans are engaged in an earnest and profound debate about the morality, legality, and practicality of physician-assisted suicide. Our holding permits this debate to continue, as it should in a democratic society."

In the wake of the Supreme Court's decisions, physician-assisted suicide remains a topic of vigorous debate at the state level. In one case, a Montana trial court held that state constitutional guarantees of individual privacy and human dignity embraced "the right of a competent, terminally ill patient to die with dignity" by ingesting a lethal dose of medication prescribed by a physician; as a corollary, the court held that the prescribing physician enjoyed constitutional protection from criminal prosecution under state homicide laws. On appeal, the Montana Supreme Court affirmed the trial court's grant of summary judgment on statutory grounds but expressly declined to address the constitutional issue. Baxter v. Montana, 224 P.3d 1211 (2009) (finding "no indication in Montana law that physician aid in dying provided to terminally ill, mentally competent adult patients is against public policy").

In 1994, Oregon voters approved the Oregon Death With Dignity Act, Or. Rev. Stat. §§ 127.800 to 127.897, which allows a competent, adult, terminally ill resident of the state to obtain and use a prescription for a self-administered lethal medication "for the purpose of ending his or her life in a humane and dignified manner." The statute includes procedural safeguards to ensure that the patient is not suffering from a psychological disorder and that the decision is voluntary and informed. No person incurs civil or criminal liability for good faith compliance with the statutory procedure, but neither can any person be compelled to assist a patient in ending his or her own life. No protection is afforded for any sort of mercy killing or active euthanasia. The Supreme Court has upheld the Oregon statute against an attempt by the U.S. Attorney General to block its implementation. See Gonzalez v. Oregon, 546 U.S. 243 (2006). Voters in Washington approved similar legislation in 2008. See Wash. Rev. Code §§ 70.245.010 to 70.245.904.

For a sampling of the burgeoning literature on legal, ethical and medical aspects of physician-assisted suicide, see Behuniak & Svenson, Physician-Assisted Suicide: The Anatomy of a Constitutional Law Issue (2003); Regulating How We Die: The Ethical, Medical, and Legal Issues Surrounding Physician–Assisted Suicide (Emanuel ed., 1998); Physician-Assisted Suicide: What Are the Issues? (Kopelman & de Ville eds., 2001); Assisted Suicide: Finding Common Ground (Snyder & Caplan eds., 2001); Urofsky, Lethal Judgments: Assisted Suicide and American Law (2000).

3. *Disposition of body.* In general, a testator's directions concerning funeral and burial or cremation are enforceable if they are unambiguously expressed in the will, even though the funeral will ordinarily be held before the will is admitted to probate. As a practical matter, of course, the testator's wishes may be frustrated by a delay in disclosing the terms of the will or by objections from surviving family members. As one court observed, the "common industry practice" among funeral home directors is "to honor the wishes

of the deceased's next of kin when there is a conflict between the wishes of the deceased and those of the next of kin with regard to the disposition of the body." Cottingham v. McKee, 821 So.2d 169 (Ala. 2001); cf. Alcor Life Extension Found. v. Richardson, 785 N.W.2d 717 (Iowa 2010) (siblings had decedent's corpse embalmed and buried, disregarding instructions for cryopreservation; court ordered application for disinterment). In the absence of testamentary directions, the surviving spouse or next of kin is generally entitled to possession of the decedent's body for purposes of burial or cremation. For a perceptive discussion of conflicts over disposition of a decedent's corporeal remains, see Foster, Individualized Justice in Disputes Over Dead Bodies, 61 Vand. L. Rev. 1351 (2008).

4. *Anatomical gifts.* Modern medicine has found many uses for human bodies and organs, including teaching, research, therapy, and transplantation. Organs suitable for transplantation include corneas, kidneys, livers, and hearts. The need is great, and many people are willing to become donors. Procedures for making anatomical gifts at death are set forth in the Uniform Anatomical Gift Act, which has been adopted in every state, either as originally promulgated in 1968 or as subsequently revised in 1987 and 2006. This Act makes it easier to make an effective gift, but the demand for transplantable organs remains far greater than the supply. Various proposals, including the purchase of organs and the introduction of legislation permitting the routine removal of organs in the absence of objections by interested parties, have been advanced as ways of increasing the supply. A majority of states have enacted "required request" laws which require that hospital administrators discuss with a deceased patient's next of kin the possibility of authorizing anatomical gifts. In 1984 Congress passed the National Organ Transplant Act, which provides for the establishment of a national "organ procurement and transplantation network" and prohibits the purchase of human organs. See 42 U.S.C. §§ 274 and 274e. See generally Hastings Center, Ethical, Legal and Policy Issues Pertaining to Solid Organ Procurement (1985).

2. HOLOGRAPHIC WILLS

A holographic will is one that is written in the testator's handwriting and signed by the testator; attestation is unnecessary. Holographic wills have their roots in the civil law tradition; they originated in Roman law and were authorized by the Code Napoleon. They were introduced to this country by Spanish and French settlers, primarily in the South and West, and today are authorized by statute in approximately half the states.[7] Under the traditional type of statute, a holographic will must be "entirely written, dated and signed by the hand of the testator himself." Former

---

[7] Holographic wills are recognized in Alaska, Arizona, Arkansas, California, Colorado, Hawaii, Idaho, Kentucky, Louisiana, Maine, Michigan, Mississippi, Montana, Nebraska, Nevada, New Jersey, North Carolina, North Dakota, Oklahoma, Pennsylvania, South Dakota, Tennessee, Texas, Utah, Virginia, West Virginia, and Wyoming; in Maryland and New York they are available only for members of the armed forces. See Restatement (Third) of Property: Wills and Other Donative Transfers, § 3.2, Statutory Note (1999).

Cal. Prob. Code § 53. Many states that recognize holographic wills, however, have substantially relaxed the traditional requirement that the document be "entirely" handwritten, and most have abandoned the date requirement altogether. The revised Uniform Probate Code provides as follows:

Uniform Probate Code (2011)

§ 2–502. Execution; . . . Holographic Wills. . . .

(b) [Holographic Wills.] A will that does not comply with subsection (a) [prescribing formal requirements for an attested or notarized will] is valid as a holographic will, whether or not witnessed, if the signature and material portions of the document are in the testator's handwriting.

(c) [Extrinsic Evidence.] Intent that the document constitute the testator's will can be established by extrinsic evidence, including, for holographic wills, portions of the document that are not in the testator's handwriting.

ASHBEL G. GULLIVER & CATHERINE J. TILSON, CLASSIFICATION OF GRATUITOUS TRANSFERS
51 Yale L.J. 1, 13 (1941).

The exemption of holographic wills from the usual statutory requirements seems almost exclusively justifiable in terms of the evidentiary function. The requirement that a holographic will be entirely written in the handwriting of the testator furnishes more complete evidence for inspection by handwriting experts than would exist if only the signature were available, and consequently tends to preclude the probate of a forged document. While it may be argued that the requirement tends to prevent fraud in the execution, since the testator would normally sign the will immediately after he had finished writing it, and, there is, therefore, less likelihood of his signing a different document, there seems no substantial guarantee of the performance of the protective function, since no effort is made to prevent other forms of imposition such as undue influence. A holographic will is obtainable by compulsion as easily as a ransom note. While there is a certain ritual value in writing out the document, casual offhand statements are frequently made in letters. The relative incompleteness of the performance of the functions of the regular statute of wills, and particularly the absence of any ritual value, may account for the fact that holographic wills are not recognized in [all] of the states, and for some decisions, in states recognizing them, requiring the most precise compliance with specified formalities.

IN RE ESTATE OF MUDER

Supreme Court of Arizona, 1988.
159 Ariz. 173, 765 P.2d 997.

CAMERON, JUSTICE. . . .

Respondent seeks review of the decision and opinion of the court of appeals, which reversed the trial court's admission of Edward Frank Muder's will to probate. . . .

We must determine whether the purported will is a valid holographic will pursuant to A.R.S. § 14–2503. . . .

Edward Frank Muder died on 15 March 1984. In September 1986, Retha Muder, the surviving spouse, submitted a purported will dated 26 January 1984 to the probate court. The purported will was on a pre-printed will form set forth as Exhibit A.

The daughters of Edward Muder by a previous wife contested the will. They were unsuccessful in the trial court and appealed to the court of appeals. A divided court of appeals reversed. In re Estate of Muder, 156 Ariz. 326, 751 P.2d 986 (1987). We granted Retha Muder's petition for review. . . .

It is apparent that this was not a proper formal will pursuant to statute because only one witness signed.

> Except as provided for holographic wills, . . . every will shall be in writing signed by the testator or in the testator's name by some other person in the testator's presence and by his direction, and shall be signed by *at least two* persons each of whom witnessed either the signing or the testator's acknowledgment of the signature or of the will. [A.R.S. § 14–2502 (emphasis added).] . . .

We agree with the court of appeals that the will is not valid under the formal will statute, A.R.S. § 14–2502. . . .

To serve as a will, the document must indicate that the testator had testamentary intent. In re Estate of Blake v. Benza, 120 Ariz. 552, 553, 587 P.2d 271, 272 (App. 1978); see also In re Estate of Harris, 38 Ariz. 1, 296 P. 267 (1931). Testamentary intent requires that the writing, together with whatever extrinsic evidence may be admissible, establish that the testator intended such writing to dispose of his property upon his death. Blake, 120 Ariz. at 553, 587 P.2d at 272.

Because this will fails under A.R.S. § 14–2502, it is only valid if it can be considered a holographic will under the statute that provides:

A will which does not comply with § 14–2502 is valid as a holographic will, whether or not witnessed, if the signature and the material provisions are in the handwriting of the testator. [A.R.S. § 14–2503.]

This section was enacted in 1973 and replaced the previous holographic will statute that stated:

A holographic will is one entirely written and signed by the hand of the testator himself. Attestation by subscribing witnesses is not necessary in the case of a holographic will. [A.R.S. § 14–123 (1956).]

Under the previous statute, no printed matter was allowed on the document. Litigation resulted because often a testator would write his holographic will on paper containing printed letterheads. Such printed matter was obviously not in the testator's handwriting. To avoid the harsh result of denying such holographic wills admission to probate, courts created the "surplusage theory." This theory held that the statutory words "wholly" or "entirely" were satisfied when the material provisions of the will were "wholly" or "entirely" in the handwriting of the testator, and that other written or printed material could accordingly be disregarded as surplusage. Arizona adopted the surplusage theory to preserve the validity of such holographic wills. See In re Estate of Schuh, 17 Ariz. App. 172, 173, 496 P.2d 598, 599 (1972); see also In re Estate of Morrison, 55 Ariz. 504, 510, 103 P.2d 669, 672 (1940) (it was important that the testamentary part of the will be wholly written by the testator and signed by him).

With the increased use of printed will forms, states with statutes similar to our previous statute requiring that a holographic will be *entirely* in the handwriting of the testator, applied the surplusage theory to the printed will forms by disregarding the printed matter and then looking to see if what was left made sense and could be considered a valid will. See Estate of Black, 30 Cal.3d 880, 641 P.2d 754, 181 Cal.Rptr. 222 (1982); Succession of Burke, 365 So.2d 858 (La.Ct.App.1978); Watkins v. Boykin, 536 S.W.2d 400 (Tex.Civ.App.1976); see also In re Estate of Johnson, 129 Ariz. 307, 630 P.2d 1039 (App. 1981).

California considered this issue because its statute required that a holographic will must be entirely written, dated, and signed by the hand of the testator himself and that any matter printed that was incorporated in the will provisions had to be considered part of the will. Estate of Black, 30 Cal.3d 880, 883, 641 P.2d 754, 755, 181 Cal.Rptr. 222, 223 (1982). The will in *Black* was a document that was handwritten on three pages of a partially preprinted stationer's form. Id. The court upheld the will by finding that none of the incorporated material was either material to the substance of the will or essential to its validity as a testamentary disposition. Id. at 885, 641 P.2d at 757, 181 Cal.Rptr. at 225. As Justice Richardson stated:

> No sound purpose or policy is served by invalidating a holograph where every statutorily required element of the will is concededly expressed in the testatrix' own handwriting and where her testamentary intent is clearly revealed in the words as she wrote them. Frances Black's sole mistake was her superfluous utilization of a small portion of the language of the preprinted form. Nullification of her carefully expressed testamentary purpose because of such error is unnecessary to preserve the sanctity of the statute. [Black, 30 Cal.3d at 888, 641 P.2d at 759, 181 Cal.Rptr. at 227.]

We believe that our legislature, in enacting the present statute, A.R.S. § 14–2503, intended to allow printed portions of the will form to be incorporated into the handwritten portion of the holographic will as long as the testamentary intent of the testator is clear and the protection afforded by requiring the material provisions be in the testator's handwriting is present.

Indeed, our statute states:

> B. The underlying purposes and policies of this title are: . . .

> 2. To discover and make effective the intent of a decedent in distribution of his property. [A.R.S. § 14–1102(B)(2).]

In the instant case, there is no question as to the testator's intent. We hold that a testator who uses a preprinted form, and in *his own handwriting* fills in the blanks by designating his beneficiaries and apportioning his estate among them and signs it, has created a valid holographic will. Such handwritten provisions may draw testamentary context from both the printed and the handwritten language on the form. We see no need to ignore the preprinted words when the testator clearly did not, and the statute does not require us to do so.

We find the words of an early California decision persuasive: "If testators are to be encouraged by a statute like ours to draw their own wills, the courts should not adopt upon purely technical reasoning a construction which would result in invalidating such wills. . . ." In re Soher's Estate, 78 Cal. 477, 482, 21 P. 8, 10 (1889) (quoted with approval by Estate of Black, 30 Cal.3d 880, 884, 641 P.2d 754, 756, 181 Cal.Rptr. 222, 224 (1982)). . . .

We vacate the opinion of the court of appeals and affirm the judgment of the trial court admitting the will to probate.

GORDON, C.J., and FELDMAN, V.C.J., concur.

EXHIBIT A

The Last Will and Testament

OF

Edward Frank Muder

I, _Edward F Muder_ _____ a resident of
Shumway, in the County of Navajo, State of Arizona
the _____, which I do declare to be my
domicile, being of sound and disposing mind and memory, do make, publish and declare this to be my last
will and testament, hereby revoking all wills or codicils to wills previously made by me.

FIRST: I direct that all my just debts and obligations, including funeral expenses, and the expenses
incident to my last illness be paid as soon after my death as practical.

SECOND: I give, devise and bequeath of this my gross estate, after all of my just debts, expenses, taxes and
administration cost of the estate have first been paid, settled or compromised. to _A My Wife_
Retha F Muder, Our home & property in
Shumway, Navajo County; Car - Pick up, Travel
Trailer, & all other Earthly possessions Belonging
To Me, Live Stock cattle, Horse etc Tacks, Savings Accounts
Checking Accounts, Retirement Benefits etc
_____
_____
_____

THIRD: I nominate, constitute and appoint my _Wife Retha F Muder_
_____ as Executor (Executrix) of my
estate.

FOURTH: I nominate, constitute and appoint my _Wife: Retha. F Muder_
_____ as guardian of the person and
property of each minor child of mine who shall survive me.

IN WITNESS HEREOF, I, _Edward F Muder_ _____ the testator
(testatrix), sign my name to this instrument this _26th_ day of _January_
19_84_ _____ and being first duly sworn, do hereby declare to the undersigned authority that I sign
and execute this instrument as my last will and that I sign it willingly, that I execute it as my free and voluntary
act for the purposes therein expressed, and that I am eighteen years of age or older, of sound mind, and under
no constraint or undue influence.

Edward F Muder
TESTATOR (TESTATRIX)

WE, _____   _____

_____   _____ . the

witnesses, sign our names to this instrument, being first duly sworn, and do hereby declare to the undersigned authority that the testator (testatrix) signs and executes this instrument as his (her) last will and that he (she) signs it willingly, and that each of us, in the presence and hearing of the testator (testatrix), hereby signs this will as witness to the testator's signing, and that to the best of our knowledge the testator (testatrix) is eighteen years of age or older, of sound mind and under no constraint or undue influence.

_____ resides at _____

_____

_____ resides at _____

_____

_____ resides at _____

_____

_____ resides at _____

_____

ACKNOWLEDGEMENT*

,

STATE OF _Arizona_   )

COUNTY OF _Maricopa_   )

SUBSCRIBED, SWORN to and acknowledged before me by, _Edward F_

Muder _____ the testator (testatrix) and subscribed and sworn to

before me by _Edward F Muder_ _____

_____

the witnesses, this ___26___ day of ___February___ ____ 19_84_

Helene P. Matley

SIGNATURE OF OFFICER

Notary   ,

OFFICIAL CAPACITY OF OFFICER

MY COMMISSION EXPIRES:

My Commission Expires Mar. 1, 1939

My Commission Expires Mar. 1, 1939

MOELLER, JUSTICE, dissenting. . . . [T]he document in this case does not comply with Arizona's holographic will statute, A.R.S. § 14–2503. The statute is clear: in a holographic will the "signature and the material provisions" must be in the handwriting of the testator. The majority reads into the statute a provision that printed portions of a form may be "incorporated" into the handwritten provisions so as to meet the statutory requirements. I am unable to discern such expansiveness in the statute. Neither was the court of appeals in the recent case of In re Estate of Johnson, 129 Ariz. 307, 630 P.2d 1039 (App. 1981), which was decided under the identical statute and in which we denied review. *Johnson*, if followed, compels the conclusion that the instrument in this case is not a valid holographic will; however, the majority opinion neither discusses, distinguishes, or disapproves of *Johnson*.

I am sympathetic to the majority's desire to give effect to a decedent's perceived testamentary intent. However, the legislature has chosen to require that testamentary intent be expressed in certain deliberate ways before a document is entitled to be probated as a will. Whether the holographic will statute should be amended to take into account the era of do-it-yourself legal forms is a subject within the legislative domain. I suspect the ad hoc amendment engrafted on the statute in this case will prove to be more mischievous than helpful. Because I believe there has been no compliance with the statute on holographic wills, I respectfully dissent.

HOLOHAN, J., joins in the dissent of MOELLER, J.

NOTES

1. *"Surplusage" approach.* Under the older statutes requiring that a holographic will be "entirely" handwritten by the testator, courts regularly held that a purported holographic will could not be probated if it contained any printed matter intended to be incorporated as part of its operative provisions. See Estate of Thorn, 192 P. 19 (Cal.1920) (name of country house inserted by rubber stamp); Estate of Christian, 131 Cal.Rptr. 841 (App. 1976) (preprinted will form). To alleviate this rather rigid interpretation of the statute, some courts determined that printed matter could be disregarded as surplusage if it was neither "material to the substance of the will" nor "essential to its validity as a testamentary disposition." Estate of Black, 641 P.2d 754 (Cal.1982) (4–3 decision); see also Estate of Teubert, 298 S.E.2d 456 (W.Va.1982).

The technique of disregarding printed matter as surplusage, originally developed to mitigate the rigors of strict compliance with the requirement that a will be entirely in the testator's handwriting, has also been applied where the statute provides that only the material portions of the will need be handwritten. In addition to the principal case, see Estate of Gonzalez, 855 A.2d 1146 (Me. 2004), reaching the same result on similar facts. The surplusage approach, if applied mechanically, sometimes leads to a denial of probate. In Will of Ferree, 848 A.2d 81 (N.J. Super. 2003), aff'd, 848 A.2d 1 (N.J. App. 2004), the testator completed a preprinted will form by hand and signed it. Applying a provision modeled on the original Uniform Probate Code and identical to the statute in *Muder*, the court observed:

> [W]hile our statute does not disqualify a holograph simply because portions are not in the testator's handwriting, it does require that only

the testator's handwritten words be considered and that those words must be intelligible without resort to words not in the testator's handwriting. All other provisions, whether pre-printed, typed or written by others, are deemed surplusage and must be ignored.

> In this case, an elimination of the pre-printed words renders the offered document meaningless. . . As can readily be seen, the handwritten portions of this document—standing alone—mean nothing. The pre-printed verbs, the pre-printed punctuation, the pre-printed directions and the pre-printed testamentary language are essential if this document is to have any meaning. Material language, necessary to reveal the writer's testamentary intent, is not in decedent's handwriting. As such, this document cannot be considered a holographic will. [848 A.2d at 88.]

See also Estate of Johnson, 630 P.2d 1039 (Ariz.App.1981), cited in the principal case. According to the *Johnson* court, the statutory requirement that the material provisions be in the testator's handwriting required that "the handwritten portion clearly express a *testamentary* intent." Disregarding the printed portions of the will form as surplusage, the court found that the handwritten portions did not sufficiently indicate testamentary intent and affirmed the denial of probate. Is the *Muder* court's analysis of the same statute more persuasive? Note that the relevant UPC provision has been renumbered and amended to permit the use of "extrinsic evidence, including, for holographic wills, portions of the document that are not in the testator's handwriting," to establish testamentary intent. UPC § 2–502(c), reproduced supra.

2. *Testator's signature.* The required signature may take the form of the testator's first name, nickname, initials, or other identifying mark made by the testator with the intent to authenticate the instrument. See Estate of Mangeri, 127 Cal.Rptr. 438 (App. 1976) (mark); Estate of Morris, 74 Cal.Rptr. 32 (App. 1969) (initials); Estate of Briggs, 134 S.E.2d 737 (W.Va.1964) (first name).

Most statutes are silent concerning the location of the signature, leaving courts free to find that the testator's handwritten name constitutes a valid signature if so intended, even if it appears in the exordium clause or elsewhere in the body of the instrument. See Estate of Siegel, 520 A.2d 798 (N.J.App.1987); Estate of Williams, 66 Cal.Rptr.3d 34 (Cal. App. 2007) (name printed in block capital letters in caption; probate allowed); cf. Estate of Erickson, 806 P.2d 1186 (Utah 1991) (name in exordium clause not intended as signature; probate denied); Kidd v. Gunter, 551 S.E.2d 646 (Va. 2001) (probate denied where testator wrote detailed instructions for property disposition in bound journal and signed her name in preprinted box inside the front cover; testamentary intent was clear, but act of signing was "equivocal"). A statute requiring that all wills be signed "at the end" may be applied rigidly or flexibly by the same court. Compare Estate of Weiss, 279 A.2d 189 (Pa.1971) (will form signed in side margin rather than in designated space;

probate denied) with Estate of Stasis, 307 A.2d 241 (Pa.1973) (will valid where testator signed in upper margin at top of reverse side of page, which was the only remaining space large enough for the signature). With specific reference to holographic wills, what purpose might be served by such a requirement?

3. *Date.* A few states retain the traditional requirement that a holographic will be dated. See, e.g., Mich. Comp. L. § 700.2502. The evidentiary value of a date is obvious, especially when more than one instrument is offered for probate. (In this connection, note that attested wills are customarily dated, though this is not a statutory requirement. What policy is served by requiring a date for holographic wills but not for attested wills?) Nevertheless, in the hands of courts requiring strict compliance, the date requirement has caused numerous wills to fail on technical grounds. Some courts require a complete day, month and year, and reject extrinsic evidence to fill in a missing element. See Estate of Hazelwood, 57 Cal.Rptr. 332 (App. 1967) ("1965"); Estate of Carson, 344 P.2d 612 (Cal.App.1959) ("May 1948"). Others allow extrinsic evidence to resolve an ambiguous date. See Succession of Boyd, 306 So.2d 687 (La.1975) (extrinsic evidence established that "2–8–72" meant February 8, 1972; extensive review of cases). Sometimes a date can be ascertained simply by taking judicial notice of the calendar, though this approach has obvious limitations. See Estate of Rudolph, 169 Cal.Rptr. 126 (App. 1980) ("Monday 26, 1978" sufficient where reference could be only to one day); Succession of Raiford, 404 So.2d 251 (La.1981) ("Monday 8, 1968" insufficient; eighth day of the month fell on a Monday three times in 1968). A few courts have adopted a substantial compliance approach, holding that a partial date suffices when no issue is presented that requires knowledge of the exact date of execution. See Estate of Wells, 497 N.W.2d 683 (Neb.1993).

4. *Written instrument.* May a sound recording of the testator's declaration of testamentary wishes be admitted to probate as a holographic will? No court has been willing to go so far. See Estate of Reed, 672 P.2d 829 (Wyo.1983) (tape recording found in sealed envelope bearing decedent's signature and handwritten instruction, "To be played in the event of my death only!"; probate denied). What function is served by the statutory requirement that a will be in writing? Might not a video recording serve just as well? See Langbein, Substantial Compliance With the Wills Act, 88 Harv. L. Rev. 489, 519 (1975).

IN RE ESTATE OF KURALT

Supreme Court of Montana, 2000.
303 Mont. 335, 15 P.3d 931.

JUSTICE TERRY N. TRIEWEILER delivered the Opinion of the Court.

Elizabeth Shannon, longtime personal companion of the deceased, Charles Kuralt, challenged the testamentary disposition of Kuralt's real and personal property in the District Court for the Fifth Judicial District in Madison County. . . . Following an evidentiary hearing, the District Court found that Kuralt executed a valid holographic codicil which expressed his testamentary intent to transfer the Madison County property to Shannon. The Estate now appeals from the order and judgment of the District Court. We affirm the District Court's order and judgment.

The parties present issues on appeal which we restate as follows:

1. Did the District Court err when it found that the June 18, 1997 letter expressed a present testamentary intent to transfer property in Madison County?

2. Did the District Court err when it held that the letter was a codicil without affording the parties an opportunity to be heard on that issue?

FACTUAL BACKGROUND

. . . Charles Kuralt and Elizabeth Shannon maintained a longterm and intimate personal relationship. Kuralt and Shannon desired to keep their relationship secret, and were so successful in doing so that even though Kuralt's wife, Petie, knew that Kuralt owned property in Montana, she was unaware, prior to Kuralt's untimely death, of his relationship with Shannon.

Over the nearly 30–year course of their relationship, Kuralt and Shannon saw each other regularly and maintained contact by phone and mail. Kuralt was the primary source of financial support for Shannon and established close, personal relationships with Shannon's three children. Kuralt provided financial support for a joint business venture managed by Shannon and transferred a home in Ireland to Shannon as a gift.

In 1985, Kuralt purchased a 20–acre parcel of property along the Big Hole River in Madison County, near Twin Bridges, Montana. Kuralt and Shannon constructed a cabin on this 20–acre parcel. In 1987, Kuralt purchased two additional parcels along the Big Hole which adjoined the original 20–acre parcel. These two additional parcels, one upstream and one downstream of the cabin, created a parcel of approximately 90 acres and are the primary subject of this appeal.

On May 3, 1989, Kuralt executed a holographic will which stated as follows:

May 3, 1989

In the event of my death, I bequeath to Patricia Elizabeth Shannon all my interest in land, buildings, furnishings and personal belongings on Burma Road, Twin Bridges, Montana.

Charles Kuralt

34 Bank St.

New York, NY 10014

Although Kuralt mailed a copy of this holographic will to Shannon, he subsequently executed a formal will on May 4, 1994, in New York City. This Last Will and Testament, prepared with the assistance of counsel, does not specifically mention any of the real property owned by Kuralt. The beneficiaries of Kuralt's Last Will and Testament were his wife, Petie, and the Kuralts' two children. Neither Shannon nor her children are named as beneficiaries in Kuralt's formal will. Shannon had no knowledge of the formal will until the commencement of these proceedings.

On April 9, 1997, Kuralt deeded his interest in the original 20–acre parcel with the cabin to Shannon. The transaction was disguised as a sale. However, Kuralt supplied the "purchase" price for the 20–acre parcel to Shannon prior to the transfer. After the deed to the 20–acre parcel was filed, Shannon sent Kuralt, at his request, a blank buy-sell real estate form so that the remaining 90 acres along the Big Hole could be conveyed to Shannon in a similar manner. Apparently, it was again Kuralt's intention to provide the purchase price. The second transaction was to take place in September 1997 when Shannon, her son, and Kuralt agreed to meet at the Montana cabin.

Kuralt, however, became suddenly ill and entered a New York hospital on June 18, 1997. On that same date, Kuralt wrote the letter to Shannon which is now at the center of the current dispute:

June 18, 1997

Dear Pat—

Something is terribly wrong with me and they can't figure out what. After cat-scans and a variety of cardiograms, they agree it's not lung cancer or heart trouble or blood clot. So they're putting me in the hospital today to concentrate on infectious diseases. I am getting worse, barely able to get out of bed, but still have high hopes for recovery . . . if only I can get a diagnosis! Curiouser and curiouser! I'll keep you informed. I'll have the lawyer visit the hospital to be sure you *inherit* the rest of the place in MT. if it comes to that.

I send love to you & [your youngest daughter,] Shannon. Hope things are better there!

Love,

C.

Enclosed with this letter were two checks made payable to Shannon, one for $8000 and the other for $9000. Kuralt did not seek the assistance of an attorney to devise the remaining 90 acres of Big Hole land to Shannon. Therefore, when Kuralt died unexpectedly, Shannon sought to probate the letter of June 18, 1997, as a valid holographic codicil to Kuralt's formal 1994 will.

The Estate opposed Shannon's Petition for Ancillary Probate based on its contention that the June 18, 1997 letter expressed only a future intent to make a will. . . . The District Court held that the June 18, 1997 letter was a valid holographic codicil to Kuralt's formal will of May 4, 1994 and accordingly entered judgment in favor of Shannon. The Estate now appeals from that order and judgment.

STANDARD OF REVIEW

The standard of review of a district court's findings of fact is whether they are clearly erroneous. . . . We review a district court's conclusions of law to determine whether the court's interpretation of the law is correct. . . .

DISCUSSION

Issue 1

Did the District Court err when it found that the June 18, 1997 letter expressed a present testamentary intent to transfer property in Madison County?

The Estate contends that the District Court made legal errors which led to a mistaken conclusion about Kuralt's intent concerning the disposition of his Montana property. The Estate argues that the District Court failed to recognize the legal effect of the 1994 will and therefore erroneously found that Kuralt, after his May 3, 1989 holographic will, had an uninterrupted intent to transfer the Montana property to Shannon. The Estate further argues that Kuralt's 1994 formal will revoked all prior wills, both expressly and by inconsistency. This manifest change of intention, according to the Estate, should have led the District Court to the conclusion that Kuralt did not intend to transfer the Montana property to Shannon upon his death. . . .

The record supports the District Court's finding that the June 18, 1997 letter expressed Kuralt's intent to effect a posthumous transfer of his Montana property to Shannon. Kuralt and Shannon enjoyed a long, close personal relationship which continued up to the last letter Kuralt wrote Shannon on June 18, 1997, in which he enclosed checks to her in the amounts of $8000 and $9000. Likewise, Kuralt and Shannon's children had a long, family-like relationship which included significant financial support.

The District Court focused on the last few months of Kuralt's life to find that the letter demonstrated his testamentary intent. The conveyance of the 20–acre parcel for no real consideration and extrinsic evidence that Kuralt intended to convey the remainder of the Montana property to Shannon in a similar fashion provides substantial factual support for the District Court's determination that Kuralt intended that Shannon have the rest of the Montana property.

The June 18, 1997 letter expressed Kuralt's desire that Shannon inherit the remainder of the Montana property. That Kuralt wrote the letter in extremis is supported by the fact that he died two weeks later. Although Kuralt intended to transfer the remaining land to Shannon, he was reluctant to consult a lawyer to formalize his intent because he wanted to keep their relationship secret. Finally, the use of the term "inherit" underlined by Kuralt reflected his intention to make a posthumous disposition of the property. Therefore, the District Court's findings are supported by substantial evidence and are not clearly erroneous. Accordingly, we conclude that the District Court did not err when it found that the letter dated June 18, 1997 expressed a present testamentary intent to transfer property in Madison County to Patricia Shannon.

Issue 2

Did the District Court err when it held that the letter was a codicil without affording the parties an opportunity to be heard on that issue?

The Estate contends that the District Court erred when it held that the June 18, 1997 letter was a valid codicil, because by definition a codicil must refer to a previous will or must itself be a valid will. Because the District Court held that the June 18, 1997 letter was a codicil without analyzing how the letter affected the provisions of the 1994 will, the Estate contends that the District Court erred and that it improperly deprived the parties of a chance to be heard on this issue.

However, we agree with the District Court's conclusion that the June 18, 1997 holograph was a codicil to Kuralt's 1994 formal will. Admittedly, the June 18, 1997 letter met the threshold requirements for a valid holographic will. . . . Moreover, the letter was a codicil as a matter of law because it made a specific bequest of the Montana property and did not purport to bequeath the entirety of the estate. . . . The District Court was therefore correct when it concluded that the June 18, 1997 letter was a codicil. . . . Accordingly, we affirm the judgment of the District Court.

NOTES

1. *Testamentary intent.* A holographic will, like any other will, must be executed with testamentary intent; that is, the instrument must represent a definitive expression of the testator's directions which are to become operative at death. In the case of an instrument executed in accordance with the statutory formalities for an attested will, testamentary intent is ordinarily evident from the face of the instrument. By contrast, it is often unclear whether an informal handwritten instrument was intended to be effective as a holographic will. For example, a signed, handwritten memorandum listing assets and beneficiaries might represent a definitive statement of testamentary intent, or merely a summary of a plan to be formalized in the future. Compare Estate of Teubert, 298 S.E.2d 456 (W.Va.1982) (valid will) with Estate of Ritchie, 389 A.2d 83 (Pa.1978) (preliminary memorandum, not valid will); Will of Smith, 528 A.2d 918 (N.J.1987) (memorandum of instructions, not valid will). As long as there is some indication of testamentary intent on the face of the instrument, courts readily consider extrinsic evidence. See Bailey v. Kerns, 431 S.E.2d 312 (Va.1993); Estate of Ramirez, 869 P.2d 263 (Mont.1994); cf. McDonald v. Petty, 559 S.W.2d 1 (Ark.1977) (extrinsic evidence not admissible where no indication of testamentary intent on face of instrument). What sort of extrinsic evidence would be relevant and admissible on the issue of testamentary intent?

Suppose that testator instructs her attorney to draw up a formal will in accordance with a detailed testamentary plan set forth in a signed, handwritten letter. Unfortunately, testator dies before she has an opportunity to execute the will. Courts routinely hold that a letter of instructions cannot be admitted to probate as a holographic will. See Estate of Moore, 277 A.2d 825 (Pa.1971); Estate of Schiwetz, 102 S.W.3d 355 (Tex. App. 2003) (letter setting forth "changes to be made in my will" not intended to operate as testamentary instrument; testator contemplated preparation of new will); Fischer v. Johnson, 441 S.W.2d 132 (Ky. 1969) (letter concluded with request to "make this as legal and binding as possible"). Would a different result be justified under the doctrine of substantial compliance? Under a statutory dispensing power? Suppose instead that the attorney prepares a formal will in accordance with testator's oral instructions. The testator does not have time to review the will or execute it, but on the day of her death she signs a handwritten letter confirming that the unsigned instrument is "my last will and as I wish it." What result? See Scott v. Gastright, 204 S.W.2d 367 (Ky. 1947).

In the principal case, is it clear that Charles Kuralt intended his letter dated June 18, 1997 to operate as a testamentary instrument? If so, why would it be necessary to "have the lawyer visit the hospital" to ensure that his friend Pat Shannon would inherit the Montana property?

Many bizarre documents are offered for probate; not all of them are accepted. See Bailey v. Kerns, 431 S.E.2d 312 (Va.1993) (note written on back of hardware store receipt; probate allowed); Estate of Wong, 47 Cal.Rptr.2d

707 (App. 1995) ("All Tai's → Xi"; probate denied); McDonald v. Petty, 559 S.W.2d 1 (Ark.1977) (sketch on back of used envelope; probate denied); see also the case reported in 26 Can. B. Rev. 1242 (1948) (will written on the fender of a tractor). Writings may be accepted as wills even though words are misspelled, the syntax confused, the handwriting illegible, and the disposition set out in a few words. See Estate of Logan, 413 A.2d 681 (Pa.1980) (review of wills written by testators with little formal education); Estate of Grobman, 635 P.2d 231 (Colo.App.1981) (will may be probated though writing appeared illegible).

2. *Letters as holographic wills.* Informal letters are frequently admitted to probate as holographic wills. Since many letters are handwritten and signed as a matter of course, the issue of testamentary intent assumes heightened importance. To appreciate the problems that confront courts in determining whether a particular letter was intended to be a will, consider the following instrument, which was accepted for probate in In re Kimmel's Estate, 123 A. 405 (Pa.1924):

Johnstown, Dec. 12

The Kimmel Bros. and Famly We are all well as you can espec fore the time of the Year. I received you kind & welcome letter from Geo & Irvin all OK gald you poot your Pork down in Pickle it is the true way to keep meet every piece gets the same, now always poot it down that way & you will not miss it & you will have good pork fore smoking you can keep it from butchern to butchern the hole year round. Boys, I wont agree with you about the open winter I think we are gone to have one of the hardest. Plenty of snow & Verry cold verry cold! I dont want to see it this way but it will will come see to the old sow & take her away when the time comes well I cant say if I will come over yet. I will wright in my next letter it may be to ruff we will see in the next letter if I come I have some very valuable papers I want you to keep fore me so if enny thing hapens all the scock money in the 3 Bank liberty lones Post office stamps and my home on Horner St goes to George Darl & Irvin Kepp this letter lock it up it may help you out. Earl sent after his Christmas Tree & Trimmings I sent them he is in the Post office in Phila working.

Will clost your Truly Father

See also Kauffman's Estate, 76 A.2d 414 (Pa.1950) ("dear bill i want you to have the farm"; probate allowed); Estate of Blake, 587 P.2d 271 (Ariz.App.1978) ("P.S. You can have my entire estate. (SAVE THIS)" at end of thank-you note; probate allowed); Estate of Olschansky, 735 P.2d 927 (Colo.App.1987) ("Whatever is left after I'm gone is all yours. So rest asured [sic] that I know where my belongings will go, to you and your family."; probate denied); Dahlgren v. First Nat'l Bank, 580 P.2d 478 (Nev.1978) ("To whom it may concern, . . . I would like Maymie Gilson to have all my personal effects, furniture and belongings."; probate denied).

3. *Conditional wills.* Many holographic wills are executed in contemplation of a journey, a medical operation, or some other event that may result in the testator's death. If the operation of a will appears to be conditioned on a particular event that does not actually occur, the question arises whether the will can nevertheless be given effect. In the leading case of Eaton v. Brown, 193 U.S. 411 (1904), a will leaving the residuary estate to the testator's adopted son began with the statement, "I am going on a journey and may not ever return. And if I do not, this is my last request." The testator returned safely from the journey and died several months later. In holding that the will was admissible to probate, the court viewed the possibility of the testator's death during the journey as "the occasion and inducement" for making the will rather than as a condition precedent to its operation. Modern authority follows the same approach. See Estate of Martin, 635 N.W.2d 473 (S.D. 2001) ("if anything should happen to me on this trip . . ."); In re Will of Cohen, 491 A.2d 1292 (N.J.App.1985) ("In the event that something should happen while I am away . . ."); Mason v. Mason, 268 S.E.2d 67 (W.Va.1980) ("I am in the hospital for surgery, and in case I do not survive . . ."); but cf. Estate of Perez, 155 S.W.3d 599 (Tex. App. 2004) (will held not operative; disposition expressly conditioned on death during surgery, which did not occur).

Testator, engaged to be married, executed a will leaving his estate "to my wife, Robyn." The will also recited that it was "prepared in anticipation of [testator's] upcoming marriage." A few weeks after executing the will and just three days before the scheduled wedding, testator died unexpectedly. Should Robyn take the estate, or did testator intend that the will take effect only if the marriage took place as planned? See Estate of Paulson, 812 N.W.2d 476 (N.D. 2012).

4. *Choice of law.* Under the usual choice-of-law rules, a holographic will that complies with the law of the place where it is executed may be given effect in other states, including those that have no statute specifically authorizing holographic wills. See Robinson's Estate, 123 N.W.2d 515 (Wis.1963) (applying the Uniform Foreign Wills Act); but cf. Fla. Stat. § 732.502 (holographic wills not recognized in Florida, no matter where executed).

3. NUNCUPATIVE WILLS

A nuncupative will is one that is declared orally by the testator in the presence of witnesses. The Statute of Frauds imposed detailed restrictions on the method of making and proving such wills, as well as on the type and amount of property they could dispose of. In this country, nuncupative wills are authorized by statute in less than half the states and are generally subject to burdensome restrictions that render them practically obsolete.

ASHBEL G. GULLIVER & CATHERINE J. TILSON, CLASSIFICATION OF GRATUITOUS TRANSFERS
51 Yale L.J. 1, 14 (1941).

In order to afford a dying man who has no opportunity to make a formal will the privilege of making a last minute oral disposition, many states, following the English Statute of Frauds, have enacted statutes authorizing nuncupative wills in the last illness, provided that numerous detailed requirements are complied with. The desirability of attempting to insure compliance with the ritual function seems to justify the requirement that the testator ask some person or persons present to bear testimony to such disposition as his will, since such a statement indicates that he intends a serious disposition and is not conversing in a purely haphazard manner. The evidentiary function seems responsible for the requirement of a reduction to writing, which tends to prevent a variation between the testator's statement and subsequent testimony owing to lapse of memory, and also for the requirement that the will be proved by more than one witness, which makes it possible for the misinterpretation of one witness to be cleared up by another witness. The protective function is exemplified in statutes requiring the witnesses to be competent and disinterested and decisions to the same effect in the absence of an expressed statutory requirement. Because of the detailed requirements for the validity of these nuncupative wills and the restrictions on the type and value of the property that may be transferred by them, they are probably rarely employed. There is very little litigation concerning them, and they are, therefore, not of great importance in a general survey of the exercise of the testamentary power in this country.

NOTES

1. *Nuncupative wills.* The number of states with statutes authorizing nuncupative wills has declined in recent years; the Uniform Probate Code makes no provision at all for oral wills. The statutes that remain differ as to details but typically require that a nuncupative will be made during the testator's "last sickness" and be witnessed by at least two witnesses at the testator's request; that the witnesses' testimony be reduced to writing within a specified time (e.g., 30 days); that the will be offered for probate within a specified time (e.g., six months); and that the will be effective only to dispose of personal property not exceeding a specified value (e.g., $1,000). Courts have traditionally defined "last sickness" to require that the testator be in such extreme circumstances as to be unable to make a written will. See McClellan's Estate, 189 A. 315 (Pa.1937) (oral will witnessed by a nurse, doctor, and friend, not entitled to probate; 33–year-old testator entered the hospital with encephalitis, became delirious and incoherent on the second day, gave instructions about the distribution of her property during a 3–hour lucid interval on the third day, and died on the fifth day). As a practical matter, nuncupative wills are useful only in situations of extreme emergency such as an

automobile accident followed by death within a few hours. There have been virtually no reported cases in recent years involving nuncupative wills.

2. *Soldiers' and sailors' wills.* Both the Statute of Frauds (1676) and the Wills Act (1837) specifically excepted from their requirements wills of personal property made by soldiers "in actual military service" or by sailors while "at sea." Several states have somewhat similar provisions. See, e.g., N.Y. EPTL § 3–2.2 (no limitation on type or amount of property, but soldier's will becomes invalid one year after discharge and sailor's will three years after it was made). Special exceptions for members of the armed services seem unnecessary today, since will forms and advice on how to use them are readily available at every base headquarters. See Note 6, supra p. 366.

B. WHAT CONSTITUTES THE WILL?

An instrument that purports to make a testamentary disposition must comply with the requirements of the local wills statute if it is to be admitted to probate and given effect as a valid will. Even when it is clear that a testator has executed a will with full statutory formalities, difficulties may arise in determining whether a particular writing is intended to be part of the will and, if so, whether it can be given effect. In identifying what constitutes the will, several doctrines may be relevant.

1. INTEGRATION

Integration refers to the process of embodying the testator's will in one or more writings which are physically present at the time of execution and are intended to be included in the will. If the will comprises several pages it is common practice, though not required by statute, to have each separate page signed at the bottom by the testator, to recite the total number of pages in the attestation clause, and to fasten all of the pages together. These steps help to ensure that the instrument is not tampered with after execution by inserting spurious pages or removing original pages. Cf. Estate of Beale, 113 N.W.2d 380 (Wis.1962) (will admitted to probate as originally executed, disregarding substituted pages). Even if the pages are not physically fastened together, a connection of language or "coherence of sense" carrying over from page to page supports an inference of integration.

In the case of a holographic will, the issue of integration takes on a new dimension. The will may consist of a letter comprising several disorganized pages, or even a series of letters written over a period of time. Modern courts recognize that all the pages may be integrated as a single will if the testator so intended, regardless of the time and place of their writing. See Randall v. Salvation Army, 686 P.2d 241 (Nev.1984) (two-page holographic will valid, even though first page was dated later than second page bearing testator's signature); Estate of Moore, 300 P.2d 110

(Cal.App.1956) (holographic will need not be made on single day, and separate pages reflecting a "continuous chain of thought" need not be physically fastened together); cf. Estate of Rigsby, 843 P.2d 856 (Okla. App. 1992) (one-page holographic will made no reference to handwritten list found folded together with it; held, list not intended to form part of will).

See generally Atkinson § 139; Evans, Incorporation by Reference, Integration, and Non–Testamentary Act, 25 Colum. L. Rev. 879 (1925); Mechem, The Integration of Holographic Wills, 12 N.C. L. Rev. 213 (1934).

2. REPUBLICATION BY CODICIL

A codicil is a written instrument, executed with the same formalities as a will, which modifies or supplements an existing will. Ordinarily, a codicil refers specifically to the underlying will, thereby indicating an intent on the part of the testator to "republish" or reaffirm the provisions of the will, as amended by the codicil. In general, republication causes the will to be treated as if it were reexecuted at the same time as the codicil. Republication is a doctrine of presumed intent; it does not apply if the result would defeat the testator's testamentary plan. The doctrine may come into play in numerous situations where the date of execution of a will or codicil has special significance. Consider the following examples.

a. *Interested witness.* *T* executes a will, witnessed by *A* and *B*, which leaves her entire estate to *A*. Under a purging statute (see supra p. 334), the bequest to *A* is invalid. One year later, however, *T* executes a codicil modifying an unrelated provision of the will. The codicil is witnessed by two disinterested witnesses. The doctrine of republication may be invoked to validate the gift to *A*.

b. *Omitted child.* *T* executes a will leaving her entire estate to her child *A*. One year later, *T* gives birth to a second child, *B*, and subsequently executes a codicil modifying an unrelated provision of the will. Under the doctrine of republication, the will may be deemed to have been reexecuted after *B*'s birth, with the result that *B* no longer qualifies as an afterborn child entitled to half of the estate. See Azcunce v. Estate of Azcunce, Note 1, supra p. 215.

c. *Incorporation by reference.* *T* executes a will which purports to incorporate by reference a separate writing "executed on the same date as this will." In fact, no such separate writing exists. One year later, however, *T* executes a separate writing and on the same date executes a codicil modifying an unrelated provision of the will. Under the doctrine of republication, the separate writing may be incorporated by reference if this was *T*'s intent. See Clark v. Greenhalge, infra p. 393.

d. *Ademption.* *T* executes a will leaving "the gold watch owned by me on the date of this will" to *A* and the rest of her estate to *B*. One year later, *T* exchanges her original gold watch for a new one, and then executes a codicil modifying an unrelated provision of the will. Under the doctrine of republication, the will may be interpreted as leaving the new watch to *A* if this was *T*'s intent; otherwise, the bequest may be adeemed and the new watch may pass to *B* along with the rest of the estate. (For more on ademption, see infra p. 471.)

The doctrine of republication may also affect the application of an anti-lapse statute (see infra p. 482). See generally Evans, Testamentary Republication, 40 Harv. L. Rev. 71 (1926).

NOTES

1. *Historical note.* The courts originally developed the doctrine of republication in response to an old rule against devises of after-acquired land. Prior to the enactment of the Wills Act (1837), a will operated only on land owned by the testator at the time the will was executed; if the testator subsequently acquired new land and failed to reexecute the will, the after-acquired land passed by intestacy. In holding that a codicil triggered a republication of the will—in effect, a deemed reexecution—the courts found a way to allow the amended will to dispose of land held at the time the codicil was executed. The doctrine of republication is no longer necessary to reach this result, since contemporary wills statutes provide that a will operates on all property owned at death. See UPC § 2–602.

2. *Validation of defective will.* Properly speaking, the doctrine of republication has no application unless there is a valid will in existence at the time the codicil is executed. If the original instrument was invalid for some reason—e.g., improper execution, lack of testamentary capacity, or undue influence—it cannot be republished. Nevertheless, the courts frequently hold that such an instrument is validated by a subsequent will or codicil, and these decisions can be justified under the doctrine of incorporation by reference, discussed infra. Even in jurisdictions that do not generally permit incorporation by reference (e.g., New York), the courts have held that a subsequent codicil can validate a properly executed will which was originally invalid solely as a result of undue influence or lack of testamentary capacity. See Cook v. White, 60 N.Y.S. 153 (App. Div. 1899), aff'd, 60 N.E. 1109 (N.Y.1901).

3. INCORPORATION BY REFERENCE

Not infrequently a will directs that the estate, or a portion thereof, be distributed in accordance with the terms of a separate writing—e.g., a memorandum, deed, or inter vivos trust agreement. Even if the separate writing is not integrated with the will and is not executed with the formalities required for a will, the disposition may be effective under the doctrine of incorporation by reference. As originally articulated by the courts, the doctrine required that (1) the separate writing must be in existence at the time the will was executed, (2) the will must refer to the separate writing as being in existence and sufficiently identify it, and (3) the will must manifest an intent to incorporate the separate writing as part of the will. See Wagner v. Clauson, 78 N.E.2d 203 (Ill.1948). So formulated, the doctrine has been viewed as requiring that the will refer to the separate writing in the present tense rather than as one "to be prepared" or "to be found" with the will in the future. See Kellom v. Beverstock, 126 A.2d 127 (N.H.1956). A few states, of which New York and Connecticut are notable examples, reject the doctrine of incorporation by reference. Booth v. Baptist Church, 28 N.E. 238 (N.Y.1891); Hatheway v. Smith, 65 A. 1058 (Conn.1907).

The doctrine is codified in UPC § 2–510, which provides: "A writing in existence when a will is executed may be incorporated by reference if the language of the will manifests this intent and describes the writing sufficiently to permit its identification." Note that this streamlined version of the doctrine does not require that the will refer to the separate writing as being presently in existence.

A testator who owns numerous items of tangible personal property (e.g., jewelry, antiques, paintings, or other collectibles) may wish to direct the disposition of such property in a separate memorandum that can be amended by the stroke of a pen (without executing a new will). Although the disposition can be framed in precatory terms that give rise to no legally enforceable rights or duties (see the illustrative will form, supra p. 443), many testators prefer that the disposition be binding. Incorporation by reference is not well suited for this purpose, since the doctrine applies only if the memorandum is in existence at the time the will is executed or republished; if the memorandum is prepared or amended thereafter, the attempted disposition may fail. To facilitate a binding disposition while affording the testator a measure of flexibility, UPC § 2–513 provides as follows:

Uniform Probate Code (2011)

§ 2–513. Separate Writing Identifying Devise of Certain Types of Tangible Personal Property.

Whether or not the provisions relating to holographic wills apply, a will may refer to a written statement or list to dispose of items of tangible personal property not otherwise specifically disposed of by the will, other than money. To be admissible under this section as evidence of the intended disposition, the writing must be signed by the testator and must describe the items and the devisees with reasonable certainty. The writing may be referred to as one to be in existence at the time of the testator's death; it may be prepared before or after the execution of the will; it may be altered by the testator after its preparation; and it may be a writing that has no significance apart from its effect upon the dispositions made by the will.

Similar provisions have been enacted in approximately half the states. Note that UPC § 2–513 permits multiple separate writings and places no limit on the value of tangible personal property that may be disposed of. Nevertheless, as a practical matter, it is generally advisable to limit such dispositions to property of modest value.

CLARK V. GREENHALGE

Supreme Judicial Court of Massachusetts, 1991.
411 Mass. 410, 582 N.E.2d 949.

NOLAN, JUSTICE.

We consider in this case whether a probate judge correctly concluded that specific, written bequests of personal property contained in a notebook maintained by a testatrix were incorporated by reference into the terms of the testatrix's will.

We set forth the relevant facts as found by the probate judge. The testatrix, Helen Nesmith, duly executed a will in 1977, which named her cousin, Frederic T. Greenhalge, II, as executor of her estate. The will further identified Greenhalge as the principal beneficiary of the estate, entitling him to receive all of Helen Nesmith's tangible personal property upon her death except those items which she "designate[d] by a memorandum left by [her] and known to [Greenhalge], or in accordance with [her] known wishes," to be given to others living at the time of her death.[8] Among Helen Nesmith's possessions was a large oil painting of a farm scene signed by T.H. Muckley and dated 1833. The value of the painting, as assessed for estate tax purposes, was $1,800.00.

In 1972, Greenhalge assisted Helen Nesmith in drafting a document entitled "MEMORANDUM" and identified as "a list of items of personal property prepared with Miss Helen Nesmith upon September 5, 1972, for the guidance of myself in the distribution of personal tangible property." This list consisted of forty-nine specific bequests of Ms. Nesmith's tangible personal property. In 1976, Helen Nesmith modified the 1972 list by interlineations, additions and deletions. Neither edition of the list involved a bequest of the farm scene painting.

Ms. Nesmith kept a plastic-covered notebook in the drawer of a desk in her study. She periodically made entries in this notebook, which bore the title "List to be given Helen Nesmith 1979." One such entry read: "Ginny Clark farm picture hanging over fireplace. Ma's room." Imogene

---

[8] The value of Ms. Nesmith's estate at the time of her death exceeded $2,000,000.00, including both tangible and nontangible assets.

Conway and Joan Dragoumanos, Ms. Nesmith's private home care nurses, knew of the existence of the notebook and had observed Helen Nesmith write in it. On several occasions, Helen Nesmith orally expressed to these nurses her intentions regarding the disposition of particular pieces of her property upon her death, including the farm scene painting. Helen Nesmith told Conway and Dragoumanos that the farm scene painting was to be given to Virginia Clark, upon Helen Nesmith's death.

Virginia Clark and Helen Nesmith first became acquainted in or about 1940. The women lived next door to each other for approximately ten years (1945 through 1955), during which time they enjoyed a close friendship. The Nesmith–Clark friendship remained constant through the years. In more recent years, Ms. Clark frequently spent time at Ms. Nesmith's home, often visiting Helen Nesmith while she rested in the room which originally was her mother's bedroom. The farm scene painting hung in this room above the fireplace. Virginia Clark openly admired the picture.

According to Ms. Clark, sometime during either January or February of 1980, Helen Nesmith told Ms. Clark that the farm scene painting would belong to Ms. Clark after Helen Nesmith's death. Helen Nesmith then mentioned to Virginia Clark that she would record this gift in a book she kept for the purpose of memorializing her wishes with respect to the disposition of certain of her belongings.[9] After that conversation, Helen Nesmith often alluded to the fact that Ms. Clark someday would own the farm scene painting.

Ms. Nesmith executed two codicils to her 1977 will: one on May 30, 1980, and a second on October 23, 1980. The codicils amended certain bequests and deleted others, while ratifying the will in all other respects.

Greenhalge received Helen Nesmith's notebook on or shortly after January 28, 1986, the date of Ms. Nesmith's death. Thereafter, Greenhalge, as executor, distributed Ms. Nesmith's property in accordance with the will as amended, the 1972 memorandum as amended in 1976, and certain of the provisions contained in the notebook.[10] Greenhalge refused, however, to deliver the farm scene painting to Virginia Clark because the

---

[9] According to Margaret Young, another nurse employed by Ms. Nesmith, Ms. Nesmith asked Ms. Young to "print[] in [the] notebook, beneath [her] own handwriting, 'Ginny Clark painting over fireplace in mother's bedroom.'" Ms. Young complied with this request. Ms. Young stated that Ms. Nesmith's express purpose in having Ms. Young record this statement in the notebook was "to insure that [Greenhalge] would know that she wanted Ginny Clark to have that particular painting."

[10] Helen Nesmith's will provided that Virginia Clark and her husband, Peter Hayden Clark, receive $20,000.00 upon Helen Nesmith's death. Under the terms of the 1972 memorandum, as amended in 1976, Helen Nesmith also bequeathed to Virginia Clark a portrait of Isabel Nesmith, Helen Nesmith's sister with whom Virginia Clark.

painting interested him and he wanted to keep it. Mr. Greenhalge claimed that he was not bound to give effect to the expressions of Helen Nesmith's wishes and intentions stated in the notebook, particularly as to the disposition of the farm scene painting. Notwithstanding this opinion, Greenhalge distributed to himself all of the property bequeathed to him in the notebook. Ms. Clark thereafter commenced an action against Mr. Greenhalge seeking to compel him to deliver the farm scene painting to her.

The probate judge found that Helen Nesmith wanted Ms. Clark to have the farm scene painting. The judge concluded that Helen Nesmith's notebook qualified as a "memorandum" of her known wishes with respect to the distribution of her tangible personal property, within the meaning of Article Fifth of Helen Nesmith's will.[11] The judge further found that the notebook was in existence at the time of the execution of the 1980 codicils, which ratified the language of Article Fifth in its entirety. Based on these findings, the judge ruled that the notebook was incorporated by reference into the terms of the will. Newton v. Seaman's Friend Soc'y, 130 Mass. 91, 93 (1881). The judge awarded the painting to Ms. Clark.

The Appeals Court affirmed the probate judge's decision in an unpublished memorandum and order, 30 Mass.App.Ct. 1109, 570 N.E.2d 184 (1991). We allowed the appellee's petition for further appellate review and now hold that the probate judge correctly awarded the painting to Ms. Clark.

A properly executed will may incorporate by reference into its provisions any "document or paper not so executed and witnessed, whether the paper referred to be in the form of . . . a mere list or memorandum, . . . if it was in existence at the time of the execution of the will, and is identified by clear and satisfactory proof as the paper referred to therein." Newton v. Seaman's Friend Soc'y, supra at 93. The parties agree that the document entitled "memorandum," dated 1972 and amended in 1976, was in existence as of the date of the execution of Helen Nesmith's will. The parties further agree that this document is a memorandum regarding the distribution of certain items of Helen Nesmith's tangible personal property upon her death, as identified in Article Fifth of her will. There is no dispute, therefore, that the 1972 memorandum was incorporated by reference into the terms of the will. Newton, supra.

The parties do not agree, however, as to whether the documentation contained in the notebook, dated 1979, similarly was incorporated into the will through the language of Article Fifth. Greenhalge advances sev-

---

[11] Article Fifth of Helen Nesmith's will reads, in pertinent part, as follows: "that [Greenhalge] distribute such of the tangible property to and among such persons *as I may designate by a memorandum left by me and known to him, or in accordance with my known wishes*, provided that said persons are living at the time of my decease" (emphasis added).

eral arguments to support his contention that the purported bequest of the farm scene painting written in the notebook was not incorporated into the will and thus fails as a testamentary devise. The points raised by Greenhalge in this regard are not persuasive. First, Greenhalge contends that the judge wrongly concluded that the notebook could be considered a "memorandum" within the meaning of Article Fifth, because it is not specifically identified as a "memorandum." Such a literal interpretation of the language and meaning of Article Fifth is not appropriate.

"The 'cardinal rule in the interpretation of wills, to which all other rules must bend, is that the intention of the testator shall prevail, provided it is consistent with the rules of law.'" Boston Safe Deposit & Trust Co. v. Park, 307 Mass. 255, 259, 29 N.E.2d 977 (1940), quoting McCurdy v. McCallum, 186 Mass. 464, 469, 72 N.E. 75 (1904). The intent of the testator is ascertained through consideration of "the language which [the testatrix] has used to express [her] testamentary designs," Taft v. Stearns, 234 Mass. 273, 277, 125 N.E. 570 (1920), as well as the circumstances existing at the time of the execution of the will. Boston Safe Deposit & Trust Co., supra 307 Mass. at 259, 29 N.E.2d 977, and cases cited. The circumstances existing at the time of the execution of a codicil to a will are equally relevant, because the codicil serves to ratify the language in the will which has not been altered or affected by the terms of the codicil. See Taft, supra 234 Mass. at 275–277, 125 N.E. 570.

Applying these principles in the present case, it appears clear that Helen Nesmith intended by the language used in Article Fifth of her will to retain the right to alter and amend the bequests of tangible personal property in her will, without having to amend formally the will. The text of Article Fifth provides a mechanism by which Helen Nesmith could accomplish the result she desired; i.e., by expressing her wishes "in a memorandum." The statements in the notebook unquestionably reflect Helen Nesmith's exercise of her retained right to restructure the distribution of her tangible personal property upon her death. That the notebook is not entitled "memorandum" is of no consequence, since its apparent purpose is consistent with that of a memorandum under Article Fifth: It is a written instrument which is intended to guide Greenhalge in "distribut[ing] such of [Helen Nesmith's] tangible personal property to and among . . . persons [who] are living at the time of [her] decease." In this connection, the distinction between the notebook and "a memorandum" is illusory.

The appellant acknowledges that the subject documentation in the notebook establishes that Helen Nesmith wanted Virginia Clark to receive the farm scene painting upon Ms. Nesmith's death. The appellant argues, however, that the notebook cannot take effect as a testamentary instrument under Article Fifth, because the language of Article Fifth limits its application to "a" memorandum, or the 1972 memorandum. We reject this strict construction of Article Fifth. The language of Article Fifth does not preclude the existence of more than one memorandum which serves the intended purpose of that article. As previously suggested, the phrase "a memorandum" in Article Fifth appears as an expression of the manner in which Helen Nesmith could exercise her right to alter her will after its execution, but it does not denote a requirement that she do so within a particular format. To construe narrowly Article Fifth and to exclude the possibility that Helen Nesmith drafted the notebook contents as "a memorandum" under that Article, would undermine our long-standing policy of interpreting wills in a manner which best carries out the known wishes of the testatrix. See Boston Safe Deposit & Trust Co., supra. The evidence supports the conclusion that Helen Nesmith intended that the bequests in her notebook be accorded the same power and effect as those contained in the 1972 memorandum under Article Fifth. We conclude, therefore, that the judge properly accepted the notebook as a memorandum of Helen Nesmith's known wishes as referenced in Article Fifth of her will.

. . . The judge found that Helen Nesmith drafted the notebook contents with the expectation that Greenhalge would distribute the property accordingly. The judge further found that the notebook was in existence on the dates Helen Nesmith executed the codicils to her will, which affirmed the language of Article Fifth, and that it thereby was incorporated into the will pursuant to the language and spirit of Article Fifth. It is clear that the judge fairly construed the evidence in reaching the determination that Helen Nesmith intended the notebook to serve as a memorandum of her wishes as contemplated under Article Fifth of her will.

Lastly, the appellant complains that the notebook fails to meet the specific requirements of a memorandum under Article Fifth of the will, because it was not "known to him" until after Helen Nesmith's death. For this reason, Greenhalge states that the judge improperly ruled that the notebook was incorporated into the will. One of Helen Nesmith's nurses testified, however, that Greenhalge was aware of the notebook and its contents, and that he at no time made an effort to determine the validity of the bequest of the farm scene painting to Virginia Clark as stated therein. There is ample support in the record, therefore, to support the judge's conclusion that the notebook met the criteria set forth in Article Fifth regarding memoranda.

We note, as did the Appeals Court, that "one who seeks equity must do equity and that a court will not permit its equitable powers to be employed to accomplish an injustice." Pitts v. Halifax Country Club, Inc., 19 Mass. App. Ct. 525, 533, 476 N.E.2d 222 (1985). To this point, we remark that Greenhalge's conduct in handling this controversy fell short of the standard imposed by common social norms, not to mention the standard of conduct attending his fiduciary responsibility as executor, particularly with respect to his selective distribution of Helen Nesmith's assets. We can discern no reason in the record as to why this matter had to proceed along the protracted and costly route that it did.

Judgment affirmed.

NOTES

1. *Subsequent separate writings.* Note that in *Clark* the reference to "a memorandum" in the testator's will, executed in 1977 and republished in 1980, is held sufficient to incorporate both the 1972 memorandum and the 1979 list. How can a will refer to and clearly identify a separate writing that is not yet in existence?

For an earlier case reaching the same result on similar facts, see Simon v. Grayson, 102 P.2d 1081 (Cal.1940). In his will dated March 25, 1932, testator left $6,000 to be distributed in accordance with "a letter that will be found in my effects which said letter will be addressed to [the executors] and will be dated March 25, 1932." The will was republished by a codicil dated November 25, 1933. After testator's death, a letter was found in his safe deposit box, addressed to the executors and dated July 3, 1933, which named the beneficiaries of the $6,000 bequest; no letter dated March 25, 1932 was found. Notwithstanding the discrepancy in dates, the court held that the letter was sufficiently identified in the will and, though apparently not in existence when the will was originally executed, was incorporated by reference when the will was subsequently republished by the codicil.

In *Clark* the court invokes the doctrine of incorporation by reference to give effect to the testator's intent expressed in an unattested writing which was not yet in existence when she originally executed her will. How would the case have been decided if the testator had not republished her will in 1980?

The case of Estate of Richardson, 50 P.3d 584 (Okla. App. 2002), presented the following facts. Testator's will, executed in 1998, made no reference to either of his two sons but did incorporate by reference an inter vivos trust instrument which expressly disinherited testator's son John. The following year, testator executed a trust amendment which expressly disinherited his son James. Testator died shortly afterward without having amended or republished his will. The court held that the original 1998 trust instrument was incorporated in the will but the subsequent amendment was not. Accordingly, under a pretermitted heir statute requiring that an intent to omit a child appear on the face of the will, John was disinherited but James was allowed to claim an intestate share as an omitted child.

2. *Holographic wills.* The doctrine of incorporation by reference raises special problems in its application to holographic wills. Courts generally recognize that a typewritten, formally attested will may be amended, revoked or republished by a subsequent holographic will or codicil. See Estate of Nielson, 165 Cal.Rptr. 319 (App. 1980) (notations written and signed by testator on original attested will constituted valid holographic codicil). Suppose, however, that a holographic will purports to incorporate an existing typewritten instrument that does not qualify as a formal will. In Estate of Smith, 191 P.2d 413 (Cal.1948), the court stated that a holographic will may incorporate "another testamentary instrument executed with different statutory formalities or an informal or unattested document" that is sufficiently identified; the court further observed that incorporated writings "do not become part of the will in the same sense as those integrated. Hence the holographic will may be regarded as entirely in the testator's handwriting, as required by the statute." See also Johnson v. Johnson, 279 P.2d 928 (Okla. 1954) (upholding holographic "codicil" written on same page as unattested typewritten will); but cf. Hinson v. Hinson, 280 S.W.2d 731 (Tex. 1955).

3. *Memorandum disposing of tangible personal property.* In her will, testator expressly reserved the right to dispose of tangible personal property by a separate list, and at her death a signed, handwritten note was found in her jewelry box stating, "I want Vernita Ellison to have these items." Does the note constitute an enforceable "written statement or list" under UPC § 2–513, reproduced supra? Does the will "refer to" the handwritten note, and does the note describe the items with "reasonable certainty"? See Jones v. Ellison, 15 S.W.3d 710 (Ark. App. 2000). If testator's last will recites an "intention to make" a separate memorandum disposing of tangible personal property, but the only such memorandum found at testator's death is attached to an earlier will which was revoked by the later will, can the disposition in the memorandum be given effect under UPC § 2–513? See Estate of Wilkins, 48 P.3d 644 (Idaho 2002).

Testator owned a valuable painting. Her will made reference to a separate memorandum which was found with the will after her death. The memorandum directed the executor to sell the painting and distribute the proceeds to a named beneficiary. Is this an enforceable bequest of tangible personal property "other than money" under UPC § 2–513? See Will of Moor, 879 A.2d 648 (Del. Ch. 2005).

4. FACTS OF INDEPENDENT SIGNIFICANCE

A will may identify the beneficiaries of the estate, as well as the property given to them, by referring to an act or event, whether occurring before or after the execution of the will, which has independent significance apart from its effect on the disposition of property in the will. See UPC § 2–512. For example, the will may include a legacy to "any person employed by me as a housekeeper at the time of my death" or a bequest of "all the furnishings in my summer home." If after executing the will the testator hires a new housekeeper or remodels the summer home, these acts will produce corresponding changes in the testamentary disposition. The reference in the will to extrinsic acts or events is permissible as long as the specified acts or events have independent, nontestamentary significance, even if they lie completely within the testator's control. By contrast, if the will purports to dispose of property in accordance with the testator's oral instructions or an unsigned memorandum to be prepared in the future for the sole purpose of supplementing the will, the attempted disposition is not enforceable. See Atkinson § 81.

The concept of independent significance has often been tested where a will refers to the contents of an envelope, safe deposit box, or other container. There is authority upholding a gift of the contents to a beneficiary named in the will, on the theory that the place and manner of storing property during life constitutes a fact of independent, nontestamentary significance. See Gaff v. Cornwallis, 106 N.E. 860 (Mass.1914) (bequest of contents of safe deposit box, including bank books, corporate stock, and mortgage note, held valid). The outcome is by no means certain, however, especially if the beneficiaries are not identified in the will. See Walsh v. St. Joseph's Home For the Aged, 303 A.2d 691 (Del.Ch.1973) (will directed that bonds in safe deposit box be distributed "as marked"; bonds were found together with handwritten memorandum listing intended beneficiaries; held, although there was no doubt about testator's intended disposition, it failed because memorandum had no independent significance and there was no way of knowing whether it was in existence when the will was executed).

Suppose the testator executes a will leaving her estate to her son if he survives her, or if he does not survive her to the residuary legatees under the son's last will. The son dies testate, survived by the testator. On similar facts, the court in First Nat'l Bank v. Klein, 234 So.2d 42 (Ala.1970), held that the testator's estate passed at her death to the son's residuary legatees, on the theory that the son's will disposed of his own property and hence had independent significance apart from the testator's will. See also In re Tipler's Will, 10 S.W.3d 244 (Tenn.App. 1998).

5. POUR–OVER WILLS

The doctrine of incorporation by reference provides the conceptual basis for pour-over wills, which have become enormously popular. Under a typical pour-over will, property owned at death (and hence included in the probate estate) is given to the trustee of an inter vivos trust, with a direction that the pour-over assets be added to the trust property and be disposed of in accordance with the terms of the trust. Usually, the trust is established by the testator as settlor, and its terms are set forth in a written instrument executed prior to or at the same time as the will.

Prior to the enactment of statutes like the uniform act reproduced below, courts regularly upheld pour-over dispositions on the theory that the written trust instrument was incorporated by reference in the will. Under this approach, it was essential that the trust instrument be in existence and sufficiently identified in the will, but there was no requirement that the trust be funded or operative before death. Problems arose, however, where the trust instrument reserved to the settlor a power to revoke or amend, especially if the power was actually exercised after the execution of the will. See President & Directors of Manhattan Co. v. Janowitz, 21 N.Y.S.2d 232 (App. Div. 1940) (refusing to incorporate original trust terms as they existed before amendment, so that pour-over failed entirely); Montgomery v. Blankenship, 230 S.W.2d 51 (Ark.1950) (upholding pour-over where trust was not actually amended). See generally Lynn, Problems With Pour–Over Wills, 47 Ohio St. L.J. 47 (1986); Palmer, Testamentary Disposition to the Trustee of an Inter Vivos Trust, 50 Mich. L. Rev. 33 (1951); Evans, Nontestamentary Acts and Incorporation by Reference, 16 U. Chi. L. Rev. 635 (1949).

Some courts eventually invoked the doctrine of "facts of independent significance" to validate a testamentary pour-over to a funded revocable trust that became operative during the testator's lifetime, even if the trust was amended after the execution of the will. See Second Bank–State Street Trust Co. v. Pinion, 170 N.E.2d 350 (Mass.1960), and authorities cited therein. This approach proved unavailing, however, if the trust remained unfunded and hence inoperative at the testator's death. See Estate of Daniels, 665 P.2d 594 (Colo.1983) (pour-over conditioned on trust being "in effect" at death failed where trust was not funded before death).

Today, pour-over wills are specifically authorized by statute in every state (including states that do not recognize incorporation by reference). The most widely followed approach is set forth in the Uniform Testamentary Additions to Trusts Act (UTATA), which was originally promulgated in 1960 and subsequently revised in 1991. The current version of the UTATA also appears as § 2–511 of the Uniform Probate Code.

Uniform Probate Code (2011)

§ 2–511. Uniform Testamentary Additions to Trusts Act (1991).

(a) A will may validly devise property to the trustee of a trust established or to be established (i) during the testator's lifetime by the testator, by the testator and some other person, or by some other person, including a funded or unfunded life insurance trust, although the settlor has reserved any or all rights of ownership of the insurance contracts, or (ii) at the testator's death by the testator's devise to the trustee, if the trust is identified in the testator's will and its terms are set forth in a written instrument, other than a will, executed before, concurrently with, or after the execution of the testator's will or in another individual's will if that other individual has predeceased the testator, regardless of the existence, size, or character of the corpus of the trust. The devise is not invalid because the trust is amendable or revocable, or because the trust was amended after the execution of the will or the testator's death.

(b) Unless the testator's will provides otherwise, property devised to a trust described in subsection (a) is not held under a testamentary trust of the testator, but it becomes a part of the trust to which it is devised, and must be administered and disposed of in accordance with the provisions of the governing instrument setting forth the terms of the trust, including any amendments thereto made before or after the testator's death.

(c) Unless the testator's will provides otherwise, a revocation or termination of the trust before the testator's death causes the devise to lapse.

Under the UTATA, a testamentary pour-over to an inter vivos trust is valid even if the arrangement does not satisfy the requirements of incorporation by reference or facts of independent significance. The trust instrument need not be in existence when the will is executed, and the trust itself need not be funded or become operative until the testator's death. The UTATA requires only that the trust be identified in the testator's will and that its terms be set forth in a written instrument in existence at the testator's death. Indeed, the trust may be subject to amendment even after the testator's death.

The impact of the UTATA is discussed in Clymer v. Mayo, 473 N.E.2d 1084 (Mass.1985). In 1973 the decedent, Clara Mayo, executed a pour-over will which left her residuary estate to the trustees named in a revocable trust agreement which she executed on the same day as the will. The trust remained "unfunded" until the decedent died in 1981. After her death, her parents, the Weisses, challenged the validity of the pour-over provision of her will. The court, however, upheld the validity of the pour-over:

The Weisses claim that the judge erred in ruling that the decedent's trust was validly created despite the fact that it was not funded until her death. They rely on the common law rule that a trust can be created only when a trust res exists. New England Trust Co. v. Sanger, 337 Mass. 342, 348, 149 N.E.2d 598 (1958). Arguing that the trust never came into existence, the Weisses claim they are entitled to the decedent's entire estate as her sole heirs at law.

In upholding the validity of the decedent's pour-over trust, the judge cited the relevant provisions of G.L. c. 203, § 3B, inserted by St. 1963, c. 418, § 1, the Commonwealth's version of the Uniform Testamentary Additions to Trusts Act.

A devise or bequest, the validity of which is determinable by the laws of the commonwealth, may be made to the trustee or trustees of a trust established or to be established by the testator . . . including a funded or unfunded life insurance trust, although the trustor has reserved any or all rights of ownership of the insurance contracts, if the trust is identified in the will and the terms of the trust are set forth in a written instrument executed before or concurrently with the execution of the testator's will . . . *regardless of the existence, size or character of the corpus of the trust* (emphasis added).

The decedent's trust instrument, which was executed in Massachusetts and states that it is to be governed by the laws of the Commonwealth, satisfies these statutory conditions. The trust is identified in the residuary clause of her will and the terms of the trust are set out in a written instrument executed contemporaneously with the will. However, the Weisses claim that G.L. c. 203, § 3B, was not intended to change the common law with respect to the necessity for a trust corpus despite the clear language validating pour-over trusts, "regardless of the existence, size or character of the corpus." The Weisses make no showing of legislative intent that would contradict the plain meaning of these words. It is well established that "the statutory language is the principal source of insight into legislative purpose." Bronstein v. Prudential Ins. Co. of Am., 390 Mass. 701, 704, 459 N.E.2d 772 (1984). Moreover, the development of the common law of this Commonwealth with regard to pour-over trusts demonstrates that G.L. c. 203, § 3B, takes on practical meaning only if the Legislature meant exactly what the statute says concerning the need for a trust corpus.

This court was one of the first courts to validate pour-over devises to a living trust. In Second Bank–State St. Trust Co. v. Pinion, 341 Mass. 366, 371, 170 N.E.2d 350 (1960), decided prior to the adoption of G.L. c. 203, § 3B, we upheld a testamentary gift to a revocable and amendable inter vivos trust established by the testator before the execution of his will and which he amended after the will's execution. Recognizing the importance of the pour-over devise in modern estate planning, we explained that such transfers do not violate the statute of wills despite the testator's ability to amend the trust and thereby change the disposition of property at his death without complying with the statute's formalities. "We agree with modern legal thought that a subsequent amendment is effective because of the applicability of the established equitable doctrine that subsequent acts of independent significance do not require attestation under the statute of wills." Id. at 369.

At that time we noted that "[t]he long established recognition in Massachusetts of the doctrine of independent significance makes unnecessary statutory affirmance of its application to pour-over trusts." Id. at 371, 170 N.E.2d 350. It is evident from *Pinion* that there was no need for the Legislature to enact G.L. c. 203, § 3B, simply to validate pour-over devises from wills to funded revocable trusts.

However, in *Pinion*, we were not presented with an unfunded pour-over trust. Nor, prior to G.L. c. 203, § 3B, did other authority exist in this Commonwealth for recognizing testamentary transfers to unfunded trusts. The doctrine of independent significance, upon which we relied in *Pinion*, assumes that "property was included in the purported inter vivos trust, prior to the testator's death." Restatement (Second) of Trusts § 54, comment f (1959). That is why commentators have recognized that G.L. c. 203, § 3B, "[m]akes some . . . modification of the *Pinion* doctrine. The act does not require that the trust res be more than nominal or even existent." E. Slizewski, Legislation: Uniform Testamentary Additions to Trusts Act, 10 Ann. Survey of Mass. Law § 2.7, 39 (1963). See Osgood, Pour Over Will: Appraisal of Uniform Testamentary Additions to Trusts Act, 104 Trusts 768, 769 (1965) ("The Act . . . eliminates the necessity that there be a trust corpus"). . . .

For the foregoing reasons we conclude, in accordance with G.L. c. 203, § 3B, that the decedent established a valid inter vivos trust in 1973 and that its trustee may properly receive the residue of her estate. We affirm the judge's ruling on this issue. . . .

The disposition of Clara Mayo's estate was further complicated by the fact that she and her husband were divorced in 1978. The court's discussion of this aspect of the case is reproduced infra at p. 443.

C. REVOCATION AND AMENDMENT

1. CONTRACTUAL RESTRICTIONS ON REVOCATION

A will is said to be ambulatory. It has no operative effect until death and remains freely revocable during the testator's life. Nevertheless, if it becomes important to ensure that a particular testamentary disposition will be given effect, a testator may make a binding promise to execute (and to refrain from revoking or amending) a will with specified terms. Such a promise, if made for valid consideration and not in violation of public policy, is enforceable in much the same manner as any other contractual obligation. Technically, the enforceability of the contract and the remedies for its breach—money damages, an equitable remedy such as a constructive trust, or restitution—are governed by the law of contracts, not by the law of wills. See generally Sparks, Contracts to Make Wills (1956).

Contracts concerning testamentary dispositions are sometimes used to provide deferred compensation in exchange for support or services furnished to the testator during life. More often, such contracts represent a means of settling marital property rights between spouses, either at the inception of the marriage or at its termination by separation or divorce. (Similar property settlement agreements between unmarried cohabitants have also become fairly common.) Even in the absence of an express contract, the wills of married couples usually reflect a shared testamentary plan or understanding. The wills themselves may take the form of a joint will or of mutual wills. A *joint will* is a single testamentary instrument executed by both parties which may be offered for probate as the will of each; *mutual wills* are separate instruments with reciprocal or parallel provisions.

There is no legal requirement that the parties declare the existence and terms of their agreement in the same instrument as their testamentary dispositions. Failure to do so, however, raises serious evidentiary problems and breeds litigation. Several states follow the Uniform Probate Code in requiring written evidence of a contract to make a will.

Uniform Probate Code (2011)

§ 2–514. Contracts Concerning Succession.

A contract to make a will or devise, or not to revoke a will or devise, or to die intestate, if executed after the effective date of this [article], may be established only by (i) provisions of a will stating material provisions of the contract, (ii) an express reference in a will to a contract and extrinsic evidence proving the terms of the contract, or (iii) a writing signed by the decedent evidencing the contract. The execution of a joint will or mutual wills does not create a presumption of a contract not to revoke the will or wills.

GARRETT V. READ

Supreme Court of Kansas, 2004.
278 Kan. 662, 102 P.3d 436.

BEIER, J.:

This dispute over the wills of the parents in a blended family requires us to decide whether the district court erred in (1) admitting a scrivener attorney's testimony about a contemporaneous oral agreement between the parents; (2) holding that the wills were contractual, rendering a later will executed by the surviving parent ineffective; and (3) imposing a constructive trust on the estate property or proceeds.

Plaintiffs Elizabeth Garrett, Calvin Humble, Dale Humble, and Patricia Humble are the children of John Humble. In 1967, their father married Sarah Puffinbarger, who had two daughters, defendants Deloris Read and Dorothy Brookhauser, and one son, Gary Lee Puffinbarger, from her previous marriage. Gary eventually predeceased his mother, leaving Sarah three of her grandchildren, third-party plaintiffs Christie Cambers, Gregory Puffinbarger, and Melanie Crumby.

In 1984, lawyer Timothy Fielder prepared nearly identical wills for Sarah and John. Each will first directed that any funeral expenses and debts be paid from the estate. Each will also provided that one of Sarah's daughters would receive a grandfather clock. The remaining estate was bequeathed to the surviving spouse "absolutely." If one spouse predeceased the other, or if the spouses died at the same time, each will provided that the rest of the estate was to be divided into sevenths. One-seventh would be distributed to each of the six surviving children of the two spouses. The remaining one-seventh would be split evenly among Gary's children.

John died in October 1984, and his entire estate passed to Sarah.

In 1993, Sarah met with Fielder and executed a new will, revoking her 1984 will. The 1993 will retained the grandfather clock provision, but it changed the disposition of the rest of Sarah's estate, directing that it be divided into only two equal shares, one for each of her daughters. John's four children and Gary's three children were disinherited.

Sarah died in October 2001.

John's children filed this lawsuit, seeking a constructive trust on four-sevenths of the estate property. They alleged the 1993 will was invalid because the 1984 wills had been contractual. Gary's children intervened as third-party plaintiffs, also arguing that the 1984 wills were contractual and that Sarah could not violate her agreement with John by denying them their one-seventh share.

Plaintiffs and third-party plaintiffs both relied on the 1984 wills' reciprocal provisions as evidence of the contract between Sarah and John. Plaintiffs also relied on Fielder's deposition testimony.

Fielder testified that an agreement existed between Sarah and John at the time they executed their 1984 wills. He had explained joint and mutual wills to them and suggested including contractual language in the documents. Although they agreed they wanted contractual wills, they wanted the surviving spouse to be able to liquidate estate assets and spend all of the proceeds, if necessary. They also believed that an equal distribution among their seven children or their offspring would best reflect the assets each had brought into the marriage; they wanted the surviving parent to be prevented from changing the shares designated for the deceased parent's children; yet they wanted the surviving parent to be able to alter the shares of that parent's own children. Fielder said this was the intention behind the use of the word "absolutely" in the wills.

Fielder also testified that, before Sarah executed her 1993 will, he informed her that she and John had entered into an agreement. Sarah told him she had taken care of John's children outside of the will by means of joint property and investments. Fielder prepared the 1993 will in reliance on this statement.

Defendants and third-party plaintiffs filed motions in limine. Defendants contended Fielder's testimony should be barred as parol evidence contradicting the wills. Third-party plaintiffs argued Fielder's testimony was admissible only to prove the agreement to leave the estate to the children and grandchildren in sevenths; they asserted any further testimony from Fielder was inadmissible parol evidence. The district court denied the motions in limine, relying on In re Estate of Chronister, 203 Kan. 366, 454 P.2d 438 (1969), and In re Estate of Tompkins, 195 Kan. 467, 407 P.2d 545 (1965). Thus all of Fielder's testimony was admitted into evidence.

All parties filed motions for summary judgment. The district court found the evidence of an agreement between Sarah and John was uncontroverted. As a result, Sarah's 1993 will could not alter the 1984 wills' designation of shares for John's children but could alter the shares designated for her own children. Thus the district court granted plaintiffs' motion for summary judgment, denied defendants' motion for summary judgment, and denied third-party plaintiffs' motion for summary judgment. The district court imposed a constructive trust in favor of plaintiffs in an amount equal to four-sevenths of the worth of Sarah's estate that had passed to the defendants.

Defendants and third-party plaintiffs appealed to the Court of Appeals, and this court transferred the case pursuant to K.S.A. 20–3018(c). . . .

ADMISSION OF ATTORNEY SCRIVENER'S TESTIMONY

Generally, "[a]ll relevant evidence is admissible. K.S.A. 60–407(f). Relevant evidence is defined as 'evidence having any tendency in reason to prove any material fact.' K.S.A. 60–401(b)." State v. Dreiling, 274 Kan. 518, 549, 54 P.3d 475 (2002). There can be no serious question in this case regarding the relevance of the scrivener's testimony.

Beyond relevance, the admission of evidence lies within the sound discretion of the trial court. An appellate court's standard of review regarding a trial court's admission of evidence is abuse of discretion. See Wendt v. University of Kansas Med. Center, 274 Kan. 966, 975, 59 P.3d 325 (2002). An abuse of discretion must be shown by the party attacking the evidentiary ruling and "exists only when no reasonable person would take the view adopted by the district court." Jenkins v. T.S.I. Holdings, Inc., 268 Kan. 623, 633–34, 1 P.3d 891 (2000).

Defendants argued that the 1984 wills were unambiguous and that Fielder's testimony therefore was barred by the parol evidence rule. In fact, our previous cases do not establish ambiguity as the analytical touchstone defendants want to make it.

This court has held:

Extrinsic evidence is admissible in connection with the instruments themselves to show that separate wills, which are mutual and reciprocal in their bequests and devises, were executed in pursuance of an agreement between the testators, notwithstanding the absence of recitals in the wills designating or referring to such agreement. Such evidence may consist of writings, acts and declarations of the parties, testimony of other persons, and evidence of all the surrounding facts and circumstances. Eikmeier v. Eikmeier, 174 Kan. 71, 254 P.2d 236 (1953).

This court has also stated that "the rule that parol evidence is never admissible to change or vary the terms and provisions of an unambiguous will does not render inadmissible extrinsic evidence that a will was executed pursuant to an agreement." In re Estate of Tompkins, 195 Kan. 467 at 474, 407 P.2d 545 (citing Eikmeier, 174 Kan. 71, 254 P.2d 236). "The admission of such evidence may result in proving the will to have been non-contractual as well as contractual. [Citations omitted.]" Tompkins, 195 Kan. at 474, 407 P.2d 545. . . .

It was not an abuse of discretion for the district court to allow Fielder's testimony. The language of the wills supported the existence of a mutual understanding between Sarah and John to leave the bulk of their estate to the surviving parent for full use during that person's lifetime, then to the six children and one set of grandchildren evenly. Testimony regarding such an agreement was not barred by the parol evidence rule. See Eikmeier, 174 Kan. 71, 254 P.2d 236; Tompkins, 195 Kan. at 474, 407 P.2d 545. Plaintiffs were not required to demonstrate first that the language of the wills was ambiguous in order to admit testimony regarding the oral agreement.

Third-party plaintiffs nevertheless continue to argue that Fielder's testimony was admissible only to the extent that it proved the existence of an agreement regarding distribution of seven equal shares. They claim Fielder's testimony about the further agreement that the surviving parent would have a right to alter the shares of his or her own children should have been inadmissible.

We disagree. Fielder's further testimony about this topic explained more than the choice of the word "absolutely." The testimony did not alter or amend the language of the wills; it further demonstrated the existence of the basic agreement to divide the bulk of the estate into sevenths; and it demonstrated the existence of a sensible limitation on that agreement, reserving to the surviving parent the right to alter the distributions to his or her own children. It was not an abuse of discretion to allow Fielder's testimony regarding this additional facet of the oral agreement between John and Sarah.

CONTRACTUAL WILLS

"Whether a will is contractual in character involves a question of fact, the determination of which must be established by competent evidence." In re Estate of Chronister, 203 Kan. 366, 454 P.2d 438. . . .

The district court accurately described the evidence regarding whether the 1984 wills were contractual as uncontroverted. The only evidence consisted of the language of the wills and Fielder's testimony.

Defendants contend that the 1984 wills were not contractual because no plural pronouns, contractual terms, or mention of consideration appear in their language. This court has stated that use of plural pronouns and contractual terms supports the presumption that wills are contractual, but this is not the end of the inquiry. This court has also held that separate wills without mention of an agreement between the testators, may be contractual wills if that interpretation is supported by the evidence. See Chronister, 203 Kan. at 371–72, 454 P.2d 438.

In *Chronister*, 203 Kan. at 367, 454 P.2d 438, Herbert and Mabel Chronister executed a joint will leaving their estate to the surviving spouse "for his or her own personal use and benefit forever" and then to the nieces and nephews of Herbert. After Herbert died, Mabel changed her will to leave a large portion of the estate to her sister and her sister's children, with the remainder to Herbert's nieces and nephews.

This court reviewed previous cases, finding that in some cases wills had contractual language contained therein, but in other cases "wills have been construed as contractual on the basis of specific provisions or terms, one of the common denominators usually being a provision for the disposition of property after the death of the survivor." 203 Kan. at 369, 454 P.2d 438. We decided the joint and mutual will of Herbert and Mabel was contractual in spite of the language stating the estate passed to the survivor forever and said: "[P]rovisions of like nature [in wills] have commonly been said to evidence, in the case of joint wills, an understanding between the joint testators by which they intended to bind themselves." 203 Kan. at 373, 454 P.2d 438. We held that identical disposition of property, the use of plural pronouns, the mutual exclusion of heirs, and a "full and explicit provision . . . for disposition of the testators' remaining property after the death of the survivor" in the joint will were indicative of the agreement between them. 203 Kan. at 373, 454 P.2d 438.

In *Tompkins*, the will left the property to the surviving spouse with a right of disposal. Although the appellants claimed that meant the survivor had an unlimited right to dispose of the property, this court held the language did not authorize the survivor to breach the agreement between testators. See 195 Kan. at 472–73, 407 P.2d 545. . . .

In an opinion affirmed and adopted by this court, the Court of Appeals set out factors that could be considered to determine whether a will is contractual. See Bell v. Brittain, 19 Kan.App.2d 1073, 880 P.2d 289 (1994), aff'd 257 Kan. 407, 893 P.2d 251 (1995). The Court of Appeals stated:

> The fact that a will does not contain a reference to a contract is not conclusive in determining whether a will is contractual. The intent of the testators to be bound by a joint and mutual will need not be expressly recited, but may be determined circumstantially by language and other expressions used in the will. Language indicating a contractual will includes: (1) a provision in the will for the distribution of property on the death of the survivor; (2) a carefully drawn provision for the disposition of any share in case of a lapsed residuary bequest; (3) the use of plural pronouns; (4) joinder and consent language; (5) the identical distribution of property upon the death of the survivor; (6) joint revocation of former wills; and (7) consideration, such as mutual promises. 19 Kan.App.2d 1073, 880 P.2d 289.

The *Bell* panel found that a mutual will meeting some of the stated provisions was contractual. 19 Kan.App.2d at 1077–80, 880 P.2d 289. Under the *Bell* facts, the will provided for a distribution at the death of the survivor, used plural pronouns, used language that "appear[ed] to qualify as joinder and consent language[,]" had identical distributions, and evidenced consideration. The will did not provide for a lapsed bequest; nor did it revoke all former wills. 19 Kan.App.2d at 1078–79, 880 P.2d 289. The panel also noted that the family of a predeceased son had been expressly disinherited. 19 Kan.App.2d at 1079, 880 P.2d 289. Based on these factors, the panel held that the will, on its face, evidenced an agreement between the testators "that the parties intended the will to be joint, mutual, and contractual." 19 Kan.App.2d at 1079–80, 880 P.2d 289. As a result, the panel upheld the district court's grant of summary judgment. 19 Kan.App.2d at 1079–80, 880 P.2d 289.

The uncontroverted facts here lead to the same conclusion. The 1984 wills were nearly identical, leaving the entire estate to the surviving parent and then to the children and one set of grandchildren, evenly divided. Both of the 1984 wills left a grandfather clock to one of Sarah's daughters, and the wills provided for the family of Sarah's predeceased son, evidencing a "full and explicit provision for the disposition" of the estate at the death of the surviving spouse. See In re Estate of Chronister, 203 Kan. 366, 373, 454 P.2d 438 (1969). Further, Fielder testified that Sarah and John communicated their wishes to be bound by their agreement with each other to leave a portion of the estate's assets to one another's children. They also wanted the freedom to change the distributions to their own children. Under the circumstances, it is apparent that John and Sarah wanted the surviving spouse to ensure that the children of the deceased parent were included if the estate was not consumed during the surviving parent's lifetime.

The uncontroverted evidence establishes that the 1984 wills were contractual and that Sarah retained the right to disinherit any of her children and grandchildren. Summary judgment in favor of plaintiffs was appropriate. Denial of summary judgment in favor of defendants and third-party plaintiffs also was appropriate.

CONSTRUCTIVE TRUST AS REMEDY

This court has stated:

> A single instrument may be both a will contractual in nature, and a contract testamentary in nature; as a will it is revocable but as a contract it is enforceable; and although a contractual will revoked by execution of a second will, cannot be probated, it may nonetheless be enforced as a contract against the estate of the testator breaching it. Reznik v. McKee, Trustee, 216 Kan. 659, 534 P.2d 243 (1975).

Sarah's revoked 1984 will was no longer in effect at the time of Sarah's death in 2001. However, because it was contractual, her estate remained subject to its terms. Because the 1984 will could not be probated, plaintiffs were correct to seek imposition of a constructive trust as their remedy.

"A constructive trust arises wherever the circumstances under which property was acquired make it inequitable that it should be retained by the person who holds the legal title." Logan v. Logan, 23 Kan.App.2d 920, 937 P.2d 967, rev. denied 262 Kan. 961 (1997). To prove a constructive trust, there must be a showing of one of the two types of fraud: actual or constructive. 23 Kan.App.2d 920, 937 P.2d 967.

Actual fraud is not at issue in this case. "Constructive fraud is a breach of a legal or equitable duty which, irrespective of moral guilt, the law declares fraudulent because of its tendency to deceive others or violate a confidence, and neither actual dishonesty or purpose or intent to deceive is necessary." 23 Kan.App.2d 920, 937 P.2d 967. Two additional elements also must be proved: "[T]here must be a confidential relationship[, and] the confidence reposed must be betrayed or a duty imposed by the relationship must be breached." 23 Kan.App.2d 920, 937 P.2d 967. . . .

. . . For "purposes of imposing a constructive trust, a confidential relationship can be based on an agreement between the owner of property and another who will distribute the owner's property in a specified manner upon the owner's death." [Heck v. Archer, 23 Kan.App.2d 57, 67, 927 P.2d 495 (1996)]. . . .

In this case, the district court found that there was an agreement between John and Sarah regarding distribution of their property after the death of the survivor. The relationship between spouses qualifies as a confidential relationship. In addition, this confidential relationship was based on John's trust in Sarah to distribute four-sevenths of the estate to his children. . . . The agreement imposed a duty upon Sarah, and she breached this duty by executing the 1993 will and disinheriting plaintiffs. The district court properly imposed a constructive trust.

Affirmed.

NOTES

1. *Wills and contracts.* A contractual will has a dual aspect. On one hand, the will is a testamentary instrument subject to the law of wills; it is freely revocable and can be admitted to probate only if it is not revoked during the testator's lifetime. On the other hand, the agreement is enforceable under the law of contracts; if a party commits a breach by revoking his or her will, the beneficiaries can pursue an appropriate remedy at law or in equity. In addition to the principal case, see Shimp v. Shimp, 412 A.2d 1228 (Md.1980) (husband, who survived wife, was entitled to revoke joint will, but binding contract between husband and wife would be enforceable at his death by an action in damages or for specific performance); Chapman v. Citizens & Southern Nat'l Bank, 395 S.E.2d 446 (S.C.App. 1990) (imposing constructive trust where wife exercised power of appointment in favor of her own children in violation of promise to let property pass to deceased husband's children as takers in default).

In the case of joint or mutual wills, each party's promise to make (or not to revoke) a will serves as consideration for the other party's reciprocal promise. Under general principles of contract law, there is no reason why such a will contract should not become irrevocable and binding on both parties immediately upon its formation—subject, of course, to modification by mutual consent while both parties are alive. Most courts, however, take the view that either party can freely abrogate a will contract by giving notice to the other party while both parties are alive; in effect, only at the death of one party does the contract become irrevocable and binding on the survivor. See Duhme v. Duhme, 260 N.W.2d 415 (Iowa 1977); Boyle v. Schmitt, 602 So.2d 665 (Fla.App. 1992). What if one party is no longer competent at the time the other gives notice of intent to revoke? See Estate of Lilienthal, 574 N.W.2d 349 (Iowa App.1997).

2. *Joint wills and mutual wills.* The weight of authority holds that the mere existence of a joint will containing reciprocal dispositive provisions is not sufficient, by itself, to establish a contractual restriction on the surviving party's power to revoke or amend the will after the other party's death. If the terms of the contract are not set out in the will or in a separate written instrument, they may be established by implication from the language of the will and from extrinsic evidence concerning the parties' intent. In such an inquiry, some courts are willing to infer a contractual restriction if the joint will includes reciprocal provisions for the surviving party, uses the plural words "we" and "our," and makes a common disposition of the parties' combined property at the survivor's death with roughly equal treatment of their respective families. See Estate of Kaplan, 579 N.E.2d 963 (Ill. App. 1991). See also Estate of Graham, 690 N.W.2d 66 (Iowa 2004) (implied restriction where joint will recited that husband and wife "agree, each in consideration of the promise and act of the other, . . . to dispose of our property in the manner hereinafter set forth"); but cf. In re Lubins, 673 N.Y.S.2d 204 (App. Div. 1998) (opposite result under statute requiring "an express statement in the will that the instrument is a joint will and that the provisions thereof are intended to constitute a contract between the parties").

Courts are not as quick to imply a contract of irrevocability in the case of mutual wills as in that of a joint will. The execution of mutual wills indicates that the testators formed a common testamentary plan, but is not sufficient by itself to support an inference that the plan was intended to be irrevocable. See Walleri v. Gorman, 853 P.2d 714 (Nev.1993); Mabry v. McAfee, 783 S.W.2d 356 (Ark. 1990); Oursler v. Armstrong, 179 N.E.2d 489 (N.Y. 1961). Thus, in Estate of Stratmann, 806 P.2d 459 (Kan. 1991), three siblings lived together and executed reciprocal wills pursuant to a common plan, leaving their property to each other or, in the absence of a survivor, to a college, a church, and a hospital. In discussions with representatives of these charitable organizations, the testators confirmed their collective intent to leave substantial bequests to each organization. After two of the testators died, however, the surviving sibling married and a few years before his death executed a new will leaving the bulk of the combined property to his wife. The charitable organizations sought to enforce the terms of the original will, but the court rejected their claims; in the absence of direct evidence of a promise supported by consideration, general statements of testamentary intent did not amount to a contract of irrevocability. Nevertheless, a contract of irrevocability, if proved, will be enforced in the same manner as in the case of a joint will. In addition to the principal case, see Alvarez v. Coleman, 642 So.2d 361 (Miss.1994); Shaka v. Shaka, 424 A.2d 802 (N.H.1980). The same analysis has been applied where a married couple executed reciprocal inter vivos revocable trusts as will substitutes. See Reznik v. McKee, 534 P.2d 243 (Kan.1975).

A husband and wife executed reciprocal wills together with a written agreement providing that neither spouse's will could be revoked or amended without the other spouse's consent. At the husband's death his will could not be found, giving rise to a presumption that he had revoked it. See Note 3, infra p. 426. As a result, the wife took the husband's entire estate by intestacy. If the wife decides to change her will, may she do so without regard to the contractual restriction? See Estate of Cohen, 629 N.E.2d 1356 (N.Y.1994) (wife not bound by contractual restriction where husband died intestate).

3. *Oral contracts.* Oral contracts concerning testamentary dispositions are viewed "with misgivings and suspicion." Fahringer v. Strine Estate, 216 A.2d 82 (Pa.1966). One court offered the following explanation:

> The genesis of the concept that this type of case requires proof beyond the usual civil rule of preponderance of the evidence lies in the very nature of the problem. The right to devolve one's estate is a valuable right and these cases arise after death has silenced the only person who actually knows the decedent's true intent. Thus, courts must look to objective facts—the actions and statements made by the deceased promissor during his lifetime—to determine the existence of an agreement. In assessing the evidence, the trier of the facts must be mindful of the elements of probable self-interest of those still living and seeking the benefits of an asserted agreement; that statements made by the decedent to disinterested parties must be tested in light of the time and circumstances existing at the time; and the countervailing equities of the contesting parties. In short, courts strive to determine whether or not the contract did in fact exist and, within the obvious limitations of proof in these cases, the trier of the facts must be convinced that it is highly probable that there was such an agreement as is asserted by the proponents of the contract. [Cook v. Cook, 497 P.2d 584, 587 (Wash.1972).]

A further obstacle to enforcement of oral will contracts arises where a statute requires written evidence of the alleged contract. See UPC § 2–514, reproduced supra. Most courts apply such statutes quite literally, in marked contrast to the Statute of Frauds, and refuse to recognize equitable exceptions that would "once again create the uncertainties and litigation that the statute was designed to reduce and eliminate." Orlando v. Prewett, 705 P.2d

593 (Mont. 1985). See also Cragle v. Gray, 206 P.3d 446 (Alaska 2009) ("a plain reading of [UPC § 2–514] indicates that oral succession contracts are unenforceable"); Newton v. Lawson, 720 S.E.2d 353 (Ga.App. 2011). How would such a statute affect the outcome in a case like Garrett v. Read?

Suppose that *T* orally offers to leave her entire estate to *A* in return for *A*'s services as housekeeper, companion and nurse. In reliance on *T*'s promise, *A* leaves her previous employer and moves in to take care of *T*. *T* subsequently dies intestate, leaving no written memorandum of her promise. Is *T*'s promise enforceable? What remedies are available to *A*? See Musselman v. Mitchell, 611 P.2d 675 (Or.App.1980) (constructive trust); Malone v. Spangler, 606 S.W.2d 218 (Mo. App. 1980) (specific performance); Williams v. Mason, 556 So.2d 1045 (Miss. 1990) (quantum meruit); Estate of White, 31 P.3d 1071 (Okla. App. 2001) (same); cf. Estate of Orr, 60 P.3d 962 (Mont. 2002) (services of relative presumed gratuitous; no recovery). What if *T* signs a typewritten instrument naming *A* as the sole beneficiary of her estate, but the instrument is unwitnessed and cannot be admitted to probate? See Estate of Fritz, 406 N.W.2d 475 (Mich. App. 1987); Estate of Spaulding, 543 N.E.2d 980 (Ill. App. 1989). Suppose instead that *T* properly executes a will in favor of *A*. Shortly afterward, however, *A* becomes disenchanted and ceases taking care of *T*. If *T* dies without revoking or amending her will, can *A* keep the estate? See Trotter v. Trotter, 490 So.2d 827 (Miss.1986). What if *T* becomes dissatisfied and dismisses *A*, and then changes her will? See Story v. Hargrave, 369 S.E.2d 669 (Va. 1988); Wyrick v. Wyrick, 349 S.E.2d 705 (Ga. 1986).

4. *Disposition by surviving testator.* Can a surviving testator circumvent a contract of irrevocability by making inter vivos gifts? In Estate of Chayka, 176 N.W.2d 561 (Wis.1970), a testator and her first husband had agreed not to revoke their joint will, but after the first husband's death the testator remarried and made substantial gifts to her second husband. The court rejected as "a mere play upon words" the argument that by leaving the will unchanged the testator had complied with the literal terms of the agreement:

> The duty of good faith is an implied condition in every contract, including a contract to make a joint will, and the transfers here violate such good faith standard by leaving the will in effect but giving away the properties which the parties agreed were to be bequeathed at the death of both to a designated party. The contract to make a will, once partially executed and irrevocable, is not to be defeated or evaded by what has been termed "completely and deliberately denuding himself of his assets after entering into a bargain." [176 N.W.2d at 564.]

The court ordered the second husband to return the property to the testator's estate and to account for property not still in his possession. Many courts agree that a contract of irrevocability imposes an implied good faith limitation on the testator's ability to dispose of property by gift or by will substitute. See Schwartz v. Horn, 290 N.E.2d 816 (N.Y. 1972) (inter vivos gift); Nile

v. Nile, 734 N.E.2d 1153 (Mass. 2000) (revocable trust); Self v. Slaughter, 16
So.3d 781 (Ala. 2008) (same); Estate of Draper v. Bank of America, N.A., 205
P.3d 698 (Kan. 2009) (irrevocable trust); Robison v. Graham, 799 P.2d 610
(Okla. 1990) (joint bank account). Others take a stricter view and refuse to
enforce any limitations not expressly stated in the contract. See Duncan v.
Duncan, 553 S.E.2d 925 (N.C. App. 2001); Meyer v. Shelley, 34 S.W.3d 619
(Tex. App. 2000).

In Garrett v. Read, according to the attorney who drafted mutual wills
for John and Sarah, both spouses agreed that the survivor should have the
right to "liquidate estate assets and spend all of the proceeds, if necessary"
and to alter the shares of his or her own children (but not those of the other
spouse's children). At John's death, his property passed to Sarah "absolutely"
under his will. Had Sarah wished to make inter vivos gifts of property that
she inherited "absolutely" from John, could she have done so? What about her
own property?

5. *Death of contract beneficiary.* Suppose that a husband and wife execute a joint and contractual will which leaves all their property to the survivor and leaves the property remaining at the survivor's death to *A.* If *A* is still
living at the death of the first spouse, but dies while the surviving spouse is
still alive, does *A*'s interest under the joint will lapse? Several courts have
held that there is no lapse, on the theory that *A*'s interest came into existence
at the first spouse's death and is not subject to any further survival requirement. See Jones v. Jones, 692 S.W.2d 406 (Mo.App.1985); Fiew v. Qua-
ltrough, 624 S.W.2d 335 (Tex.App.1981); Estate of Maloney, 381 N.E.2d 1263
(Ind.App.1978). Others, however, have held that the gift to *A* lapses unless it
is preserved for other beneficiaries by an anti-lapse statute. See Estate of
Burcham, 811 P.2d 1208 (Kan.1991); Estate of Arends, 311 N.W.2d 686 (Iowa
App.1981). The doctrine of lapse is discussed infra at p. 482.

6. *Collision of statutory and contract rights.* The rights of third-party beneficiaries under a valid will contract may collide with a surviving spouse's
elective share rights. Suppose *H* and *W* agree to leave their property to the
survivor and at the survivor's death to their descendants. *H* dies and his
property passes by will to *W* in accordance with the agreement. *W* remarries,
and eventually dies survived by her second husband, who claims an elective
share of *W*'s estate. (Elective share statutes are discussed supra at pp. 161–
184.) The descendants of *H* and *W*, however, claim that they are entitled to
W's entire estate by the terms of the will contract. Whose claim prevails? It is
sometimes suggested that the result depends on whether *W* dies in compliance with the will contract or in breach: in the former case, the descendants take as legatees under *W*'s will subject to the second husband's elective
share; in the latter case, they take the entire estate as creditors. The problem
with this approach is that it puts the descendants in a better position if *W*
breaches the contract than if she complies. See Erstein's Estate, 129 N.Y.S.2d
316 (Sur. 1954). To avoid this anomalous result, some courts find a justification in considerations of policy for giving priority to the elective share. See

Shimp v. Huff, 556 A.2d 252 (Md.1989) (contract beneficiaries' rights were "limited by the possibility that the survivor might remarry and that the subsequent spouse might elect against the will"); Patecky v. Friend, 350 P.2d 170 (Or.1960); see also Via v. Putnam, 656 So.2d 460 (Fla.1995) (statutory share of spouse who married testator after execution of will prevailed over contract beneficiaries' rights under will). Other courts, however, take the opposite view and give priority to the rights of beneficiaries under the preexisting will contract. See Gregory v. Estate of Gregory, 866 S.W.2d 379 (Ark.1993); Keats v. Cates, 241 N.E.2d 645 (Ill.App.1968); Rubenstein v. Mueller, 225 N.E.2d 540 (N.Y.1967); see also Estate of Stewart, 444 P.2d 337 (Cal. 1968) (contract beneficiaries' rights not impaired by pretermitted spouse's statutory share).

7. *Estate tax consequences.* Contractual restrictions on property passing to a surviving spouse may jeopardize the federal estate tax marital deduction in the estate of the first spouse to die. See Note 1, infra p. 1041. In preparing and filing the estate tax return, what are the legal and ethical obligations of the executor (and the estate's attorney) to disclose contractual restrictions that do not appear on the face of the will? See Redke v. Silvertrust, 490 P.2d 805 (Cal.1971) (upholding oral contract which restricted surviving spouse's rights, rejecting claim that contract was against public policy as "an attempted evasion of death taxes").

2. METHODS AND EFFECTS OF REVOCATION

Once a will has been validly executed, it is admissible to probate if it remains unrevoked at the testator's death. Modern statutes provide for two principal methods of revoking a will: by written instrument executed with testamentary formalities, or by physical act performed on the original will. The Uniform Probate Code provides as follows:

Uniform Probate Code (2011)

§ 2–507. Revocation by Writing or by Act.

(a) A will or any part thereof is revoked:

(1) by executing a subsequent will that revokes the previous will or part expressly or by inconsistency; or

(2) by performing a revocatory act on the will, if the testator performed the act with the intent and for the purpose of revoking the will or part or if another person performed the act in the testator's conscious presence and by the testator's direction. For purposes of this paragraph, "revocatory act on the will" includes burning, tearing, canceling, obliterating, or destroying the will or any part of it. A burning, tearing, or canceling is a "revocatory act on the will," whether or not the burn, tear, or cancellation touched any of the words on the will.

(b) If a subsequent will does not expressly revoke a previous will, the execution of the subsequent will wholly revokes the previous will by inconsistency if the testator intended the subsequent will to replace rather than supplement the previous will.

(c) The testator is presumed to have intended a subsequent will to replace rather than supplement a previous will if the subsequent will makes a complete disposition of the testator's estate. If this presumption arises and is not rebutted by clear and convincing evidence, the previous will is revoked; only the subsequent will is operative on the testator's death.

(d) The testator is presumed to have intended a subsequent will to supplement rather than replace a previous will if the subsequent will does not make a complete disposition of the testator's estate. If this presumption arises and is not rebutted by clear and convincing evidence, the subsequent will revokes the previous will only to the extent the subsequent will is inconsistent with the previous will; each will is fully operative on the testator's death to the extent they are not inconsistent.

In addition, certain changes in family circumstances (e.g., divorce) may operate to revoke particular provisions of a will. Revocation by operation of law is discussed infra at p. 439.

a. Revocation by Written Instrument

The usual method of revoking an existing will is by a new will containing express words of revocation. Indeed, most wills drafted by attorneys begin with a clause revoking all of the testator's previous wills. Such a clause wipes the testamentary slate clean and allows the testator to make a completely new disposition of the estate. Note that the Uniform Probate Code defines a "will" to include "any testamentary instrument that merely . . . revokes or revises another will." UPC § 1–201(57). Does this suggest the possibility of a testamentary instrument that revokes a will without affirmatively making a new disposition? The instrument in Brown v. Brown, 21 So.3d 1 (Ala. App. 2009), executed with full testamentary formalities, stated: "I . . . hereby revoke all last wills and testaments heretofore made by me; it being my intention and desire to die without a will." Despite the testator's clearly expressed intent, the court held the attempted revocation ineffective:

> By its terms, the revocation document was intended to take effect immediately, not upon the death of the decedent. Moreover, the revocation document did not determine the disposition of the decedent's property after his death. Because the revocation document is not a 'subsequent will,' we conclude that that document did not meet the statutory requirements to revoke the [earlier] will. [21 So.3d at 6.]

See also Estate of Gushwa, 197 P.3d 1 (N.M. 2008). Can the court's analysis be squared with the definition of a will in UPC § 1–201(57)?

Traditionally a codicil is used to modify specific provisions of an existing will. To avoid unintended conflicts between the codicil and the will, the codicil should expressly refer to the will, identify the provisions to be modified, set forth the new (substituted or additional) provisions, and republish the remaining provisions of the will. In the absence of express words of revocation, the codicil generally revokes the will only to the extent that the new provisions are inconsistent with the will.

GILBERT V. GILBERT

Court of Appeals of Kentucky, 1983.
652 S.W.2d 663.

PAXTON, JUDGE.

This is an appeal from a judgment of the Jefferson Circuit Court determining that a holographic instrument, consisting of two writings folded together inside a sealed envelope, was a codicil instead of a second and superseding will. Appellees are a brother of the testator, a niece and three nephews of the testator, and two beneficiaries unrelated to the testator. Appellants are the testator's sisters and remaining brothers.

Frank Gilbert died testate on June 5, 1979. Two writings were offered for probate: an eight-page typewritten instrument, prepared by an attorney, dated April 2, 1976, and the holographic instrument dated December 8, 1978. The "codicil" was written on the back of a business card and on the back of one of Frank's pay stubs. The card and stub were found folded together in a sealed envelope. On the back of the business card, Frank wrote: "12/8/78 Jim and Margaret I have appro $50,000.00 in Safe. See Buzz if anything happens [signed] Frank Gilbert." On the back of the pay stub, Frank wrote: "Jim & Margaret $20,000.00 the Rest divided Equally the other Living Survivors Bro. & Sisters [signed] Frank Gilbert 12/8/78." Written on the envelope is the following: "This day 12/8/1978 I gave to Jim and Margaret this card which I Stated what to do." "Jim and Margaret" are James Gilbert (one of the appellees) and Margaret Gilbert, brother and sister-in-law, respectively, of Frank Gilbert, the testator. The typewritten instrument and the holographic instrument were admitted to probate on September 4, 1979, the holographic instrument being admitted as a codicil.

Appellants subsequently brought a will contest action in Jefferson Circuit Court seeking to have the holographic instrument interpreted as a second and superseding will. After a hearing, the circuit court entered a judgment construing the second instrument as a codicil affecting only the

money Frank kept in his employer's safe. This appeal is from that judgment. We affirm. . . .

Appellants contend that the pay stub ("Jim & Margaret $20,000.00
the Rest divided Equally the other Living Survivors Bro. & Sisters") contains the only holographic writing that is testamentary in character; that
it is a second will which wholly revokes the eight-page typewritten will;
and that the language on the business card ("Jim and Margaret I have
appro $50,000.00 in Safe . . .") is merely informational. This interpreta-
tion would eliminate James Gilbert from sharing in any portion of his
brother's estate, except the $20,000.00 bequeathed to him and his wife,
Margaret, in the "codicil." Appellees argue, of course, that the "codicil"
pertains only to the money in the safe and that James takes both his
share under the typewritten will and one-half of the first $20,000.00 of
the money in the safe pursuant to the terms of the "codicil."

We must first determine which of the holographic writings are to be
considered testamentary acts of Frank and then decide what he meant by
what he wrote. See Kirk v. Lee, Ky., 402 S.W.2d 838, 839 (1965); Reno's
Ex'r v. Luckett, Ky., 298 S.W.2d 674, 675–76 (1956). While it is true that
both holographic writings are signed and dated, giving credence to the
argument that Frank intended them to be separate documents, the fact
that they were found folded together in a sealed envelope and are coherent in sense is sufficient to support the trial court's conclusion that the
two writings should be considered as one. Frank begins the two-part instrument by identifying the property to be distributed (the money in the
safe) and explaining how to gain access to it ("See Buzz"). He then
proceeds, on the second sheet of paper, to distribute that property. These
circumstances show the writings were "tacked together in the mind of the
testator," and that is all the law requires for integration. 79 Am. Jur. 2d
Wills § 191 (1975); see generally, Annot., 38 A.L.R.2d 477, 495 (1954).

The second instrument was probated as a codicil, but because it does
not refer to the typewritten will, we prefer to characterize it as a second
will. A testator can have more than one will effective at the same time,
each distributing part of the estate. In such a case the subsequent wills
"perform the office of codicils." Muller v. Muller, 108 Ky. 511, 516, 56 S.W.
802, 803 (1900); cf. KRS 394.010 ("will" may mean "codicil"); KRS
446.010(35) ("will" includes "codicils"). We believe that to be the situation
in this case: the second will serves as a codicil because it does not contain
a revocation clause and only distributes part of the residuary estate.

The holographic will does not revoke the typewritten one. We think it
is very unlikely that Frank intended to supplant the elaborate distribution of his estate contained in the eight-page typewritten will with a single phrase scratched out on the back of a pay stub. Furthermore, there is

no revocation clause in the second will and Kentucky courts have consistently held that one testamentary instrument revokes another only if it is the clear intent of the testator to do so, and even then the revocation is only to the extent necessary. E.g. Newell v. State Bank of Maysville, Ky., 348 S.W.2d 916 (1961); Stivers v. Mitchell, Ky., 314 S.W.2d 569 (1958); Robinson's Ex'rs v. Robinson, 297 Ky. 229, 179 S.W.2d 886 (1944); Breckinridge v. Breckinridge's Ex'rs, 264 Ky. 82, 94 S.W.2d 283 (1936); Jones v. Jones' Ex'rs, 198 Ky. 756, 250 S.W. 92 (1923). The second will in this case need only re-distribute part of the residue.

We must resolve Frank's intent by looking at the four corners of the two wills, Kirk, supra; Hall's Adm'r v. Compton, Ky., 281 S.W.2d 906 (1955), and harmonizing any conflicting provisions to give effect to every provision of each instrument. Stivers, supra; Compton, supra; Lane v. Railey, 280 Ky. 319, 133 S.W.2d 74 (1939); Breckinridge; supra; Muller, supra. Here, it is easy to harmonize the two instruments. The only way to give effect to every provision of both instruments is to adopt the trial court's interpretation, to-wit: the two holographic writings comprise a second will that distributes only the money Frank kept in his employer's safe. It was not inconsistent for him to distribute, by a second will, a portion of his estate that would have passed under the residuary clause of the first will.

The judgment of the Jefferson Circuit Court is affirmed.

NOTES

1. *Revocation by inconsistency.* The Uniform Probate Code does not explicitly distinguish a will from a codicil. See UPC § 1–201(57) (defining "will" to include a codicil). However, the Code raises different presumptions concerning revocation by inconsistency, depending on whether or not a will makes a "complete disposition" of the testator's property. A will that makes a complete disposition of the testator's estate is presumed to "replace" a previous will, revoking all its provisions by inconsistency. A will that does not make a complete disposition of the estate is presumed to "supplement" the previous will, revoking it "only to the extent the subsequent will is inconsistent with the previous will." See UPC § 2–507, reproduced supra. To test the statutory rule, suppose a testator executes a will leaving a diamond brooch to *A*, $20,000 to *B*, and the rest of her estate to *C*. Subsequently, the testator executes a new will, with no express revocatory clause, which leaves the brooch to *A*'s child, $10,000 to *B*, and the rest of the estate to *C*. Obviously, the bequest of the brooch to *A*'s child revokes the original bequest to *A*. Does the later bequest to *B* of $10,000 "replace" or "supplement" the original bequest of $20,000? Would the result be different if the second will contained no residuary clause? See UPC § 2–507 cmt. If the new will makes a complete disposition of the testator's property but fails to appoint an executor, does it

impliedly revoke the appointment of an executor in the original will? See Estate of Danford, 238 P. 76 (Cal.1925).

2. *Handwritten notations.* In states that recognize holographic wills, a testator may revoke a will, holographic or attested, by an appropriate notation written and signed by the testator. The single word "cancelled," written in the margin of the original will, followed by the testator's signature, has been held sufficient. Estate of Langan, 668 P.2d 481 (Or.App.1983); see also Estate of Kehr, 95 A.2d 647 (Pa.1953) (testator wrote "null and void," followed by her initials, in top margin of unexecuted copy of will; held, valid revocation). Indeed, a testator who has already executed a holographic will may revoke or amend the will simply by making handwritten alterations to the original executed instrument; no reexecution is required. See Estate of Archer, 239 Cal.Rptr. 137 (App. 1987); Randall v. Salvation Army, 686 P.2d 241 (Nev.1984).

Many handwritten notations fail to achieve their intended effect. For example, in Estate of Phifer, 200 Cal.Rptr. 319 (App. 1984), a testator made several handwritten alterations, each followed by his signature or initials, on a copy of his typewritten, attested will. The trial court viewed the alterations as a valid holographic codicil, but the appellate court reversed, pointing out that the handwritten changes, viewed in isolation from the typed provisions of the original will, were "wholly unintelligible" and "devoid of testamentary intent." Is this result consistent with the rationale of *Muder,* supra p. 373? See also Estate of Sola, 275 Cal.Rptr. 98 (App. 1990) (handwritten interlineations meaningless without reference to typed provisions of attested will; held, no holographic codicil); Estate of Foxley, 575 N.W.2d 150 (Neb.1998) (same); cf. Estate of Nielson, 165 Cal.Rptr. 319 (App. 1980) (handwritten notations completely expressed intent to change residuary clause; held, valid holographic codicil).

b. Revocation by Physical Act

A testator may revoke a will by intentionally performing a physical act of revocation (e.g., mutilation or destruction) on the original will. The Statute of Frauds (1676) enumerated "burning, cancelling, tearing, or obliterating" as revocatory acts; the Wills Act (1837) mentioned only "burning, tearing, or otherwise destroying." These early statutes are echoed in modern statutes such as UPC § 2–507, reproduced supra, which provides that a testator can revoke a will (or a part thereof) by "burning, tearing, canceling, obliterating, or destroying the will or any part of it" if the specified act is performed "with the intent and for the purpose of revoking the will or part." In reading the following materials, consider when, if ever, a well-advised testator might prefer to revoke a will by physical act rather than by executing a new will.

HARRISON V. BIRD

Supreme Court of Alabama, 1993.
621 So.2d 972.

HOUSTON, JUSTICE.

The proponent of a will appeals from a judgment of the Circuit Court of Montgomery County holding that the estate of Daisy Virginia Speer, deceased, should be administered as an intestate estate and confirming the letters of administration granted by the probate court to Mae S. Bird.

The following pertinent facts are undisputed:

Daisy Virginia Speer executed a will in November 1989, in which she named Katherine Crapps Harrison as the main beneficiary of her estate. The original of the will was retained by Ms. Speer's attorney and a duplicate original was given to Ms. Harrison. On March 4, 1991, Ms. Speer telephoned her attorney and advised him that she wanted to revoke her will. Thereafter, Ms. Speer's attorney or his secretary, in the presence of each other, tore the will into four pieces. The attorney then wrote Ms. Speer a letter, informing her that he had "revoked" her will as she had instructed and that he was enclosing the pieces of the will so that she could verify that he had torn up the original. In the letter, the attorney specifically stated, "As it now stands, you are without a will."

Ms. Speer died on September 3, 1991. Upon her death, the postmarked letter from her attorney was found among her personal effects, but the four pieces of the will were not found. Thereafter, on September 17, 1991, the Probate Court of Montgomery County granted letters of administration on the estate of Ms. Speer, to Mae S. Bird, a cousin of Ms. Speer. On October 11, 1991, Ms. Harrison filed for probate a document purporting to be the last will and testament of Ms. Speer and naming Ms. Harrison as executrix. On Ms. Bird's petition, the case was removed to the Circuit Court of Montgomery County. Thereafter, Ms. Bird filed an "Answer to Petition to Probate Will and Answer to Petition to Have Administratrix Removed," contesting the will on the grounds that Ms. Speer had revoked her will.

Thereafter, Ms. Bird and Ms. Harrison moved for summary judgments, which the circuit court denied. Upon denying their motions, the circuit court ruled in part (1) that Ms. Speer's will was not lawfully revoked when it was destroyed by her attorney at her direction and with her consent, but not in her presence, see Ala. Code 1975, § 43–8–136(b); (2) that there could be no ratification of the destruction of Ms. Speer's will, which was not accomplished pursuant to the strict requirements of § 43–8–136(b); and (3) that, based on the fact that the pieces of the destroyed will were delivered to Ms. Speer's home but were not found after her death, there arose a presumption that Ms. Speer thereafter revoked the will herself. However, because the trial court found that a genuine issue of material fact existed as to whether Ms. Harrison had rebutted the presumption that Ms. Speer intended to revoke her will even though the duplicate was not destroyed, it held that "this issue must be submitted for trial."

Subsequently, however, based upon the affidavits submitted in support of the motions for summary judgment, the oral testimony, and a finding that the presumption in favor of revocation of Ms. Speer's will had not been rebutted and therefore that the duplicate original will offered for probate by Ms. Harrison was not the last will and testament of Daisy Virginia Speer, the circuit court held that the estate should be administered as an intestate estate and confirmed the letters of administration issued by the probate court to Ms. Bird.

If the evidence establishes that Ms. Speer had possession of the will before her death, but the will is not found among her personal effects after her death, a presumption arises that she destroyed the will. See Barksdale v. Pendergrass, 294 Ala. 526, 319 So.2d 267 (1975). Furthermore, if she destroys the copy of the will in her possession, a presumption arises that she has revoked her will and all duplicates, even though a duplicate exists that is not in her possession. See Stiles v. Brown, 380 So.2d 792 (Ala.1980); see, also, Snider v. Burks, 84 Ala. 53, 4 So. 225 (1887). However, this presumption of revocation is rebuttable and the burden of rebutting the presumption is on the proponent of the will. See Barksdale, supra.

Based on the foregoing, we conclude that under the facts of this case there existed a presumption that Ms. Speer destroyed her will and thus revoked it. Therefore, the burden shifted to Ms. Harrison to present sufficient evidence to rebut that presumption—to present sufficient evidence to convince the trier of fact that the absence of the will from Ms. Speer's personal effects after her death was not due to Ms. Speer's destroying and thus revoking the will. See Stiles v. Brown, supra.

From a careful review of the record, we conclude, as did the trial court, that the evidence presented by Ms. Harrison was not sufficient to rebut the presumption that Ms. Speer destroyed her will with the intent to revoke it. We, therefore, affirm the trial court's judgment.

We note Ms. Harrison's argument that under the particular facts of this case, because Ms. Speer's attorney destroyed the will outside of Ms. Speer's presence, "[t]he fact that Ms. Speer may have had possession of the pieces of her will and that such pieces were not found upon her death is not sufficient to invoke the presumption [of revocation] imposed by the trial court." We find that argument to be without merit.

Affirmed.

NOTES

1. *Mutilated wills.* A testator who revokes a will by mutilating or destroying it seldom does so in the presence of an attorney or witnesses, and evidence of the surrounding circumstances is likely to be sparse. If the testator retained possession and control of a will during life and the will is discovered in a mutilated condition after death, a presumption arises that the mutilation was performed by the testator with revocatory intent. See Board of Trustees v. Calhoun, 514 So.2d 895 (Ala.1987) (page containing signatures of testator and witnesses removed from will); Estate of Bakhaus, 102 N.E.2d 818 (Ill.1951) (will found with testator's signature excised). The presumption of revocation is rebuttable. See Estate of May, 220 N.W.2d 388 (S.D.1974) (one-page holographic will torn from notebook, obliterating words at left-hand margin; presumption of revocation rebutted by testator's statement, three days before death, that he had a will); McKenzie v. Francis, 197 S.E.2d 221 (Va.1973) (will found with part of testator's signature and portions of five pages illegible due to water damage; presumption of revocation rebutted by evidence supporting inference of accident).

Although the statutes permit a will to be revoked by a third person acting at the testator's direction, the revocatory act must be performed in the testator's presence. As noted in *Harrison*, there is no effective revocation if the will is destroyed outside the testator's presence. Accord, Estate of O'Donnell, 803 S.W.2d 530 (Ark.1991) (attorney, following testator's telephone instructions, tore up will outside testator's presence); Estate of Haugk, 280 N.W.2d 684 (Wis.1979) (at request of testator, who remained in kitchen, husband burned will in basement incinerator thirteen steps away; reversing trial court's finding that destruction occurred in testator's "constructive presence").

2. *Cancellation.* In Thompson v. Royall, 175 S.E. 748 (Va.1934), the testator wished to revoke her will, and in the presence of two witnesses asked her attorney to destroy it. However, the will was not destroyed. After the testator's death, the will was found with the following notation written on the back of the manuscript cover by the attorney who drafted the will: "This will null and void and to be only held by H.P. Brittain instead of being destroyed as a memorandum for another will if I desire to make same. This 19 Sept. 1932." The testator's signature appeared beneath the notation. The court held that there was no effective act of revocation:

> [R]evocation of a will by cancellation within the meaning of the statute contemplates marks or lines across the written parts of the instrument or a physical defacement, or some mutilation of the writing itself, with the intent to revoke. If written words are used for the purpose, they must be so placed as to physically affect the written portion of the will, not merely on blank parts of the paper on which the will is written. If the

writing intended to be the act of canceling does not mutilate, or erase, or deface, or otherwise physically come in contact with, any part of written words on the will, it cannot be given any greater weight than a similar writing on a separate sheet of paper, which identifies the will referred to, just as definitely as does the writing on the back. If a will may be revoked by writing on the back, separable from the will, it may be done by a writing not on the will. This the statute forbids. [175 S.E. at 750.]

Accord, Kronauge v. Stoecklein, 293 N.E.2d 320 (Ohio App. 1972). Would the court have reached a different result if the notation had been written, in the testator's presence and by her direction, across the face of the will? On similar facts, one court held that such a notation constituted a valid cancellation even though the words of the will were not completely obliterated:

> Surely no one can be found who would say that a postage stamp is not canceled because he can still see that it is a postage stamp, nor that a provision of any document is not canceled by drawing a line through it with pen and ink although the words can still be read, nor that any banker, whatever he might think of other methods of cancellation, would pay a check canceled by writing across the face merely because he could see what the check was before cancellation. [Noesen v. Erkenswick, 131 N.E. 622, 623 (Ill.1921).]

See also Maxwell v. Dawkins, 974 So.2d 282 (Ala. 2006) (testator signed beneath lawyer's handwritten notation of revocation across top of will; held, valid revocation by physical act); cf. Estate of Dickson, 590 So.2d 471 (Fla.App.1991) (testator wrote "void" across notary seal on self-proving affidavit).

Unlike the physical act of cancellation, other acts of mutilation have been held effective to revoke a will even though none of the words of the will are physically defaced. See Crampton v. Osborn, 201 S.W.2d 336 (Mo.1947) (crumpling and slight tearing); White v. Casten, 46 N.C. 197 (1853) (slight burning). The scope of revocation by cancellation is expanded by the revised Uniform Probate Code, which provides that cancelling, like burning and tearing, constitutes a revocatory act "whether or not the burn, tear, or cancellation touched any of the words on the will." UPC § 2–507(a)(2). Would this provision, if applicable, require a different result in Thompson v. Royall?

3. *Missing wills. Harrison* illustrates the evidentiary problems that arise when the testator is known to have executed a will which cannot be found after death. If the will was last seen in the testator's possession, a presumption arises that the testator destroyed the will with intent to revoke it. See Estate of Travers, 589 P.2d 1314 (Ariz.App.1978); Estate of Millsap, 371 N.E.2d 185 (Ill.App.1977); cf. Johnson v. Cauley, 546 S.E.2d 681 (Va. 2001) (presumption not applicable where testator lacked access to lost will). The presumption may be rebutted, however, by circumstantial evidence (e.g., access by persons with a pecuniary interest in preventing probate, or state-

ments by the testator confirming that the will was not revoked) indicating that the will may have been lost or destroyed without the testator's knowledge. See Estate of Pallister, 611 S.E.2d 250 (S.C. 2005); Estate of Mecello, 633 N.W.2d 892 (Neb. 2001); McBride v. Jones, 494 S.E.2d 319 (Ga.1998).

The testator in Estate of Beauregard, 921 N.E.2d 954 (Mass. 2010), was murdered a few weeks after executing his will. Only a copy of the will was offered for probate; the original, last seen in testator's possession, could not be found and its absence remained unexplained. In holding that the presumption of revocation was not rebutted, the court made the following observation concerning the proponent's burden of proof:

> It is not necessary that the proponent establish that the will was in fact accidentally lost or destroyed, or that it was wrongfully suppressed by someone who was dissatisfied with its terms. The presumption is rebutted if a preponderance of the evidence demonstrates that the testator did not intend to revoke his will, regardless of whether the proponent can demonstrate what may ultimately have become of the will. [921 N.E.2d at 958.]

Some courts apply a more stringent evidentiary standard. See Estate of Crozier, 232 N.W.2d 554 (Iowa 1975) (presumption rebutted by clear and convincing evidence).

If the original will cannot be found, the proponent has the burden of proving that the will was properly executed and not revoked. In some states, a statute requires proof that the will was "in existence" at the testator's death or was "fraudulently destroyed" during the testator's life. Courts have interpreted these statutes with remarkable flexibility to permit probate of a will which was accidentally destroyed during the testator's life. See Estate of Irvine v. Doyle, 710 P.2d 1366 (Nev.1985); Estate of Wheadon, 579 P.2d 930 (Utah 1978) (destroyed will remained in "legal existence"); In re Will of Fox, 174 N.E.2d 499 (N.Y.1961) (will was "fraudulently destroyed" if destruction not performed by testator or by his authority during life). In addition, of course, it is necessary to prove the terms of the will.

4. *Duplicate wills.* One court had the following to say about the practice of executing wills in duplicate:

> [I]t is the popular belief that when a testator executes a will in duplicate, and leaves one with the scrivener and retains the other in his possession, he lessens by half the chances of loss and accidental destruction of the will, thinking that if either paper can be produced it can be probated without accounting for the other. But . . . one who makes a will in duplicate subjects it to a double hazard of loss or accidental destruction which cannot be accounted for; and this may result in the defeat of the testator's intentions by mere accident, or by the carelessness of a custodian of one of the duplicates, or even by the deliberate fraud of one having an in-

terest in defeating the will. . . . [Will of Robinson, 13 N.Y.S.2d 324, 326 (App. Div. 1939).]

Suppose that a testator leaves one original will with the attorney for safekeeping and retains possession of a duplicate will. At testator's death only one will can be found. Should it matter whether the missing will was the one left with the attorney or the one retained by the testator? See Stiles v. Brown, 380 So.2d 792 (Ala.1980); Estate of Shaw, 572 P.2d 229 (Okla. 1977). What if the testator retains both duplicate copies, and after death one is found intact but the other is missing or mutilated? See Etgen v. Corboy, 337 S.E.2d 286 (Va.1985); In re Will of Mittelstaedt, 112 N.Y.S.2d 166 (App. Div. 1952).

Instead of executing a will in duplicate, it is common practice in some areas of the country for the testator to keep the original executed will while the attorney retains a "conformed copy" on file. (A conformed copy is an exact copy of the unexecuted instrument with the names of the testator and witnesses and other information typed in.) In other areas the attorney may offer to hold the original executed will in safekeeping for the testator while the testator keeps only a conformed copy. Either practice avoids potential confusion between the original executed will and an exact photocopy. See Morrison v. Morrison, 655 S.E.2d 571 (Ga. 2008) (handwritten markings on copy of will not valid as physical act of revocation); Estate of Stanton, 472 N.W.2d 741 (N.D.1991) (testator crumpled photocopy instead of original will; held, no effective revocation, regardless of intent to revoke); cf. Estate of Tolin, 622 So.2d 988 (Fla.1993) (testator tore up a photocopy of a codicil, believing it to be the original executed codicil; held, constructive trust available to prevent unjust enrichment caused by testator's mistake, even in absence of wrongdoing).

5. *Custody of original will.* Is it proper for an attorney who has drafted a client's will to hold the original will in the firm's vault for safekeeping? Under one view, the attorney may offer to retain the original will, as long as the client receives a written acknowledgment that the will is held "subject to the client's order." American College of Trust & Estate Counsel, Commentaries on the Model Rules of Professional Conduct 113 (4th ed. 2006). That relatively lenient view, however, is not universally shared. In the words of one court:

> Nor do we approve of attorneys' "safekeeping" wills. In the old days this may have been explained on the ground many people did not have a safe place to keep their valuable papers, but there is little justification today because most people do have safekeeping boxes, and if not, [a state statute] provides for the deposit of a will with the register in probate for safekeeping during the lifetime of the testator. The correct practice is that the original will should be delivered to the testator, and should only be kept by the attorney upon specific unsolicited request of the client. [State v. Gulbankian, 196 N.W.2d 733, 736 (Wis.1972).]

What drawbacks or dangers might arise from the safekeeping of wills by attorney-drafters?

6. *Alterations.* Where the statute provides for revocation of a will "or any part thereof" by physical act, it is possible for a testator to delete a particular provision while leaving the rest of the will intact. See Seeley v. Estate of Seeley, 627 P.2d 1357 (Wyo.1981) (testator excised paragraph from holographic will and then taped remaining pieces back together); Estate of Bogner, 184 N.W.2d 718 (N.D.1971) (on learning of son-in-law's "depraved moral conduct," testator validly revoked bequests to son-in-law by drawing lines through his name).

If the testator attempts to substitute a new disposition—e.g., by adding the name of a different beneficiary or specifying a different type or amount of property—the new testamentary act must comply with the regular wills formalities. See Estate of Beale, 113 N.W.2d 380 (Wis.1962) (informal substitution of new pages disregarded; will given effect as originally executed); Will of Robinson, 273 N.Y.S.2d 985 (App. Div. 1966) (informal substitution of page containing all dispositive provisions treated as complete revocation, causing intestacy); Estate of Weston, 833 A.2d 490 (D.C. 2003) (informal substitution of pages listing preresiduary bequests treated as complete revocation, even though final page containing residuary clause and signatures of the testator and witnesses remained intact; as a result, the estate passed by intestacy to testator's brother, who would have received only $1 under the will).

To guard against unattested amendments in the guise of partial revocations by physical act, courts hold that such revocations must not change the meaning of the remaining terms of the will. For example, if the will leaves "Blackacre to *A* and the rest of the estate to *B*," and the testator draws a line through all but the first word and the last two words of the clause, intending to leave Blackacre to *B*, the attempted alteration will be disregarded. This approach, if carried to its logical conclusion, could be applied to deny effect to almost any partial revocation by physical act. See Dodson v. Walton, 597 S.W.2d 814 (Ark. 1980) (one name struck from residuary gift to six beneficiaries). Accordingly, some courts seek to distinguish a revocation of a preresiduary bequest which incidentally enhances the residuary estate from a more substantial alteration of the testamentary scheme which requires compliance with execution formalities. See Estate of Becklund, 497 P.2d 1327 (Wash. App. 1972) ("If the result of the partial revocation only causes an increase in the residuary estate rather than such a vital enhancement thereof as to constitute a new scheme, this is not a disparate testamentary disposition but only a consequence resulting from the exercise of the power given the testator by the statute."); Patrick v. Patrick, 649 A.2d 1204 (Md.App.1994) (testator drew lines through $5,000 bequest and through one-half residuary bequest; former effective, latter not); Estate of Malloy, 949 P.2d 804 (Wash.1998).

If the statute does not provide for partial revocation by physical act, a revocatory act that is not intended to revoke the entire will is simply disregarded. See Peterson v. Harrell, 690 S.E.2d 151 (Ga. 2010) (lines drawn through names of successor trust beneficiaries). Of course, if essential words of the original will have been completely obliterated and cannot be ascertained, the entire will may fail. See Estate of Johannes, 227 P.2d 148 (Kan.1951); but cf. Hansel v. Head, 706 So.2d 1142 (Ala.1997) (giving effect to original provisions except for obliterated legacy, which passed by intestacy). In Estate of Funk, 654 N.E.2d 1174 (Ind.App.1995), the testator wrote numerous notes and changes on the will and drew lines through the residuary clause; one page of the will was missing, and a portion of another page had been cut out and then reattached by stapling. The will was held to be unrevoked and therefore admissible to probate because the testator had not obliterated "any essential part" such as her own signature, nor had she manifested "an intent to revoke the will in its entirety."

7. *Wills and codicils.* If a testator revokes a will (for example, by mutilating it) but preserves an existing codicil intact, the codicil may be revoked if it is "necessarily interdependent or so interinvolved as to be incapable of separate existence." In re Francis' Will, 132 N.Y.S. 695 (Sur. 1911) (codicil eliminated one-third residuary share and divided it between the other two residuary shares; mutilation of will revoked codicil as well). What if the testator instead cancels the codicil and preserves the original will intact? See Estate of Hering, 166 Cal.Rptr. 298 (App. 1980); Dean v. Garcia, 795 S.W.2d 763 (Tex.App.1989).

c. Revival

The question of revival arises where a testator executes a first will, then executes a second will revoking the first will, and ultimately revokes the second will. Assuming the first will remains physically intact, does it regain testamentary force upon the revocation of the second will, or does it remain revoked? In other words, does the revocation of the second will revive the first will? In England, prior to the enactment of the Wills Act (1837), the common law courts and the ecclesiastical courts developed two divergent approaches. The common law courts held that the first will was automatically revived. The theory was that each provision of a will, including a revocatory clause, remained ambulatory until the testator's death, and so the first will was never effectively revoked by the second will. In contrast, the ecclesiastical courts held that a will of personal property was revived only if the testator's intent, as gleaned from all the circumstances, favored revival.

The Wills Act (1837) provided that "no Will or Codicil, or any Part thereof, which shall be in any Manner revoked, shall be revived otherwise than by the Re-execution thereof, or by a Codicil executed in the manner herein-before required, and showing an Intention to revive the same." 7 Wm. IV & 1 Vict., c. 26, § 22 (1837). In this country, a substantial number of states have similar anti-revival provisions. The Kentucky statute is typical:

Kentucky Revised Statutes

§ 394.100. Revoked will may be revived, how.

A will or codicil, or part thereof, that has been revoked shall be revived only by reexecution or by a codicil executed in the manner required for making a will, and then only to the extent to which an intention to revive is shown thereby.

In effect, this type of statute forecloses any inquiry into the circumstances surrounding the revocation of the second will, and requires that the first will be either reexecuted or republished if it is to be given testamentary effect. See Estate of Lagreca, 687 A.2d 783 (N.J.App.1997) (codicil that modified residuary clause was revoked by physical act; held, no revival, residuary estate passed by intestacy); Will of Farr, 175 S.E.2d 578 (N.C.1970) (similar result where codicil revoked by subsequent testamentary instrument). The testator in Estate of Greenwald, 584 N.W.2d 294 (Iowa 1998), executed her first will in 1973 and a second will in 1988 which revoked her earlier will. At her death the original second will could not be found and was presumed to have been revoked by the testator. Applying the anti-revival statute, the court held that neither will could be admitted to probate:

It might appear anomalous that a will that is denied probate, as [the 1988 will] was, may nevertheless be valid to the extent that it revokes a prior will. This, however, is the law. This is so because a revocation is effective on the execution of the subsequent will, and in this case, there is no dispute that the 1988 will was validly executed; it merely disappeared sometime afterward. [584 N.W.2d at 295.]

See also Estate of Creech, 989 A.2d 185 (D.C. 2010) (residuary gift modified by codicil which could not be found after testator's death). Under an anti-revival statute, is there a risk that a disappointed heir might seek to defeat probate of a will and obtain an intestate share by fabricating evidence of a "lost" second will that allegedly revoked the will offered for probate? See Will of McCauley, 565 S.E.2d 88 (N.C. 2002) (acknowledging that "fraud is always a concern," but noting that under a more lenient rule a beneficiary named in an earlier will might attempt to revive that will by destroying a later, revoking will). Is the risk of fraud outweighed by the convenience of a bright-line rule that avoids a case-by-case inquiry into the testator's intent?

In contrast to the anti-revival statutes, a substantial number of states follow the lead of the Uniform Probate Code which takes a more flexible approach to the question of revival. UPC § 2–509 raises a presumption for or against revival, depending on the nature of the subsequent will and the circumstances of its revocation, and allows the presumption to be rebutted by evidence of the testator's contrary intent.

Uniform Probate Code (2011)

§ 2–509. Revival of Revoked Will.

(a) If a subsequent will that wholly revoked a previous will is thereafter revoked by a revocatory act under Section 2–507(a)(2), the previous will remains revoked unless it is revived. The previous will is revived if it is evident from the circumstances of the revocation of the subsequent will or from the testator's contemporary or subsequent declarations that the testator intended the previous will to take effect as executed.

(b) If a subsequent will that partly revoked a previous will is thereafter revoked by a revocatory act under Section 2–507(a)(2), a revoked part of the previous will is revived unless it is evident from the circumstances of the revocation of the subsequent will or from the testator's contemporary or subsequent declarations that the testator did not intend the revoked part to take effect as executed.

(c) If a subsequent will that revoked a previous will in whole or in part is thereafter revoked by another, later, will, the previous will remains revoked in whole or in part, unless it or its revoked part is revived. The previous will or its revoked part is revived to the extent it appears from the terms of the later will that the testator intended the previous will to take effect.

The original version of UPC § 2–509, promulgated in 1969, raised a presumption against revival without distinguishing between complete and partial revocations. As part of the 1990 revisions, the UPC drafters inserted subsection (b), which reverses the presumption where the first will is only partially revoked by the second will (which itself is ultimately revoked by physical act). The rationale for the distinction, as explained in the Official Comment, is that "where Will #2 only partly revoked Will #1, Will #2 is only a codicil to Will #1, and the testator knows (or should know) that Will #1 does have continuing effect." Cf. Estate of Hering, 166 Cal.Rptr. 298 (App. 1980) (statutory presumption against revival inapplicable where first will was partially revoked by codicil).

In states without a revival statute, the cases generally follow one or the other of the two original English rules. See Whitehill v. Halbing, 118 A. 454 (Conn.1922) (common law rule); Pickens v. Davis, 134 Mass. 252 (1883) (ecclesiastical rule). For further discussion of revival doctrine, its historical development, and the Uniform Probate Code provisions, see Whitman, Revocation and Revival: An Analysis of the 1990 Revision of the Uniform Probate Code and Suggestions for the Future, 55 Alb. L. Rev. 1035 (1992); Bird, Revocation of a Revoking Codicil: The Renaissance of Revival in California, 33 Hast. L.J. 357 (1981).

NOTES

1. *Testator's intent.* Note that under UPC § 2–509, extrinsic evidence, including the testator's contemporaneous or subsequent declarations, can be used to rebut the statutory presumptions where the second will is revoked by physical act, but not where it is revoked by a subsequent will. What is the rationale for this distinction?

In Estate of Heibult, 653 N.W.2d 101 (S.D. 2002), the testator initially executed a will which favored a son who had stayed near and taken care of her. Later, while visiting her other children, she executed a new will which divided her estate equally among all four children. At testator's death, the second will could not be found and the son offered the earlier will for probate. Apparently the testator had deliberately misled her children by pretending to destroy the first will when she actually destroyed the second will, and she told her attorney that she wanted the first will to stand. Applying a statute identical to UPC § 2–509, the court held that testator's oral statements to her attorney were sufficient evidence of her intent to revive the earlier will.

2. *Revival by republication.* The anti-revival statutes modeled on the Wills Act (1837) produce dramatically different results depending on whether a will that revoked an earlier will is itself ultimately revoked by physical act or by subsequent written instrument. To illustrate the difference, suppose a testator executes a will which leaves some small bequests to relatives and the rest of the estate to charity. Later the testator executes a codicil leaving her residuary estate to her nephew. Still later, in the presence of witnesses, the testator destroys the codicil and announces, "I have the thing back as I want it now." Under an anti-revival statute, the original gift to charity is not revived, and the residuary estate passes by intestacy. See Parker v. Mobley, 577 S.W.2d 583 (Ark.1979). By contrast, if the testator executes a second codicil which revokes the first codicil and republishes the original will, the gift to charity is revived. See Estate of Lane, 492 So.2d 395 (Fla.App.1986). Cf. Will of Cable, 210 N.Y.S. 187 (App. Div. 1925), aff'd mem., 152 N.E. 405 (N.Y.1926) (codicil republished original will, including previous codicils that remained physically intact and attached to will, but excluding one codicil that had been destroyed).

d. Dependent Relative Revocation

Dependent relative revocation, sometimes referred to as the doctrine of conditional or ineffective revocation, is an equitable doctrine developed by courts to provide limited relief in situations where a testator has made a formally sufficient revocation of a will but the revocation turns out to be premised on a mistaken assumption of fact or law. The operation of the doctrine has been described as follows:

Restatement (Third) of Property: Wills and Other Donative Transfers (1999)

§ 4.3. Ineffective Revocation (Dependent Relative Revocation)

(a) A partial or complete revocation of a will is presumptively ineffective if the testator made the revocation:

(1) in connection with an attempt to achieve a dispositive objective that fails under applicable law, or

(2) because of a false assumption of law, or because of a false belief about an objective fact, that is either recited in the revoking instrument or established by clear and convincing evidence.

(b) The presumption established in subsection (a) is rebutted if allowing the revocation to remain in effect would be more consistent with the testator's probable intent.

Dependent relative revocation has been described as "a fictional process which consists of disregarding revocation brought about by mistake on the feigned ground that the revocation was conditional." Atkinson § 88. Thus, the revocation might be termed "dependent" and "relative" in the sense that it depends on and relates to a contrary-to-fact condition. See generally Warren, Dependent Relative Revocation, 33 Harv. L. Rev. 337 (1920).

SCHNEIDER V. HARRINGTON

Supreme Judicial Court of Massachusetts, 1947.
320 Mass. 723, 71 N.E.2d 242.

SPALDING, JUSTICE.

This is a petition for the probate of an instrument purporting to be the last will of Letitia Bliss. The judge of probate entered a decree allowing the will with the exception of certain portions which had been crossed out by the testatrix. The case comes here on the appeal of Amy E. Harrington, a sister of the testatrix, who took one third of the estate under the will as executed, but nothing under the will as allowed. Although she did not appear in opposition to the will in the court below, the appellant has a pecuniary interest affected by the decree entered there, and is entitled to appeal as a "person aggrieved." . . .

The judge made a voluntary report of the material facts, which may be summarized as follows: The will when executed provided that the entire estate, real and personal, was to be disposed of in the following manner:

1. To my niece Phyllis H. Schneider, of 2368 Washington Avenue Bronx, New York, one third (1/3).

2. One third (1/3) to my sister Margaret J. Sugarman, of 177 West 95th Street New York City, New York.

3. One third (1/3) to my sister, Amy E. Harrington, of New York City, New York.

There was no residuary clause. The testatrix at some time after the execution of the will "cancelled clause 3 in her will and attempted and intended thereby to increase the shares in clauses 1 and 2 from 1/3 to 1/2 each and to that end by pencil crossed out all of clause 3 and the figures '1/3' in clauses 1 and 2. She then inserted by pencil the figures 1/2 in clauses 1 and 2 leaving uncancelled in these clauses the words 'one third.'" There was no codicil to the will nor was it ever republished or reexecuted. The will contained the following provision: "I am intentionally omitting my other sisters and brothers for I feel that they are well taken care of."

It appears that the testatrix left no husband, and that her heirs at law and next of kin were four sisters and twenty-two nieces and nephews. The decree of the court below provided that the will was to be allowed except for clause 3 and the figures "1/3" in clauses 1 and 2; it also provided that the figures "1/2" which had been substituted for the figures "1/3" in clauses 1 and 2 were not part of the will.

By the law of this Commonwealth a will can be revoked "by burning, tearing, cancelling or obliterating it with the intention of revoking it, by the testator himself or by a person in his presence and by his direction." G.L. (Ter. Ed.) c. 191, § 8. In the case before us there was clearly a "cancelling" of the third clause of the will which, if done with the requisite revocatory intent, would constitute a revocation pro tanto; a part of a will may be cancelled, leaving the rest in full force. Bigelow v. Gillott, 123 Mass. 102, 106, 25 Am. Rep. 32. . . . For reasons that will presently appear, it is not necessary to decide whether the cancelling of the figures "1/3" in the first and second clauses, leaving the words "one third" intact, would, if coupled with the necessary intent, effect a revocation of the legacies therein provided. See Worcester Bank & Trust Co. v. Ellis, 292 Mass. 88, 91, 197 N.E. 637. . . .

The appellant argues that the cancellation of clause 3 was made conditional on the validity of the attempted substitutions in clauses 1 and 2, and that since these failed for want of proper authentication there was no revocation. The doctrine of conditional revocation (frequently, but less aptly, called dependent relative revocation) is recognized in this Commonwealth. In Sanderson v. Norcross, 242 Mass. 43, 45, 136 N.E. 170,

171, it was said, "The doctrine is widely established that a revocation of a valid will, which is so intimately connected with the making of another will as to show a clear intent that the revocation of the old is made conditional upon the validity of the new, fails to become operative if the new will is void as a testamentary disposition for want of proper execution. Revocation in its last analysis is a question of intent. A revocation grounded on supposed facts, which turn out not to exist, falls when the foundation falls." After recognizing the doctrine as part of our law, the court went on to say that "It is a principle to be applied with caution. . . . Courts have no power to reform wills. . . . Omissions cannot be supplied. . . . The only means for ascertaining the intent of the testator are the words written and the acts done by him." 242 Mass. at pages 45, 46, 136 N.E. at page 172. It has been held on the authority of Sanderson v. Norcross that where a testator cancels or obliterates portions of his will in order to substitute different provisions, and in such a way as to show a clear intent that the revocation is conditional on the validity of the substitution, and the substitution fails for want of proper authentication, the will stands as originally drawn. Thus in Walter v. Walter, 301 Mass. 289, 17 N.E.2d 199, the testatrix, after her will had been executed, obliterated the description of real estate in two devises, and then interlined different descriptions which were not properly authenticated. The decree of the Probate Court allowed the will, but disallowed the devises which had been obliterated. On appeal, this court reversed the decree, holding that the obliterations when considered with the interlineations disclosed an intent on the part of the testatrix to revoke only if the interlineations were valid as a substitute, and that parol evidence was admissible to prove the original wording of the obliterated clauses. See also Porter v. Ballou, 303 Mass. 234, 21 N.E.2d 237. . . .

We think that the principle discussed above is applicable here. It is clear that the cancellations and the substitutions were inextricably linked together as parts of one transaction; and it is evident that the testatrix intended the cancellations to be effective only if the substitutions were valid. But the substitutions, inasmuch as they were not authenticated by a new attestation as required by statute, were invalid. Consequently the cancellations never became operative. Additional support for this conclusion, if any is needed, may be found in the fact that the will contained no residuary clause, and if the decree entered in the court below should stand there would be a partial intestacy—a result which we think the testatrix did not intend. It follows that the decree of the Probate Court is reversed, and a new decree is to be entered allowing the will as worded prior to the attempted changes. . . .

So ordered.

NOTES

1. *Interlineations.* Where the testator has made an unsuccessful attempt to amend a will by striking out some provisions and writing in new ones, courts readily apply the doctrine of dependent relative revocation if the attempted disposition can be more closely approached by restoring the original terms of the will than by treating the stricken provisions as revoked. In accord with the principal case, see Oliver v. Union Nat'l Bank, 504 S.W.2d 647 (Mo.App.1974); Estate of Eastman, 812 P.2d 521 (Wash.App.1991). The application of the doctrine thus depends on several factors, including the specific terms of the attempted change. Suppose a testator, having duly executed a will which includes a bequest of $500 to *A*, crosses out "$500" and writes "$1,000" in the margin, mistakenly believing that this is effective to increase the amount of *A*'s bequest. Alternatively, suppose the testator writes "$100" in the margin. Assuming that the cancellation constitutes a formally sufficient act of partial revocation, should a court apply dependent relative revocation? See Ruel v. Hardy, 6 A.2d 753 (N.H.1939).

2. *Attempted new disposition.* Most courts draw a distinction between an "ineffective attempt" to make a new disposition and an "uncompleted plan" to do so. Dependent relative revocation is potentially applicable in the former case, but not in the latter one. See Estate of Ausley, 818 P.2d 1226 (Okla.1991) (testator cancelled original will and died before he could execute new will, naming same beneficiaries with different shares, which he had instructed attorney to prepare; doctrine not applicable, testator died intestate). Professor Palmer defends this distinction on grounds of policy:

> [U]nless a new dispositive plan has become definitive—and this does not normally occur until the decedent has executed a testamentary writing which he believes to be effective—the evidence is too uncertain that the decedent's intent to revoke is dependent upon putting the plan into effect. In addition, the existence of a writing containing the terms of the substituted disposition provides some assurance that the testator's true intentions in that regard are known. [Palmer, Dependent Relative Revocation and Its Relation to Relief for Mistake, 69 Mich. L. Rev. 989, 994 (1971).]

See also Estate of Patten, 587 P.2d 1307 (Mont.1978) (doctrine not applicable where defective 1970 will was not shown to have been executed "concurrently with or shortly after" presumed destruction of 1968 will); Mincey v. Deckle, 662 S.E.2d 126 (Ga. 2008) ("no evidence that Decedent's revocation of the 1998 Will was dependent upon the creation of a new will"); cf. Carter v. First United Methodist Church, 271 S.E.2d 493 (Ga.1980) (applying doctrine where executed will was found with lines drawn through dispositive provisions, folded together with unexecuted handwritten instrument captioned as a will); Estate of Bowers, 131 P.3d 916 (Wash. App. 2006) (applying doctrine where unexecuted new will made disposition similar to missing original will).

3. *Dispensing power*. Recall that some states have enacted a statutory dispensing power which validates a writing intended as "an addition to or an alteration of the will." UPC § 2–503, reproduced supra at p. 347. According to the UPC drafters, in cases like *Schneider*, "the evidence necessary to establish the testator's intention that the altered terms be valid should be sufficient under Section 2–503 to give effect to the will as altered, making dependent relative revocation as to the lined-out parts unnecessary." UPC § 2–507 cmt. Would a dispensing power make dependent relative revocation completely obsolete? What if there is no "clear and convincing" evidence of the testator's actual intent?

4. *Effectuating dispositive intent*. The UPC drafters describe dependent relative revocation as "the law of second best" because its application often "does not produce the result the testator actually intended." UPC § 2–507 cmt. In a similar vein, Professor Palmer argues that the sole justification for the doctrine is "to effectuate the decedent's intent as nearly as possible":

> In most cases the reason for the application of the doctrine is that the known dispositive intent cannot be given effect. Where the act of revocation went to the whole instrument, the court is left with a choice between giving effect to the dispositions contained in that instrument or letting the property go by intestacy. Usually, neither course will effectuate the decedent's intent exactly, but it will often be possible for the court to conclude that one will come closer than the other. If the testamentary disposition is closer dependent relative revocation should be applied and the will held unrevoked, but if intestacy is closer the doctrine should be held inapplicable. [Palmer, Dependent Relative Revocation and Its Relation to Relief for Mistake, 69 Mich. L. Rev. 989, 998 (1971).]

Should the doctrine be applied if the attempted new disposition departs significantly from the provisions of the original will? See Carter v. First United Methodist Church, 271 S.E.2d 493 (Ga.1980) (applying doctrine where new disposition in unexecuted handwritten instrument was "somewhat different" from cancelled terms of original will); Estate of Patten, 587 P.2d 1307 (Mont.1978) (doctrine not applicable where dissimilarities indicated revocation of earlier will was not conditioned on validity of later will, although primary beneficiary was the same under both wills); Kroll v. Nehmer, 705 A.2d 716 (Md. 1998) (doctrine not applicable where disposition in attempted new will was "very different" from original will, despite testator's notation indicating old will was "void—new will drawn up").

5. *Revocation by subsequent instrument*. Although dependent relative revocation was originally applied in cases involving revocation by physical act, the doctrine is also applied in cases of revocation by subsequent instrument. For example, courts have applied the doctrine where a testator properly executes a will which expressly revokes an earlier will while reiterating its dispositive provisions with no substantial change; if the new disposition is invalid for some reason, the revocation is disregarded and the earlier will re-

mains in effect. See La Croix v. Senecal, 99 A.2d 115 (Conn.1953) (residuary bequest to witness' wife void under purging statute); Estate of Kaufman, 155 P.2d 831 (Cal.1945) (residuary bequest to charity void under mortmain statute); Charleston Library Soc. v. Citizens & Southern Nat'l Bank, 20 S.E.2d 623 (S.C.1942) (bequest for noncharitable purpose void under rule against perpetuities); but cf. Crosby v. Alton Ochsner Medical Foundation, 276 So.2d 661 (Miss.1973) (divided court refused to apply doctrine where validly executed will contained express revocation clause). Of course, if the new will is not properly executed, the revocation clause fails along with the rest of the will and there is no need to invoke dependent relative revocation. See Estate of Laura, 690 A.2d 1011 (N.H.1997); Estate of Shelly, 399 A.2d 98 (Pa.1979).

6. *Mistake of fact.* Suppose a testator executes a will leaving her entire estate to *A* and later, mistakenly believing that *A* has died, executes a new will expressly revoking *A*'s bequest and leaving her estate to *A*'s child *B*. Under standard rules of interpretation, parol evidence is not admissible to cure a mistake or change the meaning of a will. See Gifford v. Dyer, 2 R.I. 99 (1852). Nevertheless, if the new will recites the testator's mistaken belief and indicates how she would have left her estate had she known the true facts, the courts may invoke the doctrine of dependent relative revocation and ignore the new will. The leading case is Campbell v. French, 30 Eng. Rep. 1033 (Ch. 1797). How likely is it that these requirements will be met? Compare the cases involving conditional wills, cited in Note 3, supra p. 387, and the cases involving mistake, discussed infra at pp. 454–470.

e. Revocation by Operation of Law—Changed Family Circumstances

At common law, a will executed before the testator's marriage was automatically revoked by marriage (in the case of a woman) or by marriage coupled with the birth of a child (in the case of a man). See Atkinson § 85. The common law rule may have protected spouses and children from disinheritance in some cases, but its effect was to defeat the entire will, without regard to whether the testator actually left a surviving spouse or child or made provision for them outside the will. Most states have repudiated the common law rule by statute, often in favor of more narrowly tailored statutory provisions for an omitted spouse or child. See supra Chapter 3, Section E.

Almost every state has a statute providing that divorce revokes all provisions for the testator's former spouse in a will executed before the divorce. Many of these statutes are modeled on the original version of UPC § 2–508, promulgated in 1969, which treats a divorce or annulment as revoking "any disposition or appointment of property made by the [testator's] will to the former spouse," unless the will expressly provides otherwise; the remaining provisions of the will take effect "as if the former spouse failed to survive the decedent." See, e.g., the Massachusetts statute set forth in Clymer v. Mayo, infra. Partly in response to the *Clymer* decision, the UPC drafters substantially revised, expanded, and renumbered the revocation-by-divorce provision. The revised version, reproduced below, has been adopted in several states.

Uniform Probate Code (2011)

§ 2–804. Revocation of Probate and Nonprobate Transfers by Divorce; No Revocation by Other Changes of Circumstances.

(a) [Definitions.] In this section:

(1) "Disposition or appointment of property" includes a transfer of an item of property or any other benefit to a beneficiary designated in a governing instrument.

(2) "Divorce or annulment" means any divorce or annulment, or any dissolution or declaration of invalidity of a marriage, that would exclude the spouse as a surviving spouse within the meaning of Section 2–802 [concerning effect of decree or judgment]. A decree of separation that does not terminate the status of husband and wife is not a divorce for purposes of this section.

(3) "Divorced individual" includes an individual whose marriage has been annulled.

(4) "Governing instrument" means a governing instrument executed by the divorced individual before the divorce or annulment of his [or her] marriage to his [or her] former spouse.

(5) "Relative of the divorced individual's former spouse" means an individual who is related to the divorced individual's former spouse by blood, adoption, or affinity and who, after the divorce or annulment, is not related to the divorced individual by blood, adoption, or affinity.

(6) "Revocable," with respect to a disposition, appointment, provision, or nomination, means one under which the divorced individual, at the time of the divorce or annulment, was alone empowered, by law or under the governing instrument, to cancel the designation in favor of his [or her] former spouse or former spouse's relative, whether or not the divorced individual was then empowered to designate himself [or herself] in place of his [or her] former spouse or in place of his [or her] former spouse's relative and whether or not the divorced individual then had the capacity to exercise the power.

(b) [Revocation Upon Divorce.] Except as provided by the express terms of a governing instrument, a court order, or a contract relating to the division of the marital estate made between the divorced individuals before or after the marriage, divorce, or annulment, the divorce or annulment of a marriage:

(1) revokes any revocable

(A) disposition or appointment of property made by a divorced individual to his [or her] former spouse in a governing instrument and any disposition or appointment created by law or in a governing instrument to a relative of the divorced individual's former spouse,

(B) provision in a governing instrument conferring a general or nongeneral power of appointment on the divorced individual's former spouse or on a relative of the divorced individual's former spouse, and

(C) nomination in a governing instrument, nominating a divorced individual's former spouse or a relative of the divorced individual's former spouse to serve in any fiduciary or representative capacity, including a personal representative, executor, trustee, conservator, agent, or guardian; and

(2) severs the interests of the former spouses in property held by them at the time of the divorce or annulment as joint tenants with the right of survivorship [or as community property with the right of survivorship], transforming the interests of the former spouses into equal tenancies in common.

(c) [Effect of Severance.] A severance under subsection (b)(2) does not affect any third-party interest in property acquired for value and in good faith reliance on an apparent title by survivorship in the survivor of the former spouses unless a writing declaring the severance has been noted, registered, filed, or recorded in records appropriate to the kind and location of the property which are relied upon, in the ordinary course of transactions involving such property, as evidence of ownership.

(d) [Effect of Revocation.] Provisions of a governing instrument are given effect as if the former spouse and relatives of the former spouse disclaimed all provisions revoked by this section or, in the case of a revoked nomination in a fiduciary or representative capacity, as if the former spouse and relatives of the former spouse died immediately before the divorce or annulment.

(e) [Revival if Divorce Nullified.] Provisions revoked solely by this section are revived by the divorced individual's remarriage to the former spouse or by a nullification of the divorce or annulment.

(f) [No Revocation for Other Change of Circumstances.] No change of circumstances other than as described in this section and in Section 2-803 [concerning felonious and intentional killing] effects a revocation.

(g) [Protection of Payors and Other Third Parties.]

(1) A payor or other third party is not liable for having made a payment or transferred an item of property or any other benefit to a beneficiary desig-

nated in a governing instrument affected by a divorce, annulment, or remarriage, or for having taken any other action in good faith reliance on the validity of the governing instrument, before the payor or other third party received written notice of the divorce, annulment, or remarriage. A payor or other third party is liable for a payment made or other action taken after the payor or other third party received written notice of a claimed forfeiture or revocation under this section.

(2) Written notice of the divorce, annulment, or remarriage under subsection (g)(1) must be mailed to the payor's or other third party's main office or home by registered or certified mail, return receipt requested, or served upon the payor or other third party in the same manner as a summons in a civil action. Upon receipt of written notice of the divorce, annulment, or remarriage, a payor or other third party may pay any amount owed or transfer or deposit any item of property held by it to or with the court having jurisdiction of the probate proceedings relating to the decedent's estate or, if no proceedings have been commenced, to or with the court having jurisdiction of probate proceedings relating to decedents' estates located in the county of the decedent's residence. The court shall hold the funds or item of property and, upon its determination under this section, shall order disbursement or transfer in accordance with the determination. Payments, transfers, or deposits made to or with the court discharge the payor or other third party from all claims for the value of amounts paid to or items of property transferred to or deposited with the court.

(h) [Protection of Bona Fide Purchasers; Personal Liability of Recipient.]

(1) A person who purchases property from a former spouse, relative of a former spouse, or any other person for value and without notice, or who receives from a former spouse, relative of a former spouse, or any other person a payment or other item of property in partial or full satisfaction of a legally enforceable obligation, is neither obligated under this section to return the payment, item of property, or benefit nor is liable under this section for the amount of the payment or the value of the item of property or benefit. But a former spouse, relative of a former spouse, or other person who, not for value, received a payment, item of property, or any other benefit to which that person is not entitled under this section is obligated to return the payment, item of property, or benefit, or is personally liable for the amount of the payment or the value of the item of property or benefit, to the person who is entitled to it under this section.

(2) If this section or any part of this section is preempted by federal law with respect to a payment, an item of property, or any other benefit covered by this section, a former spouse, relative of the former spouse, or any other person who, not for value, received a payment, item of property, or any other benefit to which that person is not entitled under this section is obligated to return that payment, item of property, or benefit, or is personally liable for

the amount of the payment or the value of the item of property or benefit, to the person who would have been entitled to it were this section or part of this section not preempted.

CLYMER V. MAYO

Supreme Judicial Court of Massachusetts, 1985.
393 Mass. 754, 473 N.E.2d 1084.

HENNESSEY, CHIEF JUSTICE.

This consolidated appeal arises out of the administration of the estate of Clara A. Mayo (decedent). We summarize the findings of the judge of the Probate and Family Court incorporating the parties' agreed statement of uncontested facts.

At the time of her death in November, 1981, the decedent, then fifty years of age, was employed by Boston University as a professor of psychology. She was married to James P. Mayo, Jr. (Mayo), from 1953 to 1978. The couple had no children. The decedent was an only child and her sole heirs at law are her parents, Joseph A. and Maria Weiss.

In 1963, the decedent executed a will designating Mayo as principal beneficiary. In 1964, she named Mayo as the beneficiary of her group annuity contract with John Hancock Mutual Life Insurance Company; and in 1965, made him the beneficiary of her Boston University retirement annuity contracts with Teachers Insurance and Annuity Association (TIAA) and College Retirement Equities Fund (CREF). As a consequence of a $300,000 gift to the couple from the Weisses in 1971, the decedent and Mayo executed new wills and indentures of trust on February 2, 1973, wherein each spouse was made the other's principal beneficiary. Under the terms of the decedent's will, Mayo was to receive her personal property. The residue of her estate was to "pour over" into the inter vivos trust she created that same day.

The decedent's trust instrument named herself and John P. Hill as trustees. As the donor, the decedent retained the right to amend or revoke the trust at any time by written instrument delivered to the trustees. In the event that Mayo survived the decedent, the trust estate was to be divided into two parts. Trust A, the marital deduction trust, was to be funded with [an amount specified by formula]. Mayo was the income beneficiary of Trust A and was entitled to reach the principal at his request or in the trustee's discretion. The trust instrument also gave Mayo a general power of appointment over the assets in Trust A.

The balance of the decedent's estate, excluding personal property passing to Mayo by will, or the entire estate if Mayo did not survive her, composed Trust B. Trust B provided for the payment of five initial specific bequests totalling $45,000. After those gifts were satisfied, the remaining trust assets were to be held for the benefit of Mayo for life. Upon Mayo's death, the assets in Trust B were to be held for "the benefit of the nephews and nieces of the Donor" living at the time of her death. The trustee was given discretion to spend so much of the income and principal as necessary for their comfort, support, and education. When all of these nephews and nieces reached the age of thirty, the trust was to terminate and its remaining assets were to be divided equally between Clark University and Boston University to assist in graduate education of women.

On the same day she established her trust, the decedent changed the beneficiary of her Boston University group life insurance policy from Mayo to the trustees. One month later, in March, 1973, she also executed a change in her retirement annuity contracts to designate the trustees as beneficiaries. At the time of its creation in 1973, the trust was not funded. Its future assets were to consist solely of the proceeds of these policies and the property which would pour over under the will's residuary clause. The judge found that the remaining trustee has never received any property or held any funds subsequent to the execution of the trust nor has he paid any trust taxes or filed any trust tax returns.

Mayo moved out of the marital home in 1975. In June, 1977, the decedent changed the designation of beneficiary on her Boston University life insurance policy for a second time, substituting Marianne LaFrance for the trustees.[12] LaFrance had lived with the Mayos since 1972, and shared a close friendship with the decedent up until her death. Mayo filed for divorce on September 9, 1977, in New Hampshire. The divorce was decreed on January 3, 1978, and the court incorporated into the decree a permanent stipulation of the parties' property settlement. Under the terms of that settlement, Mayo waived any "right, title or interest" in the decedent's "securities, savings accounts, savings certificates, and retirement fund," as well as her "furniture, furnishings and art." Mayo remarried on August 28, 1978, and later executed a new will in favor of his new wife. The decedent died on November 21, 1981. Her will was allowed on November 18, 1982, and the court appointed John H. Clymer as administrator with the will annexed.

What is primarily at issue in these actions is the effect of the Mayos' divorce upon dispositions provided in the decedent's will and indenture of trust. . . .

1. *The Judge's Conclusions.* . . .

On November 1, 1983, the judge issued his rulings of law. . . . The rulings that have been challenged by one or more parties on appeal are as

---

[12] Upon the decedent's death the benefits under said policy were paid to LaFrance.

follows: (1) the decedent's inter vivos trust, executed contemporaneously with her will, is valid under G.L. c. 203, § 3B, despite the fact that the trust did not receive funding until the decedent's death; (2) Mayo does not take under Trust A because that transfer was intended to qualify for a marital deduction for Federal estate tax purposes and this objective became impossible after the Mayos' divorce; (3) Mayo is entitled to take under Trust B because the purpose of that trust was to create a life interest in him, the decedent failed to revoke the trust provisions benefiting Mayo, and G.L. c. 191, § 9, operates to revoke only testamentary dispositions in favor of a former spouse; (4) J. Chamberlain, A. Chamberlain, and Hinman, the decedent's nephews and niece by marriage at the time of the trust's creation, are entitled to take under Trust B as the decedent's intended beneficiaries. . . .

2. *Validity of "Pour-over" Trust.*

[The court held, under the Massachusetts version of the Uniform Testamentary Additions to Trusts Act, "that the decedent established a valid inter vivos trust in 1973 and that its trustee may properly receive the residue of her estate." This portion of the opinion is reproduced at p. 402 supra.] . . .

4. *Termination of Trust A.*

The judge terminated Trust A upon finding that its purpose—to qualify the trust for an estate tax marital deduction—became impossible to achieve after the Mayos' divorce. Mayo appeals this ruling. It is well established that the Probate Courts are empowered to terminate or reform a trust in whole or in part where its purposes have become impossible to achieve and the settlor did not contemplate continuation of the trust under the new circumstances. Gordon v. Gordon, 332 Mass. 193, 197, 124 N.E.2d 226 (1955). Ames v. Hall, 313 Mass. 33, 37, 46 N.E.2d 403 (1943).

The language the decedent employed in her indenture of trust makes it clear that by setting off Trusts A and B she intended to reduce estate tax liability in compliance with then existing provisions of the Internal Revenue Code. Therefore we have no disagreement with the judge's reasoning. See Putnam v. Putnam, 366 Mass. 261, 267 (1974). However, we add that our reasoning below—that by operation of G.L. c. 191, § 9, Mayo has no beneficial interest in the trust—clearly disposes of Mayo's claim to Trust A.

5. *Mayo's Interest in Trust B.*

The judge's decision to uphold Mayo's beneficial interest in Trust B was appealed by the Weisses, as well as by Boston University and Clark University. The judge reasoned that the decedent intended to create a life interest in Mayo when she established Trust B and failed either to revoke or to amend the trust after the couple's divorce. The appellants argue that we should extend the reach of G.L. c. 191, § 9, to revoke all Mayo's interests under the trust. General Laws c. 191, § 9, as amended through St. 1977, c. 76, § 2, provides in relevant part:

> If, after executing a will, the testator shall be divorced or his marriage shall be annulled, the divorce or annulment shall revoke any disposition or appointment of property made by the will to the former spouse, any provision conferring a general or special power of appointment on the former spouse, and any nomination of the former spouse, as executor, trustee, conservator or guardian, unless the will shall expressly provide otherwise. Property prevented from passing to a former spouse because of a revocation by divorce shall pass as if a former spouse had failed to survive the decedent, and other provisions conferring a power of office on the former spouse shall be interpreted as if the spouse had failed to survive the decedent.

The judge ruled that Mayo's interest in Trust B is unaffected by G.L. c. 191, § 9, because his interest in that trust is not derived from a "disposition . . . made by the will" but rather from the execution of an inter vivos trust with independent legal significance. We disagree, but in fairness we add that the judge here confronted a question of first impression in this Commonwealth.

. . . In this case we must determine what effect, if any, G.L. c. 191, § 9, has on the former spouse's interest in the testator's pour-over trust.

While, by virtue of G.L. c. 203, § 3B, the decedent's trust bore independent significance at the time of its creation in 1973, the trust had no practical significance until her death in 1981. The decedent executed both her will and indenture of trust on February 2, 1973. She transferred no property or funds to the trust at that time. The trust was to receive its funding at the decedent's death, in part through her life insurance policy and retirement benefits, and in part through a pour-over from the will's residuary clause. Mayo, the proposed executor and sole legatee under the will, was also made the primary beneficiary of the trust with power, as to Trust A only, to reach both income and principal.

During her lifetime, the decedent retained power to amend or revoke the trust. Since the trust was unfunded, her co-trustee was subject to no duties or obligations until her death. Similarly, it was only as a result of the decedent's death that Mayo could claim any right to the trust assets. It is evident from the time and manner in which the trust was created and funded, that the decedent's will and trust were integrally related components of a single testamentary scheme. For all practical purposes the trust, like the will, "spoke" only at the decedent's death. For this rea-

son Mayo's interest in the trust was revoked by operation of G.L. c. 191, §
9, at the same time his interest under the decedent's will was revoked.

It has reasonably been contended that in enacting G.L. c. 191, § 9,
the Legislature "intended to bring the law into line with the expectations
of most people. . . . Divorce usually represents a stormy parting, where
the last thing one of the parties wishes is to have an earlier will carried
out giving everything to the former spouse." Young, Probate Reform, 18
Boston B.J. 7, 11 (1974). To carry out the testator's implied intent, the
law revokes "any disposition or appointment of property made by the will
to the former spouse." It is indisputable that if the decedent's trust was
either testamentary or incorporated by reference into her will, Mayo's
beneficial interest in the trust would be revoked by operation of the statute. However, the judge stopped short of mandating the same result in
this case because here the trust had "independent significance" by virtue
of c. 203, § 3B. While correct, this characterization of the trust does not
end our analysis. For example, in Sullivan v. Burkin, 390 Mass. 864, 867,
460 N.E.2d 572 (1984), we ruled prospectively that the assets of a revocable trust will be considered part of the "estate of the decedent" in determining the surviving spouse's statutory share.

Treating the components of the decedent's estate plan separately,
and not as parts of an interrelated whole, brings about inconsistent results. Applying c. 191, § 9, the judge correctly revoked the will provisions
benefiting Mayo. As a result, the decedent's personal property—originally
left to Mayo—fell into the will's residuary clause and passed to the trust.
The judge then appropriately terminated Trust A for impossibility of purpose thereby denying Mayo his beneficial interest under Trust A. Yet, by
upholding Mayo's interest under Trust B, the judge returned to Mayo a
life interest in the same assets that composed the corpus of Trust A—both
property passing by way of the decedent's will and the proceeds of her
TIAA/CREF annuity contracts.

We are aware of only one case concerning the impact of a statute similar to G.L. c. 191, § 9, on trust provisions benefiting a former spouse. In
Miller v. First Nat'l Bank & Trust Co., 637 P.2d 75 (Okla.1981), the testator also simultaneously executed an indenture of trust and will naming
his spouse as primary beneficiary. As in this case, the trust was to be
funded at the testator's death by insurance proceeds and a will pour-over.
Subsequently, the testator divorced his wife but failed to change the
terms of his will and trust. The District Court revoked the will provisions
favoring the testator's former wife by applying a statute similar to G.L. c.
191, § 9. Recognizing that "[t]he will without the trust has no meaning or
value to the decedent's estate plan," the Oklahoma Supreme Court revoked the trust benefits as well. Id. at 77. However, we do not agree with
the court's reasoning. Because the Oklahoma statute, like G.L. c. 191, § 9,

revokes dispositions of property made by will, the court stretched the doctrine of incorporation by reference to render the decedent's trust testamentary. We do not agree that reference to an existing trust in a will's pour-over clause is sufficient to incorporate that trust by reference without evidence that the testator intended such a result. See Second Bank–State St. Trust Co. v. Pinion, 341 Mass. 366, 367, 170 N.E.2d 350 (1960). However, it is not necessary for us to indulge in such reasoning, because we have concluded that the legislative intent under G.L. c. 191, § 9, is that a divorced spouse should not take under a trust executed in these circumstances. In the absence of an expressed contrary intent, that statute implies an intent on the part of a testator to revoke will provisions favoring a former spouse. It is incongruous then to ignore that same intent with regard to a trust funded in part through her will's pour-over at the decedent's death. See State St. Bank & Trust v. United States, 634 F.2d 5, 10 (1st Cir.1980) (trust should be interpreted in light of settlor's contemporaneous execution of interrelated will). As one law review commentator has noted, "[t]ransferors use will substitutes to avoid probate, not to avoid the subsidiary law of wills. The subsidiary rules are the product of centuries of legal experience in attempting to discern transferors' wishes and suppress litigation. These rules should be treated as presumptively correct for will substitutes as well as for wills." Langbein, The Nonprobate Revolution and the Future of the Law of Succession, 97 Harv. L. Rev. 1108, 1136–1137 (1984).

Restricting our holding to the particular facts of this case— specifically the existence of a revocable pour-over trust funded entirely at the time of the decedent's death—we conclude that G.L. c. 191, § 9, revokes Mayo's interest under Trust B.[13]

6. Nephews and Nieces of Donor.

According to the terms of G.L. c. 191, § 9, "[p]roperty prevented from passing to a former spouse because of revocation by divorce shall pass as if a former spouse had failed to survive the decedent. . . ." In this case, the decedent's indenture of trust provides that if Mayo failed to survive her, "the balance of 'Trust B' shall be held . . . for the benefit of the nephews and nieces of the Donor living at the time of the death of the Donor." The trustee is directed to expend as much of the net income and principal as he deems "advisable for [their] reasonable comfort, support and education" until all living nephews and nieces have attained the age of thirty. At that time, the trust is to terminate and Boston University and Clark

---

[13] As an alternative ground the appellants argue that the terms of the Mayos' divorce settlement, in which Mayo waived "any right, title or interest" in the assets that later funded the decedent's trust, amount to a disclaimer of his trust interest. We decline to base our holding on such reasoning because a disclaimer of rights "must be clear and unequivocal." Second Bank–State St. Trust Co. v. Yale Univ. Alumni Fund, 338 Mass. 520, 524, 156 N.E.2d 57 (1959), and we find no such disclaimer in the Mayos' divorce agreement.

University are each to receive fifty per cent of the trust property to assist women students in their graduate programs.

The decedent had no siblings and therefore no nephews and nieces who were blood relations.[14] However, when she executed her trust in 1973, her husband, James P. Mayo, Jr., had two nephews and one niece—John and Allan Chamberlain and Mira Hinman. Before her divorce, the decedent maintained friendly relations with these young people and, along with her former husband, contributed toward their educational expenses. The three have survived the decedent.

The Weisses, Boston University, and Clark University appeal the decision of the judge upholding the decedent's gift to these three individuals. They argue that at the time the decedent created her trust she had no "nephews and nieces" by blood and that, at her death, her marital ties to Mayo's nephews and niece had been severed by divorce. Therefore, they contend that the class gift to the donor's "nephews and nieces" lapses for lack of identifiable beneficiaries.

The judge concluded that the trust language created an ambiguity, and thus he considered extrinsic evidence of the decedent's meaning and intent. Based upon that evidence, he decided that the decedent intended to provide for her nieces and nephews by marriage when she created the trust. Because the decedent never revoked this gift, he found that the Chamberlains and Hinman are entitled to their beneficial interests under the trust. We agree. . . .

The appellants argue that . . . the Mayos' divorce left the decedent without *any* nephews and nieces—by blood or marriage—at the time of her death. They argue that even if the decedent had intended to provide for the Chamberlains and Hinman when she executed her indenture of trust, we should rule that the Mayos' divorce somehow "revoked" this gift. According to Boston University, since the beneficiaries are identified by their relationship to the decedent through her marriage and not by name, we should presume that the decedent no longer intended to benefit her former relatives once her marriage ended. General Laws c. 191, § 9, does not provide the authority for revoking gifts to the blood relatives of a former spouse. The law implies an intent to revoke testamentary gifts between the divorcing parties because of the profound emotional and financial changes divorce normally engenders. There is no indication in the statutory language that the Legislature presumed to know how these changes affect a testator's relations with more distant family members. We therefore conclude that the Chamberlains and Hinman are entitled to take as the decedent's "nephews and nieces" under Trust B. . . .

---

[14] Considering the ages of all concerned, it could not reasonably be argued that the decedent might have contemplated the possibility of siblings to be born after the trust was executed.

In sum, we conclude that the decedent established a valid trust under G.L. c. 203, § 3B; Mayo's beneficial interest in Trust A and Trust B is revoked by operation of G.L. c. 191, § 9; [and] the Chamberlains and Hinman are entitled to take the interest given to the decedent's "nephews and nieces" under Trust B, leaving the remainder to Clark University and Boston University. . . .

So ordered.

NOTES

1. *Statutory presumptions.* The revocation-by-divorce statute reflects the testator's presumed intent. Under UPC § 2–804, reproduced supra, divorce revokes only the provisions in favor of the testator's former spouse (or the former spouse's relatives), leaving the rest of the will intact, and the statute can be overridden by the "express terms" of a governing instrument, court order, or marital property agreement. Why is the statutory presumption rebuttable only by an express provision? Should the circumstances surrounding the divorce, or other extrinsic evidence, be admissible to rebut the statutory presumption? Consider the following facts. After twenty years of marriage, testator and his wife file for divorce. The proceedings are amicable, and shortly after reaching a court-approved property settlement, testator executes a will naming his wife as sole beneficiary of his estate; six weeks later, the divorce becomes final. The couple remains on friendly terms until testator dies a few years later having made no change in his will. Should the will be carried out in accordance with its terms, or does the gift to the wife fail, causing the estate to pass to testator's intestate successors? See Langston v. Langston, 266 S.W.3d 716 (Ark. 2007) (divorce automatically revokes provisions for wife; "It is not necessary for us to try to reach the intent of the testator because the statute solves that problem for us.") Does it matter whether the will recites that it is executed in contemplation of divorce?

Consider the problem that arises when two spouses enter into a separation agreement but for religious or other reasons fail to obtain a divorce. By its terms, the revocation-by-divorce statute does not apply; indeed, in most states the statute expressly excludes revocation by operation of law due to any change in family circumstances other than divorce. Nevertheless, suppose the separation agreement sets forth a comprehensive property settlement and recites that each spouse expressly waives "all rights, claims, and interests in and to any property" of the other spouse. If one spouse dies leaving a will (executed before the separation agreement) which names the other spouse as a beneficiary, is the bequest valid? See UPC § 2–213 ("complete property settlement" waives all benefits under previously executed will); cf. Estate of Maruccia, 429 N.E.2d 751 (N.Y.1981) (under New York statute providing for revocation by "wholly inconsistent" settlement, will is revoked only if spouse explicitly renounces benefit under will or agreement unequivocally manifests such an intent). If one spouse agrees as part of a marital property settlement to maintain a life insurance policy with the other spouse named as beneficiary, but dies without doing so, does the promisee have an enforceable claim against the decedent's estate for the value of the promised proceeds? See Estate of Matteson, 675 N.W.2d 366 (Neb. 2004). See generally Lynn, Will Substitutes, Divorce, and Statutory Assistance for the Unthinking Donor, 71 Marq. L. Rev. 1 (1987).

Under UPC § 2–804, does it matter whether the will was executed during the testator's marriage? Suppose that *T* executes a will naming his friend *A* as sole beneficiary. *T* and *A* subsequently marry and then divorce. Finally, *T* dies without having changed his will, and leaves no surviving heirs. What result? See Gibboney v. Wachovia Bank, 622 S.E.2d 162 (N.C. App. 2005).

2. *Nonprobate assets.* Note how carefully the *Clymer* court limited its holding to "the particular facts of this case—specifically the existence of a revocable pour-over trust funded entirely at the time of the decedent's death." Would the result or the rationale be different if Clara Mayo had funded her trust in part during life and in part at death? What if she had designated her husband as beneficiary of her life insurance policy in 1973 and then failed to change the beneficiary designation before her death?

Suppose that *H* takes out a policy of insurance on his own life and names his wife *W* as beneficiary; *H* also names *W* as beneficiary of *H*'s employer-provided pension. Several years later, in connection with their divorce, *H* and *W* enter into a property settlement which awards exclusive ownership of the policy and the pension to *H*. Still later, *H* dies intestate, without having formally changed the beneficiary designation. Who is entitled to the proceeds, *W* or *H*'s heirs? Unless *W* is found to have specifically waived her rights as beneficiary, the traditional view is that the beneficiary designation remains valid and unrevoked. See Schultz v. Schultz, 591 N.W.2d 212 (Iowa 1999) (individual retirement account); Hughes v. Scholl, 900 S.W.2d 606 (Ky.1995) (life insurance); Pepper v. Peacher, 742 P.2d 21 (Okla.1987) (retirement benefits); Bersch v. VanKleeck, 334 N.W.2d 114 (Wis.1983) (life insurance); but cf. Vasconi v. Guardian Life Ins. Co., 590 A.2d 1161 (N.J.1991) (life insurance beneficiary designation presumed revoked by divorce). To reverse this result, several states have adopted revocation-by-divorce statutes modeled on UPC § 2–804, reproduced supra, covering a wide range of revocable nonprobate transfers, including revocable trusts, transfer-on-death accounts, and beneficiary designations under life insurance policies and pension plans.

3. *Former spouse's relatives.* Sometimes a will makes provision not only for the testator's spouse but also for members of the spouse's family who are not related by blood to the testator (e.g., an unadopted stepchild). *Clymer* is typical in refusing to imply a revocation of provisions for beneficiaries other than the former spouse, where the statute does not expressly refer to such beneficiaries. See Estate of Kerr, 520 N.W.2d 512 (Minn.App.1994) (bequest to stepchild not revoked, even though testator was incompetent at time of divorce and hence had no opportunity to change will); Bloom v. Selfon, 555 A.2d 75 (Pa.1989); Bowling v. Deaton, 507 N.E.2d 1152 (Ohio App. 1986); but

cf. Estate of Hermon, 46 Cal.Rptr.2d 577 (App. 1995) (provisions for step-children presumed revoked by divorce, unless will indicates contrary intention); Friedman v. Hannan, 987 A.2d 60 (Md. 2010) (deemed revocation of provisions "relating to" former spouse "is not limited to bequests to a former spouse, and may include bequests to a former spouse's family members").

Under UPC § 2–804, reproduced supra, revocation by divorce applies equally to the decedent's former spouse and to relatives of the former spouse. According to the UPC drafters, most decedents would prefer this result because in the course of the divorce "the former spouse's relatives are likely to side with the former spouse, breaking down or weakening any former ties that may previously have developed" with the decedent. UPC § 2–804 cmt. Is the rationale for implied revocation as compelling in the case of the former spouse's relatives as in the case of the former spouse?

4. *Employee benefits.* The Employee Retirement Income Security Act of 1974 (ERISA) expressly preempts "any and all State laws" to the extent they "relate to" an employee benefit plan governed by ERISA. 29 U.S.C. § 1144(a). In Egelhoff v. Egelhoff, 532 U.S. 141 (2001), a husband named his wife as beneficiary of employer-provided life insurance and pension benefits under an ERISA-governed plan. The couple subsequently divorced, and the husband died intestate shortly afterward without having changed the beneficiary designations. Decedent was survived by his former wife and by his two children from a previous marriage. The former wife claimed the benefits as designated beneficiary, but the children argued that the beneficiary designation failed under the Washington revocation-by-divorce statute and claimed the benefits as decedent's heirs. The Supreme Court rejected the children's claim and held that the revocation-by-divorce statute was preempted. The majority found that the state law had an "impermissible connection" with ERISA plans because it required that benefits be paid "to the beneficiaries chosen by state law, rather than to those identified in the plan documents." The majority also found that the state law "interfere[d] with nationally uniform plan administration" and imposed unwarranted burdens on plan administrators, who would not be able to make payments "simply by identifying the beneficiary specified by the plan documents" but instead would have to look to state law to determine whether a named beneficiary's status had been revoked by divorce. Two dissenters saw no "direct conflict or contradiction" with the terms of the plan documents and argued that the state statute merely provided a "default rule" to fill a gap in the plan documents concerning the effect of divorce on a beneficiary designation.

Does the Supreme Court's holding in *Egelhoff* apply with equal force to other provisions of state law, such as a slayer statute, that disqualify an heir or named beneficiary from succeeding to probate or nonprobate assets? The majority considered the question but declined to answer it, noting only that "the principle underlying the [slayer] statutes . . . is well established in the law and has a long historical pedigree predating ERISA," and that "because the statutes are more or less uniform nationwide, their interference with the aims of ERISA is at least debatable."

The UPC drafters foresaw the possibility of ERISA preemption when they expanded the disqualification rules for slayers and divorce to cover nonprobate transfers. To counteract the effect of preemption, the Uniform Probate Code requires a slayer, former spouse, or other person who receives property in contravention of the disqualification rules to return the property to "the person who would have been entitled to it" in the absence of preemption. UPC §§ 2–803(i)(2) and 2–804(h)(2). The UPC drafters explain that this provision "respects ERISA's concern that federal law govern the administration of the plan, while still preventing unjust enrichment that would result if an unintended beneficiary were to receive the pension benefits." UPC § 2–804 cmt. Does the provision achieve its intended effect?

In *Egelhoff*, suppose that in connection with the divorce proceedings decedent and his wife agreed on a property settlement which awarded exclusive ownership of the life insurance and pension benefits to decedent. Moreover, as part of the property settlement the wife expressly waived her interest as designated beneficiary. Should the wife's waiver be enforceable as a matter of federal law? See Kennedy v. Plan Administrator for DuPont Savings & Investment Plan, 555 U.S. 285 (2009) (no; waiver did not satisfy plan requirements for change of beneficiary). Should it matter whether the property settlement is incorporated in the divorce decree? See 29 U.S.C. § 1056(d)(3) (enforceability of "qualified domestic relations order"). Note that ERISA does not create substantive survivorship rights but merely requires that benefits be paid to a designated beneficiary in accordance with the plan's governing documents. (If the plan documents provided for revocation on divorce, the presumed intent of employees could be carried out without running afoul of ERISA. Why might employers resist including such a provision in plan documents?)

5. *Statutory vacuum.* In the absence of a statute, the courts are divided over the effect of divorce on an existing will. See Estate of Reap, 727 A.2d 326 (D.C. 1999) (complete revocation upon divorce coupled with property settlement); Hinders v. Hinders, 828 So.2d 1235 (Miss.2002) (no automatic revocation upon divorce and property settlement; intent to revoke must be shown by clear and unequivocal evidence).

D. INTERPRETATION OF WILLS

A considerable period of time may elapse between the execution of a will and the testator's death, when the will takes effect. Circumstances may change: the testator may dispose of some assets and acquire others; asset values may fluctuate; and beneficiaries may come into existence or die. Even if circumstances do not change dramatically, the will may express the testator's intent imperfectly, as in the case of an ambiguous term or a provision included or omitted by mistake. The following materials illustrate several areas in which courts are frequently called on to interpret a will—i.e., to ascertain the meaning of the will as it applies to persons and property existing at the testator's death. In reading these materials, consider how a competent drafter might have identified and resolved the problems that ultimately led to litigation.

1. AMBIGUITY AND MISTAKE

The process of interpretation begins with the words of the will, which presumably represent the testator's deliberate and final expression of testamentary intent. To make sense of the words used by the testator, however, it may be necessary to look beyond the four corners of the will. Courts routinely admit extrinsic evidence, other than direct declarations of intent, to show the testator's circumstances at the time the will was executed. For example, evidence of the testator's habits, financial condition, personal relationships, and family composition are freely admissible to provide a background or context for interpreting the words of the will. In contrast, direct declarations of intent, such as the testator's oral comments or written instructions to the drafter, have traditionally been excluded, except in limited circumstances. See Estate of Utterback, 521 A.2d 1184 (Me. 1987) (distinguishing testator's "oral declarations of intent" from "objective circumstances" surrounding execution of will, and admitting latter but not former to resolve ambiguity).

It is often said that extrinsic evidence is inadmissible to vary or contradict the "plain meaning" of the will or to supply omitted provisions. As one court observed, the task is to discover "what the testator meant by what he said, not by what it might be supposed he intended to say or should have said." Aldridge v. First & Merchants Nat'l Bank, 60 S.E.2d 905 (Va. 1950). Both the parol evidence rule (which applies to wills as well as other "integrated" writings) and the wills statutes are invoked in support of this exclusionary rule. (Recall the "evidentiary function" of the wills formalities, discussed supra at p. 313.) At the same time, courts recognize that extrinsic evidence may be admitted to resolve an ambiguity. How should a court determine whether the words of a particular will are ambiguous?

MAHONEY V. GRAINGER

Supreme Judicial Court of Massachusetts, 1933.
283 Mass. 189, 186 N.E. 86.

RUGG, CHIEF JUSTICE.

This is an appeal from a decree of a probate court denying a petition for distribution of a legacy under the will of Helen A. Sullivan among her first cousins who are contended to be her heirs at law. The residuary clause was as follows: "All the rest and residue of my estate, both real and personal property, I give, demise and bequeath to my heirs at law living at the time of my decease, absolutely; to be divided among them equally, share and share alike. . . ."

The trial judge made a report of the material facts in substance as follows: The sole heir at law of the testatrix at the time of her death was her maternal aunt, Frances Hawkes Greene, who is still living and who was named in the petition for probate of her will. The will was duly proved and allowed on October 8, 1931, and letters testamentary issued accordingly. The testatrix was a single woman about sixty-four years of age, and had been a school teacher. She always maintained her own home but her relations with her aunt who was her sole heir and with several first cousins were cordial and friendly. In her will she gave general legacies in considerable sums to two of her first cousins. About ten days before her death the testatrix sent for an attorney who found her sick but intelligent about the subjects of their conversation. She told the attorney she wanted to make a will. She gave him instructions as to general pecuniary legacies. In response to the questions "Whom do you want to leave the rest of your property to? Who are your nearest relations?" she replied "I've got about twenty-five first cousins . . . let them share it equally." The attorney then drafted the will and read it to the testatrix and it was executed by her.

The trial judge ruled that statements of the testatrix "were admissible only in so far as they tended to give evidence of the material circumstances surrounding the testatrix at the time of the execution of the will; that the words heirs at law were words in common use, susceptible of application to one or many; that when applied to the special circumstances of this case that the testatrix had but one heir, notwithstanding the added words 'to be divided among them equally, share and share alike,' there was no latent ambiguity or equivocation in the will itself which would permit the introduction of the statements of the testatrix to prove her testamentary intention." Certain first cousins have appealed from the decree dismissing the petition for distribution to them.

There is no doubt as to the meaning of the words "heirs at law living at the time of my decease" as used in the will. Confessedly they refer alone to the aunt of the testatrix and do not include her cousins. Gilman v. Congregational Home Missionary Society, 276 Mass. 580, 177 N.E. 621; Calder v. Bryant (Mass.) 184 N.E. 440.

A will duly executed and allowed by the court must under the statute of wills . . . be accepted as the final expression of the intent of the person executing it. The fact that it was not in conformity to the instructions given to the draftsman who prepared it or that he made a mistake does not authorize a court to reform or alter it or remould it by amendments. The will must be construed as it came from the hands of the testatrix. Polsey v. Newton, 199 Mass. 450, 85 N.E. 574, 15 Ann. Cas. 139. Mistakes in the drafting of the will may be of significance in some circumstances in a trial as to the due execution and allowance of the alleged testamentary instrument. Richardson v. Richards, 226 Mass. 240, 115 N.E. 307. Proof that the legatee actually designated was not the particular person intended by the one executing the will cannot be received to aid in the interpretation of a will. Tucker v. Seaman's Aid Society, 7 Metc. 188, 210. See National Society for the Prevention of Cruelty to Children v. Scottish National Society for the Prevention of Cruelty to Children, [1915] A.C. 207. When the instrument has been proved and allowed as a will oral testimony as to the meaning and purpose of a testator in using language must be rigidly excluded. Sibley v. Maxwell, 203 Mass. 94, 104, 89 N.E. 232; Saucier v. Fontaine, 256 Mass. 107, 110, 152 N.E. 95; Calder v. Bryant (Mass.) 184 N.E. 440.

It is only where testamentary language is not clear in its application to facts that evidence may be introduced as to the circumstances under which the testator used that language in order to throw light upon its meaning. Where no doubt exists as to the property bequeathed or the identity of the beneficiary there is no room for extrinsic evidence; the will must stand as written. Barker v. Comins, 110 Mass. 477, 488; Best v. Berry, 189 Mass. 510, 512, 75 N.E. 743, 109 Am. St. Rep. 651.

In the case at bar there is no doubt as to the heirs at law of the testatrix. The aunt alone falls within that description. The cousins are excluded. The circumstance that the plural word "heirs" was used does not prevent one individual from taking the entire gift. Calder v. Bryant (Mass.) 184 N.E. 440.

Decree affirmed.

NOTES

1. *Plain meaning.* The plain meaning doctrine expounded in the principal case is still widely followed. Thus, if a will refers to the intestacy laws to identify a beneficiary or delimit a bequest, courts regularly adhere to the literal or technical meaning of the words used in the will and refuse to consider extrinsic evidence that might suggest a contrary intent. See Gustafson v. Svenson, 366 N.E.2d 761 (Mass.1977) (bequest to predeceased brother's "heirs per stirpes" went to brother's wife); Estate of Kelly, 373 A.2d 744 (Pa. 1977) (bequest to wife of intestate share disposed of entire estate, leaving nothing for named residuary beneficiary). At least one court has taken a different approach. In Estate of Taff, 133 Cal.Rptr. 737 (App. 1976), the testator left her residuary estate "to my heirs in accordance with the laws of intestate succession, in effect at my death in the State of California." Under the California intestacy laws, the residuary estate would have been divided between

the testator's relatives and those of her predeceased husband. Based on the testator's oral instructions to the drafter of the will and a letter written to her sister shortly before the will was executed, the court held that the residuary gift was "properly interpreted" to limit the takers to the testator's own relatives, despite the "seemingly clear and unambiguous language" to the contrary.

2. *Personal usage.* Courts recognize a "personal usage" exception to the plain meaning rule where a particular word or expression in the will reflects the testator's idiosyncratic use of language. A leading example is Moseley v. Goodman, 195 S.W. 590 (Tenn.1917), which involved a bequest to "Mrs. Moseley." The bequest was claimed by Mrs. Lenoir Moseley, with whom the testator was not personally acquainted. Extrinsic evidence was admitted to show that the testator habitually used "Mrs. Moseley" as a nickname for Mrs. Trimble, who took care of the testator while he was ill and whose husband was a salesman for the Moseley cigar company. Could the Massachusetts court have reached a different result in the principal case by invoking a personal usage exception?

3. *Role of attorney-drafter.* The attorney who drafted a will may be uniquely well situated to recall the testator's instructions concerning the preparation of the will and to explain any discrepancies between the intended disposition and the terms of the will as finally executed. Why might a court be reluctant to allow the attorney-drafter to testify about these matters? See Estate of Campbell, 655 N.Y.S.2d 913 (Sur. 1997) (noting possibility that an "unscrupulous draftsman" might "collude with beneficiaries to redefine the parameters of a bequest" or that testimony of an "otherwise honest practitioner" might be tainted by fear of "damage to his reputation, loss of business, or even legal action because of a perceived error in the articulation of his client's desires").

If a lawyer drafts a will which fails to carry out the disposition directed by the testator, many courts allow the disappointed beneficiary to sue the lawyer, either on a contract (third-party beneficiary) theory or on a tort (malpractice) theory. See Simpson v. Calivas, 650 A.2d 318 (N.H. 1994) (ambiguous devise of "homestead"); Hale v. Groce, 744 P.2d 1289 (Or. 1987) (omitted bequest); Ogle v. Fuiten, 466 N.E.2d 224 (Ill.1984) (omitted residuary clause). Some courts take a more restrictive view, holding that the beneficiary has standing only if the lawyer fails to "effectuate the testator's intent as expressed in the testamentary instruments." Harrigfeld v. Hancock, 90 P.3d 884 (Idaho 2004); see also Schreiner v. Scoville, 410 N.W.2d 679 (Iowa 1987); Espinosa v. Sparber, Shevin, Shapo, Rosen & Heilbronner, 612 So.2d 1378 (Fla. 1993). In a few states, the common law requirement of privity remains in full force, depriving the beneficiary of standing to sue the lawyer. See Barcelo v. Elliott, 923 S.W.2d 575 (Tex. 1996); Noble v. Bruce, 709 A.2d 1264 (Md. 1998); Schneider v. Finman, 933 N.E.2d 718 (N.Y. 2010). Does the mere existence of an ambiguous provision in a will indicate a prima facie case of negligence on the part of the drafting attorney? See Ventura County Humane Society v. Holloway, 115 Cal.Rptr. 464 (App. 1974).

4. *References.* For a comprehensive exposition of the parol evidence rule and the use of extrinsic evidence, see IX Wigmore, Evidence in Trials at Common Law §§ 2458–2478 (Chadbourn rev. 1981); see also Thayer, A Preliminary Treatise on Evidence 390–483 (1898); Hawkins, On the Principles of Legal Interpretation, With Reference Especially to the Interpretation of Wills (reproduced as Appendix C of Thayer's treatise).

IN RE ESTATE OF RUSSELL

Supreme Court of California, 1968.
69 Cal.2d 200, 444 P.2d 353, 70 Cal.Rptr. 561.

SULLIVAN, ASSOCIATE JUSTICE.

Georgia Nan Russell Hembree appeals from a judgment (Prob. Code, § 1240) entered in proceedings for the determination of heirship (§§ 1080–1082) decreeing inter alia that under the terms of the will of Thelma L. Russell, deceased, all of the residue of her estate should be distributed to Chester H. Quinn.

Thelma L. Russell died testate on September 8, 1965, leaving a validly executed holographic will written on a small card. The front of the card reads:

Turn
the card   March 18–1957
        I leave everything
        I own Real &
        Personal to Chester
        H. Quinn & Roxy Russell
        Thelma L. Russell

The reverse side reads:

        My ($10.) Ten dollar gold
        Piece & diamonds I leave
        to Georgia Nan Russell.
        Alverata, Geogia [sic]

Chester H. Quinn was a close friend and companion of testatrix, who for over 25 years prior to her death had resided in one of the living units on her property and had stood in a relation of personal trust and confidence toward her. Roxy Russell was testatrix' pet dog which was alive on the date of the execution of testatrix' will but predeceased her.[15] Plaintiff is testatrix' niece and her only heir-at-law.

In her petition for determination of heirship plaintiff alleges, inter alia, that "Roxy Russell is an Airedale dog";[16] that section 27 enumerates those entitled to take by will; that "Dogs are not included among those listed in . . . Section 27. Not even Airedale dogs"; that the gift of one-half of the residue of testatrix' estate to Roxy Russell is invalid and void; and that plaintiff was entitled to such one-half as testatrix' sole heir-at-law.

At the hearing on the petition, plaintiff introduced without objection extrinsic evidence establishing that Roxy Russell was testatrix' Airedale dog which died on June 9, 1958. To this end plaintiff, in addition to an independent witness, called defendant. . . . Upon redirect examination, counsel for Quinn then sought to introduce evidence of the latter's relationship with testatrix "in the event that your Honor feels that there is any necessity for further ascertainment of the intent above and beyond the document." Plaintiff's objections on the ground that it was inadmissible under the statute of wills and the parol evidence rule "because there is no ambiguity" . . . were overruled. Over plaintiff's objection, counsel for Quinn also introduced certain documentary evidence consisting of testatrix' address book and a certain quitclaim deed "for the purpose of demonstrating the intention on the part of the deceased that she not die intestate." Of all this extrinsic evidence only the following infinitesimal portion of Quinn's testimony relates to care of the dog: "Q. [Counsel for Quinn] Prior to the first Roxy's death did you ever discuss with Miss Russell taking care of Roxy if anything should ever happen to her? A. Yes." Plaintiff carefully preserved an objection running to all of the above line of testimony and at the conclusion of the hearing moved to strike such evidence. Her motion was denied.

The trial court found, so far as is here material, that it was the intention of the testatrix "that Chester H. Quinn was to receive her entire estate, excepting the gold coin and diamonds bequeathed to" plaintiff and that Quinn "was to care for the dog, Roxy Russell, in the event of Testatrix's death. The language contained in the Will concerning the dog, Roxy Russell, was precatory in nature only, and merely indicative of the wish,

---

[15] Actually the record indicates the existence of two Roxy Russells. The original Roxy was an Airedale dog which testatrix owned at the time she made her will, but which, according to Quinn, died after having had a fox tail removed from its nose, and which, according to the testimony of one Arthur Turner, owner of a pet cemetery, was buried on June 9, 1958. Roxy was replaced with another dog (breed not indicated in the record before us) which, although it answered to the name Roxy, was, according to the record, in fact registered with the American Kennel Club as "Russel's [sic] Royal Kick Roxy."

[16] In his "Petition for Probate of Holographic Will and for Letters of Administration with the Will Annexed," Quinn included under the names, ages and residences of the devisees and legatees of testatrix (§ 326, subd. (3)) the following: "Roxy Russell, A 9 year old Airedale dog, [residing at] 4422 Palm Avenue, La Mesa, Calif."

desire and concern of Testatrix that Chester H. Quinn was to care for the dog, Roxy Russell, subsequent to Testatrix's death."[17] The court concluded that testatrix intended to and did make an absolute and outright gift to Mr. Quinn of all the residue of her estate, adding: "There occurred no lapse as to any portion of the residuary gift to Chester H. Quinn by reason of the language contained in the Will concerning the dog, Roxy Russell, such language not having the effect of being an attempted outright gift or gift in trust to the dog. The effect of such language is merely to indicate the intention of Testatrix that Chester H. Quinn was to take the entire residuary estate and to use whatever portion thereof as might be necessary to care for and maintain the dog, Roxy Russell." Judgment was entered accordingly. This appeal followed.

Plaintiff's position before us may be summarized thusly: That the gift of one-half of the residue of the estate to testatrix' dog was clear and unambiguous; that such gift was void and the property subject thereof passed to plaintiff under the laws of intestate succession; and that the court erred in admitting the extrinsic evidence offered by Quinn but that in any event the uncontradicted evidence in the record did not cure the invalidity of the gift. . . .

First, as we have said many times: "The paramount rule in the construction of wills, to which all other rules must yield, is that a will is to be construed according to the intention of the testator as expressed therein, and this intention must be given effect as far as possible." (Estate of Wilson (1920) 184 Cal. 63, 66–67, 193 P. 581, 582.) [The] objective [of the rule] is to ascertain what the testator meant by the language he used.

When the language of a will is ambiguous or uncertain resort may be had to extrinsic evidence in order to ascertain the intention of the testator. We have said that extrinsic evidence is admissible "to explain any ambiguity arising on the face of a will, or to resolve a latent ambiguity which does not so appear." (Estate of Torregano (1960) 54 Cal. 2d 234, 246, 5 Cal. Rptr. 137, 144, 352 P.2d 505, 512. . . .) A latent ambiguity is

---

[17] The memorandum decision elaborates on this point, stating in part: "The obvious concern of the human who loves her pet is to see that it is properly cared for by someone who may be trusted to honor that concern and through resources the person may make available in the will to carry out this entreaty, desire, wish, recommendation or prayer. This, in other words, is a most logical example of a precatory provision. It is the only logical conclusion one can come to which would not do violence to the apparent intent of Mrs. Russell."

The trial court found further: "Testatrix intended that Georgia Nan Russell Hembree was not to have any other real or personal property belonging to Testatrix, other than the gold coin and diamonds." This finding also was elaborated on in the memorandum decision: "In making the will it is apparent she had Georgia on her mind. While there is other evidence in the case about Thelma Russell's frame of mind concerning her real property and her niece, which was admitted by the Court, over counsel's vigorous objection, because it concerned testatrix' frame of mind, a condition relevant to the material issue of intent, nevertheless this additional evidence was not necessary to this Court in reaching its conclusion." The additional evidence referred to included an address book of testatrix upon which she had written: "Chester, Don't let Augusta and Georgia have one penny of my place if it takes it all to fight it in Court. Thelma."

one which is not apparent on the face of the will but is disclosed by some fact collateral to it. . . .

. . . Extrinsic evidence always may be introduced initially in order to show that under the circumstances of a particular case the seemingly clear language of a will describing either the subject of or the object of the gift actually embodies a latent ambiguity for it is only by the introduction of extrinsic evidence that the existence of such an ambiguity can be shown. Once shown, such ambiguity may be resolved by extrinsic evidence. . . .

A patent ambiguity is an uncertainty which appears on the face of the will. . . . "When an uncertainty arises upon the face of a will as to the meaning of any of its provisions, the testator's intent is to be ascertained from the words of the will, but the circumstances of the execution thereof may be taken into consideration, excluding the oral declarations of the testator as to his intentions." (Estate of Salmonski, . . . 38 Cal. 2d 199, 214, 238 P.2d 966, 975.) . . .

In order to determine initially whether the terms of *any written instrument* are clear, definite and free from ambiguity the court must examine the instrument in the light of the circumstances surrounding its execution so as to ascertain what the parties meant by the words used. Only then can it be determined whether the seemingly clear language of the instrument is in fact ambiguous. "Words are used in an endless variety of contexts. Their meaning is not subsequently attached to them by the reader but is formulated by the writer and can only be found by interpretation in the light of all the circumstances that reveal the sense in which the writer used the words. The exclusion of parol evidence regarding such circumstances merely because the words do not appear ambiguous to the reader can easily lead to the attribution to a written instrument of a meaning that was never intended." (Universal Sales Corp. v. Cal., etc., Mfg. Co. (1942) 20 Cal. 2d 751, 776, 128 P.2d 665, 679 (Traynor, J., concurring).) . . . [S]ee also Corbin, The Interpretation of Words and the Parol Evidence Rule (1965) 50 Cornell L.Q. 161, 164: "[W]hen a judge refuses to consider relevant extrinsic evidence on the ground that the meaning of written words is to him plain and clear, his decision is formed by and wholly based upon the completely extrinsic evidence of his own personal education and experience". . . .

The foregoing reflects the modern development of rules governing interpretation. . . . While "still surviving to us, in many Courts, from the old formalism . . . [is] the rule that you *cannot disturb a plain meaning*" (9 Wigmore [on Evidence § 2462, at 191 (3d ed. 1940)], original emphasis) nevertheless decisions and authorities like those cited above bespeak the current tendency to abandon the "stiff formalism of earlier interpretation" and to show the meaning of words even though no ambiguity appears on the face of the document. . . .

Accordingly, we think it is self-evident that in the interpretation of a will, a court cannot determine whether the terms of the will are clear and definite in the first place until it considers the circumstances under which the will was made so that the judge may be placed in the position of the testator whose language he is interpreting. . . . Failure to enter upon such an inquiry is failure to recognize that the "ordinary standard or 'plain meaning,' is simply the meaning of the people who did *not* write the document." (9 Wigmore, op. cit. supra, § 2462, p. 191.) . . .

. . . [E]xtrinsic evidence of the circumstances under which a will is made (except evidence expressly excluded by statute) may be considered by the court in ascertaining what the testator meant by the words used in the will. If in the light of such extrinsic evidence, the provisions of the will are reasonably susceptible of two or more meanings claimed to have been intended by the testator, "an uncertainty arises upon the face of a will" . . . and extrinsic evidence relevant to prove any of such meanings [other than oral declarations of the testator as to his intentions] is admissible. . . . If, on the other hand, in the light of such extrinsic evidence, the provisions of the will are not reasonably susceptible of two or more meanings, there is no uncertainty arising upon the face of the will . . . and any proffered evidence attempting to show an intention *different* from that expressed by the words therein, giving them the only meaning to which they are reasonably susceptible, is inadmissible. In the latter case the provisions of the will are to be interpreted according to such meaning. In short, . . . it cannot always be determined whether the will is ambiguous or not until the surrounding circumstances are first considered. . . .

Examining testatrix' will in the light of the foregoing rules, we arrive at the following conclusions: Extrinsic evidence offered by plaintiff was admitted without objection and indeed would have been properly admitted over objection to raise and resolve the latent ambiguity as to Roxy Russell and ultimately to establish that Roxy Russell was a dog. Extrinsic evidence of the surrounding circumstances was properly considered in order to ascertain what testatrix meant by the words of the will, including the words: "I leave everything I own Real & Personal to Chester H. Quinn & Roxy Russell" or as those words can now be read "to Chester H. Quinn and my dog Roxy Russell."

However, viewing the will in the light of the surrounding circumstances as are disclosed by the record, we conclude that the will cannot reasonably be construed as urged by Quinn and determined by the trial court as providing that testatrix intended to make an absolute and outright gift of the entire residue of her estate to Quinn who was "to use whatever portion thereof as might be necessary to care for and maintain the dog." No words of the will gave the entire residuum to Quinn, much less indicate that the provision for the dog is merely precatory in nature. Such an interpretation is not consistent with a disposition which by its language leaves the residuum in equal shares to Quinn and the dog. A disposition in equal shares to two beneficiaries cannot be equated with a disposition of the whole to one of them who may use "whatever portion thereof as might be necessary" on behalf of the other. . . . Neither can the bare language of a gift of one-half of the residue to the dog be so expanded as to mean a gift to Quinn in trust for the care of the dog. . . .

Accordingly, since in the light of the extrinsic evidence introduced below, the terms of the will are not reasonably susceptible of the meaning claimed by Quinn to have been intended by testatrix, the extrinsic evidence offered to show such an intention should have been excluded by the trial court. Upon an independent examination of the will we conclude that the trial court's interpretation of the terms thereof was erroneous. Interpreting the provisions relating to testatrix' residuary estate in accordance with the only meaning to which they are reasonably susceptible, we conclude that testatrix intended to make a disposition of all of the residue of the estate to Quinn and the dog in equal shares; therefore, as tenants in common. . . . As a dog cannot be the beneficiary under a will . . . the attempted gift to Roxy Russell is void.[18] . . .

There remains only the necessity of determining the effect of the void gift to the dog upon the disposition of the residuary estate. That portion of any residuary estate that is the subject of a lapsed gift to one of the residuary beneficiaries remains undisposed of by the will and passes to the heirs-at-law. . . . The rule is equally applicable with respect to a void gift to one of the residuary beneficiaries. . . . Therefore, notwithstanding testatrix' expressed intention to limit the extent of her gift by will to plaintiff . . . one-half of the residuary estate passes to plaintiff as testatrix' only heir-at-law (§ 225). We conclude that the residue of testatrix' estate should be distributed in equal shares to Chester H. Quinn and Georgia Nan Russell Hembree, testatrix' niece.

The judgment is reversed and the cause is remanded with directions to the trial court to set aside the findings of fact and conclusions of law; to make and file findings of fact and conclusions of law in conformity with the views herein expressed; and to enter judgment accordingly. . . .

[The dissenting opinion of McComb, J., is omitted.]

---

[18] As a consequence, the fact that Roxy Russell predeceased the testatrix is of no legal import. As appears, we have disposed of the issue raised by plaintiff's frontal attack on the eligibility of the dog to take a testamentary gift and therefore need not concern ourselves with the novel question as to whether the death of the dog during the lifetime of the testatrix resulted in a lapsed gift. (§ 92.)

NOTES

1. *Testator's intent.* Are the words of the will in the principal case capable of bearing the meaning attributed to them by the court? Is the court correct that there is no other reasonable interpretation? Does the court's reading of the will make sense?

The New Jersey courts have developed a doctrine of "probable intent" which aims to discover and carry out the disposition that the testator probably would have wished had he or she foreseen the circumstances that actually arose. This doctrine allows courts considerable flexibility to consider the testator's direct statements of testamentary intent outside the will. See Wilson v. Flowers, 277 A.2d 199 (N.J. 1971) (admitting direct statements of intent "first to show if there is an ambiguity and second, if one exists, to shed light on the testator's actual intent"). In Engle v. Siegel, 377 A.2d 892 (N.J.1977), a married couple executed reciprocal wills which provided that, in the event the husband and wife died in a common disaster (which actually occurred), their residuary estates were to go to the husband's mother (Rose Siegel) and the wife's mother in equal shares. Rose Siegel predeceased both spouses. Relying on oral statements of intent made by the couple to the attorney who drafted their wills, the court held that Rose Siegel's share of both estates went to her surviving children rather than to the surviving residuary beneficiary. For a discussion of lapse, see infra p. 482.

2. *Misdescriptions.* Frequently wills contain garbled or mistaken descriptions of beneficiaries. To prevent a bequest from going to an unintended beneficiary, many courts admit extrinsic evidence both to discover an ambiguity and then to resolve it. See Estate of Kremlick, 331 N.W.2d 228 (Mich.1983) (residuary gift to "Michigan Cancer Society" claimed both by an organization of that name and by the American Cancer Society, Michigan Division, commonly known as the Michigan Cancer Society, in which testator took special interest); Legare v. Legare, 490 S.E.2d 369 (Ga. 1997) (residuary gift to "John Houston Legare"; testator had no relative of that name but did have two nephews, one named John Edward Legare and the other James Houston Legare); but cf. Vadman v. American Cancer Society, 615 P.2d 500 (Wash.App.1980) (no ambiguity in gift to "National Cancer Foundation"). A few courts go even further. In Estate of Gibbs, 111 N.W.2d 413 (Wis.1961), a married couple made bequests to "Robert J. Krause, now of 4708 North 46th Street, Milwaukee." Extrinsic evidence showed that the intended beneficiary was Robert W. Krause, a longtime friend and employee. The court rejected the claim of a stranger meeting the literal description in the will, and concluded that "details of identification, particularly such matters as middle initials, street addresses, and the like," should be disregarded "when the proof establishes to the highest degree of certainty that a mistake was, in fact, made."

Another technique for correcting a mistaken description is simply to strike part of the description without adding any new words. For example, if a will purports to devise property at "No. 304 Harrison Avenue," and the testator owned property at No. 317 (but not at No. 304), the court may disregard the number and give effect to the devise of property owned by the testator. See Arnheiter v. Arnheiter, 125 A.2d 914 (N.J. Super. 1956). Of course, this approach works only if the remaining words adequately express the testator's intent. Cf. Patch v. White, 117 U.S. 210 (1886) (interpreting devise of Lot No. 6 in Square 403, which testator did not own, to mean Lot No. 3 in Square 406, which he did). Why are courts inclined to cure a mistake by striking words from the will but not by substituting other words?

3. *Omitted provisions.* A recurring problem involves language that is mistakenly omitted from a will, due to clerical error or inept drafting. Courts generally refuse to admit extrinsic evidence to establish the terms of an omitted provision or to change the words of the will. See Burnett v. First Commercial Trust Co., 939 S.W.2d 827 (Ark. 1997) (omitted residuary gift); Knupp v. District of Columbia, 578 A.2d 702 (D.C. 1990) (same, resulting in escheat); Estate of Blankenship, 518 S.E.2d 615 (S.C. App. 1999) (will left entire estate to three of testator's children, subject to simultaneous death condition which did not in fact occur, and expressly disinherited fourth child; estate passed to all four children by intestacy). Occasionally, however, courts admit extrinsic evidence to correct an omission or other mistake while purporting to resolve an ambiguity. See Painter v. Coleman, 566 S.E.2d 588 (W. Va. 2002) (disregarding simultaneous death condition); Estate of Lohr, 497 N.W.2d 730 (Wis.App.1993) (botched survival condition); Wilson v. First Florida Bank, 498 So.2d 1289 (Fla.App.1986) (missing description of trust property); Estate of Ikuta, 639 P.2d 400 (Haw.1981) (reference to "oldst" instead of "youngest" child).

4. *Patent and latent ambiguities.* The court in *Russell* notes the distinction between a *patent ambiguity* appearing on the face of the will and a *latent ambiguity* which emerges only from a consideration of circumstances outside the will. For example, if a will contains two inconsistent provisions purporting to devise the same parcel of property to different beneficiaries, the ambiguity is patent. In contrast, a devise to "cousin Mary" may seem clear enough until it is revealed that the testator had two cousins with the same given name, or perhaps a niece named Mary and a cousin named Martha; here the ambiguity is latent. Some courts hold that extrinsic evidence is admissible to resolve a latent ambiguity but not a patent one. See, e.g., Estate of Mousel, 715 N.W.2d 490 (Neb. 2006); Estate of Click v. Estate of Click, 40 A.3d 1105 (Md. App. 2012). This rule, often repeated but seldom subjected to critical analysis, rests on the dubious ground that it is necessary in the former case (but not the latter) to look beyond the four corners of the will to discover the existence of the ambiguity in the first place. However, the prevailing modern trend, as the *Russell* court observed, is to allow extrinsic evidence "to explain any ambiguity arising on the face of a will, or to resolve a latent ambiguity which does not so appear." As another court stated, "the distinction between patent and latent ambiguities is not useful, and it is proper to admit extrinsic evidence to resolve any ambiguity." Univ. of Southern Indiana Found. v.

Baker, 843 N.E.2d 528 (Ind. 2006). See also Restatement (Third) of Property: Wills and Other Donative Transfers § 11.2 cmt. d (2003).

———————

Although courts demonstrate considerable agility in interpreting ambiguous testamentary provisions, they have categorically refused to reform the terms of a will to cure mistakes on the part of the testator or the attorney who drafted the will. In this regard, the statement in Mahoney v. Grainger, supra p. 454, is typical:

> A will duly executed and allowed by the court must under the statute of wills . . . be accepted as the final expression of the intent of the person executing it. The fact that it was not in conformity to the instructions given to the draftsman who prepared it or that he made a mistake does not authorize a court to reform or alter it or remould it by amendments.

(For a rare instance of a court openly granting reformation, see Matter of Snide, supra p. 302.)

In recent years the no-reformation rule has come under sustained criticism. Commentators have observed that the rule applies only to wills; if the terms of a deed of gift, inter vivos trust, beneficiary designation, or other instrument of transfer fail to express the transferor's intent accurately, courts routinely reform the terms of the instrument as an equitable remedy to prevent unjust enrichment. "Why, then," they ask, "does equity refuse to remedy unjust enrichment in the case of a mistaken will?" Langbein & Waggoner, Reformation of Wills on the Ground of Mistake: Change of Direction in American Law?, 130 U. Pa. L. Rev. 521 (1982). One possible answer involves the "inherently suspect" nature of extrinsic evidence of a deceased testator's intent, but Langbein and Waggoner point out that the same objections are met in the nonprobate context by imposing a heightened evidentiary standard, and they find "no principled way to reconcile the exclusion of extrinsic evidence in the law of wills with the rule of admissibility in the law of nonprobate transfers." In their view, the anomalous treatment of wills flows from deeply rooted judicial attitudes toward compliance with the wills act formalities. Instead of excluding extrinsic evidence and foreclosing the opportunity to rectify mistakes, they argue, courts should deal with potentially unreliable evidence "by admitting it and testing it against the higher-than-ordinary standard of proof that has worked so well in the law of nonprobate transfers."

The arguments advanced by Langbein and Waggoner have led to a reappraisal of the no-reformation rule, which no longer enjoys unquestioning acceptance. In some quarters, the rule has been expressly repudiated. Section 12.1 of the Restatement (Third) of Property: Wills and Other Donative Transfers (2003)—for which Waggoner and Langbein served as Reporter and Associate Reporter, respectively—expressly approves judicial reformation of wills and other "donative documents" to cure mistakes of fact or law. The same theme is echoed in the Uniform Probate Code and the Uniform Trust Code. See UPC 2–805; UTC § 415.

Uniform Probate Code (2011)

§ 2–805. Reformation to Correct Mistakes.

The court may reform the terms of a governing instrument, even if unambiguous, to conform the terms to the transferor's intention if it is proved by clear and convincing evidence what the transferor's intention was and that the terms of the governing instrument were affected by a mistake of fact or law, whether in expression or inducement.

NOTES

1. *Judicial reformation of wills and nonprobate transfers.* A judicial power of reformation also implies that courts may consider "direct evidence of intention contradicting the plain meaning of the text as well as other evidence of intention." Restatement (Third) of Property: Wills and Other Donative Transfers § 12.1 (2003); see id. cmt. d (disapproving "plain meaning rule" to the extent it "purports to exclude extrinsic evidence of the donor's intention"). The Restatement offers the following general rationale for a judicial power of reformation:

When a donative document is unambiguous, evidence suggesting that the terms of the document vary from intention is inherently suspect but possibly correct. The law deals with situations of inherently suspicious but possibly correct evidence in either of two ways. One is to exclude the evidence altogether, in effect denying a remedy in cases in which the evidence is genuine and persuasive. The other is to consider the evidence, but guard against giving effect to fraudulent or mistaken evidence by imposing an above-normal standard of proof. In choosing between exclusion and high-safeguard allowance of extrinsic evidence, this Restatement adopts the latter. Only high-safeguard allowance of extrinsic evidence achieves the primary objective of giving effect to the donor's intention. . . .

Equity rests the rationale for reformation on two related grounds: giving effect to the donor's intention and preventing unjust enrichment. The claim of an unintended taker is an unjust claim. Using the equitable remedy of reformation to correct a mistake is necessary to prevent unjustly enriching the mistaken beneficiary at the expense of the intended beneficiary. [Id. cmt. b.]

The expansion of judicial reformation to wills is explained as follows:

> The reformation doctrine for donative documents other than wills is well established. . . . This section unifies the law of wills and will substitutes by applying to wills the standards that govern other donative documents. Until recently, courts have not allowed reformation of wills. The denial of a reformation remedy for wills was predicated on observance of the Statute of Wills, which requires that wills be executed in accordance with certain formalities. . . . Reforming a will, it was feared, would often require inserting language that was not executed in accordance with the statutory formalities. . . .

> The trend away from insisting on strict compliance with statutory formalities is based on a growing acceptance of the broader principle that mistake, whether in execution or in expression, should not be allowed to defeat intention. A common principle underlies the principle of this section, which authorizes reformation of unambiguous donative documents (including wills) to correct mistakes, and the movement (1) to excuse defective execution . . . and (2) to authorize insertion of language to resolve ambiguities in donative documents . . . . [Id. cmt. c.]

2. *Judicial response.* Even without express statutory authorization, a few courts have showed signs of willingness to reform wills. See Estate of Herceg, 747 N.Y.S.2d 901 (Sur. 2002) (interpolating name of beneficiary inadvertently omitted from will); Trust under Will of Kamp, 790 N.Y.S.2d 852 (Sur. 2005) (reforming testamentary trust to preserve disabled beneficiary's Medicaid eligibility); see also Erickson v. Erickson, 716 A.2d 92 (Conn. 1998) (extrinsic evidence of testator's intent admissible to rebut statutory presumption that will was revoked by subsequent marriage; where testator was misled into making a testamentary disposition that would not otherwise have occurred, court saw "no discernible policy difference" between mistake induced by fraud and mistake caused by scrivener's innocent misrepresentation; in both cases "the testamentary process is distorted by the interference of a third person who misleads the testator into making a testamentary disposition that would not otherwise have occurred"). Others, however, adhere to the traditional no-reformation rule. In Flannery v. McNamara, 738 N.E.2d 739 (Mass. 2000), the only beneficiary named in the will was testator's predeceased wife. Consequently the gift lapsed and the estate passed by intestacy to testator's cousins. The court held that the will was "not ambiguous" and refused to allow the wife's sisters to introduce extrinsic evidence in support of their claim that testator intended to include them as contingent beneficiaries. In rejecting the Restatement's approach, the court stated that reformation of wills would "violate the Statute of Wills" and would "open the floodgates of litigation" for disgruntled individuals claiming that they were omitted by mistake. Had the court accepted the Restatement's approach, what sort of factual showing would the wife's sisters have had to make in order to prevail?

What sort of mistakes "in expression or inducement" are amenable to reformation? Consider the following observations concerning the scope of the judicial reformation power:

> A mistake of expression arises when a donative document includes a term that misstates the donor's intention . . . , fails to include a term that was intended to be included . . . , or includes a term that was not intended to be included . . . . A mistake in the inducement arises when a donative document includes a term that was intended to be included or fails to include a term that was not intended to be included, but the intention to include or not to include the term was the product of a mistake of fact or law . . . . [Restatement (Third) of Property: Wills and Other Donative Transfers § 12.1 cmt. i (2003).]

> Reformation is a rule governing mistakes in the content of a donative document, in a case in which the donative document does not say what the transferor meant it to say. Accordingly, reformation is not available to correct a failure to prepare and execute a document . . . . Nor is reformation available to modify a document in order to give effect to the donor's post-execution change of mind . . . or to compensate for other changes in circumstances . . . . Id. cmt. h.]

3. *Tax consequences.* In cases involving revocable trusts and other will substitutes, courts frequently grant reformation to avoid unintended tax consequences. A leading example is Berman v. Sandler, 399 N.E.2d 17 (Mass. 1980), in which the drafter of a revocable trust amendment mistakenly deleted the operative provisions of a marital trust; based on clear and convincing evidence of the settlor's intended disposition, the court reinstated the deleted provisions. See also Loeser v. Talbot, 589 N.E.2d 301 (Mass.1992) (salvaging marital deduction by transposing powers of appointment); Estate of Branigan, 609 A.2d 431 (N.J.1992) (severing trusts to obtain favorable generation-skipping transfer tax treatment). Even without express statutory authorization, a few courts go further and openly reform a will to ameliorate an unforeseen tax burden. See Estate of Keller, 46 P.3d 1135 (Kan. 2002); Shawmut Bank v. Buckley, 665 N.E.2d 29 (Mass.1996); In re Application of Choate, 533 N.Y.S.2d 272 (Sur. 1988). Why might a court be especially willing to reform a will if the mistake to be cured relates solely to tax consequences? Cf. UPC § 2–806 ("To achieve the transferor's tax objectives, the court may modify the terms of a governing instrument in a manner that is not contrary to the transferor's probable intention. The court may provide that the modification has retroactive effect.")

4. *Goals and methods of interpretation.* There is a burgeoning literature concerning the interpretation of wills. Most commentators begin by recognizing that words are at best imperfect signifiers of testamentary wishes and that the words of a will may suggest different meanings to different people. The goals and methods of interpretation give rise to numerous questions with many possible answers. In interpreting a will, should courts seek to discover

the testator's actual, subjective intent or should they focus instead on what a reasonable person would understand the testator's words to mean? Should the meaning ascribed to words depend on the particular circumstances of the testator? If so, what extrinsic evidence should be taken into account to illuminate the intended meaning? Should it matter whether the will was drafted by the testator or by an attorney? To what extent should the fairness of the outcome be taken into account? For discussions of these and other matters, see Fellows, In Search of Donative Intent, 73 Iowa L. Rev. 611 (1988) (abandoning search for subjective intent in favor of "imputed intent" guided by "equal planning under the law" and "family preference"); Robertson, Myth and Reality—Or Is It "Perception and Taste"?—in the Reading of Donative Documents, 61 Fordham L. Rev. 1045 (1993) (advocating "circumstanced external approach" based on the words of the will and circumstances surrounding its execution); Baron, Intention, Interpretation, and Stories, 42 Duke L.J. 630 (1992) (noting potential conflict between testator's "subjective thoughts and objective words" and arguing that "doctrinal obsession" with the words of the will is based on "oversimplified and inaccurate presuppositions about the connections between thought and language and between the individual and the world of others"); Greenawalt, A Pluralist Approach to Interpretation: Wills and Contracts, 42 San Diego L. Rev. 533 (2005) (arguing that "judges will sometimes resolve what counts as a text's meaning without settling the question of writer's intent" and that "proceeding in this manner is desirable").

For further discussions of doctrine and theory, see Holmes, The Theory of Legal Interpretation, 12 Harv. L. Rev. 417 (1899); Kales, Considerations Preliminary to the Practice of the Art of Interpreting Writings—More Especially Wills, 28 Yale L.J. 33 (1918); Warren, Interpretation of Wills, 49 Harv. L. Rev. 689 (1936); Chafee, The Disorderly Conduct of Words, 41 Colum. L. Rev. 381 (1941); see also Power, Wills: A Primer of Interpretation and Construction, 51 Iowa L. Rev. 75 (1965).

2. CHANGES IN PROPERTY HOLDINGS

Dispositions under a will are classified as specific, demonstrative, general, or residuary. They are defined as follows:

> (1) A *specific* devise or bequest is a gift of a specific item of property which is identifiable and distinguishable from the rest of the testator's estate. Examples include gifts of "the house and land located at 31 Garden Street," "the roll-top desk in my study," and "my savings account at the First National Bank."

> (2) A *general* devise or bequest is a gift of a certain amount or quantity which is payable from general assets of the estate and which does not require delivery of any particular property or payment from any designated source. The most common example of a general bequest is a gift of a specified sum of money.

(3) A *demonstrative* devise or bequest is a gift of a specified amount or quantity to be paid primarily from a designated source and ultimately, if necessary, from general assets of the estate. An example of a demonstrative bequest is a gift of "the sum of $10,000, payable from my savings account at the First National Bank." Demonstrative bequests, though rare, do occasionally occur. See, e.g., Estate of Lung, 692 A.2d 1349 (D.C. 1997).

(4) A *residuary* devise or bequest is a gift of whatever property remains in the estate after all other dispositions have been satisfied.

Classification of testamentary dispositions often becomes important for purposes of ademption and abatement.

a. Ademption

Ordinarily, a specific devise or bequest can be given effect only if the property which forms the subject matter of the gift exists as part of the probate estate. If the property has been destroyed or disposed of before death, the gift fails because there is no property on which the will can operate. This is the doctrine of ademption (or ademption by extinction). Note that ademption applies only to specific devises and bequests. (Review the classification of testamentary dispositions to see why this is so.) In this country, the prevailing view of ademption holds "that intent has nothing to do with the matter, and that the sole question is whether the subject matter of the specific legacy is in the testator's estate at his death, and if it is not the legacy is adeemed, and the legatee gets nothing." Atkinson § 134. This view, referred to as the "identity theory" of ademption, can be traced back to the leading case of Ashburner v. Macguire, 29 Eng. Rep. 62 (Ch. 1786), in which Chancellor Thurlow sought to overcome the confusion and uncertainty engendered by earlier decisions which focused on the testator's intent. The background and evolution of ademption are discussed in Warren, The History of Ademption, 25 Iowa L. Rev. 290 (1940); Page, Ademption by Extinction, 1943 Wis. L. Rev. 11; Paulus, Ademption by Extinction: Smiting Lord Thurlow's Ghost, 2 Tex. Tech. L. Rev. 195 (1971); Lundwall, The Case Against the Ademption by Extinction Rule: A Proposal for Reform, 29 Gonz. L. Rev. 105 (1993).

IN RE ESTATE OF NAKONECZNY
Supreme Court of Pennsylvania, 1974.
456 Pa. 320, 319 A.2d 893.

NIX, JUSTICE.

Michael Nakoneczny died testate on January 26, 1970, leaving a Will dated November 5, 1956 ... and two codicils dated May 4, 1966 and March 27, 1967 respectively. The Will and codicils were admitted to probate and an inventory and appraisement were filed showing a gross estate of $545,483.21. This is an appeal from the denial of exceptions filed to the Opinion, Order and Decree of Distribution by appellants, Paul Nakoneczny, son of testator, and his wife, Stella. The exceptions were dismissed and the Decree of the auditing judge was affirmed by the Court en banc on April 25, 1972. . . .

In paragraph four of his will testator provided:

Fourth: I give, devise and bequeath that certain parcel of real estate situate at 3039 Preble Avenue, Pittsburgh, Pennsylvania, which is presently operated as a tavern, together with all fixtures forming a part of the said realty and all equipment necessary to the operation of the said tavern, to my son, Paul Nakoneczny, if he survives me. It is my desire that my Executor secure, if at all possible, the transfer of the liquor license to my son, Paul Nakoneczny, if he is then living.

In November of 1956, testator owned the building situated at 3039 Preble Avenue, Pittsburgh. A portion of these premises was used in the operation of a restaurant and barroom by testator and the remainder served as a dwelling for him and his family. Decedent operated this business until January 1960 when he gave the business, equipment, supplies and liquor license to his son, the appellant, Paul Nakoneczny. In May of 1968, the property was acquired by the Urban Redevelopment Authority and the bulk of the proceeds were used by decedent to purchase certain bonds which he retained and remained in his possession until his death. The auditing judge found that there had been an ademption and denied appellants' claim to the bonds that had been purchased with the proceeds derived from the sale of the Preble Avenue property. We agree.

It has long since been decided in this jurisdiction that a specific legacy or devise is extinguished if the property is not in existence or does not belong to the testator at the time of his death. Soles' Estate, 451 Pa. 568, 304 A.2d 97 (1973); McFerren's Estate, 365 Pa. 490, 76 A.2d 759 (1950); Horn's Estate, 317 Pa. 49, 175 A. 414 (1934); Harshaw v. Harshaw, 184 Pa. 401, 39 A. 89 (1898); Hoke v. Herman, 21 Pa. 301 (1853); Blackstone v. Blackstone, 3 Watts 335 (1834). Testator's intent is not relevant where the property devised or bequeathed in his will is not part of his estate at death. Where the legacy has been determined to be specific "[t]he legatee is entitled to the very thing bequeathed if it be possible for the executor to give it to him; but if not, he cannot have money in place of it. This results from an inflexible rule of law applied to the mere fact that the thing bequeathed does not exist, and it is not founded on any presumed intention of the testator." Horn's Estate, supra, 317 Pa. at 55, 175 A. at 416; Hoke v. Herman, supra, 21 Pa. at 305. . . . This rule is equally applicable where the specifically devised or bequeathed property is removed from testator during his lifetime by an involuntary act or by operation of law.[19] Harshaw v. Harshaw, supra; Pleasants' Appeal, 77 Pa. 356 (1875). Thus, where it is established that the bequest or devise was specific and the nonexistence of the item in the testator's estate at the time of death, an ademption results.

The only issue crucial to the resolution of the problem presented is whether the devise of the realty in this case was specific. A specific devise is a gift by will of a specific parcel which is identified and distinguished from all other parcels of land, and which may be satisfied only by delivery of the particular parcel of property. Soles' Estate, supra 451 Pa. at 573, 304 A.2d 97; Snyder's Estate, 217 Pa. 71, 66 A. 157 (1907). Appellant first argues that this was a demonstrative devise and thus not subject to ademption. He argues that paragraphs seven[20] and eight[21] evidence a clear intention on the part of decedent to assure Paul's right to the proceeds in the event the Preble Avenue property was sold. Although, as has been stated, intention is not relevant on the question of ademption, it is relevant when the issue to be determined is whether the legacy is demonstrative or specific. Shearer's Estate, 346 Pa. 97, 29 A.2d 535 (1943); Walls v. Stewart, 16 Pa. 275, 281–282 (1851). Further, that intention must be gathered not only from the language used in creating the bequest or devise but from the provisions of the will as a whole, and if there is doubt, courts are inclined to find a demonstrative rather than a specific legacy, devise or bequest. Shearer's Estate, supra 346 Pa. at 101, 29 A.2d 535. See also Crawford's Estate, 293 Pa. 570, 574, 143 A. 214 (1928). Here, however, the language of paragraph four leaves no question of the intent to create a specific devise. Nor do we find any merit in the suggestion that paragraphs 7 and 8 in any way alters this conclusion. Clearly paragraphs 7 and 8 were merely limiting the power of the Executor to prevent the sale of the property that was designated in paragraph 4 as the subject of the specific devise provided that the property was an asset of the estate at the time of death. In our judgment, these paragraphs strengthen rather than weaken the view that testator intended a specific devise.

---

[19] "It was once thought that ademption was dependent on intention, and it was, therefore, held in old days that when a change was effected by public authority, or without the will of the testator, ademption did not follow. But for many years, that has ceased to be law. . . . What courts look to now is the fact of change. That ascertained, they do not trouble themselves about the reason for the change." In re Brann, 219 N.Y. 263, 114 N.E. 404, 405 (1916) (Cardozo, J.).

[20] "Paragraph Seventh: Subject to the provisions of Paragraphs Third and Fourth, I authorize my Executor to sell any and all real estate of which I die seised, at public or private sale, for such prices and upon such terms and conditions as it shall deem advisable, and to make, execute and deliver good and sufficient deed or deeds there."

[21] "Paragraph Eighth: Subject to the provisions of Paragraphs Third and Fourth, I authorize my Executor to make distribution of my estate in kind, in cash, or partly in kind and partly in cash, as my Executor shall believe advisable."

Appellant's reliance upon *Shearer's Estate*, supra, is misplaced. In *Shearer's Estate*, the testator created by will a trust for the benefit of his son, for and during the lifetime of the son. After describing his farm along with the stock and personal property thereon as the corpus of the trust, testator provided: "[t]he value of the said farm and contents I fix at the sum of Six Thousand Dollars, so that my said son shall receive the use and benefit of said amount out of my estate." From other provisions in the document it was clear that testator was attempting to equalize the distributions among his children. This Court there properly held:

> . . . it is quite obvious that the intention of testator was that his son Clayton should, in all events, receive the benefit of an amount of $6,000, his paramount desire being to equalize the shares of his children after taking into consideration the amounts that some of them had received in his lifetime. As Jacob had already obtained $6,000, and each daughter $2,000, he gave to each daughter $4,000 more and to Clayton the farm and its contents, the value of which he expressly fixed at the sum of $6,000 "so that my said son shall receive the use and benefit of *said amount* out of my estate." 346 Pa. at 101, 29 A.2d at 537.

As evident as testator's "demonstrative" intent was in *Shearer*, the intent of this testator to make a specific devise is equally as apparent. The fourth paragraph fails to express any intention to carry with it the proceeds from a possible sale of the subject real estate.

Appellant's reliance upon Frost's Estate, 354 Pa. 223, 47 A.2d 219 (1946) is also of no avail. In *Frost's Estate*, supra, where testatrix provided a gift to her brother and sisters of the proceeds of her General Motors stock and prior to death sold the stock, however the funds were traceable, we held that the gift was not adeemed. Our decision in *Frost* was a recognition of a distinction between a gift of stock and a gift of its proceeds. Consistent with the decisions in a number of other jurisdictions we held in the latter instance where the money can be traced the gift is not adeemed and the legatee is entitled to the proceeds. Here, however, there was not a gift of the proceeds from the sale of the realty but rather a gift of the realty itself.

Finally, appellant argues that Section 14 of the Wills Act of 1947 is applicable. This section provides:

> (17) Ademption. A specific devise or bequest shall not be adeemed when the testator or the testator's estate receives an asset in exchange for the subject of the devise or bequest and the act which otherwise would have caused the ademption occurs while the testator is an adjudged incompetent. In such case the devise or bequest shall be deemed to apply to whatever was received in exchange. . . .

Appellant attempted to demonstrate that the decedent became incompetent shortly after the sale of the subject real estate and was therefore unable to make a new Will. To the contrary, there was substantial testimony in the record that indicates decedent continued to conduct his personal affairs competently for many months after the June 1968 sale. In any event there was never an adjudication of incompetency and thus this statutory provision is inapplicable. We therefore affirm the Court en banc's ruling that the devise set forth in paragraph four of the will was adeemed.

[The court rejected the argument that the ademption of the devise resulted in a breach of a contract between the testator and his son, and also rejected the daughter-in-law's claim for housekeeping, bookkeeping, and clerical services.]

Decree affirmed. Costs to be borne by the appellants.

NOTES

1. *Identity theory.* In declaring that the testator's intent is not relevant, the court adheres to the identity theory of ademption. Accord, Estate of Donovan, 20 A.3d 989 (N.H. 2011) (sale of specifically bequeathed stock); Estate of Hume, 984 S.W.2d 602 (Tenn. 1999) (foreclosure of specifically devised land); McGee v. McGee, 413 A.2d 72 (R.I.1980) (funds withdrawn from specifically bequeathed bank account by agent acting under power of attorney); Wasserman v. Cohen, 606 N.E.2d 901 (Mass. 1993) (sale of real property in revocable trust). This approach is still followed in the majority of jurisdictions, but it occasionally produces harsh results, and signs of dissatisfaction continue to appear. See, for instance, the debate between the majority and dissenters in Newbury v. McCammant, 182 N.W.2d 147 (Iowa 1970) (testator died before receiving final installment of proceeds from sale of land). To mitigate the rigors of the identity theory, courts have discovered several avenues of escape.

(a) *Classification.* The borderline between specific and general legacies is sometimes unclear. Although a bequest of "my gold watch" shouldn't cause much trouble, how about a bequest of "100 shares of AT & T stock"? (Assume the testator owned exactly 100 shares when the will was executed.) Courts are often able to avoid ademption in doubtful cases by interpreting a bequest as general rather than specific. See Blomdahl's Will, 257 N.W. 152 (Wis.1934) (bequest of 100 shares of Ohio Oil Co. stock). This has the incidental effect, however, of exposing the gift to a greater risk of abatement. In this respect, demonstrative bequests have the best of both worlds. For purposes of ademption they are treated as general bequests, while for purposes of abatement they are treated as specific bequests. See Paulus, Special and General Legacies of Securities—Whither Testator's Intent, 43 Iowa L. Rev. 467 (1958); Mechem, Specific Legacies of Unspecific Things—Ashburner v. MacGuire Reconsidered, 87 U. Pa. L. Rev. 546 (1939).

(b) *Time-of-death construction.* A testamentary gift of specific property—e.g., "my gold watch" or "the house in which I now reside"—is normally taken to refer to property owned by the testator when the will is executed. However, where the original property is no longer in existence but the testator dies owning similar property, ademption can be avoided by interpreting the will to refer to property owned at death. See Lusk's Estate, 9 A.2d 363 (Pa.1939) ("my house and lot in which I now reside"); Estate of Cooper, 237 P.2d 699 (Cal.App.1951) ("that certain Hudson Automobile, now owned by me").

(c) *Change of form.* Another avenue of escape is found in the rule that ademption does not occur if the change in the testator's property holdings is one of form and not of substance. Courts frequently invoke this rule to avoid ademption in cases involving de minimis changes of formal ownership. See Parker v. Bozian, 859 So.2d 427 (Ala. 2003) (testator closed out numbered certificate of deposit and transferred funds to new certificates issued by same bank with longer term and higher interest rate); Estate of Geary, 275 S.W.3d 835 (Tenn. App. 2008) (securities transferred in kind from specifically identified brokerage account to new account at another firm); Will of Redditt, 820 So.2d 782 (Miss. App. 2002) (specifically devised land contributed to family corporation in exchange for stock); Estate of Austin, 169 Cal.Rptr. 648 (App. 1980) (specifically bequeathed promissory note paid off, proceeds lent to new borrower). The distinction between form and substance is murky, however, and the outcome of litigation correspondingly uncertain. See Estate of Mayberry v. Mayberry, 886 S.W.2d 627 (Ark.1994) (bequest of bank account adeemed where testator closed account and used proceeds to purchase certificates of deposit from same bank); Welch v. Welch, 113 So. 197 (Miss. 1927) (testator exchanged Packard automobile owned at time of execution for Lincoln automobile owned at death; specific bequest of Packard adeemed).

Where a testator sells specifically devised real property for a note secured by a mortgage on the property, courts generally treat the sale as a change not of form but of substance. The devise is adeemed, and the devisee is not entitled to receive the note or the mortgage as substitute property. See Chapman v. Chapman, 577 A.2d 775 (Me.1990); Estate of Reposa, 427 A.2d 19 (N.H.1981). But cf. UPC § 2–606(a)(1), reproduced infra.

2. *Non-adeeming dispositions.* In a few recurring situations, the rule of automatic ademption has been abrogated by statute or judicial decision. The most common situation arises where the testator has been declared incompetent and a guardian or conservator sells property which is the subject of a specific devise or bequest, usually to obtain funds for the testator's support and care. The courts have held that ademption does not occur, at least with respect to unexpended sale proceeds that are traceable to property in the estate. See Estate of Swoyer, 439 N.W.2d 823 (S.D. 1989); Walsh v. Gillespie, 154 N.E.2d 906 (Mass.1959). Similar results have been reached where property is sold by an agent acting on behalf of an incompetent testator under a durable power of attorney. See Estate of Graham, 533 P.2d 1318 (Kan.1975); Estate of Anton, 731 N.W.2d 19 (Iowa 2007); but see Estate of Hegel, 668

N.E.2d 474 (Ohio 1996); Estate of Bauer, 700 N.W.2d 572 (Neb. 2005). Cf. UPC § 2–606(b), reproduced below. Should the non-ademption result depend on whether the testator is shown to have been incompetent at the time of the sale? Cf. Wachovia Bank & Trust Co. v. Ketchum, 333 S.E.2d 542 (N.C.App. 1985). What if an agent acting under a durable power of attorney sells specifically devised property, knowing that any proceeds remaining at death will pass to the agent under the residuary clause in the testator's will? See Crosby v. Luehrs, 669 N.W.2d 635 (Neb. 2003).

Many courts also refuse to apply an automatic rule of ademption where the subject of a specific devise or bequest is destroyed and casualty insurance proceeds are paid to the estate after death. See Estate of Wolfe, 208 N.W.2d 923 (Iowa 1973) (testator died in automobile crash; legatee of destroyed automobile entitled to insurance proceeds); White v. White, 251 A.2d 470 (N.J.Super.1969) (devisee of house partly destroyed by fire entitled to proceeds collected after death); see also Estate of Kolbinger, 529 N.E.2d 823 (Ill.App.1988) (devisee of land damaged by fire entitled to property in estate traceable to proceeds collected during life). Cf. UPC § 2–606(a)(3), reproduced infra.

Testator's will devises Blackacre to *A*, "if I am still the owner at the time of my death," and the rest of the estate to *B*. Testator subsequently enters into a contract to sell Blackacre but dies before the closing. The executor eventually completes the sale. Is *A* entitled to the proceeds, or is the devise adeemed? See Melican v. Parker, 711 S.E.2d 628 (Ga. 2011).

3. *Change in stock or securities.* Related to ademption is the issue of whether a bequest of a specified number of shares of stock carries with it additional stock acquired in a stock split or a corporate reorganization. Under the traditional approach, if the bequest is classified as specific, the legatee receives any additional shares received in a stock split or other transaction that is viewed as a mere change of form. More recently, several courts have abandoned the initial step of classification and accepted the view that "in the absence of anything manifesting a contrary intent, a legatee of a bequest of stock is entitled to the additional shares received by a testator as a result of a stock split occurring in the interval between the execution of his will and his death." Bostwick v. Hurstel, 304 N.E.2d 186 (Mass.1973) (testator sold all her original stock, but after she became incompetent her conservator purchased identical stock, which split 2–for–1 and then 3–for–1 before her death); accord, Watson v. Santalucia, 427 S.E.2d 466 (W.Va.1993); Stickley v. Carmichael, 850 S.W.2d 127 (Tenn.1992); cf. Rosenfeld v. Frank, 546 A.2d 236 (Conn.1988). Cf. UPC § 2–605 (specifying treatment of certain changes in stock or securities).

In many states the common law doctrine of ademption is subject to statutory exceptions. The anti-ademption provision of the Uniform Probate Code is especially far-reaching.

Uniform Probate Code (2011)

§ 2–606. Nonademption of Specific Devises; Unpaid Proceeds of Sale, Condemnation, or Insurance; Sale by Conservator or Agent.

(a) A specific devisee has a right to specifically devised property in the testator's estate at the testator's death and to:

(1) any balance of the purchase price, together with any security agreement, owed by a purchaser at the testator's death by reason of sale of the property;

(2) any amount of a condemnation award for the taking of the property unpaid at death;

(3) any proceeds unpaid at death on fire or casualty insurance on or other recovery for injury to the property;

(4) any property owned by the testator at death and acquired as a result of foreclosure, or obtained in lieu of foreclosure, of the security interest for a specifically devised obligation;

(5) any real property or tangible personal property owned by the testator at death which the testator acquired as a replacement for specifically devised real property or tangible personal property; and

(6) if not covered by paragraphs (1) through (5), a pecuniary devise equal to the value as of its date of disposition of other specifically devised property disposed of during the testator's lifetime but only to the extent it is established that ademption would be inconsistent with the testator's manifested plan of distribution or that at the time the will was made, the date of disposition or otherwise, the testator did not intend ademption of the devise.

(b) If specifically devised property is sold or mortgaged by a conservator or by an agent acting within the authority of a durable power of attorney for an incapacitated principal, or a condemnation award, insurance proceeds, or recovery for injury to the property is paid to a conservator or to an agent acting within the authority of a durable power of attorney for an incapacitated principal, the specific devisee has the right to a general pecuniary devise equal to the net sale price, the amount of the unpaid loan, the condemnation award, the insurance proceeds, or the recovery.

(c) The right of a specific devisee under subsection (b) is reduced by any right the devisee has under subsection (a).

(d) For the purposes of the references in subsection (b) to a conservator, subsection (b) does not apply if after the sale, mortgage, condemnation, casualty, or recovery, it was adjudicated that the testator's incapacity ceased and the testator survived the adjudication for at least one year.

(e) For the purposes of the references in subsection (b) to an agent acting within the authority of a durable power of attorney for an incapacitated principal, (i) "incapacitated principal" means a principal who is an incapacitated person, (ii) no adjudication of incapacity before death is necessary, and (iii) the acts of an agent within the authority of a durable power of attorney are presumed to be for an incapacitated principal.

NOTE

Anti-ademption statutes. Note that UPC § 2–606 imposes an overlay of limitations and exceptions while leaving the basic doctrine of ademption uncodified. Subsections (a)(1) through (a)(4) are generally consistent with judicially created avenues of escape from the common law doctrine. Subsections (a)(5) and (a)(6) did not appear in the original version of UPC § 2–606; they were added in 1990, and they have proved considerably more controversial.

Subsection (a)(5) prevents ademption where the testator dies owning real property or tangible personal property which was acquired as a "replacement" for similar property specifically devised in the will. Suppose the will includes a specific bequest to *A* of "my 1984 Ford automobile" which testator owned at the time of execution. Testator subsequently exchanges the Ford for a 1988 Buick, then sells the Buick and buys a 1993 Chrysler which she still owns at death. Is *A* entitled to the Chrysler? See UPC § 2–606 cmt. (describing provision as "a sensible 'mere change in form' principle"). Why does subsection (a)(5) exclude intangible personal property such as stocks, bonds and mutual funds?

Subsection (a)(6) represents a decisive step away from the identity theory and opens the door to a case-by-case inquiry to determine whether ademption would contravene the testator's intent. How would subsection (a)(6) affect the outcome in a case like *Nakoneczny*? See Ascher, The 1990 Uniform Probate Code: Older and Better, or More Like the Internal Revenue Code?, 77 Minn. L. Rev. 639 (1993); Fellows, Traveling the Road of Probate Reform: Finding the Way to Your Will (A Response to Professor Ascher), 77 Minn. L. Rev. 659 (1993); Alexander, Ademption and the Domain of Formality in Wills Law, 55 Alb. L. Rev. 1067 (1992).

b. Satisfaction

A legacy under an existing will may be satisfied in whole or in part by an inter vivos gift from the testator to the legatee, if the testator so intends. Indeed, if the testator is a parent of the legatee (or stands in loco parentis), there may be a rebuttable presumption that the gift is intended to satisfy the legacy. The fact that the property given is not of the same value or nature as the property described in the will supports an inference that no satisfaction was intended, but that fact is not conclusive; an intent to satisfy the legacy may be shown from the circumstances surrounding the gift, including the testator's contemporaneous statements. Traditionally, the doctrine of satisfaction (or ademption by satisfaction) applied only to legacies of personal property, not to devises of real property. In some jurisdictions, however, this distinction has been obliterated by statute. For a general discussion of the doctrine, see Barstow, Ademption by Satisfaction, 6 Wis. L. Rev. 217 (1931).

The most obvious instance of satisfaction involves a general or residuary bequest. For example, if *T* makes an inter vivos gift of $25,000 to *A* after executing a will which includes a general bequest of $50,000 to *A*, the gift may operate as a partial satisfaction if that was *T*'s intent. What if *T* gives $25,000 to *A* and $25,000 to *A*'s spouse—is *A*'s entire bequest satisfied? In the case of a specific bequest, it is usually unnecessary to consider the doctrine of satisfaction. To see why this is so, suppose *T* makes an inter vivos gift of a painting to *B* after executing a will which includes a specific bequest of the same painting to *B*. Since *T* no longer owns the property at death, *B*'s bequest is adeemed by extinction and *B* takes no additional property under *T*'s will. Cf. YIVO Institute for Jewish Research v. Zaleski, 874 A.2d 411 (Md. 2005) (testator made gifts of stock and cash worth $100,000 to charitable organization after executing will which included specific bequest of other stock of approximately equivalent value to same organization; held, gifts satisfied specific bequest in accordance with testator's intent).

The doctrine of satisfaction reflects the same policy against double portions as does the doctrine of advancements in the case of intestacy, discussed supra at p. 138. In a substantial number of states, the common law rule has been superseded by statutes which permit satisfaction "only if (i) the will provides for deduction of the gift, (ii) the testator declared in a contemporaneous writing that the gift is in satisfaction of the devise or that its value is to be deducted from the value of the devise, or (iii) the devisee acknowledged in writing that the gift is in satisfaction of the devise or that its value is to be deducted from the value of the devise." UPC § 2–609.

c. Abatement

Before distributing any assets of the estate to beneficiaries under the will, the executor must first pay all debts and other charges, including administrative expenses, taxes, and statutory allowances. Such payments implicitly limit the assets available for distribution and may reduce or eliminate one or more entire classes of testamentary dispositions. In the absence of a contrary provision in the will, testamentary dispositions usually abate in the following order of priority: (1) property not disposed of by the will, if any (i.e., intestate assets); (2) residuary gifts; (3) general gifts (and demonstrative gifts, to the extent payable from general assets); and (4) specific gifts (and demonstrative gifts, to the extent payable from the designated source). If the estate's assets are sufficient to pay some but not all of the gifts within a particular class, the gifts in the class usually abate ratably. See UPC § 3–902. To illustrate, suppose T dies owning the following assets: Blackacre (worth $20,000), which is specifically devised to A, Greenacre (worth $30,000), which is specifically devised to B, and general assets worth $150,000, of which $10,000 are left to C, $40,000 to D, and the rest to E. If the debts and other charges amount to no more than $150,000, they are payable entirely from general assets of the estate: the first $100,000 reduce E's residuary share dollar for dollar, and the next $50,000 reduce C's and D's general bequests ratably (i.e., one-fifth from C's share and four-fifths from D's share). If the debts and other charges exceed $150,000, the next $50,000 reduce A's and B's specific devises ratably (i.e., two-fifths from A's share and three-fifths from B's share). If the debts and other charges exceed the value of all assets in the estate, the estate is insolvent.

d. Exoneration

When a testator dies owning land encumbered by a mortgage or other lien, a question may arise whether the lien is to be satisfied from the land or from general assets of the estate. The question is especially acute if the land is devised to one beneficiary and the residuary estate to another. For example, suppose T dies owning Blackacre, worth $200,000 and encumbered by a recourse mortgage in the amount of $80,000; T's other assets are worth $100,000. T's will leaves Blackacre to A and the rest of the estate to B. Does A take Blackacre subject to the mortgage with a net value of $120,000, leaving a residuary gift of $100,000 for B? Or is A entitled to take Blackacre free and clear of the mortgage, leaving B with only $20,000 after the mortgage lien is satisfied? At common law, a specific devisee of land was entitled to exoneration from the residuary estate of liens securing the decedent's personal obligations. Accordingly, under the doctrine of exoneration A would take Blackacre free and clear of the mortgage. In effect, the burden of the mortgage would fall entirely on the residuary estate.

The doctrine of exoneration is open to criticism on the ground that it reflects an outdated preference for devises of land and often defeats the testator's probable intent. Many states have abandoned the common law rule in favor of a presumption against exoneration. The Uniform Probate Code provision is typical: "A specific devise passes subject to any mortgage interest existing at the date of death, without right of exoneration, regardless of a general directive in the will to pay debts." UPC § 2–607. The statutory presumption can be overcome by evidence that the testator intended for the devisee to take the property exonerated of liens. Does a presumption against exoneration correspond more closely to the testator's probable intent? In the above example, should it matter whether T took out the mortgage loan before or after executing the will? Whether T used the loan proceeds to improve Blackacre, to invest in the stock market, or to take a round-the-world cruise?

3. LAPSE

At common law, a devise or bequest failed if the intended beneficiary died before the testator. The attempted disposition was said to *lapse* if the beneficiary's death occurred after the will was executed, or to be *void* if the beneficiary was already dead when the will was executed. Today the distinction between lapsed gifts and void gifts is of little consequence; both types of gifts are treated identically for most purposes. When a lapse occurs with respect to a specific or general gift (i.e., a preresiduary gift), the property in question usually becomes part of the residuary estate and is disposed of accordingly, unless the will directs otherwise. If the sole residuary beneficiary predeceases the testator, the residuary estate passes by intestacy.

Where the residuary estate is left to two or more beneficiaries as individuals (not as a class) and some of the residuary beneficiaries survive the testator while others do not, there is a split of authority. The traditional common law rule is that the lapsed residuary portion passes by intestacy, on the ground that there can be "no residue of a residue." See Estate of Russell, supra p. 458. Accord, Estate of McFarland, 167 S.W.3d 299 (Tenn. 2005); Estate of Turpin, 19 A.3d 801 (D.C. 2011). This rule has been roundly criticized and has been rejected by several courts. See Frolich Estate, 295 A.2d 448 (N.H.1972); Estate of Jackson, 471 P.2d 278 (Ariz.1970); Niemann v. Zacharias, 176 N.W.2d 671 (Neb.1970). Today, by statute or by judicial decision, a substantial majority of jurisdictions treat a lapsed residuary portion as passing to the remaining residuary takers in proportion to their respective interests. See UPC § 2–606(b) (1969), reproduced below.

At common law, the doctrine of lapse ordinarily had no application to a class gift. A class gift is generally defined as a gift to a group whose membership may fluctuate between the time the will is executed and the testator's death. Usually, the members of the class share some common relation or characteristic; a typical example of a class gift is a bequest to the testator's children, descendants, siblings, or nieces and nephews. In the simple case of an outright testamentary gift, the members of the class usually are ascertained at the testator's death, and the class gift is distributed to the persons who are in existence and meet the class description at that time. (The treatment of class gifts of future interests is discussed infra at p. 914.) If a person dies before the testator, that person drops out of the class and the entire gift is divided among the remaining class members. Accordingly, as long as at least one member of the class survives the testator, the class gift can be given effect in accordance with its terms without invoking concepts of lapse or substitute gifts. See Casner, Class Gifts—Effect of Failure of Class Members to Survive the Testator, 60 Harv. L. Rev. 373 (1947).

The common law rules concerning lapsed gifts are modified in significant respects by anti-lapse statutes, which have been enacted in every state except Louisiana. Strictly speaking, the term "anti-lapse" is somewhat misleading, since these statutes do not abrogate the requirement that a beneficiary must survive the testator, nor do they prevent a deceased beneficiary's gift from lapsing. Instead, the anti-lapse statutes preserve the lapsed gift and redirect it to the deceased beneficiary's surviving descendants (or some other specified group of substitute takers).[22] In effect, the anti-lapse statutes create an implied gift to the substitute takers, preempting the general rules concerning the disposition of lapsed gifts.

Anti-lapse statutes have a limited field of application. By their own terms, most statutes operate only if (1) the deceased beneficiary bears a specified relationship to the testator, and (2) the testator is survived by at least one eligible substitute taker. Furthermore, even if these threshold requirements are met, the statutes do not apply automatically but yield to a contrary intent appearing in the will. The scope and operation of the statutes vary considerably in the following respects:

(1) *Relationship between testator and deceased beneficiary.* Most statutes require that the deceased beneficiary fall within a specified group of the testator's close relatives (e.g., the testator's grandparents or their descendants). Some statutes require that the beneficiary be a child or descendant of the testator, while others require only that the beneficiary be a relative, no matter how distant. Several statutes do not require any family relationship.

(2) *Eligible substitute takers.* All but one of the statutes preserve the lapsed gift exclusively for the deceased beneficiary's descendants, if any, who survive the testator. The exception is Maryland, where a lapsed gift passes directly to the deceased beneficiary's testate or intestate successors.

---

[22] By contrast, the anti-lapse provision of the original Wills Act, 7 Wm. IV & 1 Vict., c. 26, § 33 (1837), provided that the gift passed through the predeceased beneficiary's estate to his or her testate or intestate successors.

(3) *Class gifts.* Most anti-lapse statutes apply to class gifts as well as gifts to named individual beneficiaries, either by their express terms or by judicial interpretation. If the statute is silent on the point, however, some courts take the view that a class gift automatically reapportions a deceased member's share among the remaining class members, leaving no room for a substitute gift to the deceased member's surviving descendants.

(4) *Void gifts.* Most statutes by their express terms cover void as well as lapsed gifts, but a few specifically exclude coverage in the case of a class gift where the beneficiary was already dead when the will was executed. In the absence of clear statutory language, courts have sometimes held that void gifts to individuals are also excluded.

The Uniform Probate Code provisions concerning lapsed and failed gifts have undergone significant changes since they were originally promulgated in 1969. Both provisions were renumbered, and the anti-lapse statute was dramatically expanded, in 1990 as part of a broader revision of the Code. The current version of the anti-lapse statute is discussed in Note 5, infra. The original 1969 version is reproduced here in the interest of brevity and clarity.

Uniform Probate Code (1969)

§ 2–605. [Anti-lapse; Deceased Devisee; Class Gifts.]

If a devisee who is a grandparent or a lineal descendant of a grandparent of the testator is dead at the time of execution of the will, fails to survive the testator, or is treated as if he predeceased the testator, the issue of the deceased devisee who survive the testator by 120 hours take in place of the deceased devisee and if they are all of the same degree of kinship to the devisee they take equally, but if of unequal degree then those of more remote degree take by representation. One who would have been a devisee under a class gift if he had survived the testator is treated as a devisee for purposes of this section whether his death occurred before or after the execution of the will.

§ 2–606. [Failure of Testamentary Provision.]

(a) Except as provided in Section 2–605 if a devise other than a residuary devise fails for any reason, it becomes a part of the residue.

(b) Except as provided in § 2–605 if the residue is devised to two or more persons and the share of one of the residuary devisees fails for any reason, his share passes to the other residuary devisee, or to other residuary devisees in proportion to their interests in the residue.

Problem. T executed a will leaving her residuary estate to her three siblings *A*, *B* and *C*, in equal shares. Later, *A* died without issue and *B* died survived by two children, *X* and *Y*. Finally, *T* died survived by *C*, *X* and *Y*. *T* was also survived by *Z*, the child of a fourth sibling *D* who died before the will was executed. How should *T*'s residuary estate be distributed? What difference would it make if the residuary gift took the form of a class gift to *T*'s "siblings"? To her "surviving siblings"?

IN RE ESTATE OF BURNS

Supreme Court of South Dakota, 1960.
78 S.D. 223, 100 N.W.2d 399.

RENTTO, JUDGE.

In this probate matter a petition was filed asking a construction of [paragraph] twentieth of the will. [From a decision of the county court affirming a decree of the probate court, this appeal was brought by a group of five heirs.]

The construction of paragraph twentieth presents the question of whether our statute against lapses is operative under the circumstances here presented. Both courts held that it was not. . . .

In the twentieth paragraph of her will executed on May 19, 1949, the testatrix provided:

All the rest and residue of my property, of whatsoever kind and nature, and wheresoever situated, I hereby give, devise and bequeath unto Clara Davison, Fannie Wells and Ida Hust, share and share alike; and in case of the death of any of said persons, that said rest and residue shall be divided equally between the survivors of said persons[.]

The three beneficiaries named are sisters of the decedent and all predeceased her. Ida Hust died on February 22, 1951 at the age of 86, leaving no lineal descendants. Fannie Wells died in August 1951 at the age of 90, leaving lineal descendants, the appellants herein. Clara Davison died in June 1952 at the age of 89, leaving no lineal descendants. The testatrix died on April 6, 1958 at the age of 87. The courts below held that the residuary estate lapsed and that as to such property the decedent died intestate. Accordingly, it was ordered distributed to her heirs at law. They are 21 in number, including these five appellants.

The appellants, the lineal descendants of Fannie Wells, claim that our anti-lapse statute governs the distribution of the residuary estate and by virtue of its provisions they are entitled to take such property. That section is SDC 56.0232 and provides:

If a devisee or legatee dies during the lifetime of the testator, the testamentary disposition to him fails unless an intention appears to substitute another in his place; except that when any property is devised or bequeathed to any child or other relation of the testator, and the devisee or legatee dies before the testator, leaving lineal descendants, or is dead at the time the will is executed but leaves lineal descendants surviving the testator, such descendants take the estate so given by the will in the same manner the devisee or legatee would have done had he survived the testator.

The county and circuit courts were of the view that the testatrix by using words of survivorship indicated an intention that the beneficiaries therein named would not take under this paragraph unless they survived her.

By its terms the statute does not affect a testamentary disposition if an intention appears to substitute another in place of the deceased devisee or legatee. This intent must be the testator's intent at the time he executed his will. A testator has the right to select the objects of his bounty and if he has selected a substitutionary beneficiary to take the property given to the beneficiary who predeceased him, then the statute cannot be invoked. It is equally obvious that if the testator uses words indicating an intention that the named beneficiary shall take the gift only if he outlives the testator, there is nothing upon which the statute can operate.

In Hoverstad v. First National Bank and Trust Co., 76 S.D. 119, at page 130, 74 N.W.2d 48, at page 55, 56 A.L.R.2d 938, it is written that this statute "was motivated by a purpose to protect the kindred of the testator and by a belief that a more fair and equitable result would be assured if a defeated legacy were disposed of by law to the lineal descendants of the legatees or devisees selected by the testator." This purpose and belief must be kept in mind in determining whether the statute applies to a given situation. Also it is the policy of the law to prefer that construction of a will which will prevent intestacy, either partial or total. See SDC 56.0310. When a testator makes provision for residuary devisees and legatees he manifests a desire that none of his possessions be distributed as intestate property. Schroeder v. Benz, 9 Ill. 2d 589, 138 N.E.2d 496.

It is generally presumed that the testator made his will in view of the statute and intended to have the statute apply unless the contrary intention appears. If that does not appear the statute is a part of the will. It was intended to supplement the will and not to defeat it. Union Trust Co. v. Richardson, 70 R.I. 151, 37 A.2d 777. The intent to substitute another in place of the deceased beneficiary must be clear and if there is doubt concerning the testator's intent to do so it must be resolved in favor of the operation of the statute.

An intention that the statute is not to apply is also revealed when the testator uses words indicating an intention that the named beneficiary shall take the gift only if he outlives the testator. If the gift is so conditioned there is nothing upon which the statute can operate. The intent that the gift is effective only if the recipient outlives the testators, must also be clear before the statute is ousted, and if this is doubtful, it too must be resolved in favor of the operation of the statute.

Whether a gift to two or more beneficiaries or the survivor of them shows an intention to exclude the operation of the statute, if they all die before the testator, is a question upon which there is a division of authority. Page on Wills, Lifetime, Ed., § 1423. The author of the annotation in 92 A.L.R. 846, at page 858 says: "There appears to be some difference of opinion as to what disposition should be made of a legacy given to several legatees or the survivor of them where all of the legatees predecease the testator."

It seems to us that hard and fast rules cannot be applied in this field because so many of the decisions obviously are the result of seemingly insignificant differences of language in the cases under consideration. . . .

Professor Philip Mechem in an article entitled Problems Under Anti–Lapse Statutes appearing in Vol. 19, Iowa L. Rev. p. 1 at p. 10 has this to say concerning the situation we are considering:

> It can be argued that testator contemplated non-survival and made, not a substitutional gift to issue or the like, but a gift over to the other legatee; this is inconsistent with the intention that the issue of either legatee should take. On the other hand it can be suggested that the survivorship requirement is applicable only in the case where one survives; that the testator did not contemplate or provide for the case where neither survives, and that accordingly the statute is left to operate. This has been held in several cases. Since on this view the provision about survivorship virtually becomes nugatory in the event that has happened, it should make no difference which of the legatees died first.

Under the circumstances here existing we are inclined to accept the latter position. . . .

The survivorship clause in this paragraph by its terms does not contemplate the death of all three sisters before the testatrix. It says merely, "and in case of the death of any of said persons, that said rest and residue shall be divided equally between the survivors of said persons[.]" There can be survivors to take the property only if the beneficiaries who predecease the testatrix are less than all of them. Nothing is said as to who shall take if they all predecease her. Probably this happening did not occur to her when the will was being prepared. While we appreciate respondent's position and able argument we are unable to hold that it clearly appears that the testatrix intended the statute was not to apply. Had she intended the anti-lapse statute not to apply she could have very easily shown such contrary intent. Benz v. Paulson, 246 Iowa 1005, 70 N.W.2d 570. It is not for us to do that for her. Accordingly, the distribution under this paragraph of the will must be to the lineal descendants of Fannie Wells. . . .

. . . Accordingly, the judgment entered on the petition for construction . . . is reversed. . . .

NOTES

1. *Operation of anti-lapse statute.* In the *Burns* case, why do Fannie Wells's descendants take the entire residuary estate rather than one third? What portion of the estate would they receive if one of the testator's other sisters also left surviving issue? What if the testator were survived by one of her sisters? Even if one of the sisters survived, might the gift over to "the survivors of said persons" be interpreted to refer to the surviving issue of a predeceased sister? See Polen v. Baker, 752 N.E.2d 258 (Ohio 2001).

Compare the *Burns* case with Bridges v. Taylor, 579 S.E.2d 740 (Ga. 2003), where the testator left her residuary estate to three named relatives with the proviso that the share of any predeceased beneficiary "shall lapse and shall augment proportionally the remaining shares." All three residuary beneficiaries predeceased the testator and the issue of one of them claimed the residuary estate under the anti-lapse statute. The court held that under the "plain language" of the will, the condition of survival was not met and the anti-lapse statute did not apply. Accordingly the residuary estate passed by intestacy. Accord, Estate of Snapp, 233 S.W.3d 288 (Tenn. App. 2007).

2. *Gift to named takers "or the survivor."* In the case of a residuary gift to several named individuals "or the survivor," courts routinely hold that the anti-lapse statute does not apply as long as at least one of the named individuals survives the testator. As a result, if one of the named individuals dies before the testator, the predeceased beneficiary's share is not preserved for his or her descendants but instead passes to the surviving named individuals. See Estate of Farris, 865 P.2d 1275 (Okla.App.1993); Estate of Rehwinkel, 862 P.2d 639 (Wash.App.1993); Estate of Burruss, 394 N.W.2d 466 (Mich.App.1986). This approach has been criticized as unduly mechanical where it produces an unequal disposition among the testator's descendants or collateral relatives. See French, Antilapse Statutes Are Blunt Instruments: A Blueprint for Reform, 37 Hast. L.J. 335 (1985); Roberts, Lapse Statutes: Recurring Construction Problems, 37 Emory L.J. 323 (1988). Occasionally, courts have reached a different result where other provisions in the will indicate that the words of survivorship were not intended to override the anti-lapse statute. See Estate of Kehler, 411 A.2d 748 (Pa.1980) (residuary gift to

testator's named siblings or the survivor; held, anti-lapse statute applied to deceased brother's share, notwithstanding survivorship language, where will specifically provided for lapse of general bequests to other beneficiaries).

To test whether the anti-lapse statute tends to preserve equality among different lines of succession, consider Estate of Ulrikson, 290 N.W.2d 757 (Minn.1980). The will left $1,000 apiece to each of the testator's eleven nieces and nephews (including two nieces by marriage), and left the residuary estate "to my brother Melvin Hovland, and my sister, Rodine Helger, share and share alike, and in the event that either one of them shall predecease me, then to the other surviving brother or sister." Both siblings were alive when the will was executed, but both predeceased the testator; only Melvin left issue who survived the testator. Applying a statute modeled on UPC § 2–605 (1969), reproduced supra, the court stated that the testator "simply did not contemplate that both her younger brother and sister would predecease her" and that the anti-lapse statute was "free to operate." Accordingly, Melvin's two children took the entire residuary estate. In view of the fact that Melvin's two children received the same $1,000 bequest as the testator's other nieces and nephews, might a distribution of the residuary estate to the testator's heirs by intestacy have been more consistent with the dispositive plan set out in her will? The result in *Ulrikson* has been described as "unjust and easily avoidable." French, supra, at 354. Cf. Estate of Kerr, 433 F.2d 479 (D.C.Cir. 1970).

As noted above, anti-lapse statutes are regularly held applicable to class gifts, even if the statutory language is silent on the point. See Hoverstad v. First Nat'l Bank & Trust Co., 74 N.W.2d 48 (S.D.1955). Should a bequest "to my children, *X* and *Y*, or the survivor" be treated differently under the anti-lapse statute from a bequest "to my children, *X* and *Y*"?

3. *Gift over to beneficiary's successors.* Suppose *T*'s will devises Blackacre "to *A*, and to his heirs and assigns forever." Such words are usually interpreted as "words of limitation" describing the nature of the devised estate (a fee simple absolute) rather than as "words of purchase" identifying substitute takers in the event *A* predeceases *T*. See Estate of Sessions, 153 P. 231 (Cal.1915); Hofing v. Willis, 201 N.E.2d 852 (Ill.1964). Accordingly, if *A* is not covered by the anti-lapse statute, the devise normally falls into the residuary estate. Courts occasionally strain to reach a different result. See Estate of Calden, 712 A.2d 522 (Me. 1998) (holding that devise to predeceased stepson "and his . . . heirs forever" created substitute gift in stepson's spouse and children). What if the devise were "to *A* or his estate"? See Estate of Brunet, 207 P.2d 567 (Cal.1949) (valid substitute gift in deceased devisee's heirs or devisees).

4. *Gift expressly conditioned on beneficiary's survival.* Frequently a bequest is expressly conditioned on the beneficiary's surviving the testator. Even if the will fails to name an alternative taker, courts routinely hold that an express survival condition indicates an intent to override the anti-lapse

statute and allow the lapsed bequest to pass under the residuary clause or by intestacy. See Mrocko v. Wright, 309 S.E.2d 115 (W. Va. 1983); McGowan v. Bogle, 331 S.W.3d 642 (Ky. App. 2011). A number of jurisdictions have statutory provisions to similar effect. See Cal. Prob. Code § 21110(b); Fla. Stat. § 732.603(3)(a); Tex. Prob. Code § 68(e). For a contrary constructional rule, see UPC § 2–603(b)(3), discussed in Note 5, infra; see also Ruotolo v. Tietjen, 890 A.2d 166 (Conn. App. 2006), aff'd, 916 A.2d 1 (Conn. 2007) (words of survivorship alone not sufficient to override anti-lapse statute).

5. *Uniform Probate Code revision.* In 1990 the Uniform Probate Code's anti-lapse statute was completely rewritten (and renumbered as UPC § 2–603). The revised statute, which has been enacted in several states, can fairly be described as "elaborate and intricate." Halbach & Waggoner, The UPC's New Survivorship and Antilapse Provisions, 55 Alb. L. Rev. 1091 (1992). The revised statute introduces several significant innovations.

(a) *Stepchildren.* UPC § 2–603 adds the testator's stepchildren to the list of relatives covered by the statute. Why are stepchildren treated differently from other relatives of the testator's spouse? Compare Cal. Prob. Code § 21110 (covering relatives of testator or of testator's "surviving, deceased, or former spouse"). Note that UPC § 2–603, like most anti-lapse statutes, does not apply to gifts to the testator's spouse. Why should this be so?

(b) *Contrary intent.* One of the most controversial aspects of UPC § 2–603 is its reversal of the traditional rule concerning the effect of express survivorship conditions. Under the revised statute, "words of survivorship . . . are not, in the absence of additional evidence, a sufficient indication of an intent" to prevent the statute from operating. UPC § 2–603(b)(3). The Official Comment to the provision offers the following explanation:

> A formalistic argument sometimes employed by courts adopting the view that words of survivorship automatically defeat the antilapse statute is that, when words of survivorship are used, there is nothing upon which the antilapse statute can operate; the devise itself, it is said, is eliminated by the devisee's having predeceased the testator. . . .

> Another objection to applying the antilapse statute is that mere words of survivorship somehow establish a contrary intention. The argument is that attaching words of survivorship indicates that the testator thought about the matter and intentionally did not provide a substitute gift to the devisee's descendants. At best, this is an inference only, which may or may not accurately reflect the testator's actual intention. . . .

> Even a lawyer's deliberate use of mere words of survivorship to defeat the antilapse statute does not guarantee that the lawyer's intention represents the client's intention. Any linkage between the lawyer's intention and the client's intention is speculative unless the lawyer discussed the matter with the client. . . .

In the absence of persuasive evidence of a contrary intent, however, the antilapse statute, being remedial in nature, and tending to preserve equality among different lines of succession, should be given the widest possible chance to operate and should be defeated only by a finding of intention that *directly contradicts* the substitute gift created by the statute. Mere words of survivorship—by themselves—do not directly contradict the statutory substitute gift to the descendants of a deceased devisee. . . .

In effect, UPC § 2–603 presumes that a bequest "to *A* if *A* survives me" should be interpreted to mean "to *A* if *A* survives me, or if *A* does not survive me then to *A*'s descendants who survive me." If this is not the testator's intent, consider how a competent drafter might expressly negate application of the anti-lapse statute.

(c) *Alternative devise.* Suppose that *T*'s will leaves $10,000 "to my sister *A* if she survives me, or if she does not survive me to my brother *B*." *A* predeceases *T*, who dies survived by *A*'s descendants and by *B*. Under UPC § 2–603, the express "alternative devise" to *B* takes precedence over the implied "substitute gift" to *A*'s descendants. An alternative devise is defined as

a devise that is expressly created by the will and, under the terms of the will, can take effect instead of another devise on the happening of one or more events, including survival of the testator or failure to survive the testator, whether an event is expressed in condition-precedent, condition-subsequent, or any other form. [UPC § 2–603(a)(1).]

The operative provision states:

If the will creates an alternative devise with respect to a devise for which a substitute gift is created by [the anti-lapse statute], the substitute gift is superseded by the alternative devise if: (A) the alternative devise is in the form of a class gift and one or more members of the class is entitled to take under the will; or (B) the alternative devise is not in the form of a class gift and the expressly designated devisee of the alternative devise is entitled to take under the will. [UPC § 2–603(b)(4).]

Thus, in the above example, if *B* also fails to survive *T*, the alternative devise to *B* does not supersede the substitute gift to *A*'s descendants. How would the statute apply if the bequest were "to *A* and *B* or the survivor of them," assuming *A* and *B* both predeceased *T* and only *A* left descendants who survived *T*? See UPC § 2–603 cmt. (Example 5). What if the bequest were in the form of a class gift to *T*'s siblings "or to the survivor or survivors thereof"? See Estate of Raymond, 764 N.W.2d 1 (Mich. 2009).

Suppose that *T*'s will specifically devises Blackacre to her sister *A* and leaves the rest of her property to her brother *B*. *A* predeceases *T*, who dies survived by *A*'s descendants and by *B*. Does Blackacre pass to *A*'s descendants under the anti-lapse statute or to *B* under the residuary clause? Under

UPC § 2–603, "[a] residuary clause constitutes an alternative devise with respect to a nonresiduary devise only if the will specifically provides that, upon lapse or failure, the nonresiduary devise, or nonresiduary devises in general, pass under the residuary clause." UPC § 2–603(a)(1). Thus, a simple residuary clause that disposes of "all the rest of my property" does not override the anti-lapse statute. See UPC § 2–603 cmt. (Example 2). The result would be different, however, if the residuary clause disposed of "all the rest of my property, including any lapsed or failed gifts." See id. (Example 3); Colombo v. Stevenson, 563 S.E.2d 591 (N.C. App. 2002), aff'd, 579 S.E.2d 269 (N.C. 2003) (accord); but cf. Blevins v. Moran, 12 S.W.3d 698 (Ky. App. 2000) (contra). Does an express reference to lapsed gifts reliably indicate testator's intent to override the anti-lapse statute? See Roberts, Lapse Statutes: Recurring Construction Problems, 37 Emory L.J. 323 (1988) (warning that such language "should be avoided since it creates ambiguity").

(d) *Competing substitute gifts.* The statute also includes a tie-breaking provision to establish which of two competing substitute gifts takes precedence. Suppose that *T*'s will leaves $10,000 "to my niece *A* if she survives me, or if she does not survive me to my nephew *B*." *A* and *B* predecease *T*, both of them leaving descendants who survive *T*. Since *A* would have taken in preference to *B* if both had survived *T*, the tie-breaking provision generally gives precedence to the substitute gift to *A*'s descendants (the "primary substitute gift"). UPC § 2–603(c)(1). If *B* were a descendant of *A*, however, the substitute gift to *B*'s descendants (the "younger-generation substitute gift") would take precedence. UPC § 2–603(c)(2). Why should the result turn on the relationship between *A* and *B*?

(e) *Nonprobate transfers.* The Uniform Probate Code also includes a separate provision which extends similar anti-lapse treatment to beneficiary designations under a broad range of will substitutes (e.g., life insurance policies, pension plans, pay-on-death accounts, etc.). See UPC § 2–706.

For a discussion of the revised anti-lapse statute, see Halbach & Waggoner, supra. For a debate over the goals and effects of the revisions, see the exchange between Professors Ascher and Fellows in 77 Minn. L. Rev. 639, 659 (1993).

6. *Failed gifts and disinheritance.* If a residuary gift fails and no substitute or alternative beneficiary is designated in the will or by statute, the residuary estate is likely to pass to the testator's heirs through a partial intestacy. This outcome was almost certainly not contemplated by the testator, who probably assumed that the residuary gift would take effect as written. Indeed, a partial intestacy may frustrate the testator's clearly expressed intent to disinherit the heirs. Nevertheless, most courts follow the traditional view that a will cannot alter the course of intestate succession except by making an affirmative gift to beneficiaries other than the heirs. As one court observed:

It is settled that a disinheritance clause, no matter how broadly or strongly phrased, operates only to prevent a claimant from taking under the will itself, or to obviate a claim of pretermission. Such a clause does not and cannot operate to prevent the heirs at law from taking under the statutory rules of inheritance when the decedent has died intestate as to any or all of his property. [Estate of Barnes, 407 P.2d 656, 659 (Cal. 1965).]

Thus, for example, a testator executed a will leaving her entire estate "to my mother . . . if she shall survive me by 30 days." The will failed to name an alternative taker, but expressed the testator's intent to disinherit her estranged husband. The testator and her mother died in a common disaster, and the mother was presumed not to have survived under the simultaneous death statute. The court held that the 30–day survivorship requirement prevented the anti-lapse statute from preserving the mother's share for her other issue. As a result, the entire estate passed to the husband by intestacy. Estate of Stroble, 636 P.2d 236 (Kan.App.1981).

By statute in some jurisdictions, however, "[a] decedent by will may expressly exclude or limit the right of an individual or class to succeed to property of the decedent passing by intestate succession," with the result that the excluded heir is deemed to have disclaimed his or her intestate share of the estate. UPC § 2–101(b). Suppose a testator executes a will which names his mother as sole residuary beneficiary and expressly disinherits his sister. At testator's death, both mother and sister are predeceased, and his only surviving relatives are sister's descendants. Does the clause disinheriting the sister prevent her descendants from taking the mother's lapsed residuary gift? See Estate of Samuelson, 757 N.W.2d 44 (N.D. 2008); see also Note 5, supra p. 217.

CHAPTER 6

GIFTS

■ ■ ■

A. REAL PROPERTY

The evolution of methods of conveying land in Anglo–American law falls chronologically into three periods: (1) that of the common law conveyances—primarily the feoffment, which required a ceremonial livery of seisin (delivery of possession) with both parties physically present on the land; (2) that of conveyances under the Statute of Uses, which first authorized the transfer of legal title to land by written instrument without physical delivery; and (3) that of conveyances under the Statute of Frauds, which established the general requirement of a signed writing for conveyances of interests in land.

Unlike the old charter of feoffment, which served a merely evidentiary function, the modern deed operates as a document of transfer. The conveyance is ordinarily effected by delivery of the deed, not the land. Under the original Statute of Frauds, 29 Car. II, c. 3, § 1 (1676), and its modern counterparts, any conveyance of an interest in land (other than a short-term lease) generally must be in the form of a written instrument signed by the grantor. The requirement of a written instrument also establishes the foundation for a workable system of recording and security of land titles. In addition to the requirements of the statute of frauds, modern recording statutes usually require that a deed be acknowledged before a notary or other public officer; several states also require attestation by witnesses, and a few still require a seal or its equivalent. A written instrument that satisfies the statute of frauds but is not in recordable form is effective only as between the grantor and the grantee, and does not protect the grantee from claims of subsequent purchasers. Accordingly, almost all conveyances today are effected by means of a deed in recordable form.

In general, a gift of land requires (1) donative intent on the grantor's part, (2) delivery of a written instrument that satisfies the statute of frauds, and (3) acceptance on the grantee's part. Consideration is not essential. That is, the absence of consideration usually does not affect the validity of the deed as between the parties to it. It may, of course, be material for other purposes. A gratuitous conveyance made by an insolvent grantor may be set aside by the grantor's creditors under the fraudulent transfers statute. A donee of land is not entitled to the same protection against prior equities or under the recording statutes as a bona fide purchaser for value. A donee may be barred from obtaining reformation of a deed against the donor on the ground of mistake. In jurisdictions where the common law efficacy of a seal no longer obtains, the grantor's covenants in the deed may be unenforceable if the transaction is gratuitous. Although consideration is not required, it is customary to recite consideration even in a gratuitous deed. Such a recital permits the deed to be sustained as a bargain and sale if, for any reason, it fails to comply with the statutory form. A recital of consideration, while open to contradiction for most purposes, is generally sufficient to establish conclusively the validity of a deed as between the grantor and grantee.

MERTZ V. ARENDT
Supreme Court of North Dakota, 1997.
564 N.W.2d 294.

VANDEWALLE, CHIEF JUSTICE.

Louise Arendt, Darlene Hankison, Leeland Mertz, Lawrence Mertz, Marvin Mertz, Jarred Schmitt, and Clifford Grosz, personal representative of the estate of John Mertz, Sr., appealed from a judgment quieting title to approximately 240 acres of Wells County farmland in John Mertz, Jr. We conclude the trial court's finding John Mertz, Jr., acquired the property through an executed parol gift from his parents is not clearly erroneous, and we affirm the judgment.

John Mertz, Jr., is the youngest of six children born to John Mertz, Sr., and Emilie H. Mertz, both now deceased. Part of the disputed property was owned by John Sr. and Emilie as joint tenants and the other part was owned solely by Emilie. John Sr. farmed the land until sometime in the 1940s. After John Sr. quit farming the land, John Jr.'s older brother, Lawrence, farmed it, except during a two-year period while he served in the armed forces. In 1957 Lawrence married and moved to Fessenden. John Jr. then began farming the land.

According to John Jr., in 1958 or 1959, while he was still a teenager, his parents verbally gave him the disputed property. John Jr. testified:

A. Well, I stayed home and I, my other brothers, they went out and they worked for everybody else and I spent more time at home with my folks and that there and I guess being I was a boy and my dad wanted the land to stay in the Mertz name all the time so they, my dad and mother give me the land.

John Jr. never received a deed to the property from John Sr. or Emilie, because, according to John Jr., his father told him he would receive a tax deed to the property if he paid the taxes.

John Sr. and Emilie continued to live in a house on the farmstead and John Sr. began drilling wells for an occupation. They lived there until 1973 or 1974. Emilie died in 1974 and John Sr. died in 1993. John Jr. lived on the farm with his parents until 1962, when he married and moved to Hurdsfield. John Jr. continued to farm the land from the time of the alleged gift until the spring of 1994, when the personal representative of John Sr.'s estate took possession.

At the time of John Sr.'s death, it was discovered the family had done nothing to update record title ownership of the disputed property for almost 70 years. When this action was started, record title ownership of part of the property remained in Luise Stadelman, Emilie's mother, who died in 1929. That property passed to Emilie as Luise's sole surviving heir. Upon Emilie's death and under a probate court order, the record title ownership of that part of the property was finally listed as an undivided one-half interest in John Sr.'s estate, and an undivided one-twelfth interest in each of the six children. The record title ownership of the remainder of the property showed John Sr. and Emilie as joint tenants. With the property passing to John Sr. upon Emilie's death, record title ownership was changed to show John Sr.'s estate as the record owner of that part of the property.

Following a bench trial, the trial court quieted title to all of the disputed property in John Jr. The trial court concluded John Sr. and Emilie "by their actions, had, in 1958 or 1959, executed a parol[] gift" of the property to John Jr. . . . . The defendants and appellants are John Jr.'s brothers and sisters, the personal representative of John Sr.'s estate, and the person who leased the property from the estate.

The dispositive issue in this case is whether the trial court erred in ruling John Jr. acquired title to the disputed property through an executed parol gift from his parents.

This Court long ago ruled the statute of frauds, codified in N.D.C.C. §§ 9–06–04 and 47–10–01, will not defeat a parol gift of real property.

> The fact that the gift was by parol does not necessarily avoid it. Where a vendee is placed in possession of land under a contract of sale, makes valuable improvements, and pays part of the purchase price, the fact that the requirements of the statute of frauds were not complied with in making the contract will not defeat an action for the specific performance thereof. . . . There is no good reason why a gift should not be subject to the same rules as a sale, and the cases so

hold. . . . Thus where under a parol gift of land the donee takes possession and makes improvements in reliance on the gift so it would work a substantial injustice to hold the gift void, the transaction is taken out of the statute of frauds. [Heuer v. Heuer, 64 N.D. 497, 253 N.W. 856, 858–859 (1934) (citations omitted).]

The party claiming land under an executed parol gift has the burden of proving each element of a valid gift. Hagerott v. Davis, 73 N.D. 532, 17 N.W.2d 15 (1944). Where, as here, a claim is asserted after the death of the donor, proof of each element must be by clear and convincing evidence. Schrank v. Meade, 145 N.W.2d 514 (N.D.1966). Our review of a trial court's finding whether a valid parol gift of land has occurred is governed by the "clearly erroneous" standard of N.D. R. Civ. P. 52(a). Lindvig v. Lindvig, 385 N.W.2d 466 (N.D. 1986). A finding of fact is clearly erroneous if it is induced by an erroneous view of the law, if there is no evidence to support it, or if this Court is left with a definite and firm conviction that a mistake has been made. Endresen v. Scheels Hardware and Sports, 1997 ND 38, 560 N.W.2d 225.

The trial court's finding John Jr. acquired the property by an executed parol gift from his parents in 1958 or 1959 is supported not only by John Jr.'s testimony, but by permissible inferences the trial court could have drawn from other evidence in the record. John Jr. was the only person who possessed and farmed the tillable land from the late 1950s until the personal representative took the land from him in 1994. John Jr. also possessed the pasture land except for two years in the early 1970s when he traded with his brother for other pasture land. John Jr. possessed the farmsite with the exception of the house, where his parents lived until 1973 or 1974. When they left, he fenced the farmsite into the pasture. John Jr.'s allowing his parents to live in the house while he farmed the land is not necessarily inconsistent with his having been given the property as a gift. Cf. Houdek v. Ehrenberger, 397 Ill. 62, 72 N.E.2d 837, 840 (1947) (where parent deeds property to child, the facts that "the parent occupied the premises, paid taxes and made improvements, although some evidence of the absence of an intention to make a gift, are neither sufficient to overcome the presumption of a gift nor inconsistent with the theory of an advancement").

John Jr. paid all of the real estate taxes during the years he farmed the land. Although his parents were listed in tax records as having paid the taxes some years, the trial court found John Jr. reimbursed them for those payments. John Jr. also insured the property and listed himself as the owner. John Jr. paid no rent for use of the property and took the farm products and proceeds including all government farm program payments connected with the property. . . .

John Jr. treated the property as his own and made a number of improvements. He picked rocks, buried rock piles, and drained sloughs. He rebuilt the fence on the pasture land, built a dam at a cost of approximately $6,000, rebuilt a well, placed a water tank on the property, and reshingled a granary. All of this was done without anyone's consent, approval or supervision.

Moreover, only after John Sr. died and it was discovered John Jr. had not received a deed to the property did anyone dispute John Jr.'s ownership of the property. John Jr.'s sister, who handled John Sr.'s affairs while he received nursing home care, certified in five annual medical assistance reviews that John Sr. did not own the land and received no rental income from it. In Social Security Administration documents, John Sr. also certified he did not own the land in question or receive any rental payments from it. In view of the state of the record title, it simply appears this family was not overly concerned about the formalities of record title.

The defendants argue, however, that avoidance of the gift will not work a substantial injustice because John Jr. did not use the property as his homestead. *Heuer* involved homestead property, and the court partially relied on this fact in finding substantial injustice. But, we decline to hold a substantial injustice can occur only if homestead property is the subject of the gift. Neither the case law nor logic dictate such a distinction. Certainly, substantial injustice can occur when a donee makes valuable and permanent improvements to non-homestead property. Compare Vasichek v. Thorsen, 271 N.W.2d 555 (N.D.1978) (where vendee constructed permanent grain bins on non-homestead property, summerfallowed the land, and improved drainage ditches, evidence was sufficient to show partial performance of an oral contract to remove the transaction from the statute of frauds). The improvements found by the trial court to have been made by John Jr. in this case were valuable, substantial and permanent, and were made in reliance on the gift.

The defendants point to evidence they presented at trial, which, if believed by the court, would support their contention no valid parol gift of the property occurred in this case. But it would serve no useful purpose to detail that evidence. We do not reexamine findings of fact made by the trial court on conflicting evidence, and a choice between two permissible views of the weight of the evidence is not clearly erroneous. Matter of Estate of Nelson, 553 N.W.2d 771 (N.D.1996). There was clear and convincing evidence to support the trial court's view that a parol gift of the property occurred in 1958 or 1959.

We conclude the trial court's finding John Jr. received the disputed property through an executed parol gift from his parents is not clearly erroneous. . . .

The judgment is affirmed.

NOTES

1. *Statute of frauds.* An informal writing such as a letter or memorandum may satisfy the statute of frauds even though it is not a recordable deed. The statute of frauds requires only that the writing be signed by the grantor and that it sufficiently identify the grantor, the grantee, the land, and the interest conveyed. By its terms the statute does not apply to transfers of personal property.

2. *The "part performance" exception to the statute of frauds.* Courts have long recognized several exceptions to the statute of frauds. Under the equitable doctrine of "part performance," an oral gift of land may be enforceable against the donor if the donee takes possession of the land and makes lasting and valuable improvements on it. In addition to the principal case, see Conradi v. Perkins, 941 P.2d 1083 (Or.App. 1997); cf. Jones v. Kirk, 719 S.E.2d 428 (Ga. 2011) (occupancy alone not sufficient; purported donee helped to maintain property but made no substantial and permanent improvements). In the absence of a properly recorded deed, however, the donee's equitable rights are subject to those of a subsequent bona fide purchaser for value without notice of the gift. See Ortmeyer v. Bruemmer, 680 S.W.2d 384 (Mo.App.1984). If the improvements are not sufficiently lasting or valuable, the donee may be entitled only to an equitable lien for the value thereof. Or the court may decline to grant any equitable relief whatsoever if the claimant had only an expectation of receiving a gift of the land at some future time. See Fuisz v. Fuisz, 591 A.2d 1047 (Pa.1991).

The doctrine of part performance is usually explained in evidentiary terms: The requirements that the donee take possession and make lasting and valuable improvements provide corroborating evidence of the donor's intent to make a gift of the land. Sometimes the doctrine is explained in terms of equity and fairness. In Rarry v. Shimek, 62 A.2d 46 (Pa.1948), for example, the court put it this way:

> The testimony was that, after taking possession, Shimek cemented the basement, put up partitions there for a laundry room, fruit cellar, coal bin and furnace room, installed a sink and a lavatory, built a linen closet in the bathroom, dug a water-well, dug driveways and laid cement sidewalks around the house, graded the lawn, sowed grass seed on it and planted trees and shrubbery. It is true that he obtained the material for these improvements either as gifts or at small expense, but he himself performed the necessary labor, working nights and at odd hours when not on duty. . . . Plaintiffs deprecate the importance of the improvements on the ground that they were neither valuable nor incapable of being adequately compensated in damages; they were, however, of a permanent nature and of such an extent as to render any attempted revocation of the gift unjust and inequitable. Improvements that might be deemed

inconsequential in connection with a property which was itself extremely valuable might properly be regarded as of comparatively large value when made upon a $9000 house, and, since Shimek made them by his own labor performed at various odd times, his contention would seem reasonable that compensation therefor in damages must necessarily be inadequate; the requirement of the law that the improvements be such that compensation would be inadequate does not mean, of course, that no amount of compensation, however large, would be sufficient, but that it would be impracticable, if not impossible, to determine such amount with any fair degree of accuracy by ordinary and available standards. [62 A.2d at 48–49.]

3. *Other exceptions to the statute of frauds.* The statute of frauds applies to express trusts of land but not to trusts arising by operation of law, i.e., constructive and resulting trusts. Thus, where a person acquires or retains title to land as a result of fraud, duress, or undue influence, the statute does not prevent a court from decreeing a constructive trust as a mechanism to compel the person holding legal title to convey the land to the rightful owner. Here, as elsewhere, the constructive trust has nothing to do with the donor's intent, but operates merely as an equitable remedy to prevent unjust enrichment. For further discussion of constructive trusts, see infra p. 675.

LENHART V. DESMOND
Supreme Court of Wyoming, 1985.
705 P.2d 338.

CARDINE, JUSTICE.

This is an appeal from a judgment in favor of Edward V. Desmond in which the district court declared a deed recorded by Desmond's daughter, Elizabeth A. Lenhart, invalid and restored real property to him.

We affirm. . . .

THE FACTS

In 1974 Mr. Desmond executed a warranty deed to his daughter and only child, Elizabeth A. Lenhart. This was done because Mr. Desmond was then in his 80's and he thought that he had "better make arrangements, that in case of my death, why, Elizabeth can have all of my earthly possessions." Mr. Desmond executed the deed and placed it in his safety deposit box. Then he informed Mrs. Lenhart of his intentions of her getting the house when he passed on. To facilitate this he gave her access to the box through a signature card. Further, at the time of signing of this card, Lenhart became explicitly aware of the deed in the box. Subsequently, Desmond was injured in an automobile accident in July of 1983 and hospitalized. Lenhart returned to Cheyenne to help her father which required her to retrieve some insurance policies from the safety deposit box.

After his release from the hospital, Desmond checked his box and found the deed was missing, although it had been there before the accident. The facts of exactly who removed the deed are in dispute. Mrs. Lenhart, however, recorded the deed in October of 1983.

The complaint in this action, asking that the deed recorded by appellant be declared invalid, was filed on May 22, 1984, by Edward Desmond. Mrs. Lenhart counterclaimed asking that the deed be held valid as a gift of the property. The trial court without a jury found generally in favor of Mr. Desmond entering a judgment invalidating the deed to appellant and dismissing her counterclaim.

SUFFICIENCY OF THE EVIDENCE

It is well established that this court on appeal must accept the evidence of the successful party as true, leave out of consideration entirely the evidence of the unsuccessful party in conflict therewith, and give to the evidence of the successful party every favorable inference that may fairly and reasonably be drawn from it. . . . It is also firmly established that the trial judge is in the best position to weigh and judge credibility of witnesses and to weigh the evidence. . . . Further, the findings of the trial judge must be sustained unless they are clearly erroneous or contrary to the great weight of the evidence. . . .

In the case at bar there was a direct conflict in the testimony concerning the delivery of the deed and whether Edward Desmond intended that the property should pass to Lenhart immediately or upon his death. Mrs. Lenhart claimed that her father physically handed her the deed saying, "I went down and got the deed for you." Mr. Desmond testified that he did not give the deed to his daughter nor did he intend for her to have the property before his death. Mr. Desmond was the successful party and his testimony must be taken as true.

Appellant argues, nevertheless, that the decision below must be reversed because the great weight of evidence is against appellee's position. Further, appellant claims that possession and recordation of the deed make out a prima facie case of delivery and that appellee must then establish nondelivery by clear and convincing evidence, rather than by a preponderance of the evidence. . . .

. . . The court in its decision letter found that "Plaintiff has proved by a preponderance of the evidence" that "there was no delivery of the deed." In support of this statement the court stated,

> Defendant testified that the Plaintiff had, of his own accord, gone to retrieve the deed from the safe-deposit box on a Saturday and had given the same to her with instructions to record it. The Court is

skeptical of this testimony when it is coupled with the fact that the Plaintiff has requested that Defendant deed the property back to him and she refuses to do so. Her reason for not deeding the property back to the Plaintiff was that he would mortgage the property and spend the money on strong drink.

In essence, the court rejected appellant's testimony leaving only that evidence of appellee which clearly shows nondelivery.

Reviewing the record, we find that Mr. Desmond's testimony that he never intended Mrs. Lenhart to have the property before his death and that she took and recorded the deed without his knowledge or consent, was sufficient, persuasive and clear to rebut the presumption of delivery. This is true especially when Mr. Desmond's unequivocal testimony is compared to Mrs. Lenhart's. We do not believe the trial court applied an incorrect burden of proof to the facts; but, were it so, it would not affect the result in this case for we view the evidence supporting the judgment as clear and sufficient. . . .

CONSTRUCTIVE DELIVERY

To effect a conveyance transferring title, a deed must be both executed and delivered. Hein v. Lee, Wyo., 549 P.2d 286, 292 (1976). At the time of the delivery the grantor's intent is of primary and controlling importance. Rosengrant v. Rosengrant, Okl.App., 629 P.2d 800, 802 (1981). Further, the controlling issue in determining if delivery was effective is whether the grantor manifested an intention to presently divest himself of title. Matter of Estate of Courtright v. Robertson, 99 Idaho 575, 586 P.2d 265, 269 (1978); Yunghans v. O'Toole, 224 Kan. 553, 581 P.2d 393, 396 (1978). Not only is intent a controlling factor, it is also the crucial one when constructive delivery is claimed.

> The intention of the parties is an essential and controlling element of delivery of a deed. Intention has been called the "essence of delivery," and not only is it often the determining factor among other facts and circumstances, *but is the crucial test where constructive delivery is relied upon.* Categorically stated, the rule is that it is essential to the delivery of a deed that there be a giving of the deed by the grantor and a receiving of it by the grantee, with a mutual intention to pass the title from the one to the other. (Emphasis added.) 23 Am. Jur. 2d Deeds § 123.

In the case at bar, appellant claims that delivery occurred when the deed was placed in the safety deposit box and Mr. Desmond provided Mrs. Lenhart access to it. Appellant fails to realize that these actions alone do not constitute delivery since they fail the crucial test. According to Mr. Desmond's testimony, he did not possess the present intent to divest himself irretrievably of his property. Rather, he intended that Mrs. Desmond have the property upon his death. He believed he had put his affairs in order.

Appellant points to a number of cases from other jurisdictions which she believes hold that these actions alone can constitute constructive delivery. The reliance on these cases is unfounded because they refer to similar action coupled with an uncontroverted intent or an intent to immediately pass title inferred from other evidence. In the case at bar, the intent was very much controverted. In fact, Mr. Desmond stated that he never manifested the intent necessary to pass the title of his property to his daughter while he was alive. Without the requisite intent there can be no delivery.

We need not address the third issue on appeal, the reformation of the deed, because we affirm the trial court's judgment that the deed was ineffective to pass title, it not being delivered. Thus, we hold that the evidence was sufficient to declare the deed invalid and the property was properly restored to Mr. Desmond.

Affirmed.

NOTES

1. *Delivery requirement.* In general, an inter vivos gift of land takes effect only if the grantor delivers a deed (or other writing sufficient to satisfy the statute of frauds) during life with the intent of presently conveying some interest in the land. A recorded deed raises a presumption that the conveyance is valid, although, as the principal case illustrates, the presumption is rebuttable. See also Crowder v. Crowder, 798 S.W.2d 425 (Ark.1990) (husband conveyed land to wife for purpose of defeating creditors' claims, with understanding that wife would reconvey to husband on demand; held, no valid gift). A similar presumption arises if the grantee has physical possession of the deed, even if it is not recorded during the grantor's life. See Estate of Blettell v. Snider, 834 P.2d 505 (Or.App. 1992); Salter v. Hamiter, 887 So.2d 230 (Ala. 2004) (grantor retained possession of land and requested that deed not be recorded until after death; valid gift). If the grantor retains possession of the deed until death, however, there is a presumption of nondelivery which, if not rebutted, defeats the attempted conveyance. See Estate of Dittus, 497 N.W.2d 415 (N.D.1993) (grantor placed executed deeds in safe deposit box, retaining one key and giving a duplicate key to grantee; held, no valid gift); cf. Agrelius v. Mohesky, 494 P.2d 1095 (Kan.1972) (valid gift despite joint access).

After decedent's death the following handwritten memorandum was discovered in her desk: "I sold my interest in the Home Farm to Jared W. Darlington on his 40th birthday for one dollar ($1.00). /s/ Martha Darlington." No deed was executed or delivered during the decedent's life. Is the attempted conveyance valid? See Estate of Darlington, 527 A.2d 159 (Pa.Super.1987).

2. *Delivery to third party on behalf of grantee.* A deed may be delivered to a third party with instructions for redelivery to the grantee at some future time such as the grantor's death. Such an arrangement is often referred to as an "escrow," although it differs from a traditional escrow in that the condition for redelivery—the grantor's death—is certain to occur and does not depend on any payment or performance by the grantee. Nomenclature aside, courts routinely uphold such conveyances on the ground that delivery takes place when the grantor relinquishes dominion and control of the deed, even though the grantee's interest in the land does not become possessory until the grantor's death. In effect, the grantor has made a completed conveyance of the land subject to a reserved life estate. See Herron v. Underwood, 503 N.E.2d 1111 (Ill.App.1987); cf. Howell v. Herald, 197 S.W.3d 505 (Ky. 2006). Nevertheless, if the grantor reserves a power to recall or revoke the deed, the attempted conveyance may fail for lack of delivery. See Albrecht v. Brais, 754 N.E.2d 396 (Ill.App.2001). Suppose the grantor hands an executed deed to the grantee, who immediately hands the deed back to the grantor (or the grantor's attorney) for safekeeping during the grantor's life. Should the conveyance be upheld? See Rosengrant v. Rosengrant, 629 P.2d 800 (Okla. App. 1981); cf. Payne v. Carver, 534 So.2d 566 (Ala.1988).

3. *"Testamentary" deeds.* A grantor may convey land subject to a reserved life estate, thereby creating a future interest—a remainder—in the grantee. Although the grantee will not obtain possession of the land until the grantor's death, the conveyance operates to create an interest in the grantee immediately upon delivery of the deed. See Simmons v. Buchanan, 803 S.W.2d 950 (Ark.App.1991). In contrast, if a deed has no operative effect during the grantor's life, the attempted conveyance may be attacked as "testamentary," meaning that the deed is not effective as an inter vivos transfer; the attempted transfer may fail completely, unless the deed complies with the applicable wills formalities and accordingly can be admitted to probate as a valid will.[1] For example, in Wheeler v. Rines, 375 S.W.2d 48 (Mo.1964), a deed recited that it was "not to take effect till after the [grantor's] death." The court interpreted this language to mean that the grantor "intended that no estate or interest would pass until his death," and held that the deed was a nullity. But cf. Vigil v. Sandoval, 741 P.2d 836 (N.M.App.1987) (upholding deed, delivered and recorded during grantor's life, which stated that it would "become effective only upon the death of grantor").

Suppose that a deed expressly reserves to the grantor not only a life estate but also a power to revoke. Is such a deed open to attack on the grounds that delivery requires that the grantor relinquish dominion and control, and that the grantor's power to revoke is inconsistent with this requirement? Several courts have upheld revocable deeds, reasoning that the possibility of revocation is merely a divesting condition which does not prevent the con-

---

[1] See Will of Wnuk, 41 N.W.2d 294 (Wis.1950) (deed executed with testamentary formalities, recited that it was "null and void until after [grantor's] death"; held, admissible to probate); cf. Ex parte Rucker, 702 So.2d 456 (Ala.1997) (giving effect to instrument entitled "last will" as inter vivos deed).

veyance from becoming effective during the grantor's life. See Harris v. Neely, 359 S.E.2d 885 (Ga.1987); St. Louis County Nat'l Bank v. Fielder, 260 S.W.2d 483 (Mo.1953) ("a grantor has the right to reserve the power to revoke and . . . such a reservation alone does not make a deed testamentary"); Tennant v. John Tennant Memorial Home, 140 P. 242 (Cal.1914). The traditional rule, however, was otherwise. See, e.g., Butler v. Sherwood, infra p. 539.

4. *Transfer on death deeds.* The Uniform Real Property Transfer on Death Act, promulgated in 2009, allows the owner of real property to designate one or more beneficiaries to receive the property at the owner's death pursuant to a "transfer on death deed." URPTODA § 5. The deed must be in recordable form, must state that the transfer is to occur at the transferor's death, and must be recorded in the appropriate land records office during the transferor's lifetime. Id. § 9. As long as the transferor is alive, the deed is freely revocable and has no effect on the rights or interests of the transferor, the beneficiary, or any third party. Id. §§ 6, 11 and 12. At the transferor's death, unless previously revoked, the deed takes effect according to its terms; if the beneficiary survives the transferor, the property passes directly to the designated beneficiary, subject to any conveyances, assignments, or encumbrances in effect at the transferor's death. Id. § 13. The deathtime transfer occurs outside the probate system and is expressly declared to be "nontestamentary," but if the transferor's probate estate is insufficient to pay claims and statutory allowances, the beneficiary may be liable (along with recipients of other nonprobate transfers) for contribution to make up the deficiency. Id. §§ 7 and 15. The uniform act is incorporated in Article VI of the Uniform Probate Code concerning nonprobate transfers on death. See UPC §§ 6–401 to 6–417.

A transfer on death deed under the uniform act is functionally indistinguishable from a specific devise of real property. Although the transfer occurs at the transferor's death, the required formalities are those prescribed for an inter vivos conveyance of real property rather than for a testamentary disposition. Of even greater practical significance is the avoidance of probate administration. Are there circumstances in which it might be advantageous to dispose of real property by will rather than by a transfer on death deed? If a transferor executes a transfer on death deed but fails to record it during his or her lifetime, may the deed be admitted to probate as a will? Cf. UPC § 2–502 (will duly executed if signed by testator and acknowledged before a notary public; attesting witnesses not required).

Legislation modeled on the uniform act has been enacted in a substantial number of states. For further discussion of the scope and application of the uniform act, see Gary, Transfer-on-Death Deeds: The Nonprobate Revolution Continues, 41 Real Prop. Prob. & Tr. J. 529 (2006).

B. PERSONAL PROPERTY

1. INTER VIVOS GIFTS

Conceptions of Ownership

The simplest and most innate conception of ownership is materialistic and is identified with physical control. Among young children who trade in the innumerable and diverse chattels which seem to fall into their possession, the standard and obvious way to "transfer title" is to hand the thing over. And it would hardly occur to a child who had been tortiously dispossessed to seek comfort in the thought that he or she was still the true owner. In this way of thinking, the owner is the one who has physical control; if you want to make someone else owner, you must make a physical transfer of the subject matter; and, if you lose possession, you are no longer the owner. You haven't got a thing if you haven't got it. These notions are probably widespread among many adults not accustomed to thinking in legal terms. How many people readily comprehend, or take kindly to, the legal distinction between title and possession? Are they not more likely, unless stirred by theft or other impairment of their rights, to dismiss the matter as a trivial legal quibble?

More sophisticated legal reasoning has now freed the idea of ownership from the confines of pure materialism and placed it on a more abstract plane. Ownership is popularly defined as a "bundle of rights" (Maitland, The Mystery of Seisin, 2 L.Q. Rev. 481, 489 (1886)) or as a group of legal relations, the nature of which of course varies with the interest involved. Transfer of ownership is therefore, by definition, a change of legal relations. Legal relations in turn are concepts that are useful in describing and analyzing what courts have done in the past and in predicting what they may do in the future. The statement that ownership (as thus defined) has been transferred is therefore a shorthand expression of legal opinion, convenient in the quick communication of ideas, and not a description of a factual occurrence, except in so far as the phrase may incidentally connote certain actions of the parties. Such abstractions as ownership and legal relations are, of course, not susceptible of physical transfer. Nor should the phrase "transfer of ownership" be taken literally to mean that the legal relations of the transferee are precisely identical with the previous legal relations of the transferor, since those may vary according to the terms of the transfer and the application of legal rules such as those relating to good faith purchase. But the phrase serves well enough to state the opinion that they will be substantially similar—in other words, that after the "transfer" courts will treat the transferee in about the same way that, before it, they would have treated the transferor. What proof the courts will require as prerequisite to an effective transfer under this analysis is a question of legal judgment, which depends more on considerations of policy than on some immutable requirement of a physical transfer.

These two conceptions of ownership seem to influence a large part of the law of inter vivos gifts of personal property. The materialistic attitude obviously stresses physical transfer of a tangible object. The modern notion of ownership shifts the emphasis to the functional criterion of what sort of proof courts should require before putting one person in the shoes of another with respect to a particular type of property. Under this criterion, a physical transfer is not indispensable; it is important only if it accomplishes some useful purpose. In this manner, however, the materialistic attitude, because of its intuitive appeal and widespread acceptance, finds a place in a functional approach. Thousands of gifts are made daily in this country by people based on rudimentary ideas of ownership, often without benefit of legal advice. To many people who would not consider making a will or creating a trust without going to an attorney, it may come as a surprise to learn that gifts of personalty raise legal problems. They have been giving presents all their lives without having to pay a lawyer. And, very likely, they assume without reflection that "giving" means "handing over." Functional criteria cannot neglect these typical human habits, or the materialistic assumptions underlying them, without leading to arbitrary and intent-defeating results. For an example of an attempt to formulate legal doctrine in the light of ordinary human reactions, see the excerpt from Cochrane v. Moore, quoted infra.

Evolution of the Law of Gifts

At one time, in accordance with the general emphasis on possession, the only possible method of making a gift of a chattel was by physical delivery of the chattel to the donee. A deed of gift without delivery of the subject matter of the gift was ineffectual, and the concept of constructive delivery was unknown. In the fifteenth century, however, the common law courts began to recognize that a gift could be effectuated by a deed of gift without delivery of the subject matter, apparently based on an analogy to the binding effect of a promise under seal. (At that time a deed had characteristics of both contract and conveyance, which had not yet evolved as clearly distinct concepts.) Thus in its origins at common law a deed of gift of personalty appears to have depended for its effectiveness on the presence of a seal and on the ritualistic and irrebuttable character of a sealed instrument. A donor who delivered a deed under seal reciting a gift of a chattel could not later deny the gift, which therefore was effective. In sum, as early as the fifteenth century the common law recognized two alternative methods of delivery in gifts of personalty: (1) delivery of the subject matter, and (2) delivery of a deed of gift, it being essential that the deed be under seal. A deed of gift, like other deeds, must of course be "delivered" (a term of variable content and meaning) in order to be effectual. Assuming satisfactory evidence of donative intent, necessary in any gift case, the donee could prevail on proof of either of these two forms of delivery.

Beginning in the eighteenth century, the courts began to accept the notion that a gift may be effectuated by "constructive" (as distinguished from actual) delivery. For example, where it is inconvenient or impossible to hand over physical possession of the subject matter due to its size, nature or location, a donor may accomplish a constructive delivery by handing over a key or some other object which allows the donee to take control of the subject matter. Thus the concept of constructive delivery appears to have emerged independently of, and considerably later than, the cases recognizing the validity of a deed of gift of chattels at common law.

Courts have repeatedly affirmed the traditional rule requiring delivery as an essential element of an inter vivos gift. From time to time some courts have called the delivery requirement into question, usually in dicta, and suggested that a gift should rest purely on the question of intention and that delivery should be relevant only to prove donative intent. Doubts concerning the delivery requirement were effectively silenced by the famous case of Cochrane v. Moore, 25 Q.B. Div. 57 (1890), which considered the matter in great detail and strongly reaffirmed the traditional rule requiring delivery of either the subject matter or a deed of gift. In his opinion, Lord Esher stated:

> Upon long consideration, I have come to the conclusion that actual delivery in the case of a "gift" is more than evidence of the existence of the proposition of law which constitutes a gift, and I have come to the conclusion that it is a part of the proposition itself. . . . The proposition before the Court on a question of gift or not is—that the one gave and the other accepted. . . . The one cannot give, according to the ordinary meaning of the word, without giving; the other cannot accept then and there such a giving without then and there receiving the thing given. . . . Short of these things being done, the donee could not get possession without bringing an action against the donor to force him to give him the thing. But if we are to force him to give, it cannot be said that he has given. Suppose the proposing donor offers the thing saying, "I give you this thing—take it"; and the other says, "No, I will not take it now; I will take it tomorrow." I think the proposing donor could not in the meantime say correctly to a third person, "I gave this just now to my son or my friend." The answer of the third person would (I think rightly) be: "You cannot say you gave it to him just now; you have it now in your hand." All you can say is: "That you are going to give it him to-morrow, if then he will take it." I have come to the conclusion that in ordinary English language, and in legal effect, there cannot be a "gift" without a giving and taking. The

giving and taking are the two contemporaneous reciprocal acts which constitute a "gift." They are a necessary part of the proposition that there has been a "gift." They are not evidence to prove that there has been a gift, but facts to be proved to constitute the proposition that there has been a gift. [25 Q.B. Div. at 75–76.]

In this country the courts have always recognized a general requirement of delivery in gifts of personal property. Accordingly, the typical American law may be stated as follows: To succeed in establishing an inter vivos gift of personalty, the donee must prove (1) the alleged donor's intent to make a gift, and (2) delivery of either (a) the subject matter of the gift or (b) an instrument of gift. Despite the apparent simplicity of this statement, the concept of "delivery" exhibits a protean ability to take on different meanings in different contexts.

GRUEN V. GRUEN

Court of Appeals of New York, 1986.
68 N.Y.2d 48, 496 N.E.2d 869, 505 N.Y.S.2d 849.

SIMONS, JUDGE.

Plaintiff commenced this action seeking a declaration that he is the rightful owner of a painting which he alleges his father, now deceased, gave to him. He concedes that he has never had possession of the painting but asserts that his father made a valid gift of the title in 1963 reserving a life estate for himself. His father retained possession of the painting until he died in 1980. Defendant, plaintiff's stepmother, has the painting now and has refused plaintiff's requests that she turn it over to him. She contends that the purported gift was testamentary in nature and invalid insofar as the formalities of a will were not met or, alternatively, that a donor may not make a valid inter vivos gift of a chattel and retain a life estate with a complete right of possession. Following a seven-day nonjury trial, Special Term found that plaintiff had failed to establish any of the elements of an inter vivos gift and that in any event an attempt by a donor to retain a present possessory life estate in a chattel invalidated a purported gift of it. The Appellate Division held that a valid gift may be made reserving a life estate and, finding the elements of a gift established in this case, it reversed and remitted the matter for a determination of value 104 A.D.2d 171, 488 N.Y.S.2d 401). That determination has now been made and defendant appeals directly to this court . . . from the subsequent final judgment entered in Supreme Court awarding plaintiff $2,500,000 in damages representing the value of the painting, plus interest. We now affirm.

The subject of the dispute is a work entitled "Schloss Kammer am Attersee II" painted by a noted Austrian modernist, Gustav Klimt. It was purchased by plaintiff's father, Victor Gruen, in 1959 for $8,000. On April

1, 1963 the elder Gruen, a successful architect with offices and residences in both New York City and Los Angeles during most of the time involved in this action, wrote a letter to plaintiff, then an undergraduate student at Harvard, stating that he was giving him the Klimt painting for his birthday but that he wished to retain the possession of it for his lifetime. This letter is not in evidence, apparently because plaintiff destroyed it on instructions from his father. Two other letters were received, however, one dated May 22, 1963 and the other April 1, 1963. Both had been dictated by Victor Gruen and sent together to plaintiff on or about May 22, 1963. The letter dated May 22, 1963 reads as follows:

> Dear Michael:
>
> I wrote you at the time of your birthday about the gift of the painting by Klimt.
>
> Now my lawyer tells me that because of the existing tax laws, it was wrong to mention in that letter that I want to use the painting as long as I live. Though I still want to use it, this should not appear in the letter. I am enclosing, therefore, a new letter and I ask you to send the old one back to me so that it can be destroyed.
>
> I know this is all very silly, but the lawyer and our accountant insist that they must have in their possession copies of a letter which will serve the purpose of making it possible for you, once I die, to get this picture without having to pay inheritance taxes on it.
>
> Love,
>
> s/ Victor.

Enclosed with this letter was a substitute gift letter, dated April 1, 1963, which stated:

> Dear Michael:
>
> The 21st birthday, being an important event in life, should be celebrated accordingly. I therefore wish to give you as a present the oil painting by Gustav Klimt of Schloss Kammer which now hangs in the New York living room. You know that Lazette and I bought it some 5 or 6 years ago, and you always told us how much you liked it.
>
> Happy birthday again.
>
> Love,
>
> s/ Victor.

Plaintiff never took possession of the painting nor did he seek to do so. Except for a brief period between 1964 and 1965 when it was on loan to art exhibits and when restoration work was performed on it, the painting remained in his father's possession, moving with him from New York City to Beverly Hills and finally to Vienna, Austria, where Victor Gruen died on February 14, 1980. Following Victor's death plaintiff requested possession of the Klimt painting and when defendant refused, he commenced this action.

The issues framed for appeal are whether a valid inter vivos gift of a chattel may be made where the donor has reserved a life estate in the chattel and the donee never has had physical possession of it before the donor's death and, if it may, which factual findings on the elements of a valid inter vivos gift more nearly comport with the weight of the evidence in this case, those of Special Term or those of the Appellate Division. The latter issue requires application of two general rules. First, to make a valid inter vivos gift there must exist the intent on the part of the donor to make a present transfer; delivery of the gift, either actual or constructive to the donee; and acceptance by the donee (Matter of Szabo, 10 N.Y.2d 94, 98, 217 N.Y.S.2d 593, 176 N.E.2d 395; Matter of Kelly, 285 N.Y. 139, 150, 33 N.E.2d 62 [dissenting in part opn.]; Matter of Van Alstyne, 207 N.Y. 298, 306, 100 N.E. 802; Beaver v. Beaver, 117 N.Y. 421, 428, 22 N.E. 940). Second, the proponent of a gift has the burden of proving each of these elements by clear and convincing evidence (Matter of Kelly, supra, 285 N.Y. at p. 150, 33 N.E.2d 62; Matter of Abramowitz, 38 A.D.2d 387, 389–390, 329 N.Y.S.2d 932, affd. on opn. 32 N.Y.2d 654, 342 N.Y.S.2d 855, 295 N.E.2d 654).

Donative Intent

There is an important distinction between the intent with which an inter vivos gift is made and the intent to make a gift by will. An inter vivos gift requires that the donor intend to make an irrevocable present transfer of ownership; if the intention is to make a testamentary disposition effective only after death, the gift is invalid unless made by will (see, McCarthy v. Pieret, 281 N.Y. 407, 409, 24 N.E.2d 102; Gannon v. McGuire, 160 N.Y. 476, 481, 55 N.E. 7; Martin v. Funk, 75 N.Y. 134, 137–138).

Defendant contends that the trial court was correct in finding that Victor did not intend to transfer any present interest in the painting to plaintiff in 1963 but only expressed an intention that plaintiff was to get the painting upon his death. The evidence is all but conclusive, however, that Victor intended to transfer ownership of the painting to plaintiff in 1963 but to retain a life estate in it and that he did, therefore, effectively transfer a remainder interest in the painting to plaintiff at that time. Although the original letter was not in evidence, testimony of its contents was received along with the substitute gift letter and its covering letter dated May 22, 1963. The three letters should be considered together as a single instrument (see, Matter of Brandreth, 169 N.Y. 437, 440, 62 N.E. 563) and when they are they unambiguously establish that Victor Gruen intended to make a present gift of title to the painting at that time. But there was other evidence for after 1963 Victor made several statements orally and in writing indicating that he had previously given plaintiff the painting and that plaintiff owned it. Victor Gruen retained possession of the property, insured it, allowed others to exhibit it and made necessary repairs to it but those acts are not inconsistent with his retention of a life estate. . . . Victor's failure to file a gift tax return on the transaction was partially explained by allegedly erroneous legal advice he received, and while that omission sometimes may indicate that the donor had no intention of making a present gift, it does not necessarily do so and it is not dispositive in this case.

Defendant contends that even if a present gift was intended, Victor's reservation of a lifetime interest in the painting defeated it. She relies on a statement from Young v. Young, 80 N.Y. 422 that " '[a]ny gift of chattels which expressly reserves the use of the property to the donor for a certain period, or . . . as long as the donor shall live, is ineffectual' " (id., at p. 436, quoting 2 Schouler, Personal Property, at 118). The statement was dictum, however, and the holding of the court was limited to a determination that an attempted gift of bonds in which the donor reserved the interest for life failed because there had been no delivery of the gift, either actual or constructive (see, id., at p. 434; see also, Speelman v. Pascal, 10 N.Y.2d 313, 319–320, 222 N.Y.S.2d 324, 178 N.E.2d 723). The court expressly left undecided the question "whether a remainder in a chattel may be created and given by a donor by carving out a life estate for himself and transferring the remainder" (Young v. Young, supra, at p. 440). We answered part of that question in Matter of Brandreth (169 N.Y. 437, 441–442, 62 N.E. 563, supra) when we held that "[in] this state a life estate and remainder can be created in a chattel or a fund the same as in real property." The case did not require us to decide whether there could be a valid gift of the remainder.

Defendant recognizes that a valid inter vivos gift of a remainder interest can be made not only of real property but also of such intangibles as stocks and bonds. Indeed, several of the cases she cites so hold. That being so, it is difficult to perceive any legal basis for the distinction she urges which would permit gifts of remainder interests in those properties but not of remainder interests in chattels such as the Klimt painting here. The only reason suggested is that the gift of a chattel must include a present right to possession. The application of *Brandreth* to permit a gift of the remainder in this case, however, is consistent with the distinction, well recognized in the law of gifts as well as in real property law, between ownership and possession or enjoyment (see, Speelman v. Pascal, 10 N.Y.2d 313, 318, 222 N.Y.S.2d 324, 178 N.E.2d 723, supra; McCarthy v. Pieret, 281 N.Y. 407, 409–411, 24 N.E.2d 102, supra; Matter of Brandreth, 169 N.Y. 437, 442, 62 N.E. 563, supra). Insofar as some of our cases purport to require that the donor intend to transfer both title and possession immediately to have a valid inter vivos gift (see, Gannon v. McGuire, 160 N.Y. 476, 481, 55 N.E. 7, supra; Young v. Young, 80 N.Y. 422, 430, supra), they state the rule too broadly and confuse the effectiveness of a gift with the transfer of the possession of the subject of that gift. The correct test is " 'whether the maker intended the [gift] to have *no effect* until after the maker's death, or whether he intended it to transfer *some present interest*' " (McCarthy v. Pieret, 281 N.Y. 407, 409, 24 N.E.2d 102, supra [emphasis added] . . .). As long as the evidence establishes an intent to make a present and irrevocable transfer of title or the right of ownership, there is a present transfer of some interest and the gift is effective immediately (see, Matter of Brady, 228 App. Div. 56, 60, 239 N.Y.S. 5, affd. no opn. 254 N.Y. 590, 173 N.E. 879; In re Sussman's Estate, 125 N.Y.S.2d 584, 589–591, affd. no opn. 284 A.D. 844, 134 N.Y.S.2d 586; Matter of Valentine, 122 Misc. 486, 489, 204 N.Y.S. 284; Brown, Personal Property § 48, at 133–136 [2d ed.] . . . ; see also, Farmers' Loan & Trust Co. v. Winthrop, 238 N.Y. 477, 485–486, 144 N.E. 686). Thus, in Speelman v. Pascal (supra), we held valid a gift of a percentage of the future royalties to the play "My Fair Lady" before the play even existed. There, as in this case, the donee received title or the right of ownership to some property immediately upon the making of the gift but possession or enjoyment of the subject of the gift was postponed to some future time.

Defendant suggests that allowing a donor to make a present gift of a remainder with the reservation of a life estate will lead courts to effectuate otherwise invalid testamentary dispositions of property. The two have entirely different characteristics, however, which make them distinguishable. Once the gift is made it is irrevocable and the donor is limited to the rights of a life tenant not an owner. Moreover, with the gift of a remainder title vests immediately in the donee and any possession is postponed until the donor's death whereas under a will neither title nor possession vests immediately. Finally, the postponement of enjoyment of the gift is produced by the express terms of the gift not by the nature of the instrument as it is with a will (see, Robb v. Washington & Jefferson Coll., 185 N.Y. 485, 493, 78 N.E. 359).

DELIVERY

In order to have a valid inter vivos gift, there must be a delivery of the gift, either by a physical delivery of the subject of the gift or a constructive or symbolic delivery such as by an instrument of gift, sufficient to divest the donor of dominion and control over the property (see, Matter of Szabo, 10 N.Y.2d 94, 98–99, 217 N.Y.S.2d 593, 176 N.E.2d 395, supra; Speelman v. Pascal, 10 N.Y.2d 313, 318–320, 222 N.Y.S.2d 324, supra; Beaver v. Beaver, 117 N.Y. 421, 428–429, 22 N.E. 940, supra; Matter of Cohn, 187 App. Div. 392, 395, 176 N.Y.S. 225). As the statement of the rule suggests, the requirement of delivery is not rigid or inflexible, but is to be applied in light of its purpose to avoid mistakes by donors and fraudulent claims by donees (see, Matter of Van Alstyne, 207 N.Y. 298, 308, 100 N.E. 802, supra; Matter of Cohn, supra, 187 App. Div. at pp. 395–396, 176 N.Y.S.2d 255; Mechem, Requirement of Delivery in Gifts of Chattels and of Choses in Action Evidenced by Commercial Instruments, 21 Ill. L. Rev. 341, 348–349). Accordingly, what is sufficient to constitute delivery "must be tailored to suit the circumstances of the case" (Matter of Szabo, supra, 10 N.Y.2d at p. 98, 217 N.Y.S.2d 593, 176 N.E.2d 395). The rule requires that " '[t]he delivery necessary to consummate a gift must be as perfect as the nature of the property and the circumstances and surroundings of the parties will reasonably permit' " (id.; Vincent v. Rix, 248 N.Y. 76, 83, 161 N.E. 425; Matter of Van Alstyne, supra, 207 N.Y. at p. 309, 100 N.E. 802; see, Beaver v. Beaver, supra, 117 N.Y. at p. 428, 22 N.E. 940).

Defendant contends that when a tangible piece of personal property such as a painting is the subject of a gift, physical delivery of the painting itself is the best form of delivery and should be required. Here, of course, we have only delivery of Victor Gruen's letters which serve as instruments of gift. Defendant's statement of the rule as applied may be generally true, but it ignores the fact that what Victor Gruen gave plaintiff was not all rights to the Klimt painting, but only title to it with no right of possession until his death. Under these circumstances, it would be illogical for the law to require the donor to part with possession of the painting when that is exactly what he intends to retain.

Nor is there any reason to require a donor making a gift of a remainder interest in a chattel to physically deliver the chattel into the donee's hands only to have the donee redeliver it to the donor. As the facts of this case demonstrate, such a requirement could impose practical burdens on the parties to the gift while serving the delivery requirement poorly. Thus, in order to accomplish this type of delivery the parties would have been required to travel to New York for the symbolic transfer and redelivery of the Klimt painting which was hanging on the wall of Victor Gruen's Manhattan apartment. Defendant suggests that such a requirement would be stronger evidence of a completed gift, but in the absence of witnesses to the event or any written confirmation of the gift it would provide less protection against fraudulent claims than have the written instruments of gift delivered in this case.

ACCEPTANCE

Acceptance by the donee is essential to the validity of an inter vivos gift, but when a gift is of value to the donee, as it is here, the law will presume an acceptance on his part (Matter of Kelsey, 26 N.Y.2d 792, 309 N.Y.S.2d 219, 257 N.E.2d 663, affg. on opn. at 29 A.D.2d 450, 456, 289 N.Y.S.2d 314; Beaver v. Beaver, 117 N.Y. 421, 429, 22 N.E. 940, supra). Plaintiff did not rely on this presumption alone but also presented clear and convincing proof of his acceptance of a remainder interest in the Klimt painting by evidence that he had made several contemporaneous statements acknowledging the gift to his friends and associates, even showing some of them his father's gift letter, and that he had retained both letters for over 17 years to verify the gift after his father died. Defendant relied exclusively on affidavits filed by plaintiff in a matrimonial action with his former wife, in which plaintiff failed to list his interest in the painting as an asset. These affidavits were made over 10 years after acceptance was complete and they do not even approach the evidence in Matter of Kelly (285 N.Y. 139, 148–149, 33 N.E.2d 62 [dissenting in part opn.], supra) where the donee, immediately upon delivery of a diamond ring, rejected it as "too flashy." We agree with the Appellate Division that interpretation of the affidavit was too speculative to support a finding of rejection and overcome the substantial showing of acceptance by plaintiff.

Accordingly, the judgment appealed from and the order of the Appellate Division brought up for review should be affirmed, with costs.

NOTES

1. *Donative intent.* A completed gift requires donative intent, i.e., the donor must intend to surrender dominion and control over the subject matter of the gift. This does not mean that the donor must be motivated by benevolent or generous feelings; quite the reverse may be true. See Schultz v. Schultz, 637 S.W.2d 1 (Mo.1982) (donor threw stock certificates on brother's desk and told him "to stick them . . ."; held, valid gift). Once a completed gift has occurred, donative intent cannot be repudiated at a later date if the donor changes his or her mind. See Estate of Saathoff, 295 N.W.2d 290 (Neb.1980).

2. *Delivery.* There are three types of delivery: manual delivery; constructive delivery; and symbolic delivery (e.g., by an instrument of gift). Ordinarily a donor can make a gift of tangible personal property by handing over physical possession to the donee. See Barham v. Jones, 647 P.2d 397 (N.M. 1982) (diamond rings); Estate of Kremer, 546 N.E.2d 1047 (Ill.App. 1989) (cameras). Professor Mechem suggested that the delivery requirement serves several functions in the law of gifts: (1) the act of handing over an object makes the significance of the gift "vivid and concrete" to the donor (who feels the "wrench of delivery"); (2) the act provides unequivocal evidence to witnesses that a gift has occurred; and (3) the act provides the donee with prima facie

evidence of the gift. Mechem, The Requirement of Delivery in Gifts of Chattels and of Choses in Action Evidenced by Commercial Instruments, 21 Ill. L. Rev. 341 (1926). For further analysis of the purposes of the delivery requirement, see Gulliver & Tilson, Classification of Gratuitous Transfers, 51 Yale L.J. 1 (1941); Fuller, Consideration and Form, 41 Colum. L. Rev. 799 (1941); see also Rohan, The Continuing Question of Delivery in the Law of Gifts, 38 Ind. L.J. 1 (1962).

If delivery does not occur during the donor's lifetime, the gift generally fails. See Lauerman v. Destocki, 622 N.E.2d 1122 (Ohio App. 1993) (stock certificates endorsed but not delivered); Worrell v. Lathan, 478 S.E.2d 287 (S.C. App. 1996) (check written but not delivered); Simpson v. Simpson, 723 So.2d 326 (Fla.App. 1998) (father indicated intent to give guns to son but failed to deliver them). Nevertheless, where it appears that the donor clearly manifested donative intent and took all steps within his or her power to consummate the gift but died before delivery became complete, courts occasionally strain to uphold the attempted gift. See Estate of Capuzzi, 684 N.W.2d 677 (Mich. 2004) (upholding gift where child, acting at parent's direction under power of attorney, took all necessary actions to transfer partnership interests but donor died before transfer was completed on partnership's books); Naylor v. United States Trust Co., 711 So.2d 1350 (Fla.App. 1998) (upholding gift where donor directed trustee of revocable trust to make gifts "immediately" but died before checks were issued); but cf. Estate of Rider, 713 S.E.2d 643 (S.C. App. 2011) (no completed gift where husband instructed bank to transfer mutual funds to wife but died before funds credited to her account).

3. *Constructive delivery.* The donor may make a constructive delivery by handing over a key or similar object which opens up access to the subject matter of the gift. The key to a safe deposit box, jewelry box, or locked chest is a classic example. See Carlson v. Bankers Trust Co., 50 N.W.2d 1 (Iowa 1951); Cluck v. Ford, 152 P.3d 279 (Okla. App. 2006). Handing over a key to a house has been held sufficient to sustain a gift of the furnishings and other personal property in the house. See Libel v. Corcoran, 452 P.2d 832 (Kan.1969). Delivery of car keys may constitute a gift of the car. See Estate of Lines, 201 N.Y.S.2d 290 (Sur. 1959). What are the donee's chances of getting a new registration without litigating the question of title?

Since a key is a tangible object, handing it over satisfies to some extent the materialistic common law concept of manual delivery. Nevertheless, courts that follow the more modern, functional approach often sustain gifts on a theory of constructive delivery even where there is no transfer of a tangible object. See Brown v. Metz, 393 S.E.2d 402 (Va. 1990) (terminally ill donor instructed donee to retrieve bonds from safe deposit box); Teague v. Abbott, 100 N.E. 27 (Ind. App. 1912) (disclosure of combination to safe); Waite v. Grubbe, 73 P. 206 (Or.1903) (father showed daughter location of buried cash).

On one hand, courts state that constructive delivery is available only if manual delivery is "difficult, impracticable, inconvenient or impossible" due to the size, nature, or location of the subject matter. See Hatch v. Atkinson, 56 Me. 324 (1868); Newman v. Bost, 29 S.E. 848 (N.C.1898). This restriction can be explained in terms of the functions of delivery: If the subject matter itself can easily be handed over, the delivery of a key in its place indicates an equivocal intent on the donor's part. Similarly, if the donor delivers one key to a safe deposit box while retaining a duplicate, the requisite confirmation of donative intent seems to be lacking. See Estate of Stahl, 301 N.E.2d 82 (Ill.App.1973) (equivocal intent, no delivery).

On the other hand, courts state that delivery must be "as perfect as the nature of the property and the circumstances and surroundings of the parties will reasonably permit." In re Van Alstyne, 100 N.E. 802 (N.Y.1913). This suggests a somewhat more flexible approach, at least where there is clear and convincing evidence of donative intent. Thus, in Hebrew University Ass'n v. Nye, 223 A.2d 397 (Conn.Super.1966), the donor made a valid gift of a valuable collection of books, documents, and incunabula when she gave the donee a memorandum listing its contents and publicly announced a gift of the collection, even though the contents were not manually delivered during the donor's life. See also Bellis v. Bellis, 56 S.W.3d 396 (Ark.App. 2001) (oral gift of music box to child who left it with parents for safekeeping); McCarton v. Estate of Watson, 693 P.2d 192 (Wash.App.1984) (donor dictated dispositive wishes to donee, who confirmed he knew location of stock certificates and bank books).

4. *Instrument of gift.* To make a gift of intangible personal property (e.g., stocks, bonds, or other securities), the most practicable method of delivery may be to hand over a written instrument signed by the donor, which confirms the donor's intent. A gift of tangible personal property is sometimes made by delivering an instrument of gift where manual delivery would be inconvenient or impracticable. See Estate of Genecin v. Genecin, 363 F.Supp.2d 306 (D. Conn. 2005) (painting); Carey v. Jackson, 603 P.2d 868 (Wyo.1979) (jewelry, china, and glassware); Beck v. Givens, 309 P.2d 715 (Wyo.1957) (sheep).

If a donor retains physical possession of a security certificate or promissory note and delivers an instrument of gift with an express reservation of the right to receive payments made during the donor's life, the gift may be upheld as a valid inter vivos transfer. See Estate of Monks, 655 N.Y.S.2d 296 (Sur. 1997) (stock); Thatcher v. Merriam, 240 P.2d 266 (Utah 1952) (promissory note).

Even an informal letter may be effective if it sufficiently expresses the donor's intent to make a completed gift. See Hawkins v. Union Trust Co., 175 N.Y.S. 694 (App. Div. 1919) (gift of yacht); In re Kaufman's Estate, 107 N.Y.S.2d 681 (Sur. 1951) (gift announced by letter mailed before death but received by donee thereafter; gift upheld); Lewis v. Burke, 226 N.E.2d 332 (Ind.1967) (gift of household furnishings and contents effected by letter, sustained over a vigorous dissent); cf. Humble v. Gay, 143 P. 778 (Cal.1914) (chatty letter too informal to show intent to give valuable collection of Indian rugs).

5. *Uncashed checks.* In general, a check represents an order to pay which can be revoked by a stop payment order. The check itself does not operate as an assignment of any funds in the hands of the drawee. See U.C.C. §§ 3–408 and 4–403. Accordingly, a gift of a donor's own check ordinarily remains revocable and incomplete until the check is paid, certified, accepted, or negotiated for value. See Estate of Heyn, 47 P.3d 724 (Colo.App. 2002); Creekmore v. Creekmore, 485 S.E.2d 68 (N.C.App.1997); Estate of Bolton, 444 N.W.2d 482 (Iowa 1989); but cf. Sinclair v. Fleischman, 773 P.2d 101 (Wash.App. 1989) (upholding gift where donee failed to cash check before donor's death due to circumstances beyond either party's control). See generally Restatement (Third) of Property: Wills and Other Donative Transfers § 6.2 cmt. n (2003).

Suppose *A* gives *B* a $500 check as a birthday present; shortly afterward, *A* dies while the check is still outstanding. When the check is subsequently presented, may the drawee bank properly refuse payment? See Hieber v. Uptown Nat'l Bank of Chicago, 557 N.E.2d 408 (Ill.App.1990). If the bank accepts the check and pays *B* $500, is the bank liable to *A*'s personal representative? May the personal representative recover the $500 from *B*? See U.C.C. § 4–405 (death or incompetence of customer); Woo v. Smart, 442 S.E.2d 690 (Va. 1994); see also Scherer v. Hyland, infra.

6. *Securities and other intangibles.* A transfer of stocks, bonds, or other securities represented by a certificate is normally effected by delivering the certificate to the transferee or to a third party on behalf of the transferee. As a practical matter, the certificate should be endorsed or accompanied by a separate instrument of assignment, to facilitate registration of the change of ownership on the issuer's books. Nevertheless, the act of handing over the certificate constitutes an effective delivery even without an endorsement or an instrument of assignment. See Andrews v. Troy Bank & Trust Co., 529 So.2d 987 (Ala.1988); Rogers v. Rogers, 319 A.2d 119 (Md.1974); In re McVicker's Estate, 188 N.E.2d 731 (Ill.App.1963) (but lack of endorsement may raise questions concerning donative intent).

A gift may be upheld even if the donor retains physical possession of the certificate and simply hands over a written assignment of the stock or causes the issuer to record a change of ownership on its books. See Grau v. Dooley, 431 N.E.2d 1164 (Ill.App.1981) (written assignment); Pell Street Nineteen Corp. v. Mah, 671 N.Y.S.2d 742 (App. Div.1998) (change of record ownership). The same result has been reached where the donor submits an instrument of assignment together with instructions to register the transfer on the issuer's books, but dies before the instructions are carried out. See Kintzinger v. Millin, 117 N.W.2d 68 (Iowa 1962). Nevertheless, if there is substantial doubt concerning donative intent, failure to comply fully with the usual formalities may defeat the gift entirely. See Young v. Young, 393 S.E.2d 398 (Va.1990);

Estate of Szabo, 176 N.E.2d 395 (N.Y.1961) (transfer of stock on issuer's books not complete before owner's death).

Frequently a security certificate includes an express recital that the security is transferable only on the issuer's books. Courts generally hold that such restrictions are designed to protect the issuer and may be relied on by it for questions concerning ownership of the security; however, such restrictions have no effect on the rights as between a donor and a donee, and a valid gift may be made by manual delivery of the security (or a separate instrument of transfer) without a change in the registration.

In general, any intangible personal property represented by a written instrument may be transferred by delivery of the instrument (or a separate instrument of gift) coupled with donative intent. See Mashburn v. Wright, 420 S.E.2d 379 (Ga.App. 1992) (certificate of deposit); Estate of Campbell, 939 S.W.2d 558 (Mo.App.1997) (unendorsed promissory note); Chalmers v. Chalmers, 937 S.W.2d 171 (Ark.1997) (gift of promissory note made by separate instrument); Davis v. Gillespie, 507 S.W.2d 179 (Ky.1974) (life insurance policy); Ridden v. Thrall, 26 N.E. 627 (N.Y.1891) (gift causa mortis of savings account by delivery of bank book). Why then does delivery of a personal check book fail to effect a gift of the checking account? See Brophy v. Haeberle, 221 N.Y.S. 698 (App. Div. 1927).

7. *Delivery to third person.* Sometimes the donor delivers the subject matter of the gift to a third person with instructions to redeliver it to the donee at the donor's death. In deciding whether to uphold the gift, courts often ask whether the third person is acting as a "trustee" for the donee or as an "agent" of the donor. (In this context, the term "trustee" is used loosely to mean a person acting on behalf of the donee.) The former label signifies that the gift is valid, while the latter label indicates that the gift fails for lack of delivery since the agency terminates automatically at the donor's death. For the most part, it appears that courts use the two labels simply to describe conclusions as to whether or not a gift was intended. Among the factors that may affect the outcome in a particular case are the following:

(a) *Retained control.* If the donor indicates that he or she may ask for return of the subject matter or otherwise purports to retain a power of revocation, the inference is that the third party is the donor's agent. Ironically, such a power is implied without invalidating the gift in the case of a gift causa mortis, discussed infra. A similar inference may be drawn if the donor retains other types of control or supervision over the third party. A direction not to deliver until the donor's death does not necessarily destroy the gift—again, the issue turns on whether the gift is viewed as a present transfer with possession postponed (i.e., a valid inter vivos gift) or as a transfer to be completed at death (i.e., an invalid testamentary transfer).

(b) *Reasons for indirect delivery.* If there is a valid reason (unrelated to the donor's retention of control) for making the gift through an intermediary—for example, where the donee is unavailable or incapacitated—this tends to support an inference that the third party is not the donor's agent.

(c) *Previous relationship between donor and third party.* If the third party is the donor's former lawyer or business partner, a court may find a continuing agency relationship.

On the validity of delivery to a third person, see Kesterson v. Cronan, 806 P.2d 134 (Or.App.1991) (donor instructed friend to deliver third party's promissory note to maker at donor's death in satisfaction of debt; no valid gift); Albrecht v. Brais, 754 N.E.2d 396 (Ill.App.2001) (donor deposited deed with escrow agent but retained power to revoke; no valid gift); Estate of Cristo, 446 N.Y.S.2d 555 (App. Div. 1982) (delivery to donor's accountant upheld); Malloy v. Smith, 290 A.2d 486 (Md.1972) (valid delivery to donor's friend to be turned over to donee at donor's death).

8. *Authority of agent or conservator.* An agent acting under a durable power of attorney may be expressly authorized to make gifts of the principal's property. In view of the ever-present possibility of fraud or overreaching, however, many courts are reluctant to find implied authority to make gifts, especially if the gift results in a personal benefit to the agent. See Fender v. Fender, 329 S.E.2d 430 (S.C.1985) (agent's gifts to self invalid despite purported oral authorization; power to make any gift "must be expressly granted in the instrument itself"); Bienash v. Moller, 721 N.W.2d 431 (S.D. 2006); Archbold v. Reifenrath, 744 N.W.2d 701 (Neb. 2008); Bryant v. Bryant, 882 P.2d 169 (Wash. 1994). Some courts adopt a more flexible approach and look at the surrounding facts and circumstances to determine whether a broadly worded durable power of attorney includes the power to make gifts. See Figgins v. Cochrane, 942 A.2d 736 (Md. 2008). Suppose that *A* names her child *B* as agent under a durable power of attorney which authorizes *B* "to sell, convey or otherwise dispose of" *A*'s property and "to do all things which [*A*] could do if personally present." Does *B* have authority to make gifts to herself? To *A*'s other children? To charitable organizations? Does it matter whether *A* is competent at the time of the gifts? Whether the gifts are trivial in amount or represent a substantial portion of *A*'s assets? See LeCraw v. LeCraw, 401 S.E.2d 697 (Ga.1991) (upholding gifts made by agent on behalf of competent principal to natural objects of bounty in accordance with established pattern); cf. Estate of Littlejohn, 698 N.W.2d 923 (N.D. 2005) (gifts of land authorized by broad power to convey). See generally Restatement (Third) of Property: Wills and Other Donative Transfers § 8.1 cmt. *l* (2003).

The Uniform Power of Attorney Act (2006) codifies restrictions on an agent's power to engage in active estate planning on behalf of the principal. The uniform act enumerates actions involving the principal's property that an agent can perform only pursuant to an express grant of authority in the power of attorney: for example, making gifts; creating, amending or revoking a revocable trust; and creating or changing survivorship rights and beneficiary designations. UPAA § 201(a). Moreover, a general grant of authority to make gifts extends only to the amount of the gift tax annual exclusion ($13,000 per donee per year in 2012) unless otherwise provided in the power of attorney. Id. § 217(b). In making gifts of the principal's property, the agent is directed to act consistently with the principal's known objectives or with the principal's best interest. Id. § 217(c). Although an agent, like any other fiduciary, is constrained by fundamental duties of loyalty and impartiality, those duties can be modified by the terms of the power of attorney. Id. § 114(b). Indeed, the uniform act provides the further qualification that an agent who acts with care, competence, and diligence in the principal's best interest "is not liable solely because the agent also benefits from the act or has an individual or conflicting interest" in the transaction. Id. § 114(d). Does the uniform act strike a fair balance between the goal of flexible and efficient property management and the need for protection against unscrupulous agents? For an overview of the uniform act, see Hook & Johnson, The Uniform Power of Attorney Act, 45 Real Prop. Tr. & Est. L.J. 283 (2010).

Unlike an agent acting under a durable power of attorney, a conservator or guardian must be appointed by a court and remains subject to judicial supervision in managing the affairs of an incapacitated ward. Under the doctrine of "substituted judgment," a conservator or guardian may seek judicial approval to make gifts of the ward's property in accordance with the ward's probable intent or best interests. In several cases courts have authorized substantial asset transfers in connection with Medicaid planning. See Matter of John XX, 652 N.Y.S.2d 329 (App. 1996) (authorizing gifts by guardian of more than $600,000 to ward's adult children); Matter of Labis, 714 A.2d 335 (N.J. App. 1998) (transfer of home to spouse); see also UPC § 5–427(b) (limited authority of conservator to make gifts on behalf of adult protected person); Restatement (Third) of Property: Wills and Other Donative Transfers § 8.1 cmt. k (2003).

9. *Acceptance.* In theory, a gift is valid only if the donee accepts it. Acceptance is presumed, however, if the gift is beneficial to the donee. Thus, as a practical matter, it may be more accurate to say that a gift may be defeated if the donee rejects or disclaims it. See Estate of Kelly, 33 N.E.2d 62 (N.Y.1941) (donee rejected diamond ring as "too flashy"). Suppose *A*, acting with donative intent, delivers two rings to *B*; the next day, *B* gives the rings back to *A* to wear, saying "you are just not you without them." At *A*'s death, *B* claims the rings pursuant to *A*'s original gift. What result? See Barham v. Jones, 647 P.2d 397 (N.M.1982); Newell v. National Bank of Norwich, 212 N.Y.S. 158 (App. Div. 1925).

10. *Promise to make future gift.* In general, a gratuitous promise to make a future gift is unenforceable. An expression of donative intent, without delivery, does not give rise to a completed gift, and a promise unsupported by consideration (or by detrimental reliance on the promisee's part) creates no

binding contractual obligation. See Wetmore's Estate, 343 N.E.2d 224 (Ill.App.1976); Unthank v. Rippstein, 386 S.W.2d 134 (Tex.1964) (written promise to pay friend $200 per month for five years); but cf. Faith Lutheran Retirement Home v. Veis, 473 P.2d 503 (Mont.1970) (upholding promise to make charitable gift).

Similarly, a gratuitous assignment of an expectancy is unenforceable. Thus, for example, *B*, the only child of *A*, has no transferable interest in *A*'s estate until *A*'s death and therefore cannot make a valid gift of an expected inheritance while *A* is living. On the other hand, at *A*'s death *B* inherits an interest which can be transferred by gift. See Estate of Saathoff, 295 N.W.2d 290 (Neb.1980) (valid gift of intestate share in deceased son's estate). The transfer of an expectancy for consideration is discussed supra at p. 141.

In Speelman v. Pascal, 178 N.E.2d 723 (N.Y.1961), cited in the principal case, the theatrical producer Gabriel Pascal acquired the right to prepare and produce a musical play based on George Bernard Shaw's *Pygmalion*. Several months before his death, before the musical play (which ultimately became the highly successful *My Fair Lady*) was written or produced, Pascal wrote to his executive secretary as follows:

> This is to confirm to you our understanding that I give you [a percentage of] my shares of profits of the Pygmalion Musical stage version. . . . As soon as the contracts are signed, I will send a copy of this letter to my lawyer . . . and he will confirm to you this arrangement in a legal form.

The court upheld the gift, noting that Pascal owned the production rights and "could grant to another a share of the moneys to accrue from the use of those rights by others." Furthermore, the delivery requirement was met since "there was nothing left for Pascal to do in order to make an irrevocable transfer to plaintiff of part of Pascal's right to receive royalties from the productions."

2. GIFTS CAUSA MORTIS

A gift "causa mortis," as its name indicates, is a gift made in contemplation of death for the purpose of making a final disposition of the subject matter if death occurs. Professor Story called it "a sort of amphibious gift between a gift inter vivos and a legacy." Story, Equity Jurisprudence § 606 (11th ed. 1873). Indeed, this form of transfer, as developed in England and America, resembles a will in objectives and general effect, but the required formalities are those applicable to inter vivos gifts.

The modern concept of a gift causa mortis exhibits several distinctive characteristics which set it apart from an inter vivos gift:

(a) The gift causa mortis is made in apprehension of impending death, though the donor need not be in extremis.

(b) The gift automatically fails if the donor recovers from the apprehended peril, and the donor must intend this result. If the donor intends to make an unconditional gift, it is analyzed as an inter vivos gift rather than a gift causa mortis.

(c) The gift is revocable by the donor. This point is seldom tested in litigation: if the donor dies, it is unlikely that he or she will have occasion to revoke the gift; if the donor recovers, the gift will automatically fail on that ground.

(d) The gift automatically fails if the donee predeceases the donor. This point also seldom arises in litigation, since a donee is unlikely to die before a donor who is already dying at the time of the gift.

(e) The gift is subject to claims of the donor's creditors if the probate estate is insufficient to satisfy them—i.e., if the decedent's estate is insolvent.

(f) The subject matter of the gift is limited to personal property; land cannot be transferred by a gift causa mortis.

(g) The gift is effectuated by delivery in the same manner as an inter vivos gift. Accordingly, the gift is usually viewed as passing title to the donee at the time of the gift, subject to divestment by the operation of the conditions subsequent of recovery, revocation, predecease, and liability to creditors.

SCHERER V. HYLAND
Supreme Court of New Jersey, 1977.
75 N.J. 127, 380 A.2d 698.

PER CURIAM.

Defendant, the Administrator ad litem of the Estate of Catherine Wagner, appeals from an Appellate Division decision, one judge dissenting, affirming a summary judgment by the trial court holding that Ms. Wagner had made a valid gift causa mortis of a check to plaintiff. We affirm.

The facts are not in dispute. Catherine Wagner and the plaintiff, Robert Scherer, lived together for approximately fifteen years prior to Ms. Wagner's death in January 1974. In 1970, the decedent and plaintiff were involved in an automobile accident in which decedent suffered facial wounds and a broken hip. Because of the hip injury, decedent's physical mobility was substantially impaired. She was forced to give up her job and to restrict her activities. After the accident, plaintiff cared for her and assumed the sole financial responsibility for maintaining their household.

During the weeks preceding her death, Ms. Wagner was acutely depressed. On one occasion, she attempted suicide by slashing her wrists. On January 23, 1974, she committed suicide by jumping from the roof of the apartment building in which they lived.

On the morning of the day of her death, Ms. Wagner received a check for $17,400 drawn by a Pennsylvania attorney who had represented her in a claim arising out of the automobile accident. The check represented settlement of the claim. Plaintiff telephoned Ms. Wagner at around 11:30 a.m. that day and was told that the check had arrived. Plaintiff noticed nothing unusual in Ms. Wagner's voice. At about 3:20 p.m., decedent left the apartment building and jumped to her death. The police, as part of their investigation of the suicide, asked the building superintendent to admit them to the apartment. On the kitchen table they found the check, endorsed in blank, and two notes handwritten by the decedent. In one, she described her depression over her physical condition, expressed her love for Scherer, and asked him to forgive her "for taking the easy way out." In the other, she indicated that she "bequeathed" to plaintiff all of her possessions, including "the check for $17,400. . . ." The police took possession of the check, which was eventually placed in an interest-bearing account pending disposition of this action.

Under our wills statute it is clear that Ms. Wagner's note bequeathing all her possessions to Mr. Scherer cannot take effect as a testamentary disposition. N.J.S.A. 3A:3–2. A donatio causa mortis has been traditionally defined as a gift of personal property made by a party in expectation of death, then imminent, subject to the condition that the donor die as anticipated. Establishment of the gift has uniformly called for proof of delivery.

The primary issue here is whether Ms. Wagner's acts of endorsing the settlement check, placing it on the kitchen table in the apartment she shared with Scherer, next to a writing clearly evidencing her intent to transfer the check to Scherer, and abandoning the apartment with a clear expectation of imminent death constituted delivery sufficient to sustain a gift causa mortis of the check. Defendant, relying on the principles established in Foster v. Reiss, 18 N.J. 41, 112 A.2d 553 (1955), argues that there was no delivery because the donor did not unequivocally relinquish control of the check before her death. Central to this argument is the contention that suicide, the perceived peril, was one which decedent herself created and one which was completely within her control. According to this contention, the donor at any time before she jumped from the apartment roof could have changed her mind, re-entered the apartment, and reclaimed the check. Defendant therefore reasons that decedent did not make an effective transfer of the check during her lifetime, as is required for a valid gift causa mortis. . . .

There is general agreement that the major purpose of the delivery requirement is evidentiary. Proof of delivery reduces the possibility that the evidence of intent has been fabricated or that a mere donative impulse, not consummated by action, has been mistaken for a completed gift. Since "these gifts come into question only after death has closed the lips of the donor," the delivery requirement provides a substantial safeguard against fraud and perjury. See Keepers v. Fidelity Title and Deposit Co., 56 N.J. L. 302, 308, 28 A. 585 (E. & A. 1893). In *Foster*, the majority concluded that these policies could best be fulfilled by a strict rule requiring actual manual tradition of the subject-matter of the gift except in a very narrow class of cases where "there can be no actual delivery" or where "the situation is incompatible with the performance of such ceremony." 18 N.J. at 50, 112 A.2d at 559. Justice Jacobs, in his dissenting opinion (joined by Justices Brennan and Wachenfeld) questioned the reasonableness of requiring direct physical delivery in cases where donative intent is "freely and clearly expressed in a written instrument." Id. at 56, 112 A.2d at 562. He observed that a more flexible approach to the delivery requirement had been taken by other jurisdictions and quoted approvingly from Devol v. Dye, 123 Ind. 321, 24 N.E. 246, 7 L.R.A. 439 (Sup. Ct. 1890). That case stated:

> [G]ifts causa mortis . . . are not to be held contrary to public policy, nor do they rest under the disfavor of the law, when the facts are clearly and satisfactorily shown which make it appear that they were freely and intelligently made. Ellis v. Secor, 31 Mich. 185. While every case must be brought within the general rule upon the points essential to such a gift, yet, as the circumstances under which donations mortis causa are made must of necessity be infinite in variety, each case must be determined upon its own peculiar facts and circumstances. Dickeschied v. Bank, 28 W.Va. 341; Kiff v. Weaver, 94 N.C. 274. The rule requiring delivery, either actual or symbolical, must be maintained, but its application is to be militated [sic] and applied according to the relative importance of the subject of the gift and the condition of the donor. The intention of a donor in peril of death, when clearly ascertained and fairly consummated within the meaning of well-established rules, is not to be thwarted by a narrow and illiberal construction of what may have been intended for and deemed by him a sufficient delivery. . . .

The balancing approach suggested in Devol v. Dye has been articulated in the following manner:

> Where there has been unequivocal proof of a deliberate and well-considered donative intent on the part of the donor, many courts have been inclined to overlook the technical requirements and to hold that a "constructive" or "symbolic" delivery is sufficient to vest title in

the donee. However, where this is allowed the evidence must clearly show an intention to part presently with some substantial attribute of ownership. [Gordon v. Barr, 13 Cal. 2d 596, 601, 91 P.2d 101, 104 (Sup. Ct. Cal. 1939)]

In essence, this approach takes into account the purposes served by the requirement of delivery in determining whether that requirement has been met. It would find a constructive delivery adequate to support the gift when the evidence of donative intent is concrete and undisputed, when there is every indication that the donor intended to make a present transfer of the subject-matter of the gift, and when the steps taken by the donor to effect such a transfer must have been deemed by the donor as sufficient to pass the donor's interest to the donee. We are persuaded that this approach, which does not minimize the need for evidentiary safeguards to prevent frauds upon the estates of the deceased, reflects the realities which attend transfers of this kind.

In this case, the evidence of decedent's intent to transfer the check to Robert Scherer is concrete, unequivocal, and undisputed. The circumstances definitely rule out any possibility of fraud. The sole question, then, is whether the steps taken by the decedent, independent of her writing of the suicide notes, were sufficient to support a finding that she effected a lifetime transfer of the check to Scherer. We think that they were. First, the act of endorsing a check represents, in common experience and understanding, the only act needed (short of actual delivery) to render a check negotiable. The significance of such an act is universally understood. Accordingly, we have no trouble in viewing Ms. Wagner's endorsement of the settlement check as a substantial step taken by her for the purpose of effecting a transfer to Scherer of her right to the check proceeds. Second, we note that the only person other than the decedent who had routine access to the apartment was Robert Scherer. Indeed, the apartment was leased in his name. It is clear that Ms. Wagner before leaving the apartment placed the check in a place where Scherer could not fail to see it and fully expected that he would take actual possession of the check when he entered. And, although Ms. Wagner's subsequent suicide does not itself constitute a component of the delivery of this gift, it does provide persuasive evidence that when Ms. Wagner locked the door of the apartment she did so with no expectation of returning. When we consider her state of mind as it must have been upon leaving the apartment, her surrender of possession at that moment was complete. We find, therefore, that when she left the apartment she completed a constructive delivery of the check to Robert Scherer. In light of her resolve to take her own life and of her obvious desire not to be deterred from that purpose, Ms. Wagner's failure manually to transfer the check to Scherer is understandable. She clearly did all that she could do or thought necessary to do to surrender the check. Her donative intent has been conclusively demonstrated by independent evidence. The law should effectuate that intent rather than indulge in nice distinctions which would thwart her purpose. Upon these facts, we find that the constructive delivery she made was adequate to support a gift causa mortis.

Defendant's assertion that suicide is not the sort of peril that will sustain a gift causa mortis finds some support in precedents from other jurisdictions. E.g., Ray v. Leader Federal Sav. & Loan Ass'n, 40 Tenn. App. 625, 292 S.W.2d 458 (Ct.App.1953). See generally Annot., "Nature and validity of gift made in contemplation of suicide," 60 A.L.R.2d 575 (1958). We are, however, not bound by those authorities nor do we find them persuasive. While it is true that a gift causa mortis is made by the donor with a view to impending death, death is no less impending because of a resolve to commit suicide. Nor does that fixed purpose constitute any lesser or less imminent peril than does a ravaging disease. Indeed, given the despair sufficient to end it all, the peril attendant upon contemplated suicide may reasonably be viewed as even more imminent than that accompanying many illnesses which prove ultimately to be fatal. Cf. Berl v. Rosenberg, 169 Cal. App. 2d 125, 336 P.2d 975, 978 (Dist.Ct.App. 1959) (public policy against suicide does not invalidate otherwise valid gift causa mortis). And, the notion that one in a state of mental depression serious enough to lead to suicide is somehow "freer" to renounce the depression and thus the danger than one suffering from a physical illness, although it has a certain augustinian appeal, has long since been replaced by more enlightened views of human psychology. In re Van Wormer's Estate, 255 Mich. 399, 238 N.W. 210 (Sup. Ct. 1931) (melancholia ending in suicide sufficient to sustain a gift causa mortis). We also observe that an argument that the donor of a causa mortis gift might have changed his or her mind loses much of its force when one recalls that a causa mortis gift, by definition, can be revoked at any time before the donor dies and is automatically revoked if the donor recovers.

Finally, defendant asserts that this gift must fail because there was no acceptance prior to the donor's death. Although the issue of acceptance is rarely litigated, the authority that does exist indicates that, given a valid delivery, acceptance will be implied if the gift is unconditional and beneficial to the donee. See, e.g., Sparks v. Hurley, 208 Pa. 166, 57 A. 364, 366 (Sup. Ct. 1904); Graham v. Johnston, 243 Iowa 112, 49 N.W.2d 540, 543 (Sup. Ct. 1951). The presumption of acceptance may apply even if the donee does not learn of the gift until after the donor's death. Taylor v. Sanford, 108 Tex. 340, 344, 193 S.W. 661, 662 (Sup. Ct. 1917) (assent to gift of deed mailed in contemplation of death but received after grantor's death should be presumed unless a dissent or disclaimer appears). A donee cannot be expected to accept or reject a gift until he learns of it and unless a gift is rejected when the donee is informed of it the presumption of acceptance is not defeated. See id. at 344, 193 S.W. at 662. Here the gift was clearly beneficial to Scherer, and he has always expressed his acceptance.

Judgment affirmed.

NOTES

1. *Apprehension of death.* On one hand, requiring that a gift causa mortis be made in apprehension of death serves to establish a foundation for implying divesting conditions in accordance with the donor's probable intent. On the other hand, some courts defeat attempted gifts by applying this requirement quite strictly. For instance, there is authority suggesting that the donor must die of the apprehended peril, which raises difficult problems of proof. Most modern authority, however, adopts a less rigid approach. See Ridden v. Thrall, 26 N.E. 627 (N.Y.1891) (upholding gift made in anticipation of hernia operation where donor died two weeks later from heart attack); cf. Antos v. Bocek, 452 P.2d 533 (Ariz.App.1969) (purported gift of automobile failed where donor returned from hospital, resumed use of automobile, and died two weeks later from drug overdose). A gift in contemplation of a surgical operation may qualify as a valid gift causa mortis even if the donor voluntarily submits to the operation. See Adcock v. Bishop, 218 S.W.2d 52 (Ky.1949). The validity of gifts made in contemplation of suicide is discussed in the principal case.

2. *Conditional intent.* Where a donor makes a gift in contemplation of death but survives the apprehended peril, it is open to the donee to show that the gift was intended to be final whether the donor lived or died and that it is therefore valid as an inter vivos gift. See Newell v. National Bank of Norwich, 212 N.Y.S. 158 (App. Div. 1925). The label may be important in determining the outcome of the litigation.

Traditional doctrine holds that a gift is valid only if some interest passes from the donor to the donee at delivery. In the case of a gift causa mortis, the gift is subject to divestment if the donor revokes or recovers. A non-lawyer may have difficulty in appreciating the difference between the operation of a gift causa mortis and a will. (So may a lawyer.) The validity of the gift may turn on whether the donor says, "When I die these are yours" or "These are yours, but if I recover I may want them back." Compare Van Pelt v. King, 154 N.E. 163 (Ohio App. 1926) (donor stated that "if he did not return from the hospital they were hers"; gift failed for lack of intent to make present transfer) with In re Newland's Estate, 70 N.E.2d 238 (Ohio App. 1946) (donor stated, "if I get well I want it back"; valid gift causa mortis).

3. *Delivery.* Given the functional similarities between a gift causa mortis and a will, some courts scrutinize gifts causa mortis with particular care out of a perceived need to safeguard the integrity of the statute of wills. For example, in Foster v. Reiss, 112 A.2d 553 (N.J.1955), decedent, in hospital for major surgery, left a letter in her bedside table for her husband which di-

rected the disposition of cash and other personal property. Her husband arrived at the hospital and picked up the note while decedent was unconscious in the operating room. A divided court held the attempted gift invalid for lack of delivery, despite the decedent's clearly expressed donative intent:

> We must not forget that since a gift causa mortis is made in contemplation of death and is subject to revocation by the donor up to the time of his death, it differs from a legacy only in the requirement of delivery. Delivery is in effect the only safeguard imposed by law upon a transaction which would ordinarily fall within the statute of wills. To eliminate delivery from the requirements for a gift causa mortis would be to permit any writing to effectuate a testamentary transfer, even though it does not comply with the requirements of the statute of wills. [112 A.2d at 560.]

With this strict view of delivery, compare the opinion in the principal case; see also Estate of Smith, 694 A.2d 1099 (Pa. Super. 1997) (valid gift causa mortis of checks mailed by donor but not received by donee before death); Whisnant v. Whisnant, 928 P.2d 999 (Or.App. 1996) (valid gift causa mortis where husband instructed broker to sell bonds and use proceeds to pay off mortgage on property owned jointly with wife). In *Scherer*, suppose that Ms. Wagner went out for a walk, leaving the endorsed check on the kitchen table for Mr. Scherer with a cover note, and met her death by accident. Would the transfer be valid as an inter vivos gift?

4. *Gifts in contemplation of marriage.* By analogy to gifts causa mortis, gifts made in contemplation of marriage are subject to an implied condition of divestment if the marriage does not in fact take place. The issue usually arises when the engagement is broken off and the donor demands the return of an engagement ring or other valuable property previously given to the intended spouse. Traditionally, the donor is entitled to recover the gift if the parties dissolve the engagement by mutual consent or if the donee unjustifiably breaks off the engagement, but not if the donor is at fault in breaking off the engagement. See Curtis v. Anderson, 106 S.W.3d 251 (Tex. App. 2003); Albinger v. Harris, 48 P.3d 711 (Mont. 2002). In recent years, however, many courts have discarded the traditional rule in favor of a no-fault rule which allows the donor to recover the gift if the marriage does not take place, regardless of which party is responsible for terminating the engagement. In Aronow v. Silver, 538 A.2d 851 (N.J. Super. 1987), the court offered the following rationale:

> What fact justifies the breaking of an engagement? The absence of a sense of humor? Differing musical tastes? Differing political views? The painfully-learned fact is that marriages are made on earth, not in heaven. They must be approached with intelligent care and should not happen without a decent assurance of success. When either party lacks that assurance, for whatever reason, the engagement should be broken. No

justification is needed. Either party may act. Fault, impossible to fix, does not count. [538 A.2d at 853–54.]

Accord, Lindh v. Surman, 742 A.2d 643 (Pa. 1999); Heiman v. Parrish, 942 P.2d 631 (Kan.1997). In any event, recovery may be denied, on grounds of public policy, if one of the parties is already married to someone else at the time of the gift. See Hooven v. Quintana, 618 P.2d 702 (Colo.App.1980) (gift to married donee).

3. GIFTS TO MINORS

In general, a minor is capable of owning property but lacks legal capacity to engage in property transactions. Therefore, a direct gift of property to a minor may give rise to serious practical difficulties if it becomes necessary to sell the property. In the case of securities, for example, brokers, banks, issuers, and transfer agents deal with the minor at their peril: Upon reaching majority, the minor may disaffirm the sale and hold them liable for any loss suffered as a result of the transaction.

Although a guardian may be appointed in formal court proceedings to sell, lease, pledge, or otherwise deal with property on behalf of a minor, guardianships are expensive, cumbersome, and relatively inflexible. For example, a guardian is generally required to furnish a fiduciary bond and to file periodic accountings with the court. Furthermore, in many jurisdictions a guardian has limited powers and cannot sell property without approval from the court.

One alternative to direct ownership by the minor is a full-fledged trust, in which a trustee holds legal title to property and manages it for the benefit of the minor beneficiary under the terms established by the settlor of the trust. Another alternative is a custodianship established under the Uniform Transfers to Minors Act (UTMA), which supersedes the original Uniform Gifts to Minors Act and has been enacted in one version or another throughout the country. A custodianship can be created with respect to any type of property, real or personal, tangible or intangible, simply by transferring property "to A as custodian for B under the [State] Uniform Transfers to Minors Act." UTMA § 9. In practical effect, a custodianship resembles a statutory trust for a single beneficiary. Technically, however, the custodial property is vested in the minor; the custodian has substantial fiduciary powers and duties, but not legal title. Id. § 11(b). The custodian is under a duty to take control of the custodial property and manage it in accordance with "the standard of care that would be observed by a prudent person dealing with the property of another." Id. § 12. The custodian has broad administrative powers, id. § 13, and also has authority to deliver or pay to the minor or expend for the minor's benefit so much of the custodial property as the custodian considers advisable for the use and benefit of the minor, without court order and without regard to (i) the duty or ability of the custodian personally or of any other person to support the minor, or (ii) any other income or property of the minor which may be applicable or available for that purpose. [Id. § 14(a).]

The statute does not require periodic accountings by the custodian, but does give the minor and certain other persons standing to petition the court for an accounting. Id. § 19. In general, the custodian is under a duty to turn over the custodial property to the minor when the minor reaches age 21. Id. § 20(1).

For federal tax purposes, the custodianship is not recognized as a separate taxpayer; the custodial property and any income therefrom are treated as owned directly by the minor. The Internal Revenue Service also recognizes that UTMA gifts qualify as present interests for purposes of the gift tax annual exclusion. See Rev. Rul. 59–357, 1959–2 C.B. 212. However, if a parent puts property in his or her name as custodian and then dies while acting in that capacity, the custodial property is includible in the parent's gross estate for estate tax purposes. See id.; Estate of Prudowsky v. Commissioner, 465 F.2d 62 (7th Cir. 1972). For this reason, it may be desirable to name a third person as custodian.

C. CONTRACTUAL AND SURVIVORSHIP ARRANGEMENTS

1. CONTRACTUAL ARRANGEMENTS

Conceptually and historically, the law of contracts has evolved separately from the law of property and gifts. In general, a valid contract requires a promise or agreement supported by consideration; donative intent and delivery are irrelevant. From a functional perspective, however, a contract that provides benefits to a third party often serves as a convenient substitute for a gift or a will.

The leading example is a life insurance policy, which by its terms obligates the issuer to pay proceeds at the insured party's death to a designated beneficiary. Payment of the proceeds to the beneficiary represents the performance by the issuer of its contractual obligation; there is no transfer of property directly from the policy owner to the beneficiary. Accordingly, the proceeds normally do not constitute probate assets (unless the insured party's estate is designated as beneficiary). Moreover, by statute in most jurisdictions, the policy and proceeds are exempt in whole or in part from claims of the insured party's creditors. Typically, the policy provides that the owner may revoke or amend the beneficiary designation at any time during the insured party's life but the proceeds automatically become payable at the insured party's death in accordance with the beneficiary designation then on file with the issuer. Most insurance policies offer a range of "settlement options" concerning the form of payment, including (1) a lump sum payment, (2) periodic payments of principal and interest over a fixed period or a specified lifetime (i.e., an annuity), and (3) payments of interest for a fixed period or a specified lifetime followed by a lump sum payment of principal.

The validity of beneficiary designations under life insurance policies is well established. See Gordon v. Portland Trust Bank, 271 P.2d 653 (Or.1954) (life insurance payable to trust or other designated beneficiary). In other contexts, as well, courts often give effect to contractual provisions requiring payment of cash or other property to a third-party beneficiary at the death of one of the parties. See E.F. Hutton & Co., Inc. v. Wallace, 863 F.2d 472 (6th Cir.1988) (pay-on-death beneficiary of individual retirement account); Estate of Verbeek, 467 P.2d 178 (Wash.App.1970) (self-cancelling mortgage note); Estate of Hillowitz, 238 N.E.2d 723 (N.Y.1968) (deceased partner's interest passed to widow under partnership agreement); Kansas City Life Ins. Co. v. Rainey, 182 S.W.2d 624 (Mo.1944) (contract to pay interest for life to depositor and principal at death to designated beneficiary).

The validity of pay-on-death beneficiary designations remains doubtful in some areas, however. In the absence of a validating statute, there is a risk that a court may brand such a designation as a futile attempt to make a "testamentary" disposition of property in violation of the prescribed wills formalities. See Miller v. Cothran, 280 S.W.3d 580 (Ark.App. 2008) (pay-on-death provision in lease); Will of Collier, 381 So.2d 1338 (Miss. 1980) (certificate of deposit); Truax v. Southwestern College, 522 P.2d 412 (Kan.1974) (bank accounts); Waitman v. Waitman, 505 P.2d 171 (Okla.1972) (same). Even where there is statutory authority for a pay-on-death designation, failure to comply with the applicable statutory requirements may defeat the attempted disposition. See Estate of Waitkevich, 323 N.E.2d 545 (Ill.App.1975) (requirement of "written agreement" not met where designation was typed on ledger card previously signed by depositor); cf. Corning Bank v. Rice, 645 S.W.2d 675 (Ark.1983) (bank liable for failure to comply with statutory formalities for pay-on-death designation requested by depositor).

NOTES

1. *Life insurance policies and other contracts.* At the death of an insured party, suppose the issuer agrees, at the beneficiary's request, to pay interest at a fixed rate on the proceeds to the beneficiary for life and then to pay the proceeds to another person designated by the beneficiary. The agreement is invariably upheld if it is viewed as part of the original life insurance policy or

a supplement thereto, rather than as a separate free-standing deposit contract. See Hall v. Mutual Life Ins. Co. of New York, 122 N.Y.S.2d 239 (App. Div. 1953); Toulouse v. New York Life Ins. Co., 245 P.2d 205 (Wash.1952); cf. Wilhoit v. Peoples Life Ins. Co., 218 F.2d 887 (7th Cir.1955). Why should the validity of a pay-on-death provision depend on whether it appears in a life insurance policy or in some other type of contract?

2. *Change of life insurance beneficiary.* Life insurance policies typically provide that the owner may revoke or amend a beneficiary designation by giving written notice to the issuer during the insured party's life. If an owner (who is also the insured party) took all reasonable steps to designate a new beneficiary but died before the change was recorded on the issuer's books, courts routinely invoke the doctrine of substantial compliance to give effect to the change as between the competing beneficiaries, on the theory that the formal requirements are intended solely for the benefit of the issuer. Is the doctrine of substantial compliance available where the owner-insured submitted an unsigned change-of-beneficiary form? See Davis v. Combes, 294 F.3d 931 (7th Cir. 2002). Where the owner signed a change-of-beneficiary form but failed to submit it to the issuer before death? See IDS Life Ins. Co. v. Estate of Groshong, 736 P.2d 1301 (Idaho 1987). Where the owner gave oral instructions for a new beneficiary designation but never signed a change-of-beneficiary form? See Estate of Golas, 751 A.2d 229 (Pa. Super. 2000); Prudential Ins. Co. v. Schmid, 337 F.Supp.2d 325 (D. Mass. 2004). What if the owner-insured named a new beneficiary by will? See McCarthy v. Aetna Life Ins. Co., 704 N.E.2d 557 (N.Y. 1998); Stone v. Stephens, 99 N.E.2d 766 (Ohio 1951). If it is uncertain which of two competing claimants is entitled to proceeds payable at the death of the insured party, what steps may the issuer take to avoid double liability?

3. *Revocation by divorce.* The revocation-by-divorce rule of UPC § 2–804 applies not only to bequests in the testator's will but also to revocable beneficiary designations under life insurance policies and other nonprobate transfers. Suppose that, prior to the enactment of UPC § 2–804, *H* took out an insurance policy on his own life and named his wife *W* as sole beneficiary. A few years after the statute took effect, the marriage ended in divorce and *H* subsequently died without having designated a new beneficiary. Does the application of UPC § 2–804 to a pre-enactment insurance policy on *H*'s life impair the parties' constitutionally protected contractual rights? See Estate of De-Witt, 54 P.3d 849 (Colo. 2002) (no, rule of construction affects only donative aspects of policy, not contractual aspects); Mearns v. Scharbach, 12 P.3d 1048 (Wash. App. 2000) (accord; beneficiary designation deemed revoked despite owner's orally expressed contrary intent); but see Aetna Life Ins. Co. v. Schilling, 616 N.E.2d 893 (Ohio 1993); Parsonese v. Midland Nat'l Ins. Co., 706 A.2d 814 (Pa. 1998).

4. *Nonprobate transfers.* UPC § 6–101 provides:

A provision for a nonprobate transfer on death in an insurance policy, contract of employment, bond, mortgage, promissory note, certificated or uncertificated security, account agreement, custodial agreement, deposit agreement, compensation plan, pension plan, individual retirement plan, employee benefit plan, trust, conveyance, deed of gift, marital property agreement, or other written instrument of a similar nature is nontestamentary. This subsection includes a written provision that:

(1) money or other benefits due to, controlled by, or owned by a decedent before death must be paid after the decedent's death to a person whom the decedent designates either in the instrument or in a separate writing, including a will, executed either before or at the same time as the instrument, or later;

(2) money due or to become due under the instrument ceases to be payable in the event of death of the promisee or the promisor before payment or demand; or

(3) any property controlled by or owned by the decedent before death which is the subject of the instrument passes to a person the decedent designates either in the instrument or in a separate writing, including a will, executed either before or at the same time as the instrument, or later.

According to the UPC drafters, this statute is intended "to prevent the transfers authorized here from being treated as testamentary." UPC § 6–101 cmt. Consequently, the instrument of transfer need not be executed with the formalities required for a will, and the transfer is executed outside the probate system. Of the various types of transfer described in UPC § 6–101, which ones depend on the statute for their validity and which ones would be valid even without statutory authorization? See McCouch, Will Substitutes Under the Revised Uniform Probate Code, 58 Brook. L. Rev. 1123 (1993).

Suppose *A* executes a deed, absolute on its face, naming *B* as grantee of Blackacre; the deed remains undelivered during *A*'s life, but after *A*'s death *B* retrieves it and records it. Does UPC § 6–101 validate the conveyance, or should it fail for lack of delivery? Compare Estate of O'Brien, 749 P.2d 154 (Wash.1988) (upholding conveyance under original version of statute) with First Nat'l Bank of Minot v. Bloom, 264 N.W.2d 208 (N.D.1978) (contra). See UPC § 6–101 cmt. (disapproving the result in *O'Brien* and stating that the statute was not intended "to relieve against the delivery requirement of the law of deeds").

Consider the following possibility. *A* and *B* enter into a written agreement, signed by both parties but not executed with testamentary formalities, providing that upon the death of either of them the survivor will collect the decedent's property and distribute it in accordance with the decedent's written directions. Should the arrangement be upheld as a valid nonprobate transfer under UPC § 6–101? See Creviston v. Aspen Products, Inc., 168

S.W.3d 700 (Mo.App. 2005) (agreement directing payment at death held "testamentary in character and hence invalid due to lack of compliance with the formalities of a will"); Hibbler v. Knight, 735 S.W.2d 924 (Tex. App. 1987).

2. JOINT–AND–SURVIVOR ARRANGEMENTS

The joint tenancy developed at common law as a form of concurrent ownership of real property by two or more individuals. Today, this form of ownership (and, in the case of a married couple, the tenancy by the entirety) remains popular as vehicle for shared ownership while both joint tenants are alive and for succession without probate when one tenant dies survived by the other. Conceptually, each joint tenant has an equal, undivided interest in the entire property from the inception of the joint tenancy coupled with survivorship rights. When one joint tenant dies survived by the other, the decedent's interest simply expires, leaving the survivor as sole, absolute owner of the property. Accordingly, no interest passes at death from the decedent to the survivor, and the provisions of the decedent's will have no effect on the devolution of property held in joint tenancy. The survivor receives full ownership of the property by operation of law, not through the probate system. By similar reasoning, it is widely held that after the death of a joint tenant the decedent's general creditors cannot reach the property to satisfy their claims.

The joint tenancy also has significant consequences while both tenants are alive. From inception, all joint tenants are equally entitled to possess and enjoy the entire property and any net income it produces. Moreover, each joint tenant is free to dispose of his or her interest at any time during life, and creditors of a living joint tenant can reach his or her interest. A transfer of any joint tenant's interest during life automatically severs the joint tenancy and converts it to a tenancy in common with no right of survivorship. Thus, although the right of survivorship cannot be revoked or altered by will, it can be destroyed by the unilateral act of either joint tenant while both are alive.

Today a joint tenancy with right of survivorship can be created in personal property as well as real property. Applying traditional joint tenancy doctrine to an account in a financial institution, however, raises special problems. In theory, each party to a joint account has an equal, undivided interest in the account coupled with survivorship rights. Thus, if A opens a bank account in the names of "A or B" and contributes all of the funds in the account, A may really intend to give B an immediate right to withdraw up to half the balance without liability to account to A, as well as the right to take any balance remaining at A's death if B survives A. But it is also possible that this is not at all what the parties intended. At least two other possible explanations come to mind. First, A may have established the account solely as a matter of convenience, intending simply to authorize B to withdraw funds on behalf of A during A's life, with no present beneficial interest and no survivorship rights. Alternatively, *A* may have intended to give *B* survivorship rights at *A*'s death without any present beneficial interest, in which case the joint account is merely a disguised pay-on-death beneficiary designation.

In most states, by statute or judicial decision, at the death of one party an account in joint-and-survivor form is presumed to belong to the survivor. A substantial number of states have statutes, modeled on the original 1969 version of the Uniform Probate Code, providing that the survivorship presumption is rebuttable by clear and convincing evidence of a different intent. See UPC § 6–104 (1969). In other states, courts hold that an express survivorship provision in the terms of the account is conclusive in the absence of fraud, duress, undue influence, or lack of capacity. See Estate of Metz, 256 P.3d 45 (Okla. 2011); Wright v. Bloom, 635 N.E.2d 31 (Ohio 1994); Robinson v. Delfino, 710 A.2d 154 (R.I. 1998). In most states, while both parties are alive each party is presumed to have beneficial rights in proportion to his or her own net contributions (i.e., amounts deposited, plus a proportional share of interest received, less amounts withdrawn); a party who withdraws amounts in excess of his or her beneficial share is liable to account therefor to the other party. See UPC § 6–211. In some states, however, each party owns half the amounts on deposit. See Banko v. Malanecki, 451 A.2d 1008 (Pa.1982); Kleinberg v. Heller, 345 N.E.2d 592 (N.Y.1976).

NOTES

1. *Survivorship rights.* Where one party establishes an account in joint-and-survivor form and contributes all of the funds in the account, the question of beneficial ownership often does not arise until the death of that party. A rebuttable presumption of survivorship rights invites litigation over the decedent's intent at the time the account was established. If the decedent's executor rebuts the presumption, the account passes as part of the estate. See Franklin v. Anna Nat'l Bank of Anna, 488 N.E.2d 1117 (Ill.App.1986); Desrosiers v. Germain, 429 N.E.2d 385 (Mass.App.1981); Johnson v. Herrin, 250 S.E.2d 334 (S.C.1978). If the presumption is not rebutted, the account belongs to the surviving party. See Estate of Anderson, 988 A.2d 977 (Me. 2010); Estate of Sipe, 422 A.2d 826 (Pa.1980). Should the terms of a written deposit agreement be conclusive evidence of the parties' intent? Should financial institutions be encouraged to offer standard account forms with optional survivorship and agency features to be selected when the account is created?

In 1989, the drafters of the Uniform Probate Code rewrote the provisions concerning multiple-party accounts and adopted a new classification scheme with standard forms. The Code no longer recognizes the traditional joint bank account as a discrete category. Instead, the current version of the Code requires that all bank accounts (including those established before the effective date of the statute) be classified as "either a single-party account or a multiple-party account, with or without right of survivorship, and with or without a POD designation or an agency designation." UPC § 6–203; see also UPC § 6–204 (standard forms). Any bank account with more than one party is presumed to create a right of survivorship unless the terms of the account indicate a contrary intent. See UPC § 6–212. Thus, if an account is held in the names of "*A* and *B* as joint tenants," with no mention of survivorship, the balance remaining on deposit at the death of either party belongs conclusively to the survivor. Assume that the account was funded entirely by *A*, who died survived by *B*. Is it open to *A*'s executor to argue that the account was not intended to create any beneficial interest in *B* but merely to allow *B* to withdraw funds on behalf of *A* during *A*'s lifetime? For a thoughtful discussion of the revised provisions, see McGovern, Nonprobate Transfers Under the Revised Uniform Probate Code, 55 Alb. L.Rev. 1329 (1992).

2. *Lifetime rights.* Most disputes over joint bank accounts involve the question of survivorship rights at the death of one party. Occasionally, though, the question of beneficial ownership may arise while both parties are still alive. If each party is entitled to withdraw his or her net contributions, the arrangement is functionally equivalent to a revocable transfer by each party. Tracing the parties' respective net contributions, of course, may present difficult problems of proof.

In the case of a joint tenancy of other property (e.g., land, tangible personal property, stock, or securities), the question is whether the party who contributed the underlying property intended to confer present rights on the other party. If so, each party is entitled to an equal, undivided interest upon severance of the joint tenancy. If not, the joint tenancy was not validly created and each party is entitled to recover his or her proportional contribution. See Blanchette v. Blanchette, 287 N.E.2d 459 (Mass.1972) (husband purchased stock in names of himself and wife as "joint tenants" without donative intent, solely to avoid probate; in subsequent divorce proceeding, court held husband was sole owner of stock, emphasizing that "nothing we say here is intended to impair the right of the survivor to joint bank accounts or to share certificates in joint names, where the donor has died without manifesting an intention to defeat the gift").

3. *Withdrawals from joint bank accounts.* Suppose that *A* and her nephew *B* establish a joint bank account with funds contributed solely by *A*. As *A*'s health begins to fail, *B* closes out the joint account and deposits the balance in his own separate account. *A* subsequently dies intestate, leaving a child *C* as her sole heir. *C*, who has qualified as executor of the estate, demands that *B* return the funds withdrawn from the joint account, but *B* insists that he is entitled to keep them. What result? See Vaughn v. Bernhardt, 547 S.E.2d 869 (S.C. 2001); Estate of Lennon v. Lennon, 29 P.3d 1258 (Wash. App. 2001); Sandler v. Jaffe, 913 So.2d 1205 (Fla. App. 2005); cf. Estate of Bligh, 30 S.W.3d 319 (Tenn.App. 2000). Alternatively, suppose that the funds are misappropriated not by *B* but by *D*, acting as *A*'s agent under a durable power of attorney. Clearly *D* cannot keep the funds. But should the funds be

paid to *C* (as *A*'s successor) or to *B* (as surviving owner of the joint account)? See Estate of Beckley, 961 So.2d 707 (Miss. 2007).

4. *Safe deposit boxes.* If two individuals jointly rent a safe deposit box, courts generally hold that the joint rental, without more, does not create a joint tenancy of the contents of the box. See Estate of Silver, 1 P.3d 358 (Mont. 2000); Longstreet v. Decker, 717 S.E.2d 513 (Ga. App. 2011). However, if the agreement expressly recites that the lessees hold the contents as joint tenants with right of survivorship, a valid joint tenancy may be created if the parties so intend. See Kulbeth v. Purdom, 805 S.W.2d 622 (Ark.1991).

5. *References.* On the uses and misuses of joint tenancies, see Hines, Real Property Joint Tenancies: Law, Fact, and Fancy, 51 Iowa L. Rev. 582 (1966); Hines, Personal Property Joint Tenancies: More Law, Fact and Fancy, 54 Minn. L. Rev. 509 (1970); Effland, Estate Planning: Co–Ownership, 1958 Wis. L. Rev. 507. On joint bank accounts, see Kepner, The Joint and Survivorship Bank Account: A Concept Without a Name, 41 Cal. L. Rev. 596 (1953); Kepner, Five More Years of the Joint Bank Account Muddle, 26 U. Chi. L. Rev. 376 (1959). On pay-on-death arrangements, see McGovern, The Payable on Death Account and Other Will Substitutes, 67 Nw. U. L. Rev. 7 (1972).

D. THE ELUSIVE DISTINCTION BETWEEN LIFE AND DEATH TRANSFERS

A core problem running throughout the law of gratuitous transfers is the distinction between transfers completed during life and those occurring at death. Transfers of the latter type are often described as "testamentary," a conclusionary label which signifies that the transfer is valid only if it complies with the statute of wills. On the other hand, the validity of lifetime transfers depends on different criteria. The issue comes up frequently, because a number of flexible devices (e.g., the revocable trust) allow property owners to give away property in a formal sense while retaining much of the substance of beneficial ownership until death. Parents who make lifetime gifts to their children may feel a warm glow of satisfaction from seeing their children enjoy an accession of wealth, or may simply hope to avoid the tax burdens and probate costs that sometimes accompany deathtime transfers. At the same time, they may have nagging doubts about the children's capacity to manage the property wisely, or may insist on retaining some control over their property as a precaution against possible misfortune. If they reconcile these apparently inconsistent aims by creating an inter vivos trust for their children over which they retain substantial control, the question may arise whether the trust is effective at creation or only at death.

In terms of property law, the basic question is whether a particular transfer is valid or invalid. The principal cases reproduced below prompt several additional questions. How, if at all, are these cases to be reconciled? Why should there be a penalty for trying to avoid the statute of wills? What function does this statute perform that justifies such solicitude for safeguarding its integrity? If an attempted lifetime transfer fails, the property passes by will or by intestacy. Is there a reason for preferring this disposition to the one the owner chose? The dividing line between lifetime and deathtime transfers can be highly abstract and conceptual. Furthermore, solutions are not uniform; a transfer may be effective for some purposes but for others.

BUTLER V. SHERWOOD

Supreme Court of New York, Appellate Division, 1921.
196 A.D. 603, 188 N.Y.S. 242, aff'd mem., 233 N.Y. 655, 135 N.E. 957 (1922).

WOODWARD, J.

Ella F. Sherwood, being about to undergo an operation for a cancer, made and executed an instrument in writing, in form a quitclaim deed, of all her real estate and personal property, to her husband. This instrument bears date of January 25, 1916. The plaintiff is the brother and only heir at law of Ella F. Sherwood, and brings this action to set aside the said instrument, on the ground that it was procured by undue influence, and that there was never any transfer of the property under the instrument. Upon the trial of the action there does not appear to have been any serious contention of conduct amounting to fraud, and there is little room for doubt that Ella F. Sherwood intended to place her property where it would be vested in her husband, this defendant, upon her death. If she has failed in this purpose, it is because she has sought to accomplish an entirely legal result by an illegal method—because she has attempted to accomplish by an instrument in the form of a deed that which could be accomplished only by a will. The learned court at Special Term has found that the instrument relied upon by the defendant was of a testamentary character, and did not comply with the statutory requirements of a will, and that it was therefore void. 114 Misc. Rep. 483, 186 N.Y. Supp. 712. . . . The defendant appeals.

The instrument in question provides that it is between Ella Francis Sherwood and Edward H. Sherwood, and that "the said party of the first part, in consideration of the sum of one dollar, love and affection, and other good and valuable considerations," does hereby "remise, release and forever quitclaim unto the said party of the second part, his heirs and assigns forever," all of the real estate of the said Ella F. Sherwood, wherever situate, "to have and to hold the same unto the party of the second part, his heirs, executors, administrators and assigns forever," and "for the same considerations, I do hereby sell, assign, transfer, convey and set over unto the party of the second part, all personal property, bills, notes, deposits in bank, certificates of stock, and all choses in action, evidences of indebtedness due me, and all my personal property of whatever name or kind the same may be and wheresoever situate, to have and to hold the same unto the party of the second part, his executors, administrators and assigns forever."

If the instrument had ended here, and had been executed and delivered, it would, of course, have operated to divest Ella F. Sherwood of her property and to have vested it in Edward H. Sherwood. But this would not have accomplished the purpose which Ella F. Sherwood had in mind; she wanted to hold the ownership and possession of her property until her death, and then to vest it in her husband. She had, however, been through a will contest in connection with the estate of a former husband, and, as she told her friends, she had no faith in wills; she wanted to fix her property where it would be disposed of without a contest, and, of course, invited one. She provided that "this conveyance and transfer are made upon the condition that the party of the second part, my husband, survive me, and the same is intended to vest and take effect only upon my decease and until said time the same shall be subject to revocation upon the part of the party of the first part."

This instrument was delivered to the defendant, but what did it convey? It could not be determined at any time prior to her death whether her husband survived her, and unless he survived her there was clearly no intention of conveying to him. Moreover, she provided that the conveyance and transfer "are intended to vest and take effect only upon my decease"; so that there was no time prior to her death when the instrument could have any effect, and when that event took place the law determined the disposition to be made of her estate, in the absence of a valid will. There was no moment from the time of making the instrument down to the very instant of dissolution when any rights could vest under the intent or language of this deed, and beyond this it was provided that, "until said time, the same shall be subject to revocation upon the part of the party of the first part"; so that the supposed grantor was in full control of the property during all of her life subsequent to the making of the deed, with the right reserved to revoke the instrument itself. No right whatever passed to the defendant under the terms of the deed; it was not to take effect until the decease of the party of the first part, and then only upon the condition that the defendant survived her. This is not the case of a deed executed and delivered to a third party, with instructions not to record or deliver the same until the death of the grantor. Such a deed, absolute in form and to take effect immediately, divests the grantor of his interest in the property, making its enjoyment to depend upon the date of his death; but here the instrument is, by its terms, to take effect only upon the decease of the grantor, and at a time when the law operates to prevent a transfer otherwise than by a last will and testament.

It is impossible to sustain this transaction as an executed gift of the personal property, for that was subject to the same conditions and limitations as the real estate. "It is an elementary rule," say the court in Young v. Young, 80 N.Y. 422, 435 (36 Am. Rep. 634), "that such a gift cannot be made to take effect in possession in futuro. Such a transaction amounts only to a promise to make a gift, which is nudum pactum. Pitts v. Mangum, 2 Bailey (S.C.) 588. There must be a delivery of possession with a view to pass a present right of property. 'Any gift of chattels which expressly reserves the use of the property to the donor for a certain period, or (as commonly appears in the cases which the courts have had occasion to pass upon) as long as the donor shall live, is ineffectual.' Schouler on Pers. Prop., vol. 2, p. 118, and cases cited; Vass v. Hicks, 3 Murphy (N.C.) 494. This rule has been applied, even where the gift was made by a written instrument or deed purporting to transfer the title, but containing the reservation." In the case here under consideration the instrument itself is limited to take effect upon the death of the donor if the donee shall survive her, and there is no pretense that any of the personal property itself was ever delivered to the defendant. Delivery by the donor, either actual or constructive, operating to divest the donor of possession of and dominion over the thing, is a constant and essential factor in every transaction which takes effect as a completed gift. Instruments may be ever so formally executed by the donor, purporting to transfer title to the donee, or there may be the most explicit declaration of intention to give, or of an actual present gift, yet, unless there is a delivery, the intention is defeated. Beaver v. Beaver, 117 N.Y. 421, 429, 22 N.E. 940, 6 L.R.A. 403, 15 Am. St. Rep. 531.

While there is a recital of a consideration of $1, and every legal mode of acquisition of real property except by descent is denominated in law a purchase, and the person who thus acquires it is a purchaser, there is no doubt that the transaction here under consideration possesses all of the essential qualities of a gift, as distinguished from a valuable consideration supporting a bargain and sale . . . , and as this gift was not to take effect until the death of the grantor, upon the survival of the named grantee, and even the instrument itself might be revoked, it must be clear that Ella F. Sherwood undertook to accomplish by a deed what the law requires to be done by will, and, of course, she has failed. The judgment appealed from should be affirmed.

Judgment affirmed, without costs. All concur.

NOTES

1. *Dispositive outcome.* Under the New York intestacy laws in effect when the principal case arose, decedent's husband would have received only $2,000 and one-half of any remaining personal property; her brother would have taken the rest of her personal property and all her real property. A hus-

band's rights in his wife's real property under the estate of curtesy, as it then existed in New York, became effective only if a child was born of the marriage.

2. *Gift of personal property taking effect at death.* At one time it was assumed that a donor could not make an outright gift of chattels subject to a retained life estate, and the court relied in part on this "elementary rule" in concluding that Mrs. Sherwood's attempted gift was invalid. More recently, that rule has been widely repudiated. Modern authority recognizes that future interests can be created and transferred in chattels as well as in intangibles or real property. Recall, for example, a father's gift to his son of a remainder interest in a painting in Gruen v. Gruen, supra p. 509. Nevertheless, a gift which is intended to take effect at the donor's death may fail if the donor lacks present donative intent or retains a power of revocation. See Estate of Bessett, 39 P.3d 220 (Or.App. 2002) (note found in decedent's safe deposit box directing cancellation of debts at death, held unenforceable); Estate of Yorty, 761 A.2d 187 (Pa. Super. 2000) (promissory note payable at death to sister in gratitude for past assistance, held unenforceable as gift or as contract). But see UPC § 6–101, Note 4, supra p. 533.

3. *Deed of land taking effect at death.* In the early years of the twentieth century, as property owners became increasingly aware of the burdens attendant on testamentary transfers, they began to use more sophisticated methods of transfer by which they hoped to rid themselves of legal title while retaining substantially undiminished dominion and control of their property. Among other devices, they made use of inter vivos deeds of land, which sometimes fared considerably better in the courts than Mrs. Sherwood's. See, e.g., Montgomery v. Reeves, 146 S.E. 311 (Ga.1929) (deed stated it was "not to take effect until after the death of the maker, he reserving to himself the right to control same and the rents and profits thereof as long as he lives"; court construed deed as passing immediate title with enjoyment postponed until grantor's death); Mays v. Burleson, 61 So. 75 (Ala.1913); Pelt v. Dockery, 3 S.W.2d 62 (Ark.1928) (deed stated it was to "take effect and be in force after my death, and . . . the title to said land is to remain in me so long as I may live"). Indeed, legislation in a number of states now expressly authorizes such arrangements. See Note 4, supra p. 505. On the formal distinction between lifetime gifts and testamentary transfers and its doctrinal ramifications, see Browder, Giving or Leaving—What Is a Will?, 75 Mich. L. Rev. 845 (1977); Ritchie, What Is a Will?, 49 Va. L. Rev. 759 (1963); Gulliver & Tilson, Classification of Gratuitous Transfers, 51 Yale L.J. 1 (1941).

FARKAS V. WILLIAMS

Supreme Court of Illinois, 1955.
5 Ill.2d 417, 125 N.E.2d 600.

HERSHEY, JUSTICE.

This is an appeal from a decision of the Appellate Court, First District, which affirmed a decree of the circuit court of Cook County finding that certain declarations of trust executed by Albert B. Farkas and naming Richard J. Williams as beneficiary were invalid and that Regina Farkas and Victor Farkas, as coadministrators of the estate of said Albert B. Farkas, were the owners of the property referred to in said trust instruments, being certain shares of capital stock of Investors Mutual, Inc.

Said coadministrators, herein referred to as plaintiffs, filed a complaint in the circuit court of Cook County for a declaratory decree and other relief against said Richard J. Williams and Investors Mutual, Inc., herein referred to as defendants. The plaintiffs asked the court to declare their legal rights, as coadministrators, in four stock certificates issued by Investors Mutual Inc. in the name of "Albert B. Farkas, as trustee for Richard J. Williams" and which were issued pursuant to written declarations of trust. The decree of the circuit court found that said declarations were testamentary in character, and not having been executed with the formalities of a will, were invalid, and directed that the stock be awarded to the plaintiffs as an asset of the estate of said Albert B. Farkas. Upon appeal to the Appellate Court, the decree was affirmed. (See 3 Ill.App.2d 248.) We allowed defendants' petition for leave to appeal.

Albert B. Farkas died intestate at the age of sixty-seven years, a resident of Chicago, leaving as his only heirs-at-law brothers, sisters, a nephew and a niece. Although retired at the time of his death, he had for many years practiced veterinary medicine and operated a veterinarian establishment in Chicago. During a considerable portion of that time, he employed the defendant Williams, who was not related to him.

On four occasions (December 8, 1948; February 7, 1949; February 14, 1950; and March 1, 1950) Farkas purchased stock of Investors Mutual, Inc. At the time of each purchase he executed a written application to Investors Mutual, Inc., instructing them to issue the stock in his name "as trustee for Richard J. Williams." Investors Mutual, Inc., by its agent, accepted each of these applications in writing by signature on the face of the application. Coincident with the execution of these applications, Farkas signed separate declarations of trust, all of which were identical except as to dates. The terms of said trust instruments are as follows:

Declaration of Trust—Revocable. I, the undersigned, having purchased or declared my intention to purchase certain shares of capital stock of Investors Mutual, Inc. (the Company), and having directed that the certificate for said stock be issued in my name as trustee for Richard J. Williams as beneficiary, whose address is 1704 W. North Ave. Chicago, Ill., under this Declaration of Trust Do Hereby Declare that the terms and conditions upon which I shall hold said stock in trust and any additional stock resulting from reinvestments of cash dividends upon such original or additional shares are as follows:

(1) During my lifetime all cash dividends are to be paid to me individually for my own personal account and use; provided, however, that any such additional stock purchased under an authorized reinvestment of cash dividends shall become a part of and subject to this trust.

(2) Upon my death the title to any stock subject hereto and the right to any subsequent payments or distributions shall be vested absolutely in the beneficiary. The record date for the payment of dividends, rather than the date of declaration of the dividend, shall, with reference to my death, determine whether any particular dividend shall be payable to my estate or to the beneficiary.

(3) During my lifetime I reserve the right, as trustee, to vote, sell, redeem, exchange or otherwise deal in or with the stock subject hereto, but upon any sale or redemption of said stock or any part thereof, the trust hereby declared shall terminate as to the stock sold or redeemed, and I shall be entitled to retain the proceeds of sale or redemption for my own personal account and use.

(4) I reserve the right at any time to change the beneficiary or revoke this trust, but it is understood that no change of beneficiary and no revocation of this trust except by death of the beneficiary, shall be effective as to the Company for any purpose unless and until written notice thereof in such form as the Company shall prescribe is delivered to the Company at Minneapolis, Minnesota. The decease of the beneficiary before my death shall operate as a revocation of this trust.

(5) In the event this trust shall be revoked or otherwise terminated, said stock and all rights and privileges thereunder shall belong to and be exercised by me in my individual capacity.

(6) The Company shall not be liable for the validity or existence of any trust created by me, and any payment or other consideration made or given by the Company to me as trustee or otherwise, in connection with said stock or any cash dividends thereon, or in the event of my death prior to revocation, to the beneficiary, shall to the extent

of such payment fully release and discharge the Company from liability with respect to said stock or any cash dividends thereon.

The applications and declarations of trust were delivered to Investors Mutual, Inc., and held by the company until Farkas' death. The stock certificates were issued in the name of Farkas as "trustee for Richard J. Williams" and were discovered in a safety-deposit box of Farkas after his death, along with other securities, some of which were in the name of Williams alone.

The sole question presented on this appeal is whether the instruments entitled "Declaration of Trust—Revocable" and executed by Farkas created valid *inter vivos* trusts of the stock of Investors Mutual, Inc. The plaintiffs contend that said stock is free and clear from any trust or beneficial interest in the defendant Williams, for the reason that said purported trust instruments were attempted testamentary dispositions and invalid for want of compliance with the statute on wills. The defendants, on the other hand, insist that said instruments created valid *inter vivos* trusts and were not testamentary in character.

It is conceded that the instruments were not executed in such a way as to satisfy the requirements of the statute on wills; hence, our inquiry is limited to whether said trust instruments created valid *inter vivos* trusts effective to give the purported beneficiary, Williams, title to the stock in question after the death of the settlor-trustee, Farkas. To make this determination we must consider: (1) whether upon execution of the so-called trust instruments defendant Williams acquired an interest in the subject matter of the trusts, the stock of defendant Investors Mutual, Inc., (2) whether Farkas, as settlor-trustee, retained such control over the subject matter of the trusts as to render said trust instruments attempted testamentary dispositions.

First, upon execution of these trust instruments did defendant Williams presently acquire an interest in the subject matter of the intended trusts?

If no interest passed to Williams before the death of Farkas, the intended trusts are testamentary and hence invalid for failure to comply with the statute on wills. Oswald v. Caldwell, 225 Ill. 224, 80 N.E. 131; Troup v. Hunter, 300 Ill. 110, 133 N.E. 56; Restatement of the Law of Trusts, section 56.

But considering the terms of these instruments we believe Farkas did intend to presently give Williams an interest in the property referred to. For it may be said, at the very least, that upon his executing one of these instruments, he showed an intention to presently part with some of the incidents of ownership in the stock. Immediately after the execution of each of these instruments, he could not deal with the stock therein referred to the same as if he owned the property absolutely, but only in accordance with the terms of the instrument. He purported to set himself up as trustee of the stock for the benefit of Williams, and the stock was registered in his name as trustee for Williams. Thus assuming to act as trustee, he is held to have intended to take on those obligations which are expressly set out in the instrument, as well as those fiduciary obligations implied by law. In addition, he manifested an intention to bind himself to having this property pass upon his death to Williams, unless he changed the beneficiary or revoked the trust, and then such change of beneficiary or revocation was not to be effective as to Investors Mutual, Inc., unless and until written notice thereof in such form as the company prescribed was delivered to them at Minneapolis, Minnesota. An absolute owner can dispose of his property, either in his lifetime or by will, in any way he sees fit without notifying or securing approval from anyone and without being held to the duties of a fiduciary in so doing.

It seems to follow that what incidents of ownership Farkas intended to relinquish, in a sense he intended Williams to acquire. That is, Williams was to be the beneficiary to whom Farkas was to be obligated, and unless Farkas revoked the instrument in the manner therein set out or the instrument was otherwise terminated in a manner therein provided for, upon Farkas' death Williams was to become absolute owner of the trust property. It is difficult to name this interest of Williams, nor is there any reason for so doing so long as it passed to him immediately upon the creation of the trust. As stated in 4 Powell, The Law of Real Property, at page 87: "Interests of beneficiaries of private express trusts run the gamut from valuable substantialities to evanescent hopes. Such a beneficiary may have any one of an almost infinite variety of the possible aggregates of rights, privileges, powers and immunities."

An additional problem is presented here, however, for it is to be noted that the trust instruments provide: "The decease of the beneficiary before my death shall operate as a revocation of this trust." The plaintiffs argue that the presence of this provision removes the only possible distinction which might have been drawn between these instruments and a will. Being thus conditioned on his surviving, it is argued that the "interest" of Williams until the death of Farkas was a mere expectancy. Conversely, they assert, the interest of Farkas in the securities until his death was precisely the same as that of a testator who bequeaths securities by his will, since he had all the rights accruing to an absolute owner.

Admittedly, had this provision been absent the interest of Williams would have been greater, since he would then have had an inheritable interest in the lifetime of Farkas. But to say his interest would have been greater is not to say that he here did not have a beneficial interest, properly so-called, during the lifetime of Farkas. The provision purports to set up but another "contingency" which would serve to terminate the trust. The disposition is not testamentary and the intended trust is valid, even though the interest of the beneficiary is contingent upon the existence of a certain state of facts at the time of the settlor's death. Restatement of the Law of Trusts, section 56, comment f. In an example contained in the previous reference, the authors of the Restatement have referred to the interest of a beneficiary under a trust who must survive the settlor (and where the settlor receives the income for life) as a contingent equitable interest in remainder.

This question of whether any interest passed immediately is also involved in the next problem considered, namely, the quantum of power retained by a settlor which will cause an intended *inter vivos* trust to fail as an attempted testamentary disposition. . . .

Second, did Farkas retain such control over the subject matter of the trust as to render said trust instruments attempted testamentary dispositions?

In each of these trust instruments, Farkas reserved to himself as settlor the following powers: (1) the right to receive during his lifetime all cash dividends; (2) the right at any time to change the beneficiary or revoke the trust; and (3) upon sale or redemption of any portion of the trust property, the right to retain the proceeds therefrom for his own use.

Additionally, Farkas reserved the right to act as sole trustee, and in such capacity, he was accorded the right to vote, sell, redeem, exchange or otherwise deal in the stock which formed the subject matter of the trust.

We shall consider first those enumerated powers which Farkas reserved to himself as settlor.

It is well established that the retention by the settlor of the power to revoke, even when coupled with the reservation of a life interest in the trust property, does not render the trust inoperative for want of execution as a will. . . .

A more difficult problem is posed, however, by the fact that Farkas is also trustee, and as such, is empowered to vote, sell, redeem, exchange and otherwise deal in and with the subject matter of the trusts.

That a settlor may create a trust of personal property whereby he names himself as trustee and acts as such for the beneficiary is clear. Restatement of the Law of Trusts, section 17.

Moreover, the later cases indicate that the mere fact that the settlor in addition to making himself sole trustee also reserves a life interest and a power of revocation does not render the trust invalid as testamentary in character. 32 A.L.R. 2d 1286. In 1 Scott, The Law of Trusts, it is stated at pages 353–354: "The owner of property may create a trust not only by transferring the property to another person as trustee, but also by declaring himself trustee. Such a declaration of trust, although gratuitous, is valid. . . . Suppose, however, that the settlor reserves not only a beneficial life interest but also a power of revocation. It would seem that such a trust is not necessarily testamentary. The declaration of trust immediately creates an equitable interest in the beneficiaries, although the enjoyment of the interest is postponed until the death of the settlor, and although the interest may be divested by the exercise of the power of revocation. The disposition is not essentially different from that which is made where the settlor transfers the property to another person as trustee. It is true that where the settlor declares himself trustee he controls the administration of the trust. As has been stated, if the settlor transfers property upon trust and reserves not only a power of revocation but also power to control the administration of the trust, the trust is testamentary. There is this difference, however: the power of control which the settlor has as trustee is not an irresponsible power and can be exercised only in accordance with the terms of the trust." See also Restatement of the Law of Trusts, section 57, comment b.

In the instant case the plaintiffs contend that Farkas, as settlor-trustee, retained complete control and dominion over the securities for his own benefit during his lifetime. It is argued that he had the power to deal with the property as he liked so long as he lived and owed no enforceable duties of any kind to Williams as beneficiary. . . .

That the retention of the power by Farkas as trustee to sell or redeem the stock and keep the proceeds for his own use should not render these trust instruments testamentary in character becomes more evident upon analyzing the real import and significance of the powers to revoke and to amend the trust, the reservation of which the courts uniformly hold does not invalidate an *inter vivos* trust.

It is obvious that a settlor with the power to revoke and to amend the trust at any time is, for all practical purpose, in a position to exert considerable control over the trustee regarding the administration of the trust. For anything believed to be inimicable to his best interests can be thwarted or prevented by simply revoking the trust or amending it in such a way as to conform to his wishes. Indeed, it seems that many of those powers which from time to time have been viewed as "additional powers" are already, in a sense, virtually contained within the overriding power of revocation or the power to amend the trust. Consider, for example, the following: (1) the power to consume the principal; (2) the power to sell or mortgage the trust property and appropriate the proceeds; (3) the power to appoint or remove trustees; (4) the power to supervise and direct investments; and (5) the power to otherwise direct and supervise the trustee in the administration of the trust. Actually, any of the above powers could readily be assumed by a settlor with the reserved power of revocation through the simple expedient of revoking the trust, and then, as absolute owner of the subject matter, doing with the property as he chooses. Even though no actual termination of the trust is effectuated, however, it could hardly be questioned but that the mere existence of this power in the settlor is sufficient to enable his influence to be felt in a practical way in the administration of the trust. . . .

In the case at bar, the power of Farkas to vote, sell, redeem, exchange or otherwise deal in the stock was reserved to him as trustee, and it was only upon sale or redemption that he was entitled to keep the proceeds for his own use. Thus, the control reserved is not as great as in those cases where said power is reserved to the owner as settlor. For as trustee he must so conduct himself in accordance with standards applicable to trustees generally. It is not a valid objection to this to say that Williams would never question Farkas's conduct, inasmuch as Farkas could then revoke the trust and destroy what interest Williams has. Such a possibility exists in any case where the settlor has the power of revocation. Still, Williams has rights the same as any beneficiary, although it may not be feasible for him to exercise them. Moreover, it is entirely possible that he might in certain situations have a right to hold Farkas's estate liable for breaches of trust committed by Farkas during his lifetime. In this regard, consider what would happen if, without having revoked the trust, Farkas as trustee had given the stock away without receiving any consideration therefor, had pledged the stock improperly for his own personal debt and allowed it to be lost by foreclosure or had exchanged the stock for another security or other worthless property in such manner as to constitute gross impropriety and gross negligence. In such instances, it would seem in accordance with the terms of these instruments that Williams would have had an enforceable claim against Farkas's estate for whatever damage had been suffered. Contrast this with the rights of a legatee or devisee under a will. The testator could waste the property or do anything with it he wished during his lifetime without incurring any liability to those designated by the will to inherit the property. In any event, if Farkas as settlor could reserve the power to sell or otherwise deal with the property and retain the proceeds, which the cases indicate he could, then it necessarily follows that he should have the right to sell or otherwise deal with the property as trustee and retain the proceeds from a sale or redemption without having the instruments rendered invalid as testamentary dispositions.

Another factor often considered in determining whether an *inter vivos* trust is an attempted testamentary disposition is the formality of the transaction. Restatement of the Law of Trusts, section 57, comment g. . . . Historically, the purpose behind the enactment of the statute on wills was the prevention of fraud. The requirement as to witnesses was deemed necessary because a will is ordinarily an expression of the secret wish of the testator, signed out of the presence of all concerned. The possibility of forgery and fraud are ever present in such situations. Here, Farkas executed four separate applications for stock of Investors Mutual, Inc., in which he directed that the stock be issued in his name as trustee for Williams, and he executed four separate declarations of trust in which he declared he was holding said stock in trust for Williams. The stock certificates in question were issued in his name as trustee for Williams. He thus manifested his intention in a solemn and formal manner.

For the reasons stated, we conclude that these trust declarations executed by Farkas constituted valid *inter vivos* trusts and were not attempted testamentary dispositions. It must be conceded that they have, in the words of Mr. Justice Holmes in Bromley v. Mitchell, 155 Mass. 509, 30 N.E. 83, a "testamentary look." Moreover, it must be admitted that the line should be drawn somewhere, but after a study of this case we do not believe that point has here been reached.

The judgment of the Appellate Court affirming the decree of the circuit court of Cook County is reversed, and the cause is remanded to the circuit court of Cook County, with directions to enter a decree in favor of the defendants.

Reversed and remanded, with directions.

NOTES

1. *Present transfer of interest.* The court in Nichols v. Emery, 41 P. 1089 (Cal.1895), stated the proposition as follows:

> The essential characteristic of an instrument testamentary in its nature is, that it operates only upon and by reason of the death of the maker. Up to that time it is ambulatory. By its execution the maker has parted with no rights and divested himself of no modicum of his estate, and, *per contra* no rights have accrued to and no estate has vested in any other person. . . .

> Upon the other hand, to the creation of a valid express trust it is essential that some estate or interest should be conveyed to the trustee, and, when the instrument creating the trust is other than a will, that estate or interest must pass immediately. . . . By such a trust, therefore, something of the settlor's estate has passed from him and into the trustee for the benefit of the *cestui*, and this transfer of interest is a present

one and in no wise dependent upon the settlor's death. But it is important to note the distinction between the interest transferred and the enjoyment of that interest. The enjoyment of the *cestui* may be made to commence in the future and to depend for its commencement upon the termination of an existing life or lives or of an intermediate estate. . . . [41 P. at 1091.]

In *Farkas*, the court upholds Mr. Farkas's trust declarations as "valid inter vivos trusts," explaining that upon execution they created an equitable interest in the beneficiary and imposed fiduciary duties on the settlor. The elements of a trust and the methods by which it is created will be treated in more detail in Chapter 7. For the moment, however, consider the hypothetical example offered by the *Farkas* court to demonstrate the passing of an interest to Mr. Williams and the duties imposed on Mr. Farkas as trustee. The court observes that if Mr. Farkas, without having revoked the trust, had squandered or lost the trust property through "gross impropriety and gross negligence," he would have incurred liability to Williams for breach of trust, noting that "Williams [had] rights the same as any beneficiary, although it [might] not be feasible for him to exercise them." In the absence of fiduciary misconduct, how can it be determined whether Williams acquired any enforceable rights during Mr. Farkas's life?

In this regard, the Uniform Trust Code provides that as long as a trust remains subject to the settlor's power of revocation, the "rights of the beneficiaries are subject to the control of, and the duties of the trustee are owed exclusively to, the settlor." UTC § 603(a). In effect, this provision makes it impossible for a remainder beneficiary to sue the trustee of a revocable trust for any breach occurring while the settlor is alive and competent to revoke the trust. See Ex parte Synovus Trust Co., 41 So.3d 70 (Ala. 2009); Gunther Revocable Living Trust, 350 S.W.3d 44 (Mo. App. 2011); Moon v. Lesikar, 230 S.W.3d 800 (Tex. App. 2007) (bargain sale of trust property treated as constructive partial revocation). Can the denial of beneficiary standing under UTC § 603(a) be reconciled with the *Farkas* court's rationale for upholding the trust declarations as valid inter vivos trusts?

2. *Validity of revocable trusts.* During the first half of the twentieth century the validity of revocable inter vivos trusts was tested and upheld in a large number of cases. See In re Shapley's Deed of Trust, 46 A.2d 227 (Pa.1946); Bolles v. Toledo Trust Co., 58 N.E.2d 381 (Ohio 1944); National Shawmut Bank v. Joy, 53 N.E.2d 113 (Mass.1944); Cramer v. Hartford–Connecticut Trust Co., 147 A. 139 (Conn.1929). The issue still surfaces occasionally. See Welch v. Crow, 206 P.3d 599 (Okla. 2009); McMahon v. Standard Bank & Trust Co., 550 N.W.2d 727 (Wis.App.1996). However, it is unlikely that any court would seriously question the validity of Mr. Farkas's trusts today. See 1 Scott and Ascher on Trusts § 8.2.2, which states: "[T]he unmistakable trend in the United States has long been to uphold clearly expressed inter vivos trusts, no matter how extensive the interests or powers are that the settlor has reserved." The Restatement (Third) of Trusts § 25(1)

summarizes the matter as follows: "A trust . . . is not rendered testamentary merely because the settlor retains extensive rights such as a beneficial interest for life, powers to revoke and modify the trust, and the right to serve as or control the trustee, . . . or because the trust is intended to serve as a substitute for a will."

3. *Practical advantages of revocable trusts.* Revocable trusts play an important role in modern estate planning. Such trusts function as nearly perfect will substitutes: they can be created and revoked quite easily, with relatively few formalities; they can be funded with almost any type of property, ranging from a nominal amount of cash (e.g., ten dollars) to stocks, securities, or life insurance policies of substantial value; the individual who creates the trust (the settlor) may also be the sole trustee and primary beneficiary. Typically, in connection with the creation of a revocable trust the settlor also executes a "pour-over" will which directs that the settlor's residuary estate be added to the trust at the settlor's death. Early doubts about the validity of pour-over arrangements have been dispelled by judicial decision or by statute in virtually all states. See the Uniform Testamentary Additions to Trusts Act, supra p. 401.

A revocable trust affords no tax advantages; as long as the settlor has an absolute power of revocation, he or she is generally treated as the owner of the trust property for tax purposes. See I.R.C. §§ 676 (income tax) and 2038 (estate tax); see also Treas. Reg. § 25.2511–2(c) (gift tax). Among the non-tax reasons for creating an inter vivos trust are the following:

1. *Privacy.* The terms of an inter vivos trust, unlike those of a testamentary trust, are not a matter of public record in the probate court. (If the trust property includes land, however, it may be necessary as a practical matter to record the trust instrument.)

2. *Incapacity.* An inter vivos trust can name one or more successor trustees who can take over responsibility for managing the trust property in the event the settlor becomes incapacitated, without the need for formal guardianship proceedings. (In this respect, compare a trust arrangement with a durable power of attorney.)

3. *Convenience.* An inter vivos trust ensures continuity of management and prompt access to the trust property at the settlor's death, and removes the trust property from the probate process. Note, however, that assets added to the trust at death under the settlor's will must first go through the probate process.

4. *Administration.* An inter vivos trust, unlike a testamentary trust, is not automatically subject to supervision by a probate court. The trustees may be appointed without judicial approval; they usually do not have to furnish a fiduciary bond; and they may be authorized to account in a streamlined form.

5. *Choice of law.* Compared to a testamentary trust, an inter vivos trust offers considerable flexibility in designating the law of a particular jurisdiction to govern matters of trust administration.

See Westfall, Estate Planning 43 (2d ed. 1982).

4. *The "nonprobate revolution."* One prominent commentator has written critically of the analytical process by which a court must be able to classify a transfer as a present gift in order to sustain it. He asks: "Why insist on finding a present interest that is lacking?" Langbein, The Nonprobate Revolution and the Future of the Law of Succession, 97 Harv. L. Rev. 1108 (1984). He points out that will substitutes, such as revocable trusts, joint bank accounts, life insurance, and pensions are now widespread and that the volume of wealth passing in this manner far exceeds the value of wealth passing by will or intestate succession. He argues that acceptance of these devices does not contravene the policies that traditionally have justified probate and administration. He concludes that, instead of pretending that will substitutes are lifetime transfers, we should simply recognize them as "wills" that need not comply with the statute of wills.

CHAPTER 7

TRUSTS

■ ■ ■

A. INTRODUCTION

1. THE NATURE, UTILITY, AND CLASSIFICATION OF TRUSTS

The trust concept is essentially quite simple. It involves the idea of one person (the trustee) holding legal title to certain property (the res or subject-matter) for the benefit of another person (the cestui or beneficiary), whose interest is equitable. After the merger of law and equity, it may seem unfortunate to continue using the terms "legal" and "equitable," but the idea that the trustee is recognized as the sole owner at law, and that the beneficiary's interest is recognized only in equity, is so fundamental to the reasoning of so many trust cases that it would be difficult, if not impossible, to understand the development and utility of the trust device without appreciating this traditional division of title. From a functional viewpoint, the effect of the division of title is to allocate the burdens of property ownership to the trustee, and to allocate its benefits (except for any compensation the trustee may earn) to the beneficiary.

Our chief emphasis here is on the utility of the trust in the gratuitous disposition of property, but this is by no means the trust's only role. In both England and America we employ the trust to accomplish a large variety of results. Its simplicity and flexibility make it actually or potentially applicable to many diverse situations. We use it extensively in business, as well as in non-commercial transactions. We also employ it under various circumstances as part of the reasoning by which we require defendants to conform to the equitable standard of fairness; i.e., we force people who, by strict legal doctrine, would otherwise be entitled to retain property to give it up if the court thinks that it would be unjust for them to keep it. We sometimes make remedies against tortfeasors more effectual by calling them trustees. These are merely examples; they are hardly an exhaustive catalogue of the trust's functions. See Langbein, The Secret Life of the Trust: The Trust as an Instrument of Commerce, 107 Yale L.J. 165 (1997); Arnold, The Restatement of the Law of Trusts, 31 Colum. L.

Rev. 800 (1931); Scott, The Trust as an Instrument of Law Reform, 31 Yale L.J. 457 (1922).

Trusts are traditionally classified as express, constructive, or resulting. The conceptual distinction between express and constructive trusts is analogous to that between the concepts of express contract and quasi-contract. The ideas of both constructive trust and quasi-contract took an established formula out of its existing context for the purpose of remedying injustice. Though the common law enforced quasi-contractual obligations, the results achieved and the methods of achieving them had a distinctly equitable character. Theoretically, the express trust, like the express contract, is an intent-enforcing mechanism. In a contract action, the court acts on the theory that the defendant has manifested an intention to assume an obligation, and if the defendant breaches that obligation, the court may hold the defendant liable. So also, when a trustee has agreed to act as trustee, the court may order the trustee to act in accordance with the terms of the trust. For more on the contractual underpinnings of the law of trusts, see Langbein, The Contractarian Basis of the Law of Trusts, 105 Yale L.J. 625 (1995). In contrast, the constructive trust, like the quasi-contract, is theoretically a remedial device that is in no way dependent upon the defendant's intention to undertake an obligation. If a court compels a thief to transfer to a victim the proceeds of sale of stolen property, either on a quasi-contractual theory or on the ground that the thief is a constructive trustee, the court is not employing an intent-enforcing device; normally, it would be fantastic to assume that a thief intended to return either the property or its proceeds to the victim. In any event, ascertainment of the thief's intention is immaterial. The constructive trust is an equitable device courts utilize to prevent unjust enrichment. "A constructive trust is the formula through which the conscience of equity finds expression. When property has been acquired in such circumstances that the holder of the legal title may not in good conscience retain the beneficial interest, equity converts him into a trustee." Beatty v. Guggenheim Exploration Co., 122 N.E. 378 (N.Y.1919) (Cardozo, J.).

It is difficult, even conceptually, to define the resulting trust in terms of its essential nature. Decisions relying on the theory of the resulting trust seem in part to conceive of it as a remedial device and in part to emphasize the intention of the parties. Perhaps one can most easily grasp the idea of the resulting trust by considering the three situations in which it is or was most often employed. (1) The resulting trust on a gratuitous conveyance (now largely obsolete) was imposed under certain circumstances for the grantor's benefit on the grantee of land gratuitously transferred. (2) A purchase money resulting trust may arise when A pays B the purchase price of land that B conveys to C. Under certain circumstances, C holds the land on resulting trust for A. (3) A resulting trust may arise for the benefit of the settlor or the settlor's successors (e.g., the heirs or residuary beneficiaries of a deceased settlor) upon the complete or partial failure of an express trust or its termination before the expiration of the trustee's legal title. For discussions of the classification of trusts, see Costigan, The Classification of Trusts as Express, Resulting and Constructive, 26 Harv. L. Rev. 437 (1914).

2. THE ORIGINS OF THE TRUST

The trust idea, the development and extensive use of which some scholars believe are the greatest achievement of Anglo–American law, is not present in all legal systems.[1] English and American lawyers are so accustomed to thinking in terms of the trust device, both in situations to which it is technically applicable and in others for which it furnishes a convenient metaphor, that there may be a tendency to consider it an inevitable part of our legal system. This, however, is by no means self-evident. The concept of the trust owes its development to a number of accidental factors, both political and historical. If it had not happened to grow as it did, some other device might have been adapted to perform similar functions.

The unique character of the Anglo–American trust is fundamentally due to the existence of its prototype, the use, and to the dual system of law and equity that made the use possible. Indeed, Maitland said that it was "absolutely impossible for one to speak of trusts . . . without speaking first of uses." Mait. Eq. 36. Though uses are now largely obsolete, a basic understanding of their origin and development contributes considerably to an understanding of the modern law of trusts.

There is nothing complicated about the basic idea of the use. It was merely a transfer of property from *A* to *B* for certain purposes, *A* trusting *B* to carry out those purposes. Thus, if *A* wished *C* to have the benefit of a use, *A* would enfeoff *B*, *B* agreeing to hold the land to the use (i.e., for the benefit) of *C*. *A* would be the "feoffor to uses" (corresponding to the settlor of the modern trust), *B* the "feoffee to uses" (corresponding to the trustee of the modern trust), and *C* the "cestui que use" (corresponding to the cestui que trust, or beneficiary, of the modern trust).

The beginning of uses in England is obscure, but they were certainly being used by the thirteenth century. For about the first two centuries of its existence, the use probably had no legal significance. That is, the feoffment in our hypothetical case would transfer legal title to the land to

---

[1] Trusts did not exist in Louisiana, for example, due to its civil law heritage, until authorized by statute in 1920. Other legal systems, however, sometimes accomplish similar results by employing different concepts and theories. See Fratcher, Trusts, in 6 Int'l Encyclopedia of Comparative Law (Lawson ed. 1974); De Wulf, The Trust and Corresponding Institutions in the Civil Law (1965).

B, but *B*'s agreement to hold it for *C*'s benefit was unenforceable. Because the common law courts refused to recognize it, its efficacy depended upon *B*'s trustworthiness. Nevertheless, the scheme apparently worked well enough to become popular, even without judicial assistance. Petitions to the Chancellor requesting enforcement of uses are extant from just before 1400. It is probable that the Chancellor gave relief early in the fifteenth century, though no recorded decree in favor of a cestui que use seems to exist before 1445. Whenever it was, it was a significant development. The effect was to separate the benefits of property ownership from its burdens, and that is the defining characteristic of the modern trust.

At first, the Chancellor probably acted on simple ethical grounds. The original use looked much like a modern contract. In consideration of the receipt of the land from *A*, *B* promised *A* to deal with the land in a certain way. Speaking in modern terms, there was certainly consideration for this promise; the conception of bargain is now flexible enough to cover a transfer in reliance on the transferee's promise, even if the transferee receives no benefit. Today, enforcement of *B*'s promise seems obviously proper. In the early days, the Chancellor probably considered it only fair to compel *B* to live up to the agreement; certainly the Chancellor did not reason in terms of the modern doctrine of consideration, which had not yet been formulated. The disloyal feoffee to uses did not conform to the equitable standard of morality, and the common law afforded no remedy. Thus began probably the most permanently important branch of equity jurisdiction. See 1 Holds. 454; 4 Holds. 414–20; 2 P. & M. 235–39; Mait. Eq. 29; Scott, supra, at 458.

The use's great value lay in the fact that it enabled a person to escape the unfortunate consequences of technical legal ownership and yet enjoy the benefits of ownership. Once the Chancellor began to enforce the use, its efficacy and popularity increased dramatically; thereafter, this form of ownership was no longer solely dependent on the feoffee's honesty. Moreover, though Chancery thereafter protected the cestui que use, who therefore had "equitable title," the law courts continued to refuse to recognize the interest. Thus, the escape from the disadvantages of "legal" (as distinguished from equitable) ownership continued to be effective. In this way, the dual system of law and equity made possible the convenient though curious situation in which one person, in reality only a dummy, was recognized in the law courts as sole owner with all the legal consequences recognized by the common law, while the beneficiary enjoyed protection in Chancery free of those consequences, except insofar as the Chancellor wished to follow the doctrines of the common law.

Of all the causes of the widespread employment of uses, however, the most important and influential was the desire to make a will of land. From the thirteenth century until 1540, the law courts ruled that wills of real property were not possible. However, in an age when land was the chief form of wealth, there was widespread interest in avoiding primogeniture, by which the eldest son took all of a decedent's land. Without a will, it was impossible for a dying landowner to provide adequately for daughters or younger sons, or to provide for charity. Another important factor in the development of uses, also influential in promoting the desire to make a will, was the wish to escape the onerous feudal incidents that attached on the death intestate of a landowner. See Fratcher, Uses of Uses, 34 Mo. L. Rev. 39 (1969).

The typical use arrangement accomplished both of these ends—the testamentary gift of land and the avoidance of feudal incidents. The feoffor would enfeoff not one but several feoffees (e.g., six or more) as joint tenants, to the use of the feoffor. These feoffees would agree to allow the feoffor to use the land and to transfer the title to whomever the feoffor might designate. Thereafter, the feoffor could in effect make a will by instructing the feoffees to transfer legal title to designated takers after the feoffor's death. More often than not, the directions for the post-mortem disposition of the land actually appeared in the feoffor's will. In the law courts, however, this was not a testamentary disposition of the land. The subject matter was the feoffor's use interest, which the law courts did not recognize. Thus, there was no testamentary disposition of legal title, unless one were willing to look through form to substance—and the law courts were not. Ignoring the use interest, as the law courts did, there was no basis for prohibiting these transfers. The use also avoided the feudal incidents. Again, the law courts shut their eyes to the use interest; thus, it generated no feudal incidents. True, the cestuis que use and not the feoffees were the practical owners, but there was no rule prohibiting a legal owner from allowing somebody else to enjoy the land. Feudal incidents did not attach at the death of any one feoffee, because the feoffees held title as joint tenants; at the death of any *one*, the survivors continued to own the entire estate. To avoid the untoward possibility that a lone surviving joint tenant might die (in which case intestate succession would occur, and the feudal incidents would attach), feoffees to uses assiduously replenished their own ranks; if their number became low, they added more joint tenants. In this way, they kept legal title free not only of feudal incidents but also of dower and of the possibility of escheat in the event of a feoffee's death without heirs. So popular was this arrangement that, by about 1500, almost all the land in England was held to uses.[2] See 4 Holds. 416–17, 436–44, 521–24; 2 P. & M. 231, 238; Mait. Eq. 25–27.

---

[2] For several reasons, uses were much less common in disposing of personal property. First, it was permissible to dispose of personalty by will. Second, while the rigidity of the common law of real property precluded recognition of a use interest, the law of personal property afforded adequate legal remedies to those for whose use chattels were held. Third, personal property was then a comparatively unimportant form of wealth and often consisted of perishables that were unlikely subjects of long-term uses. See 4 Holds. 412–14, 420–21.

The one person who suffered from the development of the use was the King. Other landowners, as feudal lords, would lose through evasion of feudal incidents, but they would also gain as feudal tenants. The King, as feudal lord over all and tenant to none, would always lose and never gain. The spread of uses therefore seriously diminished the crown's revenue. The situation eventually came to a head in 1535, when Henry VIII, by threat and diplomacy, secured enactment of the famous Statute of Uses (27 Hen. 8, c. 10):

> That where any Person or Persons stand or be seised . . . of and in any Honours, Castles, Manors, Lands, Tenements, Rents, Services, Reversions, Remainders or other Hereditaments, to the Use, Confidence or Trust of any other Person or Persons, or of any Body Politick . . . ; that in every such Case, all and every such Person and Persons, and Bodies Politick . . . shall from henceforth stand and be seised, deemed and adjudged in lawful Seisin, Estate and Possession of and in the same Honours, Castles, Manors, Lands, Tenements, Rents, Services, Reversions, Remainders, and Hereditaments, with their Appurtenances, to all Intents, Constructions and Purposes in the Law, of and in such like Estates as they had or shall have in Use, Trust or Confidence of or in the same; . . . .

The Statute's basic purpose was to extinguish the seisin or legal estate of the feoffees to uses and relocate it in the cestui que use. The Statute thereby sought to abolish dual ownership and prevent evasion of the common law by making the cestui the legal owner, subject to the usual liabilities. In other words, the Statute did not abolish the system of uses; it merely "executed" uses by turning them into legal estates. If *A* enfeoffed *B* in fee to the use of *C* in fee, the Statute vested *B*'s legal estate in *C*, who thus became the fee simple owner at law. See 4 Holds. 446–67; Mait. Eq. 34–36; Holdsworth, The Political Causes Which Shaped the Statute of Uses, 26 Harv. L. Rev. 108 (1912). Though the Statute would probably have been unpopular merely because it was a revenue measure, its attempt, by turning equitable interests into legal estates, to abolish the power to devise land provoked immediate hostility. Henry therefore restored the power to devise land in 1540 by securing enactment of the original Statute of Wills, under which the King asserted his rights to feudal incidents as to devises of land.

The survival of the use (or trust) is due to the fact that the Statute of Uses did not apply to three types of uses. First, the Statute did not apply to *uses of personal property*. As we have already seen, chattels played no significant part in the development of uses, and the Statute covered only the typical case.[3] As personal property increased in importance as a form of wealth, the Chancellor thus acquired a significant branch of jurisdiction. Second, the Statute did not apply to *active uses.* The Chancellor's retention of jurisdiction over this exception was the most important factor in the development of the modern trust. Today, most trusts are active: the trustee has active duties, and retention by the trustee of "legal" title is essential to carrying out the trust purposes. Perhaps the best explanation of why the Statute of Uses did not execute active uses is that it focused primarily on the typical use, the passive use, under which the feoffee to uses was a dummy who held legal title while the cestui was in possession and enjoyed all practical benefits of ownership. Third, the Statute did not apply to a *use on a use,* which was an attempt to give two contemporaneous use interests in the same property, as when *A* enfeoffed *B* in fee to the use of *C* in fee to the use of *D* in fee.[4] See 4 Holds. 463, 468–73, 476; 5 Holds. 307–09; 6 Holds. 641–42; 7 Holds. 135; Mait. Eq. 37–38, 41–42. These uses thus continued after and flourished under the Statute of Uses, and certain aspects of the law governing them eventually evolved into what is now called the law of trusts.

3. THE DISTINCTION BETWEEN ACTIVE AND PASSIVE TRUSTS

Today, in America, the primary significance of the Statute of Uses is the distinction, perhaps fading, between active and passive trusts. As Restatement (Third) of Trusts § 2 (2003), infra p. 562, makes clear, it is essential to the existence of a trust that the trustee be subject to duties with respect to property for the benefit of one or more beneficiaries. If a "trustee" holds title to property for the benefit of one or more "beneficiaries" but has no duties with respect to the property, there is no trust. When the property consists exclusively of real property, one can reach this conclusion by reference to the Statute of Uses, which, most believe, continues to apply, even in this country, unless abolished statutorily or judicially. See Restatement (Third) of Trusts § 6, cmt. b (2003).

Most trusts today, however, involve primarily or even exclusively personal property, as to which the Statute of Uses never did apply. As to these trusts, the analog to the Statute of Uses is the passive trust doctrine. Under this doctrine, no trust exists, and the "beneficiary" owns the property outright and free of trust, if the "trustee" has no "active duty" with respect to the property. See, e.g., Estate of Mannara, 785 N.Y.S.2d 274 (Sur. 2004); Penney v. White, 594 S.W.2d 632 (Mo.App.1980); N.Y.

---

[3] The Statute applied only when one person was "seised" to the use of another, and seisin had by then come to apply only to freehold estates in real property. The statute therefore did not apply when one person was "possessed" of chattels to the use of another.

[4] In such a case, *D*'s interest would be the use of (or "on") a use. Actually, it was not until a hundred years after the Statute of Uses that the Chancellor began to enforce the second use.

EPTL § 7–1.2. Increasingly, however, modern courts seem ready to grasp at almost any straw to find an "active duty" on the part of the trustee, thereby justifying the conclusion that the relationship under scrutiny is, in fact, a trust. See, e.g., McMahon v. Standard Bank & Trust Co., 550 N.W.2d 727 (Wis.App.1996); Smith v. Wright, 779 S.W.2d 177 (Ark.1989); Odum v. Henry, 334 S.E.2d 304 (Ga.1985). For more on active and passive trusts, see Restatement (Third) of Trusts § 6 (2003); 1 Scott and Ascher on Trusts §§ 3.4 to 3.4.7.

4. METHODS OF CREATING TRUSTS

Today, there are two primary methods of creating a trust during the settlor's lifetime. The first is a *transfer in trust*. This occurs when *A*, the settlor, transfers property to *B*, the trustee, in trust for *C*, the beneficiary. This is the modern counterpart of a use created by a feoffment. The second is a *declaration of trust*. This occurs when *A*, the owner of property, declares himself or herself trustee of the property for the benefit of *C*, the beneficiary.

A testamentary declaration of trust is, of course, impossible, since a will is not effective until the testator is dead and, therefore, unable to act as trustee. Instead, testamentary trusts, of which there are many, more resemble transfers in trust, in that they come into existence upon the transfer at death of property from a testator to a third party, who is to act as trustee for the benefit of one or more beneficiaries.

5. THE UNIFORM TRUST CODE

As we have seen, the law of trusts has for centuries been the bailiwick of the courts. Almost exclusively, it has been judge-made law. Increasingly, though, the law of trusts is being codified. Every year, state legislatures throughout the United States add to the statutory coverage of the law of trusts and try improve on what already exists. Undoubtedly, the three Restatements of Trusts (1935, 1959, and 2003-2012) have eased, if not prompted, that process. But during the last few decades, the single most influential force in American trust law has almost certainly been the National Conference of Commissioners on Uniform State Laws (NCCUSL). A selective list of the many Uniform Laws that relate to the law of trusts includes: three separate versions of the Uniform Principal and Income Act (1931, 1962, and 1997), the Uniform Probate Code, the Uniform Prudent Investor Act, the Uniform Statutory Rule Against Perpetuities, the Uniform Testamentary Additions to Trusts Act, the Uniform Transfers to Minors Act, and the Uniform Trustees' Powers Act. In addition, in 2000, NCCUSL promulgated the Uniform Trust Code (UTC), the first nationwide attempt to codify the entire law of trusts (or most of it anyway). See English, The Uniform Trust Code (2000): Significant Provisions and Policy Issues, 67 Mo. L. Rev. 143 (2002) (written by reporter for UTC). Already, twenty-four jurisdictions have enacted it, and it seems likely that, over time, at least a few more will join the UTC ranks. In addition, the UTC has influenced the law in countless ways in many other jurisdictions. Thus, the UTC already is, and seems destined for the indefinite future to remain, a major force in American trust law. See generally Langbein, Why Did Trust Law Become Statute Law in the United States?, 58 Ala. L. Rev. 1069 (2007).

B. THE EXPRESS TRUST

Restatement (Third) of Trusts (2003)

§ 2. Definition of Trust

A trust, as the term is used in this Restatement, when not qualified by the word "resulting" or "constructive," is a fiduciary relationship with respect to property, arising from a manifestation of intention to create that relationship and subjecting the person who holds title to the property to duties to deal with it for the benefit of charity or for one or more persons, at least one of whom is not the sole trustee.

1. DECLARATION OF TRUST

TALIAFERRO V. TALIAFERRO

Supreme Court of Kansas, 1996.
260 Kan. 573, 921 P.2d 803.

LARSON, JUSTICE:

[P]roponents of the Will C. Taliaferro Trust appeal from a trial court decision that the trust was invalid because the settlor had not transferred title to property he owned to himself as trustee. We reverse and hold that where the settlor of a trust executes a declaration of trust, no transfer of legal title to the trust property is required to fund the trust.

On March 29, 1990, while in the hospital, Will C. Taliaferro executed two revocable trust indentures, a will, and various other documents. The trust documents had been prepared by his nephew, an attorney, who had little estate planning experience. The first trust [not in issue here] was called the Taliaferro & Browne Trust. It covered the ownership of Will C. Taliaferro's business venture, the Taliaferro & Browne, Inc., engineering firm, and the proceeds of a life insurance policy on his life. . . .

The second trust was a personal revocable inter vivos trust, the Will C. Taliaferro Trust, and is the subject of this action. Section One of the Will C. Taliaferro Trust provides in part:

I, Will Cedric Taliaferro, as Grantor, hereby declare the establishment of the Will C. Taliaferro Trust (hereinafter sometimes referred to as "the trust"). I hereby declare that I have appointed myself as Trustee of the Trust (hereinafter sometimes referred to as "the Trustee") and declare, further, that as the Trustee, I accept and hold in trust all of the property described in Schedule A, which is attached hereto and incorporated herein by reference. Such property, together with any other property that may later become subject to this trust, shall constitute the trust estate, and shall be held, administered and distributed by the Trustee as herein provided.

The trust property was described in Schedule A to the trust indenture:

The following described property of Will C. Taliaferro is held in trust and made subject to the terms and provisions of the foregoing Declaration of Trust for the Will C. Taliaferro Trust:

1. All Douglass Bank stock that is solely or separately owned by Grantor.

2. Grantor's entire interest in Equitable Insurance Company Policy number 34–590–634 MSC/KSM, a policy of insurance on the life of Carl Buckner.

3. All of Grantor's household goods, the contents of Grantor's safe deposit box, and all other tangible personal property owned by Grantor at the time of execution of this agreement, subject to disposition at the Trustee's discretion from this date forward, and all such property hereinafter acquired by Grantor and delivered to Trustee as of the date of death of Grantor.

Will C. Taliaferro was the income beneficiary of this trust during his life. After his death, the successor trustee was to distribute the accrued income and corpus among a number of named beneficiaries, with the remainder to go to Betty Taliaferro, who was Will C. Taliaferro's wife, his sole heir, the executor named in his will, the designated successor trustee of the Will C. Taliaferro Trust, and the opponent of the trust herein.

Will C. Taliaferro died September 1, 1990. The present case is a declaratory judgment action brought by Betty Taliaferro to determine the validity of the Will C. Taliaferro Trust. In her petition, Betty Taliaferro contended that Will C. Taliaferro never transferred any of the property allegedly subject to the trust into the trust because none of the property in Schedule A had been assigned to the trust or to Will C. Taliaferro as trustee. She further alleged that Will C. Taliaferro did not treat the property as trust property during his lifetime but rather as if he owned it individually. . . .

[T]he trial court found the Will C. Taliaferro trust to be invalid. It held the evidence did not show that Will C. Taliaferro had intended to transfer property to the corpus of the trust. The trial court held that Pizel v. Pizel, 7 Kan. App. 2d 388, 643 P.2d 1094, rev. denied, 231 Kan. 801 (1982) laid down three requirements the trust had to meet to be a valid inter vivos trust: "(1) an explicit declaration and intention to create a trust; (2) definite property or subject matter of the trust; and (3) the acceptance and handling of the subject matter by the trustee as a trust."

The trial court found there was a sufficient declaration of trust and intent to create a trust to meet the first *Pizel* requirement—an explicit declaration and intention to create a trust—and that the second requirement—that there be definite property or subject matter of the trust—was satisfied by the Douglass Bancorp stock owned by Will C. Taliaferro, the life insurance policy on Carl Buckner, and Will C. Taliaferro's personal jewelry and clothing.

However, the trial court found that the evidence failed to establish the third requirement of a valid trust it attributed to *Pizel.* The court found the evidence did not establish that the trustee, Will C. Taliaferro, had accepted and handled the subject matter of the trust as trust property, nor had Will C. Taliaferro, as settlor, effected the transfer of the property to the trust. . . .

The court also based its decision on its conclusion that whatever Will C. Taliaferro's original intentions were when executing the trust document, he changed his mind about creating a trust in the months following. This holding was drawn primarily from the fact that Will C. Taliaferro had transferred the stock subject to the Taliaferro & Browne Trust to himself as trustee but took no similar action with respect to property subject to the Will C. Taliaferro Trust. . . .

Did Will C. Taliaferro transfer definite property sufficient to create a trust?

As a preliminary matter, it is important to note that the Will C. Taliaferro Trust is purported to be created by a declaration of trust, rather than by the transfer of the trust property to a separate trustee. Restatement (Second) of Trusts § 17 (1959) teaches us that "[a] trust may be created by (a) a declaration by the owner of property that he holds it as trustee for another person; or (b) a transfer inter vivos by the owner of property to another person as trustee for the transferor or for a third person." . . .

The trial court explicitly based its final judgment that the Will C. Taliaferro Trust was invalid on its finding that Will C. Taliaferro made "no present and irrevocable transfer of title of any of the property mentioned in Schedule A of the Trust Declaration." . . .

The trial court's legal conclusion is erroneous because there is no requirement that a settlor who also serves as trustee of a trust established by declaration must transfer legal title to the trust property.

Although the present transfer of property to the trustee is crucial when the settlor is not also the trustee, or when the settlor attempts to establish the trust solely by transfer, this requirement has not been included in the requirement for establishment of a trust because it is not necessary in every trust. . . .

Where the present transfer of legal title to property is required, it is because common sense and logic dictate that the requirements of a valid trust cannot be fulfilled without it. Before property can be said to be held in trust by a trustee, the trustee must have legal title. Without legal title the trustee holds nothing in trust. Furthermore, the backbone of trust law is the concept of separate ownership of equitable and legal interests. See I Scott on Trusts § 1, p. 4 (4th ed. 1987); . . . Restatement (Second) Trusts § 2, Comment f (in trusts there is a separation of legal and equitable interests in the subject matter). Ordinarily, transfer of legal title to the trust property to a trustee accomplishes the separation of legal and equitable interests.

However, a trust can exist where the settlor is both trustee and life beneficiary. See In re Estate of Ingram, 212 Kan. 218, 510 P.2d 597 (1973). Where, as here, the settlor and the trustee are the same person, no transfer of legal title is required, since the trustee already holds legal title. The important question in such cases is whether an equitable interest has been divested to a cestui que trust by the settlor. If such a transfer of an equitable interest is made, the separation of equitable and legal interests required to support a trust is present, and the settlor-trustee holds legal title to the trust property subject to the trust.

In the present case, the settlor declared the property to be held in trust. "The declaration is a conveyance of an equitable interest." Bogert, Trusts & Trustees § 147, p. 62 (2d ed. rev. 1979). A declaration of trust is considered in a court of equity as equivalent to an actual transfer of legal interest in a court of law. Milholland v. Whalen, 89 Md. 212, 214, 43 A. 43 (1899).

Bogert, Trusts & Trustees § 141 (2d ed. rev. 1979) states:

It is sometimes stated that the transfer by the settlor of legal title to the trustee is essential to the creation of an express trust. This statement is inaccurate in one respect. Obviously, if the trust is to be created by declaration there is no real transfer of any property interest to a trustee. The settlor holds a property interest before the trust declaration, and after the declaration he holds bare legal interest in the same property with the equitable or beneficial interest in the beneficiary. No new property interest has passed to the trustee. The settlor has merely remained owner of part of what he formerly owned.

The Comment on Clause (a) of Restatement (Second) of Trusts § 17 states directly: "If the owner of property declares himself trustee of the property, a trust may be created without a transfer of title to the property." . . .

Thus, the mere declaration that real estate is held in trust, without the transfer of a deed, is sufficient. Estate of Heggstad, 16 Cal. App. 4th 943, 950, 20 Cal. Rptr. 2d 433 (1993). The same is true as to a policy of life insurance, without reference to whether the named beneficiary of the policy itself is changed: "Where a policy of life insurance is payable to the insured or his estate, he can effectively declare himself trustee of his rights under the policy." IA Scott on Trusts § 82.1, p. 461 (4th ed. 1987).

Pizel v. Pizel, 7 Kan. App. 2d 388, 643 P.2d 1094, on which the trial court relied, is distinguishable as it involved a trust the settlor attempted to create by a failed deed rather than by declaration. In *Pizel*, the purported settlor executed a document entitled "Charles Pizel Revocable Trust." Although the settlor was named as one of several trustees, the document was not a declaration of trust but was accompanied by a separate deed purporting to convey the subject matter of the trust, 1,760 acres of land, from Charles Pizel, settlor, to the trustees of the Charles Pizel Revocable Trust. Both the deed and the trust were held by Pizel's attorneys until his death. Several years after executing the original trust document, Pizel, by amendment of the trust document, replaced himself as trustee with Herbert Pizel and executed a second deed purporting to convey the same 1,760 acres of land from himself as settlor to the reconstituted group of trustees. Again, these documents remained with Pizel's attorneys. The trial court and the Court of Appeals found that Pizel never had the requisite intent to establish a trust, he never transferred the trust property to the trustees, and no named trustee had accepted the property as trustee. Those facts are materially different from those we face herein.

Pizel illustrates the rule set forth by Bogert, Trusts & Trustees § 202, p. 12 (2d ed. rev. 1992):

If a voluntary settlor intends to create a trust by way of transfer to a trustee but his conduct in order to accomplish his purpose is wholly ineffective to transfer any legal interest to the trustee or any equitable interest to the beneficiary, equity will not treat such conduct as amounting to a declaration of trust with the settlor as trustee, even though such a declaration could have been accomplished without formality. Thus if settlor never delivers the deed of transfer, and so it is a nullity as an instrument of transfer, equity will not treat the undelivered instrument as a declaration of trust by the settlor. . . .

We hold that Will C. Taliaferro clearly declared himself as trustee of the property described in schedule A, which was attached to and made a part of the trust document. No further document transferring title to the property was required.

Did Will C. Taliaferro manifest a present intent to transfer an equitable interest in his property and thereby create a trust through his declaration of trust?

In a case where a trust is purported to have been created by declaration, to determine whether the trust is valid the factfinder must ascertain whether at the time the declaration was executed, there was a present intent to transfer an equitable interest to the cestui que trust and thereby create a trust. . . .

The trial court put great weight on Will C. Taliaferro's conduct after executing the declaration of trust in determining no trust had been created. However, subsequent behavior inconsistent with the creation of a trust is of no importance to the question of whether a trust came into being if there was a present intent to create a trust and transfer an equitable interest contemporaneous with the declaration.

"The declaration of trust immediately creates an equitable interest in the beneficiaries, although the enjoyment of the interest is postponed until the death of the settlor, and although the interest may be divested by the exercise of the power of revocation." IA Scott on Trusts § 57.6, pp. 189–90 (4th ed. 1987). Once the trust is established, the settlor's declarations thereafter in derogation are immaterial unless they rise to the level of a revocation. See Elliott v. Gordon, 70 F.2d 9, 13 (10th Cir. 1934).

The fact that a trustee exceeded his or her power and violated his or her trust would not terminate the trust, but merely would "provide justification for the removal of the trustee and appointment of a successor." In re Estate of Yetter, 183 Kan. 340, 349, 328 P.2d 738 (1958). Therefore, the subsequent mindset of the settlor-trustee, unless it is accompanied by a revocation of the trust, is immaterial where the conveyance and establishment of an equitable interest were made in the first instance.

Although the settlor-trustee's subsequent treatment of trust property without regard to the duties imposed by the trust might be consistent with the absence of an intent to create a trust *ab initio*, it is equally consistent with the conclusion that a trust which was created was subsequently breached. Thus, it is the commended practice to execute documents of transfer. Such documents may help prove the settlor intended a declaration to be operative to create a trust, help prevent a challenge to the trust as a testamentary disposition, and avoid the necessity of probating the property, but they are not required by the law of trusts. . . .

The intent to create a trust can be manifested through a plain affirmative declaration by a person that he or she holds property for the benefit or use of another person. Johnson v. Capitol Federal Savings & Loan Assoc., 215 Kan. 286, 524 P.2d 1127. Contrary to the appellee's argument, where the trust is purportedly created by declaration, a settlor's intent may be established from the face of the instrument. In re Estate of Morton, 241 Kan. 698, 703, 769 P.2d 616 (1987). . . .

The trust instrument purporting to create the Will C. Taliaferro Trust on its face unequivocally and unambiguously evidences Will C. Taliaferro's intent to create a present trust at the time it was executed and to assume the duties of a trustee. Under the parol evidence rule, the trial court erred in considering extrinsic evidence to rebut the clear language of the trust declaration:

> If the owner of property by a written instrument declares that he holds the property upon a particular trust, extrinsic evidence, in the absence of fraud, duress, mistake or other ground for reformation or rescission, is not admissible to show that he intended to hold the property upon a different trust or to hold it free of trust.

Restatement (Second) of Trusts § 38(4) (1959).

Even if the instrument had not clearly established trust intent and was sufficiently ambiguous to permit the court to look to the settlor's subsequent conduct, the factors relied on by the trial court in this case were erroneous as a matter of law.

The trial court noted that Will C. Taliaferro

> did not change the name of the owner of the Equitable Insurance Company life insurance policy to himself as trustee. . . . He did not vote the stock he owned as trustee. He opened no bank accounts in the name of the trust. Premiums on the life insurance policy were paid from his personal account. Most importantly, he did not change his stock certificates from his name to himself as trustee. . . .

The fact that Will C. Taliaferro on one occasion voted the Douglass Bancorp shares held in trust individually without specifying he was acting as trustee is not inconsistent with his role as trustee. The law of trusts does not require that securities be transferred to the settlor "as trustee." See Bogert, Trusts & Trustees § 142(b) (2d ed. rev. 1979) ("The owner of shares of stock in a corporation may make himself trustee of the shares for another by oral or written declaration of the trust, without delivery of any document to the beneficiary or change on the corporation stock records."). Moreover, the trust declaration itself grants the trustee the power "[t]o cause to be registered in its name, individually *or* as Trustee . . . any securities . . . from time to time held by it."

In addition, the fact that the proceeds of a life insurance policy are declared to be equitably conveyed is independent of who pays the premiums and it is immaterial that the insured, or in this case the settlor individually, continued to pay the premiums. See IA Scott on Trusts § 57.3, pp. 152–54 (4th ed. 1987). The trial court's conclusion to the contrary is erroneous.

Finally, although no bank account was opened in the trust's name, the record reveals no exigency for the creation of one.

In finding the trust invalid, the trial court also relied on its conclusion that after conferring with a second attorney, Will C. Taliaferro reissued the stock in Taliaferro & Browne, Inc., but failed to do so as to the Douglass Bancorp stock described in Schedule A of the Will C. Taliaferro Trust. The only direct evidence on this issue is the specific wording of the trust declaration. Evidence of inconsistent actions or a different action in dealing with one trust than another does nothing to invalidate a transfer which was completed upon execution of the trust instrument. Under the provisions of the trust document, revocation of the trust could be accomplished only by a "duly executed instrument." There is no evidence Will C. Taliaferro ever executed any instrument revoking the trust. In addition, the trial court's conclusion that Will C. Taliaferro changed his mind is not supported by any substantial competent evidence.

Did Will C. Taliaferro agree to act as trustee?

Did Will C. Taliaferro do what is required to meet the third element of a trust and accept, as trustee, the subject matter as trust property? We find that the undisputed facts in the record establish as a matter of law that he did. The focus of this element is on the *acceptance* by the trustee of the property as trust property, not the subsequent treatment of the property. . . .

In this case, Will C. Taliaferro's acceptance of the property as trust property and his willingness to act as trustee is proved by the unambiguous signed trust instrument in which he swore he was holding the property *as trustee of trust property*. . . . Again, not only does the parol evidence rule restrict the extrinsic evidence that may impeach this sworn declaration, but also, even if Will C. Taliaferro's subsequent actions were considered, they were not inconsistent with having conveyed a present revocable equitable interest, the enjoyment of which was delayed, and accepting the responsibilities of trustee of that property at that time. . . .

The decision of the trial court is reversed.

NOTES

1. *Transfers in trust.* There are two ways to create an inter vivos trust. One, as in *Taliaferro*, is by a declaration of trust. See UTC § 401(2). For a declaration of trust, all that is ordinarily required is that the settlor declare that he or she is holding property in trust for one or more beneficiaries, at least one of whom is not the settlor. Because the settlor-trustee already owns the property prior to the declaration of trust, it is impossible and, therefore, unnecessary for the settlor to "transfer" the property to himself or herself, as trustee.

The other way to create an inter vivos trust is by a transfer in trust, in which the settlor transfers title to property to a third party, who is to serve as trustee for one or more beneficiaries. See UTC § 401(1). In general, it is essential to the effectiveness of a transfer in trust that the transfer actually occur. See Pizel v. Pizel, 643 P.2d 1094 (Kan.App.1982).

2. *Statute of Frauds. Taliaferro* asserts that "the mere declaration that real estate is held in trust, without the transfer of a deed, is sufficient." If the res is land, however, the Statute of Frauds requires that a writing (not necessarily a deed) properly evidence the trust. See Section E of this Chapter, infra. The settlor-declarant may sign such a writing "before or at the time of the declaration," or "after the time of the declaration but before the declarant has transferred the property." Restatement (Third) of Trusts § 23(1) (2003). In Chebatoris v. Moyer, 757 N.W.2d 212 (Neb. 2008), the court upheld a revocable trust of both real and personal property where the transfer was evidenced by nothing more than the trust agreement itself.

A declaration of trust of personalty ordinarily need not be in writing, but, in order to secure more enduring evidence of the terms of the trust, careful lawyers always insist on written declarations. Cf. UTC § 407 ("the creation of an oral trust and its terms may be established only by clear and convincing evidence").

3. *Defective gifts. Taliaferro* discusses a situation in which a property owner wishes to create a trust and attempts unsuccessfully to transfer property to another, as trustee. From time to time courts have attempted to salvage the situation by treating the failed transfer as a declaration of trust, despite the fact that the property owner, *who sought to give the property away*, never undertook to hold it in trust. See Ex parte Pye, 34 Eng. Rep. 271

(Ch. 1811). Generally, however, the courts have declined to sustain defective gifts as declarations of trust. See Richards v. Delbridge, L.R. 18 Eq. 11, 14–15 (Ch. 1874), in which the court stated:

> The principle is a very simple one. A man may transfer his property, without valuable consideration, in one of two ways: he may either do such acts as amount in law to a conveyance or assignment of the property, and thus completely divest himself of the legal ownership, in which case the person who by those acts acquires the property takes it beneficially, or on trust, as the case may be; or the legal owner of the property may, by one or other of the modes recognized as amounting to a valid declaration of trust, constitute himself a trustee, and, without an actual transfer of the legal title, may so deal with the property as to deprive himself of its beneficial ownership, and declare that he will hold it from that time forward on trust for the other person. It is true he need not use the words, "I declare myself a trustee," but he must do something which is equivalent to it, and use expressions which have that meaning; for, however anxious the Court may be to carry out a man's intention, it is not at liberty to construe words otherwise than according to their proper meaning. . . .

> The true distinction appears to me to be plain, and beyond dispute: for a man to make himself a trustee there must be an expression of intention to become a trustee, whereas words of present gift shew an intention to give over property to another, and not retain it in the donor's own hands for any purpose, fiduciary or otherwise.

The modern American rule appears in Restatement (Third) of Trusts § 16 (2003), as follows:

> (1) If a property owner undertakes to make a donative inter vivos disposition in trust by transferring property to another as trustee, an express trust is not created if the property owner fails during life to complete the contemplated transfer of the property. In some circumstances, however, the trust intention of such a property owner who dies or becomes incompetent may be given effect by constructive trust in order to prevent unjust enrichment of the property owner's successors in interest.

> (2) If a property owner intends to make an outright gift inter vivos but fails to make the transfer that is required in order to do so, the gift intention will not be given effect by treating it as a declaration of trust.

Compare Love, Imperfect Gifts as Declarations of Trust: An Unapologetic Anomaly, 67 Ky. L.J. 309 (1979).

For more on defective gifts, see Farmers' Loan & Trust Co. v. Winthrop, infra p. 590.

4. *Stashes.* Because the requirements for a valid declaration of trust are imprecise, the situation in which survivors find particular items of property set aside among a decedent's possessions, marked for a particular person, have elicited varying judicial responses. Relevant factors seem to include, among others: how the decedent used the property after the alleged transfer, the extent to which the decedent communicated his or her intent, the value of the items in comparison to the estate as a whole, and the identity of the parties. Compare Govin v. De Miranda, 27 N.Y.S. 1049 (App.Div. 1894) ("In no case has it ever been held as yet that a party may, by transferring his property from one pocket to another, make himself a trustee."), with Estate of Smith, 22 A. 916 (Pa.1891) (envelope containing 13 bonds worth $1,000 apiece was trust for nephew, rather than part of million-dollar estate). A more recent case, finding a declaration of trust, is Ridge v. Bright, 93 S.E.2d 607 (N.C.1956).

5. *Separation of legal and equitable title.* In Morsman v. Commissioner, 90 F.2d 18 (8th Cir.1937), an unmarried, childless settlor declared himself trustee of certain property for his own benefit. Upon his death, the trust was to continue for the benefit of his issue, if any; otherwise, the trust was to terminate in favor of his widow, if any, or his heirs. The court held that no trust arose; the settlor had failed to separate legal and equitable title:

> [I]t is settled that a trust cannot exist where the same person possesses both the legal and equitable titles to the trust fund at the same time. In such a case the two titles are said to merge. . . . The result, of course, is different where one person conveys property to another who agrees to hold in trust for the grantor. . . . In such a case there is an immediate severance of the legal and equitable titles, and a trust arises at once. . . .

> [I]t has been held in several cases that a present trust may be created where the beneficiary of an express trust is an unborn child. . . . The rationale of such a case is that the instrument has the effect of creating an immediate resulting trust for the settlor (which will cease if the expected child is born) "with an express trust for the child springing up when and if such child ever materializes." Bogert, Trusts and Trustees, § 163. In such a case, where the trustee is a third person, if no child is born within the period of the rule against perpetuities, the legal and equitable interests both merge in the settlor at the end of the period; but, if the settlor is himself the trustee, the two interests are not severed by the purported declaration. . . . The distinction . . . between the case where *A* declares himself trustee for his unborn issue and where he conveys to *B* to hold in trust for such issue is vital. . . . The possibility of issue does not of itself have the effect of presently severing the legal and equitable interests. It can operate in futuro at best. [90 F.2d at 23–25.]

Morsman is noteworthy for its assertion that a declaration of trust (i.e., the settlor declares that he or she holds certain property in trust) may not be effective in some situations in which a transfer in trust (i.e., the settlor transfers various property to another person in trust) clearly is effective.

The Restatement seems, in general terms, contrary to *Morsman*:

> A trust or trust provision may be created, and once created may continue, for the benefit of a person or persons not in existence or not ascertainable at the time of the creation or continuation of the trust if they and their interests will be ascertainable, or the beneficial interests will fail, within the period and the terms of the applicable rule against perpetuities. Thus, a child who has not been born or conceived at the time of the creation of a trust can be a beneficiary of the trust.

Restatement (Third) of Trusts § 44, cmt. c (2003). But none of the Restatement's illustrations mirrors the *Morsman* fact pattern; the closest involves a childless bachelor who creates a trust by a transfer to a third party. Id. illus. 3. See Fratcher, Trustor as Sole Trustee and Only Ascertainable Beneficiary, 47 Mich. L. Rev. 907 (1949).

6. *Transfers to minors.* Historically, questions concerning the validity of a declaration of trust often arose in an attempted transfer for one or more minor children or grandchildren. Now, however, the Uniform Transfers to Minors Act provides a simple and inexpensive method for making gifts to minors and holding the property during their minority. See supra p. 530.

2. TRUSTS CREATED BY PRECATORY WORDS

MATTER OF ESTATE OF BOLINGER
Supreme Court of Montana, 1997.
284 Mont. 114, 943 P.2d 981.

NELSON, JUSTICE. . . .

Harry Albert Bolinger, III, (Decedent), died March 23, 1995. Decedent's estate was initially commenced as an intestacy proceeding with Deborah [Reichman] being nominated by Decedent's three adult children (the children) and subsequently being appointed as personal representative. On July 13, 1995, however, H.A. Bolinger (Hal), father of Decedent, filed a petition for formal probate of will and a request to be appointed personal representative. The November 15, 1984 will so offered for probate devised all Decedent's estate to Hal, or, in the event that Hal predeceased Decedent, to Hal's wife (Decedent's step-mother), Marian. Specifically, the Fifth paragraph of the will, the language of which is at issue here, provides:

> I intentionally give all of my property and estate to my said father, H.A. Bolinger, in the event that he shall survive me, and in the event he shall not survive me, I intentionally give all of my property and estate to my step-mother, Marian Bolinger, in the event she shall

survive me, and in that event, I intentionally give nothing to my three children, namely: Harry Albert Bolinger, IV, Wyetta Bolinger and Travis Bolinger, or to any children of any child who shall not survive me. I make this provision for the reason that I feel confident that any property which either my father or my step-mother, Marian Bolinger, receive from my estate will be used in the best interests of my said children as my said beneficiaries may determine in their exclusive discretion.

The will nominated Hal as personal representative with Marian as the alternate. Hal subsequently renounced his right to serve as personal representative and suggested the appointment of Marian, who petitioned to be appointed on November 6, 1995. Decedent's children objected, contending, among other things, that . . . the will created a trust on behalf of the children.

The children moved for summary judgment. [T]he court ruled that the will, through the language in the Fifth paragraph, created an express trust in favor of Decedent's children. Because Marian would be the trustee under the Fifth paragraph of the will and because of the admitted hostility between her and the children, the court also ruled that the trust should be terminated and the trust corpus distributed to them with Deborah continuing to act as the personal representative. . . .

[T]he District Court found that both Hal and Marian believed that the language in the Fifth paragraph of Decedent's will created a trust. . . . The court also found that Marian believed that at the time Decedent's will was drafted and executed, the children were minors and that Decedent used the language in the will to prevent his ex-wife from obtaining control over his estate. The court also [found] that, when read in its entirety, the Fifth paragraph of the will expressed Decedent's intention that all of his property must be used in the best interests of his children. The court found that the subject or res of the trust was all of Decedent's property and that the testator's purpose in creating the trust was to ensure that his assets would be used in his children's best interests. . . .

On appeal from the District Court's decision, Marian argues that . . . devises, bequests and gifts that do not contain any restrictions on use or disposition of the property involved do not create an express trust. She contends that the use of "precatory" words by a testator, that is words which express only a wish or recommendation as to the disposition of property, are not sufficient to establish an intention to create a trust. . . .

In support of the District Court's decision, the children argue that where the testator manifests his intention to create a trust, no particular form of words or conduct is necessary, and that, providing that the trustor indicates with reasonable certainty the subject, purpose and beneficiary of the trust, an express trust is created. The children contend that, under the facts here and under these criteria, the language used by Decedent in the Fifth paragraph of his will created an express trust in their favor. . . .

[A] trust is created only if the testator demonstrates that he or she intends that a trust be created. . . .

[We follow] the general rule that . . . it is the trustor's intent that controls and that to determine that intent we look to the language of the trust agreement. . . .

Furthermore, "[n]o particular form of words or conduct is necessary for the manifestation of intention to create a trust," Restatement (Second) of Trusts § 24 (1959), and "words of trusteeship are not necessarily conclusive," George T. Bogert, Trusts § 11 at 24 (6th ed.1987). . . .

From th[e] language [of the Fifth paragraph of Decedent's will] it is clear that Decedent intended to accomplish several things. . . . First, he "intentionally" devised outright all of his property and estate to his father, and in default of that bequest, then to his step-mother, Marian. Second, it is also clear that Decedent "intentionally" devised nothing to his three children. Third, Decedent desired to make some explanation as to why he disposed of his estate in the foregoing manner. To this end, he added to the otherwise unequivocal language of the first sentence of the Fifth paragraph, a second sentence with the explanation that he made this provision because he felt "confident" that any property which either his father or his step-mother, Marian, received from his estate would ["will"] be used in the best interests of his said children as Hal or Marian may determine in their exclusive discretion. It is the language in this second sentence which is at issue and which the District Court determined created an express trust in favor of the children.

The use of this latter sort of qualifying language in a will or instrument is referred to as "precatory" language. As stated in Bogert, supra § 19 at 41:

> Usually, if a transferor of property intends the transferee to be a trustee, he directs him to act in that capacity, but sometimes he merely expresses a wish or recommendation that the property given be used in whole or in part for the benefit of another. Words of this latter type are called "precatory" and are generally construed not to create a trust but instead to create at most an ethical obligation. . . .

> In weighing the effect of precatory expressions the courts consider the entire document and the circumstances of the donor, his family, and other interested parties.

The author of this treatise notes that the primary question in construing precatory language is whether the testator meant merely to advise or influence the discretion of the devisee, or himself control or direct the disposition intended. Bogert, supra § 19 at 42. Here, in Marian's favor, the author notes that "the settlor must have explicitly or impliedly expressed an intent to impose obligations on the trustee and not merely to give the donee of the property *an option to use it for the benefit of another*." Bogert, supra § 19 at 42 (emphasis added). Put another way, considering the language of the entire instrument and the situation of the alleged settlor, his family, and the supposed beneficiaries at the time the will was executed, "was it natural and probable that the donor intended the donee to be bound by an enforceable obligation *or was he to be free to use his judgment and discretion?*" Bogert, supra § 19 at 42 (emphasis added). Moreover, "[w]here a donor first makes an absolute gift of property, without restriction or limitation, and later inserts precatory language in a separate sentence or paragraph, the courts are apt to find that there was no intent to have a trust." Bogert, supra § 19 at 43. . . .

[T]he language used by Decedent clearly and unambiguously makes an outright gift to his father, and in default of that gift, to his step-mother and specifically excludes his children. Then, in a separate sentence, Decedent explains the reason for this distribution, expressing his "confidence" that the devisees will use his estate for the children's "best interests" in the devisees' "exclusive discretion." This language does not impose any sort of clear directive or obligation (other than, perhaps, a moral or ethical one) on either Hal or Marian. The purported trustee is given no direction as to how the supposed settlor intends his estate to be used to further the "best interests" of the children and neither does Decedent provide any guidance as to what those best interests might include. Decedent imposes no restrictions on the purported trustee, but, rather, leaves in that person the "exclusive discretion" as to how the estate will be used for the children's best interests, expressing his "confidence" that will be accomplished. Decedent's statement of reasons for devising his estate to Hal and Marian, neither limits nor restricts the gift to them. . . . The bottom line is that, under the precatory language used by Decedent, his devisees had complete discretion as to how to use the property given them outright.

Furthermore, . . . the facts found by the court and relied on by the children in the case at bar do not support the conclusion that Decedent intended that his expression of confidence in his father and step-mother would create a legally enforceable express trust. First, the trial court and the children focus on deposition testimony of Marian that she . . . and Hal believed that the will created a trust. How Marian and Hal may have construed the language is not the issue, however. The real issue is what Decedent intended when he used the language which he did. . . . Second, while Marian believed that Decedent may have been concerned that his first wife would obtain control over his estate while the children were minors, *her* personal belief of what motivated Decedent is not evidence of what Decedent actually intended. . . .

Furthermore, we note that the Third paragraph of Decedent's will makes an unconditional, outright devise of all of Decedent's estate to Hal and that the Fourth paragraph of the will makes an unconditional, outright devise of the same property to Marian, should Hal die before Decedent. Also, we note that the Sixth paragraph of the will appoints Hal as the personal representative with Marian as the alternate, both without bond, and gives both unrestricted power to sell any or all of the estate property without court order at public or private sale, with or without notice. Again, Decedent's unequivocal, outright and unrestricted gifts to Hal and alternatively to Marian, and his appointment of them as the personal representative and alternate without bond and without restriction on their powers, supports the conclusion that the one precatory sentence in the Fifth paragraph was advisory only and was not intended to create a legal, express trust obligation. . . .

. . . Whether a trust will be found from the use of any precatory word or phrase, whether that be "desire," "wish," "hope," "recommend," "in confidence" or "rely," cannot be concluded merely from the particular word or phrase used. Bogert, supra § 19 at 41–42. . . .

[R]eviewing Decedent's will as a whole, taking the words and phrases used by Decedent in their ordinary and grammatical sense and considering the facts found by the District Court, [we cannot conclude] that Decedent clearly and directly expressed his intention to create an express trust in favor of the children through his use of precatory language in the Fifth paragraph of his will. . . .

Reversed and remanded.

TURNAGE, C.J., and GRAY, REGNIER, and TRIEWEILER, JJ., concur.

[The dissenting opinion of LEAPHART, J., joined in by HUNT, J., is omitted.]

LEVIN V. FISCH

Court of Civil Appeals of Texas, 1966.
404 S.W.2d 889.

COLLINGS, JUSTICE.

Laura Fisch brought suit against Suzanne Cohen Levin and Jay Howard Cohen, individually and as independent executors of the estate of Bertha Cohen, deceased. Plaintiff, a sister of the deceased, claimed that she had an interest in said estate under the provisions of the last will and testament of Bertha Cohen. Defendants are the children of Bertha Cohen, deceased. It was stipulated that Bertha Cohen died on November 28, 1959, in Houston, Harris County, Texas, that the last will and testament of Bertha Cohen, dated April 11, 1958, was admitted to probate on January 27, 1960 by the Probate Court of Harris County, Texas, and that the defendants are the duly appointed and acting independent executors of the estate of Bertha Cohen, deceased. Both plaintiff and defendants filed motions for summary judgment urging that no genuine issue as to any material fact existed. Plaintiff contended that under the pleadings, the language of the will, considered with her ex parte affidavit and stipulations, she was entitled to judgment as a matter of law. Defendants contended that they were entitled to judgment, as a matter of law, because the provision of the will relied upon by plaintiff was precatory in nature and not mandatory and amounted, in effect, to only the expression of a wish on the part of the testatrix. The court overruled defendants' motion for summary judgment, sustained plaintiff's motion and rendered judgment for the plaintiff. The defendants have appealed.

The will provided for specific bequests to appellants. In addition to the provision for specific bequests, paragraph V of the will, the interpretation of which is here in controversy, is as follows:

> All of my other property of whatsoever nature, real, personal, or mixed, I give, devise and bequeath to my two children, Suzanne Cohen Levin and Jay Howard Cohen, to be divided equally between them so that each shall receive an equal share with the other in said property. It is my desire that each year out of the annual rent proceeds, rents and revenues from such property during such year so received by my said daughter and son they pay to my sister Mrs. Laura Fisch the sum of $2,400.00, provided such net proceeds, rents and revenues, received by them from such property for such year is sufficient to meet such payment. In the event the net revenues from such property for any given year should be insufficient to meet such payment for such year, then the amount of the payment to my said sister for such year should be reduced in the amount of such deficiency. It is my desire that my children continue such payments during the remainder of my said sister's life time provided that should my sister Laura Fisch get married, then my said children should not, after the date of such marriage continue such payment. In the event my said sister should marry, then the payment to her during the year of such marriage, should be prorated as of the date of such marriage.

Appellants present one point of error contending the court erred in overruling appellants' motion for summary judgment, and in sustaining appellee's motion for summary judgment and rendering judgment thereon, for the reason that paragraph V of the last will and testament of Bertha Cohen is clearly precatory in nature and not mandatory, and amounts only to a wish on the part of the testatrix and does not express a mandatory bequest to appellee, or devise or bequeath to appellee any interest whatsoever in the estate of Bertha Cohen, deceased, which the appellants, or either of them, either individually or as independent executors, are, as a matter of law required to recognize, honor or pay.

Appellants point out that the testatrix Bertha Cohen unequivocally devised and bequeathed to appellants all of her property not theretofore devised. Appellants contend that the phrase "It is my desire" considered in connection with the language used "within the four corners of the instrument," is not ambiguous, and should be given its ordinary and natural meaning, and should not be interpreted as a bequest or a mandatory instruction to appellants to pay to her sister, Mrs. Fisch, the $2,400.00 annual payment indicated in the will. Appellants contend that if Bertha Cohen had intended to bestow upon her sister, Laura Fisch, any right to the annual net rents and revenues from the properties which she had previously and unequivocally devised to appellants, she would have directed appellants in their capacity as executors to make such distribution. The word "desire" in its ordinary and primary meaning is precatory, but is often construed when used in a will as directive or mandatory when it clearly appears that such was the intention of the testator from a consideration of the instrument as a whole and the surrounding circumstances.

In support of the judgment appellee relies upon Colton v. Colton, 127 U.S. 300, 8 S. Ct. 1164, 32 L. Ed. 138 (1888). In that case the testator devised and bequeathed to his wife all of his estate, both real and personal, and then continued as follows: "I recommend to her the care and protection of my mother and sister, and request her to make such gift and provision for them as in her judgment will be best." In discussing the question of whether the above provision was precatory or mandatory the court stated:

> According to its context and manifest use, an expression of desire or wish will often be equivalent to a positive direction, where that is the evident purpose and meaning of the testator. . . . And in such a case as the present, it would be but natural for the testator to suppose that a request, which, in its terms, implied no alternative, addressed to his widow and principal legatee, would be understood and obeyed as strictly as though it were couched in the language of direction and command. . . .

The applicable rule in such cases was stated to be as follows:

> The object . . . of a judicial interpretation of a will is to ascertain the intention of the testator, according to the meaning of the words he has used, deduced from a consideration of the whole instrument and

a comparison of its various parts in the light of the situation and circumstances which surrounded the testator when the instrument was
framed.

The record in this case which is not disputed shows the following
facts and circumstances surrounding the testator when the will was executed. The deceased, Bertha Cohen and the appellee Laura Fisch were
sisters. Appellants are the children of Bertha Cohen. On April 11, 1958,
when Bertha Cohen executed the will she and Laura Fisch were both widows, approximately fifty years of age. Bertha Cohen owned property of
the value of approximately one million dollars, and the value of property
owned by Laura Fisch was approximately Twenty-five Thousand Dollars.
The appellant Cohen was twenty years of age and appellant Levin was
twenty-five years old. Appellants had one year previously inherited from
their father property of the approximate value of one million dollars. For
two years prior to her death Bertha Cohen paid appellee the sum of
$200.00 per month. She also made other gifts to appellee and her daugh-
ter of clothing and money. The record shows that appellee was in poor
health and unable to work full time, and that her income was approximately $300.00 per month.

Appellants rely principally on Byars v. Byars et al., 143 Tex. 10, 182
S.W.2d 363 (Sup. Ct. 1944), in which it was held that the word "request"
in its ordinary or natural meaning when used in a will is precatory and
not mandatory. Our Supreme Court in that case noted the statement of
the rule set out in the *Colton* case, supra, and then distinguished the facts
in the *Byars* case as follows:

> No facts are presented in this case, as in Colton v. Colton, 127 U.S.
> 300, 8 S. Ct. 1164, 32 L. Ed. 138, showing the situation of the testator
> when the will was drawn and the circumstances of the surviving wife
> and the other persons named, from which the inference might be
> drawn that the precatory paragraph of the will was intended to be
> mandatory. There is the single circumstance that the request is by
> the husband to the surviving wife. . . .

In 95 C.J.S. Wills § 602 b the rule which in our opinion is applicable
in Texas is stated as follows:

> Whether Precatory or Mandatory. In determining whether particular
> words are to be construed as precatory or mandatory, the court will
> look to the expressed intent of the testator, as found from the context
> of the will and surrounding circumstances; and words which, in their
> ordinary meaning, are precatory will be construed as mandatory only
> when it is evident that such was the testator's intent. . . .

The trial court correctly found that there was no genuine issue of fact in the case. Based upon the rule announced in the above cited cases and authorities it is our opinion that it was the intention of the testatrix that the words of "desire" as used in the will were a positive directive and imposed an obligation on appellants to comply therewith. The provision of the will for the payment to appellee of $2,400.00 annually was set out specifically as well as the desire or direction of the testatrix that such payments should be discontinued in certain specified contingencies. The language in question considered in context and in connection with the language of the will as a whole, and the surrounding facts and circumstances is in our opinion more clearly mandatory than that of the *Colton* case. The court properly entered summary judgment in favor of appellee, Laura Fisch.

The judgment is affirmed.

NOTES

1. *Intent to create a trust.* It is not necessary to use words such as "trust" or "trustee" in order to create a trust. Conversely, use of such words does not guarantee creation of a trust if essential characteristics of a trust are not present. See Restatement (Third) of Trusts § 13, cmt. b (2003); Estate of Damon, 869 P.2d 1339 (Haw. 1994); Marshall v. Grauberger, 796 P.2d 34 (Colo.App.1990).

In one case, a settlor conveyed land "to Mary Pursiful for the use and benefit of Moses A. Cottrell, during his natural life—if said Moses A. Cottrell should leave children in lawful wedlock it shall go to them." Although the deed did not explicitly refer to Ms. Pursiful as trustee, the court determined that, in accordance with the settlor's intent, she held the property on trust:

Th[is] case is on a par with the celebrated bear case (Prewitt v. Clayton, 5 T.B. Mon. 5), where it was said:

A bear well painted and drawn to the life is yet a picture of a bear, although the painter may omit to write over it, "This is the bear."

Fox v. Faulkner, 1 S.W.2d 1079, 1080 (Ky.1927).

2. *Precatory or mandatory language.* Recent cases tend to depart from the older view that precatory words, such as "wish" and "desire," are presumptively mandatory. Instead, the recent cases inquire whether the words and the factual context reveal an intention to impose legally enforceable obligations on the transferee. Restatement (Third) of Trusts § 13, cmt. d (2003) states:

The inference normally to be drawn from precatory language accompanying a transfer, suggesting that the transferee use or dispose of the property in a certain manner, is that the transferor intends to leave it to the transferee to decide whether or not to follow the suggestion. It is no longer the case, as it once appeared to be in England, that the wish of a testator, like that of a sovereign, is to be taken as a command. And no trust is created if the transferor manifests an intention merely to impose a moral obligation on the transferee.

Compare Estate of Brill v. Phillips, 76 So. 3d 695 (Miss. 2011) (not mandatory), and Pittman v. Thomas, 299 S.E.2d 207 (N.C.1983) (not mandatory), with In re Bair Family Trust, 183 P.3d 61 (Mont. 2008) (mandatory), and Estate of Pearson, 275 A.2d 336 (Pa.1971) (mandatory).

See generally McElwee, Precatory Language in Wills: Mere Utterances of the Sibyl?, 11 Prob. L.J. 145 (1992).

3. *Equitable charge.* Though the court in *Levin v. Fisch* held that the presumptively precatory word "desire," taken in context, was mandatory, the result was not that the testator's children held the property in trust. Instead, they held it subject to an *equitable charge.* See also Howell v. Sykes, 526 S.E.2d 183 (N.C. App. 2000) (bequest of stock "subject to" payment of salary to former employee created equitable charge).

Suppose that in *Levin* the testator had left her residuary estate to her two children in equal shares, *on condition that* they pay a specified annuity to their aunt. Such an arrangement lacks the usual indicia of a trust because there is no indication that the children are to take the property as trustees for the benefit of their aunt. Instead, the children seem to take the property outright. Nor, in the absence of an express forfeiture condition, is a court likely to imply such a condition. Instead, the court might well find that the testator had created an equitable charge—a security interest (rather than a beneficial interest in trust property)—for the aunt.

For more on the distinction between trusts, conditions, and equitable charges, see Restatement (Third) of Trusts § 5, cmt. h (2003).

3. DISTINGUISHING A TRUST FROM A CONTRACT

PIEROWICH V. METROPOLITAN LIFE INSURANCE CO.

Supreme Court of Michigan, 1937.
282 Mich. 118, 275 N.W. 789.

CHANDLER, JUSTICE.

The appellee, on September 15, 1931, issued a policy of life insurance on the life of Dan Pierowich, in which his wife was named beneficiary. Subsequently the parties were divorced and during the pendency of the proceedings the insured changed the policy and named his two minor sons, Alex and James, age eight and ten respectively, as the beneficiaries.

On November 23, 1934, the insured executed and delivered to appellee the following:

Policy No. 7288571—A

To the Metropolitan Life Insurance Company, New York, New York.

I hereby direct that in the event either of my sons, Alex Pierowich, born 5/9/1924, and James Pierowich, born 2/1926, the beneficiaries of record, shall survive me but shall not have attained the age of 21 years at the time of my death, the amount payable under the said policy upon my death, to such son, shall be retained by the Company and interest thereon at the rate which the Company may each year declare on such funds (but at no less rate than three and one-half per centum per annum) shall be compounded annually at the end of each year until such child shall have attained the age of 21 years when his share, together with the interest then accumulated thereon, shall be paid at once in one sum to him.

Provided, however, in the event that either of my said sons shall survive me but shall die before attaining the age of 21 years, his share, together with the interest then accumulated thereon, shall be paid at once in one sum to the executors or administrators of such deceased son.

And I hereby further direct that neither of my said sons shall have the right to withdraw any of the amount retained by the Company, except as hereinbefore provided, nor the right to assign or encumber any payment hereunder.

Provided, however, that the foregoing directions shall not apply to the share of either of my said sons who shall predecease me or who shall not be a beneficiary of record at the time of my death or who shall have attained the age of 21 years at the time of my death.

The right to cancel the foregoing directions by written notice to the Home Office of the Metropolitan Life Insurance Company of New York, New York, is reserved.

Dated at Hamtramck, Mich. Nov. 23, 1934

Insured Dan Pierowich.

Witness

L.M. Locianoures

Dan Pierowich died on June 18, 1935, and thereafter appellee, upon surrender of the policy, delivered to each of the beneficiaries a supplemental contract providing for payment of the proceeds of the policy in exact accordance with the directions given by the insured in his lifetime and set forth above.

The mother of Alex and James filed her bill in equity as guardian of said minors alleging that she is without sufficient funds with which to properly maintain and educate the children, and prayed for a decree ordering appellee to pay her for this purpose such sums from the proceeds of the policy as the court found necessary. The trial court dismissed the bill.

Whether or not a trust was created must depend upon the intention of the insured in providing for the disposition of the proceeds of the policy in the manner which he instructed and whether the necessary requisites to the creation of a trust were observed. In Equitable Trust Co. v. Milton Realty Co., 261 Mich. 571, 246 N.W. 500, 502, we held that: "To create a trust, there must be an assignment of designated property to a trustee with the intention of passing title thereto, to hold for the benefit of others. There must be a separation of the legal estate from the beneficial enjoyment."

We are unable to find from an examination of the evidence the essential element of intent to create a trust. Although not decisive, the provision for the payment of interest on the fund held by appellee, together with the fact that there was no designation or segregation of any particular fund from which payment was to be made, are of interest in determining the intent, and are not indicative of the trust relationship. The supplemental agreements executed by appellee which in terms specifically incorporate the insured's directions appear to be no more than contracts containing a promise to pay the proceeds of the policy in such a manner as the contingencies therein expressed shall command. We fail to find that the fund was assigned from the appellee as debtor to the appellee as trustee as is contended by appellants. The relationship existing is that of debtor and creditor rather than that of trustee and cestui que trust. . . .

Appellant further contends that, even though no trust relationship appears, the facts are such as to warrant the interference of a court of equity to grant the desired relief. In support of this position, testimony was introduced establishing the indigent circumstances of the family and the lack of funds claimed necessary to properly provide for the support and education of the beneficiaries. Although in certain circumstances an advancement will be allowed from a trust fund for such purposes as are relied upon in the instant case, Post v. Grand Rapids Trust Co., 255 Mich. 436, 238 N.W. 206, we do not find this rule to be applicable here. The disposition of the property has been fixed by contract, and this court cannot alter the terms thereof even in view of the changed now existing conditions.

The decree is affirmed, with costs to appellee.

NOTE

The distinction. As *Pierowich* illustrates, different remedies may be available, depending on whether an arrangement is a trust or a contract. Courts sometimes permit acceleration of trust funds under circumstances similar to those in *Pierowich*. See UTC § 412; 5 Scott and Ascher on Trusts § 33.4. But see New York Life Ins. Co. v. Conrad, 107 S.W.2d 248 (Ky.1937) (no deviation allowed though insurance company held the proceeds "in trust").

In *Pierowich*, would there have been a trust if the insurance company had agreed to hold the proceeds of the policy "in trust" for the purpose of making the payments the insured specified?

How do you suppose Metropolitan Life Insurance Company viewed its role in this litigation—as passive stakeholder or as interested party strenuously opposing the guardian's petition? Consider the differences in responsibility between the payor on a deferred payment contract and the trustee of a trust. Even if the insurance contract refers to the company as "trustee" of the proceeds, the fine print inevitably removes practically all the traditional fiduciary duties by establishing a fixed rate of return and payment schedule, permitting commingling with general assets, waiving additional compensation as trustee, and the like.

4. TOTTEN TRUSTS

IN RE RODGERS' ESTATE
Supreme Court of Pennsylvania, 1953.
374 Pa. 246, 97 A.2d 789.

ALLEN M. STEARNE, JUSTICE.

Did Elizabeth M. Rodgers revoke either during her lifetime or by will the tentative trust which she had established for her sister, Martha B. Rodgers? This is the single question presented by the appeal.

The issue is raised by the petition of John J. Mitchell, Jr., Esq., executor of the will of Elizabeth Rodgers, for a citation directed to the guardian of the estate of Martha B. Rodgers, incompetent, and to the Beneficial Saving Fund Society, to show cause why the fund on deposit in that society in an account entitled "Elizabeth M. Rodgers in trust for sister Martha B. Rodgers" should not be paid to the executor. After answer on the merits the matter was referred for hearing to a master who concluded in an exhaustive report that the trust had been revoked and that the fund should be awarded to the executor as part of the decedent's estate. Exceptions were argued in the orphans' court and the matter referred back to the master for a further finding. The master affirmed his earlier conclusion in a second report, and this was approved by the orphans' court in banc. This appeal followed.

The doctrine of tentative trusts was evolved by the courts of New York in what Justice (later Chief Justice) Schaffer described as "an effort to retain for the depositor the complete control of the fund during his life and yet secure to the beneficiary any balance standing in the account at the death of the depositor." In re Scanlon's Estate, 313 Pa. 424, 427, 169 A. 106, 108. In that case we adopted the New York rule as the law of Pennsylvania, quoting as follows from In re Totten, 179 N.Y. 112, 71 N.E. 748, 70 L.R.A. 711 [1904]:

> . . . A deposit by one person of his own money in his own name as trustee for another, standing alone, does not establish an irrevocable trust during the lifetime of the depositor. It is a tentative trust merely, revocable at will, until the depositor dies or completes the gift in his lifetime by some unequivocal act or declaration, such as delivery of the passbook or notice to the beneficiary. In case the depositor dies before the beneficiary without revocation, or some decisive act or declaration of disaffirmance, the presumption arises that an absolute trust was created as to the balance on hand at the death of the depositor.

Since then, despite some criticism of the rule, see, e.g., dissenting opinion of Mr. Justice Bell in In re Ingels' Estate, 372 Pa. 171, 182, 92 A. 2d 881, it has become an integrated part of our jurisprudence and has been applied time and again by our appellate courts and courts of first instance. . . .

Our decisions have repeatedly acknowledged the New York origin of the rule and have adverted to the reports of that state for guidance in exploring its many ramifications. On the question of revocation now before us, we once again find no definitive authority in Pennsylvania but a number of decisions in New York. The latter cases have been concisely summarized in a recent opinion of the Surrogate's Court of Kings County, In re Koster's Will, 119 N.Y.S.2d 2, at pages 4, 5:

> It has been held that, among other means, a tentative trust may be revoked: (1) by a transfer of the form of the deposit; (2) by the terms of a will of a depositor, Moran v. Ferchland, 113 Misc. 1, 184 N.Y.S. 428; Matter of Brazil's Estate, 127 Misc. 288, 216 N.Y.S. 430; Matter of Schrier's Estate, 145 Misc. 593, 260 N.Y.S. 610; Matter of Beck's Estate, 260 App. Div. 651, 23 N.Y.S.2d 525; In re Shelley's Estate, Sur., 50 N.Y.S.2d 570; Walsh v. Emigrant Industrial Savings Bank, 106 Misc. 628, 176 N.Y.S. 418, affirmed 192 App. Div. 908, 182

N.Y.S. 956, affirmed 233 N.Y. 512, 135 N.E. 897; (3) by the depositor's unequivocal act or declaration of disaffirmance, Walsh v. Emigrant Industrial Savings Bank, supra; Matter of Beagan's Estate, 112 Misc. 292, 183 N.Y.S. 941; Matter of Richardson's Estate, 134 Misc. 174, 235 N.Y.S. 747; Cf. Matter of Halpern's Estate, 303 N.Y. 33, 100 N.E.2d 120; and (4) by facts and circumstances resulting in inadequacy of the estate assets to satisfy the testamentary gifts, funeral and administration expenses, taxes and other charges. Matter of Murray's Estate, 143 Misc. 499, 256 N.Y.S. 815; Matter of Mannix' Estate, 147 Misc. 479, 264 N.Y.S. 24; Matter of Beagan's Estate, supra; Matter of Reich's Estate, 146 Misc. 616, 262 N.Y.S. 623.

The master and the learned court below found that revocation had been accomplished in the present case by either of the last two of the four means above enumerated.

Such decision does not rest upon New York authority alone. The Restatement of Trusts definitely supports the same view in the following excerpts from the comment to sec. 58:

> b. *Revocation of tentative trust.* A tentative trust of a savings deposit in a bank can be revoked by the depositor at any time during his lifetime, by a manifestation of his intention to revoke the trust. *No particular formalities are necessary to manifest such an intention.* (latter italics ours)

> A tentative trust of a savings deposit can be revoked by the depositor by his will. It is so revoked where by will he makes a disposition of the bank deposit in favor of anyone other than the beneficiary. It is also revoked where by will he makes a disposition of his property which cannot be carried out except by using the deposit, as for example where he leaves no other property than the deposit.

Indeed, the original statement of the *Totten* rule quoted in Re Scanlon's Estate, supra, clearly implies that revocation may be accomplished by " 'some decisive act or declaration of disaffirmance.' " Implied recognition of the right to revoke orally is also found In re Krewson's Estate, 154 Pa. Super. 509, at page 511, 36 A.2d 250, at page 251 . . . :

> The alleged oral statements made by the decedent . . . were not sufficiently clear and unambiguous to constitute a parol revocation of the written declaration of trust made with the deposit.

What was the evidence of oral revocation which satisfied the master and the orphans' court in banc in the present case? Mr. Mitchell, the executor, a reputable member of the bar of Philadelphia county, was the scrivener of the will. He was permitted to testify to his conversations with the testatrix leading to the preparation of her will. This testimony was admitted over the objection of the appellants, who contended that the will was clear and unambiguous and not subject to oral explanation. We agree with this contention of appellants and would exclude the testimony if it were offered only as explanation of the will. In re Mizener's Estate, 262 Pa. 62, 105 A. 46; Prime's Petition, 335 Pa. 218, 6 A.2d 530. But, as above stated, the creator of a tentative trust has power to revoke it by oral declarations, and the testimony of testatrix's attorney was clearly admissible to show her intention that the trust be revoked, entirely apart from any question of interpretation of the written will. Testatrix told Mr. Mitchell that her sister Martha was the prime object of her bounty, that Martha was sole beneficiary under an earlier will but was now " . . . infirm mentally and physically . . . can't look after things for herself, and somebody will have to look after her in case I go first." She approved the attorney's suggestion of a trust for maintenance and support with power to invade principal and discussed with him, without reaching any definite conclusion, the Catholic charities to whom she would bequeath the remainder. According to Mr. Mitchell's testimony, she then described the property which would be the subject of this trust as follows: " ' . . . we have some stocks and we own the property we live in at 1805 Wylie Street,' and she said, 'my money is on deposit at the Beneficial Saving Fund Society.' " It is undisputed that the only money which testatrix had on deposit at that bank was the tentative trust fund in question. Unless she was referring to that fund when she spoke of her money on deposit at the Beneficial, her words were meaningless. Hence this conversation with the scrivener constitutes a clear declaration by the decedent of her desire to revoke the tentative trust and with that money make more appropriate arrangements for the care of her failing sister.

Furthermore, we agree with the court below that the will itself was sufficient to effect a revocation by the fourth means referred to in In re Koster's Will, supra. Findings of fact by the master to which no exceptions were taken establish that at the time of the making of the will, decedent's only assets other than the savings fund account were approximately $500 in cash, fractional interests in real estate worth about $2,000, an expectancy of a legacy of about $2,000, and joint ownership with her sister of securities stated to be small in value and a checking account of about $300. It requires no legal or financial expert to conclude that after payment of her own debts and funeral and administration expenses, her assets other than the savings account in dispute would be pitifully inadequate for the establishment of a trust for maintenance and support. It would be ascribing extraordinarily poor judgment to testatrix to suppose that she went to the trouble of creating an elaborate testamentary trust for the relatively small assets she possessed outside the savings account and yet intended the fund which comprised the bulk of her estate to go to the sister absolutely. This account contained $34,356.30.

Appellants also argue that, because the parties lived together sharing all expenses, had reciprocal wills and reciprocal tentative trusts with common possession of the pass books, the trusts which they created were irrevocable. The master and the court below found these circumstances inadequate to justify an inference that the sisters intended to make their trusts irrevocable. We are entirely in accord with this conclusion. We recently had occasion to discuss the quantum of evidence necessary to establish that a settlor intended to impart a quality of irrevocability to a tentative trust. In re Ingels' Estate, 372 Pa. 171, 92 A.2d 881. The circumstantial evidence here present falls far short of the standard we there established; viz., " 'clear and unambiguous language or conduct' indicating that [settlor] intended to make the tentative trust irrevocable." . . .

This tentative trust was revoked by testatrix in her lifetime by her oral declarations. But in any event the decedent by her will by establishing a testamentary scheme whereunder her assets would have been wholly inadequate, likewise disclosed an unequivocal intent of such revocation since her scheme failed unless the trust fund was included.

Decree affirmed; costs to be paid out of the fund.

NOTES

1. *The development of Totten trusts.* Many states initially refused to recognize tentative trusts of savings accounts, finding them "testamentary." See, e.g., Cazallis v. Ingraham, 110 A. 359 (Me.1920). Now, almost all states recognize Totten trusts, or their modern-day equivalents, either judicially or by statute. See generally 1 Scott and Ascher on Trusts §§ 8.3 to 8.3.5.

A parallel development, which has effectively replaced the Totten trust in many jurisdictions, is the POD ("pay on death") bank account. Indeed, the Uniform Probate Code now treats Totten trusts as interchangeable with POD accounts. See UPC § 6–203, cmt. Where permitted, a POD bank account accomplishes exactly what the Court of Appeals of New York created the Totten trust to do, i.e., to provide a simple and inexpensive will substitute for savings accounts. The depositor continues as exclusive "owner" of the account during life, but, upon the death of the depositor, any amount remaining on deposit becomes payable to the surviving beneficiary (rather than the depositor's estate). For the UPC coverage, which governs multiple-person accounts generally, see UPC §§ 6–201 to 6–227.

2. *Death of beneficiary.* In the absence of special circumstances, a Totten trust terminates, and the depositor holds the deposit free of trust, if the depositor survives the beneficiary. See UPC § 6–212.

3. *Oral revocation.* If *Rodgers* holds that the testator's statement to her lawyer was enough to revoke her Totten trust, query whether it opens the way to fraud. Can any apparently disinterested perjurer throw a Totten de-

posit into the residue? In New York, the possibility of oral revocation gave rise to so much litigation that the legislature eventually enacted EPTL § 7–5.2(1), which permits modification or revocation of a Totten trust during the lifetime of the depositor in only two ways: (1) withdrawal of the funds, or (2) by filing with the financial institution a writing that specifically names both the beneficiary and the financial institution. See Cianciulli v. Smyth, 678 N.Y.S.2d 881 (Sup. 1998) (completed withdrawal request sent to bank before death but received and processed after death; held, no valid revocation). Similarly, UPC § 6–213(a) states:

> Rights at death of a party under Section 6–212 are determined by the terms of the account at the death of the party. A party may alter the terms of the account by a notice signed by the party and given to the financial institution to change the terms of the account or to stop or vary payment under the terms of the account. To be effective, the notice must be received by the financial institution during the party's lifetime.

The Restatement, however, provides: "A tentative trust can properly be revoked by the depositor at any time during life by a manifestation of intention to do so. No particular formalities are necessary to manifest that intention." Restatement (Third) of Trusts § 26, cmt. c (2003). Thus, under the Restatement, there is apparently still room for oral revocation and the litigation necessary to prove it.

4. *Revocation by will.* The possibility of revoking a Totten trust by will leads to another litigation quagmire. Here again, to achieve greater predictability, the New York legislature intervened, by enacting EPTL § 7–5.2(2), which permits modification or revocation of a Totten trust by will only if the will describes the account "as being in trust for a named beneficiary in a named financial institution," and employs either "express words of revocation" or "a specific bequest of the trust account, or any part of it, to someone other than the beneficiary." The Uniform Probate Code employs an even brighter line: "A right of survivorship . . . may not be altered by will." UPC § 6–213(b). The Restatement, however, continues to permit a depositor to revoke a Totten trust by will, without restriction. Restatement (Third) of Trusts § 26, cmt. c (2003).

5. THE TRUST RES (PROPERTY)

FARMERS' LOAN & TRUST CO. v. WINTHROP

Court of Appeals of New York, 1924.
238 N.Y. 477, 144 N.E. 686.

CARDOZO, J.

On February 3, 1920, Helen C. Bostwick executed her deed of trust to the Farmers' Loan & Trust Company as trustee. . . . By [this deed] she gave to her trustee $5,000, "the said sum, and all other property hereafter delivered to said trustee as hereinafter provided," to be held upon the trusts and limitations therein set forth. The income was to be paid to her own use during life, and the principal on her death was to be divided into two parts—one for the benefit of the children of a deceased son, Albert; the other for the benefit of a daughter, Fannie, and the children of said daughter. The donor reserved "the right, at any time and from time to time during the continuance of the trusts, . . . to deliver to said trustee additional property to be held by it" thereunder. She reserved also a power of revocation.

At the date of the execution of this deed, a proceeding was pending in the Surrogate's Court for the settlement of the accounts of the United States Trust Company as trustee of a trust under the will of Jabez A. Bostwick. The effect of the decree, when entered, would be to transfer to Mrs. Bostwick money, shares of stock, and other property of the value of upwards of $2,300,000. The plan was that this property, when ready to be transferred, should be delivered to the trustee, and held subject to the trust. On February 3, 1920, simultaneously with the execution of the trust deed, three other documents, intended to effectuate this plan, were signed by the donor. One is a power of attorney whereby she authorized the Farmers' Loan & Trust Company as her attorney "to collect and receive any and all cash, shares of stock and other property" to which she might "be entitled under any decree or order made or entered" in the proceeding above mentioned. A second is a power of attorney authorizing the Farmers' Loan and Trust Company to sell and transfer any and all shares of stock then or thereafter standing in her name. A third is a letter, addressed to the Farmers' Loan & Trust Company, in which she states that she hands to the company the powers of attorney just described, and in which she gives instructions in respect of the action to be taken thereunder: "My desire is and I hereby authorize you to receive from the United States Trust Company of New York all securities and property coming to me under the decree on the settlement of its account and to transfer such securities and property to yourself as trustee under agreement of trust bearing even date herewith executed by me to you."

The decree in the accounting proceeding was entered March 16, 1920. It established the right of Helen C. Bostwick to the payment or transfer of shares of stock and other property of the market value (then or shortly thereafter) of $2,327,353.70. On April 27, 1920, a representative of the Farmers' Loan & Trust Company presented the power of attorney to the United States Trust Company and stated that he was authorized to receive such securities as were ready for delivery. Shares of stock having a market value of $856,880 were handed to him then and there. No question is made that these became subject to the provisions of the deed of trust. The controversy arises in respect of the rest of the securities, $1,470,473.70 in value, which were retained in the custody of the United States Trust Company, apparently for the reason that they were not yet ready for delivery. During the night of April 27, 1920, Helen C. Bostwick died. She left a will, appointing the Farmers' Loan & Trust Company executor, and disposing of an estate of the value of over $20,000,000. The securities retained, as we have seen, in the custody of the United States Trust Company, were delivered on or about July 13, 1920, to the executor under the will. Conflicting claims of ownership are made by the legatees under the will and the remaindermen under the deed.

We think, with the majority of the Appellate Division, that the gift remained inchoate at the death of the donor. There is no occasion to deny that in the setting of other circumstances a power of attorney, authorizing a donee to reduce to possession the subject of a gift, may be significant as evidence of a symbolical delivery. We assume, without deciding, that such effect will be allowed if, apart from the power, there is established an intention that the title of the donor shall be presently divested and presently transferred. The assumption ignores difficulties not to be underestimated (cf. Young v. Young, 80 N.Y. 422, 36 Am. Rep. 634; Beaver v. Beaver, 117 N.Y. 421, 22 N.E. 940, 6 L.R.A. 403, 15 Am. St. Rep. 531; Augsbury v. Shurtliff, 180 N.Y. 138, 72 N.E. 927), but we pass them over for the purpose of the argument, and treat them as surmounted. Even so, the basic obstacle remains that there is here no expression of a purpose to effectuate a present gift. The power of attorney, standing by itself, results, as all concede, in the creation of a revocable agency. Hunt v. Rousmanier, 8 Wheat. 174, 5 L. Ed. 589; Farmers' Loan & Trust Co. v. Wilson, 139 N.Y. 284, 34 N.E. 784, 36 Am. St. Rep. 696.

If something more was intended, if what was meant was a gift that was to be operative at once, the expression of the meaning will have to be found elsewhere, in the deed of trust or in the letter. Neither in the one, however, nor in the other, can such a purpose be discerned. Deed and letter alike are framed on the assumption that the gift is executory and future, and this though the addition of a few words would have established it beyond cavil as executed and present. In the deed there is a present transfer of $5,000 and no more. This wrought, there is merely the reservation of a privilege to augment the subject-matter of the trust by deliveries thereafter. The absence of words of present assignment is emphasized when we consider with what simplicity an assignment could have been stated. All that was needed was to expand the description by a phrase:

> The right, title, and interest of the grantor in the securities and other property due or to become due from the United States Trust Company as trustee under the will.

The deed and the other documents, we must remember, were not separated in time. They were parts of a single plan, and were executed together. In these circumstances, a present transfer, if intended, would naturally have found its place in the description of the deed itself. If omitted for some reason there, the least we should expect would be to find it in the letter. Again words of present transfer are conspicuously absent. What we have instead is a request, or at best a mandate, incompetent without more to divest title, or transfer it, serving no other purpose than a memorandum of instructions from principal to agent as a guide to future action. Harris v. Clark, 3 N.Y. 93, 51 Am. Dec. 352; Gerry v. Howe, 130 Mass. 350; Welch v. Henshaw, 170 Mass. 409, 49 N.E. 659, 64 Am. St. Rep. 309. Deed and documents were prepared by counsel learned in the law. With industrious iteration, they rejected the familiar formulas that would have given unmistakable expression to the transfer of a present title. With like iteration, they chose the words and methods appropriate to a gift that was conceived of as executory and future. We must take the transaction as they made it. The very facility with which they could have made it something else is a warning that we are not at liberty, under the guise of construction, to make it other than it is. Matter of Van Alstyne, 207 N.Y. 298, 309, 310, 100 N.E. 802. They were willing to leave open what they might readily have closed. Death overtook the signer before the gap was filled.

Viewed thus as a gift, the transaction was inchoate. An intention may be assumed, and indeed is not disputed, that what was incompetent at the moment should be completed in the future. The difficulty is that the intention was never carried out. Mrs. Bostwick remained free (apart from any power of revocation reserved in the deed of trust) to revoke the executory mandate, and keep the property as her own. Very likely different forms and instrumentalities would have been utilized, if she or her counsel had supposed that death was to come so swiftly. We might say as much if she had left in her desk a letter or memorandum expressing her resolutions for the morrow. With appropriate forms and instrumentalities available, she chose what the course of events has proved to be the wrong one. The court is without power to substitute another. Hunt v. Rousmanier, supra; Young v. Young, supra; Beaver v. Beaver, supra.

The transaction, failing as a gift, because inchoate or incomplete, is not to be sustained as the declaration of a trust. Beaver v. Beaver, supra; Matter of Crawford, 113 N.Y. 560, 566, 21 N.E. 692, 5 L.R.A. 71; Wadd v. Hazelton, 137 N.Y. 215, 33 N.E. 143, 21 L.R.A. 693, 33 Am. St. Rep. 707. The donor had no intention of becoming a trustee herself. The donee never got title, and so could not hold it for another.

There was no equitable assignment. Equity does not enforce a voluntary promise to make a gift thereafter. . . .

The judgment of the Appellate Division should be modified [on another issue], and, as so modified affirmed. . . .

Notes

1. *Dispositive outcome.* It appears from the opinion below, 202 N.Y.S. 456 (App. Div. 1923), that Mrs. Bostwick's will left one-fourth of her residuary estate to her son's children and three-fourths to her daughter's children.

2. *More on defective gifts.* In Hardy v. Robinson, 170 S.W.3d 777 (Tex. App. 2005), in an instrument creating a durable power of attorney, the decedent directed that the proceeds of a pending personal injury lawsuit be placed in trust for his children, with his sister as trustee. After the decedent's death, the court held that this did not give rise to a valid transfer in trust.

In Estate of Collins, 149 Cal.Rptr. 65 (App. 1978), the decedent, shortly prior to death, signed an application to create a Totten trust at Bank *A*. He deposited no funds but signed a sight draft directing Bank *B* to deliver to Bank *A* the proceeds of a savings account in Bank *B*. Before Bank *B* honored the draft, he died. The court held that no Totten trust arose.

For another case that refused to convert a defective gift into a trust, see Cate–Schweyen v. Cate, 15 P.3d 467 (Mont. 2000).

Restatement (Third) of Trusts § 16(1) (2003) acknowledges that failure to complete a contemplated transfer of property in trust generally does not result in the creation of a trust. But, the Restatement continues, "In some circumstances . . . the trust intention of such a property owner who dies or becomes incompetent may be given effect by constructive trust in order to prevent unjust enrichment of the property owner's successors in interest." Id. Does the Restatement thereby suggest a different result in *Winthrop*? See id. cmt. c, illus. 8. (Restatement (Third) of Trusts § 16 is reproduced, in full, supra, at p. 571.)

3. *Property.* Property is an essential element of a trust. See Restatement (Third) of Trusts § 2, cmt. i (2003) ("A trust cannot be created unless there is trust property in existence and ascertainable at the time of the creation of the trust."). Any type of property interest will do. Id. § 40 ("[A] trustee may hold in trust any interest in any type of property."). But there must be *property*. Id. § 41 ("An expectation or hope of receiving property in the future, or an interest that has not come into existence or has ceased to exist, cannot be held in trust."). Thus, In re Gurlitz, 172 N.Y.S. 523 (Sur. 1918), modified sub nom. In re Lynde's Estate, 175 N.Y.S. 289 (Sur.), aff'd mem., 179 N.Y.S. 933 (App. Div. 1919), held that a gratuitous assignment of an expectancy to a trustee was merely an unenforceable promise to create a trust in the future. See also Bowden v. Teague, 159 So.2d 844 (Ala.1963). But see Warne v. Warne, 275 P.3d 238 (Utah 2012) (upholding transfer of "after-acquired property" in trust).

In contrast, a promise, for consideration, to create a trust in the future is enforceable even if the res is not yet in existence. See Penney v. White, 594 S.W.2d 632 (Mo.App.1980). Suppose that *A*, who is a legatee under *B*'s existing will, assigns, during *B*'s life, *A*'s expectancy to *S* for value; and that *S*, after the assignment, but still during *B*'s life, attempts to assign *S*'s interest in *A*'s expectancy gratuitously to *T* in trust for *C*. Does a trust exist? Compare In re Baker, 13 F.2d 707 (6th Cir.), cert. denied, 273 U.S. 733 (1926), with Note, 36 Yale L.J. 272 (1926).

4. *Life insurance trusts as nontestamentary.* The argument that a life insurance trust is an invalid testamentary transfer has been frequently made and almost always rejected. See, e.g., Koziell Trust, 194 A.2d 230 (Pa.1963); Prudential Insurance Co. v. Gatewood, 317 S.W.2d 382 (Mo.1958). Courts almost invariably hold insurance trusts to be nontestamentary on either or both of two theories. Often the court declares that the execution of the trust agreement, and the performance of present duties under it, results in an immediate transfer of an interest. In short, the insurance beneficiary designation *itself* qualifies as trust property. See, e.g., Estate of Herron, 237 So.2d 563 (Fla.App.1970). Except in the rare situation where it makes a difference *when* the insurance trust comes into existence, there is a simpler reason for rejecting the contention that it is void as a testamentary transfer. See, e.g., In re Albert Anderson Life Ins. Trust, 293 N.W. 527, 529 (S.D.1940):

> We are concerned here with a trust res which never was the property of the insured and which came into existence only after his death. We are not here concerned with the policy of insurance as such or the rights of the beneficiary in such policy. We are concerned only with the funds which the insurance companies paid to the bank, the title to which funds never was in Anderson. The transaction that here appears, is that Albert Anderson named the bank as beneficiary in the policy, and in consideration for this designation the bank declared the trust in the proceeds of the policy to which it acquired title upon the death of Albert Anderson.

Often courts use both theories indiscriminately. See, e.g., Connecticut General Life Ins. Co. v. First Nat'l Bank of Minneapolis, 262 N.W.2d 403 (Minn.1977); Gordon v. Portland Trust Bank, 271 P.2d 653 (Or.1954); Gurnett v. Mutual Life Ins. Co., 191 N.E. 250 (Ill.1934).

In cases in which the designated beneficiary of the insurance policy is an individual who has promised to give all or part of the proceeds to others, it is possible to advance an additional theory. Constructive trust doctrine does not permit the beneficiary of the policy to go back on his or her promise. See, e.g., Voelkel v. Tohulka, 141 N.E.2d 344 (Ind.), cert. denied, 355 U.S. 891 (1957).

5. *Life insurance beneficiary designations as "property."* Are there any functional differences between the interest of the beneficiary of a life insurance policy on the life of a living person and the interest of a legatee in the will of a living testator? See Vance, The Beneficiary's Interest in a Life Insur-

ance Policy, 31 Yale L.J. 343, 358 (1922); Brown's Estate, 119 A.2d 513 (Pa. 1956).

6. *Terminology.* The term "life insurance trust" can be confusing because, in common parlance, it can refer to either of two quite different devices. The first, and more precise, use of the term refers to a particular type of private express trust: a trust company or other third party, whom the owner of a life insurance policy has named as policy beneficiary, agrees to hold the proceeds for one or more trust beneficiaries after the death of the insured. Such trusts are either "funded" or "unfunded." In a funded life insurance trust, the settlor-insured not only designates the trust company or other third party as beneficiary of the policy, but also delivers *additional* trust property (possibly including the policy itself) to the trustee. Depending on the extent of the funding, and the nature and yield of the assets, the trustee of a funded life insurance trust may be able to pay all or a portion of the policy premiums while the insured is still alive. In contrast, the trustee of an unfunded life insurance trust has no property with which to pay premiums. Thus, the settlor-insured (or someone else) must continue to pay the premiums, or the policy will lapse. Funded trusts are less prevalent, because they require substantial capital outlays prior to death.

A second, less precise, use of the term "life insurance trust" refers to a provision in a life insurance policy purporting to make the insurance company itself "trustee" of the policy proceeds. This device is almost always merely a contractual settlement option, not a trust. See Pierowich v. Metropolitan Life Ins. Co., supra p. 582.

C. ALIENABILITY OF A BENEFICIARY'S INTEREST

1. SPENDTHRIFT TRUSTS

SLIGH V. FIRST NATIONAL BANK OF HOLMES COUNTY

Supreme Court of Mississippi, 1997.
704 So.2d 1020.

MILLS, JUSTICE, FOR THE COURT:

This case comes on appeal from the Chancery Court of Holmes County, where Will and Lucy Sligh sought to garnish Gene Lorance's beneficial interest in two spendthrift trusts in order to partially satisfy a tort judgment for damages resulting from injuries sustained by Will Sligh in an automobile accident with Gene Lorance. On December 15, 1995, the chancellor dismissed the Slighs' complaint, ruling that the assets of spendthrift trusts may not be garnished to satisfy the claims of tort judgment creditors. Aggrieved, the Slighs appeal to this Court. . . .

FACTS

On January 30, 1993, William B. Sligh was involved in an automobile accident with Gene A. Lorance, an uninsured motorist who was operating a vehicle while intoxicated. As a result, Will Sligh suffered a broken spine and resulting paralysis, including loss of the use of both legs, loss of all sexual functions and loss of the ability to control bowel and urinary functions. Lorance was convicted of the felony of driving under the influence and causing bodily injury to another, for which he was sentenced to serve ten years, with six years suspended, in the custody of the Mississippi Department of Corrections.

On April 2, 1993, Will and his wife, Lucy M. Sligh, filed in the Circuit Court of Holmes County an action against Lorance alleging gross negligence resulting in personal injury, property damage and loss of consortium, for which they sought compensatory and punitive damages. Lorance failed to respond, and after entry of default and a hearing on the Slighs' Motion for Writ of Inquiry on January 25, 1994, the circuit court entered default judgment against Lorance for $5,000,000 in compensatory and punitive damages.

Lorance has no assets other than his interest as beneficiary of two spendthrift trusts established by his mother in 1984 and 1988, respectively, before she died in 1993. Both trusts, whose trustee is First National Bank of Holmes County ("First National Bank"), provide as follows:

> 1. My said Trustee shall have full and complete authority to expend all or any part of the income or corpus of said trust property for the benefit of myself and my said son, Gene Lorance, and shall have the right to make payments directly to me and to my said son or to anyone for myself or my said son.

> 2. . . . My said Trustee shall . . . pay to me or the said Gene Lorance such sums and at such times as my said Trustee thinks in my or his best interest. *No part of this trust, either principal or income, shall be liable for the debts of the said Gene Lorance, nor shall the same be subject to seizure by any creditor of his* and he shall not have the right to sell, assign, transfer, encumber or in any manner anticipate or dispose of his interest in said property, or any part of same, or the income produced from said trust or any part thereof.

(emphasis added). Lorance is the lifetime beneficiary of the two trusts, which each have two remaindermen, Virginia Tate and William C. Bardin.

On June 29, 1994, Will and Lucy Sligh filed in the Circuit Court of Holmes County a Suggestion for Writ of Garnishment as to First National

Bank, either in its corporate capacity or in its capacity as trustee of the two trusts. A Writ of Garnishment was issued and served upon First National Bank, who, in its answer filed on June 30, 1994, admitted that it was indebted to Lorance in the amount of $313,677.48, but asserted that such sum was held in trust for Lorance and was not subject to seizure. After the Slighs filed a motion for judgment on the answer and First National Bank filed its response, First National Bank moved for a dismissal or, in the alternative, for a transferal of the garnishment proceeding to chancery court. On October 5, 1994, the circuit court transferred the proceeding to the Chancery Court of Holmes County.

On October 25, 1994, the Slighs filed in that court their complaint naming as defendants First National Bank, Gene Lorance, Viginia Tate and William Bardin. The Slighs alleged, in addition to the aforementioned facts, that Lorance's mother, Edith Lorance, had actual knowledge of the following facts: her son was an habitual drunkard who had been unsuccessfully treated for alcoholism; he was mentally deficient and had been previously committed to mental institutions; he had impaired facilities due to his alcoholism and mental disorders; he regularly operated motor vehicles while intoxicated; he was a reckless driver who had been involved in numerous automobile accidents; and he had been arrested and convicted on numerous occasions for driving under the influence. The complaint alleged that despite her actual knowledge of these facts, Mrs. Lorance established the two trusts as part of her intentional plan and design to enable her son to continue to lead his intemperate, debauched, wanton and depraved lifestyle while at the same time shielding his beneficial interest in the trusts from the claims of his involuntary tort creditors. The Slighs alleged that it was a violation of public policy to enforce and give priority to spendthrift trust provisions over involuntary tort judgments against the beneficiary, and they urged the court to recognize and enforce a public policy exception to the spendthrift trust doctrine in favor of involuntary tort creditors by subjecting Lorance's beneficial interests to the payment of their tort judgment. . . .

After the defendants filed their respective answers, First National Bank filed a Motion for Dismissal on October 27, 1995. On December 15, 1995, the chancellor granted the motion, ruling that the Slighs failed to state a claim upon which relief can be granted. The chancellor ruled that "a tort judgment creditor may not garnish the trustee of a spendthrift trust in which the tort judgment defendant is a mere lifetime discretionary income beneficiary, nor are the assets of such trust subject to the claims of the tort judgment creditor."

DISCUSSION . . .

II. Whether the Chancellor Erred in Failing to Recognize and Establish a Public Policy Exception to the Spendthrift Trust Doctrine in Favor of the Beneficiary's Involuntary Tort Creditors. . . .

B. The Spendthrift Trust Doctrine

The spendthrift trust doctrine is codified by statute in some states and is a judicially created doctrine in others. In Mississippi, where the doctrine was judicially created, our main authority on point is the case of Leigh v. Harrison, 69 Miss. 923, 11 So. 604 (1892).

In that case, Regina Harrison left a testamentary trust for the support of her insolvent son, Thomas, whose judgment creditor filed a bill in chancery to reach Thomas' beneficial interest. Leigh, 69 Miss. at 927, 11 So. at 604. Although the trust contained no spendthrift language, the Court held that under the circumstances, it could only have been Mrs. Harrison's intent that the trust should be protected from her son's creditors, lest "a devise to him would be, in effect, a devise to them." Id. at 937, 11 So. at 607. In holding the trust to be immune from the claims of Thomas' creditors, the Court discussed the rights of creditors as follows:

> We confess our inability to perceive how a creditor can be said to be injured or defrauded by the recognition of power in a donor to limit his bounty according to his own will. The creditor has no right to the property in the hands of the donor, and no equity, that we can perceive, in any disposition which the owner may make of it. If Mrs. Harrison had given Thomas nothing, upon what principle could his creditors complain? How are their rights (if they had none) infringed by any limitations she chose to impose upon the bequest she did make? It must be admitted that the right to make a will is not a natural right, and that no unlawful disposition may be made of the property devised. But what law is violated by disposing of property with a limitation which confines its benefit to the person of the donee? It cannot be said that it is against public policy for a testator to provide a support for a spendthrift child, for the interest of the public is that such child shall not become a public burden. Our statutes upon the subject of exemptions indicate a clear public policy that exemption from personal pauperism is of greater concern than the rights of creditors. A donation by will or deed with limitation against liability to the debts of the donee, cannot invite to undue credit being given to the donee, for such instruments are required to be recorded, and third persons may, by examination of the public records, learn the terms on which the bounty is to be enjoyed.

Id. at 933–34, 11 So. at 606. On the policy of enforcing the wishes of donors, the Court quoted the following passage by the U.S. Supreme Court:

> We do not see . . . that the power of alienation is a necessary incident to a life-estate in real property, or that the rents and profits of real property and the interest and dividends of personal property may not be enjoyed by an individual without liability for his debts being attached as a necessary incident to such enjoyment. The doctrine is one which the English chancery court has ingrafted upon the common law for the benefit of creditors, and is comparatively of modern origin. We concede that there are limitations which public policy or general statutes impose upon all dispositions of property—such as those designed to prevent perpetuities and accumulations of real estate in corporations and ecclesiastical bodies. We also admit that there is a just and sound policy, peculiarly appropriate to the jurisdiction of courts of equity, to protect creditors against frauds upon their rights, whether they be actual or constructive frauds. But the doctrine that the owner of property, in the free exercise of his will in disposing of it, cannot so dispose of it, but that the object of his bounty, who parts with nothing in return, must hold it subject to the debts due his creditors, though that may soon deprive him of all the benefits sought to be conferred by the testator's affection or generosity, is one which we are not prepared to announce as the doctrine of this court.

Id. at 934–35, 11 So. at 606 (quoting Nichols v. Eaton, 91 U.S. 716, 725, 23 L.Ed. 254 (1875)). . . .

In the case of Calhoun v. Markow, 168 Miss. 556, 151 So. 547 (1933), the beneficiary's bankruptcy trustee filed a bill in chancery to attach the beneficiary's interest in a spendthrift trust in order to satisfy the claims of the beneficiary's creditors. On appeal after the chancery court denied the claim, this Court held:

> We think the chancellor was correct in his holding that neither the property nor the income were subject to [the beneficiary's] debts. The property covered by the trust instrument belonged to [the donor], and she could deal with it as she pleased, provided it did not infringe any of the provisions of law; and the decisions in this state show that a trust of this kind is lawful and that it is permissible for a parent to place property in the hands of a trustee to secure a child from poverty, want, or misfortune, and to provide for the necessities of life for such child. A creditor has no right to look to property in such a trust for the satisfaction of his demands. Creditors are charged with a knowledge of the law and the provisions of such trusts.

Calhoun, 168 Miss. at 565–66, 151 So. at 549.

These two cases, standing for the broad principle that spendthrift trust assets are not subject to the claims of the beneficiary's creditors, comprise almost the entire extent of this Court's pronouncements on the matter. In another case, we held that the spendthrift trust doctrine does not protect the beneficiary's interest from his creditors where the trust is a self-settled trust, i.e., where the trust is for the benefit of the donor. Deposit Guaranty Nat'l Bank v. Walter E. Heller & Co., 204 So.2d 856, 859 (Miss.1967). Although this Court has had no opportunity to establish any other exceptions to the doctrine, there are four other exceptions which have been recognized in other jurisdictions and are stated in the Restatement (Second) of Trusts § 157 (1959) as follows:

> Although a trust is a spendthrift trust or a trust for support, the interest of the beneficiary can be reached in satisfaction of an enforceable claim against the beneficiary,
>
> (a) by the wife or child of the beneficiary for support, or by the wife for alimony;
>
> (b) for necessary services rendered to the beneficiary or necessary supplies furnished to him;
>
> (c) for services rendered and materials furnished which preserve or benefit the interest of the beneficiary;
>
> (d) by the United States or a State to satisfy a claim against the beneficiary.

Although the rule does not list an exception for involuntary tort creditors, the comment on the scope of the rule provides:

> The enumeration in this Section of situations in which the interest of the beneficiary of a spendthrift trust or of a trust for support can be reached is not necessarily exclusive. The interest of a beneficiary of a spendthrift trust or a trust for support may be reached in cases other than those herein enumerated, if considerations of public policy so require. Thus it is possible that a person who has a claim in tort against the beneficiary of a spendthrift trust may be able to reach his interest under the trust.

Restatement (Second) of Trusts § 157 cmt. (a) (1959).

In *The Law of Trusts*, Austin W. Scott explained as follows:

> There is little authority on the question whether the interest of the beneficiary of a ... spendthrift trust can be reached by persons against whom he has committed a tort. In the absence of authority it was felt by those who were responsible for preparation of the Res-

tatement of Trusts that no categorical statement could be made on the question. It is believed, however, that there is a tendency to recognize that the language of the earlier cases to the effect that no creditor can reach the interest of a spendthrift trust is too broad, and that in view of the cases that have been cited in the previous sections allowing various classes of claimants to reach the interest of the beneficiary, the courts may well come to hold that the settlor cannot put the interest of the beneficiary beyond the reach of those to whom he has incurred liabilities in tort.

Austin W. Scott, The Law of Trusts § 157.5 (4th ed. 1987).

Legal scholars for years have called for the recognition of a public policy exception to the spendthrift trust doctrine in favor of tort judgment creditors.[5] However, there is little case law on the matter. In Thackara v. Mintzer, 100 Pa. 151, 154–55 (1882), the Pennsylvania Supreme Court, in upholding the validity of a spendthrift trust, declared in dicta that "[w]hether the judgment be for a breach of contract or for a tort, matters not." In Kirk v. Kirk, 254 Or. 44, 456 P.2d 1009 (1969), the Oregon Supreme Court held that the interest of a spendthrift trust created by the United States for the Klamath Tribe of American Indians was unreachable by the Indian beneficiary's tort judgment creditor. However, at least one state, Louisiana, has recognized an exception to the spendthrift trust doctrine in favor of tort judgment creditors, which doctrine and exception were codified by the Louisiana Legislature.[6]

C. Public Policy Considerations

Upon examination of the two Mississippi cases, *Leigh* and *Calhoun*, one can identify three public policy considerations observed by this Court when enforcing spendthrift trust provisions: (1) the right of donors to dispose of their property as they wish; (2) the public interest in protecting spendthrift individuals from personal pauperism, so that they do not become public burdens; and (3) the responsibility of creditors to make themselves aware of their debtors' spendthrift trust protections. Upon consideration of these public policy concerns in the present context, we find that

---

[5] See Laurene M. Brooks, Comment, A Tort–Creditor Exception to the Spendthrift Trust Doctrine: A Call to the Wisconsin Legislature, 73 Marq. L. Rev. 109 (1989); Frank A. Gregory, Note, Trusts: Tort Claims as an Exception to the Spendthrift Trust Doctrine, 17 Okla. L. Rev. 235 (1964); Antonis, Spendthrift Trusts, Attachability of a Beneficiary's Interests in Satisfaction of a Tort Claim, 28 Notre Dame L. Rev. 509 (1952); Costigan, Those Protective Trusts Which Are Miscalled "Spendthrift Trusts" Reexamined, 22 Cal. L. Rev. 471 (1934); Griswold, Reaching the Interest of [the Beneficiary of] a Spendthrift Trust, 43 Harv. L. Rev. 63 (1929).

[6] The Louisiana Trust Code provides that the beneficiary's interest in a spendthrift trust may be seized to satisfy a judgment for "[[d]amages arising from a felony criminal offense committed by the beneficiary which results in a conviction or a plea of guilty." La. Rev. Stat. Ann. § 9:2005(3).]

they do not weigh in favor of enforcing spendthrift trust provisions as against the claims of tort creditors or those found liable for gross negligence.

Regarding the responsibility of creditors when entering into transactions with spendthrift trust beneficiaries, Austin W. Scott stated in *The Law of Trusts*:

> In many of the cases in which it has been held that by the terms of the trust the interest of a beneficiary may be put beyond the reach of his creditors, the courts have laid some stress on the fact that the creditors had only themselves to blame for extending credit to a person whose interest under the trust had been put beyond their reach. The courts have said that before extending credit they could have ascertained the extent and character of the debtor's resources. Certainly, the situation of a tort creditor is quite different from that of a contract creditor. A man who is about to be knocked down by an automobile has no opportunity to investigate the credit of the driver of the automobile and has no opportunity to avoid being injured no matter what the resources of the driver may be.

Scott, supra. Likewise, George T. Bogert reasoned in *Trusts and Trustees*:

> It is true that a tort creditor has had no chance to choose his debtor and cannot be said to have assumed the risk of the collectibility of his claim. The argument for the validity of spendthrift trusts based on notice to the business world of the limited interest of the beneficiary does not apply. It may be argued that the beneficiary should not be permitted to circumvent the case and statute law as to liability for wrongs by taking advantage of the spendthrift clause.

George T. Bogert, Trusts and Trustees § 224 (2d ed. Rev. 1992). As these scholars point out, it is plain to see that one of the main reasons for enforcing spendthrift trust provisions—the responsibility of creditors to be aware of the law and of the substance of such provisions—simply does not apply in the case of tort judgment creditors.

As for the public interest in protecting spendthrift individuals from personal pauperism, we believe that this interest is not as strong in the case of tort judgment creditors, where the inability to collect on their claims may well result in their own personal pauperism. While it is true that most contract creditors do not risk becoming insolvent if they do not collect on a particular claim, such is often not the case with tort judgment creditors, particularly those who have suffered such devastating and expensive injuries as did the Slighs. The public interest against individuals becoming public burdens would not be served by protecting a spendthrift tortfeasor from personal pauperism where such protection would result merely in the pauperism of his victim. If one must choose whom to reduce to personal pauperism in such a case, the spendthrift tortfeasor or the innocent tort judgment creditor, we are inclined to choose the party at fault, especially where that fault rises to the level of gross negligence or intentional conduct.

This limitation on the public interest in protecting individuals from personal pauperism is reflected in our federal bankruptcy laws, whose very purpose is to protect debtors from pauperism. Under the Federal Bankruptcy Act, debtors may not discharge their debts to tort victim creditors whose claims are based on "willful and malicious" injuries. 11 U.S.C.A. § 523(a)(6) (West 1993). Thus, it has been recognized that the rights of intentional tort creditors are greater than the public interest in protecting debtors from personal pauperism.

Perhaps the most important policy consideration in favor of enforcing spendthrift trust provisions is the right of donors to dispose of their property as they wish. On this subject, Austin W. Scott stated in *The Law of Trusts*:

> It may be argued that the settlor can properly impose such restrictions as he chooses on the property that he gives. But surely he cannot impose restrictions that are against public policy. It is true that the tortfeasor may have no other property than that which is given him under the trust, and that the victim of the tort is no worse off where the tortfeasor has property that cannot be reached than he would [be] if the tortfeasor had no property at all. Nevertheless, there seems to be something rather shocking in the notion that a man should be allowed to continue in the enjoyment of property without satisfying the claims of persons whom he has injured. It may well be held that it is against public policy to permit the beneficiary of a spendthrift trust to enjoy an income under the trust without discharging his tort liabilities to others.

Scott, supra.

Clearly, the right of donors to place restrictions on the disposition of their property is not absolute, for as discussed above, there are several generally recognized exceptions to the spendthrift trust doctrine. Rather, a donor may dispose of his property as he sees fit so long as such disposition does not violate the law or public policy. We find that it is indeed against public policy to dispose of property in such a way that the beneficiary may enjoy the income from such property without fear that his interest may be attached to satisfy the claims of his gross negligence or intentional torts.

Our tort doctrine has evolved into two types of torts, ordinary torts and intentional torts. Public policy deems it so important to deter the commission of intentional torts or acts of gross negligence, that we allow victims of gross negligence or intentional torts to recover damages above and beyond what is necessary to compensate them for their injuries, i.e., punitive damages. However, the intended deterrent effect would be completely lost upon individuals whose interests are immune from the satisfaction of such claims.

The Slighs have alleged facts to the effect that Lorance's mother intended that her son should be able to commit acts of gross negligence or intentional torts without fear that his beneficial interests would be attached as a result thereof. However, in cases such as this where the donor has died, such facts may often be difficult, if not impossible, to prove. We hold that plaintiffs need not prove such facts but that such intent shall be presumed where a party has obtained a judgment based upon facts evidencing gross negligence or an intentional tort against the beneficiary of a spendthrift trust. Furthermore, we state the natural corollary that when assessing punitive damages against a tortfeasor found to have committed gross negligence or an intentional tort who is a spendthrift trust beneficiary, the beneficiary's interest should be taken into account as a factor in determining his monetary worth. However, in order to uphold spendthrift trust provisions so much as is reasonably possible, we hold that the beneficiary's interest in a spendthrift trust should not be attached in satisfaction of a claim until all of his other available assets have first been exhausted.

D. Interests of the Remaindermen

The parties agree that the trusts' two remaindermen, Virginia Tate and William Bardin, have vested remainders. The trusts provide that First National Bank "shall have full and complete authority to expend *all or any part* of the income or corpus of said trust property for the benefit of myself and my said son." (emphasis added). Therefore, the interests of Ms. Tate and Mr. Bardin are vested remainders subject to complete defeasance in the event that all of the trust assets are expended to satisfy the interest of Lorance. Put another way, Lorance has a beneficial interest in all of the trust assets. Accordingly, we hold that all of the trust assets should be subject to the Slighs' claim, thereby defeating the interests of the two remaindermen. . . .

CONCLUSION

We find, as a matter of public policy, that a beneficiary's interest in spendthrift trust assets is not immune from attachment to satisfy the claims of the beneficiary's intentional or gross negligence tort creditors, and that such claims take priority over any remainder interests in such assets. Accordingly, we reverse and render.

[The dissenting opinion of Prather, P.J., is omitted.]

NOTES

1. *General principles.* In the absence of a restriction in the trust instrument or applicable law, the interest of a trust beneficiary is as transferable as any other property. In the great majority of states, however, the settlor may make the beneficiary's interest inalienable. See, e.g., UTC § 502; Scott v. Bank One Trust Co., 577 N.E.2d 1077 (Ohio 1991) (accepting spendthrift trust doctrine). If the governing instrument includes language that makes the beneficiary's interest inalienable, the beneficiary may not voluntarily transfer the interest, and the interest may be unreachable in whole or in part by the beneficiary's creditors. Such a trust, often referred to as a "spendthrift trust," is now widely accepted throughout the United States but never has been permitted in England. Even in America, however, it has always been the subject of considerable controversy. See generally Griswold, Spendthrift Trusts (2d ed. 1947); Danforth, Article Five of the UTC and the Future of Creditors' Rights in Trusts, 27 Cardozo L. Rev. 2551 (2006); Newman, Spendthrift and Discretionary Trusts: Alive and Well Under the Uniform Trust Code, 40 Real Prop. Prob & Tr. J. 567 (2005); Hirsch, Spendthrift Trusts and Public Policy: Economic and Cognitive Perspectives, 73 Wash. U.L.Q. 1 (1995).

2. *Sligh update.* In 1998, the Mississippi legislature overruled *Sligh* in at least two crucial respects. First, under Miss. Code Ann. §§ 91–9–503 and 91–9–509, the only exception to the protection afforded by spendthrift language is in the case of a self-settled trust. As to self-settled trusts, see infra pp. 626–641. Second, Miss. Code Ann. § 91–9–507 now makes clear what should have been clear even without the statute, i.e., that although a creditor who has a claim against the beneficiary of a discretionary trust may be able to access the beneficiary's beneficial interest, such a creditor cannot access the trust property itself, at least if the beneficiary is not also the settlor. See UTC § 504; Restatement (Third) of Trusts § 60 (2003). For more on discretionary trusts, see infra pp. 620–626.

In Sligh v. First Nat'l Bank of Holmes County, 735 So.2d 963 (Miss. 1999), the court held that the trustee was not liable in tort for the trust beneficiary's actions.

3. *More on the tort exception.* Like the Second Restatement, the Third Restatement sets forth no black-letter exception to the protection afforded by spendthrift language for tort claims. In commentary, however, the Third Restatement provides:

... The exceptions to spendthrift immunity stated in this Section are not exclusive. Special circumstances or evolving policy may justify recognition of other exceptions. ...

The nature or a pattern of tortious conduct by a beneficiary, for example, may on policy grounds justify a court's refusal to allow spendthrift immunity to protect the trust interest and the lifestyle of that beneficiary, especially one whose willful or fraudulent conduct or persistently reckless behavior causes serious harm to others.

Restatement (Third) of Trusts § 59, cmt. a(2) (2003). For statutes implementing such policies, see, in addition to that of Louisiana cited in *Sligh,* Cal. Prob. Code § 15305.5 (restitution for commission of a felony and money damages for conduct for which beneficiary has been convicted of a felony) and Ga. Code Ann. § 53-12-80 (tort judgments, as well as judgments and restitution for conduct for which beneficiary has been convicted criminally).

On the other hand, the tort exception has plainly been rejected by the legislature in Mississippi (see Note 2). More generally, as state legislatures codify the law relating to spendthrift trusts, they often fail to include an exception for tort claims. See, e.g., UTC § 503 & cmt. Moreover, several recent cases have refused to recognize such an exception. See Jackson v. Fidelity & Deposit Co., 608 S.E.2d 901 (Va. 2005) ("because the statute specifically lists exceptions to spendthrift protection, those exceptions are the only ones allowed by law"); Duvall v. McGee, 826 A.2d 416 (Md. 2003) (tort claim based on battery and murder; specifically rejecting rationale of *Sligh*); Scheffel v. Krueger, 782 A.2d 410 (N.H. 2001) (refusing to expand existing statutory exceptions).

4. *Child support.* Restatement (Second) of Trusts § 157 (1959), quoted in *Sligh,* set forth various exceptions to the effectiveness of spendthrift provisions. One of the most widely accepted exceptions was that in § 157(a), which provided that a plaintiff asserting a child support claim against a trust beneficiary could recover against the beneficiary's interest in the trust, notwithstanding otherwise effective spendthrift language in the governing instrument. See, e.g., Ex parte Boykin, 656 So.2d 821 (Ala. App. 1994); Matt v. Matt, 473 N.E.2d 1310 (Ill.1985); Shelley v. Shelley, 354 P.2d 282 (Or.1960); Zouck v. Zouck, 104 A.2d 573 (Md.1954). A number of states have codified this exception. See, e.g., UTC § 503(b)(1); Cal. Prob. Code § 15305; Tex. Fam. Code § 154.005. Restatement (Third) of Trusts § 59(a) (2003) is to similar effect. Can you explain the exception for child support in terms of the policy justifications for spendthrift trusts?

5. *Former spouses.* Restatement (Second) of Trusts § 157(a) (1959) also set forth an exception for the claims of former spouses for alimony. A number of courts have followed in this regard, as well. See, e.g., Flaherty v. Flaherty, 638 A.2d 1254 (N.H.1994); Bacardi v. White, 463 So.2d 218 (Fla.1985); Wife, J.B.G. v. Husband, P.J.G., 286 A.2d 256 (Del.Ch.1971). So have some legisla-

tures. See, e.g., UTC § 503(b)(1); Cal. Prob. Code § 15305. But other courts have rejected the Restatement position insofar as it relates to alimony. See, e.g., Miller v. Miller, 643 N.E.2d 288 (Ill.App.1994), appeal denied, 647 N.E.2d 1011 (Ill.1995); Ex parte Boykin, 656 So.2d 821 (Ala. App. 1994); Erickson v. Erickson, 266 N.W. 161 (Minn.1936). Still others have allowed recovery of court-ordered alimony but denied recovery of spousal support under a separation agreement. Compare Safe Deposit & Trust Co. of Baltimore v. Robertson, 65 A.2d 292 (Md.1949) (alimony pursuant to court decree), with Hitchens v. Safe Deposit & Trust Co., 66 A.2d 97 (Md.1949) (support payments pursuant to separation agreement). Here again, Restatement (Third) of Trusts § 59(a) (2003) follows the Second Restatement. Can you articulate any reason, based in policy or otherwise, why a court might allow recovery of child support but not alimony? See generally Dessin, Feed a Trust and Starve a Child: The Effectiveness of Trust Protective Techniques Against Claims for Support and Alimony, 10 Ga. St. U.L. Rev. 691 (1994).

SCHREIBER V. KELLOGG

United States Court of Appeals, Third Circuit, 1995.
50 F.3d 264.

SCIRICA, CIRCUIT JUDGE.

This diversity case requires us to interpret the scope of a purported spendthrift provision in a trust created in the early part of the century. In so doing, we face an issue of first impression under the laws of Pennsylvania and most other states: the applicability of section 157(c) of the Restatement (Second) of Trusts, which allows creditors to reach a spendthrift trust interest in limited circumstances. The district court found the trust contained a spendthrift provision protecting the interest of the beneficiary and that Pennsylvania courts would not apply the Restatement exception under the circumstances of this case. Schreiber v. Kellogg, 849 F. Supp. 382, 389, 394 (E.D.Pa.1994). We will affirm in part and reverse in part.

I.

In 1928, Rodman Wanamaker died, leaving a will and codicils that established trusts for his children and their descendants. At issue in this case is a $120 million trust created in Paragraph Third of his will.

For half a century, the trust consisted of the stock in the John Wanamaker department store. In March 1978, Carter, Hawley, Hale, Inc. offered the trust $40 million for the Wanamaker stock. Christopher G. Kellogg, one of Wanamaker's great-grandchildren and a contingent income beneficiary of the trust,[7] engaged attorney Palmer K. Schreiber to

---

[7] Although the will did not expressly provide that Wanamaker's great-grandchildren would succeed to their parents' interests in the trust, Judge Alfred L. Taxis, Jr., of the Montgomery County Orphans' Court ruled two decades ago that the failure to include such specific language was an oversight of the drafter. In re Wanamaker Estate, No. 38,456 (Montgomery County Or-

increase the purchase price of the stock. Partially as a result of those efforts, the stock was sold for $60 million, about $20 million more than the original offer. For his services, the Montgomery County Orphans' Court awarded Schreiber $117,000 in counsel fees and interest from the corpus of the trust, and he later received a judgment of nearly $88,000, plus counsel fees and interest, against another attorney involved in the stock sale for breach of a fee-sharing agreement.

In October 1978, after the stock was sold, Schreiber filed a surcharge action on behalf of Kellogg against the trustees of the Wanamaker trust, alleging negligence, mismanagement, and breach of fiduciary duty. In May 1981, the parties settled the suit. The trustees agreed to hold regular meetings, make certain information available to beneficiaries, and file a plan for the creation of a retirement age for trustees. For his part, Kellogg agreed to pay his own counsel fees and to obtain a release of any claims against the trust from his counsel. Schreiber and Kellogg then signed a fee agreement that provided for Kellogg to pay Schreiber $80,000, plus interest at a "commercially competitive" rate.

When Kellogg failed to pay the amount due, Schreiber filed this suit for breach of contract. The district court awarded him $512,864 for counsel fees and interest, and we affirmed. Schreiber v. Kellogg, 37 F.3d 1488 (3d Cir.1994).

During the pendency of the appeal, Schreiber asked the district court to execute on Kellogg's interest in the trust to satisfy the judgment. The court denied the motion, holding that Wanamaker had intended to provide spendthrift protection for his great-grandchildren and Kellogg's interest in the trust was protected. . . . The court also ruled that Pennsylvania courts would not apply, under the circumstances of this case, section 157(c) of the Restatement (Second) of Trusts (1959), which permits judgment creditors that preserve or benefit an interest in a spendthrift trust to reach that interest to enforce valid claims. . . . Schreiber appealed. . . .

II.

[W]e look to Pennsylvania law to determine whether Schreiber may execute on Kellogg's interest in the Wanamaker trust.

---

phans' Ct. Feb. 27, 1975). Thus, Kellogg became a contingent beneficiary as a result of this 1975 decision; he became an income beneficiary upon the death of his mother in August 1989. . . . He receives $31,500 per month in income from the trust. . . .

A.

In general, "[t]rusts in which the interest of a beneficiary cannot be assigned by him or reached by his creditors have come to be known as 'spendthrift trusts.'" 2A Austin W. Scott & William F. Fratcher, The Law of Trusts § 151, at 83 (4th ed. 1987).[8] No specific wording is required under Pennsylvania law to create a spendthrift trust. If a spendthrift trust is created, courts will sustain its validity, except in a few limited circumstances.

. . . Because the trust here was created in the Wanamaker will, we look to the language of that will to determine the validity of the purported spendthrift provision.

B.

The relevant provisions of the will are Paragraphs Third and Eighth. Paragraph Third established the stock trust and divided certain proceeds between Wanamaker's children "for their sole and separate use, not to be anticipated, or assigned by them, in any manner whatever, nor subject to any attachment, alienation or sequestration for their debts, contracts or engagements." There is no dispute that this language established a spendthrift trust protecting Wanamaker's children.

Paragraph Eighth stipulated that the trust established in Paragraph Third also shall provide for descendants of the Wanamaker children "subject to the provisions herein previously contained." The fundamental disagreement in this case is whether this language extends the spendthrift protection from Paragraph Third to cover the bequest to Wanamaker's grandchildren and great-grandchildren in Paragraph Eighth. The district court held that it did, thereby providing spendthrift protection to Kellogg's interest. . . . But Schreiber contends the phrase merely means that a gift made in a preceding paragraph takes precedence over a gift stated later in the will.

To resolve this dispute, we must look to the language and structure of the entire will. . . . After the first two paragraphs made unrelated bequests, Paragraph Third created the stock trust and divided the proceeds into three general categories. First, between one-half and two-thirds of the income from the trust was to pay outstanding debts of the John Wanamaker corporate entities. Second, the remainder of the stock income was to be shared by Rodman Wanamaker's three children, subject to the spendthrift provisions noted earlier. Upon the death of the Wanamaker children, their children were to split one-half of their parent's share.

---

[8] . . . The beneficiary of a spendthrift trust, however, need not be a spendthrift. . . .

Third, the other half share would be accumulated to fund various charities.

Paragraph Seventh noted that if, under Paragraph Third, the first category of money was not needed to pay Wanamaker corporate debts, then the entire income of the trust should be divided among the Wanamaker children. "[B]ut the provisions as to the amount which shall go to my children's children, in the event of the decease of the former, shall remain as provided for in the paragraph heretofore." The final relevant section, Paragraph Eighth, directed the trust income to the Wanamaker children's descendants "subject to the provisions herein previously contained."

Although Schreiber contends the limiting phrase in Paragraph Eighth merely prioritizes among gifts made in the will, we believe it means something more. Paragraph Third created a detailed scheme of distribution to different categories of beneficiaries subject to certain conditions and restrictions, and the paragraphs following made bequests according to that scheme. We believe the restrictive phrase in Paragraph Eighth was meant to subject the bequests made therein to all applicable provisions of the previous paragraphs; the phrase was meant to state that the descendants of Rodman Wanamaker would receive the trust income under the scheme as established in Paragraph Third and followed in the other relevant paragraphs. That scheme included a spendthrift provision for the individual beneficiaries. We see no reason why that provision should not be among those to which the bequests in Paragraph Eighth were explicitly made "subject."

Other provisions of the will support this interpretation. For example, Paragraph Fifth mandated the creation of an artisans school and adopted "[t]he same method of creating a principal sum" as used to fund a children's home established in Paragraph Third. Paragraph Sixth provided for a sanitarium with funding "[a]s provided under the last paragraph, and fully set forth in the third paragraph." Thus, it appears Rodman Wanamaker created a detailed funding mechanism from stock income in Paragraph Third of his will and envisioned that bequests made in the paragraphs following would conform to the rules applicable to that category of income.

Pennsylvania case law also supports this result. In Ball v. Weightman, 273 Pa. 120, 116 A. 653 (1922), the Pennsylvania Supreme Court upheld spendthrift protection for a testator's great-grandchildren, even though the will specifically included such protection only for the testator's grandchildren. Repeatedly noting that it examined the "entire will" for an indication of the testator's intent, the court stated it saw:

nothing to indicate an intent to discriminate between beneficiaries, or to require the trustees to distribute the income direct to some, and not so to others. Testator's manifest purpose was to secure the income of his estate for the personal use of his descendants during the life of the trust, and such protection is no more essential to a child or grandchild than to a great-grandchild. . . .

Id., 116 A. at 654. Similarly, the Supreme Court in Riverside Trust Co. v. Twitchell, 342 Pa. 558, 20 A.2d 768 (1941), decided that a deed of trust explicitly granting spendthrift protection over the principal of the trust, but not to the income, was meant to cover both. . . . From these cases, it appears the Pennsylvania Supreme Court broadly construes spendthrift provisions when the testator has indicated a desire to incorporate such protection into a trust, but has failed to clearly define the scope of coverage. . . .

Therefore, . . . we . . . hold that the spendthrift provision here encompasses Kellogg's interest in the trust.

III.

Because a spendthrift provision is involved, we must decide whether Pennsylvania would adopt section 157(c) of the Restatement (Second) of Trusts, which permits creditors to reach spendthrift trust interests to satisfy claims for services or materials that preserved or benefitted the beneficiary's interest in the trust. No Pennsylvania court has resolved this question. Indeed, neither the parties nor this court could locate more than one reported decision from any jurisdiction addressing this issue. Accordingly, we must determine whether the Pennsylvania Supreme Court would adopt section 157(c) and, if so, whether it is applicable under the facts of this case. . . .

A.

Section 157 of the Restatement (Second) of Trusts provides:

Although a trust is a spendthrift trust or a trust for support, the interest of the beneficiary can be reached in satisfaction of an enforceable claim against the beneficiary,

    (a) by the wife or child of the beneficiary for support, or by the wife for alimony;

    (b) for necessary services rendered to the beneficiary or necessary supplies furnished to him;

    (c) for services rendered and materials furnished which preserve or benefit the interest of the beneficiary;

(d) by the United States or a State to satisfy a claim against the beneficiary.

(emphasis added).

Section 157(c) has two fundamental purposes. First, it was intended to prevent unjust enrichment of a beneficiary,[9] and second, to ensure that beneficiaries were able to obtain necessary resources to protect their interests.[10]

B.

As the state credited with first recognizing the validity of spendthrift trusts,[11] Pennsylvania has more than 150 years' worth of jurisprudence on the issue. Originally, "spendthrift trusts were upheld in their entirety by Pennsylvania courts on the theory that property rights include the right to place any type of restriction on . . . disposition." *Wills—Spendthrift Clause—Legacies—Assignment,* Fiduciary Rev., June 1941, at 1. Yet, as time passed, Pennsylvania courts began recognizing exceptions to the spendthrift trust rule . . . , even when that meant overruling prior case law. . . .

This evolution of spendthrift trust law in Pennsylvania is consistent with the law's development in the majority of American jurisdictions. As one treatise explained:

> [T]he trend of the last twenty-five years has been to limit and qualify spendthrift trusts, either by statute or by judicial decisions which create exceptions. . . . The spirit of nineteenth century individualism which originally validated these trusts is meeting opposition of a socially-minded character.

George G. Bogert & George T. Bogert, Handbook of the Law of Trusts § 40, at 154 (5th ed. 1973). . . .

---

[9] Restatement (Second) of Trusts § 157(c) cmt. d ("In such a case the beneficiary would be unjustly enriched if such a claim were not allowed"); Scott & Fratcher, supra, § 157.3, at 208 ("The purpose of the settlor in imposing restrictions on the alienation of the beneficiary's interest is to prevent him from losing his interest by his own improvidence. There is no reason, however, why his interest under the trust should be exempt from the claims of those who have by their services conferred a benefit on his interest. He should not be permitted to profit at their expense.").

[10] See Erwin N. Griswold, Spendthrift Trusts § 346, at 410 (2d ed. 1947) ("Without such a remedy, needy beneficiaries may be wholly unable to enforce their interests or to obtain protection in case the trust is not properly administered."). . . .

[11] See, e.g., . . . Griswold, supra, § 26, at 22 . . . ("These early Pennsylvania cases not only were the foundation of spendthrift trusts in that state, but they were also frequently cited and relied on in other jurisdictions. They formed the principal basis of the dictum in Nichols v. Eaton [91 U.S. 716, 23 L. Ed. 254 (1875)] which was the greatest single factor in the establishment of spendthrift trusts in the United States."). . . .

C.

As we have noted, no Pennsylvania court has considered whether section 157(c) should be adopted. In fact, only one state's court apparently has decided the issue. Evans & Luptak v. Obolensky, 194 Mich. App. 708, 487 N.W.2d 521, appeal denied, 441 Mich. 909, 496 N.W.2d 289 (1992), involved a situation similar to this case. In *Evans*, the trust beneficiary hired a law firm to secure the best price for the primary assets of the trust, but failed to pay the firm after the sale occurred. The firm obtained a judgment against the beneficiary, and a lower court denied execution on the trust proceeds. The Michigan Court of Appeals, in adopting section 157(c), reversed and remanded. . . .

Schreiber contends that, as in *Evans*, the state courts in Pennsylvania have adopted all the other subsections of section 157. Subsection (a), which permits trust assets to be reached to satisfy alimony or support claims, has been substantially—if not entirely—adopted in Pennsylvania. For more than sixty years, the Pennsylvania Supreme Court has permitted wives to reach the assets of spendthrift trusts to satisfy claims for support. See In re Moorehead's Estate, 289 Pa. 542, 137 A. 802 (1927). . . .

. . . Furthermore, the state now has a broad statute that provides:

Income of a trust subject to spendthrift or similar provisions shall nevertheless be liable for the support of anyone whom the income beneficiary shall be under a legal duty to support.

20 Pa. Cons. Stat. Ann. § 6112 (1975). . . .

As for Restatement section 157(b), the Pennsylvania Supreme Court cited the subsection with approval in Lang v. Commonwealth of Pa., Dep't of Public Welfare, 515 Pa. 428, 528 A.2d 1335, 1341–42 (1987). In *Lang*, the Supreme Court noted that "[a] support trust, though containing an implied spendthrift provision, can generally be reached to satisfy claims for necessary services rendered to the beneficiary. See Restatement (Second) of Trusts, § 157 (1959)." Because *Lang* involved a support trust, however, the district court held the case did not stand for the proposition that interests in a spendthrift trust could be reached under section 157(b). We disagree. Section 157, by its terms, encompasses both spendthrift and support trusts. The *Lang* court did not express any intention to distinguish between those types of trusts in determining the applicability of the Restatement; it simply cited section 157 with approval.

Furthermore, in Quigley Estate, 22 Pa. D. & C. 2d 598 (Montgomery County Orphans' Ct. 1960), Judge Alfred L. Taxis, Jr., approved a beneficiary's assignment of her interest in a spendthrift trust to the Pennsylvania Department of Welfare. The court, in upholding the "right of the

Commonwealth to recover for furnishing the legatee with such fundamental necessities of life," expressly cited section 157 as support for its decision. Id. at 599. . . .

Quigley Estate and similar cases adopt the reasoning not only of section 157(b), but also of section 157(d), which allows spendthrift trust interests to be reached in satisfaction of government claims. Another Pennsylvania case upholding the application of section 157(d) is Scott Estate, 11 Pa. D & C.2d 589 (Montgomery County Orphans' Ct. 1957), in which the Treasury Department served a writ of attachment on the executors of a trust to recover unpaid taxes of the beneficiary. Judge Taxis noted the applicability of section 157(d), but stated he did "not assume to decide the effectiveness of this attachment." Id. at 592. Nevertheless, relying in part on section 157(d), the court permitted the amount of the unpaid taxes to be retained, pending a resolution of the attachment. . . .[12]

. . . We have found no Pennsylvania case that has expressly declined to follow Restatement section 157 or even criticized it. In fact, Pennsylvania courts routinely cite as authority for their decisions the Restatement of Trusts, including sections of the Restatement governing spendthrift trusts. Given the rationale underlying section 157(c), and the favorable treatment Pennsylvania courts have afforded other subsections of section 157 and the Restatement overall, we believe the Pennsylvania Supreme Court would adopt section 157(c).

IV.

Although we hold that the Pennsylvania Supreme Court would adopt Restatement section 157(c), we still must determine whether the district court properly ruled that Pennsylvania courts would not apply the Restatement "under the circumstances of this case." . . .

A.

As an initial matter, we consider whether this type of case, involving an attorney seeking reimbursement for services rendered in connection with a trust interest, generally fits within section 157(c). We believe it does. . . .

---

[12] For decades, commentators have cited Scott Estate for the proposition that Pennsylvania permits the United States to attach spendthrift trust interests to recover unpaid taxes. . . . Furthermore, it is doubtful whether Pennsylvania even has the power to shield interests in a spendthrift trust from federal tax liens. See First Northwestern Trust Co. v. Internal Revenue Serv., 622 F.2d 387, 390 (8th Cir.1980) (noting the "well established legal principle that the income from a spendthrift trust is not immune from federal tax liens, notwithstanding any state laws or recognized exemptions to the contrary"); United States v. Rye, 550 F.2d 682, 685 (1st Cir.1977) ("In the area of spendthrift trusts, the courts have consistently held that a restraint on transferability, whether arising from the trust instrument or from state law, does not immunize the beneficiary's interest from a federal tax lien.").

Furthermore, one commentator cited this situation as an example of the proper application of the principles underlying section 157(c):

> Although an attorney, so far as payment for his general services is concerned, stands no better than an ordinary creditor in reaching the interest in a spendthrift trust, he is, nevertheless, entitled in New York to recover from his client's income for services rendered in connection with the client's interest in the trust. These cases seem to be a proper application of the principle that the beneficiary's interest in a spendthrift trust may be alienated for the purpose of preserving or improving its value.

Erwin N. Griswold, Spendthrift Trusts § 346, at 409–10 (2d ed. 1947) . . . ; see also Scott & Fratcher, supra, § 157.3, at 209. But see Griswold, supra, § 346, at 410 (noting that "attorneys have not been so successful" in some states in recovering under this theory).

B.

In considering the applicability of section 157(c), the district court conducted an evidentiary hearing and held that Pennsylvania courts would not apply Restatement section 157(c) to this case. . . . Specifically, the court determined that, because Rodman Wanamaker had expressly indicated he wished the trustees to remain free from interference by the beneficiaries, invasion of the spendthrift trust interest here would "negate the wishes of Rodman Wanamaker." . . .[13] . . .

If a testator's intent controlled whether an exception to spendthrift protection was allowed, then none of the Restatement section 157 exceptions could ever apply. This is so because if a testator had intended the result mandated by the section 157 exceptions, then presumably he would have said so in the will, and there would be no need to look beyond the will for policy reasons that warrant invasion of the trust. Despite the usual importance of a testator's intent in construing the terms of a will or trust, Pennsylvania courts have not hesitated to disregard such intent when public policy requires. See, e.g., In re Moorehead's Estate, 289 Pa. 542, 137 A. 802, 806 (1927) ("A testator has a right . . . to dispose of his own property with such restrictions and limitations not repugnant to law, as he sees fit, and his intentions ought to be carried out, unless they contravene some positive rule of law or are against public policy.").

---

[13] The district court divided Schreiber's representation of Kellogg into two time periods: representation during the sale of the Wanamaker stock and representation during the subsequent surcharge action against the trustees. As for the representation during the sale of the stock, the district court held that Schreiber had discharged Kellogg for all liability for that period. . . . Because Schreiber did not appeal this portion of the district court's ruling, the only representation at issue is Schreiber's work for Kellogg during the surcharge action against the trustees. . . .

Thus, we believe the district court must determine whether Schreiber's work for Kellogg did "preserve or benefit the interest of the beneficiary." Schreiber contends that this analysis does not require the court to decide whether an actual preservation or benefit to the beneficiary's interest occurred, but instead whether a good-faith attempt to preserve or benefit the interest was made. We disagree. By its terms, section 157(c) does not require merely an action that might preserve or benefit the beneficiary's interest, but instead mandates that the action achieve the result of preserving or benefitting the interest in the trust. See § 157(c) ("the interest of the beneficiary can be reached . . . for services rendered and materials furnished which preserve or benefit the interest of the beneficiary"); see also Griswold, supra, § 366, at 445 ("[T]he creditor should be allowed to recover at least to the extent that his labor and materials have improved the value of the beneficiary's interest.").

The purposes behind section 157(c) support this interpretation. Section 157(c) permits the attachment of spendthrift interests because a beneficiary "should not be permitted to profit at [his creditor's] expense." Scott & Fratcher, supra, § 157.3, at 208. Similarly, the Restatement notes that section 157(c) is necessary because "the beneficiary would be unjustly enriched if such a claim were not allowed." Restatement § 157(c) cmt. d. In cases in which the beneficiary's interest is not actually preserved or benefitted, however, the beneficiary has received no "profit" at all; thus, he cannot have been "unjustly enriched." . . .

Nevertheless, Schreiber contends this interpretation would emasculate one of the policies underlying section 157(c), namely, ensuring that needy beneficiaries obtain the necessary resources to protect their interests in a trust. Without a standard allowing recovery for "good-faith" attempts, Schreiber argues, few attorneys or other creditors would ever agree to help beneficiaries in these circumstances. Schreiber cites no legal authority for this proposition. We believe his argument is answered by the widespread acceptance of the most common practice designed to ensure that those in need obtain proper representation: contingency fee agreements, which require a favorable result to generate fees. . . . This approach is also similar to that embodied in the various federal fee-shifting statutes: Attorneys can recover their fees in certain cases, but only when they represent the "prevailing party." . . . Like Restatement section 157(c), these statutes reward only those efforts that actually succeed in benefitting a plaintiff, not those that are well-intentioned but fail. . . . Accordingly, we do not believe it unfair to require Schreiber to demonstrate that the surcharge action actually "preserve[d] or benefit[ted]" Kellogg's interest in the trust.[14]

---

[14] Whether creditors may recover for a non-pecuniary preservation or benefit to a trust interest is a more difficult question. We note that in other contexts we have not always required

This construction of section 157(c) does not mean that those who unsuccessfully attempt to benefit an interest in a spendthrift trust should not be paid for their services. It merely means that the equities of the situation are not so far in their favor as to warrant ... an invasion of a spendthrift trust interest. Such creditors still may pursue alternative measures to collect debts.

V.

Based upon the foregoing, we will reverse and remand this case to the district court for a determination of whether Schreiber's work for Kellogg did "preserve or benefit the interest of the beneficiary," within the meaning of Restatement § 157(c). In all other respects, we will affirm the judgment of the district court.

[The concurring opinion of Circuit Judge Lewis is omitted.]

NOTES

1. *Schreiber update.* On remand, the lower court ruled that Restatement (Second) of Trusts § 157(c) (1959) encompassed non-pecuniary benefits to a trust beneficiary. Schreiber v. Kellogg, 194 B.R. 559 (E.D.Pa.1996), aff'd in part and rev'd in part without opinion, 124 F.3d 188 (3d Cir.1997). In particular, the lower court allowed $140,000 as reasonable compensation for "obtaining the important but limited result of increasing the information flow to the beneficiaries of the Wanamaker trust." 194 B.R. at 567.

2. *Exception for services provided to protect a beneficial interest.* As did the Second Restatement, both UTC § 503(b)(2) and Restatement (Third) of Trusts § 59(b) (2003) set forth an exception to the effectiveness of spendthrift language for claims for services provided to protect the beneficiary's interest in the trust. What sort of service provider is most likely to qualify under this exception?

3. *Exception for necessities.* As did Restatement (Second) of Trusts § 157(b) (1959), the Third Restatement continues to set forth an exception to the effectiveness of spendthrift language for claims for services or supplies provided for necessities. What sort of service provider is most likely to qualify under this exception? See Restatement (Third) of Trusts § 59(b), cmt. c (2003). UTC § 503 deliberately omits this exception. See id. cmt.

4. *Exception for governmental claims.* Governmental claims constitute another exception to the effectiveness of spendthrift provisions. See UTC § 503(a)(3); Restatement (Second) of Trusts § 157(d) (1959). Until lately, this exception has mostly recognized the authority of governmental creditors to

---

attorneys to prove a pecuniary benefit in order to recover fees. But we have required that the benefit must be real. . . .

collect beneficiaries' taxes. Currently it may have greater significance in its recognition of governmental creditors' authority to recoup Medicaid or other public assistance benefits. See, e.g., Estate of Gist, 763 N.W.2d 561 (Iowa 2009) (allowing governmental recovery from discretionary support trust on account of Medicaid expenditures for former beneficiary, notwithstanding spendthrift restrictions). The Third Restatement omits this exception from the black-letter, but the commentary explains: "It is implicit in the rule of this Section, as a statement of the common law, that governmental claimants . . . may reach the interest of a beneficiary of a spendthrift trust to the extent provided by federal law or an applicable state statute." Restatement (Third) of Trusts § 59, cmt. a(1) (2003).

5. *Beneficiary serving as trustee.* Spendthrift provisions are also ineffective to insulate a beneficiary's interest from a surcharge, i.e., personal liability for breaches of trust committed while serving as trustee. See Restatement (Third) of Trusts § 59, cmt. a(2) (2003); Chatard v. Oveross, 101 Cal. Rptr. 3d 883 (App. 2009).

6. *Restrictions on voluntary/involuntary alienation.* For spendthrift language to be effective, it must restrain both voluntary and involuntary alienation of a beneficiary's interest. See UTC § 502(a); Restatement (Third) of Trusts § 58, cmt. b(2) (2003). Why should this be so?

7. *Actual distributions.* Once a beneficiary receives a distribution, the property distributed is no longer subject to any spendthrift restriction the trust instrument may contain. It is thus subject to attachment by creditors, along with any of the beneficiary's other property, subject to local rules. See UTC § 502, cmt.; Restatement (Third) of Trusts § 58, cmt. d(2) (2003). Until distribution, however, the beneficiary's creditors must ordinarily wait. Indeed, in Fannie Mae v. Heather Apartments Ltd. P'ship, 811 N.W.2d 596 (Minn. 2012), the court held that it was error to enter an injunction barring a beneficiary from disposing of property that was neither distributed nor due.

8. *Pending distributions.* Though the point was once subject to debate, it is now settled that spendthrift language can protect beneficial interests in income, principal, or both. See UTC § 502, cmt.; Restatement (Third) of Trusts § 58, cmt. d(2) (2003). Nonetheless, "property that has become distributable to a beneficiary but is retained by the trustee beyond a time reasonably necessary to make distribution to the beneficiary, and thus to which the beneficiary has a right to demand immediate distribution," is subject to attachment. Id. See also UTC § 506. Why should the alienability of trust property depend on whether the beneficiary is currently entitled to receive it?

9. *Ownership equivalence.* Though the trust instrument includes spendthrift language, if a beneficiary has the equivalent of outright ownership of part or all of the trust property, the property in question is assignable by the beneficiary and subject to claims of the beneficiary's creditors. See Restatement (Third) of Trusts § 58 & cmt. b (2003). Among the clearest examples of

ownership equivalents are unrestricted rights of withdrawal and unrestricted presently exercisable general powers of appointment. See UTC § 505; In re Hoff, 644 F.3d 244 (5th Cir. 2011). How much further the concept should extend is difficult to say. See Scott & Ascher on Trusts § 15.2.8. In Miller v. Kresser, 34 So. 3d 172, 174 (Fla. App. 2010), the court denied a creditor access to the assets of a discretionary trust, notwithstanding the fact that the beneficiary's brother, as trustee, "simply rubber-stamped [the beneficiary's] decisions and 'serve[d] as the legal veneer to disguise [the beneficiary's] exclusive dominion and control of the trust assets.'"

10. *Practical effect of invalid assignment.* Even though a beneficiary's interest is non-assignable, if the beneficiary does assign it, the assignment is effective "as a revocable authorization to the trustee to pay to the assignee the income as it accrues, and to the extent that such accrued income is paid to the assignee before revocation by the beneficiary, the trustee is protected in making the payment and the assignee can keep the amount so paid to him." 3 Scott and Ascher on Trusts § 15.2.3. See also UTC § 502, cmt.

11. *Testamentary disposition.* Some beneficial interests, including, for example, indefeasibly vested remainders, survive the beneficiary's death. There is authority for the proposition that the beneficiary of such an interest may dispose of it by will or intestate succession, and that upon the beneficiary's death it becomes subject to the claims of the beneficiary's creditors, notwithstanding spendthrift language in the terms of the trust. See Restatement (Third) of Trust § 58 cmt. g (2003); In re Townley Bypass Unified Credit Trust, 252 S.W.3d 715 (Tex. App. 2008). The rationale is that spendthrift restrictions protect beneficiaries only while alive.

12. *Statutes.* Increasingly, statutes govern the creation and characteristics of spendthrift trusts. See, e.g., UTC §§ 501 to 507; N.Y. EPTL § 7–1.5 (all mandatory income trusts are spendthrift unless the trust instrument provides otherwise, but certain assignments of income in excess of $10,000 per year are possible).

2. DISCRETIONARY TRUSTS

UNITED STATES V. O'SHAUGHNESSY

Supreme Court of Minnesota, 1994.
517 N.W.2d 574.

WAHL, JUSTICE.

The United States District Court, District of Minnesota, certified to this court . . . the following question of state law:

> Under Minnesota law, does the beneficiary of a discretionary trust with the provisions described herein have "property" or any "right to property" in nondistributed trust principal or income before the trus-

tees have exercised their discretionary powers of distribution under
the trust agreement?

According to the facts set out in the Order, Lawrence P.
O'Shaughnessy is a beneficiary of two separate identical trusts established by his grandparents, I.A. O'Shaughnessy and Lillian G.
O'Shaughnessy on December 26, 1951 (the 1951 Trusts) for their 16 (later
17) grandchildren. First Trust National Association (First Trust), Lawrence M. O'Shaughnessy, and Donald E. O'Shaughnessy (Co–Trustees)
are the current trustees of the 1951 Trusts.

The 1951 Trust Agreements allow the trustees, in their discretion, to
distribute the principal and income of the Trusts to the beneficiaries. Article III provides, in part:

> The Trustees in their discretion may pay to [Lawrence P.
> O'Shaughnessy], or for his benefit, all or such part of the principal or
> the annual net income of the trust estate as they shall see fit during
> his lifetime. . . .

> Net income not paid out shall be accumulated and at the end of
> each calendar year added to the principal of the trust estate.

> The Trustees in their sole discretion may pay to [Lawrence P.
> O'Shaughnessy's father], all or any part of the principal and accumu-
> lated income of the trust estate at such time or times and in such
> amounts as they deem advisable, and if pursuant to this provision all
> of the principal and accumulated income of the trust are paid over to
> [Lawrence P. O'Shaughnessy's father], the trust shall thereupon
> terminate.

Article VIII of the Trust Agreements further provides that:

> If at any time or times in the opinion of the Trustees it is advisable to
> do so, the Trustees may pay to or expend for any beneficiary such
> sum from the principal of such beneficiary's share of the trust estate
> as the Trustees in their sole discretion deem wise, and the discretion
> so given to the Trustees shall be absolute and binding upon all per-
> sons in interest.

Although the trustees have the discretion to distribute or withhold
trust assets during Lawrence P. O'Shaughnessy's lifetime, the 1951 Trust
Agreements give him a limited power of appointment exercisable only by
his last will and testament to a certain class of individuals. If Lawrence
P. O'Shaughnessy dies without exercising his power of appointment, Article III dictates the distribution of the principal and undistributed income at his death.

In October 1989, a delegate of the Secretary of the Treasury assessed a $412,921.27 federal income tax deficiency against Lawrence P. O'Shaughnessy for the years 1983 through 1986. On August 1, 1990, First Trust was served with a Notice of Levy upon "property or rights to property" belonging to Lawrence P. O'Shaughnessy and held by First Trust to satisfy the deficiency. No distribution of principal or income from the 1951 Trusts was pending when the levy was served.

The government filed suit in federal court on April 26, 1993, seeking judicial enforcement of the levy. First Trust and the Co–Trustees moved to dismiss the complaint pursuant to Fed. R. Civ. P. 12(b)(6) asserting that at the time the levy was served, they did not hold property or rights to property belonging to Lawrence P. O'Shaughnessy. After a hearing, the federal district court determined that the issue raised by the Motion to Dismiss presented a question of state law appropriate for certification to this court.

The United States has a lien for the amount of any tax deficiency, including interest, upon "all property and rights to property, whether real or personal, belonging to [the delinquent taxpayer]." 26 U.S.C. § 6321 (1988). Although the federal courts decide whether a federal tax lien can attach to a particular interest, the threshold question of whether a taxpayer possesses "property" or "rights to property" must be resolved by reference to state law. Aquilino v. United States, 363 U.S. 509, 512–13, 80 S. Ct. 1277, 1279–80, 4 L. Ed. 2d 1365 (1960).

An express trust creates two separate interests in the subject matter of the trust—a legal interest vested in the trustee and an equitable interest vested in the beneficiary. Farmers State Bank of Fosston v. Sig Ellingson & Co., 218 Minn. 411, 16 N.W.2d 319, 322 (1944). Under a discretionary express trust, "a beneficiary is entitled only to so much of the income or principal as the trustee in his uncontrolled discretion shall see fit to [distribute] . . . [the beneficiary] cannot compel the trustee to pay him or to apply for his use any part of the trust property." IIA Austin W. Scott & William F. Fratcher, The Law of Trusts § 155 (4th ed. 1987) [hereinafter Scott on Trusts]. Because discretionary trusts give the trustee complete discretion to distribute all, some, or none of the trust assets, the beneficiary has a "mere expectancy" in the nondistributed income and principal until the trustee elects to make a payment. George G. Bogert & George T. Bogert, The Law of Trusts and Trustees § 228 (1992). Creditors, who stand in the shoes of the beneficiary, have no remedy against the trustee until the trustee distributes the property. Id.

We are unpersuaded by the government's claim that the 1951 Trusts are not discretionary. The Trust Agreements do not direct the trustees to distribute the trust assets to Lawrence P. O'Shaughnessy. Rather, the agreements state that the trustees "*may* pay . . . all or such part of the principal or the annual net income of the trust estate as they shall see fit during his lifetime." (Emphasis added). This use of precatory language reveals the settlors' intent to create a discretionary trust. Moreover, even though the trustees do not have express authority to exclude Lawrence P. O'Shaughnessy from receiving any trust income or principal, the "sole discretion" given the trustees is "absolute and binding upon all persons in interest." While the trustees cannot exercise their discretion in a way that defeats the intent of the settlors or the purpose of the 1951 Trusts, this fact does not change the nature of the 1951 Trusts. Even where trustees have absolute, unlimited, or uncontrolled discretion, any attempt to violate the settlor's intent or the trust's purpose is considered an abuse of that discretion. Restatement (Second) on Trusts § 187 cmt. j (1959). So long as the trustees act in good faith, from proper motives, and within the bounds of reasonable judgment, the court will not interfere with their decisions. Scott on Trusts § 187. Finally, the intent of the settlors is revealed not only by the clear language of the trust documents but also by the provision allowing the trustees to pay out all of the income and principal to Lawrence P. O'Shaughnessy's father, thereby terminating the Trust and excluding Lawrence P. O'Shaughnessy from the trust assets.

The parties agree that Lawrence P. O'Shaughnessy has an equitable interest in the 1951 Trusts that entitles him to bring suit to compel the trustees to perform their duties, to enjoin the trustees from committing a breach of trust, or to remove the trustees altogether. See Restatement (Second) of Trusts § 199; Farmers State Bank, 16 N.W.2d at 322. It is also undisputed that the 1951 Trusts give Lawrence P. O'Shaughnessy a testamentary power of appointment. The parties disagree, however, as to whether these interests rise to the level of property rights.

Property is broadly defined by the Minnesota Probate Code as "real and personal property or any interest therein . . . [or] anything that may be the subject of ownership." Minn. Stat. § 524.1–201(29) (1992). This definition, however, is little help in discerning the nature of undistributed discretionary trust assets. More on point is a recent court of appeals decision addressing the nature of undistributed discretionary trust assets in the context of state-funded medical assistance. In re Leona Carlisle Trust Created Under the Trust Agreement Dated February 9, 1985, 498 N.W.2d 260 (Minn.App.1993). In *In re Leona Carlisle Trust*, the court of appeals held that the assets of a discretionary trust were not available assets for the purpose of determining a person's eligibility for public medical assistance. Id. at 266. The court recognized that support trusts, which direct the trustee to distribute trust income or principal as necessary for the support of the beneficiary, usually are considered available assets while discretionary trusts are not. Id. at 264. The court explained that this was because beneficiaries of support trusts legally can compel the trustee to distribute trust assets while beneficiaries of discretionary trusts cannot. Id. See Restatement (Second) of Trusts § 198 cmt. c.

Cases from other states support the holding in *In re Leona Carlisle Trust*. See, e.g., Chenot v. Bordeleau, 561 A.2d 891 (R.I.1989) (discretionary trust assets not available because trustees have discretion to withhold payments); First Nat'l Bank of Md. v. Dept. of Health & Mental Hygiene, 284 Md. 720, 399 A.2d. 891 (1979) (state could not compel trustees of discretionary trust to pay for beneficiary's stay in state hospital); Town of Randolph v. Roberts, 346 Mass. 578, 195 N.E.2d 72 (1964) (state welfare agency could not recover from discretionary trust for disability payments). Additionally, some states have enacted statutes that preclude creditors from reaching nondistributed discretionary trust proceeds. See Mont. Code Ann. § 72–33–304(1) (1993) (creditor cannot compel trustee to exercise discretion); Nev. Rev. Stat. § 166.110 (1993) (trustee's discretion "shall never be interfered with for any consideration of the needs, station in life or mode of life of the beneficiary, or for uncertainty, or on any pretext whatever"). Even in California, where the legislature gave courts the authority to order trustees to distribute discretionary trust assets to reimburse the state for public assistance payments, Cal. Prob. Code § 15306(a)(2) (West 1991), there is no similar provision for tax obligations.

We reject the government's claim that Lawrence P. O'Shaughnessy's equitable interest in the trust and his power of appointment are both property interests subject to taxation under Minnesota law. . . .

Under Minnesota law the beneficiary of a discretionary trust with the provisions described in the 1951 Trust Agreements does not have "property" or any "right to property" in nondistributed trust principal or income before the trustees have exercised their discretionary powers of distribution under the trust agreement.

Certified Question answered in the negative.

NOTES

1. *Terminology.* A mandatory-income trust is one in which the trustee is required to distribute all of the trust's income on a regular basis. A discretionary trust is one in which the trustee has discretion, i.e., authority, to make, or not to make, certain types of distributions.

A spendthrift trust is a trust whose governing instrument contains language prohibiting alienation by the beneficiary and immunizing the beneficiary's interest from the claims of creditors. A trust can be both a mandatory-income trust and a spendthrift trust. Or a trust can be both discretionary and spendthrift. Almost any type of trust can be a spendthrift trust.

2. *General principles.* Ordinarily, neither the beneficiary nor the beneficiary's assignees and creditors can compel the trustee of a discretionary trust to distribute anything. See UTC § 504; Medical Park Hospital v. Bancorp South, 166 S.W.3d 19 (Ark. 2004); Doksansky v. Norwest Bank, 615 N.W.2d 104 (Neb. 2000); Restatement (Third) of Trusts § 60, cmt. e (2003). Indeed, in *O'Shaughnessy,* the court concluded that the beneficiary lacked the requisite statutory property interest in either the income or the principal that remained in the trustee's hands. The trustee, therefore, correctly resisted the government's efforts to levy directly on the trust assets. The court also acknowledged, however, that the beneficiary had "an equitable interest" in the trusts that allowed him to enforce them. See also Scanlan v. Eisenberg, 669 F.3d 838 (7th Cir. 2012) (beneficiary of discretionary trust had standing to sue trustees for breach of trust). In the absence of spendthrift restrictions, perhaps the government should have levied on the beneficial interest itself. To be sure, doing so would not have allowed the government to force the trustees to distribute anything, but it would have given the government a powerful advantage in seeking to recover the beneficiary's unpaid taxes. Do you see how?

An assignee or creditor may have more bargaining power against the beneficiary of a discretionary trust (unless it is also spendthrift) than against the beneficiary of a spendthrift trust. Again, do you see how?

When the beneficiary whose creditor seeks to compel payment is also the trustee and, as such, has discretion to make or not to make distributions to himself or herself, the Third Restatement takes the position that the creditor can "reach from time to time the maximum amount the trustee-beneficiary can properly take." Restatement (Third) of Trusts § 60, cmt. g (2003). Regardless of whether the beneficiary is also the trustee, the result is the same if the beneficiary has the right to demand the payment of trust property, as when the beneficiary has a "right of withdrawal" or an inter vivos general power of appointment. See id. cmts. a, g.

3. *Scope of discretion.* Even if the governing instrument purports to confer "absolute discretion" on the trustee, the trustee remains subject to judicial control to prevent an abuse of discretion. See, e.g., UTC § 814 & cmt.; Estate of Stillman, infra p. 841; Restatement (Third) of Trusts § 50(1) (2003). In some circumstances a court may instruct a trustee with broad discretion on how to proceed or even order a particular distribution. See Old Colony Trust Co. v. Rodd, 254 N.E.2d 886 (Mass.1970); In re Chusid's Estate, 301 N.Y.S.2d 766 (Sur. 1969). See generally Halbach, Problems of Discretion in Discretionary Trusts, 61 Colum. L. Rev. 1425 (1961).

4. *Forfeiture restraints.* In England and the few American states that do not enforce spendthrift restrictions, forfeiture restraints serve much the same role. A forfeiture restraint derives from language in the trust instrument providing that any attempt on the part of a beneficiary to assign his or her interest, or any attempt by a beneficiary's creditor to attach it, will cause the

interest to terminate. If this happens, the beneficiary "forfeits" the interest. On the other hand, the terms of the trust may, and frequently do, also provide that, upon such an event, the trust is to become a discretionary trust for the benefit of one or more beneficiaries, likely including the beneficiary whose previous interest has ended. For an example of an instrument employing a forfeiture restraint, see In re Villar, infra p. 927.

3. SELF–SETTLED TRUSTS

COHEN V. COMMISSIONER OF DIVISION OF MEDICAL ASSISTANCE

Supreme Judicial Court of Massachusetts, 1996.
423 Mass. 399, 668 N.E.2d 769, cert. denied, 519 U.S. 1057,
117 S.Ct. 687, 136 L.Ed.2d 611 (1997).

FRIED, JUSTICE.

These . . . cases raise a common issue in the administration of the Medicaid program that has recurred in virtually identical form throughout the United States. In [them], the Division of Medical Assistance (division) denied the plaintiffs' eligibility for Medicaid benefits because it deemed that the plaintiffs had available to them sufficient resources of their own. . . .

I

A

The Medicaid program was established in 1965 as Title XIX of the Social Security Act, 42 U.S.C. §§ 1396 et seq., to provide health care to needy persons. The program, which makes funds available to individuals and those who furnish services to them, is administered by the States, but the State programs must comply with Federal statutes and regulations in order to qualify for the Federal funds which pay for a significant part of the program. . . . The issue presented in these cases arises from the wish of persons with some means, perhaps even considerable means, to preserve their assets in the face of the large medical expenses faced particularly by elderly persons. While the Medicare program, 42 U.S.C. §§ 1395 et seq. (1994), is designed to provide medical insurance for elderly and disabled persons generally, the coverage of that program is not complete. Supplemental private insurance is expensive and rarely comprehensive, and certain expenses—particularly long-term institutional care—confront especially elderly individuals and their families with expenses that are likely to deplete their resources entirely. . . . Many of those same expenses, though perhaps on a less generous scale, are covered for the indigent by Medicaid. . . .

In response, attorneys and financial advisers hit upon the device of having a person place his or her assets in trust so that those assets would provide for that person's comfort and well being, maybe even leaving something over to pass on his or her death, while creating eligibility for public assistance. See H.R. Rep. No. 265, 99th Cong., 1st Sess., pt. 1, at 71–72 (1985) (Committee on Energy and Commerce). The theory behind this maneuver was that, because the assets are in trust, they do not count as the grantor's assets and thus do not raise the grantor above the level of indigency needed to qualify for public assistance.[15] Courts in this State and elsewhere had ruled in various contexts that, if an individual settled assets in an irrevocable trust and the disposition of those assets was at the discretion of a trustee, no beneficiary of the trust would have a right to call for them, and so the assets could not be considered available to the beneficiary. See Randolph v. Roberts, 346 Mass. 578, 579–580, 195 N.E.2d 72 (1964) (creditor denied access to assets of testamentary spendthrift trust to reimburse itself for beneficiary's welfare disability charges); Pemberton v. Pemberton, 9 Mass. App. Ct. 9, 19–20, 411 N.E.2d 1305 (1980) (court cannot compel trustee to expend assets of spendthrift trust created by father to satisfy husband's arrearages and continuing support orders); Zeoli v. Commissioner of Social Servs., 179 Conn. 83, 425 A.2d 553 (1979) (parent settled assets in trust for child; court holds assets not available to child for Medicaid purposes); Tidrow v. Director, Missouri State Div. of Family Servs., 688 S.W.2d 9 (Mo.Ct.App.1985) (same); Hoelzer v. Blum, 93 A.D.2d 605, 462 N.Y.S.2d 684 (N.Y.1983) (same). The parties have not cited any case in any jurisdiction that has applied this reasoning to a trust in which the grantor or settlor is also the beneficiary, a so-called self-settled trust, nor have we decided such a case. Indeed, as we show below, . . . the law as to self-settled trusts is to the contrary. Nevertheless, individuals faced with health care costs that threatened to deplete their assets seized upon this jurisprudence as sanctioning their seeming impoverishment through self-settled trusts. Thus, a grantor: was able to qualify for public assistance without depleting his assets; could once more enjoy those assets if he no longer needed public assistance; and, if such a happy time did not come, could let them pass intact pursuant to the terms of the trust to his heirs. The grantor was able to have his cake and eat it too.

There was considerable dissatisfaction with the ensuing state of affairs. The bill containing the provisions now before this court was referred

---

[15] The regulations implementing the Commonwealth's codification of the Medicaid program, G.L. c. 118E (1994 ed.), establish a modest ceiling of resources said to be "available" to an applicant above which the individual is determined not to be sufficiently needy to qualify for public assistance from the program. See 106 Code Mass. Regs. § 505.110 (1991), now codified at 130 Code Mass. Regs. § 505.110 (1995) ("total value of countable assets owned by or available to persons . . . may not exceed": for one person, $2,000; for two persons, $3,000, as of July, 1995).

in 1985 to the House Committee on Energy and Commerce. In its report recommending passage, the committee wrote:

> The Committee feels compelled to state the obvious. Medicaid is, and always has been, a program to provide basic health coverage to people who do not have sufficient income or resources to provide for themselves. When affluent individuals use Medicaid qualifying trusts and similar "techniques" to qualify for the program, they are diverting scarce Federal and State resources from low-income elderly and disabled individuals, and poor women and children. This is unacceptable to the Committee.

H.R. Rep. No. 265, 99th Cong., 1st Sess., pt. 1, at 72 (1985).

The provisions, as finally enacted in 1986 and referred to here as the MQT statute, are the same in all relevant respects to those reported by the committee.[16] ... Building on the predicate that a person's eligibility for Medicare assistance depends on whether the resources available to that person exceed a specified maximum, the MQT statute first provides that:

> In the case of a medicaid qualifying trust [described in paragraph (2)], the amounts from the trust deemed available to a grantor, for purposes of subsection (a)(17), is the maximum amount of payments that may be permitted under the terms of the trust to be distributed to the grantor, assuming the full exercise of discretion by the trustee or trustees for the distribution of the maximum amount to the grantor. For purposes of the previous sentence, the term "grantor" means the individual referred to in paragraph (2).

42 U.S.C. § 1396a(k)(1). Subsection (2) then goes on to define the term "medicaid qualifying trust":

> (2) For purposes of this subsection, a "medicaid qualifying trust" is a trust, or similar legal device, established (other than by will) by an individual (or an individual's spouse) under which the individual may be the beneficiary of all or part of the payments from the trust and the distribution of such payments is determined by one or more trustees who are permitted to exercise any discretion with respect to the distribution to the individual. . . .

In 1993, Congress amended the provision relating to irrevocable MQTs to provide:

---

[16] The Committee on Energy and Commerce indicated in its report that the MQT statute applies retroactively. See H.R. Rep. No. 265, 99th Cong., 1st Sess., pt. 1, at 73 (1985) ("Medicaid qualifying trusts that have already been established, as well as those that may be created in the future, would be subject to the [MQT statute]"). . . .

(i) if there are any circumstances under which payment from the trust could be made to or for the benefit of the individual, the portion of the corpus from which, or the income on the corpus from which, payment to the individual could be made shall be considered re- sources available to the individual, and payments from that portion of the corpus or income—

(I) to or [for] the benefit of the individual, shall be consi- dered income of the individual, and

(II) for any other purpose, shall be considered a transfer of assets by the individual subject to subsection (c); and

(ii) any portion of the trust from which, or any income on the corpus from which, no payment could under any circumstances be made to the individual shall be considered, as of the date of estab- lishment of the trust (or, if later, the date on which payment to the individual was foreclosed) to be assets disposed by the individual for purposes of subsection (c), and the value of the trust shall be deter- mined for purposes of such subsection by including the amount of any payments made from such portion of the trust after such date.

42 U.S.C. § 1396p(d)(3)(B).

This amendment, which, unlike the MQT statute, explicitly applies only to trusts established after the effective date of the statute, see Pub. L. 103–66, § 13611(e)(2)(C), 107 Stat. 627 (1993),[17] resolves in favor of the Commonwealth beyond any possibility of argument the issue presented in these cases: if, in any circumstances any amount of money might be paid to a beneficiary, the maximum of such amount is deemed to be available to the beneficiary. The 1993 amendment does not, however, shed any light on the intentions of the earlier Congress. It may be said with equal plausibility that the 1993 amendment confirms the Commonwealth's in- terpretation of the MQT statute by stating it more explicitly, or that the later Congress intended a change therefore implying that some less strin- gent interpretation of the earlier provision was assumed. . . .

B

The issue posed by these cases is simply stated, although how the au- thoritative materials resolve that issue has been the subject of much con- troversy. In each of these cases, the grantor of an irrevocable trust, of which the grantor (or spouse) is a beneficiary and to which the grantor has transferred substantial assets, claims eligibility for Medicaid assis- tance because the trust, while according the trustee substantial discretion

---

[17] The 1993 amendment also repealed the 1986 MQT statute. Pub. L. 103–66, § 13611(d)(1)(C), 107 Stat. 627 (1993). . . .

in a number of respects, explicitly seeks to deny the trustee any discretion to make any sums available to the grantor if such availability would render the grantor ineligible for public assistance. Thus, all these trusts seek to limit the trustees' discretion just insofar as the exercise of that discretion may make the grantor ineligible for public assistance. The grantors and their representatives argue that, since no funds are available by the terms of the trust if such funds would render the beneficiary ineligible for Medicaid under the provisions of the MQT statute and the implementing State regulations, the grantors' eligibility is assured. The Commonwealth argues that this device has no purpose other than to frustrate the stated purpose of Congress in enacting the MQT statute. Accordingly, from the time of the adoption of the regulations in 1989, it has undertaken to review the Medicaid eligibility of all persons who are beneficiaries of self-settled trusts and has denied eligibility to persons who benefit from trusts with provisions such as we have described. The consequence of holding these persons ineligible has been to require them to spend down the resources in their trusts. Several Superior Court decisions have addressed the issue we face here today, all ruling that the trust assets are available to the grantors thereby rendering them ineligible for Medicaid assistance to the extent of such assets. Decisions in Minnesota, Matter of Kindt, 542 N.W.2d 391 (Minn.Ct.App.1996), Kansas, Williams v. Kansas Dep't of Social & Rehabilitation Servs., 258 Kan. 161, 171–173, 899 P.2d 452 (1995), Michigan, Ronney v. Department of Social Servs., 210 Mich. App. 312, 532 N.W.2d 910 (1995), and Florida, Hatcher v. Department of Health & Rehabilitative Servs., 545 So. 2d 400, 402 (Fla.Dist.Ct.App.1989), have reached the same conclusion. Only one decision, arguably distinguishable, Miller v. Ibarra, 746 F. Supp. 19 (D.Colo.1990), favors the trust beneficiaries.

II

The plaintiffs argue that the plain words of the statute support their position. They take as their premises that: (1) the MQT statute provides that the amount deemed available to the grantor is limited to "the maximum amount of payments that may be permitted under the terms of the trust to be distributed to the grantor, assuming the full exercise of discretion by the trustee or trustees for the distribution of the maximum amount to the grantor"; and (2) that, in one way or another under the terms of these trusts, the trustees have no discretion to pay anything but benefits supplementary to, or for purposes other than those covered by, public assistance, or to make any payments that would render the grantor ineligible for public assistance. From these premises, they reason that, under the terms of the trusts, there is no discretion to pay monies that would make the grantors ineligible for assistance under the program, and that therefore the trusts assets are not available to the beneficiaries. . . .

The Commonwealth argues that trusts of the sort in issue here do not get trust assets or income out from under the terms of the MQT statute since the purpose of the statute is to identify when, because of trustee discretion, trust assets are available to the beneficiary, while the terms of the trusts assume eligibility and define discretion so as not to disturb it. To allow such a device, the Commonwealth asserts, would "allow grantors of trusts to make their own Medicaid eligibility rules." This argument, which reappears in all the cases, is said to show that the grantors' move in these trusts is somehow illogical or at least illegitimate. See, e.g., Williams v. Kansas Dep't of Social & Rehabilitation Servs., 258 Kan. 161, 172, 899 P.2d 452 (1995), quoting Forsyth vs. Rowe, Conn. Super. Ct. No. CV91–0396327–S, 1995 WL 152124 (Mar. 23, 1995). There are, however, other instances in the law where instruments are specifically drafted to take advantage of available government benefits or facilities, even making explicit reference to the statutory facility which is meant to be enjoyed. It is entirely familiar, for instance, for trusts to be drafted to take advantage of the provisions in Federal estate taxation that allow assets to be passed down and enjoyed through two generations, while being subject to lesser inheritance taxes. In the case of such "generation skipping" trusts, not only may the trust specifically define the trustees' discretion in terms of retaining eligibility for the more favorable tax treatment, but this court has reformed trust documents to overcome drafting errors that might have defeated this tax-minimizing purpose. See, e.g., Shawmut Bank v. Buckley, 422 Mass. 706, 711, 665 N.E.2d 29 (1996). It might be said that this is an example of a facility which the law contemplates and thus does not seek to impede, while the trust device in issue here is a misuse of the law. Unfortunately that argument begs the question by assuming that the trusts in question frustrate the purpose of the statute, and therefore all doubts should be indulged against them. But this is just what needs to be shown.

It is the text of the statute itself that leads to the conclusion that the grantors in all of these cases cannot render themselves eligible for Medicaid assistance by these devices. The clause "under the terms of the trust," on which plaintiffs place such heavy emphasis, nestles between the phrase "the maximum amount of payments that may be permitted" and "to be distributed to the grantor, assuming the full exercise of discretion by the trustee or trustees for the distribution of the maximum amount to the grantor." The clause is most naturally read to measure the maximum amount (principal or income) to be deemed available to the grantor, asking what is the greatest amount the trustees in any circumstances have discretion to disburse. The plaintiffs read the clause as not only measuring the maximum amount available to grantors but also as carrying forward to the determination of availability the circumstances in which that amount might be paid. But the clause does not say this, and making it say this is a less natural reading than the alternative. Once we have identified the maximum amount trustees in any circumstances have discretion to pay, we then proceed to ask whether that amount is so large as to render the grantor ineligible. . . .

Drawing these strands together, we interpret the statute to define what is an MQT. See 42 U.S.C. § 1396a(k)(2). And that is any trust established by a person (or that person's spouse) under which that person may receive any payments. This general definition is qualified only by the requirement that the trustees must be permitted to exercise some discretion—that is, the conditions for distribution may not be completely fixed for all circumstances. If there is an MQT, then subsection (1) of the MQT statute, with which we have been occupied, tells us how much money is to be deemed to be available. That amount is the greatest amount that the trustees in any set of circumstances might have discretion to pay out to the beneficiary. Thus, if there is a peppercorn of discretion, then whatever is the most the beneficiary might under any state of affairs receive in the full exercise of that discretion is the amount that is counted as available for Medicaid eligibility.[18]

We are confirmed in this reading by something akin to legislative history: a consideration of the source from which the legislative language appears to have been taken. . . . Restatement (Second) of Trusts § 156 (1959) provides:

> Where the Settlor is a Beneficiary . . . (2) Where a person creates for his own benefit a trust for support or a discretionary trust, his transferee or creditors can reach the maximum amount which the trustee under the terms of the trust could pay to him or apply for his benefit.

The plaintiffs suggest that this provision was a likely model for the Congressional enactment, and a comparison of the purpose and the language of the provisions confirms their suggestion. Section 156 of the Restatement deals with a device, like the MQT, concocted for the purpose of having your cake and eating it too: the self-settled, spendthrift trust. Under such a trust, a grantor puts his assets in a trust of which he is the beneficiary, giving his trustee discretion to pay out monies to gratify his needs but limiting that discretion so that the trustee may not pay the grantor's debts. Thus, the grantor hopes to put the trust assets beyond the reach of his or her creditors. Like the MQT statute, § 156 defeats this unappetizing maneuver by providing that, even if those assets are sought to be shielded by the discretion of a trustee, or if the trust simply declares assets unavailable to creditors, the full amount of the monies that the trustee could in his or her discretion "under the terms of the trust" pay to the

---

[18] It is the requirement of that peppercorn of discretion that the 1993 amendment removes, providing that eligibility is to be measured by the maximum amount available under the trust under any circumstances, whether or not the trustee enjoys any discretion. . . .

grantor, is the amount available to the grantor and thus to his or her creditors. Not only the courts of this State, but those of many other jurisdictions have long followed this Restatement principle. See Ware v. Gulda, 331 Mass. 68, 70, 117 N.E.2d 137 (1954); Merchants Nat'l Bank v. Morrissey, 329 Mass. 601, 605, 109 N.E.2d 821 (1953). . .[19] We do not innovate here, nor do we see any reason to be the least bit squeamish about interpreting the analogous Federal statute in an analogous way to accomplish an analogously just result.[20]

III

We now proceed to apply these generalities to the specific cases before us.

1. *Cohen.* In June, 1983, the plaintiff established the Mary Ann Cohen Trust. She was the grantor and the sole lifetime beneficiary of the irrevocable trust. The trust provides that:

> The Trustees may, from time to time and at any time, distribute to or expend for the benefit of the beneficiary, so much of the principal and current or accumulated net income as the Trustees may in their sole discretion, determine. . . . The Trustees, however, shall have no authority whatsoever to make any payments to or for the benefit of any Beneficiary hereunder when the making of such payments shall result in the Beneficiary losing her eligibility for any public assistance or entitlement program of any kind whatever. It is the specific intent of the Grantor hereof that this Trust be used to supplement all such public assistance or entitlement programs and not defeat or destroy their availability to any beneficiary hereunder.

On October 27, 1993, Cohen was admitted to a nursing home. She applied for Medicaid on November 26, 1993. The division denied her application on January 11, 1994, and a welfare appeals referee affirmed the division's

---

[19] The plaintiffs argue that trust law supports their position and cite Randolph v. Roberts, 346 Mass. 578, 195 N.E.2d 72 (1964), and Pemberton v. Pemberton, 9 Mass. App. Ct. 9, 411 N.E.2d 1305 (1980). But these cases concerned trusts established by individuals for the benefit of another. When the trust is not a self-settled trust, the language of the trust, even to the extent of a spendthrift clause, is honored. See Randolph, supra at 579–580, 195 N.E.2d 72. The rule, however, is the opposite for self-settled trusts, see Ware v. Gulda, 331 Mass. 68, 70, 117 N.E.2d 137 (1954), and, as we have noted, the Medicaid statute only reaches trusts created by the grantor (or spouse). See 42 U.S.C. § 1396a(k)(2). See also Restatement (Second) Trusts § 156(2) & comment f (1959).

[20] The Restatement provides further analogies to the reading of the MQT statute we adopt here. Restatement (Second) of Trusts § 157(b) (1959) provides that in the case of a spendthrift trust or a trust for support—a genus of which the trusts in question here are a species—the beneficiary's interest is available to those who render necessary services or furnish necessary supplies to the beneficiary. Of course that is just what Medicaid does for the grantors in these cases. . . . Thus, trust attorneys are likely to be familiar with the notion that the law is anything but hospitable to arrangements such as an MQT that is designed to allow a beneficiary to have his cake and eat it too.

denial on March 10, 1994. A Superior Court judge affirmed the division's denial of her application.

This is the pure case of a trust with no other purpose than to defeat Medicaid ineligibility standards. The trustee has complete discretion to pay income, accumulated income, and principal to the settling beneficiary, save only that the trustee has no discretion to make any payments that may result in loss of public assistance. Since there is "under the terms of the trust" the discretion to pay to the beneficiary the full amount in the trust, then that is the amount deemed available to the beneficiary for the purpose of determining Medicaid eligibility. The judgment of the Superior Court is affirmed. . . .

3. *Walker.* On March 24, 1990, Walker created "The Clark Family Trust," an irrevocable trust of which her daughter is the trustee. Walker is the lifetime beneficiary of the trust and her three children are remainderpersons. The trust's principal is over $100,000.

Article two, paragraph A of the trust provides that the trustee "shall expend as much of the income and principal of the trust property as she in her sole discretion deems necessary for the comfortable maintenance of [Walker] subject to the restrictions contained in paragraph B of this Article." Paragraph B states:

> The Trustee is prohibited from spending sums of interest or principal to [Walker] for her benefit for services which are otherwise available under any public entitlement program of the United States of America, the Commonwealth of Massachusetts, or any political subdivision thereof. The exercise of a discretionary power to make a distribution for [Walker's] health care, which would result in trust assets being used in substitution of public entitlement benefits is a breach of the fiduciary duties imposed on the Trustees [sic] under this indenture.

In July, 1991, Walker entered a nursing home. She applied for Medicaid benefits on February 26, 1993, and the division denied Walker's application. On April 20, 1993, the division denied her appeal. On January 27, 1994, a Probate and Family Court judge pursuant to a petition for instructions issued a judgment declaring that the trust limits the trustee's discretion to distribute monies from the trust if doing so would cause Walker to become ineligible for Medicaid. Nevertheless, a Superior Court judge affirmed the division's decision.

Since the measure of the monies deemed available to the beneficiary under the terms of the trust is the amount the trustee under any circumstances has discretion to disburse, and since that discretion reaches the full amount of the principal and income, the division correctly ignored the limitation on the trustee's discretion and ruled that Walker was ineligible for Medicaid benefits. The judgment of the Superior Court is affirmed. . . .

NOTES

1. *Self-settled trusts.* There is no prohibition against creating a trust for one's own benefit; indeed, the revocable inter vivos trust, which is exceedingly popular these days, is a prime example of a self-settled trust. In most states, however, spendthrift provisions are ineffective against the settlor's creditors. See UTC § 505; Cal. Prob. Code § 15304; Tex. Prop. Code Ann. § 112.035(d); Restatement (Third) of Trusts § 58(2) (2003). Why should this be so? See Griswold, Spendthrift Trusts 644–45 (2d ed. 1947). In other words, the settlor's creditors can reach whatever interests the settlor has retained. If, for example, the settlor has retained only an income interest, creditors can reach only the settlor's income interest. If, on the other hand, the settlor has retained an unrestricted right to revoke the entire trust or an unrestricted presently exercisable power of appointment over all of the trust assets, creditors can reach the entire trust estate. When what the settlor has retained is the right to receive what the trustee in its discretion chooses to distribute, as in *Cohen,* creditors can reach the maximum amount that the trustee could properly distribute, notwithstanding the existence of other beneficiaries. See UTC § 505; Restatement (Third) of Trusts § 60 cmt. f (2003). So also, the courts have sometimes concluded that when the settlor has retained a *testamentary* general power of appointment, creditors could reach the entire trust estate. See, e.g., Phillips v. Moore, 690 S.E.2d 620 (Ga. 2010).

2. *Asset protection trusts.* Recently, a number of states, led by Alaska and Delaware, but also including Missouri, Nevada, Oklahoma, Rhode Island, South Dakota, and Utah, have enacted legislation that seems to allow effective spendthrift limitations even against certain types of claims of the *settlor's* own creditors. Why would a state enact such legislation? See Blattmachr & Hompesch, Alaska v. Delaware: Heavyweight Competition in New Trust Laws, Prob. & Prop., Jan./Feb. 1998, at 32; Hompesch, Rothschild & Blattmachr, Does the New Alaska Trusts Act Provide an Alternative to the Foreign Trust?, J. Asset Protection, July/Aug. 1997, at 9.

A number of countries (mostly small islands with unfamiliar names) permit self-settled trusts with enforceable spendthrift provisions. See Duckworth, The Trust Offshore, 32 Vand. J. Transnat'l L. 879 (1999); Marty–Nelson, Offshore Asset Protection Trusts: Having Your Cake and Eating It Too, 47 Rutgers L. Rev. 11 (1994). These countries have served for years as "safe havens" for wealthy foreigners concerned with protecting current assets against future debts. Examples are doctors and lawyers worried about future malpractice liability.

Whether it is good policy to permit such trusts is perhaps not yet fully settled. Both the UTC and the Restatement (Third) of Trusts adhere to the traditional view (see Note 1), under which such trusts are not permitted. For the opposing view, see Hirsch, Fear Not the Asset Protection Trust, 27 Cardozo L. Rev. 2685 (2006); Danforth, Rethinking the Law of Creditors' Rights in Trusts, 53 Hast. L.J. 287 (2002); Rothschild, Rubin & Blattmachr, Self-Settled Spendthrift Trusts: Should a Few Bad Apples Spoil the Bunch?, 32 Vand. J. Transnat'l L. 763 (1999). Just how successful such trusts will prove in insulating trust assets from the settlor's own creditors is also not clear. For a trio of cases in which it seems safe to say that the hoped-for protection did not fully pan out, see In re Lawrence, 279 F.3d 1294 (11th Cir. 2002); Federal Trade Comm'n v. Affordable Media, 179 F.3d 1228 (9th Cir. 1999); and In re Mortensen, 2011 WL 5025249 (Bankr. D. Alaska May 26, 2011).

3. *Medicaid planning.* As *Cohen* makes clear, the existence of a self-settled trust generally disqualifies its settlor from Medicaid benefits. See also Shaak v. Pennsylvania Dep't of Public Welfare, 747 A.2d 883 (Pa. 2000). Pursuant to 42 U.S.C. § 1396p(d)(4), it is possible to place certain assets (such as a personal injury recovery) in a self-settled trust without affecting the settlor's Medicaid qualification. Under the terms of the governing instrument, however, the state must be entitled to whatever remains of the trust property upon the death of the settlor-beneficiary, up to the value of the medical care the state has provided. See, e.g., Cal. Prob. Code §§ 3604, 3605; Department of Social Services v. Saunders, 724 A.2d 1093 (Conn. 1999); N.Y. EPTL § 7–1.12. These self-settled trusts are often referred to as "special needs trusts."

As *Cohen* also makes clear, trusts established by someone other than the institutionalized beneficiary need not interfere with Medicaid qualification, if properly designed. See Young v. Ohio Dep't of Human Serv., 668 N.E.2d 908 (Ohio 1996); Hecker v. Stark County Social Serv. Bd., 527 N.W.2d 226 (N.D.1994). Unfortunately, these third-party trusts are also often referred to as "special needs trusts."

See generally Krooks, Individuals With Special Needs, Tr. & Est., July 2011, at 30.

STATE STREET BANK AND TRUST COMPANY V. REISER

Appeals Court of Massachusetts, 1979.
7 Mass.App.Ct. 633, 389 N.E.2d 768.

KASS, JUSTICE.

State Street Bank and Trust Company (the bank) seeks to reach the assets of an inter vivos trust in order to pay a debt to the bank owed by the estate of the settlor of the trust. We conclude that the bank can do so. . . .

Wilfred A. Dunnebier created an inter vivos trust on September 30, 1971, with power to amend or revoke the trust and the right during his lifetime to direct the disposition of principal and income. He conveyed to the trust the capital stock of five closely held corporations. Immediately following execution of this trust, Dunnebier executed a will under which he left his residuary estate to the trust he had established.

About thirteen months later Dunnebier applied to the bank for a $75,000 working capital loan. A bank officer met with Dunnebier, examined a financial statement furnished by him and visited several single family home subdivisions which Dunnebier, or corporations he controlled, had built or were in the process of building. During their conversations, Dunnebier told the bank officer that he had controlling interests in the corporations which owned the most significant assets appearing on the financial statement. On the basis of what he saw of Dunnebier's work, recommendations from another bank, Dunnebier's borrowing history with the bank, and the general cut of Dunnebier's jib, the bank officer decided to make an unsecured loan to Dunnebier for the $75,000 he had asked for. To evidence this loan, Dunnebier, on November 1, 1972, signed a personal demand note to the order of the bank. The probate judge found that Dunnebier did not intend to defraud the bank or misrepresent his financial position by failing to call attention to the fact that he had placed the stock of his corporations in the trust.

Approximately four months after he borrowed this money Dunnebier died in an accident. His estate has insufficient assets to pay the entire indebtedness due the bank.

Under Article Fourteen of his inter vivos trust, Dunnebier's trustees " . . . may in their sole discretion pay from the principal and income of this Trust Estate any and all debts and expenses of administration of the Settlor's estate." The bank urges that, since the inter vivos trust was part of an estate plan in which the simultaneously executed will was an integrated document, the instruction in Dunnebier's will that his executor pay his debts[21] should be read into the trust instrument. This must have been Dunnebier's intent, goes the argument.

Leaving to one side whether the precatory language in the will could be read as mandatory, and whether the language of that separate, albeit related, instrument, constitutes a surrounding circumstance . . . which could guide us in interpreting the trust, we find the trust agreement manifests no such intent by Dunnebier. Article Fourteen speaks of the sole discretion of the trustees. Subparagraphs A and B of Article Five, by contrast, direct the trustees unconditionally to pay two $15,000 legacies provided for in Dunnebier's will if his estate has insufficient funds to do so. It is apparent that when Dunnebier wanted his trustees unqualifiedly to discharge his estate's obligations, he knew how to direct them. As to those matters which Dunnebier, as settlor, left to the sole discretion of his trustees, we are not free to substitute our judgment for theirs as to what is

---

[21] "It is my wish that all my just debts . . . be fully paid."

wise or most to our taste. The court will substitute its discretion only on those relatively rare occasions when it is necessary to prevent an abuse of discretion. Sylvester v. Newton, 321 Mass. 416, 421–422, 73 N.E.2d 585 (1947) . . . . Restatement (Second) of Trusts § 187 (1959) (see particularly comment [j], which says that where such adjectives as "absolute" or "un-limited" or "uncontrolled" modify the word "discretion" the trustees may act unreasonably, so long as not dishonestly or from a motive other than the accomplishment of the purposes of the trust). Here, the trustees could have considered preservation of the trust corpus for the benefit of the be-neficiaries as most consistent with the trust purpose.

During the lifetime of the settlor, to be sure, the bank would have had access to the assets of the trust. When a person creates for his own benefit a trust for support or a discretionary trust, his creditors can reach the maximum amount which the trustee, under the terms of the trust, could pay to him or apply for his benefit. Ware v. Gulda, 331 Mass. 68, 70, 117 N.E.2d 137 (1954). Restatement (Second) of Trusts § 156(2) (1959). This is so even if the trust contains spendthrift provisions. Pacific Natl. Bank v. Windram, 133 Mass. 175, 176–177 (1882). Merchants Natl. Bank v. Morrissey, 329 Mass. 601, 605, 109 N.E.2d 821 (1953). Restatement (Second) of Trusts § 156(1) (1959). Under the terms of Dunnebier's trust, all the income and principal were at his disposal while he lived.

We then face the question whether Dunnebier's death broke the vital chain. His powers to amend or revoke the trust, or to direct payments from it, obviously died with him, and the remainder interests of the bene-ficiaries of the trust became vested. The contingencies which might defeat those remainder interests could no longer occur. Greenwich Trust Co. v. Tyson, 129 Conn. 211, 225, 27 A.2d 166 (1942). In one jurisdiction, at least, it has been held that when the settlor of a revocable living trust dies, the property is no longer subject to his debts. Schofield v. Cleveland Trust Co., 135 Ohio St. 328, 334, 21 N.E.2d 119 (1939). See generally McGovern, The Payable on Death Account and Other Will Substitutes, 67 Nw. L. Rev. 7, 26–29 (1972). Cf. Griswold, Spendthrift Trusts § 475 (2d ed. 1947).

Traditionally the courts of this Commonwealth have always given full effect to inter vivos trusts, notwithstanding retention of powers to amend and revoke during life, even though this resulted in disinheritance of a spouse or children and nullified the policy which allows a spouse to waive the will and claim a statutory share, G.L. c. 191, § 15. See National Shawmut Bank of Boston v. Joy, 315 Mass. 457, 474–475, 53 N.E.2d 113 (1944); Kerwin v. Donaghy, 317 Mass. 559, 567, 59 N.E.2d 299 (1945); Ascher v. Cohen, 333 Mass. 397, 400, 131 N.E.2d 198 (1956). It might then be argued that a creditor ought to stand in no better position where, as here, the trust device was not employed in fraud of creditors.

There has developed, however, another thread of decisions which takes cognizance of, and gives effect to, the power which a person exercises in life over property. When a person has a general power of appointment, exercisable by will or by deed, and exercises that power, any property so appointed is, in equity, considered part of his assets and becomes available to his creditors in preference to the claims of his voluntary appointees or legatees. Clapp v. Ingraham, 126 Mass. 200, 202 (1879); Shattuck v. Burrage, 229 Mass. 448, 452, 118 N.E. 889 (1918); State St. Trust Co. v. Kissel, 302 Mass. 328, 333, 19 N.E.2d 25 (1939). . . . These decisions rest on the theory that as to property which a person could appoint to himself or his executors, the property could have been devoted to the payment of debts and, therefore, creditors have an equitable right to reach that property. It taxes the imagination to invent reasons why the same analysis and policy should not apply to trust property over which the settlor retains dominion at least as great as a power of appointment. The Restatement of Property has, in fact, translated the doctrine applicable to powers of appointment to trusts: "When a person transfers property in trust for himself for life and reserves a general power to appoint the remainder and creates no other beneficial interests which he cannot destroy by exercising the power, the property, though the power is unexercised, can be subjected to the payment of the claims of creditors of such person and claims against his estate to whatever extent other available property is insufficient for that purpose." Restatement of Property, § 328 (1940). . . .

As an estate planning vehicle, the inter vivos trust has become common currency. . . . Frequently, as Dunnebier did in the instant case, the settlor retains all the substantial incidents of ownership because access to the trust property is necessary or desirable as a matter of sound financial planning. Psychologically, the settlor thinks of the trust property as "his," as Dunnebier did when he took the bank's officer to visit the real estate owned by the corporation whose stock he had put in trust. . . . In other circumstances, persons place property in trust in order to obtain expert management of their assets, while retaining the power to invade principal and to amend and revoke the trust. It is excessive obeisance to the form in which property is held to prevent creditors from reaching property placed in trust under such terms. See Restatement of Property, § 328, Comment a (1940).

This view was adopted in United States v. Ritter, 558 F.2d 1165, 1167 (4th Cir.1977). In a concurring opinion in that case Judge Widener observed that it violates public policy for an individual to have an estate to live on, but not an estate to pay his debts with. . . . The Internal Revenue Code institutionalizes the concept that a settlor of a trust who retains administrative powers, power to revoke or power to control beneficial enjoyment "owns" that trust property and provides that it shall be included in the settlor's [gross] estate. I.R.C. §§ 2038 and 2041.

We hold, therefore, that where a person places property in trust and reserves the right to amend and revoke, or to direct disposition of principal and income, the settlor's creditors may, following the death of the settlor, reach in satisfaction of the settlor's debts to them, to the extent not satisfied by the settlor's estate, those assets owned by the trust over which the settlor had such control at the time of his death as would have enabled the settlor to use the trust assets for his own benefit. Assets which pour over into such a trust as a consequence of the settlor's death or after the settlor's death, over which the settlor did not have control during his life, are not subject to the reach of creditors since, as to those assets, the equitable principles do not apply which place assets subject to creditors' disposal.

The judgment is reversed, and a new judgment is to enter declaring that the assets owned by the trust . . . up to the time of Dunnebier's death can be reached and applied in satisfaction of a judgment entered in favor of the plaintiff against the estate of Dunnebier, to the extent assets of the estate are insufficient to satisfy such a judgment.

NOTES

1. *Creditors' rights in revocable trust assets. State Street Bank* differs from most of the other cases in this section, in that it does not involve the effectiveness of spendthrift language. It does, however, ask a related and extremely important question, i.e., whether it is possible to insulate assets from the claims of creditors after death simply by transferring them during life to a revocable trust. The assets a decedent owns at death make up his or her probate estate, and one of probate's central missions is to ensure payment of decedents' creditors. It seems perverse to expect that transferring assets to a trust over which the settlor retains a power of revocation would yield the opposite result; yet this seems to have been the traditional understanding. See Restatement (Second) of Trusts § 330, cmt. o (1959). *State Street Bank* is significant in that it unequivocally holds otherwise. To the same effect are UTC § 505(a)(3); Cal. Prob. Code § 19001; Estate of Nagel, 580 N.W.2d 810 (Iowa 1998); Commerce Bank v. Bolander, 239 P.3d 83 (Kan. App. 2007); and Restatement (Third) of Trusts § 25(2) & cmt. e (2003).

If *State Street Bank* and its ilk are sound, what are the implications for the "nonprobate revolution"? One of the primary reasons for probate's unpopularity is the delay it can entail. Yet the delay is in part the byproduct of procedures that have evolved over centuries to ensure orderly handling of creditors' claims. If the assets of revocable trusts are similarly subject to the claims of creditors, prudent trustees may find it necessary to investigate the existence and validity of claims against the settlor and postpone distributions to beneficiaries in the meantime. Over time, therefore, post mortem administration of revocable trusts may begin to look more like probate. Already, states are beginning to enact statutes, similar to probate non-claim provisions, detailing procedures for dealing with creditors' claims against revocable trust assets. See, e.g., UTC § 604; Cal. Prob. Code § 19003. See generally Blaustein & Ward, The Future of Revocable Intervivos Trusts: Are the Lines Between Wills and Trusts Blurring? Prob. & Prop., Sept./Oct. 1995, at 46; Kruse & Kent, Creditors' Rights in Probate Avoidance Trusts—A Model Statute, Prob. & Prop., Jan./Feb. 1995, at 61; Kruse, Revocable Trusts: Creditors' Rights After Settlor–Debtor's Death, Prob. & Prop., Nov./Dec. 1993, at 40.

2. *Other nonprobate assets.* The availability of nonprobate assets to a decedent's creditors currently varies widely from one type of asset to another. Statutes in many states exempt all or part of the proceeds of insurance policies on the life of a decedent, particularly when payable to certain close relatives. Similarly, real estate passing by right of survivorship has traditionally passed free of the claims of the creditors of the first co-owner to die. UPC § 6–102, on the other hand, permits creditors of a decedent to reach POD or joint bank accounts, but only if the probate estate is insufficient. Why do creditors' rights in nonprobate assets vary so widely? As the "nonprobate revolution" spreads, the pressure on this disorderly body of law will no doubt increase.

See generally Fisher, Creditors of a Joint Tenant: Is There a Lien After Death?, 99 W. Va. L. Rev. 637 (1997); McCouch, Will Substitutes Under the Revised Uniform Probate Code, 58 Brook. L. Rev. 1123 (1993); Effland, Rights of Creditors in Nonprobate Assets, 48 Mo. L. Rev. 431 (1983).

D. TERMINATION OF TRUSTS

1. TERMINATION PURSUANT TO THE TERMS OF THE TRUST

Most trusts terminate pursuant to their own terms. See UTC § 410(a); Restatement (Third) of Trusts § 61 (2003). Ordinarily, this is all quite unremarkable. For example, if the terms of the trust are "income to my surviving spouse for life, remainder to my children," the trust ordinarily terminates upon the death of the settlor's surviving spouse, whereupon the remainder becomes payable, after a reasonable period of time for the trustee to wind up administration, to the settlor's children.

Alternatively, a trust may end when one who has the power to revoke or terminate it exercises that power. See UTC § 410(a); Restatement (Third) of Trusts § 63 (2003). Many, perhaps most, trusts created these days are revocable by their settlors.

BARNETTE V. MCNULTY

Court of Appeals of Arizona, 1973.
21 Ariz.App. 127, 516 P.2d 583.

HOWARD, JUDGE.

The appellant-plaintiff in this case disputed the testamentary disposition by her deceased husband of certain property and contended that the property was her sole and separate property upon her husband's death by virtue of an inter vivos trust. This appeal was undertaken when the trial court disagreed with appellant's position and entered judgment in favor of appellee.

Appellant's questions for review revolve around three general areas: (1) Did the deceased create a valid inter vivos trust? (2) Did the deceased revoke the trust? (3) Did the court err in the admission of certain oral testimony?

. . . Appellant and her deceased husband, Wilson M. Barnette, were married on September 17, 1967. They took up residence at the home owned by appellant prior to their marriage. Mr. Barnette was the owner and operator of a moving and storage business incorporated as Van Pack of Arizona, Inc., and appellant was unemployed at the time of the marriage. Appellant was subsequently employed by the corporation and became secretary-treasurer. As such, she kept the books, made the deposits and acted generally as office manager. Her starting salary of $75 per week was raised to $125 per week, which continued until shortly after Mr. Barnette died. Prior to his death, appellant was removed as secretary-treasurer of the corporation even though she continued to receive a salary.

In early March of 1970, Mr. Barnette was hospitalized with high blood pressure and diabetes. On March 12th he executed a power of attorney to appellant so she could continue to run the business. In the spring of 1970, appellant discussed with Mr. Barnette a book that she had read written by a man called Dacey, entitled "How To Avoid Probate." They discussed the book and the creation of a "Dacey Trust" while Mr. Barnette was in the hospital and again when he came home. On March 25, 1970, Mr. Barnette executed a form contained in the book entitled "Declaration of Trust." In this declaration of trust Mr. Barnette declared himself to be the trustee of his shares of the capital stock of Van Pack of Arizona, Inc., for the use and benefit of the appellant. It also provided that upon Mr. Barnette's death, appellant was to be appointed as successor trustee—the successor trustee was to transfer all of his shares of the trust to the beneficiary. Another provision stated:

6. I hereby reserve unto myself the power and right at any time during my lifetime, before actual distribution to the beneficiary hereunder, to revoke in whole or in part or to amend the Trust hereby created without the necessity of obtaining the consent of the beneficiary and without giving notice to the beneficiary. Any one of the following acts shall be conclusive evidence of such revocation of this Trust:

(a) The delivery to the issuer or transfer agent of the shares by me of written notice that this Trust is revoked in whole or in part;

(b) the transfer by me of my right, title and interest in and to said Shares;

(c) the delivery by me to the issuer or transfer agent of the Shares of written notice of the death of the beneficiary hereunder. . . .

At the time of the execution of the trust document and up to the time of trial there was issued an outstanding certificate No. 6 dated February 18, 1968, for 201 shares of the capital stock of Van Pack of Arizona, Inc., in the name of Mr. Barnette. The stock was not transferred on the books of the corporation to Mr. Barnette as trustee nor was the assignment on the back of the stock certificate executed by Mr. Barnette.

In June of 1970, appellant became ill and it was not long before marital difficulties arose between the parties. Mr. Barnette filed a divorce action in Cochise County and appellant filed a divorce action on July 15, 1970, in Pima County. On July 9, 1970, Mr. Barnette consulted with his attorney, James F. McNulty, Jr., and discussed both his will and his marital problems. Mr. Barnette told Mr. McNulty that Van Pack of Arizona, Inc. was his corporation, that his efforts had created it, that it was separate property, that his wife owned no interest, and that he wanted his son to succeed to his interest. By Mr. Barnette's explicit direction the will drafted by Mr. McNulty and subsequently executed by Mr. Barnette specifically referred to the Van Pack Corporation as being owned solely by Mr. Barnette.

In July of 1970, Mr. Barnette consulted with Mr. Fred Talmadge, an attorney in Cochise County, concerning his domestic problems and as a result Mr. Talmadge filed on his behalf a divorce complaint in Cochise County on July 17, 1970. Mr. Talmadge testified that in his consultations leading up to the filing of the divorce complaint Mr. Barnette told him that the Van Pack Corporation belonged to him; that he understood the appellant might be filing for divorce herself and that he was sure she would attempt to take his interest in Van Pack from him, they were separated, he was keeping her on the corporation payroll as an employee because she was still his wife and he was under a legal obligation to support her whether he liked it or not.

Mr. Barnette died in the hospital on July 23, 1970 with appellant at his bedside.[22]

WAS A VALID TRUST CREATED?

The essential elements of a trust are: (a) A competent settlor and trustee; (b) clear and unequivocal intent to create a trust; (c) an ascertainable trust res and (d) sufficiently identifiable beneficiaries. Appellee contends that no trust was created in this instance because the settlor, Mr. Barnette, failed to have the stock transferred on the corporation books to himself as trustee and did not execute the assignment on the reverse side of the stock certificates. We do not agree with this contention. The owner of shares of stock in a corporation may make himself trustee of the shares for another by oral or written declaration of the trust without a delivery of any document to the beneficiary or any change in the corporation's records. . . . Where the settlor is also the trustee, Scott on Trusts, 3rd Ed. § 32.5 states:

> We have been considering the situation that arises when the owner of property conveys it to another person as Trustee. Where he declares himself Trustee of the property, however, it is obvious that the delivery of the subject matter to the beneficiary is neither necessary nor appropriate. Since his intention is to retain title to the property, although he is to hold it for the benefit of another, it is clear that it would be inconsistent with his intention for him to surrender the property.

Further, Restatement (Second) of Trusts, § 17 at 59 states: "A trust may be created by: (a) a declaration by the owner of property that he holds it as Trustee for another person; . . ." The comment on clause (a) states that "if the owner of property declares himself trustee of the property, a trust may be created without a transfer of title to the property." It is therefore clear that Mr. Barnette created a valid trust.

WAS THE TRUST REVOKED?

Appellant contends that the trust in this case was not revoked since Mr. Barnette did not attempt to revoke the same according to the mandate of the trust document. This contention is without merit. Although the trust provisions set forth certain acts which would be deemed conclusive evidence of revocation, they are by no means the exclusive

---

[22] Appellant did not deliver the trust instrument to the executor of the estate of her deceased husband because she did not remember that it existed until about a month after the death when she found it in her desk drawer.

ways in which the trust could be revoked by Mr. Barnette. Restatement (Second) of Trusts, § 330 comment i at 139, states:

> . . . If the settlor reserves a power to revoke the trust but does not specify any mode of revocation, the power can be exercised in any manner which sufficiently manifests the intention of the settlor to revoke the trust . . . It may be sufficient that he manifest his decision to revoke the trust by communicating it to the beneficiaries or to third parties. . . .

Turning our attention to the terms of the trust instrument we note that it gives the settlor the power to revoke without the necessity of obtaining the consent of and/or giving notice to the beneficiary. As set forth in Restatement (Second) of Trusts, § 330, comment i, the settlor can revoke a trust by communicating his decision to do so to the trustee. In the case sub judice, the settlor is also the trustee. It would be absurd to require the settlor to call himself up on the telephone as trustee and tell himself that he is revoking the trust. It would be equally absurd to have the settlor send himself a letter as trustee to inform himself as trustee that the trust is to be terminated. The appellee in this case merely had to show that Mr. Barnette intended to terminate the trust and some communication on his part to the beneficiary or to a third party manifesting his decision to revoke.

Since the trust instrument stated that revocation could occur only during the lifetime of the settlor and since the will he executed did not take effect during his lifetime, we cannot consider the provisions of the will as a revocation of the trust. Leahy v. Old Colony Trust Company, 326 Mass. 49, 93 N.E.2d 238 (1950) . . . . We do believe, however, that the statements made by the deceased to Mr. McNulty prior to the time the will was executed and to Mr. Talmadge, his attorney in the divorce action, manifested his decision to revoke the trust and support the judgment of the trial court.

Since one of the issues in this case was whether Mr. Barnette manifested an intent to revoke the trust by making oral declarations to a third person, appellant's contention that the court erred in allowing the appellee and attorney Fred Talmadge to testify as to what Mr. Barnette had told them about his ownership of the shares is without merit. The communications to appellee and Talmadge do not come within the rules relating to hearsay testimony. These communications were verbal facts to be proved as any other fact and therefore it was not error to permit such testimony. . . . Where a material issue was whether certain words were spoken without reference to their truth or falsity the evidence is admissible though it would otherwise be hearsay. . . .

Appellant contends that assuming the deceased intended to revoke the trust, he could only do so in writing. As authority for this proposition appellant cites Restatement (Second) of Trusts § 38(4). We find that appellant's reliance on that authority is inappropriate. That section of the Restatement deals with the creation of a trust and states that if the owner of property makes a written declaration of trust he cannot introduce parol evidence in the absence of grounds for rescission or reformation to show that he really did not intend to create a trust. The cited authority has nothing to do whatsoever with the method of revoking a written trust when it contains a reservation of the power to revoke but does not state how the revocation is to be effected. The apposite section of the Restatement is § 330 and comment i. See also Gifford Estate, 18 Pa. D. & C. 2d 769, 9 Fiduciary 631 (1959) which holds that where no method of revoking a revocable trust is set forth in the instrument the trust may be revoked informally and orally.

The judgment is affirmed.

NOTES

1. *Major change in default rule.* Restatement (Second) of Trusts § 330 (1959) provided that the settlor had the power to revoke the trust "if and to the extent that by the terms of the trust he reserved such a power" and that the settlor could not revoke the trust "if by the terms of the trust he did not reserve a power of revocation." In sharp contrast, UTC § 602(a) provides, "Unless the terms of a trust expressly provide that the trust is irrevocable, the settlor may revoke or amend the trust." This has long been the rule in California and Texas. See Cal. Prob. Code § 15400; Tex. Prop. Code Ann. § 112.051(a). The Third Restatement splits the difference: "If the settlor has failed expressly to provide whether the trust is subject to a retained power of revocation or amendment, the question is one of interpretation." Restatement (Third) of Trusts § 63(2) (2003). In commentary, the Third Restatement continues:

> Where the settlor has failed expressly to provide whether a trust is subject to revocation or amendment, if the settlor has retained no interest in the trust (other than by resulting trust . . .), it is rebuttably presumed that the settlor has no power to revoke or amend the trust. If, however, the settlor has failed expressly to provide whether the trust is revocable or amendable but has retained an interest in the trust (other than by resulting trust), the presumption is that the trust is revocable and amendable by the settlor. For these purposes, a power of appointment retained by the settlor (including a power of withdrawal . . .) is a retained interest. . . .

Id. cmt c.

2. *Formalities for revocation or amendment.* Unless the governing instrument provides otherwise, no particular formality is necessary to revoke a trust or to amend a trust instrument. Under the Second Restatement, all that was necessary was that the method chosen "sufficiently manifest" the settlor's intent. Restatement (Second) of Trusts §§ 330, cmt. i, 331, cmt. c (1959). Under the UTC and the Third Restatement, the method chosen must provide "clear and convincing evidence" of the settlor's intent. See UTC § 602(c)(2)(B); Restatement (Third) of Trusts § 63(3) (2003).

On the other hand, "[i]f the terms of the trust reserve to the settlor a power to revoke or amend the trust *exclusively* by a particular procedure, the settlor can exercise the power only by substantial compliance with the method prescribed." Id. cmt. i (emphasis in the original). See also UTC § 602(c)(1); Salem United Methodist Church v. Bottorff, 138 S.W.3d 788 (Mo. App. 2004) (terms of trust provided for revocation by written instrument; tearing out pages containing dispositive provisions did not revoke them); In re Reid Living Trust, 46 P.3d 188 (Okla. App. 2002) (trust instrument provided for amendment during settlor's lifetime by writing delivered to trustee; amendment delivered after settlor's death not effective); Estate of Tosh, 920 P.2d 1230 (Wash.App.1996) (terms of trust provided for amendment by written instrument delivered to trustee; substituting new page in revocable trust agreement, without more, did not effectively amend it). But see Paul v. Arvidson, 123 P.3d 808 (Okla. App. 2005) (conveyance of trust property to new trust effectively removed property from original trust; "when the grantor and the trustee are the same person, requiring strict compliance with formal delivery of written notice would be unnecessary and absurd"); Estate of Mueller, 933 S.W.2d 903 (Mo. App. 1996) (waiving requirement that trustee sign amendment, because trustee had actual notice of changes and acquiesced in them).

In Godley v. Valley View State Bank, 89 P.3d 595 (Kan. 2004), the terms of the trust permitted amendment by written instrument delivered to the trustee and required the trustee's consent as to any amendment changing the trustee's right or duties. The trustee refused to consent to an amendment delivered during the settlor's lifetime. The court held that the amendment was valid as to changes in dispositive provisions. Requiring trustee consent served only to protect the trustee, and not to limit the settlor's power to change the dispositive provisions.

3. *Revocation by will.* A valid, witnessed will can revoke a revocable trust if the terms of the trust are not to the contrary: "[T]he power [to revoke] can be exercised by a will or codicil that is executed after the creation of the trust and remains unrevoked at the settlor's death, and that refers expressly to the trust or the power or that otherwise clearly manifests the settlor-testator's intent to exercise the power." Restatement (Third) of Trusts § 63, cmt. h (2003). See also UTC § 602(c)(2)(A); Gardenhire v. Superior Court, 26 Cal.Rptr.3d 143 (App. 2005); Restatement (Third) of Property: Wills and Other Donative Transfers § 7.2, cmt. e (2003). But many cases have held that a

valid will did not revoke a revocable trust. Some reasoned that the power of revocation was exercisable only during the settlor's lifetime. See *Barnette*; Gabel v. Manetto, 427 A.2d 71 (N.J.Super.1981). Others found that revocation by will was inconsistent with the terms of the governing instrument. See Wright v. Rains, 106 S.W.3d 678 (Tenn. App. 2003); Matter of Estate of Sanders, 929 P.2d 153 (Kan.1996). See also In re Will of Tamplin, 48 P.3d 471 (Alaska 2002) (retroactive application of statute barring revocation by will).

4. *Oral revocation.* On the issue of whether it is possible orally to revoke a trust that owns real property, compare Coleman v. Coleman, 61 P.2d 441 (Ariz.1936), with Gabel v. Manetto, 427 A.2d 71 (N.J.Super.1981).

5. *Amendment.* The courts usually interpret a power of revocation as authorizing the settlor to amend the terms of the trust without first revoking the trust. See Restatement (Third) of Trusts § 63, cmt. g (2003).

6. *While the trust is revocable.* UTC § 603(a) provides: "While a trust is revocable [and the settlor has capacity to revoke the trust], rights of the beneficiaries are subject to the control of, and the duties of the trustee are owed exclusively to, the settlor." Thus, not only can the settlor of a revocable trust revoke or amend the trust, the settlor can consent to a breach of trust by the trustee, and thereby bind the beneficiaries, or unilaterally approve the trustee's account. See Linthicum v. Rudi, 148 P.3d 746 (Nev. 2006) (during settlor's lifetime, beneficiaries of revocable trust lacked standing to challenge amendment). UTC § 603(b) provides that while the power may be exercised, the holder of a power of withdrawal has rights similar to those of the settlor of a revocable trust, to the extent of the property subject to the power. On both points, Restatement (Third) of Trusts § 74 (2007) is to similar effect. Several states have modified the UTC provision so that the trustee's duties run exclusively to the settlor or power holder without regard to his or her capacity. See, e.g., Fla. Stat. Ann. § 736.0603; Ohio Rev. Code Ann. § 5806.03; 20 Pa. Cons. Stat. § 7753. Indeed, the bracketed portion of the UTC provision is now "optional."

In JP Morgan Chase Bank v. Longmeyer, 275 S.W.3d 697 (Ky. 2009), a former trustee informed the former beneficiaries of a previously revocable trust that the settlor had revoked it under questionable circumstances, executed a new will, and created a new trust with a new trustee and very different terms. After the settlor's death, the former beneficiaries contested the will, contending that both it and the revocation were the result of undue influence. After entering into a substantial settlement, the new trustee/executor sued the former trustee for breach of confidentiality in disclosing the changes. The court held that, in doing so, the former trustee fulfilled its duty to the former beneficiaries and violated no duty to the settlor. A strong dissent questioned the timing of the notification, which occurred not only after the former trustee decided to honor the revocation, but also after the new trustee terminated an investment agreement with the former trustee. Subsequently, the legislature amended Ky. Rev. Stat. Ann. § 386.715 to provide that the duties of the trustee of a revocable trust run only to the settlor as long as the trustee reasonably believes that the settlor still has the capacity to revoke.

See generally Foster, Trust Privacy, 93 Cornell L. Rev. 555 (2008); Newman, Revocable Trusts and the Law of Wills: An Imperfect Fit, 43 Real. Prop. Tr. & Est. L.J. 523 (2008); Gallanis, The Trustee's Duty to Inform, 85 N.C. L. Rev. 1595 (2007).

7. *Capacity to revoke or amend.* In Maimonides School v. Coles, 881 N.E.2d 778 (Mass. App. 2008), the court held that the capacity necessary to amend a revocable trust is the same as that necessary to execute a will, not the higher level necessary to make a contract. On a parallel track, both Restatement (Third) of Trusts § 11(2) (2003) and UTC § 402 cmt. provide that, in order to *create* a revocable trust, the settlor must have *testamentary* capacity.

8. *Multiple settlors.* For better or for worse, trusts sometimes have more than one settlor. Generally, the settlors are married; often, they live in community property states. If the trust is revocable, any number of questions may arise. May either settlor, acting alone, revoke or amend, or must they act jointly? After the death of one, may the survivor revoke or amend? Restatement (Third) of Trusts § 63, cmt. k (2003), offers thoughtful guidance. Certainly, the terms of the trust ought to provide answers, and if they do, they control. If not, each settlor may revoke or amend only as to the portion of the trust attributable to that settlor's contribution, regardless of whether the other has died. With respect to trusts funded with community property, the Restatement takes the position, again in the absence of answers in the governing instrument, that while both settlors are still alive, either may revoke, restoring the property to both of them as community property free of trust, but that joint action is necessary to amend. UTC § 602(b) is to similar effect. The cases, such as they are, often rely on language in the governing instrument that does not unambiguously answer the question. For an example of a case in which the court found that the surviving settlor could revoke or amend, see In re Cable Family Trust, 231 P.3d 108 (N.M. 2010). For the opposite result, see L'Argent v. Barnett Bank, 730 So. 2d 395 (Fla. App. 1999).

2. TERMINATION BY COMPLETION OF PURPOSE

FROST NATIONAL BANK OF SAN ANTONIO V. NEWTON

Supreme Court of Texas, 1977.
554 S.W.2d 149.

STEAKLEY, JUSTICE.

The Frost National Bank of San Antonio, Independent Executor of the will of Louise M. Cozby, deceased, and Trustee of the trust estate created in the will, brought this declaratory judgment suit to determine whether the trust estate created by Mrs. Cozby in her will should be terminated. The district court rendered a judgment terminating the trust, and the Court of Civil Appeals affirmed that judgment. See Frost National Bank of San Antonio v. Newton, 543 S.W.2d 196 (Tex.Civ.App.—Waco 1976). We reverse the judgments of the lower courts.

The will in question was drafted by Rexford Cozby, an attorney and the husband of the testatrix. Paragraph One appointed the Frost National Bank Independent Executor of the estate, Paragraph Two provided for certain specific bequests, and Paragraphs Three and Four provided for the creation and administration of the trust estate. Pertinent to the resolution of this case are the following provisions:

PARAGRAPH NUMBER THREE.

Trust Estate:

I hereby give, devise and bequeath unto the Frost National Bank of San Antonio, as Trustee, in trust for the following beneficiaries and for the uses and purposes hereinafter set forth, . . . all of the residue and remainder of my property and estate, . . . all of which property will be hereinafter referred to as the "Trust Estate," and is to be held, managed, controlled and disposed of by said Bank as Trustee, as hereinafter provided.

The said Trust . . . shall continue in force and effect during the remainder of the lifetime of the last survivor of the following named three beneficiaries, viz: Rexford S. Cozby, Karolen Newton and Louise Purvis, and shall terminate upon the date of death of the last survivor of said three last named beneficiaries. Provided, however, that said Trustee shall have the right, at its option, to sooner terminate said Trust in the event the income from the trust property shall hereafter cease to be sufficient in amount to justify the further continuance of such Trust, in the opinion of the Trustee. . . .

During the entire existence of the term of said Trust, the said Trustee is directed to pay, out of said Trust funds, to or for the use and benefit of the following named respective beneficiaries the following periodical payments:

One-third (1/3) of the net income from said Trust Estate shall be by said Trustee paid to my husband, Rexford S. Cozby, during the remainder of his lifetime; and the remaining two-thirds (2/3) of said net income from said Trust Estate (plus such portions of the principal thereof as the Trustee may deem necessary) shall be applied to the payment of the expenses incident to: (a)—The support and education through high school and college of my great-nephew, Warren S. Wilkinson, Jr., so long as he may attend and continue in school or college during the term of said Trust; and (b)—The support and education through college of my great-niece, Susan Arnette, so long as she may attend and continue in college during the term of said Trust; and (c)—The support and education through college of my great-niece, Karolen (Lyn) Wilkinson, so long as she may attend and continue in college during the term of said Trust; and (d)—If, as and when any one or more of said three student beneficiaries shall, during the term of said Trust, obtain a college degree, he or she shall be paid by said Trustee the sum of $1,000.00 in cash out of the interest or principal of said two-thirds (2/3) of said total Trust Estate, as a graduation present.

The payments of net income which are to be so paid by the Trustee to or for the use and benefit of the respective beneficiaries above named shall be so paid in monthly installments, or in such other periodical installments as the Trustee may determine, and the respective proportionate amounts of the principal payments to be so paid to or for the benefit of my said great-nephew and great-nieces for educational purposes, out of the said two-thirds (2/3) of the total net income from the entire Trust Estate, shall be left to the discretion of and shall be determined by the Trustee according to the needs of each of said three student beneficiaries, and need not be in equal proportions. Such payments may be made direct to said student beneficiaries, regardless of their minority, or may be made to any other person or persons for any such beneficiary's use and benefit.

If at any time during the term of said Trust the net income from said two-thirds (2/3) of said Trust Estate shall be insufficient to pay the expenses incident to a college education for said last named three beneficiaries, or any of them, then in such event the Trustee shall have the right to pay any excess amount needed for said purposes out of the principal of said two-thirds (2/3) share of said entire net Trust Estate; and in the event their said proportionate share of said net income shall be more than sufficient to pay for their college education as aforesaid, then any such excess amount thereof shall be by the Trustee, from time to time, paid in equal shares thereof to Louise Purvis and Karolen Newton at such times and in such installments as the Trustee may determine.

In the event of the death of my husband, Rexford S. Cozby, before the expiration of the term of said Trust, then his one-third (1/3) of the net income from the entire Trust Estate shall be thenceforth added to and become a part of the proportionate two-thirds (2/3) part of the net income from the Trust Estate which is hereinabove provided for the college education of my said great-nieces and great-nephew above named.

PARAGRAPH NUMBER FOUR.

Upon the final termination of said Trust Estate all of the property then comprising said Trust Estate, and all of the remainder and residue of my property and estate, if any, not hereinabove otherwise disposed of, I hereby give, devise and bequeath to the following named ultimate beneficiaries, in equal shares, an undivided one-half (1/2) to each, viz: Karolen Newton and Louise Purvis. If either one of said last named beneficiaries be not living at the time of the final termination of the Trust Estate above provided for, then the share of my estate which such deceased beneficiary would be otherwise entitled to receive if living, shall go to and vest in her then living children, in equal shares. . . .

The will was executed on August 25, 1965. Mrs. Cozby died in December 1967, her husband having predeceased her. All other beneficiaries of the will survived Mrs. Cozby. The Bank administered the trust as provided in the will, making the specified payments to the student beneficiaries and disbursing the excess income to Louise Purvis and Karolen Newton, the nieces of the testatrix. Warren Wilkinson, Jr., the last of the beneficiaries to be entitled to the educational benefits provided for in the trust, graduated from college in 1971 and received the stipulated one thousand dollars as a graduation present.

In 1974 the Bank brought this declaratory judgment suit to determine whether the trust had terminated upon the completion of the payments to the student beneficiaries or whether the trust remained in effect until the death of the last to survive of Karolen Newton and Louise Purvis. . . .

Karolen Newton, Louise Purvis, and their children entered into an agreement urging the court to terminate the trust and releasing the Bank from all responsibilities in connection with such termination. [T]he trial court rendered a judgment terminating the trust on the ground that, while the trust estate was sufficient in amount to justify its continuance, its primary purposes had been accomplished and fulfilled. . . . The court ordered the Bank to deliver the funds comprising the trust estate to the ultimate beneficiaries, Karolen Newton and Louise Purvis. The Court of Civil Appeals affirmed the trial court judgment, agreeing that the primary purposes of the trust had been accomplished and that its termination would not subvert the wishes of the testatrix.

The Bank and the guardian ad litem for the unborn and unadopted children of Karolen Newton and Louise Purvis here contend the lower courts erred in decreeing termination of the trust. They argue the language of the will is unambiguous and clearly states that, unless the Bank voluntarily terminates the trust due to insufficient income, the trust is to terminate only upon the death of the last to survive of Karolen Newton and Louise Purvis. Newton and Purvis, they assert, are "ultimate beneficiaries" only in the sense that they would be entitled to the corpus of the trust in the event the Bank terminated it because of insufficient income. Furthermore, according to the Bank and the guardian ad litem, the primary purposes of the trust have not been fulfilled because the provision for the payment of excess income to Karolen Newton and Louise Purvis is not incidental and is a continuing obligation of the Bank as trustee. The beneficiaries argue the two primary purposes of the trust have been accomplished and that therefore termination of the trust as decreed by the lower courts is proper and does not defeat the intent of the testatrix. . . .

Louise Cozby could not have stated more clearly her intention regarding the termination of the Trust. Paragraph Three of the will states:

> The said Trust . . . shall continue in force and effect during the remainder of the lifetime of the last survivor of the following named three beneficiaries, viz: Rexford S. Cozby; Karolen Newton and Louise Purvis, and shall terminate upon the date of death of the last survivor of said three last named beneficiaries.

The will then provides that the Frost National Bank, as trustee, could terminate the trust if in its opinion the income from the trust property was insufficient to justify the continuation of the trust. The trial court found the income of the trust was sufficient to justify the continued existence of the trust, and that finding is undisputed here. That being the case, it is clear the trust established under the will of Louise Cozby will terminate upon the death of the last to survive of Karolen Newton and Louise Purvis unless circumstances dictate an earlier termination due to insufficient income.

The beneficiaries assert that the payment of "excess income" to Karolen Newton and Louise Purvis is merely an incidental purpose of the trust and that, since the primary purposes of the trust have been accomplished, the trust can be terminated prior to the time specified in the will. See Alamo National Bank of San Antonio v. Daubert, 467 S.W.2d 555 (Tex.Civ.App.—Beaumont 1971, writ ref'd n.r.e.); G. Bogert, Trusts and Trustees § 1002 (2d ed. 1962). To accept such a contention would require a determination of what the testatrix considered to be the principal purposes of the trust and what she considered only incidental. Such a determination would take the court beyond the express language of the will into the realm of conjecture and speculation, for it is by no means clear that the provision for excess income distribution was merely an incidental purpose of the testatrix. It is consistent with the estate plan of Louise Cozby to infer that after the death of her husband and the education of the student beneficiaries, the trust was to continue in effect, with periodical payments of excess income to Karolen Newton and Louise Purvis, until the death of the last to survive of Purvis and Newton. In construing an unambiguous will, the cardinal rule is to give effect to the intentions of the testator or testatrix as they are expressed within the four corners of the instrument. . . . Absent an express declaration of purpose in the instrument, a court cannot go beyond the face of the will to make an ad hoc and speculative assessment of which purposes the trustor or testator considered "primary" and which he considered merely "incidental." Thus the trust established by Louise Cozby in her will cannot be judicially terminated on the ground that its primary purposes have been accomplished where, as in the instant case, the trust expressly provides for its termination upon the happening of specified events. To the extent Alamo National Bank of San Antonio v. Daubert, supra, is inconsistent with this opinion, it is disapproved. . . .

The judgments of the lower courts are reversed and judgment is here rendered that the trust remain in effect until the death of the last to survive of Karolen Newton and Louise Purvis or until the trustee, in its discretion, determines that the income of the trust is insufficient to justify its continuation. . . .

GREENHILL, CHIEF JUSTICE, dissenting.

I respectfully dissent.

The terms of Louise Cozby's will clearly indicate her primary purposes in establishing the trust estate were twofold: (1) to provide an income for life for Rexford Cozby in the event he survived the testatrix; and (2) to provide for the education of the three student beneficiaries, Warren Wilkinson, Jr., Susan Arnette and Karolen Wilkinson Dittmar. If Rexford Cozby died before the expiration of the term of the trust, as indeed he did, the proportion of the trust principal reserved for his use was to be aggregated with the proportionate share reserved for the students and the income generated thereby was to be used to defray their college expenses. If the income from the trust property was insufficient to pay the expenses of the student beneficiaries, the trustee was authorized to invade the trust principal in order to provide the funds necessary to cover the expenses. If, on the other hand, the income from the trust property exceeded that necessary to pay the educational expenses of the three designated beneficiaries, the trustee was authorized to distribute such excess to Louise Purvis and Karolen Newton in equal shares.

The first purpose of Louise Cozby in establishing the trust, the provision of income for her husband, was rendered impossible of performance by his death prior to the death of the testatrix. The second purpose, the provision of educational benefits for the great-nieces and great-nephew of Louise Cozby, was accomplished with the 1971 graduation from college of

Warren S. Wilkinson, Jr. In support of its judgment terminating the trust the trial court found the purposes of the trust had been accomplished. The Court of Civil Appeals concurred in this finding, specifying that at best the provision for the payment of excess income to Louise Purvis and Karolen Newton was an incidental or minor purpose of the trust.

The structure and terms of the will support these findings. The language of Paragraph Three directs the trustee to pay "to or for the use and benefit of the following named respective beneficiaries the following periodical payments . . ." The remainder of the sentence specifies the nature of the payments to be made to Rexford Cozby and to the student beneficiaries. It says nothing of the possible payments to Karolen Newton and Louise Purvis and does not, in this section of the will, refer to them as beneficiaries of the trust.

The succeeding paragraph directs the bank to make the payments to the beneficiaries "in monthly installments, or in such other periodical installments as the Trustee may determine." Again, there is no mention of the contingent payments to Purvis and Newton.

The next paragraph provides the only mention of the payments, and dictates that if the income is more than sufficient to cover the educational expenses, then and only then is the bank authorized to distribute the excess to Louise Purvis and Karolen Newton "from time to time, . . . at such times and in such installments as the Trustee may determine." The will mandates that any such excess income payments "shall" be made by the bank, but the frequency and amount of such payments are left to the discretion of the trustee. It is clear from these provisions that the testatrix did not intend to provide continuing, regular payments for Louise Purvis and Karolen Newton during the term of the trust, and that any benefits due them were an incidental and minor purpose of the trust. . . .

I would affirm the judgments of the trial court and the Court of Civil Appeals.

DANIEL and JOHNSON, JJ., join in this Dissent.

NOTES

1. *Termination by completion of purpose.* Similar in effect to the argument the beneficiaries made in *Frost National Bank* is N.Y. EPTL § 7–2.2, which states: "When the purpose for which an express trust is created ceases, the estate of the trustee also ceases." See also Restatement (Third) of Trusts § 61 (2003) ("termination will occur in whole or in part when the purposes(s) of the trust or severable portion thereof are accomplished"). One of the problems with any such formulation, however, is the assumption that a trust (or a portion thereof) may or must have only a definite (and presumably small) num-

ber of purposes. Instead, most trusts have several, or even numerous, purposes, not necessarily of equal importance, and rarely equally well articulated by the settlor. See Work v. Central National Bank & Trust Co., 151 N.W.2d 490 (Iowa 1967), which denied termination because a secondary purpose had not been accomplished.

2. *Impossibility.* Restatement (Third) of Trusts § 30 (2003) provides: "If all of the purposes for which a private trust is created are or become impossible of accomplishment, the trust will be terminated."

3. *Illegality.* Restatement (Third) of Trusts § 29(a) (2003) provides that an intended trust or trust provision is invalid if "its purpose is unlawful or its performance calls for the commission of a criminal or tortious act." The Restatement continues:

> In general, the fact that a trust purpose is not enforceable or that the settlor directs or suggests an unlawful means of performing a trust does not invalidate the trust if it has a substantial purpose that is valid and can be achieved by methods that are not unlawful. This is not the case, however, if the purpose or method directed is so essential to the settlor's objective(s) that the permissible and impermissible purposes cannot be separated.

Id. cmt. e.

4. *UTC formulation.* This is the way UTC § 410(a) puts it: "[A] trust terminates to the extent . . . no purpose of the trust remains to be achieved, or the purposes of the trust have become unlawful, contrary to public policy, or impossible to achieve."

3. TERMINATION BY CONSENT

IN RE BAYLEY TRUST

Supreme Court of Vermont, 1969.
127 Vt. 380, 250 A.2d 516.

HOLDEN, CHIEF JUSTICE.

This is an appeal by the trustee from an order of the probate court, directing partial termination of the testamentary trust established by Charles H. Bayley. Mr. Bayley, who resided at Newbury, Vermont, died January 28, 1928. His will was established and allowed by the probate court for the district of Bradford.

The testator bequeathed the residue of his estate to the First National Bank of Boston in trust. In substance, the will directed the trustee to pay one-half the annual gross income to Laura Morse Bayley, the surviving widow. Provided the widow received an annual net income of not less than $12,000, the remaining income was to be expended to certain specified relatives and to four annuitants for charitable uses—The First Congregational Church, the Tenney Memorial Library, the Ox–Bow Cemetery, all of Newbury, and the Mary Hitchcock Memorial Hospital of Hanover, New Hampshire.

The will provides that the "trust hereby created shall be terminated upon the death of the last surviving life beneficiary hereinbefore mentioned. . . ." Upon the termination of the trust, the trustee was directed to pay a bequest to the Mary Hitchcock Memorial Hospital and establish four separate trusts to continue the benefit of the charity specified above and provide income to be paid to the town for the maintenance of the Village Common and shade trees.

The will then follows:

> All the rest, residue and remainder of my estate, of every name and nature, both real and personal, of which I may die seised and possessed, or to which I may be entitled at the time of my decease, or which may fall into the said rest and residue of my estate, as hereinbefore provided, I give, devise and bequeath to the Museum of Fine Arts, located in said Boston, and its successors, the same to be held by it as a separate and permanent fund to be known as the "Charles H. Bayley Picture and Painting Fund," the income only to be expended in the purchase of pictures and paintings for said Museum of Fine Arts.

Mrs. Bayley died on February 7, 1963. Only two of the life beneficiaries are now living—Margaret C. Fabyan and Dorothy Chamberlin Robinson. Under the terms of the will, these annuitants receive $2,000 and $1,000 annually. With the income payable to the charities during the life of these beneficiaries, the total income distributed by the trustee is $5,500.

On December 31, 1966, the market value of the trust estate was $6,856,081.08. Since the death of Mrs. Bayley the trustee has accumulated more than $600,000 from income, beyond that required to pay the annuities, adding an average of $200,000 to the principal each year.

On October 21, 1966, all of the surviving beneficiaries under the will joined in an agreement to petition the probate court to terminate the trust as to that part of the estate which is not necessary to provide the income required for the annuities specified in the instrument. The agreement provides for setting aside sufficient funds to increase the annuity of Margaret C. Fabyan from $2,000 to $3,000, and that of Dorothy Chamberlin Robinson from $1,000 to $1,750 during their respective lives. The share to be distributed to the Mary Hitchcock Memorial Hospital is increased from $10,000 to $25,000. The separate trust estates for the benefit of each of the charities in Newbury are also enlarged to provide increased income to those beneficiaries. The agreement provides that upon the setting apart of these sums, the Trustee shall forthwith pay over, transfer and deliver the remainder of the residuary trust fund, held by it under the will, to the Museum to be received by it for the purposes set forth in the residuary clause of the will. Subject to these changes, the entire trust estate is to be distributed, as provided in the will, upon the termination of the trust at the death of the last surviving life beneficiary.

In accordance with its stipulation, the agreement of the beneficiaries was presented to the probate court for the district of Bradford by petition of the Museum of Fine Arts. The trustee and the attorney general of Vermont were cited before the court with the several beneficiaries. The case was submitted on agreed facts.

After hearing, the court determined that the trust created under the will of Charles H. Bayley was not a spendthrift trust. It was further determined that no lawful restriction imposed by the testator and no ascertainable purpose of his will would be nullified or disturbed by the court's approval of the agreement of the beneficiaries. The court found that the life expectancies of the living annuitants, Margaret C. Fabyan and Dorothy Chamberlin Robinson, as of July 31, 1968, were 9.63 and 9.15 [years] respectively.

Other findings of the court establish that since the death of the testator, particularly in the last ten years, the scarcity of paintings and pictures of high quality, desirable for acquisition, has been subject to extraordinary and continuing increase. The prices required to purchase such works of art will continue to increase in the foreseeable future. The purchasing power of the dollar has declined substantially since the death of the testator. The court also found that all parties to the proceedings will be substantially benefitted by carrying out the agreement of the beneficiaries and that this is especially true of the Museum of Fine Arts. The agreement will enable this beneficiary to purchase paintings and pictures of high quality at prevailing prices and before these works of art are permanently removed from the market. Upon these considerations, the probate court approved the agreement of the beneficiaries and issued its decree in substantial compliance with its terms.

In these proceedings the trustee, the First National Bank of Boston, has assumed the posture of a stakeholder, without urging either the adoption of the agreement or adherence to the literal terms of the Bayley will. To make certain that the decree issued by the probate court is effective and binding and insure proper performance of its duties under the trust, the trustee brings this appeal. . . .

The remaining question is whether [the probate court] had the legal authority to accelerate the operation of the residuary clause in the manner provided by the agreement of all the beneficiaries. We think it did.

The postponement of the distribution was principally designed to protect the interest of the testator's widow and, incidently, that of the surviving life beneficiaries. The provision that the widow is to receive one-half the annual income, but in no event less than $12,000, clearly indicates the testator did not foresee the bountiful accumulations that now prevail. However that may be, Mrs. Bayley is now deceased. The other life beneficiaries, who have survived, have agreed to the partial termination of the original trust and join the other beneficiaries to urge that the probate decree be affirmed. Their life interests are adequately secured. The design of the agreement and the scheme of the will are entirely compatible. In the present inflationary economy, the agreement promotes the objectives of the testator's bounty and is in no way discordant with his interest.

When all the beneficiaries of a trust desire to terminate it in part, they can compel that result unless the continuation of the entire trust estate is necessary to carry out a material purpose of the trust. Davis v. Goodman, 17 Del. Ch. 231, 152 A. 115, 117; Welch v. Trustees of Episcopal Theological School, 189 Mass. 108, 75 N.E. 139, 140; Ames v. Hall, 313 Mass. 33, 46 N.E.2d 403; Harlow v. Weld, R.I., 104 A. 832; Restatement, Trusts 2d § 337, comment p; Scott, Trusts (Third Ed.) § 337.8.

Continuation of the entire trust estate is not essential to the purpose of the trust. To the contrary, the facts presented demonstrate that partial termination and acceleration of the remaining trusts will serve the testator's ultimate objective and promote the interests of those he sought to protect by the postponement.

Decree affirmed.

NOTES

1. *General principles.* Restatement (Third) of Trusts § 65 (2003) is as follows:

§ 65. Termination or Modification by Consent of Beneficiaries

(1) Except as stated in Subsection (2), if all of the beneficiaries of an irrevocable trust consent, they can compel the termination or modification of the trust.

(2) If termination or modification of the trust under Subsection (1) would be inconsistent with a material purpose of the trust, the beneficiaries cannot compel its termination or modification except with the con-

sent of the settlor or, after the settlor's death, with authorization of the court if it determines that the reason(s) for termination or modification outweigh the material purpose.

UTC § 411 is to similar effect.

2. *Material purpose.* The doctrine that termination by consent is unavailable when it would frustrate a material purpose of the settlor derives from Claflin v. Claflin, 20 N.E. 454 (Mass.1889). The testator in *Claflin* left property in trust to be paid to his son in installments—$10,000 at age 21, $10,000 at age 25, and the balance at age 30. Prior to reaching age 30, the son sought to compel the trustees to distribute the trust property. The court refused, noting that "a testator has a right to dispose of his own property with such restrictions and limitations, not repugnant to law, as he sees fit, and . . . his intentions ought to be carried out, unless they contravene some positive rule of law, or are against public policy." Id. at 456.

Not all jurisdictions embrace the *Claflin* doctrine. In England, all the beneficiaries can compel termination, even if doing so defeats a material purpose of the settlor. See In re Courtourier, 1 Ch. 470 (1907); Saunders v. Vautier, 41 Eng. Rep. 482 (Ch. 1841). This may also be true in Missouri. See Hamerstrom v. Commerce Bank of Kansas City, 808 S.W.2d 434 (Mo.App.1991) (construing Mo. Rev. Stat. § 456.590(2)).

Sometimes it is easy to determine whether a given purpose is material. For example, the settlor's intent to provide for multiple beneficiaries in succession is not, alone, a material purpose. See Restatement (Third) of Trusts § 65, cmt. d (2003). Otherwise, termination by consent would almost never be available. In contrast, the settlor's intent to deny possession or enjoyment until a beneficiary attains a particular age almost always is a material purpose. See Estate of Bonardi, 871 A.2d 103 (N.J. App. 2005); *Claflin*, supra. As to other purposes, however, the answer is less clear. There is ample authority, for example, for the proposition that the settlor's intent to subject the beneficiaries' interests to spendthrift restrictions is a material purpose. See, e.g., In re Trust Under Will of Darby, 234 P.3d 793 (Kan. 2010); Restatement (Second) § 337, cmt. l (1959). Yet UTC § 411(c) (optional provision) and Restatement (Third) of Trusts § 65, cmt. e (2003), are to the contrary.

No doubt the difficulty of determining whether termination would be inconsistent with a material purpose limits the actual availability of termination by consent, in the absence of judicial approval. Nor is judicial approval always available. See, e.g., McEver v. First Union Bank of Rome, 383 S.E.2d 889 (Ga.1989); Estate of Brown, 528 A.2d 752 (Vt.1987).

See generally Alexander, The Dead Hand and the Law of Trusts in the Nineteenth Century, 37 Stan. L. Rev. 1189 (1985); Bird, Trust Termination: Unborn, Living, and Dead Hands—Too Many Fingers in the Trust Pie, 36 Hast. L.J. 563 (1985).

3. *Signifying consent.* Suppose that a beneficiary, who takes no position on a proposed termination, fails to object. Has the beneficiary consented for purposes of terminating the trust? See Sundquist v. Sundquist, 639 P.2d 181 (Utah 1981).

HATCH V. RIGGS NATIONAL BANK

United States Court of Appeals, District of Columbia Circuit, 1966.
361 F.2d 559.

LEVENTHAL, CIRCUIT JUDGE.

Appellant seeks in this action to obtain modification of a trust she created in 1923. The income terms of the trust instrument are of a spendthrift character, directing the trustees to pay to the settlor for life all the income from the trust estate "for her own use and benefit, without the power to her to anticipate, alienate or charge the same. . . ." Upon the death of the settlor-life tenant, the trustees are to pay over the corpus as the settlor may appoint by will; if she fails to exercise this testamentary power of appointment, the corpus is to go to "such of her next of kin . . . as by the law in force in the District of Columbia at the death of the . . . [settlor] shall be provided for in the distribution of an intestate's personal property therein." No power to appoint the corpus by deed, nor any power to revoke, alter, amend or modify the trust, was expressly retained by appellant, and the instrument states that she conveys the property to the trustees "irrevocably."

Appellant does not claim that the declaration of trust itself authorizes her to revoke or modify the trust. In effect she invokes the doctrine of worthier title, which teaches that a grant of trust corpus to the heirs of the settlor creates a reversion in the settlor rather than a remainder in his heirs. She claims that since she is the sole beneficiary of the trust under this doctrine, and is also the settlor, she may revoke or modify under accepted principles of trust law.

The District Court, while sympathizing with appellant's desire to obtain an additional stipend of $5000 a year, out of corpus, "to accommodate recently incurred expenses, and to live more nearly in accordance with her refined but yet modest tastes,"[23] [denied relief]. We affirm.

I

. . . The doctrine of worthier title had its origins in the feudal system which to a large extent molded the English common law which we inherited. In its common law form, the doctrine provided that a conveyance of

---

[23] . . . The District Court found that there was "no suggestion of extravagance" in appellant's way of life or in her request for additional funds. She now lives in a one-bedroom apartment in a modest residential section of Long Beach, California, and has no assets except limited jewelry, furniture, personal effects, and a medium-priced automobile.

land by a grantor with a limitation over to his own heirs resulted in a reversion in the grantor rather than creating a remainder interest in the heirs. It was a rule of law distinct from, though motivated largely by the same policies as, the Rule in Shelley's Case. Apparently the feudal overlord was entitled to certain valuable incidents when property held by one of his feoffees passed by "descent" to an heir rather than by "purchase" to a transferee. The doctrine of worthier title—whereby descent is deemed "worthier" than purchase—remained ensconced in English law, notwithstanding the passing of the feudal system, until abrogated by statute in 1833.[24]

The doctrine has survived in many American jurisdictions, with respect to inter vivos conveyances of both land and personalty, as a common law "rule of construction" rather than a "rule of law." In Doctor v. Hughes, 225 N.Y. 305, 122 N.E. 221 (1919), Judge Cardozo's landmark opinion reviewed the common-law history of the doctrine and concluded that its modern relevance was as a rule of construction, a rebuttable presumption that the grantor's likely intent, in referring to his own heirs, was to reserve a reversion in his estate rather than create a remainder interest in the heirs. Evidence might be introduced to show that the grantor really meant what he said when he spoke of creating a remainder in his heirs. "Even at common law," wrote Cardozo, "a distinction was taken between grants to the heirs as such, and grants where the reference to heirs was a mere *descriptio personarum*." But to overcome the presumption that a reversion rather than a remainder was intended, "the intention to work the transformation must be clearly expressed." 122 N.E. at 222.

In the decades that followed, the worthier title doctrine as a rule of construction with respect to inter vivos transfers won widespread acceptance.[25] The "modern" rationale for the rule is well stated in an opinion of the Supreme Court of California:

> It is said that where a person creates a life estate in himself with a gift over to his heirs he ordinarily intends the same thing as if he had given the property to his estate; that he does not intend to make a gift to any particular person but indicates only that upon his death the residue of the trust property shall be distributed according to the general laws governing succession; and that he does not intend to create in any persons an interest which would prevent him from exercising control over the beneficial interest. . . . Moreover, this rule of construction is in accord with the general policy in favor of the free

---

[24] 3 & 4 Wm. IV, ch. 106, § 3. For more detailed discussion of the evolution of the doctrine of worthier title at common law, see . . . Doctor v. Hughes, 225 N.Y. 305, 122 N.E. 221 (1919); In re Burchell's Estate, 299 N.Y. 351, 87 N.E.2d 293, 296 (1949).

[25] See Restatement, Property, § 314(1) (1940); Restatement (Second), Trusts, § 127 Comment b (1959). . . .

alienability of property, since its operation tends to make property more readily transferable.[26]

While the weight of authority, as just indicated, supports the retention of the doctrine of worthier title (unlike its common-law brother, the Rule in Shelley's Case) as a rule of construction, there has been substantial and increasing opposition to the doctrine.[27]

The views of the critics of the doctrine, which we find persuasive against its adoption, and borne out by the experience of the New York courts in the series of cases which have followed Doctor v. Hughes, supra, may be summarized as follows. The common-law reasons for the doctrine are as obsolete as those behind the Rule in Shelley's Case.[28] Retention of the doctrine as a rule of construction is pernicious in several respects.

First, it is questionable whether it accords with the intent of the average settlor. It is perhaps tempting to say that the settlor intended to create no beneficial interest in his heirs when he said "to myself for life, remainder to my heirs" when the question is revocation of the trust, or whether creditors of the settlor's heirs should be able to reach their interest. But the same result is far from appealing if the settlor-life beneficiary dies without revoking the trust and leaves a will which makes no provision for his heirs-at-law (whom he supposed to be taken care of by the trust). In short, while the dominant intent of most such trusts may well be to benefit the life tenant during his life, a subsidiary but nevertheless significant purpose of many such trusts may be to satisfy a natural desire to benefit one's heirs or next of kin. In the normal case an adult has a pretty good idea who his heirs will be at death, and probably means exactly what he says when he states in the trust instrument, "remainder to my heirs."

It is said that the cases in which such is the grantor's intent can be discerned by an examination into his intent; the presumption that a gift over to one's heirs creates a reversion can thereby be rebutted in appropriate cases. But the only repository of the settlor's intent, in most cases, will be the trust instrument itself. Nor would it be fruitful or conducive to orderly and prompt resolution of litigation to engage in searches for other sources of intent. In the typical case of this genre—a stark, unqualified "to myself for life, remainder to my heirs"—the instrument will send forth

---

[26] Bixby v. California Trust Co., 33 Cal. 2d 495, 202 P.2d 1018, 1019 (1949). . . .

[27] See, e.g., Simes, Fifty Years of Future Interests, 50 Harv. L. Rev. 749, 756 (1937). . . . A recent study of the subject by Professor Verrall of the University of California, under the auspices of the California Law Revision Commission, resulted in a strong condemnation of the doctrine. Verrall, The Doctrine of Worthier Title: A Questionable Rule of Construction, 6 U.C.L.A. L. Rev. 371 (1959).

[28] The Rule in Shelley's Case (1 Coke Rep. 104) has been abolished by statute in the District of Columbia. D.C. Code § 45–203 (1961 ed.).

no signals of contrary intent to overcome the presumption that only a reversion was intended. Yet this is precisely the class of cases in which settlors are likely to have intended to create beneficial interests in their heirs.

A lengthier document may send forth more signals, but they may well be murky. Where other indicia of intent can be discovered in the trust instrument, with the aid of ingenious counsel, the result, as the New York cases have demonstrated, is a shower of strained decisions difficult to reconcile with one another and generative of considerable confusion in the law.[29] After three decades of observing the New York courts administer the rule of construction announced in Doctor v. Hughes, supra, Professor Powell of Columbia observed that "there were literally scores of cases, many of which reached the Appellate Division, and no case involving a substantial sum could be fairly regarded as closed until its language and circumstances had been passed upon by the Court of Appeals. . . . This state of uncertainty was the product of changing an inflexible rule of law into a rule of construction."[30]

An excellent example of this confusion is the effect to be given the fact that, as in the case at bar, the settlor has reserved the power to defeat the heirs' interest by appointing the taker of the remainder by will. One might well think that the reservation of a power of appointment was an index of intent which buttressed the presumption of a reversion by demonstrating that the settlor did not wish to create firm interests or expectations among his heirs, but intended to retain control over the property. Most courts, including the New York Court of Appeals in its most recent pronouncement on the subject, have disagreed, albeit over the voice of dissent.[31] They have reasoned that the retention of the testamentary power of appointment confirms the intent to create a remainder in the heirs, since the settlor would not have retained the power had he not thought he was creating a remainder interest in the heirs.

We see no reason to plunge the District of Columbia into the ranks of those jurisdictions bogged in the morass of exploring, under the modern doctrine of worthier title, "the almost ephemeral qualities which go to prove the necessary intent."[32] The alleged benefit of effectuating intent must be balanced against the resulting volume of litigation and the diversity and difficulty of decision.[33] We are not persuaded that the policy of

---

[29] The New York cases are admirably summarized and discussed in Verrall, [supra], at 374–387.

[30] Powell, Cases on Future Interests 88 n.14 (3d ed. 1961).

[31] In re Burchell's Estate, 299 N.Y. 351, 361, 87 N.E.2d 293, 297 (1949). . . .

[32] In re Burchell's Estate, supra, 299 N.Y. at 361, 87 N.E.2d at 297 (1949).

[33] These results led Judge Fuld to call for "clarifying legislation." Dissent in In re Burchell's Estate, supra. . . .

upholding the intention of creators of trusts is best effectuated by such a rule of construction, with its accompanying uncertainty.

The rule we adopt, which treats the settlor's heirs like any other remaindermen, although possibly defeating the intention of some settlors, is overall, we think, an intent-effectuating rule. It contributes to certainty of written expression and conceptual integrity in the law of trusts. It allows heirs to take as remaindermen when so named, and promises less litigation, greater predictability, and easier drafting. These considerations are no small element of justice.

We hold, then, that the doctrine of worthier title is no part of the law of trusts in the District of Columbia, either as a rule of law or as a rule of construction. Any act or words of the settlor of a trust which would validly create a remainder interest in a named third party may create a valid remainder interest in the settlor's heirs. It follows that the District Court was correct in granting summary judgment for appellees in this case, since appellant's action is based on the theory that she was the sole beneficiary and hence could revoke the "irrevocable" trust she had created.

II

Appellant's invocation of worthier title was premised in part on the injustice alleged to result in many cases from holding such a trust irrevocable. The irrevocability was supposed to be riveted into the trust by the impossibility of obtaining consent to revocation from all the beneficiaries, since some of them are still unborn. Appellant's argument reflects a misunderstanding of the consequence of the judgment of the District Court.

It is hornbook law that any trust, no matter how "irrevocable" by its terms, may be revoked with the consent of the settlor and all beneficiaries.

The beneficiaries of the trust created by appellant are herself, as life tenant, and her heirs, as remaindermen. Her heirs, if determined as of the present time, are her two sisters. There is no assurance that they will in fact be the heirs who take the remainder under the trust; appellant might survive one or both. Yet their consent is necessary, we think, to revocation, since they are at least the persons who would be beneficiaries if the settlor died today.[34]

In addition, it is necessary to protect the interests of those additional persons, both living and unborn, who may, depending on circumstances, be members of the class of heirs at the time the corpus is distributed. We

---

[34] One of the sisters is not *sui juris*. In referring to her consent, we do not mean to exclude consent by her guardian ad litem.

think that upon an adequate showing, by the party petitioning to revoke or modify the trust, that those who are, so to speak, the heirs as of the present time consent to the modification, and that there is a reasonable possibility that the modification that has been proposed adequately protects the interests of those other persons who might be heirs at the time the corpus is to be distributed, the District Court may appoint a guardian ad litem to represent the interest of those additional persons.

Although the question has not been previously discussed by this court we think basic principles of trust law are in accord with appointment of a guardian ad litem to represent interests of unborn or unascertained beneficiaries, for purposes of consent to modification or revocation of a trust. This use of a guardian ad litem is not uncommon in other jurisdictions. In a number of states authority for such appointments is provided by statute.[35] These statutes reflect a broad sentiment of the approaches that are consistent with the Anglo–American system of law and adopted to promote the objective of justice. . . . Here we are certainly in a field where it is not inappropriate for courts to act without statutory foundation, as appears from the well-considered authority cited in the margin.[36] "Courts of justice as an incident of their jurisdiction have inherent power to appoint guardians ad litem."[37] The efficacy of a guardian ad litem appointed to protect the interests of unborn persons is no different whether he be appointed pursuant to statute or the court's inherent power. Given such protection, the equitable doctrine of representation embraces the flexibility, born of convenience and necessity, to act upon the interests of unborn contingent remaindermen to the same effect as if they had been *sui juris* and parties.

The use of guardians ad litem to represent interests of unborn and/or otherwise unascertainable beneficiaries of a trust seems to us wholly appropriate. Though the persons whose interests the guardian ad litem represents would be unascertainable as individuals, they are identifiable as a class and their interest, as such, recognizable.

The settlor seeking to revoke or modify the trust may supplement his appeal to equity with a quid pro quo offered to the heirs for their consent. In many cases it may well be consistent with or even in furtherance of the interest of the heirs to grant such consent. The case at bar provides a

---

[35] [See] Restatement, Property § 182, Comment e (1936). . . .

[36] Peoples Nat. Bank v. Barlow, 235 S.C. 488, 112 S.E.2d 396, 398–399 (1960). A few courts have held, to the contrary, that no guardian ad litem for the interests of unborn beneficiaries may be appointed in the absence of express statutory authorization. . . . The Restatement expressly takes no position as to whether the general power of equity, apart from statute, includes the power to appoint such a guardian. Restatement, Property, § 182, Comment e (1936).

[37] Mabry v. Scott, 51 Cal. App. 2d 245, 124 P.2d 659, 665, cert. denied 317 U.S. 670] (1942). See also Smith v. Lamb, 103 Ga. App. 157, 118 S.E.2d 924, 927 (1961) (power to appoint guardian ad litem an "incident of courts"); 27 Am. Jur., Infants § 120, pp. 840–41 ("The power to appoint a guardian ad litem is inherent in every court of justice."). . . .

good example. Here the interest of all heirs is contingent, since appellant can defeat their remainder by exercising her testamentary power of appointment. If the modification agreed upon not only increased the annual income of the life tenant but also transferred assets in trust for the benefit of the heirs, without any power of alteration in the settlor, the heirs' remainder interest would be secure, and accordingly more valuable than it is now. The pattern of such a modification is clearly available where the remaindermen of a trust are specific named persons, and, we think, should also be available where the remaindermen are recognizable as a class even though the members of the class are not now individually ascertainable.

Appellant, proceeding on a different theory, has not taken steps to obtain the consent of heirs. We think it important to make clear that, in rejecting the doctrine of worthier title, we do not mean to put settlors and life tenants of trusts in which the remaindermen are the settlor's heirs at an unwarranted disadvantage with respect to legitimate efforts to modify trust arrangements concluded largely for their own benefit. Our affirmance of the judgment for appellees is without prejudice to a future submission by appellant on such a basis.

Affirmed.

NOTES

1. *Subsequent history.* The settlor in *Hatch* followed the court's suggestion and obtained appointment of a guardian ad litem for her unborn heirs. Thereafter, the guardian ad litem and the settlor's presumptive heirs consented to a modification of the trust. The lower court approved the arrangement, over the trustee's objection that the court lacked statutory authority to appoint a guardian ad litem. Hatch v. Riggs Nat'l Bank, 284 F.Supp. 396 (D.D.C.1968) (Sirica, J.).

2. *When there is only one beneficiary.* When there is only one beneficiary who is adult and competent, he or she may compel termination of the trust if termination would not be inconsistent with a material purpose. When such a beneficiary is also the settlor, he or she may compel termination regardless of whether termination would be inconsistent with a material purpose. See Phillips v. Lowe, 639 S.W.2d 782 (Ky.1982); Matter of Harbaugh's Estate, 646 P.2d 498 (Kan.1982). Occasionally, however, the court shows signs of discomfort in following these rules. For example, in Johnson v. First Nat'l Bank of Jackson, 386 So.2d 1112 (Miss. 1980), the sole beneficiary of a trust was also its settlor. At the age of 25, she decided to terminate the trust and give everything to the Church of Scientology. The court held that she was entitled to do so:

> ... Johnson may not create a spendthrift trust for herself in this case, i.e., she may not place this money in trust to remove it from the

reach of her creditors. . . . Even if this Court were to determine that it would not be "in the best interest" of Johnson to terminate or revoke this trust, she may in effect revoke it herself. For example, she may borrow money equal to the amount of the money of the corpus of the trust, donate this amount to the Church of Scientology, and her creditors would then be able to proceed against the corpus of the trust. Our view is that, unless Johnson is determined judicially to be of unsound mind (which has not been done) under the general rule stated above, she has the right to revoke and terminate this trust and dispose of the money.

It may be said of this case that FNB and the chancellor made a noble effort to protect the appellant from herself, but we are unwilling to say that they have a legal right to do so. The mere fact that a person has done or attempted to do something with her money which is considered foolish by society is not sufficient reason for an equity court to invoke its power. [386 So.2d at 1115.]

3. *Virtual representation.* The traditional rule was that termination by consent was available only upon the consent of *all* of the beneficiaries. See, e.g., Matter of Schroll, 297 N.W.2d 282, 284 (Minn.1980) ("While the interests of unborn beneficiaries are contingent . . . , they may not be disregarded."). Thus, whenever there was *any* beneficiary who was incompetent, a minor, unborn, or unascertainable, termination by consent was not possible. Yet most trusts provide, at some point or another, for distribution among a group of relatives, variously described in class terminology. See Restatement (Third) of Trusts § 65, cmt. b (2003). So most trusts, at any given time, have at least one beneficiary who is either incompetent, a minor, unborn, or unascertainable. As a result, under the traditional rule, termination by consent was often not possible.

Over the last several decades, both the courts and the legislatures have struggled to make termination by consent more readily available, without too severely affecting the rights of beneficiaries whose consent is unavailable not because they do not agree, but because their consent is legally ineffective or it is impossible to ascertain their wishes. One option is to permit the appointment of a guardian ad litem to represent one or more beneficiaries. On this option, in addition to *Hatch*, see UTC § 305 (appointment of "representative"); Restatement (Third) of Trusts § 65, cmt. b (2003). Such appointments are, however, expensive, and it is sometimes difficult to obtain consent from a guardian ad litem. See generally Begleiter, The Guardian Ad Litem in Estate Proceedings, 20 Willamette L. Rev. 643 (1984).

Another option is simply to ignore certain types of beneficiaries. N.Y. EPTL § 7–1.9, as interpreted, dispenses with the need to obtain the consent of unborn beneficiaries for trust termination. See, e.g., Application of Roth, 423 N.Y.S.2d 25 (App. Div. 1979).

Perhaps the most promising, and certainly the most flexible, option is virtual representation. The notion is that there may be someone adult and competent who can appropriately give or withhold consent on behalf of an incompetent, minor, unborn, or unascertainable beneficiary. For example, UTC § 303 permits conservators and guardians to consent on behalf of their wards. If a minor or unborn child has no such fiduciary, UTC § 303 permits a parent to consent on the child's behalf. The rationale is that the representative's fiduciary obligations or parental instincts will adequately protect the beneficiary's interests. UTC § 304 permits a beneficiary who has a "substantially identical interest" to consent on behalf of an incompetent, minor, unborn, or unascertainable beneficiary. Here, the rationale is that if a beneficiary who is adult and competent is willing to consent on his or her own behalf, it is likely that any other similarly situated beneficiary would reach the same conclusion. In addition, UTC § 302 permits the holder of a general testamentary power of appointment to represent anyone whose interest is subject to the power. In each of these cases the UTC requires that there be no conflict of interest between the representative and the person represented. Compare N.Y. SCPA § 315. See generally Begleiter, Serve the Cheerleader–Serve the World, 43 Real Prop. Tr. & Est. L.J. 311 (2008).

4. *Trusts that produce insufficient income. Hatch* illustrates an all-too-common problem: the trust that does not produce enough income to support the income beneficiary. N.Y. EPTL § 7–1.6 was enacted to allow limited invasions of principal in certain circumstances, but it is a poor substitute for language in the governing instrument authorizing the trustee to invade principal for the benefit of the income beneficiary when appropriate.

5. *Doctrine of worthier title.* UPC § 2–710 provides:

The doctrine of worthier title is abolished as a rule of law and as a rule of construction. Language in a governing instrument describing the beneficiaries of a disposition as the transferor's "heirs," "heirs at law," "next of kin," "distributees," "relatives," or "family," or language of similar import, does not create or presumptively create a reversionary interest in the transferor.

Most states have abolished the doctrine of worthier title. See 2 Scott and Ascher on Trusts § 12.14.1.

E. THE STATUTE OF FRAUDS; CONSTRUCTIVE AND RESULTING TRUSTS

Many states follow the English Statute of Frauds in requiring that express trusts of land, but not express trusts of personal property, be in writing. There is, however, no requirement that either a constructive or a resulting trust be in writing. Indeed, the original Statute of Frauds itself was expressly inapplicable to these trusts, which are created by operation of law. See generally 1 Scott and Ascher on Trusts §§ 6.1 to 6.15.

1. ORAL TRUSTS

FAIRCHILD V. RASDALL

Supreme Court of Wisconsin, 1859.
9 Wis. 379.

PAINE, J. This suit was brought by the plaintiffs as administrator and administratrix of the estate of Abel Rasdall, deceased, to enjoin the defendant from proceeding in a suit to recover possession of certain real estate in the city of Madison, and to compel a conveyance by him to the plaintiffs. The grounds set forth for relief are that the plaintiffs' intestate, having in a personal encounter in 1843, dangerously wounded a man named Smith, and being apprehensive of arrest and prosecution, and desirous to so arrange his affairs that he might escape from the country, conveyed the property in question to the defendant, who was his brother; and that although the deed was absolute on its face, and purported to be for the consideration of $2,000, yet that it was without consideration, and that the defendant agreed to hold the property in trust, for the use and benefit of the deceased and his heirs. . . .

We have no doubt, from the evidence presented, that the conveyance was made by the deceased under the circumstances, and with the understanding set forth in the bill, though this is denied by the answer. And were this evidence proper to be received, it would fully sustain the decision of the court below. But it was parol evidence, and was all objected to by the defendant's counsel, and the objection is fatal.

It is one of those cases where the real merits and justice of the matter create a strong desire to escape from the application of the stern rule of law, which prohibits an inquiry by means of parol evidence. But the barrier is too strong to be broken over; and while it restrains us, furnishes its own justification in the fact, that though, in individual instances like the present, it may work hardship, yet in the main it promotes private security and the general good.

We do not feel called upon to cite authorities, to show that in the absence of fraud, accident, or mistake, parol evidence cannot be received to prove that a deed, absolute on its face, was given in trust for the benefit of the grantor; and we have not been able to find anything in this case to make it an exception. We cannot see why, if this evidence is to be received to establish this trust, every other deed in the state may not be shown by parol to have been given upon trust, and the statute of frauds be entirely annulled.

But the counsel for the complainants, seeming conscious of the difficulty of sustaining the admissibility of this evidence for the purpose of establishing the trust, yet contended that although inadmissible for that purpose directly, it should be admitted, and the relief granted, on the ground of fraud. This presents a question of very great importance, and in view of the authorities on the subject, of no little difficulty. There is no doubt that if any fraud had been alleged, by means of which the defendant procured the conveyance from his brother to himself, or any mistake, by which the instrument was made absolute, instead of expressing the trust intended, parol evidence would have been admissible to show such fraud or mistake. This conveyance would thus stand upon the same footing with all other contracts, and come within the conceded power of courts of equity to inquire, by parol evidence, into frauds or mistakes in their procurement or execution.

But no such fraud or mistake is alleged here. On the contrary, it appears from the whole tenor of the complaint, that the conveyance was made by Abel Rasdall, upon his own motion, and without any solicitation or instigation of the defendant, and that it was intended to be, as it is, absolute on its face.

The only fraud alleged, therefore, is that of the defendant's now claiming the property in violation of the parol trust, and whether that constitutes such a fraud, as will justify a court of equity in overturning the written contract of the parties upon parol evidence, is the question presented.

It cannot be denied that if the court can, by any legal means, arrive at the existence of the parol trust, then the violation of it by the defendant, in wresting their inheritance from the family of his dead brother, is most grossly fraudulent. And to avoid such injustice, courts of equity have frequently seized upon the slightest circumstances connected with the procurement of the conveyance, to avoid the operation of the statute of frauds. And there are cases, the principle of which would warrant the assertion that the attempt by the defendant to claim the rights which this deed, on its face, gives him, contrary to the parol trust, is such a fraud as would justify the relief upon parol evidence. But I confess my inability to see how, upon principle, this position can be sustained, consistently with a due observance of the statute. Placing the relief in such cases upon the ground of fraud, is implied by admitting that the parol evidence cannot be admitted to establish the trust, for the purpose of enforcing it, directly as a trust. And this is also expressly admitted. But it seems apparent to my mind that to say, in such a case, it shall be admitted to establish the fraud, is equally a violation of the statute. Because the fraud consists only in the refusal to execute the trust. The court, therefore, cannot say that there is a fraud, without first saying that there is a trust. And the parol evidence, if admitted, must be admitted to establish the trust, in order that the court may charge the party with fraud in setting up his claim against it. Conceding then, that they cannot execute the trust directly in such case, because it cannot be proved by parol, is it not a mere evasion of the statute to say that they will allow it to be proved by parol for the purpose of enforcing it indirectly, by charging the party with fraud for refusing to execute it? Such a course does not relieve the court from the charge of violating the statute, but subjects it to the odium of an attempted, but unsuccessful evasion.

It may be said that fraud ought not to be tolerated. That is very true, but that is not the question. The question is, whether the court, without violating the law, can get at the fraud. There is no doubt that trusts ought to be enforced; but that is not a sufficient reason for admitting parol evidence to establish them. When the party offers this, the court says no; the law forbids it.

So, however desirable it may be to prevent fraud, if the fraud cannot be established, except by first showing a trust by parol, is not the same answer equally applicable? If not, it is difficult to see that the statute of frauds is to have any practical effect; for although trusts and agreements contrary to the written contracts of parties, cannot be proved by parol so as to be enforced as such, yet they may be proved and held of sufficient force to charge the party with fraud in not observing them. And the result is practically the same. It is for courts to say to the parties, "These agreements are not valid, not binding; we cannot compel you to observe them; yet if you do not observe them without being compelled, we will hold that to be a fraud on your part, and for the fraud, will compel you to execute them."

It is impossible to reconcile with principle very many of the adjudications upon the statute of frauds. Courts seem to have been so intent upon administering justice in the particular case, that they have frequently lost sight of its provision, and their action has often amounted to little less than the exercise of the right to repeal, or suspend its operation whenever they deemed that the real justice of the case required it. But the progress of adjudication upon the subject has been marked by many strong protests against the wide departure from principle, and the regrets expressed by courts that it had ever obtained. And the current of modern authority is in favor of returning to the due observance of the provisions of this law, according to their obvious intent.

But the distinction between fraud in procuring a conveyance, and that which arises only from the refusal to execute a parol trust or agreement, connected with a conveyance obtained without fraud, is not only clear upon principle, but is not without sanction. . . .

In the cases of Dean v. Dean et al., 6 Conn., 284; Bandor v. Snyder, 5 Barb. S.C. Rep., 63; Lathrop v. Hoyt, 7 id., 59, and other similar cases which might be cited, the hardship of enforcing the statute was equally great as in this case, and in some of them the courts expressed their willingness to escape from its application if possible. But there was no suggestion that the mere refusal of the defendants to execute the parol trusts, was such a fraud as would take the case out of its provisions. . . .

[W]e must hold that as the deed was made absolute to the defendant without any mistake, or fraud on his part, his mere refusal to perform the trust, is not such a fraud as will justify the admission of parol evidence, and the enforcement of the trust. The reason is, that the law forbids us to be informed that there was a trust by that kind of evidence. It may and does undoubtedly work hardship in this case, and that we regret; but if parties will, in face of the positive provisions of the statute, risk their interests upon the honor or justice of others, and the security fails them, they have no right to ask courts to violate the law to furnish relief. . . .

We are compelled, therefore, upon the whole case, to reverse the judgment of the court below, and direct a decree to be entered dismissing the complaint. At the same time we may express the hope that the defendant's conscience, to which his brother has trusted, may not suffer him so far to violate that trust, as to detain their just inheritance from his wife and children.

NOTES

1. *Constructive trusts and the Statute of Frauds. Fairchild* starkly poses the conflict between the policy of the Statute of Frauds and the policy against dishonesty. In most cases, the only evidence of unfair dealing is the oral promise to hold the property in trust, proof of which the Statute of Frauds forbids. See, e.g., Troutman v. Troutman, 676 S.E.2d 787 (Ga. App. 2009).

The English courts have had little trouble dealing with the conflict. They have long been willing to decree a reconveyance from the grantee to the grantor if the grantee, without more, fails to keep an oral promise to hold for, or reconvey to, the grantor. They theorize that the grantee is a constructive (not express) trustee for the grantor, and the Statute of Frauds is expressly inapplicable to constructive trusts. See Haigh v. Kaye, L.R. 7 Ch. App. C. 469 (Ch. 1872); Davies v. Otty, 35 Beav. 208 (Ch. 1865) ("I am of the opinion that it is not honest to keep the land.").

In the United States the courts have traditionally been less ready—at least in theory—to gut the Statute of Frauds. But they have fashioned a number of "exceptions." For example, if there is fraud in the procurement of title to land, American courts readily find a constructive trust. See, e.g., Rajanna v. KRR Investments, Inc., 810 S.W.2d 548 (Mo.App.1991); Guy v. Guy, 411 S.E.2d 403 (N.C.App.1991). American courts are also generally willing to find a constructive trust when there is a confidential relationship between the transferor and the transferee. See, e.g., Baizley v. Baizley, 734 A.2d 1117 (Me. 1999) (grandmother and grandson); Alvarez v. Coleman, 642 So.2d 361

(Miss.1994); Zanakis v. Zanakis, 629 So.2d 181 (Fla.App.1993); Sinclair v. Purdy, 139 N.E. 255 (N.Y.1923) ("Here was a man transferring to his sister the only property he had in the world. He was transferring it in obedience to advice that embarrassment would be avoided if he put it in her name. He was doing this, as she admits, in reliance upon her honor.").

2. *Restatement (Third) of Trusts.* Restatement (Third) of Trusts § 24 (2003) offers the following summary:

§ 24. Result of Noncompliance with Statute of Frauds

(1) Where a property owner creates an oral inter vivos trust for which a statute of frauds requires a writing, the trustee

(a) can properly perform the intended express trust, or

(b) can be compelled to perform the intended express trust if it later becomes enforceable on the basis of part performance.

(2) Where an owner of property transfers it to another upon an inter vivos trust for which a statute of frauds requires a writing, but no writing is properly signed (§ 23) evidencing the intended trust (§ 22), and the transferee refuses and cannot be compelled to perform it as an express trust under Clause (b) of Subsection (1), the transferee holds upon a constructive trust for the intended beneficiaries and purposes if

(a) the transfer was procured by fraud, undue influence, or duress, or

(b) the transferee at the time of the transfer was in a confidential relation to the transferor.

(3) Where an owner of property transfers it to another upon an inter vivos trust for which a statute of frauds requires a writing, but no writing is properly signed (§ 23) evidencing the intended trust (§ 22) and the rule of Subsection (2) does not apply, and the transferee refuses and cannot be compelled under Clause (b) of Subsection (1) to perform the intended express trust, the transferee can be compelled to hold the property either upon resulting trust or upon constructive trust for the transferor, except when the transferor is incompetent or dead and a constructive trust for the intended beneficiaries and purposes is necessary as a means of preventing unjust enrichment of successors in interest of the transferor.

(4) Where an owner of property orally declares a trust that is unenforceable because of a statute of frauds and cannot be compelled to perform the trust under Clause (b) of Subsection (1), the declarant holds the property free of enforceable trust, except when the declarant is incompetent or dead and a constructive trust for the intended beneficiaries and

purposes is necessary as a means of preventing unjust enrichment of successors in interest of the declarant.

In certain respects, the Restatement position is more lenient than the traditional American rule. Under it, how would you resolve the principal case?

2. CONSTRUCTIVE TRUSTS AND UNJUST ENRICHMENT

Our concern with the constructive trust in the previous subsection was with its use as a device for effectuating oral express trusts that would otherwise fail under the Statute of Frauds. But the constructive trust is not a true trust; instead, it is a remedial device available to prevent unjust enrichment in a wide variety of situations, most of which do not involve express trusts.

SULLIVAN V. ROONEY
Supreme Judicial Court of Massachusetts, 1989.
404 Mass. 160, 533 N.E.2d 1372.

WILKINS, JUSTICE.

This case is another, in what appears likely to be an increasing number of cases, concerned with unraveling the property interests of two unmarried people who became disaffected after living together for a long time as if husband and wife. Here, we conclude that the defendant holds a one-half interest in residential premises in Reading in constructive trust for the plaintiff. We thus affirm the judgment entered in the Probate and Family Court directing the defendant to convey the premises to the plaintiff and himself as tenants in common.

We recite the facts from the judge's findings, supplemented in certain respects by the defendant's testimony and by testimony of the plaintiff, to whose truthfulness the defendant admitted at trial. The parties had had a thirteen or fourteen-year relationship, during seven of which they lived together and were engaged to be married at some indefinite future date. The plaintiff gave up her position as a flight attendant in order to maintain a home for the defendant. In 1977, while they were living in an apartment in Medford, they discussed buying a house, and, after some months of searching, they settled on purchasing the Reading home of the defendant's sister and her husband. Each thought of the transaction as a joint purchase of a home that would belong to both of them. On the way to the Registry of Deeds for the passing of papers, the defendant told the plaintiff that, in order to get 100% Veterans' Administration financing, he would have to take title in his name alone. The deed was so recorded.

The parties lived together in the Reading house from January, 1978, to December, 1980, when the defendant, a career army officer who had been admitted to the bar of the Commonwealth, was transferred to Washington, D.C. While living in Reading, the defendant worked full-time during the day as an R.O.T.C. instructor and attended law school at night. He paid the mortgage obligations, taxes, utilities, and insurance on the house. The plaintiff, a waitress, put all her earnings and savings into the house, paying for the food and household supplies and for much of the furniture. She did all the housework, the decorating, and the entertaining of the defendant's colleagues. The defendant promised at various times to place the property in joint ownership, but he never did.

In June, 1982, the plaintiff agreed, on the defendant's urging, to join the defendant in the Washington, D.C. area, where again she kept house while he paid their expenses. The defendant told the plaintiff that they should rent out the Reading house rather than sell it, so they would have a home to go back to in a few years and to which they could retire. After a year, the plaintiff, unhappy in Virginia, moved back to Massachusetts. The relationship deteriorated, and the two separated in late 1983. The plaintiff wished to move back into what she considered her home, the house in Reading, but the defendant told her she could not because it was rented.

In 1984, the plaintiff brought this action to obtain title to the house as tenant in common with the defendant. The judge found that the defendant had promised to convey joint title at the time of the purchase, that he had reiterated that promise on several occasions up through early 1984 (when he told the plaintiff to send him a deed to sign), and that he admitted to having made these promises. The judge further found that, in reliance on these promises, the plaintiff was induced to stay in the relationship, to contribute her earnings and services, and to give up her home to move to Virginia. The judge also found that the plaintiff had made these contributions to her detriment, because she gave up her position as a flight attendant and lost career opportunities and job benefits. The judge ruled that the defendant would be unjustly enriched if he were allowed to keep sole title to the house. The judgment ordered the defendant to convey to the plaintiff a half-interest in the house. We transferred the defendant's appeal here.

We are unable to identify the principle of law on which the judge relied in awarding the plaintiff a tenancy in common in the Reading property. The judge's rulings of law speak of compensation for services and "a quantum meruit theory." Even if we were to recognize that the plaintiff was entitled to recover the fair value of her services, without offsetting the value of her services against the fair value of the defendant's contributions during their relationship, there are no findings, nor any evidence that would warrant findings, concerning the fair value of the plaintiff's services or the fair value of one-half of the equity in the Reading property at the time of the trial.

The plaintiff argues here that the defendant's oral promises to give her one-half the property are enforceable in the circumstances despite the defendant's reliance on the Statute of Frauds, and, alternatively, that the defendant holds one-half the property on a constructive trust in favor of the plaintiff. We accept the plaintiff's argument that the evidence and the judge's findings demonstrate that the judgment should be upheld on the theory of a constructive trust.[38]

The judge's unchallenged findings of fact demonstrate that there was a fiduciary relationship between the parties and that the defendant violated his fiduciary duty to the plaintiff. Equitable principles impose a constructive trust on property to avoid the unjust enrichment of a party who violates his fiduciary duty and acquires that property at the expense of the person to whom he owed that duty. See Barry v. Covich, 332 Mass. 338, 342–343, 124 N.E.2d 921 (1955); Hatton v. Meade, 23 Mass. App. Ct. 356, 363, 502 N.E.2d 552 (1987). Here the plaintiff was less educated (a high school graduate) and less experienced (she is a waitress) than the defendant (a career army officer attending law school at the time of the purchase of the house). She relied on him over a long period in important matters. See Kelly v. Kelly, 358 Mass. 154, 156, 260 N.E.2d 659 (1970). That reliance was reasonable, and the defendant knew of and accepted the plaintiff's trust in him. See Hatton v. Meade, supra, 23 Mass. App. Ct. at 365, 502 N.E.2d 552, which has many factual parallels to this case. . . .

It would be unjust not to impose a constructive trust in this case. The plaintiff gave up her career as a flight attendant and undertook to maintain a home for the defendant while he advanced his career. She contributed her earnings and services to the home. The defendant's assurances to the plaintiff that they would own the property together (although title would be taken only in his name), his later promises to transfer title to

---

[38] We need not, therefore, consider the plaintiff's other claim: that her partial performance of the agreement, including a substantial change in her circumstances to her detriment made in reasonable reliance on the defendant's admitted oral promises, estops him from relying on the Statute of Frauds as a defense and entitles her to specific performance. See Davis v. Downer, 210 Mass. 573, 576, 97 N.E. 90 (1912); Glass v. Hulbert, 102 Mass. 24, 35–36, 43 (1869). The principles expressed in Restatement (Second) of Contracts § 129 (1981) are said to be consistent with the law of Massachusetts [:]

> A contract for the transfer of an interest in land may be specifically enforced notwithstanding failure to comply with the Statute of Frauds if it is established that the party seeking enforcement, in reasonable reliance on the contract and on the continuing assent of the party against whom enforcement is sought, has so changed his position that injustice can be avoided only by specific enforcement.

See also § 129 comment d.

As will be seen, the circumstances that demonstrate a constructive trust in this case are remarkably similar to circumstances that would deny the defendant the right to rely on the Statute of Frauds on principles of estoppel.

joint ownership, and the plaintiff's reasonable reliance on those promises made by one in whom she reasonably placed special confidence call for the imposition of a constructive trust in the plaintiff's favor on one-half the Reading property.

Judgment affirmed.

NOTES

1. *Constructive trust as equitable remedy.* A recent black-letter formulation of the law of constructive trusts is as follows:

> (1) If a defendant is unjustly enriched by the acquisition of title to identifiable property at the expense of the claimant or in violation of the claimant's rights, the defendant may be declared a constructive trustee, for the benefit of the claimant, of the property in question and its traceable product.

> (2) The obligation of a constructive trustee is to surrender the constructive trust property to the claimant, on such conditions as the court may direct. [Restatement (Third) of Restitution and Unjust Enrichment § 55 (2011).]

The nomenclature, however, has long seemed confusing:

> It is commonly repeated that a constructive trust is "not a real trust" since it is "only a remedy." One might go further and explain that the term "constructive trust" . . . is only a manner of speaking. Abandoning the metaphor, every judicial order recognizing that "B holds X in constructive trust for A" may be seen to comprise, in effect, two remedial components. The first of these is a declaration that B's legal title to X is subject to A's superior equitable claim. The second is a mandatory injunction directing B to surrender X to A or to take equivalent steps. . . .

> The composite remedy designated by the term "constructive trust" was first developed in the context of express trusts. If B (as trustee for A) acquired X in breach of trust . . . the most effective mode of restitution might be simply to treat X as trust property, making B the "constructive" trustee of X for the benefit of A. [I]n the modern law of constructive trust there is no requirement that the parties have ever occupied a fiduciary or confidential relation. [Id. cmt. b.]

2. *Tracing.* Subjecting ill-gotten gains to a constructive trust is fairly easy when the original property is still intact. When it has been sold and the proceeds invested in other property, however, difficult problems of "tracing" may arise. On this subject, see Ayers v. Fay, 102 P.2d 156, 158–59 (Okla.1940):

It has long been a fundamental concept of English law that a change in the form of a thing which is owned does not change the ownership. Derived from and based upon this concept is the rule that the equitable owner of trust property is entitled to that which arises out of such property by sale, exchange or otherwise. This rule is, in many instances, effectuated by a device known as "tracing," meaning nothing more nor less than identification, by the cestui, of the trust or its avails in the hands of the trustee or a third person not a bona fide purchaser. A majority of the courts require the cestui, seeking to follow trust property, to convince the court that the fund or property in the hands of the trustee or another not a bona fide purchaser is either all of, part of, or was produced by the original trust res. Volume 4, Bogert, "Trusts & Trustees," § 921.

Early cases tended to impose on the cestui the unbearable burden of specifically identifying even coins and bills claimed subject to the original trust. But the more modern and certainly the more practical view is that trust funds have been sufficiently traced when it is shown they entered a mass of cash and have remained there. As stated in Massey v. Fisher, C.C., 62 F. 958, 959, "It is sufficient to trace it into the bank's vaults, and find that a sum equal to it (and presumably representing it), continuously remained there until the receiver took it. The modern rules of equity require no more." See, also, 65 C.J. 973, where it is stated sufficient proof is made if the cestui " . . . can show the particular fund or mass into which the trust money has gone, such as an individual bank account of the trustee." And where a trustee has commingled trust funds with his own, the cestui may recover, to the extent of the trust fund, the lowest balance to which the mass has been depleted. The trustee is presumed to have used his own funds first, so that the remainder is sufficiently identified as the trust fund, 65 C.J. 975.

See also Restatement (Third) of Restitution and Unjust Enrichment § 55 cmt. g (2011).

3. *Divorce and life insurance.* Divorce decrees and settlements sometimes require one spouse who owns an insurance policy on his or her own life to designate the other spouse or the children of that marriage as the beneficiaries of the policy. Often, the insured then fails to make the required designation or, having done so, makes a different designation later. Upon the death of the insured, the question may arise whether the non-conforming designation (typically in favor of a later spouse or different children) is effective. In a long line of cases, the courts have almost always imposed a constructive trust on the insurance proceeds in favor of those designated in the divorce decree or settlement. See, e.g., Flanigan v. Munson, 818 A.2d 1275 (N.J. 2003); Holt v. Holt, 995 S.W.2d 68 (Tenn. 1999). See generally Dickinson, Divorce and Life Insurance: Post Mortem Remedies for Breach of a Duty to Maintain a Policy for a Designated Beneficiary, 61 Mo. L. Rev. 533 (1996).

4. *More constructive trust cases.* For more constructive trust cases, see, e.g., Matter of O'Rourke, 648 N.Y.S.2d 704 (App. Div. 1996); Namow Corp. v. Egger, 668 P.2d 265 (Nev.1983); Provencher v. Berman, 699 F.2d 568 (1st Cir.1983); Latham v. Father Divine, supra p. 293.

3. RESULTING TRUSTS

The constructive trust is *implied in law*, i.e., a court may impose it on a transaction despite the intent of the parties. The resulting trust is *implied in fact* in three types of situations: (1) when a trust (private or charitable) has become impossible of fulfillment, e.g., Evans v. Abney, infra p. 698; (2) when a trust (private or charitable) is fully performed without exhausting the trust property; (3) when one person pays the consideration for property and directs the transfer of title to another. The first two are the equitable analog of the possibility of reverter. The third, the "purchase money resulting trust," is of immediate interest because it sometimes serves the same purpose as the constructive trust, i.e., effectuation of an oral express trust that would otherwise fail under the Statute of Frauds. Like the constructive trust, the resulting trust is not subject to the Statute of Frauds, a fact that may explain the courts' tendency to treat them interchangeably. See, e.g., Askins v. Easterling, 347 P.2d 126 (Colo.1959).

The Restatement (Third) of Trusts § 9 (2003) offers the following summary of purchase money resulting trust doctrine:

§ 9. Purchase–Money Resulting Trusts

(1) Except as stated in Subsection (2), where a transfer of property is made to one person and the purchase price is paid by another, a resulting trust arises in favor of the person by whom the purchase price is paid unless

(a) the latter manifests an intention that no resulting trust should arise, or

(b) the transfer is made to accomplish an illegal purpose, in which case a resulting trust does not arise if the policy against unjust enrichment of the transferee is outweighed by the policy against giving relief to a person who has entered into an illegal transaction.

(2) Where a transfer of property is made to one person and the purchase price is paid by another and the transferee is a spouse, descendant, or other natural object of the bounty of the person by whom the purchase price is paid, a resulting trust does not arise unless the latter manifests an intention that the transferee should not have the beneficial interest in the property.

The origins of the purchase money resulting trust are obscure. Some commentators assume that the presumption arose at the same time and for the same reasons as the presumption of a resulting use on a gratuitous conveyance. See Costigan, The Classification of Trusts as Express, Resulting, and Constructive, 27 Harv. L. Rev. 437 (1914); Ames, Constructive Trusts Based Upon the Breach of an Express Oral Trust of Land, 20 Harv. L. Rev. 549 (1907). It is plausible that the presumption originated out of the general practice of holding land to the use of another, since a purchaser of land under such a practice would probably have title conveyed to a dummy. Thus, Ames argued that there was no reason to continue the purchase money resulting trust presumption after the Statute of Uses had changed the land-holding customs. That is, Ames felt that there was no longer any more justification for this presumption than for the presumption of a resulting trust on a gratuitous conveyance, and that the proper assumption, in the absence of evidence to the contrary, was that the grantor intended the grantee to take absolutely. A number of states have followed the Ames view and abolished the presumption by statute. See, e.g., N.Y. EPTL § 7–1.3. In contrast, Professor Scott argued that, in a variety of situations, the presumption reflects the probable intentions of the parties. See Scott, Resulting Trusts Arising Upon the Purchase of Land, 40 Harv. L. Rev. 669 (1927).

F. THE BENEFICIARY

1. INDEFINITENESS

MORICE V. THE BISHOP OF DURHAM

Chancery, 1804.
9 Ves. Jr. 399, 32 Eng. Rep. 656, aff'd, 10 Ves. Jr. 522, 32 Eng. Rep. 947 (1805).

Ann Cracherode by her Will, dated the 16th of April 1801, and duly executed to pass real estate, after giving several legacies to her next of kin and others, some of which she directed to be paid out of the produce of her real estate, directed to be sold, bequeathed all her personal estate to the Bishop of Durham, his executors, & c., upon trust to pay her debts and legacies, & c.; and to dispose of the ultimate residue to such objects of benevolence and liberality as the Bishop of Durham in his own discretion shall most approve of; and she appointed the Bishop her sole executor.

The bill was filed by the next of kin, to have the Will established, except as to the residuary bequest; and that such bequest may be declared void. The Attorney General was made a Defendant. The Bishop by his answer expressly disclaimed any beneficial interest in himself personally. . . .

THE MASTER OF THE ROLLS [Sir W. Grant].

The only question is, whether the trust upon which the residue of the personal estate is bequeathed, be a trust for charitable purposes. That it is upon some trust, and not for the personal benefit of the Bishop, is clear from the words of the Will; and is admitted by his Lordship, who expressly disclaims any beneficial interest. That it is a trust, unless it be of a charitable nature, too indefinite to be executed by this Court, has not been, and cannot be, denied. There can be no trust, over the exercise of which this Court will not assume a control; for an uncontrollable power of disposition would be ownership, and not trust. If there be a clear trust, but for uncertain objects, the property that is the subject of the trust, is undisposed of, and the benefit of such trust must result to those to whom the law gives the ownership in default of disposition by the former owner. But this doctrine does not hold good with regard to trusts for charity. Every other trust must have a definite object. There must be somebody in whose favour the Court can decree performance. But it is now settled, upon authority, which it is too late to controvert, that, where a charitable purpose is expressed, however general, the bequest shall not fail on account of the uncertainty of the object: but the particular mode of application will be directed by the King in some cases, in others by this Court.

Then is this a trust for charity? Do purposes of liberality and benevolence mean the same as objects of charity? That word, in its widest sense, denotes all the good affections men ought to bear towards each other; in its most restricted and common sense, relief of the poor. In neither of these senses is it employed in this Court. Here its signification is derived chiefly from the Statute of Elizabeth (Stat. 43 Eliz. c. 4). Those purposes are considered charitable, which that Statute enumerates, or which by analogies are deemed within its spirit and intendment; and to some such purpose every bequest to charity generally shall be applied. But it is clear liberality and benevolence can find numberless objects, not included in that statute, in the largest construction of it. The use of the word "charitable" seems to have been purposely avoided in this will, in order to leave the Bishop the most unrestrained discretion. Supposing the uncertainty of the trust no objection to its validity, could it be contended to be an abuse of the trust to employ this fund upon objects which all mankind would allow to be objects of liberality and benevolence; though not to be said, in the language of this Court, to be objects also of charity? By what rule of construction could it be said, all objects of liberality and benevolence are excluded, which do not fall within the Statute of Elizabeth? The question is, not whether he may not apply it upon purposes strictly charitable, but whether he is bound so to apply it? I am not aware of any case, in which the bequest has been held charitable, where the testator has not either used that word to denote his general purpose, or specified some particular purpose, which this Court has determined to be charitable in its nature. . . .

. . . But here there is no specific purpose pointed out, to which the residue is to be applied: the words "charity" and "charitable" do not occur: the words used are not synonymous: the trusts may be completely executed without bestowing any part of this residue upon purposes strictly charitable. The residue therefore cannot be said to be given to charitable purposes; and, as the trust is too indefinite to be disposed of to any other purpose, it follows, that the residue remains undisposed of; and must be distributed among the next of kin of the testatrix.

[This decree was affirmed, 10 Ves. Jr. 522, 32 Eng. Rep. 947 (1805), by Lord Chancellor Eldon. Excerpts from that opinion follow.]

The question then is entirely, whether this is according to the intention a gift to purposes of charity in general, as understood in this Court: such, that this Court would have held the Bishop bound, and would have compelled him, to apply the surplus to such charitable purposes as can be answered only in obedience to decrees, where the gift is to charity, in general: or is it, or may it be according to the intention, to such purposes, going beyond those, partially, or altogether, which the Court understands by "charitable purposes"; and, if that is the intention, is the gift too indefinite to create an effectual trust, to be here executed? . . . It is not contended, and it is not necessary, to support this decree, to contend, that the trustee might not consistently with the intention, have devoted every shilling to uses, in that sense charitable, and of course a part of the property. But the true question is, whether, if upon the one hand he might have devoted the whole to purposes, in this sense charitable, he might not equally according to the intention have devoted the whole to purposes benevolent and liberal, and yet not within the meaning of charitable purposes, as this Court construes those words; and, if according to the intention it was competent to him to do so, I do not apprehend, that under any authority upon such words the Court could have charged him with maladministration, if he had applied the whole to purposes, which according to the meaning of the testator are benevolent and liberal; though not acts of that species of benevolence and liberality, which this Court in the construction of a Will calls charitable acts.

. . . But the question is, whether, according to the ordinary sense, . . . this testatrix meant by these words to confine the Defendant to such acts of charity or charitable purposes as this Court would have enforced by decree, and reference to a Master. I do not think, that was the intention; and, if not, the intention is too indefinite to create a trust. But it was the intention to create a trust; and the object being too indefinite, has failed. The consequence of Law is, that the Bishop takes the property upon trust to dispose of it, as the Law will dispose of it: not for his own benefit, or any purpose this Court can effectuate. I think, therefore, this decree is right.

NOTES

1. *Indefiniteness of beneficiary or purpose.* Why was the trust in *Morice* invalid as

      (a) A private trust?

      (b) A charitable trust?

Nichols v. Allen, 130 Mass. 211 (1881), is the leading American analog of *Morice*. In *Nichols* the testator left the residue of her estate to her executors "to be by them distributed to such persons, societies or institutions as they may consider most deserving." The court began:

> Two general rules are well settled: 1st. When a gift or bequest is made in terms clearly manifesting an intention that it shall be taken in trust, and the trust is not sufficiently defined to be carried into effect, the donee or legatee takes the legal title only, and a trust results by implication of law to the donor and his representatives, or to the testator's residuary legatees or next of kin. . . . 2d. A trust which by its terms may be applied to objects which are not charitable in the legal sense, and to persons not defined, by name or by class, is too indefinite to be carried out. [Citing *Morice*.]

130 Mass. at 212. Applying these rules, the court held that the testator had intended, but failed, to create a trust. The failure occurred because she had not "defined the trust sufficiently to enable the court to execute it." Id. at 221. Therefore, her heirs took the property upon resulting trust.

The use of vague general terms describing the purposes of the trust, such as "benevolent," "liberal," "utilitarian," "public," "deserving," "worthy," and "patriotic," is, of course, highly unfortunate. Even if the trust is not ultimately held void, such words invite litigation. Moreover, in many such instances, the settlor could have fully achieved the desired outcome simply by using the word "charitable" or one of the more specific standard charitable purposes. Thus, in *Morice*, if the testator had left her estate to the Bishop of Durham for "such *charitable* purposes as the Bishop of Durham in his own discretion shall most approve of," or for "such *church* purposes as the Bishop of Durham in his own discretion shall most approve of," she would have succeeded in creating a valid charitable trust. See Estate of Clementi, 82 Cal. Rptr. 3d 685 (App. 2008) (bequest to fund "a charitable foundation or trust in my name" valid without more specific purpose); Mangines v. Ermisch, 704 A.2d 1174 (Conn. 1998) (bequest to named bishop "for church needs").

In Chichester Diocesan Fund v. Simpson, [1944] A.C. 341, the House of Lords affirmed the view that the word "benevolent" is not synonymous with "charitable." Not all American courts, however, agree. See 6 Scott and Ascher on Trusts § 39.4.1.

In Clark v. Campbell, 133 A. 166 (N.H.1926), the will left certain items of tangible personal property to trustees "to make disposal by the way of a memento from myself, of such articles to such of my friends as they, my trustees, shall select." The court held that the property passed instead under the residuary clause, because the purported trust failed due to indefiniteness of beneficiaries.

In contrast, in Leach v. Hyatt, 423 S.E.2d 165 (Va.1992), the will authorized the executor to appoint certain property to anyone other than himself. The court called this a "limited power of appointment" and permitted the executor to dispose of the property accordingly. To similar effect is Restatement (Third) of Trusts § 46(2) (2003), which recognizes a power to distribute property to the members of an "indefinite class."

2. *Trust for non-charitable purposes.* Assuming that the court in *Morice* was correct in holding that neither a private nor a charitable trust arose, and assuming further that the court could identify "objects of benevolence and liberality," is there any way it might have allowed the Bishop to carry out the testator's intent, while still being subject to judicial scrutiny if he failed to devote the property to those objects?

Restatement (Third) of Trusts § 47(1) (2003) provides:

If the owner of property transfers it in trust for indefinite or general purposes, not limited to charitable purposes, the transferee holds the property as trustee with the power but not the duty to distribute or apply the property for such purposes; if and to whatever extent the power (presumptively personal) is not exercised, the trustee holds the property for distribution to reversionary beneficiaries implied by law.

See also UTC § 409(1) ("A trust may be created for a noncharitable purpose without a definite or definitely ascertainable beneficiary or for a noncharitable but otherwise valid purpose to be selected by the trustee. The trust may not be enforced for more than [21] years."); UPC § 2–907(a) (to similar effect).

3. *Outright bequest.* In *Morice*, would the result have been the same if there had been an outright bequest to the Bishop, accompanied by such language as: "I request the Bishop of Durham to dispose of the ultimate residue to such objects of benevolence and liberality as he in his own discretion shall most approve of, not intending, however, to impose any obligation upon him to carry out this request"?

In Ralston's Estate, 37 P.2d 76 (Cal.1934), the will gave the entire estate to the executor "in trust" with "absolute authority to dispose of this my entire estate as he may see fit." The court held that the property passed by intestacy, the dissenting judge expressing the opinion that the will made an absolute gift to the executor.

4. *More on indefiniteness and trusts for purposes.* See 2 & 6 Scott and Ascher on Trusts §§ 12.1, 12.7 to 12.12, 41.1, 41.1.1, 41.7; Hirsch, Bequests for Purposes: A Unified Theory, 56 Wash. & Lee L. Rev. 33 (1999); Fratcher, Bequests for Purposes, 56 Iowa L. Rev. 773 (1971).

5. *"Secret" and "semi-secret trusts."* When a decedent dies intestate or leaves property by will relying on the promise of the intestate taker or devisee to hold the property in trust, but no writing evidences the promise and nothing in the will, if any, evidences an intent to create a trust, the arrangement is called a "secret trust." When a testator devises property relying on the promise of the devisee to hold the property in trust and the will refers to the trust but fails to set forth its purposes and beneficiaries and no other writing evidences the promise, the arrangement is called a "semi-secret trust." Under the applicable statute of wills, such arrangements necessarily fail as express trusts. According to Restatement (Third) of Trusts § 18 (2003), the intestate taker or devisee holds the property on constructive trust for the intended purposes and beneficiaries. An alternate resolution, which the American courts have often preferred in the case of semi-secret trusts, is that the devisee holds the property on resulting trust for the decedent's estate. See, e.g., Pickelner v. Adler, 229 S.W.3d 516 (Tex. App. 2007); Olliffe v. Wells, 130 Mass. 221 (1881).

2. CHARITABLE TRUSTS AND GIFTS SUBJECT TO CHARITABLE RESTRICTIONS

a. Charitable Purposes

In *Morice*, the Master of the Rolls cited the 1601 Statute of Charitable Uses, 43 Eliz. c. 4, as the chief guide to the meaning of "charitable" purposes. The preamble to that statute listed a number of typical charities:

> . . . some for relief of aged, impotent and poor people, some for maintenance of sick and maimed soldiers and mariners, schools of learning, free schools, and scholars in universities, some for repair of bridges, ports, havens, causeways, churches, sea-banks and highways, some for education and preferment of orphans, some for or towards relief, stock or maintenance for houses of correction, some for marriages of poor maids, some for supportation, aid and help of young tradesmen, handicraftsmen and persons decayed, and others for relief or redemption of prisoners or captives, and for aid or ease of any poor inhabitants concerning payments of fifteens, setting out of soldiers and other taxes. . . .

Subject to the general requirement of benefit to the public at large or a substantial segment of it, courts usually hold that gifts for purposes that fit within or are closely analogous to one or more of the purposes of the Statute of Elizabeth are charitable per se, without extensive inquiry as to the public value of the particular gift. The statutory enumeration did not purport to be exhaustive, however, and courts have also held other purposes of public value to be charitable. The Third Restatement of Trusts, after denominating as charitable the relief of poverty, the advancement of knowledge or education, the advancement of religion, the promotion of health, and governmental or municipal purposes, adds the following catch-all: "other purposes that are beneficial to the community." Restatement (Third) of Trusts § 28 (2003). See also id. cmt. a; UTC § 405(a) ("other purposes the achievement of which is beneficial to the community"); Evangelical Lutheran Charities Society v. South Carolina Nat'l Bank, 495 S.E.2d 199 (S.C. 1997) (trust to restore and preserve historic properties was charitable, though properties were not open to general public on regular basis and were rented to private individuals).

Not surprisingly, judicial appraisal of community benefit is to some extent a function of time and place. Jackson v. Phillips, 96 Mass. 539 (1867), though holding that trusts for opposition to slavery and aid to fugitive slaves were charitable, held that a trust "to secure the passage of laws granting women, whether married or unmarried, the right to vote, to hold office, to hold, manage and devise property, and all other civil rights enjoyed by men" was not. Id. at 571. Compare Register of Wills for Baltimore City v. Cook, 216 A.2d 542 (Md.1966), holding charitable a trust "to help further the passage of and enactment into law of the Equal Rights Amendment to the Constitution of the United States."

Astonishing advances in technology have led modern courts to be fairly open-minded with respect to the possibility of further advances. In Pierce v. Tharp, 430 S.W.2d 787 (Tenn.App.1967), rev'd as to attorney fees, 455 S.W.2d 145 (Tenn.1970), cert. denied, 402 U.S. 929 (1971), the court confronted a testamentary trust to pay the annual net income "as an award to the individual, or team, who, during the year . . . has contributed most toward the solution of the problem of alcoholism" and to deliver the corpus to whoever should "solve the problem of alcoholism whereby alcoholics can ingest alcohol without the concomitant allergy of the body and obsession of the mind." 430 S.W.2d at 790. Though there was "a vast amount of testimony . . . that it is impossible for an alcoholic to be cured so that he can become a social drinker," the court wrote:

> Even that may be possible, however, in the future. As was said by the learned Chancellor in his opinion, "A devise or bequest made fifty years ago to reward the first person who lands on the moon, probably would have been held unenforceable and therefore void, but certainly it would not be so held today." [430 S.W.2d at 793.]

Sometimes, however, the purpose is simply too "nutty" to be charitable. Thus, one court held that a trust to accumulate the income and ultimately distribute $1 million to every adult American, though benevolent and generous, was not charitable. Marsh v. Frost Nat'l Bank, 129 S.W.3d 174 (Tex. App. 2004). Another held that a trust for the typing, editing, and distribution of the testator's "Random Scientific Notes Seeking the Essentials in Place and Space" was not charitable, finding that the Notes were irrational, unintelligible, and of no scientific or other value—in other words, that there was no public benefit. Wilber v. Asbury Park Nat'l Bank & Trust Co., 59 A.2d 570 (N.J.Ch.1948), aff'd, 65 A.2d 843 (N.J.1949). See also Fidelity Title & Trust Co. v. Clyde, 121 A.2d 625 (Conn.1956), a similar case with the same outcome, though more doubtful because the court seems to have been influenced less by a lack of scientific or literary merit than by the nature of the writings, which it characterized as pornographic. Yet another court, however, held that a trust for "the promotion and/or publication of my late husband's compositions" was charitable, on the ground that the purpose was the entertainment and education of the public. Matter of Manschinger, 343 N.Y.S.2d 426 (Sur. 1973).

One must distinguish the "purpose" of a gift from the motivation of its giver. The charitable nature of a purpose depends not on its subjective basis, but on the objective standard of benefit to the community or a sizeable part of it. It is immaterial that a selfish motive, such as a desire to perpetuate one's own memory, prompts a gift; many, if not most, charitable gifts spring to some degree from selfish motivations of this type. See, e.g., Runser v. Lippi, 664 N.E.2d 1355 (Ohio App. 1995) (upholding bequest to county foundation to provide scholarships for needy students, with preference for testator's nieces and nephews). However, limiting the benefits to too small a class can render a gift non-charitable, even though the nature of the benefits fits into a traditionally charitable category. For example, the establishment and maintenance of a public park is ordinarily charitable. See, e.g., Kentucky v. Isaac W. Bernheim Foundation, 505 S.W.2d 762 (Ky.1974). If, however, the park is for the exclusive benefit of purchasers of lots on a 500–acre tract of the settlor's land, it may not be charitable. Butler v. Shelton, 408 S.W.2d 530 (Tex. App. 1966).

Superficially, it might seem that a trust to award annual prizes to individuals would benefit too small a group to qualify as a charity. The courts have taken a broader view, holding such trusts charitable when the prizes are incentives to accomplishments that are beneficial to the community. See, e.g., In re Harmon's Will, 80 N.Y.S.2d 903 (Sur. 1948) (trust to award Harmon aviation trophies held charitable, as promoting world peace). Likewise, a trust to endow a professorial chair, or to supplement a minister's salary, is charitable even though the particular incumbents are few; the gift also aids the school or church by relieving it of a financial burden. 6 Scott and Ascher on Trusts §§ 38.3, 38.4.1. Traditionally, courts held that bequests for masses or other religious services for a deceased testator were noncharitable, because they were solely for the benefit of the testator. See, e.g., Chelsea Nat'l Bank v. Our Lady Star of the Sea, 147 A. 470 (N.J.Ch.1929). Today, however, many courts strain to uphold such bequests, treating them as gifts to the religious institution itself. E.g., Matter of Connolly, 243 N.Y.S.2d 727 (Sur. 1963); Matter of Klein, 242 N.Y.S.2d 241 (Sur. 1963) (Jewish memorial services).

Tennessee Division of the United Daughters of the Confederacy v. Vanderbilt University

Court of Appeals of Tennessee, 2005.
174 S.W.3d 98.

William C. Koch, Jr., P.J., M.S., delivered the opinion of the court
. . . .

This appeal involves a dispute stemming from a private university's decision to change the name of one of its dormitories. An organization that donated part of the funds used to construct the dormitory filed suit . . . asserting that the university's decision to rename the dormitory breached its seventy-year-old agreement with the university . . . . The trial court . . . determined that the university should be permitted to modify the parties' agreement regarding the dormitory's name because it would be "impractical and unduly burdensome" to require the university to continue to honor the agreement. . . . We have determined that . . . the university has breached the conditions placed on the donor's gift and, therefore, that [it] should be required to return the present value of the gift to the donor if it insists on renaming the dormitory.

I.

[In the early 1900's, Peabody College purchased several properties adjacent to Vanderbilt University, on which it proceeded to build a campus.] On January 21, 1913, the [Tennessee Division of the United Daughters of the Confederacy ("Tennessee U.D.C.")] entered into a contract with the Peabody College trustees to raise $50,000 for the construction of a women's dormitory on the new campus. In return . . . the trustees agreed to allow women descendants of Confederate soldiers nominated by the Tennessee U.D.C. to live in the dormitory rent-free . . . . The 1913 contract specifically stated that the purpose of the . . . contract was to evidence the agreement by which the Tennessee U.D.C. undertook to raise the construction fund and "the conditions which will be attached to the gift of the said fund" to Peabody College.

The fundraising campaign proceeded slowly at first. By 1927 . . . the Tennessee U.D.C. had collected little more than a third of the $50,000 . . . . The Tennessee U.D.C. desired to turn over these funds to Peabody College but also desired to retain a right to recall them in the event the fundraising campaign ultimately failed. Thus, on June 17, 1927, the Tennessee U.D.C. entered into a second written contract with Peabody College.

The second contract stated that both parties desired that a "Confederate Memorial Hall" building be constructed on Peabody College's campus. The Tennessee U.D.C. agreed to pay over . . . the $17,421.47 it had already raised and to turn over further sums when they were collected. In return, the college agreed that when the funds reached a sufficient amount, it would construct a building on its property conforming to plans and specifications to be agreed upon by the parties . . . .

In spite of the Great Depression, during the next six years the Tennessee U.D.C. managed . . . to meet its original $50,000 goal. By that time, the Tennessee U.D.C. and Peabody College had decided that although a small women's dormitory could be constructed for $50,000, they would both prefer to use the $50,000 as partial funding for the construction of a larger women's dormitory to be located on the campus quadrangle. Peabody College estimated that the larger dormitory would cost approximately $150,000 . . . .

Sometime in September of 1933, the Tennessee U.D.C. and Peabody College entered into a third written contract . . . . The Tennessee U.D.C. agreed to allow the college to use the original $50,000 . . . for the construction of a larger building, the plans and specifications of which had been examined, approved, and signed by representatives of the Tennessee U.D.C. The Tennessee U.D.C. agreed to this modification on the condition . . . that the college place on the building an inscription naming it "Confederate Memorial." . . .

On June 8, 1934, the Peabody College trustees voted to borrow $100,000 from the school's permanent endowment to supplement the funds raised by the Tennessee U.D.C. On July 12, 1934, the contract for the construction of the new dormitory was awarded . . . for a guaranteed price of $131,294 or less. Construction drawings dated July 12, 1934 show the words "Confederate Memorial Hall" in incised lettering on the pediment on the front of the building. . . .

From 1935 until the late 1970's, women descendants of Confederate soldiers . . . lived in Confederate Memorial Hall rent-free. However, by the late 1970's, Peabody College found itself in increasingly dire financial straits. In the spring of 1978, the trustees of the college decided to lease two dormitories, including Confederate Memorial Hall, to Vanderbilt as a way to raise revenue. . . .

Peabody College's financial situation continued to deteriorate, and it soon became evident that the college would either have to merge with another institution or face bankruptcy. . . .

On April 28, 1979, the trustees of Vanderbilt and Peabody College entered into an agreement effectuating [a] merger. Under the terms of the merger agreement, Vanderbilt succeeded to all of Peabody's legal obligations.

By the time of the merger, only four students nominated by the Tennessee U.D.C. were still living in Confederate Memorial Hall. [A]fter they graduated, no other students nominated by the Tennessee U.D.C. were allowed to live in Confederate Memorial Hall rent-free or at a reduced rate.[39]

In 1987 and 1988, Vanderbilt spent approximately $2.5 million to renovate and upgrade Confederate Memorial Hall. During the following academic year, there was much discussion on the Vanderbilt campus regarding the propriety of retaining the name "Confederate Memorial Hall." . . .

Within a few months, the Vanderbilt Student Government Association passed a resolution recommending that Vanderbilt install a plaque on Confederate Memorial Hall explaining why it was named "Confederate." . . . The plaque was installed in 1989.

Controversy over the name of Confederate Memorial Hall arose again in the spring of 2000 when the Vanderbilt Student Government Association passed a resolution calling on the administration to change the name of the building. . . .

E. Gordon Gee became the new chancellor of Vanderbilt in July 2000. In conversations with Vanderbilt students, faculty, and alumni over the next two years, the name of Confederate Memorial Hall was repeatedly identified as a major impediment to the progress of the university. In June 2002, Chancellor Gee discussed the matter with the executive committee of the Vanderbilt board of trust . . . . Chancellor Gee, without consulting the Tennessee U.D.C., then decided to change the name of "Confederate Memorial Hall" to "Memorial Hall" . . . .

Since then, Vanderbilt has changed its maps, website, and correspondence to reflect the building's new name of "Memorial Hall." Vanderbilt has not yet removed the name "Confederate Memorial Hall" from the pediment on the front of the building but has indicated its unequivocal

---

[39] Vanderbilt has continued to use the building as a dormitory to the present day.

intention to do so. The 1989 plaque describing the history of the building and the contributions of the Tennessee U.D.C. remains in place . . . .

III. THE NATURE OF THE LEGAL RELATIONSHIP BETWEEN PEABODY COLLEGE AND THE TENNESSEE U.D.C.

[W]e must first determine the precise nature of the legal relationship formed between the Tennessee U.D.C. and Peabody College by the 1913, 1927, and 1933 agreements. Although all three agreements use the word "contract," they do not purport to establish a typical commercial arrangement in which one party provides certain goods or services in return for a sum to be paid by the other party. Instead, the agreements indicate that the $50,000 to be raised by the Tennessee U.D.C. was to be transferred to Peabody College as a gift. . . .

The 1913, 1927, and 1933 contracts do not, however, describe the proposed transfer to Peabody College as a gift with no strings attached. The three contracts attach specific conditions to the gift, and the 1927 contract expressly reserves to the Tennessee U.D.C. the right to recall the gift if Peabody College fails or ceases to comply with these conditions. Where a party makes a donation to a charitable organization accompanied by conditions and a right to reclaim the donation if the conditions are not met, the law treats the arrangement between the parties as either a revocable charitable trust or a charitable gift subject to conditions. Southwestern Presbyterian Univ. v. City of Clarksville, 149 Tenn. 256, 281, 259 S.W. 550, 558 (1923); George Gleason Bogert & George Taylor Bogert, The Law of Trusts and Trustees § 324, at 379-80 (rev. 2d ed. 1992) [hereinafter Bogert on Trusts]; 4A Scott on Trusts § 351, at 52-54 . . . .

The courts must look to the intent of the donating party to determine whether a particular transaction involves the creation of a revocable charitable trust or simply the giving of a charitable gift subject to conditions. 4A Scott on Trusts § 351, at 52-53 . . . . A donating party will be deemed to have created a trust only if the party has expressed with certainty its intent to create a trust. . . . Bogert on Trusts § 45, at 483; 4A Scott on Trusts § 351, at 49 . . . . Moreover, the expression of trust intent must be definite and particular, i.e., the donating party must express a particular intent to confer benefits through the medium of a trust rather than through some related or similar device. Ratto v. Nashville Trust Co., 178 Tenn. 457, 462, 159 S.W.2d 88, 90 (1942); Bogert on Trusts § 46, at 489-91 . . . . The mere expression of a donative intent, or a statement of the purpose for which a gift is given, does not constitute an expression of trust intent. Bogert on Trusts § 46, at 492, 494. Absent a finding of an intent to create a trust, the transaction will be analyzed as a gift subject to conditions. Compare Bogert on Trusts § 324, at 382-86 & n.15 (listing cases where trusts found based on sufficient expression of trust intent) with § 324, at 382 & n.14 (listing cases where absolute or conditional gifts found because of insufficient expression of trust intent).

In many cases, the donating party is a natural person who has died by the time litigation arises concerning the appropriate characterization of the transaction. In such cases, it can be extremely difficult to discern whether the donating party possessed the intent necessary to create a revocable charitable trust or instead simply made a gift to charity subject to conditions. In this case, however, the donating party is a corporate entity that is still in existence . . . . The Tennessee U.D.C. does not claim that it intended to create a revocable charitable trust . . . and Vanderbilt has presented no evidence suggesting a trust intent on the part of the Tennessee U.D.C. Accordingly, we have no difficulty concluding, as a matter of law, that the 1913, 1927, and 1933 contracts reflect a charitable gift subject to conditions rather than the creation of a revocable charitable trust.

IV. THE CONDITIONS OF THE GIFT

Donors often seek to impose conditions on gifts to charitable organizations. . . . In the case of inter vivos transfers, the conditions are generally embodied in a gift agreement or a deed of conveyance. . . . In the case of transfers to take place on the death of the donor, the conditions are generally contained in the terms of the donor's will. . . .

A conditional gift is enforceable according to the terms of the document or documents that created the gift. . . . If the recipient fails or ceases to comply with the conditions, the donor's remedy is limited to recovery of the gift. *Southwestern Presbyterian Univ. v. City of Clarksville,* 149 Tenn. at 269, 259 S.W. at 554 ("One may attach such conditions to his contributions as to support his right to withdrawal thereof, upon a violation of such conditions, but his rights, or those of a group so situated, must be so limited."); . . . . Because noncompliance results in a forfeiture of the gift, the conditions must be created by express terms or by clear implication and are construed strictly. *Southwestern Presbyterian Univ. v. City of Clarksville,* 149 Tenn. at 282, 259 S.W. at 558 . . . .

Taking all three contracts together, the gift from the Tennessee U.D.C. to Peabody College was subject to three specific conditions. First, Peabody College was required to use the gift to construct a dormitory on its campus conforming to plans and specifications approved by the Tennessee U.D.C. Second, Peabody College was required to allow women descendants of Confederate soldiers . . . to live [in] the dormitory without paying rent . . . . Third, Peabody College was required to place on the dormitory an inscription naming it "Confederate Memorial." The contracts do not specify the duration of these conditions. In such circumstances, the court must determine whether a duration can be inferred from the nature and circumstances of the transaction. . . . Given the nature of the project and the content of the conditions, we conclude that these conditions were not meant to bind Peabody College forever but instead were to be limited to the life of the building itself. Thus, as long as the building stands, these three conditions apply to the gift.

V. VANDERBILT'S COMPLIANCE WITH THE CONDITIONS

In its complaint, the Tennessee U.D.C. claimed that Vanderbilt had already violated the condition requiring an inscription on the building naming it "Confederate Memorial" by publicly and privately announcing its intention to rename the building "Memorial Hall" and that Vanderbilt planned to violate the condition further by removing or altering the inscription on the pediment. In its answer, Vanderbilt admitted its plans to rename the building "Memorial Hall" and to remove the word "Confederate" from the inscription on the pediment . . . . Vanderbilt argues that . . . Vanderbilt and Peabody College substantially performed their obligations under the contracts, that the Tennessee U.D.C. has already received full consideration for its original contribution, and that principles of academic freedom require that Vanderbilt be allowed to change the name of Confederate Memorial Hall without any further obligation to the Tennessee U.D.C. We find no merit in these arguments.

Vanderbilt's claim that the placement of a plaque by the entrance to the building describing the contributions of the Tennessee U.D.C. to the original construction constitutes substantial performance with the inscription condition cannot be taken seriously. The determination of whether a party has substantially performed depends on what it was the parties bargained for in their agreement. . . . Here, the 1933 contract expressly and unambiguously required Peabody College to place an inscription on the building naming it "Confederate Memorial," and we have already concluded that the parties intended the inscription to remain until the building was torn down. . . .

Vanderbilt's argument that it should be excused from complying with the inscription condition contained in the 1933 contract because the Tennessee U.D.C. has already received enough value for its original contribution to the construction of the building is likewise without merit. The courts must interpret contracts as they are written . . . and will not make a new contract for parties who have spoken for themselves. . . . The courts do not concern themselves with the wisdom or folly of a contract . . . and are not at liberty to relieve parties from contractual obligations simply because these obligations later prove to be burdensome or unwise. . . .

The same is true of conditions contained in a gift agreement. By entering into the 1913, 1927, and 1933 contracts, Peabody College necessarily agreed that the value of the gift it was receiving was worth the value of full performance of the conditions of the gift. . . . In short, Vanderbilt's unilateral assessment that Peabody College gave away too much in the 1913, 1927, and 1933 agreements does not constitute a legal defense that would excuse Vanderbilt from complying with the conditions of the original gift.

Vanderbilt's assertion that principles of academic freedom allow it to keep the gift from the Tennessee U.D.C. while ignoring the conditions attached to that gift is equally unavailing. As Vanderbilt correctly notes in its brief on appeal, the United States Supreme Court has long been solicitous of the independence of private colleges from government control. See, e.g., Trs. of Dartmouth Coll. v. Woodward, 17 U.S. 518, 4 L. Ed. 629 (1819). However, the source of the obligation at issue in this case is not the government but Vanderbilt itself. The original obligation to place the inscription on Confederate Memorial Hall is contained in a private gift agreement voluntarily entered into between Peabody College and the Tennessee U.D.C. Vanderbilt's legal obligation to comply with the conditions of that gift agreement arises not from any action on the part of the government but from Vanderbilt's own decision to enter into a merger agreement with Peabody College in 1979 in which it agreed to succeed to Peabody College's legal obligations.

Moreover, we fail to see how the adoption of a rule allowing universities to avoid their contractual and other voluntarily assumed legal obligations whenever, in the university's opinion, those obligations have begun to impede their academic mission would advance principles of academic freedom. To the contrary, allowing Vanderbilt and other academic institutions to jettison their contractual and other legal obligations so casually would seriously impair their ability to raise money in the future by entering into gift agreements such as the ones at issue here.

VI. THE TENNESSEE U.D.C.'S REMEDY

As noted above, where a donee fails or ceases to comply with the conditions of a gift, the donor's remedy is limited to recovery of the gift. However, it would be inequitable to allow Vanderbilt to "return" the gift at issue here simply by paying the Tennessee U.D.C. the same sum of money the Tennessee U.D.C. donated in 1933 because the value of a dollar today is very different from the value of a dollar in 1933. To reflect the change in the buying power of the dollar, the amount Vanderbilt must pay to the Tennessee U.D.C. in order to return the gift should be based on the consumer price index published by the Bureau of Labor Statistics of the United States Department of Labor. . . . Thus, on remand, if Vanderbilt continues to elect not to comply with the terms of the gift, it must pay the Tennessee U.D.C. in today's dollars the value of the original gift in 1933.

In settling on this method of accounting for the changed value of the Tennessee U.D.C.'s original contribution, we have considered and rejected an approach that would require Vanderbilt to pay simple or compound interest on the original contribution. Any requirement that Vanderbilt pay interest on the original donation would necessarily be premised on the idea that the Tennessee U.D.C. was deprived of all beneficial use of the funds from the time of the original donation to the present. Such an approach would invite an offset defense by Vanderbilt and would require the trial court to attempt to quantify the value to the Tennessee U.D.C. not only of the housing awards, but also of having the inscription on the pediment of the building for the past seventy years. Determining the value of an inscription is not a matter that is subject to easy proof or to reasonably definite calculation, and any attempt to do so would lead to a calculation of damages that was impermissibly speculative in nature. . . .

VII.

[T]he undisputed facts establish that the Tennessee U.D.C. gave a monetary gift to Vanderbilt's predecessor-in-interest subject to conditions and that Vanderbilt's predecessor-in-interest accepted the gift as well as the conditions that accompanied it. It is further undisputed that Vanderbilt now declines to abide by the conditions attached to the gift. Thus, because Vanderbilt has presented no legal basis for permitting it to keep the gift while refusing to honor the conditions attached to it, Vanderbilt must now either return the present value of the gift to the Tennessee U.D.C. or reverse its present course and agree to abide by the conditions originally placed on the gift.

Accordingly, we reverse the summary judgment entered in favor of Vanderbilt . . . . We have also determined that, if Vanderbilt insists on changing the name of Confederate Memorial Hall, the Tennessee U.D.C. has demonstrated that it is entitled to a judgment as a matter of law on its motion for partial summary judgment. We remand the case with directions to calculate the present value of the Tennessee U.D.C.'s gift to Peabody College, to enter a judgment in favor of the Tennessee U.D.C. in that amount, and to make whatever further orders may be required. . . .

[The concurring opinion of William B. Cain, J., is omitted.]

NOTES

1. *General principles.* As the principal case indicates, a gift subject to a charitable restriction is not a charitable trust. See also Persan v. Life Concepts, Inc., 738 So.2d 1008 (Fla. App. 1999) ("Making a gift to a charity for a specific project or purpose does not create a charitable trust."); Lefkowitz v. Cornell University, 316 N.Y.S.2d 264 (App. Div. 1970). The Attorney General

can, however, enforce the restrictions, and cy pres may be available if the restrictions turn out badly.

2. *Donor standing.* Traditionally, only the attorney general, a co-trustee, or someone with a "special interest" (such as the current holder of an endowed chair) could enforce either a charitable trust or restrictions on a charitable gift. See Rhone v. Adams, 986 So. 2d 374 (Ala. 2007) (eligible charities lacked standing to enforce trust for unspecified charities in specified counties; "potential beneficiaries" lack "sufficient special interest"); In re Milton Hershey School, 911 A.2d 1258 (Pa. 2006) (alumni association lacked standing to intervene in litigation concerning amendments to school's governing instruments); State ex rel. Nixon v. Hutcherson, 96 S.W.3d 81 (Mo. 2003) (eligible children lacked standing to enforce trust for education of needy children in specified counties); Restatement (Second) of Trusts § 391 (1959). Notably, this has often meant that even the settlor lacked standing. See Prentis Family Foundation v. Karmanos Cancer Institute, 698 N.W.2d 900 (Mich. App. 2005); Herzog Foundation v. University of Bridgeport, 699 A.2d 995 (Conn. 1997). The trend, however, is to make donor standing more widely available. In addition to the principal case, see UTC § 405(c) ("The settlor of a charitable trust, among others, may maintain a proceeding to enforce the trust."); Smithers v. St. Luke's–Roosevelt Hospital Center, 723 N.Y.S.2d 426 (App. Div. 2001) (donor's administrator); Restatement (Third) of Trusts § 94(2) (2012). But see Hardt v. Vitae Foundation, 302 S.W.3d 133 (Mo. App. 2009) (UTC § 405(c) confers standing on settlors of charitable trusts but not on donors of gifts subject to charitable restrictions). See generally Weisbord & DeScioli, The Effects of Donor Standing on Philanthropy: Insights From the Psychology of Gift-Giving, 45 Gonzaga L. Rev. 225 (2010) ("donor standing is unlikely to increase, and might actually decrease, charitable giving"); Schlesinger & Goodman, Enforcement of Charitable Transfers: A Question of Standing, Est. Plan., Aug. 2009, at 37; Brody, From the Dead Hand to the Living Dead: The Conundrum of Charitable-Donor Standing, 41 Ga. L. Rev. 1183 (2007); Chester, Grantor Standing to Enforce Charitable Transfers under Section 405(c) of the Uniform Trust Code and Related Law: How Important Is It and How Extensive Should It Be?, 37 Real Prop. Prob. & Tr. J. 611 (2003).

The Attorney General always has standing and is ordinarily an indispensable party in any matter involving a charitable trust. Persons with no special interest may sometimes petition the Attorney General to institute a suit to enforce a charitable trust, and bring a derivative action if the Attorney General refuses, but they may have to assume the responsibility for costs.

3. *More on charity and charitable trusts.* See 5 & 6 Scott and Ascher on Trusts §§ 37.1 to 37.1.4, 37.3.10, 38.1 to 38.11; Gary, The Problems With Donor Intent: Interpretation, Enforcement, and Doing the Right Thing, 85 Chi.-Kent L. Rev. 977 (2010); Klick & Sitkoff, Agency Costs, Charitable Trusts, and Corporate Control: Evidence From Hershey's Kiss-Off, 108 Colum. L. Rev. 749 (2008); Eason, Private Motive and Perpetual Conditions in Charita-

ble Naming Gifts: When Good Names Go Bad, 38 U.C. Davis L. Rev. 375 (2005).

b. Cy Pres

EVANS V. ABNEY

Supreme Court of the United States, 1970.
396 U.S. 435, 90 S.Ct. 628, 24 L.Ed.2d 634.

MR. JUSTICE BLACK delivered the opinion of the Court.

Once again this Court must consider the constitutional implications of the 1911 will of United States Senator A.O. Bacon of Georgia which conveyed property in trust to Senator Bacon's home city of Macon for the creation of a public park for the exclusive use of the white people of that city. As a result of our earlier decision in this case which held that the park, Baconsfield, could not continue to be operated on a racially discriminatory basis, Evans v. Newton, 382 U.S. 296 (1966), the Supreme Court of Georgia ruled that Senator Bacon's intention to provide a park for whites only had become impossible to fulfill and that accordingly the trust had failed and the parkland and other trust property had reverted by operation of Georgia law to the heirs of the Senator. 224 Ga. 826, 165 S.E. 2d 160 (1968). Petitioners, the same Negro citizens of Macon who have sought in the courts to integrate the park, contend that this termination of the trust violates their rights to equal protection and due process under the Fourteenth Amendment. We granted certiorari because of the importance of the questions involved. . . . For the reasons to be stated, we are of the opinion that the judgment of the Supreme Court of Georgia should be, and it is, affirmed.

The early background of this litigation was summarized by Mr. Justice Douglas in his opinion for the Court in Evans v. Newton, 382 U.S., at 297–298:

> In 1911 United States Senator Augustus O. Bacon executed a will that devised to the Mayor and Council of the City of Macon, Georgia, a tract of land which, after the death of the Senator's wife and daughters, was to be used as "a park and pleasure ground" for white people only, the Senator stating in the will that while he had only the kindest feeling for the Negroes he was of the opinion that "in their social relations the two races (white and negro) should be forever separate." The will provided that the park should be under the control of a Board of Managers of seven persons, all of whom were to be white. The city kept the park segregated for some years but in time let Negroes use it, taking the position that the park was a public facility which it could not constitutionally manage and maintain on a segregated basis.

Thereupon, individual members of the Board of Managers of the park brought this suit in a state court against the City of Macon and the trustees of certain residuary beneficiaries of Senator Bacon's estate, asking that the city be removed as trustee and that the court appoint new trustees, to whom title to the park would be transferred. The city answered, alleging it could not legally enforce racial segregation in the park. The other defendants admitted the allegation and requested that the city be removed as trustee.

Several Negro citizens of Macon intervened, alleging that the racial limitation was contrary to the laws and public policy of the United States, and asking that the court refuse to appoint private trustees. Thereafter the city resigned as trustee and amended its answer accordingly. Moreover, other heirs of Senator Bacon intervened and they and the defendants other than the city asked for reversion of the trust property to the Bacon estate in the event that the prayer of the petition were denied.

The Georgia court accepted the resignation of the city as trustee and appointed three individuals as new trustees, finding it unnecessary to pass on the other claims of the heirs. On appeal by the Negro intervenors, the Supreme Court of Georgia affirmed, holding that Senator Bacon had the right to give and bequeath his property to a limited class, that charitable trusts are subject to supervision of a court of equity, and that the power to appoint new trustees so that the purpose of the trust would not fail was clear. 220 Ga. 280, 138 S.E.2d 573.

The Court in Evans v. Newton, supra, went on to reverse the judgment of the Georgia Supreme Court and to hold that the public character of Baconsfield "requires that it be treated as a public institution subject to the command of the Fourteenth Amendment, regardless of who now has title under state law." 382 U.S., at 302. Thereafter, the Georgia Supreme Court interpreted this Court's reversal of its decision as requiring that Baconsfield be henceforth operated on a nondiscriminatory basis. "Under these circumstances," the state high court held, "we are of the opinion that the sole purpose for which the trust was created has become impossible of accomplishment and has been terminated." Evans v. Newton, 221 Ga. 870, 871, 148 S.E.2d 329, 330 (1966). Without further elaboration of this holding, the case was remanded to the Georgia trial court to consider the motion of Guyton G. Abney and others, successor trustees of Senator Bacon's estate, for a ruling that the trust had become unenforceable and that accordingly the trust property had reverted to the Bacon estate and to certain named heirs of the Senator. The motion was opposed by petitioners and by the Attorney General of Georgia, both of whom argued that the trust should be saved by applying the *cy pres* doctrine to amend the terms of the will by striking the racial restrictions and opening Bacons-field to all the citizens of Macon without regard to race or color. The trial court, however, refused to apply *cy pres*. It held that the doctrine was inapplicable because the park's segregated, whites-only character was an essential and inseparable part of the testator's plan. Since the "sole purpose" of the trust was thus in irreconcilable conflict with the constitutional mandate expressed in our opinion in Evans v. Newton, the trial court ruled that the Baconsfield trust had failed and that the trust property had by operation of law reverted to the heirs of Senator Bacon. On appeal, the Supreme Court of Georgia affirmed.

We are of the opinion that in ruling as they did the Georgia courts did no more than apply well-settled general principles of Georgia law to determine the meaning and effect of a Georgia will. At the time Senator Bacon made his will Georgia cities and towns were, and they still are, authorized to accept devises of property for the establishment and preservation of "parks and pleasure grounds" and to hold the property thus received in charitable trust for the exclusive benefit of the class of persons named by the testator. Ga. Code Ann., c. 69–5 (1967); Ga. Code Ann. §§ 108–203, 108–207 (1959). These provisions of the Georgia Code explicitly authorized the testator to include, if he should choose, racial restrictions such as those found in Senator Bacon's will. The city accepted the trust with these restrictions in it. When this Court in Evans v. Newton, supra, held that the continued operation of Baconsfield as a segregated park was unconstitutional, the particular purpose of the Baconsfield trust as stated in the will failed under Georgia law. The question then properly before the Georgia Supreme Court was whether as a matter of state law the doctrine of *cy pres* should be applied to prevent the trust itself from failing. Petitioners urged that the *cy pres* doctrine allowed the Georgia courts to strike the racially restrictive clauses in Bacon's will so that the terms of the trust could be fulfilled without violating the Constitution.

The Georgia *cy pres* statutes upon which petitioners relied provide:

> When a valid charitable bequest is incapable for some reason of execution in the exact manner provided by the testator, donor, or founder, a court of equity will carry it into effect in such a way as will as nearly as possible effectuate his intention. Ga. Code Ann. § 108–202 (1959).

> A devise or bequest to a charitable use will be sustained and carried out in this State; and in all cases where there is a general intention manifested by the testator to effect a certain purpose, and the particular mode in which he directs it to be done shall fail from any cause, a court of chancery may, by approximation, effectuate the pur-

pose in a manner most similar to that indicated by the testator. Ga. Code Ann. § 113–815 (1959).

The Georgia courts have held that the fundamental purpose of these *cy pres* provisions is to allow the court to carry out the general charitable intent of the testator where this intent might otherwise be thwarted by the impossibility of the particular plan or scheme provided by the testator. Moss v. Youngblood, 187 Ga. 188, 200 S.E. 689 (1938). But this underlying logic of the *cy pres* doctrine implies that there is a certain class of cases in which the doctrine cannot be applied. Professor Scott in his treatise on trusts states this limitation on the doctrine of *cy pres* which is common to many States as follows:

> It is not true that a charitable trust never fails where it is impossible to carry out the particular purpose of the testator. In some cases . . . it appears that the accomplishment of the particular purpose and only that purpose was desired by the testator and that he had no more general charitable intent and that he would presumably have preferred to have the whole trust fail if the particular purpose is impossible of accomplishment. In such a case the cy pres doctrine is not applicable. 4 A. Scott, The Law of Trusts § 399, p. 3085 (3d ed. 1967).

In this case, Senator Bacon provided an unusual amount of information in his will from which the Georgia courts could determine the limits of his charitable purpose. Immediately after specifying that the park should be for "the sole, perpetual and unending, use, benefit and enjoyment of the white women, white girls, white boys and white children of the City of Macon," the Senator stated that "the said property under no circumstances . . . (is) to be . . . at any time for any reason devoted to any other purpose or use excepting so far as herein specifically authorized." And the Senator continued:

> I take occasion to say that in limiting the use and enjoyment of this property perpetually to white people, I am not influenced by any unkindness of feeling or want of consideration for the Negroes, or colored people. On the contrary I have for them the kindest feeling, and for many of them esteem and regard, while for some of them I have sincere personal affection.

> I am, however, without hesitation in the opinion that in their social relations the two races . . . should be forever separate and that they should not have pleasure or recreation grounds to be used or enjoyed, together and in common.

The Georgia courts, construing Senator Bacon's will as a whole . . . , concluded from this and other language in the will that the Senator's charitable intent was not "general" but extended only to the establishment of a segregated park for the benefit of white people. The Georgia trial court found that "Senator Bacon could not have used language more clearly indicating his intent that the benefits of Baconsfield should be extended to white persons only, or more clearly indicating that this limitation was an essential and indispensable part of his plan for Baconsfield." App. 519. Since racial separation was found to be an inseparable part of the testator's intent, the Georgia courts held that the State's *cy pres* doctrine could not be used to alter the will to permit racial integration. See Ford v. Thomas, 111 Ga. 493, 36 S.E. 841 (1900); Adams v. Bass, 18 Ga. 130 (1855). The Baconsfield trust was therefore held to have failed, and, under Georgia law, "[w]here a trust is expressly created, but [its] uses . . . fail from any cause, a resulting trust is implied for the benefit of the grantor, or testator, or his heirs." Ga. Code Ann. § 108–106(4) (1959). The Georgia courts concluded, in effect, that Senator Bacon would have rather had the whole trust fail than have Baconsfield integrated.

When a city park is destroyed because the Constitution requires it to be integrated, there is reason for everyone to be disheartened. We agree with petitioners that in such a case it is not enough to find that the state court's result was reached through the application of established principles of state law. No state law or act can prevail in the face of contrary federal law, and the federal courts must search out the fact and truth of any proceeding or transaction to determine if the Constitution has been violated. . . . Here, however, the action of the Georgia Supreme Court declaring the Baconsfield trust terminated presents no violation of constitutionally protected rights, and any harshness that may have resulted from the state court's decision can be attributed solely to its intention to effectuate as nearly as possible the explicit terms of Senator Bacon's will.

Petitioners first argue that the action of the Georgia court violates the United States Constitution in that it imposes a drastic "penalty," the "forfeiture" of the park, merely because of the city's compliance with the constitutional mandate expressed by this Court in Evans v. Newton. Of course, Evans v. Newton did not speak to the problem of whether Baconsfield should or could continue to operate as a park; it held only that its continued operation as a park had to be without racial discrimination. But petitioners now want to extend that holding to forbid the Georgia courts from closing Baconsfield on the ground that such a closing would penalize the city and its citizens for complying with the Constitution. We think, however, that the will of Senator Bacon and Georgia law provide all the justification necessary for imposing such a "penalty." The construction of wills is essentially a state-law question, Lyeth v. Hoey, 305 U.S. 188 (1938), and in this case the Georgia Supreme Court, as we read its opinion, interpreted Senator Bacon's will as embodying a preference for termination of the park rather than its integration. Given this, the Georgia court had no alternative under its relevant trust laws, which are long standing and neutral with regard to race, but to end the Baconsfield trust and return the property to the Senator's heirs.

A second argument for petitioners stresses the similarities between this case and the case in which a city holds an absolute fee simple title to a public park and then closes that park of its own accord solely to avoid the effect of a prior court order directing that the park be integrated as the Fourteenth Amendment commands. Yet, assuming *arguendo* that the closing of the park would in those circumstances violate the Equal Protection Clause, that case would be clearly distinguishable from the case at bar because there it is the State and not a private party which is injecting the racially discriminatory motivation. In the case at bar there is not the slightest indication that any of the Georgia judges involved were motivated by racial animus or discriminatory intent of any sort in construing and enforcing Senator Bacon's will. Nor is there any indication that Senator Bacon in drawing up his will was persuaded or induced to include racial restrictions by the fact that such restrictions were permitted by the Georgia trust statutes. . . . On the contrary, the language of the Senator's will shows that the racial restrictions were solely the product of the testator's own full-blown social philosophy. Similarly, the situation presented in this case is also easily distinguishable from that presented in Shelley v. Kraemer, 334 U.S. 1 (1948), where we held unconstitutional state judicial action which had affirmatively enforced a private scheme of discrimination against Negroes. Here the effect of the Georgia decision eliminated all discrimination against Negroes in the park by eliminating the park itself, and the termination of the park was a loss shared equally by the white and Negro citizens of Macon since both races would have enjoyed a constitutional right of equal access to the park's facilities had it continued.

Petitioners also contend that since Senator Bacon did not expressly provide for a reverter in the event that the racial restrictions of the trust failed, no one can know with absolute certainty that the Senator would have preferred termination of the park rather than its integration, and the decision of the Georgia court therefore involved a matter of choice. It might be difficult to argue with these assertions if they stood alone, but then petitioners conclude: "Its [the court's] choice, the anti-Negro choice, violates the Fourteenth Amendment, whether it be called a 'guess,' an item in 'social philosophy,' or anything else at all." We do not understand petitioners to be contending here that the Georgia judges were motivated either consciously or unconsciously by a desire to discriminate against Negroes. In any case, there is, as noted above, absolutely nothing before this Court to support a finding of such motivation. What remains of petitioners' argument is the idea that the Georgia courts had a constitutional obligation in this case to resolve any doubt about the testator's intent in favor of preserving the trust. Thus stated, we see no merit in the argument. The only choice the Georgia courts either had or exercised in this regard was their judicial judgment in construing Bacon's will to determine his intent, and the Constitution imposes no requirement upon the Georgia courts to approach Bacon's will any differently than they would approach any will creating any charitable trust of any kind. Surely the Fourteenth Amendment is not violated where, as here, a state court operating in its judicial capacity fairly applies its normal principles of construction to determine the testator's true intent in establishing a charitable trust and then reaches a conclusion with regard to that intent which, because of the operation of neutral and nondiscriminatory state trust laws, effectively denies everyone, whites as well as Negroes, the benefits of the trust.

Another argument made by petitioners is that the decision of the Georgia courts holding that the Baconsfield trust had "failed" must rest logically on the unspoken premise that the presence or proximity of Negroes in Baconsfield would destroy the desirability of the park for whites. This argument reflects a rather fundamental misunderstanding of Georgia law. The Baconsfield trust "failed" under that law not because of any belief on the part of any living person that whites and Negroes might not enjoy being together but, rather, because Senator Bacon who died many years ago intended that the park remain forever for the exclusive use of white people.

Petitioners also advance a number of considerations of public policy in opposition to the conclusion which we have reached. In particular, they regret, as we do, the loss of the Baconsfield trust to the City of Macon, and they are concerned lest we set a precedent under which other charitable trusts will be terminated. It bears repeating that our holding today reaffirms the traditional role of the States in determining whether or not to apply their *cy pres* doctrines to particular trusts. Nothing we have said here prevents a state court from applying its *cy pres* rule in a case where the Georgia court, for example, might not apply its rule. More fundamentally, however, the loss of charitable trusts such as Baconsfield is part of the price we pay for permitting deceased persons to exercise a continuing control over assets owned by them at death. This aspect of freedom of testation, like most things, has its advantages and disadvantages. The responsibility of this Court, however, is to construe and enforce the Constitution and laws of the land as they are and not to legislate social policy on the basis of our own personal inclinations. . . .

The judgment is affirmed.

Mr. Justice Marshall took no part in the consideration or decision of this case.

[The dissenting opinion of Mr. Justice Douglas is omitted.]

MR. JUSTICE BRENNAN, dissenting. . . .

No record could present a clearer case of the closing of a public facility for the sole reason that the public authority that owns and maintains it cannot keep it segregated. This is not a case where the reasons or motives for a particular action are arguably unclear . . . nor is it one where a discriminatory purpose is one among other reasons . . . nor one where a discriminatory purpose can be found only by inference. . . . The reasoning of the Georgia Supreme Court is simply that Senator Bacon intended Baconsfield to be a segregated public park, and because it cannot be operated as a segregated public park any longer . . . the park must be closed down and Baconsfield must revert to Senator Bacon's heirs. This Court agrees that this "city park is [being] destroyed because the Constitution require[s] it to be integrated. . . ." . . . It is therefore quite plain that but for the constitutional prohibition on the operation of segregated public parks, the City of Macon would continue to own and maintain Baconsfield.

I have no doubt that a public park may constitutionally be closed down because it is too expensive to run or has become superfluous, or for some other reason, strong or weak, or for no reason at all. But under the Equal Protection Clause a State may not close down a public facility solely to avoid its duty to desegregate that facility. . . . When it is as starkly clear as it is in this case that a public facility would remain open but for the constitutional command that it be operated on a nonsegregated basis, the closing of that facility conveys an unambiguous message of community involvement in racial discrimination. Its closing for the sole and unmistakable purpose of avoiding desegregation, like its operation as a segregated park, "generates [in Negroes] a feeling of inferiority as to their status in the community that may affect their hearts and minds in a way unlikely ever to be undone." Brown v. Board of Education, 347 U.S. 483, 494 (1954). It is no answer that continuing operation as a segregated facility is a constant reminder of a public policy that stigmatizes one race, whereas its closing occurs once and is over. That difference does not provide a constitutional distinction: state involvement in discrimination is unconstitutional, however short-lived.

The Court, however, affirms the judgment of the Georgia Supreme Court on the ground that the closing of Baconsfield did not involve state action. The Court concedes that the closing of the park by the city "solely to avoid the effect of a prior court order directing that the park be integrated" would be unconstitutional. However, the Court finds that in this case it is not the State or city but "a private party which is injecting the racially discriminatory motivation". . . . The exculpation of the State and city from responsibility for the closing of the park is simply indefensible on this record. This discriminatory closing is permeated with state action:

at the time Senator Bacon wrote his will Georgia statutes expressly authorized and supported the precise kind of discrimination provided for by him; in accepting title to the park, public officials of the City of Macon entered into an arrangement vesting in private persons the power to enforce a reversion if the city should ever incur a constitutional obligation to desegregate the park; it is a *public* park that is being closed for a discriminatory reason after having been operated for nearly half a century as a segregated *public* facility; and it is a state court that is enforcing the racial restriction that keeps apparently willing parties of different races from coming together in the park. That is state action in overwhelming abundance. . . .

In 1911, only six years after the enactment of §§ 69–504 and 69–505, Senator Bacon, a lawyer, wrote his will. When he wrote the provision creating Baconsfield as a public park open only to the white race, he was not merely expressing his own testamentary intent, but was taking advantage of the special power Georgia had conferred by §§ 69–504 and 69–505 on testators seeking to establish racially segregated public parks. . . . This state-encouraged testamentary provision is the sole basis for the Georgia courts' holding that Baconsfield must revert to Senator Bacon's heirs. The Court's finding that it is not the State of Georgia but "a private party which is injecting the racially discriminatory motivation" inexcusably disregards the State's role in enacting the statute without which Senator Bacon could not have written the discriminatory provision.

This, then, is not a case of private discrimination. It is rather discrimination in which the State of Georgia is "significantly involved," and enforcement of the reverter is therefore unconstitutional. . . .

I would reverse the judgment of the Supreme Court of Georgia.

TRAMMELL V. ELLIOTT
Supreme Court of Georgia, 1973.
230 Ga. 841, 199 S.E.2d 194.

HAWES, JUSTICE.

The appeal here is from an order of the Superior Court of DeKalb County entered on motion for summary judgment in a case brought by the executor of the estate of Miss Clem Boyd seeking construction of her will and direction from the court.

. . . In Item X of the will of Clem Boyd, there is recorded the desire that an educational scholarship fund be established in memory of the deceased's parents. This provision is, in its entirety, as follows: "All funds remaining after the aforementioned bequests are made or set aside, I wish made into an Endowment or Scholarship Fund in memory of my parents, the late William and Frances McCord Boyd, of Newton County, Georgia, said fund to be known as the Boyd–McCord Memorial Scholarship and placed with the Trustees of the Georgia Institute of Technology, Emory University, and Agnes Scott College, in equal proportions, to manage and keep reports on same. This scholarship is set aside *for benefit of deserving and qualified poor white boys and girls*, and interest only is to be used for said scholarships. However, should any proven descendant of my parents qualify and apply for benefits of this scholarship, it is my desire that they be given preference, and, if need be, go into the principal to the amount of $500.00 per scholastic year of four years for said descendant if earnestness is indicated and courses taken leading to a degree." (Emphasis supplied.) Although two of the named universities to act as trustees of the funds are private institutions, the Attorney General representing the Board of Regents of the University System of Georgia has conceded the requisite state interest with regard to the trust administration on behalf of the Georgia Institute of Technology. We proceed, therefore, on the basis that there is sufficient state action involved to invoke the strictures of the Fourteenth Amendment of the United States Constitution and that the racial restrictions in the devise may not be enforced save in violation of equal protection of law. Evans v. Newton, 382 U.S. 296, 86 S. Ct. 486, 15 L. Ed. 2d 373 (1966). . . . The single issue before the court with regard to the devise is whether the trial court erred in applying the doctrine of *cy pres* to exclude the offensive and discriminatory classification of the beneficiaries of the trusts and to effectuate the devise on the basis of an otherwise nondiscriminatory administration of the trusts.

The rule of law commonly termed the doctrine of *cy pres* is codified in the law of Georgia in two separate sections of the Code. These sections are as follows: "When a valid charitable bequest is incapable for some reason of execution in the exact manner provided by the testator, donor, or founder, a court of equity will carry it into effect in such a way as will as nearly as possible effectuate his intention." Code § 108–202. "A devise or bequest to a charitable use will be sustained and carried out in this State; and in all cases where there is a general intention manifested by the testator to effect a certain purpose, and the particular mode in which he directs it to be done shall fail from any cause, a court of chancery may, by approximation, effectuate the purpose in a manner most similar to that indicated by the testator." Code § 113–815.

The public policy expressed in these provisions favoring the validation of charitable trusts is supported by the longstanding rule of construction of this court by which forfeitures because of restrictive conditions attached to grants or devises of property are not favored, and as well by related Code provisions immunizing such trusts from the Georgia law against perpetuities. Code Ann. § 85–707. . . .

As a general rule, the doctrine of *cy pres* is applied in cases (1) where there is the presence of an otherwise valid charitable grant or trust; that is, one that has charity as its purpose and sufficiently offers benefits to an indefinite public; (2) where the specific intention of the settlor may not be legally or practicably carried into effect; and (3) where there is exhibited a general charitable intent on the part of the settlor. See, e.g., Creech v. Scottish Rite Hospital for Crippled Children, 211 Ga. 195, 84 S.E.2d 563 (1954); Moss v. Youngblood, 187 Ga. 188, 200 S.E. 689 (1938); Goree v. Georgia Industrial Home, 187 Ga. 368, 200 S.E. 684 (1938); Restatement, Second, Trusts Vol. 2, § 399, p. 297. . . . In determining at the outset whether there is exhibited a valid charitable purpose, the court is to look to Code § 108–203 wherein are listed the legitimate subjects of charity in Georgia. This Code provision includes, for example, for purposes of this appeal, "1. Relief of aged, impotent, diseased, or poor people. 2. Every educational purpose," among other legitimate subjects. Secondly, the court is to consider, from the instrument itself, whether there is exhibited a general charitable intent. See Hines v. Village of St. Joseph, Inc., 227 Ga. 431, 181 S.E.2d 54 (1971). The existence of a general charitable intent is inferred upon the establishment that the grant conforms in subject matter to any of the legitimate subjects of charity described in Code § 108–203. However, in deference to the intent of the testator, *cy pres* will not be applied where there is demonstrated an intention of the settlor contrary to the inference of general charitable intent that the property should be applied exclusively to the purpose which is or has become impracticable or illegal. Evans v. Abney, 224 Ga. 826, 165 S.E.2d 160 (1968). See, also, Restatement, Second, Trusts Vol. 2, § 399 Comment c, p. 299, and IV Scott, Trusts § 399.2 (3d ed. 1967). In view of the public policy expressed in Code §§ 108–202 and 113–815 favoring the effectuation of charitable grants promoting the public good and our own rule disfavoring forfeitures, such demonstration of a specific intent of the settlor as would result in a failure of the devise must be clear, definite, and unambiguous. In such event the trust will fail, and a resulting trust will be implied for the benefit of the testator or his heirs. Code § 108–106.

In viewing the will of Clem Boyd, the trusts established in Item X conformed in subject matter to those legitimate subjects of charity as found in Code § 108–203, being for the poor and for educational purposes. The purpose was one which offered a benefit to the general community, thereby qualifying as a public trust even though a preference is given to the relatives of the testator. . . . We infer from this that the testatrix possessed the requisite charitable intent as would authorize the use of *cy pres* to remove the discriminatory classification of the beneficiaries.

The appellant has argued on the basis of Evans v. Abney, 224 Ga. 826, 165 S.E.2d 160, supra, however, that the mere existence of the racial classification was sufficient to rebut the inference of general charitable intent. This argument is not, we believe, of substance. In *Evans* we held that from the contents of the will, in addition to the provision for racial restrictions on the use of a park, there was exhibited an intention on the part of the testator which would preclude the use of such park in any manner except that as exclusively and clearly demanded by the testator. *Evans*, therefore, upon its facts, stood for the recognized exception in the use of *cy pres* whereby from the will the specific intent of the testator conclusively negated any general charitable intention.

The will in the present case did not contain language by which the testatrix intended that the charitable trusts be administered exclusively in the manner prescribed. Other evidence supportive of the establishment of a specific and exclusive intention was also absent from the will, for there was no provision in the devise, for example, for a reverter clause or an alternative gift over in the event of a failure of the grant. On the other hand, in other parts of the will, the testatrix indicated strongly that she desired that no provision of the will should fail and the funds as set aside revert to her heirs. In Item IX, she noted in this regard that "Adults do not need my life's earnings, and the children who need a college education are the ones who interest me most."

We conclude from the foregoing that the evidence on summary judgment was conclusive of the trial court's finding of a general charitable intent on the part of the testatrix and that the doctrine of *cy pres* was correctly applied in excluding the illegal racial classification from the charitable grant. . . .

Judgment affirmed.

All the Justices concur except JORDAN, J. . . .

MATTER OF ESTATE OF WILSON

Court of Appeals of New York, 1983.
59 N.Y.2d 461, 465 N.Y.S.2d 900, 452 N.E.2d 1228.

COOKE, CHIEF JUDGE.

These appeals present the question whether the equal protection clause of the Fourteenth Amendment is violated when a court permits the administration of private charitable trusts according to the testators' intent to finance the education of male students and not female students. When a court applies trust law that neither encourages, nor affirmatively promotes, nor compels private discrimination but allows parties to engage in private selection in the devise or bequest of their property, that choice will not be attributable to the State and subjected to the Fourteenth Amendment's strictures.

I

The factual patterns in each of these matters are different, but the underlying legal issues are the same. In each there is imposed a decedent's intention to create a testamentary trust under which the class of beneficiaries are members of one sex.

In Matter of Wilson, article eleventh of Clark W. Wilson's will provided that the residuary of his estate be held in trust (Wilson Trust) and that the income "be applied to defraying the education and other expenses of the first year at college of five (5) young men who shall have graduated from the Canastota High School, three (3) of whom shall have attained the highest grades in the study of science and two (2) of whom shall have attained the highest grades in the study of chemistry, as may be certified to by the then Superintendent of Schools for the Canastota Central School District." Wilson died in June, 1969 and for the next 11 years the Wilson Trust was administered according to its terms.

In early 1981, the Civil Rights Office of the United States Department of Education received a complaint alleging that the superintendent's acts in connection with the Wilson Trust violated title IX of the Education Amendments of 1972 (U.S. Code, tit. 20, § 1681 et seq.), which prohibits gender discrimination in Federally financed education programs. The Department of Education informed the Canastota Central School District that the complaint would be investigated. Before the investigation was completed, the school district agreed to refrain from again providing names of students to the trustee. The trustee, Key Bank of Central New York, initiated this proceeding for a determination of the effect and validity of the trust provision of the will.

The Surrogate's Court, 108 Misc. 2d 1066, 439 N.Y.S.2d 250, held that the school superintendent's co-operation with the trustee violated no Federal statute or regulation prohibiting sexual discrimination, nor did it implicate the equal protection clause of the Fourteenth Amendment. The court ordered the trustee to continue administering the trust.

A unanimous Appellate Division, 87 A.D.2d 98, 451 N.Y.S.2d 891, Third Department, modified the Surrogate's decree. The court affirmed the Surrogate's finding that the testator intended the trust to benefit male students only and, noting that the school was under no legal obligation to provide the names of qualified male candidates, found "administration of the trust according to its literal terms is impossible." . . . The court then exercised its cy pres power to reform the trust by striking the clause in the will providing for the school superintendent's certification of the names of qualified candidates for the scholarships. The candidates were permitted to apply directly to the trustee.

Matter of Johnson also involves a call for judicial construction of a testamentary trust created for the exclusive benefit of male students. By a will dated December 13, 1975, Edwin Irving Johnson left his residuary estate in trust (Johnson Trust). Article sixth of the will provided that the income of the trust was to "be used and applied, each year to the extent available, for scholarships or grants for bright and deserving young men who have graduated from the High School of [the Croton–Harmon Union Free] School District, and whose parents are financially unable to send them to college, and who shall be selected by the Board of Education of such School District with the assistance of the Principal of such High School."

Johnson died in 1978. In accordance with the terms of the trust, the board of education, acting as trustee, announced that applications from male students would be accepted on or before May 1, 1979. Before any scholarships were awarded, however, the National Organization for Women, filed a complaint with the Civil Rights Office of the United States Department of Education. This complaint alleged that the school district's involvement in the Johnson Trust constituted illegal gender-based discrimination.

During the pendency of the Department of Education's investigation, a stipulation was entered into between the executrix of the will, the president of the board of education, and the Attorney–General. The parties sought "to avoid administering the educational bequest set forth in Article Sixth in a manner which is in conflict with the law and public policy prohibiting discrimination based on sex." The stipulation provided that "all interested parties agree to the deletion of the word 'men' in Article Sixth of the Will and the insertion of the word 'persons' in its place." The Attorney–General then brought this proceeding by petition to the Surrogate's Court to construe article sixth of the will.

The Surrogate found that the trustee's unwillingness to administer the trust according to its terms rendered administration of the trust impossible. The court, however, declined to reform the trust by giving effect to the stipulation. Rather, it reasoned that the testator's primary intent to benefit "deserving young men" would be most closely effected by replacing the school district with a private trustee.

A divided Appellate Division, 93 A.D.2d 1, 460 N.Y.S.2d 932, Second Department, reversed, holding that under the equal protection clause of the Fourteenth Amendment, a court cannot reform a trust that, by its own terms, would deny equal protection of law. The court reasoned that inasmuch as an agent of the State had been appointed trustee, the trust, if administered, would violate the equal protection clause. Judicial reformation of the trust by substituting trustees would, in that court's view, itself constitute State action in violation of the Fourteenth Amendment. The court determined that administration of the trust was impossible and, in an exercise of its cy pres power, reformed the trust by eliminating the gender restriction.

II

On these appeals, this court is called upon to consider the testators' intent in establishing these trusts, evaluate the public policy implications of gender restrictive trusts generally, and determine whether the judicial reformation of these trusts violates the equal protection clause of the Fourteenth Amendment.

There can be no question that these trusts, established for the promotion of education, are for a charitable purpose within the meaning of the law (see EPTL 8–1.1; . . . 4 Scott, Trusts [3d ed.], § 370). Charitable trusts are encouraged and favored by the law . . . and may serve any of a variety of benevolent purposes. . . . Among the advantages the law extends to charitable trusts are their exemption from the rules against perpetuities (see EPTL 9–1.1 . . .) and accumulations (EPTL 8–1.7) and their favorable tax treatment. . . . Moreover, unlike other trusts, a charitable trust will not necessarily fail when the settlor's specific charitable purpose or direction can no longer be accomplished.

When a court determines that changed circumstances have rendered the administration of a charitable trust according to its literal terms either "impracticable or impossible," the court may exercise its cy pres power to reform the trust in a manner that "will most effectively accomplish its general purposes" (EPTL 8–1.1, subd. [c]). In reforming trusts pursuant to this power, care must be taken to evaluate the precise purpose or direction of the testator, so that when the court directs the trust towards another charitable end, it will "give effect insofar as practicable to the full design of the testator as manifested by his will and codicil" (Matter of Scott, 8 N.Y.2d 419, 427, 208 N.Y.S.2d 984, 171 N.E.2d 326 . . .).

The court, of course, cannot invoke its cy pres power without first determining that the testator's specific charitable purpose is no longer capable of being performed by the trust (see, e.g., Matter of Scott, supra; Matter of Swan, 237 App. Div. 454, 261 N.Y.S. 428, affd. sub nom. Matter of St. Johns Church of Mt. Morris, 263 N.Y. 638, 189 N.E. 734; Matter of Fairchild, 15 Misc. 2d 272, 178 N.Y.S.2d 886). In establishing these trusts, the testators expressly and unequivocally intended that they provide for the educational expenses of male students. It cannot be said that the accomplishment of the testators' specific expression of charitable intent is "impossible or impracticable." So long as the subject high schools graduate boys with the requisite qualifications, the testators' specific charitable intent can be fulfilled.

Nor are the trusts' particular limitation of beneficiaries by gender invalid and incapable of being accomplished as violative of public policy. It is true that the eradication in this State of gender-based discrimination is an important public policy. Indeed, the Legislature has barred gender-based discrimination in education ..., employment ..., housing, credit, and many other areas. ... The restrictions in these trusts run contrary to this policy favoring equal opportunity and treatment of men and women. A provision in a charitable trust, however, that is central to the testator's or settlor's charitable purpose, and is not illegal, should not be invalidated on public policy grounds unless that provision, if given effect, would substantially mitigate the general charitable effect of the gift (see 4 Scott, Trusts [3d ed.], § 399.4).

Proscribing the enforcement of gender restrictions in private charitable trusts would operate with equal force towards trusts whose benefits are bestowed exclusively on women. "Reduction of the disparity in economic condition between men and women caused by the long history of discrimination against women has been recognized as ... an important governmental objective" (Califano v. Webster, 430 U.S. 313, 317, 97 S. Ct. 1192, 1194, 51 L. Ed. 2d 360). There can be little doubt that important efforts in effecting this type of social change can be and are performed through private philanthropy (see, generally, Commission on Private Philanthropy and Public Needs, Giving in America: Toward a Stronger Voluntary Sector [1975]). And, the private funding of programs for the advancement of women is substantial and growing (see ... Ford Foundation, Financial Support of Women's Programs in the 1970's [1979] ...). Indeed, one compilation of financial assistance offered primarily or exclusively to women lists 854 sources of funding (see Schlacter, Directory of Financial Aids for Women [2d ed., 1981] ...). Current thinking in private philanthropic institutions advocates that funding offered by such institutions and the opportunities within the institutions themselves be directly responsive to the needs of particular groups (see Ford Foundation, op cit., at pp. 41–44 ...). It is evident, therefore, that the focusing of private philanthropy on certain classes within society may be consistent with public policy. Consequently, that the restrictions in the trusts before this court may run contrary to public efforts promoting equality of opportunity for women does not justify imposing a per se rule that gender restrictions in private charitable trusts violate public policy.

Finally, this is not an instance in which the restriction of the trusts serves to frustrate a paramount charitable purpose. In Howard Sav. Inst. v. Peep, 34 N.J. 494, 170 A.2d 39, for example, the testator made a charitable bequest to Amherst College to be placed in trust and to provide scholarships for "deserving American born, Protestant, Gentile boys of good moral repute, not given to gambling, smoking, drinking or similar acts." Due to the religious restrictions, the college declined to accept the bequest as contrary to its charter. The court found that the college was the principal beneficiary of the trust, so that removing the religious restriction and thereby allowing the college to accept the gift would permit administration of the trust in a manner most closely effectuating the testator's intent (see, also, Matter of Hawley, 32 Misc. 2d 624, 223 N.Y.S.2d 803; Coffee v. Rice Univ., 408 S.W.2d 269 [Tex. Civ. App.]).

In contrast, the trusts subject to these appeals were not intended to directly benefit the school districts. Although the testators sought the school districts' participation, this was incidental to their primary intent of financing part of the college education of boys who attended the schools. Consequently, severance of the school districts' role in the trusts' administration will not frustrate any part of the testators' charitable purposes. Inasmuch as the specific charitable intent of the testators is not inherently "impossible or impracticable" of being achieved by the trusts, there is no occasion to exercise cy pres power.

Although not inherently so, these trusts are currently incapable of being administered as originally intended because of the school districts' unwillingness to co-operate. These impediments, however, may be remedied by an exercise of a court's general equitable power over all trusts to permit a deviation from the administrative terms of a trust and to appoint a successor trustee.

A testamentary trust will not fail for want of a trustee (see EPTL 8–1.1; see, also, Matter of Thomas, 254 N.Y. 292, 172 N.E. 513) and, in the event a trustee is unwilling or unable to act, a court may replace the trustee with another (see EPTL 7–2.6; SCPA 1502; see, also, Matter of Andrews, 233 App. Div. 547, 253 N.Y.S. 590; 2 Scott, Trusts [3d ed.], § 108.1). Accordingly, the proper means of continuing the Johnson Trust would be to replace the school district with someone able and willing to administer the trust according to its terms.

When an impasse is reached in the administration of a trust due to an incidental requirement of its terms, a court may effect, or permit the trustee to effect, a deviation from the trust's literal terms. . . . This power differs from a court's cy pres power in that "[t]hrough exercise of its deviation power the court alters or amends administrative provisions in the trust instrument but does not alter the purpose of the charitable trust or change its dispositive provisions" (Bogert, Trusts and Trustees [rev. 2d ed.], § 394, p. 249; see, e.g., Trustees of Sailors' Snug Harbor v. Carmody, 211 N.Y. 286, 105 N.E. 543; Matter of Bruen, 83 N.Y.S.2d 197; Matter of Godfrey, 36 N.Y.S.2d 414, affd. no opn. 264 App. Div. 885, 36 N.Y.S.2d 244). The Wilson Trust provision that the school district certify a list of students is an incidental part of the trust's administrative requirements, which no longer can be satisfied in light of the district's refusal to cooperate. The same result intended by the testator may be accomplished by permitting the students to apply directly to the trustee. Therefore, a deviation from the Wilson Trust's administrative terms by eliminating the certification requirement would be the appropriate method of continuing that trust's administration.

III

It is argued before this court that the judicial facilitation of the continued administration of gender-restrictive charitable trusts violates the equal protection clause of the Fourteenth Amendment. . . . The strictures of the equal protection clause are invoked when the State engages in invidious discrimination. . . . Indeed, the State itself cannot, consistent with the Fourteenth Amendment, award scholarships that are gender restrictive. . . .

The Fourteenth Amendment, however, "erects no shield against merely private conduct, however discriminatory or wrongful." (Shelley v. Kraemer, 334 U.S. 1, 13, 68 S. Ct. 836, 842, 92 L. Ed 1161 . . . ; Evans v. Abney, 396 U.S. 435, 445, 90 S. Ct. 628, 633, 24 L. Ed. 2d 634). Private discrimination may violate equal protection of the law when accompanied by State participation in, facilitation of, and, in some cases, acquiescence in the discrimination (see, e.g., . . . Shelley v. Kraemer, . . . supra). Although there is no conclusive test to determine when State involvement in private discrimination will violate the Fourteenth Amendment . . . , the general standard that has evolved is whether "the conduct allegedly causing the deprivation of a federal right [is] fairly attributable to the state" (Lugar v. Edmondson Oil Co., 457 U.S. 922, 937, 102 S. Ct. 2744, 2754, 73 L. Ed. 2d 482). Therefore, it is a question of "state responsibility" and "[o]nly by sifting facts and weighing circumstances can the . . . involvement of the State in private conduct be attributed its true significance" (Burton v. Wilmington Parking Auth., 365 U.S. 715, 722, 81 S. Ct. 856, 860, 6 L. Ed. 2d 45 . . .). . . .

The State generally may not be held responsible for private discrimination solely on the basis that it permits the discrimination to occur (see Flagg Bros. v. Brooks, 436 U.S. 149, 164, 98 S. Ct. 1729, 1737, 56 L. Ed. 2d 185 . . . ; Evans v. Abney, . . . supra). Nor is the State under an affirmative obligation to prevent purely private discrimination (see Reitman v. Mulkey, 387 U.S. 369, 376, 377, 87 S. Ct. 1627, 1631, 1632, 18 L. Ed. 2d 830 . . .). Therefore, when the State regulates private dealings it may be responsible for private discrimination occurring in the regulated field only when enforcement of its regulation has the effect of compelling the private discrimination (see Flagg Bros. v. Brooks, supra . . . ; Shelley v. Kraemer, . . . supra . . .).

In Shelley v. Kraemer (supra), for example, the Supreme Court held that the equal protection clause was violated by judicial enforcement of a private covenant that prohibited the sale of affected properties to "people of Negro or Mongolian Race." When one of the properties was sold to a black family, the other property owners sought to enforce the covenant in State court and the family was ordered to move from the property. The Supreme Court noted "that the restrictive agreements standing alone cannot be regarded as violative of any rights guaranteed to petitioners by the Fourteenth Amendment. So long as the purposes of those agreements are effectuated by voluntary adherence to their terms, it would appear clear that there has been no action by the State and the provisions of the Amendment have not been violated" (334 U.S., at p. 13, 68 S. Ct. at p. 842). The court held, however, that it did [not] have before it cases "in which the States have merely abstained from action leaving private individuals free to impose such discriminations as they see fit. Rather, these are cases in which the States have made available to such individuals the full coercive power of the government to deny petitioners, on the grounds of race or color, the enjoyment of property rights" (id., at p. 19, 68 S. Ct. at p. 845). It was not the neutral regulation of contracts permitting parties to enter discriminatory agreements that caused the discrimination to be attributable to the State. Instead, it was that the State court's exercise of its judicial power directly effected a discriminatory act. . . .

A court's application of its equitable power to permit the continued administration of the trusts involved in these appeals falls outside the ambit of the Fourteenth Amendment. Although the field of trusts is regulated by the State, the Legislature's failure to forbid private discriminatory trusts does not cause such trusts, when they arise, to be attributable to the State (see Flagg Bros. v. Brooks, . . . supra; see, also, Evans v. Abney, 396 U.S. 435, 458, 90 S. Ct. 628, 640, 24 L. Ed. 2d 634 [Brennan, J., dissenting] . . .). It naturally follows that, when a court applies this trust law and determines that it permits the continued existence of private discriminatory trusts, the Fourteenth Amendment is not implicated.

In the present appeals, the coercive power of the State has never been enlisted to enforce private discrimination. Upon finding that requisite formalities of creating a trust had been met, the courts below determined the testator's intent, and applied the relevant law permitting those intentions to be privately carried out. The court's power compelled no discrimination. That discrimination had been sealed in the private execution of the wills. Recourse to the courts was had here only for the purpose of facilitating the administration of the trusts, not for enforcement of their discriminatory dispositive provisions.

This is not to say that a court's exercise of its power over trusts can never invoke the scrutiny of the Fourteenth Amendment. This court holds only that a trust's discriminatory terms are not fairly attributable to the State when a court applies trust principles that permit private discrimination but do not encourage, affirmatively promote, or compel it.

The testators' intention to involve the State in the administration of these trusts does not alter this result, notwithstanding that the effect of the courts' action respecting the trusts was to eliminate this involvement. The courts' power to replace a trustee who is unwilling to act as in *Johnson* or to permit a deviation from an incidental administrative term in the trust as in *Wilson* is a part of the law permitting this private conduct and extends to all trusts regardless of their purposes. It compels no discrimination. Moreover, the minimal State participation in the trusts' administration prior to the time that they reached the courts for the constructions under review did not cause the trusts to take on an indelible public character (see Evans v. Newton, 382 U.S. 296, 301, 86 S. Ct. 486, 489, 15 L. Ed. 2d 373; Commonwealth of Pennsylvania v. Brown, 392 F.2d 120).

In sum, the Fourteenth Amendment does not require the State to exercise the full extent of its power to eradicate private discrimination. It is only when the State itself discriminates, compels another to discriminate, or allows another to assume one of its functions and discriminate that such discrimination will implicate the amendment.

Accordingly, in Matter of Wilson, the order of the Appellate Division should be affirmed. . . .

In Matter of Johnson, the order of the Appellate Division should be reversed . . . and the decree of the Surrogate's Court, Westchester County, reinstated.

[The opinion of JUDGE MEYER, who concurred in Matter of Wilson and dissented in Matter of Johnson, is omitted.]

NOTES

1. *State action.* For a case reaching a different result than that in *Wilson*, see In re Certain Scholarship Funds, 575 A.2d 1325 (N.H.1990) (affirming trial court's use of cy pres to reform wills creating male-only scholarship funds by replacing the words "boy" and "protestant boy" with the word "student"; use of "equitable powers of deviation to reform the trust[s] by striking the language requiring the participation of public officials and appointing private persons to act in their absence, thereby terminating any State participation," would have been impermissible under the New Hampshire constitution).

Over the years, a number of judicial opinions have expressed concern that application of the equal protection clause to charitable trusts would destroy a wide variety of beneficial enterprises. In particular, these opinions have envisioned a threat to trusts in support of religious activities. For example, Justice Bell, concurring in In re Girard's Estate, 127 A.2d 287 (Pa.1956), rev'd sub nom. Pennsylvania v. Board of Directors of City Trusts, 353 U.S. 230 (1957), warned:

> If the present contention of the City is correct, its effect will be catastrophic on testamentary church and charitable bequests. . . . The constitutional prohibition against discrimination—the Fourteenth Amendment—is not confined to color; *it prohibits the States* from making any discrimination because of race, creed or color. It follows logically and necessarily that if an individual cannot constitutionally leave his money to an orphanage or to a private home and college for poor white male orphans, he cannot constitutionally leave his money to a Catholic, or Episcopal, or Baptist, or Methodist, or Lutheran or Presbyterian Church; or to a Synagogue for Orthodox Jews; or to a named Catholic Church or to a named Catholic priest for Masses for the repose of his soul, or for other religious or charitable purposes. That would shock the people of Pennsylvania and the people of the United States more than a terrible earthquake or a large atomic bomb. [127 A.2d at 318 (emphasis in the original).]

In fact, the courts have, by and large, refused to expand the concept of state action to include supervision of a charitable trust by either the court or the attorney general. In addition to the *Wilson* decision, see Lockwood v. Killian, 375 A.2d 998 (Conn.1977), which involved a testamentary charitable trust to grant college scholarships to beneficiaries chosen by a special selection committee from among "needy, deserving boys from the graduating classes of the preceding month of June from the high schools of the County of Hartford and State of Connecticut, whose high school marks for their individual and respective entire high school course shall have been at least an average of seventy (70) points . . . or better, who are members of the Caucasian race and who have severally, specifically professed themselves to be of the Protestant Congregational Faith." Members of the selection committee requested judicial instructions because there was an insufficient number of applicants for the scholarships. The trial court applied cy pres and removed the racial and gender restrictions. On appeal by the Attorney General from the refusal of the trial court to strike the religious qualification as unlawful, the Supreme Court of Connecticut upheld the restriction as a private discrimination not involving state action notwithstanding the "necessary participation" of the Attorney General in a cy pres proceeding brought by the selection committee. The Court reaffirmed its position, following remand. 425 A.2d 909 (Conn.1979). See also First Nat'l Bank of Kansas City v. Danforth, 523 S.W.2d 808 (Mo.), cert. denied, 421 U.S. 992 (1975), in which a testator left approximately $8,500,000 in trust with the income to be used for the "maintenance and support of Protestant Christian Hospitals . . . contributing to the maintenance, support and care of sick and infirm patients in said Hospitals, born of white parents in the United States of America." The Missouri Supreme Court held that this description of the beneficiaries was unambiguous and that because no state action was involved the trust was not invalidated by the Fourteenth Amendment.

Courts have usually held that religious eligibility standards for individual bequests or benefits under private trusts (e.g., requirements that a beneficiary must marry, raise children, etc. within a specified religion to receive benefits) are not subject to the equal protection clause of the Fourteenth Amendment. See, e.g., Shapira v. Union Nat'l Bank, 315 N.E.2d 825 (Ohio Com. Pleas 1974); Gordon v. Gordon, 124 N.E.2d 228 (Mass.1955), cert. denied, 349 U.S. 947 (1955); United States Nat'l Bank v. Snodgrass, supra p. __.

See generally Petrucci, The Cy Pres Doctrine—Is It State Action?, 18 Cap. U.L. Rev. 383 (1989); Macey, Private Trusts for the Provision of Private Goods, 37 Emory L.J. 295 (1988); Luria, Prying Loose the Dead Hand of the Past: How Courts Apply Cy Pres to Race, Gender, and Religiously Restricted Trusts, 21 U.S.F. L. Rev. 41 (1987); Swanson, Discriminatory Charitable Trusts: Time for a Legislative Solution, 48 U. Pitt. L. Rev. 153 (1986); Leacock, Racial Preferences in Educational Trusts: An Overview of the United States Experience, 28 How. L.J. 715 (1985); Annot., Validity of Charitable Gift or Trust Containing Gender Restrictions on Beneficiaries, 90 A.L.R.4th 836 (1991).

2. *Tax law.* In Bob Jones University v. United States, 461 U.S. 574 (1983), the Supreme Court upheld, on statutory grounds, the Internal Revenue Service's denial of tax exemptions for both a university and a private school with racially discriminatory admissions policies. Both schools justified their policies on religious grounds. Although in *Bob Jones* the Court found statutory authority for IRS denial of tax exemptions for racially discriminatory schools, and upheld the constitutionality of the statutes involved, it shed little light on the constitutionality of various discriminatory practices or even the constitutionality of tax statutes that grant exemptions to racially discriminatory institutions. Thus, the question remains open whether federal and state tax exemptions for charitable trusts and foundations, or the administrative relationships between these charities and the taxing authorities, constitute state action.

The Second Circuit, en banc, has divided on the question. The majority held that, upon remand to the trial court, a sifting of the facts and a weighing of the circumstances might well lead to a conclusion that the defendant foundations were "substantially dependent upon their exempt status, that the regulatory scheme [was] both detailed and intrusive, that the scheme carrie[d] connotations of government approval . . . , and that they serve[d] some public function" and that, as a consequence, a finding of state action might be appropriate. Jackson v. Statler Foundation, 496 F.2d 623, 634 (2d Cir.1973). Judge Friendly argued in dissent:

The interest in preserving an area of untrammeled choice for private philanthropy is very great. Even among philanthropic institutions, the activities of charitable family foundations, receiving no government benefit other than tax exemption, should be the last to be swept, under a "sifting of facts and exercise of judgment," within the concept of state action. There are hundreds of thousands of foundations ranging from the giants to the pigmies. While most foundations, particularly large ones, give mainly to institutions serving all races and creeds, although hardly in the completely nondiscriminatory way required of public institutions, I see nothing offensive, either constitutionally or morally, in a foundation's choosing to give preferentially or even exclusively to Jesuit seminaries, to Yeshivas, to black colleges or to the NAACP. Indeed, I find it something of a misnomer to apply the pejorative term "racial discrimination" to a *failure* to make a charitable gift. . . . Donors are not going to be willing to spend their time and money, or to have directors and staffs of foundations spend theirs, in defending actions like this one. If the federal courts take over the supervision of philanthropy, there will ultimately be no philanthropy to supervise. [496 F.2d at 639–40.]

The majority relied on McGlotten v. Connally, 338 F.Supp. 448 (D.D.C.1972), as authority for the proposition that tax benefits constitute federal subsidies and make the recipient subject to constitutional obligations and federal civil rights legislation. In that case a three-judge district court held that a fraternal order that excluded nonwhites from membership was not entitled to tax exemptions; nor were gifts to it for charitable purposes deductible by the donors. An article thereafter warned:

If full sway is given to the *McGlotten* theory that tax allowances are equivalent to direct grants of public funds and hence impose constitutional obligations on the recipient, no one will be immune. As we have pointed out, the Internal Revenue Code is a pudding with plums for everyone.

Bittker & Kaufman, Taxes and Civil Rights: "Constitutionalizing" the Internal Revenue Code, 82 Yale L.J. 51, 86 (1972).

SIMMONS V. PARSONS COLLEGE

Supreme Court of Iowa, 1977.
256 N.W.2d 225.

LeGRAND, JUSTICE.

This declaratory judgment action was brought to construe the will of Lester Morgan Wells as it relates to two trusts established for the education of needy students at Drake University and Parsons College.

The will was executed on August 15, 1969. Lester Morgan Wells died on January 3, 1974. After the execution of the will but prior to the testator's death, Parsons College became bankrupt. It no longer operates as an educational institution.

The action was brought by Dorothy Simmons, Executor of the estate of Lester Morgan Wells. Parsons College (and its trustee in bankruptcy), Drake University, and the heirs at law of the decedent were made defendants. The trial court held the trust established for Parsons College students failed and the testator's heirs at law were entitled to take the property which would otherwise have gone to Parsons College as trustee.

Parsons College has filed a disclaimer and is not a party to this appeal. The heirs at law, of course, do not appeal. The sole appellant is Drake University (Drake), and our discussion is limited accordingly. We affirm the trial court.

We set out the controversial provision of decedent's will:

> *Fourth*: All the rest of my estate and the assets thereof, I give, devise and bequeath, subject to the provisions of the Fifth Paragraph of this will, to Drake University of Des Moines, Iowa, and Parsons College of Fairfield, Iowa, in equal shares, for scholarship purposes only. Such funds shall be held in a permanent trust by each institution, which shall be known as the Lester Morgan Wells Trust, and only the income therefrom shall be used to assist needy students to receive a college education and the same shall be paid to such persons and in such amounts as the respective colleges shall determine, but the principal is to be kept intact and properly invested as a permanent trust fund; said institutions are not required to give bond.

> It is my wish and desire, but not mandatory, that the trust fund herein established and devised for Parsons College of Fairfield, Iowa, be used for the benefit of students seeking a college education who reside in Jefferson County, Iowa, or in the vicinity thereof, which shall include the State of Iowa but not beyond.

> If either or both of said institutions should fail to faithfully carry out the provisions of the Fourth Paragraph of this will, then said trust or trusts shall fail and shall stand cancelled and revoked and the principal thereof I will, devise and bequeath to my legal heirs at law who may be living at that time and as may be determined by the laws of the State of Iowa, said heirs to be determined as of the date of my death.

Several codicils were executed later, but they are unimportant to the issues raised on this appeal.

Although Drake poses a number of questions to be answered, the sole issue presented is whether the doctrine of cy pres should be applied to the Parsons College trust in view of that institution's inability to carry out the trust purposes. Drake says we should apply cy pres and urges us to let it serve as trustee for the entire fund. Otherwise, Drake argues, that portion of the funds left to Parsons College will revert to numerous collateral heirs whom the testator did not know and whom he did not intend to benefit.

Cy pres is a doctrine which literally means "as near as may be." Hodge v. Wellman, 191 Iowa 877, 882, 179 N.W. 534, 536 (1920). . . . It is applicable only to charitable trusts and then only when the trust established by a testator fails, no alternative disposition of the property has been made, and the general trust purposes may be accomplished by permitting it to be administered in a way different from, but closely related to, the testator's plan.

The doctrine is stated this way in Restatement (Second) Trusts, § 399 (1959):

> *Failure of Particular Purpose Where Settlor Had General Charitable Intention. The Doctrine of Cy Pres.*
>
> If property is given in trust to be applied to a particular charitable purpose, and it is or becomes impossible or impracticable or illegal to carry out the particular purpose, and if the settlor manifested a more general intention to devote the property to charitable purposes, the trust will not fail but the court will direct the application of the property to some charitable purpose which falls within the general charitable intention of the settlor.

While charitable trusts are favored by the law . . . courts may not ignore the testator's intent in order to give effect to doubtful trust provisions by invoking the doctrine of cy pres. Cy pres is simply a liberal rule of construction used to carry out, not defeat, the testator's intent. In re Estate of Staab, 173 N.W.2d 866, 870 (Iowa 1970); Hodge v. Wellman, supra, 191 Iowa at 882, 179 N.W. at 536.

The cy pres doctrine is inapplicable when the testator has anticipated the possible failure of the trust and has made alternative disposition of his property to meet that contingency. Under such circumstances the testamentary intent may be ascertained without such extrinsic help. . . .

Although Drake argues otherwise, the testator made such alternative disposition in the event either Parsons or Drake was unable to administer the trust. He said unequivocally the assets which would have gone to the trust should then go to his heirs at law.

This was the basis for the trial court's ruling that the cy pres doctrine was not applicable. We hold this conclusion was correct. We have reviewed all of the authorities relied on by Drake. None of them afford substantial support for its position.

We are told the case is stronger in favor of cy pres because the trust failed at the outset rather than after it had been under administration for some time. The authorities are to the contrary. The doctrine is more reluctantly resorted to under such circumstances. See Restatement (Second) Trusts § 399, Comment "i". . . .

We hold the bequest to Parsons College in trust for the purposes set out in the Fourth Paragraph of decedent's will has failed because Parsons College is unable to administer the trust. We further find that the last will of Lester Morgan Wells provides the designated trust property under such circumstances should go to his heirs at law.

The judgment of the trial court is affirmed.

NOTES

1. *Leading case.* The classic American cy pres case is Jackson v. Phillips, 96 Mass. 539 (1867), involving a trust under the will of a decedent who died in 1861. Its stated purpose was "for the preparation and circulation of books, newspapers, the delivery of speeches, lectures, and such other means, as, in [the trustees'] judgment, will create a public sentiment that will put an end to negro slavery in this country." Id. at 541. President Lincoln emancipated the slaves in 1863, and, in 1865, the Thirteenth Amendment abolished slavery. Thus, by 1867, the testator's particular charitable purpose had already been accomplished, and, absent cy pres, the trust would have failed.

In searching for evidence of general charitable intent, the Court found comfort in the following language from the will: "I hope and trust that [the trustees] will receive the services and sympathy, the donations and bequests, of the friends of the slave." Id. at 541, 558, 594–96. This the Court took as evidence that the testator wanted not only to eliminate slavery, but also to help the slaves themselves. The Court also noted the will's elaborate mechanisms for ensuring a self-perpetuating body of trustees. These mechanisms allowed the Court to infer that the testator must have been willing to embrace changed circumstances. The Court held that the testator's "immediate purpose" was "moral education of the people," and that his "ultimate object" was "to better the condition of the African race in this country." Id. at 595. The Court therefore allowed application of the trust assets cy pres pursuant to a scheme to be framed by a master. The master, in turn, reported that "the intention nearest to that of emancipating the slaves was by educating the emancipated slaves to render them capable of self-government." This the master aimed to accomplish by paying over the trust funds to the New England Branch of the American Freedmen's Union Commission, which had as its object "the relief, education and elevation of the freedmen of the United

States." Id. at 598. With minor modifications, the Court accepted and confirmed the master's report.

2. *Typical cases.* Typical situations in which courts have applied cy pres include:

   a. insufficient funds, see Will of Porter, 447 A.2d 977 (Pa.Super.1982); Estate of Thompson, 414 A.2d 881 (Me.1980);

   b. surplus funds, see United States on Behalf of United States Coast Guard v. Cerio, 831 F.Supp. 530 (E.D.Va.1993); Estate of Puckett, 168 Cal.Rptr. 311 (App. 1980);

   c. prior accomplishment of charitable purpose, see Board of Trustees of the University of North Carolina at Chapel Hill v. Unknown Heirs of Prince, 319 S.E.2d 239 (N.C.1984); Jackson v. Phillips, supra;

   d. impossibility or refusal of trustee or third person to cooperate, see Kolb v. City of Storm Lake, 736 N.W.2d 546 (Iowa 2007); Weninger Estate v. Canadian Diabetes Ass'n, 109 D.L.R.4th 232 (Ont. Ct. 1993);

   e. nonexistence of named charitable corporation or association, see Obermeyer v. Bank of America, 140 S.W.3d 18 (Mo. 2004); Mark Twain Kansas City Bank v. Kroh Brothers Development Co., 863 P.2d 355 (Kan.1992); and

   f. unsuitability of premises devised for charitable purpose, see Wigglesworth v. Cowles, 648 N.E.2d 1289 (Mass.App.), review denied, 651 N.E.2d 410 (Mass.1995).

3. *General charitable intent no longer necessary.* The stated goal of cy pres is to carry out the settlor's wishes as nearly as possible. Thus, under traditional doctrine, if a settlor had no "general" charitable intent, the trust *should* fail upon failure of the settlor's particular purpose. See Restatement (Second) of Trusts § 399 (1959). It was, however, often difficult to determine whether the settlor (usually dead) had general charitable intent, or whether, upon failure of the initial particular charitable purpose, the settlor would have preferred a resulting trust (the equitable equivalent of a reversion). When the governing instrument contained a gift over, the courts generally found that there was no general charitable intent. In addition to Simmons v. Parsons College, see, e.g., L.C. Wagner Trust v. Barium Springs Home, 409 S.E.2d 913 (N.C.1991); Hermitage Methodist Homes of Virginia, Inc. v. Dominion Trust Co., 387 S.E.2d 740 (Va.), cert. denied, 498 U.S. 907 (1990) (refusing to apply cy pres to avoid gift over, despite presence of racial restriction). But see In re Lucas Charitable Gift, 261 P.3d 800 (Haw. App. 2011) (notwithstanding gift over, when both primary and secondary charitable purposes proved impracticable, court applied cy pres, reasoning that alternative charitable purposes indicated general charitable intent). Even when there was no gift over, the courts, as in Evans v. Abney, supra, sometimes found

that the settlor lacked general charitable intent. See, e.g., American Nat'l Bank & Trust Co. v. Auman, 746 S.W.2d 464 (Tenn.App.1987). See generally Note, Phantom Selves: The Search for a General Charitable Intent in the Application of the Cy Pres Doctrine, 40 Stan. L. Rev. 973 (1988).

Restatement (Third) of Trusts § 67 (2003) omits any reference to general charitable intent and makes cy pres available "[u]nless the terms of the trust provide otherwise." The Restatement reasons that trust law "favors an interpretation that would sustain a charitable trust and avoid the return of the trust property to the settlor or successors in interest." Id. cmt. b. UTC § 413(b) goes even further, providing that a gift over that would result in the property of a charitable trust going to a noncharitable beneficiary prevails over the court's power to apply cy pres *only if* "the trust property is to revert to the settlor and the settlor is still living" or "fewer than 21 years have elapsed since the date of the trust's creation." Thus, under the UTC, except in the relatively unusual case in which the failure of the initial particular charitable purpose occurs shortly after the creation of the trust, cy pres is mandatory, notwithstanding the clearest of indications that the settlor's intent was to the contrary.

4. *Charitable purposes that are wasteful.* Cy pres has generally been available only when it was "impossible or impracticable or illegal" to carry out the initial charitable purpose. Restatement (Second) of Trusts § 399 (1959). See, e.g., In re R.B. Plummer Memorial Loan Fund Trust, 661 N.W.2d 307 (Neb. 2003) (charitable trust created to make student loans sought permission to grant scholarships; denied, as original purpose was neither impossible nor impracticable); Museum of Fine Arts v. Beland, 735 N.E.2d 1248 (Mass. 2000) (charitable trust for exhibition of certain paintings sought authorization to sell some of the paintings; denied, as original purpose was neither impossible nor impracticable).

Restatement (Third) of Trusts § 67 (2003) extends cy pres to situations in which it would be "wasteful to apply all of the property to the designated purpose." See also UTC § 413(a). This change responds in part to a prominent case in which the settlor created a large trust (that grew to more than $300 million) to "provid[e] care for the needy" and "for other non-profit charitable, religious, or educational purposes" in one of the nation's most affluent areas, Marin County, California. For the otherwise unpublished Superior Court opinion, which refused to apply cy pres so as to permit the trustee also to spend trust income in the four other Bay Area counties, see In the Matter of the Estate of Beryl H. Buck, 21 U.S.F. L. Rev. 691 (1987) ("Neither 'inefficiency' nor 'ineffective philanthropy' constitute impracticability. . . ."). See generally Note, Relaxing the Dead Hand's Grip: Charitable Efficiency and the Doctrine of Cy Pres, 74 Va. L. Rev. 635 (1988); Simon, American Philanthropy and the Buck Trust, 21 U.S.F. L. Rev. 641 (1987); Comment, Cy Pres Inexpediency and the Buck Trust, 20 U.S.F. L. Rev. 577 (1986).

5. *Standing.* When a particular charitable purpose fails, the settlor (or the settlor's successor) ordinarily has standing to oppose application of cy pres and argue for a resulting trust. Compare Note 2, supra p. 697. In some states, a living settlor even has the power to veto cy pres. See N.Y. EPTL § 8–1.1(c). In contrast, as we have seen, under the UTC cy pres is often mandatory. See Note 3. In any event, the Attorney General always has standing and is ordinarily an indispensable party in any cy pres proceeding.

6. *Gifts subject to charitable restrictions.* Cy pres is also available as to outright gifts subject to charitable restrictions. See Restatement (Third) of Trusts §§ 28 cmt. a, 67 cmt. e (2003); Georgia O'Keeffe Found. v. Fisk Univ., 312 S.W.3d 1 (Tenn. App. 2009).

7. *More on cy pres.* See 6 Scott and Ascher on Trusts ch. 39; Atkinson, The Low Road to Cy Pres Reform: Principled Practice to Remove Dead Hand Control of Charitable Assets, 58 Case W. L. Rev. 97 (2007); Chester, Cy Pres or Gift Over?: The Search for Coherence in Judicial Reform of Failed Charitable Trusts, 23 Suffolk U.L. Rev. 41 (1989).

8. *Equitable deviation.* Even as to private trusts, to which cy pres does not apply, the courts can authorize deviation from the literal terms of the trust instrument, in order to accommodate new circumstances the settlor has not foreseen. See Restatement (Third) of Trusts § 66 (2003); infra pp. 849–856. This power also exists as to charitable trusts. See Matter of Estate of Craig, 848 P.2d 313 (Ariz.App.1992). See generally Goldman, Just What the Doctor Ordered? The Doctrine of Deviation, the Case of Doctor Barnes's Trust and the Future Location of the Barnes Foundation, 39 Real Prop. Prob. & Tr. J. 711 (2005); Schweizer, Settlor's Intent vs. Trustee's Will: The Barnes Foundation Case, 29 Colum. J.L. & Arts 63 (2005).

3. HONORARY TRUSTS

IN RE THOMPSON

Chancery Division, 1933.
[1934] Ch. 342, [1933] All Eng. Rep. 805.

CLAUSON, J.

The testator, who was a member of Trinity Hall, [in the University of] Cambridge [and died on August 21, 1932], by his will dated December 14, 1904, bequeathed a legacy of 1000*l.* to his friend George William Lloyd, who is also a member of the same college, to be applied by him in such manner as he should in his absolute discretion think fit towards the promotion and furthering of fox-hunting [and devised and bequeathed his residuary estate to Trinity Hall in the University of Cambridge to be applied by the Master and Fellows thereof in such manner as they should deem best for the benefit of the college as therein more particularly mentioned]. In the first place, it is clear that Mr. Lloyd is not entitled to the legacy for his own benefit nor indeed does he so claim it, but he is anxious to carry out the testator's expressed wishes, if and so far as he lawfully may do so. No argument has been put forward which could justify the Court in holding this gift to be a gift in favour of charity, although it may well be that a gift for the benefit of animals generally is a charitable gift: but it seems to me plain that I cannot construe the object for which this legacy was given as being for the benefit of animals generally. In my judgment the object of the gift has been defined with sufficient clearness and is of a nature to which effect can be given. The proper way for me to deal with the matter will be, not to make, as it is asked by the summons, a general declaration, but, following the example of Knight Bruce V.-C. in Pettingall v. Pettingall [11 L.J. (Ch.) 176], to order that, upon the defendant Mr. Lloyd giving an undertaking (which I understand he is willing to give) to apply the legacy when received by him towards the object expressed in the testator's will, the plaintiffs do pay to the defendant Mr. Lloyd the legacy of 1000*l*.; and that, in case the legacy should be applied by him otherwise than towards the promotion and furthering of fox-hunting, the residuary legatees are to be at liberty to apply.

NOTES

1. *Honorary trusts.* Arrangements such as that at issue in *Thompson* are sometimes referred to as "honorary trusts." Common types of honorary trusts include those for:

>   a. the erection or maintenance of tombs, monuments, and graves;

>   b. the saying of masses (though some states regard such trusts as charitable); and

>   c. the benefit of specific animals.

See generally 2 Scott and Ascher on Trusts §§ 12.11 to 12.11.8.

2. *Black-letter summary.* Restatement (Third) of Trusts § 47(2) (2003) provides:

> If the owner of property transfers it in trust for a specific noncharitable purpose and no definite or ascertainable beneficiary is designated, unless the purpose is capricious, the transferee holds the property as trustee with power, exercisable for a specified or reasonable period of time normally not to exceed 21 years, to apply the property to the designated purpose; to whatever extent the power is not exercised (although this power is *not* presumptively personal), or the property exceeds what reasonably may be needed for the purpose, the trustee holds the property, or the excess, for distribution to reversionary beneficiaries implied by law.

(italics in original).

3. *Enforcement.* In Phillips v. Estate of Holzmann, 740 So.2d 1 (Fla. App. 1998), the testator left a $25,000 bequest to a friend, for the care of the testator's dogs. Shortly after the testator's death, the dogs were euthanized. The court held that the friend held the bequest on resulting trust for the testator's residuary beneficiaries.

4. *From "honorary trust" to "trust."* Increasingly, state legislatures are recognizing, by statute, various types of honorary trusts, calling them "trusts," and providing for their enforcement. For example, N.Y. EPTL § 8–1.5 accords charitable trust status to trusts "for the purpose of the perpetual care, maintenance, improvement or embellishment of cemeteries or private burial lots." More generally, UTC § 409(1) provides: "A trust may be created for a noncharitable purpose without a definite or definitely ascertainable beneficiary or for a noncharitable but otherwise valid purpose to be selected by the trustee. The trust may not be enforced for more than [21] years." UPC § 2–907(a) is similar.

5. *Trusts for pets.* Many clients wish to provide for their pets. Not long ago, the best advice in such a situation was often a specific bequest of the pet, along with a general bequest in more than a token amount, to a trusted friend or relative. The hope was that respect for the wishes of a departed friend or family member, coupled with the consciousness of having received an unexpected and otherwise undeserved windfall, would suffice to ensure the pet's longevity. In the last few decades, however, most states have enacted statutes that authorize trusts for pets. See UTC § 408(a) ("A trust may be created to provide for the care of an animal alive during the settlor's lifetime."); UPC § 2–907(b); Cal. Prob. Code § 15212; Fla. Stat. Ann. § 736.0408; 760 Ill. Comp. Stat. 5/15.2; N.Y. EPTL § 7–8.1; Tex. Prop. Code Ann. § 112.037.

CHAPTER 8

FIDUCIARY ADMINISTRATION

■ ■ ■

A. JURISDICTION

1. THE DECEDENT IN A FEDERAL SYSTEM: DOMICILE

Consider the case of a wealthy and mobile couple who own a home in New York, a summer place in Maine, a hunting lodge in Georgia, and a business in Delaware. In their younger days, they divided most of their time between Delaware and New York. In their later years, they spent more and more of their time in Maine and Georgia. During life, this dispersal of self and resources created few problems. But at death, the status of each of them, and the situs of their property, became fixed. An enlightened system of law would provide for a single, unified administration of each of their estates. That is the theoretical ideal. The reality is the subject matter of this subsection.

Restatement (Second) of Conflict of Laws (1971)

§ 314. Where Will May Be Probated and Representative Appointed

The will of a decedent will customarily be admitted to probate and an executor or administrator appointed in a state

(a) where the decedent was domiciled at the time of his death; or

(b) where there are assets of the estate at the time of the decedent's death or at the time of the appointment of the executor or administrator; or

(c) where there is jurisdiction over the person or property of one who is alleged to have killed the decedent by his wrongful act, if the statute under which recovery is sought permits suit by an executor or administrator appointed in that state.

§ 315. Where Administrator May Be Appointed in Case of Intestacy

An administrator will customarily be appointed in the case of intestacy in any state in which a will would have been admitted to probate.

§ 11. Domicil

(1) Domicil is a place, usually a person's home, to which the rules of Conflict of Laws sometimes accord determinative significance because of the person's identification with that place.

(2) Every person has a domicil at all times and, at least for the same purpose, no person has more than one domicil at a time.

NOTES

1. *Multi-state jurisdiction.* Under the Restatement, jurisdiction over the administration of a decedent's estate may lie in more than one state, even if there is no dispute with respect to where the decedent died domiciled. See also Estate of Marcos, 963 P.2d 1124 (Haw. 1998) (jurisdiction requires either domicile or ownership of property).

2. *Domicile.* Under the Restatement, the state in which a decedent dies domiciled (among others) has jurisdiction over the administration of the estate. A decedent's domicile is, however, a conclusion about which survivors (or their lawyers) can disagree. Such disagreements are particularly likely if there are reasons for the survivors to disagree about which state is the most attractive forum. For example, the substantive law of one state may be more attractive to a given survivor than that of another, as when a disinherited surviving spouse learns that the elective share in one state is one-half of the augmented estate, whereas, in another, it is one-third of the probate estate. Or there may be differences in the relevant statutes of limitation, rules of procedure, or taxes, to name only a few. Then again, the survivors may simply disagree about which state is more *convenient*, because not all live in the same locality.

In short, disputes over the domicile of wealthy decedents do occur. Riley v. New York Trust Co., 315 U.S. 343 (1942), involved a decedent very much like the one described in the introduction. The Georgia courts, affirmed by the Supreme Court of Georgia, found that the decedent was a Georgia domiciliary. Despite the inherent logical inconsistency, the New York courts subsequently found that the decedent was a New York domiciliary. Both states appointed fiduciaries, and both claimed decedent's shares of Coca–Cola, a Delaware corporation. Coca–Cola filed a bill of interpleader in Delaware. The Supreme Court of Delaware found that the decedent had, in fact, died domiciled in New York and held that the full faith and credit clause of the United States Constitution did not require adherence to the Georgia decree. The Supreme Court of the United States affirmed, holding that, because the Georgia decree did not bind the New York fiduciary, the Delaware courts were free to make their own finding of domicile in determining ownership of the shares. Implicit in *Riley* is the notion that the United States Constitution requires only a fair trial on the issue of domicile—not consistent results. Thus, as in *Riley*, both inconsistent claims and inconsistent determinations of domicile are possible.

3. *Uniform Probate Code.* One "solution" to the problem of inconsistent determinations of domicile would be uniform enactment by states of statutes that avoided the possibility. In this regard, the Uniform Probate Code is exemplary. UPC § 3–202 vests responsibility for making the determination of domicile in the first court to take jurisdiction:

> If conflicting claims as to the domicile of a decedent are made in a formal testacy or appointment proceeding commenced in this state, and in a testacy or appointment proceeding after notice pending at the same time in another state, the court of this state must stay, dismiss, or permit suitable amendment in, the proceeding here unless it is determined that the local proceeding was commenced before the proceeding elsewhere. The determination of domicile in the proceeding first commenced must be accepted as determinative in the proceeding in this state.

Thus, if everyone plays by the rules, it is impossible for an inconsistent finding of domicile to arise from a UPC court. See Cuevas v. Kelly, 873 So.2d 367 (Fla. App. 2004) (determination of domicile in one jurisdiction, properly obtained, binds parties and bars them from seeking inconsistent ruling in another jurisdiction).

4. *Testator's choice of governing law.* Another possible "solution" is for the testator to designate, by will, the state whose law is to apply. N.Y. EPTL § 3–5.1(h), for example, authorizes such a provision:

> Whenever a testator, not domiciled in this state at the time of death, provides in his will that he elects to have the disposition of his property situated in this state governed by the laws of this state, the intrinsic validity, including the testator's general capacity, effect, interpretation, revocation or alteration of any such disposition is determined by the local law of this state.

Sometimes such a provision works. In Estate of Renard, 439 N.E.2d 341 (N.Y.1982), the decedent, a French domiciliary but a long-time New York resident, left her New York property to charities, stating in her will that New York law was to determine the will's validity and effect. Decedent's son, who held both American and French citizenship and lived in California, asserted that French law, under which he was entitled to a forced share equal to half the estate, should apply. The court denied the son's claim, applying New York, rather than French, law. But *Renard* is difficult to reconcile with an earlier case by the same court involving a spouse's elective share. In Estate of Clark, 236 N.E.2d 152 (N.Y.1968), the decedent, a Virginia domiciliary, left a $23 million estate, mostly securities on deposit with a New York bank. His will satisfied the widow's elective share rights under New York law, but not under Virginia law. Despite language in the will requiring application of New York law, the court granted the widow a right of election in accordance with Virginia law. The court reasoned that the predecessor of EPTL § 3–5.1(h) did not apply, because the disposition of property in question was by statute, rather than by will. Compare UPC § 2–703, which permits a testator to select the state whose law is to determine the "meaning and legal effect of a governing instrument" but denies effectiveness to such a provision with respect to: (1) the spouse's elective share, (2) exempt property and allowances, and (3) "any other public policy of this state otherwise applicable to the disposition." See generally Scoles, Choice of Law in Trusts: Uniform Trust Code, Sections 107 and 403, 67 Mo. L. Rev. 213 (2002).

5. *State death taxes.* All of the states, at one time or another, have imposed some type of tax, variously referred to as a "death," "succession," "inheritance," or "estate" tax, on the transfer of property at death. In general, a state has jurisdiction to tax only property located within its own borders. In contrast, the state in which a decedent dies domiciled has jurisdiction to tax (basically) all the decedent's property, anywhere in the world, except real property and tangible personal property outside its borders. See Treichler v. Wisconsin, 338 U.S. 251 (1949); State Tax Commission v. Aldrich, 316 U.S. 174 (1942); Curry v. McCanless, 307 U.S. 357 (1939); Frick v. Pennsylvania, 268 U.S. 473 (1925); Bittker, The Taxation of Out-of-State Tangible Property, 56 Yale L.J. 640 (1947); Note, Problematic Definitions of Property in Multistate Death Taxation, 90 Harv. L. Rev. 1656 (1977).

Obviously, states can and do disagree among themselves over the domicile, for tax purposes, of a given decedent. In one heavily litigated instance, the Pennsylvania courts held that a decedent died domiciled in Pennsylvania and upheld imposition of a domiciliary inheritance tax exceeding $14 million. Dorrance's Estate, 163 A. 303 (Pa.), cert. denied, 287 U.S. 660 (1932). Subsequently, the New Jersey courts upheld imposition of a similar domiciliary tax exceeding $12 million on the same estate. In re Dorrance's Estate, 170 A. 601 (N.J.Prerog.1934), sustained per curiam sub nom. Dorrance v. Martin, 176 A. 902 (N.J.Sup.1935), aff'd per curiam, 184 A. 743 (N.J.), cert. denied, 298 U.S. 678 (1936). The Supreme Court of the United States refused to resolve the conflicting claims. New Jersey v. Pennsylvania, 287 U.S. 580 (1933); Hill v. Martin, 296 U.S. 393 (1935).

A Massachusetts executor attempted to obtain a definitive determination of the decedent's domicile for tax purposes by interpleading, under the Federal Interpleader Act, the tax authorities of Massachusetts and California. The Supreme Court held that the Eleventh Amendment barred the action. Worcester County Trust Co. v. Riley, 302 U.S. 292 (1937).

In Texas v. Florida, 306 U.S. 398 (1939), the Supreme Court did determine a decedent's domicile. In that case, the combined tax claims of *four* states (all claiming domicile), plus that of the federal government, threatened substantially to exceed the entire $42 million estate. The Supreme Court took original jurisdiction.

In 1977 California gave the Supreme Court an opportunity to reexamine this unruly body of law, when it sought leave to file a complaint under the court's original jurisdiction regarding whether Howard Hughes had died domiciled in California or Texas. (Nevada also had grounds to claim Hughes as a domiciliary, but it was not a necessary party because, at that time, Nevada had no death tax.) California asserted that the combined marginal tax rates of the two states, combined with that of the federal government, totaled 101%. Thus, taxes could totally deplete the estate, giving rise to a "controversy" between the states, as in Texas v. Florida. The court denied the motion without opinion, although four Justices separately expressed the opinion that Worcester County Trust Company v. Riley was no longer "a bar against the use of federal interpleader by estates threatened with double taxation because of possible inconsistent adjudications of domicile." Three Justices opined that Texas v. Florida was wrongly decided and should be overruled, because there was no "controversy" between the states until they had reduced their tax claims to money judgments and the estate's insufficiency had been demonstrated. California v. Texas, 437 U.S. 601 (1978).

Accepting this invitation, the administrator of the Hughes estate brought a statutory interpleader action in a district court in Texas. On review, a majority of the Supreme Court reaffirmed Worcester County Trust Company v. Riley. Cory v. White, 457 U.S. 85 (1982). In a companion case, the Supreme Court granted California's renewed motion to invoke the Court's original jurisdiction. California v. Texas, 457 U.S. 164 (1982). There were dissents in both actions, arguing for reversal of the landmark decisions and recognition of federal interpleader as an appropriate remedy. The action was, however, discontinued, as the two states settled, dividing an estimated $169 million in inheritance taxes. Washington Post, Aug. 30, 1984, § C, at 1.

For the moment, the status quo seems to have prevailed. But the margin of its support seems sufficiently narrow to suggest that the Supreme Court may yet some day define a federal role in resolving competing claims to a decedent's domicile. See generally Report of the Committee on State Death Tax Problems of Estates and Trusts, Multi–State Death Tax Problems of Estates and Trusts, 21 Real Prop. Prob. & Trust J. 527 (1986).

In the absence of dependable assistance from the federal judiciary in resolving conflicting claims over decedents' domiciliary status, a number of states have enacted relevant legislation. In particular, the Uniform Interstate Compromise of Death Taxes Act (1943) and the Uniform Interstate Arbitration of Death Taxes Act (1943) seek to fill the vacuum the Supreme Court has created.

In the absence of relevant legislation, an executor facing multiple domiciliary tax claims may seek to persuade the tax officials of one state to enter an appearance in the courts of the other state and obtain a determination of domicile binding on all parties. The Connecticut commissioner once followed this procedure in New York and won. Matter of Trowbridge, 194 N.E. 756 (N.Y.1935).

6. *Estate planning for snowbirds.* Not infrequently, successful business or professional people who have amassed their wealth in one of the large northern urban centers wish to retire to a warmer climate. They move to the Sunbelt, into an apartment, club, hotel, or house, which they may have purchased, execute new wills declaring themselves domiciliaries of the new state, and remain there for much of the year. Still, they visit their children and grandchildren throughout the country, go north for the summer, and make periodic stops at their original home—to visit friends, go to the theater, and take care of business, banking, legal, or medical problems. The tax authorities of the original domicile are understandably reluctant to concede domicile to a "retirement haven" when such people die.

To avoid such disputes, or, worse, multi-state imposition of domiciliary taxes, anyone seeking to change domicile should sever as many connections with the original home as cleanly as possible. A few of many relevant suggestions include: obtain a driver's license in the new state, vote (only) in the new state, pay income taxes as a domiciliary of the new state, register all cars in the new state, and dispose of all residences in the old state. Because "domicile" turns in large part on one's own notion of where "home" is, one seeking to avoid post-mortem controversy over domicile may also want to discuss his or her notions of "home" with those who are likely to survive him or her and might have reason to remember the conversation. See generally Michaels et al., Domicile: Estate Planning Issues for the Mobile Client, N.Y. St. B.A. J., July/Aug. 2006, at 37; Schmoker, Minimizing State Death Taxes; Domicile; Tax Situs of Various Assets, 41 N.Y.U. Inst. on Fed. Tax'n 45–1 (1983).

2. THE FIDUCIARY IN A FEDERAL SYSTEM: ANCILLARY ADMINISTRATION

Happily, cases in which two or more states claim the same decedent as a domiciliary are relatively rare. When states persist in such claims, unified administration is impossible.

The more frequent situation involves a decedent who dies incontestably domiciled in one state but owns property elsewhere. Traditionally, each non-domiciliary state in which a decedent owns property has been entitled to require separate administration, generally called "ancillary administration," of all property within its borders. This duplication of administration necessarily entails additional inconvenience, delay, and expense. Ancillary administration, however, does not necessarily lead to anarchy, as in cases of multiple domicile. Those in charge of the various proceedings usually manage to summon up a measure of cooperation.

When things go well, all states in which ancillary administration is proceeding defer to the domiciliary administration.

NOTES

1. *Rationale for ancillary administration.* The necessity for ancillary administration stems in part from the notion that the authority of a personal representative cannot extend beyond the jurisdiction of the appointing tribunal. Thus, traditionally, personal representatives have not had the capacity to sue or to give valid discharges outside the appointing jurisdiction. See In re Stern, 696 N.E.2d 984 (N.Y. 1998) (Surrogate's Court lacks subject matter jurisdiction over out-of-state assets in ancillary administration proceeding). Another reason for ancillary administration is "to protect local creditors (and perhaps local distributees) whenever it is within the power of the courts of the forum to do so." Beale, Conflict of Laws § 471.1 (1935). For critical analysis, see Lerner, The Need for Reform in Multistate Estate Administration, 55 Tex. L. Rev. 303 (1977); Currie, The Multiple Personality of the Dead: Executors, Administrators, and the Conflict of Laws, 33 U. Chi. L. Rev. 429 (1966) (arguing for appointment of a universal administrator with nationwide powers).

2. *When ancillary administration is necessary.* When ancillary administration is necessary is not always clear. Consider the following excerpt from Alford, Collecting a Decedent's Assets without Ancillary Administration, 18 Sw. L.J. 329, 331–32 (1964):

> . . . States of both "domicile" and "business" situs may impose inheritance taxes upon intangible personal property. Tangibles are taxable where situated. To avoid multiple taxation, the domiciliary personal representative usually is pushed to recover as much of the personal estate of the decedent as he can legitimately without subjecting it to crippling local tax blows. If an ancillary administration is commenced, it is assured that local taxes will be imposed upon the property.

> Since good and sufficient reasons exist to cut ancillary administration to the bare minimum, it is disconcerting that so many ancillary administrations apparently are conducted. In the writer's opinion, many domiciliary personal representatives blunder into ancillary administrations through ignorance, although many judicial officers have been known to give kindly guidance to the wayward. Some of the administrations arise through references to lawyers to collect foreign assets. For example, the local practitioner who is to collect debts without exact knowledge of the existence of local creditors may be inclined to seek ancillary letters for his own protection. Also, corporate fiduciaries may seek to avoid conflicts with their professional competitors in other states.

> Some ancillary administrations clearly may be necessary. Perhaps title to foreign land must be cleared by elimination of creditor claims in

the situs jurisdiction. A debtor may refuse to pay without a receipt from a local administrator. The biography of the decedent may be so obscure that neither his assets nor his debts in other states can be discovered with certainty without a formal administration. Also it is an unfortunate fact that some domiciliary fiduciaries lack the competence to be permitted to collect debts and to pay creditors without the supervision a judicial officer in a foreign state can provide.

When ancillary administration *is* necessary, it helps to have the domiciliary personal representative qualify as ancillary administrator in each ancillary state. Unfortunately, some states still find it necessary to re-proclaim their sovereignty (and incidentally to channel business to local fiduciaries) through statutes barring non-residents from service as fiduciaries. See Annot., Executors—Requirement of Residency, 9 A.L.R.4th 1223 (1981).

3. *Land.* The situs of land prevails over the decedent's domicile, both as a basis for ancillary administration and in questions of choice of law. In fact, the law of the situs generally prevails even when the people involved have had only minimal contacts with the situs. See generally Hancock, Full Faith and Credit to Foreign Laws and Judgments in Real Property Litigation: The Supreme Court and the Land Taboo, 18 Stan. L. Rev. 1299 (1966).

4. *Situs of intangible personal property as basis for ancillary administration.* The situs of intangible personal property can serve as a basis for ancillary administration. There remains, however, the question where such property is located. Albuquerque Nat'l Bank v. Citizens Nat'l Bank, 212 F.2d 943 (5th Cir. 1954), recites, as the "majority rule," that the situs of shares of stock is the place of incorporation. See also Pomerance, The "Situs" of Stock, 17 Corn. L.Q. 43 (1931). But see Restatement (Second) of Conflict of Laws §§ 324, 325 (1971) (situs of shares of stock represented by a share certificate not in the lawful possession of a foreign fiduciary is the state in which the certificate is located; situs of shares not represented by a share certificate is the state of incorporation). The situs of a debt owed the decedent is ordinarily the debtor's domicile. With respect to debts of the federal government, however, the rule appears to be otherwise: situs "for the purpose of founding administration is at the domicile of the creditor." Diehl v. United States, 438 F.2d 705, 710 (5th Cir.1971) (income tax refund was payable at decedent's domicile and therefore California rather than Texas had jurisdiction over it).

5. *Statutory reform.* Many states have enacted statutes that have modified, in various respects, the traditional rule that a personal representative lacks capacity to sue outside the appointing jurisdiction. E.g., N.Y. EPTL § 13–3.5.

If no local administration is pending in an ancillary state, the Uniform Probate Code permits a domiciliary foreign personal representative to "exercise as to assets in this state all powers of a local personal representative and [to] maintain actions and proceedings in this state subject to any conditions imposed upon nonresident parties generally," after filing proof of appointment. UPC §§ 4–204, 4–205. Thus, if all the ancillary jurisdictions have enacted the UPC or comparable legislation, it may be possible to avoid administration in any state other than that in which the decedent died domiciled. Of course, there is a "cost" of avoiding ancillary administration by proceeding in this fashion. Any foreign personal representative who files proof of appointment, receives money or delivery of personal property, or does any act that would have given the state jurisdiction over the representative as an individual, submits personally to the jurisdiction of the courts of the ancillary state. UPC § 4–301. The General Comment to Article IV of the Uniform Probate Code states that its provisions relating to administration of estates of non-residents "are designed to coerce respect for domiciliary procedures and administrative acts to the extent possible."

3. STATUTORY JURISDICTION OF THE PROBATE COURT

Speaking generally, there are three categories of probate courts. In some states, such as California, courts of general jurisdiction serve both the trial and the probate functions. Other states, such as New York, have separate probate courts that occupy a place in the overall judicial structure more or less equal to that of a court of general jurisdiction. Finally, in a number of states, the probate court is a separate court relegated to an inferior position in the judicial hierarchy. In states of this last category, probate judges may not even have legal training. In any state in which the probate court is not a court of general jurisdiction, various sorts of problems may arise during estate administration that require resort to *other* courts. For example, it may be necessary to litigate a tort, contract, or wrongful-death claim in the court that regularly handles the claim, rather than in the probate court.

Most states have organized their probate court systems on a county or district basis. Venue for probate of a will and for administration generally lies in the county or district where the decedent died domiciled or, if the decedent was a non-domiciliary, where the decedent's property is located. See UPC § 3–201.

B. ESTABLISHING THE VALIDITY OF THE WILL

1. THE NECESSITY AND EFFECT OF PROBATE

The first step in administering a testate estate is to file, with the probate court, a petition for admission of the will to probate. Typically, the person nominated in the will as executor brings this petition, but any interested person is generally eligible to do so. Anyone in possession of a will is under a duty to produce it. In some states there is criminal liability for suppression of a will. Typically, a petition for appointment as executor or administrator accompanies the probate petition. The procedure is similar for intestate estates, with a finding of intestacy replacing the probate decree. The next section describes the various types of formal and informal procedures used throughout the country to probate wills, determine heirs in intestacy, and appoint fiduciaries.

There is an important distinction between probate and construction proceedings. The probate proceeding establishes the validity of the will, including due execution in accordance with statutory formalities, the capacity of the testator, and the fact that it is the genuine and last formal expression of the testator's intent. In the probate proceeding the court does not concern itself with what the will says. It has been held, for instance, that a will should have been admitted to probate even though intervening circumstances had negated the effectiveness of its provisions except for a revocation of earlier wills and a direction for cremation. Estate of Schumann, 308 A.2d 375 (N.J.App. 1973). Moreover, it has been held not to be a proper ground for denying probate that the will's execution revoked a prior will in violation of an agreement making the prior will irrevocable, as the proper procedure was to bring an action to enforce the contract. Estate of Schultz, 193 N.W.2d 655 (Wis.1972). Inquiry into the validity and meaning of the will's language ordinarily must await a construction proceeding, which typically occurs after probate.

HAUSEN v. DAHLQUIST
Supreme Court of Iowa, 1942.
232 Iowa 100, 5 N.W.2d 321.

BLISS, J.

[On June 24, 1940, plaintiff-appellee initiated a partition action, alleging ownership in fee simple of a two-fifteenths interest in land under the terms of her father's will, which was not, however, admitted to probate until November 17, 1941. This is an appeal from the March 8, 1941, denial of defendant's motion to dismiss.]

The first point which the appellants argue as a ground for reversal is that at the time the petition was filed, and when the order appealed from was entered, the will of the testator had not been admitted to probate in Iowa. They rely upon section 11882, Code of Iowa, 1939, which provides that wills, foreign or domestic, shall not be carried into effect until admitted to probate. We find no merit in this contention. The rights of all parties to this suit, with respect to at least two thirds of the real estate, are based upon the will of the testator. It is fundamental law that a will speaks from the death of the testator, and the rights of the parties hereto accrued at that time. Proof of the probate of that will may be necessary in establishing those rights, but such proof was not a condition precedent to the commencement of the suit. In Otto v. Doty, 61 Iowa 23, 26, 15 N.W. 578, 579, a like contention was made. In disposing of it, the court said:

We reach the conclusion, then, that there is no valid objection either to the will or the probate thereof. It is objected by the defendants, however, that the admission of the will to probate in the circuit court of Story county was too late. This action, it seems, had already been commenced. The defendants' theory is that at the time the plaintiff commenced her action she had no cause of action. But, in our opinion, the most that can be said is that at that time she merely lacked the means of proof. Her title vested at the death of the testator. To prove it, however, it was necessary for her to put in evidence the will; and to do that, it was necessary that it should be probated, not only in Tennessee, but in Iowa. We think that it was sufficient that the will had been so probated at the time it was offered in evidence.

Probate of a will is the statutory method of establishing the proper execution of the instrument, but it is, nevertheless, a valid instrument before and independent of such proof, and while the probate of a will is necessary to perfect it as an instrument of title, yet without probate it is capable of conveying an interest in land. . . .

An amendment to the abstract, which has not been challenged in any way, shows that the will has now been duly admitted to probate in the district court of Montgomery County, Iowa.

[Affirmed.]

NOTES

1. *When and to whom does title pass?* The traditional view is that title to personal property passes, upon death of the owner, to his or her personal representative. Compare UPC § 3–101. As to real property:

Contrary to the present state of the law in England, neither statutes nor decisions in America have uprooted the basic tenet of the common law that title to a decedent's realty passes at once on his death to his heirs or devisees and not to his personal representatives. . . .

The common law concept is still basic in American law. It is true that land is here universally liable for the decedent's debts, and in almost all states it can be applied by the personal representative for this purpose under statutory power of sale. In some jurisdictions the personal representative has statutory powers of sale for other purposes. Statutes sometimes give the latter the right of possession to decedent's land and the right to the rents and profits, at least where these may be necessary for payment of debts. Finally, some statutes contemplate that the personal representative will distribute the decedent's land to the heirs or devisees, or that a decree of the court will determine this matter and operate as a muniment of title. In particular regards the common law rule is thus, in effect, abrogated or is almost a mere empty shell. Still it is the principle upon which American courts must proceed, and they depart therefrom only to the extent that there is statutory authority. Important manifestations of the common law rule remain, notably the right of the heir or devisee to enjoy immediate possessory rights unless or until the personal representative has exercised his statutory powers.

3 Am. L. Prop. § 14.7. Thus, the devisee or heir, rather than the executor, is generally the proper party to bring or defend actions pertaining to land. See McCarthy v. Landry, 678 N.E.2d 172 (Mass.App.), review denied, 682 N.E.2d 1362 (Mass.1997); Collins v. Scott, 943 P.2d 20 (Colo.App.1996). A devisee's title is, however, subject to an executor's power to sell the property to satisfy debts or in accordance with the terms of the will. See DeLong v. Scott, 217 N.W.2d 635 (Iowa 1974).

2. *What does probate do?* Probating a will "is essentially a formal validation of the property interests which came into existence upon the death of the testator. [P]robate is title-accommodating rather than interest-creating." Jenkins v. United States, 428 F.2d 538, 548 (5th Cir.), cert. denied, 400 U.S. 829 (1970). It is generally accepted that an unprobated will does not constitute evidence of title. But see UPC §§ 3–102, 3–1201 (permitting collection of personal property by affidavit under certain circumstances). If the will is not probated within the time limit fixed by a local statute, it may be impossible to establish title. See Estate of Zimmerman, 485 P.2d 215 (Kan.1971). Thus, administration may be necessary to establish title, even as to personal property. Administration may also be necessary to discharge debts owed by or to the estate.

ECKLAND V. JANKOWSKI

Supreme Court of Illinois, 1950.
407 Ill. 263, 95 N.E.2d 342.

SIMPSON, CHIEF JUSTICE.

Appellant, Charles J. Eckland, claims to be the owner of an undivided one-half interest, as devisee of Thorwald Hegstad, deceased, in the premises occupied by appellees under a deed from the heirs-at-law of the decedent. An amended complaint for partition of the premises was filed in the circuit court of Cook County. A hearing on the merits resulted in a decree dismissing the amended complaint for want of equity. A direct appeal has been perfected to this court, a freehold being involved.

Thorwald Hegstad died January 23, 1945. At that time he was the owner of the premises described in the amended complaint for partition. Soon after his death proceedings for the administration of his estate were commenced, the estate was duly administered and the administrator finally discharged on August 14, 1946. Thereafter, on November 30, 1946, the heirs-at-law of Thorwald Hegstad, in consideration of the sum of $12,000, conveyed the real estate in question to Louis Berland and Gudrun Berland. These persons, on February 8, 1947, conveyed the premises to the appellees for the sum of $13,000. Approximately six months after appellees acquired title to the premises, through the heirs of Thorwald Hegstad, appellant found a receipt showing the existence and whereabouts of a will of Thorwald Hegstad. On December 10, 1947, almost three years after the death of Thorwald Hegstad, and slightly more than a year after the heirs had conveyed the premises, the will was admitted to probate in the probate court of Cook County. Under the provisions of the will, appellant was devised a one-half interest in the premises while the other one-half interest was devised to Garman Hegstad, one of the heirs of Thorwald Hegstad, who had previously joined in the conveyance to appellees' predecessors in title.

It is the contention of appellant that when the will was admitted to probate he became vested with the title to the premises in question; that his title relates back to the moment of the death of the testator; and that the conveyance of the premises by the heirs-at-law of the testator was absolutely void and conveyed no title to appellees' predecessors in title. Appellees contend that they are innocent purchasers for value without any notice or knowledge of the existence of the will; that the will was not effective to pass any title to appellant until it had been admitted to probate; and that the probate of the will was ineffectual to relate back to the date of death of the testator and divest title previously acquired by an innocent purchaser for value from the lawful heirs of the testator.

At the time appellees acquired their conveyance of the premises in question, Thorwald Hegstad had been deceased for more than two years. His estate had been administered upon as intestate property, and he was shown to be the last owner of the record title to the premises. The probate court found that he died intestate and declared his heirship. It was not until after the administration proceedings had been concluded that the premises were conveyed by the heirs-at-law. The controversy is one of law, namely, whether under the facts as above set out in substance, the appellant, as devisee in the will, is the owner of a one-half interest in the property in question, or whether appellees, claiming title by purchase through the heirs of Thorwald Hegstad before they had any knowledge of the existence of said will, are the owners.

Section 53 of the Probate Act, Ill. Rev. Stat. 1949, chap. 3, par. 205, provides that every will when admitted to probate as provided by the act is effective to transfer the real estate of the testator devised therein. A devisee, however, cannot assert his title to land devised to him unless the will is probated and made a matter of record in accordance with the applicable statutes of our State. Barnett v. Barnett, 284 Ill. 580, 120 N.E. 532; Stull v. Veatch, 236 Ill. 207, 86 N.E. 227. The will of Thorwald Hegstad, therefore, could not become effective to vest title in appellant until it had been probated in the probate court of Cook County and made a matter of record in that county.

Section 33 of the act concerning conveyances, Ill. Rev. Stat. 1949, chap. 30, par. 32, provides as follows:

> All original wills duly proved, or copies thereof duly certified, . . . may be recorded in the same office where deeds and other instruments concerning real estate may be required to be recorded; and the same shall be notice from the date of filing. . . .

The only effect of recording a duly authenticated copy of a will in the office of the recorder of deeds . . . is to give constructive notice to all persons of the contents of the will. . . . The section, however, does not apply to a domestic will for the reason that the probate of a domestic will of itself constitutes constructive notice of the effect of the will on real estate affected by it, in the county where it is probated.

A purchaser of land is charged with constructive notice not only of whatever is shown in the records of the office of the recorder of deeds, but in addition, with matters affecting the title of the land which appear in the records in the circuit, probate, and county courts in the county where the land is situated. Clark v. Leavitt, 335 Ill. 184, 166 N.E. 538. It is the duty of a purchaser of land to examine the record and he is chargeable with notice of whatever is shown by the record. Blake v. Blake, 260 Ill. 70, 102 N.E. 1007. . . .

The right to take property, either real or personal, is purely a statutory right which rests wholly within legislative enactment, and the State, by appropriate legislation, may regulate and control its devolution. Jahnke v. Selle, 368 Ill. 268, 13 N.E.2d 980. Under the Statute of Descent of this State, the heir-at-law of a person who dies intestate acquires an absolute interest in the intestate's realty, although he cannot convey it to the prejudice of the rights of creditors of the decedent. Ill. Rev. Stat. 1949, chap. 3, par. 162; Neuffer v. Hagelin, 369 Ill. 344, 16 N.E.2d 715.

The object of the heirship proceedings in the probate court was to find upon whom the laws of this State had cast the estate of the intestate decedent. George v. Moorhead, 399 Ill. 497, 78 N.E.2d 216. At the time appellees obtained a conveyance to the premises, there was nothing upon record which would give them actual or constructive notice of the existence of the will, or that anyone other than those persons designated by the Statute of Descent had any interest in the premises. An examination of the record in the recorder's office would then have disclosed that Thorwald Hegstad was the owner of the record title at the time of his death and would show no transfers from him. Appellees were bound to know the law with reference to the descent of property. The records of the probate court at that time disclosed that Thorwald Hegstad had died intestate, and a finding of his heirship was included in the administration proceedings. The claims against the estate of the decedent were paid and the administrator discharged.

Under the Statute of Descent the heirs-at-law of Thorwald Hegstad had succeeded to the ownership of his real estate. The will of Thorwald Hegstad was not discovered until several months after the real estate had been conveyed by his heirs. There was no notice, either actual or constructive, as to the existence or contents of the will. Appellees had the right to rely on the devolution of title shown by the record. Under the facts and circumstances appearing of record, we conclude that the conveyance to appellees, who are admitted to be *bona fide* innocent purchasers for value, should prevail as against appellant, a devisee in the will subsequently discovered and admitted to probate.

The decree of the circuit court of Cook County is accordingly affirmed.

NOTES

1. *What does probate involve?* If no one contests the will, probate is a simple affair. The proponent submits proof of death, jurisdiction, notice, due execution, and testamentary capacity. Testimony of one or more of the attesting witnesses, if available, generally suffices on the latter two points. If the will is self-proved, even that may be unnecessary. See UPC §§ 2–504, 3–406(b). Even if the will is not self-proved, the witnesses often need not appear in court; their affidavits may suffice. See UPC § 3–405; N.Y. SCPA § 1406. Or, if one or more of the witnesses are dead or otherwise unavailable, probate is generally possible upon submission of other proof, such as proof of the genuineness of the signatures appearing on the will. See UPC § 3–405; N.Y. SCPA § 1405. Procedures may also be available to probate a lost or destroyed will. See N.Y. SCPA § 1407.

2. *Notice.* Generally, all interested persons (e.g., legatees, devisees, intestate takers, executors, trustees, guardians, creditors, and the state attorney-general if the will contains a charitable trust) must receive notice of a probate proceeding. See UPC § 3–403. As to those who are "known or readily ascertainable," notice by publication is constitutionally insufficient. Tulsa Professional Collection Services, Inc. v. Pope, 485 U.S. 478 (1988) (creditors). According to the Supreme Court, all such persons must receive "notice by mail or other means." Local requirements may be stricter. See, e.g., Estate of Lemke, 216 N.W.2d 186 (Iowa 1974) (mailed notice inadequate). Some states require personal service upon persons who are within the jurisdiction.

UPC § 1–401 stipulates as a general matter that notice be given by mail or delivery to any interested person at least fourteen days before a hearing or, if the address or identity of the person is not known and cannot be discovered with reasonable diligence, by publication at least once a week for three consecutive weeks in a general circulation newspaper. UPC notice requirements differ, however, depending on the nature of the proceeding. For a formal testacy proceeding, the petitioner must give notice to interested parties in advance of the hearing. UPC § 3–403. In contrast, the proponent in an informal probate proceeding or in a proceeding for a declaration of universal succession need only give notice to interested persons within thirty days after issuance of the informal probate or universal succession order. UPC §§ 3–306(b), 3–319.

3. *Family settlements.* If there is a dispute over the will, may all the interested parties enter into a compromise agreement setting forth a different dispositive scheme? UPC § 3–1101 encourages compromises and provides that, after formal court approval, such agreements are binding on all the parties, including those who are unborn or unascertained or cannot be located. See also UPC § 3–912 (private agreement). Even in the absence of statutory authorization, courts generally treat settlements favorably. See, e.g., Brewer v. Brewer, 872 A.2d 48 (Md. 2005); First Nat'l Bank v. Brown, 251 So.2d 204 (Ala.1971).

2. ADMINISTRATION OF ESTATES WITH A MINIMUM OF COURT SUPERVISION

Formal administration of estates under the supervision of a probate court has been frequently criticized as being unnecessarily time-consuming and expensive, involving overly complex and archaic laws and procedures, existing primarily for the benefit of lawyers and probate judges, and performing a useful function only in the rare instances when controversy occurs. These charges have not just appeared in professional journals; nor has the debate been confined to bar association meetings and legislative halls. A paperback by Norman F. Dacey, entitled How to Avoid Probate, published in 1965, sold 670,000 copies by mid–1967 and was first on the nonfiction best-seller list in late 1966. In fact, much of the client interest in inter vivos trusts and joint tenancies stems from the fact that these forms of property ownership keep the assets out of probate.

The Uniform Probate Code starts from the proposition that basic probate reforms are necessary. It offers, in lieu of the traditional procedures, a flexible system under which estate administration is available in uncontested estates, at the option of the parties, without judicial supervision. See generally Wellman, Recent Developments in the Struggle for Probate Reform, 79 Mich. L. Rev. 501 (1981). Twenty states, more or less, have adopted major components of the Code. But the significance of the UPC's innovations lies not alone in the fundamental change it has effectuated in those states. The UPC has also contributed to the national debate over the pros and cons of unsupervised versus supervised administration of decedents' estates. The opposition, which lies mainly within the legal profession, has proven formidable, and the drive to enact the UPC has slowed significantly. In response to political obstacles to enactment of the full UPC, a number of states have enacted partial measures, seeking to achieve some simplification of the administration process. It is likely that future developments will depend on the experiences UPC states have with the new procedures. If these states find that administration of estates is quicker and cheaper, with no increase in fraud and embezzlement, public pressure in favor of the goals the UPC seeks to achieve may eventually secure more widespread enactment.

Prior to the UPC, a number of procedures allowed administration of certain estates with little, if any, judicial contact. Indeed, the UPC is in many respects a logical extension of these prototypes.[1]

a. Immediate Distribution of Family Property

States typically authorize immediate distribution to spouse and children, without court intervention, of certain kinds of "exempt property," including, for example, wages, bank deposits, savings and loan deposits, insurance and other death benefits, various types of tangible personal property, and motor vehicles. Sometimes these items are, however, part of the estate for purposes of tax and/or creditors' claims. Other statutes may make available to spouse and children homestead property, exempt property, and/or a family allowance (to provide maintenance of the spouse and children during administration), free of creditors' claims. See generally Statutory Allowances, supra p. 154.

b. Administration of Small Estates

Many states have procedures that dispense with or simplify the administration of small estates. In California, an estate that does not exceed $150,000 in gross value may qualify for disposition as a small estate without the aid of either probate or administration. Cal. Prob. Code § 13100. If the total net value of the estate over liens, encumbrances, and homestead interest does not exceed $20,000, the court, upon petition and notice to interested parties, may distribute the estate to the surviving spouse and/or minor children and close the proceedings. Cal. Prob. Code § 6602.

---

[1] Undoubtedly, private settlement of estates, within the decedent's family, occurs often. For example, we rarely read accounts of the probate of a gangster's will. But when there is no administration, the certainty of the successors' title necessarily awaits passage of limitation periods. See A.B.A. Committee on Administration and Distribution of Decedents' Estates, Clearing Titles of Heirs to Intestate Real Property, 10 Real Prop. Prob. & Tr. J. 454 (1975). See also the discussion of the "do-nothing" option under the UPC, infra.

c. Probate in the Common Form

The English ecclesiastical courts (which had jurisdiction over wills of personal property only) allowed two types of probate—probate in the common form and probate in the solemn form. The former was a summary proceeding without notice to anyone; the will was often proved on the oath of the executor alone. The procedure was administrative rather than judicial; as a consequence, it was open to contest by any interested party at any time. (Some authorities suggest that there was a thirty-year limitation.) Probate in the solemn form required notice to interested parties, was a formal judicial proceeding in which questions of validity were litigated, and was final in the manner of any judicial decree. See Fratcher, Fiduciary Administration in England, 40 N.Y.U. L. Rev. 12 (1965).

A number of non-UPC states authorize use of the common form procedure and thereby admit wills to probate without notice to the parties or a formal hearing. The validity of the will remains subject to challenge after the initial probate, however, by an aggrieved party (e.g., a disinherited intestate taker, a beneficiary under an earlier will, or, if the state has an interest, the attorney-general) for a period that typically runs from six months to a year. See Levy, Probate in Common Form in the United States: The Problem of Notice in Probate Proceedings, 1952 Wis. L. Rev. 420. The UPC's informal probate proceedings are an adaptation of the common form approach, expanded to eliminate any need during administration for court intervention. In contrast, the personal representative in non-UPC states may continue to be subject to probate court supervision, for such purposes as review of an inventory or a final account.

d. Pre–Code Systems for Non–Intervention Administration

Prior to promulgation of the UPC, several states, including Arizona, Idaho, and Texas, permitted a personal representative to administer an estate without court supervision if the testator authorized the procedure by will. The fiduciary then had the option of using the procedure or pursuing traditional administration. The court, at the request of a beneficiary or creditor, could for cause deny non-intervention administration. The statutes are collected in Parker, No–Notice Probate and Non–Intervention Administration under the Code, 2 Conn. L. Rev. 546, 559–60 (1970).

Arizona and Idaho have adopted the UPC, which has even more extensive options for administration without court supervision. Texas has amended its statute to expand the opportunities for independent administration, which is now available to intestate estates and estates governed by wills that do not expressly prohibit it. Tex. Prob. Code § 145.

e. The Uniform Probate Code

About the origins of the UPC, Professor Richard V. Wellman, its Chief Reporter, has written: "The basic scheme is not very original. . . . The idea is to offer the various major features of the different probate systems presently followed in our fifty states, as options, in a single system." Wellman, The Uniform Probate Code: A Possible Answer to Probate Avoidance, 44 Ind. L.J. 191, 198 (1969). Still, the UPC does break radically with tradition by making non-intervention probate and administration the norm, rather than an infrequent exception. Court-supervised administration remains available, but an interested party must specifically request it. "The Code accepts the proposition that the probate court's proper role in regard to settlement of estates is to answer questions which parties want answered rather than to impose its authority when it is not requested. . . ." Id. at 199.

The UPC leaves it to the interested parties to decide the extent to which the court is to play a role in the process. These options include no role, a spot role in adjudicating specific issues, or the traditional role, in which the court supervises administration from probate to final distribution. As Professor Wellman has observed: "The state has no greater interest in enforcing the substantive rules of inheritance than it has in enforcing the rules governing contracts, trusts and other property arrangements controlling private wealth." Wellman, Recent Developments in the Struggle for Probate Reform, 79 Mich. L. Rev. 501, 509 (1981). According to 1 Uniform Probate Code Practice Manual 189, 203–04, 239–41 (2d ed. 1977), the UPC offers six options for estate settlement:

(i) *Survivors Take No Action of Any Sort.* Members of the family or others, entitled to the estate by will or intestacy, may simply take possession of the estate's assets, UPC § 3–101 vesting title in them subject to administration, and do nothing else. An interested party who brings a successful petition for appointment of a personal representative within three years of decedent's death will dispossess them, but, in the absence of such an action, the estate is, by and large, settled at the end of the limitation period. See UPC § 3–108. Proceedings to probate a will or appoint a representative are still possible, but not for the benefit of unsecured creditors. See UPC § 3–108(a)(4). In addition, the three-year limitation period is specifically inapplicable to proceedings to determine heirs by intestacy. See UPC § 3–108(b). It follows that settling an estate by inaction does not afford complete protection to those in possession because they may forfeit the estate within three years of the decedent's death, or even thereafter. Moreover, they are not "distributees" under UPC § 1–201(13) and thus cannot pass marketable title to a good-faith purchaser.

(ii) *Informal Probate Only.* The parties may submit decedent's will to the registrar for probate but not seek appointment of a personal representative. Advance notice to interested parties is not required, UPC § 3–306, but the registrar has discretion to deny probate if, for example, jurisdiction is lacking or the document does not satisfy statutory formalities. As in the "do-nothing" option, the devisees cannot retain estate property as against the demand of a duly appointed personal representative. In addition, an informally probated will is subject to challenge in formal proceedings brought within three years of the decedent's death or one year after the grant of informal probate, whichever is longer. See UPC § 3–108(a)(3). After this limitation period has run, however, the devisees can convey marketable title.

(iii) *Informal Probate with Administration, or Administration in Intestacy Without Formal Testacy Proceeding.* Under this option, the parties petition the registrar for informal probate (or file a statement that no will exists) and request appointment of a personal representative (either the fiduciary designated in the will or the person eligible under UPC § 3–203). Assuming that no one initiates a formal testacy proceeding within the limitation period, the personal representative has full control of estate assets and authority to settle creditors' claims, give marketable title, and make distribution. The personal representative may take these steps without further judicial contact, although reference to the court may be necessary to resolve a controversy, construe the will, or secure absolution from future liability. This is probably the way most estates will be settled. Professor Wellman cites as its advantages: the role of the court is at a minimum; succession to family wealth is mostly a private matter; and there is a minimum of red tape, cost, and delay. Wellman, supra, 79 Mich. L. Rev. at 508–10.

(iv) *Formal Testacy Proceeding Without Administration.* This option offers the parties the opportunity to obtain a judicial adjudication of the will's validity, or a judicial determination of intestacy, but without administration. The parties might select this option when, for instance, the circumstances suggest that a definitive hearing is necessary to resolve disputes over the identity of the beneficiaries. After resolution of these disputes, however, the parties may feel no need for administration.

(v) *Formal Testacy Proceeding at Beginning of Administration.* This option, too, offers the parties the opportunity to obtain a judicial adjudication of the will's validity, or a judicial determination of intestacy, but also offers a formal proceeding for appointment of a personal representative. The parties might select this option when, for instance, the circumstances suggest that a definitive hearing is necessary to resolve disputes over the identity of both the beneficiaries and the fiduciaries. After resolution of these disputes, however, the personal representative may proceed as in the third option, with the assurance that no one will interrupt his, her, or its authority by petitioning for formal probate or appointment.

(vi) *Supervised Administration*. Supervised administration is formal administration of the traditional sort, including a court adjudication, following prior notice to interested parties, of the will's validity, a formal proceeding for appointment of a personal representative, court orders to authorize distributions, and judicial review of accounts. Except in very large or highly contentious estates, there is little incentive for the parties to select this option.

Except under the "do-nothing" option, the UPC places responsibility for administration on the personal representative. Critics have suggested that, without judicial oversight, the personal representative has the opportunity to commit fraud and embezzlement without detection. The UPC, however, imposes criminal and civil penalties for intentional misrepresentations. In addition, the UPC imposes personal liability on any personal representative who misappropriates or otherwise misuses estate assets and establishes procedures for accountability to the decedent's creditors and successors.

In 1982 a new UPC option appeared, at §§ 3–312 to 3–322. This option would eliminate the personal representative from routine estate administration. Known as *Universal Succession,* this option enables the intestate takers or the residuary devisees to become universal successors, with authority to settle and distribute the estate without court supervision, unless they need judicial resolution of specific issues. Application is to the registrar, who issues a "statement of universal succession" upon satisfaction of the conditions set forth in UPC § 3–314. After appointment, the successors must notify interested parties and assume personal liability for administration expenses, death taxes, the decedent's debts, and all unpaid legacies or shares owing to other persons. At the end of the limitation period, assuming satisfaction of all claims against the estate and the absence of any application for informal or formal administration, the successors have full ownership of their respective shares of the assets and can convey marketable title. See Scoles, Succession Without Administration: Past and Future, 48 Mo. L. Rev. 371 (1983).

3. FINALITY OF PROBATE DECREES

Allen v. Dundas

Court of King's Bench, 1789.
100 Eng. Rep. 490, [1775–1802] All Eng. Rep. 398

This was an action on the case for money had and received to the use of the intestate, and to the use of the plaintiff as administrator: to which the defendant pleaded the general issue. And on the trial a special verdict was found, stating in substance as follows. The defendant, as Treasurer of the Navy, was indebted to the intestate in his lifetime in 58£, 13s. 6d. for money had and received to his use. Priestman died on the 2d of June

1784, and on the 13th of August 1785, one Robert Brown proved in the Prerogative Court of the Archbishop of Canterbury, a forged paper writing, dated the 18th of May 1784, purporting to be the last will of Priestman, otherwise Handy; whereby he was supposed to have appointed Brown the sole executor thereof; and a probate of that supposed will issued in due form of law, under the seal of that Court, on the same day, in favour of Brown. The defendant, not knowing the will to have been forged, and believing Brown to be the rightful executor, on Brown's request paid him 58£. 13s. 6d. being the whole balance then due from the defendant to Priestman. On the 21st of July 1787, Brown was called by citation, at the suit of John Priestman the father, and next of kin of the deceased, in the Prerogative Court of the Archbishop of Canterbury, touching the validity of such supposed will; and such proceedings were thereupon had in that Court, that the will and probate were declared null and void; that Thomas Priestman died intestate; and that John Priestman the father was his next of kin. And on the 31st of March 1788, letters of administration of the goods, & c. of Thomas Priestman were granted by that Court in due form of law to the plaintiff, as attorney of John Priestman.

ASHHURST, J.—I am of opinion that the plaintiff has no right to call on the defendant to pay this money a second time, which was paid to a person who had at that time a legal authority to receive it. It is admitted, that if he had made this payment under the coercion of a suit in a Court of Law, he would have been protected against any other demand for it: but I think that makes no difference. For as the party to whom the payment was made had such authority as could not be questioned at the time, and such as a Court of Law would have been bound to enforce, the defendant was not obliged to wait for a suit, when he knew that no defense could be made to it: this therefore cannot be called a voluntary payment. This is different from payments under forged bonds or bills of exchange; for there the party is to exercise his own judgment, and acts at his peril: a payment in such a case is a voluntary act, though perhaps the party is not guilty of any negligence in point of fact. But here the defendant acted under the authority of a Court of Law; every person is bound to pay deference to a judicial act of a Court having competent jurisdiction. Here the Spiritual Court had jurisdiction over the subject matter; and every person was bound to give credit to the probate till it was vacated. The case of a probate of a supposed will during the life of the party may be distinguished from the present; because during his life the Ecclesiastical Court has no jurisdiction, nor can they inquire who is his representative; but when the party is dead, it is within their jurisdiction. . . . But the foundation of my opinion is, that every person is bound by the judicial acts of a Court having competent authority: and during the existence of such judicial act, the law will protect every person obeying it. . . .

Judgment for the defendant.

NOTES

1. *Late probate.* It is generally possible to offer a will for probate, even after complete administration under an earlier will or the laws of intestate succession. See In re Elliott's Estate, 156 P.2d 427 (Wash.1945). The principles of Allen v. Dundas, however, protect a debtor who has paid the original personal representative, or a bona fide purchaser for value whose title derives from the first proceeding. See Eckland v. Jankowski, supra p. 740. The beneficiaries of the second will do, of course, have rights of action against the distributees of the first administration. See In re Cecala's Estate, 232 P.2d 48 (Cal.App.1951). Whether, in a given instance, those rights are worth anything is another matter. The moral of these cases seems to be that prompt administration of a decedent's estate has distinct advantages.

2. *Statutes of limitation.* Statutes may impose time limits on the probate of a will. Many, however, are subject to exceptions or probate court discretion. See, e.g., UPC § 3–108; Estate of Chartier, 866 A.2d 125 (Me. 2005).

3. *Fraud, accident, or mistake.* A probate court decree, following notice to the interested parties and a hearing, is a final judgment, subject only to appeal. After the appeal period has run, the decree can only be upset on a showing of fraud, accident, or mistake "lying at the very basis of the decree." Miller v. McNamara, 66 A.2d 359 (Conn.1949). With respect to fraud, UPC § 1–106 establishes as the appropriate procedure an action against the perpetrator or an action for restitution from any person, whether innocent or not (except a bona fide purchaser for value), benefitting from the fraud. In general, such a proceeding must be commenced within two years of *discovery* of the fraud, but no such proceeding may be brought against anyone other than the perpetrator of the fraud later than five years from the *commission* of the fraud. See Matter of Estates of Cahoon, 633 P.2d 607 (Idaho 1981).

4. *Finality in non-intervention administration.* Under the traditional view, finality never attached to the actions of a personal representative who administered an estate without judicial supervision. But the UPC recognizes that, for a non-intervention system to have widespread appeal, it must offer finality at *some* point, after which challenges to the informal actions of a personal representative are no longer timely. Thus, UPC § 3–108(a)(3) limits these challenges to those brought within the later of one year after informal probate or three years after the decedent's death.

C. THE FIDUCIARY

1. APPOINTMENT AND QUALIFICATION

The will or the trust agreement should always specify one or more individuals and/or a corporate fiduciary to act as personal representative or trustee. When choosing fiduciaries, testators and settlors often ask their lawyers for advice. Sometimes they ask, "Should I name a corporate fiduciary?" Corporate fiduciaries offer permanence, expert management, continuity, and freedom from concerns relating to dishonesty and insolvency but, on the whole, have a bad reputation for "playing it safe" with overly conservative investment practices and institutional inattention and insensitivity to personal and family concerns. See Gilman, Trustee Selection: Corporate vs. Individual, Tr. & Est., June 1984, at 29. More frequently clients ask, "Should I name my spouse or eldest child?" A trust beneficiary who has certain types of powers over the trust may incur unnecessary tax burdens. See Pennell, Estate Planning: Drafting and Tax Considerations in Employing Individual Trustees, 60 N.C. L. Rev. 799 (1982). If the testator or settlor decides on an individual, the next question is likely to be, "Should I name more than one?" Many documents name multiple fiduciaries in an effort to ameliorate concerns about dishonesty, competence, expertise, or interest, or purely to avoid hurting someone's feelings through omission. Yet multiple fiduciaries often raise thorny problems involving division of responsibility, disagreements over policy, and the proliferation and sharing of compensation. A lawyer should certainly advise the testator or settlor to name successor fiduciaries, to guard against the primary nominee's death, incapacity, or unwillingness to serve. Finally, a lawyer should remind the testator to nominate a guardian of the person and property of any minor children.

Judicial appointment of trustees of inter vivos trusts is rarely necessary. Traditionally, however, judicial appointment has been mandatory for personal representatives and testamentary trustees. Usually, there are statutory eligibility requirements. See, e.g., UPC § 3–203(f)(1) (age); N.Y. SCPA § 707(1) (inter alia, age, place of domicile, criminal record, and history of substance abuse). Though there may also be statutory discretion in the court to disqualify nominees on other grounds, see, e.g., UPC § 3–203(f)(2), N.Y. SCPA § 707(2), courts have traditionally been reluctant to substitute their own assessment of a nominee's merits for that of the testator. Thus, the court generally appoints whomever the will names, with little additional inquiry.

If there is no will, if the will fails to nominate an eligible fiduciary, or if none of the fiduciaries nominated in the will is eligible, willing, and able to serve, the court appoints one in accordance with statutory priorities. Typically, persons with high statutory priority include the surviving spouse, children, devisees, and intestate takers. See, e.g., UPC § 3–203(a).

NOTES

1. *Appointment.* Under the traditional view, the court may not deny appointment of the testator's nominee, except on particular, statutory grounds. See, e.g., Rose v. O'Reilly, 841 P.2d 3 (Or.App.1992) (refusal to appoint beneficiary nominated as successor trustee was improper); Estate of Nagle, 317 N.E.2d 242 (Ohio App. 1974) (court refused to disqualify nominee who had

been decedent's lover for twenty years, despite objection by decedent's wife and children); In re Foss' Will, 125 N.Y.S.2d 105 (App. Div. 1953) (nominee had apparent conflict of interest, but court refused disqualification because testator was presumably aware of nominee's conflict). But see Estate of Henne, 421 N.E.2d 506 (Ohio 1981) (denying appointment of nominee whose personal interests were adverse to those of the estate's beneficiaries).

Similarly, the courts have generally found that statutes establishing priorities for appointment as personal representative are mandatory. See, e.g., Estate of Weaver, 520 P.2d 1330 (Kan.1974). But see Estate of Shorter, 444 A.2d 954 (D.C. 1982) (probate court has some discretion to deviate from statutory guidelines).

Can the beneficiaries join together and veto appointment of the testator's nominee for reasons other than the nominee's competency and capacity to serve, such as personal animus or a desire to save fees? The usual response, stressing the need to honor the testator's intent, has been in the negative. See, e.g., State ex rel. First Nat'l Bank & Trust Co. of Racine v. Skow, 284 N.W.2d 74 (Wis.1979) (probate court cannot disqualify nominee bank merely because beneficiaries prefer a personal representative who would not charge fees).

How much intelligence must the nominee possess? Just sufficient wit to hire a good lawyer? In Matter of Leland, 114 N.E. 854 (N.Y.1916), the court upheld the authority of the Surrogate to deny appointment of the only remaining nominee, who was 63 years old, had suffered two strokes of apoplexy, was partially paralyzed, and was in such mental and physical condition that he could not engage in active work. The court, however, cautioned:

> The test of incompetency should be applied with caution to cases where inability intelligently to discharge the duties of the trust arises from bodily disease resulting in permanent impairment of mental and physical ability. . . . The courts will not undertake to make a better will nor name a better executor for the testator. They will not add disqualifications to those specified by the statute, nor disregard testator's wishes by too liberal an interpretation of the specific disqualifications, nor consider the size and condition of the estate, except as a minor consideration. Where the ties of kindred and long acquaintanceship lead the testator to choose the inexperienced wife or friend rather than the modern trust company, the relative advantage to the beneficiaries will not justify a judicial veto on such choice. Every executor is entitled to have the aid of counsel learned in the law. [114 N.E. at 856.]

2. *Non-residents.* Statutes in some states deny appointment to a non-resident. Some apply only to foreign corporations, even those authorized to do business in the state; some release from the prohibition close non-domiciliary relatives of the decedent; and some make non-residence a ground for exercise of judicial discretion in making the appointment. These statutes have been

attacked as violative of the equal protection and due process clauses of the fourteenth amendment and the privileges and immunities clause. They have, however, generally been upheld. See Estate of Greenberg, 390 So.2d 40 (Fla.1980), appeal dismissed, 450 U.S. 961 (1981) (upholding, as constitutional, Florida statute barring appointment of unrelated non-residents; dismissing Fain v. Hall, infra, as "wholly unpersuasive"); In re Emery, 391 N.E.2d 746 (Ohio App. 1978) (Ohio statute barring non-resident banks constitutional). But see Fain v. Hall, 463 F.Supp. 661 (M.D.Fla.1979) (Florida statute unconstitutional). A number of states have statutes allowing appointment of foreign corporations only if the state of the corporation's domicile accords the same privilege to corporations of the forum state.

3. *Attorney designations.* Provisions in a will naming an attorney to represent the personal representative during estate administration are generally ineffective. As the relationship between client and attorney is personal and one of mutual trust, the personal representative must be able to select an attorney of his, her, or its own choosing. Moreover, if the nominee lawyer has drafted the will, it is only natural to suspect overreaching.

4. *Bonding.* Statutes have traditionally required an appointee to post a bond. In most states today, however, the will may waive the bond. Indeed, in some states the statutes themselves now dispense with bonding unless the will specifically requires it or there are special circumstances. See UPC § 3–603; N.Y. SCPA §§ 708, 710, 806.

2. REMOVAL AND RESIGNATION

The court may remove a fiduciary for malfeasance, breach of duty, or unfitness to serve, if doing so is in the best interests of the estate or its beneficiaries. See UPC § 3–611; UTC § 706; N.Y. SCPA § 711; Estate of Jones, 93 P.3d 147 (Wash. 2004) (removing executor for personal use of estate property, commingling estate funds, and failing to keep beneficiaries informed). Still, removal is a drastic action, which courts generally take only when the fiduciary's conduct endangers the estate. See Estate of Quinlan, 273 A.2d 340 (Pa.1971).

Alternatively, a fiduciary can petition to resign prior to completion of administration. See UPC § 3–610; UTC § 705; N.Y. SCPA §§ 715, 716. Before the court will accept a fiduciary's resignation, however, the fiduciary generally must account and turn over all property and papers to a successor. Because of the necessary complications involving the accounting, compensation, and title, the courts can be properly unreceptive to a petition for resignation from a fiduciary who pleads personal inconvenience or overwork. Petitions alleging old age or physical infirmities, as well as those alleging strained relationships between the fiduciary and beneficiaries, are normally granted.

Appointment of a successor fiduciary may follow any one of a number of courses: (a) the will nominates a successor; (b) the surviving fiduciary or fiduciaries continue without a new appointment; (c) the will names someone who is to nominate a successor; or (d) the court fills the vacancy. Upon assuming the position, the successor must ordinarily take reasonable steps to discover and redress any errors in the previous administration. See Restatement (Third) of Trusts § 76 cmt. d (2007); O'Connor v. Redstone, 896 N.E.2d 595 (Mass. 2008).

3. COMPENSATION

A number of states have enacted statutory fee schedules, which fix a fiduciary's fee solely or primarily by reference to the value of the estate assets. See, e.g., N.Y. SCPA § 2307 (unless the will provides otherwise). Other jurisdictions provide simply that fiduciaries are entitled to reasonable compensation. UPC § 3–719, for example, states:

> A personal representative is entitled to reasonable compensation for his services. If a will provides for compensation of the personal representative and there is no contract with the decedent regarding compensation, he may renounce the provision before qualifying and be entitled to reasonable compensation. A personal representative also may renounce his right to all or any part of the compensation. A written renunciation of fee may be filed with the court.

See also UTC § 708 (trustee entitled to reasonable compensation). In fact, customary rates seem to have developed in many of the so-called reasonable compensation jurisdictions that are nearly as fixed as those in states with statutory schedules. Under either statutory approach, therefore, the fees that fiduciaries claim often seem disproportionate to responsibilities undertaken. In a reasonable compensation jurisdiction, however, the court has the final say. See, e.g., Estate of Weeks, 950 N.E.2d 280 (Ill. App. 2011) (fees should be based on time spent, complexity of work performed, and ability; executor claimed $120,000 (3% of estate); court allowed $37,500 (500 hours at $75/hr.)).

NOTES

1. *Minimum fee schedules.* It was once common practice for bar associations to publish minimum fee schedules, based on a percentage of the estate, to be charged by fiduciaries. The Supreme Court, in Goldfarb v. Virginia State Bar, 421 U.S. 773 (1975), held that a minimum fee schedule for title searches, published by a county bar association, constituted price-fixing in violation of the Sherman Act. Thus, it is now clear that neither bar groups nor lawyers acting in concert can dictate adherence to a minimum fee schedule. *Goldfarb* does not, however, proscribe use by individual lawyers of their own percentage fee schedules (rather than charging at an hourly rate, for ex-

ample), so long as they do not arrive at the percentages in concert with other lawyers. Nor, apparently, does *Goldfarb* prohibit development of purely advisory fee schedules.

2. *Determining the fee.* One variable that almost inevitably enters into the calculation of a personal representative's fee, regardless of whether the state is a reasonable compensation jurisdiction or has a statutory schedule, is the value of estate assets. But what counts as an estate asset for this purpose varies widely from state to state. Typically, statutory schedule states fix a personal representative's compensation solely by reference to the value of the probate estate. In contrast, reasonable compensation jurisdictions tend to count all assets, including non-probate assets, such as insurance, survivorship property, Totten trusts, employee benefit plans, and the like, in arriving at a reasonable fee.

In many statutory schedule jurisdictions, additional fees may be available for "extraordinary services" necessary to administer an estate properly. Examples of such services include managing a decedent's business or litigating contested creditor or tax claims.

3. *Multiple fiduciaries.* N.Y. SCPA §§ 2307 & 2313 establish rules for fees allowable to multiple fiduciaries. Most states leave it to the court to award compensation in proportion to each fiduciary's contribution, even if the total thereby exceeds the amount a single fiduciary would have received. See, e.g., Hayward v. Plant, 119 A. 341 (Conn.1923) (in $36 million estate five co-executors received, respectively, $135,000, $120,000, $120,000, $30,000, and $30,000).

4. *Renunciation of compensation fixed in will.* Ordinarily, a personal representative may renounce any compensation prescribed by the will and claim, instead, the usual fee. See, e.g., UPC § 3–719. This option assumes that the testator would have preferred the nominee at a full fee to a stranger of the court's choosing. However, a fiduciary may be limited to the stipulated compensation if the fiduciary accepts appointment without first objecting to the compensation. See Marks v. Marks, 465 P.2d 996 (Haw.1970).

5. *Lawyers' fees.* In a number of states, statutory schedules also determine the fee of an estate's attorney, but, in the majority, attorneys receive reasonable compensation for their services. See, e.g., N.Y. SCPA § 2110. In determining reasonableness, variables include time spent, size of the estate, difficulty of issues, degree of skill required, extent of responsibilities assumed, and results obtained. Thus, the number of hours billed is ordinarily not alone determinative. See Estate of Bush, 230 N.W.2d 33 (Minn.1975) (awarding $710,000, plus expenses, to attorneys who represented executors for six years in complex estate worth $125 million); Matter of Shalman, 414 N.Y.S.2d 70 (App. Div. 1979) (objectants "placed undue emphasis on the time clock approach despite ample legal precedent to the contrary"). But see Es-

tate of Weeks, supra (lawyer claimed more than $170,000; court allowed $75,000 (300 hours at $250/hr.)).

6. *Lawyers serving in dual roles.* It was the rule at common law, predicated on the policy against self-dealing, that fiduciaries could not compensate themselves for legal services rendered to the estate. In some jurisdictions today, however, attorney-fiduciaries receive separate compensation for each function they perform. See, e.g., Estate of Hackett, 366 N.E.2d 1103 (Ill.App.1977). Largely in response to consumerist concerns about overreaching and "double-dipping" lawyers, however, courts and legislatures in some jurisdictions are making it difficult, if not impossible, for lawyers to receive compensation in both capacities. See, e.g., Estate of Weinstock, 351 N.E.2d 647 (N.Y.1976); Estate of Downing, 184 Cal.Rptr. 511 (Cal.App.1982); Estate of Thron, 530 N.Y.S.2d 951 (Sur. 1988); N.Y. SCPA § 2307–a (requiring written acknowledgment by client of specified disclosures).

7. *Deductibility for estate tax purposes.* Of course, no one likes paying administration expenses, whether as compensation to a personal representative or as a fee to the personal representative's lawyer. Both expenses, however, are ordinarily deductible for federal estate tax purposes. See I.R.C. § 2053(a)(2). Alternatively, they may be deductible for federal income tax purposes. See I.R.C. §§ 212, 642(g). In addition, they are generally deductible, one way or another, for state death or income tax purposes. Thus, those succeeding to a decedent's property often bear nothing like the full brunt of administration expenses. Deductibility is clearly a spoonful of sugar that can help to make the medicine of administration expenses go down.

D. CREDITORS

1. INVENTORY

Traditionally, one of the personal representative's first responsibilities has been to prepare an inventory of estate assets. UPC § 3–706 continues this duty:

> Within three months after his appointment, a personal representative . . . shall prepare and file or mail an inventory of property owned by the decedent at the time of his death, listing it with reasonable detail, and indicating as to each listed item, its fair market value as of the date of the decedent's death, and the type and amount of any encumbrance that may exist with reference to any item.

> The personal representative shall send a copy of the inventory to interested persons who request it. He may also file the original of the inventory with the court.

NOTES

1. *Why an inventory?* The inventory requirement tends to serve the purpose of having the fiduciary pull together and organize the estate early on. Variables include the time within which the inventory must be filed, the property to be included, and the qualifications of appraisers. Two additional reasons have been cited for requiring an inventory. "The first is to serve as a basis of computation for the representative's intermediate and final accounts. The second is to furnish information for the benefit of the beneficiaries, creditors and others interested in the estate." Atkinson § 115.

2. *Disadvantages of the inventory requirement.* In an estate of sufficient size to require the personal representative to file an estate or inheritance tax return, the inventory requirement is somewhat redundant, because there will eventually be full disclosure of the estate assets on the tax return. On the other hand, the inventory often is due prior to the tax return. Moreover, tax returns typically have narrow circulation.

If there is a requirement that the personal representative file the inventory with the probate court, the family's assets automatically become a matter of public record. Most families would prefer to keep such information private. UPC § 3–706, supra, therefore requires the personal representative to mail the inventory, with market values, to "interested persons who request it" but does not require the personal representative to file it with the court. New York does not require an inventory unless the court orders it on the petition of an interested party. See N.Y. SCPA §§ 2101, 2102.

2. CLAIMS OF CREDITORS

a. In General

Uniform Probate Code

Section 3–803. Limitations on Presentation of Claims.

(a) All claims against a decedent's estate which arose before the death of the decedent, including claims of the state and any political subdivision thereof, whether due or to become due, absolute or contingent, liquidated or unliquidated, founded on contract, tort, or other legal basis, if not barred earlier by another statute of limitations or non-claim statute, are barred against the estate, the personal representative, the heirs and devisees, and non-probate transferees of the decedent, unless presented within the earlier of the following:

(1) one year after the decedent's death; or

(2) [the later of four months after publication or sixty days after mailing or other delivery] for creditors who are given actual notice, and

within [four months after publication] for all creditors barred by publication.

(b) A claim described in subsection (a) which is barred by the non-claim statute of the decedent's domicile before the giving of notice to creditors in this state is also barred in this state.

(c) All claims against a decedent's estate which arise at or after the death of the decedent, including claims of the state and any subdivision thereof, whether due or to become due, absolute or contingent, liquidated or unliquidated, founded on contract, tort, or other legal basis, are barred against the estate, the personal representative, and the heirs and devisees of the decedent, unless presented as follows:

(1) a claim based on a contract with the personal representative, within four months after performance by the personal representative is due; or

(2) any other claim, within the later of four months after it arises, or the time specified in subsection (a)(1).

(d) Nothing in this section affects or prevents:

(1) any proceeding to enforce any mortgage, pledge, or other lien upon property of the estate;

(2) to the limits of the insurance protection only, any proceeding to establish liability of the decedent or the personal representative for which he is protected by liability insurance; or

(3) collection of compensation for services rendered and reimbursement for expenses advanced by the personal representative or by the attorney or accountant for the personal representative of the estate.

NOTES

1. *Non-claim statutes.* Most states have non-claim statutes similar to that of the UPC, absolutely barring untimely claims. See, e.g., Estate of Fleming, 786 So.2d 660 (Fla. App. 2001) (non-claim statute is "absolute bar"; no exception for fraud or estoppel). In a few states the statute does not finally bar late claims; instead, the statute assigns them a lower priority for payment. In New York, for instance, the personal representative can pay legacies and timely claims without accountability to late creditors for doing so. See N.Y. SCPA § 1802.

Non-claim statutes run the gamut, in the types of claims they bar, from the comprehensive phrase, "all claims," to limited formulas, such as "claims arising out of contract." In the main, any claim founded on a decedent's personal obligation, which would have been the basis of an in personam action against the decedent, is within the non-claim proscription, unlike claims for recovery of property that are in rem in nature.

2. *Secured creditors.* Secured creditors need not file claims to protect their security. If, however, the amount of the obligation exceeds the value of the property securing it, even a secured creditor must file a claim as to the excess. See Jones v. McLauchlin, 299 So.2d 723 (Ala.1974).

3. *Contingent and unmatured obligations.* Contingent obligations (which may never come into existence, such as an agreement by the decedent to go surety on another person's debt) and unmatured obligations (which are in existence but not yet due) present special problems. Many statutes do not require the filing of such claims, in which case they continue as claims against the distributees if and when they materialize. If, as under the UPC, they are specifically within the non-claim statute, several methods of payment are available. One method requires determination of a present value and payment of that amount. See, e.g., UPC § 3–810(b)(1) (if claimant consents). Alternatively, it may be necessary for the personal representative to retain a reserve fund or otherwise provide for the possibility of future liability. See, e.g., UPC § 3–810(b)(2).

4. *Allowance and compromise of claims.* After determining the validity of a claim, the personal representative may allow or disallow it. Upon disallowance, the claimant may bring an action for a judicial determination, within a further statutory time period. The personal representative generally has power to compromise claims, in the best interest of the estate. Some statutes, however, require judicial approval of all compromises. A personal representative who allows a claim that should have been disallowed may be personally liable for it. In other words, the personal representative, when accounting, may not receive credit for its payment. See generally Shaffer, Fiduciary Power to Compromise Claims, 41 N.Y.U. L. Rev. 528 (1966).

5. *Notice.* Statutes have long required notice to a decedent's creditors by publication in a local newspaper. Creditors who failed to submit their claims promptly thereafter were barred. In Tulsa Professional Collection Services, Inc. v. Pope, 485 U.S. 478 (1988), however, the Supreme Court ruled that the due process clause of the fourteenth amendment requires that "known or readily ascertainable" creditors receive "notice by mail or other means" prior to the barring of their claims under such a statutory format. In response, there have been substantial amendments to the UPC. UPC § 3–801 now makes both actual notice and notice by publication optional as to creditors, but UPC § 3–803(a)(2) applies especially short statutes of limitation, running from the giving of notice, only to those creditors who receive actual notice or as to whom notice by publication is effective. Alternatively, UPC § 3–803(a)(1) bars all claims one year after a decedent's death, without regard to notice. See Estate of Ongaro, 998 P.2d 1097 (Colo. 2000) (self-executing non-claim statute barred claim submitted more than one year after decedent's death, even though decedent's daughter continued to make payments on the

note and failed to notify the creditor of decedent's death). The aim of the UPC seems to be to allow a personal representative the option of providing no notice of any kind to creditors, or to provide notice by publication only, even when there are known or ascertainable creditors, if the personal representative is willing to wait an entire year for a bar on creditors' claims. Although some commentators have expressed doubts about the validity of the UPC approach, e.g., Reutlinger, State Action, Due Process, and the New Nonclaim Statutes: Can No Notice be Good Notice if Some Notice is Not?, 24 Real Prop. Prob. & Tr. J. 433 (1990), a number of courts have upheld it against constitutional challenge. E.g., State ex rel. Houska v. Dickhaner, 323 S.W.3d 29 (Mo. 2010), cert. denied, 131 S. Ct. 2106 (U.S. 2011); Estate of Ongaro, supra.

6. *Environmental clean-up costs.* Under the Comprehensive Environmental Response, Compensation, and Liability Act of 1980 (CERCLA), 42 U.S.C. §§ 9601–9657, anyone who owns contaminated real property is liable (along with others) for the costs of cleaning it up. This includes fiduciaries who own contaminated land. See City of Phoenix v. Garbage Services Co., 827 F.Supp. 600 (D.Ariz.1993). In Witco Corp. v. Beekhuis, 38 F.3d 682 (3d Cir.1994), however, the court held that CERCLA did not preempt state nonclaim statutes. Thus, the trial court properly dismissed CERCLA claims asserted against an estate after the applicable non-claim statute had run. On the other hand, distributees of estate property may hold it "in trust" for payment of environmental clean-up costs. See State ex rel. Howes v. W.R. Peele, Sr. Trust, 876 F.Supp. 733 (E.D.N.C.1995); Steego Corp. v. Ravenal, 830 F.Supp. 42 (D.Mass.1993). See generally Graham & Lindquist, The Application of CERCLA and Other Strict Liability Environmental Statutes to Fiduciary Relationships—Putting *City of Phoenix* in Context, 29 Real Prop. Prob. & Tr. J. 1 (1994); Rodosevich, The Expansive Reach of CERCLA Liability: Potential Liability of Executors of Wills and Inter Vivos and Testamentary Trustees, 55 Alb. L. Rev. 143 (1991).

b. Post–Death Creditors

ONANIAN V. LEGGAT

Appeals Court of Massachusetts, 1974.
2 Mass.App.Ct. 623, 317 N.E.2d 823.

ROSE, JUSTICE.

The defendant appeals from a decree of the Superior Court in which the plaintiff was declared entitled to the payment of a sum of money, with interest, in lieu of specific performance of an agreement for the purchase of certain real property from the defendant. . . .

On July 17, 1970, the defendant qualified as executor under the will of one L. Francis F. Knowles. The will devised the decedent's real property to certain persons, but conferred a power of sale thereof upon the defendant as executor. The defendant received at least two offers to purchase the real property, one of which was from the plaintiff. During the last week of November, 1970, the plaintiff and the defendant executed an agreement for the purchase and sale of the property (the agreement) for $32,500, title to pass on or before January 1, 1971. The agreement was in typical form, but contained the following provision: "This conveyance is subject to and contingent upon the issuance of a license to sell from the Probate Court for Middlesex County in the Estate of L. Francis F. Knowles."

On December 3, 1970, the defendant filed a petition in the Probate Court for Middlesex County in which he represented that "an advantageous offer for the purchase of said real estate ha[d] been made to [him] in the sum of [$32,500]" and prayed that he "may be licensed to sell said real estate . . . at private sale in accordance with said offer or for a larger sum. . . ." The defendant also filed documents signed by each of the devisees assenting to the "petition for license to sell real estate for the sum of $32,500 without further notice to me." On December 15 a judge of the Probate Court entered a decree to the effect that the defendant be licensed to sell the property "at private sale in accordance with said offer or for a larger sum, or at public auction, if he shall think best so to do. . . ."

By a letter dated December 29, 1970, the defendant informed the plaintiff that the license had been obtained. In the same letter, however, the defendant stated that another prospective purchaser was interested in the property and that it would be sold to the highest bidder on January 4, 1971. The plaintiff filed his bill in equity on December 31, 1970, seeking specific performance of the agreement and other relief, but, without waiving his rights under the agreement, submitted a bid to the defendant in the amount of $35,155, and obtained title to the property for that price during the pendency of this suit. The decree appealed from declared the defendant indebted to the plaintiff for the difference between that price and the contract price of $32,500, with interest from December 31, 1970.

We are uncertain whether the thrust of the defendant's argument is that his agreement with the plaintiff was not binding upon him or that a condition to which his obligation thereunder was subject was not fulfilled. Under either interpretation the argument is without merit.

1. Under the first of these interpretations, the defendant is contending that because he was under a duty to obtain the highest possible price for the property, he was excused from performing the agreement when a higher offer than the plaintiff's was received. The first of these propositions is unquestionably true. . . . But the second proposition does not inevitably follow from it. The fiduciary duty of an executor or administrator is separate and distinct from the contractual duty he may incur when he enters into agreements with third persons. The first is owed to and enfor-

ceable by the beneficiaries of the estate, while the second is owed to and enforceable by a stranger to the estate. And, with a few exceptions not here material . . . , an executor or administrator is liable on contracts he makes for the benefit of the estate, if at all, individually and not in his representative capacity. . . . Thus, the two types of duties are enforceable *by* different persons and, in the eyes of the law, *against* different persons. See Eaton v. Walker, 244 Mass. 23, 30–32, 138 N.E. 798 (1923). The executor or administrator, of course, is entitled to reimbursement for expenses reasonably and necessarily incurred for the benefit of the estate. . . . But whether he can obtain such reimbursement is a question to be answered by the Probate Court in the settlement of his account, a separate proceeding which is not before us . . . , and as to which we make no comment. . . .

That the contracts of an executor or administrator are enforceable in an action at law, however improvident they may be from the standpoint of the estate, is well settled. . . . It has been said that personal liability attaches even where the fiduciary entering into such a contract lacks authority to perform it in accordance with its terms. Dresel v. Jordan, 104 Mass. 407, 414 (1870). Additionally, where he has authority to sell a decedent's real property (contrast Dresel v. Jordan, supra), has entered into a contract to do so (compare Weinstein v. Green, 347 Mass. 580, 199 N.E.2d 310 [1964]) and his obligation thereunder has become unconditional (contrast Grennan v. Pierce, 229 Mass. 292, 293–294, 118 N.E. 301 [1918]), the contract may well be specifically enforceable against him. See Justice v. Soderlund, 225 Mass. 320, 322–324, 114 N.E. 623 (1916); O'Neill v. Niccolls, 324 Mass. 382, 384–385, 86 N.E.2d 522 (1949). We need not decide whether the plaintiff could have obtained a decree ordering the defendant to convey the property, however, as no such decree was necessary. Having already acquired title to the property, the plaintiff received by the decree what amounts to nothing more than money damages in the nature of a refund of the excess of the price he paid over the price stipulated in the agreement—which he could just as well have recovered in an action at law.

It has been suggested that an executor or administrator can escape such personal liability to third persons by an agreement exempting himself therefrom. Anglo–American Direct Tea Trading Co. v. Seward, 294 Mass. 349, 351, 2 N.E.2d 448 (1936). Reilly v. Whiting, 332 Mass. 745, 746–747, 127 N.E.2d 567 (1955). But the agreement in the present case contains no provision purporting to grant such an exemption. The fact that the defendant is identified in the opening clause of the agreement as "Executor u/w/o L. Francis F. Knowles" and that his signature is followed by the abbreviation "Execr." is insufficient to protect him against personal liability. Reilly v. Whiting, supra. . . . Nor is it of any consequence that the defendant may have understood the agreement as affording him such protection, especially where as here, he was its draftsman. No such mistake of law on the defendant's part can free him from liability. Scirpo v. McMillan, 355 Mass. 657, 660, 247 N.E.2d 368 (1969). Rather, his liability is governed by "[t]he general rule . . . that . . . one who signs a written agreement is bound by its terms whether he reads and understands it or not. . . ." Spritz v. Lishner, 355 Mass. 162, 164, 243 N.E.2d 163, 164 (1969).

2. If the defendant's argument is interpreted as one that his obligation under the agreement was conditional upon his not receiving a higher offer for the property, it must also fail. There was no evidence of any antecedent understanding between the parties in this regard. There was nothing in the agreement itself expressly relieving the defendant of liability upon receipt of a higher offer. The defendant seems to argue, however, that the provision making his obligation conditional upon obtaining a license from the Probate Court impliedly had this effect.

[The court rejected defendant's argument.]

3. We note that the defendant is characterized in the pleadings and the decree of the Superior Court as "executor." For the reasons previously stated he is properly before the Superior Court only as an individual, and we treat the bill as having been brought against him in that capacity, the word "executor" being surplusage. . . . Since the identification of the defendant in the decree ("as he is the Executor of the Will of L. Francis F. Knowles") might be susceptible of misinterpretation, the decree is to be modified by striking the quoted words therefrom. . . .

The decree as modified is affirmed.

VANCE V. ESTATE OF MYERS
Supreme Court of Alaska, 1972.
494 P.2d 816.

CONNOR, JUSTICE.

The central question in this case concerns the liability of an estate for the torts of a trustee, executor, or administrator.

Appellant brought a tort action against the administrator of the appellee's estate. The action was filed shortly before the superior court discharged the administrator, thus terminating the administration of the estate. Appellant moved to set aside the decree of discharge and reinstate the administrator until the tort action could be concluded. Appellant's motion was denied. The issue on appeal is whether the court erred in refusing to set aside its decree of discharge.

Charles O. Myers died in Fairbanks, Alaska, on May 3, 1969. Shortly thereafter Howard E. Holbert was appointed administrator of the estate. By court order Holbert was allowed to operate the business owned by the decedent, Chuck's Corner Bar, in Nenana, Alaska.

On June 1, 1970, Holbert filed a petition for settling final account, distribution and discharge. In an order of July 16, 1970, the court approved the accounting and found that the administrator should be discharged, after paying expenses and making distribution of the estate.

The final distribution, leaving no funds of the estate in the hands of Holbert, was accomplished on August 20, 1970. On August 31, 1970, a request was made by the sole beneficiary of the estate that the administrator be discharged. This request included a statement of satisfaction with the disbursements made by the administrator. On September 22, 1970, the administrator submitted a second supplement to his final accounting and petitioned for discharge. This was granted by order of the superior court on September 25, 1970.

On August 31, 1970, the appellant filed suit against several persons, including Holbert as administrator of the estate of Myers. The complaint alleges that appellant's husband, for whom she is suing as guardian ad litem, was physically injured in an altercation in Chuck's Corner Bar on June 5, 1970. It is alleged that the injuries resulted, in part, from the actions of the administrator and an employee of the administrator in that they served drinks to John Vance, when Vance was already intoxicated. The complaint further alleges that this rendered Vance incapable of caring for his own safety, that the employee assisted in dragging Vance to the street outside the bar after Vance had been beaten by another person in the bar, and that the employee failed to protect Vance from being beaten in the bar while Vance was in a helpless condition. An amended complaint, stipulated by the parties as part of the record, but as yet unfiled, also asserts that Holbert was negligent in failing to obtain insurance covering the operation of the bar.

Holbert was served with the complaint on September 6, 1970. A copy of the complaint was sent to the probate master on September 14, 1970. The superior court was aware of the pending tort action at the time it granted the discharge.

Appellant argues that the estate should not have been closed and the administrator discharged while a tort action was pending against it, relying upon Dunn v. Lindsey, 68 N.M. 288, 361 P.2d 328 (1961). But that case is quite distinguishable. There the cause of action was based upon the conduct of the decedent himself, not that of the executor. In the present case the claim relates entirely to the alleged negligence of the administrator in his operation and management of the assets of the estate. We must consider, therefore, whether those assets can be subjected directly to liability for the alleged torts of the administrator. Preliminarily it should be observed that in the area we are treating no distinction exists between a decedent's estate and a trust estate.

Under the traditional rule a trustee, executor, or administrator was normally liable for torts committed by him or his servants in the administration of the trust or estate. But such torts did not result in the imposition of direct liability upon the assets of the trust or estate. Kirchner v. Muller, 280 N.Y. 23, 19 N.E.2d 665 (1939); Brown v. Guaranty Estates Corp., 239 N.C. 595, 80 S.E.2d 645 (1954); Barnett v. Schumacher, 453 S.W.2d 934 (Mo.1970); A. Scott, Liabilities Incurred in the Administration of Trusts, 28 Harv. L. Rev. 725 (1915). The orthodox view, still adhered to in a great number of jurisdictions, is that the person to whom the trustee has incurred liability in the administration of the trust must bring an action against the trustee personally, but not in his representative capacity. The claimant may not reach the trust estate directly and apply it to the satisfaction of his claim.

The personal liability of the trustee or executor for torts of his agents is now generally qualified, however, by allowing the executor or trustee to obtain reimbursement from the assets of the estate when he is personally without fault. Restatement 2d, Trusts, § 247. If the claim against the trustee is uncollectible, it is generally recognized that the plaintiff may then reach the trust assets to the extent of the trustee's right to reimbursement. Restatement 2d, Trusts, § 268; H. Stone, A Theory of Liability of Trust Estates for the Contracts and Torts of the Trustee, 22 Colum. L. Rev. 527 (1922). In some jurisdictions, when the trustee's right to reimbursement is clear, the courts have allowed suit against the trustee in his representative capacity, thus avoiding circuity of action. Ewing v. Wm. L. Foley, Inc., 115 Tex. 222, 280 S.W. 499 (1926); Dobbs v. Noble, 55 Ga. App. 201, 189 S.E. 694 (1937); Smith v. Coleman, 100 Fla. 1707, 132 So. 198 (1931).

One of the original principles underlying the basic rule was that the trustee had an obligation to the trust beneficiaries to manage the estate without fault. Trust property should not be impaired or dissipated through wrongdoing of the trustee. This is, of course, a sound principle where the trustee acts outside the scope of his authority. It evolved at a time when the administration of trusts and estates was relatively passive and seldom required active management of a business enterprise. In much of the earlier case law the courts seem to be concerned exclusively with protecting the estate and the beneficiaries from the acts of reckless and improvident fiduciaries. Parmenter v. Barstow, 22 R.I. 245, 47 A. 365 (1900); Birdsong v. Jones, 222 Mo. App. 768, 8 S.W.2d 98 (1928). Little thought seems to have been given to the plight of the tort victim for harms done to him by the operation of a business enterprise.

Where the trustee's wrongful acts or omissions occur within the general scope of his authority to manage trust assets, and more particularly when the trustee himself has no appreciable assets, the impact of the traditional rule has been perceived as unjust. For this reason the courts have sought mechanisms, described above, by which the claimants in these circumstances could ultimately reach the assets of the estate. Many of the resulting decisions represent only a partial solution to the problem. Circuity of action is still often required, suit being filed first against the trustee, and only when collection against the trustee has been exhausted and proved futile is enforcement allowed against the estate directly. Kirchner v. Muller, supra; Schmidt v. Kellner, 307 Ill. 331, 138 N.E. 604 (1923). Even that procedure assumes that the trustee has a right to be exonerated out of the estate for the liability he has incurred, which is not always the case even when the trustee's tort was committed within the scope of his authority. Reimbursement may be denied to the trustee when he is personally at fault. . . .

The traditional rule and its exceptions have been criticized by recognized scholars and jurists as being inadequate and unfair to the tort creditor. Dean, later Chief Justice, Harlan Fiske Stone pointed out fifty years ago in a salient law review article that the traditional rule was premised upon theories which were untenable. The trustee's right to indemnity should not be the measure of the plaintiff's rights against the assets of the trust for this leads to uneven results based solely upon the criterion of whether the trustee was or was not personally at fault. The true reason for reaching the assets of the estate should be the policy of casting the economic loss resulting from the trustee's tort upon the estate, rather than upon the tort victim. This would bring the law of trust liability into harmony with the modern doctrine that an economic enterprise should bear the burden of the losses caused by it, including actionable personal injuries which result from its operations. H. Stone, op. cit., 542–545. To the same effect are the penetrating analyses and conclusions found in C. Fulda & W. Pond, Tort Liability of Trust Estates, 41 Colum. L. Rev. 1332 (1941).

In 1937 the Commissioners on Uniform State Laws proffered one solution to the problem in the Uniform Trusts Act. Section 14 of that act provides that the trustee may be sued in his representative capacity and collection may be had directly from the trust assets if "the tort was a common incident of the kind of business activity in which the trustee or his predecessor was properly engaged for the trust." This provision has been adopted in several states. . . . But it is not necessary that a statute be enacted in order to bring this standard into being. The basic rule was the product of common law decision. It can be altered in the same manner.

One of the current reasons advanced for perpetuating the traditional rule is that if the tort claimant is allowed to sue the trustee in his representative capacity, the beneficiaries may not be adequately represented. That is, a conflict can exist between the trustee as an individual and the trustee in his official capacity, for often he will be named a party defendant in both those capacities. Johnston v. Long, 30 Cal. 2d 54, 181 P.2d 645 (1947). But this problem can be minimized by the appointment of a special representative to protect the interests of the estate and beneficiaries when such a conflict between the estate and the fiduciary appears. In re Estate of Gregory, 487 P.2d 59, 63 (Alaska 1971).

Other courts have held that the trustee may be sued in his representative capacity in cases such as the one before us. Miller v. Smythe, 92 Ga. 154, 18 S.E. 46 (1893); Smith v. Coleman, 100 Fla. 1707, 132 So. 198 (1931); Carey v. Squire, 63 Ohio App. 476, 27 N.E.2d 175 (1939). We are convinced this is the right result. It should be recognized that in respect to tort liability a trustee acting within the general scope of his authority can subject the estate to liability, in the same manner as could an agent acting on behalf of an ordinary principal. That the estate lacks legal personality is true. But that factor should not be a roadblock to achieving realistic justice. See commentary, Restatement 2d, Trusts, § 271A, comment a.–c. at 23.

We hold that an administrator, executor, or trustee may be sued in his representative capacity, and collection may be had from the trust assets, for a tort committed in the course of administration, if it is determined by the court that the tort was a common incident of the kind of business activity in which the administrator, executor, or trustee was properly engaged on behalf of the estate. It follows that appellant's action against appellee was proper. . . .

We must reverse the denial of appellant's motion to set aside the decree of discharge and to reinstate the administrator until the tort action can be concluded, and we must remand for proceedings consistent with this opinion.

Reversed.

NOTES

1. *The traditional rule.* As both *Onanian* and *Vance* make clear, the traditional rule required claimants, whether their claims sounded in tort or in contract, to sue an executor, administrator, guardian, or trustee in the fiduciary's personal capacity, rather than *as fiduciary* (in which case the action

would have been directly against the estate or trust). This rule derived from the refusal of the common law courts to recognize the existence of the trust. As *Vance* also makes clear, however, there have long been critics of the traditional rule. See, e.g., Johnston, Developments in Contract Liability of Trusts and Trustees, 41 N.Y.U. L. Rev. 483 (1966); Stone, A Theory of Liability of Trust Estates for the Contracts and Torts of the Trustee, 22 Colum. L. Rev. 527 (1922).

2. *The modern trend.* The UPC continues in the tradition of the Uniform Trusts Act (quoted in *Vance*) and makes the estate initially responsible for torts and contracts. UPC § 3–808 provides:

> (a) Unless otherwise provided in the contract, a personal representative is not individually liable on a contract properly entered into in his fiduciary capacity in the course of administration of the estate unless he fails to reveal his representative capacity and identify the estate in the contract.

> (b) A personal representative is individually liable for obligations arising from ownership or control of the estate or for torts committed in the course of administration of the estate only if he is personally at fault.

> (c) Claims based on contracts entered into by a personal representative in his fiduciary capacity, on obligations arising from ownership or control of the estate or on torts committed in the course of estate administration may be asserted against the estate by proceeding against the personal representative in his fiduciary capacity, whether or not the personal representative is individually liable therefor.

> (d) Issues of liability as between the estate and the personal representative individually may be determined in a proceeding for accounting, surcharge or indemnification or other appropriate proceeding.

UPC § 7–306 and UTC § 1010 adopt similar rules for trustees. See generally 4 Scott and Ascher on Trusts §§ 26.1 to 26.7. For critical analysis of the movement away from the traditional rule, see Curtis, The Transmogrification of the American Trust, 31 Real Prop. Prob. & Tr. J. 251 (1996).

3. *Decedents' contracts.* A decedent's contracts generally bind the estate, unless they involve a type of personal service that only the decedent could have performed. Compare Estate of Spann, 520 S.W.2d 286 (Ark.1975) (executor must employ necessary farm help to complete large contract for sale of cotton), with Farnon v. Cole, 66 Cal.Rptr. 673 (Cal.App.1968) (contract with popular singer, Nat King Cole, terminated by his death), and Kowal v. Sportswear by Revere, Inc., 222 N.E.2d 778 (Mass.1967) (contract with salesman was personal and did not survive his death).

4. *Estates winding up businesses.* Assume that the decedent was in the construction business and that, at death, a number of projects were under-

way. The personal representative faces a dilemma. A personal representative who breaches contracts and thereby incurs liability may be surchargeable for any resulting loss to the estate. On the other hand, a personal representative who attempts to fulfill the contracts may end up personally liable for the costs of completion (e.g., labor and materials), regardless of whether the estate has sufficient funds to pay them. Not surprisingly, there is authority both ways as to whether the personal representative's initial responsibility is to fulfill the contracts. Compare Exchange Nat'l Bank v. Betts' Estate, 176 P. 660 (Kan.1918), with In re Burke's Estate, 244 P. 340 (Cal.1926), and Didier v. American Casualty Co., 68 Cal.Rptr. 217 (Cal.App.1968).

Unless the will or a court order provides otherwise, a personal representative who carries on the decedent's business longer than is reasonably necessary may well be found to have violated one or more fiduciary duties. No matter how long the business continues, the personal representative must actively supervise its management. See Estate of Baldwin, 442 A.2d 529 (Me.1982) (corporate executor surchargeable for failure to oversee operation of decedent's general store). See generally Schwartzel, Continuing a Decedent's Business: Selected Creditors' Rights and Fiduciary Liability Issues, 26 Real Prop. Prob. & Tr. J. 775 (1992).

E. THE FIDUCIARY AND THE BENEFICIARIES

For fiduciaries, the principal threat of liability does not come from the occasional third person who acquires a claim against the trust or the estate; it comes from the beneficiaries. The focus of this section is on the nature of a fiduciary's obligations to the beneficiaries and problems of fiduciary management. For this purpose, the term "fiduciary" includes both personal representatives (executors and administrators) and trustees. Their functions and powers differ, and therefore the imposition of liability varies, depending upon the capacity in which the fiduciary is serving. Still, the basic fiduciary duties governing the use and management by one person of property in which another has rights of beneficial enjoyment are remarkably constant.

1. THE FIDUCIARY DUTY OF LOYALTY

Fiduciaries derive their powers from various sources, including the terms of the governing instrument, statutes, and case law. In the exercise of these powers there are certain duties fiduciaries cannot violate without rendering themselves liable for the resulting losses. Among these duties are the duty with respect to delegation of fiduciary obligations; the duty to keep and render accounts; the duty to exercise reasonable care and skill; the duty to retain control of and preserve the property; the duty to enforce claims; the duty to keep the property earmarked and separate from their own and others' property; the duty to make the property productive; the duty to deal impartially with the beneficiaries; and the duty to minimize taxes. See generally 3 Scott and Ascher on Trusts §§ 17.1 to 17.16. The most fundamental fiduciary duty, however, may be the duty of loyalty, which requires that a fiduciary make no profit (except compensation for serving as fiduciary) and take no personal advantage of the position. See generally Scott, The Trustee's Duty of Loyalty, 49 Harv. L. Rev. 521 (1936).

RUSSELL D. NILES, A CONTEMPORARY VIEW OF LIABILITY FOR BREACH OF TRUST
114 Trusts & Estates 12 (1975).

There are two general trends observable and they seem to go in opposite directions. First there is a trend toward strict liability or accountability wherever a fiduciary has made an unauthorized profit out of the property which he has been entrusted to manage. He must yield up this profit even if he has not been guilty of a breach of trust, even if he has not been conscious of any fault, and even if he has not caused any damage to his principal. This trend is clearly recognizable not only in the law of trusts but is being extended to an ever increasing number of other fiduciary relationships.

The other trend is toward narrowing and ameliorating the law of strict liability where a trustee, who has acted without conscious fault, is asked to pay out of his own resources for a loss suffered by the trust estate or to compensate the estate for profits that might have been made. In this branch of the subject, while liability without fault is retained for breaches of special danger, the trend is toward limiting liability for compensatory damages to cases where there is proof of wrongdoing and of the causal relation between fault and injury.

There may be an incipient trend away from personal fault toward institutionalizing or socializing some of the risks inherent in trust management. If so, this trend is largely for the future. For the present the two trends to be considered are, first, toward taking the profit out of fiduciary management, and, second, toward restricting compensatory damages to the consequences of provable fault.

MATTER OF ESTATE OF ROTHKO
Court of Appeals of New York, 1977.
43 N.Y.2d 305, 401 N.Y.S.2d 449, 372 N.E.2d 291.

COOKE, JUDGE.

Mark Rothko, an abstract expressionist painter whose works through the years gained for him an international reputation of greatness, died testate on February 25, 1970. The principal asset of his estate consisted of 798 paintings of tremendous value, and the dispute underlying this appeal involves the conduct of his three executors in their disposition of these works of art. In sum, that conduct as portrayed in the record and sketched in the opinions was manifestly wrongful and indeed shocking.

Rothko's will was admitted to probate on April 27, 1970 and letters testamentary were issued to Bernard J. Reis, Theodoros Stamos and Morton Levine. Hastily and within a period of only about three weeks and by virtue of two contracts each dated May 21, 1970, the executors dealt with all 798 paintings.

By a contract of sale, the estate executors agreed to sell to Marlborough A.G., a Liechtenstein corporation (hereinafter MAG), 100 Rothko paintings as listed for $1,800,000, $200,000 to be paid on execution of the agreement and the balance of $1,600,000 in 12 equal interest-free installments over a 12–year period. Under the second agreement, the executors consigned to Marlborough Gallery, Inc., a domestic corporation (hereinafter MNY), "approximately 700 paintings listed on a Schedule to be prepared," the consignee to be responsible for costs covering items such as insurance, storage, restoration and promotion. By its provisos, MNY could sell up to 35 paintings a year from each of two groups, pre–1947 and post–1947, for 12 years at the best price obtainable but not less than the appraised estate value, and it would receive a 50% commission on each painting sold, except for a commission of 40% on those sold to or through other dealers.

Petitioner Kate Rothko, decedent's daughter and a person entitled to share in his estate by virtue of an election under [former] EPTL 5–3.3 [imposing restrictions on charitable bequests], instituted this proceeding to remove the executors, to enjoin MNY and MAG from disposing of the paintings, to rescind the aforesaid agreements between the executors and said corporations, for a return of the paintings still in possession of those corporations, and for damages. She was joined by the guardian of her brother Christopher Rothko, likewise interested in the estate, who answered by adopting the allegations of his sister's petition and by demanding the same relief. The Attorney–General of the State, as the representative of the ultimate beneficiaries of the Mark Rothko Foundation, Inc., a charitable corporation and the residuary legatee under decedent's will, joined in requesting relief substantially similar to that prayed for by petitioner. On June 26, 1972 the Surrogate issued a temporary restraining order and on September 26, 1972 a preliminary injunction enjoining MAG, MNY, and the three executors from selling or otherwise disposing of the paintings referred to in the agreements dated May 21, 1970, except for sales or dispositions made with court permission. The Appellate Division modified the preliminary injunction order by increasing the amount of the bond and otherwise affirmed. By a 1974 petition, the Attorney–General, on behalf of the ultimate charitable beneficiaries of the Mark

Rothko Foundation, sought the punishment of MNY, MAG, Lloyd and Reis for contempt and other relief.

Following a nonjury trial covering 89 days and in a thorough opinion, the Surrogate found: that Reis was a director, secretary and treasurer of MNY, the consignee art gallery, in addition to being a coexecutor of the estate; that the testator had a 1969 *inter vivos* contract with MNY to sell Rothko's work at a commission of only 10% and whether that agreement survived testator's death was a problem that a fiduciary in a dual position could not have impartially faced; that Reis was in a position of serious conflict of interest with respect to the contracts of May 21, 1970 and that his dual role and planned purpose benefited the Marlborough interests to the detriment of the estate; that it was to the advantage of coexecutor Stamos as a "not-too-successful artist, financially," to curry favor with Marlborough and that the contract made by him with MNY within months after signing the estate contracts placed him in a position where his personal interests conflicted with those of the estate, especially leading to lax contract enforcement efforts by Stamos; that Stamos acted negligently and improvidently in view of his own knowledge of the conflict of interest of Reis; that the third coexecutor, Levine, while not acting in self-interest or with bad faith, nonetheless failed to exercise ordinary prudence in the performance of his assumed fiduciary obligations since he was aware of Reis' divided loyalty, believed that Stamos was also seeking personal advantage, possessed personal opinions as to the value of the paintings and yet followed the leadership of his coexecutors without investigation of essential facts or consultation with competent and disinterested appraisers, and that the business transactions of the two Marlborough corporations were admittedly controlled and directed by Francis K. Lloyd. It was concluded that the acts and failures of the three executors were clearly improper to such a substantial extent as to mandate their removal under SCPA 711 as estate fiduciaries. The Surrogate also found that MNY, MAG and Lloyd were guilty of contempt in shipping, disposing of and selling 57 paintings in violation of the temporary restraining order dated June 26, 1972 and of the injunction dated September 26, 1972; that the contracts for sale and consignment of paintings between the executors and MNY and MAG provided inadequate value to the estate, amounting to a lack of mutuality and fairness resulting from conflicts on the part of Reis and Stamos and improvidence on the part of all executors; that said contracts were voidable and were set aside by reason of violation of the duty of loyalty and improvidence of the executors, knowingly participated in and induced by MNY and MAG; that the fact that these agreements were voidable did not revive the 1969 *inter vivos* agreements since the parties by their conduct evinced an intent to abandon and abrogate these compacts. The Surrogate held that the present value at the time of trial of the paintings sold is the proper measure of damages as to MNY, MAG, Lloyd, Reis and Stamos. He imposed a civil fine of $3,332,000 upon MNY,

MAG and Lloyd, same being the appreciated value at the time of trial of the 57 paintings sold in violation of the temporary restraining order and injunction. It was held that Levine[2] was liable for $6,464,880 in damages, as he was not in a dual position acting for his own interest and was thus liable only for the actual value of paintings sold MNY and MAG as of the dates of sale, and that Reis, Stamos, MNY and MAG, apart from being jointly and severally liable for the same damages as Levine for negligence, were liable for the greater sum of $9,252,000 "as appreciation damages less amounts previously paid to the estate with regard to sales of paintings." . . . The liabilities were held to be congruent so that payment of the highest sum would satisfy all lesser liabilities including the civil fines and the liabilities for damages were to be reduced by payment of the fine levied or by return of any of the 57 paintings disposed of, the new fiduciary to have the option in the first instance to specify which paintings the fiduciary would accept.

The Appellate Division, in an opinion by Justice Lane, modified to the extent of deleting the option given the new fiduciary to specify which paintings he would accept. Except for this modification, the majority affirmed on the opinion of Surrogate Midonick, with additional comments. Among others, it was stated that the entire court agreed that executors Reis and Stamos had a conflict of interest and divided loyalty in view of their nexus to MNY and that a majority were in agreement with the Surrogate's assessment of liability as to executor Levine and his findings of liability against MNY, MAG and Lloyd. The majority agreed with the Surrogate's analysis awarding "appreciation damages". . . .

In seeking a reversal, it is urged that an improper legal standard was applied in voiding the estate contracts of May, 1970, that the "no further inquiry" rule applies only to self-dealing and that in case of a conflict of interest, absent self-dealing, a challenged transaction must be shown to be unfair. The subject of fairness of the contracts is intertwined with the issue of whether Reis and Stamos were guilty of conflicts of interest. Scott is quoted to the effect that "[a] trustee does not necessarily incur liability merely because he has an individual interest in the transaction. . . . In Bullivant v. First Nat. Bank [246 Mass. 324, 141 N.E. 41] it was held that . . . the fact that the bank was also a creditor of the corporation did not make its assent invalid, *if it acted in good faith and the plan was fair*" (2 Scott, Trusts, § 170.24, p. 1384 [emphasis added]), and our attention has been called to the statement in Phelan v. Middle States Oil Corp., 220 F.2d 593, 603, 2 Cir., cert. den. sub nom. Cohen v. Glass, 349 U.S. 929, 75 S. Ct. 772, 99 L. Ed. 1260, that Judge Learned Hand found "no decisions that have applied [the no further inquiry rule] inflexibly to every occasion

---

[2] Mr. Levine was at the time a professor and head of the anthropology department at Fordham University.—EDS.

in which the fiduciary has been shown to have had a personal interest that might in fact have conflicted with his loyalty."

These contentions should be rejected. First, a review of the opinions of the Surrogate and the Appellate Division manifests that they did not rely solely on a "no further inquiry rule," and secondly, there is more than an adequate basis to conclude that the agreements between the Marlborough corporations and the estate were neither fair nor in the best interests of the estate. This is demonstrated, for example, by the comments of the Surrogate concerning the commissions on the consignment of the 698 paintings (see 84 Misc. 2d 830, 852–853, 379 N.Y.S.2d 923, 947–948) and those of the Appellate Division concerning the sale of the 100 paintings (see 56 A.D.2d, at pp. 501–502, 392 N.Y.S.2d, at pp. 872–873). The opinions under review demonstrate that neither the Surrogate nor the Appellate Division set aside the contracts by merely applying the no further inquiry rule without regard to fairness. Rather they determined, quite properly indeed, that these agreements were neither fair nor in the best interests of the estate.

To be sure, the assertions that there were no conflicts of interest on the part of Reis or Stamos indulge in sheer fantasy. Besides being a director and officer of MNY, for which there was financial remuneration, however slight, Reis, as noted by the Surrogate, had different inducements to favor the Marlborough interests, including his own aggrandizement of status and financial advantage through sales of almost one million dollars for items from his own and his family's extensive private art collection by the Marlborough interests (see 84 Misc. 2d, at pp. 843–844, 379 N.Y.S.2d, at pp. 939–940). Similarly, Stamos benefited as an artist under contract with Marlborough and, interestingly, Marlborough purchased a Stamos painting from a third party for $4,000 during the week in May, 1970 when the estate contract negotiations were pending (see 84 Misc. 2d, at p. 845, 379 N.Y.S.2d, at p. 941). The conflicts are manifest. Further, as noted in Bogert, Trusts and Trustees (2d ed.), "The duty of loyalty imposed on the fiduciary prevents him from accepting employment from a third party who is entering into a business transaction with the trust" (§ 543, subd. [S], p. 573). "While he [a trustee] is administering the trust he must refrain from placing himself in a position where his personal interest or that of a third person does or may conflict with the interest of the beneficiaries" (Bogert, Trusts [Hornbook Series—5th ed.], p. 343). Here, Reis was employed and Stamos benefited in a manner contemplated by Bogert (see, also, Meinhard v. Salmon, 249 N.Y. 458, 464, 466–467, 164 N.E. 545, 547–548; Schmidt v. Chambers, 265 Md. 9, 33–38, 288 A.2d 356). In short, one must strain the law rather than follow it to reach the result suggested on behalf of Reis and Stamos.

Levine contends that, having acted prudently and upon the advice of counsel, a complete defense was established. Suffice it to say, an executor who knows that his coexecutor is committing breaches of trust and not only fails to exert efforts directed towards prevention but accedes to them is legally accountable even though he was acting on the advice of counsel (Matter of Westerfield, 32 App. Div. 324, 344, 53 N.Y.S. 25, 39; 3 Scott, Trusts [3d ed.], § 201, p. 1657). When confronted with the question of whether to enter into the Marlborough contracts, Levine was acting in a business capacity, not a legal one, in which he was required as an executor primarily to employ such diligence and prudence to the care and management of the estate assets and affairs as would prudent persons of discretion and intelligence (King v. Talbot, 40 N.Y. 76, 85–86), accented by "[n]ot honesty alone, but the punctilio of an honor the most sensitive" (Meinhard v. Salmon, 249 N.Y. 458, 464, 164 N.E. 545, 546, supra). Alleged good faith on the part of a fiduciary forgetful of his duty is not enough (Wendt v. Fischer, 243 N.Y. 439, 443, 154 N.E. 303, 304). He could not close his eyes, remain passive or move with unconcern in the face of the obvious loss to be visited upon the estate by participation in those business arrangements and then shelter himself behind the claimed counsel of an attorney (see Matter of Niles, 113 N.Y. 547, 558, 21 N.E. 687, 689 . . .).

Further, there is no merit to the argument that MNY and MAG lacked notice of the breach of trust. The record amply supports the determination that they are chargeable with notice of the executors' breach of duty.

The measure of damages was the issue that divided the Appellate Division (see 56 A.D.2d, at p. 500, 392 N.Y.S.2d, at p. 872). The contention of Reis, Stamos, MNY and MAG, that the award of appreciation damages was legally erroneous and impermissible, is based on a principle that an executor authorized to sell is not liable for an increase in value if the breach consists only in selling for a figure less than that for which the executor should have sold. For example, Scott states:

> The beneficiaries are not entitled to the value of the property at the time of the decree if it was not the duty of the trustee to retain the property in the trust and the breach of trust consisted *merely* in selling the property for too low a price. (3 Scott, Trusts [3d ed.], § 208.3, p. 1687 [emphasis added]).

> If the trustee is guilty of a breach of trust in selling trust property for an inadequate price, he is liable for the difference between the amount he should have received and the amount which he did receive. He is not liable, however, for any subsequent rise in value of the property sold. (Id., § 208.6, pp. 1689–1690.)

A recitation of similar import appears in Comment d under Restatement, Trusts 2d (§ 205):

> d. Sale for less than value. If the trustee is authorized to sell trust property, but in breach of trust he sells it for less than he should receive, he is liable for the value of the property at the time of the sale less the amount which he received. If the breach of trust consists *only* in selling it for too little, he is not chargeable with the amount of any subsequent increase in value of the property under the rule stated in Clause (c), as he would be if he were not authorized to sell the property. See § 208. (Emphasis added.)

However, employment of "merely" and "only" as limiting words suggests that where the breach consists of some misfeasance, other than solely for selling "for too low a price" or "for too little," appreciation damages may be appropriate. Under Scott (§ 208.3, pp. 1686–1687) and the Restatement (§ 208), the trustee may be held liable for appreciation damages if it was his or her duty to retain the property, the theory being that the beneficiaries are entitled to be placed in the same position they would have been in had the breach not consisted of a sale of property that should have been retained. The same rule should apply where the breach of trust consists of a serious conflict of interest—which is more than merely selling for too little.

The reason for allowing appreciation damages, where there is a duty to retain, and only date of sale damages, where there is authorization to sell, is policy oriented. If a trustee authorized to sell were subjected to a greater measure of damages he might be reluctant to sell (in which event he might run a risk if depreciation ensued). On the other hand, if there is a duty to retain and the trustee sells there is no policy reason to protect the trustee; he has not simply acted imprudently, he has violated an integral condition of the trust.

> If a trustee in breach of trust transfers trust property to a person who takes with notice of the breach of trust, and the transferee has disposed of the property . . . [i]t seems proper to charge him with the value at the time of the decree, since if it had not been for the breach of trust the property would still have been a part of the trust estate. (4 Scott, Trusts [3d ed.], § 291.2 . . .).

This rule of law which applies to the transferees MNY and MAG also supports the imposition of appreciation damages against Reis and Stamos, since if the Marlborough corporations are liable for such damages either as purchaser or consignees with notice, from one in breach of trust, it is only logical to hold that said executors, as sellers and consignors, are liable also *pro tanto*.

. . . Here, the executors, though authorized to sell, did not merely err in the amount they accepted but sold to one with whom Reis and Stamos had a self-interest. To make the injured party whole, . . . the quantum of damages [must be appropriate]. In other words, since the paintings cannot be returned, the estate is therefore entitled to their value at the time of the decree, i.e., appreciation damages. These are not punitive damages in a true sense, rather they are damages intended to make the estate whole. Of course, as to Reis, Stamos, MNY and MAG, these damages might be considered by some to be exemplary in a sense, in that they serve as a warning to others (see Reynolds v. Pegler, 123 F. Supp. 36, 38, D.C., affd. 223 F.2d 429, 2 Cir., cert. den. 350 U.S. 846, 76 S. Ct. 80, 100 L. Ed. 754), but their true character is ascertained when viewed in the light of overriding policy considerations and in the realization that the sale and consignment were not merely sales below value but inherently wrongful transfers which should allow the owner to be made whole (see Menzel v. List, 24 N.Y.2d 91, 97, 298 N.Y.S.2d 979, 982, 246 N.E.2d 742, 744 . . .).

The decree of the Surrogate imposed appreciation damages against Reis, Stamos, MNY and MAG in the amount of $7,339,464.72—computed as $9,252,000 (86 works on canvas at $90,000 each and 54 works on paper at $28,000 each) less the aggregate amounts paid the estate under the two rescinded agreements and interest. Appellants chose not to offer evidence of "present value" and the only proof furnished on the subject was that of the expert Heller whose appraisal as of January, 1974 (the month previous to that when trial commenced) on a painting-by-painting basis totaled $15,100,000. There was also testimony as to bona fide sales of other Rothkos between 1971 and 1974. Under the circumstances, it was impossible to appraise the value of the unreturned works of art with an absolute certainty and, so long as the figure arrived at had a reasonable basis of computation and was not merely speculative, possible or imaginary, the Surrogate had the right to resort to reasonable conjectures and probable estimates and to make the best approximation possible through the exercise of good judgment and common sense in arriving at that amount. . . . This is particularly so where the conduct of wrongdoers has rendered it difficult to ascertain the damages suffered with the precision otherwise possible. . . .

Accordingly, the order of the Appellate Division should be affirmed, with costs to the prevailing parties against appellants. . . .

NOTES

1. *Short statements of the duty of loyalty.* UTC § 802(a) provides: "A trustee shall administer the trust solely in the interests of the beneficiaries." Uniform Prudent Investor Act § 5 is to similar effect.

"[T]he duty of loyalty, far from violating the postulate of self-interested behavior, is based upon it. The duty of loyalty must be understood as the law's attempt to create an incentive structure in which the fiduciary's self-interest directs her to act in the best interest of the beneficiary." Cooter & Freedman, The Fiduciary Relationship: Its Economic Character and Legal Consequences, 68 N.Y.U. L. Rev. 1045 (1991).

2. *Recovery of property from third parties.* In *Rothko* the court held that a beneficiary could pursue property sold to a third person if the third person took the property with notice that the sale was in breach of trust. See Kline v. Orebaugh, 519 P.2d 691 (Kan.1974); 5 Scott and Ascher on Trusts §§ 29.1.8 to 29.1.8.9.

3. *Appreciation damages.* The court's award of appreciation damages in *Rothko* has been criticized as not clearly supported by authority and as creating a precedent that will operate as a "threat of severe penalties," adding "unacceptable legal costs to honest administration—costs that cannot be justified as a means of deterring undesirable conduct." Wellman, Punitive Surcharges Against Disloyal Fiduciaries—Is *Rothko* Right?, 77 Mich. L. Rev. 95 (1978). That being said, in many jurisdictions appreciation damages are now available even in the absence of self-dealing, although the terminology often differs. See, e.g., Cal. Prob. Code § 16440(a)(3) ("any profit that would have accrued to the trust"); Restatement (Third) of Trusts § 100(a) (2012) ("amount required to restore the values of the trust estate and trust distributions to what they would have been").

4. *Rothko update.* In a later proceeding, the Surrogate approved an award of legal fees to the four law firms that handled *Rothko*. They requested $8.6 million, and the Surrogate approved $3.2 million. The lion's share, $2.6 million, went to the attorneys for decedent's daughter Kate. Estate of Rothko, 414 N.Y.S.2d 444 (Sur. 1979).

I.R.C. § 4941 imposes stiff excise taxes (including a tax equal to 200% of the "amount involved") on any manager of a private foundation who engages in self dealing. Under this and other provisions, the Internal Revenue Service subsequently assessed staggering deficiencies against the two faithless Rothko fiduciaries. See Estate of Reis v. Commissioner, 87 T.C. 1016 (1986) (more than $21 million); Stamos v. Commissioner, 87 T.C. 1451 (1986) (more than $23 million).

5. *Other examples.*

a. In Hall v. Schoenwetter, 686 A.2d 980 (Conn.1996), an executor discovered a stolen Stradivarius violin among the decedent's possessions. She negotiated with Lloyd's of London, who had acquired title to the violin upon paying the legitimate owner the amount for which it was insured, for a finder's fee of more than $250,000. She failed to include the fee as an estate asset, treating it as her own. The court, rejecting her accounting, required her to return the fee to the estate:

The [executor's] argument that a thief should not benefit from his crime strikes a dissonant note in light of the facts of this case. Although morally compelling in the abstract, the [executor's] argument is logically inconsistent with her actions since, by negotiating for and accepting the finder's fee on her own behalf, [she] appropriated to herself, in breach of her fiduciary duty, whatever value the violin had to the estate. . . . The [executor] had no right or title to the violin except as [executor]. The only possible party that possessed better title than the decedent was Lloyd's. The [executor], however, did not accede to the interest of Lloyd's or acquire privity of title with Lloyd's when she misappropriated the violin from the estate.

In sum, the [executor] was under a fiduciary duty to act not in her own self-interest, but in the best interests of the estate. She failed to do so and she may not justify the breach of her fiduciary duty in 1988 by virtue of the fact that the decedent may have stolen the violin in 1936. No matter how the [violin] was obtained, it was a possession of the decedent's estate, and once the [executor] chose to negotiate with Lloyd's for the finder's fee her fiduciary duty required that she negotiate on behalf of the estate, not herself. [686 A.2d at 985–86.]

b. In Renz v. Beeman, 589 F.2d 735 (2d Cir. 1978), cert. denied, 444 U.S. 834 (1979), Mr. and Mrs. Beeman, as trustees of several family trusts, held a substantial number of the shares of a family corporation. The trusts, which were for the benefit of two distinct branches of the family, thus had voting control of the corporation. Thereafter, Mr. Beeman negotiated a purchase from a third party, on behalf of Mrs. Beeman in her individual capacity, of a substantial number of additional shares of the same corporation. This purchase shifted voting control of corporation to the Beemans' side of the family. The court held that, in making the purchase, the Beemans violated the duty of loyalty:

It is true . . . that the trustee never dealt with the shares which were in the corpus of the trust. In that sense Mr. Beeman may have been an exemplary trustee. But the absence of self-dealing does not measure the limit of the fiduciary obligation. The trust possessed an intangible asset which was to be free of competition from its fiduciary. An opportunity for purchase that comes to him while in a fiduciary capacity compels the trustee to give a right of first refusal to his trust estate if the opportunity fits the purpose of the trust. . . . See Restatement (Second) of Trusts § 170, comment k. When the trust is settled by two branches of a family, who jointly own control of a family company, the chancellor will insist that a trustee with ties to one branch should not disfavor the other. To upset the balance of control for selfish gain is to commit a breach of the high fiduciary duty of undivided loyalty. 589 F.2d at 746–47.]

The court also held, however, that the statute of limitations barred the claim.

c. In Paradee v. Paradee, 2010 Del. Ch. LEXIS 212 (Oct. 5, 2010), the settlor had a son, Charles, Jr., and a grandson, Trey. Troubles promptly arose between Charles, Jr., and the settlor's much younger second wife, Eleanor. Nonetheless, the settlor created a life insurance trust for Trey and named as trustee the settlor's long-time insurance agent, one Sterling. The sole trust asset was a fully paid, single-premium second-to-die policy on the lives of the settlor and Eleanor, with a face value in excess of $1 million. Both before and after the settlor's death, Eleanor repeatedly tried to revoke the trust, surrender the policy, and recover the policy's cash surrender value, notwithstanding the fact that the trust was irrevocable. Failing in that endeavor, she persuaded Sterling to make a large unsecured loan to her and the aging settlor. Sterling obtained the funds by borrowing against the cash surrender value of the policy at a higher rate of interest than Eleanor and the settlor agreed to pay the trust. After the settlor's death, the loan to the trust become due in full, Eleanor stopped paying interest on it, and Sterling made no collection efforts. As a result, Sterling lacked funds to repay the trust's own loan, and the policy eventually lapsed. Under the terms of the trust, Trey had the right to name himself trustee upon reaching age 30, but neither Sterling nor anyone else so informed him. Finding that Sterling acted primarily to curry favor with Eleanor and the settlor, the court held that Sterling violated the duty of loyalty: "Instead of evaluating what was in the best interests of the Trust, he evaluated whether he could please his long-time clients, the Paradees. Sterling should have asked himself whether the Trust Loan was good for the Trust." Eleanor, the court found, knowingly participated in Sterling's breaches of trust; indeed, she "aided and abetted them." In addition, she herself violated the duty of loyalty because, after Sterling's death, she named herself trustee, failed to inform Trey of his rights, continued not to make payments on the loan, and allowed the policy to lapse. Among the court's findings: "Eleanor consciously, intentionally, and vengefully refused to take any action to protect or preserve the Policy because she did not want Trey to benefit."

6. *Conflicting fiduciary duties.* In cases involving corporations, particularly closely-held corporations, a trustee who is also a corporate officer may owe fiduciary obligations not only to the trust beneficiaries but also to the corporation and other stockholders. See Matter of Hubbell, 97 N.E.2d 888 (N.Y.1951). Trustees in this dual capacity may find themselves in a no-win situation as, for instance, when they must vote dividends to obtain income for the income beneficiaries but their best business judgment tells them to reinvest the assets in furtherance of the company's continued growth.

In Childs v. National Bank of Austin, 658 F.2d 487 (7th Cir. 1981), a corporate fiduciary held in trust a majority of the shares of a closely-held corporation. As trustee, the bank voted the shares to install its own chairman as chairman of the corporation. The court held that the conflicts of interest thus created did not require removal of the bank's chairman as chairman of the corporation, but the court did require him to account to the trust for any compensation received from the corporation.

7. *Other types of fiduciaries.* Not only executors and trustees are subject to the fiduciary duty of loyalty. Almost all fiduciaries are. See, e.g., Matter of Bond & Mortgage Guar. Co., 103 N.E.2d 721 (N.Y. 1952) (trustee's lawyers); Estate of Ferrara, 852 N.E.2d 138 (N.Y. 2006) (in making gifts under durable power of attorney, attorneys-in-fact must act in principal's best interest).

8. *Liability without fault.* The Restatement (Third) of Trusts sometimes imposes liability even in the absence of a breach of trust:

§ 99. Absence of Breach of Trust

Absent a breach of trust, a trustee

(a) is not liable for a loss or depreciation in the value of trust property or a failure to make a profit greater than actually generated, but

(b) is accountable for any profit made arising from the administration of the trust.

Comment: . . .

c. *Accountability for profit.* When the administration of a trust produces a profit, whether there has or has not been a breach of trust, the trustee is accountable for the profit, including any income, realized gains, and unrealized appreciation in the value of trust property. This accountability reflects the fundamental principle that value generated by the trust estate and trust activities belongs to the trust, not to the trustee personally, and is to be held or applied for trust purposes.

JOHN H. LANGBEIN, QUESTIONING THE TRUST LAW DUTY OF LOYALTY: SOLE INTEREST OR BEST INTEREST?
114 Yale L.J. 929, 931–34 (2005).

The duty of loyalty requires a trustee "to administer the trust solely in the interest of the beneficiary."[3] . . .

The sole interest rule . . . applies not only to cases in which a trustee misappropriates trust property, but also to cases in which no such thing has happened—that is, to cases in which the trust "incurred no loss" or in which "actual benefit accrued to the trust" from a transaction with a conflicted trustee.

The conclusive presumption of invalidity[4] under the sole interest rule has acquired a distinctive name: the "no further inquiry" rule. What that

---

[3] Restatement (Second) of Trusts § 170(1) (1959); accord Unif. Trust Code § 802(a) (2000) . . . ("A trustee shall administer the trust solely in the interests of the beneficiaries.").

label emphasizes, as the official comment to the Uniform Trust Code of 2000 explains, is that "transactions involving trust property entered into by a trustee for the trustee's own personal account [are] voidable without further proof."[5] Courts invalidate a conflicted transaction without regard to its merits. . . . Courts have boasted of their "stubbornness and inflexibility," their "[u]ncompromising rigidity,"[6] in applying the sole interest rule. Remedies include rescission, disgorgement of gain, and consequential damages.

The underlying purpose of the duty of loyalty, which the sole interest rule is meant to serve, is to advance the best interest of the beneficiaries. This Article takes the view that a transaction prudently undertaken to advance the best interest of the beneficiaries best serves the purpose of the duty of loyalty, even if the trustee also does or might derive some benefit. A transaction in which there has been conflict or overlap of interest should be sustained if the trustee can prove that the transaction was prudently undertaken in the best interest of the beneficiaries. In such a case, inquiry into the merits is better than "no further inquiry."

. . . A main theme is that the severity of the sole interest rule is premised on assumptions that have become outmoded. Two centuries ago, when trust law settled on the sole interest rule, grievous shortcomings in the fact-finding processes of the equity courts placed a premium on rules that avoided fact-finding. Subsequently, however, the reform of civil procedure and the fusion of law and equity have equipped the courts that enforce trusts with effective fact-finding procedures. I also point to improvements in the standards, practices, and technology of trust record-keeping, as well as enhanced duties of disclosure, which have largely defused the old concern that a trustee operating under a potential conflict could easily conceal wrongdoing. Discussing the claim that the sole interest rule is needed to deter trustee wrongdoing, I point to cases in which the resulting overdeterrence harms the interests of trust beneficiaries. I compare the trust law duty of loyalty with the law of corporations, which originally shared the trust law sole interest rule but abandoned it in favor of a regime that undertakes to regulate rather than prohibit conflicts.

What has made the harshness of the trust law sole interest rule tolerable across the last two centuries is that its bark has been worse than

---

[4] "Such transactions are irrebuttably presumed to be affected by a conflict between personal and fiduciary interests. It is immaterial whether the trustee acts in good faith or pays a fair consideration." Unif. Trust Code § 802 cmt. . . . .

[5] Id. (explaining the "no further inquiry" rule).

[6] Meinhard v. Salmon, 164 N.E. 545, 546 (N.Y. 1928) (Cardozo, J.). Richard Posner has called this case the "most famous of Cardozo's moralistic opinions." Richard A. Posner, Cardozo: A Study in Reputation 104 (1990). Meinhard v. Salmon was not in fact a trust case; it concerned the fiduciary duties of commercial joint venturers, but it is incessantly invoked in the trust law loyalty cases. . . .

its bite. A group of excusing doctrines and a further group of categoric transactional exceptions . . . have drastically reduced the scope of the sole interest rule. Those devices allow the well-counseled trustee to escape much of the mischief that would otherwise result from the overbreadth of the rule. Of these excusing doctrines, the rule allowing a trustee to petition for advance judicial approval of a conflicted transaction is particularly revealing. When deciding whether to authorize the transaction, the court inquires whether it is in the best interest of the beneficiary. Thus, practice under the advance-approval doctrine supports the theme of this Article, that conflicted transactions that are beneficial to trust beneficiaries ought to be allowed.

[There are now] exceptions to the sole interest rule that have developed to legitimate particular classes of conflicted transactions. These categoric exceptions are mostly rooted in statute. Many reflect the business practices of bank trust departments and other institutional trustees—for example, allowing the deposit of trust funds in the trustee's commercial banking division or investing trust funds in trustee-sponsored investment pools such as mortgage participations, common trust funds, and mutual funds. Institutional trustees did not exist in the early nineteenth century, when the English and American courts settled the sole interest rule. Modern trusteeship is increasingly embedded in commerce, from which the patterns of mutual advantage that are characteristic of bilateral exchange are being absorbed into fiduciary administration. The common thread that runs through the categoric exceptions is that they facilitate the best interest of the beneficiary, even though the trustee also benefits or may benefit.

I recommend . . . reformulating the trust law duty of loyalty in light of these developments. I would generalize the principle now embodied in the exclusions and exceptions, which is that the trustee must act in the beneficiary's best interest, but not necessarily in the beneficiary's sole interest. Overlaps of interest that are consistent with the best interest of the beneficiary should be allowed. What is needed to cure the overbreadth of the sole interest rule is actually quite a modest fix: reducing from conclusive to rebuttable the force of the presumption of invalidity that now attaches to a conflicted transaction. Under a rule thus modified, the trustee would be allowed to defend a breach-of-loyalty case by proving that a conflicted transaction was prudently undertaken in the best interest of the beneficiary.

NOTES

1. *More on the no further inquiry rule.* In Uzyel v. Kadisha, 116 Cal. Rptr. 3d 244, 275-76 (App. 2010), the court emphatically endorsed the no further inquiry rule:

> A trustee is strictly prohibited from administering the trust with the motive or purpose of serving interests other than those of the beneficiaries. . . . A trustee also is strictly prohibited from engaging in transactions in which the trustee's personal interests may conflict with those of the beneficiaries without the express authorization of either the trust instrument, the court, or the beneficiaries. . . . It is no defense that the trustee acted in good faith, that the terms of the transaction were fair, or that the trust suffered no loss or the trustee received no profit. This is known as the no further inquiry rule. . . . Such a transaction is voidable at the election of the beneficiaries, and other remedies may be available, including an award of profits that the trust would have made if not for the breach of trust. . . . The rule is prophylactic and is justified in part by its deterrent effect. . . . [116 Cal. Rptr. 3d at 275-76.]

See also Estate of Hines, 715 A.2d 116 (D.C. 1998) (voiding personal representative's purchase of estate property without regard to fairness of transaction and adequacy of purchase price). For a perspective contrary to Professor Langbein's, see Leslie, In Defense of the No Further Inquiry Rule, 47 Wm. & Mary L. Rev. 541 (2005).

2. *The terms of the trust.* The settlor, by express language in the governing instrument, can authorize a fiduciary to do that which would otherwise constitute a breach of the duty of loyalty. See UTC § 802(b)(1); Schildberg v. Schildberg, 461 N.W.2d 186 (Iowa 1990); Kerper v. Kerper, 780 P.2d 923 (Wyo.1989); Restatement (Third) of Trusts § 78, cmt. c(2) (2007). Alternatively, the settlor may exculpate a fiduciary from liability, even with respect to a breach of the duty of loyalty. See Texas Commerce Bank v. Grizzle, 96 S.W.3d 240 (Tex. 2002). As to exculpatory clauses, see infra p. 840.

Even in the absence of express authorization or exculpation, the courts have sometimes ruled in favor of fiduciaries when the settlor has put them in positions of conflict between self-interest and obligation to the trust. See, e.g., Clement v. Larkey, 863 S.W.2d 580 (Ark.1993) (no violation of the duty of loyalty occurred when the trustee proposed a slightly disproportionate distribution of closely-held corporate shares (offset by cash) to two equally entitled beneficiaries, when the effect was to equalize corporate holdings between two family branches, despite the fact that the beneficiary to whom the larger number of shares would go was the trustee's son); Goldman v. Rubin, 441 A.2d 713 (Md.1982) (no self-dealing when testator's will placed four personal representatives who were directors of family corporation in a position of conflict when they sold stock to the corporation to pay taxes and expenses); Rosencrans v. Fry, 95 A.2d 905 (N.J.1953) (testator's will gave the trustee who ran the business an option to buy any or all of the stock in the trust corpus at its par value; court allowed the trustee to exercise the option despite the objections of the co-trustee-widow); In re Flagg's Estate, 73 A.2d 411 (Pa.1950) (approving redemption of stock held in trust when trustees controlled redeeming corporation, despite possible reduction in trust income).

3. *Court approval.* The court may approve conduct that would otherwise constitute a breach of the duty of loyalty. See UTC § 802(b)(2); Matter of Abdella, 476 N.Y.S.2d 400 (App. Div. 1984); Restatement (Third) of Trusts § 78, cmt. c(1) (2007); infra p. 841.

4. *Beneficiaries' consent.* Informed beneficiaries who are adult and competent may consent to or ratify conduct that would otherwise constitute a breach of the duty of loyalty. See UTC § 802(b)(4); Matter of Lifgren, 827 N.Y.S.2d 753 (App. Div. 2007); Restatement (Third) of Trusts § 78, cmt. c(3) (2007). For more on the effect of beneficiaries' consent, see infra p. 839.

5. *Corporate fiduciary depositing trust funds in its own bank.* The authorities were once divided as to whether a corporate executor or trustee could properly deposit cash, temporarily in its possession, in its own commercial banking department. Now, legislation ordinarily permits the practice. See Uniform Trustees' Powers Act § 3(c)(6); UTC § 802(h)(4); Restatement (Third) of Trusts § 78, cmt. c(6) (2007).

6. *Corporate fiduciary investing in proprietary mutual funds.* Statutes now widely permit corporate fiduciaries to invest trust funds in their own proprietary mutual funds. See UTC § 802(f); Restatement (Third) of Trusts § 78, cmt. c(8) (2007).

7. *Corporate fiduciary holding or investing in its own shares.* Ordinarily, a corporate trustee cannot properly hold, or invest trust funds in, shares of its own stock, unless the terms of the trust provide otherwise. See 3 Scott and Ascher on Trusts § 17.2.14.5.

2. DUTIES WITH RESPECT TO FIDUCIARY INVESTMENT

a. The Prudent Investor Rule

In the first part of the twentieth century, trust administration was, by today's standards, simple. A trustee's responsibility began and practically ended with investing the trust corpus in government bonds, first mortgages, and, occasionally, high-grade industrial bonds. Because these investments combined security with high yields, there were few calls for more diversified portfolios. The Great Depression demonstrated the faultiness of this approach, however. Real estate mortgages proved unreliable storehouses of value, as defaults forced trustees to buy in, at foreclosure, practically valueless land. In addition, income from the standard investments fell off, from a then handsome five or six percent (or more), to little or nothing. After World War II, trustees faced yet another set of problems, in the form of high personal income taxes on beneficiaries and a seemingly never-ending inflationary trend, while prosperous business conditions and a constantly rising stock market offered new investment opportunities. Predictably, the principles of fiduciary investment changed in response to these (and other) changing circumstances.

Two famous cases supplied underpinning for the principles of fiduciary investment that, until recently, applied in virtually every state. The first was Harvard College v. Amory, 26 Mass. (9 Pick.) 446 (1830), which stated:

> All that can be required of a trustee to invest, is, that he conduct himself faithfully and exercise a sound discretion. He is to observe how men of prudence, discretion, and intelligence manage their own affairs, not in regard to speculation, but in regard to the permanent disposition of their funds, considering the probable income, as well as the probable safety of the capital to be invested. [26 Mass. (9 Pick.) at 461.]

The second was King v. Talbot, 40 N.Y. 76 (1869), in which the court observed:

> My own judgment, after an examination of the subject, and bearing in mind the nature of the office, its importance, and the considerations, which alone induce men of suitable experience, capacity, and responsibility to accept its usually thankless burden, is, that the just and true rule is, that the trustee is bound to employ such diligence and such prudence in the care and management, as in general, prudent men of discretion and intelligence in such matters, employ in their own like affairs.
>
> This necessarily excludes all speculation, all investments for an uncertain and doubtful rise in the market, and of course everything that does not take into view the nature and object of the trust and the consequences of a mistake in the selection of the investment to be made. [40 N.Y. at 85–86.]

From these remarkably similar statements emerged two thoroughly different rules. The Massachusetts case spawned the prudent person rule—a rule that almost always took the form of the language in the Court's opinion. The New York case, on the other hand, served as prologue to the adoption of a statutory legal list of permissible investments. The prudent person rule allowed investment in "seasoned" common stock, while legal lists prohibited any investment in stock unless the will authorized such an investment. The legal list approach, which sought preservation of principal at its initial dollar level, proved highly unsatisfactory in times of inflation. As a result, by the middle of the twentieth century, the more flexible prudent person rule had almost completely displaced the legal list approach.[7]

Despite the fact that, by the 1970s, almost every state had adopted the prudent person rule,[8] it has been the subject of intense criticism. See, e.g., Longstreth, Modern Investment Management and the Prudent Man Rule (1986); Gordon, The Puzzling Persistence of the Constrained Prudent Man Rule, 62 N.Y.U. L. Rev. 52 (1987); Hirsch, Inflation and the Law of Trusts, 18 Real Prop. Prob. & Tr. J. 601 (1983). Much of this criticism focuses on the consequences of a pair of aspects of the rule, as applied. Both Harvard College v. Amory and King v. Talbot indicate that a fiduciary must not "speculate." This prohibition naturally caused careful and well-counseled fiduciaries to eschew "risky" investments. Moreover, courts tended to analyze a fiduciary's prudence in making or retaining each investment on an investment-by-investment basis, almost in isolation from the design (or even the performance) of the portfolio as a whole. Thus, it became widely accepted that a fiduciary would be personally liable for any loss resulting from a "speculative" investment, and that, in evaluating a fiduciary's conduct, gains from other investments would not offset losses. These operating principles proved pernicious, in that they caused fiduciaries, particularly corporate or otherwise well-counseled fiduciaries, to be extremely cautious. Lest they be liable for the loss on any given investment, fiduciaries often featured in their investment portfolios only "safe" investments they hoped would preserve principal, with insufficient concern for growth of principal to reflect true value (as opposed to original dollar value), and avoided small and untried ventures. In short, many trustees tried to make each and every investment as secure as possible. Of course, return generally varies inversely with security, and fiduciaries therefore often achieved miserable investment results.

In the 1980s, with Professor Halbach as Reporter, the American Law Institute launched an effort to rationalize the legal principles relating to fiduciary investment. The result was the Restatement (Third) of Trusts

---

[7] See, e.g., UPC § 7–302 ("Except as otherwise provided by the terms of the trust, the trustee shall observe the standards in dealing with the trust assets that would be observed by a prudent man dealing with the property of another . . . .") (withdrawn 2010); Restatement (Second) of Trusts § 227 (1959) ("In making investments of trust funds the trustee is under a duty . . . to make such investments and only such investments as a prudent man would make of his own property having in view the preservation of the estate and the amount and regularity of the income to be derived. . . .").

In some states, vestiges of legal lists may still remain. Now, however, such lists are usually permissive, providing safe havens (prudence is still wise policy) within which trustees may invest, but not prohibiting other investments. New York did not abandon its legal list until 1970.

[8] In 1974, the prudent person rule received a significant new assignment. The Employee Retirement Income Security Act of 1974 requires administration of pension funds "with the care, skill, prudence, and diligence under the circumstances then prevailing that a prudent man acting in a like capacity and familiar with such matters would use in the conduct of an enterprise of a like character and with like aims." 29 U.S.C. § 1104(a)(1)(B).

(Prudent Investor Rule), which was adopted by the A.L.I. in 1990.[9] Shortly thereafter, the Uniform Prudent Investor Act appeared. It has now been adopted by virtually every state.[10]

Uniform Prudent Investor Act (1994)

Section 2. Standard of Care; Portfolio Strategy; Risk and Return Objectives.

(a) A trustee shall invest and manage trust assets as a prudent investor would, by considering the purposes, terms, distribution requirements, and other circumstances of the trust. In satisfying this standard, the trustee shall exercise reasonable care, skill, and caution.

(b) A trustee's investment and management decisions respecting individual assets must be evaluated not in isolation but in the context of the trust portfolio as a whole and as a part of an overall investment strategy having risk and return objectives reasonably suited to the trust.

(c) Among circumstances that a trustee shall consider in investing and managing trust assets are such of the following as are relevant to the trust or its beneficiaries:

(1) general economic conditions;

(2) the possible effect of inflation or deflation;

(3) the expected tax consequences of investment decisions or strategies;

(4) the role that each investment or course of action plays within the overall trust portfolio, which may include financial assets, interests in closely held enterprises, tangible and intangible personal property, and real property;

(5) the expected total return from income and the appreciation of capital;

(6) other resources of the beneficiaries;

(7) needs for liquidity, regularity of income, and preservation or appreciation of capital; and

(8) an asset's special relationship or special value, if any, to the purposes of the trust or to one or more of the beneficiaries.

---

[9] First published as a separate volume, Restatement (Third) of Trusts: Prudent Investor Rule (1992), the material relating to the prudent investor rule now appears in Restatement (Third) of Trusts ch. 17 (2007).

[10] It appears that each of the few states that have not adopted the Uniform Prudent Investor Act has in fact adopted the prudent investor rule, albeit by non-uniform statutory language.

(d) A trustee shall make a reasonable effort to verify facts relevant to the investment and management of trust assets.

(e) A trustee may invest in any kind of property or type of investment consistent with the standards of this [Act].

(f) A trustee who has special skills or expertise, or is named trustee in reliance upon the trustee's representation that the trustee has special skills or expertise, has a duty to use those special skills or expertise.

NOTES

1. *Trustee's conduct not to be evaluated by hindsight.* Restatement (Third) of Trusts § 90, cmt. b (2007), states:

> The trustee's compliance with these fiduciary standards is to be judged as of the time the investment decision in question was made, not with the benefit of hindsight or by taking account of developments that occurred after the time of a decision to make, retain, or sell an investment. The question of whether a breach of trust has occurred turns on the prudence and propriety of the trustee's conduct, not on the eventual results of investment decisions. The trustee is not a guarantor of the trust's investment performance.

See also Uniform Prudent Investor Act § 8 ("Compliance with the prudent investor rule is determined in light of the facts and circumstances existing at the time of a trustee's decision or action and not by hindsight."); In re Cochran Irrevocable Trust, 901 N.E.2d 1128 (Ind. App. 2009). This, however, was also true under the prudent person rule. See, e.g., In re Chase Manhattan Bank, 809 N.Y.S.2d 360 (App. Div. 2006) ("In our view, the Surrogate's determination that the trustee should have sold the stock on January 31, 1974 is impermissibly based on nothing more than hindsight. . . ."); In re Morgan Guaranty Trust Co., 396 N.Y.S.2d 781 (Sur. 1977) (the test is one of prudence, not performance).

2. *Executors.* Traditionally, executors have had no duty to invest estate funds. Their primary duties were to collect the decedent's assets, pay the decedent's debts, and distribute the remainder in accordance with the will or the law of intestate succession as soon as reasonably possible. These are liquidation functions, inconsistent with a long-term investment strategy. With the rise of secure but highly liquid investments (such as Treasury bills and interest-bearing checking accounts), however, it seems natural to expect that courts will require at least some minimal level of investment activity on the part of executors, during administration, with respect to idle estate funds. See generally Estate of McCrea, 380 A.2d 773 (Pa.1977); Estate of Beach, 542 P.2d 994 (Cal.1975).

3. *"Social investing."* Connecticut provides various forms of statutory guidance for its state treasurer, in investing state trust funds (which include

the state and municipal employees' retirement funds, the teachers' pension fund, and similar funds for former government workers):

> Among the factors to be considered by the Treasurer with respect to all securities may be the social, economic and environmental implications of investments of trust funds in particular securities or types of securities. In the investment of the state's trust funds the Treasurer shall consider the implications of any particular investment in relation to the foreign policy and national interests of the United States.

Conn. Gen. Stat. § 3–13d(a). See also Conn. Gen. Stat. § 3–13g(c) (state treasurer "may divest, decide to not further invest state funds or not enter into any future investment in any company doing business in Iran" and "shall divest and not further invest in any security or instrument issued by Iran").

Nor is Connecticut unique in this regard. Other states and a number of municipalities, including New York, Philadelphia, Boston, and the District of Columbia, have enacted similar laws. One of the causes they backed was opposition to apartheid in South Africa. For a review of many of these statutes and an analysis of their legality and effect, see McCarroll, Socially Responsible Investment of Public Pension Funds: The South Africa Issue and State Law, 10 N.Y.U. Rev. of Law and Social Change 407 (1981). Similarly, many contracts between unions and industry contain provisions calling for social investment in activities to buttress local economies or particular industries. See Murrmann, Schaffer & Wokutch, Social Investing by State Public Employee Pension Funds, 35 Lab. Law J. 360 (1984).

Does a trustee who accepts a reduction in return on investments to foster political, social, or other noneconomic objectives thereby violate the prudent investor rule? For arguments in favor of social investing by fiduciaries, see Hylton, "Socially Responsible" Investing: Doing Good Versus Doing Well in an Inefficient Market, 42 Am. U.L. Rev. 1 (1992); Dobris, Arguments in Favor of Fiduciary Divestment of "South African" Securities, 65 Neb. L. Rev. 209 (1986); Ravikoff & Curzan, Social Responsibility in Investment Policy and the Prudent Man Rule, 68 Cal. L. Rev. 518 (1980). For the view that social investing violates a fiduciary's duties unless the beneficiaries can opt out of the socially-invested fund and into a fund managed solely to achieve economic return, see Langbein & Posner, Social Investing and the Law of Trusts, 79 Mich. L. Rev. 72 (1980), which suggests the variety of investments that can appear on a prohibited list:

> It is not easy to specify the portfolio adjustments that an investor committed to social investing would have to make, because the social principles are poorly specified. There is no consensus about which social principles to pursue and about which investments are consistent or inconsistent with those principles. At a time when most of the social activism in investing was liberal or radical rather than conservative, there was some agreement among the activists as to the types of companies

that should be avoided and the types that should be embraced. The ranks of the disapproved included companies lending to or having branches or subsidiaries in the Republic of South Africa, big defense contractors, nonunion companies, and prominent or recurrent violators of federal discrimination, pollution, safety, and antitrust laws. More recently, the nuclear power and herbicide industries have also fallen into disfavor. The ranks of the approved included companies that manufactured anti-pollution equipment, or used especially clean technologies, or invested in the inner cities. . . . With the rapid rise of right-wing social activism, we can expect social-investment advocates to appear who will urge investment managers not to invest in corporations that manufacture contraceptive devices, or publish textbooks that teach the theory of evolution, or do business with the Soviet Union. [Id. at 83–84.]

Restatement (Third) of Trusts § 90, cmt. c (2007) states:

[I]n managing the investments of a trust, the trustee's decisions ordinarily must not be motivated by a purpose of advancing or expressing the trustee's personal views concerning social or political issues or causes. Such considerations, however, may properly influence the investment decisions of a trustee to the extent permitted by the terms of the trust or by consent of the beneficiaries. . . . In addition, social considerations may be taken into account in investing the funds of charitable trusts to the extent the charitable purposes would justify an expenditure of trust funds for the social issue or cause in question or to the extent the investment decision can be justified on grounds of advancing, financially or operationally, a charitable activity conducted by the trust.

Existing authority seems to allow a public fiduciary to engage in social investing, at least to the extent that it does not substantially impair the trust's economic prospects. See Harries v. Church Commissioners, [1992] 1 W.L.R. 1241, [1993] 2 All E.R. 300 (Ch. 1991) (permitting charitable trustees to take into account moral positions when making investments, but only to the extent doing so does not "involve a risk of significant financial detriment"); Board of Trustees of Employees' Retirement System of City of Baltimore v. Mayor and Council of Baltimore City, 562 A.2d 720 (Md.1989), cert. denied, 493 U.S. 1093 (1990) (upholding ordinances requiring city pension fund trustees to divest themselves of corporations doing business in South Africa).

4. *References.* For more on the prudent investor rule and modern portfolio theory, see generally Schanzenbach & Sitkoff, Did Reform of Prudent Trust Investment Laws Change Trust Portfolio Allocation?, 50 J.L. & Econ. 681 (2007) ("[T]he trust institutions in our sample increased stock holdings by 1.5-4.5 percentage points—an increase of 3-10 percent—after the adoption of the new prudent-investor rule."); Langbein, The Uniform Prudent Investor Act and the Future of Trust Investing, 81 Iowa L. Rev. 641 (1996); Halbach, Trust Investment Law in the Third Restatement, 77 Iowa L. Rev. 1151 (1992); Macey, An Introduction to Modern Financial Theory (2d ed. 1998)

(American College of Trust & Estate Counsel Foundation). For a contrarian perspective, see Sterk, Rethinking Trust Law Reform: How Prudent Is Modern Prudent Investor Doctrine?, 95 Cornell L. Rev. 851 (2010).

b. The Duty to Diversify

MATTER OF ESTATE OF JANES

Court of Appeals of New York, 1997.
90 N.Y.2d 41, 659 N.Y.S.2d 165, 681 N.E.2d 332.

LEVINE, JUDGE.

Former State Senator and businessman Rodney B. Janes (testator) died on May 26, 1973, survived solely by his wife, Cynthia W. Janes, who was then 72 years of age. Testator's $3,500,000 estate consisted of a $2,500,000 stock portfolio, approximately 71% of which consisted of 13,232 shares of common stock of the Eastman Kodak Company. The Kodak stock had a date-of-death value of $1,786,733, or approximately $135 per share.

Testator's 1963 will and a 1969 codicil bequeathed most of his estate to three trusts. First, the testator created a marital deduction trust consisting of approximately 50% of the estate's assets, the income of which was to be paid to Mrs. Janes for her life. In addition, it contained a generous provision for invasion of the principal for Mrs. Janes's benefit and gave her testamentary power of appointment over the remaining principal. The testator also established a charitable trust of approximately 25% of the estate's assets which directed annual distributions to selected charities. A third trust comprised the balance of the estate's assets and directed that the income therefrom be paid to Mrs. Janes for her life, with the remainder pouring over into the charitable trust upon her death.

On June 6, 1973, the testator's will and codicil were admitted to probate. Letters testamentary issued to petitioner's predecessor, Lincoln Rochester Trust Company, and Mrs. Janes, as coexecutors, on July 3, 1973. Letters of trusteeship issued to petitioner alone. By early August 1973, petitioner's trust and estate officers, Ellison Patterson and Richard Young had ascertained the estate's assets and the amount of cash needed for taxes, commissions, attorneys' fees, and specific bequests.

In an August 9, 1973 memorandum, Patterson recommended raising the necessary cash for the foregoing administrative expenses by selling certain assets, including 800 shares of Kodak stock, and holding "the remaining issues . . . until the [t]rusts [were] funded." The memorandum did not otherwise address investment strategy in light of the evident primary objective of the testator to provide for his widow during her lifetime. In a September 5, 1973 meeting with Patterson and Young, Mrs. Janes, who had a high school education, no business training or experience, and who had never been employed, consented to the sale of some 1,200 additional shares of Kodak stock. Although Mrs. Janes was informed at the meeting that petitioner intended to retain the balance of the Kodak shares, none of the factors that would lead to an informed investment decision was discussed. At that time, the Kodak stock traded for about $139 per share; thus, the estate's 13,232 shares of the stock were worth almost $1,840,000. The September 5 meeting was the only occasion where retention of the Kodak stock or any other investment issues were taken up with Mrs. Janes.

By the end of 1973, the price of Kodak stock had fallen to about $109 per share. One year later, it had fallen to about $63 per share and, by the end of 1977, to about $51 per share. In March 1978, the price had dropped even further, to about $40 per share. When petitioner filed its initial accounting in February 1980, the remaining 11,320 shares were worth approximately $530,000, or about $47 per share. Most of the shares were used to fund the trusts in 1986 and 1987.

In addition to its initial accounting in 1980, petitioner filed a series of supplemental accountings that together covered the period from July 1973 through June 1994. In August 1981, petitioner sought judicial settlement of its account. Objections to the accounts were originally filed by Mrs. Janes in 1982, and subsequently by the Attorney–General on behalf of the charitable beneficiaries (collectively, "objectants"). In seeking to surcharge petitioner for losses incurred by the estate due to petitioner's imprudent retention of a high concentration of Kodak stock in the estate from July 1973 to February 1980, during which time the value of the stock had dropped to about one third of its date-of-death value, objectants asserted that petitioner's conduct violated EPTL 11–2.2(a)(1), the so-called "prudent person rule" of investment. When Mrs. Janes died in 1986, the personal representative of her estate was substituted as an objectant.

Following a trial on the objections, the Surrogate found that petitioner, under the circumstances, had acted imprudently and should have divested the estate of the high concentration of Kodak stock by August 9, 1973. The court imposed a $6,080,269 surcharge against petitioner and ordered petitioner to forfeit its commissions and attorneys' fees. In calculating the amount of the surcharge, the court adopted a "lost profits" or "market index" measure of damages espoused by objectants' expert—what the proceeds of the Kodak stock would have yielded, up to the time of trial, had they been invested in petitioner's own diversified equity fund on August 9, 1973.

The Appellate Division modified solely as to damages, holding that "the Surrogate properly found [petitioner] liable for its negligent failure to diversify and for its inattentiveness, inaction, and lack of disclosure, but that the Surrogate adopted an improper measure of damages" (Matter of Janes, 223 A.D.2d 20, 22, 643 N.Y.S.2d 972). In a comprehensive opinion by Presiding Justice M. Dolores Denman, the Court held that the Surrogate's finding of imprudence, as well as its selection of August 9, 1973 as the date by which petitioner should have divested the estate of its concentration of Kodak stock, were "well supported" by the record. Id., at 29, 643 N.Y.S.2d 972. The Court rejected the Surrogate's "lost profits" or "market index" measure of damages, however, holding that the proper measure of damages was "the value of the capital that was lost"—the difference between the value of the stock at the time it should have been sold and its value when ultimately sold (Id., at 34, 643 N.Y.S.2d 972). Applying this measure, the Court reduced the surcharge to $4,065,029. We . . . affirm.

I. PETITIONER'S LIABILITY

Petitioner argues that New York law does not permit a fiduciary to be surcharged for imprudent management of a trust for failure to diversify in the absence of additional elements of hazard. . . . Relying on Matter of Balfe, 152 Misc. 739, 749, 274 N.Y.S. 284, mod. 245 App. Div. 22, 280 N.Y.S. 128, petitioner claims that elements of hazard can be capsulized into deficiencies in the following investment quality factors:

> (i) the capital structure of the company; (ii) the competency of its management; (iii) whether the company is a seasoned issuer of stock with a history of profitability; (iv) whether the company has a history of paying dividends; (v) whether the company is an industry leader; (vi) the expected future direction of the company's business; and (vii) the opinion of investment bankers and analysts who follow the company's stock.

Evaluated under these criteria, petitioner asserts, the concentration of Kodak stock at issue in this case, that is, of an acknowledged "blue chip" security popular with investment advisors and many mutual funds, cannot be found an imprudent investment on August 9, 1973 as a matter of law. In our view, a fiduciary's duty of investment prudence in holding a concentration of one security may not be so rigidly limited.

New York followed the prudent person rule of investment during the period of petitioner's administration of the instant estate. This rule provides that "[a] fiduciary holding funds for investment may invest the same in such securities as would be acquired by prudent [persons] of discretion and intelligence in such matters who are seeking a reasonable income and the preservation of their capital" (EPTL 11–2.2[a][1]).[11] Codi-

---

[11] The recently enacted Prudent Investor Act requires a trustee "to diversify assets unless the trustee reasonably determines that it is in the interests of the beneficiaries not to diversify, taking into account the purposes and terms and provisions of the governing instrument" (EPTL

fied in 1970 . . . , the prudent person rule's New York common-law antecedents can be traced to King v. Talbot, 40 N.Y. 76, wherein this Court stated:

> [T]he trustee is bound to employ such diligence and such prudence in the care and management [of the trust], as in general, prudent men of discretion and intelligence in such matters, employ in their own like affairs.

> This necessarily excludes all speculation, all investments for an uncertain and doubtful rise in the market, and, of course, *everything that does not take into view the nature and object of the trust, and the consequences of a mistake in the selection of the investment to be made.* . . .

> *[T]he preservation of the fund, and the procurement of a just income therefrom, are primary objects* of the creation of the trust itself, and are to be primarily regarded (id., at 85–86 [emphasis supplied]).

No precise formula exists for determining whether the prudent person standard has been violated in a particular situation; rather, the determination depends on an examination of the facts and circumstances of each case. . . . In undertaking this inquiry, the court should engage in " 'a balanced and perceptive analysis of [the fiduciary's] consideration and action in light of the history of each individual investment, viewed at the time of its action or its omission to act' " (Matter of Donner, 82 N.Y.2d 574, 585, 606 N.Y.S.2d 137, 626 N.E.2d 922 [quoting Matter of Bank of N.Y., 35 N.Y.2d 512, 519, 364 N.Y.S.2d 164, 323 N.E.2d 700]). And, while a court should not view each act or omission aided or enlightened by hindsight (see, Matter of Bank of N.Y., supra, at 519, 364 N.Y.S.2d 164, 323 N.E.2d 700 . . .), a court may, nevertheless, examine the fiduciary's conduct over the entire course of the investment in determining whether it has acted prudently. . . . Generally, whether a fiduciary has acted prudently is a factual determination to be made by the trial court. . . .

As the foregoing demonstrates, the very nature of the prudent person standard dictates against any absolute rule that a fiduciary's failure to diversify, in and of itself, constitutes imprudence, as well as against a rule invariably immunizing a fiduciary from its failure to diversify in the absence of some selective list of elements of hazard. . . . Indeed, in various cases, courts have determined that a fiduciary's retention of a high concentration of one asset in a trust or estate was imprudent without reference to those elements of hazard (see, Matter of Donner, supra, at 585–

11–2.3[b][3][C]). The act applies to investments "made or held" by a trustee on or after January 1, 1995 and, thus, does not apply to the matter before us (EPTL 11–2.3 [a]).

586, 606 N.Y.S.2d 137, 626 N.E.2d 922 . . .). The inquiry is simply whether, under all the facts and circumstances of the particular case, the fiduciary violated the prudent person standard in maintaining a concentration of a particular stock in the estate's portfolio of investments.

[A]s commentators have noted, one of the primary virtues of the prudent person rule *"lies in its lack of specificity,* as this permits the propriety of the trustee's investment decisions to be measured in light of the business and economic circumstances existing at the time they were made" (Laurino, Investment Responsibility of Professional Trustees, 51 St. John's L. Rev. 717, 723 [1977] [emphasis supplied]).

Petitioner's restrictive list of hazards omits such additional factors to be considered under the prudent person rule by a trustee in weighing the propriety of any investment decision, as: "the amount of the trust estate, the situation of the beneficiaries, the trend of prices and of the cost of living, the prospect of inflation and of deflation" (Restatement [Second] of Trusts § 227, comment e). Other pertinent factors are the marketability of the investment and possible tax consequences (id., comment o). The trustee must weigh all of these investment factors as they affect the principal objects of the testator's or settlor's bounty, as between income beneficiaries and remainder persons, including decisions regarding "whether to apportion the investments between high-yield or high-growth securities" (Turano and Radigan, New York Estate Administration ch. 14, § P, at 409 [1986]).

Moreover, and especially relevant to the instant case, the various factors affecting the prudence of any particular investment must be considered in the light of the "circumstances of the trust itself rather than [merely] the integrity of the particular investment" (9C Rohan, N.Y. Civ. Prac.—EPTL ¶ 11–2.2[5], at 11–513, n.106 [1996]). As stated in a leading treatise:

> The trustee should take into consideration the circumstances of the particular trust that he is administering, both as to the size of the trust estate and the requirements of the beneficiaries. He should consider each investment *not as an isolated transaction but in its relation to the whole of the trust estate* (3 Scott, Trusts § 227.12, at 477 [4th ed.]).

Our case law is entirely consistent with the foregoing authorities. Thus, in Matter of Bank of N.Y., 35 N.Y.2d 512, 364 N.Y.S.2d 164, 323 N.E.2d 700, supra, although we held that a trustee remains responsible for imprudence as to each individual investment in a trust portfolio, we stated:

The record of any individual investment is not to be viewed exclusively, of course, as though it were in its own water-tight compartment, since to some extent individual investment decisions may properly be affected by considerations of the performance of the fund as an entity, as in the instance, for example, of individual security decisions based in part on considerations of diversification of the fund or of capital transactions to achieve sound tax planning for the fund as a whole. The focus of inquiry, however, is nonetheless on the individual security as such and factors relating to the entire portfolio are to be weighed only along with others in reviewing the prudence of the particular investment decisions (35 N.Y.2d, at 517, 364 N.Y.S.2d 164, 323 N.E.2d 700, supra [emphasis supplied]).

Thus, [petitioner's] elements of hazard . . . suffer from two major deficiencies under the prudent person rule. First, petitioner's risk elements too narrowly and strictly define the scope of a fiduciary's responsibility in making any individual investment decision, and the factors a fiduciary must consider in determining the propriety of a given investment.

A second deficiency in petitioner's elements of hazard list is that all of the factors relied upon by petitioner go to the propriety of an individual investment "exclusively . . . as though it were in its own water-tight compartment" (Matter of Bank of N.Y., supra, at 517, 364 N.Y.S.2d 164, 323 N.E.2d 700), which would encourage a fiduciary to treat each investment as an isolated transaction rather than "in its relation to the whole of the trust estate" (3 Scott, op. cit., at 477). Thus, petitioner's criteria for elements of hazard would apply irrespective of the concentration of the investment security under consideration in the portfolio. That is, the existence of any of the elements of risk specified by petitioner in a given corporate security would militate against the investment even in a diversified portfolio, obviating any need to consider concentration as a reason to divest or refrain from investing. This ignores the market reality that, with respect to some investment vehicles, concentration itself may create or add to risk, and essentially takes lack of diversification out of the prudent person equation altogether.

Likewise, contrary to petitioner's alternative attack on the decisions below, neither the Surrogate nor the Appellate Division based their respective rulings holding petitioner liable on any absolute duty of a fiduciary to diversify. Rather, those courts determined that a surcharge was appropriate because maintaining a concentration in Kodak stock, under the circumstances presented, violated certain critical obligations of a fiduciary in making investment decisions under the prudent person rule. First, petitioner failed to consider the investment in Kodak stock in relation to the entire portfolio of the estate . . . , i.e., whether the Kodak concentration itself created or added to investment risk. The objectants' experts testified that even high quality growth stocks, such as Kodak, possess some degree of volatility because their market value is tied so closely to earnings projections. . . . They further opined that the investment risk arising from that volatility is significantly exacerbated when a portfolio is heavily concentrated in one such growth stock.

Second, the evidence revealed that, in maintaining an investment portfolio in which Kodak represented 71% of the estate's stock holdings, and the balance was largely in other growth stocks, petitioner paid insufficient attention to the needs and interests of the testator's 72–year-old widow, the life beneficiary of three quarters of his estate, for whose comfort, support and anticipated increased medical expenses the testamentary trusts were evidently created. Testimony by petitioner's investment manager, and by the objectants' experts, disclosed that the annual yield on Kodak stock in 1973 was approximately 1.06%, and that the aggregate annual income from all estate stockholdings was $43,961, a scant 1.7% of the $2.5 million estate securities portfolio. Thus, retention of a high concentration of Kodak jeopardized the interests of the primary income beneficiary of the estate and led to the eventual need to substantially invade the principal of the marital testamentary trust.

Lastly, there was evidence in the record to support the findings below that, in managing the estate's investments, petitioner failed to exercise due care and the skill it held itself out as possessing as a corporate fiduciary (. . . Restatement [Second] of Trusts § 227, Comment on Clause [a]). Notably, there was proof that petitioner (1) failed initially to undertake a formal analysis of the estate and establish an investment plan consistent with the testator's primary objectives; (2) failed to follow petitioner's own internal trustee review protocol during the administration of the estate, which advised special caution and attention in cases of portfolio concentration of as little as 20%; and (3) failed to conduct more than routine reviews of the Kodak holdings in this estate, without considering alternative investment choices, over a seven-year period of steady decline in the value of the stock.

Since, thus, there was evidence in the record to support the foregoing affirmed findings of imprudence on the part of petitioner, the determination of liability must be affirmed. . . .

II. DATE OF DIVESTITURE

As we have noted, in determining whether a fiduciary has acted prudently, a court may examine a fiduciary's conduct throughout the entire period during which the investment at issue was held. . . . The court may then determine, within that period, the "reasonable time" within which divestiture of the imprudently held investment should have occurred. . . .

What constitutes a reasonable time will vary from case to case and is not fixed or arbitrary. . . .

Again, there is evidentiary support in the record for the trial court's finding, affirmed by the Appellate Division, that a prudent fiduciary would have divested the estate's stock portfolio of its high concentration of Kodak stock by August 9, 1973. . . . Petitioner's own internal documents and correspondence, as well as the testimony of Patterson, Young, and objectants' experts, establish that by that date, petitioner had all the information a prudent investor would have needed to conclude that the percentage of Kodak stock in the estate's stock portfolio was excessive and should have been reduced significantly, particularly in light of the estate's over-all investment portfolio and the financial requirements of Mrs. Janes and the charitable beneficiaries.

III. DAMAGES

Finally, as to the calculation of the surcharge, we conclude that the Appellate Division correctly rejected the Surrogate's "lost profits" or "market index" measure of damages. Where, as here, a fiduciary's imprudence consists solely of negligent retention of assets it should have sold, the measure of damages is the value of the lost capital (see, Matter of Garvin, 256 N.Y. 518, 521, 177 N.E. 24 . . .). Thus, the Surrogate's reliance on Matter of Rothko in imposing a "lost profit" measure of damages is inapposite, since in that case the fiduciary's misconduct consisted of deliberate self-dealing and faithless transfers of trust property. . . .

In imposing liability upon a fiduciary on the basis of the capital lost, the court should determine the value of the stock on the date it should have been sold, and subtract from that figure the proceeds from the sale of the stock or, if the stock is still retained by the estate, the value of the stock at the time of the accounting (see, Matter of Garvin, supra, at 521, 177 N.E. 24 . . .). Whether interest is awarded, and at what rate, is a matter within the discretion of the trial court (see . . . SCPA 2211[1]; . . . 3 Scott, op. cit., § 207, at 255–256). Dividends and other income attributable to the retained assets should offset any interest awarded (see, Matter of Garvin, supra, at 521, 177 N.E. 24).

Here, uncontradicted expert testimony established that application of this measure of damages resulted in a figure of $4,065,029, which includes prejudgment interest at the legal rate, compounded from August 9, 1973 to October 1, 1994. The Appellate Division did not abuse its discretion in adding to that figure prejudgment interest from October 1, 1994 through August 17, 1995, $326,302.66 previously received by petitioner for commissions and attorneys' fees, plus postjudgment interest, costs, and disbursements.

Accordingly, the order of the Appellate Division should be affirmed, without costs.

Notes

1. *The duty to diversify.* Uniform Prudent Investor Act § 3 states: "A trustee shall diversify the investments of the trust unless the trustee reasonably determines that, because of special circumstances, the purposes of the trust are better served without diversifying." There is no shortage of cases holding trustees liable for failure to diversify trust holdings. See, e.g., Estate of Saxton, 712 N.Y.S.2d 225 (App. Div. 2000) (testamentary trust held IBM stock exclusively for over 30 years); Estate of Rowe, 712 N.Y.S.2d 662 (App. Div. 2000) (trustee retained concentrated position in IBM stock with little more than routine reviews and no attention to trust's particular circumstances).

2. *Why diversify?* Long before the Uniform Prudent Investor Act, it was generally, but not universally, understood that trustees ordinarily had a duty to diversify investments, in order to minimize risk of loss. See 4 Scott and Ascher on Trusts § 19.2. Under the prudent investor rule, however, the duty to diversify now plays a greater role than just avoiding loss:

> Investment values are based on projections of future return, which take account of changes in market price as well as cash receipts. Value depends, however, not only on expectations concerning average return from an asset but also on volatility and the risk of departures ("variance") from that average. For example, common stocks can be expected to outperform bonds in the long run but yet to have poorer returns—even negative returns—during some periods. Because investors are risk averse, they require extra compensation for increased risk. The investor's reward for accepting a greater likelihood of volatile returns follows from the lower market price at which the investor is able to purchase the investment.

> Events affecting the economy do not affect the value of all investments in the same way. Thus, effective diversification depends not only on the number of assets in a trust portfolio but also on the ways and degrees in which their responses to economic events tend to cancel or neutralize one another. Consequently, an otherwise dubious, volatile investment can make a major contribution to risk management if the shifts in its returns tend not to correlate with the movements of other investments in the portfolio. This is a major reason why diversification is valued and why the prudence of a trustee's investment is to be judged by its role in the trust portfolio rather than in isolation. . . .

> As a result of the tendency of the value fluctuations of different assets to offset one another, a portfolio's *risk* is less than the weighted average of the risk of its individual holdings. A portfolio's *expected return,*

on the other hand, is simply a weighted average of the expected returns of the individual assets. Thus, the expected return is not affected by the portfolio's reduced level of what is often called "specific" or "unique" risk—insofar as those terms are used to refer to risks that can be reduced by diversification. Other types of risk, however, are generally compensated through market pricing, so that the expected return from an investment or portfolio is directly affected by the level of these risks that cannot be diversified away—the so-called "market" or "systematic" risks. Accordingly, a trustee's duty of prudent investing normally calls for reasonable efforts to reduce diversifiable risks, while no such generalization can be made with respect to market risk. . . .

The rationale of the trust law's requirement of diversification is more than conservatism or a duty of caution, which admonishes trustees not to take excessive risks—that is, not to take risks higher than suitable to a trust's purposes, return requirements, and other circumstances. The general duty to diversify further expresses a warning to trustees, predicated on the duty to exercise care and skill, against taking bad risks—ones in which there is unwarranted danger of loss, or volatility that is not compensated by commensurate opportunities for gain. Thus, while risk-taking cannot realistically be forbidden, or subjected to an arbitrary ceiling, it is required to be done prudently. A central feature of such prudence ordinarily is the reduction of uncompensated risk through diversification.

Restatement (Third) of Trusts § 90, cmt. g (2007).

3. *Retention of securities originally acquired by settlor.* As in *Janes,* it frequently occurs that a trustee retains stock originally acquired by the settlor, despite a decline in value, sometimes catastrophic. Under the prudent person rule, trustees occasionally avoided liability on such facts by arguing that the settlor had particular confidence in the investment and that they were, therefore, justified in retaining it, even during a market decline. There comes a point, however, when the prudent person must abandon a losing enterprise. Identifying that point is often difficult. Cf. Estate of Knipp, 414 A.2d 1007 (Pa.1980) (not imprudent to hold Sears stock while it dropped from $117 to $88 per share in fifteen months; dissent found performance did not meet the standards of a corporate fiduciary); Stark v. United States Trust Co., 445 F.Supp. 670 (S.D.N.Y. 1978) ("It is not inherently negligent for a trustee to retain stock in a period of declining market values, . . . nor is there any magic percentage of decline which, when reached, mandates sale. . . .").

Under the prudent investor rule, the propriety of the fiduciary's conduct is not supposed to depend upon analysis of any given investment in isolation. There is, however, a special duty relating to original investments: "The trustee has a duty, within a reasonable time after the creation of the trust, to review the contents of the trust estate and to make and implement decisions concerning the retention and disposition of original investments in order to conform to the requirements of §§ 90 and 91." Restatement (Third) of Trusts § 92 (2007).

4. *Market conditions.* When there is little or no market for the investment in which the trust's holdings are concentrated, the trustee may be able justify retention on the grounds that diversification would have been imprudent or impossible. See In re Hyde, 845 N.Y.S.2d 833 (App. Div. 2007) (stock in closely held family corporation "with an unusual capital structure" was "particularly unmarketable"); Estate of Stetson, 345 A.2d 679 (Pa.1975).

5. *The need for prudence in diversification.* In re Scheidmantel, 868 A.2d 464 (Pa. Super. 2005), involved a trust that was to terminate upon the death of the income beneficiary. Just prior to the death of the income beneficiary, whose "physical and mental health were deteriorating rapidly," the corporate fiduciary commenced an aggressive program of diversification, which continued even after the income beneficiary's death. The court found that the trustee had acted imprudently and held it liable for the losses incurred as a result of the diversification. The court added: "We do not disagree with the trustee that diversification generally is a good idea. However, diversification cannot become a goal in and of itself. Rather, diversification is a tool that can provide the means to effectuate a settlor's goals for a trust, if used properly and prudently with due regard to the specific facts and circumstances that exist in a particular case." Id. at 490.

6. *The terms of the trust.* There is ample authority for the proposition that the terms of the trust may modify or eliminate the duty of a trustee to diversify the trust's holdings. See Uniform Prudent Investor Act § 1(b) ("The prudent investor rule, a default rule, may be expanded, restricted, eliminated, or otherwise altered by the provisions of a trust. A trustee is not liable to a beneficiary to the extent that the trustee acted in reasonable reliance on the provisions of the trust."); Nelson v. First Nat'l Bank & Trust Co., 543 F.3d 432 (8th Cir. 2008) (no breach for retaining 90-percent concentration when terms of trust provided that "any investment made or retained by the trustee in good faith shall be proper despite any resulting risk or lack of diversification or marketability" and settlor directed retention); Americans for the Arts v. Ruth Lilly Charitable Remainder Annuity Trust, 855 N.E.2d 592 (Ind. App. 2006) (no duty to diversify when terms of trust authorized trustee "to retain indefinitely any property received" and provided that "any investment made or retained by the trustee in good faith shall be proper despite any resulting risk or lack of diversification"); In re Chase Manhattan Bank, 809 N.Y.S.2d 360 (App. Div. 2006) (no breach for retaining concentration in Kodak stock when will directed retention, exonerated trustee for any resulting loss, and authorized disposition only for "some compelling reason other than diversification"; neither drop in value nor low dividend yield compelled sale); Atwood v. Atwood, 25 P.3d 936 (Okla. App. 2001) (trustee not liable for retaining concentration in single publicly traded stock; boilerplate language authorized retention).

On the other hand, trustees have often been held liable for failing to diversify, notwithstanding language in the governing instrument that was arguably intended to permit the trustee to retain certain holdings. See, e.g., Wood v. U.S. Bank, 828 N.E.2d 1072 (Ohio App. 2005) (authorization to retain inception assets did not negate duty to diversify trust's concentration in corporate fiduciary's stock); Robertson v. Central Jersey Bank & Trust Co., 47 F.3d 1268 (3d Cir. 1995) (corporate trustee liable for retaining 95 percent of trust assets in its own stock, despite express authorization to retain its own stock and to retain securities without regard to diversification; "authorization to retain investments enhances the trustee's discretion, but does not wholly insulate it from liability for its exercise of a power to retain assets"); First Alabama Bank v. Spragins, 515 So.2d 962 (Ala. 1987) (will authorized corporate fiduciary to invest in property it deemed suitable "regardless of any lack of diversification, risk or nonproductivity"; trustee liable for retaining concentration in its own stock). See generally Cooper, Speak Clearly and Listen Well: Negating the Duty to Diversify Trust Investments, 33 Ohio N.U. L. Rev. 903 (2007).

JOHN H. LANGBEIN, MANDATORY RULES IN THE LAW OF TRUSTS

98 Northwestern U. L. Rev. 1105, 1106–07, 1111–17 (2004).

The law of trusts consists overwhelmingly of default rules that the settlor who creates the trust may alter or negate. There are, however, some mandatory rules, which the settlor is forbidden to vary. . . .

The Code. The mandatory rules have gained new prominence as the result of a pair of coordinated law revision projects, both quite recently concluded. The Uniform Trust Code of 2000 ("the Code") is the first comprehensive national codification of the American law of trusts. The Code contains a novel provision, section 105, which . . . provides that all trust law is default law, apart from the mandatory rules that are specially scheduled in section 105(b). . . .

The Third Restatement. The other major development . . . is the refinement of the benefit-the-beneficiaries requirement in the Restatement (Third) of Trusts. Section 27 requires that "a private trust, its terms, and its administration must be for the benefit of its beneficiaries. . . ." . . . The Code, which was prepared in close coordination with the drafting of the Third Restatement, absorbs this benefit-the-beneficiaries requirement.[12]

Rules of general application. Several of the mandatory rules rest on self-evident principles of legal process that are broadly shared with the rest of private law. The settlor may not, for example, interfere with the

---

[12] UTC § 404 & cmt.

court's routine powers of judicial administration,[13] nor may the settlor enlarge or diminish the rights of creditors or other third parties.[14] [These are] familiar limits on private ordering. [There is also] the rule against trusts for illegal purposes,[15] a principle shared with every branch of private and organizational law. A scheme to overthrow the government or to sell dope or to operate a bordello is no more enforceable as a trust than as a contract, a corporation, or a partnership.

I. RESTRAINING THE DEAD HAND

A. Benefit the Beneficiaries

The rule that the trust and its terms must be for the benefit of the beneficiaries reworks an older doctrine, the rule against "capricious purposes."[16] . . .

B. Investment Directions

The characteristic sphere for the application of the anti-dead-hand rule has been the fringe world of the eccentric settlor: the crackpot who wants to brick up her house, or build statues of himself, or dictate children's marital choices. In the future, however, I believe that the benefit-the-beneficiaries rule will set limits upon a more common form of settlor direction, the value-impairing investment instruction. The benefit-the-beneficiaries requirement will interact with the growing understanding of sound fiduciary investing practices to restrain the settlor's power to direct a course of investment imparting risk and return objectives contrary to the interests of the beneficiaries.

To take an extreme example, suppose that the settlor were to leave a modest trust fund for the support of his otherwise destitute widow and orphans and were to require that the fund be entirely invested in, say, shares of the bankrupt Enron Corporation. Suppose further that the settlor were to leave an account of his thinking, explaining that, depending

---

[13] E.g., id. § 105(b)(4) (referencing § 415, the court's power to reform a trust instrument to correct mistaken terms); id. § 105(b)(6) (court's power to require or waive bond); id. § 105(b)(12) (limitations periods); id. § 105(b)(13) (court's power to take action and exercise jurisdiction that is "necessary in the interests of justice"); id. § 105(b)(14) (rules of jurisdiction and venue).

[14] Id. § 105(b)(5) (creditor rights); id. § 105(b)(11) (rights of a person other than trustee or beneficiary). The question remains quite contentious of whether various classes of privileged creditors (e.g., suppliers of necessaries; former spouses and other holders of domestic relations awards; tort creditors; and governmental entities) should be excepted from the enforcement of spendthrift restraints in a trust instrument. What the mandatory rule of section 105(b)(5) provides is simply that once those matters are resolved as a matter of spendthrift law (in the case of the Code, under section 503), they are not subject to alteration by unilateral act of the settlor.

[15] The second clause of UTC § 105(b)(3) lists "the requirement . . . that the trust have a purpose that is lawful, not contrary to public policy, and possible to achieve," which tracks the language of UTC § 404, which in turn follows Restatement (Second) of Trusts §§ 60–65 (1959); accord Restatement (Third) of Trusts § 29 (2003).

[16] Restatement (Third) of Trusts § 29 cmt. h (2003) (preserving the old rule). . . .

upon the course of the bankruptcy proceeding, these shares have the potential to increase greatly in value. No court would enforce such a direction, even though the principles of trust investment law with which the direction conflicts (especially the duty to diversify trust investments and, more generally, the duty of prudent investing) are default rules that the settlor may waive.[17] There are circumstances (discussed below) in which the settlor can abridge the diversification and prudent-investing norms without violating the benefit-the-beneficiaries requirement. However, in [my example], the resulting underdiversification and volatility levels would be so contrary to the risk-and-return profile of the beneficiaries that the direction could not satisfy an objective standard of benefit under the benefit-the-beneficiaries rule.

The deeper lesson from this example is that, even though most rules of trust law (such as the duties to diversify and to invest prudently) are default rules rather than mandatory rules, it does not follow that the settlor is free to authorize any conceivable departure from the default rules. A default rule is one that the settlor can abridge, but only to the extent that the settlor's term is "for the benefit of [the] beneficiaries."[18] The requirement that there be benefit to the beneficiaries sets outer limits on the settlor's power to abridge the default law. Trust law's deference to the settlor's direction always presupposes that the direction is beneficiary-regarding.

1. Blue Chips.—What should happen in a case in which, instead of requiring the portfolio to be in Enron shares, the settlor requires it to be invested entirely in shares of a seasoned blue chip? In my view, such a direction should also be seen as a violation of the requirement that trust terms must be for the benefit of the beneficiaries. . . .

Modern portfolio theory instructs us that the investor who diversifies thoroughly virtually always improves the odds of doing better than a one-stock portfolio, regardless of what the stock is. Failure to diversify imposes upon the portfolio what is called uncompensated risk, risk that can be costlessly avoided by spreading the investment across many asset classes and many distinct security issues.

. . . The advantages of diversifying an investment portfolio broadly are so great that it is usually folly not to do it, and folly is not how to benefit beneficiaries.

To be sure, there are circumstances that can make it prudent for a trust fund not to diversify, which is why the duty has been formulated as

---

[17] "The prudent investor rule, a default rule, may be expanded, restricted, eliminated, or otherwise altered by the provisions of a trust." [UPIA] § 1(b).

[18] UTC § 105(b)(3). . . .

a default rule. When, for example, the trust in question is but one of many for the same beneficiaries, or when the trust otherwise represents only a small portion of the total wealth available to the beneficiaries, the trustee may appropriately take into account the beneficiaries' other trust and nontrust resources in deciding whether and how to diversify the trust.[19] Moreover, there will sometimes be cases in which the tax cost of diversifying a low-basis asset may outweigh the gain.[20] Yet another circumstance in which an underdiversified portfolio may be quite justified occurs when trust assets are not being held for investment (or not wholly for investment). Such "programmatic" investing is common in certain kinds of charitable trusts—for example, in a trust that holds land as a bird sanctuary or nature preserve. There are analogues to programmatic investing in personal trusts, as when the settlor directs that the family residence be retained as a home for the widow or that vacation property be held for the recreational use of family members.

When, however, trust assets are held for investment, and are easily diversifiable at no cost or at acceptable cost, I believe that the courts will come to view the advantages of diversification as so overwhelming that the settlor's interference with effective diversification will be treated as inconsistent with the requirement that the trust terms must be for the benefit of the beneficiaries. Settlor-directed underdiversification is an avoidable harm, akin to the harm that the courts have prevented by intervening against settlors' directions to waste or destroy trust property.

2. Family Enterprises.—A recurrent setting in which we sometimes see a settlor impose a value-impairing investment restriction arises in connection with the disposition of a family enterprise. It is common for a trust to be used as part of the succession arrangements for a family firm. When the settlor directs the trustee to retain the firm, that direction brings the trust into tension not only with the duty to diversify,[21] but also with the branch of the duty of prudent investing that . . . discourages investments that require trustees to engage in active entrepreneurship. . . .

The aversion to conducting entrepreneurship within a trust fund is mere default law, which the settlor can override. Sometimes the settlor has sound reasons for thinking that the beneficiaries will derive more benefit from retaining the family firm than from selling or dissolving it. For example, a family firm sometimes occupies a market niche that pro-

---

[19] The Uniform Prudent Investor Act includes "other resources of the beneficiaries" among the "circumstances that a trustee shall consider in investing and managing trust assets." UPIA § 2(c)(6).

[20] "If a tax-sensitive trust owns an underdiversified block of low-basis securities, the tax costs of recognizing the gain may outweigh the advantages of diversifying the holding." Id. § 3 cmt.

[21] "The wish to retain a family business is another situation in which the purposes of the trust sometimes override the conventional duty to diversify." UPIA § 3 cmt.

duces returns superior to those readily available to fiduciaries in the investment markets. There are circumstances in which a family firm that would not realize much if sold or liquidated can continue to be a profitable source of employment and income for family members. Sometimes what motivates the settlor's direction to retain is the belief that operating the family firm can be the source of influence, prestige, and perquisites for family members that may outweigh the superior expected investment returns of a diversified portfolio. We see such thinking in the strategies that have been used to perpetuate family control of such prominent institutions as the New York Times and the Ford Motor Company, as well as many smaller and less storied firms.

Sometimes, however, what lurks behind a settlor's direction to retain a family firm is the settlor's aspiration to perpetuate his or her notions about the conduct of the enterprise and thus to steer the firm's and the family's affairs from the grave. The grave is not, however, a good place from which to adjust to the pace of modern commerce. The family business is sometimes the alter ego of the decedent, too dependent upon the decedent's entrepreneurial skills to be viable after his or her death, in which case the interests of the beneficiaries would be best served by selling or liquidating it. When a family firm falls into a trust without any direction to retain it, the duty of prudence requires the trustee to investigate the alternatives with care, including such factors as the business prospects of the firm; the abilities of its management; and the abilities, relationships, and financial and other circumstances of the beneficiaries. The trustee's determination to retain a family firm is a fiduciary act that the trustee must continually revisit, because the balance of circumstances that initially supported the decision can change over time.

When, however, the trust instrument requires the trustee to retain the family firm, that course of conduct is potentially so risky that, in my view, the benefit-the-beneficiaries standard now requires a prudent trustee to examine closely whether to oblige. In the event that the trustee determines that the direction to retain the asset is not in the interests of the beneficiaries, the trustee has a duty to resist the direction. If the trustee adheres to the trust term in such circumstances, the trustee risks liability to the beneficiaries for breach of trust. Procedurally, the appropriate step would be for the trustee to petition the court to modify the direction, consistent with the benefit-the-beneficiaries standard.[22]

NOTES

1. *Uniform Trust Code.* UTC § 105 is as follows:

---

[22] See UTC § 410(b) (authorizing such proceedings). See generally Restatement (Second) of Trusts § 259 (1959) (application to court for instructions). . . .

§ 105. Default and Mandatory Rules.

(a) Except as otherwise provided in the terms of the trust, this [Code] governs the duties and powers of a trustee, relations among trustees, and the rights and interests of a beneficiary.

(b) The terms of a trust prevail over any provision of this [Code] except:

    (1) the requirements for creating a trust;

    (2) the duty of a trustee to act in good faith and in accordance with the terms and purposes of the trust and the interests of the beneficiaries;

    (3) the requirement that a trust and its terms be for the benefit of its beneficiaries, and that the trust have a purpose that is lawful, not contrary to public policy, and possible to achieve;

    (4) the power of the court to modify or terminate a trust under Sections 410 through 416;

    (5) the effect of a spendthrift provision and the rights of certain creditors and assignees to reach a trust as provided in [Article] 5;

    (6) the power of the court under Section 702 to require, dispense with, or modify or terminate a bond;

    (7) the power of the court under Section 708(b) to adjust a trustee's compensation specified in the terms of the trust which is unreasonably low or high;

    [(8) the duty under Section 813(b)(2) and (3) to notify qualified beneficiaries of an irrevocable trust who have attained 25 years of age of the existence of the trust, of the identity of the trustee, and of their right to request trustee's reports;]

    [(9) the duty under Section 813(a) to respond to the request of a [qualified] beneficiary of an irrevocable trust for trustee's reports and other information reasonably related to the administration of a trust;]

    (10) the effect of an exculpatory term under Section 1008;

    (11) the rights under Sections 1010 through 1013 of a person other than a trustee or beneficiary;

    (12) periods of limitation for commencing a judicial proceeding; [and]

    (13) the power of the court to take such action and exercise such jurisdiction as may be necessary in the interests of justice [; and

(14) the subject-matter jurisdiction of the court and venue for commencing a proceeding as provided in Sections 203 and 204].

2. *Are fiduciary duties something more than default rules?* Professor Leslie has argued against thinking of fiduciary duties as mere default rules:

> In steadily increasing numbers, trust scholars are embracing the view that fiduciary duties are mere default rules, freely waivable by the parties to the trust document. . . .

> . . . The default rule paradigm has increasingly influenced doctrine and permeates the recently promulgated Uniform Trust Code ("UTC").

> Of course, parties to a trust instrument may, to a considerable extent, tailor a trustee's fiduciary duties to facilitate the settlor's objectives. But it is a long leap from the proposition that fiduciary duties can be tailored to further individual objectives to the conclusion that fiduciary duties are merely gap-filling default rules, similar to those found [U.C.C.] Article Two. As even default rule proponents recognize, trustees' fiduciary duties are not, and never have been, completely waivable. For example, no court would uphold a trust provision purporting to eliminate the trustee's duty of loyalty in its entirety. In addition, by statute or common law some states invalidate or sharply circumscribe parties' power to eviscerate the trustee's duty of care through a clause that exculpates the trustee from liability for ordinary or gross negligence. These doctrinal rules are inconsistent with a pure default rule paradigm. . . . Scholars have not offered an account that explains why trust law differs from contract law in this important respect. . . .

> This Article argues that characterizing trustees' fiduciary duties as pure "default rules" too easily equates trusts with contracts and blinds academics and courts to the need to develop a coherent theory about the extent to which fiduciary duties can be modified. Any such theory must take into account the trust mechanism's unique characteristics. . . . Information asymmetries between trust settlors and professional trustees make it unlikely that certain types of express waivers incorporated in trust documents reflect a settlor's judgment that the provision would be value-maximizing.

> Finally, labeling fiduciary duties "default rules" threatens to strip fiduciary rules of their moral content. Fiduciary duties are most effective when they function both as legal rules and moral norms. A label that equates the duty of loyalty with, say, a U.C.C. provision allocating risk of loss undermines the duty's normative force. The erosion of the social norm may create significant external costs for all future settlors and beneficiaries, in two respects. First, destigmatizing opportunist behavior may encourage trustees to stretch the boundaries of acceptable conduct. Second, erosion of the form will create uncertainty about the content of

the fiduciary standard, which will increase transaction costs for all settlors.

Leslie, Trusting Trustees: Fiduciary Duties and the Limits of Default Rules, 94 Geo. L.J. 67, 68–70 (2005).

3. *Actual case involving Enron stock.* In McGinley v. Bank of America, 109 P.3d 1146 (Kan. 2005), the settlor of a revocable trust reserved the right to direct investments and signed a letter directing the trustee to retain Enron stock. The letter also relieved the trustee of responsibility for analyzing or monitoring the stock and exonerated the trustee from liability for any loss resulting from its retention. Both the trust instrument and the letter of instructions were prepared by the settlor's own lawyer. In 2001, the value of the trust's Enron stock plunged from nearly $800,000 to less than $5,000, wiping out three-quarters of the trust's value. The court held that the trustee was not liable.

IN RE TRUST CREATED BY INMAN
Supreme Court of Nebraska, 2005.
269 Neb. 376, 693 N.W.2d 514.

STEPHAN, J.

Robert H. Brackett, as trustee of a revocable trust created by his grandfather, Harold Inman, now deceased, petitioned the county court for Douglas County for authority to sell certain real property held by the trust to himself. After an evidentiary hearing at which several beneficiaries of the trust appeared in opposition to the proposed sale, the court denied Brackett's petition. . . .

Inman, as settlor, executed a revocable trust agreement dated March 9, 1994, naming himself as the initial trustee. The beneficiaries of the trust included Inman's two daughters and seven grandchildren, including Brackett, who was also named as successor trustee. Brackett became the trustee upon Inman's death. . . .

. . . The trust assets also included approximately 189 acres of farmland located in Washington County, Nebraska. The trust instrument directed that Elizabeth Peters, one of Inman's surviving daughters, was to receive rental income from 55 acres of this land during her lifetime and that upon her death, Brackett was to receive the income during his lifetime. The trust instrument further provided that Brackett was to receive income from the remainder of the farmland and that upon his death, it was to be divided among the other beneficiaries or their issue.

Brackett executed a real estate purchase agreement dated September 30, 2002, whereby he agreed to purchase from "Robert Brackett as Trustee of the Inman Living Trust" a portion of the Washington County land held by the trust, consisting of 42 acres. . . . On April 14, 2003, Brackett . . . petitioned the court to approve the proposed sale. . . . All nine beneficiaries . . . were listed in the petition as interested parties. Brackett alleged in his verified petition that he had purchased a home and moved it "onto the real property he proposes to sale [sic] to himself." He further alleged that if the court approved the sale at a price of $84,000, a reasonable rate of return on the proceeds would exceed the income being generated by the subject property. Five of the beneficiaries thereafter filed a written objection to the proposed sale. . . .

An evidentiary hearing on the proposed sale was held on August 15, 2003. Brackett testified that the only assets held by the trust . . . were the 189 acres of Washington County farmland, which included the 42 acres he proposed to sell, and $300 in cash. . . . Brackett testified that the proposed purchase price of $84,000 was based upon an appraised value of $2,000 per acre. Frederick Wohlenhaus, a licensed real estate appraiser, testified that he appraised the 189–acre tract in the fall of 1999, in March 2002, and in early August 2003. He also examined the 42–acre parcel which was the subject of the proposed sale. Wohlenhaus concluded that the highest and best use of the land was agricultural and that the fair market value of the 42–acre parcel was $2,000 per acre.

Brackett testified that he purchased an old farmhouse at auction and moved it onto the 42–acre parcel in June 2002, prior to seeking court approval of the sale. He further acknowledged that as a condition of the proposed sale, he would grant a permanent easement for ingress and egress to the remaining property which is located generally northeast and southwest of the 42 acres. Brackett believed, but was not certain, that the rate of return on the farmland was approximately 2 1/3 percent, based upon its appraised value. Although he professed no experience in investing, he believed that the proceeds from the sale of the land could be invested to earn a greater return. He testified that if the sale were authorized, he would employ a broker to invest the proceeds. . . . Brackett testified that he had previously attempted to sell the entire parcel of land held by the trust but received no offers.

Dr. David Volkman testified on behalf of Brackett as an expert in economics and finance. . . . Volkman opined that because the assets of the trust were not diversified, the standards of the Nebraska Uniform Prudent Investor Act were not met. Volkman analyzed the diversification of the trust in relation to the return and risk of the investments and compared the rate of return on farmland as opposed to other types of investments. Asked to evaluate the risk associated with the trust assets as then held, Volkman stated:

The greatest risk is that it's not diversified. It's invested all in one asset. And when you invest in one asset, you significantly increase the probability of not receiving the return that you would like to [get from] it. It would be similar if you went out and bought one stock and put all of your savings in one stock. There's a high probability you may not get the return that you want from that one stock.

Volkman further testified that farmland has a lower rate of return and higher risk for rate of return compared to the Dow Jones index, a higher rate of return and higher risk than treasury notes, and a significantly lower rate of return but also less risk than the NASDAQ Composite Index. He testified that the overall risk to the beneficiaries could be reduced by having a portion of the corpus invested in farmland and other portions in investments which would yield a higher rate of return.

Maryann Tremaine, Inman's other surviving daughter, testified as a spokesperson for the five beneficiaries who filed a written objection to the sale. She opposed the sale because of her belief that Inman intended the farmland to remain in trust for all of the beneficiaries and that it would increase in value over time. Another beneficiary who joined in the written objection testified that she opposed the sale for generally the same reasons. Two beneficiaries who did not file written objections also testified in opposition to the sale. Peters opposed the sale because she believed the property should remain "in the family" and was satisfied with the current income. One of Inman's granddaughters who is a beneficiary of the trust testified that she opposed the sale because "I truly believe my grandfather left the property for everybody to enjoy. It has sentimental value to the whole family, not just one person."

In its order denying Brackett authority to execute the proposed sale, the county court found that "seven of the nine trust beneficiaries oppose the sale; that there is no persuasive evidence that the proposed sale would enhance or protect the interests of the beneficiaries and that there is a likelihood that the sale would lessen the value of those interests." . . .

Brackett [argues] that by denying him authority to sell the trust property to himself, the probate court (1) failed to allow him to diversify the assets of the trust in compliance with the Nebraska Uniform Prudent Investor Act and (2) erroneously allowed principles against self-dealing to trump statutory law and trust provisions that authorized the requested sale. . . .

The Nebraska Uniform Trust Code (NUTC) was enacted in 2003 and became operative on January 1, 2005, during the pendency of this judicial proceeding. . . . Because we perceive no prejudice to any party in analyzing this issue under the NUTC, we do so. . . .

Resolution of the issue prescribed by this appeal requires an examination of the relationship between two separate legal duties owed by a trustee to the beneficiaries of the trust. The first is the duty of loyalty, which is substantially the same under the NUTC and prior law. Under the NUTC, "[a] trustee shall administer the trust solely in the interests of the beneficiaries." § 30–3867(a). . . . Similar substantive provisions of the Nebraska Uniform Prudent Investor Act . . . are also now included in the NUTC. . . . Accordingly, . . . we shall refer to the provisions of the NUTC in discussing the trustee's duties of loyalty and compliance with the prudent investor rule.

The record reflects that Brackett has purely personal reasons for seeking to acquire the 42–acre parcel from the trust. . . . Brackett argues, however, that the county court should nevertheless have approved the sale because investment of the proceeds in something other than agricultural real estate would provide diversification of trust assets in a manner consistent with the prudent investor rule, thereby benefiting all the beneficiaries.

The prudent investor rule applicable to trustees [includes] the principle that a "trustee shall diversify the investments of the trust unless the trustee reasonably determines that, because of special circumstances, the purposes of the trust are better served without diversifying." § 30–3885. On the record before us, we conclude that there was no absolute duty to diversify the trust assets which would compel court approval of the proposed sale. The prudent investor rule is a "default rule" which "may be expanded, restricted, eliminated, or otherwise altered by the provisions of a trust." § 30–3883(b). It is true, as Brackett argues, that the trust instrument in this case gave the trustee broad powers in dealing with trust assets, including the power "to receive, hold, manage and care for the property held in trust," and "to sell publicly or privately for cash or on time, property, real or personal, held in trust. . . ." However, the trust instrument also conferred upon the trustee the power

> to retain any property, whether consisting of stocks, bonds, other securities, participations in common trust funds, or of any other type of personal property or of real property, taken over by it as a portion of the trust, *without regard to the proportion such property or property of a similar character so held may bear to the entire amount of the trust*, whether or not such property is of the class in which trustees generally are authorized to invest by law or rule of court; *intending thereby to authorize the Trustee to act in such manner as will be for the best interest of the trust beneficiaries*, giving due consideration to the preservation of principal and the amount and regularity of the income to be derived therefrom.

(Emphasis supplied.) With respect to assets originally placed in trust, this provision modifies the general duty to diversify by authorizing the trustee to retain nondiversified assets if retention would be in the best interests of the beneficiaries.

Furthermore, the trustee's statutory duty to diversify trust assets is subject to the general "prudent investor" standard of care which requires a trustee to consider various circumstances relevant to the trust or its beneficiaries in investing and managing trust assets. § 30–3884(c). These circumstances include "an asset's special relationship or special value, if any, to the purposes of the trust or to one or more of the beneficiaries." § 30–3884(c)(8). We agree with a commentator who has noted that a similar provision in the Nebraska Uniform Prudent Investor Act could be utilized as a basis for justifying "non-diversification" of a family farm or ranch held in trust in favor of retaining the asset "for future generations of the family." Ronald R. Volkmer, *The Latest Look in Nebraska Trust Law*, 31 Creighton L. Rev. 221, 246 (1997). Brackett's professed "sentimental" attachment to the farmland which has been in his family for many years is clearly shared by the other family members who are beneficiaries of the trust. Those who filed an objection or testified in opposition to the proposed sale expressed the view that excising a 42–acre parcel from the 189–acre farm would have a detrimental effect upon their special relationship with the asset without achieving any appreciable benefit. . . .

Historically, the law has looked with disfavor upon a trustee selling trust assets to himself. . . . While such transactions are not absolutely prohibited under current law, they are voidable by a beneficiary unless specifically authorized by the trust instrument, approved by a court, or consented to or ratified by the beneficiary. . . . It logically follows that a court should not approve such a transaction over the objection of a beneficiary unless it can be clearly demonstrated that the transaction is consistent with the trustee's duty to administer the trust solely in the interests of the beneficiaries. See Restatement (Third) of Trusts § 170, comment *f.* at 196 (1992) (noting that "court will permit a trustee to purchase trust property only if in its opinion such purchase is for the best interest of the beneficiary"). We agree with the county court that the evidence in this case does not meet this test. Brackett presented no specific plan for investment of the proceeds from the proposed sale, and thus, any potential benefit to the beneficiaries in the nature of increased income without a corresponding increase in risk to the principal is speculative. There is no evidence that additional income is needed in order to carry out any specific purpose of the trust, and the beneficiaries have articulated a legitimate interest in maintaining the geographic integrity of the farm that has been in their family for many years.

We conclude that the judgment of the county court conforms to the law, is supported by competent evidence, and is neither arbitrary, capricious, nor unreasonable. Finding no error appearing on the record, we affirm.

NOTE

Other trust purposes. Weldon Revocable Trust v. Weldon, 231 S.W.3d 158 (Mo. App. 2007), involved a trust for the settlor's benefit. Upon her death, the trust assets were to be divided among her three children. Among the substantial trust assets was an opulent horse farm. Although the farm occasionally yielded a profit, it usually lost about $1 million a year. After the settlor became incapacitated, two of three co-trustees proposed selling the farm, to preserve the trust estate for the benefit of all of the beneficiaries. The other co-trustee sought to enjoin the sale. The court held that the settlor's intent was that the farm remain available after her death for distribution to one or more of the remainder beneficiaries, and that, until then, the trustees lacked authority to sell it. The court relied on provisions in the governing instrument detailing the treatment of the horses after the settlor's death. The court acknowledged that the trustees were authorized to sell the farm if necessary to accomplish the trust's primary purposes. The court found, however, that the trust estate was ample to provide for the settlor's needs and that credible efforts were underway to diminish the losses.

c. The Duty to Conserve Trust Property

IN RE TRUSTEESHIP AGREEMENT WITH MAYO

Supreme Court of Minnesota, 1960.
259 Minn. 91, 105 N.W.2d 900.

DELL, CHIEF JUSTICE.

Appeals from orders of the district court denying the petitions of Esther Mayo Hartzell, as beneficiary, for orders authorizing the trustees of two separate trusts created by the late Dr. Charles H. Mayo on August 17, 1917, and March 28, 1919, to deviate from identical investment restrictions in the trust instruments or to construe the term "other forms of income bearing property" as used therein as authorizing investment of trust funds in corporate stock. The donor died May 26, 1939.

The petitions were opposed by the trustees. Roderick D. Peck was appointed guardian ad litem and appeared for all "unknown, unascertained, minor and incompetent beneficiaries" with respect to both trusts. . . .

With reference to investments the provisions of both trusts are in substance as follows:

. . . The Trustees shall hold said property as a trust fund and collect the interest, income and profits therefrom as the same accrue; *manage, care for and protect said fund all in accordance with their best judgment and discretion*, invest and re-invest the same in *real estate mortgages, municipal bonds or any other form of income bearing property (but not real estate nor corporate stock)*, ... (Italics supplied.)

At the time of the hearing the value of the assets of the first trust was approximately $1,000,000, invested mostly in municipal bonds and in 1,944 shares of common stock of the Kahler Corporation, the latter coming into the trust at the time of its creation from the donor. The value of the assets of the second trust at the time of the hearing was approximately $186,000 invested mostly in municipal bonds. The first trust by its terms will continue until 21 years after the death of the petitioner, who was 51 years of age at the time of the hearing; while the second trust by its terms will partially terminate as each surviving child of petitioner attains the age of 30 years and will fully terminate when the last of such children attains such age; but in the event of certain alternatives it will not continue longer than 21 years after the death of all of donor's children.

In support of the petition, evidence was submitted that an inflationary period, which could not have been foreseen, had commenced shortly after the donor's death in 1939; that it had reduced the real value of the trust assets by more than 50 percent; that a further inflationary period or a permanent "creeping inflation," which the donor could not have foreseen, must be expected; that on December 30, 1940, when the trustees filed their first accounting, the value of the assets of the first trust was $957,711.60; that in October 1958, at the trustees' most recent accounting, the value of such assets was $968,893.08, which in terms of 1940 dollar values meant that in 1958 the assets of the first trust were worth only $456,139.67; that the same percentage of shrinkage was experienced in the second trust; that the provisions of the trust prohibiting investments in real estate and corporate stocks had caused such shrinkage; and that the market value of common stocks had almost doubled since 1939 while the actual value of bonds, in terms of purchasing power, had been cut almost in half since that time. Appellants state that even in the short period between March 1959 and November 1959 the Consumer Price Index of the Bureau of Labor Statistics has increased from 123.7 to 125.6, representing an increase of almost 2 percent in 8 months.

Petitioner urges that the donor's ultimate and dominant intention was to preserve the value of the trust corpus and that this will be circumvented unless the court authorizes the trustees to deviate from the investment provisions of the trust and invest part of the funds in corporate stocks; that it is common practice of trustees of large trusts which have no restrictive investment provisions (including the First National Bank of Minneapolis, one of the trustees in both trusts here) to invest substantial proportions of trust assets in corporate stocks to protect such trusts against inflation, and she asserts that if no deviation is permitted and the next 20 years parallel the last 20 years the ultimate beneficiaries of these trusts will be presented with assets having less than one-fourth of the value which they had at the time of the donor's death.

In opposition to the petition, the trustees refer to the donor's clear intention, as expressed in the trust instruments, that no part of the trust funds should be invested in real estate or corporate stocks, and urge that, since no emergency or change of circumstances which could not have been foreseen or experienced by the donor during his lifetime has been shown, no deviation from the donor's clearly expressed intention would be justified. They urge that the rule is well established that where prospective changes of conditions are substantially known to or anticipated by the settlor of a trust the courts will not grant a deviation from its provisions. They point out that the donor here had survived some 20 years after the creation of the trusts during a period in which there had been both a great inflation and a severe depression; that after creating such trusts he had observed the inflation of the post–World–War–I period, the stock market fever of the pre–1929 era, the market crash of 1929, and the subsequent depression and lowering of bond interest rates during the late 1930's; that despite these economic changes he had never altered the investment restrictions in these trusts; and that he was always aware of his right to amend the trust instruments and, in fact, had consented to minor departures from the provisions of one of the trusts in 1932 and had once amended another trust to permit acquisition of common stocks, but had never requested any change in the investment provisions of the trusts now under consideration and apparently was satisfied with them exactly as they had been drawn and executed. Petitioner offered expert testimony favoring deviation and respondents' expert testimony was to the contrary. The lower court found in favor of respondents and these appeals followed. . . .

In our opinion the evidence here, together with economic and financial conditions which may properly be judicially noticed, compels us to hold that unless deviation is ordered the dominant intention of the donor to prevent a loss of the principal of the two trusts will be frustrated. When the trusts were created and for many years prior thereto, the dollar, based upon the gold standard, remained at a substantially fixed value. On March 9, 1933, the United States went off the gold standard and has since that time remained off from it domestically. While some inflation shortly thereafter followed, it was not until after the death of the donor that inflation commenced to make itself really known and felt. Since then it has gradually increased until at the time of the trial of this case the purchasing power of the dollar, measured by the Consumer Price Index of the U.S. Bureau of Labor Statistics, had depreciated to one-half of its 1940 value. While the experts called by the respective parties disagreed as to when inflation, which they felt was then dormant, would start again and at what percentage it would proceed, there was no disagreement between them that further inflation "in the foreseeable future" could be expected. There was testimony that there would possibly be none for the next year or two and that then it would "increase so that over the period of ten years, on the average, the trend line would be between one and a half and two per cent. . . ." But from the date of trial to November 1959 there was an increase of almost 2 percent in the cost of living index.

At the time these trusts were created it was common practice for business men, in protecting their families through the creation of trusts, to authorize investments to be made by their trustees only in high-grade bonds or first mortgages on good real estate. Many of the states then had statutes preventing trustees from investing in corporate stocks or real estate. Since that time many of the states, including Minnesota, have enacted statutes permitting trustees to invest in corporate stocks and real estate. In recent years most trust companies have encouraged donors, when naming the companies as trustees, to permit investment in common stocks as well as bonds and mortgages. And these trustees maintain competent and efficient employees, well acquainted with the various aspects of corporations having listed stocks, so as to enable them to make reasonably safe and proper corporate-stock purchases.

Throughout the trial considerable reference was made to the 1929 stock-market crash as a reason why deviation would not be granted. There are many reasons, however, why the market action of that period is not a controlling factor today. At that time, many of the corporations, including some of the very best, did not maintain sufficient current assets in relation to current liabilities. And several of them then carried a large funded indebtedness drawing high interest rates with comparatively early maturities. Many companies also, during that period, declared and paid higher dividends than should have been paid. As a result they did not retain and build up a sufficient surplus for future use in the business. When the crash came, many of them, because of such practices, had great difficulty for a long period of time in extricating themselves from their unfortunate financial positions. Dividends from many of such companies were stopped or greatly reduced. A few of them failed altogether. This caused the market value of stocks for a long period of time to greatly decline. But even so, almost all of the companies having corporate stock classified as "good, sound investment stocks" not only survived but have been paying regular and substantial dividends. Many of them are now considered outstanding, safe, investment stocks. Now almost all of these companies maintain a high ratio between their current assets and their current liabilities. They have also built up and retain large surpluses for use in their business. Many of them now have no funded debt at all; and those that do, in most instances, have fixed maturity dates well ahead in years with a satisfactory rate of interest.

Officers and directors of companies registered and listed on the New York and American Stock Exchanges, as well as beneficial owners of more than 10 percent of any of its securities, must now, under the Securities Exchange Act of 1934, 15 U.S.C.A. § 78a et seq., file a statement with the exchange where the stock is registered and listed, and a duplicate original thereof with the Securit[ies] Exchange Commission, indicating their ownership at the close of the calendar month and such changes in their ownership as have occurred during such calendar month. Such statements must be in the hands of the commission and the exchange before the 10th day of the month following that which they cover. The information thus made available is published for the benefit of the public. Large investment companies have been organized under the Investment Company Act of 1940, 15 U.S.C.A. § 80a–1 et seq. They now buy, sell, and own large amounts of corporate stocks in various companies. This assists in stabilizing the market in difficult financial times.

In 1929 there was no Securit[ies] Exchange Commission to regulate and control corporate stock purchases or sales. Many of the people of that era were not investing in stocks at all but were gambling in them. At that time the margin requirement was only 10 percent and brokers' loans reached an alltime high of approximately $8,500,000,000. Until recently margin requirements were, as fixed within the framework of the Securities Exchange Act, 90 percent. As a result there has been very little speculation and brokers' loans have been relatively small. In 1929 large speculators pooled their resources with a premeditated plan to buy and force certain stocks upward. This upward surge prompted uninformed people to purchase those stocks. When the stocks had reached a predetermined value, the pool operators sold out, the stocks declined, and the people took the losses. During that period promoters were dealing in public utilities stocks, merging companies together without proper relation one to the other geographically or otherwise. When the crash came those stocks suffered greatly. Some of the companies never recovered at all. And it took many of those that did recover several years to reestablish themselves again. Several of them were required to divest themselves of their complex and wide holdings under the Public Utility Holding Company Act of 1935, 15 U.S.C.A. § 79a et seq. These practices are no longer permissible under that act and the rules and regulations of the Securit[ies] Exchange Commission. Since 1932, because of heavy Federal expenditures, the national debt has grown from a high of approximately $25,400,000,000 at the end of World War I to approximately $258,600,000,000 at the end of World War II and to approximately $290,000,000,000 at the present time.[23] Inflation has been steadily increasing. None of this was foreseeable by an ordinary prudent investor at the time these trusts were created, nor at the time of the donor's death in 1939, since these inflationary practices did not become noticeably fixed and established until after his death.

It appears without substantial dispute that if deviation is not permitted the accomplishment of the purposes of the trusts will be substantially impaired because of changed conditions due to inflation since the trusts were created; that unless deviation is allowed the assets of the trusts, within the next 20 years, will, in all likelihood, be worth less than one-fourth of the value they had at the time of the donor's death. To avoid this we conclude that in equity the trustees should have the right and be authorized to deviate from the restrictive provisions of the trusts by permitting them, when and as they deem it advisable, to invest a reasonable amount of the trust assets in corporate stocks of good, sound investment issues. Through an investment in bonds and mortgages of the type designated by the donor, plus corporate stocks of good, sound investment issues, in our opinion, the trusts will, so far as possible, be fortified against inflation, recession, depression, or decline in prices. Corporate trustees [regularly manage] trusts consisting of corporate stocks, bonds, and mortgages, on a successful basis. There appears to be no sound reason why they cannot do the same thing here.

Reversed and remanded for further proceedings in conformity with this opinion.

NOTES

1. *The opposite result.* For the opposite result, see Toledo Trust Co. v. Toledo Hospital, 187 N.E.2d 36 (Ohio 1962); Stanton v. Wells Fargo Bank, 310 P.2d 1010 (Cal.App.1957) (in absence of emergency, investment restriction is effective).

2. *Changing economic conditions and the law of fiduciary investment.* *Mayo* is a dramatic example of how changing economic conditions affect investment strategy. The prudent investor rule itself is in many ways a response to such changes.

JOHN H. LANGBEIN, THE UNIFORM PRUDENT INVESTOR ACT AND THE FUTURE OF TRUST INVESTING
81 Iowa L. Rev. 641, 663–65 (1996).

INCREASED SCRUTINY OF UNECONOMIC SETTLOR INSTRUCTIONS

I would also predict that the greater clarity of the new trust investment law will result in less deference to the wishes of the trust settlor in

---

[23] In 2012, the national debt exceeded $16,000,000,000,000 ($16 trillion).—EDS.

an uncommon but troubling case—the case in which the settlor attempts to impose a manifestly stupid investment restriction on the trust.

Take as the starting point the proposition . . . that almost all trust law is default law, rules that yield to the contrary wishes of the settlor. Trust law presumes that the settlor has the best interests of the beneficiaries at heart when the settlor imposes restrictions on the disposition of trust property. If, for example, I leave my summer cottage on Lake Adams in trust for my children with instructions that it not be sold but kept in the family for recreational use, that instruction will be honored even if the beneficiaries would rather not set foot on the shores of Lake Adams ever again. Under conventional American trust law, the settlor's property rights are indulged. As settlor, I am entitled to decide what is best for my beneficiaries, subject only to the rule against perpetuities.

There are, however, limitations. If I devise property to a trust directing that the trustee erect equestrian statues of me in public squares in Iowa, that provision will be invalidated. A private trust must be for the benefit of the beneficiaries; a charitable trust must satisfy standards of public benefit. The trust to endow Iowa with bronze, equestrian Langbeins achieves neither.

Even when the settlor's instruction is not manifestly loony, the deviation doctrine allows a court to alter an unwise investment restriction "if necessary to carry out the purposes of the trust."[24] The leading case involved a trust set up by Joseph Pulitzer for his children, in which he forbad the trustees to sell the *New York World* newspaper. When the paper became unprofitable, the trustees received judicial approval to sell it anyhow.[25] The reasoning in such cases is that subsequent experience has revealed a conflict between the settlor's dominant purpose, which is to benefit the trust beneficiaries; and the settlor's subsidiary purpose, which is to benefit them in a particular way—in *Pulitzer*, by keeping the *New York World* in the trust. The court is simply preferring the dominant purpose, in order to carry out the settlor's presumed intent.

Suppose, however, that the trust instrument in *Pulitzer* had foreseen and recited the danger that the paper might become unprofitable, and had directed retention of the investment in any event. I have no doubt that the court in *Pulitzer* would have ordered the trustees to sell the newspaper despite the settlor's direction to retain it. The settlor's instruction to retain the newspaper at all costs would come to resemble my instruction to litter the Iowa landscape with equestrian statues. If the settlor directs an objectively stupid investment policy, the court will direct

---

[24] Restatement (Second) of Trusts § 167(1) (1959).

[25] In re Pulitzer, 249 N.Y.S. 87 (N.Y. Sur. Ct. 1931), aff'd mem., 260 N.Y.S. 975 (N.Y.App.Div.1932).

deviation even though the settlor anticipates the circumstance.[26] The settlor is presumed to intend to benefit the beneficiaries, but if it can be shown that a term of the trust manifestly harms their interests, the court will order deviation from it. A private trust must be for the benefit of the beneficiaries.

Now consider a type of investment instruction that is closer to reality. The settlor has worked all his life for, let us say, IBM. Through stock options and company sponsored investment plans, he has accumulated a large block of IBM common stock. He dies, leaving the block in trust with instructions not to sell it. The block is the only substantial asset of the trust, and because the settlor's death results in a stepped-up basis, selling the block incurs no tax cost. Suppose, further, that the settlor leaves a letter explaining his thinking. "I worked for IBM for 35 years, they were wonderful to me, they helped me buy the stock, and the stock zoomed in value throughout my career. You just cannot do better."

What is happening in this case is that the settlor is imposing his supposed investment wisdom on the trust in circumstances in which the investment strategy is objectively stupid and imprudent. We now know that the advantages of diversifying a portfolio of securities are so great that it is folly not to do it. I am not saying that you can never have an underdiversified trust fund. It will remain common to place a family firm or a family farm in trust, notwithstanding that such a trust will often be underdiversified. There's nothing wrong with using a trust as part of the succession arrangements for a family enterprise. I further concede, following the official Comment to the Uniform Prudent Investor Act,[27] that there will remain cases in which the tax cost of diversifying a low-basis asset may outweigh the gain. When, however, the trust assets are cash or cash-equivalent, in the sense that diversification can be achieved at little cost, I believe that the courts will come to view the advantages of diversification as so overwhelming that the settlor's interference with effective diversification will be found to be inconsistent with the requirement that a private trust must be for the benefit of the beneficiary.

NOTES

1. *Another fiduciary duty?* Given the zest with which both the court in *Mayo* and Professor Langbein in his article attack uneconomic restrictions, do you have any advice for the trustee who is subject to an uneconomic restriction? Might a court find that a trustee who has failed to seek judicial authority to deviate from such a restriction has violated the fiduciary duty to conserve trust assets? See Restatement (Third) of Trusts § 66(2) (2003).

---

[26] E.g., Colonial Trust Co. v. Brown, 135 A. 555, 564 (Conn.1926) (holding void certain restrictions as to the height of buildings to be erected on trust real estate because "the restrictions are opposed to the interests of the beneficiaries of the trust").

[27] UPIA § 3 cmt.

2. *Deviation from dispositive provisions.* As *Mayo* suggests, judicial relief may be available if the terms of a trust include administrative provisions that are archaic or unduly restrictive. Traditionally, the courts have been much slower to authorize deviations from the dispositive provisions of private trusts. See infra pp. 849-856.

3. *The fiduciary duty to minimize taxes.* The duty to conserve trust property also imposes on fiduciaries heavy responsibilities with respect to taxes. See generally Ascher, The Fiduciary Duty to Minimize Taxes, 20 Real Prop. Prob. & Tr. J. 663 (1985).

d. The Duty to Treat Beneficiaries Impartially

DENNIS V. RHODE ISLAND HOSPITAL TRUST CO.

United States Court of Appeals, First Circuit, 1984.
744 F.2d 893.

BREYER, CIRCUIT JUDGE.

The plaintiffs are the great-grandchildren of Alice M. Sullivan and beneficiaries of a trust created under her will. They claimed in the district court that the Bank trustee had breached various fiduciary obligations owed them as beneficiaries of that trust. The trust came into existence in 1920. It will cease to exist in 1991 (twenty-one years after the 1970 death of Alice Sullivan's last surviving child). The trust distributes all its income for the benefit of Alice Sullivan's living issue; the principal is to go to her issue surviving in 1991. Evidently, since the death of their mother, the two plaintiffs are the sole surviving issue, entitled to the trust's income until 1991, and then, as remaindermen, entitled to the principal.

The controversy arises out of the trustee's handling of the most important trust assets, undivided interests in three multi-story commercial buildings in downtown Providence. The buildings (the Jones, Wheaton–Anthony, and Alice Buildings) were all constructed before the beginning of the century, in an area where the value of the property has declined markedly over the last thirty years. During the period that the trust held these interests the buildings were leased to a number of different tenants, including corporations which subsequently subleased the premises. Income distribution from the trust to the life tenants has averaged over $34,000 annually.

At the time of the creation of the trust in 1920, its interests in the three buildings were worth more than $300,000. The trustee was authorized by the will to sell real estate. When the trustee finally sold the buildings in 1945, 1970, and 1979, respectively, it did so at or near the lowest point of their value; the trust received a total of only $185,000 for its interests in them. These losses, in plaintiffs' view, reflect a serious mishandling of assets over the years.

The district court, 571 F. Supp. 623, while rejecting many of plaintiffs' arguments, nonetheless found that the trustee had failed to act impartially, as between the trust's income beneficiaries and the remaindermen; it had favored the former over the latter, and, in doing so, it had reduced the value of the trust assets. To avoid improper favoritism, the trustee should have sold the real estate interests, at least by 1950, and reinvested the proceeds elsewhere. By 1950 the trustee must have, or should have, known that the buildings' value to the remaindermen would be small; the character of downtown commercial Providence was beginning to change; retention of the buildings would work to the disadvantage of the remaindermen. The court ordered a surcharge of $365,000, apparently designed to restore the real value of the trust's principal to its 1950 level. . . .

I

a. The trustee first argues that the district court's conclusions rest on "hindsight." It points out that Rhode Island law requires a trustee to be "prudent and vigilant and exercise sound judgment," Rhode Island Hospital Trust Co. v. Copeland, 39 R.I. 193, 98 A. 273, 279 (1916), but "[n]either prophecy nor prescience is expected." Stark v. United States Trust Co. of New York, 445 F. Supp. 670, 678 (S.D.N.Y.1978). It adds that a trustee can indulge a preference for keeping the trust's "inception assets," those placed in trust by the settlor and commended to the trustee for retention. See Peckham v. Newton, 15 R.I. 321, 4 A. 758, 760 (1886); Rhode Island Hospital Trust Co. v. Copeland, supra. How then, the trustee asks, can the court have found that it should have sold these property interests in 1950?

The trustee's claim might be persuasive had the district court found that it had acted imprudently in 1950, in retaining the buildings. If that were the case, one might note that every 1950 sale involved both a pessimistic seller and an optimistic buyer; and one might ask how the court could expect the trustee to have known then (in 1950) whose prediction would turn out to be correct. The trustee's argument is less plausible, however, where, as here, the district court basically found that in 1950 the trustee had acted not imprudently, but unfairly, between income beneficiaries and remaindermen.

Suppose, for example, that a trustee of farmland over a number of years overplants the land, thereby increasing short run income, but ruining the soil and making the farm worthless in the long run. The trustee's duty to take corrective action would arise from the fact that he knows (or plainly ought to know) that his present course of action will injure the remaindermen; settled law requires him to act impartially, "with due regard" for the "respective interests" of both the life tenant and the remainderman. Restatement (Second) of Trusts § 232 (1959). See also A. Scott, The Law of Trusts § 183 (1967); G.G. Bogert & G.T. Bogert, The Law of Trusts and Trustees § 612 (1980). The district court here found that a sale in 1950 would have represented one way (perhaps the only practical way) to correct this type of favoritism. It held that instead of correcting the problem, the trustee continued to favor the life tenant to the "very real disadvantage" of the remainder interests, in violation of Rhode Island law. See Industrial Trust Co. v. Parks, 57 R.I. 363, 190 A. 32, 38 (1937); Rhode Island Hospital Trust Co. v. Tucker, 52 R.I. 277, 160 A. 465, 466 (1932).

To be more specific, in the court's view the problem arose out of the trustee's failure to keep up the buildings, to renovate them, to modernize them, or to take other reasonably obvious steps that might have given the remaindermen property roughly capable of continuing to produce a reasonable income. This failure allowed the trustee to make larger income payments during the life of the trust; but the size of those payments reflected the trustee's acquiescence in the gradual deterioration of the property. In a sense, the payments ate away the trust's capital.

The trustee correctly points out that it did take certain steps to keep up the buildings; and events beyond its control made it difficult to do more. In the 1920's, the trustee, with court approval, entered into very longterm leases on the Alice and Wheaton–Anthony buildings. The lessees and the subtenants were supposed to keep the buildings in good repair; some improvements were made. Moreover, the depression made it difficult during the 1930's to find tenants who would pay a high rent and keep up the buildings. After World War II the neighborhood enjoyed a brief renaissance; but, then, with the 1950's flight to the suburbs, it simply deteriorated.

Even if we accept these trustee claims, however, the record provides adequate support for the district court's conclusions. There is considerable evidence indicating that, at least by 1950, the trustee should have been aware of the way in which the buildings' high rents, the upkeep problem, the changing neighborhood, the buildings' age, the failure to modernize, all together were consuming the buildings' value. There is evidence that the trustee did not come to grips with the problem. Indeed, the trustee did not appraise the properties periodically, and it did not keep proper records. It made no formal or informal accounting in 55 years. There is no indication in the record that the trust's officers focused upon the problem or consulted real estate experts about it or made any further rehabilitation efforts. Rather, there is evidence that the trustee did little more than routinely agree to the requests of the trust's income beneficiaries that it manage the trust corpus to produce the largest possible income. The New Jersey courts have pointed out that an impartial trustee must view the overall picture as it is presented from all the facts, and not close its eyes to any relevant facts which might result in excessive burden to the one class in preference to the other. Pennsylvania Co. v. Gillmore, 137 N.J. Eq. 51, 43 A.2d 667, 672 (1945). The record supports a conclusion of failure to satisfy that duty.

The district court also found that the trustee had at least one practical solution available. It might have sold the property in 1950 and reinvested the proceeds in other assets of roughly equivalent total value that did not create a "partiality" problem. The Restatement of Trusts foresees such a solution, for it says that

> the trustee is under a duty to the beneficiary who is ultimately entitled to the principal not to . . . retain property which is certain or likely to depreciate in value, although the property yields a large income, unless he makes adequate provision for amortizing the depreciation.

Restatement (Second) of Trusts § 232, comment b. Rhode Island case law also allows the court considerable discretion, in cases of fiduciary breach, to fashion a remedy, including a remedy based on a hypothetical, earlier sale. In, for example, Industrial Trust Co. v. Parks, 190 A. at 42, the court apportioned payments between income and principal "in the same way as they would have been apportioned if [certain] rights had been sold by the trustees immediately after the death of the testator" for a specified hypothetical value, to which the court added hypothetical interest. In the absence of a showing that such a sale and reinvestment would have been impractical or that some equivalent or better curative steps might have been taken, the district court's use of a 1950 sale as a remedial measure of what the trustee ought to have done is within the scope of its lawful powers.

In reaching this conclusion, we have taken account of the trustee's argument that the buildings' values were especially high in 1950 (though not as high as in the late 1920's). As the trustee argues, this fact would make 1950 an unreasonable remedial choice, other things being equal. But the record indicates that other things were not equal. For one thing, the district court chose 1950, not because of then-existing property values, but because that date marks a reasonable outer bound of the time the trustee could plead ignorance of the serious fairness problem. And, this conclusion, as we have noted, has adequate record support. For another thing, the district court could properly understand plaintiffs' expert witness as stating that the suburban flight that led to mid–1950's downtown decline began before 1950; its causes (increased household income; more cars; more mobility) were apparent before 1950. Thus, the court might reasonably have felt that a brief (1948–52) downtown "renaissance" should not have appeared (to the expert eye) to have been permanent or longlasting; it did not relieve the trustee of its obligation to do something about the fairness problem, nor did it make simple "building retention" a plausible cure. Finally, another expert testified that the trustee should have asked for power to sell the property "sometime between 1947 and 1952" when institutional investors generally began to diversify portfolios. For these reasons, reading the record, as we must, simply to see if it contains adequate support for the district court's conclusion as to remedy (as to which its powers are broad), we find that its choice of 1950 as a remedial base year is lawful.

Contrary to the trustee's contention, the case law it cites does not give it an absolute right under Rhode Island law to keep the trust's "inception assets" in disregard of the likely effect of retention on classes of trust beneficiaries. Cf. Peckham v. Newton, supra (original holdings should be retained but only so long as there is no doubt as to their safety). . . . The district court's conclusion that the trustee should have sold the assets if necessary to prevent the trust corpus from being consumed by the income beneficiaries is reasonable and therefore lawful. . . .

c. The trustee challenges the district court's calculation of the surcharge. The court assumed, for purposes of making the trust principal whole, that the trustee had hypothetically sold the trust's interests in the Wheaton–Anthony and the Alice buildings in 1950, at their 1950 values (about $70,000 and $220,000, respectively). It subtracted, from that sum of about $290,000, the $130,000 the trust actually received when the buildings were in fact sold (about $40,000 for the Wheaton–Anthony interest in 1970 and about $90,000 for the Alice interest in 1979). The court considered the difference of $160,000 to be a loss in the value of the principal, suffered as a result of the trustee's failure to prevent the principal from eroding. The court then assumed that, had the trustee sold the buildings in 1950 and reinvested the proceeds, the trustee would have been able to preserve the real value of the principal. It therefore multiplied the $160,000 by 3.6 percent, the average annual increase in the consumer price index from 1950 to 1982, and multiplied again by 32, the number of full years since 1950. Finally, the court multiplied again by an annual 0.4 percent, designed to reflect an "allowance for appreciation." It added the result ($160,000 × 4 percent × 32), about $205,000, to the $160,000 loss and surcharged the trustee $365,000. We are aware of a number of mathematical problems with this calculation. (Why, for example, was no account taken of inflation when subtracting sale receipts from 1950 values?) But, in the context of this specific litigation, fairness as between the parties requires us to restrict our examination to the two particular challenges that the trustee raises.

First, the trustee claims that the court improperly ascertained the 1950 values of the trust's interests because it simply took a proportionate share of the buildings' values. That is to say, it divided the total value of the Alice Building by four to reflect the fact that the trust owned a 1/4 undivided interest. The trustee argues that the building's values should have been discounted further to reflect the facts that the trust owned a fractional interest in the buildings and that fractional interests (with their consequent problems of divided control) typically sell at a discount.

This particular matter in this case, however, was the subject of conflicting evidence. On the one hand, the trustee showed that the marketplace ordinarily discounted the value of fractional interests. On the other hand, the plaintiffs introduced an expert study giving the 1950 values of the trust's interests at precisely the figure shown by the district court. When the trustee finally sold the trust's interests (in 1970 and 1979), their value was not significantly discounted. And, since the trustee also controlled (as a trustee) other fractional interests in the same building, the trustee arguably could have arranged to sell the entire building in 1950 as it did in 1970 and 1979. Evaluating this evidence and the merits of these arguments is a matter for the district court. We see no abuse of the district court's powers to make reasonable judgments as to hypothetical values in its efforts to devise an appropriate remedy for the trustee's breach of duty.

Second, the trustee argues that the district court should not have applied to the 1950 hypothetical sales value a 4 percent interest factor—a factor designed to compensate for 3.6 percent average annual inflation and for 0.4 percent "appreciation." We do not agree with the trustee in respect to the 3.6 percent.

Rhode Island law simply requires that the court's approach be reasonable and its calculations grounded in the record's facts. . . . The trustee does not claim that it requires the court to follow any one particular calculation method, such as that, for example, contained in Restatement (Second) of Trusts § 241. And, we believe the inflation adjustment meets Rhode Island's broader requirements.

For one thing, it seems reasonable for the court—in devising a remedy for the trustee's violation of its duty of impartiality—to assume that a fair trustee would have maintained the property's real value from 1950 through 1982. Cf. In re Trusteeship under Agreement with Mayo, 105 N.W.2d 900 (Minn.1960) (ordering modification in trust terms where inflation was reducing real value of trust). Such an assumption is consistent with basic trust law policies of providing income to income beneficiaries while preserving principal for the remaindermen, and, consequently, of avoiding investment in wasting assets. . . . Moreover, it is consistent with readily ascertainable general economic facts that wages and many asset values as well as prices have on average kept pace with inflation. See generally K. Hirsch, Inflation and the Law of Trusts, 18 Real Prop., Prob. & Tr. J. 601 (Win. 1983). . . . While the value of long term bonds has fallen, the value of common stocks and much property has risen. See generally R. Ibbotson & R. Sinquefield, Stocks, Bonds, Bills and Inflation: The Past and the Future (1982); J. Wiedemer, Real Estate Investment (1979). Where a court is trying to create, not a measure of the trustee's duty, but simply a plausible reconstruction of what would have occurred to a hypothetical 1950 reinvestment, we see nothing unreasonable in assuming that the value of the corpus would have kept pace with inflation.

We reach a different conclusion, however, in respect to the additional 0.4 percent, designed to reflect "appreciation." Neither the court nor the parties have provided us with any reason to believe that the trustee would have outperformed inflation. There is no evidence in the record suggesting that a hypothetical reinvestment of hypothetical proceeds from a hypothetical 1950 property sale would have yielded real appreciation over and above inflation's nominal increase. We have found no information about the performance of an average, or typical, trust. And the general publicly available sources offer insufficient support for a claim of likely real increase. See R. Ibbotson & R. Sinquefield, supra. [We] conclude that, in adding 0.4 percent interest for real appreciation, the district court exceeded its broad remedial powers. Our recalculation, omitting the 0.4 percent, reduces the surcharge from $365,781.67 to $345,246.56.

The trustee objects to the court's having removed it as trustee. The removal of a trustee, however, is primarily a matter for the district court. A trustee can be removed even if "the charges of his misconduct" are "not made out." Petition of Statter, 108 R.I. 326, 275 A.2d 272, 276 (1971). The issue here is whether "ill feeling" might interfere with the administration of the trust. The district court concluded that the course of the litigation in this case itself demonstrated such ill feeling. Nothing in the record shows that the court abused its powers in reaching that conclusion. . . .

The judgment of the district court is modified and as modified affirmed.

NOTES

1. *Black-letter formulations.* Uniform Prudent Investor Act § 6 provides: "If a trust has two or more beneficiaries, the trustee shall act impartially in investing and managing the trust assets, taking into account any differing interests of the beneficiaries." Restatement (Third) of Trusts § 79 (2007) provides:

(1) A trustee has a duty to administer the trust in a manner that is impartial with respect to the various beneficiaries of the trust, requiring that:

(a) in investing, protecting, and distributing the trust estate, and in other administrative functions, the trustee must act impartially and with due regard for the diverse beneficial interests created by the terms of the trust; and

(b) in consulting and otherwise communicating with beneficiaries, the trustee must proceed in a manner that fairly reflects the diversity of their concerns and beneficial interests.

(2) If a trust is created for two or more beneficiaries or purposes in succession and if the rights of any beneficiary or the expenditures for a charitable purpose are defined with reference to trust income, the trustee's duty of impartiality includes a duty to so invest and administer the trust, or to so account for principal and income, that the trust estate will produce income that is reasonably appropriate to the purposes of the trust and to the diverse present and future interests of its beneficiaries.

2. *Conflicts between income and principal.* Trustees, required to treat income and remainder beneficiaries equitably, face a dilemma. Income beneficiaries often urge investment strategies that emphasize bonds. Though fixed-dollar investments have, from time to time, yielded substantially more income than common stocks, such investments ordinarily offer little potential for appreciation, to offset the effects of inflation. Remainder beneficiaries, on the other hand, often urge an emphasis on growth stocks, which promise substantially more appreciation and are widely regarded as superior in preserving the real, not just the nominal, value of the principal. Yet many successful and expanding corporations distribute little or nothing in the way of cash dividends. Some occasionally declare stock dividends, but principal and income law generally treats stock dividends as principal, rather than income.

A sampling of decisions indicates that the courts try to hold trustees to a middle course. Demands by income beneficiaries that the trustee maximize income have generally not been successful. See, e.g., Estate of Hamill, 410 A.2d 770 (Pa.1980) (upholding bank's refusal to accept widow's instructions to invest in U.S. Treasury notes or high-quality industrial bonds; 6 percent income return reasonable); State of Delaware ex rel. Gebelein v. Belin, 456 So.2d 1237 (Fla.App.1984) (3 percent return on $805 million charitable trust created by Alfred I. duPont resulted from reasonable exercise of trustees' discretion); Estate of Stillman, infra p. 841 (approving investment practices that yielded modest income as principal grew from $2 million in 1944 to $8.5 million in 1977). The courts have also often rejected demands by remainder beneficiaries that the trustee invest for growth. See, e.g., SunTrust Bank v. Merritt, 612 S.E.2d 818 (Ga. App. 2005); In re Trust of Martin, 664 N.W.2d 923 (Neb. 2003); Law v. Law, 753 A.2d 443 (Del. 2000). (Query whether, under the Prudent Investor Rule, such cases remain good law.) In one case, the trustee successfully defended a surcharge action for investing in low-yield, tax-exempt government bonds by contending that such a portfolio better met the needs of the high-bracket income beneficiaries. Commercial Trust Co. v. Barnard, 142 A.2d 865 (N.J.1958).

For an example of this ever-present conflict between beneficiaries interested in income and those interested in principal, see Estate of Cooper, 913 P.2d 393 (Wash.App.), review denied, 928 P.2d 414 (Wash.1996). *Cooper* is especially interesting because it also involved a prudent investor statute. An individual trustee was also the trust's income beneficiary. His daughter, a remainder beneficiary, complained that he had favored his own interest (income), at the expense of principal, by investing 87 percent of the portfolio in fixed-income securities. One of the trustee's arguments was that the applicable Washington prudent investor statute protected him from liability. That statute required, in evaluating fiduciary conduct, "due consideration [of] the role that the proposed investment or investment course of action plays within the overall portfolio of assets." (Washington subsequently enacted the Uniform Prudent Investor Act.) Because the overall investment performance of the trust portfolio exceeded that of the corporate co-trustee's trust department, so the trustee argued, there were no grounds for holding him liable on account of his investment strategy. The court disagreed, affirming imposition of a surcharge:

> We hold the prudent investor rule focuses on the performance of the trustee, not the results of the trust. The trial court here then appropriately considered individual assets, and groups of assets, in finding that the trustee had improperly weighed trust assets in favor of himself, the income beneficiary. [913 P.2d at 395.]

The court also noted that the trust's overall investment performance had been "boosted dramatically" by sale of a single stock at a staggering gain, which the trustee "could not have anticipated" when he formulated his investment strategy.

Under a prudent investor statute, a fiduciary who invests for total return may choose to invest in assets whose blend of income and appreciation seems to favor principal over income. This could happen, for example, by investing heavily in stocks, particularly so-called "growth" stocks, which generally pay no or very low dividends. (Of course, a fiduciary's investment policy could, instead, favor income over principal, as in *Cooper*.) Yet, as *Cooper* indicates, the duty of impartiality continues to require even-handed treatment of all beneficiaries, even under a prudent investor statute. Uniform Principal and Income Act § 104 (1997) provides a fiduciary who operates under prudent investor principles a method by which to comply with the duty of impartiality. Such a fiduciary may "adjust between principal and income to the extent the trustee considers necessary." See Note 2, infra p. 867.

3. *The procedural aspect of the duty of impartiality.* There is also a procedural aspect of the duty of impartiality. See Restatement (Third) of Trusts § 79(1)(b) (2007), supra Note 1. Thus, in McNeil v. McNeil, 798 A.2d 503 (Del. 2002), the court held that the trustees violated the duty of impartiality by failing to inform an estranged child of his beneficial interest and failing to provide him with the same information they provided to the other beneficiaries.

4. *Equitable adjustments.* Tax laws, both federal and state, impose major responsibilities on fiduciaries. One such responsibility is to make various elections involving such crucial and diverse issues as whether to claim a marital deduction (I.R.C. § 2056(b)(7)), whether to deduct a given expense on the estate tax return or the income tax return (I.R.C. § 642(g)), when to value estate assets (I.R.C. § 2032), and whether to pay an avoidable tax (I.R.C. § 643(e)(3)), among many others. Fiduciaries must conserve estate assets, minimize taxes, treat beneficiaries impartially, and refrain from self-dealing, but the exercise of any one of these elections almost invariably results in a benefit to one set of beneficiaries at the expense of others. Thus, tax elections frequently put a fiduciary, particularly one who is also a beneficiary, in apparent violation of one or more fiduciary duties. See Ascher, The Quandary of Executors Who Are Asked to Plan the Estates of the Dead: The Qualified Terminable Interest Property Election, 63 N.C. L. Rev. 1 (1984).

In such circumstances, must the fiduciary effect an equitable adjustment among the beneficiaries to compensate for disproportionate allocation of tax burdens resulting from a fiduciary election? This issue has received relatively widespread attention, both judicially and legislatively, in the context of one particular tax election, that available under I.R.C. § 642(g). Under that provision, a fiduciary can elect to deduct certain administration expenses, normally deductible for federal estate tax purposes under I.R.C. § 2053, on the fiduciary income tax return instead. It seems reasonable to expect that a fiduciary would seek to use the election to reduce an estate's overall tax burden. But because administration expenses ordinarily reduce principal, and fiduciary income taxes ordinarily reduce income, electing to deduct these expenses for income tax purposes can have the effect of denying the principal beneficiaries the tax benefits of the expenses principal has borne, thereby providing the income beneficiaries with a windfall of sorts. In a 1955 decision, the New York Surrogate's Court became the first court to rule that income must reimburse principal in the amount of the tax savings that would have resulted had the fiduciary declined to make the election and deducted the expenses for estate tax purposes. Estate of Warms, 140 N.Y.S.2d 169 (Sur. 1955). See also Bixby's Estate, 295 P.2d 68 (Cal.App.1956); Uniform Principal and Income Act § 506(b) (1997) (modified *Warms* adjustment).

Occasionally courts or statutes have authorized or required adjustments in the aftermath of other tax elections, but uniform practices seem not to have developed. See generally Carrico & Bondurant, Equitable Adjustments: A Survey and Analysis of Precedents and Practices, 36 Tax Law. 545 (1983);

Dobris, Limits on the Doctrine of Equitable Adjustment in Sophisticated Postmortem Tax Planning, 66 Iowa L. Rev. 273 (1981); Dobris, Equitable Adjustments in Postmortem Income Tax Planning: An Unremitting Diet of *Warms*, 65 Iowa L. Rev. 103 (1979). Uniform Principal and Income Act § 506 (1997) authorizes adjustments in a wide variety of contexts but requires them in only one very narrow instance. Because the number and variety of conflicts that can result from a fiduciary's exercise of tax elections are practically limitless, prudence suggests inclusion of specific directions in wills and trust agreements, absolving the fiduciary from liability for making or failing to make equitable adjustments.

e. The Duty With Respect to Delegation of Fiduciary Obligations

It has often been said that a fiduciary has a duty not to delegate fiduciary obligations. Fiduciaries, however, have long felt free to hire attorneys, accountants, investment advisers, and other agents, and to allow them to provide services on behalf of the estate or trust, when doing so seemed reasonable. The cases cited in support of this vaguely-defined duty often involved a fiduciary who had hired a faithless attorney, to whom the fiduciary had entrusted administration, and over whom the fiduciary had exercised little, if any, supervision. When the attorney absconded with the estate assets, the hapless fiduciary was left holding the bag, in which nothing remained for the beneficiaries. The courts in such circumstances often imposed liability on the fiduciary for the full amount of the loss and curtly blamed the fiduciary for having "delegated" fiduciary obligations. See, e.g., Laramore v. Laramore, 64 So.2d 662 (Fla.1953); Kaufman v. Kaufman's Administrator, 166 S.W.2d 860 (Ky.1942). In actuality, the error of the victimized fiduciary was not delegation of fiduciary obligations, but, instead, negligent selection and/or inadequate supervision. More modern authority therefore generally tests a fiduciary's actions against a standard of due care in the selection and supervision of agents, attorneys, and advisers. See, e.g., O'Neill v. O'Neill, 865 N.E.2d 917 (Ohio App. 2006).

Restatement (Third) of Trusts (2007)

§ 80. Duty with Respect to Delegation

(1) A trustee has a duty to perform the responsibilities of the trusteeship personally, except as a prudent person of comparable skill might delegate those responsibilities to others.

(2) In deciding whether, to whom, and in what manner to delegate fiduciary authority in the administration of a trust, and thereafter in supervising or monitoring agents, the trustee has a duty to exercise fiduciary discretion and to act as a prudent person of comparable skill would act in similar circumstances.

General Comment: . . .

b. Advice or consultation distinguished. A trustee, in acting personally and without the effect of delegation, may consult with and receive advice from others, such as accountants, legal counsel, and financial advisers. On the duty sometimes to do so, see § 77, Comment b. . . .

Comment on Subsection (1):

c. Resignation; delegation of entire administration. . .

A trustee cannot properly commit the entire administration of the trust to an agent or other person, except as permitted to do so by the terms of the trust.

This prohibition does not preclude even extensive temporary delegation on a prudent basis by the trustee for a reasonable period of absence or during the trustee's inability to perform the duties of the trusteeship. Delegation of this type may be justified when it would not be practical or in the interest of sound administration to require appointment of a substitute or temporary trustee or a trustee ad litem. Extensive temporary delegation may be appropriate, for example, to enable the trustee to take reasonable vacations, including overseas travel, or to cover the trustee's absence due to illness or the necessities of other employment that is not inappropriate to the responsibilities and circumstances of the trusteeship. . . .

d. General fiduciary duty and discretion. . . .

Decisions of trustees concerning delegation are matters of fiduciary judgment and discretion. Therefore, these decisions are not to be controlled by a court except to prevent abuse of that discretionary authority. . . .

d(1). Imprudent failure to delegate. A trustee's discretionary authority in matters of delegation may be abused by imprudent failure to delegate as well as by making an imprudent decision to delegate. See § 77, Comment *b.*

d(2). Prudence in delegation. Abuse of discretion may also be found in failure to exercise prudence in the degree or manner of delegation. Prudence thus requires the trustee to exercise reasonable care, skill, and caution in the selection and retention of agents and in negotiating and establishing the terms of the delegation.

Significant terms of a delegation range from matters of agent compensation, and matters relating to the duration, termination, and other conditions of the delegation, to providing the agent with substantive direction and guidance. . . . Significant terms also include those providing the arrangements for supervision or for reporting and reviewing the agent's activities. . . .

The trustee then has a further duty to act with prudence in supervising or monitoring the agent's performance and compliance with the terms of the delegation. Upon discovering a breach of duty by the agent . . . the trustee has a duty to take reasonable steps to remedy it. . . .

Comment on Subsection (2):

e. Permissible delegation: in general. Although the administration of a trust may not be delegated in full (Comment *c*), a trustee may for many purposes delegate fiduciary authority to properly selected, instructed, and supervised or monitored agents.

Prudent delegation is not limited to the performance of ministerial acts. In appropriate circumstances delegation may extend, for example, to the selection of trust investments or the management of specialized investment programs, and to other activities of administration involving significant judgment.

It is not possible precisely to define acts that a trustee can properly delegate or the circumstances and conditions of proper delegation. A delegation of fiduciary authority is proper when it is prudently arranged and is reasonably intended to further sound administration of the trust. . . .

NOTES

1. *Statutory formulation.* Uniform Prudent Investor Act § 9 provides:

(a) A trustee may delegate investment and management functions that a prudent trustee of comparable skills could properly delegate under the circumstances. The trustee shall exercise reasonable care, skill, and caution in:

(1) selecting an agent;

(2) establishing the scope and terms of the delegation, consistent with the purposes and terms of the trust; and

(3) periodically reviewing the agent's actions in order to monitor the agent's performance and compliance with the terms of the delegation.

(b) In performing a delegated function, an agent owes a duty to the trust to exercise reasonable care to comply with the terms of the delegation.

(c) A trustee who complies with the requirements of subsection (a) is not liable to the beneficiaries or to the trust for the decisions or actions of the agent to whom the function was delegated. . . .

More general but to substantially similar effect is UTC § 807.

2. *Evaluating developments.* The old ban on delegation served useful objectives in safeguarding trusts from having to pay twice for the same services and in compelling the trustee to use care in selecting agents but was subject to sound criticism as unrealistic, particularly when it came to putting together a modern trust portfolio. See Langbein & Posner, Market Funds and Trust–Investment Law, 1976 A.B.F. Res. J. 1, 18–24; Cary & Bright, The Delegation of Investment Responsibility for Endowment Funds, 74 Colum. L. Rev. 207 (1974). Thus, for some time it has been common practice for fiduciaries, corporate as well as individual, to seek assistance from outside advisers and market analysts in designing investment strategies. It may, however, be necessary for the trustee to pay the adviser's fee out of the trustee's commission. See Chase v. Pevear, 419 N.E.2d 1358 (Mass.1981) (payment to adviser approved when trustee took no separate trustee's fee).

For differing assessments of the changes in the duty with respect to delegation, compare Langbein, Reversing the Nondelegation Rule of Trust–Investment Law, 59 Mo. L. Rev. 105 (1994), with Curtis, The Transmogrification of the American Trust, 31 Real Prop. Prob. & Tr. J. 251 (1996).

3. *Investment in mutual funds.* Early authority concluded that a fiduciary who invested in a mutual fund violated the duty not to delegate discretionary responsibilities, but an influential article, Shattuck, The Legal Propriety of Investment by American Fiduciaries in the Shares of Boston–Type Open–End Investment Trusts, 25 B.U. L. Rev. 1 (1945), and an Ohio decision, In re Rees' Estate, 85 N.E.2d 563 (Ohio App. 1949), reversed the trend. Most states now authorize such investments by statute. See 4 Scott and Ascher on Trusts § 19.1.10. The trustee of a relatively small fund may find that mutual funds offer the only investment that provides an adequate return, ample diversification, and full employment of funds.

f. The Duty to Earmark and the Prohibition Against Commingling

Restatement (Third) of Trusts (2007)

§ 84. Duty to Segregate and Identify Trust Property

The trustee has a duty to see that trust property is designated or identifiable as property of the trust, and also a duty to keep the trust property separate from the trustee's own property and, so far as practical, separate from other property not subject to the trust.

Comment:

a. Duty in general. It is ordinarily the duty of the trustee: to earmark the trust property as property of the trust . . . ; to keep the trust property separate from the trustee's own property . . . ; and to keep the trust property separate from property held by the trustee upon other trusts. . . .

b. Duty not to commingle trust property with trustee's own. A trustee has a duty not to commingle property of the trust with the trustee's own property. Thus, it is improper for a trustee to deposit money of the trust in the trustee's personal account in a bank. . . .

c. Duty not to mingle property of separate trusts. It is ordinarily the duty of a trustee not to mingle property held upon one trust with property held upon another trust, whether the two or more trusts are created by the same or different settlors. . . .

NOTE

Common trust funds. Almost all states now permit (many by the Uniform Common Trust Fund Act), a corporate fiduciary to hold the assets of various trusts in a common trust fund. See 4 Scott and Ascher on Trusts § 19.1.9.

3. VARIABLES AFFECTING THE IMPOSITION OF LIABILITY

a. Identification of the Fiduciary

(i) *Multiple Fiduciaries.* Traditionally, co-trustees of private trusts have had to act unanimously. Thus, a trustee's liability did not necessarily depend on his or her direct participation in a breach of trust. Moreover, in situations in which the unanimity rule still applies, it effectively gives each trustee a veto, in the absence of judicial instruction. To address both of these concerns, the terms of trusts that have more than two trustees commonly provide for majority rule.

Moreover, the unanimity rule is in decline. Restatement (Third) of Trusts § 39 (2003) provides: "Unless otherwise provided by the terms of the trust, if there are two trustees their powers may be exercised only by concurrence of both of them, absent an emergency or a proper delegation; but if there are three or more trustees their powers may be exercised by a majority." Likewise, UTC § 703(a) provides: "Cotrustees who are unable to reach a unanimous decision may act by majority decision."

Regardless of whether the unanimity rule applies, no trustee can be purely passive and leave the burdens of administration to the others. Such a trustee may be liable for failing to police the others or for wrongfully delegating his or her authority to them. Because of these independent responsibilities, a minority trustee may hire an attorney of his or her own choice at the trust's expense. See Belcher v. Conway, 425 A.2d 1254 (Conn.1979).

The unanimity rule does not apply to co-executors or co-administrators. Each is ordinarily competent to act for the estate. Personal representatives are therefore less strictly accountable for each other's defaults, though, in the case of a default, they do have an obligation to seek redress on behalf of the estate. See Estate of Rothko, supra p. 771.

(ii) *Degree of Expertise.* Uniform Prudent Investor Act § 2(f), supra p. 790; UTC § 806; and Restatement (Third) of Trusts § 77(3) (2007) all provide that a trustee who has special skills or makes representations of special skills is under a duty to use those special skills. Thus, a corporate fiduciary may be judged by a higher standard than an ordinarily prudent individual fiduciary. See, e.g., In re Mendenhall, 398 A.2d 951 (Pa.1979). See generally Leslie, Common Law, Common Sense: Fiduciary Standards and Trustee Identity, 27 Cardozo L. Rev. 2713 (2006).

b. Consent of the Beneficiaries

If a beneficiary knows, in advance, of a fiduciary's proposed conduct and consents to it, the consenting beneficiary may not thereafter challenge the fiduciary's conduct. Likewise, if a beneficiary learns, after the fact, of a fiduciary's conduct and ratifies it, the ratification estops that beneficiary from contesting the fiduciary's conduct. It appears, however, that the beneficiary's knowledge of the fiduciary's conduct or proposed conduct must be quite complete. See John R. Boyce Family Trust v. Snyder, 128 S.W.3d 630 (Mo. App. 2004); In re Hunter, 739 N.Y.S.2d 916 (Sur. 2002). Moreover, silence does not constitute acquiescence. See Renz v. Beeman, 589 F.2d 735 (2d Cir.1978), cert. denied, 444 U.S. 834 (1979). Nor are casual conversations likely to give rise to a finding of beneficiary consent. See, e.g., Estate of Cooper, 913 P.2d 393 (Wash.App.) ("Daddy, I want you to take care of everything just as you always have," did not waive daughter's right to require prudent trust management from her father), review denied, 928 P.2d 414 (Wash.1996); Estate of Janes, 630 N.Y.S.2d 472 (Sur. 1995), modified on other grounds, 643 N.Y.S.2d 972 (App. Div. 1996), aff'd, 681 N.E.2d 332 (N.Y.1997) ("loose statements [by beneficiary that she 'loved Kodak'] can hardly be equated with a consent to the retention" of Kodak stock).

In states that apply the doctrine of virtual representation, consent or ratification by adult beneficiaries may bind contingent beneficiaries who are not yet ascertained or are minors, so long as the adults have no conflict of interest or other hostility toward those whom they represent. See, e.g., Estate of Lange, 383 A.2d 1130 (N.J.1978).

c. Advice of Counsel

The fiduciaries in *Rothko*, supra p. 771, argued, as a defense, that they had acted on the advice of counsel. This did not, however, immunize them from the consequences of their defaults. Reliance on advice of counsel may help to establish that the fiduciary has acted in good faith and with due diligence, but it certainly does not confer blanket immunity. See, e.g., In re Trust of Mintz, 282 A.2d 295 (Pa.1971).

d. Exculpatory Clauses

Wills and trust agreements frequently contain language, generally referred to as "exculpatory clauses," that purport to immunize fiduciaries from liability for various breaches of duty. It is a contradiction in terms, of course, to suggest that a fiduciary is totally exempt from accountability; otherwise, the fiduciary would own the property outright. Accordingly, the courts have generally construed and applied exculpatory clauses strictly. Usually, an exculpatory clause saves a fiduciary from liability only if the breach in question falls precisely within the scope of an immunity clearly conferred. Moreover, to the extent that an exculpatory clause purports to confer too broad an immunity, the clause itself may violate public policy. See, e.g., UTC § 1008; N.Y. EPTL § 11–1.7; Tex. Prop. Code § 114.007(a). No doubt one of the reasons for the frosty judicial reception is that exculpatory clauses are often drafted and included at the request of corporate or professional fiduciaries who also insist on handsome compensation. Notwithstanding these limitations, exculpatory clauses remain extremely popular with both testators and settlors, who are generally keenly interested in doing everything they can to protect family members and close friends whom they have asked to serve as fiduciaries from lawsuits, frivolous or otherwise.

At least in theory, exculpatory provisions are distinct from grants of discretionary power. An exculpatory clause is "not an enlargement of power, but a limitation of liability. As such it is more in the nature of an affirmative defense than a factor bearing on the standard of care." Moore, A Rationalization of Trust Surcharge Cases, 96 U. Pa. L. Rev. 647, 674–75 (1948). The distinction between immunizing a fiduciary for committing a breach of duty and authorizing a fiduciary to do that which would otherwise constitute a breach of duty, however, is extremely thin. Cf. Tex. Prop. Code § 114.007(c) (distinguishing a term of a trust "that may otherwise relieve a trustee from liability for a breach of trust" from one "relieving the trustee from a duty or restriction imposed by this subtitle or by common law"). So it should come as no surprise that there is also authority for the proposition that an exculpatory clause can reduce the degree of care and prudence required of a fiduciary. See, e.g., Estate of Niessen, 413 A.2d 1050 (Pa.1980).

See generally Leslie, Trusting Trustees: Fiduciary Duties and the Limits of Default Rules, 94 Geo. L.J. 67 (2005).

e. Court Approval

Fiduciaries need not act at their peril; generally, they can seek the instructions of a court in advance. See 3 Scott and Ascher on Trusts § 16.8. The New York Court of Appeals has applied this principle even in cases involving the most sacrosanct trust duty: "[T]he rule against self-dealing has not been applied, and does not apply, to interdict the purchase of trust property by a trustee where the court, after conducting a full adversary hearing at which all interested parties are represented, approves and authorizes the sale." Matter of Scarborough Properties Corp., 255 N.E.2d 761 (N.Y.1969).

4. THE SUPERVISORY ROLE OF THE COURT

a. Abuse of Fiduciary Discretion

ESTATE OF STILLMAN

Surrogate's Court, New York County, 1980.
107 Misc.2d 102, 433 N.Y.S.2d 701.

MILLARD L. MIDONICK, SURROGATE.

The central issue in this proceeding is this: At what point does an "absolute and uncontrolled" discretion of trustees to withhold invasion of principal become an unreasonable abuse of that discretion?

The petitioners here, Guy Stillman and Dr. James Stillman, are grandsons of the testator James Stillman. They are income beneficiaries of two trusts under article Seventh of the will of the testator. Each of them complains of the failure on the part of the trustees of their respective trusts to invade principal requested in 1977, particularly for $145,000 requested by Guy Stillman and $150,000 requested by Dr. James Stillman.

Whatever interest the six children of Guy Stillman and the six children of Dr. James Stillman may have as remaindermen, they have been cited, and they have defaulted to the extent of the issues involved before me now. A contingent remainderman appears by counsel, who approves of the accounting in all respects and supports the trustees as not having abused their discretion to withhold principal invasions and as not having been imprudent in investment policies.

The testator James Stillman died in 1918 leaving one third of his residuary estate to his son, James A. Stillman, for his life, and provided that upon his death, which occurred in 1944, his issue should become income beneficiaries of equal shares of James A. Stillman's trust. James A. Stillman's trust commenced with a fund of approximately $9,000,000 in value in 1918. At the time of his death in 1944, this trust was split into four separate trusts as the will provided, for his four children, three grandsons and a granddaughter. Each of these four trusts was funded in 1944 with the amount of about $2,000,000. Each of the two trusts for the two complaining grandsons before me now is valued at approximately $8,500,000. (In 1977 Guy Stillman's trust approximated $8,370,000 and Dr. James Stillman's trust approximated $8,670,000.) From these, the two grandsons, petitioners, have derived income in excess of $300,000 annually in 1977 and in 1979 of approximately $425,000 annually, from each of their respective trusts.

Also in issue is the objection by the same two income beneficiaries, to the trustees' account in respect to what proportion of each of these trusts should be devoted to income-tax-free investments. Approximately one third of the principal of the trusts has been invested by this time in tax exempt income-producing securities, which these beneficiaries complain is inadequate in proportion to the entire corpus. The income beneficiaries' evidence places the tax-exempt income close to 20% of the total income. After deliberation, the court hereby rules favorably to the trustees whose judgment cannot be found to be improvident with respect to investment policies under the circumstances of this particular case. Essentially, the trustees have convinced the court that they have been fair to both the income beneficiaries with respect to the amount and character of the income, including the proportion which is tax exempt, and they have been equally fair to the presumptive remaindermen and the contingent remaindermen who are more interested in the preservation and appreciation of the principal than in the size of the income. . . .

With respect to the most vigorously contested issue in this proceeding, we return now to the problem whether the trustees have acted correctly in refusing to invade principal of Guy Stillman's trust to the extent of the $145,000 last requested of them by him and to invade principal of Dr. James Stillman's trust to the extent of the $150,000 last requested of them by him.

In order to frame the problem, we turn to the invasion article of the will, paragraph Tenth, which reads in its entirety:

> I. Upon any grandson of mine attaining the age of twenty-five years, during the continuance of a Trust hereunder for his benefit, I authorize and empower my said Trustees, if, in their absolute and uncontrolled discretion, they deem it advisable to do so, to convey, transfer and pay over to such grandson, out of the principal of the Trust, held for his benefit, property of the reasonable value, in the judgment of my said Trustees, of one-fifth, or of any less part, of the share so held for him.

II. Upon any grandson of mine attaining the age of thirty years, during the continuance of a Trust hereunder for his benefit, I authorize and empower my said Trustees, if, in their absolute and uncontrolled discretion, they deem it advisable to do so, to convey, transfer and pay over to such grandson, out of the principal of the Trust, held for his benefit, property of the reasonable value, in the judgment of my said Trustees, of two-fifths, or of any less part, of the share so held for him.

III. Upon any grandson of mine attaining the age of thirty-five years, during the continuance of a Trust hereunder for his benefit, I authorize and empower my said Trustees if, in their absolute and uncontrolled discretion, they deem it advisable to do so, to convey, transfer and pay over to such grandson, out of the principal of the Trust held for his benefit, property of the reasonable value, in the judgment of my said Trustees, of one-fifth, or of any less part, of the share so held for him.

IV. Upon any grandson of mine attaining the age of forty years, during the continuance of a Trust hereunder for his benefit, I authorize and empower my said Trustees if, in their absolute and uncontrolled discretion, they deem it advisable to do so, to convey, transfer and pay over to such grandson, the whole or any part of the remainder of the principal of the Trust held for his benefit.

The paramount consideration resolves itself to the basic intention of the testator concerning invasions and whether the trustees have deviated from the testator's plan. . . . The question here is whether the above language when read together with the entire instrument evidenced any condition for the invasion, such as need, or whether invasion was unconditional and equal to the right of petitioners to principal upon attaining various ages, or whether the trustees' "absolute and uncontrolled discretion" was intended by the testator to be based upon considerations neither of maturity of the life beneficiaries alone, nor of need alone, but upon those and other additional circumstances which the trustees have unreasonably disregarded.

In the case at bar, principal was to be disbursed at ages 25, 30, 35 and 40, i.e., ages of maturity, if in their "absolute and uncontrolled discretion, they deem it advisable to do so. . . ." These two grandsons have now attained the age of 62 in the case of Guy Stillman and of 76 in the case of Dr. James Stillman. Despite their advanced ages and obvious maturity, Dr. James Stillman has never received any principal of his $8,500,000 trust and Guy Stillman has received only $230,000 in 1974 of his $8,500,000 trust.

Upon receiving requests for invasion by each of these grandsons of the testator, the trustees used as their criterion for decision a relatively restrictive standard as the basis on which to measure and consider the purposes for which each grandson wished to have this principal.

In 1974, Guy Stillman advised that he wished to buy land adjoining a plantation he owns in Hawaii in order to profit from sugar cane farming. The trustees proceeded to employ independent business advisors who warned that a nearby sugar mill was about to close and that the business of sugar cane farming would not be profitable as a result. Guy Stillman responded that he could use a distant mill profitably. He also informed the trustees that in case it would not prove feasible to plant sugar cane, he could resort to a cattle-feeding crop. The trustees granted his request, and he used the $230,000 to acquire some but not all of the land specified, and to fund a farming project on his Hawaiian property. The nearby mill thereafter closed as he had been warned, and he found that he could not profitably transport any sugar cane as he had told the trustees he had intended to do. After 1974 when he resumed his efforts, now in dispute, for further invasion about 1977, the trustees discovered that his cash flow problem stemmed from his having planted macadamia nut trees on his Hawaiian land rather than following either of the plans he had outlined in 1974. Since those trees had not come to production, his low tax write off and high upkeep costs were compelling him in 1977 to convert his home in Scottsdale, Arizona, into a commercial enterprise and to build another home with more moderate upkeep problems; he planned to use the $145,000 that he was requesting in 1977 for this purpose.

The trustees rejected the request for $145,000 in 1977 on the ground that Guy Stillman was able to manage without this money by using his own funds and by mortgage borrowing, and although this is disputed, perhaps on the further ground that he had shown fallible business judgment in respect to the use of the previous invasion money.

Similar criteria were used to reject Dr. James Stillman's request for $150,000 since the trustees found on the basis of net worth, his income tax returns, and his own assertions, that he could manage the conversion of his beach house in Texas into commercial purposes by using his own funds and by obtaining mortgage loans.

Apparently, no real consideration was given by the trustees to the essential plan of the testator to be derived from the terms of his will probated in 1918. Those purposes stand out quite clearly and the court finds the intent of the testator to have been different from the standards that the trustees have been using in considering invasion. The purpose that the testator had in mind for his grandsons were those of a careful testator intending to protect his then immature grandsons (Guy was then *en ven-*

tre sa mere, as yet unborn; James was then about 14) from creditors of every kind. As the years went by, the taxing authorities became one kind of potential creditor, perhaps the most depleting of all. This typical invasion language at ages 25, 30, 35 and 40, emphasizing uncontrolled and absolute discretion on the part of the trustees, constitutes more an urging of the trustees to invade than a restraint against invasion except for limited protective purposes. This is especially the case where a series of ages is set forth in the will for permitted partial cumulative distributions at which times the trustees are enabled to dispose to grandsons of an entire estate in stages culminating at age 40. . . .

It would be therefore a matter of questionable judgment for these trustees or income beneficiaries to extract excessive amounts of principal, because upon the deaths of these income beneficiaries, their estates will be subject to estate tax on such principal whereas no estate tax will be due on the principal if the respective trust continues to hold the principal. Apparently, the income beneficiaries are well aware of this problem because they have been quite modest in their requests for invasion, and their personal net worth is relatively modest compared to each trust's value of about $8,500,000. Indeed, Guy Stillman testified that his children are well cared for by his trust, but his personal net worth leaves his wife relatively less financially secure in the event of his death. He gives this concern for his wife as one reason why he requests $145,000 of invasion. He has gone ahead by other means, such as mortgaging, to build a home in Scottsdale, Arizona, without the help of the trustees' invasion and that home cost him approximately $360,000. Presumably, the $145,000 he is asking for will reduce or eliminate such mortgage and increase his net worth by that relatively modest amount. He points out that $145,000 constitutes less than two per cent of the principal of his trust.

Similar considerations seem to apply to Dr. James Stillman's request which was also turned down by the trustees because of lack of need and because of his ability to finance his Texas beach house conversion into a commercial enterprise through other means. Indeed, he informed the trustees that he could and would go ahead with such plan, even if the trustees would not help him by a contribution of $150,000. He, in fact, so acted.

The two trustees who testified agree in effect that the amounts requested and the purposes of the requests were reasonable but were not needed and were not economically feasible to produce income. The difficulty with the trustees' standards is that they do not conform with the plan set forth in the will of the grandfather of these income beneficiaries. It is quite clear that the trustees, one of which is an important banking institution, are applying standards to these grandsons almost as though they were lending them money which is bound to be returned as in a banking transaction, or as though these income beneficiaries are themselves fiduciaries who are required to be prudent and to avoid speculative investments.

Clearly there was no such condition to the invasion intended by the decedent. Moreover, there is no duty on the part of Guy Stillman or Dr. James Stillman as envisioned by the will to be infallible in business transactions or to be prudent in the sense that they are protecting other people's money as fiduciaries. It was their grandfather's intention that they be reasonably comfortable as well as free of creditors, including creditors in the form of unnecessary tax liabilities. These two Stillman grandsons seem to have conducted their lives financially in such a way as to avoid such pitfalls and they have attained ages 62 and 76 with their relatively modest property intact. They have not anticipated income or assigned income, nor are they being hounded by creditors of any sort. . . .

For all of these reasons the court hereby finds that the trustees quite innocently have misconstrued the testator's will and therefore have abused so-called absolute and uncontrolled discretion to withhold principal in these two instances.

> If discretion is conferred upon the trustee in the exercise of a power, the court will not interfere unless the trustee in exercising or failing to exercise the power acts dishonestly, or with an improper even though not a dishonest motive, or fails to use his judgment, or acts beyond the bounds of a reasonable judgment.

(Restatement, Trusts 2d, § 187, Comment e . . .).

The trustees have overprotected these beneficiaries contrary to the intention expressed by the testator in his will. That intention is essentially that invasion of principal shall be favorably considered, after stated ages of grandsons, if such invasion will, on balance, enhance the quality of the lives of such grandsons, by benefiting them rather than creditors of any kind.

The fact that the trustees have thus abused their discretion, but in good faith, makes it clear that there is no need to remove these trustees. The fine record of the trustees in enhancing the equity of these trusts while earning substantial income, also persuades the court of the wisdom of retaining their services as fiduciaries.

. . . Nothing in this opinion, however, can be construed as compelling the trustees to comply with future invasion requests or demands, however moderate; this decision rules only upon the current requests, leaving future requests for invasion still subject to the absolute and uncontrolled discretion of the majority of the trustees, short of their unreasonably abusing their testamentary mandate.

[The Surrogate overruled the objections of the two income beneficiaries to the amount of attorneys' fees, payment of them out of the trust, and payment to the trustees of their statutory commissions] because they have done a commendable job by way of investments and equity appreciation, and because they have in good faith pursued their decisional duties with respect to invasions even though they have been too restrictive in respect to the two current requests for principal invasions.

NOTES

1. *Black-letter formulation.* Restatement (Third) of Trusts § 87 (2007) puts it this way: "When a trustee has discretion with respect to the exercise of a power, its exercise is subject to supervision by a court only to prevent abuse of discretion." In commentary, the Restatement continues:

> A court will not interfere with a trustee's exercise of a discretionary power (or decision not to exercise the power) when that conduct is reasonable, not based on an improper interpretation of the terms of the trust, and not otherwise inconsistent with the trustee's fiduciary duties. . . . Thus, judicial intervention is not warranted merely because the court would have differently exercised the discretion.

> On the other hand, a court may be called upon to intervene for the purpose of preventing a trustee's abuse (including by misinterpretation) of discretionary authority. What constitutes an abuse of discretion depends on the terms and purposes of the trust, and particularly on the terms and purposes of the power and any standards or guidance provided for its exercise, as well as on applicable principles of fiduciary duty. . . . Also relevant is the extent of the discretion conferred upon the trustee. . . . [Id. cmt. b.]

Cases abound in which the courts describe their function as policing, not usurping, the discretion of the trustee. In *Stillman*, should Surrogate Midonick have set out the parameters within which the trustees were to exercise their discretion and then sent the matter back to them to set the actual dollar amount?

2. *Standards.* Settlors who authorize their trustees to make distributions to or for the benefit of one or more beneficiaries often employ "standards" to inform or limit the trustees' discretion. In a "support trust," for example, the trustee may or must make distributions to or for the benefit of one or more beneficiaries *for their support.* An alternative is a trust to maintain one or more beneficiaries "in the style to which they have become accustomed." Other trusts are for the education of one or more beneficiaries. Standards such as these are said to be "ascertainable," because they provide both the trustee

and the court with relatively clear guidance. A great many trusts include ascertainable standards relating to the distributees' health, education, maintenance, or support ("HEMS") because federal tax law excludes powers to distribute thus limited from its definition of a general power of appointment. See Note 1, infra p. 1032. Other standards are considerably less restrictive, as, for example, in the case of a power to distribute for a beneficiary's *comfort*. Whatever the standard, the trustee must try to understand it fully and apply it faithfully. See Estate of Wallens, 877 N.E.2d 960 (N.Y. 2007) ("even when the trust instrument vests the trustee with broad discretion to make decisions regarding the distribution of the trust funds, a trustee is still required to act reasonably and in good faith in attempting to carry out the terms of the trust"); *Stillman*, supra. Questions of interpretation often arise. Among them is whether the trustee, in deciding whether to make a distribution, and in determining its size, may or must take into account the beneficiary's own resources. For example, may or must the trustee of a support trust make distributions to or for the support of a beneficiary who is capable of supporting himself or herself? Perhaps precisely because the question is one of interpretation, the cases go both ways. See Harootian v. Douvadjian, 954 N.E.2d 560 (Mass. App. 2011) (trustee-beneficiary who had other resources did not abuse discretion in making distributions to herself); In re Goodman, 790 N.Y.S.2d 837 (Sur. 2005) (construing will as requiring trustees to consider beneficiary's other resources), aff'd, 821 N.Y.S.2d 918 (App. Div. 2006); Scott and Ascher on Trusts § 13.2.4.

3. *Invasions of principal.* An invasion of principal reduces the amount available to generate income and for future distribution. Thus, even when the governing instrument authorizes invasions, the trustee may face a difficult decision. In Emmert v. Old Nat'l Bank of Martinsburg, 246 S.E.2d 236 (W.Va.1978), one of two brothers, both income beneficiaries, petitioned the trustee to exercise its discretion to invade corpus on his behalf in the amount of $100,000. He argued that he was "necessitous," because he suffered from an incurable disease that made it impossible for him to work and had incurred $48,000 of medical bills. The trustee refused, primarily because it would have had to make a similar distribution of $100,000 to the other brother, thereby reducing the $230,000 corpus to $30,000, thus greatly reducing the trust's future income stream and practically eliminating contingent remainder interests. There was additional evidence that the petitioning brother had squandered monies he had previously received from the trust. The appellate court reversed the trial court's order sustaining the trustee's decision, ordered protection of the other brother's interests by dividing the corpus into two trusts, and remanded:

> [W]e come to the question of appellant's needs. Having determined that The Old National Bank of Martinsburg, as trustee, has abused its discretion in refusing to make principal distributions to Frank S. Emmert, we are remanding this case to the Circuit Court of Berkeley County for a hearing to determine the frequency and amount of principal distributions. The circuit court should consider all the evidence concerning

the appellant's assets, liabilities, and available financial resources. It is the present needs of the appellant and not his past extravagances that should control the court's determination. At the same time, blind approval of appellant's demand for $100,000 should not be given because it is the amount necessary for comfort and support and not what the beneficiary desires that is controlling. The court can easily determine support but meaning must also be given to "comfort." The circuit court should keep in mind that comfort is not a "mere quantum sufficient to eat, to drink and to wear . . ." but that it denotes whatever is necessary to give security from want, including reasonable physical, mental and spiritual fulfillment. A meager distribution might not fulfill the testator's intentions, but at the same time one too large could cause detriment to the beneficiary himself. The court should weigh the possibility that too rapid a reduction of principal could leave the beneficiary in want later in life (contrary to the testator's intention that he be provided for) and at the same time consider the beneficiary's needs and his station in life. Furthermore the bank should consider the probable life expectancy of Frank Emmert and the maximum benefit which combined interest and principal can provide him during his remaining life in the event that he is totally destitute of other sources of income.

We hope the hearing fairly accommodates all the competing interests of existing and contingent beneficiaries, is faithful to the testator's intent, and is just under all the circumstances. We hope that it marks the end of protracted and expensive litigation in this case, but we cannot say that in the event of some extraordinary and unanticipated circumstances the appellant's needs may not change. In such event we hope the trustee will voluntarily exercise its discretion to increase the distributions if the appellant's needs are greater, and we hope the appellant will voluntarily accept a reduction in the principal if the circumstances warrant. [246 S.E.2d at 244–45.]

See also First Nat'l Bank of Beaumont v. Howard, 229 S.W.2d 781 (Tex.1950) (upholding invasion for need as to one sister but denying it as to second sister).

b. Modification, Reformation, and Equitable Deviation

SMITH V. HALLUM

Supreme Court of Georgia, 2010.
286 Ga. 834, 691 S.E.2d 848.

HUNSTEIN, CHIEF JUSTICE.

This case involves the equitable modification of a trust pursuant to OCGA § 53-12-153. The trust in issue is the J.D. Smith Irrevocable Trust created in 1990 by John Dewey Smith ("Settlor"). As OCGA § 53-12-153 mandates, modification is warranted only where it is established by clear and convincing evidence that, "owing to circumstances not known to or anticipated by the settlor, compliance would defeat or substantially impair the accomplishment of the purposes of the trust." Id. Because the trial court abused its discretion in concluding that appellee Judith Hallum, in her capacity as trustee, carried her burden of showing by clear and convincing evidence that modification of the J.D. Smith Irrevocable Trust ("Trust") was warranted, we reverse.

"[T]he cardinal rule in construing a trust instrument . . . is to discern the intent of the settlor and to effectuate that intent within the language used and within what the law will permit. [Cits.]" Miller v. Walker, 270 Ga. 811, 815, 514 S.E.2d 22 (1999). The trial court found, and appellee admitted in verified pleadings, that Settlor established the Trust for the purpose of providing for his descendants when he and his wife are no longer living. The Trust's sole asset is a life insurance policy in the face amount of $800,000 on the joint lives of Settlor and his wife, Inez Smith. It is uncontroverted that appellant Alden Smith, as the son of Settlor's only child, is a descendant of Settlor.[28]

Settlor died in 2003; Inez Smith is still alive. In October 2004, Inez Smith survived an attack in her home during which she was shot and also stabbed over 20 times. Appellant has been charged with aggravated assault, aggravated battery and other offenses in connection with the attack. However, those charges remain pending and issues regarding appellant's competency to stand trial on those charges have not been resolved.

In May 2005 appellee filed a petition to amend the Trust pursuant to OCGA § 53-12-153 in order to "forego any distributions of Trust property to" appellant. [T]he trial court, without any opposition by appellee, granted the motion filed by appellant's attorney on his behalf for the appointment of a guardian ad litem for an incapacitated adult. The grounds for the motion included the representations that appellant "suffers from a psychotic disorder that includes paranoid delusions" and that a forensic psychologist who examined appellant had determined that appellant's "psychotic disorder has the effect of rendering him incapable to assist counsel in this matter as a result of the pervasive delusions which are [i]ntertwined with the fact pattern underlying [appellant's] behavior."

The record reveals that the litigation was continued several times pending resolution of the criminal charges, a delay that included the trial court's recognition in April 2007 that the criminal trial court had found appellant "to be presently incompetent to stand trial" and had ordered him to be evaluated to determine whether he "is competent to stand trial in his criminal case or whether there is a substantial probability that [he] will at some future time obtain mental competency to stand trial." The

---

[28] The child predeceased Settlor, who also has a granddaughter by that same child. She is the mother of Settlor's two great-grandchildren.

record also reveals that, notwithstanding appellee's argument that modification was necessary because Settlor's intent was not to "incentivize [sic] his grandson to attack his grandmother to speed his receipt of Trust benefits," at the time this matter was heard by the trial court in January 2009, there had been no evidentiary determination in appellant's criminal proceedings regarding his intent in allegedly attacking Inez Smith. Moreover, even if we assume . . . that clear and convincing evidence exists that appellant actually perpetrated the attack on Inez Smith, the transcript of the January 2009 hearing clearly establishes that appellee adduced no evidence . . . to establish that appellant's attack was motivated by his greed for the Trust receipts rather than as the result of the alleged paranoid delusions that had justified the trial court's appointment of a guardian ad litem for appellant.

OCGA § 53-12-153 "gives courts equitable powers of modification in extraordinary circumstances to change administrative or other terms, but only when the intent of the settlor would be defeated by circumstances unanticipated or unknown at the time of the trust's establishment." Friedman v. Teplis, 268 Ga. 721, 722(1), 492 S.E.2d 885 (1997). Based on the assumption above that appellant committed the attack on Inez Smith, we recognize that the evidence would support the trial court's conclusion that this attack was a circumstance unanticipated by Settlor, inasmuch as it is uncontroverted that appellant was only seven years old at the time the Trust was created. However, the unknown or unanticipated event requirement in OCGA § 53-12-153 is only part of the equation. Equitable modification is authorized only when such action is also necessary to *avoid* the defeat or substantial impairment of the trust's purpose. Friedman, supra; see also 3 Scott and Ascher on Trusts, § 16.4 (5th ed.). Given that the purpose of the Trust in this case is to provide financially for Settlor's descendants when he and his wife are no longer living, the modification approved by the trial court actively *promotes* the defeat of the Trust's purpose in that, by artificially treating one of Settlor's descendants as having predeceased him, it removes that descendant from among those entitled to receive Trust proceeds.

Moreover, even assuming . . . that removal of a beneficiary in this manner is a proper subject of modification under OCGA § 53-12-153,[29]

---

[29] Even though a review of the law and learned treatises has revealed a "staggering range of changes that have been conceptualized as deviations relating to trustees' powers," (footnote omitted), 5 Scott and Ascher on Trusts, supra, § 33.4, p. 2172, research has failed to uncover a single case in which a trust was modified so as to exclude a beneficiary based on the beneficiary's criminal conduct towards others. Because of the evidentiary flaws in this case, however, we need not resolve the question whether the power to modify granted the courts by OCGA § 53-12-153 extends to altering the dispositive provisions of trusts by removing beneficiaries in this manner. See Bogert and Radford, The Law of Trust and Trustees, Secs. 975-1030, § 994, p. 189 (3rd ed.) (the power of the court to modify does not extend to altering the dispositive provisions by introducing new beneficiaries, or removing old ones, or changing the shares of the beneficiaries). Compare Restatement (Third) of Trusts § 66(1) (court may modify an administrative or distributive provision of a trust, or direct or permit the trustee to deviate from an administrative or dis-

there is no clear and convincing evidence that it would "defeat or substantially impair" the purpose of the Trust for appellant to receive Trust funds. Appellee claims that appellant attacked Inez Smith in order to accelerate his receipt of the Trust funds and . . . speculates that Settlor would have wanted the Trust modified to prevent appellant from profiting from his wrongdoing. We need not speculate whether . . . Settlor's intent in creating the Trust would have been substantially impaired thereby. That is because appellee failed to adduce *any* evidence to establish that appellant intentionally attacked Smith for this reason. Given the strong evidence in the record that appellant is suffering from a serious mental illness, e.g., the trial court's appointment of a guardian ad litem for appellant as an incapacitated adult, the lack of any opposition thereto, and the trial court's own recognition of the unresolved competency issues in the criminal proceedings against appellant, the possibility remains that appellant's attack on Smith was not motivated by greed but instead arose out of a paranoid delusion caused by a psychotic disorder. Hence, despite the attack, Settlor might well have wanted appellant, his only grandson, to receive Trust proceeds in order to facilitate treatment for his illness.

"[T]he most important issue for the trial court is whether the denial of the modification will impair the purpose of the trust." (Footnote omitted.) Friedman, supra, 268 Ga. at 722(1), 492 S.E.2d 885. Because the record does not contain the clear and convincing evidence required by OCGA § 53-12-153 to establish that it would defeat or substantially impair the purpose of the Trust for appellant (should he survive Inez Smith) to receive his share of the Trust funds, we conclude that the trial court abused its discretion by ordering equitable modification of the trust at issue. . . .

Judgment reversed.

CARLEY, PRESIDING JUSTICE, dissenting.

. . . The majority relies in part on the apparent absence of precedent from any state authorizing the use of judicial modification to disinherit a named beneficiary based on alleged instances of misconduct. However, unlike the traditional rule in most states precluding any deviation from the distributive provisions of a trust, the Georgia statute "is not . . . limited to administrative terms." Comment to OCGA § 53-12-153. See also Restatement (Third) of Trusts § 66 reporter's notes on cmt. b (2003). The particular misconduct alleged in this case can certainly be described as extraordinary. I believe that the trial court was authorized to find by clear and convincing evidence that appellant shot and repeatedly stabbed

---

tributive provision, if because of circumstances not anticipated by the settlor the modification or deviation will further the purposes of the trust).

the very person whose death would trigger the distribution to him of $400,000 in Trust property. Under Georgia law, if Mrs. Smith had not managed to survive the attack or if Appellant had conspired with another to kill her, the trial court's modification would have been mandatory. OCGA § 53-1-5. See also OCGA § 33-25-13. The circumstances would, in effect, have been considered extraordinary as a matter of law. Although Georgia law does not mandate modification of the Trust as a result of the assault and serious injury of Mrs. Smith, those circumstances are nearly as grievous as felonious homicide or conspiracy to kill, and the trial court's decision to modify the Trust cannot be overturned absent an abuse of discretion. Friedman v. Teplis, 268 Ga. 721, 723(2), (3), 492 S.E.2d 885 (1997).

"[T]he courts have recognized a variety of 'unanticipated circumstances' that may support modification, including a change in tax or other laws [cits.] and a settlor's mistaken view regarding the effect of tax laws. [Cit.]" Friedman v. Teplis, supra at 722(1), 492 S.E.2d 885. If those types of circumstances justify modification, then surely modification is permissible where a beneficiary assaults and severely injures the settlor's wife, whose death would cause distribution of the trust property. That occurrence could not have been anticipated by Settlor when he established the Trust, at which time Appellant was seven years old. Likewise, it cannot be said that Settlor anticipated the severe attack on Mrs. Smith merely because he specifically provided for beneficiaries suffering from disability and there is evidence that Appellant is mentally incompetent. [T]he mere fact that Settlor supported Appellant by hiring an attorney when he was charged with nonviolent crimes does not necessarily show that Settlor anticipated an assault on Mrs. Smith. The trial court did not abuse its discretion in finding "by clear and convincing evidence that [Appellant's] assault on his grandmother is a circumstance that was unanticipated by [Settlor]." With respect to that issue, this Court has observed that "no hard and fast rules exist; rather, the most important issue for the trial court is whether the denial of the modification will impair the purpose of the trust. [Cit.]" Friedman v. Teplis, supra. Thus, I now turn to a consideration of this latter issue.

Initially I observe that modification of the trust would not frustrate its purpose to provide for Settlor's lineal descendants per stirpes, by eliminating not only Appellant, but also his unborn descendants, from receipt of Trust property. To the contrary, the trial court's treatment of Appellant as predeceased is narrowly tailored to prevent him from receiving a distribution of Trust property and does not affect any of his potential descendants. . . If Appellant has any children before Mrs. Smith dies, they will take under the Trust as modified. If he has any children after she dies, they would not take under the Trust either with or without the modification, because only descendants living at the time of Mrs. Smith's death will be eligible to participate in the distribution. . . .

Moreover, the Trust provides for the descendants of both Mrs. Smith and Settlor, and therefore benefits Mrs. Smith by relieving her of the full burden of that undertaking. Thus, denial of modification would undermine this purpose of the Trust by providing Appellant with a continuing financial incentive to hasten the death of his grandmother and by placing her in fear thereof. Therefore, the trial court did not abuse its discretion in finding, by clear and convincing evidence, that "the purpose of the Trust would be substantially impaired if [Appellant] were permitted to receive benefits from this Trust." . . .

NOTE

1. *More on equitable deviation.* The courts have long hesitated to authorize deviations from the dispositive provisions of a private trust. See Ladysmith Rescue Squad, Inc. v. Newlin, 694 S.E.2d 604 (Va. 2010); 5 Scott and Ascher on Trusts § 33.4. In particular, the courts have rarely authorized invasions not provided for in the governing instrument, added or subtracted beneficiaries, or permitted early termination, without the consent of all of the beneficiaries. It is true that when the sole current beneficiary is also eventually entitled to take the entire trust principal, the courts have sometimes allowed acceleration. Still, in the case of private trusts, the main function of equitable deviation has been to relieve trustees of archaic or unduly restrictive administrative provisions. See supra pp. 816–824. The clear trend, however, is to extend equitable deviation to dispositive provisions as well, even in private trusts. See UTC § 412; Restatement (Third) of Trusts § 66(1) (2003) (permitting judicial modification of, or deviation from, either administrative or dispositive provisions "if because of circumstances not anticipated by the settlor the modification or deviation will further the purposes of the trust"). Equitable deviation thus seems destined to play a role in the case of private trusts analogous to that which cy pres has long played in the case of charitable trusts. See supra pp. 698–726.

In re Riddell Testamentary Trust, 157 P.3d 888 (Wash. App. 2007), involved trusts created by the settlors for their son, his wife, and their children. The trusts were to terminate, following the deaths of the son and his wife, when the grandchildren turned 35. Unbeknownst to the settlors, one of the grandchildren suffered from schizophrenia and bipolar disorder and was eventually institutionalized. As to her, the court reversed a ruling by the trial court refusing to authorize deviation for the creation of a "special needs trust." See Note 3, supra p. 636.

2. *Reformation on account of mistake.* The courts often reform trust terms that fail to reflect the settlor's true intentions as the result of a mistake of either fact or law. Almost invariably, the courts require clear and convincing evidence of both the mistake and the settlor's true intent. See UTC §

415; Restatement (Third) of Trusts § 62 & cmt. b (2003); Restatement (Third) of Property: Wills and Other Donative Transfers § 12.1 (2003). The typical case involves a "scrivener's error," i.e., one or more terms in a lawyer-prepared trust instrument that do not reflect the client's true intentions. See, e.g., Gassmann Revocable Living Trust v. Reichert, 802 N.W.2d 889 (N.D. 2011) ("Evidence from the attorney who drafted the trust that a specific drafting error occurred and, as a result, the trust language did not conform to the settlor's true intent may, if believed by the trier of fact, constitute clear and convincing evidence sufficient to warrant reformation of the trust."). There is even authority to the effect that the settlor, though neither a beneficiary nor a trustee, has standing to seek reformation for mistake. See Bilafer v. Bilafer, 73 Cal. Rptr. 3d 880 (App. 2008).

In re Trust of Isvik, 741 N.W.2d 638 (Neb. 2007), presented the following facts. The settlor of a revocable trust, dissatisfied with the corporate trustee, wrote the trustee: "I am revoking my trust as of this date. Consider this my notice . . . . Make no further transactions . . . and convey all materials pertaining to and including my holdings to me immediately." After the settlor's death, the trial court treated the letter as a trust term subject to reformation and admitted extrinsic evidence to show that the settlor never intended to revoke the trust but only to remove the bank and substitute herself as trustee. The supreme court reversed, holding that the evidence of mistake was not clear and convincing.

3. *Changes in the tax laws.* Do changes in the tax laws justify judicial modification of specific terms of a governing instrument? Compare Davison v. Duke University, 194 S.E.2d 761 (N.C.1973) (yes as to investment powers), with Givens v. Third Nat'l Bank in Nashville, 516 S.W.2d 356 (Tenn.1974) (no as to payment of undistributed income to remainder beneficiaries).

4. *Changes to take advantage of tax laws.* Frequently a will or trust agreement is less tax-efficient than it could have been, had it been designed or drafted differently. Reasons explaining the existence of the less efficient document may include: a deliberate and well-informed client decision to forgo the more efficient path (perhaps because the dispositive scheme necessary to achieve the more efficient result was unacceptable); failure of the client or the client's adviser to consider the more efficient alternative; and failure of the client's scrivener to secure the more efficient alternative, though chosen by the client. If discovery of the inefficiency occurs in time to remedy the tax situation, should a court "reform" the document? Traditionally, the courts have been willing to rewrite a trust instrument only on strong evidence that the document, as and when written, failed to comply with the client's intent. See, e.g., In re Trust Under Will of Darby, 234 P.3d 793 (Kan. 2010). Recently, however, some courts have "reformed" badly drafted and even badly conceived documents on the basis of little more than the assumption that the client would have wanted to minimize taxes, notwithstanding the fact that the requested modification involved an extensive rearrangement of beneficial interests. See, e.g., Simches v. Simches, 671 N.E.2d 1226 (Mass.1996). See

also UTC §§ 415 (reformation to correct mistakes), 416 (modification to achieve settlor's tax objectives); Restatement (Third) of Property: Wills and Other Donative Transfers § 12.2 (2003) ("A donative document may be modified, in a manner that does not violate the donor's probable intention, to achieve the donor's tax objectives."). For the effect of such a decree on the actual tax outcome, see Commissioner v. Estate of Bosch, 387 U.S. 456 (1967).

5. INCOME AND PRINCIPAL

a. Basic Principles

Uniform Principal and Income Act (1997)

Section 404. Principal Receipts. A trustee shall allocate to principal:

(1) to the extent not allocated to income under this [Act], assets received from a transferor during the transferor's lifetime, a decedent's estate, a trust with a terminating income interest, or a payer under a contract naming the trust or its trustee as beneficiary;

(2) money or other property received from the sale, exchange, liquidation, or change in form of a principal asset, including realized profit, subject to this [article]; . . . .

Section 405. Rental Property. To the extent that a trustee accounts for receipts from rental property pursuant to this section, the trustee shall allocate to income an amount received as rent of real or personal property, including an amount received for cancellation or renewal of a lease. An amount received as a refundable deposit, including a security deposit or a deposit that is to be applied as rent for future periods, must be added to principal and held subject to the terms of the lease and is not available for distribution to a beneficiary until the trustee's contractual obligations have been satisfied with respect to that amount.

Section 406. Obligation to Pay Money.

(a) An amount received as interest, whether determined at a fixed, variable, or floating rate, on an obligation to pay money to the trustee, including an amount received as consideration for prepaying principal, must be allocated to income without any provision for amortization of premium.

(b) A trustee shall allocate to principal an amount received from the sale, redemption, or other disposition of an obligation to pay money to the trustee more than one year after it is purchased or acquired by the trustee, including an obligation whose purchase price or value when it is acquired is less than its value at maturity. If the obligation matures within one year after it is purchased or acquired by the trustee, an amount received in excess of its purchase price or its value when acquired by the trust must be allocated to income. . . .

NOTE

Expenses. Sections 501 to 506 of the Uniform Principal and Income Act (1997) allocate the liability for court costs, attorney's fees, trustee's compensation, repairs, depreciation, taxes, and other expenses between income and principal.

b. Corporate Distributions

TAIT V. PECK

Supreme Judicial Court of Massachusetts, 1963.
346 Mass. 521, 194 N.E.2d 707.

CUTTER, JUSTICE.

Letitia M. Tait (the widow) seeks a declaratory decree with respect to an inter vivos trust (the trust) executed in 1935 by her late husband (the settlor). She asks the court to determine whether a certain distribution of capital gains to the trust, made by Broad Street Investing Corporation (Broad Street) in December, 1961, is to be treated as principal or income of the trust. The widow, life beneficiary of the trust, asserts that the capital gains distribution is income. The individual remaindermen and the trustees assert that it is a return of capital and hence should be added to principal. The parties filed an "Agreement as to the Evidence and All Material Facts," constituting a case stated. The probate judge reported the case, without decision, for the consideration of the full court. The facts as agreed are set forth below.

On December 9, 1935, the settlor transferred to the trustees, subject to the trust, 100 shares of Linden Associates (Linden) a Massachusetts trust. He "provided . . . that in the event of . . . liquidation of . . . Linden . . . during the [widow's] life . . . the [t]rustees . . . shall receive from . . . Linden . . . 'the distributive share in the assets of . . . Linden . . . properly allocable to them' " in trust "to pay over the net income . . . monthly to . . . [the widow] during her life, and upon her death to pay over . . . [the] trust fund . . . to" others. The settlor died on September 20, 1940. The holders of the vested remainder interests have been determined by an earlier court decree.

"Linden . . . was liquidated following the sale, as of July 12, 1961, of all its assets to Broad Street." The trust received 55,434 shares of Broad Street in exchange for the shares of Linden then held by it. In 1961, subsequent to July 12, Broad Street paid to the trustees of the trust two cash dividends from income and in addition, in December, 1961, Broad Street delivered to the trustees 1,463 additional shares of Broad Street as "distributions of gain," as distinguished from "dividend from income," on the shares then held by the trustees. The trustees paid to the widow the 1961 dividends from income paid to them by Broad Street in 1961 (less expenses and taxes) "but refused and still refuse to transfer" to the widow the 1,463 shares of Broad Street (less any expenses or taxes thereto allocable). The trustees, in support of their position, state that under Int. Rev. Code of 1954, § 852, the trustees must pay a Federal capital gains tax . . . on these shares of Broad Street so received as "distributions of gain."

"In the past quarter of a century or so, there . . . [have] grown up . . . in our investment economy so-called [m]utual [i]nvestment [t]rusts, wherein each share of the [t]rust . . . held . . . represents a share in the ownership of a number of [diversified] companies . . . [so that] the investor has a broad spread of risk and the benefit of the general investment management of the [m]utual [t]rust. It derives its earning from net income received in the form of dividends and interest paid on securities . . . held by the [investment] company, and also from net profits realized on the sale of [its] investments. . . . Broad Street . . . is such a . . . [company], subject to the operation of the Investment Company Act of 1940 . . . . It is so classified for tax purposes under the Internal Revenue Code" (Subchapter M—Regulated Investment Companies, Int. Rev. Code of 1954, §§ 851–855).

In its statements to the public, Broad Street says that its investments have two goals—(1) favorable current income, and (2) long term growth in both income and capital value. Dividends payable out of net income are paid quarterly, whereas distributions of gain realized on the sale of investments are paid at the end of each year. Since 1945, except for 1949, Broad Street has paid dividends from income. It has also paid distributions of capital gain to its shareholders either in stock, or in cash, at the option of the shareholder, except for the years 1936, 1937, and 1944 when capital gain distributions were paid in cash. The 1,463 shares were paid to the trustees in December, 1961, at their request. At their option, they could have received the equivalent of these shares in cash.

1. No party contends that the inter vivos trust shows what the settlor's intent was with respect to capital gains dividends. There are no special provisions concerning the allocation of receipts as between principal and income. Cf. Dumaine v. Dumaine, 301 Mass. 214, 222–224, 16 N.E.2d 625, 118 A.L.R. 834. Because the original trust fund consisted of shares of Linden, there may be (wholly apart from the usual investment powers of a trustee in Massachusetts) special indication of the settlor's approval of investment trust shares as a trust investment. See Loring, Trustee's Handbook (Farr Rev.) § 81. The settlor included in the trust no discretionary power to expend principal for the widow, which would have been a natural provision for him to make if he had intended that she be given more than the normal benefits afforded to a life beneficiary. Beyond these slight indications of the settlor's views, interpretation of the trust instru-

ment seems to us to be of no assistance. See Scott, Trusts (2d ed.) § 236.3, pp. 1819–1821.

2. The usual Massachusetts rule for the allocation of dividends was stated in Minot v. Paine, 99 Mass. 101, 108,

> A trustee needs some plain principle to guide him; and the cestuis que trust ought not to be subjected to the expense of going behind the action of the directors, and investigating the concerns of the corporation, especially if it is out of our jurisdiction. A simple rule is, to regard cash dividends, however large, as income, and stock dividends, however made, as capital.

See Lyman v. Pratt, 183 Mass. 58, 60, 66 N.E. 423. This simple rule, in practice, has come to be based in some degree, in certain instances, upon the substance, rather than the form alone, of the transaction as carried out by the entity declaring the dividend. . . . Dividends in cash in substance paid out of capital or in liquidation have been treated as belonging to principal. . . . The substance of a transaction has been examined to determine whether it was equivalent to a stock dividend. . . . Where the trustee, as shareholder, is given the option to receive a dividend in stock or in cash, the later cases, in effect, treat the dividend as a cash dividend and as income. . . . We look at the substance of the capital gain distribution made by Broad Street in December, 1961, against the background of these authorities. No prior Massachusetts case has presented the question whether such a distribution, received by a trustee, is to be treated as capital or income.

Decisions outside of Massachusetts have generally treated such capital gain dividends as income rather than principal. . . .

Some commentators have felt that dividends from net capital gains from the sales of securities held in a mutual fund's portfolio are income from the ordinary conduct of the fund's business, that the portfolio holdings are bought and sold like inventory or other corporate property of a business corporation, and that distributions from such gains, at least where there is opportunity to receive the distribution in cash, should be treated as income. Weight is given by these commentators to the circumstances that investors in investment companies rely on both income and capital gains as a part of the expected yield. It is suggested by at least one author (Professor Bogert) [Trusts and Trustees (2d ed.) § 858] that to invest in mutual funds would be a breach of trust, about which the life beneficiary could complain, unless the investment produced a normal trust investment yield. The contrary view is that the sale of a security in an investment company portfolio involves the sale of a capital item, so that, if the gain is distributed the capital is necessarily reduced. In some years such a company may experience net losses. It is argued that if capital gain distributions of other years have been paid to the income beneficiary, the trust principal will inevitably suffer in years of losses, which must be expected even in an era generally inflationary, so that, in effect, the investment company shares may become a wasting investment. It is also urged that a trustee's investment in an investment company is in substance nothing more than a fractional ownership in a diversified portfolio of securities, as to which the trustee should account as if he held the portfolio securities directly. The special character of regulated investment companies and their specialized tax treatment under the Internal Revenue Code also have some tendency to give capital gains distributions the aspect of principal.

If the dividends and distributions of a regulated investment company should be regarded as inherently the same as those of an ordinary industrial company, then the rule of Smith v. Cotting, 231 Mass. 42, 48–49, 120 N.E. 77, should be applied to Broad Street's 1961 capital gain distribution, which the trustees, at their option, could have received either in cash or in shares. It seems to us, however, that, when a fiduciary invests in investment company shares, he is entering into an arrangement more closely like participation in a common trust fund . . . than like an investment in the shares of an industrial company. His purpose generally will be to obtain for his trust beneficiaries (usually of a small trust) the same type of spread of investment risk which the trustee of a common trust fund can obtain for its participating trusts, or which the trustee of a large trust fund can obtain by a well conceived program of diversified direct investment.[30]

The arguments against the soundness of the analogy between investments in mutual funds and in a common trust fund (see e.g. Bogert, Trusts and Trustees [2d ed.] § 858, pp. 557–558 . . .) are to us unconvincing. It may be a sound reason for a trustee to refrain from investing in investment company shares that the return from dividends paid from ordinary income of such companies is low, so that the life beneficiary will suffer unless he receives also the capital gain distributions. It may be also that appropriate downward adjustment in the rate of trustee's fees should be made, if he invests substantially in investment company shares (because he is not burdened with investment management), with the consequence that the income return to the life beneficiary will be improved pro tanto. See discussion in Scott, Trusts (2d ed.) § 227.9A; Bogert, Trusts and Trustees (2d ed.) § 679, pp. 311–313. These matters we need not determine. The possible meager return does not change the substance of the

---

[30] Broad Street as of December 31, 1962, is reported by a standard manual to have had $249,079,948, invested in the common shares of 99 companies, in the preferred shares of seven companies, and in the bonds of twenty-four companies, plus some government bonds. See Wiesenberger, Investment Companies (1963 ed.) part 5, p. 12. Such an investment diversification could not possibly be directly achieved by any trustee unless the trust res was extraordinarily large.

investment as a reasonable attempt at risk diversification similar to that of the common trust fund. To say that the realized gains of a common trust fund are not distributed to the participating trust, whereas those of an investment company are distributed (primarily for tax reasons) to fiduciaries who are shareholders, is merely to state the obvious fact that a common trust is administered by the trustee itself, whereas the regulated investment company is a separate entity from the trustee who invests in its shares. If a trustee elects to take shares of the investment company in payment of any distribution made to him of capital gains, he will be able to achieve the same substantive result as that achieved by the common trust fund.

The method of determining the purchase and sale prices of investment company shares, in relation to the net asset value of shares, is consistent with the concept that the trustee is obtaining diversification by an indirect participation in the investment company's portfolio. It is apparent that if a fiduciary were to redeem his shares at a profit just before a capital gain distribution, he would necessarily allocate any gain to principal. No practical reason requires treating the capital gain distribution, when made, in any different way, or prevents retaining it as a part of the principal of the trust.

One major virtue of our Massachusetts rule for allocation between principal and income has been its simplicity as a rule of convenience. See Minot v. Paine, 99 Mass. 101, 108; Third Natl. Bank & Trust Co. v. Campbell, 336 Mass. 352, 354–355, 145 N.E.2d 703. To treat capital gains distributions of regulated investment companies as principal will not impair the simplicity of our rule, for no inquiry need be made as to the source of the distribution. The source must be announced, as it was in respect of Broad Street's capital gain distribution in December, 1961.

Since no binding precedent controls our decision, we are guided by the substance of the situation. We adopt the rule that distributions by a regulated investment company, from capital gains (whether made in the form of cash or shares or an option to take or purchase new shares), are to be allocated to principal. This is essentially the view adopted by the Commissioners on Uniform State Laws in 1962 after full deliberation. . . . The Commissioners' action can be taken as reflecting a considered current view of what is in the public interest. In effect, we think that the regulated company, from the standpoint of a trustee investing in its shares, is merely a conduit of its realized gains to the trust fund and that, in the hands of the trustee, the gains should retain their character as principal.

3. A decree is to be entered in the Probate Court (a) that the distribution of capital gains by Broad Street in December, 1961, in the hands of the trustees of the settlor's trust is to be treated as principal and not as

income, and (b) that future similar distributions to the trustees of capital gains by Broad Street also are to be allocated to principal. . . .

NOTES

1. *Uniform Principal and Income Act approach.* Uniform Principal and Income Act § 401 (1997) provides:

(a) In this section, "entity" means a corporation, partnership, limited liability company, regulated investment company, real estate investment trust, common trust fund, or any other organization in which a trustee has an interest [subject to certain exceptions].

(b) Except as otherwise provided in this section, a trustee shall allocate to income money received from an entity.

(c) A trustee shall allocate the following receipts from an entity to principal:

(1) property other than money;

(2) money received in one distribution or a series of related distributions in exchange for part or all of a trust's interest in the entity;

(3) money received in total or partial liquidation of the entity; and

(4) money received from an entity that is a regulated investment company or a real estate investment trust if the money distributed is a capital gain dividend for federal income tax purposes. . . .

2. *The impact of the uniform principal and income acts.* Both the original Uniform Principal and Income Act (1931) and the Revised Uniform Principal and Income Act (1962) were widely adopted, but the 1997 version of the Uniform Principal and Income Act has proven even more successful. Already, it has been enacted in forty-six states. Principal and income law continues to vary from state to state, however, in part because many states have enacted variations on the design or wording of the uniform act.

c. Equitable Adjustments

ENGLUND V. FIRST NATIONAL BANK OF BIRMINGHAM

Supreme Court of Alabama, 1980.
381 So.2d 8.

FAULKNER, JUSTICE. . . .

On December 12, 1929, Morris W. Bush executed his last will and testament, and appointed the American Trader National Bank of Birmingham (now The First National Bank of Birmingham) as executor and trustee. Under the terms of the will, Miss A. L. Williams, Bush's aunt received the net income for her life from one-fourth of the residuary estate, held in trust by the Bank. Bush's wife, Margaret Gage Bush, received the net income for her life from three-fourths of the estate for her support and comfort. In addition, if the trustee were satisfied that the net income from her share of the trust was not sufficient for her "proper support and comfort" it was authorized to pay to her any additional sum or sums out of the principal of said trust "as to it may seem necessary or desirable for such purposes." Upon the death of Mrs. Bush, the will provides that the

> . . . trustee shall hold the trust estate in trust for the equal use and benefit of my children living at decease of my said wife. . . .

> The Trustee shall hold the share of each child entitled to share in the trust estate upon the decease of my said wife in trust for such child for and during his or her lifetime, and shall pay over to such child, or use and apply for his or her support, education and comfort, the entire net income from his or her share of said trust estate and so much of the principal thereof as to the Trustee may seem necessary or desirable for such purposes; . . . .

The will further provides that upon the death of a child leaving descendants, those descendants (grandchildren of Morris Bush) shall receive the trust estate in equal shares if they are "of age"—if not they receive the net income from the trust, and so much of the principal as the trustee deems necessary or desirable for their support, education, and comfort, until they become "of age."

Mr. Bush died January 24, 1932, survived by his wife, one daughter, Gage, and his aunt, Miss Williams. The trust was established on December 10, 1933, with the Bank as trustee.

Miss Williams died in February, 1932. Mrs. Bush, therefore, became the sole income beneficiary. She died on June 27, 1971, survived by her daughter, Gage Bush Englund, and two granddaughters, Alixandra Gage Englund and Rachael Rutherford Englund.

At the time of Mr. Bush's death, the principal assets of his estate consisted of shares of capital stock of the Alabama By–Products Corporation and Alabama Chemical Products Company. In June, 1971, when Gage became the sole life beneficiary, the market value of the stock in Alabama By–Products and Alabama Chemical was about $10,535,000. On October 16, 1977, the trustee agreed to sell all of the stock in Alabama By–Products and Alabama Chemical to the Drummond Company for $31,090,400. After expenses and taxes, the trustee realized net proceeds of $17,628,513 from the sale.

From the sale of the stock, Gage Englund requested the trustee to allocate $900,000 to income instead of principal and distribute that money to her as income. She made that request under this provision of the will:

> The Trustee hereunder shall have the power to determine whether any money or property coming into its hands shall be treated as a part of the principal of this trust estate, or a part of the income therefrom, and to apportion between such principal and income any loss or expenditure in connection with the trust estate as to it may seem just and equitable.

This request was considered by the Trust Committee of the Bank, who adopted a resolution stating that the proposed allocation was a proper exercise of the trustee's power. They determined that the trustee would treat as income $900,000 in after-tax dollars of the capital gain resulting from the sale, subject to obtaining a declaratory judgment, and instruction from the Circuit Court that the trustee had the allocatory power.

The First National Bank as trustee filed a complaint on June 13, 1978, requesting instructions from the court and a declaratory judgment as to the proper construction of the clause. The trustee contended that this provision gave it authority to allocate trust receipts between income and principal in its absolute discretion. A guardian ad litem was appointed for the minor remaindermen and for any members of the class of remaindermen which might become entitled to any interest in the trust estate.

[T]he trial court adjudged that the trust instrument did not authorize the trustee to determine whether trust receipts were to be allocated to income or principal as the trustee might find to be just and equitable, except where there was reasonable doubt as to the character of the receipt in question. The trial court ruled that the proposed allocation of a portion of the capital gain realized on the sale of the stock to income would constitute an abuse of discretion. . . .

I.

On appeal we are asked to determine if the testator intended to give his trustee the discretionary power to determine whether money or property that it obtained should be treated as principal or income, without regard to rules of allocation which would apply in the absence of an expression of settlor's intent, [and] if the proposed allocation was an abuse of discretion. . . .

Even prior to the passage of the Alabama Principal and Income Act, courts recognized that profits on the sale of shares of stock which comprise a part of the trust corpus are ordinarily to be treated as principal.

Sherman v. Sherman, 5 Ohio St. 2d 27, 213 N.E.2d 360 (1966); G. Bogert, The Law of Trusts and Trustees, §§ 816, 823 (2d ed. 1962); 3 A. Scott, Law of Trusts, § 233.1 (3rd ed. 1967). . . .

Whether the above trust provision gives the trustee, FNB, the authority to determine which receipts are principal and which are income in its absolute and unfettered discretion or only the authority to make such a determination when the character of the receipt is unclear or doubtful, is the crux of this case.

In American Security & Trust Co. v. Frost, 73 App. D.C. 75, 117 F.2d 283 (D.C.Cir.1940), the testatrix provided in her will for a residuary trust leaving the income to her children and grandchildren for life and the corpus ultimately to be distributed to her descendants living at the time specified for final distribution. The executors/trustees sold certain securities which were a part of the trust estate, and also received a stock dividend during the estate administration. They decided that a portion of the proceeds of the stock sale and some of the shares received as a stock dividend were income which should be distributed to the life beneficiaries. On appeal, the Circuit Court considered whether Will Clause Eleven authorizing the executors/trustees "to decide finally any question that may arise as to what constitutes income and what principal . . ." empowered the trustees to allocate the funds and stock as income. The court first determined that there was no general intention expressed throughout the will as a whole to allow such a departure from the established rules regarding trusts. The court decided that the trial judge's interpretation of Clause Eleven was too broad:

> To say that Clause 11 empowers the trustees to "decide" contrary to local "rules of construction," proves too much. In a sense, every item of property is controlled by a "rule of construction." E.g., bonds received from the original estate would be corpus, the interest on those bonds, income. This is a "rule of construction" derived from the customs of the community. Surely, it would not be said that under the power given in Mrs. Lincoln's will, the trustees could override this rule. And yet if they may override some rules of construction and not others, there would be complicated questions of degree, e.g., whether one rule or another was so certain that the trustees must not overstep it.

There being no genuine question concerning the category in which the fund or stock fell, the court reversed the trial court's decision.

In the present case, an examination of the entire will does not reflect a clearly indicated intention on the part of Morris Bush to violate any rules of construction and give his trustee the power to make the requested allocation. Although he granted the trustee broad powers in other areas, he expressly provided a standard for the invasion of the principal of the trust on behalf of his daughter, Mrs. Englund—invasion to the extent that it seemed necessary or desirable to the trustee for Mrs. Englund's *support, education, or comfort*. It was estimated that in 1978 Mrs. Englund would receive approximately $1,000,000 in income from the trust and her purpose in requesting the $900,000 allocation was to provide a separate estate for her husband and to repay an interest-free $300,000 debt to the trust. It would have been an abuse of discretion for the trustee to have made the proposed allocation pursuant to the clause allowing invasion for support, education, or comfort as the trustee admitted no such need existed and that it could not and did not rely on this clause. Because of the presence of this clause allowing invasion of the principal pursuant to a fixed standard, we cannot say that the will as a whole reflected a general intention to allow the proposed allocation.

Although the clause in American Security & Trust Co. v. Frost, supra, is worded differently from the provision in Morris Bush's will, it expresses the same grant of authority to the trustee. In both instances the character of the receipt is clear; proceeds from the sale of trust securities are principal. Where proper allocation is not "a matter of honest doubt" the trustees are not authorized to make allocations between principal and income. See, Commissioner of Internal Revenue v. O'Keeffe, 118 F.2d 639, 642 (1st Cir.1941). The trial judge was correct in his decision that the trust provision in question did not authorize the allocation. We affirm this part of the decree. . . .

Affirmed in part, reversed [on another issue], and remanded.

TORBERT, C. J., and JONES, ALMON, and SHORES, JJ., concur. . . .

BEATTY, JUSTICE (concurring in part and dissenting in part):

I disagree with the conclusions of the majority on its interpretation of the language of this instrument.

It is true that profits on the sale of shares of stock are ordinarily to be allocated to principal. See First National Bank of Tuskaloosa v. Hill, 241 Ala. 606, 4 So. 2d 170 (1941); see also Code of 1975, §§ 19–3–271, –272. However, this proposition holds true only if there is no expression of a different intention on the part of the settlor, for it is well settled in this jurisdiction that *"[t]he intention of the settlor is the law of the trust* and if the nature, subject matter and objects are reasonably ascertainable and the scheme not inconsistent with some established rule of law or public policy, that intention must control and the courts will sustain and give it effect." (Emphasis added.) Stariha v. Hagood, 252 Ala. 158, 40 So. 2d 85 (1949). . . .

The provision of the trust instrument under which the trustee sought to allocate the $900,000 to income instead of principal gave to the trustee "the power to determine whether any money or property coming into its hands shall be treated as a part of the principal of the trust estate, or a part of the income therefrom. . . ." The language utilized by the testator in the provision quoted above clearly and unambiguously grants the trustee the authority to use its discretion in determining whether property received by the trust is to be held as principal or distributed as income. The trust document as a whole supports this conclusion, for an examination of that instrument reveals that the settlor sought to vest in the trustee a large amount of discretion in dealing with the trust estate. For example, the trustee was given the power to invest as it saw fit, regardless of any restrictions which would otherwise have been imposed by law. It was also given the power to form a corporation to which it could transfer all trust assets.

The majority's reliance on the provision allowing invasion of the corpus of the trust for the support, education, or comfort of the beneficiary is misplaced under the circumstances of this case. Although that provision would seem to serve as a limitation on the trustee's power to distribute principal, I fail to perceive its relationship to the trustee's power to determine what constitutes principal. The former power comes into being only after the exercise of the latter. As a result, the trustee under the will of Morris W. Bush had the authority to classify the property received by the trust as income. Cases from other jurisdictions support this position. See, e.g., Sherman v. Sherman, 5 Ohio St. 2d 27, 213 N.E.2d 360 (1966); Hopkins v. Cleveland Trust Co., 120 N.E.2d 457 (Ohio App. 1954); Dumaine v. Dumaine, 301 Mass. 214, 16 N.E.2d 625 (1938). . . .

BLOODWORTH, MADDOX and EMBRY, JJ., concur.

NOTES

1. *The conflict between "total return" investing and traditional notions of principal and income.* One of the central teachings of the prudent investor rule is that a fiduciary, investing for total return, should generally focus on the portfolio as a whole, rather than on its individual components. Yet, under traditional notions of principal and income, the source of each individual receipt determines its character. The fiduciary who exploits the investment flexibility of modern portfolio theory to maximize total return (consistent with an appropriate level of risk), but who must then allocate receipts between income beneficiaries and remainder beneficiaries in accordance with the rules defining income and principal, is very likely to short-change one or the other, thereby violating the duty of impartiality.

2. *Equitable adjustments.* The 1997 Uniform Principal and Income Act authorizes a fiduciary investing in accordance with the prudent investor rule

to depart from traditional notions of principal and income, by adjusting between principal and income, in order to avoid violating the duty of impartiality:

Section 103. Fiduciary Duties; General Principles.

(a) In allocating receipts and disbursements to or between principal and income . . . a fiduciary:

(1) shall administer a trust or estate in accordance with the terms of the trust or the will, even if there is a different provision in this [Act];

(2) may administer a trust or estate by the exercise of a discretionary power of administration given to the fiduciary by the terms of the trust or the will, even if the exercise of that power produces a result different from a result required or permitted by this [Act];

(3) shall administer a trust or estate in accordance with this [Act] if the terms of the trust or the will do not contain a different provision or do not give the fiduciary a discretionary power of administration; and

(4) shall add a receipt or charge a disbursement to principal to the extent that the terms of the trust and this [Act] do not provide a rule for allocating the receipt or disbursement to or between principal and income.

(b) In exercising the power to adjust under Section 104(a) or a discretionary power of administration regarding a matter within the scope of this [Act], whether granted by the terms of a trust, a will, or this [Act], a fiduciary shall administer a trust or estate impartially, based on what is fair and reasonable to all of the beneficiaries, except to the extent that the terms of the trust or the will clearly manifest an intention that the fiduciary shall or may favor one or more of the beneficiaries. A determination in accordance with this [Act] is presumed to be fair and reasonable to all of the beneficiaries.

Section 104. Trustee's Power to Adjust.

(a) A trustee may adjust between principal and income to the extent the trustee considers necessary if the trustee invests and manages trust assets as a prudent investor, the terms of the trust describe the amount that may or must be distributed to a beneficiary by referring to the trust's income, and the trustee determines, after applying the rules in Section 103(a), that the trustee is unable to comply with Section 103(b).

(b) In deciding whether and to what extent to exercise the power conferred by subsection (a), a trustee shall consider all factors relevant to the trust and its beneficiaries, including the following factors to the extent they are relevant:

(1) the nature, purpose, and expected duration of the trust;

(2) the intent of the settlor;

(3) the identity and circumstances of the beneficiaries;

(4) the needs for liquidity, regularity of income, and preservation and appreciation of capital;

(5) the assets held in the trust; the extent to which they consist of financial assets, interests in closely held enterprises, tangible and intangible personal property, or real property; the extent to which an asset is used by a beneficiary; and whether an asset was purchased by the trustee or received from the settlor;

(6) the net amount allocated to income under the other sections of this [Act] and the increase or decrease in the value of the principal assets, which the trustee may estimate as to assets for which market values are not readily available;

(7) whether and to what extent the terms of the trust give the trustee the power to invade principal or accumulate income or prohibit the trustee from invading principal or accumulating income, and the extent to which the trustee has exercised a power from time to time to invade principal or accumulate income;

(8) the actual and anticipated effect of economic conditions on principal and income and effects of inflation and deflation; and

(9) the anticipated tax consequences of an adjustment. . . .

(f) Terms of a trust that limit the power of a trustee to make an adjustment between principal and income do not affect the application of this section unless it is clear from the terms of the trust that the terms are intended to deny the trustee the power of adjustment conferred by subsection (a).

See generally Schaengold, New Uniform Principal and Income Act in Progress, Tr. & Est., Dec. 1994, at 42; Dobris, The Probate World at the End of the Century: Is a New Principal and Income Act in Your Future?, 28 Real Prop. Prob. & Tr. J. 393 (1993).

3. *Abandoning traditional notions of principal and income.* Traditional notions of principal and income need not interfere with fiduciary administration. For example, if the trustee has discretion to distribute either income or

principal to the current beneficiaries, defining principal and income is much less important. This is perhaps one of many reasons why discretionary trusts have become popular. Alternatively, if the current beneficiaries are entitled to periodic distributions of fixed amounts (possibly subject to readjustment by formula), rather than "all income," traditional notions of principal and income lose much of their capacity to distort investment policy. Indeed, if the settlor has not provided otherwise, statutes in many states now authorize the trustee of a mandatory income trust, under various conditions, to convert the trust to a unitrust, i.e., a trust in which the current beneficiaries are entitled annually to a fixed percentage of the current value of the trust assets. These statutes ordinarily either fix the percentage or prescribe a narrow range within which the trustee may choose. See, e.g., Cal. Prob. Code § 16336.4 (4 percent, subject to variation by the court or, after conversion, by the parties); Fla. Stat. Ann. § 738.1041 (3–5 percent); N.Y. EPTL § 11-2.4 (4 percent). See generally Wolf, Defeating the Duty to Disappoint Equally—The Total Return Trust, 32 Real Prop. Prob. & Tr. J. 45 (1997); Dobris, Why Trustee Investors Often Prefer Dividends to Capital Gain and Debt Investments to Equity—A Daunting Principal and Income Problem, 32 Real Prop. Prob. & Tr. J. 255 (1997).

6. ACCOUNTING

Upon termination of a trust or completion of administration of an estate, the fiduciary generally must file an accounting with the court, prior to discharge from office.[31] An accounting is a detailed summary of the fiduciary's conduct during administration, describing all items of property received, all income earned, all disbursements for taxes, claims, and administration expenses, and all proposed distributions of any property that remains. Thus, if a fiduciary seeks credit for payment of an administration expense that is questionable either in its nature or in its amount, one or more of the beneficiaries may request denial of the credit. If there is no settlement, the court must hear and decide the issue. Denial of the credit would result in the court surcharging the fiduciary with the amount denied. After approval of the final accounting, the fiduciary makes all remaining distributions to the beneficiaries and is discharged from office. Trustees may file interim accountings before the trust terminates, in order to receive judicial approval of their conduct up to the time of the accounting. (Fiduciaries can also seek approval of specific actions without an accounting.) Courts regularly allow waivers of accountings on the agreement of all interested parties. See generally Westfall, Nonjudicial Settlement of Trustees' Accounts, 71 Harv. L. Rev. 40 (1957). But a provision in a trust instrument purporting to eliminate the duty to account or requiring the trustee to account only to certain beneficiaries (e.g., current income beneficiaries) and purporting to eliminate any duty to account to

---

[31] All persons who have an interest in the estate or trust must ordinarily receive notice, so that they may challenge the accounting. See Gaynor v. Payne, 804 A.2d 170 (Conn. 2002) (contingent remainder beneficiary).

others (e.g., the remainder beneficiaries) may be invalid, as contrary to public policy. See Wilson v. Wilson, 690 S.E.2d 710 (N.C. App. 2010) (provision that trustee need not account); Estate of Thomas, 28 So. 3d 627 (Miss. App. 2009) (although testator waived accounting, court may require accounting "where there are charges of mismanagement or maladministration"); Johnson v. Johnson, 967 A.2d 274 (Md. App. 2009) ("a trustor cannot, by including limitations in the Trust instrument, circumscribe the trustee's duty to account to beneficiaries"), vacated on other grounds, 32 A.3d 1072 (Md. 2011); Vena v. Vena, 899 N.E.2d 522 (Ill. App. 2008) (provision for approval of accounts by majority of income beneficiaries); In re Trust of Malasky, 736 N.Y.S.2d 151 (App. Div. 2002) (provision that trustees of revocable trust need account only to income beneficiaries was valid only during settlor's lifetime; remainder beneficiaries had standing to challenge trustee's accounting for actions taken after settlor's death).

The effect of an accounting has been described as follows:

> In general, the judicial settlement of a trustee's account renders *res judicata* all matters in dispute and determined by the court in settling the account, as well as all matters which were open to dispute but not actually disputed, regardless of whether the account was intermediate or final. Even after an account has been settled, however, the account may be reopened if the trustee is guilty of fraudulent concealment or misrepresentation in presenting the account or in obtaining the court's approval.

4 Scott and Ascher on Trusts § 24.25 (footnotes omitted).

CHAPTER 9

FUTURE INTERESTS

■ ■ ■

A. INTRODUCTION

What are future interests? The first thing to note about future interests is that the term is somewhat misleading. Future interests are, in fact, present rights to future possession (or enjoyment[1]) of property. By the time students take this course, most will have taken a basic course in property, in which they will have learned that one way of measuring ownership of property is along the plane of time. So measured, the ultimate in ownership is the fee simple or, as it is sometimes called, the fee simple absolute.[2] Ownership in fee simple may be something less than total; the rights of the owner may be subject to covenants, zoning laws, mortgages, etc.; they are certainly subject to taxation. But for these purposes, ownership in fee simple, because it is infinite in duration, is complete ownership.

A fee simple is a present—or "possessory"—interest, i.e., a right to present possession. Since it is infinite in duration, when a person owns a fee simple there can be no future interests in that property. So, too, when the owner of a fee simple transfers his or her entire interest to another, no future interest comes into existence. However, if the owner of a fee simple transfers anything less—whether by design or inadvertence—one or more future interests do come into existence. And, of course, the owner of the fee simple may create future interests by transferring part of the fee simple interest to one person and the rest to someone else. One must always be able to account temporally for infinity of ownership. Unless some person (or group of persons, e.g., tenants in common) owns a fee simple, future interests exist.

---

[1] If the future interest is an income interest in trust, the owner may be entitled to enjoyment but not possession.

[2] This book uses the shorter term "fee simple" as the equivalent of "fee simple absolute" and as excluding other forms of fee simple such as the "fee simple determinable," the "fee simple subject to a condition subsequent," and the "fee simple subject to an executory limitation."

A second thing to note about future interests is that they may be substantial or very insubstantial. The right to future possession[3] may be certain to ripen in the near future, or it may be subject to the prior occurrence of one or more highly improbable and distant events. Whether substantial or insubstantial, a future interest (in contrast to a "mere expectancy," such as the interest of a potential taker under the will of a living person) has many of the attributes of "property." With rare exceptions, future interests may be transferred inter vivos or by will, inherited, taxed, and subjected to the claims of creditors.

B. CLASSIFICATION OF FUTURE INTERESTS

Theoretically, future interests could come in infinite variety. In practice, they come in standard forms capable of classification by standard, if not universally accepted, criteria. Future interests law—and particularly its terminology—is rooted in land law, but many of the interests common in land law of an earlier era occur only infrequently in wills and trusts (and even in real estate transactions) today. Accordingly, this book devotes no time to the interests following defeasible fees (see footnote 2, supra). Instead, it concentrates on those interests following life estates, i.e., remainders, executory interests, and reversionary interests.

For purposes of the Rule against Perpetuities, the first important distinction is between interests created in third parties and those created in the transferor or the transferor's estate.[4] The latter—collectively, reversionary interests—are not subject to the Rule against Perpetuities. The explanation is historical, rather than rational, but there it is. Some interests in third parties are subject to the Rule, however, and it is necessary to distinguish among them. Two broad classifications exist: remainders and executory interests. The distinction between remainders and executory interests appears infra at pp. 876-878. A traditional classification of remainders is as follows:

Indefeasibly Vested Remainders;

Remainders Vested Subject to Open;

Remainders Vested Subject to Complete Defeasance; and

Contingent Remainders.

---

[3] For these purposes one may enjoy a right to possession personally, or vicariously through one's estate.

[4] It is assumed that the future interest is created by the same instrument as the preceding interest (the "particular estate"). If the interests are transferred by different instruments, a different classification may ensue. For example, if A transfers by one instrument to B for life, then to C, C gets a vested remainder; but if A transfers to B for life, and then A by a later instrument gives C the right to possession after B's life estate, the second instrument is an assignment by A to C of the reversion left in A after the first transfer.

Before turning to a discussion of particular types of remainders, a few general observations are in order. The word "vest" is, it has been said, a four letter word that has given rise to the use of many other four letter words. Whether an interest is "vested" can be of critical importance, however, since, except for the remainder vested subject to open, the Rule against Perpetuities does not apply to vested interests. Unfortunately, the term does not have a fixed meaning and is used to describe a number of quite different things. Many cases that discuss the difference between vested and contingent remainders really turn on whether there is or is not a requirement of survival. In its normal connotation, "vest" probably connotes becoming possessory; but in future interests parlance, the term usually requires that an interest vest "in interest," rather than in possession. One might think that the term ought to mean that an interest has become certain—no longer subject to contingency—but it clearly does not mean that, as the "remainder vested subject to complete defeasance" proves. The truth is that one can only define "vest" in terms of specific interests.

A second general observation is that an interest cannot vest in an unborn or unascertained person. In the limitation A to B for life, remainder to the children of B, the remainder cannot vest until a child of B is born. So, too, in the limitation A to B for life, remainder to the last survivor of the children of B, none of B's children can have a vested remainder until all but one has died (and B is no longer living).

A third general observation is that traditionally the courts have not inferred a requirement of survival where none was stated—except that it has been necessary to survive to the effective date of the instrument creating the interest. Thus, absent evidence of contrary intent, in the limitation A to B for life, remainder to C, there is no requirement that C survive B in order to take "possession" of the property.[5] Traditionally it has not mattered that C's possession might be vicarious, i.e., through C's estate.

Finally, one should note that the classification of a future interest occurs as of a particular moment—usually the effective date of the creating

---

[5] See, e.g., Harbour v. SunTrust Bank, 685 S.E.2d 838 (Va. 2009); In re Townley Bypass Unified Credit Trust, 252 S.W.3d 715 (Tex. App. 2008); Estate of Silsby, 914 A.2d 703 (Me. 2006); Blue Ridge Bank & Trust Co. v. McFall, 207 S.W.3d 149 (Mo. App. 2006); In re Will of Uchtorff, 693 N.W.2d 790 (Iowa 2005); In re Hobert, 794 N.Y.S.2d 783 (Sur. 2004). Likewise, the beneficiary of a trust that is revocable by the settlor ordinarily need not survive the settlor. See, e.g., Baldwin v. Branch, 888 So.2d 482 (Ala. 2004).

Article II of the UPC would change all this. UPC § 2–707 requires survival unless the governing instrument clearly provides otherwise. For critical analysis, see Dukeminier, The Uniform Probate Code Upends the Law of Remainders, 94 Mich. L. Rev. 148 (1995); Cunningham, The Hazards of Tinkering with the Common Law of Future Interests: The California Experience, 48 Hastings L.J. 667 (1997); Becker, Uniform Probate Code Section 2–707 and the Experienced Estate Planner: Unexpected Disasters and How to Avoid Them, 47 UCLA L. Rev. 339 (1999).

instrument or the end of the permissible period of the Rule against Perpetuities. But it is also important to remember that the leopard can change its spots; e.g., a contingent interest can become vested, and an interest vested subject to defeasance can become indefeasibly vested.

The indefeasibly vested remainder. The typical example of such a remainder is the limitation *A* to *B* for life, remainder to *C*. As the name implies, this type of remainder vests an interest, to become possessory after the end of the life estate, which is not subject to divestment. Either *C* during life, if *C* outlives *B* (or if the life estate of *B* terminates prematurely during *C*'s life), or *C*'s estate, will come into possession when the life estate ends. Ordinarily there should be no difficulty in identifying this sort of remainder.

The remainder vested subject to open. The typical example of such a remainder is the limitation *A* to *B* for life, remainder to the children of *B*, when *B* has at least one living child. As the name implies, this type of remainder vests an interest in a member of a class, subject to the "opening" of the class to admit new members. Once the interest vests, the owner of the interest has an indefeasibly vested interest in *some* share of the property, but the size of the share must await determination of the number of class members who share in the gift. For example, in the limitation above, to determine the size of any one child's share, we need to know the number of children born to *B*. Here again, classification should not be difficult. Provided that at least one member of the class is in existence, the remainder is vested; if not, the entire remainder is contingent. As will appear below, however, the difference may not matter much, as both the remainder vested subject to open and the contingent remainder are subject to the Rule against Perpetuities.

The remainder vested subject to complete defeasance, and the contingent remainder. Serious problems of classification arise with these types of remainder. The difficulty lies in the fact that, in both cases, whether the holder of the interest will ever be entitled to possession depends on the happening of a presently unpredictable contingency—usually outliving some other person or surviving to a particular age—although the contingency may be of any kind. Yet classification of these interests is critical, since if the remainder is vested—even if subject to complete defeasance—it is not subject to the Rule against Perpetuities; if, on the other hand, the remainder is contingent, it is subject to the Rule against Perpetuities. Thus, at least in theory, classification of substantively indistinguishable interests may determine whether they are valid or void.

The surest guide is probably the *language* creating the interest. According to Professor Gray, "whether a remainder is vested or contingent depends upon the language employed. If the conditional element is incorporated into the description of, or into the gift to, the remainderman, then the remainder is contingent; but if, after words giving a vested interest, there is an additional clause divesting it, the remainder is vested." Gray § 108. Take, for example, the limitation *A* to *B* for life, remainder to *C*, but if *C* predeceases *B*, to *D*. In this limitation the language seems initially to give an unconditional remainder to *C*—if the limitation stopped after "*A* to *B* for life, remainder to *C*," *C* would have an indefeasibly vested remainder. But the language continues, attaching a condition, i.e., that *C* outlive *B*, and thereby takes away that which the previous language seems to give. Classical analysis would almost certainly classify the remainder to *C* as vested subject to divestment if *C* fails to outlive *B*. Contrast the limitation *A* to *B* for life, remainder to *C* if *C* outlives *B*, otherwise to *D*. This limitation does not give and then take away the remainder (or so one may argue). *C* is only to take the remainder if *C* outlives *B*—in Gray's words, "the conditional element is incorporated into the gift." Here, classical analysis would classify the remainder to *C* as contingent. This distinction, based on slight differences in language, has, of course, counterparts in other areas of real property law. The classification of a fee interest as "fee simple determinable" or "fee simple subject to an executory interest" may similarly depend on particular words. Whether courts actually give such weight to language seems doubtful, however. In the last analysis, their job is to give effect to the intention of the person creating the interest, and it hardly seems likely that the average donor would understand that such small differences in language could be so important.

The distinction between remainders and executory interests. A final distinction is that between remainders and executory interests. Executory interests are defined—not very helpfully—as all interests in third persons, other than remainders. Historically, executory interests are those interests whose creation the Statute of Uses (1535) and the Statute of Wills (1540) made possible. Those interests, with such exotic names as "shifting" and "springing" "uses" and "devises," were extremely important in the development of the Rule against Perpetuities; however, their importance today—as a category of interest separate from the contingent remainder—is more doubtful.

Professor Gulliver defined an executory interest as follows:

An executory interest is a future interest in a transferee that will either (1) certainly be preceded by a gap, or (2) operate by divesting an interest of another transferee. An example of the first type of executory interest would be: *A* to *B* for life and one year after *B*'s death to *C*. It is absolutely certain that a gap will precede *C*'s possession, since no *transferee* would come into possession during the one-year period. An example of the second type of executory interest would be: the interest of *C* in a transfer from A to B, but if C pay B \$25,000, then to C. The executory interest is a divesting one because, if effective, it would terminate a fee simple prior to its normal infinite duration.

Executory interests that follow gaps are easy to identify. They are also rare. When the interest is executory because it divests a prior interest, identification may be more difficult. If the preceding interest is a possessory interest, a life estate, or a defeasible fee, there should be little difficulty. In the limitation A to B for life, but if B remarries, then to C, the interest of C, if it ever becomes possessory, will cut short B's life estate. So, too, in the limitation A to B, but if B dies without having had issue, to C, the interest of C is clearly divesting, and so executory. But defeasible fees are not apt to be of great importance in the study of trusts and estates. Interests that divest life estates are more frequent (probably most often in marital property agreements), but the classification of such interests as executory—rather than as contingent remainders—seems to have no consequences.

When, however, the interest divested is itself a future interest, the situation becomes fairly murky. Take, for example, the limitation set forth above: A to B for life, remainder to C, but if C predeceases B, then to D. On traditional analysis, the interest of C is vested subject to divestment by the executory interest in D. Let us suppose now the slightly different limitation: A to B for life, remainder to C if C outlives B, otherwise to D. Here, traditional analysis would classify both C's and D's interests as contingent remainders—assuming of course that both B and C are alive. To the untrained eye it is hard to see how in one case the interest of D divests the interest of C, and hence is an executory interest, but in the second case there is no divestment. The practice of attaching significance to such slight differences in language is criticized in Halbach, Vested and Contingent Remainders: A Premature Requiem for Distinctions between Conditions Precedent and Subsequent, Essays for Austin Wakeman Scott 152 (1964). Indeed, the distinction between executory interests and contingent remainders, although once important, may be disappearing. See Dukeminier, Contingent Remainders and Executory Interests: A Requiem for the Distinction, 43 Minn. L. Rev. 13 (1958).

To satisfy the Rule against Perpetuities, an interest must be certain either to vest or to disappear within the period of the Rule. For purposes of the Rule, vesting in interest is enough; vesting in possession is not necessary. However, classical doctrine says that a characteristic of executory interests, as distinguished from remainders, is that they cannot vest in interest until they vest in possession. Thus, for perpetuities purposes, an executory interest must be certain to vest in possession within the prescribed period, whereas a contingent remainder need only be certain to vest in interest (or fail). Insofar as the executory interest in question operates to divest a possessory interest, the classical doctrine is probably correct. But when the interest to be divested is a remainder, the difference is probably meaningless. For example, in the limitation above of *A* to *B* for life, remainder to *C* but if *C* dies before *B*, to *D*, while *D*'s interest can never become a vested executory interest, it will, on *C*'s death before *B*, become a vested remainder. All in all, it seems likely that the distinction between executory interests and contingent remainders matters little today. On the other hand, it seems unlikely that the term executory interest will disappear any time soon.

Why do we care? Classification for its own sake may be of interest to collectors of stamps or butterflies, but the classification of future interests does not matter unless different legal consequences ensue. In fact, classification of an interest can be critically important for purposes of the Rule against Perpetuities. In addition, classification may have other consequences affecting the transferability of an interest during life or at death, the rights of creditors, and the rights of successive owners. Some of these differences are disappearing. Others are of little importance in the context of trusts, and today most future interests are in trust. Against the background of these fading distinctions, consider the following, from Lynn, The Modern Rule Against Perpetuities 157 (1966):

> Gray made the common-law Rule Against Perpetuities a rule against remoteness of vesting, and urged remorseless application of the Rule. . . . Applying Gray's Rule presupposes classification of future interests in the dispositive instrument as a prerequisite to determining validity under the Rule, and indeed that is true irrespective of the form that the Rule takes. The rub is that meticulous characterization of future interests is not typical of modern perpetuities cases. Limitations are not standardized and readily recognizable as falling within a particular category in the future interests hierarchy. Ambiguities frequently abound and it is sometimes almost impossible to assimilate the half-articulated expressions of the grantor, settlor, or testator to the ideal types used in this book to illustrate application of the black-letter rule.

There is, moreover, some reason to believe that change may be coming to the law of future interests. See generally Gallanis, The Future of Future Interests, 60 Wash. & Lee L. Rev. 513 (2003); Barros, Toward a Model Law of Estates and Future Interests, 66 Wash. & Lee L. Rev. 3 (2009).

C. THE RULE AGAINST PERPETUITIES

1. THE OBJECTIVE OF THE RULE

The "common law" Rule against Perpetuities did not appear as a comprehensive rule all at once. After its first formulation in the Duke of

Norfolk's case, 3 Ch. Cas. 1 (1682), the English courts took more than two hundred years to work out the details; they did not settle on the *duration* of the period of the rule until 1833, in Cadell v. Palmer, 1 Cl. & F. 373. And it was not until 1890, in In re Hargreaves, 43 Ch. Div. 401, that they agreed on the rule's *objective*.

The general idea is to invalidate *ab initio* certain future interests that might otherwise remain in existence too long. The two chief policies are to curtail "dead hand" domination and to facilitate marketability of property. The former seems far more compelling today.[6]

Any division of property ownership affects alienability. Take the simple transfer by *A* (holding property in fee simple) to *B* for life, remainder to *C*, when both *B* and *C* are *sui juris*. While *A* owns the property, the decision to sell or otherwise transfer it is *A*'s alone. In contrast, when *B* and *C* collectively own the property, they must agree on any decision to sell or transfer the property. In theory, *B* can sell the life estate—or *C* the remainder—but the uncertainties of *B*'s life expectancy make the purchase too chancy for most buyers, and those who do buy are likely to insist on a price that reflects the uncertainty. *B* and *C* together can sell—there is no legal impediment to a sale—but they are apt to disagree about the wisdom of a sale and almost certain to disagree about how to split the purchase price. *B* will regard the life expectancy tables as much too conservative, and *C* may feel that they wildly overstate *B*'s actual life expectancy.

If the division of ownership affects alienability in the simple situation in which *B* has a life estate and *C* an indefeasibly vested remainder, how much worse is it apt to be when *C*'s interest is vested subject to defeasance, or contingent. Consider the case of the limitation *A* to *B* for life, remainder to *C* if *C* survives *B*, or if *C* predeceases *B*, to *D*. *B*, *C*, and *D* can collectively convey a fee simple title to the property to anyone, but will they ever be able to agree on a sale or a price?

In the examples above, the effect on marketability is practical; there are always people in existence who, together, can convey good fee simple title to the property. In other cases, however, the interference with marketability is not only practical but legal. In the limitation *A* to *B* for life, remainder to the first child of *B* to reach 21, when *B* has no children or no child who has reached 21, there is no combination of people who can transfer good fee simple title. The ultimate taker may be a presently unborn child of *B* or, if no child of *B* ever reaches 21, *A* or *A*'s successor in interest.

---

[6] The Rule also backstops the federal estate tax by limiting "generation-skipping" tax-free transfers. See I.R.C. § 2041(a)(3), infra p. 1029. This role is now arguably somewhat less important, given the generation-skipping transfer tax. See infra p. 1048.

Yet in a trust (and most future interests are in trust) a trustee ordinarily has the power to sell any of the trust assets. The result is that, as to any particular item of property, there is usually someone who has the power to convey good title. Thus, as to each item of property held in trust, there generally is no restriction of the power of alienation. Nonetheless, the Rule against Perpetuities generally applies, regardless of the trustee's ability to alienate each and every trust asset.

Today, most observers agree that the primary justification for the Rule is to limit "dead-hand" control. See, for example, Simes and Smith § 1117:

> It is believed . . . that, today, the principal reason for the rule against perpetuities is not to secure alienability for the purpose of productivity. . . .
>
> The compelling reasons for the rule against perpetuities are believed to be these. First, it strikes a fair balance between the satisfaction of the wishes of members of the present generation to tie up their property and those of future generations to do the same. The desire of property owners to convey or devise what they have by the use of trusts and future interests is widespread, and the law gives some scope to that almost universal want. But if it were permitted without limit, then members of future generations would receive this property already tied up with future interests and trusts, and could not give effect to their desires for the disposition of the property. Thus, the law strikes a balance between these desires of the present generation and of future generations.
>
> A further reason is that, other things being equal, society is better off, if property is controlled by its living members than if controlled by the dead. Thus, one policy back of the rule against perpetuities is to prevent too much dead hand control of property.

The classic statement of the Rule is that of Professor John Chipman Gray: "No interest is good unless it must vest, if at all, not later than twenty-one years after some life in being at the creation of the interest." Gray § 201. Professor Leach suggested modifying the Gray formulation by adding the words "Generally speaking" at the beginning and putting the word vest in quotation marks. Leach, Perpetuities in a Nutshell, 51 Harv. L. Rev. 638, 639 (1938). Many others have criticized Gray's formulation, but, even today, the Rule is almost always stated the way Gray did.

2. THE PERIOD OF THE RULE

The period of time within which an interest must be certain to vest, *if at all* (a very important qualification), generally runs from the creation of the interest, i.e., the date of death in the case of a will, or the date of trust declaration or delivery of the instrument of transfer in the case of an inter vivos transfer. There are three different units of "perpetuities time": lives in being; periods of gestation; and the 21–year period "in gross." Except for the ascertainment of which lives are usable as "measuring lives," the concept of lives in being should cause no difficulty; the lives must be human, rather than animal or corporate, and one may use any number, provided the number is not so large as to make ascertainment of death too difficult, as an administrative matter. For example, a gift to vest at the death of the survivor of all people now citizens of the United States would be void under the Rule, not because they are not lives in being, but because it would be administratively impossible to give effect to the gift. Even assuming a multi-million-dollar estate sufficient to finance the years of investigation that would be necessary, it would be impossible for the fiduciary to trace all such people through the years for the purpose of determining who the survivor was and whether he or she had died. Subject to this administrative limitation, however, the rule assumes that the expectancy of the survivor of a group does not vary enough with the size of the group to warrant the inconveniences of limiting the permissible lives in being to a specific number.

The so-called "period in gross" is a flat 21–year period that may either be used independently of any life in being (for example, a gift to "the issue of *B* living twenty-one years from today,") or added onto the end of lives in being. However, the 21–year period cannot precede measuring lives. Thus, a gift to vest on the death of the survivor of all issue of the testator born within 21 years after the testator's death is void. The measuring lives must be "lives in being" at the effective date of the instrument, not 21 years thereafter. One of the functional justifications of the period in gross is to permit dispositions that tie up property during the lives of the children of the testator and until the testator's grandchildren reach the age of majority; no such justification exists for allowing a reversal of the order of measuring lives and the period in gross.

Finally, the period may include such periods of gestation as actually exist. (Thus, one cannot add a flat period of nine months to the 21–year period in gross.) What this amounts to is that the Rule regards a person as having been in being from the moment of conception. The actual period of gestation may also save a gift to a person whose attainment of the age of 21 is a condition precedent, if otherwise the contingency would not occur until more than 21 years after a life in being.

THOMAS V. HARRISON

Probate Court of Ohio, Cuyahoga County, 1962.
24 Ohio. Op.2d 148, 191 N.E.2d 862.

MERRICK, PRESIDING JUDGE. . . .

The will directs in Item IV(3) that half of the residuary estate is to be held in trust for the benefit of testatrix's son, Jean B. Harrison, his wife, and his issue. The trustees are given absolute discretion to expend so much of the income and/or principal of the trust as they deem necessary to alleviate the financial burdens of, or to provide education for, any or all of the designated beneficiaries and to accumulate in any year the income not so spent. The trust is to continue as long as any of the beneficiaries who are born within twenty years after testatrix's death remain alive. This Court is asked to determine whether the provisions of this trust violate the rule against perpetuities. . . .

It has been said that the fundamental policy behind the rule is to preserve the freedom of alienation of property. . . . But Professor Gray, in his famous treatise, states that the immediate purpose of the rule is to prevent the creation of interests which may vest too remotely. Gray, The Rule Against Perpetuities Secs. 1–4 (4th ed. 1942). Consequently, the rule applies only to the *vesting* of interests. It applies to equitable as well as legal interests. . . . Let us first see then, whether the interests created under this trust are vested.

An interest is not vested if, in order for it to come into possession, the fulfillment of some condition precedent other than the determination of the preceding estate is necessary. . . . Gray, The Rule Against Perpetuities, supra Sec. 101; Restatement Property Sec. 157 comment a. A remainder may be contingent because it is to take effect upon the happening of some event not certain to occur which is independent of the termination of the preceding estate. . . . It may also be contingent because the person to whom the remainder is limited is not yet ascertained or not yet in being. . . .

In a discretionary trust the beneficiary has no definitely ascertainable interest. He cannot compel the trustee to give him any portion of the income where the trust gives the trustee absolute discretion as to the amounts of income to distribute. See Scott on Trusts Sec. 128.3 (2d ed. 1956). The beneficiary cannot be certain that he will ever enjoy any of the proceeds of the trust. Consequently, where the extent of the interest of the beneficiary is dependent upon the exercise of discretion by the trustee, that interest is contingent. Thomas v. Gregg, 76 Md. 169, 24 A. 418 (1892); Andrews v. Lincoln, 95 Me. 541, 50 A. 898, 56 L.R.A. 103 (1901); Moore v. Moore, 59 N.C. (6 Jones Eq.) 132 (1860); Angell v. Angell, 28 R.I. 592, 68 A. 583 (1908); Denny v. Hyland, 162 Wash. 68, 297 P. 1083

(1931); . . . Gray, Perpetuities, supra, Sec. 246; Restatement, Trusts 2d Sec. 62q. Such interest does not vest until the trustee exercises his discretion.

Viewed in another way, the discretion in a trustee to distribute principal and income to any or all members of a designated class is tantamount to a special power of appointment. Simes and Smith, The Law of Future Interests 216 Sec. 1277 (2d ed. 1956); VI American Law of Property Sec. 24.30 (1952). The exercise of the power is a condition precedent to the vesting of any interest in a beneficiary of the trust. Simes & Smith, supra, Sec. 1274; Gray, Perpetuities, supra Sec. 515.

Thus it is obvious that the interests of Jean B. Harrison, his wife, and his issue, are contingent. Their interests in the income and principal of the trust are wholly dependent upon the trustee's discretion. The interests of all the beneficiaries are contingent because they are subject to a condition precedent. In addition, they are contingent because the beneficiaries are unascertained, in the sense that the trustee may select one or more of them to receive proceeds from the trusts, or unborn in the case of possible further issue of Jean.

Having determined that these interests are contingent, it still remains to be seen whether these interests must vest within the period of the rule. The Ohio statute, echoing the common law, says that interests must vest, if at all, not later than twenty-one years *after lives in being at the creation of the interest.* Ohio Rev. Code Sec. 2131.08. As the statute expressly states, and as the authorities unanimously proclaim, the twenty-one year period must *follow,* not precede, the lives in being by which the period of the rule is measured. Simes & Smith, supra, Sec. 1225; Restatement, Property Sec. 374, comment e, Illus. 6, comment o; VI American Law of Property, supra, Sec. 24.14. Furthermore the measuring lives must be lives *in being at the creation of the interest,* i.e. in the case of a testamentary trust, at the death of the testator. . . .

A simple illustration will indicate that the interests created under the testamentary trust of Mrs. Harrison will not necessarily vest within the period of the rule. Mrs. Harrison was survived by her son, Jean, his wife and their three children. Since the death of Mrs. Harrison, four more children have been born to Jean. Let us suppose that tomorrow Jean, his wife, and the three children who were alive at the death of Clara Harrison are all killed in a common accident. Let us suppose further that the inheritance of the four surviving children of Jean is adequate to take care of their needs for twenty-five years; therefore, the trustees of the Clara Harrison trust deem it unnecessary to distribute any income or principal to the children until that time. The interests of the children would not vest until twenty-five years from now. This would be more than twenty-one years after the expiration of lives in being at the death of Mrs. Harrison. Consequently, the rule against perpetuities would be violated.

It is no defense that the probabilities are greater that the interests under the trust will vest within the period of the rule. The statute says the interests *must* vest within the prescribed time. If there is any possibility that the interests will not vest within lives in being plus twenty-one years then the interests are void ab initio. . . .

There is no question of severability of interests here. That is, the contingent interests of Jean, his wife and his issue who were alive at the time of Mrs. Harrison's death, cannot be separated from the interests of later born issue. To eliminate the after born issue would warp the testamentary scheme. It would deprive the trustees of their full discretion by narrowing the class of beneficiaries. Therefore, the entire trust fails. . . . The Trustees hold upon a resulting trust for Mrs. Harrison's heirs at law. . . .

———————

How to identify "measuring lives." One of the most frequent questions of students first wrestling with the Rule is, "How do I decide who are the measuring lives?" Usually the person who asks the question wants to know whether the life of a particular person or class of persons mentioned in the will or trust instrument may be used as a measuring life or lives. Almost always the question betrays a basic misunderstanding of the operation of the common law Rule against Perpetuities. The question to ask is not whether the life of a particular person *may* be the measuring life but whether there is anyone whose life may be used to demonstrate compliance with the Rule.

Professor Gray says:

For the purpose of sustaining a limitation, reference may be made by the Court to the lives of any persons living at the testator's death, whose lives have a necessary relation to the event on which the limitation vests, whether or not those persons take any interest in the property . . . or are mentioned in the will. [Gray § 219.2 n.2.]

Professor Dukeminier gives a somewhat different formulation:

The answer [to the question, "Who is a life in being?"] is that it can be any person alive (or in the womb) at the creation of the interest, so long as his death or some event which will necessarily happen or fail to happen within his life will *insure* vesting or failure of the interest within twenty-one years of his death. The lives in being "may be any lives which play a part in the ultimate disposition of the property."

They need not be given any beneficial interest in the property nor be referred to in the instrument, but the causal connection which insures vesting must be express or implied. [Dukeminier, Perpetuities Law in Action 7–8 (1962).]

The editors prefer a third way of putting it. Ask yourself, "Is there a living person or group of persons to whom you can point and say that within twenty-one years after his, her, or their deaths the contingency as to the future interest's becoming or not becoming vested will *necessarily* be resolved?"

All these formulations lead to the same result. They take into account the so-called "remote possibilities test," i.e., the proposition that under the common law Rule against Perpetuities we are not interested in what actually happens, but what might happen, even by the remotest possibility, according to circumstances as they exist at the effective date of the instrument. Under the common law Rule, if the contingency is not *certain* to be resolved within the period, the interest is void. Any possibility, no matter how improbable, that the contingency will not be resolved is enough. If there is any life (or group of lives) that will certainly suffice, it is the measuring life (or lives). If there is not, the interest is void.

3. THE REMOTE POSSIBILITIES TEST

a. The Fertile Octogenarian

JEE v. AUDLEY

Chancery, 1787.

1 Cox 324, 29 Eng. Rep. 1186.

Edward Audley, by his will, bequeathed as follows, "Also my will is that £1000 shall be placed out at interest during the life of my wife, which interest I give her during her life, and at her death I give the said £1000 unto my niece Mary Hall and the issue of her body lawfully begotten, and to be begotten, and in default of such issue I give the said £1000 to be equally divided between the daughters *then* living of my kinsman John Jee and his wife, Elizabeth Jee."

It appeared that John Jee and Elizabeth Jee were living at the time of the death of the testator, had four daughters and no son, and were of a very advanced age. Mary Hall was unmarried and of the age of about 40; the wife was dead. The present bill was filed by the four daughters of John and Elizabeth Jee to have the £1000 secured for their benefit upon the event of the said Mary Hall dying without leaving children. And the question was, whether the limitation to the daughters of John and Elizabeth Jee was not void as being too remote; and to prove it so, it was said that this was to take effect on a general failure of issue of Mary Hall; and although it was to the daughters of John and Elizabeth Jee, yet it was not confined to the daughters living at the death of the testator, and consequently it might extend to after-born daughters in which case it would not be within the limit of a life or lives in being and 21 years afterwards, beyond which time an executory devise is void.

On the other side it was said, that though the late cases had decided that on a gift to children generally, such children as should be living at the time of the distribution of the fund should be let in, yet it would be very hard to adhere to such a rule of construction so rigidly, as to defeat the evident intention of the testator in this case, especially as there was no real possibility of John and Elizabeth Jee having children after the testator's death, they being then 70 years old; that if there were two ways of construing words, that should be adopted which would give effect to the disposition made by the testator; that the cases, which had decided that after-born children should take, proceeded on the implied intention of the testator, and never meant to give an effect to words which would totally defeat such intention. . . .

MASTER OF THE ROLLS [Sir Lloyd Kenyon]. Several cases determined by Lord Northington, Lord Camden, and the present Chancellor, have settled that children born after the death of the testator shall take a share in these cases; the difference is, where there is an immediate devise, and where there is an interest in remainder: in the former case the children living at the testator's death only shall take: in the latter those who are living at the time the interest vests in possession; and this being now a settled principle, I shall not strain to serve an intention at the expense of removing the land marks of the law; it is of infinite importance to abide by decided cases, and perhaps more so on this subject than any other. The general principles which apply to this case are not disputed: the limitations of personal estate are void, unless they necessarily vest, if at all, within a life or lives in being and 21 years or 9 or 10 months afterwards. This has been sanctioned by the opinion of judges of all times, from the time of the Duke of Norfolk's case to the present, it is grown reverend by age, and is not now to be broken in upon; I am desired to do in this case something which I do not feel myself at liberty to do, namely to suppose it impossible for persons in so advanced an age as John and Elizabeth Jee to have children; but if this can be done in one case it may in another, and it is a very dangerous experiment, and introductive of the greatest inconvenience to give a latitude to such sort of conjecture. Another thing pressed upon me, is to decide on the events which have happened; but I cannot do this without overturning very many cases. The single question before me, is, not whether the limitation is good in the events which have happened, but whether it was good in its creation; and if it were not, I cannot make it so. Then must this limitation, if at all, *necessarily* take place within the limits prescribed by law? The words are "in default of such issue I give the said £1000 to be equally divided between the daughters *then* living of John Jee and Elizabeth his wife." It if had been to "daughters now living," or "who should be living at the time of my death," it would have been very good; but as it stands, this limitation may take in after-born daughters; this point is clearly settled by Ellison v. Airey, [1 Ves. 111] and the effect of law on such limitation cannot make any difference in construing such intention. If then this will extended to after-born daughters, is it within the rules of law? Most certainly not, because John and Elizabeth Jee might have children born ten years after the testator's death, and then Mary Hall might die without issue 50 years afterwards; in which case it would evidently transgress the rules prescribed. I am of opinion, therefore, though the testator might possibly mean to restrain the limitation to the children who should be living at the time of the death, I cannot, consistently with decided cases, construe it in such restrained sense, but must intend it to take in after-born children. This therefore not being within the rules of law, and as I cannot judge upon subsequent events, I think the limitation void. Therefore dismiss the bill, but without costs.

NOTES

1. *Background.* Mr. Audley apparently intended to give Mary Hall a fee tail. But since the interest was in personal property, rather than real property, the effect was to create in Mary a fee simple, subject to an executory interest in the daughters of John and Elizabeth Jee. Even then, it was unusual to attempt to create a legal future interest in personal property, without a trust. The case arose when the Jee daughters filed a bill "to have the £1000 secured for their benefit." In other words, they sought to compel a bond as security against dissipation of the principal. Because the gift was void, they had no interest to protect, and the court dismissed the bill.

Everyone should read Professor Leach's clear and entertaining analysis of this poorly argued and vaguely decided, but nevertheless extremely influential, case, in Perpetuities and Class Gifts, 51 Harv. L. Rev. 1329, 1338–41 (1938).

2. *Failure of issue.* There are at least three possible constructions of the phrase "die without issue," as in a grant from *A to B and his heirs, but if B die without issue, then to C and his heirs*. (1) An unusual but possible construction is that this means that the gift to C is to take effect if, but only if, B never has any issue born to B. If so, the gift to C fails if B at any time has a child born alive, whether or not such child survives B. For example, B has a child, X; the gift to C immediately fails under this construction, because B has had issue, and this remains true even if X dies the next day and B lives for many more years. (2) The *"definite failure of issue"* construction. Failure of issue means, of course, non-existence of issue. "Definite failure of issue" means nonexistence of issue at a definite time. A gift to C "if there are no issue of B living on May 1, 2014," or at any other stipulated time, specifically provides for a definite failure of issue as the condition precedent to C's gift. In

the case above, although no time is explicitly stated, the definite failure of issue construction supplies one, by interpreting "if *B* die without issue" as *"if B die without issue living at B's death."* Under this construction, if *B* dies leaving a child *X* surviving, *C's* gift fails, regardless of later events. This is the most reasonable interpretation of the language, and modern American statutes favor it. (3) The *"indefinite failure of issue"* construction is that the gift to *C* is to become effective whenever *B's* issue become extinct. Under this construction, *C's* interest does not fail if *B* dies leaving a child *X* surviving. Even if *X* has a long line of lineal descendants, the last survivor of whom does not die for several centuries, this construction is that *C* or *C's* successors in interest are to take whenever the last survivor of *X's* descendants eventually dies. Although the indefinite failure of issue interpretation seems warped and may today have intent-defeating consequences, it is the one the English common law preferred. See Warren, Gifts Over on Death Without Issue, 39 Yale L.J. 342 (1930). To accord a gift on failure of issue its more natural construction, many states have enacted statutes preferring a definite failure of issue construction.

3. *Construction.* It was here argued (second paragraph of statement of facts) and apparently assumed by the court that the gift to the Jee daughters was on a "general" (indefinite) failure of Mary's issue. If the court had construed "in default of such issue" as meaning "if Mary Hall dies without issue living at the time of her death" (definite failure), would the gift to the Jee daughters have been void?

4. *Hypothetical gifts.* Assuming an indefinite failure construction, would the gift be valid if made to

> (a) "the daughters of John and Elizabeth Jee living at my death"?

> (b) "the daughters of John and Elizabeth Jee living at my death who are also living at the time of failure of Mary's issue"?

Note the dictum of the court on this question.

5. *"What might happen."* The opinion states that counsel for the Jee daughters urged the court "to decide on the events which have happened," without specifying what they were. Perhaps, between the death of the testator and the time of this suit, Mary Hall had died without issue, or John or Elizabeth Jee had died without producing any more daughters. Why would the occurrence of any of these events have insured that the interests of the Jee daughters would "in fact" vest within the period of the Rule?

The court is orthodox in stating that it cannot take into consideration events happening after the operative date of the instrument, even if they occur before commencement of the suit. By the standard case law rule, the interest is void if, at the time of its creation, there is any possibility that it may vest too remotely. Consider this proposition in connection with the contrary "wait and see" philosophy of recent legislation, infra p. 932.

6. *Lives in being.* Counsel for the Jee daughters seems to have argued that the court should interpret the will as if it read like the hypothetical gift in Note 4(b), supra.

(a) Assuming that the will (the date of which does not appear) was executed within a few years of the testator's death, how could one argue that the testator intended to confine the beneficiaries to the four living daughters of John and Elizabeth Jee? See Bankers Trust Co. v. Pearson, 99 A.2d 224 (Conn. 1953).

(b) Would the testator's use of "daughters," rather than "children," in describing the beneficiaries, be significant on this issue?

See Leach, Perpetuities and Class Gifts, 51 Harv. L. Rev. 1329, 1339 (1938). For the most part, however, the courts have followed Jee v. Audley in refusing to save gifts of this type by construing the intent of the transferor to restrict the beneficiaries to lives in being.

7. *The fertile octogenarian.* Counsel for the Jee daughters also argued that, since John and Elizabeth Jee were 70 years old at the testator's death, "there was no real possibility" that they would produce any more daughters. In other words, even if one assumes that the testator intended to include after-born daughters as beneficiaries (suppose, e.g., that the testator executed the will 40 years before death), the court should hold that the birth of any such daughters had already become a physiological impossibility when the will became operative at the testator's death. For the purpose of the Rule against Perpetuities, one always construes an instrument in light of the facts that exist at the time it becomes effective. If Elizabeth Jee had predeceased the testator, the gift would have been valid, because all possible takers would then necessarily be lives in being. Why should not the court have held that Elizabeth, aged 70, was as good as dead for reproductive purposes?

This decision, refusing to inquire into such matters, established the conclusive presumption of fertility, or, in Professor Leach's phrase, the "fertile octogenarian" doctrine, i.e., that any living person is capable of having children. The more unrealistic applications of this proposition have usually, as in this case, involved women of advanced age. But it could logically apply at the other end of the scale, so as to assume a one-year-old child capable of reproduction. See Professor Leach's entertaining account of the "Case of the Precocious Toddler" in Perpetuities in Perspective: Ending the Rule's Reign of Terror, 65 Harv. L. Rev. 721, 732 (1952). This was Re Gaite's Will Trusts, [1949] 1 All E.R. 459 (Ch.), involving a gift which would be void if it were assumed that, all in the space of five years, a 67–year–old widow could have a child and that child in turn could have a child who could take as a beneficiary. The court did not consider two such rapid-fire births a physical impossibility, but saved the gift on the theory that the hypothetical child would be too young to marry legally, and that the hypothetical grandchild would thus be illegitimate and incapable of taking under the gift. For certain other matters, courts have sometimes received evidence of impossibility of issue. See Gray § 215.1 n.4. But the conclusive presumption of fertility is settled doctrine for purposes of the Rule against Perpetuities. "The possibility of childbirth is never extinct." Turner v. Turner, 196 S.E.2d 498, 501 (S.C.1973).

8. *Adoption.* England did not recognize adoption until 1926, so that possibility did not influence the English cases formulating these rules. The American jurisdictions once varied as to whether and, if so, under what circumstances, an adopted child might take under a gift to "children", "issue", etc., but the trend is definitely inclusive. See Note 9, supra p. 97. Any possibility that adoption of a child born after a testator's death by another could result in inclusion tends to support the desirability of the present rule, since inquiry into the testator's physiological situation would be academic if an afterborn adopted child could qualify as a beneficiary.

9. *Statutory rules of construction.* N.Y. EPTL § 9-1.3(e) deals with the "fertile octogenarian" as follows:

> (1) Where the validity of a disposition depends upon the ability of a person to have a child at some future time, it shall be presumed, subject to subparagraph (2), that a male can have a child at fourteen years of age or over, but not under that age, and that a female can have a child at twelve years of age or over, but not under that age or over the age of fifty-five years.

> (2) In the case of a living person, evidence may be given to establish whether he or she is able to have a child at the time in question.

> (3) Where the validity of a disposition depends upon the ability of a person to have a child at some future time, the possibility that such person may have a child by adoption shall be disregarded.

> (4) The provisions of subparagraphs (1), (2) and (3) shall not apply for any purpose other than that of determining the validity of a disposition under the rule against perpetuities where such validity depends on the ability of a person to have a child at some future time. A determination of validity or invalidity of a disposition under the rule against perpetuities by the application of subparagraph (1) or (2) or (3) shall not be affected by the later occurrence of facts in contradiction to the facts presumed or determined or the possibility of adoption disregarded under subparagraphs (1) or (2) or (3).

10. *Class gifts.* The cases (unidentified) referred to in the first sentence of the opinion in Jee v. Audley and, presumably, in the third sentence from the end, involve an important aspect of class gifts—the time at which a class "closes." See infra p. 916.

b. The Slothful Executor

IN RE CAMPBELL'S ESTATE

District Court of Appeal of California, 1938.
28 Cal.App.2d 102, 82 P.2d 22.

BARNARD, PRESIDING JUSTICE.

Wesley S. Campbell died on October 4, 1935, leaving a will containing the following clause:

> All the rest, residue, and remainder of my estate, of whatsoever kind and nature and wheresoever situated, I give, devise and bequeath to the four chair officers of San Diego Lodge No. 168 Benevolent and Protective Order of Elks, being the four chair officers in office at the time of distribution of my estate, designated as "Exalted Ruler," "Exalted Leading Knight," "Lecturing Knight" and "Loyal Knight." Such officers shall take the same free of any trust, but it is my expectation that they will employ the same for charitable purposes conformable to the policies of such San Diego Lodge No. 168, and I earnestly request them to make such use thereof. I particularly commend to them my friend May Skinner, if she should survive me, with the purpose that her needs be provided for should her own resources be insufficient.

The will was admitted to probate and in due course a final account and petition for distribution, with objections thereto, came on for hearing, it being stipulated that "the four chair officers" of this lodge were elected annually, and that the individuals who occupied those positions at that time were not the same individuals who had occupied them at the date of decedent's death. The court found that the quoted clause of the will is invalid and void as in contravention of the provisions of sections 715 and 716 of the Civil Code, and that the said Campbell died intestate as to the residue of his estate, and ordered the same distributed to his heirs at law. The four individuals who at that time held the designated positions in this lodge have appealed from the decree of distribution.

The sole question presented is whether this provision of the will is invalid because of a possibility that distribution of the estate might not take place for more than twenty-five years after the death of the testator. If distribution should be thus delayed the provision in question would contravene the rule against perpetuities (sec. 9, art. 20, State Constitution), and also section 716 of the Civil Code, which reads in part: "Every future interest is void in its creation which, by any possibility, may suspend the absolute power of alienation for a longer period than is prescribed in this chapter." This includes the provision of section 715 of that code that such a power shall not be suspended for more than twenty-five years from the time of the creation of the suspension, which in this case would be the date of the decedent's death.

The appellant relies particularly on the case of Belfield v. Booth, 63 Conn. 299, 27 A. 585. That case involved a provision of a will which left certain property in trust, the trust to continue for fourteen years after the executor "has settled with the judge of probate." In considering this provision, under the common-law rule against perpetuities, it was held that the time set for the division of the trust estate was not so remote as to contravene that rule. In so holding the court interpreted the will as, in effect, providing that the fourteen-year trust period was to commence "at the expiration of such reasonable time after his decease as will suffice for the proper settlement of his estate," and stated that it was not to be presumed that such settlement would be delayed longer than that. To follow this reasoning in the instant case would be not only to read into the will something which is not there but to flatly disregard the provision of our statute which makes void any future interest which by any possibility may suspend the absolute power of alienation for a period longer than that prescribed.

In considering a problem similar to the one now before us the supreme court of Illinois in Johnson v. Preston, 226 Ill. 447, 80 N.E. 1001, 10 L.R.A., N.S., 564, said (page 1004):

> It is clear, from the language of the will itself, that whatever interest the executor took under it could not vest in him until the probate of the will, and while this event would, in the ordinary and usual course of events, probably occur within a few months, or at most a few years, after the death of the testatrix, yet it cannot be said that it is a condition that must inevitably happen within 21 years from the death of the testatrix. Since a bare possibility that the condition upon which the estate is to vest may not happen within the prescribed limits is all that is necessary to bring the devise in conflict with the rule, we see no escape from the conclusion that the devise to the executor offends the rule against perpetuities, and is therefore void.

That decision quoted from the case of Husband v. Epling, 81 Ill. 172, 25 Am. Rep. 273, as follows:

> The event here is: "When the estate of Thomas Mason is settled up." Can it be said to have been morally certain, when the instrument was executed, that the estate ever would be settled up? The law requires estates to be settled, and fixes a period within which it shall be done; but it does not, of and by itself, settle them. The presumption is that the law in this regard, as in others, will be obeyed. But this presumption does not amount to absolute certainty. The enforcement of the law, depending on human agencies, is liable to be af-

fected or controlled by many circumstances, and instances where it is not only not fully enforced, but is openly violated, are within the experience of all, so that it is impossible to predict with moral certainty that a thing will be done simply because it is the command of the law that it shall be.

Similar principles have been applied, although upon very different facts, in People v. Simonson, 126 N.Y. 299, 27 N.E. 380, and in Cruikshank v. Chase et al., 113 N.Y. 337, 21 N.E. 64, 4 L.R.A. 140.

In Estate of Troy, 214 Cal. 53, 3 P.2d 930, the court said (page 932):

It has frequently been stated that the provisions of section 716 of the Civil Code do not permit us to wait and see what happens in order to determine the validity or invalidity of the limitation. It is the possibility of the event that will suspend unlawfully the power of alienation which serves to void the limitation at the time of its creation.

The question before us narrows down to whether or not it can be said that this estate must of necessity have been distributed within twenty-five years after the testator's death and that such distribution could not "by any possibility" have been longer delayed. One possibility, which cannot be overlooked, is that probate proceedings might not have been started for many years. Cases are not unknown where parties, through ignorance or neglect, have continued to occupy and use for a long period property left by a decedent before resorting to probate. Property in the form of bank deposits has remained unclaimed for years before probate proceedings were commenced. The closing of many estates has been delayed for years both through neglect and by intention, because of circumstances and conditions. A long delay by reason of protracted litigation is a very real possibility. All of these possibilities, not to mention others, might become realities in a particular case, causing a delay beyond the time limited. While it can be said that the reasonable probabilities were in favor of a distribution of this estate well within the time required, to hold that such a result, with the consequent vesting of interest, was certain to occur and would inevitably take place would be to disregard the statute by accepting a high degree of probability as a certainty.

While statutes of the kind here in question may at times seem unnecessarily harsh in a particular case, they are adopted with a definite aim and purpose in view. These particular statutes are a part of the expression of well-defined public policy. In so far as material here the language therein used is not ambiguous and to interpret the phrase "by any possibility" as in effect meaning "by any probability" would be to alter a plain provision of the statute. Such a change in statutory law should come, if at all, from the legislature and not from the court.

The judgment and decree is affirmed.

NOTES

1. *Administrative contingencies.* What would be the arguments for or against the validity of the following bequests?

(a) After payment of my debts and funeral and administration expenses, I give the rest, residue, and remainder of my estate to *B.* See Collis v. Walker, 172 N.E. 228 (Mass.1930) (valid).

(b) I give $50,000 to such of *B*'s issue as are living at the date of my death, per stirpes, to be paid to them at the time of distribution of my estate. Cf. Trautz v. Lemp, 46 S.W.2d 135 (Mo.1932) (residuary estate to trustees on trust "to commence immediately upon the termination of the administration of my estate"; valid).

(c) I give $50,000 to such of *B*'s issue as are living at the date of distribution of my estate. Cf. In re Campbell's Estate, supra.

(d) I give $5,000 to my sister Susie, to be paid immediately after probate of my will. My purpose in desiring that the payment of this legacy be accelerated is to provide greatly needed funds to my said sister, who has been an invalid for many years. Cf. Union Trust Co. of Springfield v. Nelen, 186 N.E. 66 (Mass.1933) (stock in trust to "be assigned and transferred to said trustee as soon as expedient after the probate" of will; valid).

(e) I give $5,000 to my sister Susie, to be paid immediately after probate of my will, if she is still alive at the time of such payment.

2. *A different view.* The most famous decision to the contrary is Belfield v. Booth, 27 A. 585 (Conn.1893), to which the principal case refers. That decision was iconoclastic in two respects: (1) holding that 14 years after the settlement of the executor's final account would not exceed 21 years, since the time when the executor's accounts "are, or should be, settled in the due course of administration . . . cannot be delayed so long as seven years" after the testator's death; (2) apparently holding that, even if the period were too long, the gift to a class to be ascertained at the end of the period would nevertheless be valid because some members of the class had a vested interest at the testator's death; "the estate, having vested at his decease in a definite class, cannot be divested by any change in the membership of that class. It remains the same class, though composed, from time to time, of different individuals." The latter holding is, of course, the antithesis of the usual rule. Professor Gray deplored the decision. Gray §§ 205.3, 214.2–214.5. But Professor Leach liked the first holding. See Leach, Perpetuities in a Nutshell, 51 Harv. L. Rev. 638, 645 (1938).

3. *Statutory rules of construction.* N.Y. EPTL § 9–1.3(d) deals with the "slothful executor" as follows:

Where the duration or vesting of an estate is contingent upon the probate of a will, the appointment of a fiduciary, the location of a distributee, the payment of debts, the sale of assets, the settlement of an estate, the determination of questions relating to an estate or transfer tax or the occurrence of any specified contingency, it shall be presumed that the creator of such estate intended such contingency to occur, if at all, within twenty-one years from the effective date of the instrument creating such estate.

c. The Unborn Widow

PERKINS V. IGLEHART

Court of Appeals of Maryland, 1944.
183 Md. 520, 39 A.2d 672.

MARBURY, CHIEF JUDGE.

This case arose through a trustee's petition filed in the Circuit Court for Baltimore County, asking for a construction of the will of Lucy James Dun. She died in 1921, a widow with one child, a son, William James Rucker. All parties thought by the trustee to have a possible interest in the estate were brought in by summons or order of publication. . . .

Mrs. Dun had been twice married. Her first husband was Major William A. Rucker. William James Rucker was the son of this marriage. Major Rucker died in 1893, and in 1899 Mrs. Rucker married her second cousin, James Dun, who died in 1908. There were no children of this marriage. The estate which Mrs. Dun left was a valuable one, consisting very largely of an interest she had in the business of R.G. Dun and Co. . . . This interest became part of her residuary estate, was subsequently disposed of by the trustee, and the proceeds invested in securities which now constitute the estate which is to be distributed in these proceedings.

Mrs. Dun, in her will, gave various specific and pecuniary bequests, and then by the fourteenth clause provided as follows:

14. All the rest and residue of my property of every kind, I give, devise and bequeath to the Safe Deposit and Trust Company of Baltimore, in trust to hold the same, with full power to the said Trustee, both as to this trust and as to the trust created by the second clause of this my will, to make and change investments from time to time in its discretion and to sell the whole or any part of the trust estate for any purpose which, in its discretion, may be for the best interest of the same, without obligation on the part of any purchaser to see to the application of the purchase money, and to collect the income of the said trust estate and, after deducting taxes and expenses of administration, to pay over the net income thereof in monthly or quarterly installments, as it may deem best, to my son William James

Rucker, during his life, into his own hands and not into the hands of another and without power of anticipation, or, if my said Trustee shall deem it to be for the best interest of my said son, to apply the said net income for his benefit and for the benefit of his family in its discretion, during his life; and from and after the death of my said son to set apart one-third of said trust estate and pay the net income thereof to his widow during her life or widowhood, and to hold the remaining two-thirds of said trust estate for the benefit of his child or children living at the time of his death and the descendants then living of his deceased children, per stirpes and not per capita, and to pay over and transfer the same, free of any trust, to such of them as shall attain the age of twenty-one years, the original share of each therein to be paid when such age is attained, and any addition thereto, accruing by reason of the death under such age of any beneficiary, to be paid upon such event or as soon thereafter as the person hereby entitled to receive the same is of full age, and until each of them shall attain such age, to apply his or her share, original or accruing, of the net income of said trust estate to and for his or her benefit, maintenance and education, in its discretion; but, if my son shall die without children or descendants him surviving, or if all of them shall die before attaining the age of twenty-one years, then to divide, pay over and transfer the same, free of any trust, to and among the persons who may be the next of kin of my said son according to the laws of Maryland at the time of his death; and from and after the death or remarriage of the widow of my said son, to hold the one-third part of the trust estate, so as above set apart for her, for the benefit of the child or children of my said son then living and the descendants then living of his deceased children, per stirpes and not per capita, under the same limitations as are herein above set forth as to the two-thirds part of the trust estate; but if there shall be no such children or descendants then surviving, or if all of them shall die before attaining the age of twenty one years, to divide, pay over and transfer the same, free of any trust, to and among the persons who would be the next of kin of my said son according to the laws of Maryland if he were living at the time of the death or remarriage of his widow. I authorize and empower my said Trustee to invest fifty thousand ($50,000.00) dollars of the trust estate, or so much thereof as may be requisite, in the purchase for my said son and his family of a home such as he may desire and select, the house and land so purchased to continue however as a part of the trust estate.

The son, William J. Rucker, was twice married; both wives predeceased him. He was a resident of Virginia and died there December 19, 1941, testate, and without issue. W. Allen Perkins and George Pausch were made his executors. They are parties herein, and appellants in No. 4. The appellants in Nos. 5 and 6 are, respectively, a first cousin of William J. Rucker on his father's side, and the executor of a similar first cousin who has died since William J. Rucker's death. The appellants in No. 7 are the widow and administratrix and only child of another first cousin on the Rucker side, who, however, predeceased William J. Rucker. The appellees are three first cousins of William J. Rucker on his mother's side. They are nieces of the testatrix, Mrs. Dun. Other facts in the case will be mentioned and discussed when the parts of this opinion to which they are pertinent are reached.

All of the questions here involved concern that part of the residuary clause of Mrs. Dun's will which disposes of one-third of the residuary estate, after the death of the testatrix's son. There is no dispute that the two-thirds, after the death of the son without leaving any children or descendants, went to the next of kin of the son at the time of his death, and we are advised that it has already been so distributed. The remaining one-third, however, is set apart under separate provisions, and it is in respect to this one-third that the parties have conflicting theories.

It is contended by the Rucker executors that the two gifts over, each to take effect from and after the death or remarriage of the son's widow, violate the rule against perpetuities. This rule is stated by Gray on Perpetuities, Fourth Edition, page 191, paragraph 201 as follows: "No interest is good unless it must vest, if at all, not later than 21 years after some life in being at the creation of the interest." The decisions of this Court follow this rule. It is stated in Graham v. Whitridge, 99 Md. 248, 274, 275, 57 A. 609, 671, 58 A. 36, 66 L.R.A. 408: "The period fixed and prescribed by law for the future vesting of an estate or interest is a life or lives in being at the time of its commencement, and 21 years and a fraction of a year beyond, to cover the period of gestation; and, where property is rendered inalienable or its vesting is deferred for a longer period, the law denounces the devise, the bequest, or the grant as a perpetuity, and declares it void." This statement is quoted with approval in the case of Gambrill v. Gambrill, 122 Md. 563, 89 A. 1094, and the Court further said, 122 Md. at page 569, 89 A. at page 1095: "In determining this question of remoteness, there is an invariable principle that regard is to be had to possible, and not merely actual, events. It is not determined by looking back on events which have occurred and seeing whether the estate has extended beyond the prescribed limit, but by looking forward from the time the limitation was made and seeing whether, according to its terms, there was then a possibility that it might so extend. . . . The event upon the happening of which the remainder is to vest must be one that is certain to happen within the prescribed period, or the limitation will be bad." . . .

The contention of the Rucker executors is that the widow of the son of the testatrix might have been born after the death of the testatrix, and might have lived longer than 21 years and the period allowed for gestation after the death of the son. Therefore, the gift over to the children and descendants, and the gift over to the next of kin in the absence of children and descendants are both void, because both might fail to vest within the required period. This view, which was adopted by the chancellor, seems to be correct, if we read the residuary clause as it is written. It is, however, strenuously resisted for various reasons by other parties to the case. We will take up their contentions in the order which seems most logical. Before doing so, however, it may be well to restate the general rules of construction of wills, so that they may be borne in mind. The whole intention of the testatrix is to be ascertained from the entire will, as well as any specific intention shown in the particular clause under discussion. This intention is to be gathered not only from the will, but from pertinent circumstances surrounding the testatrix at the time of making the will. In cases where it is claimed that the rule against perpetuities is violated, the Court first decides what the will means, and then determines whether the will so interpreted violates the rule. There is a presumption against intestacy, especially where there is a residuary clause, indicating that the testatrix intended to dispose of her entire estate. If there are two constructions, either of which can be adopted without straining the words of the will, the court will adopt that one which disposes of the entire estate, rather than one which results in a total or partial intestacy. But the Court will not write a new will, nor attempt to surmise what the testatrix would have done had she thought of the contingency which has arisen. Nor will the Court substitute its own judgment for hers, as to what she should have done. It will interpret what she said, in the light of the circumstances which have arisen, and determine, from the will itself, what she meant.

The general intention of the residuary clause before us seems to be to provide for the son of the testatrix, his widow, his descendants and his next of kin. The entire clause revolves around the son. No question arises, or could arise, as to the estate given to the son's widow during her unmarried life. It vests within the required period. The question arises as to the two subsequent bequests of the one-third taking effect "from and after the death or remarriage of the widow." The first of these directs the one-third residuary estate to be held for the benefit of the child or children of the son "then living," and the descendants "then living," of his deceased children per stirpes and not per capita. It has been suggested in connection with this bequest that it comes within the rule that a contingent estate to a class vests immediately upon the birth of a member of that class, and becomes vested as to him, with the possibility of his being divested as to part by the subsequent birth of other members of the class. . . . The argument for its application to the present case is that any children of the son must have been in being at his death, or within the usual period of gestation thereafter, and therefore the gift must have taken effect within the period. This view, however, does not take into account the fact that the bequest is not only to the children, but to descendants of deceased children and the further fact that the time of ascertainment of the beneficiaries is fixed at the death or remarriage of the widow. Descendants of deceased children might be the only persons of the class in existence at the death or remarriage of the widow, and they might not have been born during the lifetime of William James Rucker or 21 years thereafter. "If a gift is to a class in this technical sense, and the gift is good as to some members of the class, but is within the rule against perpetuities as to other members, the entire gift must fall. The general rule is that if a gift is void as to any of a class, it is void as to all the class." Miller on Construction of Wills, paragraph 328, page 932. "Assuming then that the devise is not to vest until the remote period, the devise to the whole class is bad; and it is immaterial that some persons are in esse who should they reach 25 would be entitled to share." Gray on Perpetuities, 4th Edition, paragraph 373, page 394, and paragraph 537, page 522. . . . The principle that a contingent gift to a class vests on the birth of a member of the class cannot be applied to make a void estate valid, because it would then conflict with the rule that whether an estate is void as a perpetuity must be determined by what might happen, rather than by what has happened.

It is contended by the appellants in all four appeals that neither the bequest to the children and descendants, nor that to the next of kin are void because the word "widow" in the will does not mean widow in the usually accepted sense of a surviving wife, but means Sally Woods who was engaged to the son at the time the will was made on April 7, 1910, and who married him 21 days later. She was in being at the death of the testatrix, dying on December 20, 1932. The surrounding circumstances which we are asked to consider in connection with this contention are that the will was made at the time when Mrs. Dun had come to Baltimore to take part in the festivities in connection with her son's approaching marriage to Sally Woods; that she undoubtedly had no other thought except that Sally Woods would ultimately become her son's wife, and might become his widow; that she did not name Sally Woods because of a natural delicacy under the circumstances, but that she meant Sally Woods when she used the word "widow." Maryland cases and cases from other jurisdictions are cited in support of this contention. The Maryland case principally relied on is Lavender v. Rosenheim, 110 Md. 150, 72 A. 669, 132 Am. St. Rep. 420. In that case a mother left her estate to a trustee to pay income to her son during his life, and upon his death to pay the principal to his children. In the event no children survived, the principal of the trust estate was given absolutely to "the wife of my said son." The son, at the time the will was made, was married. His wife subsequently divorced him and married another man. The son died, leaving no children, and the Court held that his former wife was entitled to the estate. Other cases which hold that if at the time of the making of the will, there is a person who would fully answer the description of a widow should she survive her husband such person is meant by the word "widow" are Mercantile T. & D. Co. v. Brown, 71 Md. 166, 17 A. 937; In re Solms' Estate, 253 Pa. 293, 98 A. 596; . . . Van Brunt v. Van Brunt, 111 N.Y. 178, 19 N.E. 60; . . . Willis v. Hendry, 127 Conn. 653, 20 A.2d 375. It is, of course, well recognized that a beneficiary may be designated by description rather than by name, and that who is intended can be determined by who would answer that description had the contingency upon which the estate to such person is limited, happened at the time of making the will. That is all these cases hold. In each case the widow was the wife at the time of the making of the will. Had her husband's death occurred at that time, she would have been the widow. In the case before us we are asked to go much further. We are asked to hold that a person who is not married to the testatrix's son is the person she means by her son's widow. It so happened that this person did marry the son, that she died before he did, and that he then married another wife who also predeceased him, and that he died leaving no widow at all. If we should say that Mrs. Dun meant Sally Woods by the word "widow" she used, and if it should have happened that Sally Woods had not married the son at all, but that he had married someone else who survived him, it would necessarily follow that Sally Woods would get the bequest although she had never actually become connected with the testatrix by marriage to her son. The real widow would not take at all. This possible contingency illustrates the instability of the contention. What Mrs. Dun was interested in doing was to take care of her son and his relations. He was taken care of for his life, his widow was taken care of for her unmarried life, his children and descendants and finally his next of kin were attempted to be taken care of. All the residuary clause related to the son, and all the beneficiaries were to take by virtue of their relationship to the son. It was the relationship to the son, and not any particular friendship for Sally Woods which motivated the bequest. Mrs. Dun said she was providing for her son's widow. We must assume that was what she was doing, and not that she was trying to take care of a particular person, even though she thought that person might some day be the widow of her son. . . .

We, therefore, have here an absolute estate in the trustee for the duration of the life of the son and for the duration of the unmarried life of the widow, and then an indefeasibly vested reversion in the heir of the testatrix at the time of her death. That is the effect of an intestacy caused by a void bequest. . . . In Graham v. Whitridge, 99 Md. 248, at page 281, 57 A. 609, at page 614, 58 A. 36, 66 L.R.A. 408, the Court said: "Where an interest or estate is given by deed or will, with a limitation over on a specified contingency, such limitation, if it violates the rule against perpetuities, is for the purpose of determining the effect on the prior disposition of the property, to be considered as stricken out, leaving the prior disposition to operate as if a limitation over had never been made." This quotation was approved in the case of Turner v. Safe Deposit & Trust Co., 148

Md. 371, 129 A. 294. If it is applied to the present case in which the prior limitations were only for life, we have the same situation as if the estate were granted only to the trustee for the life of the son and for the unmarried life of the widow, leaving no granted estate beyond, but a reversion to the heir of the testatrix at the time of her death, who was her son. This, of course, goes to his personal representatives who are the executors of William J. Rucker.

NOTES

1. *Widow's income interest.* The opinion (eighth paragraph) states: "No question arises, or could arise, as to the estate given to the son's widow during her unmarried life."

(a) What is the explanation of the next statement in the opinion: "It vests within the required period"?

(b) Would this provision have been valid if the will had read "pay such income as the trustee shall in its absolute and uncontrolled discretion determine to his widow during her life or widowhood," instead of "pay the net income thereof to his widow during her life or widowhood"?

2. *Remote contingent interests.* On what grounds did the court hold invalid the provision to take effect on the death or remarriage of the son's widow for the benefit of—

(a) The son's descendants?

(b) The son's next of kin?

3. *Hypothetical gift.* What effect, if any, would the Rule against Perpetuities have on a testamentary trust to pay the net income to testator's son John for life, and after his death to pay the net income for her life to such person as should at the date of his death be his surviving widow, and after her death to transfer the principal to John's children?

4. *Construction.* What argument could one make for the validity of the provisions in Note 2 if testatrix's son William had been married to Sally when the will was executed?

To what extent does the force of such argument depend on whether—

(a) The will referred to the son's "wife," or to the son's "widow"?

(b) Sally were in fact William's surviving widow, or Sally should predecease William, who should then remarry and leave Mary as his surviving widow?

See generally Leach, Perpetuities in a Nutshell, 51 Harv. L. Rev. 638, 644 (1938); Leach, Perpetuities in Perspective: Ending the Rule's Reign of Terror, 65 Harv. L. Rev. 721, 731 (1952); Gray § 214.

5. *Statutory rules of construction.* N.Y. EPTL § 9–1.3(c) deals with the "unborn widow" as follows:

> Where an estate would, except for this paragraph, be invalid because of the possibility that the person to whom it is given or limited may be a person not in being at the time of the creation of the estate, and such person is referred to in the instrument creating such estate as the spouse of another without other identification, it shall be presumed that such reference is to a person in being on the effective date of the instrument.

Would this statute save the invalid interests in Perkins v. Iglehart? Suppose, instead, that the widow were in fact unborn at the time of the creation of the interests. Would these interests nonetheless be valid?

———————

"Vest if at all." One point of frequent confusion about the Rule stems from the requirement that the interest be certain to vest *if at all* within the permissible period. The Rule does not require that the interest be certain to vest within the period, but only that it be certain to vest *or disappear* within the period. The vice at which the Rule aims is not the postponement of enjoyment but the possibility that an interest may remain contingent too long; the Rule is satisfied either if the interest must become vested or if the interest is so limited that it cannot remain contingent beyond the period.

An illustration of how the phrase "vest if at all" comes into play is the hypothetical in Note 4(b), supra p. 888. Suppose the limitation in Jee v. Audley had been "to the daughters of John and Elizabeth Jee living at my death who are also living at the time of failure of Mary's issue." Assuming that the court would construe the gift to Mary as one on indefinite failure of issue, when would the gift to the daughters take effect? Can we be sure that Mary's issue will fail within 21 years after some life in being? Assuming that your answer is "no" (it should be), is the gift to the daughters void? Why not?

4. MISCELLANEOUS ASPECTS OF THE RULE

a. The Effect of the Rule Against Perpetuities on Trust Duration

Case law imposes no limit on the duration of either legal or equitable interests. The Rule against Perpetuities invalidates interests that may remain contingent for longer than the period of the Rule; it does not curtail the length of enjoyment of interest. If it did, the most obvious interest to be struck down would be the longest in duration, i.e., a fee simple, which, on the contrary, is exactly the sort of ownership the Rule seeks to promote.

There is no common law rule that directly limits the duration of either a private trust or a charitable trust. Charitable trusts may, and many do, last indefinitely. It is, however, impossible, under the common law version of the Rule against Perpetuities, to create a perpetual private trust. Just as all income interests necessarily end at the death of the income beneficiary, so also, there necessarily comes a point after which all succeeding beneficial interests must vest (or fail) remotely. Though a mandatory income interest for the benefit of both a living person and his or her children is valid, notwithstanding the fact that it may endure for longer than the perpetuities period, extending the interest to more remote generations would likely run afoul of the Rule against Perpetuities.

NOTES

1. *Applying the common law Rule.* Are the interests of B, B's oldest surviving child, and C in the following limitation valid under the common law Rule against Perpetuities?

A by will transfers property to *T*, in trust to pay the income to *B* for *B*'s life, on *B*'s death to pay the income to the oldest child of *B* living at *B*'s death for his life, remainder to *C*. When *A* died, *B* and *C* were both alive.

2. *Accumulations.* It was held in the famous case of Thellusson v. Woodford, 32 Eng. Rep. 1030 (Ch. 1805), that a direction to accumulate income for the permissible period of the Rule against Perpetuities was valid. Although in many jurisdictions, including England, there have been statutory departures from that decision, it still remains the general rule. See White v. Fleet Bank, 739 A.2d 373 (Me. 1999); 2 Scott and Ascher on Trusts § 9.3.10; Sitkoff, The Lurking Rule Against Accumulations of Income, 100 Nw. U. L. Rev. 501 (2006).

b. The Effect of Invalidating Interests Under the Rule

The effect of the Rule on an interest not certain to vest in time is to make the interest void *ab initio*. What is the effect of the Rule on interests that precede or follow the void interest but are themselves valid under the Rule?

LOVERING V. WORTHINGTON

Supreme Judicial Court of Massachusetts, 1870.
106 Mass. 86.

MORTON, J.

This is a bill in equity, brought by the trustees under the will of Joseph Lovering, to obtain the instructions of the court as to their duties under said will.

The thirteenth article of the will devises certain real estate to the trustees upon the following trusts: To pay the net rents and profits to Nancy Gay, a daughter of the testator, during her life, "and on this further trust, upon the decease of said Nancy Gay, to pay the net income of said two stores in State Street, and said house in Tremont Street, to her children, half yearly or oftener, if convenient to said trustees, during the lives of said children. And as the children of said Nancy shall successively decease, said stores in State Street, and said house in Tremont Street, are to be conveyed in fee, or in case the same be sold, the proceeds are to be paid and distributed, to and among the heirs at law of all the children of said Nancy, that is to say, that, as said Nancy's children shall successively decease, a proportion of said estates or the proceeds are to be conveyed or distributed to and among the respective heirs at law of each child so deceasing, said Nancy's grandchildren to take in right of representation of their deceased parents."

At the date of the will, and at the death of the testator, the said Nancy Gay was a widow having eight children, and she died in 1870 leaving the same eight children.

The first question presented by the trustees is, whether the limitations of said trust estates are valid beyond the life estate limited to the said Nancy Gay, or are void as tending to create perpetuities.

The will presents a case of a devise to Nancy Gay for her life, with a limitation over of a life estate to her children, and a further limitation over of a fee in the heirs at law of such children. The rule as to perpetuities is fully established, and has been recognized and applied in numerous recent decisions of this court. . . . Applying the rule to this case, we see no ground upon which it can be held that the devise of life estates to the children of Mrs. Gay is invalid. If we assume that this devise includes children born after the death of the testator, and therefore that it is contingent and executory, yet it is not void for remoteness. The devise takes effect, and the life estate in each child necessarily becomes absolute, at the death of Mrs. Gay. If, as is claimed by the defendants, the gift over of the fee to the grandchildren is void, then at the death of Mrs. Gay the remainder in fee would vest either in the residuary devisees or in the heirs at law of the testator. In either event, there were persons in being who by joining with the tenants for life could convey the whole estate. In other words, if this devise is upheld, it does not render the estate incapable of alienation for a longer period than the life of Mrs. Gay, and therefore it is not within the rule against perpetuities.

If the limitation over of the fee to the heirs at law of the children of Mrs. Gay is void, it is clear that the effect of such invalidity is not to defeat the prior life estates. The general rule is, that, if a limitation over is void for remoteness, it places all prior gifts in the same situation as if the devise over had been wholly omitted. If the prior gift was in fee, the estate is vested in the first taker discharged of the limitation over; if for life, it takes effect as a life estate. Brattle Square Church v. Grant, 3 Gray, 142. Lewis on Perpetuities, 657. In 1 Jarman on Wills, 240, the rule is stated to be, that "if a testator devise his lands to his son A. for life, with remainder to the children of A. for life, with remainder to the children of such children in fee, the last limitation would certainly be void; but it is clear that the prior devises to the testator's son and his children would be valid, and the reversion in fee, subject to those devises, and that only, would descend to the testator's heir at law as real estate undisposed of. So, if the personal estate were bequeathed in a similar manner, the gifts to A. and his children successively for life would be good, and the ulterior interest only would devolve to the next of kin." The rule is based upon the paramount consideration in the construction of wills, that the intentions of the testator are to be carried into effect as far as they can be consistently with the rules of law.

We have considered the case as though the devises were directly to Mrs. Gay and her children. The fact that trustees are appointed by the will to hold the legal title does not affect the principle. The estate is not thereby made incapable of alienation. At any time after the death of Mrs. Gay, the persons beneficially interested may, with the consent of the trustees, terminate the trust and convey the estate. . . .

We have not deemed it necessary to consider the other questions argued by the counsel. Our decision determines fully all the present duties of the trustees. The other questions may never be litigated, and if litigated may involve the rights of parties not now before the court. We, therefore, refrain from expressing an opinion upon them.

The result is, that the limitation of life estates to the children of Mrs. Gay is valid, and they are entitled to the net income of the trust estate during their lives.

Decree accordingly.

NOTES

1. *Time of adjudication.* The Massachusetts courts have generally declined to rule on the validity of a subsequent interest until all prior interests have expired. See Dewire v. Haveles, 534 N.E.2d 782 (Mass.1989); B.M.C. Durfee Trust Co. v. Taylor, 89 N.E.2d 777 (Mass.1950).

2. *Secondary life estates.* Why would the gifts to Nancy's children be independently valid?

3. *Each interest considered separately.* In holding that, even if the gift to the heirs of Nancy's children were void, the invalidity of that gift would not affect the otherwise valid interests of Nancy's children, *Lovering* follows the usual rule. In other words, life estates, including income interests, are separable from remainders, and the former are not invalid simply because the latter are. See Gray § 249.1.

4. *Rationale.* Is there any reason, other than some general conception that a disposition should be salvaged as far as possible, for assuming that a transferor would prefer to have life estates or income interests stand, even if the ultimate gift is void?

5. *Infectious invalidity.* Occasionally, the courts have found that invalidation of one interest would so distort the estate plan as to require the voiding of other, completely separate, interests. In Richards v. Stone, 278 N.W. 657 (Mich.1938), the testator left one-third of his estate to his daughter, outright. He left the other two-thirds in trust for his two sons and their issue, but in a manner that violated the Rule against Perpetuities. The three siblings were his sole heirs. The effect of invalidating only the trusts would be a partial intestacy of two-thirds of the estate, in which event the daughter would receive five-ninths and the sons two-ninths each. The court, finding a general intention to treat the children equally, struck the outright bequest as well, so that the entire estate passed, by intestate succession, to the three children in equal shares.

6. *Effect on successive interests.* Subject to Note 5 supra, a valid interest that follows one or more void interests is usually unaffected by the invalidity of the prior interests. In a common law jurisdiction, however, an interest that follows a remote interest is likely also to vest remotely.

7. *A different approach.* When an interest appears to be invalid under the Uniform Statutory Rule Against Perpetuities, infra pp. 934–936, § 3 thereof directs the court to reform the disposition "in the manner that most closely approximates the transferor's manifested plan of distribution" and is within the period of the rule.

c. The Rule Against Perpetuities and Destructible Interests

RYAN v. WARD

Court of Appeals of Maryland, 1949.
192 Md. 342, 64 A.2d 258.

MARBURY, CHIEF JUDGE.

On April 16, 1928, John R. Ward of Baltimore City executed and delivered a deed of trust to the Baltimore Trust Company conveying to the latter certain personal property consisting of stocks and bonds. The record does not show the value of this personal property at the date of the deed of trust, but it appears that the corpus of the estate, as of September 26, 1945, was approximately $32,500. John R. Ward died on October 27, 1928, and Frank R. Ward, who was given a life estate by the terms of the deed of trust, died on September 26, 1945. . . . In 1934 the Baltimore Trust Company was removed as trustee and the Baltimore National Bank was appointed substituted trustee. The latter filed its bill of complaint in the Circuit Court of Baltimore City in 1946, asking for a construction of the deed of trust, and naming as parties all the living parties who might possibly have an interest in the matter, as well as the administratrix d.b.n.c.t.a. of the estate of John R. Ward. By the will of John R. Ward, all of his estate and property was left to his son, Frank R. Ward, if the latter survived him, which was the case. Frank R. Ward, who was a resident of New Jersey, left a will by which all of his estate was left to his wife, Olive Maria Ward, provided she survived him, which was the case. He also left three children, Ruth E. Ward, David E. Ward, and John F. Ward. Olive M. Ward is the executrix of the estate of Frank R. Ward and also the administratrix d.b.n.c.t.a. of the estate of John F. Ward. James J. Ryan was appointed by the court as guardian ad litem for all persons not in being whose interests might be affected by the proceedings. [T]he chancellor filed his decree holding some of the future interests good and some void. From this decree the guardian ad litem appeals here, and cross appeals were filed by all other parties.

The deed of trust gives the trustee full and complete power to manage, sell, reinvest, and otherwise deal with the trust estate, and to collect the dividends and profits and to pay over the entire net income in monthly installments to the grantor, John R. Ward, during the term of his natural life. It is further provided that " . . . during the life of the Grantor he shall have the right by one or more instruments in writing, personally signed by him and delivered to the Trustee, to withdraw from the operation of this Deed of Trust such sum or sums as he may in his absolute discretion see fit, such withdrawals, however, shall not be in excess of the sum of Fifteen Hundred Dollars ($1500.00) per annum during his lifetime, and to the extent of any sum or sums so withdrawn, the principal of the trust hereby created shall be reduced accordingly, or expended entirely." It is further provided by the deed of trust:

> From and after the death of the Grantor, the Trustee shall pay over the net income derived therefrom in monthly instalments unto Frank R. Ward, son of the Grantor, during his lifetime, and upon the death of the Grantor's said son, Frank R. Ward, or from and after the Grantor's death in case his said son should predecease him, the Trustee shall pay the net income derived from the trust fund unto the lineal descendants, per stirpes, from time to time living, of the Grantor's said son until the death of the last surviving child of the Grantor's said son, who shall be living at the time of the Grantor's death, and upon the death of the last surviving child of the Grantor's said son, who shall be living at the time of the death of the Grantor, the trust hereby created shall terminate, and the corpus or principal thereof shall be by the Trustee conveyed, delivered and paid over absolutely free, clear and discharged of any further trust, in equal and even shares unto the then living children of the Grantor's said son, and unto the issue then living of each then deceased child of the Grantor's said son, so that each then living child of the Grantor's said son shall take and receive, absolutely, one equal share thereof, and the issue then living of each then deceased child of the Grantor's said son shall take and receive, per stirpes and not per capita, one equal share thereof absolutely.

There is a spendthrift provision for both principal and income, applicable after the death of the grantor, and it is also provided that the Trustee shall have authority to receive any other funds granted, devised, or bequeathed by the grantor or any other person for the uses of the trust created, with a proviso that during the life of the grantor, at his written request, the Trustee is directed to pay over to him the principal of any funds or property, or any part thereof, which may be received by the Trustee as an addition to the original principal of the trust. This right of withdrawal is limited to the additions to the trust fund.

The question before the court is whether any of the estates attempted to be created by this deed of trust are in violation of the rule against perpetuities. This rule requires that an interest or an estate, to be good, must vest not later than twenty-one years, plus the usual period of gestation, after some life in being at the time of its creation. In determining its applicability, the court looks forward from the time of the taking effect of the instrument in question to determine whether a possible interest is certain to vest within the prescribed period. . . .

Where an interest or an estate is created by will, the question is determined by looking forward from the date of the taking effect of the will which is, of course, the death of the testator, and not the date of the will. Gray's The Rule Against Perpetuities, 3rd Ed., Paragraph 231, p. 205; 4th Ed., Paragraph 231, p. 235. Where the interest or estate is created by deed, its effectiveness vel non is determined as of the time "when the deed became operative." Bowerman v. Taylor, 126 Md. 203 at page 212, 94 A. 652, 654. . . .

The appellant Ryan suggests (without any citation of authority) that since there is an element of revocability in the deed, the effective date from which we must consider the succeeding estates is not the date of the execution and delivery of the deed, but the date of the death of the grantor. The element of revocability is the right of withdrawal of the original trust fund, not, however, to be "in excess of the sum of $1500.00 per annum during his lifetime" and the unlimited right of withdrawal of any funds or property, or any part thereof, which may have been added to the trust estate from time to time. The terms of the provision authorizing the withdrawal of the original principal do not clearly indicate whether this right is cumulative or not, that is, whether the right must be exercised each year, if at all, or whether the grantor could withdraw at any time, not only the $1500 allowed during that year, but also $1500 for each previous year in which he had not exercised the right. Since, however, the grantor attempted to put a limitation upon his own actions, and did not reserve to himself the right to withdraw any or all of the original principal at any time he saw fit, while reserving that right as to subsequent additions, we hold that the right should be construed as non-cumulative, and lost as to the amount authorized to be withdrawn in any year, if not exercised during that year. We are not advised what was his age at the time he created it. No matter what it was, we cannot assume, viewing it prospectively, that he would not live long enough to withdraw the entire principal. Until the grantor actually died, therefore, he had the possible right to destroy the trust estate by withdrawals, although this destruction could be only partial until the end of twenty-two years.

Professor Gray, in his work "The Rule Against Perpetuities" (3rd Ed., Paragraph 203, p. 175; 4th Ed., Paragraph 203, p. 193), states that " . . . a future interest, if destructible at the mere pleasure of the present owner of the property, is not regarded as an interest at all and the Rule does not concern itself with it." . . . In paragraph 524.1 a case is suggested where a conveyance is made to A for life, with a power of revocation, A being the settlor, and, in default of exercise, to A's children at 25. If the period of the rule against perpetuities runs from the date of the conveyance, the ultimate limitation is too remote, but the author states that it seems to be correct to take A's death as the critical date, because A is at liberty to destroy the future interest. He cites the prevailing doctrine that the remoteness of limitations under a general power to appoint by deed is to be reckoned from the exercise of the power, as a reason why the same construction, by analogy, should be used in a revocable deed. In that connection he approves the reasoning of the Supreme Court of Hawaii in the case of Manufacturers Life Insurance Company v. von Hamm–Young Company, 34 Hawaii 288. The case, decided in 1937, involves the application of the rule against perpetuities to a life insurance trust agreement. The settlor reserved the right to revoke the trust agreement or to change the beneficiary. If the trust became effective at the time of its execution, there was a possibility that the future interest might not vest within the required period after that date. On the other hand, if the future interest did not come into being until the death of the settlor, no transgression of the rule could occur. The court, on the authority of Gray and of other cases, determined that the effective date from which to view the future interest was the death of the settlor, on the ground that such interest was destructible at his pleasure up until that time.

... In the case of Pulitzer v. Livingston, 89 Me. 359, 36 A. 635, the court held that the rule against perpetuities did not apply to future interests which were destructible at the will and pleasure of the present owner. The deeds in question in that case contained express powers of revocation, and the court held that they were thereby removed from the operation of the rule against perpetuities. . . . In Lewis on Law of Perpetuity, Law Library Ed., Ch. XX, p. 483, it is stated that "the great aim of the laws against remoteness is secured in the immediate and unrestrained alienability of the property by means of a power of appointment." In an article in 45 Harvard Law Review, beginning at p. 896, the effect of the rule against perpetuities on insurance trusts is discussed, and the conclusion is reached that in calculating the period of perpetuity the courts have wisely excluded that period during which the property was subject to the absolute control of a single person. In another article in 51 Harvard Law Review by W. Barton Leach, entitled "Perpetuities in a Nutshell," at p. 638, it is stated: "So long as one person has the power at any time to make himself the sole owner (of the trust estate) there is no tying-up of the property and no violation of the policy of the rule against perpetuities." In 86 Univ. of Pa. Law Review 221, the decision of the Hawaii court above quoted is discussed and is stated to be the first decision on the question. The writer says that "unhampered by precedent, the Hawaiian court has enunciated a salutory [sic] rule which should be followed in this country." . . .

Restatement, Property, Section 373, states "The period of time during which an interest is destructible, pursuant to the uncontrolled volition, and for the exclusive personal benefit of the person having such a power of destruction is not included in determining whether the limitation is invalid under the rule against perpetuities." Comment d states that the required destructibility exists only when some person possesses a complete power of disposition over the subject matter of the future interests,

and can exercise this power of disposition for his own exclusive benefit.
. . .

These cases and statements from recognized authorities amply sustain the proposition that, where a settlor has power during his lifetime to revoke or destroy the trust estate, the question whether interests, or any of them, created by a deed of trust are void because in violation of the rule against perpetuities, is to be determined as of the date of the settlor's death, and not as of the date when the deed of trust takes effect. It will be observed, however, that the cases cited involve situations where the trust is revocable at will, or could be destroyed by a single act of the settlor such as a change of beneficiary in an insurance policy, or a sale of the trust property and the use of the proceeds. It is stated in the article in 51 Harvard Law Review, already referred to, at p. 663:

> The situation is analogous to future interests after an estate tail, where the period of perpetuities is computed from the date of expiration of the estate tail; the power to disentail makes the tenant in tail the substantial owner and causes interests after the estate tail to be in substance gifts by the last tenant in tail at the time of expiration of his estate. The situation is also analogous to gifts in default of the exercise of a general power by deed or will, the period of perpetuities being computed from the expiration of the power—i.e., the death of the donee.

There is no case, so far as we have been able to find, which deals with a strictly limited power of withdrawal which can be exercised only over a period of years, and which cannot be used to destroy the entire estate until a number of years has elapsed. In the case before us, as we have shown, the estate could not be entirely destroyed during the first twenty-two years of its existence. There is some difference of opinion among the text writers whether the power to encroach upon the corpus is the same as the power to revoke. . . . The cases we have cited indicate that it is not the method of destruction but the destructibility which is the controlling factor. That being so, we are unable to say that in a case such as the one before us, the trust estate is destructible, as that word is used in connection with the Rule against Perpetuities. There is a possibility of ultimate destruction, but the estate is not destructible at the time of its creation, or at any one time thereafter. Any destruction must be by a gradual diminishing of the corpus, until, at the last, there is left only a balance equal to the amount which can be withdrawn in any year. At that time, the grantor can destroy the trust, but his right to do so is contingent upon the previous withdrawals, and does not become absolute until he has completed all such withdrawals, over a period of years. What would be the situation if the settlor were given power to revoke after twenty-two years, or power to withdraw the entire trust estate at that time, need not be decided, because we have no such situation here. It is our conclusion, there-fore, that the rule against perpetuities operates upon the estates created, as of the date of the execution and delivery of the deed of trust.

There is, of course, no question that the beneficial life estate of Frank R. Ward, son of the grantor, was valid. Thereafter, the net income is to be paid *unto the lineal descendants per stirpes from time to time living* of Frank R. Ward until the death of the last surviving child of said Frank R. Ward who shall be living at the time of the death of the grantor. At that time, the trust is to terminate, and the residuary estates are to com-mence. It is apparent that Frank R. Ward could have had a son born prior to the death of John R. Ward, who could have been living at the death of John R. Ward, and who could have lived more than twenty-one years af-ter the death of Frank R. Ward. The death of such child, if he were the last survivor of the children of Frank R. Ward, would fix the date of the ending of the trust estate and the commencement of the estates in re-mainder created by the deed of trust. It was quite within the bounds of possibility, at the time of the creation of the trust, that this date might be beyond a life and lives then in being and twenty-one years thereafter, plus the usual period of gestation. Consequently, it is agreed by everyone, and the court so held, that the remainders, after the termination of the trust estate, were void.

The gift of the beneficial estates pur autre vie, after the death of Frank R. Ward which gift, as we have shown, is to the lineal descendants per stirpes, *from time to time living,* of the grantor's son, might vest in one of those lineal descendants who was born more than twenty-one years after the death of Frank R. Ward, but before the death of his last surviv-ing child. This is a class gift. In such a case, it is well recognized that if it "is good as to some members of the class, but is within the rule against perpetuities as to other members, the entire gift must fail. The general rule is that if a gift is void as to any of a class, it is void as to all of the class." Miller, Construction of Wills, Paragraph 328. . . .

[W]e hold that the gifts pur autrie [sic] vie are void and the trust es-tate has now ended. As John R. Ward, by his will, left all his property to Frank R. Ward, who was his only child, the trust property belongs to the latter's estate. [T]here is no necessity for the property to be administered through the estate of John R. Ward, thereby multiplying the costs and expenses. Distribution can be made directly by the trustee to Olive M. Ward, Executrix of the estate of Frank R. Ward, and such distribution will relieve the trustee of further responsibilities. Decree reversed. . . .

NOTES

1. *Trust instrument effective at settlor's death.* If the court had held that the effective date of the trust was the date of death of the settlor, John R.

Ward (Oct. 27, 1928), rather than that of the delivery of the trust deed (Apr. 16, 1928), would that holding have validated—

(a) The income interest for the lineal descendants of Frank R. Ward?

(b) The gift of the principal to the issue of Frank R. Ward?

2. *Trust instrument effective on delivery.* Assuming that the effective date of the trust was that of the delivery of the trust deed—

(a) Why was it "agreed by everyone" (third-to-last paragraph of the opinion) that the gift of the principal was void?

(b) What event or events would have to occur during the period specified for the income interest for Frank's lineal descendants, in order to give any such descendant a "vested" right to the income?

3. *Power to revoke.* Suppose that *A*, by an irrevocable inter vivos trust, reserves a life estate and gives the remainder to *A*'s children at age 25. Is the remainder valid? Suppose instead that *A* reserves, expressly or by operation of law, the power to revoke the trust. Is the result the same? On the effect of a power of revocation on the Rule against Perpetuities, see Cook v. Horn, 104 S.E.2d 461 (Ga.1958); Fitzpatrick v. Mercantile–Safe Deposit & Trust Co., 155 A.2d 702 (Md.1959).

4. *Share payable at specified age.* One of the issues in the problem in Note 3, supra, is whether "at age 25" requires survival to age 25. Under the traditional rule, a gift or bequest "at" a given age requires survival to the stated age. Thus, if a donee or legatee fails to survive to the stated age, the gift or bequest fails. In contrast, a gift or bequest "to be paid at" or "payable at" a given age does not require survival to the stated age; moreover, a gift or bequest "at" a given age "to be paid with interest" does not require survival. Gifts and bequests of the latter types may therefore vest earlier than those of the former type. These exceedingly arbitrary rules derive from Clobberie's Case, 86 Eng. Rep. 476 (Ch. 1677). In contrast, the Third Restatement of Property provides: "Unless the language or circumstances establish that the transferor had a different intention, a future interest that is distributable upon reaching a specified age is conditioned on the beneficiary's living to that age." Restatement (Third) of Property: Wills and Other Donative Transfers § 26.6 (2011).

5. *Power to withdraw principal.* Assuming that the trust contained no power of revocation as such, what would be the effect of the settlor's reserving the power to withdraw any or all of the principal at any time?

By statute in Pennsylvania, the period of the Rule "shall be measured from the expiration of any time during which one person while living has the unrestricted power to transfer to himself the entire legal and beneficial interest in the property." 20 Pa. Cons. Stat. § 6104(c). The accompanying commentary states: "For revocable trusts the period would begin as of the settlor's death."

d. Application of the Rule Against Perpetuities to Charitable Gifts

Vague statements often appear to the effect that the Rule against Perpetuities does not apply to gifts to charity. Such statements may simply be erroneous, overly broad restatements of the settled rule that there is no limit on the duration of charitable trusts, which may, and often do, last indefinitely. Nonetheless, the following propositions are well established:

(a) A future interest for a charitable purpose is exempt from the Rule against Perpetuities if it follows a present interest for a charitable purpose. See, e.g., Trustees of the Storrs Agricultural School v. Whitney, 8 A. 141 (Conn.1887), in which the court said:

> The gift of property first to one charitable use and then to another upon the determination of the first trustee no longer to use, as was done in this case, does not offend the statute of perpetuities. The law favors charitable uses. It does so with knowledge that in most cases they are intended to be practically perpetual; and it is willing to permit what of evil results from the devotion to such length of use in consideration of the beneficent results flowing therefrom. As one charitable use may be perpetual, the gift to two in succession can be of no longer duration nor of greater evil. The property is taken out of commerce, but it instantly goes into perpetual servitude to charity. [8 A. at 143.]

(b) A future interest for a charitable purpose is subject to the Rule against Perpetuities if it follows a present interest for a noncharitable purpose. See, e.g., Institution for Savings in Roxbury and Its Vicinity v. Roxbury Home for Aged Women, 139 N.E. 301 (Mass.1923).

(c) A future interest for a noncharitable purpose is subject to the Rule against Perpetuities even if it follows a present interest for a charitable purpose. See, e.g., Proprietors of Church in Brattle Square v. Grant, 69 Mass. (3 Gray) 142 (1855).

5. CLASS GIFTS

a. Creation and Construction of Class Gifts

Most trusts include at least one class gift. Indeed, the typical gift of principal following an income interest is to a class, rather than to named individuals. Gifts to classes present special problems under the Rule against Perpetuities. But before turning to those problems, we need a preliminary understanding of class gifts.

Definition and illustration. A gift to a class is a gift of property to a number of persons collectively described, the share of each member of the class depending on the total number of members of the class as finally ascertained; i.e., if five members are ultimately entitled to share, each takes one-fifth, if six, each takes one-sixth, etc. A class gift differs from a gift of individual interests to several persons, as to which the governing instrument fixes the share of each. Suppose that a testator bequeaths $150,000 "to my brothers, *B*, *C*, and *D*," and gives the residuary estate to *X*; and that *B* predeceases the testator, so that *B*'s interest in the gift lapses. This legacy, if construed as a gift of individual interests, would be a gift of a one-third interest in the fund ($50,000) to each beneficiary; and, under such a construction, *C* and *D* could not profit from the lapse of *B*'s interest, but would merely take $50,000 apiece, *B*'s share going to the residuary legatee *X*, as a lapsed legacy. If the legacy were construed as a gift to a class, however, the share of each member of the class would be determined (in this case) at the testator's death, and *C* and *D*, the qualifying members of the class, would share the fund, each taking $75,000. (Anti-lapse statutes may or may not apply in this context.)

Dispositions describing a group of persons generally and collectively are usually construed as gifts to classes. Typical examples are gifts to "my issue," "*B*'s children," "*C*'s heirs," "*D*'s brothers and sisters." If, however, the beneficiaries are designated solely by their names, as "to *B*, *C*, and *D*," the gift is usually held to be one of individual interests, rather than a gift to a class. On the borderline are dispositions that use both a collective and an individual description ("to my brothers, *B*, *C*, and *D*"); in such situations, the cases are hard to reconcile.

It is useful to approach the subject of class gifts by asking a series of questions. The first is whether the settlor intended a gift to a class. This question is seldom difficult to answer. The second is, assuming that the settlor intended a class gift, what is the primary meaning of the class term used? For example, suppose a gift to "the children of *J*." Would the class of *J*'s children include an adopted child, a nonmarital child, or someone raised as his child by *J* but unrelated and never adopted? The answer depends on the intention of the transferor and is determined in the same manner as other problems of construction.

In this connection it is necessary to distinguish classes of "children," "issue," and the like from classes of "heirs," "next of kin," "distributees," or similarly described groups. In the case of gifts to "heirs," etc., the makeup of the class generally depends on the applicable intestate succession statute as it exists at the time of death of the person whose heirs make up the class. Thus, the share of each taker depends on the statutory scheme, rather than on the rule of equality that applies to classes of relatives such as "children" or "brothers."[7] See generally Casner, Construction of Gifts to Heirs and the Like, 53 Harv. L. Rev. 207 (1939).

The "closing" of the class. Assuming that the settlor intended a class gift, and determination of the primary meaning of the class, the next question is, how soon must a person be born in order to have a chance to share in the distribution? If *A* by will makes a gift to "my grandchildren," does *A* mean only those grandchildren alive when *A* makes his will, only those grandchildren born before *A*'s death, or all grandchildren whenever born? The question is sometimes phrased, in this book and elsewhere, in terms of when the class closes. The statement that a class closes at a certain time means that nobody born after that time can share, except that a child who is later born alive is treated as having been in being from the date of conception. It is important to realize that the statement that a class is closed means nothing else. It does not mean that a person must be alive when the class closes in order to take, since the estate of a person who dies before then may nonetheless be entitled to a share. Nor does it insure that those living at the time will take, since their interest may still be subject to some unfulfilled condition.

The time for closing a class is determined in one of three ways. It may be (and ought to be) fixed by the instrument creating a gift. For example, *A* may by will make a gift "to my grandchildren living at my death." Unfortunately, testators and settlors (and their lawyers) do not have a good track record on this score. A second way to fix the time for closing a class is to ask when the class closes physiologically. In the case of a gift to the children of *B*, the class is certain to close on the death of *B*, or (if *B* is a man) within a period of gestation thereafter. A third way to determine the time of closing is by reference to a "rule of construction." Such a rule can close the class before it closes physiologically. Doing so sometimes carries out the testator's or settlor's presumed intent. Sometimes, however, it serves merely as a "rule of convenience," to expedite distribution and enjoyment of property earlier than would otherwise be the case. One can have the best of both worlds by assuming that the testator or settlor desired early distribution and enjoyment. In fact, the rule of convenience is not entirely consistent with either a theory of presumed intent or a theory of early distribution and enjoyment. It is, instead, somewhat arbitrary. See generally Becker, A Critical Look at Class Gifts and the Rule of Convenience, 42 Real Prop. Prob. & Tr. J. 491 (2007).

The general "rule of convenience" is that, in the absence of an expression of contrary intent, *the class closes whenever any member is entitled to immediate possession and enjoyment of a share of principal.* This rule, in the case of personalty, permits immediate distribution of at least a mini-

---

[7] Members of classes of "issue" and "descendants" may also take unequally, e.g., by right of representation.

mum share to the first member who qualifies. In the case of realty, it tends to make title more marketable by identifying potential parties in interest and eliminating claims by those born thereafter.

The following examples of a gift "to the children of B" illustrate the operation of the rule of convenience. Assume in all cases that B is still alive, since, if B were dead, the class would have closed physiologically at B's death.

(1) In the case of an outright gift "*to the children of B*," the beneficiaries are entitled to enjoyment immediately on the operative date of the instrument (death of testator in case of a will; date of delivery in case of a deed), and the class therefore closes at that time. Suppose a legacy of $100,000 to the children of B, and that, at the death of the testator, B has two children, X and Y. Since the class closes then, no child of B born thereafter can share, and X and Y receive immediate distributions of $50,000 apiece. If the class remained open until the death of B, it would be impossible to determine immediately even the minimum share of X and Y, since it would be impossible to predict how many more children B might have. This would make any distribution to X and Y unsafe and would prejudice X and Y by making it impossible for them to predict even the minimum amount of their interests. No careful fiduciary would risk guessing that B would not have more than five children and thus distributing $20,000 apiece to X and Y, since, if the class remained open, there might ultimately be ten children of B entitled to share, reducing each share to $10,000, and making it necessary for the fiduciary to try to get back from X and Y the excess of $10,000 apiece, which they might by then have dissipated. To avoid these difficulties, the courts have held that, in the absence of any manifestation of contrary intent, the class closes at the death of the testator or the date of deed delivery. In other words, the transferor's apparent intention to make an immediate and irrevocable gift overrides any apparent (conflicting) intention that all children of B, whenever born, share in the gift. An exception to this general rule applies if, on the effective date of the instrument, there are no members of the class, e.g., in the example above, if B has no children when the testator dies. In that case, the class does not close until B's death.

(2) In the case of a gift "*to X for life, and then to the children of B*," the class closes at the death of X, since that is when the remainder beneficiaries are entitled to possession and enjoyment of principal. (Here, too, if B has had no children, the class does not close until B's death.) But the statement that the class closes at the death of X merely means that no children of B born thereafter share. It does not mean that all who are alive at the end of the life estate will share. The class-closing rules do not determine whether the estate of a member of a class who dies before the end of the life estate is entitled to share; that depends on whether the

language of the gift makes *survival* to the end of the life estate a condition. In the above example, the estate of a child of *B* who was alive at the operative date of the instrument but who predeceased *X* would (in the absence of a statute to the contrary) be entitled to a share, since nothing in the language requires survival. If, however, the gift had been "to *X* for life and then to the children of *B* then living," the interest of any child of *B* who predeceased *X* would be extinguished upon that child's death.

(3) In the case of a gift "*to the children of B, payable at 21*," the class closes as soon as any child of *B*, or the estate of any child of *B*, is entitled to possession. If *B*'s oldest child reaches 21, the class closes then. If *B*'s oldest child dies under 21, the first problem is to determine whether death extinguishes the interest. With the above language, it probably would not ("payable at 21" being construed as merely specifying the time of payment, rather than requiring survival to the specified age). Thus, the estate of such child of *B* would be entitled to a share, and the class would close at the time when the estate became entitled to possession. Under some circumstances, the estate of the child would be entitled at the child's death (at the age of 18, for example); under others, the estate would not take until the 21st anniversary of the child's birth. If the disposition had read "to such children of *B* as reach the age of 21," death would extinguish the interest of any child who died under 21. In other words, the class would close on attainment of the age of 21 by the first child of *B* to reach that age. Again, the class-closing rule would merely mean that children of *B* born thereafter would not share. It would not mean that all children of *B* then alive would share. If, when the first child of *B* reached 21, there was another child aged 18 and that other child were to die at 19, death would extinguish the interest. The class-closing rule merely fixes the maximum, not the ultimate, number of members of the class, and the minimum, not the ultimate, size of the share of the first member of the class to qualify. The object of the rule is not to permit immediate final and complete distribution (though this would be the effect of it in case 1, supra), but merely immediate distribution of the minimum present share to the first to qualify.

(4) In the case of a gift "*to X for life, and then to the children of B, payable at 21*," the death of *X* and one of the conditions to immediate enjoyment described in case 3, supra, must occur before the class closes. For example, the class does not close when the oldest child of *B* reaches 21, if this occurs before the end of the life estate. Instead, it remains open until the life estate terminates, since until then no child of *B* is entitled to possession and enjoyment of principal.

Limitations to children (or others) when "the youngest" reaches a particular age pose special problems. Possible constructions are: (a) the youngest refers to the youngest alive on the effective date of the creating instrument; (b) the youngest means the last child in fact born, i.e., the class does not close until no other children can be born; (c) the youngest means the youngest alive when all those living at a particular time have reached the stated age. Generally speaking, the last is the favored construction, and the class closes when all the children alive have reached the stated age. For the reasons underlying this choice, and the effect of the Rule against Perpetuities in sometimes dictating the choice of alternative (a), see Casner, Class Gifts to Others than to "Heirs" or "Next of Kin": Increase in the Class Membership, 51 Harv. L. Rev. 254 (1937).

It is important to understand that a class gift is not merely one to a group collectively described, but also one of an *aggregate amount* of property to be divided among the group. For example, a legacy of *"$10,000 apiece to each child of B, payable at 21"* is not a gift to a class for the purpose of the above rule. In the case of such a disposition, the usual rule is that no child of B born after the testator's death can share, whether or not there are any children of B living at his death. The difference between this situation and the regular class gift is this: in the regular class gift, the problem is to determine the minimum distributable share of the first member of the class to qualify; here, however, it would be impossible to distribute *any part of the residuary estate* unless the potential beneficiaries of the legacy were limited to those living at the testator's death, because it would be impossible to determine how much of the total estate would have to be retained by the fiduciary to pay the legacy. If, for example, the entire distributable estate were $100,000, there would be no balance if ten children of B could share, but there would be a balance of $90,000 if only one could. This differs from a regular class gift of $50,000 to the children of B, payable at 21, where a fixed amount is available to the class and the balance is immediately distributable.

b. Class Gifts and the Rule Against Perpetuities

LEAKE V. ROBINSON

Chancery, 1817.
2 Mer. 363, 35 Eng. Rep. 979.

[This case involved a trust under the will of the testator, John Milward Rowe. The trustees were to use the income to support the testator's grandson, William Rowe Robinson, until he reached 25; to pay him the income thereafter during his life; and after his death to pay the income to his children until they reached 25 (or, if a daughter, previously married with the consent of her parent or guardian) and to pay the principal to "such children . . . who shall attain" age 25 (or, if a daughter, shall be previously married with such consent). The will then proceeded with the alternative gift of the principal described in the next paragraph, which was the clause in issue. The plaintiffs were the trustees.]

The testator then directed as follows: that "in case the said William Rowe Robinson shall happen to die without leaving issue, living at the time of his decease, or leaving such, they shall all die before any of them shall attain twenty-five, if sons, and if daughters, before they shall attain such age, or be married as aforesaid;" then the plaintiffs should pay, apply, and transfer the said principal sums of stock, ground-rents, estates and mortgage moneys, "unto and amongst all and every the brothers and sisters of the said William Rowe Robinson, share and share alike, upon his, her, or their attaining twenty-five, if a brother or brothers, and if sister or sisters, at such age or marriage, with such consent as aforesaid." . . .

On the 17th of June, 1790, when the testator made this will, his grandson William Rowe Robinson, had one brother and three sisters living. Between the date of the will and the testator's death, he had another sister born.

On the 9th of February, 1792, the testator died. Between the death of the testator and the death of William Rowe Robinson, the said William Rowe Robinson had two other brothers born. On the 10th of October, 1800, William Rowe Robinson died; having attained twenty-five without issue, unmarried and intestate; and another sister was born after his death. . . .

Under these circumstances, the question for the decision of the court was, whether, in the event which happened, of the death of William Rowe Robinson without issue, the limitation to his Brothers and Sisters, to take effect on their attainment of the age of twenty-five, or marriage as aforesaid, was a good and effectual limitation, or was void, as being too remote. And this principally depended on the determination of two other questions, viz. first, what classes of persons were those intended by the Testator to take, in the event of William Rowe Robinson dying without issue, or without issue living to attain the age of twenty-five, under the description of "all and every the Brothers and Sisters of the said William Rowe Robinson;" because, if that limitation were held to extend to all the Brothers and Sisters who might be born, and (in the event which happened) actually were born, after the death of the Testator, and the period of vesting was postponed by the will till their attainment of the age of twenty-five, it is obvious that more than twenty-one years (the period beyond which a limitation by way of executory devise cannot take effect) might pass after the death of the Testator before the arrival of the limited time; and this, consequently, gave rise to the second question; which was, whether the attainment of twenty-five was in fact the period assigned for the vesting of the several shares, or was to be taken only as the time fixed for the payment of the several shares which had already vested at some antecedent period. . . .

THE MASTER OF THE ROLLS [Sir William Grant]. The first point to be determined in this case is, Who are included in the description of brothers and sisters of William Rowe Robinson . . . whether those only who were in being at the time of the testator's death, or all who might come *in esse* during the lives of the respective tenants for life. Upon that point I do not see how a question can possibly be raised. Not only is the rule of construction completely settled, but in this case, I apprehend the actual intention of the testator to be perfectly clear. . . .

. . . According to the established rule of construction, and what I conceive to have been the actual intention of the testator, all who were living at the time of William Rowe Robinson's death must be held to be comprehended in the description.

Having ascertained the persons intended to take, the next question is at what time the interests given to them were to vest.

There is no direct gift to any of these classes of persons. It is only through the medium of directions given to the trustees, that we can ascertain the benefits intended for them. . . .

As to the capital, there being, as I have already said, no direct gift to the grandchildren, we are to see in what event it is that the trustees are to make it over to them. There is, with regard to this, some difference of expression in the different parts of the will. In some instances the testator directs the payment to be to such child or children as shall attain twenty-five. In others the payment is to be made upon attainment of the age of twenty-five. . . . But I think the testator in each instance means precisely the same thing, and that none were to take vested interests before the specified period. The attainment of twenty-five is necessary to entitle any child to claim a transfer. It is not the enjoyment that is postponed; for there is no antecedent gift . . . of which the enjoyment could be postponed. The direction to pay is the gift, and that gift is only to attach to children that shall attain twenty-five. . . .

It was supposed that the clauses in the will, where the word *such* is left out, might be construed differently from those in which it is inserted; and that, although the payment is to be to *such* child or children as shall attain twenty-five, nothing could vest in any not answering that description, yet where the payment is to be to children upon the attainment of twenty-five, or from and after their attaining twenty-five, the vesting is not postponed. If there were an antecedent gift, a direction to pay upon the attainment of twenty-five certainly would not postpone the vesting. But if I give to persons of any description *when* they attain twenty-five, or upon their attainment of twenty-five, or from and after their attaining twenty-five, is it not precisely the same thing as if I gave to *such* of those persons as should attain twenty-five? None but a person who can predicate of himself that he has attained twenty-five, can claim anything under such a gift. . . .

Then, assuming that after-born grandchildren were to be let in, and that the vesting was not to take place till twenty-five, the consequence is, that it might not take place till more than twenty-one years after a life or lives in being at the death of the testator. It was not at all disputed that the bequests must for that reason be wholly void, unless the court can distinguish between the children born before, and those born after, the testator's death. Upon what ground can that distinction rest? Not upon the intention of the testator; for we have already ascertained that all are included in the description he has given the objects of his bounty. And all who are included in it were equally capable of taking. It is the period of vesting, and not the description of the legatees, that produces the incapacity. Now, how am I to ascertain in which part of the will it is that the testator has made the blunder which vitiates his bequests? He supposed that he could do legally all that he has done;—that is, include after-born grandchildren, and also postpone the vesting till twenty-five. But, if he had been informed that he could not do both, can I say that the alteration he would have made would have been to leave out the after-born grandchildren, rather than abridge the period of vesting? I should think quite the contrary. It is very unlikely that he should have excluded one half of the family of his daughters, in order only that the other half might be kept four years longer out of the enjoyment of what he left them. It is much more probable that he would have said, "I do mean to include all my grandchildren, but as you tell me that I cannot do so, and at the same time postpone the vesting till twenty-five, I will postpone it only till twenty-one." If I could at all alter the will, I should be inclined to alter it in the way in which it seems to me probable that the testator himself would have altered it. That alteration would at least have an important object to justify it; for it would give validity to all the bequests in the will. The other alteration would only give them a partial effect; and that too by making a distinction, which the testator himself never intended to make, between those who were the equal objects of his bounty. In the latter case, I should be new-modelling a bequest which, standing by itself, is perfectly valid; while I left unaltered that clause which alone impedes the execution of the testator's intention in favour of all his grandchildren. Perhaps it might have been as well if the Courts had originally held an executory devise transgressing the allowed limits to be void only for the excess, where that excess could, as in this case it can, be clearly ascertained. But the law is otherwise settled. . . .

To induce the court to hold the bequests in this will to be partially good, the case has been argued as if they had been made to some individuals who are, and to some who are not, capable of taking. But the bequests in question are not made to individuals, but to classes; and what I have to determine is, whether the class can take. I must make a new will for the testator, if I split into portions his general bequest to the class, and say, that because the rule of law forbids his intention from operating in favor of the whole class, I will make his bequests, what he never intended them to be, viz. a series of particular legacies to particular individuals, or what he had as little in his contemplation, distinct bequests, in each instance, to two different classes, namely to grandchildren living at his death, and to grandchildren born after his death.

If the present case were an entirely new question, I should doubt very much whether this could be done. But it is a question which appears to me to be perfectly settled by antecedent decisions, and in cases in which there were grounds for supporting the bequests that do not here exist. In Jee v. Audley, 1 Cox, 324, there were no after-born children—no distinction therefore to be made between persons capable and persons incapable—(all were capable)—no difficulty, consequently, in adjusting the proportions that the capable children were to take, or in determining the manner, or the period, of ascertaining those proportions. I am asked why the existence of incapable children should prevent capable children from taking. But in Jee v. Audley, the mere possibility that there might have been incapable children was sufficient to exclude those who were capable. It is said, the devise there was future. Certainly; but only in the same sense in which these bequests are future; that is, so conceived as to let in after-born children; which was the sole reason for its being held to be void. Unless my decision on the first point be erroneous, the bequests in this case do equally include after-born children of the testator's daughters, and are therefore equally void.

NOTES

1. *"Bad as to one; bad as to all."* This is the leading case for the proposition that a class gift is inseparable for purposes of the Rule against Perpetuities; it will not be split so as to uphold what would be the independently valid interests of some members of the class. In other words, if there is any possibility that the interest of any present or potential member of the class may vest too remotely, the entire class gift fails. Note this court's reliance on Jee v. Audley, supra p. 885. As the court says, the void interests that were assumed in that case to invalidate the whole gift were those for a group (after-born Jee daughters) whose existence, while legally possible, was physiologically purely hypothetical.

This proposition is part of traditional perpetuities doctrine in both England and America. Decisions that do not discuss the question often assume it; others have specifically adopted it. Professor Leach, who disapproved of any such automatic rule, was hopeful that the tide might turn in America by decisions to the contrary in the many states that had no explicit holding on the point, but there are no indications of such a shift. Everyone should read his attack on this doctrine in Perpetuities and Class Gifts, 51 Harv. L. Rev. 1329 (1938).

2. *Reducing offensive age restrictions.* Note the court's expression of a personal inclination to validate the gift by a judicial alteration of the age to be attained from 25 to 21. "But the law is otherwise settled." That is, the courts will not rewrite a disposition in this way to validate a gift. As a result, many gifts are invalid because the scrivener forgets about the Rule against Perpetuities and simply accedes to the client's natural desire to postpone receipt of principal until the beneficiaries are not merely legally adults but also mature enough to handle property carefully and intelligently.

For many years the only judicial departure was in New Hampshire. In Edgerly v. Barker, 31 A. 900 (N.H.1891), the will gave the residuary estate (after trusts for the testator's daughter, son, daughter-in-law, and grandchildren) to such grandchildren of the testator as should be living, and the children then living of any grandchild then dead, when the testator's youngest grandchild should arrive at the age of 40. The court, in a lengthy and learned opinion of Chief Justice Charles Doe, reduced the age from 40 to 21 and held the gift valid. The opinion relies on the theory of cy pres, or approximation, traditionally applicable to charitable gifts. The court concluded, from all the provisions of the will, which were detailed and included such conditions as that the testator's son should "become and remain temperate, sober, and correct in his habits" before receiving payments from the trustees, that the testator desired his grandchildren to receive the principal in preference to his two children, who would take it by intestacy if the gift were void. The court found that postponement of the interests of the grandchildren was secondary to this major objective. Therefore, in the language of cy pres, the specific intent to postpone their taking until the youngest reached 40 being void, the court carried out the general intent that they should have the property cy pres (as near as possible to the inoperative specific intent) by reducing 40 to 21, thus validating the gift. The opinion admitted that cy pres generally did not apply to private gifts but felt it proper to utilize cy pres, even in the case of a private gift, when the intent of the testator was clear. The opinion concluded:

> [T]his will is competent and sufficient evidence that if he had been informed (when he gave instructions for drafting it) that his intent that his grandchildren should have the remainder could not stand with his intent that they should not have it till the youngest was 40 years old, and had been asked which of these intents should prevail, he would have given an answer that is comprehended in his intent on the subject of approximation. The law determines not what will he would have made if he had known that the last 19 of the 40 years were too remote, but what will he did make in ignorance of this flaw in his appointment of time. His intent that the grandchildren shall not have the remainder till the youngest arrives at the age of 40 years is modified by his intent that they shall have it, and that the will shall take effect as far as possible. The 40 years are

reduced to 21 by his general approximating purpose, which is a part of the will. [31 A. at 916.]

This deviation from the norm disturbed Professor Gray. See Gray §§ 857–893. The fact that other judges for a long time declined to follow Chief Justice Doe disturbed Professor Leach. See Leach, Perpetuities in Perspective: Ending the Rule's Reign of Terror, 65 Harv. L. Rev. 721, 734–36 (1952). There are now, however, additional cases to similar effect. See Carter v. Berry, 140 So.2d 843 (Miss.1962); Estate of Chun Quan Yee Hop, 469 P.2d 183 (Haw.1970).

Statutes in a number of states now reduce age restrictions as necessary to avoid violation of the Rule against Perpetuities. For example, Me. Rev. Stat. tit. 33, § 102, provides:

> If an interest in real or personal property would violate the rule against perpetuities . . . because such interest is contingent upon any person attaining or failing to attain an age in excess of 21, the age contingency shall be reduced to 21 as to all persons subject to the same age contingency.

See also Conn. Gen. Stat. § 45a–504; N.Y. EPTL § 9–1.2; Matter of Estate of Kreuzer, 674 N.Y.S.2d 505 (App. Div. 1998) (applying statute).

3. *Class gifts and the Rule.* In dealing with class gifts under the Rule against Perpetuities, the first question to ask is: when will the class close? Unless the class is certain to close within the permissible period, the gift (assuming the all or nothing approach of Leake v. Robinson) is void. If the class is certain to close within the period *and* there are no conditions attached to an interest other than being born, then the gift is good. If, however, as in Leake v. Robinson, there is an additional condition (e.g., reaching age 25), it is not enough that the class will certainly close within the period; in addition, it must be certain that each potential class member will either satisfy, or fail to satisfy, the additional condition (reaching age 25) within the period.

6. MODERN APPROACHES TO THE RULE AGAINST PERPETUITIES

a. Drafting Generally; Perpetuities Saving Clauses in Particular

Lawyers and courts sometimes convey the impression that the Rule against Perpetuities is a malevolent force against which they are powerless. In fact, one can avoid most potential violations of the Rule by careful drafting. Some of the precautions are obvious. In the case of Ryan v. Ward, supra p. 907, the problem seems to have arisen because the scrivener used a form appropriate for a will, instead of a form appropriate for an inter vivos trust. By the same token, the scrivener can avoid many, if

not most, class gift problems by specifying that the class is to close immediately, i.e., at the date of the testator's death or on the effective date of
an inter vivos trust.

Some booby traps are less obvious, but use of perpetuities saving
clauses can avoid them, too. Professor Leach suggested the following:

> In any disposition in this instrument, or an instrument exercising a
> power of appointment created herein, I do not intend that there shall
> be any violation of the Rule Against Perpetuities or any related rule.
> If any such violation should inadvertently occur, it is my wish that
> the appropriate court shall reform the gift or appointment in such a
> way as to approximate most closely my intent or the intent of the ap-
> pointor, within the limits permissible under such rule or related rule.

Leach, Perpetuities: The Nutshell Revisited, 78 Harv. L. Rev. 973, 986
(1965). If the scrivener of the will in Perkins v. Iglehart, supra p. 895, had
used this sort of saving clause, the possibility that the life tenant might
be survived by an "unborn widow" would have empowered the court to
create a valid alternate dispositive plan. Use of such a clause, however, is
no substitute for careful drafting. It may save the will, but the court's
disposition of the property may not be what the testator would have
wanted if he or she had considered the matter. Moreover, a construction
proceeding necessarily imposes on both the trust and its beneficiaries
avoidable expenses, inconvenience, and publicity.

In fact, there are much better saving clauses. These days, most experienced estate planners use a clause that seeks to prevent any violation of
the Rule from occurring, rather than one that seeks merely to pick up the
pieces after a violation has occurred. An example:

> The trust hereby created shall terminate in any event not later than
> 21 years after the death of the last survivor of my descendants who
> are in being at the time this instrument becomes effective, and unless
> sooner terminated by the terms hereof, the trustee shall, at the ter-
> mination of such period, make distribution to the persons then en-
> titled to the income of this trust, and in the same shares and propor-
> tions as they are so entitled.

Gallanis & Waggoner, Estates, Future Interests, and Powers of Appointment in a Nutshell 145 (4th ed. 2010). Note how the clause operates. If
the trust would not otherwise terminate in a timely fashion, the clause
terminates the trust "ahead of schedule," so that all future interests necessarily vest within the period of the Rule. Indeed, such clauses are sometimes referred to as "perpetuities termination clauses," rather than "perpetuities saving clauses." If the scrivener of the will in Perkins v. Iglehart
had used this sort of clause, there would have been no violation of the

Rule, no opportunity for the court to fashion a new dispositive plan, and no litigation. For an example of such a clause in operation, see Norton v. Georgia Railroad Bank & Trust, 322 S.E.2d 870 (Ga. 1984). See generally McGovern, Perpetuities Pitfalls and How Best to Avoid Them, 6 Real Prop. Prob. & Tr. J. 155 (1971).

IN RE VILLAR

Chancery, 1929.
[1929] 1 Ch. 243.

Appeal from a decision of ASTBURY, J.

By his will dated June 14, 1921, a testator appointed the Public Trustee and the testator's adult sons ordinarily resident in England his executors and trustees.

He defined the meaning of certain expressions used in his will as follows:—

"The period of restriction" shall mean the period ending at the expiration of 20 years from the day of the death of the last survivor of all the lineal descendants of Her Late Majesty Queen Victoria who shall be living at the time of my death.

"Participating issue" shall mean all my issue for the time being living who shall not have any ancestor (being issue of mine) living.

A beneficiary forfeited his interest in income on bankruptcy or alienation.

After certain specific gifts he devised and bequeathed all his property to his trustees upon trust out of the income to pay expenses of management and insurance and to pay his wife an annuity of £1000 a year during widowhood and a life annuity of £500 a year on remarriage, each annuity being free of all deductions (including income tax).

Subject thereto and to the provisions thereinafter contained the trustees were during the period of restriction to pay and divide the income equally per stirpes among the testator's participating issue.

The testator then declared: First, that if any person who if living would be one of the participating issue died leaving children they should take their parent's share of income. Secondly, that if a son died he might by will appoint up to one-half of his income to his wife for her life or widowhood. Thirdly, he created a discretionary trust giving a protected life interest to any beneficiary who forfeited his original interest in income by bankruptcy or alienation.

The testator then declared that from and after the expiration of the period of restriction his trustees should hold his residuary trust estate on the trusts following—namely, if any share of income was then subject to the discretionary trust the trustees were to hold a proportionate share of corpus upon trust for such one or more of the participating issue then living (including the forfeiting beneficiary) and the children of the forfeiting beneficiary as the trustees should within six calendar months after the testator's death[8] nominate and in such shares as they should in like manner specify. And the trustees should hold the rest of the corpus upon trust for the participating issue living at the expiration of the period of restriction (other than and except any forfeiting beneficiary) in proportion to their previous shares of income.

By a codicil dated February 2, 1926, the testator gave his wife an additional annuity of £200 during widowhood and a £10 life annuity to Louisa Jane Langdon and confirmed his will.

The testator died on September 6, 1926, and his will was proved by the Public Trustee and a son Arthur, who was qualified to be an executor. He left a widow, three sons, a spinster daughter and a married daughter with two infant children.

There was great difficulty in ascertaining the descendants of Queen Victoria living on September 6, 1926. It appeared, however, from an affidavit of A.T. Butler, Portcullis Pursuivant of Arms, that in 1922 there were about 120 descendants who had then to be sought in England, Germany, Russia, Sweden, Denmark, Norway, Spain, Greece, Jugo–Slavia and Rumania, and many of whom had probably become scattered over the entire continent of Europe, and might even have gone much further afield. It was not certain whether any of the late Tsaritsa's children were living, and owing to the war many of the continental descendants might fall into penury and obscurity, rendering any future tracing extremely difficult, if not impossible. The expense of a strictly proved pedigree of the descendants living at the testator's death would be very heavy.

In these circumstances the Public Trustee issued this summons on October 10, 1927, to determine (inter alia) whether the trusts of the income during the period of restriction and the trusts of the corpus at the expiration of that period were void for uncertainty or on any other ground. The summons also asked that if the trusts were valid an inquiry might be directed to ascertain who were Queen Victoria's lineal descendants living at the testator's death and whether any and which of them had since died.

---

[8] So in original. Probably should read "after the expiration of the period of restriction."— EDS.

Astbury, J., said that although it would be extremely difficult and expensive to ascertain the period when the capital became distributable twenty years after the death of the survivor of the lineal descendants of Queen Victoria living on September 6, 1926, he could not say that it would be impracticable or beyond the scope of legal testimony. He must hold, therefore, that the trust was valid.

The testator's three sons and spinster daughter appealed. . . .

LORD HANWORTH, M.R. This is an appeal from Astbury, J., who had to determine whether or not in the main the will of the testator ought to be declared ineffective and that the proposed trust disposition of his residuary estate failed on the ground that it was void for uncertainty, or, in other words, that it was impracticable. [His Lordship then stated the facts and continued:] It is said that the terms of the residuary gift which are easy to carry out as regards the payment of income at the present time are to be treated as invalid, because of the period of restriction to the end of which distribution of the capital was postponed. The argument is that as the ascertainment of the end of this period will create serious difficulty in time to come, the residuary gift ought to be set aside as invalid. The period of restriction is defined as "the period ending at the expiration of 20 years from the day of the death of the last survivor of all the lineal descendants of Her Late Majesty Queen Victoria who shall be living at the time of my death." We have the evidence of a member of the College of Arms, who says the descendants of Queen Victoria numbered not less than 120 in 1922, and that they might have increased in number by 1926. On the other hand, I suppose they might have decreased in number, for I do not know whether the births of new descendants between 1922 and 1926 were sufficient to fill the vacancies among the descendants caused by death. However it is quite clear that there were a large number of descendants of Queen Victoria in being on September 6, 1926, and obviously there may be great difficulty in ascertaining whether and when the last of these lineal descendants had passed away. That is what has to be ascertained, and it depends on the existence of one single life out of many others. I recognize that serious difficulty might well arise in the future in ascertaining the date when that life ceased. . . .

[I]t is said that the Courts ought to take into consideration the difficulty that will arise in the future when, it may be 100 years hence, their successors will be faced with the problem of finding out who is the last survivor of this body of 120 or 130 persons and when he died. That is a difficulty which may arise by reason of the vicissitudes of life, but it may not. It is possible that 120 years hence the Court may find a number of problems relating to the births, marriages and deaths of various persons; but they appear to me to be matters which we ought not to take into account. The difficulties are not insurmountable, and they may in fact never arise. Therefore I return to the view that the only matter I have to consider is whether the residuary gift of the testator can be declared invalid on the ground that it has transgressed some rule of law at the present time. The answer must be that it has not so transgressed, and, if so, we cannot by reference to difficulties that may arise hereafter make a new will for the testator.

I regret the decision, as there is no reason for such a fanciful disposition; but testing it by the rules which have to be applied, I can find no breach of the existing law, and the will must therefore stand. The appellant has suggested that the whole residuary gift should be set aside, but at the present time there is no difficulty in dealing with the estate as directed by the testator. It seems impossible to set aside a gift which works well in the present but which may in the future cause difficulty. I think that the decision of Astbury J. was right, and that the appeal must be dismissed.

[The concurring opinions of LAWRENCE, L.J., and RUSSELL, L.J., are omitted.]

NOTES

1. *Background.* The statement, "It was not certain whether any of the late Tsaritsa's children were living" presumably refers to the controversy as to whether the Grand Duchess Anastasia, daughter of the Tsar, survived the execution of the Russian imperial family at Ekaterinburg in 1918. Her mother, Empress Alexandra, was a granddaughter of Queen Victoria.

One of the arguments in favor of the trust in the lower court was that it followed a popular form book, and that a decision to invalidate the interests in this case would require similar disruption of many other dispositions. In re Villar, [1928] Ch. 471, 474.

The purpose of the provisions forfeiting the interest of a beneficiary who should become bankrupt or attempt to alienate the interest, and thereupon converting the trust for that beneficiary from a mandatory trust to a discretionary trust, was to prevent any creditor of a beneficiary from reaching that beneficiary's interest in advance of actual payment to the beneficiary by the trustee. How could the scrivener have accomplished this objective more directly in the United States? See Chapter 7, Section C, supra.

2. *Rationale.* What would be the reason for holding the specified "period of restriction" invalid?

3. *Subsequent developments.* A later Chancery case followed *Villar*, with obvious reluctance, on the basis that, since the testator in that case died in 1925, one year before the testator died in *Villar*, stare decisis required the result. In re Leverhulme, 169 L.T.R. 294 (1943). The court remarked:

I hope that no draftsman will think that because of my decision today he will necessarily be following a sound course if he adopts the well-known formula referring to the descendants living at the death of the testator of her late Majesty Queen Victoria. When that formula was first adopted there was, no doubt, little difficulty in ascertaining when the last of them died. . . . I do not at all encourage anyone to use the formula in the case of a testator who dies in the year 1943 or any later date. [169 L.T.R. at 298.]

b. Miscellaneous Reform Efforts

Nor are the courts helpless. It is frequently possible to construe a provision so as to avoid a violation of the Rule. In theory, the courts are supposed to construe wills and trusts without reckoning the consequences of the Rule: "[E]very provision in a will or settlement is to be construed as if the Rule did not exist, and then to the provision so construed the Rule is to be remorselessly applied." Gray § 629. But intuition suggests, and experience confirms, that the courts have long been willing to consider the outcome before construing a provision. See, e.g., Estate of Damon, 869 P.2d 1339 (Haw. 1994); Joyner v. Duncan, 264 S.E.2d 76 (N.C. 1980). Indeed, if a provision is reasonably susceptible of alternative constructions, one that would violate the Rule and the other that would not, should not the court ordinarily prefer the latter construction? Many times, construction enables the court to reach the result the testator probably intended but the scrivener inadequately expressed. For example, in Worcester County Trust Co. v. Marble, 55 N.E.2d 446 (Mass.1944), the court construed a gift to the testator's nephews and nieces as meaning nephews living at his death and as not including any who might subsequently be born to his 82–year-old, childless sister. Sometimes, however, construction yields a result that does not seem to reflect the testator's probable wishes. Examples are the cases in which the court indulges in the "preference for early vesting." Although the preference sometimes does save interests from the Rule against Perpetuities, it also sometimes causes more property to pass through dead persons' estates. This, in turn, increases probate costs and sometimes even additional death taxes. Thus, the preference has been the subject of criticism. See, e.g., Rabin, The Law Favors the Vesting of Estates. Why?, 65 Colum. L. Rev. 467 (1965).

For another salvage device, applicable to class gifts, see the famous case of Cattlin v. Brown, 68 Eng. Rep. 1218 (Ch. 1853). In that case, a provision in A's will gave property to B for life, then to the children of B who survived B in equal shares during their lives, and, on the death of any such child, her share to her children. When A died, B was alive and had five living children. At common law, the gift to B for life would clearly be good, as would the gift to B's children for their lives, since all would vest no later than the death of B. What about the remainders to B's grandchildren? If the class of grandchildren constitutes a single class, the gift fails, since the makeup of the class may not be complete within the period of the Rule. Consider, instead, treating it not as a single class gift, but as separate class gifts of shares to the children of each child of *B*, to take effect upon that child's death. So viewed, some of the class gifts are perfectly fine, i.e., those to the children of children who are lives in being when *A* dies. If, however *B* has more children after *A*'s death, the gifts to *their* children are void. Following the lead of Cattlin v. Brown, courts have not applied the "all or nothing rule" to cases in which they have found an intent to make separable gifts to "sub-classes." See, e.g., Lanier v. Lanier, 126 S.E.2d 776 (Ga. 1962); Second Bank–State Street Trust Co. v. Second Bank–State Street Trust Co., 140 N.E.2d 201 (Mass. 1957).

Despite the availability of these (and other) devices, considerable dissatisfaction with the Rule has persisted, and legislatures and courts have fashioned a number of new approaches. One of the most simple is to enlarge the period in gross. Another is to reduce offending age contingencies to 21. See Note 2 at p. 924, supra. Yet another is to create presumptions that avoid the more bizarre applications of the remote possibilities test. See Note 9 at p. 890, supra (fertile octogenarian); Note 3 at p. 894, supra (slothful executor); and Note 5 at p. 902, supra (unborn widow). There are, in addition, several more complicated approaches.

Wait and see. The basic idea of "wait and see" is simple. Instead of invalidating an interest that *might*, under some hypothetical circumstances, vest too remotely, why not wait and see if, in fact, it does? At first glance, wait and see may seem the least radical of departures from the common law Rule. It does not require the court to rewrite the will, as when a court reduces an age contingency. Nor does it require the court to indulge in one or more fanciful presumptions, or to distort the normal meaning of language. Indeed, the courts have, occasionally, implemented wait and see on their own. For example, in Merchants Nat'l Bank v. Curtis, 97 A.2d 207 (N.H.1953), the court wrote:

> [W]e come to the crucial question whether we are justified in deciding the perpetuities issue on the facts which actually occurred rather than on facts that might have happened viewed as of the death of the testator. There is little case authority for deciding upon facts occurring after the testator's death in a case such as the one before us. However, recognized modern commentators present convincing arguments for doing so. Leach, Perpetuities in Perspective: Ending the Rule's Reign of Terror, 65 Harv. L. Rev. 721 (1952); 6 American Law of Property (1952) § 24.10; and a full study by a Pennsylvania law revision commission resulted in a statute that permits such events to be considered. Pa. Estates Act of 1947, § 4, Pa. Stat. Ann. (Purdon, 1947) tit. 20, § 301.4. There is no precedent in this state

that compels us to close our eyes to facts occurring after the death of the testator.

In the present case we are called on to determine the validity of a clause of a will that did not in fact tie up property beyond the permissible limit of lives in being plus twenty-one years. There is no logical justification for deciding the problem as of the date of the death of the testator on facts that might have happened rather than the facts which actually happened. It is difficult to see how the public welfare is threatened by a vesting that might have been postponed beyond the period of perpetuities but actually was not. [T]he glacial force of the rule [should] be avoided where the interests actually vest within the period of perpetuities. 6 American Law of Property, § 24.35. When a decision is made at a time when the events have happened, the court should not be compelled to consider only what might have been and completely ignore what was. . . .

At the death of the survivor of the life tenants, Edward Harrington and Delana B. Curtis, both of whom were lives in being at testatrix' death, it became certain that no grandchildren of the testatrix would be born after her death. This in turn made it certain that the gift in clause sixth of the will would in fact vest at the death of Margaret May Curtis Reynolds Vreeland, also a life in being at testatrix' death. Consistent with the principles above stated, the facts existing at the death of the two life tenants are taken into consideration in applying the rule.

We therefore conclude that clause sixth does not violate the rule against perpetuities. . . . [97 A.2d at 212.]

Yet merely embracing wait and see leaves unanswered the most important question it raises, i.e., how long are we to wait? In essence, this is the same as asking what lives we are to use as measuring lives. Unlike the common law rule, under which the terms of the gift dictate the choice of measuring lives, under wait and see, ascertainment of those lives can be extremely difficult. Moreover, the major substantive objection to wait and see is that it undermines a basic objective of the rule—alienability of property—by postponing the determination of ownership. Whereas the common law Rule permits an immediate test of the validity of contingent future interests, the determination (at least the determination of invalidity) cannot occur in a wait and see jurisdiction until a later—perhaps much later—time. Until then, no one can know whether the interest is valid or void.

The debate over "wait and see" has been long and heated. It reached a climax in the meeting of the American Law Institute in 1978, when Professor Richard R.B. Powell, Reporter for the First Restatement of Property, led an attack on a proposal to adopt wait and see in the Second Restatement. See Proceedings of the 55th Annual Meeting of the American Law Institute 222–307 (1978). Professor Powell and his supporters favored efforts like those of New York (see Note 9 at p. 890, supra; Note 3 at p. 894, supra; and Note 5 at p. 902, supra) to ameliorate the harsher aspects of the remote possibilities test, but drew the line at wait and see. Adoption in 1979 of wait and see by the Second Restatement was a sign of things to come; in particular, the Uniform Statutory Rule Against Perpetuities, infra p. 934.

Cy pres. Another approach is to rely on the courts to reform instruments as necessary, to avoid violations of the Rule, regardless of whether the instruments themselves include such authorization. Statutes in many states now so authorize the courts. This "unlimited cy pres" approach includes, but goes well beyond, reducing offensive age contingencies. See Note 2, supra p. 924. The following excerpt from the Second Restatement is typical:

§ 1.5 Consequences of the Failure of an Interest Under the Rule Against Perpetuities in a Donative Transfer

If under a donative transfer an interest in property fails because it does not vest or cannot vest within the period of the rule against perpetuities, the transferred property shall be disposed of in the manner which most closely effectuates the transferor's manifested plan of distribution and which is within the limits of the rule against perpetuities.

Like "wait and see," cy pres has been the subject of considerable debate. Cy pres does seem unduly dependent upon litigation. See generally Schuyler, The Statute Concerning Perpetuities, 65 Nw. L. Rev. 3, 22–25 (1970).

Given the low level of competence on the subject that lawyers and courts frequently exhibit, the existence of salvage devices is no doubt reassuring. But whenever there is litigation over a provision's meaning or effect, the scrivener has failed in one of his or her most important objectives.

c. The Uniform Statutory Rule Against Perpetuities

Uniform Statutory Rule Against Perpetuities

§ 1. Statutory Rule Against Perpetuities.

(a) **[Validity of Nonvested Property Interest.]** A nonvested property interest is invalid unless:

(1) when the interest is created, it is certain to vest or terminate no later than 21 years after the death of an individual then alive; or

(2) the interest either vests or terminates within 90 years after its creation.

(b) [Validity of General Power of Appointment Subject to a Condition Precedent.] A general power of appointment not presently exercisable because of a condition precedent is invalid unless:

(1) when the power is created, the condition precedent is certain to be satisfied or become impossible to satisfy no later than 21 years after the death of an individual then alive; or

(2) the condition precedent either is satisfied or becomes impossible to satisfy within 90 years after its creation.

(c) [Validity of Nongeneral or Testamentary Power of Appointment.] A nongeneral power of appointment or a general testamentary power of appointment is invalid unless:

(1) when the power is created, it is certain to be irrevocably exercised or otherwise to terminate no later than 21 years after the death of an individual then alive; or

(2) the power is irrevocably exercised or otherwise terminates within 90 years after its creation.

(d) [Possibility of Post-death Child Disregarded.] In determining whether a nonvested property interest or a power of appointment is valid under subsection (a)(1), (b)(1), or (c)(1), the possibility that a child will be born to an individual after the individual's death is disregarded. . . .

§ 2. When Nonvested Property Interest or Power of Appointment Created.

(a) Except as provided in subsections (b) and (c) . . . the time of creation of a nonvested property interest or a power of appointment is determined under general principles of property law.

(b) For purposes of this [Act], if there is a person who alone can exercise a power created by a governing instrument to become the unqualified beneficial owner of (i) a nonvested property interest or (ii) a property interest subject to a power of appointment described in Section 1(b) or 1(c), the nonvested property interest or power of appointment is created when the power to become the unqualified beneficial owner terminates. . . .

(c) For purposes of this [Act], a nonvested property interest or a power of appointment arising from a transfer of property to a previously funded trust or other existing property arrangement is created when the nonvested property interest or power of appointment in the original contribution was created.

§ 3. Reformation.

Upon the petition of an interested person, a court shall reform a disposition in the manner that most closely approximates the transferor's manifested plan of distribution and is within the 90 years allowed by Section 1(a)(2), 1(b)(2), or 1(c)(2) if:

(1) a nonvested property interest or a power of appointment becomes invalid under Section 1 (statutory rule against perpetuities);

(2) a class gift is not but might become invalid under Section 1 (statutory rule against perpetuities) and the time has arrived when the share of any class member is to take effect in possession or enjoyment; or

(3) a nonvested property interest that is not validated by Section 1(a)(1) can vest but not within 90 years after its creation.

NOTES

1. *Operation of USRAP.* USRAP combines several distinct perpetuity reform devices, including both wait and see and cy pres. An interest may be valid under either the traditional rule or the 90–year wait and see option. Moreover, for any interest that manages to fail under both of these possibilities, USRAP mandates judicial cy pres. See Abrams v. Templeton, 465 S.E.2d 117 (S.C.App.1995).

2. *USRAP enactments.* At its high-water mark, about half the states had adopted USRAP. Since then, however, several have modified it quite substantially.

d. The Movement to Abolish the Rule Against Perpetuities

JESSE DUKEMINIER, THE UNIFORM STATUTORY RULE AGAINST PERPETUITIES: NINETY YEARS IN LIMBO
34 UCLA L. Rev. 1023, 1025–27 (1987).

II. THE UNIFORM STATUTE PUTS THE RULE AGAINST PERPETUITIES IN THE DEEP FREEZER FOR 90 YEARS, FROM WHICH IT MAY NEVER EMERGE ALIVE

[Under USRAP], no interest . . . can be declared in violation of the Rule against Perpetuities for 90 years after the date of its creation. All interests are valid for this period. At the end of 90 years, a court will take down the old books on the Rule against Perpetuities, determine what then existing contingent interests did not satisfy the common law Rule upon creation some 90 years earlier, and, as to any such interests, reform them to vest at once.

It is an extraordinary thing to declare a whole body of prohibitory law to be in abeyance for 90 years, with no violation of the law possible for that period of time. I can think of nothing in the whole history of English or American law that is comparable. . . . It is so bizarre that the mind boggles at the very thought of what will happen in 90 years, when the Rule against Perpetuities is scheduled to be revived and then to be applied to interests created by instruments effective more than 90 years previously.

Ninety years is a long, long time. Everyone reading this Article in the year of its publication will be dead. . . . Can the Rule against Perpetuities really survive 90 years in desuetude?

I do not see how it can. If the Rule cannot strike down any interest for 90 years, I predict it will not be taught and knowledge of it will be lost to lawyers. It will become a piece of history, like the Rule in Shelley's Case. . . .

What is likely to happen is that teachers will teach only the 90–year rule: "You can have a trust for 90 years. . . ." The fertile octogenarian and other wraiths may be trotted out for a laugh. . . . I think I can safely predict, however, that most of the Rule against Perpetuities will be completely ignored in the classroom.

Perpetuities saving clauses in their present form will probably continue to be routinely inserted in trusts for many years, since lawyers are creatures of habit. With the passage of time, however, fewer and fewer will understand why such clauses work. A saving clause may come to be regarded as the seal was in the late nineteenth century, a token of obeisance to the past that must be added without anyone really understanding exactly why. Far more likely—since lawyers realize that time is money— lawyers will increasingly draft trusts to end within 90 years, either because they have not been taught the Rule against Perpetuities or because it takes too much time to remember it and, by using a 90–year period, they can be certain everything is valid.

At the end of 90 years, I cannot believe that anything as complicated as *Gray on Perpetuities* will be brought back to life. If, at the end of 90 years, there are contingent interests more than 90 years old, is it realistic to think that lawyers and judges will dig into the crumbling books of their great-grandparents to see whether these interests have vested . . . ? Surely the bar will . . . formally abolish the Rule at that point in time.

If the future does shape up this way, the effect of adopting the Uniform Statute is to keep the Rule against Perpetuities formally on the books, but in abeyance, for 90 years, after which we can expect the Rule to be discarded as an obsolete, overcomplicated relic of the Industrial Age, to be wholly replaced by a 90–year limitation on the dead hand. . . .

NOTES

1. *Will the Rule disappear?* Professor Dukeminier paints a dark future for the Rule against Perpetuities. In general, his predictions seem hard to fault. If anything, he may have overestimated how long it would take for the Rule to go the way of the buggy whip. Already nearly thirty states have repealed the Rule, either literally or in practical effect. Some states, including Idaho, Kentucky, New Jersey, Rhode Island, South Dakota, and Wisconsin, no longer have a Rule against Perpetuities. Others, including Delaware, Missouri, North Carolina, and Pennsylvania, have exempted trusts generally, or certain trusts, from the operation of the Rule. Yet others, including the District of Columbia, Illinois, Maine, Maryland, Nebraska, New Hampshire, Ohio, and Virginia, have made application of the Rule optional. Still others have extended the period in which interests must vest or fail for such lengthy periods of time that the effect is much the same as repeal. These states include Alaska, Colorado, Utah, and Wyoming (1,000 years), Arizona (500 years), Nevada (365 years), Alabama, Florida, Michigan, and Tennessee (360 years), and Washington (a mere 150 years). See generally Dukeminier & Krier, The Rise of the Perpetual Trust, 50 UCLA L. Rev. 1303 (2003); Note, Dynasty Trusts and the Rule Against Perpetuities, 116 Harv. L. Rev. 2588 (2003).

2. *Perpetuity reform.* The reform proposals of the late twentieth century came in response to a wave of critical commentary that exposed the excesses of the common law Rule against Perpetuities. Whether the common law Rule was actually as destructive as its critics claimed remains debatable. Most of the reported violations involve unwitting failure to take into account the more extreme applications of the remote possibilities test or the postponement of vesting beyond age twenty-one. Thus, some still believe that reform should be limited to curing these "technical" violations. Others feel (USRAP and the Second and Third Restatements of Property are in accord) that reform should cure all violations. In some respects, the argument is between those who believe that testators who don't understand the Rule (or whose lawyers don't) should suffer the consequences (or at least their beneficiaries should) and those who believe the law should provide everyone the protection that a sophisticated lawyer ordinarily provides. On this question and other aspects of this debate, see Waggoner, Perpetuity Reform, 81 Mich. L. Rev. 1718 (1983) (author served as reporter for USRAP and Third Restatement of Property).

3. *The abolition movement.* The movement to abolish the Rule against Perpetuities (see Note 1 supra), unlike its immediate predecessor, the move-

ment to reform the Rule (see Note 2 supra), seems largely unconcerned with whether the Rule does its job well or poorly. Instead, the abolition movement seems to be a by-product of fierce interstate competition among banks, trust companies, and perhaps estate planners themselves, to create, in their own states, legal systems that are so friendly to the creation of certain types of trusts, including the so-called "dynastic trust," that they can hope not only to retain all of the business of their own states' residents, but also to lure away the business of the residents of other states. See Schanzenbach & Sitkoff, Perpetuities or Taxes? Explaining the Rise of the Perpetual Trust, 27 Cardozo L. Rev. 2465 (2006); Sitkoff & Schanzenbach, Jurisdictional Competition for Trust Funds: An Empirical Analysis of Perpetuities and Taxes, 115 Yale L.J. 356 (2005); Sterk, Jurisdictional Competition to Abolish the Rule Against Perpetuities: R.I.P. for the R.A.P., 24 Cardozo L. Rev. 2097 (2003); Bloom, The GST Tax Tail Is Killing the Rule Against Perpetuities, 87 Tax Notes 569 (Apr. 24, 2000) ("The rule is being repealed so that wealthy individuals will be able to create perpetual dynasty trusts to exploit the generation-skipping transfer (GST) tax system."). Compare the contemporaneous but (to this point, anyway) substantially less successful effort to persuade state legislatures to relax the rule against the effectiveness of spendthrift limitations in self-settled trusts (see Note 2, supra p. 635).

4. *Problems of perpetual private trusts.* Setting aside all questions relating to whether the Rule does its job well or poorly, is it clear that it is good policy to permit settlors to create private trusts that will or may be perpetual? Would you like to serve as, or be counsel to, the trustee of a private trust created in 1776 or 1215 (to say nothing of 4000 B.C.)? Is it a good idea to let certain people, and not others, be the beneficiaries of such trusts? According to one recent estimate, the average settlor will have about 450 live descendants 150 years after creating a trust, 7000 after 250 years, 114,500 after 350 years, and 1.8 million after 450 years. Restatement (Third) of Property: Wills and Other Donative Transfers ch. 27, Intro. Note (2011). Yet, at some point, not far beyond grandchildren, such beneficiaries would have no real claim on the settlor's bounty sounding in either affinity or consanguinity, much less familiarity. Might it not be fair to refer to such beneficiaries as the winners of a genetic lottery run amok? For these and other reasons, the American Law Institute recently announced its "considered judgment" that the statutory movement allowing perpetual or near-perpetual private trusts was "ill advised." Id.

One may safely predict that there will always be children to educate and poor and sick people to care for. Thus, permitting the creation of perpetual trusts for charitable purposes has always made sense. In contrast, permitting the creation of perpetual trusts for the settlor's descendants raises the possibility that, at some point, the settlor will have so many descendants that administration of the trust, at least in conventional terms, becomes next to impossible. Certainly, in states that permit the creation of perpetual private trusts, there are many reasons to suggest that the terms of *every* such trust should grant the trustee wide discretion, broad powers, and extensive flexibility to respond to changes of all sorts, including changes in the settlor's family tree, the family fortunes, the economy, the tax system, and society generally. They should probably also permit, in various ways and under various circumstances, a combination of the trustee and certain of the beneficiaries to terminate the trust, and to determine the disposition of any remaining trust assets.

5. *Limiting the duration of private trusts.* As you may by now have learned, the Rule against Perpetuities is complex and prickly, and it sometimes acts in ways that seem highly arbitrary. What would you think of replacing the Rule with: "No private trust may endure longer than [90] years."?

The Third Restatement of Property recently debuted yet another approach. The Rule would continue, but the permissible period would expire upon the death of "the last living measuring life." Ordinarily, these measuring lives would include only the settlor, beneficiaries related to the settlor but no more than two generations younger than the settlor, and beneficiaries unrelated to the settlor but no more than the equivalent of two generations younger than the settlor. In the case of a trust for the sole current benefit of a named individual more than two generations younger than the settlor (or the equivalent), the named individual would be the measuring life. At the end of the permissible period, the trust would ordinarily terminate. As thus reformulated, the Rule would no longer be a rule against remote vesting but would instead directly limit the duration of private trusts. See Restatement (Third) of Property: Wills and Other Donative Transfers §§ 27.1 to 27.3 (2011).

D. POWERS OF APPOINTMENT

1. INTRODUCTION

A power of appointment is a power created by one person (the donor) in another (the donee), or reserved by the donor to himself or herself, to determine the transferees of property (the appointees) or the shares the appointees are to take. Instruments creating powers should also make gifts in default of appointment to those who are to receive the property if the power is not effectively exercised (the takers in default).

Powers of appointment, which were rare in the United States at the turn of the last century, are now important estate planning devices. For seemingly arbitrary reasons they are not "future interests," but they involve many of the same problems, such as the fact that they are subject to the Rule against Perpetuities. We take up the perpetuities aspects of powers of appointment in Subsection 2. Subsection 3 deals with various non-perpetuities aspects of the creation and exercise of powers.

The treatment of powers of appointment for tax, perpetuities, and other purposes depends upon an elaborate classification system, which has developed over the years. The central distinction is that between general and special powers. Broadly speaking, a general power is one that is exercisable in favor of anybody, including, most importantly, the donee. In contrast, a special power is one that is exercisable only in favor of a limited group, or class of permissible appointees, including neither the donee nor the donee's estate. An example would be a power to appoint among the donee's children. These definitions work well enough for most purposes, but they are not comprehensive. Under these definitions, a power to appoint to anybody in the world other than the donee or the donee's estate is neither a general power, because of the exclusion of the donee and the donee's estate, nor a special power, because the appointees are otherwise unlimited.

The Internal Revenue Code defines (with certain exceptions) a general power as "a power which is exercisable in favor of the decedent, his estate, his creditors, or the creditors of his estate. . . ." I.R.C. § 2041. The Code does not use the term "special power," although tax advisors often use the term to refer (colloquially) to any power not described in § 2041, which, as a result, has significant tax advantages. Given the importance of tax considerations in estate planning, it is not surprising that powers are now frequently exercisable in favor of anyone other than the donee or the donee's estate, or the creditors of either. Presumably in response, both the Second and Third Restatements of Property employ the Internal Revenue Code definition of a general power. They also abandon the term "special power of appointment," in favor of "nongeneral power," which includes all powers not exercisable in favor of the donee, the donee's estate, or the creditors of either. See Restatement (Third) of Property: Wills and Other Donative Transfers § 17.3 (2011). This terminology has the virtue of avoiding the gap in the traditional dichotomy—a class of powers not satisfying either definition. It has the drawback of requiring, as to some aspects of special powers, a sub-classification of nongeneral powers exercisable only in favor of a defined limited class. It also abandons the traditional terminology without much gain; thus, although the new terminology may eventually carry the day, we continue to use the traditional term, special power of appointment.

Another important distinction is that between powers "presently exercisable" and powers that, at the time in question, are not exercisable until the occurrence of an event or the passage of a specified period of time. In theory, powers "not presently exercisable" could come in infinite variety; in practice, the characteristic that makes them "not presently exercisable" is almost always that they are exercisable only by the will of the donee. Accordingly, this book uses the term "testamentary" as the complement of "presently exercisable."

The basic common law theory underlying the exercise of a power of appointment was that the appointee took under the instrument creating the power, rather than under the instrument exercising it. This is the "relation back" doctrine, under which the exercise of the power relates back to its creation and operates as if it appeared in the instrument creating it. The theory arose when powers of appointment first became popular, in connection with the system of uses. A major reason for the popularity of that system was that it enabled landowners to achieve the effect of a will, despite the rule in England from the thirteenth century until the Statute of Wills of 1540 that one could not devise real property. An owner's reservation of a power of appointment that would leave him or her free to choose successors at any time prior to his or her death closely approximated a will.

The general function of a power of appointment today is to make a disposition more flexible than it would be if it finally and irrevocably named all takers, either as individuals or as a class. Certainly, no one can foresee the future. A father may create a trust to pay the income to his daughter for life and the principal on her death to her surviving issue per stirpes or in default of such issue to his son. But events may occur during the daughter's lifetime that would make the disposition inappropriate. Or general economic or legal conditions may change. The extent to which different children or grandchildren of the daughter may ultimately need or deserve property or be capable of handling it may differ dramatically. Any number of unpredictable eventualities may occur. Giving the daughter a power of appointment enables her to adjust the disposition to the situation that exists when she exercises it. If the father wished to project his control to the extent of ensuring that the principal would go to the daughter's surviving issue (if she had any), but also to allow her to vary their shares, he could give her a special power to appoint among her issue, with a gift in default of appointment to her issue or in default of such issue to his son. Or, if the father wished to yield all control over the principal to his daughter (if she chose to assert it), but wanted to prevent her from making any final disposition until her death, so that she could adjust the appointment to changing conditions during her lifetime, he could give her a general testamentary power of appointment, with similar gifts in default. The combination of a trust and a power of appointment thus enables the transferor to prescribe for those whose circumstances and characteristics the transferor currently knows and to indicate general preferences for ultimate distribution, but at the same time to avoid irrevocable and perhaps unduly rigid restrictions.

2. POWERS OF APPOINTMENT AND THE RULE AGAINST PERPETUITIES

For a variety of reasons, it seems preferable to deal with the application of the Rule to powers of appointment mainly through textual exposition, rather than through cases. This Subsection attempts to classify the problems in orderly sequence, stating and quoting from leading decisions, and suggesting simple "rules" that should help in analyzing these problems.

The first step in understanding the application of the Rule to powers of appointment is to realize that there are two ways in which the Rule may invalidate a disposition: (1) the Rule may make the power itself void, in the sense that no valid appointment is possible; or (2) even though the power is valid, a given exercise may violate the Rule.

For both questions—the validity of the power itself, and the validity of the appointed interests under any given exercise of the power—it is necessary to distinguish between a general power "presently exercisable"[9] and *all* other powers of appointment, namely, general testamentary powers and special powers, whether testamentary or presently exercisable. Since the donee of a general power presently exercisable can appoint to himself or herself at any time, such a power is the equivalent of ownership of a fee simple for purposes of the Rule. However, the great majority of American decisions have refused to apply the "equivalent of ownership" theory to a general testamentary power. The logic of the American rule depends on the associated rule that a contract involving the exercise of a testamentary power is unenforceable. See infra p. 958. This Subsection follows prevailing American practice and classifies (for purposes of the Rule) general testamentary powers with special powers, rather than with general powers presently exercisable.

a. Validity of the Power

(i) General Powers Presently Exercisable

A general power presently exercisable is valid if it is *certain to become exercisable* within the period of the Rule. How would the Rule against Perpetuities affect the following powers?

(1) Testamentary trust to pay the income to *B* (who survived the testator) for life, and on *B*'s death to pay the income in equal shares to *B*'s surviving children for their lives, and on the death of any such child of *B* to pay a proportionate part of the principal equal to the child's share of the income to such person or persons as the child shall appoint. See Leach, Perpetuities in a Nutshell, 51 Harv. L. Rev. 638, 653 (1938).

---

[9] The term "presently exercisable" is somewhat awkward in analyzing the validity of a power of appointment under the Rule, as the question often is when the power will become exercisable. Nevertheless, for the sake of consistency, this book uses "presently exercisable," rather than the more descriptive (in this context) term "exercisable by deed." For perpetuities purposes, the critical element is that the power be exercisable during the lifetime of the donee, and not by will only. In addition, "presently exercisable" includes, for these purposes, a power exercisable both by deed and by will.

(2) Testamentary trust to pay the income to *B* (who was living and childless at the testator's death) for life, and on *B*'s death to pay the income in equal shares to *B*'s surviving children for their lives, and on the death of any such child of *B* to pay a proportionate part of the principal equal to the child's share of the income to such person or persons as the child shall, if and after the child attains the age of 25, appoint.

(3) Testamentary trust to pay the income to *B* (who survived the testator) for life, and on *B*'s death to pay the income in equal shares to *B*'s surviving children for their lives, and on the death of the last life tenant to pay all of the principal to such person or persons as the last surviving life tenant shall appoint.

(ii) General Testamentary Powers and Special Powers

A general testamentary power or a special power, whether testamentary or presently exercisable, is invalid if it *might be exercised* beyond the permissible period of the Rule. For example, in Burlington County Trust Co. v. Di Castelcicala, 66 A.2d 164 (N.J.1949), a will gave the residuary estate in trust to pay the income to testatrix's husband for life, then to divide the income equally between her two daughters (her only children) during their lives; on the death of either daughter to pay her share of the income to her children during their lives, "with the power of disposal by will of the mother's share of the principal." The court held all the life estates valid, but the power void; it interpreted the quoted language as giving the testamentary power to dispose of one-half of the principal to the survivor of the children of each daughter. The court stated:

> A power is subject to the rule against perpetuities and is, when created by will, void unless, by its authorizing language, it must be exercised within a life or lives in being and twenty-one years thereafter. . . . If a power can be exercised at a time beyond life or lives in being plus twenty-one years from its creation, it is bad. . . . If it be, as we have found, that the gift of the life estates to grandchildren was not to living individuals but to a class which might be augmented at an undetermined date after the testatrix' death . . . it follows that the death of the survivor and therefore the exercise of the power of disposition might come at a period too remote to be effective; and that spells the invalidity of the power. [66 A.2d at 169.]

Such powers are valid only if it is certain that they will be exercised, if at all, within the period of the Rule. It is not necessary, however, that it also be certain that any appointment will also comply with the Rule. In other words, the validity of appointments under a power that must be exercised within the period of the Rule is determined by the appointments actually made, and not on the basis of the possibility existing at the time of the creation of the power that such appointments might be too remote. Given the courts' tendency to invalidate a disposition if there is any possibility of its creating interests that may vest too remotely, why have not the courts invalidated powers ab initio if there is a chance that appointments under them might violate the Rule?

b. Validity of the Appointed Interests

If the power of appointment is invalid, no valid appointment is possible. If the power is valid, the next question is whether the appointed interests are valid. Here again, it is important to distinguish between general powers presently exercisable and all other powers.

(i) General Powers Presently Exercisable

In the case of general powers presently exercisable, the validity of the appointed interests depends on the date of exercise, i.e., there is no difference under the Rule between interests created pursuant to such a power and interests created in property owned outright.

A leading American case is Mifflin's Appeal, 15 A. 525 (Pa.1888). The actual dispositions are too complicated to justify reproduction here, but, simplified, they were: An inter vivos trust of land for Sarah Mifflin for life gave Sarah the power to transfer the land to any person or persons either during her lifetime or by will. Sarah later died, leaving a will in which she exercised the power by appointing the property as follows: in trust to pay one-seventh of the income to each of Sarah's seven children during their lives and on the death of any such child a one-seventh interest in the land to his or her surviving issue (with various other alternative gifts over). The decision would support the validity of the gift to the issue of Sarah's children, whether or not such children were in being at the date of the inter vivos trust creating the power; one son of Sarah's was born several years after that trust was created. The court followed the orthodox view that the validity of an appointment by one holding a general power presently exercisable depends on the date of the exercise of the power. Since Sarah exercised the power at her death, this would make all Sarah's children lives in being, so that gifts vesting at the deaths of such children would be valid. If, on the other hand, the period of the Rule were to run from the date of the inter vivos trust creating the power, the gift to the issue of Sarah's children would be void, at least as to the issue of such children as were not in being at the date of that trust. The lower court opinion (affirmed on appeal) read in part:

> In whatever words an estate is conferred, and although it be only for life, it cannot . . . be a perpetuity, if the holder is clothed with power that will enable him to set aside the limitations imposed by the original grantor and confer an absolute interest on himself or on another person. Such a tenant is, so far as he himself is concerned, and in

every essential particular, as much an owner as if he had the fee. . . . He can at any moment loose the bonds by which it is fettered and render it as available for the purposes of life and business as if there were no settlement. It is not therefore surprising that the English courts should have held that when property is settled on *A.* for life, with power to will and convey, he may make any disposition of it which would be valid if he were absolutely the owner; and, in determining whether the limitations which he creates contravene the rule against perpetuities, the computation will date from the period when the power is exercised, and not from the execution of the instruments by which the power was conferred. [121 Pa. at 205.]

The appellate court, speaking of Sarah Mifflin's power, said:

As a matter of course, if Mrs. Mifflin had actually executed the power of sale and caused the title to be conveyed to herself in fee simple, as she had the plain right to do, the limitations of her will would have to be determined upon their own merits, regarding her as the owner in fee and disregarding the previous state of the title. But so far as the application of the rule against perpetuities is concerned, the situation is precisely the same as if she had executed the power. . . . It was entirely within her power to become the owner in fee simple of the estates granted and to totally defeat any ulterior limitations. It proves nothing to say she did not exercise her power[10] and that therefore the situation is the same as though she never had the power. For certain purposes and in certain cases that, of course, is true. But in considering merely the application of the rule against perpetuities, it is not true, because that rule requires that the estates in question should be indestructible, and an estate which can be destroyed by the person who holds it for the time being is not indestructible. [15 A. at 528.]

(ii) General Testamentary Powers and Special Powers

For all other powers, the normal rule is that the perpetuities period begins to run on the effective date of the creation of the power. However, in testing the validity of an appointed interest, circumstances are ascertained as they actually exist at the time of exercise. This latter aspect—the "second look doctrine"—has some of the effect of a wait and see approach, but it is not the same.

Treating the appointed interests as though the donor created them is, of course, entirely consistent with the relation back doctrine. See Gray § 514; Leach, Perpetuities in a Nutshell, 51 Harv. L. Rev. 638, 653 (1938).

---

[10] By this the court means that she did not exercise the power to transfer to herself during her lifetime, as distinguished from the appointment she made in her will.—Eds.

The exhaustive opinion in Minot v. Paine, 120 N.E. 167 (Mass.1918), reads in part:

> The nature of the power created by will and conferred upon a donee to appoint property by will has been considered by this court in several different aspects. . . .

> [I]n all other respects where the question has arisen, the property appointed is regarded as the property of the donor and is treated as passing under his will, manifested by the words employed by the person upon whom he has conferred the power to express his testamentary design in specified particulars. It seems difficult to say, in view of the reasoning upon which these decisions rest, that, when the rule against perpetuities is to be applied, the ground is to be shifted and the property is to be regarded as that of the donee and disposed of by his will.

> . . . As was said by Chief Justice Baldwin in Bartlett v. Sears, 81 Conn. 34, 44, 70 A. 33, 37 (1908): "One to whom a power of appointment is given by will stands to the testator substantially in the position of an agent toward his principal. An agent cannot do that which the principal cannot do." The essential nature of his act in exercising the power is that he is speaking for the original testator in directing the devolution of the property of the latter. . . .

> The donee in exercising the power is in effect writing the will of the donor respecting the appointed property. The donee in doing this in reason is bound by the same limitations of the law as bound the original testator. The donee can take advantage of facts of which the donor was ignorant because they were not in existence when he made his will. But the donee cannot free himself from the rules of law which limited the power of the donor. The will of the donor and that of the donee so far as it exercises the power of appointment in a sense together constitute the complete testamentary design of the donor respecting the donor's estate. The words used by the donee in exercising the power are to be construed and interpreted as to their meaning in the light of the facts as they are at the time the power is exercised. The will of the donor is projected forward to the time of the exercise of the power so as to receive the benefit of the facts which have appeared since his decease. . . .

> Both on principle and on authority our conclusion is that the remoteness of an appointment, made in the exercise of a power to appoint by will alone, so far as affected by the rule against perpetuities must be measured from the time of creation and not the exercise of the power. [120 N.E. at 169–71.]

Both the Second and Third Restatements of Property are to similar effect. See Restatement (Third) of Property: Wills and Other Donative Transfers § 19.19 cmt. g (2011). This view is not, however, unanimous. See Industrial Nat'l Bank of Rhode Island v. Barrett, 220 A.2d 517 (R.I.1966) (adopting minority rule under which validity of interests appointed pursuant to general testamentary power depends on date of exercise).

It is sometimes said that appointed interests are "read back" into the will of the donor (or other creating instrument). This is a reasonably descriptive phrase for most purposes, but it does not take into account the second look doctrine. See In re Warren's Estate, 182 A. 396 (Pa.1936), which states:

> Suppose *A* bequeaths his estate to *B* for life, and after *B*'s death to *B*'s children for the life of the survivor with provision that upon the death of any of *B*'s children so possessing a life estate, their children should take the deceased parent's share until the decease of the surviving child, with remainder over to the issue of all children. Obviously, the substitutionary provisions for the disposition of the income until the death of the surviving child would be void as too remote. It would be possible that one of *B*'s children might die over 21 years after *B*'s death, and then let in a new estate. Therefore, the whole provision as to the substitutionary gift of income would be void, as would the remainder. On the other hand, if *A* gives his estate to *B* for life with a general power of appointment, and *B* gives the estate to her children for life of the survivor (who are all living at the death of *A*) and under exactly the same provisions as above stated, then the whole disposition is valid. The naming of these children, so living, is but "lighting another candle" which is burning during the lives of *A* and *B*. It is still necessary to look to the original will or deed, and to read into it the terms of the appointment. However, where it appears that the appointment in fact names persons in being in the lifetime of the donor, the disposition is valid and is not rendered void because it might have been possible to appoint otherwise. [182 A. at 397.]

In re Warren's Estate represents the prevailing American and English point of view. What would be the doctrinal basis for determining this issue based only on the circumstances that existed at the time the power was created? Is there any justification for distinguishing for this purpose between ordinary gifts and those made by exercising a power, so as to permit the court in the latter case to take into consideration circumstances existing at the time of the appointment? See Gray §§ 523–523.6.

The following appointments would be valid under the prevailing view. Why?

(a) *A*'s will created a testamentary trust to pay the income to *B* for life, and to pay the principal on *B*'s death to such persons as *B* should by will appoint. *B* later died, leaving a will appointing the property to a trustee in trust to pay the income to *B*'s husband for life, and from his death until the death of the last surviving child of *B* to pay the income in equal shares per stirpes to *B*'s living children and to the living issue of any deceased child of *B*; and on the death of *B*'s last surviving child, to divide the principal per stirpes among the issue then living of *B*'s deceased children. *B* had two children, *X* and *Y*, both of whom survived *B* and both of whom were born before the death of *A*.

(b) *A*'s will created a testamentary trust to pay the income to *B* for life, and on *B*'s death to hold the property in trust for such issue of *B*, and on such terms and in such shares, as *B* should by will appoint. *B* later died, leaving a will appointing the property in further trust to pay the income in equal shares per stirpes to *B*'s living children and to the living issue of any deceased child of *B* until *B*'s youngest child should reach the age of 30 or die under that age; and when *B*'s youngest child should reach the age of 30 or die under that age to divide the principal per stirpes among *B*'s issue then living. *B* had three children, *X*, *Y*, and *Z*, all of whom were conceived and born after *A*'s death, and all of whom survived *B*. At *B*'s death, *X* was 29 years old, *Y* was 28, and *Z* was 25.

(c) *A*'s will created a testamentary trust to pay the income to *B* for life, and to pay the principal on *B*'s death to such persons as *B* should by will appoint. *B*'s son, *S*, was conceived and born after *A*'s death, but *S* predeceased *B* leaving two surviving children. *B* later died, leaving a will appointing the property in equal shares to "the children of my son, *S*." If *B*'s appointment to *S*'s children would give the latter the right to possession at *B*'s death, would the appointment be valid if *S* survived *B*?

c. Validity of Gifts in Default of Appointment

The final problem in this area is that of the appropriate criteria for determining the validity under the Rule against Perpetuities of a gift in default of appointment, in the event that the power of appointment expires (by, e.g., the death of the donee) without exercise.

(i) If the donee of a *general power presently exercisable* dies without exercising it, what is the argument for judging the validity of the gift in default by running the period from, and considering the circumstances existing at, the time of the donee's death? Restatement of Property § 373 cmt. c, and Am. L. Prop. § 24.36, favor this approach. The latter authors, for example, would sustain the validity of the gift in default in a case like the following:

A's will created a testamentary trust to pay the income to *B* for life, and then to transfer the principal to such person or persons as *B* should by deed appoint, and in default of appointment to pay the principal to such of *B*'s children as should reach the age of 30. *B* later died without making any appointment. *B* had two children, *X* and *Y*, both of whom were conceived and born after *A*'s death. At the time of *B*'s death, *X* was 5 years of age, and *Y* was 3. What would be the argument in such a case for allowing *X* and *Y* to take the property if they reach 30?

(ii) If the donee of a *general testamentary power* or of a *special power* dies without exercising it, the period of the Rule presumably runs for the purpose of determining the validity of a gift in default from the effective date of the instrument creating the power and making such gift in default, since this would be true if the power were exercised. Would the circumstances determining whether such a gift in default was void be those at the time of the instrument making the gift in default also? Or would the court consider the circumstances existing at the time when the power expired by the donee's death?

In Sears v. Coolidge, 108 N.E.2d 563 (Mass.1952), an inter vivos trust created in 1913, following certain income interests, gave the principal in equal shares to the settlor's issue who should be living at the first to occur of two events: (1) the death of the survivor of the settlor's issue who should be living at the settlor's death, or (2) the attainment of age 50 by the settlor's youngest surviving grandchild who should be living at the settlor's death. The trust deed then reserved to the settlor the power to change the trust in any manner "except such as will vest in myself the trust property or any beneficial interest therein," and to appoint the property to persons other than those specified in the deed; any such change or appointment to be made by deed of the settlor delivered to the trustee. The court treated this as the equivalent of "a special power to appoint by deed." Id. at 566. The settlor died in 1920 without exercising the power, and the second of the two alternative conditions occurred in 1951, when the youngest grandchild living at the settlor's death attained the age of fifty.

At the time of the trust deed, the settlor was a widower aged 81, and two of his four children had died; his two living children were daughters aged 59 and 55 respectively; his ten living grandchildren ranged in age from 7 to 35; no more grandchildren were born after the trust deed, which is scarcely surprising. However, the opinion does not refer to any argument that the settlor would contemplate only his grandchildren existing at the time of the trust deed, so as to make the youngest grandchild to reach 50 a life in being and validate the gift on the second alternative contingency.

The court, however, validated the gift in default with the following reasoning: since the circumstances existing at the time of exercise of a special power are relevant in determining the validity of an appointment, it is reasonable to consider the circumstances at the time when such a power expires in determining the validity of a gift in default; operating on that theory, the gift in default was valid because it was known at the death of the settlor that any grandchild then living (whose attainment of 50 would cause the second alternative contingency to occur) would also have been living at the date of the trust deed (and was thus a life in being who would have to attain 50 within his own lifetime). The opinion read in part:

> In the case of the trust instrument under consideration until it became too late for the settlor to exercise the reserved power no one could tell what might be the ultimate disposition of the trust property. As long as there remained a right to change, alter, and make new appointments, no instruction to the trustees or declaratory decree would ordinarily have been given as to the validity of the settlor's limitations. . . . Upon his death it could be learned for the first time what definitely were to be the terms of the trust. . . . The appellees strongly urge that the doctrine of a "second look" has no place in reading the original limitations in default of appointment, which were capable of examination when created, and which should retain the same meaning throughout. They argue that its adoption would be a nullification of the rule "that executory limitations are void unless they take effect ex necessitate and in all possible contingencies" within the prescribed period. Hall v. Hall, 123 Mass. 120, 124. But this rule, while recognized, was assuaged as to the exercise of a power of appointment in Minot v. Paine, 230 Mass. 514, 522 [120 N.E. 167, 170]. It was there deemed wise not to apply unmodified a remorseless technical principle to a case which it did not fit. That principle seems equally inappropriate here. [108 N.E.2d at 567.]

Should the result differ in the following cases?

A's will leaves property in trust to pay the income to *B* for life, and on *B*'s death to pay the principal as *B* shall by will appoint or in default of appointment to such of *B*'s children as attain the age of 25. *B* has no children at *A*'s death, but later has two children born, *X* and *Y*. At *B*'s death, *X* is 20 and *Y* is 15. *X* and *Y* both later reach 25. Should their rights to the property be affected by whether

    (1) *B* leaves a will appointing to "such of my children as attain the age of 25," or

(2) *B* leaves a will stating, "I make no appointment under the power given to me by *A*'s will because I desire the property to go in default of appointment under *A*'s will," or

(3) *B* leaves no will?

See Am. L. Prop. § 24.36.

For the relationship between the Rule against Perpetuities and powers of appointment in general, see Gray § 473–561.7; Leach, Perpetuities in a Nutshell, 51 Harv. L. Rev. 638, 651–656 (1938).

d. Discretionary Trusts

A beneficial interest in a discretionary trust is void if its terms authorize distributions after the expiration of the period of the Rule against Perpetuities, regardless of whether the permissible distributions are from income or principal. Thomas v. Harrison, supra p. 882. For example, a trust to pay over to *B*'s children until the death of the survivor of *B*'s children such income as the trustee shall in its absolute and uncontrolled discretion determine would be void if *B* were alive at the effective date of the trust. A justifiable explanation of this result is that the trustee has a special power to appoint the income among a class, and that, since the power need not be exercised within the period of the Rule, it is void ab initio. Thus, no effective appointment is possible. See Restatement (Third) of Property: Wills and Other Donative Transfers § 17.1 cmt. g (2011) (treating the trustee's discretion as a power of appointment).

e. Administrative Powers

It is common these days to give the trustee broad administrative powers, including the power to sell, invest, reinvest, mortgage, and lease trust assets. Charitable trusts may last indefinitely, and, even where the Rule remains in force, private trusts may endure beyond the expiration of the period of the Rule if the beneficial interests vest within the period (e.g., mandatory income interest for *B*'s children during their lives, assuming that *B* was still living when the trust was created).

Are administrative powers vulnerable under the Rule, on the ground that exercise might occur remotely? The cases are scarce. Some English decisions cast doubt on the validity of such powers. While, of course, one can argue that such powers permit the creation of new interests in property after the period expires, it seems nonsense in terms of policy to hold such powers void. As the court said in Melvin v. Hoffman, 235 S.W. 107 (Mo.1921): "The power to lease, sell and reinvest, instead of impeding, facilitates the transfer of property, and is the very purpose the rule against perpetuities seeks to promote." Id. at 116. See Leach, Powers of

Sale in Trustees and the Rule against Perpetuities, 47 Harv. L. Rev. 948 (1934). Restatement (Third) of Property: Wills and Other Donative Transfers § 17.1 cmt. h (2011), takes the position that administrative powers are not powers of appointment.

3. POWERS OF APPOINTMENT— MISCELLANEOUS ASPECTS

a. Creation of Powers of Appointment

The general rule is that no particular language is necessary to create a power of appointment. Although occasionally a question arises as to whether a power was or was not created (see, e.g., Matter of Clark, 80 N.Y.S.2d 1 (App. Div. 1948)), problems of this kind are rare. N.Y. EPTL § 10–4.1 establishes the following modest "rules for creation of a power of appointment":

(a) The donor of a power of appointment:

(1) Must be a person capable of transferring the appointive property.

(2) Must have created or reserved the power by a written instrument executed by him in the manner required by law.

(3) Must manifest his intention to confer the power on a person capable of holding the appointive property. . . .

Notwithstanding the lack of formal requirements, the instrument creating the power should leave no doubt about the extent of the power, the property subject to it, the identity of the donee or donees, the identity of the permissible appointees, the identity of the takers in default of exercise, and any designated manner of exercise. To prevent inadvertent exercise under statutes like that in New York (infra p. 957), it is a good idea to designate a specific manner of exercise.

b. Exercise of Powers of Appointment

If the document creating the power designates a particular manner of exercise, e.g., by a will specifically referring to the creating instrument, the courts ordinarily require compliance with the donor's direction. Even an expression of the donee's intention to exercise "all powers of appointment" does not suffice. See Schede Estate, 231 A.2d 135 (Pa.1967).

If the creating instrument requires no particular formality or mode of expression, none is ordinarily necessary to exercise a power, provided that the donee sufficiently manifests the intent to exercise the power. Here again, it does not need emphasizing that the donee should express the intention to exercise in precise terms. Cf. Wetherill v. Basham, 3 P.3d 1118 (Ariz. App. 2000) (attempted amendment of trust was "effective, albeit inadvertent, exercise" of settlor's retained general power).

A question that frequently arises is whether the making of a will, which makes no reference to the power, constitutes an exercise.

IN RE PROESTLER'S WILL

Supreme Court of Iowa, 1942.
232 Iowa 640, 5 N.W.2d 922.

MILLER, JUSTICE. . . .

Henry T. Proestler died July 4, 1919, leaving his widow, Mathilde B. Proestler, but no children, surviving him. His will was admitted to probate September 11, 1919. It provided for the payment of his debts and funeral expenses, made a number of bequests, following which, Item 13 of the will provided as follows:

> All the rest, residue and remainder of the property, real, personal or mixed, of which I die seized or possessed, or to which I may be entitled, I give, devise and bequeath to Matilda B. Proestler and William Heuer in trust for the following uses and purposes: I direct that the net income from this trust fund shall be paid to my wife, Matilda B. Proestler, during her lifetime. I direct that my wife, Matilda B. Proestler, shall have the right to dispose by will of Twenty Thousand ($20,000.00) Dollars of said trust fund. All the rest, residue and remainder of said trust fund, after the death of my wife, Matilda B. Proestler, I give, devise and bequeath as follows:

(Following are set forth a number of bequests for the disposition of said trust fund.)

On September 15, 1919, the widow filed an election to take under the will and, with William Heuer, qualified as executor. The executors' final report was approved and the executors discharged January 22, 1921. The trustees named in the will carried out the provisions of the trust. On October 26, 1935, the widow died testate. Her will was admitted to probate and provides as follows:

> I, Mathilde B. Proestler, of Davenport, Scott County, Iowa, being of sound and disposing mind and memory, do hereby make, publish and declare the following as and for my Last Will and Testament, hereby revoking all former Wills.

> I. It is my will that all my just debts be first paid out of my Estate.

II. All the rest, residue and remainder of my Estate of whatever kind and wherever situated, I will, devise and bequeath to my nephew, Werner H. Grabbe, with the request, however, that the income derived therefrom be used for the benefit, during her lifetime, of my sister, Christiane Hensen.

III. I nominate, constitute and appoint my said Nephew, Werner H. Grabbe, Executor of this my Last Will and Testament, and exempt him from giving any bond, and I hereby grant and delegate to him as Executor full power and authority to sell and convey, mortgage or otherwise encumber, any real or personal property, should he deem it advisable, and to do any and all things as freely and fully as I myself might do, were I living, without the necessity of first obtaining an Order of Court.

In Testimony Whereof, I have hereunto set my hand at Davenport, Iowa, this 13th day of February, A.D. 1933.

(Signed) Mathilde B. Proestler.

On March 28, 1937, Paul A. Tornquist, trustee under the will of Henry T. Proestler, appointed to succeed William Heuer, deceased, made application for instructions as to the distribution of certain funds in the trust estate, asserting among other things as follows: "That this Trustee is unable to determine whether or not the said Mathilde B. Proestler by her will did dispose of Twenty Thousand ($20,000.00) Dollars of said trust fund. Consequently, this Trustee is unable to determine how the money should be distributed which he has on hand ready for distribution." Various petitions of intervention were filed. One of the interveners, Werner H. Grabbe, the sole legatee under the will of Mathilde B. Proestler, asserted "that said Mathilde B. Proestler intended by the terms of her said Will to devise and bequeath the said Twenty Thousand ($20,000.00) Dollars to this Intervenor and that by the terms of her said Will the said Twenty Thousand ($20,000.00) Dollars was so devised and bequeathed to him."
. . .

[O]ral testimony was offered for the purpose of showing that Mathilde B. Proestler intended by the terms of her will to devise and bequeath to Werner H. Grabbe the $20,000 referred to in her husband's will. Timely objection was interposed to the competency of such testimony. At the close of the trial, the court made the following findings:

That there is no ambiguity in the will of Mathilde B. Proestler; nor a word nor an expression of doubtful or uncertain meaning; and hence no evidence is necessary or admissible, to clear up any doubt, or to show any surrounding facts or circumstances, or to explain or make more certain any of the wording contained in her said will.

That the power of appointment, the right of disposal of $20,000.00 of the trust fund given to her under the provisions of the will of Henry T. Proestler, deceased, is not, and was not exercised by the will of Mathilde B. Proestler, and there is nothing in the language of her will to show that she intended to exercise it.

Pursuant to the foregoing, the decree determined

that Paul A. Tornquist, Trustee under the Will of Henry T. Proestler, deceased, be and is hereby ordered and directed, as to all the moneys now on hand in said trust and all that may hereafter be on hand and ready for distribution, to distribute the same in strict accord with the terms and provisions of the will of said Henry T. Proestler, deceased, exactly in the manner the same should and would be distributed if there had been no provision in said will giving the widow of said testator the power of disposal of $20,000.00 of said trust estate.

The intervener, Werner H. Grabbe, has appealed to this court. . . .

Both parties concede, and our investigation confirms the fact, that there is no Iowa statute upon the precise question here presented for our decision. . . .

The general common law principle is set forth in paragraph 343 of the Restatement of the Law of Property (Vol. 3, page 1913) as follows: "When the donee by his will makes a gift of the residue of his estate or otherwise manifests an intent to pass all of his property, this of itself does not manifest an intent to exercise any power." This statement is in accord with repeated pronouncements of various text books and annotators to the effect that, in the absence of statute, it is generally held that a power of appointment is not executed by the residuary clause in a will unless an intent to exercise the power appears in addition thereto from the terms of the will. . . . This principle of the common law has been repeatedly recognized and applied in at least a dozen of the several states. . . .

Many well established principles of the common law are recognized and applied in the application of the rule above referred to. One principle is applied herein, namely, that, where the will is unambiguous, its interpretation is for the court and oral testimony is not admissible as a basis for the interpretation of the will. Another principle is that the will is to be interpreted from the language used therein and the words used are to be understood to mean what they say, no less and no more. Where a power of appointment is vested in one who has become deceased, it is usually held that the will of the decedent will constitute an exercise of the power in three classes of cases, to-wit: (1) Where there is a reference to the power in the will, (2) where there is a reference to the property which is the subject on which it is to be executed, and (3) where the provisions of the will would otherwise be ineffectual. In the absence of any of these three requirements, it is usually held that the power of appointment does not constitute a part of the estate and therefore a general devise of "all the rest, residue and remainder" of the estate does not constitute an exercise of the power of appointment. Accordingly, the will relied upon by the appellant herein was insufficient to constitute an exercise of the power of appointment granted to Mrs. Proestler by the will of her deceased husband. Under the principles of common law, recognized and applied in the jurisdictions above referred to, the decree of the trial court was clearly right. . . .

By reason of the foregoing, the decree of the trial court herein must be, and it is, affirmed.

NOTES

1. *Exercise by residuary clause.* The overwhelming majority of American decisions have held that, in the absence of a statute, a general clause in a will purporting to convey all of the testator's property does not exercise a testamentary power of appointment. See Restatement (Second) of Property: Donative Transfers § 17.3 (1986). Many states, however, now have relevant legislation. The original version of the Uniform Probate Code, for example, followed the common law:

> A general residuary clause in a will, or a will making general disposition of all of the testator's property, does not exercise a power of appointment held by the testator unless specific reference is made to the power or there is some other indication of intention to include the property subject to the power. [UPC § 2–610 (1969).]

The most recent version of the Code provides that a residuary clause exercises a power of appointment "only if (i) the power is a general power and the creating instrument does not contain a gift if the power is not exercised or (ii) the testator's will manifests an intention to include the property subject to the power." UPC § 2-608. See also Restatement (Third) of Property: Wills and Other Donative Transfers § 19.4 (2011). Some statutes reverse the presumption. For example, N.Y. EPTL § 10–6.1 provides:

> (a) Subject to paragraph (b), an effective exercise of a power of appointment does not require an express reference to such power. A power is effectively exercised if the donee manifests his intention to exercise it. Such a manifestation exists when the donee:
>
> > (1) Declares in substance that he is exercising all the powers he has;

(2) Sufficiently identifying the appointive property or any part thereof, executes an instrument purporting to dispose of such property or part;

(3) Makes a disposition which, when read with reference to the property he owned and the circumstances existing at the time of its making, manifests his understanding that he was disposing of the appointive property; or

(4) Leaves a will disposing of all of his property or all of his property of the kind covered by the power, unless the intention that the will is not to operate as an execution of the power appears expressly or by necessary implication.

(b) If the donor has expressly directed that no instrument shall be effective to exercise the power unless it contains a specific reference to the power, an instrument not containing such reference does not validly exercise the power.

See generally French, Exercise of Powers of Appointment: Should Intent to Exercise Be Inferred From a General Disposition of Property?, 1979 Duke L.J. 749.

2. *Permissible appointments.* The donee of a general power of appointment can create any interest in the appointive property that the donee could have created if the donee had owned the property outright. Thus, the donee may appoint the appointive property outright or in trust or may (subject to the Rule against Perpetuities) create a power, general or special, in another. When the power is special, of course, the donee may appoint only to an object of the power. Thus, some decisions have held that the donee of a special power cannot appoint in further trust or create a new power of appointment. Restatement (Third) of Property: Wills and Other Donative Transfers § 19.14 (2011), however, provides that, in the absence of contrary intent by the donor, the donee of a special power may appoint in trust and may create a new power in another, but that the new power may only benefit permissible appointees of the original power.

c. Contracts to Appoint and Releases of Powers of Appointment

(i) Contracts to Appoint

As a general rule, contracts to appoint property under a testamentary power, whether general or special, are unenforceable. See Estate of Brown, 306 N.E.2d 781 (N.Y.1973); Carmichael v. Heggie, 506 S.E.2d 308 (S.C. App. 1998). In Farmers' Loan & Trust Co. v. Mortimer, 114 N.E. 389 (N.Y.1916), Judge Cardozo articulated the following rationale:

The exercise of the power was to represent the final judgment, the last will, of the donee. Up to the last moment of his life, he was to have the power to deal with the share as he thought best. . . . To permit him to bargain that right away would be to defeat the purpose of the donor. Her command was that her property should go to her son's issue unless at the end of his life it remained his will that it go elsewhere. It has not remained his will that it go elsewhere; and his earlier contract cannot nullify the expression of his final purpose. [114 N.E. at 390.]

Thus, specific enforcement of such a contract is rarely available. Whether damages for breach of contract are available is less clear. In Northern Trust Co. v. Porter, 13 N.E.2d 487 (Ill.1938), the court, after holding that an ineffective appointment void under the rule against perpetuities would constitute a breach of the contract in that case to exercise a general testamentary power of appointment, held that the promisees could not recover damages from the donee's estate:

It is conceded that the contract is not specifically enforceable.

The donor, in giving a general power of appointment by will, only, intends that the donee shall retain his discretion as to who shall receive the property subject to appointment, until the time of his death. The purpose of giving such power is to allow the exercise of such power to represent the final judgment of the donee. To permit a contract to appoint in a certain way to be binding would be, in effect, to change the power from a general testamentary power to a power to appoint by deed or will. The intention of the donor must not be thus circumvented. . . .

Moreover, the knowledge that damages would be given in case she did not comply with the contract would make the donee reluctant to breach the contract and thus to exercise her freedom of choice up to the last moment of her life,—a thing which the donor intended. In other words, if damages are allowed against the estate of the donee, it has the effect of exerting coercion of a threatened judgment to compel voluntary performance of an act which could not be judicially enforced by specific performance. For this reason, damages may be recovered from neither the individual estate of the donee nor from the appointive fund. [13 N.E.2d. at 492.]

Restatement (Third) of Property: Wills and Other Donative Transfers § 21.2 (2011), too, would deny both damages and specific performance but would permit restitution of any value given in exchange for the promise. In contrast, in In re Parkin, [1892] 3 Ch. Div. 510, the court denied specific performance but allowed damages in a decision assuming, rather than justifying, the propriety of doing so. And in Estate of O'Rourke, 648

N.Y.S.2d 704 (App. Div. 1996), the court enforced a constructive trust in favor of the takers in default against those in whose favor a general testamentary power of appointment had been exercised, based on the donee's promise not to exercise the power.

The objections to enforcing a contract to exercise a testamentary power apply to neither a contract to exercise a presently exercisable power (Restatement (Third) of Property: Wills and Other Donative Transfers § 21.1 (2011)) nor a contract to leave individually owned property by will.

(ii) Releases of Powers of Appointment

The donee of a power of appointment may, if he or she acts in time, refuse to accept the power, i.e., "disclaim" or "renounce" it. Even if the donee initially accepts the power, he or she may (in most circumstances) later give up the right to exercise it, i.e., "release" it. See Restatement (Third) of Property: Wills and Other Donative Transfers §§ 20.1, 20.2 (2011).

If the takers in default are the same people as the intended beneficiaries of a contract to appoint, one can argue that the contract to appoint is really a release of the power. In Wood v. American Security & Trust Co., 253 F.Supp. 592 (D.D.C.1966), the court sustained as a release of the power an agreement as to the ultimate disposition of property subject to a power among three life tenants, when there was a testamentary power of appointment in the "surviving" life tenant. But the more usual result is not to treat a contract to appoint as a release, because of the obvious differences in the intentions of the parties to the contract, in comparison with those of a donee who releases a power. For example, in Seidel v. Werner, 364 N.Y.S.2d 963 (Sup. Ct.), aff'd, 376 N.Y.S.2d 139 (App. Div. 1975), the court refused to conflate the two concepts, not only because the beneficiaries of the contract were not identical to the takers in default, but also because the nature of the interest (i.e., outright or in further trust) promised under the contract differed from the nature of the interests to which the takers in default were entitled. See also O'Hara v. O'Hara, 44 A.2d 813 (Md.1945).

Unfortunately, there are serious logical inconsistencies in refusing to enforce contracts to exercise testamentary powers but allowing the donee of *any* power to release it. Consider, for example:

A transfers property to *B* for life, then to such persons as *B* shall by will appoint and in default of appointment to *C*.

(a) *B* contracts to appoint the property to *X*. Subject to the as yet somewhat uncertain question as to whether *X* could recover damages for breach of contract, the contract is unenforceable.

(b) *B* executes a release of the power. The release is probably effective, either by statute or by case law. See Lyon v. Alexander, 156 A. 84 (Pa.1931) (general testamentary power released by life tenant-donee joining in deed to another; no recognition of any distinction between testamentary powers and those exercisable inter vivos).

Can the results in (a) and (b) be reconciled in terms of the donor's intent or any other factor? See Gray, Release and Discharge of Powers, 24 Harv. L. Rev. 511, 531 (1911).

d. Characteristics of Special Powers of Appointment

IN RE CARROLL'S WILL

Court of Appeals of New York, 1937.
274 N.Y. 288, 8 N.E.2d 864.

Proceeding in the matter of the petition of Harold A. Content, as one of the executors under the last will and testament of Elsa C. Milliken, deceased, for a construction of the last will and testament of William Carroll, deceased, with respect to a power of appointment therein given and attempted to be exercised by Elsa C. Milliken. From an order (247 App. Div. 11, 286 N.Y.S. 307) modifying a decree of the Surrogate's Court, New York County (153 Misc. 649, 275 N.Y.S. 911), determining that a bequest to Paul Allan Curtis by Elsa C. Milliken was entirely void, Ralph C. Carroll, individually, Grace Carroll and the Central Hanover Bank & Trust Company, as trustees under the will of William Carroll, Ralph C. Carroll, Jr., and others, by Benjamin F. Schreiber, special guardian, appeal.

The surrogate held that a bequest of $250,000 made to the respondent, Paul A. Curtis, by the terms of the will of Elsa C. Milliken, deceased, as a purported exercise of the said power of appointment, was void in its entirety as a fraud upon such power. The modification by the Appellate Division consisted of an adjudication that the bequest was valid to the extent of $150,000.

HUBBS, JUDGE. In 1910 William Carroll died leaving a will by the fourth paragraph of which he devised and bequeathed the residue of his estate to his executors in trust to pay the income to his wife during her life. By the fifth paragraph he directed that upon the death of the wife the residuary trust be divided into two equal shares, the proceeds of one to be for the use and benefit of his daughter, Elsa, during her life, and the proceeds of the other share for the use and benefit of his son, Ralph, during his life. In the fifth paragraph he gave his daughter power by her last will and testament to dispose of the property so set aside for her use "to and among her children or any other kindred who shall survive her and in such shares and manner as she shall think proper." A similar power of appointment was given to Ralph to dispose of his share "to and among his kindred or wife." With respect to the share set aside for the use of the daughter, Elsa, the will provided that, in the absence of any valid disposition of the corpus by her, it should pass "to her then surviving child or children, descendant or descendants" and, should there be no surviving child or descendant of the daughter, then the share on her decease should pass to the donor's "surviving heirs or next-of-kin, according to the nature of the estate."

Elsa died on June 26, 1933, without leaving any child or descendant her surviving. The mother, Grace Carroll, survived her and was living at the time of the trial, as was also the brother, Ralph. Elsa left a will by which she left $5,000 to her brother, and $250,000 to one Paul Curtis, a cousin, such bequest to go to his son if he predeceased her. The remainder of her share of the estate of her father she gave to her executors in trust.

When Elsa's will was drawn, the petitioning executor, Content, as her attorney, prepared the will and attended to its execution and also prepared a letter directed to Elsa by the legatee Paul Curtis, which letter read as follows:

> I am informed that by your last will and testament you have given and bequeathed to me the sum of Two Hundred and Fifty Thousand Dollars ($250,000). In the event that you should predecease me and I should receive the bequest before mentioned, I hereby promise and agree, in consideration of the said bequest, that I will pay to your husband, Foster Milliken, Jr., the sum of One Hundred Thousand Dollars ($100,000) out of the said bequest which you have given to me by your said will.

It is not contended by any of the parties to this proceeding that Foster Milliken, Jr., husband of Elsa, was of her kindred, and, therefore, a proper object of the power granted to his wife in her father's will. The question here involved is as to the effect of the attempted provision for her husband upon the bequest to Paul Curtis.

Content testified that he had advised Elsa that she could not lawfully make her husband a beneficiary of any part of her father's estate; that she had drawn a previous will in which she had given the residue of the estate of her father to her brother, Ralph, with a request that he pay to her husband the sum of $10,000 per annum; that he advised her that that provision could not be enforced; that on October 6, 1931, she told him that she was not satisfied; that she was growing away from her brother and that she wanted to increase the bequest to her cousin Paul Curtis; that she had given Curtis $50,000 in a prior will; that she wanted to leave him $250,000 and that he prepared the will with the prior will before him and on October 13 she and Mrs. Elliott came to his office where she executed the will; that after the will was executed she told him: "Paul would like to do something for Foster. He would like to leave him some of this money I am leaving to him, and Paul is perfectly willing to put this in writing to show his good faith." He then talked with Paul, dictated the letter, and had it signed. He was not sure whether the letter was delivered to Elsa or whether he kept it for her. Curtis testified that several days before the will was executed Elsa told him she was going to make a new will; that she knew if her brother, Ralph, heard about it he would probably start a row with her mother; that she had previously left Curtis $50,000 and his son $50,000, and that she was going to leave him $150,000, and add to it $100,000 which she would like him to give to Mr. Milliken; that he told her if she wanted him to do so, he would sign a paper to that effect; that she said she did not know whether it would be necessary but if she wanted him to she would make a date for him to go down to Mr. Content's office; that she called him upon the day the will was executed and asked him to meet her there; that he was not present when the will was executed but that he went in afterwards and heard the letter dictated and signed it.

The surrogate determined that the promise made by Curtis so vitiated and permeated the bequest to him that the appointment constituted a fraud upon the power and made the bequest to him void.

The Appellate Division, two justices dissenting, decided that the only reasonable interpretation to be placed upon the transaction is that Elsa desired to appoint $150,000 to her cousin and an additional $100,000 to her husband; accordingly, that the lawful appointment of $150,000 to Curtis is separable from the unlawful appointment of $100,000 to him for the benefit of the husband.

It seems to us that the conclusion is inescapable that the testimony of Content, the attorney who drew the instruments, and of Curtis, who was the legatee, do not affect the true intent and purpose of the letter. Stress is laid upon the fact as testified to by Content that the testatrix, Elsa, did not tell him of the understanding with Curtis until after the will had been executed. Nevertheless, it appears from the testimony of Curtis that she had an understanding with him prior to the execution of the will and the writing constituted only a record of the actual prior agreement. The surrogate had the benefit of hearing the witnesses testify and of observing their conduct. He found nothing in their testimony to detract from the force of the letter signed by Curtis. Concededly, the attempted bequest for the benefit of the husband was not valid. Curtis alone testified that he was to receive $150,000 and the husband $100,000. Content testified that she told him she wanted to leave Curtis $250,000, and that he did not know until after the will was drawn of the understanding between Curtis and the testatrix. The letter says that the agreement to pay the husband $100,000 is in consideration of a bequest of $250,000. No one can say whether she would have left Curtis $100,000, $150,000, or a lesser or greater sum had it not been for the agreement to take care of her husband. Only by speculation can it be said that she would have left him $150,000 had it not been for that agreement. Had it not been for her continued possession either personally or by her attorney of the promise on the part of Curtis, no one can say but what she might have changed the will. Curtis was a party to the attempted fraud on the power. If the bequest to him be sustained to the extent of $150,000 on his own testimony, he suffers no penalty. It seems to us that on the facts, the conclusion of the surrogate was correct; that the entire bequest is involved in the intent to defeat the power and that it is impossible to separate and sustain the bequest to Curtis to the extent of $150,000.

Upon the general question the law of England is correctly stated in Halsbury's Laws of England (Vol. 23 [1st ed.], pp. 58–62):

> A person having a limited power must exercise it bona fide for the end designed; otherwise the execution is a fraud on the power and void. Fraud in this connection does not necessarily imply any moral turpitude, but is used to cover all cases where the purpose of the appointor is to effect some bye or sinister object, whether such purpose be selfish or, in the appointor's belief, a more beneficial mode of disposition of the property and more consonant with that which he believes would be the real wish of the creator of the power under the circumstances existing at the date of the appointment. In all cases of fraudulent execution, the fraud consists in the exercise of the power for purposes foreign to those for which it was created and the exercise of the power may be held fraudulent on any of the three following grounds:
>
> (1) If the execution was made for a corrupt purpose.
>
> (2) If it was made in pursuance of an antecedent agreement by the appointee to benefit persons not objects of the power, even although the agreement in itself is unobjectionable. An appointment to a child an object of the power, and a contemporaneous settlement by him of the appointed fund, is, however, valid unless it can be shown that the appointment was made in pursuance of a contract inducing the appointment.
>
> (3) If it was made for purposes foreign to the power, although such purposes are not communicated to the appointee before the appointment and although the appointor gets no personal benefit. . . . Appointments cannot be severed, so as to be good to the extent to which they are bona fide exercises of the power, but bad as to the remainder, unless (1) some consideration has been given which cannot

be restored, or (2) the court can sever the intentions of the appointor and distinguish the good from the bad.

In a footnote on page 60 it is said:

The fact that the appointor knows that the object intends to dispose of the fund in favour of a stranger to the power does not necessarily vitiate the appointment, but it may have that effect if it can be shown that the appointment would not have been made but for the agreement. Pryor v. Pryor, 2 DeGex, J. & S. 205, C.A.; Daniel v. Arkwright, 2 Herm. & M. 95; Re Foote and Purdon's Estate (1910) 1 I.R. 365. The question in each case is the character in which the appointee takes the property; if it is for his absolute benefit the appointment is good, but if this is not the appointor's purpose it is bad. Langston v. Blackmore, Amb. 289; FitzRoy v. Richmond, Duke (No. 2), 27 Beav. 190; Birley v. Birley, 25 Beav. 299; Pryor v. Pryor, supra; Cooper v. Cooper, L.R. 8 Eq. 312; Roach v. Trood, 3 Ch. Div. 429, C.A.; In re Turner's Settled Estates, 28 Ch. Div. 205, C.A. . . .

In the case at bar we have written evidence which is corroborative of a prior agreement. It seems to us that the surrogate was quite correct in concluding that it is impossible to separate the valid from the invalid disposition. To say that it clearly appears that the donee would have given $150,000 to Curtis had the bargain not been made is not justified. It clearly appears that an object of the appointment to Curtis was to secure a benefit to the husband of the donee who was excluded by the donor of the power from being an appointee or benefitting from the exercise of the power. The purpose of the donee was to accomplish by an agreement with Curtis an end entirely foreign to the intent of the donor of the power. Her act constituted a fraud on the power in which Curtis actively participated. There was a bargain between the donee and Curtis by which, in consideration of the appointment, he agreed to dispose of a part of the legacy in favor of a person who was not an object of the power. That bargain resulted in vitiating not only the provision for donee's husband but also the bequest to Curtis within the meaning of the authorities heretofore cited.

The wording of the letter which he signed was "in consideration of the said bequest" he would pay to donee's husband $100,000 "out of the said bequest" of $250,000. It is hard to see how those plain words can be construed otherwise than a bargain to share his bequest of $250,000 with another not an object of the power. Such a bargain under all the authorities makes the entire bequest void. . . .

The appellant Ralph C. Carroll contends that, in permitting the donee to appoint to any of her kindred, the donor used the word "kindred" in a narrow sense and intended to limit the possible beneficiaries of the power to her next of kin. If correct in that contention, since the donee died without children, the result would be that she could appoint only to her brother, the appellant Ralph Carroll. There is no inconsistency or ambiguity in the will of William Carroll evidenced by the fact that he gave to his daughter a power of appointment to her children or any other of her kindred. Kindred has a well-established meaning, "blood relatives," as distinguished from that limited number of blood relatives embraced under the term "next of kin." William Carroll in his will used the words next of kin where it is apparent that it was his intention that the property was to pass as in the case of intestacy. The surrogate has determined that kindred was used in the generally accepted meaning of the word. That determination has been affirmed by the Appellate Division and there appears no reason for according to it a limited application. . . .

The order of the Appellate Division should be modified in accordance with this opinion, and, as so modified, affirmed, without costs.

CRANE, C.J., and O'BRIEN, LOUGHRAN, FINCH, and RIPPEY, JJ., concur.

LEHMAN, J., dissents and votes to affirm.

NOTES

1. *"Fraud" on a power.* There are many ways by which the donee of a special power may try to exercise it for his or her own benefit, or for that of another impermissible appointee. For example, the donee of a power to appoint among the donee's children may execute an instrument that purports instead to appoint all or part of the property to the donee's spouse. Such an exercise is obviously ineffective. See Restatement (Third) of Property: Wills and Other Donative Transfers § 19.15 (2011). Even if an exercise seems, on its face, to benefit only a permissible appointee, and therefore to be entirely proper, the appointment may nonetheless be wholly or partly ineffective if other evidence shows that the donee's purpose was to benefit a non-object. See id. § 19.16. Attempts of both sorts to escape the limitations of the special power have long been described as "frauds on the power." The terminology, however, is misleading, as indicated by the excerpt from Halsbury in the principal case and by the following language in the opinion in Vatcher v. Paull, [1915] A.C. 372:

> The term fraud in connection with frauds on a power does not necessarily denote any conduct on the part of the appointor amounting to fraud in the common law meaning of the term or any conduct which could be properly termed dishonest or immoral. It merely means that the power has been exercised for a purpose, or with an intention, beyond the scope of or not justified by the instrument creating the power. Perhaps the most common instance of this is where the exercise is due to some bargain between the appointor and appointee, whereby the appointor, or some other person not an object of the power, is to derive a benefit. But

such a bargain is not essential. It is enough that the appointor's purpose and intention is to secure a benefit for himself, or some other person not an object of the power. In such a case the appointment is invalid, unless the Court can clearly distinguish between the quantum of the benefit bona fide intended to be conferred on the appointee and the quantum of the benefit intended to be derived by the appointor or to be conferred on a stranger. . . . [Id. at 378.]

2. *Severability.* If an exercise purports to benefit permissible objects of the power, as well as non-objects, the issue arises as to whether the exercise is *entirely* void. The solution to this problem should probably depend on whether the donee desired the permissible objects to take, even upon failure of the improper purpose.

In the principal case, what would be the reasons for concluding that, contrary to the holding of the Court of Appeals, Paul Curtis should be entitled to $150,000, even though the attempted provision of $100,000 for the donee's husband failed? See the opinion of the majority of the Appellate Division, 286 N.Y.S. at 314.

3. *Exclusive powers.* The question may arise whether a special power is "exclusive" (in which case the donee may exercise it in favor of one or more of the permissible objects, to the exclusion of others) or "non-exclusive" (in which case the donee must appoint some of the property to each of the permissible objects). If the power is non-exclusive, the further question may arise as to how large a share each appointee must receive, in order to prevent the appointment from being "illusory." As Simes and Smith point out (§ 982), "there would appear to be no valid reason for creating a non-exclusive power"; thus, the courts are likely to find an exclusive power absent a specific direction by the donor. Restatement (Third) of Property: Wills and Other Donative Transfers § 17.5 (2011) takes the position that powers are exclusive "unless the terms of the power expressly provide that an appointment must benefit each permissible appointee or one or more designated permissible appointees." See also Ferrell–French v. Ferrell, 691 So.2d 500 (Fla. App.1997) ("We hold that a power of appointment is exclusive, unless the donor expressly manifests a contrary intent."). But see Hargrove v. Rich, 604 S.E.2d 475 (Ga. 2004) (finding intent to create non-exclusive power). A number of states have relevant statutes, most preferring the construction that a special power is exclusive. See Restatement (Second) of Property: Donative Transfers § 21.1, Statutory Note (1986). N.Y. EPTL § 10–6.5 disposes of the problem of illusory appointments by providing that, "[u]nless the donor expressly provides otherwise . . . [t]he donee of a non-exclusive power must appoint in favor of all of the appointees equally."

Implied Gifts in Default of Appointment

A's will leaves property in trust to pay the income to *B* for life and then the principal to such children of *B* as *B* shall appoint but makes no express gift in default of appointment. *B* later dies without exercising the power. One may reasonably infer from the absence of any gift in default, coupled with the specification of appointees in the creation of the special power, that *A* intended that *B*'s children would receive the property and expected that *B* would exercise the power in their favor. One may assume that, if *A* had envisaged the possibility of *B*'s not exercising the power, *A* would have made an express gift in default of appointment to *B*'s children in equal shares. Operating on these premises, decisions in both England and America have awarded the property under these circumstances to *B*'s children in equal shares. See Restatement (Third) of Property: Wills and Other Donative Transfers § 19.23 (2011).

Note on Lapse

At common law, an appointment lapsed if the appointee was not alive at the death of the donee. Restatement of Property § 349. At least in the case of general powers, however, the courts have tended to employ anti-lapse statutes to redirect gifts to substitute takers, and have applied any statutory relationship test in terms of that between the appointee and the donee, rather than that between the appointee and the donor. See Thompson v. Pew, 102 N.E. 122 (Mass.1913); Restatement of Property § 350. How may one explain this result in view of the relation back theory? See French, Application of Antilapse Statutes to Appointments Made by Will, 53 Wash. L. Rev. 405 (1978).

Few cases have dealt with the application of anti-lapse statutes to special powers of appointment. Uniform Probate Code § 2–707, however, extends anti-lapse treatment to appointments under both general and special powers. See also Restatement (Third) of Property: Wills and Other Donative Transfers § 19.12 (2011).

e. Appointive Property as Assets of the Donee

In the case of special powers of appointment, the relation-back doctrine works pretty well. Since the donee of a special power—by definition—cannot have a beneficial interest in the property subject to the power, one can conveniently regard the property as belonging to the donor, with the donee merely exercising delegated authority. In the case of general powers, however, it is more difficult to sustain the fiction that the property subject to the power is not an asset of the donee for at least some purposes. One obvious case is tax liability—discussed in the next chapter.

Apart from tax considerations, if the donee does not exercise the power, and no claims of the donee's creditors (or surviving spouse) are involved, treatment of the property as the donor's seems reasonable. In such a case, if there is a provision for a gift in default of appointment, the property goes to the taker or takers in default; if there is no such provision, the property goes back to the donor or the donor's estate.

But what about the case in which an ineffective exercise occurs, or in which the donee's creditors are in the picture? The answers to these questions may vary with the jurisdiction.

(i) Rights of Creditors of the Donee

There has long been authority for the proposition that, even in the case of a general power of appointment (not created by the donee), the donee's creditors could reach the appointive property only upon an exercise of the power, regardless of whether the power was presently exercisable or testamentary. Upon an exercise of such a power by will, some American decisions (the English rule was in accord) followed the so-called "equitable assets" doctrine and allowed creditors of the donee of a general[11] power to reach the appointive property, even if the appointment was to neither the creditors themselves nor the donee's estate. Other decisions permitted creditors to reach the property only upon an exercise of the power in favor of the donee's creditors or estate.

Increasingly, there is authority for the proposition that the donee's creditors can reach any property that is subject to a presently exercisable general power of appointment, whether the donee has exercised it or not. See, e.g., Cal. Prob. Code § 682(a); N.Y. EPTL § 10–7.2. This is also true in bankruptcy. See 11 U.S.C. § 541. There is even authority for the proposition that after the death of the donee of a testamentary general power of appointment, the appointive property is subject to the claims of creditors, to the extent that the donee's estate is insufficient. See Cal. Prob. Code § 682(b); Restatement (Third) of Trusts § 56 cmt. b (2003); Restatement (Third) of Property: Wills and Other Donative Transfers § 22.3 (2011).

(ii) "Capture" of Appointive Property

In some states, if the donee of a general power attempts to exercise the power, but the exercise is ineffective because of such reasons as invalidation of interests under the Rule against Perpetuities, lapse of an interest because of the appointee's predeceasing the testator, failure of a trust for indefiniteness, or nullification by a purging statute of a testamentary gift to an attesting witness, the appointive property does not necessarily go to the takers in default—or back to the donor's estate—but

---

[11] Unless the power is general, the creditors cannot reach the property, even if the power is exercised.

may be *captured* for the donee's estate. See, e.g., Cal. Prob. Code § 672(b); Talbot v. Riggs, 191 N.E. 360 (Mass.1934). This is the so-called "capture doctrine." It was endorsed by the Restatement (Second) of Property: Donative Transfers § 23.2 (1986).

A major difficulty with capture is that it turns on a manifestation of intent by the donee "to assume control of the appointive property for all purposes." Id. Unfortunately, clear manifestation of such an intent is rare. For this and other reasons, the Third Restatement of Property has essentially abandoned the doctrine. Upon an ineffective appointment by the donee of a general power of appointment, the appointive property passes to the takers in default, regardless of the donee's intent. Only when the donor has not provided takers in default, or the gift in default is ineffective, would the ineffectively appointed property pass to the donee's estate. See Restatement (Third) of Property: Wills and Other Donative Transfers § 19.21 (2011).

———————

It should be obvious that the scrivener must be alert to the problems that can arise with respect to appointive assets and expressly provide for them. Obviously, the first step is to ascertain whether the testator has any powers of appointment; the second is to decide whether to exercise them. What should the scrivener do about undiscovered powers or after-acquired powers? Should the donee exercise them "blindly"? Experts differ. See Rabin, Blind Exercise of Powers of Appointment, 51 Corn. L.Q. 1 (1965). If the decision is to exercise all powers, the "natural" disposition would seem to be to treat the donee's own property and the appointive assets alike for all purposes. However, the scrivener must take care that the disposition does not create perpetuities or other problems.

CHAPTER 10

FEDERAL ESTATE AND GIFT TAXATION

■ ■ ■

A. INTRODUCTION

This chapter provides an introduction to the federal taxation of gratuitous transfers—i.e., the estate, gift, and generation-skipping transfer taxes—with a very brief glimpse of the income taxation of trusts and estates. In recent years the impact of these taxes has been sharply curtailed by falling tax rates and rising exemptions. Nevertheless, these taxes have serious implications, which no practitioner can afford to ignore, for the planning and implementation of a broad range of gratuitous transfers. Moreover, as noted at the outset of this book, estate taxation responds to concerns about concentrations of inherited wealth and imposes at least a mild constraint on the general principle of testamentary freedom.

It would be impossible in an introductory course to provide full coverage of the federal and state systems of wealth transfer taxation, and these materials are by no means a substitute for a specialized tax course. On the other hand, almost every topic discussed in prior chapters raises actual or potential tax issues which require some familiarity with the basic structure of wealth transfer taxation. Indeed, as a practical matter, some transactions make sense only when viewed as techniques for reducing or eliminating taxes.

Accordingly, this chapter aims to introduce a range of tax considerations that should be of concern to a general practitioner in planning an estate of moderate size—up to a few million dollars—which is large enough to present significant tax saving opportunities yet not so large as to call for long-term generation-skipping trusts. For larger estates, the general practitioner should probably consult an estate planning specialist.

1. GENERAL BACKGROUND

The central component of the wealth transfer tax system is the federal *estate tax*, which was originally enacted in 1916. As its name implies, the estate tax is imposed on the privilege of transferring property at death and is graduated according to the size of the decedent's entire estate. (Many states have also adopted an estate tax, often with provisions conforming closely to the federal statute. In contrast, several states have an *inheritance tax*, which is imposed on the privilege of receiving property from a decedent and is graduated for each beneficiary according to the beneficiary's relationship to the decedent and the size of his or her share.) During its formative years, prior to the enactment of the gift tax, the estate tax became established as the workhorse of the federal wealth transfer tax system. To fulfill its mission effectively, the estate tax reaches not only transfers which are "testamentary" in the usual sense (i.e., property passing from a decedent by will or intestacy), but also various nonprobate transfers occurring at death and certain lifetime transfers that are treated for tax purposes as testamentary substitutes.

To prevent easy avoidance of the estate tax by means of lifetime gifts, Congress enacted the federal *gift tax* in 1932. The gift tax reaches gratuitous transfers of property made in each year during the donor's life, and functions primarily as a backstop to the estate tax. For many years the estate and gift taxes operated as components of a dual system, with each tax having its own separate exemption and rate schedule. Since the gift tax rates were substantially lower than the estate tax rates, the dual system offered substantial tax advantages to wealthy taxpayers who could afford to make large lifetime gifts. In 1976, Congress finally enacted a "unified" system which applies a single schedule of graduated rates to all cumulative taxable transfers, whether made during life or at death, above a specified exempt amount. Under the unified gift and estate tax system, a donor's taxable gifts in each year are cumulated with his or her taxable gifts for preceding years and are taxed at progressively higher marginal rates under the graduated rate schedule; at death, the taxable estate is similarly cumulated with the decedent's lifetime taxable gifts and is taxed under the same rate schedule.

Transfers made by one spouse to the other are generally sheltered from gift and estate taxes by the *marital deduction*. Congress first enacted the marital deduction in 1948 (along with the gift-splitting election and the joint income tax return), to allow married couples in separate property states to enjoy the benefits of gift and estate "splitting" on more or less the same terms as their counterparts in community property states. In its original form, the marital deduction was limited to one-half of the value of separate property transferred from one spouse to the other. However, this limitation was removed in 1981, and today spouses can make unlimited transfers of property to each other during life or at death without incurring gift or estate tax liability. Effective use of the marital deduction lies at the heart of contemporary estate planning for married couples. There is also an unlimited *charitable deduction* for transfers made during life or at death to qualifying charitable organizations. As a result, such transfers escape gift and estate tax entirely.

The final component of the wealth transfer tax system is the *generation-skipping transfer tax* (GST tax), which was enacted in 1986. (The current GST tax replaces an earlier version enacted in 1976 in connection with the unification of the estate and gift taxes.) As its name implies, the GST tax is intended to ensure that wealth does not escape tax as it passes from one generation to the next. The GST tax reaches transfers that shift property to beneficiaries two or more generations below the transferor without attracting a gift or estate tax at the level of the intervening (or "skipped") generation. The GST tax functions as a supplement to the estate and gift taxes, but it has its own special exemption and rate structure. The GST tax can have a significant impact on the planning and drafting of long-term trusts for successive generations of beneficiaries.

Taken together, the estate, gift and GST taxes constitute a free-standing system of wealth transfer taxation which operates separately from, and for the most part independently of, the federal income tax. Nevertheless, it is important to remember that the wealth transfer taxes coexist with the income tax (as well as payroll and excise taxes) as integral parts of a larger federal fiscal system.

2. THE UNIFIED GIFT AND ESTATE TAX SYSTEM

Since 1976 the estate and gift taxes have been "unified" in the sense that they share a cumulative base, a single graduated rate schedule, and a single exemption. At the same time, the two taxes remain formally separate. The estate tax appears in Chapter 11 of the Internal Revenue Code (I.R.C. §§ 2001 et seq.); the gift tax appears in Chapter 12 (I.R.C. §§ 2501 et seq.). Largely due to their separate historical evolution, the two taxes are not perfectly correlated with each other, and they occasionally overlap in their application to a single transfer. Nevertheless, the mechanics of computing gift and estate tax liability under the unified system are relatively straightforward.

a. Gift Tax

The gift tax is imposed annually on the "transfer of property by gift" by an individual donor during each calendar year. I.R.C. § 2501. The concept of a "gift" is defined broadly for gift tax purposes (see infra p. 983), but not all gifts are taxable. The total amount of gifts made by the donor during the year must be reduced by allowable *exclusions* and *deductions* to arrive at the donor's *taxable gifts.* I.R.C. § 2503.

The *annual exclusion* allows a donor to make tax-free gifts up to a specified dollar amount per donee per year. The exclusion amount—

$14,000 in 2013—is indexed for inflation. Thus, in that year a donor could make tax-free gifts of up to $14,000 to each donee, with no limit on the number of donees. (This amount can be doubled in the case of a married donor, if the donor's spouse makes a "gift-splitting" election and thereby consents to be treated as making one-half of the donor's gifts.) In addition, the gift tax allows an unlimited exclusion for payments of qualified educational and medical expenses on behalf of any donee. Note that amounts covered by these exclusions are completely removed from the gift tax base and do not count against the gift tax exemption described below. The gift tax exclusions are discussed infra at p. 997.

The gift tax allows deductions for gifts made to the donor's spouse or to a qualified charitable organization, thereby removing such gifts from the taxable base. The marital deduction and the charitable deduction are discussed infra at pp. 1034–1046.

The donor's taxable gifts for the current year must be cumulated with his or her taxable gifts for all preceding years, to ensure that successive gifts are taxed at progressively higher rates under the unified rate schedule. This is accomplished by computing a "tentative tax" under the rate schedule on the total amount of the donor's taxable gifts for the current year and all preceding years, and then subtracting a "tentative tax" computed under the same rate schedule on the total amount of the donor's taxable gifts for all preceding years. I.R.C. § 2502. In effect, each year's taxable gifts are stacked on top of those made in preceding taxable years and then subjected to tax under the unified rate schedule.

Each individual transferor is allowed a gift tax exemption in the form of a *unified credit*. I.R.C. § 2505. The unified credit applies to offset the gift tax computed under the graduated rate schedule on taxable gifts up to a specified amount. The unified credit is cumulative; it is allowed only to the extent not used in preceding years. Furthermore, the credit is not elective; it applies automatically against the gift tax imposed on the donor's taxable gifts in each year until it is exhausted. In 2011, the unified credit was set at a level that was equal to the amount of gift tax that would be imposed on a taxable gift of $5 million under the graduated rate schedule. In effect, the credit is equivalent to an exemption for cumulative taxable gifts up to $5 million, and the amount sheltered from tax by the credit is often referred to as the "exemption equivalent" (or the "applicable exclusion amount").[1] By casting the exemption in the form of a credit rather than a deduction, Congress ensured that the exemption would apply at the lowest brackets of the graduated rate schedule and would

---

[1] The exemption equivalent amount is indexed for inflation. In 2012 the exemption equivalent was $5,120,000. In the interest of clarity and simplicity, the illustrative computations given in text assume an unadjusted exemption equivalent of $5 million.

provide a uniform tax benefit to all donors regardless of their marginal rate brackets.

The unified credit eliminates gift tax liability on cumulative taxable gifts up to $5 million and thereby effectively establishes a zero rate bracket for the first $5 million of taxable gifts. All taxable gifts in excess of that amount are subject to tax at a flat 40 percent rate, as specified in the unified rate schedule set forth in I.R.C. § 2001(c).[2]

In general, a donor who makes any taxable gifts during a calendar year is required to file a gift tax return and to pay any resulting gift tax by April 15 of the following year. A gift tax return must be filed even if the tax is entirely offset by the unified credit, so as to document the cumulative amounts of taxable gifts made and credit used by the donor. However, no return is required for gifts that are entirely covered by an available exclusion (e.g., the annual exclusion).

b. Estate Tax

The estate tax is imposed on the "transfer" of a decedent's "taxable estate." I.R.C. § 2001. The starting point in computing the estate tax is the *gross estate*, which includes property actually owned by the decedent at death as well as other enumerated transfers that are deemed for this purpose to occur at death (e.g., revocable trusts, joint tenancies, and life insurance proceeds). I.R.C. § 2031. From the gross estate certain *deductions* are allowed, including administration expenses, creditors' claims, and amounts passing to a surviving spouse or to a qualified charitable organization, to arrive at the *taxable estate*. I.R.C. § 2051.

The estate tax computation resembles the cumulative gift tax computation described above. The decedent's taxable estate is cumulated with all "adjusted taxable gifts" (i.e., post–1976 taxable gifts that are not otherwise included in the gross estate), and a "tentative tax" is computed under the unified rate schedule. This tentative tax is then reduced by the amount of gift tax that would have been "payable" on the total amount of the decedent's post–1976 taxable gifts, computed under the same rate schedule in effect at death. I.R.C. § 2001(b). In effect, the taxable estate is treated as a single, final deathtime transfer which is stacked on top of the decedent's (post–1976) taxable lifetime gifts and then subjected to tax under the unified rate schedule.

The final step in computing the amount of estate tax due is to apply any available estate tax credits against the tax determined under the uni-

---

[2] The rate schedule set forth in § 2001(c) provides for graduated marginal rates beginning at 18 percent on taxable transfers up to $10,000 and rising to 40 percent on taxable transfers in excess of $1,000,000. Under current law, the lower rate brackets are completely eclipsed by the unified credit which eliminates all tax on taxable transfers up to $5 million.

fied rate schedule. The most important credit is the unified credit (I.R.C. § 2010), which is available to the extent not already used during life. In addition to the unified credit, the estate tax allows credits for estate taxes paid on certain prior transfers to the decedent (I.R.C. § 2013) and for foreign death taxes imposed on property included in the gross estate (I.R.C. § 2014).[3]

An estate tax return must be filed if the decedent's gross estate (combined with any adjusted taxable gifts) exceeds the estate tax exemption equivalent. Accordingly, a return may be required even if no estate tax is due—for example, where allowable deductions reduce the taxable estate below the exemption equivalent. The decedent's personal representative has primary responsibility for filing the estate tax return and paying any tax. The deadline for filing the estate tax return and paying the estate tax, if any, is nine months after the decedent's death, but extensions for filing and payment are available in some circumstances.

c. Illustrative Computations

At this point it may be helpful to illustrate the operation of the gift and estate taxes with a basic example. To keep matters as simple as possible, we assume that the exemption equivalent remains fixed at $5 million (ignoring inflation adjustments) and that all taxable transfers in excess of that amount are subject to tax at a flat 40 percent rate. Suppose that *A*, an unmarried individual, having made no prior taxable gifts, makes taxable gifts of $1 million in 2013, makes additional taxable gifts of $5 million in 2014, and then dies in 2018 leaving a taxable estate of $10 million.

A's gifts in 2011 are fully covered by her available gift tax exemption. Accordingly, she owes no gift tax for that year, but she must still file a gift tax return reporting her taxable gifts ($1 million), the resulting gift tax ($345,800), and the amount of unified credit to be applied against the tax ($345,800). Note that the unified credit applies automatically; *A* cannot elect to pay a gift tax now and save her unified credit for another year. Accordingly, *A*'s gift tax of $345,800 is completely offset by an equivalent amount of unified credit, yielding a gift tax payable of zero.

A's gifts in 2014 exhaust her remaining gift tax exemption and give rise to a gift tax liability of $400,000, calculated as follows:

---

[3] Beginning in 2005, the credit formerly allowed under I.R.C. § 2011 for state death taxes was replaced by a deduction for such taxes under I.R.C. § 2058.

tentative tax on cumulative taxable gifts made in current year and all prior years ($6,000,000)	$2,345,800
less tentative tax on cumulative taxable gifts made in all prior years ($1,000,000)	−345,800
tax on 2014 taxable gifts	$2,000,000
less available unified credit ($1,945,800 − $345,800)	−1,600,000
gift tax payable	$400,000

When *A* dies in 2018 with a taxable estate of $10 million, the estate tax is calculated in a similar manner under the unified rate schedule. *A* incurs an estate tax liability of $4,000,000, calculated as follows:

tentative tax on sum of taxable estate and adjusted taxable gifts ($16,000,000)	$6,345,800
less gift tax payable on cumulative post–1976 taxable gifts ($6,000,000), after unified credit	−400,000
less unified credit[4]	−1,945,800
estate tax payable	$4,000,000

Aside from illustrating the unified rate schedule and the unified credit in action, these computations prompt two further general observations. One observation concerns the method of computing the gift and estate taxes. The gift tax is imposed on the net value of the transferred property exclusive of the gift tax, while the estate tax applies to a base that includes the amount of the estate tax. In tax parlance, the gift tax is "tax-exclusive" and the estate tax is "tax-inclusive." Although both taxes use the same rate schedule, the gift tax imposes a lighter burden than the estate tax. To illustrate the difference, suppose that gift and estate taxes are imposed at a flat 50 percent rate. If a donor makes a taxable gift of $100, the resulting gift tax is $50 ($100 × 50%); the donor's total out-of-pocket cost is $150, and the donee receives $100 after tax. In contrast, if the same donor dies with a taxable estate of $150, the resulting estate tax is $75 ($150 × 50%); the decedent's total out-of-pocket cost is again $150, but the beneficiary receives only $75 after tax. In effect, the gift tax is

---

[4] At first glance it may seem odd to allow a full unified credit of $1,945,800 (equivalent to a $5 million exemption) in the estate tax computation, since a credit in the same amount was previously allowed in the gift tax computation. However, there is no double counting. To see why this is so, recall that the tentative estate tax is reduced by the sum of (1) the gift tax "payable" on post–1976 taxable gifts (taking the gift tax unified credit into account) and (2) the full amount of the estate tax unified credit. Another way of expressing the same computation is to reduce the tentative estate tax by the sum of (1) the gift tax on post–1976 taxable gifts (ignoring the gift tax unified credit) and (2) the estate tax unified credit less any gift tax unified credit used during life. The statutory language calls for the former approach in the estate tax computation, but the latter approach produces the same result. In each case the unified credit allowed at death is adjusted, directly or indirectly, for the amount of credit used during life.

paid with pre-tax dollars, while the estate tax is paid with after-tax dollars.

The second observation concerns the imperfect coordination of the gift and estate tax rules governing the timing of completed transfers. Although most transfers can be clearly classified either as lifetime transfers subject to gift tax or deathtime transfers subject to estate tax, in some situations a single transfer may be subject to both taxes. In the above example, if *A*'s 2014 transfer took the form of a contribution to an irrevocable trust under which *A* retained a life income interest, the transfer would be treated as a completed gift for gift tax purposes (hence subject to gift tax), but the same property would be drawn back into the gross estate and subjected to estate tax at *A*'s death. (See I.R.C. § 2036, infra p. 1013.) Although this might reflect poor tax planning on *A*'s part, the result would not be "double taxation" of the same transfer. Instead, the property would be included in *A*'s gross estate (at its deathtime value) and would be excluded from *A*'s "adjusted taxable gifts" (defined in I.R.C. § 2001(b) as taxable gifts made after 1976 *that are not otherwise included in the gross estate*). If the property, originally worth $5 million at the time of the lifetime gift, appreciated to $8 million by the time of *A*'s death, the estate tax computation would be as follows:

tentative tax on sum of taxable estate and adjusted taxable gifts ($19,000,000)	$7,545,800
less gift tax payable on cumulative post–1976 taxable gifts ($6,000,000), after unified credit	−400,000
less unified credit	−1,945,800
estate tax payable	$5,200,000

The net result is that the full value of the property at *A*'s death is included in the estate tax base, but the gift tax paid during life is allowed as an offset against the resulting estate tax under I.R.C. § 2001(b). The net increase of $1,200,000 in the estate tax is entirely attributable to the $3 million of appreciation between the time of the lifetime gifts and the time of *A*'s death ($3,000,000 × 40% = $1,200,000). In effect, the gift tax paid during *A*'s life is treated as a downpayment on the estate tax liability. To avoid the problem of overlapping gift and estate taxation, experienced estate planners usually are careful to structure a transfer so that it is subject to one tax or the other but not to both.

More generally, it should be observed that despite the unification of the estate and gift taxes, lifetime gifts are often taxed differently from deathtime transfers. Lifetime gifts enjoy some obvious tax advantages, such as the annual exclusion and the exclusion for qualified educational and medical transfers, which are found only in the gift tax (see infra p.

997). Another, less obvious advantage is implicit in the structure of the tax base—despite the unified rate schedule, lifetime gifts subject to the tax-exclusive gift tax are in effect taxed at lower rates than deathtime transfers subject to the tax-inclusive estate tax. These and other features of the tax system undoubtedly induce some taxpayers to make larger or more frequent gifts than they would otherwise do, but studies suggest that most people prefer to retain ownership and control of the bulk of their wealth until death, even at the cost of incurring a somewhat heavier estate tax burden. This instinctive reluctance to give away property during life is reinforced to some extent by several tax provisions that tend to favor deathtime transfers. For example, the provisions allowing a fresh-start income tax basis, special use valuation for farm or business real property, and deferred payment for closely held business interests, are available only for property passing from a decedent.

NOTES

1. *Constitutional status.* Technically, the gift and estate taxes are excise taxes levied on the transfer of property by a donor or decedent rather than "direct" taxes on the transferred property itself. The distinction, while exceedingly formalistic, has constitutional significance. An excise tax on the transfer of property—unlike a direct tax on property—need not be apportioned among the states. As Justice Holmes observed, "Upon this point a page of history is worth a volume of logic." New York Trust Co. v. Eisner, 256 U.S. 345 (1921) (rejecting constitutional challenge to estate tax).

2. *Effect on income tax basis.* A gratuitous transfer of property is generally not a taxable event for federal income tax purposes. The transferor generally realizes no gain or loss, and the transferred property is expressly excluded from the recipient's gross income under I.R.C. § 102. Nevertheless, the transfer has collateral income tax consequences, particularly in determining the recipient's tax cost ("basis") in the transferred property. For federal income tax purposes, property acquired from a decedent generally takes a "fresh-start" basis equal to its fair market value at the date of death. I.R.C. § 1014. (This is often referred to as a "stepped-up" basis, even though the basis may actually be stepped down if the value of the property at the decedent's death is less than its basis in the decedent's hands.) In effect, the fresh-start basis launders out any pre-death appreciation for income tax purposes; on a subsequent sale or disposition of the property, the beneficiary's taxable gain is limited to post-death appreciation. By contrast, there is no basis step-up in the case of a lifetime gift; the donee generally takes a "carryover" basis equal to the donor's basis in the property (adjusted for gift taxes paid). I.R.C. § 1015. While the income tax benefits of a basis step-up may justify holding appreciated property until death, those benefits should be weighed against the offsetting wealth transfer tax benefits of making lifetime gifts.

3. ROLE OF WEALTH TRANSFER TAXATION

The estate tax was originally enacted in 1916, primarily to raise revenue for the national war effort as the United States prepared to enter World War I, and for several years the estate tax (and eventually the gift tax) provided a modest but significant source of federal revenues. Since World War II, however, the contribution of the wealth transfer taxes has rarely exceeded two percent of annual federal revenues. In 2009, these taxes yielded around $25 billion, out of total federal revenues of more than $2 trillion. While $25 billion is not a trivial amount, it pales in comparison to the yield of the income and payroll taxes (or even the excise taxes on alcohol and tobacco). Compared to the broad impact of the income and payroll taxes, the wealth transfer taxes are concentrated among a small but relatively wealthy group of taxpayers. In 2009 the number of taxable estate tax returns was less than 15,000, representing less than one percent of adult deaths. In view of their narrow impact and limited revenue yield, the wealth transfer taxes cannot be expected to play a major role as an instrument of fiscal policy.

As an instrument of social policy, the wealth transfer taxes may be viewed as a means of limiting concentrations of inherited wealth and enhancing equality of opportunity. In fact, however, there is little evidence to suggest that these taxes have had a significant impact on the concentration of wealth in the United States; if anything, the trend since the 1980s appears to be toward increasing inequality of wealth and income. Nevertheless, these inequalities would presumably be even more pronounced in the absence of the wealth transfer taxes. An additional argument for maintaining and strengthening these taxes is that they contribute to the progressivity of the overall tax system and compensate for imperfections in the income tax system.

In recent years the wealth transfer taxes have come under sustained attack by opponents who seek to repeal them altogether. One charge often leveled against these taxes is that they constitute unfair "double taxation" of earnings that have already been subjected to income taxation, though this argument is undermined by the fact that many large fortunes subject to the estate tax consist in large part of unrealized appreciation that would otherwise go completely untaxed due to the "stepped-up" basis rule for property acquired from a decedent (see Note 2, supra p. 979). Another charge is that the wealth transfer taxes threaten the existence of family-owned farms and businesses because these enterprises must be sold to pay the tax imposed at the owner's death. Seldom mentioned, however, are the relief provisions of existing law that allow special use valuation and deferred payment for family-owned farms and businesses, or the small proportion of taxable estates that actually face liquidity problems, or the overwhelming non-tax factors that challenge the economic viability of such enterprises. Yet another charge is that the wealth transfer taxes are unduly complex and costly to administer, but there is no reason to believe that these taxes fare any worse in this regard than, say, the income tax.

Arguably the most serious charge against wealth transfer taxation is that it discourages work, saving and investment, and thereby impedes capital formation and economic growth. This argument undoubtedly has some force, but in reality the situation is not nearly so simple. A parent facing a heavy estate tax burden may seek to avoid the tax by retiring early and consuming his or her accumulated wealth (the "substitution effect"), but the opposite result is equally plausible; the parent may be spurred to overcome the tax burden by working harder and saving more (the "wealth effect"). In addition, it is possible that the estate tax encourages work, saving and investment on the part of a child whose inheritance is reduced by the tax. In other words, in the absence of the tax, a child who received a larger inheritance might opt for more leisure and higher consumption. Furthermore, the government's use of tax revenue should be compared with alternative uses of the same funds by taxpayers. If the government uses those funds to build infrastructure or pay down the national debt, the net result may be to stimulate capital formation and economic growth. Finally, wealth transfer taxes cannot be evaluated in isolation; they must be viewed in the larger context of federal budget decisions. If the existing taxes were repealed, the lost revenue would presumably have to be made up from other taxes, imposed either currently or in the future, which might well prove to be no more conducive to capital formation and economic growth. Given the current state of theoretical and empirical research concerning the incidence of the wealth transfer taxes, the behavior of wealthy individuals, and alternative uses of tax revenue, it is hardly surprising that the economic impact of these taxes remains uncertain and hotly contested.

For an excellent discussion of the role of wealth transfer taxation, see Graetz, To Praise the Estate Tax, Not to Bury It, 93 Yale L.J. 259 (1983). The economic effects of the taxes are discussed in Aaron & Munnell, Reassessing the Role for Wealth Transfer Taxes, 45 Nat'l Tax J. 119 (1992); Gale & Slemrod, Overview, in Rethinking Estate and Gift Taxation (Gale et al. eds., 2001); and the essays by Boskin and Jantscher in Death, Taxes and Family Property (Halbach ed., 1977).

4. THE UNCERTAIN FUTURE OF ESTATE AND GIFT TAXATION

In recent years the estate and gift taxes appear to have become increasingly unpopular, not only among farmers and small business owners but also among the population at large. Polls indicate that two out of three respondents say they favor complete repeal of the estate tax. What accounts for the widespread disapproval of a tax that directly reaches the estates of only the wealthiest one or two percent of decedents and imposes no burden on the vast majority of taxpayers? In an illuminating account of the roots of opposition to estate taxation, Professors Michael Graetz and Ian Shapiro point to several contributing factors. Most Americans routinely overestimate their own relative wealth and upward mobility. (According to some polls, 20 percent of the population believe themselves to be in the wealthiest 1 percent and another 20 percent expect that they will soon join that select group.) In addition, many people hold wildly inaccurate views of the estate tax, believing that it applies across the board to small estates as well as large ones. Most importantly, in a deft twist on its populist origins, opponents of the estate tax (which they invariably call the "death tax") have invoked the mythology of the "American dream" in challenging the morality and fairness of the tax. See Graetz & Shapiro, Death by a Thousand Cuts: The Fight Over Taxing Inherited Wealth (2005).

In 2001 Congress enacted significant changes in the estate and gift taxes, gradually reducing the top marginal rate from 55 percent to 35 percent and increasing the exemption equivalent from less than $1 million to $3.5 million between 2002 and 2009. Had the 2001 legislation taken effect as originally written, the estate tax (but not the gift tax) would have been completely repealed in 2010. At the same time, the rule of I.R.C. § 1014, which has long provided a fresh-start income tax basis for property acquired from a decedent, would have been replaced by a modified carryover basis rule set forth in new I.R.C. § 1022. None of these changes were permanent, however. Under a special "sunset" provision, the substantive changes enacted in 2001 were scheduled to expire automatically at the end of 2010, thereby reinstating prior law for 2011 and subsequent years. (The sunset provision made it possible to minimize projected revenue losses and to avoid a procedural challenge under the Senate budget rules.) In effect, the 2001 legislation called for a temporary one-year repeal of the estate tax and left open the controversial question of whether to make the repeal permanent.

In 2010 Congress intervened at the eleventh hour to keep the estate tax in place during 2011 and 2012 with a top marginal rate capped at 35 percent and an increased exemption equivalent of $5 million (indexed for inflation). Again, however, these changes were only temporary; the effective date of the sunset provision was moved back to the end of 2012. Finally, in 2013 Congress acted to prevent the estate and gift taxes from reverting to pre–2001 levels. The 2013 legislation set the top marginal rate at 40 percent and the exemption equivalent at $5 million (indexed for inflation).

After more than a decade of turmoil, the federal estate and gift taxes remain largely unchanged in their essential features. Given the deteriorating federal budget outlook and the pressing revenue demands for national security, health care, and Social Security, it seems unlikely that opponents of these taxes will achieve their goal of complete repeal in the foreseeable future. Nevertheless, opposition to the taxes (and to taxes on capital in general) remains a resilient and potent political force, and any prediction concerning the future of the estate and gift taxes should be taken with a grain of salt. The rest of this chapter focuses on those taxes as they exist under current law.

B. THE GIFT TAX

1. TRANSFERS BY GIFT

I.R.C. § 2501(a)(1) imposes the gift tax on the "transfer of property by gift." The statute does not attempt to define with any precision what constitutes a transfer by gift for this purpose, but merely states that the tax applies "whether the transfer is in trust or otherwise, whether the gift is direct or indirect, and whether the property is real or personal, tangible or intangible." I.R.C. § 2511(a). The legislative history confirms the expansive reach of the gift tax, noting that the term "property" is used in the "broadest and most comprehensive sense" to embrace "every species of right or interest protected by law and having an exchangeable value." S. Rep. No. 665, 72d Cong., 1st Sess. (1932), reprinted in 1939–1 (pt. 2) C.B. 496, 524.

The regulations provide that "any transaction in which an interest in property is gratuitously passed or conferred upon another, regardless of the means or device employed, constitutes a gift subject to tax." Reg. § 25.2511–1(c)(1). For example, a gift subject to tax may arise from "the creation of a trust, the forgiving of a debt, the assignment of a judgment, the assignment of the benefits of an insurance policy, or the transfer of cash, certificates of deposit, or Federal, State or municipal bonds." Reg. § 25.2511–1(a). The tax applies only to a "transfer of a beneficial interest in property"; it does not apply to a "transfer of bare legal title to a trustee." Reg. § 25.2511–1(g)(1).

To determine the federal tax consequences of a particular transaction, it is usually necessary to ascertain the interests and rights of the parties under applicable state law. "State law creates legal interests and rights. The federal revenue acts designate what interests or rights, so created, shall be taxed." Morgan v. Commissioner, 309 U.S. 78, 80 (1940). Note that a transaction need not be classified as a "gift" under state law to constitute a "transfer by gift" for federal tax purposes. For example, a taxable gift may occur if a parent sells property to a child at a below-market price or pays a debt incurred by the child. In Dickman v. Commissioner, 465 U.S. 330 (1984), the Supreme Court held that interest-free demand loans between family members gave rise to taxable gifts, and explained its reasoning as follows:

> [A] parent who grants to a child the rent-free, indefinite use of commercial property having a reasonable rental value of $8,000 a month has clearly transferred a valuable property right. The transfer of $100,000 in cash, interest-free and repayable on demand, is similarly a grant of the use of valuable property. Its uncertain tenure may reduce its value, but it does not undermine its status as property. In either instance, when the property owner transfers to another the right to use the object, an identifiable property interest has clearly changed hands. ... We can assume that an interest-free loan for a fixed period, especially for a prolonged period, may have greater value than such a loan made payable on demand, but it would defy common human experience to say that an intrafamily loan payable on demand is not subject to accommodation; its value may be reduced by virtue of its demand status, but that value is surely not eliminated. [465 U.S. at 336–37.]

The loans in *Dickman* involved several hundred thousand dollars of outstanding principal, with substantial amounts of forgone interest each year. Under the Court's rationale, does a family member's rent-free use of a vacation house or a car constitute a transfer of property for gift tax purposes? What if a lawyer drafts a will for a family member free of charge? If a gift occurs, how should its value be measured? For the treatment of below-market loans under current law, see I.R.C. § 7872.

Gift tax issues may also arise if a person nominated in a decedent's will as executor or trustee decides to waive the fiduciary commissions to which he or she would ordinarily be entitled under state law. Does a refusal to claim compensation give rise to a transfer by gift to the beneficiaries of the estate or trust whose shares are thereby enlarged? See Rev. Rul. 66–167, 1966–1 C.B. 20.

2. COMPLETED GIFTS

The gift tax applies only to completed transfers. For gift tax purposes, a transfer generally becomes complete when the donor relinquishes dominion and control, retaining no power to revoke the transfer or change the beneficial interests in the underlying property. Note that the test of completion focuses on the *donor*'s dominion and control; there is no requirement that the *donees* be identified or their respective shares ascertained.

The Supreme Court established the basic principles governing completion of gifts in a pair of early decisions. The first case, Burnet v. Guggenheim, 288 U.S. 280 (1933), involved two inter vivos trusts created by a settlor for his children in 1917, before the enactment of the first federal gift tax. Under the initial deeds of trust, the settlor reserved a power of revocation, but he subsequently cancelled this power in 1925 (while the short-lived gift tax of 1924 was still in effect). The Court, speaking through Justice Cardozo, held that the settlor's relinquishment of his power in 1925 gave rise to a completed gift of the underlying trust property (then worth nearly $13 million):

> "Taxation is not so much concerned with the refinements of title as it is with the actual command over the property taxed—the actual benefit for which the tax is paid." Corliss v. Bowers, 281 U.S. 376, 378. . . . While the powers of revocation stood uncanceled in the deeds [of trust], the gifts, from the point of view of substance, were inchoate and imperfect. . . . By the execution of deeds and the creation of trusts, the settlor did indeed succeed in divesting himself of title and transferring it to others . . . , but the substance of his dominion was the same as if these forms had been omitted. Corliss v. Bowers, supra. He was free at any moment, with reason or without, to revest title in himself, except as to any income then collected or accrued. As to the principal of the trusts and as to income to accrue thereafter, the gifts were formal and unreal. They acquired substance and reality for the first time in July, 1925, when the deeds became absolute through the cancellation of the power. [288 U.S. at 283–84.]

If the settlor had retained his power of revocation until death, would the trust property escape gift tax altogether? Cf. I.R.C. § 2038, discussed infra at p. 1008.

The second landmark case, Estate of Sanford v. Commissioner, 308 U.S. 39 (1939), involved a revocable inter vivos trust created in 1913. In 1919, before the enactment of the gift tax of 1924, the settlor gave up his absolute power of revocation but retained a power to "designate new beneficiaries other than himself." He finally relinquished the last vestige of his retained powers in 1924, shortly after the gift tax came into force. The Court upheld the imposition of a gift tax on the settlor's 1924 relinquishment of his "nonbeneficial" power (so called because he could not exercise it to benefit himself directly), noting that if he had retained the power until death the trust property would have been includible in his gross estate:

> There is nothing in the language of the statute, and our attention has not been directed to anything in its legislative history to suggest that Congress had any purpose to tax gifts before the donor had fully parted with his interest in the property given, or that the test of the completeness of the taxed gift was to be any different from that to be applied in determining whether the donor has retained an interest

such that it becomes subject to the estate tax upon its extinguishment at death.[5] The gift tax was supplementary to the estate tax. The two are in *pari materia* and must be construed together. Burnet v. Guggenheim, supra, 286. An important, if not the main, purpose of the gift tax was to prevent or compensate for avoidance of death taxes by taxing the gifts of property *inter vivos* which, but for the gifts, would be subject in its original or converted form to the tax laid upon transfers at death. [308 U.S. at 44.]

The Court's holdings in *Guggenheim* and *Sanford* have had a profound influence on the structure of the gift tax. The gift tax regulations (Reg. § 25.2511–2) set forth the following rules concerning gift completion:

. . . (b) As to any property, or part thereof or interest therein, of which the donor has so parted with dominion and control as to leave in him no power to change its disposition, whether for his own benefit or for the benefit of another, the gift is complete. But if upon a transfer of property (whether in trust or otherwise) the donor reserves any power over its disposition, the gift may be wholly incomplete, or may be partially complete and partially incomplete, depending upon all the facts in the particular case. Accordingly, in every case of a transfer of property subject to a reserved power, the terms of the power must be examined and its scope determined. . . .

(c) A gift is incomplete in every instance in which a donor reserves the power to revest the beneficial title to the property in himself. A gift is also incomplete if and to the extent that a reserved power gives the donor the power to name new beneficiaries or to change the interests of the beneficiaries as between themselves unless the power is a fiduciary power limited by a fixed or ascertainable standard. . . .

(d) A gift is not considered incomplete, however, merely because the donor reserves the power to change the manner or time of enjoyment. . . .

(e) A donor is considered as himself having a power if it is exercisable by him in conjunction with any person not having a substantial adverse interest in the disposition of the transferred property or the income therefrom. . . .

(f) The relinquishment or termination of a power to change the beneficiaries of transferred property, occurring otherwise than by the

---

[5] In the next paragraph of the opinion, however, the Court concedes that the estate and gift taxes are "not always mutually exclusive," as in the case of certain gifts which are "complete and taxable when made, and are also required to be included in the gross estate for purposes of the death tax." Cf. Smith v. Shaughnessy, infra p. 989.—EDS.

death of the donor (the statute being confined to transfers made by living donors), is regarded as the event which completes the gift and causes the tax to apply. . . . The receipt of income or of other enjoyment of the transferred property by the transferee or by the beneficiary (other than by the donor himself) during the interim between the making of the initial transfer and the relinquishment or termination of the power operates to free such income or other enjoyment from the power, and constitutes a gift of such income or of such other enjoyment taxable as of the [year] of its receipt. . . .

(g) If a donor transfers property to himself as trustee (or to himself and some other person, not possessing a substantial adverse interest, as trustees), and retains no beneficial interest in the trust property and no power over it except fiduciary powers, the exercise or nonexercise of which is limited by a fixed or ascertainable standard, to change the beneficiaries of the transferred property, the donor has made a completed gift and the entire value of the transferred property is subject to the gift tax. . . .

NOTES

1. *Gift of donor's own check.* Under applicable state law, a gift of a donor's own check ordinarily becomes complete only when the check is paid, certified, accepted, or negotiated for value; until then, the donor can revoke the gift by issuing a stop payment order (see Note 5, supra p. 518). This rule also has significance for federal gift tax purposes. Suppose that *A* writes a check for $500 to her favorite nephew and sends it to him as a birthday present. The nephew receives the check on December 28, 2012 and cashes it on January 3, 2013. Has *A* made a completed gift in 2012 or 2013? What if *A* dies on January 2, 2013? See Rev. Rul. 96–56, 1996–2 C.B. 161, modifying Rev. Rul. 67–396, 1967–2 C.B. 351; Estate of Metzger v. Commissioner, 38 F.3d 118 (4th Cir.1994); Estate of Dillingham v. Commissioner, 903 F.2d 760 (10th Cir.1990); Rosano v. United States, 245 F.3d 212 (2d Cir. 2001), cert. denied, 534 U.S. 1135 (2002); Estate of Gagliardi v. Commissioner, 89 T.C. 1207 (1987).

2. *Self-settled trusts.* A settlor who creates an inter vivos trust, retaining neither the right to receive distributions nor the power to affect beneficial enjoyment by others, ordinarily makes a completed gift of the trust property. The result may be different, however, if applicable state law allows the settlor's creditors to reach the trust property to satisfy claims against the settlor. See Restatement (Third) of Trusts § 60 & cmt. f (2003) (settlor's creditors can reach maximum amount that trustee of self-settled discretionary trust could pay to settlor). Even though the settlor may have no right to receive distributions directly from the trust, in theory the settlor could obtain the economic benefit of the trust property simply by going into debt and relegating creditors to the trust as a source of repayment. On this rationale, courts have held that the creation of a self-settled discretionary trust does not give

rise to a completed gift to the extent the trust property remains subject to claims of the settlor's creditors. See Outwin v. Commissioner, 76 T.C. 153 (1981).

3. *Joint tenancies.* The House Ways and Means Committee has described the gift tax treatment of joint interests as follows (H.R. Rep. No. 1380, 94th Cong., 2d Sess. (1976), reprinted in 1976–3 C.B. 735, 752–53):

> For gift tax purposes, a completed transfer is a prerequisite to the imposition of the tax. If a joint tenant, who has furnished all the consideration for the creation of the joint tenancy, is permitted to draw back to himself the entire joint property (as in a typical joint bank account), the transfer is not complete and there is no gift at that time. If the creation of a joint tenancy has resulted in a completed transfer, the value of the gift will depend upon whether, under applicable local law, the right of survivorship may be defeated by either owner unilaterally. If either joint tenant, acting alone, can bring about a severance of his interest, the value of the gift will be one-half the value of the jointly held property. If the right of survivorship is not destructible except by mutual consent, then the value of the gift requires a calculation which takes into account the ages of the donor and the other concurrent owner. This calculation is necessary because the younger of the tenants, who has a greater probability of surviving and taking all the property, has a more valuable interest.

A gift may be partially complete and partially incomplete. That is, a donor may make a completed gift of certain interests in property while retaining other interests in the same property. The most flexible and commonly used device for splitting up beneficial ownership of property in this manner is a trust. It should come as no surprise that, from the earliest days of the estate and gift taxes, transfers in trust have figured prominently in the arsenal of sophisticated tax avoidance techniques. Indeed, certain types of trusts have achieved widespread popularity—or notoriety, as the case may be—on account of their actual or supposed tax benefits.

The gift tax regulations provide:

> If a donor transfers by gift less than his entire interest in property, the gift tax is applicable to the interest transferred. The tax is applicable, for example, to the transfer of an undivided half interest in property, or to the transfer of a life estate when the grantor retains the remainder interest, or vice versa. . . . [Reg. § 25.2511–1(e).]

SMITH V. SHAUGHNESSY

Supreme Court of the United States, 1943.
318 U.S. 176, 63 S.Ct. 545, 87 L.Ed. 690.

MR. JUSTICE BLACK delivered the opinion of the Court.

The question here is the extent of the petitioner's liability for a tax under [the predecessor of I.R.C. §§ 2501 and 2511], which imposes a tax upon every transfer of property by gift, "whether the transfer is in trust or otherwise, whether the gift is direct or indirect, and whether the property is real or personal, tangible or intangible; . . . ."

The petitioner, age 72, made an irrevocable transfer in trust of 3,000 shares of stock worth $571,000. The trust income was payable to his wife, age 44, for life; upon her death, the stock was to be returned to the petitioner, if he was living; if he was not living, it was to go to such persons as his wife might designate by will, or in default of a will by her, to her intestate successors under applicable New York law. The petitioner, under protest, paid a gift tax of $71,674.22, assessed on the total value of the trust principal, and brought suit for refund in the district court. Holding that the petitioner had, within the meaning of the Act, executed a completed gift of a life estate to his wife, the court sustained the Commissioner's assessment on $322,423, the determined value of her life interest; but the remainder was held not to be completely transferred and hence not subject to the gift tax. 40 F. Supp. 19. The government appealed and the Circuit Court of Appeals reversed, ordering dismissal of the petitioner's complaint on the authority of its previous decision in Herzog v. Commissioner, 116 F.2d 591. We granted certiorari because of alleged conflict with our decisions in Helvering v. Hallock, 309 U.S. 106, and Sanford v. Commissioner, 308 U.S. 39. In these decisions, and in Burnet v. Guggenheim, 288 U.S. 280, we have considered the problems raised here in some detail, and it will therefore be unnecessary to make any elaborate resurvey of the law.

Three interests are involved here: the life estate, the remainder, and the reversion. The taxpayer concedes that the life estate is subject to the gift tax. The government concedes that the right of reversion to the donor in case he outlives his wife is an interest having value which can be calculated by an actuarial device, and that it is immune from the gift tax. The controversy, then, reduces itself to the question of the taxability of the remainder.

The taxpayer's principal argument here is that under our decision in the *Hallock* case, the value of the remainder will be included in the grantor's gross estate for estate tax purposes; and that in the *Sanford* case we intimated a general policy against allowing the same property to be taxed both as an estate and as a gift.

This view, we think, misunderstands our position in the *Sanford* case. As we said there, the gift and estate tax laws are closely related and the gift tax serves to supplement the estate tax. We said that the taxes are not "always mutually exclusive," and called attention to [the predecessor of I.R.C. § 2012] which charts the course for granting credits on estate taxes by reason of previous payment of gift taxes on the same property. The scope of that provision we need not now determine. It is sufficient to note here that Congress plainly pointed out that "some" of the "total gifts subject to gift taxes . . . may be included for estate tax purposes and some not." House Report No. 708, 72d Cong., 1st Sess., p. 45. Under the statute the gift tax amounts in some instances to a security, a form of down-payment on the estate tax which secures the eventual payment of the latter; it is in no sense double taxation as the taxpayer suggests.

We conclude that under the present statute, Congress has provided as its plan for integrating the estate and gift taxes this system of secured payment on gifts which will later be subject to the estate tax.[6]

Unencumbered by any notion of policy against subjecting this transaction to both estate and gift taxes, we turn to the basic question of whether there was a gift of the remainder. The government argues that for gift tax purposes the taxpayer has abandoned control of the remainder and that it is therefore taxable, while the taxpayer contends that no realistic value can be placed on the contingent remainder and that it therefore should not be classed as a gift.

We cannot accept any suggestion that the complexity of a property interest created by a trust can serve to defeat a tax. For many years Congress has sought vigorously to close tax loopholes against ingenious trust instruments. Even though these concepts of property and value may be slippery and elusive they cannot escape taxation so long as they are used in the world of business. The language of the gift tax statute, "property . . . real or personal, tangible or intangible," is broad enough to include property, however conceptual or contingent. And lest there by any doubt as to the amplitude of their purpose, the Senate and House Committees, reporting the bill, spelled out their meaning as follows:

> The terms "property," "transfer," "gift," and "indirectly" [in the predecessor of I.R.C. § 2511] are used in the broadest and most comprehensive sense; the term "property" reaching every species of right or interest protected by law and having an exchangeable value.

---

[6] It has been suggested that the congressional plan relating the estate and gift taxes may still be incomplete. See e.g., Griswold, A Plan for the Coordination of the Income, Estate, and Gift Tax Provisions etc., 56 Harv. L. Rev. 337; Magill, The Federal Gift Tax, 40 Col. L. Rev. 773, 792. . . .

The Treasury regulations, which we think carry out the Act's purpose, made specific provisions for application of the tax to, and determination of the value of, "a remainder . . . subject to an outstanding life estate."

The essence of a gift by trust is the abandonment of control over the property put in trust. The separable interests transferred are not gifts to the extent that power remains to revoke the trust or recapture the property represented by any of them, Burnet v. Guggenheim, supra, or to modify the terms of the arrangement so as to make other disposition of the property, Sanford v. Commissioner, supra. In the *Sanford* case the grantor could, by modification of the trust, extinguish the donee's interest at any instant he chose. In cases such as this, where the grantor has neither the form nor substance of control and never will have unless he outlives his wife, we must conclude that he has lost all "economic control" and that the gift is complete except for the value of his reversionary interest.

The judgment of the Circuit Court of Appeals is affirmed with leave to the petitioner to apply for modification of its mandate in order that the value of the petitioner's reversionary interest may be determined and excluded.

It is so ordered.

MR. JUSTICE ROBERTS:

I dissent. I am of opinion that, except for the life estate in the wife, the gift *qua* the donor was incomplete and not within the sweep of [the predecessor of I.R.C. §§ 2501 and 2511]. A contrary conclusion might well be reached were it not for Helvering v. Hallock, 309 U.S. 106. But the decisions in Burnet v. Guggenheim, 288 U.S. 280, and Sanford v. Commissioner, 308 U.S. 39, to which the court adheres, require a reversal in view of the ruling in the *Hallock* case.

The first of the two cases ruled that a transfer in trust, whereby the grantor reserved a power of revocation, was not subject to a gift tax, but became so upon the renunciation of the power. The second held that where the grantor reserved a power to change the beneficiaries, but none to revoke or to make himself a beneficiary, the transfer was incomplete and not subject to gift tax. At the same term, in Porter v. Commissioner, 288 U.S. 436, the court held that where a decedent had given property *inter vivos* in trust, reserving a power to change the beneficiaries but no power to revoke or revest the property in himself, the transfer was incomplete until the termination of the reserved power by the donor's death and hence the corpus was subject to the estate tax.

When these cases were decided, the law, as announced by this court, was that where, in a complete and final transfer *inter vivos*, a grantor provided that, in a specified contingency, the corpus should pass to him, if living, but, if he should be dead, then to others, the gift was complete when made, he retained nothing which passed from him at his death, prior to the happening of the contingency, and that no part of the property given was includible in his gross estate for estate tax. McCormick v. Burnet, 283 U.S. 784; Helvering v. St. Louis Union Trust Co., 296 U.S. 39; Becker v. St. Louis Union Trust Co., 296 U.S. 48. So long as this was the law the transfer might properly be the subject of a gift tax for the gift was, as respects the donor, complete when made.

In 1940 these decisions were overruled [by *Hallock*] and it was held that such a transfer was so incomplete when made, and the grantor retained such an interest, that the cessation of that interest at death furnished the occasion for imposing an estate tax. Thus the situation here presented was placed in the same category as those where the grantor had reserved a power to revoke or a power to change beneficiaries. By analogy to the *Guggenheim* and *Sanford* cases, I suppose the gift would have become complete if the donor had, in his life, relinquished or conveyed the contingent estate reserved to him.

In the light of this history, the *Sanford* case requires a holding that the gifts in remainder, after the life estate, create no gift tax liability. The reasoning of that decision, the authorities, and the legislative history relied upon, are all at war with the result in this case. There is no need to quote what was there said. A reading of the decision will demonstrate that, if the principles there announced are here observed, the gifts in question are incomplete and cannot be the subject of the gift tax.

It will not square with logic to say that where the donor reserves the right to change beneficiaries, and so delays completion of the gift until his death or prior relinquishment of the right, the gift is incomplete, but where he reserves a contingent interest to himself the reverse is true,—particularly so, if the criterion of estate tax liability is important to the decision of the question, as the *Sanford* case affirms.

The question is not whether a gift which includes vested and contingent future interests in others than the donor is taxable as an entirety when made, but whether a reservation of such an interest in the donor negatives a completion of the gift until such time as that interest is relinquished.

All that is said in the *Sanford* case about the difficulties of administration and probable inequities of a contrary decision there, applies here with greater force. Indeed a system of taxation which requires valuation of the donor's retained interest, in the light of the contingencies involved, and calculation of the value of the subsequent remainders by resort to higher mathematics beyond the ken of the taxpayer, exhibits the artificiality of the Government's application of the Act. This is well illustrated in the companion cases of *Robinette* and *Paumgarten*, infra. . . . Such results argue strongly against the construction which the court adopts.

NOTES

1. *Valuation of life estates and remainders.* For gift and estate tax purposes, when beneficial ownership of property is carved up into successive beneficial interests (e.g., a life estate and remainder), the value of the separate interests is generally determined using actuarial principles. The regulations provide valuation tables which vastly simplify the necessary calculations. See I.R.C. § 7520; Reg. §§ 25.2512–5(d) and 20.2031–7(d). The tables reflect some crucial simplifying assumptions concerning the life expectancy of individuals, the value of property and the income stream it produces, and the value of the use of money (i.e., the interest rate). These assumptions may depart dramatically from actual expectations in particular cases (e.g., where the life tenant is terminally ill or the underlying property produces no current income). Nevertheless, as a matter of administrative convenience, the government as well as the taxpayer is ordinarily required to use the tables in cases where they apply.

2. *Valuation of annuities.* An annuity is the right to receive fixed periodic payments for a stipulated period—e.g., $1,000 payable on July 1 each year for ten years; $100 on the 15th day of each month for 120 months. The most commonly encountered type of annuity is a *term annuity* lasting for a predetermined period of months or years. The duration of the fixed payments can also be measured by one or more lives—a *life annuity* being different from a *life estate* in that the latter represents the right to receive the income from property, whatever the income turns out to be, rather than a fixed amount.

The present value (P) of an annuity can be expressed in terms of the number of periodic payments (n), the amount payable at the end of each period (A), and the interest rate (r), by the following formula:

$$P = (a \div r) \times [1 - \frac{1}{(1+r)^n}]$$

For example, the present value of a $100 annuity, payable at the end of each year for a five-year term, assuming an interest rate of 6 percent (compounded annually), is ($100 \div 0.06) \times [1 - (1 \div 1.06^5)]$, or $421.24.[7] The valuation of life

---

[7] In other words, $421.24 is the principal amount which, together with 6 percent interest (compounded annually), will be sufficient to cover the scheduled payments of $100 at the end of each year for five years:

estates and remainders under the tables is based on similar formulas, setting n equal to the life expectancy of the life tenant.

3. *Limits on actuarial valuation.* Some types of interests are especially difficult to value due to special conditions, limitations or broad discretionary powers. For example, in Robinette v. Helvering, 318 U.S. 184 (1943), decided the same day as the principal case, a settlor created an inter vivos trust, retaining a reversion which would become possessory only if his 30–year-old daughter should die leaving no issue who reached age 21. In the absence of any recognized method for valuing the settlor's retained interest, the Court upheld the imposition of a gift tax on the full value of the trust property:

> It may be true, as the petitioners argue, that trust instruments such as these before us frequently create "a complex aggregate of rights, privileges, powers and immunities and that in certain instances all these rights, privileges, powers and immunities are not transferred or released simultaneously." But before one who gives his property away by this method is entitled to deduction from his gift tax on the basis that he had retained some of these complex strands it is necessary that he at least establish the possibility of approximating what value he holds. Factors to be considered in fixing the value of this contingent reservation as of the date of the gift would have included consideration of whether or not the daughter would marry; whether she would have children; whether they would reach the age of 21; etc. Actuarial science may have made great strides in appraising the value of that which seems to be unappraisable, but we have no reason to believe from this record that even the actuarial art could do more than guess at the value here in question. [318 U.S. at 188–89.]

The *Robinette* holding is now reflected in the gift tax regulations. See Reg. § 25.2511–1(e).

4. *Special valuation rules.* The special valuation rules of I.R.C. § 2702, enacted in 1990, significantly alter the traditional gift tax treatment of a donor's retained interests and powers. The special rules apply where a donor carves up beneficial ownership of property into successive interests and gives one or more interests to a family member (for this purpose, the donor's family includes his or her spouse, ancestors, descendants, siblings and certain in-laws) while retaining another interest in the same property. Under the spe-

Year	Beginning Principal	+	Interest	−	Annuity Payment	=	Ending Principal
1	$421.24		$25.27		$100.00		$346.51
2	346.51		20.79		100.00		267.30
3	267.30		16.04		100.00		183.34
4	183.34		11.00		100.00		94.34
5	94.34		5.66		100.00		0.00

cial rules, subject to specified exceptions,[8] the value of the donor's retained interest is treated as zero for gift tax purposes, with the result that the entire value of the underlying property is subject to gift tax.

To illustrate the effect of § 2702, consider the trust involved in Smith v. Shaughnessy, under which the settlor transferred a life income interest to his wife, with a contingent remainder to her appointees or heirs, retaining a reversion conditioned on the settlor surviving his wife. Today, the entire value of the trust property would be subject to gift tax when the trust was created, since the special rules would prescribe a gift tax value of zero for the settlor's retained interest. Note that the special rules apply only for gift tax purposes; they do not change the estate tax treatment of the trust. Thus, if the settlor died before his wife, the trust property might still be subject to estate tax (with an adjustment for the earlier gift tax).

A donor who wishes to avoid the reach of § 2702 can readily do so, either by making a completed gift of all interests in the property (i.e., retaining nothing) or by retaining sufficient dominion and control over all interests to prevent any completed gift from occurring.

3. CONSIDERATION

A transfer of property by gift is ordinarily valued for gift tax purposes at the time the gift becomes complete. The amount of the gift is equal to the value of the transferred property, reduced by any consideration "in money or money's worth" received by the donor. I.R.C. § 2512(a). If the donor receives "full and adequate consideration in money or money's worth," the gift tax does not apply. See Reg. § 25.2511–1(g)(1).

The gift tax concept of "consideration" differs in important ways from its common law cousin in the field of contract law. Consideration, as used in the gift tax, has nothing to do with determining the enforceability of a promise; instead, its primary function is to measure the net decrease in the donor's net worth (or in the case of a sale for full and adequate consideration, to negate the existence of a gift). In the absence of statutory guidance, it has fallen largely to the courts to construct a definition of consideration for gift tax purposes.

The Supreme Court laid the groundwork in a pair of cases, authored by Justice Frankfurter, involving marriage settlements made by one spouse in favor of the other. In Commissioner v. Wemyss, 324 U.S. 303 (1945), the taxpayer transferred a block of stock to his fiancée to compensate her for the loss (by reason of their marriage) of her income interest in a trust created by her first husband. The Court upheld the imposition of a

---

[8] Certain interests (e.g., a qualified annuity or unitrust interest) remain eligible for valuation under actuarial principles.

gift tax on the full value of the transferred stock and rejected the argument that the gift tax could not apply in the absence of donative intent:

> . . . Had Congress taxed "gifts" *simpliciter*, it would be appropriate to assume that the term was used in its colloquial sense, and a search for "donative intent" would be indicated. But Congress intended to use the term "gifts" in its broadest and most comprehensive sense. . . . Congress chose not to require an ascertainment of what too often is an elusive state of mind. For purposes of the gift tax it not only dispensed with the test of "donative intent." It formulated a much more workable external test, that where "property is transferred for less than an adequate and full consideration in money or money's worth," the excess in such money value "shall, for the purpose of the tax imposed by this title, be deemed a gift. . . ." And Treasury Regulations have emphasized that common law considerations were not embodied in the gift tax.

> To reinforce the evident desire of Congress to hit all the protean arrangements which the wit of man can devise that are not business transactions within the meaning of ordinary speech, the Treasury Regulations make clear that no genuine business transaction comes within the purport of the gift tax by excluding "a sale, exchange, or other transfer of property made in the ordinary course of business (a transaction which is *bona fide*, at arm's length, and free from any donative intent)." Treas. Reg. 79 (1936 ed.), Art. 8. Thus on finding that a transfer in the circumstances of a particular case is not made in the ordinary course of business, the transfer becomes subject to the gift tax to the extent that it is not made "for an adequate and full consideration in money or money's worth." . . .

> If we are to isolate as an independently reviewable question of law the view of the Tax Court that money consideration must benefit the donor to relieve a transfer by him from being a gift, we think the Tax Court was correct. . . . To allow detriment to the donee to satisfy the requirement of "adequate and full consideration" would violate the purpose of the statute and open wide the door for evasion of the gift tax. . . . [324 U.S. at 306–08.]

In the second case, Merrill v. Fahs, 324 U.S. 308 (1945), the Court, relying on a parallel estate tax provision, held that one spouse's relinquishment of inchoate marital property rights (i.e., dower) in the other spouse's property did not constitute "adequate and full consideration in money or money's worth."

NOTES

1. *Binding promise.* Suppose that *A* promises to give her favorite nephew $10,000 as a present upon his graduation from college. At common law, in the absence of consideration, *A*'s promise is initially unenforceable; however, if *A* changes her mind and refuses to pay the promised sum after the nephew graduates from college, the nephew may be able to compel payment under the doctrine of promissory estoppel. If *A* makes her promise in 2013, the nephew graduates in 2014, and *A* finally pays the $10,000 in 2018, has *A* made a gift? If so, in which year does the gift occur? What if *A* dies before making payment? See Rev. Rul. 79–384, 1979–2 C.B. 344; Rev. Rul. 84–25, 1984–1 C.B. 191.

2. *Marriage, separation and divorce.* The holdings of *Wemyss* and *Merrill* are now reflected in Reg. § 25.2512–8:

> A consideration not reducible to a value in money or money's worth, such as love and affection, promise of marriage, etc., is to be wholly disregarded, and the entire value of the property transferred constitutes the amount of the gift. Similarly, a relinquishment or promised relinquishment of dower or curtesy, or of a statutory estate created in lieu of dower or curtesy, or of other marital rights in the spouse's property or estate, shall not be considered to any extent a consideration in money or money's worth.

> In contrast, if a husband and wife enter into a written agreement relative to their marital and property rights, and divorce occurs within a specified period, any transfer of property to either spouse in settlement of his or her marital or property rights pursuant to the agreement is deemed to be made for full and adequate consideration in money or money's worth. See I.R.C. § 2516.

Why should a relinquishment of marital property rights in contemplation of divorce be treated differently for gift tax purposes from a similar relinquishment in contemplation of marriage?

3. *Business transactions.* The regulations declare that "a sale, exchange, or other transfer of property made in the ordinary course of business (a transaction which is bona fide, at arm's length, and free from any donative intent), will be considered as made for an adequate and full consideration in money or money's worth." Reg. § 25.2512–8. If a customer buys an odd lot of books from a junk dealer for $100, and the lot turns out to include a rare first edition worth $5,000, presumably there is no gift. Should the result be different if the customer is the junk dealer's child?

4. ANNUAL EXCLUSION

Despite the expansive scope of the gift tax, not all gifts are taxable. In general, the term "taxable gifts" means the total amount of gifts made by the donor during the taxable year, less allowable deductions for gifts to charity or a spouse.[9] I.R.C. § 2503(a). The statute goes on, however, to allow certain gifts to be excluded in calculating the donor's taxable gifts: "In the case of gifts (other than gifts of future interests in property) made to any person by the donor during the calendar year, the first $10,000 of such gifts to such person shall not . . . be included in the total amount of gifts made during such year." I.R.C. § 2503(b)(1).[10]

The "annual exclusion" was originally justified on grounds of administrative convenience. According to the legislative history, the exclusion was intended "on the one hand, . . . to obviate the necessity of keeping an account of and reporting numerous small gifts, and, on the other, to fix the amount sufficiently large to cover in most cases wedding and Christmas gifts and occasional gifts of relatively small amounts." S. Rep. No. 665, 72d Cong., 1st Sess. (1932), reprinted in 1939–1 (pt. 2) C.B. 496, 525–26. Over the years, however, the exclusion has become an important tool in estate planning. It allows a donor to give $10,000 each year (indexed for inflation) to an unlimited number of donees without even filing a gift tax return. The utility of the exclusion is enhanced for married couples by the "gift-splitting" provisions of I.R.C. § 2513, which treat any gift made by a married donor to a donee (other than his or her spouse) for gift tax purposes as made one-half by the donor and one-half by the spouse, if both spouses consent. Thus, a married individual with two children and six grandchildren can make gifts of $160,000 or more per year with no gift or estate tax consequences (other than filing a gift tax return containing the spouse's consent to gift-splitting).

Note that the annual exclusion does not apply to gifts of "future interests in property." Although an outright gift of property ordinarily qualifies for the exclusion without difficulty, gifts in trust require careful planning. In Helvering v. Hutchings, 312 U.S. 393 (1941), the Supreme Court established that the "donees" of a gift in trust are the trust beneficiaries rather than the trust itself. On the same day, in United States v. Pelzer, 312 U.S. 399 (1941), the Court held that no annual exclusion was available for a gift in trust where "the beneficiaries had no right to the present enjoyment of the corpus or of the income" during the first 10 years of the trust term; the beneficiaries' interests were "future interests" for gift tax purposes, regardless of their classification under state property law. A "future interest," as defined in the current gift tax regulations, includes any interest which is "limited to commence in use, possession, or enjoyment at some future date or time." Reg. § 25.2503–3(a). Although a

---

[9] The gift tax deductions for gifts to charity or a spouse closely resemble the parallel estate provisions, which are discussed infra at pp. 1034–1046.

[10] Since 1999 the $10,000 exclusion amount has been indexed for inflation, with the amount of any increase rounded down to the nearest $1,000. I.R.C. § 2503(b)(2). In 2012 I.R.C. § 2503(b)(2). In 2013 the exclusion amount was $14,000.

right to receive payments in the future under a contractual obligation (e.g., a bond or insurance policy) is not a future interest for this purpose, "a future interest or interests in such contractual obligations may be created by the limitations contained in a trust or other instrument of transfer used in effecting a gift." Id. The regulations also state the converse proposition: "An unrestricted right to the immediate use, possession, or enjoyment of property or the income from property (such as a life estate or term certain) is a present interest in property. An exclusion is allowable with respect to a gift of such an interest. . . ." Reg. § 25.2503–3(b).

Gifts to minors raise special concerns. Most donors are reluctant to make substantial outright gifts directly to minors (although there is no legal impediment to doing so). One alternative is a custodianship under the Uniform Transfers to Minors Act, which has been enacted in one version or another throughout the country (see supra p. 530). The Internal Revenue Service has ruled that such gifts are eligible for the annual exclusion. See Rev. Rul. 59–357, 1959–2 C.B. 212. (Note, however, that if the donor dies while acting as custodian before the donee reaches the age of majority, the property will be subject to estate tax.) In the case of a large gift, the donor may prefer to use a trust, which provides considerably more flexibility than a custodianship. A trust which would otherwise violate the present-interest requirement of I.R.C. § 2503(b) may nevertheless qualify for the annual exclusion if it comes within the safe harbor of § 2503(c), which states:

> **(c) Transfer for the benefit of minor.** No part of a gift to an individual who has not attained the age of 21 years on the date of such transfer shall be considered a gift of a future interest in property for purposes of [the annual exclusion] if the property and the income therefrom—
>
> (1) may be expended by, or for the benefit of, the donee before his attaining the age of 21 years, and
>
> (2) will to the extent not so expended—
>
> (A) pass to the donee on his attaining the age of 21 years, and
>
> (B) in the event the donee dies before attaining the age of 21 years, be payable to the estate of the donee or as he may appoint under a general power of appointment. . . .

This provision permits the settlor of a trust for a beneficiary under age 21 to lodge control of the trust property in the hands of a trustee with broad discretion, without losing the tax benefit of the annual exclusion.

NOTES

1. *Stretching the annual exclusion.* During the current year *A* has given her favorite nephew several modest presents on his birthday and other occasions; she now proposes to give him $10,000 at year-end as a token of esteem. Does the $10,000 qualify for the annual exclusion? Does it matter whether the earlier gifts took the form of (a) a $100 check, (b) a silk tie, or (c) a dinner out on the town? The practice of many estate planners seems to be to ignore such gifts, but the statute seems clearly to the contrary.

2. *Demand rights.* The creation of a discretionary trust ordinarily does not generate an annual exclusion for the settlor because the beneficiaries have only future interests (within the meaning of § 2503(b)). This obstacle can be overcome, however, if one or more beneficiaries have an immediate, unrestricted right, under the terms of the trust, to withdraw property from the trust. Whether or not exercised, such demand rights create present interests which can qualify for the annual exclusion. This form of trust is often called a "*Crummey* trust," after the leading case of Crummey v. Commissioner, 397 F.2d 82 (9th Cir.1968), which allowed annual exclusions based on unexercised demand rights held by minor beneficiaries. See also Estate of Cristofani v. Commissioner, 97 T.C. 74 (1991) ($70,000 transfer in trust fully excludable, based on demand rights held by two primary beneficiaries and five contingent remaindermen).

Technically, a demand right is a general power of appointment which would ordinarily subject the underlying property to gift or estate tax in the holder's hands. See I.R.C. §§ 2514 and 2041, discussed infra at p. 1028. I.R.C. § 2514(e), however, provides a special exception for certain powers which lapse during the holder's life. For this reason, demand rights are usually designed to lapse within a limited time after they become exercisable. For the Internal Revenue Service's position on lapsing demand rights, see Rev. Rul. 81–7, 1981–1 C.B. 474; Rev. Rul. 83–108, 1983–2 C.B. 167.

3. *Educational and medical expenses.* In addition to the annual exclusion, I.R.C. § 2503(e) allows a gift tax exclusion for certain educational and medical expenses paid on behalf of an individual beneficiary. The exclusion covers amounts paid directly to an educational organization as tuition for the beneficiary's education or training, as well as amounts paid directly to a medical care provider as payment for the beneficiary's medical care. The exclusion is unlimited in amount.

5. DISCLAIMER

In general, state property law authorizes the recipient of an unwanted inter vivos or testamentary gift to disclaim the gift and let it pass instead to an alternative taker. (See supra page 142). For federal tax purposes, a "qualified disclaimer" may offer significant tax benefits. The operative language of the federal disclaimer statute, I.R.C. § 2518(a), provides that "if a person makes a qualified disclaimer with respect to any interest in property, [the federal wealth transfer taxes] shall apply with respect to such interest as if the interest had never been transferred to such person." As a result, the disclaimed interest is treated as passing directly from the original transferor to the ultimate taker in a single transfer. Note that § 2518 controls only the federal tax treatment of the qualified disclaimer; the dispositive effect of a disclaimer (whether qualified or non-qualified) is governed by state property law.

To illustrate the operation of § 2518, suppose that *A* dies intestate, leaving her brother *B* as her sole heir; *B* disclaims his intestate share, which passes (under the applicable state disclaimer statute) to *B*'s descendants. If *B* has made a qualified disclaimer, *A*'s estate will be treated for gift, estate, and GST tax purposes as passing directly to *B*'s descendants. By contrast, if *B*'s disclaimer is not qualified, the transaction will be taxed as if *B* had accepted his intestate share and then retransferred it to his descendants by gift. In either case *A*'s estate will be subject to estate tax, but only if *B*'s disclaimer is not qualified will the property attract a separate gift tax in *B*'s hands.

Section 2518(b) defines a qualified disclaimer as "an irrevocable and unqualified refusal by a person to accept an interest in property" which meets the following four requirements:

(1) such refusal is in writing,

(2) such writing is received by the transferor of the interest, his legal representative, or the holder of the legal title to the property to which the interest relates not later than the date which is 9 months after the later of—

(A) the day on which the transfer creating the interest in such person is made, or

(B) the day on which such person attains age 21,

(3) such person has not accepted the interest or any of its benefits, and

(4) as a result of such refusal, the interest passes without any direction on the part of the person making the disclaimer and passes either—

(A) to the spouse of the decedent, or

(B) to a person other than the person making the disclaimer.

A qualified disclaimer may have important tax consequences for the original transferor. For example, if a decedent's surviving spouse disclaims a bequest, which passes instead to other beneficiaries, the disclaimed bequest will not be eligible for a marital deduction. The reverse is also true; if the decedent's child disclaims a bequest, which passes instead to the decedent's surviving spouse, the bequest may become eligible for a marital deduction. See Estate of Monroe v. Commissioner, 124 F.3d 699 (5th Cir.1997). If the disclaimed interest passes to the original transferor's grandchildren or more remote descendants, the transfer may become subject to a GST tax.

NOTES

1. *Time limitation.* Suppose a settlor created a testamentary trust to pay income to the settlor's child for life, with remainder at the child's death to the child's issue then living. Years later, while the income beneficiary is still living, the settlor's 25–year-old grandchild learns of the existence of the trust and proposes to disclaim her remainder interest; under applicable state law, the disclaimer would be effective to pass the disclaimed interest to the disclaimant's own issue. See Uniform Disclaimer of Property Interests Act § 6 (1999). Will the proposed disclaimer be a qualified disclaimer under § 2518? See Jewett v. Commissioner, 455 U.S. 305 (1982) (applying prior law).

2. *Prior law.* Section 2518 applies to disclaimers of interests created by transfers occurring after 1976. For the rules governing disclaimers of pre–1976 interests, see Reg. § 25.2511–1(c)(2).

C. THE ESTATE TAX

1. THE GROSS ESTATE

The estate tax calculation begins with the *gross estate*, from which various deductions are subtracted to arrive at the taxable estate. The gross estate includes not only property actually owned by the decedent at death and passing by will or intestacy but also various types of transfers passing outside the probate system—e.g., joint tenancies, life insurance, survivor annuities, and general powers of appointment—which are treated as testamentary substitutes for estate tax purposes. In addition, if the decedent transferred property during life while retaining certain interests or powers (e.g., a life estate or a power to revoke) the property may be drawn back into the gross estate. In general, all property included in the gross estate is valued at its fair market value as of the date of death. See I.R.C. § 2031(a); Reg. §§ 20.2031–1 to–9.

a. Property Owned at Death

The central component of the gross estate consists of property owned at death. The operative provision is I.R.C. § 2033, which includes "all property to the extent of the interest therein of the decedent" at death. This provision applies to property of all kinds—real property, personal effects, cash, stocks and bonds—in which the decedent had a beneficial interest (as opposed to bare legal title) at death. It also includes various items earned but not yet collected by the decedent at death (e.g., wages due, accrued interest, and dividends payable to the decedent as stockholder of record). Section 2033 applies only to transmissible interests, i.e., those which survive the death of the decedent. For example, a life estate which terminates at the decedent's death is not included under this provision, nor is a contingent remainder which is defeated by the decedent's death.

From an early date, the courts have viewed § 2033 as reaching more or less the same assets as those which form part of the decedent's probate estate. Had the courts taken a more expansive view of this provision (along the lines of "dominion and control" or "substantial ownership" under the income tax), it might have been possible to dispense with several of the inclusionary provisions discussed below.

NOTES

1. *Lottery winnings.* A bought a lottery ticket and told a friend that she was holding it for her favorite nephew. One week later, the ticket won the jackpot; A died the same day. Are the lottery winnings includible in A's gross estate under § 2033?

2. *Stolen property.* At the time of his death, decedent, a former U.S. serviceman, had in his possession several works of art (with an estimated value of $50 to $100 million) which he had stolen while stationed in Europe. When his heirs attempted to sell the works, the true owners came forward and reclaimed them, paying a $2.75 million "finder's fee" to the heirs. What interest, if any, did decedent own at death, and what amount is includible in his gross estate under § 2033? See Tech. Adv. Memo. 9152005 (Aug. 30, 1991).

b. Joint Tenancies

A substantial amount of property is held in joint tenancy with right of survivorship (or tenancy by the entirety, in the case of a married couple). The joint tenancy probably owes much of its popularity to its reputation as a convenient will substitute; by virtue of the survivorship feature, at the death of one tenant the surviving tenant takes the property without any probate proceeding (see supra p. 535). Unfortunately, many people who use joint tenancies as will substitutes overlook other features which may produce unpleasant surprises during life and at death. For example, a person who retitles his or her own property in joint tenancy, intending to provide for a loved one at death, may discover belatedly that the loved one has walked off with half of the property during life. Furthermore, the creation of the joint tenancy may give rise to a taxable gift (see Note 3, supra p. 988), adding insult to injury.

At the death of one joint tenant, all or part of the value of property held in joint tenancy may be includible in the decedent's gross estate under I.R.C. § 2040. Except in the case of spousal joint tenancies, discussed below, the general rule of § 2040(a) requires inclusion of the full value of the joint tenancy property "except such part thereof as may be shown to have originally belonged to [the surviving joint tenant] and never to have been received or acquired by the latter from the decedent for less than an adequate and full consideration in money or money's worth." Thus, the includible amount may be expressed as $V \times [1 - (p_s \div p_t)]$, where V is the value of the joint tenancy property at the decedent's death, p_s is the surviving joint tenant's contribution toward the purchase price, and p_t is the total purchase price of the property. In theory, once the respective contributions of the decedent and the surviving tenant toward the purchase price are known, it is a simple matter to compute the includible portion of the property's deathtime value.[11] However, the estate has the burden of proving the surviving joint tenant's contributions, and in the absence of meticulous recordkeeping this burden may be difficult to sustain.

To illustrate the operation of § 2040(a), suppose that *A*, using $100,000 of her own funds, purchases Blackacre for herself and her favorite nephew as joint tenants with right of survivorship. The creation of the joint tenancy results in a completed gift of $50,000 (which constitutes a present interest for purposes of the annual exclusion). *A* dies a few years later, when Blackacre is worth $150,000. The full deathtime value of Blackacre is includible in *A*'s gross estate, but the resulting estate tax is partially offset by the gift tax that *A* paid when she created the joint tenancy (see I.R.C. § 2001(b)). In effect, the full value of Blackacre is taxed in two stages, with a portion payable during life and the balance at death. If the nephew subsequently dies owning Blackacre, it will be includible in his gross estate under § 2033.

Section § 2040(b) provides a special rule for spousal joint tenancies. At the death of the first spouse, half of the joint tenancy property is includible in the decedent's gross estate, regardless of the spouses' respective contributions. Since an equivalent amount automatically qualifies for the unlimited marital deduction, however, the net effect is an inclusion of

---

[11] If the decedent and the surviving joint tenant originally acquired the joint tenancy property by "gift, bequest, devise, or inheritance," a ratable share of the property is includible in the decedent's gross estate, just as if the joint tenants had made equal contributions toward the purchase price.

zero in the taxable estate. Thus, under current law, spousal joint tenancies have little or no significance for gift and estate tax purposes.[12]

NOTE

In the above example, suppose that the nephew dies unexpectedly survived by *A*. In that case, unless there is adequate documentation of *A*'s contribution to the purchase price, the full deathtime value of Blackacre will be includible in the nephew's gross estate. What if *A* and the nephew die in circumstances which make it impossible to determine the order of death? See Rev. Rul. 76–303, 1976–2 C.B. 266.

c. Annuities

Under the somewhat misleading title "annuities," I.R.C. § 2039 includes in a decedent's gross estate the value of certain survivor benefits payable to beneficiaries under a "contract or agreement." The statute applies only if the contract or agreement also provided for an "annuity or other payment" to the decedent during life. The main purpose of this provision, when it was added in 1954, was to clarify the treatment of survivor benefits payable under employee benefit plans. The statute originally contained a special exemption for amounts payable under qualified pension and profit-sharing plans, but this exemption was prospectively repealed in 1984. In its current form, § 2039 covers most survivor benefits provided by employee benefit plans as well as amounts payable under commercial survivorship annuities.

d. Life Insurance

I.R.C. § 2042 governs the estate tax treatment of proceeds of insurance on the decedent's life. In view of the nature of life insurance, one might expect that the proceeds of any insurance on a decedent's life would be includible in his gross estate; and, where the proceeds are payable to the estate, that is the case. If, however, the insurance is payable to some other beneficiary (as it usually is), the proceeds are includible only if the decedent possessed at death any of the "incidents of ownership" in the policy. The regulations provide:

> [For this purpose], the term "incidents of ownership" is not limited in its meaning to ownership of the policy in the technical legal sense. Generally speaking, the term has reference to the right of the insured or his estate to the economic benefits of the policy. Thus, it includes the right to change the beneficiary, to surrender or cancel the policy, to assign the policy, to revoke an assignment, to pledge the policy for

---

[12] The amount included in the decedent's gross estate is relevant, however, in determining the surviving spouse's income tax basis in the property under I.R.C. § 1014.

a loan, or to obtain from the insurer a loan against the surrender value of the policy, etc. [Reg. § 20.2042–1(c)(2).]

The term "incidents of ownership" also includes a reversionary interest in the policy or its proceeds if immediately before death the value of the interest exceeded 5 percent of the value of the policy.

Prior to 1954, life insurance proceeds were includible in the gross estate, regardless of whether the decedent possessed any incidents of ownership at death, if the decedent had paid the premiums on the policy during life. Since the repeal of the "premium payment test" in 1954, life insurance has come to play a prominent role in estate planning. Today, an insured person can transfer an insurance policy on his or her life to another person, retaining no incidents of ownership, and continue to pay all of the premiums on the policy; as long as the insured person survives for at least three years, the proceeds will escape inclusion in the gross estate. Moreover, if the gift of the policy is outright rather than in trust, the transfer of the policy as well as the subsequent premium payments are eligible for the annual exclusion. See Reg. § 25.2503–3(a) and (c); Rev. Rul. 55–408, 1955–1 C.B. 113.

NOTE

Deathbed transfers. If an insured person transfers a life insurance policy or relinquishes incidents of ownership and then dies within three years, the proceeds of the policy may be fully includible in the gross estate under § 2035 (see infra p. 1026). Suppose, however, that the insured person arranges for a third person (e.g., a spouse) to take out the insurance policy; the insured person, who pays all of the premiums but possesses no incidents of ownership, dies within three years. What result? See Estate of Perry v. Commissioner, 927 F.2d 209 (5th Cir.1991).

e. Lifetime Transfers

From the outset it was recognized that if wholesale avoidance was to be prevented, some provision had to be made for taxing transfers which, although technically operative during life, functioned as testamentary substitutes. Prior to the enactment of the gift tax, such transfers would go completely untaxed unless they were included in the gross estate. Accordingly, the original estate tax statute drew two types of transfers made by the decedent during life back into the gross estate at death: transfers "intended to take effect in possession or enjoyment at or after death" (the predecessor of §§ 2036–2038) and transfers made "in contemplation of death" (the predecessor of § 2035).

The original postponed-possession-or-enjoyment provision was aimed at lifetime transfers which remained "incomplete" in some respect until death due to interests or powers held by the decedent. Had the courts interpreted this provision in light of its underlying policy, the statutory language ("intended to take effect in possession or enjoyment at or after death") should have caused no greater difficulty here than in the state inheritance tax statutes from which it was borrowed. Instead, a series of early Supreme Court decisions practically eviscerated the provision and set in motion a protracted and extraordinarily complicated process of statutory revision and judicial reinterpretation. The original postponed-possession-or-enjoyment provision was gradually replaced with three considerably more detailed provisions, I.R.C. §§ 2036–2038, which cover more or less the same territory under current law.[13] Section 2036 deals with transfers as to which the decedent retained rights and interests in the property or its income for life. Section 2037 deals with transfers as to which the decedent retained a reversionary interest and the interests of other beneficiaries are conditioned on surviving the decedent. Section 2038 deals with transfers as to which the decedent reserved a power affecting beneficial enjoyment. Each of these provisions, like their common predecessor, is predicated on a "transfer" (not necessarily a completed transfer subject to gift tax) of property made by the decedent during life which left the decedent holding some specified taxable "string" (e.g., a life estate or power to revoke). The three provisions are not mutually exclusive; indeed, they often overlap, e.g., where a decedent retained both a life estate and a power to revoke. The amount includible in the gross estate may vary depending on the type of interest or power involved.

The original contemplation-of-death provision was aimed at lifetime transfers motivated by testamentary concerns, and required a case-by-case inquiry into the decedent's subjective state of mind. As the Supreme Court explained in United States v. Wells, 283 U.S. 102 (1931):

> It is recognized that the reference is not to the general expectation of death which all entertain. It must be a particular concern, giving rise to a definite motive. The provision is not confined to gifts *causa mortis*, which are made in anticipation of impending death, are revocable, and are defeated if the donor survives the apprehended peril. . . . Death must be "contemplated," that is, the motive which induces the transfer must be of the sort which leads to testamentary disposition. [283 U.S. at 115–17.]

To stem the resulting flood of colorful but pointless litigation over "life" motives (see, e.g., Kniskern v. United States, 232 F.Supp. 7 (S.D. Fla. 1964), holding that gifts by a 99–year-old man one year before his death were not made in contemplation of death), the 1976 Act replaced the re-

---

[13] The focus here is primarily on current law. However, many trusts established long ago are still in existence today and remain subject to the provisions of prior law. Given the checkered history of the estate tax provisions (especially I.R.C. §§ 2036–2038), the tax consequences of a particular transfer may vary substantially depending on when the transfer was made.

buttable presumption with a bright-line rule requiring inclusion of gifts made within three years of death. In addition, to eliminate the tax advantages of deathbed transfers, the 1976 Act required that the gross estate be "grossed up" by gift taxes paid by the decedent within three years of death. With the unification of the estate and gift taxes, it soon became clear that there was little reason to draw most deathbed gifts back into the gross estate as long as the gross-up provision captured the gift tax on such gifts. The 1981 Act therefore repealed the 3–year inclusionary rule for most transfers, leaving the gross-up provision intact. The current version of the 3–year rule appears in § 2035, discussed infra at p. 1026.

(i) Revocable Transfers

In 1924 Congress added a new provision to the estate tax statute covering a decedent's power to "alter, amend, or revoke" a transfer made during life. This provision, which has been amended from time to time, appears in current law in I.R.C. § 2038(a), as follows:

> **(a) In general.** The value of the gross estate shall include the value of all property . . . [t]o the extent of any interest therein of which the decedent has at any time made a transfer (except in case of a bona fide sale for an adequate and full consideration in money or money's worth), by trust or otherwise, where the enjoyment thereof was subject at the date of his death to any change through the exercise of a power (in whatever capacity exercisable) by the decedent alone or by the decedent in conjunction with any other person (without regard to when or from what source the decedent acquired such power), to alter, amend, revoke, or terminate, or where any such power is relinquished during the 3–year period ending on the date of the decedent's death. . . .

In Porter v. Commissioner, 288 U.S. 436 (1933), cited in Smith v. Shaughnessy, supra p. 989, the Supreme Court held the predecessor of this provision applicable where a settlor created inter vivos trusts subject to a retained "nonbeneficial" power (i.e., one not exercisable for his own benefit). A few years later, in Commissioner v. Chase Nat'l Bank, 82 F.2d 157 (2d Cir.), cert. denied, 299 U.S. 552 (1936), the provision was held applicable where the settlor of an irrevocable inter vivos trust retained no power exercisable during life but held a special testamentary power to appoint the trust property among her descendants.

OLD COLONY TRUST CO. v. UNITED STATES

United States Court of Appeals, First Circuit, 1970.
423 F.2d 601.

ALDRICH, CHIEF JUDGE.

The sole question in this case is whether the estate of a settlor[14] of an inter vivos trust, who was a trustee until the date of his death, is to be charged with the value of the principal he contributed by virtue of reserved powers in the trust. The executor paid the tax and sued for its recovery in the district court. All facts were stipulated. The court ruled for the government, 300 F.Supp. 1032, and the executor appeals.

The initial life beneficiary of the trust was the settlor's adult son. Eighty per cent of the income was normally to be payable to him, and the balance added to principal. Subsequent beneficiaries were the son's widow and his issue. The powers upon which the government relies to cause the corpus to be includible in the settlor-trustee's estate are contained in two articles. . . .

Article 4 permitted the trustees to increase the percentage of income payable to the son beyond the eighty per cent, "in their absolute discretion . . . when in their opinion such increase is needed in case of sickness, or desirable in view of changed circumstances." In addition, under Article 4 the trustees were given the discretion to cease paying income to the son, and add it all to principal, "during such period as the Trustees may decide that the stoppage of such payments is for his best interests."

Article 7 gave broad administrative or management powers to the trustees, with discretion to acquire investments not normally held by trustees, and the right to determine, what was to be charged or credited to income or principal, including stock dividends or deductions for amortization. It further provided that all divisions and decisions made by the trustees in good faith should be conclusive on all parties, and in summary, stated that the trustees were empowered, "generally to do all things in relation to the Trust Fund which the Donor could do if living and this Trust had not been executed."

The government claims that each of these two articles meant that the settlor-trustee had "the right . . . to designate the persons who shall possess or enjoy the [trust] property or the income therefrom" within the meaning of section 2036(a)(2) of the Internal Revenue Code of 1954, 26 U.S.C. § 2036(a)(2), and that the settlor-trustee at the date of his death possessed a power "to alter, amend, revoke, or terminate" within the meaning of section 2038(a)(1) (26 U.S.C. § 2038(a)(1)).

---

[14] Actually, the decedent was a donor to three trusts, similar in form, previously established by his wife—differences which we ignore as inconsequential.

If State Street Trust Co. v. United States, 1 Cir., 1959, 263 F.2d 635, was correctly decided in this aspect, the government must prevail because of the Article 7 powers. There this court, Chief Judge Magruder dissenting, held against the taxpayer because broad powers similar to those in Article 7 meant that the trustees "could very substantially shift the economic benefits of the trusts between the life tenants and the remaindermen," so that the settlor "as long as he lived, in substance and effect and in a very real sense . . . 'retained for his life . . . the right . . . to designate the persons who shall possess or enjoy the property or the income therefrom; . . . .'" 263 F.2d at 639–640, quoting 26 U.S.C. § 2036(a)(2). We accept the taxpayer's invitation to reconsider this ruling.

It is common ground that a settlor will not find the corpus of the trust included in his estate merely because he named himself a trustee. Jennings v. Smith, 2 Cir., 1947, 161 F.2d 74. He must have reserved a power to himself that is inconsistent with the full termination of ownership. The government's brief defines this as "sufficient dominion and control until his death." Trustee powers given for the administration or management of the trust must be equitably exercised, however, for the benefit of the trust as a whole. Blodget v. Delaney, 1 Cir., 1953, 201 F.2d 589; United States v. Powell, 10 Cir., 1962, 307 F.2d 821; Scott, Trusts §§ 183, 232 (3d ed. 1967); Rest. 2d, Trusts §§ 183, 232. The court in *State Street* conceded that the powers at issue were all such powers, but reached the conclusion that, cumulatively, they gave the settlor dominion sufficiently unfettered to be in the nature of ownership. With all respect to the majority of the then court, we find it difficult to see how a power can be subject to control by the probate court, and exercisable only in what the trustee fairly concludes is in the interests of the trust and its beneficiaries as a whole, and at the same time be an ownership power.

The government's position, to be sound, must be that the trustee's powers are beyond the court's control. Under Massachusetts law, however, no amount of administrative discretion prevents judicial supervision of the trustee. Thus in Appeal of Davis, 1903, 183 Mass. 499, 67 N.E. 604, a trustee was given "full power to make purchases, investments and exchanges . . . in such manner as to them shall seem expedient; it being my intention to give my trustees . . . the same dominion and control over said trust property as I now have." In spite of this language, and in spite of their good faith, the court charged the trustees for failing sufficiently to diversify their investment portfolio.

The Massachusetts court has never varied from this broad rule of accountability, and has twice criticized *State Street* for its seeming departure. Boston Safe Deposit & Trust Co. v. Stone, 1965, 348 Mass. 345, 351, n.8, 203 N.E.2d 547; Old Colony Trust Co. v. Silliman, 1967, 352 Mass. 6, 8–9, 223 N.E.2d 504. . . . We make a further observation, which the court in *State Street* failed to note, that the provision in that trust (as in the case at bar) that the trustees could "do all things in relation to the Trust Fund which I, the Donor, could do if . . . the Trust had not been executed," is almost precisely the provision which did not protect the trustees from accountability in Appeal of Davis, supra.

We do not believe that trustee powers are to be more broadly construed for tax purposes than the probate court would construe them for administrative purposes. More basically, we agree with Judge Magruder's observation that nothing is "gained by lumping them together." State Street Trust Co. v. United States, supra, 263 F.2d at 642. We hold that no aggregation of purely administrative powers can meet the government's amorphous test of "sufficient dominion and control" so as to be equated with ownership.

This does not resolve taxpayer's difficulties under Article 4. Quite different considerations apply to distribution powers. Under them the trustee can, expressly, prefer one beneficiary over another. Furthermore, his freedom of choice may vary greatly, depending upon the terms of the individual trust. If there is an ascertainable standard, the trustee can be compelled to follow it.[15] If there is not, even though he is a fiduciary, it is not unreasonable to say that his retention of an unmeasurable freedom of choice is equivalent to retaining some of the incidents of ownership. Hence, under the cases, if there is an ascertainable standard the settlor-trustee's estate is not taxed, United States v. Powell, supra; Jennings v. Smith, supra; Estate of Budd, 1968, 49 T.C. 468; Estate of Pardee, 1967, 49 T.C. 140, but if there is not, it is taxed. Henslee v. Union Planters Nat'l Bank & Trust Co., 1949, 335 U.S. 595, 69 S. Ct. 290, 93 L. Ed. 259; Hurd v. Com'r, 1 Cir., 1947, 160 F.2d 610; Michigan Trust Co. v. Kavanagh, 6 Cir., 1960, 284 F.2d 502.

The trust provision which is uniformly held to provide an ascertainable standard is one which, though variously expressed, authorizes such distributions as may be needed to continue the beneficiary's accustomed way of life. Ithaca Trust Co. v. United States, 1929, 279 U.S. 151, 49 S. Ct. 291, 73 L. Ed. 647; cf. United States v. Commercial Nat'l Bank, 10 Cir., 1968, 404 F.2d 927, cert. denied 393 U.S. 1000, 89 S. Ct. 487, 21 L. Ed.2d 465; Blodget v. Delaney, 1 Cir., 1953, supra. On the other hand, if the trustee may go further, and has power to provide for the beneficiary's "happiness," Merchants Nat'l Bank v. Com'r of Internal Revenue, 1943, 320 U.S. 256, 64 S. Ct. 108, 88 L. Ed. 35, or "pleasure," Industrial Trust Co. v. Com'r of Internal Revenue, 1 Cir., 1945, 151 F.2d 592, cert. denied 327 U.S. 788, 66 S. Ct. 807, 90 L. Ed. 1014, or "use and benefit," Newton

---

[15] See, e.g., Old Colony Trust Co. v. Rodd, 1970 Mass. A.S. 25, 254 N.E.2d 886, trustee of trust to provide "comfortable support and maintenance," rebuked for "parsimonious" exercise of judgment.

Trust Co. v. Com'r of Internal Revenue, 1 Cir., 1947, 160 F.2d 175, or "reasonable requirement[s]," State Street Bank & Trust Co. v. United States, 1 Cir., 1963, 313 F.2d 29, the standard is so loose that the trustee is in effect uncontrolled.

In the case at bar the trustees could increase the life tenant's income "in case of sickness, or [if] desirable in view of changed circumstances." Alternatively, they could reduce it "for his best interests." "Sickness" presents no problem. Conceivably, providing for "changed circumstances" is roughly equivalent to maintaining the son's present standard of living. But see Hurd v. Com'r of Internal Revenue, supra. The unavoidable stumbling block is the trustees' right to accumulate income and add it to capital (which the son would never receive) when it is to the "best interests" of the son to do so. Additional payments to a beneficiary whenever in his "best interests" might seem to be too broad a standard in any event. In addition to the previous cases see Estate of Yawkey, 1949, 12 T.C. 1164, where the court said, at p. 1170,

> We cannot regard the language involved ["best interest"] as limiting the usual scope of a trustee's discretion. It must always be anticipated that trustees will act for the best interests of a trust beneficiary, and an exhortation to act "in the interests and for the welfare" of the beneficiary does not establish an external standard.

Power, however, to decrease or cut off a beneficiary's income when in his "best interests," is even more troublesome. When the beneficiary is the son, and the trustee the father, a particular purpose comes to mind, parental control through holding the purse strings. The father decides what conduct is to the "best interests" of the son, and if the son does not agree, he loses his allowance. Such a power has the plain indicia of ownership control. The alternative, that the son, because of other means, might not need this income, and would prefer to have it accumulate for his widow and children after his death, is no better. If the trustee has power to confer "happiness" on the son by generosity to someone else, this seems clearly an unascertainable standard. Cf. Merchants Nat'l Bank v. Com'r of Internal Revenue, supra, 320 U.S. at 261–263, 64 S. Ct. 108.

The case of Hays' Estate v. Com'r of Internal Revenue, 5 Cir., 1950, 181 F.2d 169, is contrary to our decision. The opinion is unsupported by either reasoning or authority, and we will not follow it. With the present settlor-trustee free to determine the standard himself, a finding of ownership control was warranted. To put it another way, the cost of holding onto the strings may prove to be a rope burn. State Street Bank & Trust Co. v. United States, supra.

Affirmed.

NOTES

1. *Power affecting time or manner of enjoyment.* I.R.C. § 2038 applies to "any power affecting the time or manner of enjoyment of property or its income, even though the identity of the beneficiary is not affected." Reg. § 20.2038–1(a). Thus, if a settlor creates an irrevocable inter vivos trust for the sole benefit of his minor child, and retains a fiduciary power to accumulate income or distribute corpus, the trust property is includible in the settlor's gross estate. See Lober v. United States, 346 U.S. 335 (1953).

Similarly, if a person creates a custodianship for a minor child under the Uniform Transfers to Minors Act and then dies while serving as custodian before the child reaches the age of majority, the custodianship property is includible in the gross estate under § 2038. See Rev. Rul. 59–357, 1959–2 C.B. 212; Estate of Prudowsky v. Commissioner, 465 F.2d 62 (7th Cir.1972).

2. *Power exercisable with consent of another person.* By its terms § 2038 applies to a power held by the decedent alone or "in conjunction with any other person." It is immaterial whether the other person has a substantial beneficial interest which would be adversely affected by the exercise of the power. Thus, for example, if a settlor creates an inter vivos trust, reserving a power of revocation exercisable only with the consent of the trustee and one of the beneficiaries, and then dies holding the reserved power, the trust property is includible in the settlor's gross estate. See Helvering v. City Bank Farmers Trust Co., 296 U.S. 85 (1935). What if the trust can be altered, amended, or terminated by another person but only with the settlor's consent? See Estate of Thorp, 164 F.2d 966 (3d Cir.1947), cert. denied, 333 U.S. 843 (1948); Rev. Rul. 70–513, 1970–2 C.B. 194.

Nevertheless, § 2038 does not apply to a power held by the decedent if the power is exercisable "only with the consent of all parties having an interest (vested or contingent) in the transferred property" and "adds nothing to the rights of the parties under local law." Reg. § 20.2038–1(a). This provision reflects the holding in Helvering v. Helmholz, 296 U.S. 93 (1935).

3. *Power exercisable solely by another person.* Section 2038 does not apply to "a power held solely by a person other than the decedent." Reg. § 20.2038–1(a). In some cases, however, a power held by another person may be attributed to the decedent. For example, if the decedent held "an unrestricted power to remove or discharge a trustee at any time and appoint himself as trustee," the decedent would be treated as holding the powers vested in the trustee. Id. Suppose that the decedent created a trust, naming a corporate trustee, and retained a power to remove the trustee and appoint another corporate trustee. What result? See Rev. Rul. 95–58, 1995–2 C.B. 191.

(ii) Transfers With Retained Life Interest

In Burnet v. Northern Trust Co., 283 U.S. 782 (1931), the Supreme Court held that the original postponed-possession-or-enjoyment provision did not reach an inter vivos trust in which the settlor had retained a life income interest. One day later, on March 3, 1931 Congress amended the estate tax statute to reverse the holding for transfers made after the date of enactment. In its current form, I.R.C. § 2036(a) provides:

> (a) **General rule.** The value of the gross estate shall include the value of the property to the extent of any interest therein of which the decedent has at any time made a transfer (except in case of a bona fide sale for an adequate and full consideration in money or money's worth), by trust or otherwise, under which he has retained for his life or for any period not ascertainable without reference to his death or for any period which does not in fact end before his death—
>
> > (1) the possession or enjoyment of, or the right to the income from, the property, or
> >
> > (2) the right, either alone or in conjunction with any person, to designate the persons who shall possess or enjoy the property or the income therefrom.

ESTATE OF RAPELJE V. COMMISSIONER
United States Tax Court, 1979.
73 T.C. 82.

DAWSON, JUDGE:

[In August 1969 the decedent transferred his personal residence in Saratoga Springs, New York, to his two daughters, Mrs. Mulligan and Mrs. Wright. Except for a vacation in Florida from November 1969 to May 1970, he continued to live in the house until his death in November 1973.]

The issue presented here is whether the value of decedent's residence must be included in his gross estate pursuant to section 2036. . . .

This section requires property to be included in the decedent's estate if he retained the actual possession or enjoyment thereof, even though he may have had no enforceable right to do so. Estate of Honigman v. Commissioner, 66 T.C. 1080, 1082 (1976); Estate of Linderme v. Commissioner, 52 T.C. 305, 308 (1969). Possession or enjoyment of gifted property is retained when there is an express or implied understanding to that effect among the parties at the time of transfer. Guynn v. United States, 437 F.2d 1148, 1150 (4th Cir.1971); Estate of Honigman v. Commissioner, supra at 1082; Estate of Hendry v. Commissioner, 62 T.C. 861, 872 (1974); Estate of Barlow v. Commissioner, 55 T.C. 666, 670 (1971).[16] The burden

---

[16] We note here that under sec. 2036 it is irrelevant whether the parties *intended* at the time of transfer that the decedent would retain possession and enjoyment *for his life*. The statute requires only that the decedent retain possession or enjoyment "for any period which does not *in fact* end before his death." See Estate of Honigman v. Commissioner, 66 T.C. 1080 (1976). Thus, even if the donees in the present case understood at the time of transfer that decedent would

is on the petitioner to disprove the existence of any implied agreement or understanding, and that burden is particularly onerous when intrafamily arrangements are involved. Skinner's Estate v. United States, 316 F.2d 517, 520 (3d Cir.1963); Estate of Hendry v. Commissioner, supra at 872; Estate of Kerdolff v. Commissioner, 57 T.C. 643, 648 (1972).

In the present case, there was no express agreement allowing decedent to retain possession and enjoyment of the home. Respondent, however, contends that the facts support an inference of an implied understanding between the decedent and his daughters whereby decedent was allowed to live in the house until he was able to locate a new home. Petitioners maintain that although such an understanding may have arisen after decedent suffered his stroke, there was no such agreement in existence at the time of the gift. [In July 1970, decedent suffered a stroke that left him paralyzed on his right side and unable to speak.] Based on our review of the record before us, we conclude that petitioners have failed to meet their burden of proving that a tacit agreement did not arise contemporaneously with the transfer.

In determining whether there was an implied understanding between the parties, all facts and circumstances surrounding the transfer and subsequent use of the property must be considered. The continued exclusive possession by the donor and the withholding of possession from the donee are particularly significant factors. Guynn v. United States, supra at 1150; compare Estate of Linderme v. Commissioner, supra at 309, with Estate of Gutchess v. Commissioner, 46 T.C. 554, 557 (1966). In the present case, the donor maintained almost exclusive occupancy of the residence until his death in 1973. The transfer took place in August 1969. Decedent continued to live there alone until September 1969. Sometime in September, Mrs. Mulligan's niece moved in with her husband and they stayed until January 1970. In November 1969, the decedent went to Florida and did not return until May 1970. From May 1970 until September 1971, the decedent lived alone at the residence. In September 1971, Mrs. Mulligan's daughter moved in and stayed for several months. Thereafter, the decedent was the sole occupant of the residence.

A plausible argument could be made that the donees were making indirect use of the property by allowing their relatives to stay there, particularly if they did so over the decedent's objection. There is nothing in the record, however, to support that proposition. Decedent may have been wholly indifferent to their use of the property, or he may even have invited them himself. Even if he had violently opposed the presence of the guests, that would only tend to show an intent by the donees to exercise

---

remain in the house only until he found a new home, there would still be inclusion under sec. 2036 because he retained possession or enjoyment of the property up to the time of his death.

dominion and control over the property, which is only one factor to be considered in deciding whether decedent retained possession pursuant to an implied agreement.

In spite of the donees' continued residence in their original houses after the gift, petitioners argue that the conduct of the parties subsequent to the transfer negates the existence of any implied agreement. For example, they contend that the primary purpose of decedent's 6–month sojourn in Florida soon after the transfer was to purchase a new house. We disagree. Although decedent did look at one house for sale in Fort Lauderdale, the record does not reveal any extensive house hunting activity. Moreover, the decedent had made identical winter trips to Florida every year for the past 10 years. Thus, we are not convinced that the decedent felt any compelling need to locate a new home on this particular visit.

Petitioners also maintain that Mrs. Mulligan intended to move into the residence in 1971 when her husband was due to retire. In anticipation of this event, the couple visited the home frequently on weekends and vacations and made some repairs. Mrs. Mulligan also notified her employer in Buffalo that she would be leaving in 1971. This planned move was abandoned, of course, when the decedent suffered his stroke. We think that Mrs. Mulligan did intend to move into the residence eventually, but the facts suggest to us that the move was implicitly conditioned on the successful conclusion of the decedent's search for a new home.

There are other facts which support an inference of an implied understanding between the parties. The decedent paid no rent to his daughters for the continued use of the property. Although Mrs. Wright did pay some utility bills relating to the property, the decedent continued to pay the real estate taxes. Neither daughter made any attempt to sell her own house. Nor did they ever attempt to sell or rent the residence prior to the decedent's death. The plain fact of the matter is that with the exception of the change in record title, the gift of the property did not effect any substantial changes in the relationship of the parties to the residence. Thus, we find that there was an implied understanding between the parties arising contemporaneously with the transfer whereby the decedent was allowed to retain possession or enjoyment of the residence for a period which did not in fact end before his death.

Accordingly, we hold that under section 2036 the value of the residence must be included in decedent's gross estate. . . .

NOTES

1. *Retained possession or enjoyment.* In the case of income-producing property, § 2036(a) treats a retained right to income from the property as equivalent to retained ownership of the underlying property. In the case of

property that does not produce income in the usual sense (e.g., a work of art), it is the decedent's retained "possession or enjoyment" of the property itself which causes inclusion in the gross estate.

2. *Amount includible.* Note that the amount included in the gross estate under § 2036(a) is not the value of the decedent's retained interest or right (which ordinarily expires at death) but rather the value of the underlying property in which the decedent retained the interest or right. The regulations explain as follows:

> If the decedent retained or reserved an interest or right with respect to all of the property transferred by him, the amount to be included in his gross estate under section 2036 is the value of the entire property, less only the value of any outstanding income interest which is not subject to the decedent's interest or right and which is actually being enjoyed by another person at the time of the decedent's death. [Reg. § 20.2036–1(a).]

Suppose a settlor creates an irrevocable trust to pay income to his spouse for life, then to the settlor for life (if he survives his spouse), with remainder at the death of the survivor to their issue then living. If the settlor survives his spouse, the entire trust property is includible in his gross estate under § 2036(a). How much is includible if he dies before his spouse? See Marks v. Higgins, 213 F.2d 884 (2d Cir.1954).

3. *Discharge of legal obligations.* For purposes of § 2036(a), a decedent is treated as having retained possession and enjoyment of property "to the extent that the use, possession, right to the income, or other enjoyment is to be applied toward the discharge of a legal obligation of the decedent, or otherwise for his pecuniary benefit." Reg. § 20.2036–1(b)(2). Suppose that a settlor creates an irrevocable inter vivos trust for the benefit of his minor children, authorizing the trustee to distribute income for the children's support, care, welfare, and education. If the settlor dies before the children reach the age of majority, is the trust property wholly or partially includible in his gross estate? See Estate of Gokey v. Commissioner, 72 T.C. 721 (1979), aff'd on this issue, 735 F.2d 1367 (7th Cir.1984). Does it matter whether the trustee has discretion to make or withhold distributions? See Estate of Mitchell v. Commissioner, 55 T.C. 576 (1970).

4. *Retention for life.* Section 2036(a) applies where the decedent retained the requisite interest or right for life "or for any period not ascertainable without reference to his death or for any period which does not in fact end before his death." To illustrate the application of the quoted phrase, consider the following situations.

(a) An irrevocable inter vivos trust provides for income to be paid to the settlor in semi-annual installments for life, except for income accruing after the last semi-annual payment up to the settlor's death, which is to be paid to the next income beneficiary.

(b) Settlor, age 70, creates an irrevocable inter vivos trust for her issue, retaining the right to receive the income from the trust for 10 years. Settlor dies five years later.

See H.R. Rep. No. 708, 72d Cong., 1st Sess. (1932), reprinted in 1939–1 (pt. 2) C.B. 457, 490–91; Reg. § 20.2036–1(b)(1).

5. *Retained powers over income.* Concerning the scope of a power "to designate the persons who shall possess or enjoy the property or the income therefrom" under § 2036(a)(2), the regulations provide:

> With respect to such a power, it is immaterial (i) whether the power was exercisable alone or only in conjunction with another person or persons, whether or not having an adverse interest; (ii) in what capacity the power was exercisable by the decedent or by another person or persons in conjunction with the decedent; and (iii) whether the exercise of the power was subject to a contingency beyond the decedent's control which did not occur before his death (e.g., the death of another person during the decedent's lifetime). The phrase, however, does not include a power over the transferred property itself which does not affect the enjoyment of the income received or earned during the decedent's life. (See, however, section 2038 for the inclusion of property in the gross estate on account of such a power.) Nor does the phrase apply to a power held solely by a person other than the decedent. But, for example, if the decedent reserved the unrestricted power to remove or discharge a trustee at any time and appoint himself as trustee, the decedent is considered as having the powers of the trustee. [Reg. § 20.2036–1(b)(3).]

6. *Retained right to vote stock.* For purposes of § 2036(a)(1), "the retention of the right to vote (directly or indirectly) shares of stock of a controlled corporation shall be considered to be a retention of the enjoyment of transferred property." I.R.C. § 2036(b) (applicable where the decedent or certain related parties held at least 20 percent of the combined voting power of all classes of stock). This provision was added by the 1976 Act to overrule United States v. Byrum, 408 U.S. 125 (1972), in which the Supreme Court ruled that § 2036(a) did not reach a decedent's lifetime transfers of closely held stock subject to retained voting rights.

UNITED STATES V. ESTATE OF GRACE

Supreme Court of the United States, 1969.
395 U.S. 316, 89 S.Ct. 1730, 23 L.Ed.2d 332.

MR. JUSTICE MARSHALL delivered the opinion of the Court.

This case involves the application of [the predecessor of I.R.C. § 2036(a)] to a so-called "reciprocal trust" situation. After Joseph P. Grace's death in 1950, the Commissioner of Internal Revenue determined that the value of a trust created by his wife was includible in his gross estate. A deficiency was assessed and paid, and, after denial of a claim for a refund, this refund suit was brought. The Court of Claims, with two judges dissenting, ruled that the value of the trust was not includible in decedent's estate under [the predecessor of I.R.C. § 2036(a)] and entered judgment for respondent. Estate of Grace v. United States, 183 Ct. Cl. 745, 393 F.2d 939 (1968). We granted certiorari because of an alleged conflict between the decision below and certain decisions in the courts of appeals and because of the importance of the issue presented to the administration of the federal estate tax laws. 393 U.S. 975 (1968). We reverse.

I.

Decedent was a very wealthy man at the time of his marriage to the late Janet Grace in 1908. Janet Grace had no wealth or property of her own, but, between 1908 and 1931, decedent transferred to her a large amount of personal and real property, including the family's Long Island estate. Decedent retained effective control over the family's business affairs, including the property transferred to his wife. She took no interest and no part in business affairs and relied upon her husband's judgment. Whenever some formal action was required regarding property in her name, decedent would have the appropriate instrument prepared and she would execute it.

On December 15, 1931, decedent executed a trust instrument, hereinafter called the Joseph Grace trust. Named as trustees were decedent, his nephew, and a third party. The trustees were directed to pay the income of the trust to Janet Grace during her lifetime, and to pay to her any part of the principal which a majority of the trustees might deem advisable. Janet was given the power to designate, by will or deed, the manner in which the trust estate remaining at her death was to be distributed among decedent and their children. The trust properties included securities and real estate interests.

On December 30, 1931, Janet Grace executed a trust instrument, hereinafter called the Janet Grace trust, which was virtually identical to the Joseph Grace trust.[17] The trust properties included the family estate and corporate securities, all of which had been transferred to her by decedent in preceding years.

The trust instruments were prepared by one of decedent's employees in accordance with a plan devised by decedent to create additional trusts before the advent of a new gift tax expected to be enacted the next year. Decedent selected the properties to be included in each trust. Janet Grace, acting in accordance with this plan, executed her trust instrument at decedent's request.

---

[17] That is, the Janet Grace trust included provisions for Joseph Grace which were similar to those made for Janet Grace in the Joseph Grace trust.—EDS.

Janet Grace died in 1937. The Joseph Grace trust terminated at her death. Her estate's federal estate tax return disclosed the Janet Grace trust and reported it as a nontaxable transfer by Janet Grace. The Commissioner asserted that the Janet and Joseph Grace trusts were "reciprocal" and asserted a deficiency to the extent of mutual value. Compromises on unrelated issues resulted in 55% of the smaller of the two trusts, the Janet Grace trust, being included in her gross estate.

Joseph Grace died in 1950. The federal estate tax return disclosed both trusts. The Joseph Grace trust was reported as a nontaxable transfer and the Janet Grace trust was reported as a trust under which decedent held a limited power of appointment. Neither trust was included in decedent's gross estate.

The Commissioner determined that the Joseph and Janet Grace trusts were "reciprocal" and included the amount of the Janet Grace trust in decedent's gross estate. A deficiency in the amount of $363,500.97, plus interest, was assessed and paid.

II.

[The predecessor of § 2036(a)] provided that certain transferred property in which a decedent retained a life interest was to be included in his gross estate. The general purpose of the statute was to include in a decedent's gross estate transfers that are essentially testamentary—i.e., transfers which leave the transferor a significant interest in or control over the property transferred during his lifetime. See Commissioner v. Estate of Church, 335 U.S. 632, 643–644 (1949).

The doctrine of reciprocal trusts was formulated in response to attempts to draft instruments which seemingly avoid the literal terms of [the predecessor of § 2036(a)], while still leaving the decedent the lifetime enjoyment of his property. The doctrine dates from Lehman v. Commissioner, 109 F.2d 99 (C.A. 2d Cir.), cert. denied, 310 U.S. 637 (1940). In *Lehman*, decedent and his brother owned equal shares in certain stocks and bonds. Each brother placed his interest in trust for the other's benefit for life, with remainder to the life tenant's issue. Each brother also gave the other the right to withdraw $150,000 of the principal. If the brothers had each reserved the right to withdraw $150,000 from the trust that each had created, the trusts would have been includible in their gross estates as interests of which each had made a transfer with a power to revoke. When one of the brothers died, his estate argued that neither trust was includible because the decedent did not have a power over a trust which he had created.

The Second Circuit disagreed. That court ruled that the effect of the transfers was the same as if the decedent had transferred his stock in trust for himself, remainder to his issue, and had reserved the right to withdraw $150,000. The court reasoned:

> The fact that the trusts were reciprocated or "crossed" is a trifle, quite lacking in practical or legal significance. . . . The law searches out the reality and is not concerned with the form. 109 F.2d, at 100.]

The court ruled that the decisive point was that each brother caused the other to make a transfer by establishing his own trust.

The doctrine of reciprocal trusts has been applied numerous times since the *Lehman* decision. . . . The present case is, however, this Court's first examination of the doctrine.

The Court of Claims was divided over the requirements for application of the doctrine to the situation of this case. Relying on some language in *Lehman* and certain other courts of appeals' decisions, the majority held that the crucial factor was whether the decedent had established his trust as consideration for the establishment of the trust of which he was a beneficiary. The court ruled that decedent had not established his trust as a *quid pro quo* for the Janet Grace trust, and that Janet Grace had not established her trust in exchange for the Joseph Grace trust. Rather, the trusts were found to be part of an established pattern of family giving, with neither party desiring to obtain property from the other. Indeed, the court found that Janet Grace had created her trust because decedent requested that she do so. It therefore found the reciprocal trust doctrine inapplicable.

The court recognized that certain cases had established a slightly different test for reciprocity. Those cases inferred consideration from the establishment of two similar trusts at about the same time. The court held that any inference of consideration was rebutted by the evidence in the case, particularly the lack of any evidence of an estate tax avoidance motive on the part of the Graces. In contrast, the dissent felt that the majority's approach placed entirely too much weight on subjective intent. Once it was established that the trusts were interrelated, the dissent felt that the subjective intent of the parties in establishing the trusts should become irrelevant. The relevant factor was whether the trusts created by the settlors placed each other in approximately the same objective economic position as they would have been in if each had created his own trust with himself, rather than the other, as life beneficiary.

We agree with the dissent that the approach of the Court of Claims majority places too much emphasis on the subjective intent of the parties in creating the trusts and for that reason hinders proper application of the federal estate tax laws. It is true that there is language in *Lehman* and other cases that would seem to support the majority's approach. It is also true that the results in some of those cases arguably support the decision below. Nevertheless, we think that these cases are not in accord with this Court's prior decisions interpreting related provisions of the federal estate tax laws.

Emphasis on the subjective intent of the parties in creating the trusts, particularly when those parties are members of the same family unit, creates substantial obstacles to the proper application of the federal estate tax laws. As this Court said in Estate of Spiegel v. Commissioner, 335 U.S. 701, 705–706 (1949):

> Any requirement . . . [of] a post-death attempt to probe the settlor's thoughts in regard to the transfer, would partially impair the effectiveness of . . . [the predecessor of § 2036(a)] as an instrument to frustrate estate tax evasions.

We agree that "the taxability of a trust corpus . . . does not hinge on a settlor's motives, but depends on the nature and operative effect of the trust transfer." Id., at 705. . . .

We think these observations have particular weight when applied to the reciprocal trust situation. First, inquiries into subjective intent, especially in intrafamily transfers, are particularly perilous. The present case illustrates that it is, practically speaking, impossible to determine after the death of the parties what they had in mind in creating trusts over 30 years earlier. Second, there is a high probability that such a trust arrangement was indeed created for tax-avoidance purposes. And, even if there was no estate-tax-avoidance motive, the settlor in a very real and objective sense did retain an economic interest while purporting to give away his property.[18] Finally, it is unrealistic to assume that the settlors of the trusts, usually members of one family unit, will have created their trusts as a bargained-for exchange for the other trust. "Consideration," in the traditional legal sense, simply does not normally enter into such intrafamily transfers.[19]

For these reasons, we hold that application of the reciprocal trust doctrine is not dependent upon a finding that each trust was created as a *quid pro quo* for the other. Such a "consideration" requirement necessarily involves a difficult inquiry into the subjective intent of the settlors. Nor do we think it necessary to prove the existence of a tax-avoidance motive.

---

[18] For example, in the present case decedent ostensibly devised the trust plan to avoid an imminent federal gift tax. Instead of establishing trusts for the present benefit of his children, he chose an arrangement under which he and his wife retained present enjoyment of the property and under which the property would pass to their children without imposition of either estate or gift tax.

[19] The present case is probably typical in this regard. Janet Grace created her trust because decedent requested that she do so; it was in no real sense a bargained-for *quid pro quo* for his trust. . . .

As we have said above, standards of this sort, which rely on subjective factors, are rarely workable under the federal estate tax laws. Rather, we hold that application of the reciprocal trust doctrine requires only that the trusts be interrelated, and that the arrangement, to the extent of mutual value, leaves the settlors in approximately the same economic position as they would have been in had they created trusts naming themselves as life beneficiaries.[20]

Applying this test to the present case, we think it clear that the value of the Janet Grace trust fund must be included in decedent's estate for federal estate tax purposes. It is undisputed that the two trusts are interrelated. They are substantially identical in terms and were created at approximately the same time. Indeed, they were part of a single transaction designed and carried out by decedent. It is also clear that the transfers in trust left each party, to the extent of mutual value, in the same objective economic position as before. Indeed, it appears, as would be expected in transfers between husband and wife, that the effective position of each party *vis-à-vis* the property did not change at all. It is no answer that the transferred properties were different in character. For purposes of the estate tax, we think that economic value is the only workable criterion. Joseph Grace's estate remained undiminished to the extent of the value of his wife's trust and the value of his estate must accordingly be increased by the value of that trust.

The judgment of the Court of Claims is reversed and the case is remanded for further proceedings consistent with this opinion.

It is so ordered.

MR. JUSTICE STEWART took no part in the consideration or decision of this case.

MR. JUSTICE DOUGLAS, dissenting.

The object of a reciprocal trust, as I understand it, is for each settlor to rid himself of all taxable power over the corpus by exchanging taxable powers with the other settlor. Yet Joseph P. Grace and his wife did not exchange taxable powers. Each retained a sufficient power over the corpus to require the inclusion of the corpus in his or her taxable estate. Each settlor, as one of the three trustees, reserved the right to alter the trust by paying to the chief beneficiary "any amounts of the principal of the said trust, up to and including the whole thereof, which the said Trus-

---

[20] We do not mean to say that the existence of "consideration," in the traditional legal sense of a bargained-for exchange, can never be relevant. In certain cases, inquiries into the settlor's reasons for creating the trusts may be helpful in establishing the requisite link between the two trusts. We only hold that a finding of a bargained-for consideration is not necessary to establish reciprocity.

tees or a majority of them may at any time or from time to time deem advisable." I have quoted from Janet Grace's trust. But an almost identical provision is in the trust of Joseph P. Grace.

I would conclude from the existence of this reserved power that the corpus of the Janet Grace trust was includible in her estate for purposes of the estate tax. Lober v. United States, 346 U.S. 335.

That is to say the use of a reciprocal trust device to aid the avoidance of an estate tax is simply not presented by this case.

I would dismiss the petition as improvidently granted.

(iii) Transfers Taking Effect at Death

I.R.C. § 2037 is the direct descendant of the original postponed-possession-or-enjoyment provision. The original language remained substantially unchanged until 1949, when it was completely rewritten. Further revisions occurred in 1954, but no significant changes have been made since then. The operative language of § 2037(a) provides:

> **(a) General rule.** The value of the gross estate shall include the value of all property to the extent of any interest therein of which the decedent has at any time . . . made a transfer (except in case of a bona fide sale for an adequate and full consideration in money or money's worth), by trust or otherwise, if—
>
>> (1) possession or enjoyment of the property can, through ownership of such interest, be obtained only by surviving the decedent, and
>>
>> (2) the decedent has retained a reversionary interest in the property (but in the case of a transfer made before October 8, 1949, only if such reversionary interest arose by the express terms of the instrument of transfer), and the value of such reversionary interest immediately before the death of the decedent exceeds 5 percent of the value of such property.

For purposes of this provision, the value of a reversionary interest immediately before the death of the decedent is to be determined, without regard to the fact of the decedent's death, by "usual methods of valuation, including the use of tables of mortality and actuarial principles," as prescribed in the regulations. I.R.C. § 2037(b).

The type of transfer at which § 2037 is aimed is illustrated by Helvering v. Hallock, 309 U.S. 106 (1940). There, a settlor created an inter vivos trust to pay income to his wife for life, with corpus payable to himself if he survived her, but if not to his children. To one unversed in the law of future interests, it would seem reasonably clear that the transfer to the children was "intended to take effect in possession or enjoyment at or after [the settlor's] death." Some of the Supreme Court's earlier decisions, however, indicated that the estate tax consequences might depend on whether the children's interests were regarded under state property law as subject to a "condition precedent" or a "condition subsequent." In *Hallock* the Supreme Court repudiated its earlier decisions and established that the value of the children's interests were indeed includible in the settlor's gross estate, regardless of the "elusive and subtle casuistries" of classification under state property law. Although the *Hallock* decision breathed new life into the postponed-possession-or-enjoyment provision, it left several questions unanswered, as described in Bittker, The *Church* and *Spiegel* Cases: Section 811(c) Gets a New Lease on Life, 58 Yale L.J. 825, 828 (1949):

> (1) Is the transfer taxable if the settlor's reversionary interest is not expressly reserved, as in the *Hallock* case, but arises "by operation of law"? This occurs, for example, when the settlor provides that the remaindermen must be living at his death to receive the corpus, but neglects to name an alternate taker. Consequently, a "resulting trust" (a reversionary interest) may arise in favor of the settlor.

> (2) Is the transfer taxable no matter how slim the settlor's chance of reacquiring the property? In the *Hallock* case, the corpus would revert to him if he survived his wife. But what if the return of the corpus to the settlor depends upon an unlikely contingency, such as his survivorship of children and grandchildren?

> (3) In what sense must the transfer have been "intended" to take effect in possession or enjoyment at or after death? Suppose, for example, the reversionary interest, especially if remote, exists only because the drafter of the trust instrument (without the settlor's knowledge) either overlooked the possibility of a resulting trust or, out of an excess of caution, provided for return of the corpus upon the failure of the intended disposition?

In Estate of Spiegel v. Commissioner, 335 U.S. 701 (1949), the Supreme Court held that property was includible in the gross estate regardless of intent, whether the reversionary interest was expressly reserved or arose by operation of law, and no matter how remote the likelihood that the property would revert to the decedent. Indeed, in *Spiegel*, at the moment before his death the decedent had 16 chances out of 100,000 of getting the property and the value of his reversionary interest was $85; the cost of retaining that tiny interest proved to be around $450,000 in additional estate taxes.

In 1949, after the *Spiegel* decision, Congress finally repealed the postponed-possession-and-enjoyment provision and replaced it with a new provision which (as amended in 1954) now appears as § 2037.

NOTES

1. *Transfers taking effect at death.* Consider the applicability of § 2037 in the following situations (taken from Reg. § 20.2037–1(e), Examples 1–4):

     (a) Decedent created an irrevocable inter vivos trust to pay income to his spouse for life, with corpus at her death to his issue then living, or if there are none to decedent or his estate.

     (b) Decedent created an irrevocable inter vivos trust to accumulate income during his life, with corpus and accumulated income to be paid at his death to his issue then living, or if there are none to *X* Charity.

     (c) Decedent created an irrevocable inter vivos trust to pay income to his spouse for life, with corpus at her death to decedent, or, if he is not then living, to his child or the child's estate. Assume that the decedent is survived by his spouse and by his child.

     (d) Decedent created an irrevocable inter vivos trust to pay income to his spouse for life, with principal at her death to his child, or, if the child is not then living, to decedent, or, if decedent is not then living, to *X* Charity. Assume that the decedent is survived by his spouse and by his child (and that *X* Charity is in existence).

2. *Value of reversionary interest.* Under § 2037, the reversionary interest is valued immediately *before* death; thus, it has value even if the decedent's death extinguishes it. (By contrast, under § 2033, a future interest is valued *at* death and is includible only if it is not extinguished by death.) For purposes of the 5–percent test, "the value of the reversionary interest is compared with the value of the transferred property, including interests therein which are not dependent on survivorship of the decedent." Reg. § 20.2037–1(c)(4).

3. *Includible amount.* The amount included in the gross estate under § 2037 is not the value of the reversionary interest (which may have been extinguished by death) but rather the value of the other beneficiaries' interests which can be possessed or enjoyed "only by surviving the decedent." See Reg. § 20.2037–1(d).

(iv) Transfers Within Three Years of Death

As noted at p. 1007 supra, the original contemplation-of-death provision was rewritten in 1976 to require inclusion in the gross estate of transfers made within three years of death as well as the amount of any gift taxes paid by the decedent with respect to such transfers. The 1981 Act repealed the 3–year rule for all but a few enumerated types of transfers, while leaving the "gross-up" provision in effect. The current version of I.R.C. § 2035 provides, in relevant part, as follows:

(a) Inclusion of certain property in gross estate. If—

(1) the decedent made a transfer (by trust or otherwise) of an interest in any property, or relinquished a power with respect to any property, during the 3–year period ending on the date of the decedent's death, and

(2) the value of such property (or an interest therein) would have been included in the decedent's gross estate under section 2036, 2037, 2038, or 2042 if such transferred interest or relinquished power had been retained by the decedent on the date of his death,

the value of the gross estate shall include the value of any property (or interest therein) which would have been so included.

(b) Inclusion of gift tax on gifts made during 3 years before decedent's death. The amount of the gross estate (determined without regard to this subsection) shall be increased by the amount of any [gift] tax paid . . . by the decedent or his estate on any gift made by the decedent or his spouse during the 3–year period ending on the date of the decedent's death. . . .

(d) Exception. Subsection (a) shall not apply to any bona fide sale for an adequate and full consideration in money or money's worth. . . .

NOTES

1. *Included transfers.* Section 2035(a) operates in conjunction with four enumerated provisions (§§ 2036–2038 and 2042) to reach certain transfers which would otherwise escape inclusion in the gross estate. For example, if the decedent once held incidents of ownership in a life insurance policy on his own life but relinquished them within three years before death, the proceeds are fully includible in the gross estate, just as if he had held them until death (see Note, supra p. 1006). Given the unification of the estate and gift taxes, what purpose does § 2035(a) serve?

The 3–year rule of § 2035(a) also applies where the decedent initially transferred property subject to a retained "string" of the type described in §§ 2036–2038 and then cut the string within three years of death. For example, if the decedent at age 50 transferred property subject to a retained life estate, then at age 70 released the remaining life estate and died within three years thereafter, the full value of the underlying property is includible in the gross estate. Should the result be different if the decedent received money's-worth consideration equal to the value of the remaining life estate in exchange for releasing the life estate at age 70? See United States v. Allen, 293 F.2d 916 (10th Cir.), cert. denied, 368 U.S. 944 (1961); for decisions involving a similar issue under § 2036(a), see Gradow v. United States, 897 F.2d 516 (Fed.Cir. 1990); Estate of D'Ambrosio v. Commissioner, 101 F.3d 309 (3d Cir.1996), cert. denied, 520 U.S. 1230 (1997); Wheeler v. United States, 116 F.3d 749 (5th Cir.1997).

2. *Gift tax gross-up.* Section 2035(b) requires that the gross estate be "grossed up" by the amount of gift taxes paid by the decedent on gifts made within three years of death, regardless of whether the underlying gift is also drawn back into the gross estate. This provision puts deathbed gifts more or less on a par with testamentary transfers by neutralizing the benefit of the tax-exclusive gift tax base.

Suppose that *H* made a gift of $100,000 to his wife *W*, and *W* immediately used the funds to create an irrevocable life insurance trust for the couple's children. *W* reported the creation of the trust as a taxable gift and filed a return showing a gift tax liability of $40,000. *H* transferred an additional $40,000 to *W*, who immediately used the funds to pay the gift tax. *H* dies less than three years after the date of the gift. What amount, if any, is includible in *H*'s gross estate? See Brown v. United States, 329 F.3d 664 (9th Cir.), cert. denied, 540 U.S. 878 (2003).

f. Powers of Appointment

Unlike §§ 2035–2038, which are concerned with rights reserved by a decedent in connection with lifetime transfers of his or her own property, I.R.C. § 2041 is concerned with powers of appointment created in the decedent by another person with respect to property originally owned by the latter.

In order to appreciate the importance of powers of appointment in estate taxation one must remember that, prior to the enactment of the tax on generation-skipping transfers, the shift in beneficial enjoyment from a life tenant to a remainderman at the expiration of the life estate was not (except for situations covered by § 2036) a taxable event. Thus, if *A* bequeathed property outright to her child *B* and *B* in turn bequeathed it to her child *C*, the property was (and still is) taxable in the estates of both *A* and *B*. If, however, *A* left the property to *B* for life, with remainder to *C*, the property would be taxed only in *A*'s estate and not in *B*'s estate. Furthermore, the obvious non-tax drawbacks to such a disposition could be eliminated if *A* gave *B* a life estate plus a testamentary power to appoint the property among members of the next generation. Could *B* hold such a power without incurring a second round of estate tax? The answer turned on whether the holder of a power was regarded for tax purposes as the "owner" of the property subject to the power or merely as the "agent" of the person who created the power.

From an early date, the federal estate tax has departed to some extent from the agency theory by taxing the *exercise* of a general power (including one exercisable only by will). For a long time, however, the agency theory prevailed to the extent that mere *possession* at death of a general power of appointment was not taxable. Today, except as to powers created on or before October 21, 1942, the estate tax no longer distinguishes the possession of a power from its exercise, and the estate of a decedent who dies holding a general power of appointment, whether or not exercised, is subject to tax on all property subject to the power.

On the other hand, non-general powers (those not exercisable in favor of the decedent, his estate, his creditors, or the creditors of his estate) are not taxed (except in special circumstances) even if exercised. As to them, the agency theory persists.

Section 2041 provides in relevant part as follows:

> **(a) In general.** The value of the gross estate shall include the value of all property— . . .

> > **(2) Powers created after October 21, 1942.** To the extent of any property with respect to which the decedent has at the time of his death a general power of appointment created after October 21, 1942, or with respect to which the decedent has at any time exercised or released such a power of appointment by a disposition which is of such nature that if it were a transfer of property owned by the decedent, such property would be includible in the decedent's gross estate under sections 2035 to 2038, inclusive. . . .

> > **(3) Creation of another power in certain cases.** To the extent of any property with respect to which the decedent—

> > > (A) by will, or

> > > (B) by a disposition which is of such nature that if it were a transfer of property owned by the decedent such property would be includible in the decedent's gross estate under section 2035, 2036, or 2037,

> > exercises a power of appointment created after October 21, 1942, by creating another power of appointment which under the applicable local law can be validly exercised so as to postpone the vesting of any estate or interest in such property, or suspend the absolute ownership or power of alienation of such property, for a period ascertainable without regard to the date of the creation of the first power.

> **(b) Definitions.** For purposes of subsection (a)—

> > **(1) General power of appointment.** The term "general power of appointment" means a power which is exercisable in favor of the dece-

dent, his estate, his creditors, or the creditors of his estate; except that—

(A) A power to consume, invade, or appropriate property for the benefit of the decedent which is limited by an ascertainable standard relating to the health, education, support, or maintenance of the decedent shall not be deemed a general power of appointment. . . .

(C) In the case of a power of appointment created after October 21, 1942, which is exercisable by the decedent only in conjunction with another person—

(i) If the power is not exercisable by the decedent except in conjunction with the creator of the power—such power shall not be deemed a general power of appointment.

(ii) If the power is not exercisable by the decedent except in conjunction with a person having a substantial interest in the property, subject to the power, which is adverse to exercise of the power in favor of the decedent—such power shall not be deemed a general power of appointment. For the purposes of this clause a person who, after the death of the decedent, may be possessed of a power of appointment (with respect to the property subject to the decedent's power) which he may exercise in his own favor shall be deemed as having an interest in the property and such interest shall be deemed adverse to such exercise of the decedent's power.

(iii) If (after the application of clauses (i) and (ii)) the power is a general power of appointment and is exercisable in favor of such other person—such power shall be deemed a general power of appointment only in respect of a fractional part of the property subject to such power, such part to be determined by dividing the value of such property by the number of such persons (including the decedent) in favor of whom such power is exercisable.

For purposes of clauses (ii) and (iii), a power shall be deemed to be exercisable in favor of a person if it is exercisable in favor of such person, his estate, his creditors, or the creditors of his estate.

(2) **Lapse of Power.**—The lapse of a power of appointment created after October 21, 1942, during the life of the individual possessing the power shall be considered a release of such power. The preceding sentence shall apply with respect to the lapse of powers during any calendar year only to the extent that the property, which could have been appointed by exercise of such lapsed powers, exceeded in value, at the time of such lapse, the greater of the following amounts:

(A) $5,000, or

(B) 5 percent of the aggregate value, at the time of such lapse, of the assets out of which, or the proceeds of which, the exercise of the lapsed powers could have been satisfied. . . .

The term "power of appointment," for estate and gift tax purposes, does not include reserved powers but does encompass powers created by another person, usually in connection with a transfer in trust, which permit the holder of the power to affect the beneficial enjoyment of the underlying property. The regulations offer the following examples:

For example, if a trust instrument provides that the beneficiary may appropriate or consume the principal of the trust, the power to consume or appropriate is a power of appointment. Similarly, a power given to a decedent to affect the beneficial enjoyment of trust property or its income by altering, amending, or revoking the trust instrument or terminating the trust is a power of appointment. . . . A power in a donee to remove or discharge a trustee and appoint himself may be a power of appointment. For example, if under the terms of a trust instrument, the trustee or his successor has the power to appoint the principal of the trust for the benefit of individuals including himself, and the decedent has the unrestricted power to remove or discharge the trustee at any time and appoint any other person including himself, the decedent is considered as having a power of appointment. However, the decedent is not considered to have a power of appointment if he only had the power to appoint a successor, including himself, under limited conditions which did not exist at the time of his death, without an accompanying unrestricted power of removal. Similarly, a power to amend only the administrative provisions of a trust instrument, which cannot substantially affect the beneficial enjoyment of the trust property or income, is not a power of appointment. The mere power of management, investment, custody of assets, or the power to allocate receipts and disbursements as between income and principal, exercisable in a fiduciary capacity, whereby the holder has no power to enlarge or shift any of the beneficial interests therein except as an incidental consequence of the discharge of such fiduciary duties is not a power of appointment. [Reg. § 20.2041–1(b)(1).]

The holder of a power of appointment can exercise it, release it, or allow it to lapse (e.g., by dying without exercising the power). In the case of a post-October 21, 1942 general power, any of these events may give rise to a gift or estate tax (or both, in some cases). If the holder of a general power exercises it in favor of another person or releases it during life, the exercise or release is treated for gift tax purposes as a transfer of the underlying property. See I.R.C. § 2514, which mirrors the provisions of § 2041 for gift tax purposes. A lifetime exercise or release may also give rise to an estate tax under § 2041(a)(2), if the disposition is "of such a nature that if it were a transfer of property owned by the decedent, such property would be includible in the decedent's gross estate under sections 2035 to 2038." For example, suppose that the decedent, who had a general power over trust property as well as a life income interest in the trust, released the power but continued to receive trust income until death. In addition to gift tax on the release of the power, the trust property would be drawn back into the gross estate at death (just as if the decedent had made a transfer of his or her own property subject to § 2036). Finally, if the holder retained the power until death, the underlying property is includible in the gross estate whether the holder exercised it or not.

The statutory provisions concerning lapse (§§ 2041(b)(2) and 2514(e)) come into play only where a power lapses by its terms during the holder's life (e.g., a power to withdraw property from a trust before a specified age, or during a limited period of time following a particular event). The lapse of a power during the holder's life is treated as a release of the power, but only to the extent that the property subject to the lapsed power for the calendar year exceeds the greater of $5,000 or 5 percent of the value of the property subject to the power. This special "5-or-5" provision makes it possible to set up a trust in which the income beneficiary holds a non-cumulative power to withdraw the greater of $5,000 or 5 percent of the trust corpus in any year without any adverse gift or estate tax consequences (except in the year of death) to the holder of the power.

NOTES

1. *Powers limited by ascertainable standard.* Section 2041(b)(1)(A) provides that a power which is limited by an "ascertainable standard relating to the health, education, support, or maintenance of the decedent" is not a general power of appointment. The regulations offer the following guidance:

> A power is limited by such a standard if the extent of the holder's duty to exercise and not to exercise the power is reasonably measurable in terms of his needs for health, education, or support (or any combination of them). As used in this subparagraph, the words "support" and "maintenance" are synonymous and their meaning is not limited to the bare necessities of life. A power to use property for the comfort, welfare, or happiness of the holder of the power is not limited by the requisite standard. Examples of powers which are limited by the requisite standard are powers exercisable for the holder's "support," "support in reasonable comfort," "maintenance in health and reasonable comfort," "support in his accustomed manner of living," "education, including college and professional education," "health," and "medical, dental, hospital and nursing expenses and expenses of invalidism." [Reg. § 20.2041–1(c)(2).]

2. *Powers of appointment and estate planning.* Consider how you might draft a power of appointment which provides maximum flexibility without subjecting the underlying property to gift or estate tax in the holder's hands. If the holder of a power can be given so much control over property without adverse tax consequences, why would anyone intentionally create a general power?

3. *Successive powers.* In certain cases the exercise of a non-general power may constitute a taxable event. See I.R.C. §§ 2041(a)(3) and 2514(d). These provisions are aimed at situations in which a chain of successive non-general powers might be used to postpone the vesting of interests (or suspend ownership or alienability) for an indefinite period. For example, suppose that under the will of her deceased parent *A*, *B* holds a non-general power of appointment, which she exercises to create a new non-general power in her child *C* (born after *A*'s death). Although the creation of *C*'s new power would be void under the common law version of the Rule against Perpetuities (see supra p. 944), it would be valid in a jurisdiction (e.g., Delaware) where the perpetuities period runs from the date of a non-general power's exercise rather than its creation. See, e.g., Del. Code tit. 25, § 501. To make sure that such powers do not escape gift and estate tax indefinitely, the statute treats *B*'s exercise of her power as a transfer for estate and gift tax purposes.[21] In a jurisdiction (e.g., Alaska or South Dakota) which permits perpetual trusts, can the estate and gift taxes be avoided indefinitely through the use of non-general powers of appointment?

2. DEDUCTIONS

To arrive at the taxable estate, the estate tax statute provides deductions from the gross estate for the following items: funeral and administration expenses and indebtedness (I.R.C. § 2053); losses (I.R.C. § 2054); charitable transfers (I.R.C. § 2055); transfers to the decedent's surviving spouse (I.R.C. § 2056); and state death taxes (I.R.C. § 2058).[22] The deductions for expenses and indebtedness, losses, and state death taxes reflect the principle that the estate tax is imposed on the net amount passing from the decedent to beneficiaries. The charitable and marital deductions in effect allow a decedent to leave an unlimited amount of property free of tax to eligible charitable organizations or to a surviving spouse, as long as such transfers are made in qualifying form.

---

[21] Note that *B* is taxed even if she exercises her power to create a presently-exercisable general power in *C* (which is valid under the common law version of the Rule against Perpetuities). Why should this be so?

[22] The deduction for state death taxes in § 2058 replaces the limited credit formerly allowed under § 2011. While the credit was in effect, almost all states had "pick-up" death taxes geared to the allowable amount of the credit. The pick-up taxes did not impose any additional net tax burden, since they generated a dollar-for-dollar credit against the federal estate tax; in effect, they merely shifted a portion of the estate tax revenue from the federal government to the states. With the repeal of the credit, the pick-up taxes have automatically disappeared as well, and many states have moved to enact independent death taxes.

The estate tax is imposed on the taxable estate under the cumulative computation provided in I.R.C. § 2001(b) (see supra p. 975). The resulting estate tax is then reduced by the "unified credit" (I.R.C. § 2010) and by other available credits, as noted supra at p. 976.

a. Charitable Deduction

From an early date the estate tax statute has allowed a deduction for transfers made by the decedent to charitable organizations or for charitable purposes. The operative provisions appear in I.R.C. § 2055(a):

> **(a) In general.** For purposes of the tax imposed by section 2001, the value of the taxable estate shall be determined by deducting from the value of the gross estate the amount of all bequests, legacies, devises, or transfers—
>
> (1) to or for the use of the United States, any State, any political subdivision thereof, or the District of Columbia, for exclusively public purposes;
>
> (2) to or for the use of any corporation organized and operated exclusively for religious, charitable, scientific, literary, or educational purposes, . . . no part of the net earnings of which inures to the benefit of any private stockholder or individual, which is not disqualified for tax exemption under section 501(c)(3) by reason of attempting to influence legislation, and which does not participate in, or intervene in (including the publishing or distributing of statements), any political campaign on behalf of (or in opposition to) any candidate for public office;
>
> (3) to a trustee or trustees, or a fraternal society, order, or association operating under the lodge system, but only if such contributions or gifts are to be used by such trustee or trustees, or by such fraternal society, order, or association, exclusively for religious, charitable, scientific, literary, or educational purposes, . . . such trust, fraternal society, order, or association would not be disqualified for tax exemption under section 501(c)(3) by reason of attempting to influence legislation, and such trustee or trustees, or such fraternal society, order, or association, does not participate in, or intervene in (including the publishing or distributing of statements), any political campaign on behalf of (or in opposition to) any candidate for public office; or
>
> (4) to or for the use of any veterans' organization incorporated by Act of Congress, or of its departments or local chapters or posts, no part of the net earnings of which inures to the benefit of any private shareholder or individual. . . .

The corresponding gift tax provisions appear in I.R.C. § 2522.

If the organization or purpose for which a "charitable" contribution is made satisfies the statutory criteria, there is no limit on the amount which may be given. Outright gifts seldom give rise to serious difficulties.

If the decedent attempts to combine private and public purposes, however, several problems may arise.

One area which has proved especially troublesome over the years involves gifts of charitable remainders following income interests in private beneficiaries. For many years, the actuarial value of the charitable remainder was deductible if the remainder was unconditional (e.g., to *A* for life, remainder to *X* Charity). If the remainder was subject to a condition, either precedent or subsequent, the deduction was allowed only if the possibility that the charitable interest might fail was so remote as to be negligible—it was not enough that the value of the charity's interest could be determined actuarially. See Commissioner v. Estate of Sternberger, 348 U.S. 187 (1955) (no deduction for remainder contingent on death without issue of 27–year-old woman who was unmarried and childless).[23]

The Tax Reform Act of 1969 added a completely new set of rules governing the charitable deduction for "split-interest" transfers made after 1969. The statute (I.R.C. § 2055(e)(2)) now provides (with limited exceptions) that *no* deduction is allowed for the value of a charitable remainder unless the transfer takes the form of a "charitable remainder annuity trust" or a "charitable remainder unitrust" (see I.R.C. § 664(d)) or a "pooled income fund" (see I.R.C. § 642(c)(5)).

In very general terms, a charitable remainder trust is a trust which provides for distributions (payable at least annually) to one or more noncharitable beneficiaries for life or a term of up to 20 years, followed by a charitable remainder interest. The remainder interest must be irrevocable and not subject to any power of invasion (except for the required periodic distributions to noncharitable beneficiaries). The value of the remainder interest must initially be at least 10 percent of the net fair market value of the underlying trust property. The periodic distributions to

---

[23] In this context, unlike that of the Rule against Perpetuities, the remoteness of the possibility is open to proof; a woman past the age of childbearing is not presumed to be fertile. See City Bank Farmers' Trust Co. v. United States, 74 F.2d 692 (2d Cir.1935). In Hamilton Nat'l Bank of Chattanooga v. United States, 236 F.Supp. 1005, 1016–17 (D.Tenn.1965), aff'd, 367 F.2d 554 (6th Cir.1966), the court stated:

Upon the death of his father, W.R. Long, Jr., was a 54 year old bachelor, living alone in a trailer in El Paso, Texas. He had been married in 1928 but shortly thereafter was divorced and had never remarried. He had never had children and was unknown to have had any association of any kind with the opposite sex since 1928. He was described as being very dirty, unkempt, and offensive in his personal habits, and was described as an "odd character" and as a "hobo." His only occupation appears to have been the collecting of junked automobile batteries. His medical history reflected that he was a heavy cigarette smoker, had a persistent cough and was obese with very poor dietary habits. Between 1956 and 1959 he had received medical treatment for a congenital back condition described as spina bifida, a stomach ulcer which had resulted in internal bleeding, and had been examined for blood in his urine from a cause then unknown. He was described as a very uncooperative patient and given to self-medication and home remedies, including the use of creosote for his cough and lung condition. The Court is of the opinion that upon this state of the record the evidence was sufficient to present a jury issue as to the negligible possibility of W.R. Long, Jr., having issue.

noncharitable beneficiaries may be either in the form of an annuity (i.e., a fixed amount equal to at least 5 percent but not more than 50 percent of the initial value of the trust property) or a unitrust interest (i.e., a fixed percentage—at least 5 percent but not more than 50 percent—of the value of the trust property, valued annually).

The mirror image of a charitable remainder trust is a so-called "charitable lead" trust in which the charitable interest takes the form of an annuity or unitrust interest preceding a remainder interest in noncharitable beneficiaries.

A pooled income fund is a trust or other fund maintained by a charitable organization as a vehicle for contributions of remainder interests following life income interests in the donor or other beneficiaries. The charitable remainder interest must be irrevocable; the property contributed by each donor must be commingled with similar contributions made by others; and each income beneficiary must receive a proportionate share of the annual income earned by the fund.

The statutory provisions and regulations are very detailed and strictly enforced. For more on split-interest transfers, see 4 Bittker & Lokken, Federal Taxation of Income, Estates and Gifts ¶ 82.1.2 (3d ed. 2001).

b. Marital Deduction

(i) Background

The estate tax marital deduction was enacted in 1948, along with a parallel gift tax deduction and the split-income provision in the income tax, for the purpose of equalizing the federal tax treatment of married couples in separate property and community property states. In its original form, the estate tax marital deduction provided tax-free treatment for certain transfers to a decedent's surviving spouse, up to a limit of one-half the "adjusted gross estate" (i.e., the gross estate reduced by deductible expenses, indebtedness and losses under I.R.C. §§ 2053 and 2054).

The 1976 Act increased the maximum marital deduction to equal the greater of $250,000 or one-half the adjusted gross estate; the 1981 Act went further and eliminated the quantitative limit altogether. The 1981 Act also made significant changes in the original qualitative restrictions on the types of transfers which qualify for the marital deduction. Taken together, these changes reflect a view of the married couple as a "taxable unit": each spouse can transfer an unlimited amount of property to the other without any adverse gift or estate tax consequences; it is only when property leaves the marital unit that it becomes subject to tax.

I.R.C. § 2056 provides, in relevant part, as follows:

(a) Allowance of marital deduction. For purposes of the tax imposed by section 2001, the value of the taxable estate shall, except as limited by subsection (b), be determined by deducting from the value of the gross estate an amount equal to the value of any interest in property which passes or has passed from the decedent to his surviving spouse, but only to the extent that such interest is included in determining the value of the gross estate.

(b) Limitation in the case of life estate or other terminable interest.

(1) General rule. Where, on the lapse of time, on the occurrence of an event or contingency, or on the failure of an event or contingency to occur, an interest passing to the surviving spouse will terminate or fail, no deduction shall be allowed under this section with respect to such interest—

    (A) if an interest in such property passes or has passed (for less than an adequate and full consideration in money or money's worth) from the decedent to any person other than such surviving spouse (or the estate of such spouse); and

    (B) if by reason of such passing such person (or his heirs or assigns) may possess or enjoy any part of such property after such termination or failure of the interest so passing to the surviving spouse.
    . . .

(3) Interest of spouse conditional on survival for limited period. For purposes of this subsection, an interest passing to the surviving spouse shall not be considered as an interest which will terminate or fail on the death of such spouse if—

    (A) such death will cause a termination or failure of such interest only if it occurs within a period not exceeding 6 months after the decedent's death, or only if it occurs as a result of a common disaster resulting in the death of the decedent and the surviving spouse, or only if it occurs in the case of either such event; and

    (B) such termination or failure does not in fact occur. . . .

(5) Life estate with power of appointment in surviving spouse. In the case of an interest in property passing from the decedent, if his surviving spouse is entitled for life to all the income from the entire interest, or all the income from a specific portion thereof, payable annually or at more frequent intervals, with power in the surviving spouse to appoint the entire interest, or such specific portion (exercisable in favor of such surviving spouse, or of the estate of such surviving spouse, or in favor of either, whether or not in each case the power is exercisable in favor of others), and with no power in any other person to appoint any part of the interest, or such specific portion, to any person other than the surviving spouse—

(A) the interest or such portion thereof so passing shall, for purposes of subsection (a), be considered as passing to the surviving spouse, and

(B) no part of the interest so passing shall, for purposes of paragraph (1)(A), be considered as passing to any person other than the surviving spouse.

This paragraph shall apply only if such power in the surviving spouse to appoint the entire interest, or such specific portion thereof, whether exercisable by will or during life, is exercisable by such spouse alone and in all events. . . .

(7) Election with respect to life estate for surviving spouse.

(A) In general. In the case of qualified terminable interest property—

(i) for purposes of subsection (a), such property shall be treated as passing to the surviving spouse, and

(ii) for purposes of paragraph (1)(A), no part of such property shall be treated as passing to any person other than the surviving spouse.

(B) Qualified terminable interest property defined. For purposes of this paragraph—

(i) In general. The term "qualified terminable interest property" means property—

(I) which passes from the decedent,

(II) in which the surviving spouse has a qualifying income interest for life, and

(III) to which an election under this paragraph applies.

(ii) Qualifying income interest for life. The surviving spouse has a qualifying income interest for life if—

(I) the surviving spouse is entitled to all the income from the property, payable annually or at more frequent intervals, or has a usufruct interest for life in the property, and

(II) no person has a power to appoint any part of the property to any person other than the surviving spouse.

Subclause (II) shall not apply to a power exercisable only at or after the death of the surviving spouse. . . .

(iii) Property includes interest therein. The term "property" includes an interest in property.

(iv) Specific portion treated as separate property. A specific portion of property shall be treated as separate property.

(v) Election. An election under this paragraph with respect to any property shall be made by the executor on the return of tax imposed by section 2001. Such an election, once made, shall be irrevocable. . . .

(ii) The Terminable Interest Rule and Its Exceptions

In the years since their original enactment, the marital deduction provisions have given rise to a large amount of litigation. Most of the litigation concerns the so-called "terminable interest rule" of § 2056(b)(1), which denies the deduction if three conditions are met: (1) the spouse's interest may terminate or fail upon the occurrence (or non-occurrence) of some event or condition; (2) an interest in the same property passes from the decedent to another beneficiary; and (3) the other beneficiary's interest may become possessory after the termination of the spouse's interest. The simplest example of a nondeductible terminable interest is a bequest to the surviving spouse "for life" with remainder over to another beneficiary. As a result of the terminable interest rule, such a bequest, without more, does not qualify for the marital deduction—the full value of the property, including the value of the spouse's life estate, would be taxable. The same result would hold in the case of a bequest to the spouse "for ten years," or "until remarriage."

The terminable interest rule is premised on the notion that the marital deduction should be available only if the surviving spouse will ultimately become the beneficial owner of the property passing from the decedent. (Note that the rule does not apply if the spouse or the spouse's estate is certain to take the property after an intervening income interest in another beneficiary. If the decedent leaves property to *A* for life with remainder at *A*'s death to the spouse or the spouse's estate, the value of the remainder qualifies for the marital deduction.) Thus, in theory at least, the terminable interest rule ensures that any property which escapes tax in the decedent's estate by virtue of the marital deduction will eventually become subject to tax in the hands of the surviving spouse. (Is this necessarily so? Consider the possibility that the surviving spouse may make substantial tax-free lifetime gifts, or remarry and pass on property to a new spouse.)

The terminable interest rule can produce harsh results. In the leading case of Jackson v. United States, 376 U.S. 503 (1964), the Supreme Court held that no marital deduction was allowable for amounts paid to a surviving spouse as a statutory support allowance (see supra p. 154), because under applicable state law the allowance would have terminated upon the spouse's death or remarriage (which did not in fact occur) within two years after the decedent's death. The Court noted that the terminable interest rule applies "as of the time of the testator's death rather than at a later time when the condition imposed may be satisfied," and observed:

> Petitioners contend, however, that the sole purpose of the terminable-interest provisions of the Code is to assure that interests deducted from the estate of the deceased spouse will not also escape taxation in the estate of the survivor. This argument leads to the conclusion that since it is now clear that unless consumed or given away during Mrs. Richards' life, the entire $72,000 will be taxed to her estate, it should not be included in her husband's. But as we have already seen, there is no provision in the Code for deducting all terminable interests which become nonterminable at a later date and therefore taxable in the estate of the surviving spouse if not consumed or transferred. . . .

> We are mindful that the general goal of the marital deduction provisions was to achieve uniformity of federal estate tax impact between those States with community property laws and those without them. But the device of the marital deduction which Congress chose to achieve uniformity was knowingly hedged with limitations, including the terminable-interest rule. These provisions may be imperfect devices to achieve the desired end, but they are the means which Congress chose. [376 U.S. at 509–10.]

To mitigate the rigors of the terminable interest rule, the statute provides several exceptions of crucial significance for the drafting of wills and trusts. Prior to the 1981 Act, the most widely used exception to the terminable interest rule was § 2056(b)(5), which requires that the surviving spouse receive a life income interest coupled with a general power of appointment exercisable "alone and in all events" in favor of the spouse or the spouse's estate. Such a disposition is commonly made in trust, but a legal life estate coupled with the requisite power of appointment also suffices. In either case, the surviving spouse receives beneficial rights which may be viewed as an approximate equivalent of outright ownership, thereby supporting a marital deduction for the full value of the underlying property. Moreover, the spouse's general power of appointment ensures that the marital deduction in the decedent's estate will eventually be matched by a corresponding inclusion in the spouse's gift or estate tax base.

NOTES

1. *Joint and mutual wills.* As discussed in Chapter 5, Section C, a joint will or mutual wills executed by a married couple may impose a contractual obligation on the surviving spouse to dispose of property in a particular way. Such a contractual restriction, if enforceable under applicable state law, may jeopardize the availability of the marital deduction. See Estate of Opal v. Commissioner, 450 F.2d 1085 (2d Cir.1971); see generally Hess, The Federal Transfer Tax Consequences of Joint and Mutual Wills, 24 Real Prop. Prob. & Tr. J. 469 (1990).

2. *Six-month survivorship requirement.* A bequest "to my spouse, but if she fails to survive me by 30 days to my issue then living" would ordinarily constitute a nondeductible terminable interest because it is not certain, as of the moment of the decedent's death, whether the spouse will survive for 30 days. The special rule of § 2056(b)(3) allows such a bequest to qualify for the marital deduction—provided, of course, that the spouse actually survives for the required period. Suppose the bequest is "to my spouse provided she survives the distribution of my estate." Is the spouse's interest a terminable interest? Does it qualify for the marital deduction? See Estate of Bond v. Commissioner, 104 T.C. 652 (1995).

3. *Life income interest.* To satisfy the requirement that the surviving spouse be "entitled for life to all the income," care must be taken to avoid giving the trustee any discretion to accumulate income; indeed, any limitation on the spouse's right to income may be hazardous. If the trustee is directed to apply income for the spouse's "support, welfare and comfort" or to maintain the spouse's "accustomed standard of living," does this satisfy the income requirement of § 2056(b)(5)? See Estate of Mittelman v. Commissioner, 522 F.2d 132 (D.C.Cir.1975); Estate of Nicholson v. Commissioner, 94 T.C. 666 (1990).

4. *"Estate trust."* Decedent's will establishes a trust which provides for discretionary distributions to the surviving spouse during life, with any corpus and accumulated income remaining at death to be paid to the spouse's estate. Such an "estate trust" may qualify for the marital deduction even though the spouse is not entitled to annual distributions of income. Why? See Rev. Rul. 68–554, 1968–2 C.B. 412.

5. *General power exercisable "alone and in all events."* Section 2056(b)(5) requires that the surviving spouse be given a general power of appointment which is exercisable by the spouse "alone and in all events." A simple power to invade or consume principal for the spouse's support, comfort or personal use may be inadequate. See Estate of Carpenter v. Commissioner, 52 F.3d 1266 (4th Cir.1995) (power of sale "in case my wife wants cash for her personal health, needs, trips or anything relating to my wife"); Estate of Foster v. Commissioner, 725 F.2d 201 (2d Cir.1984) (power to consume limited by

good faith standard). Might such a power nevertheless constitute a taxable general power of appointment under § 2041?

––––––––––––

As noted above, the general scheme of the marital deduction is to allow a deduction for property passing to the surviving spouse where that property—if retained by the spouse until his or her death—will necessarily be taxable in the spouse's estate. Prior to the 1981 Act, this meant that a transfer could qualify for the marital deduction only if the spouse had unfettered control over the ultimate disposition of the property. This requirement was not unduly burdensome where both spouses were in general agreement about how to pass on the family property to the next generation. However, even in first marriages that is not always the case and in many second marriages—especially if one or both of the parties have children from a prior marriage—there is a potential conflict of interest between the older and newer families. Not infrequently, a testator wishes to give a life income interest in property to his or her spouse while making sure that the property will ultimately go to the testator's own descendants at the death of the surviving spouse. Under prior law, such a testator was confronted with the delicate question of how to take full advantage of the marital deduction and still ensure that the spouse would not divert the property to the spouse's own family—or friends—instead of the testator's. The answer was that there was no way to be certain of accomplishing both objectives. Unless the surviving spouse was given an unrestricted power—at least by will—to dispose of the property, the marital deduction would not be available. If the testator gave the spouse sufficient control to obtain the marital deduction, the spouse would be completely free to dispose of the property as he or she saw fit.

The 1981 Act added the "qualified terminable interest property" (QTIP) provisions of § 2056(b)(7), which make the marital deduction available even if the surviving spouse has no control over the ultimate disposition of the property. Today, the testator can obtain the marital deduction simply by giving the surviving spouse a life income interest, without any power to dispose of the underlying property. In effect, the QTIP provisions represent a legal fiction by which the spouse's life income interest—the quintessential terminable interest—is deemed *for tax purposes* to represent complete ownership of the property. The full value of the underlying property qualifies for the marital deduction in the decedent's estate, and—in accordance with the general scheme mentioned above—the value of the same property is eventually subject to estate tax at the spouse's death (I.R.C. § 2044) or to gift tax if the spouse disposes of the income interest before death (I.R.C. § 2519).

NOTES

1. *Qualifying income interest for life.* Section 2056(b)(7) requires that the surviving spouse receive a "qualifying income interest for life." The required income interest is defined in much the same way as under § 2056(b)(5) (see Note 3, supra p. 1041). Suppose that the "stub" income accruing between the last distribution date and the spouse's death is payable to the remainder beneficiary rather than to the spouse's estate. Does the spouse have a qualifying income interest for life? See Estate of Shelfer v. Commissioner, 86 F.3d 1045 (11th Cir.1996); Reg. § 20.2056(b)–7(d)(4).

In addition, "no person"—not even the spouse—may have "a power to appoint any part of the property to any person other than the surviving spouse" during the spouse's life. I.R.C. § 2056(b)(7)(B)(ii). Suppose that a testator gave a life income interest to the surviving spouse, with a gift over to another beneficiary if the executor failed to elect QTIP treatment. Does this amount to a power in the executor to appoint the income interest to a person other than the spouse? See Estate of Clack v. Commissioner, 106 T.C. 131 (1996); Reg. § 20.2056(b)–7(d)(3).

2. *QTIP election.* An attractive feature of the QTIP provisions—for estate planners and their clients—is that the marital deduction is available, in whole or in part, at the election of the decedent's executor. Balancing the competing interests of the spouse and other beneficiaries, however, may present serious difficulties for the executor. See Ascher, The Quandary of Executors Who Are Asked to Plan the Estates of the Dead: The Qualified Terminable Interest Property Election, 63 N.C. L. Rev. 1 (1984).

3. *Another perspective.* According to the legislative history, the QTIP provisions were intended to spare the decedent from being "forced to choose between surrendering control of the entire estate to avoid imposition of estate tax at his death or reducing his tax benefits at his death to insure inheritance by the children." Allowing the decedent to obtain a marital deduction without giving up control over the ultimate disposition of property was justified on the grounds "that the tax laws should be neutral and that tax consequences should not control an individual's disposition of property." H.R. Rep. No. 201, 97th Cong., 1st Sess. (1981), reprinted in 1981–2 C.B. 352, 378.

From the surviving spouse's perspective, the QTIP provisions may be seen as offering an inducement (i.e., the marital deduction) to testators to limit the surviving spouse to a life income interest. See Gerzog, The Marital Deduction QTIP Provisions: Illogical and Degrading to Women, 5 UCLA Women's L.J. 301 (1995) (arguing that the QTIP provisions "encourage husbands to transfer less than a full property interest to their wives").

(iii) Planning Considerations

Using the unlimited marital deduction, a married couple can easily arrange to avoid incurring any estate tax at the death of the first spouse, but it is not always advisable to do so. Whether it makes sense to take advantage of the marital deduction at all, and if so, to what extent, will depend on the circumstances of the particular case. Consider how the marital deduction might be used in the following cases, assuming that H and W are married, that neither of them makes any lifetime gifts, and that H dies first:

> (1) H has property worth $6 million and W has nothing;

> (2) H has property worth $6 million and W has property of equal value;

> (3) H has property worth $6 million and W has property worth $12 million.

In each case, to avoid wasting H's unified credit, the standard estate planning approach is to make sure that H has a taxable estate at least equal to the exemption equivalent (see supra p. 974), which in turn implies a ceiling on the amount of property that H should leave to W in deductible form. (If H wants to give W more, how might the transfer be structured so as to avoid a marital deduction in H's estate and inclusion in W's estate?)

Under a progressive tax rate schedule, it appears that the overall tax burden can be minimized—if this is the primary goal—by equalizing the spouses' respective estates (e.g., through deductible gifts from the richer spouse to the poorer spouse), so that neither ends up in a higher marginal tax bracket than the other. However, a strategy of estate equalization—which must be implemented no later than the death of the first spouse—requires a good deal of guesswork about future events which cannot be predicted with confidence: How long will the surviving spouse live? Will the value of the survivor's property go up or down over time? Will the survivor acquire substantial additional property through personal effort, astute investment, inheritance, or blind luck? Will the survivor run up large expenses for support or medical care? Will the survivor make substantial tax-free gifts during life? Will Congress make further changes in tax rates and exemptions? Perhaps, in view of these imponderables, it is not surprising that many couples forgo the potential tax benefits of estate equalization and settle instead for a strategy of tax deferral, i.e., leaving just enough property to the surviving spouse to produce a zero estate tax in the first spouse's estate.

In drafting a will or trust, it is common practice to define the size of the marital bequest by means of a formula clause, which may be phrased either in terms of an amount of property (a pecuniary clause) or a fractional share of the estate (a fractional share clause). This allows the drafter to specify the size of the marital bequest in terms of the desired tax result, despite the inevitable uncertainties concerning the size and composition of the estate at the time of the testator's death. The following is an example of a pecuniary marital bequest:

> If my spouse survives me, I give to my spouse an amount equal to the minimum marital deduction necessary to eliminate (or reduce as far as possible) the federal estate tax on my estate, after taking into account all other property passing to my spouse under this will or outside this will that is includible in my federal gross estate and qualifies for the federal marital deduction, and after taking into account the federal unified credit.

Another variation involves the establishment of a "credit shelter trust" to use up any available unified credit, followed by a gift of the residuary estate to the surviving spouse. The choice among various types of formula clauses, and the drafting of particular clauses, involve a host of federal income, estate, gift, and GST tax issues as well as considerations of estate and trust administration under state law.

For general discussions of the use of the marital deduction in estate planning, see Kurtz, Marital Deduction Estate Planning Under the Economic Recovery Tax Act of 1981: Opportunities Exist But Watch the Pitfalls, 34 Rutgers L. Rev. 591 (1982); Dobris, Marital Deduction Estate Planning: Variations on a Classic Theme, 20 S. Diego L. Rev. 801 (1983); Llewellyn, Estate Planning for the Married Couple, 28 Vill. L. Rev. 491 (1983).

NOTES

1. *Portability of exemption.* Beginning in 2011, if one spouse dies without using all of his or her exemption equivalent, the unused amount may be used by the surviving spouse, in addition to his or her own exemption equivalent, if the decedent's executor so elects on a timely filed estate tax return. I.R.C. § 2010(c). This "portability" feature provides considerable flexibility in tax planning for married couples and reduces the need for the decedent to make full use of his or her exemption equivalent. Note that the portability provision requires a timely filed estate tax return. How likely is it that this requirement will be met in the case of an estate worth less than $5 million that otherwise would not have to file a return? Is it possible for a person who has been married more than once to accumulate unused exemption equivalents from multiple predeceased spouses? See I.R.C. § 2010(c)(4) (defining "deceased spousal unused exclusion amount"). Why is portability available only to married couples? Should a decedent's unused exemption equivalent be freely transferable?

2. *Qualified disclaimers.* A qualified disclaimer may prove useful in salvaging a defective marital trust provision, for example, where the drafter inadvertently included a power to invade trust corpus for the benefit of a per-

son other than the surviving spouse. A qualified disclaimer may also permit the surviving spouse to fine-tune the amount of the marital deduction after the death of the first spouse. In Estate of Rolin v. Commissioner, 588 F.2d 368 (2d Cir.1978), a wife died four months after her husband, who had created a marital deduction trust for her benefit. The wife's estate was substantially larger than the husband's, and the court approved a disclaimer (made on behalf of the wife by her executors) of her interest in the trust, resulting in a net estate tax saving of around $64,000.

3. *Reformation.* Some courts readily reform trust instruments to cure drafting errors affecting the marital deduction. In Pond v. Pond, 678 N.E.2d 1321 (Mass.1997), the drafter of an inter vivos trust neglected to include any provisions for distributions of income to the surviving spouse after the settlor's death, but indicated that the trust was intended to be eligible for a QTIP election under § 2056(b)(7). The court approved a reformation of the trust to give the surviving spouse not only a qualifying income interest for life but also a discretionary interest in corpus. In such cases, the state court's order determines the property rights of the litigants under state law. May the federal government—which ordinarily does not participate in the state court proceedings—look behind the state court order and recharacterize the transaction for federal tax purposes? See Commissioner v. Estate of Bosch, 387 U.S. 456 (1967); Bennett v. Commissioner, 100 T.C. 42 (1993). See Caron, The Role of State Court Decisions in Federal Tax Litigation: *Bosch, Erie,* and Beyond, 71 Or. L. Rev. 781 (1992); Wolfman, *Bosch,* Its Implications and Aftermath: The Effect of State Court Adjudications on Federal Tax Litigation, 3 Inst. on Est. Plan. ch. 2 (1969).

4. *Taxes payable from marital share.* If property passes to the surviving spouse in a manner qualifying for the marital deduction, but such property is burdened by liability for death taxes, § 2056(b)(4) requires a corresponding reduction in the allowable marital deduction. For this reason, it is common practice to include a tax apportionment clause exonerating the property passing to the spouse from liability for death taxes. If the surviving spouse claims an elective share, the burden of death taxes is generally determined under state law. See Kahn, The Federal Estate Tax Burden Borne by a Dissenting Widow, 64 Mich. L. Rev. 1499 (1966).

3. ESTATE TAX APPORTIONMENT

Although Congress could have enacted a comprehensive scheme for apportioning liability for the federal estate tax among the various recipients of property passing from the decedent, it has not done so. The federal estate tax statute provides that the tax "shall be paid by the executor," but in general leaves the ultimate burden of the tax to be determined under state law. I.R.C. § 2002.

Under the traditional rule, the estate tax, like administration expenses and debts of the decedent, was payable entirely from the share of the residuary beneficiaries—often the decedent's surviving spouse or issue. To alleviate the resulting hardship, most states today by statute or judicial decision have adopted some form of "equitable apportionment." In the absence of a contrary provision in the decedent's will, most states require that all beneficiaries bear a proportionate share of the taxes attributable to their respective interests. Some states, however, provide for apportionment only in the case of property passing outside the will, with the result that taxes attributable to probate assets remain payable from the residuary estate.

Many states have enacted one version or another of the Uniform Estate Tax Apportionment Act, which was initially promulgated in 1958 and was subsequently revised in 1964 and 2003 in response to changes in tax laws and estate planning practices. Broadly speaking, the uniform act provides a rule of equitable apportionment for federal and state estate taxes (but not state inheritance or gift taxes), so that the burden of the tax falls on the beneficiaries of the taxable estate in proportion to the value of their interests. Because property qualifying for a marital or charitable deduction does not give rise to any estate tax burden, the benefit of those deductions inures to the recipients of such property. In the case of a transfer involving successive beneficial interests (e.g., a life estate followed by a remainder), any resulting tax is generally charged to the corpus of the property without apportionment, even if this reduces the amount of a deduction that would otherwise be allowable (e.g., in the case of a charitable remainder trust). The statutory rules are default rules which can be overridden if the decedent directs a different method of apportionment. For a discussion of recent revisions to the uniform act, see Kahn, The 2003 Revised Uniform Estate Tax Apportionment Act, 38 Real Prop. Prob. & Tr. J. 613 (2004).

Federal law gives the decedent's personal representative the right to recover the amount of federal estate tax attributable to certain property from the recipient of such property. The federal right of recovery applies only in the case of life insurance proceeds (I.R.C. § 2206), property subject to a general power of appointment (I.R.C. § 2207), qualified terminable interest property upon disposition by the surviving spouse (I.R.C. § 2207A), and property in which the decedent retained a life estate (I.R.C. § 2207B). In each case, the right of recovery can be overridden by a contrary direction in the decedent's will.

In drafting a tax apportionment clause, it is important to specify which taxes are covered as well as which property or beneficiaries are to be exonerated and how the tax burden is to be apportioned among the remaining property or beneficiaries. For more on tax apportionment clauses, see Death Tax Clauses in Wills and Trusts: Discussion and Sample Clauses, 19 Real Prop. Prob. & Tr. J. 495 (1984).

D. THE GENERATION–SKIPPING TRANSFER TAX

1. OVERVIEW

For many years, the shift of beneficial enjoyment from an income beneficiary to a remainderman was not treated as a taxable event. As a result, it was possible to shelter dynastic wealth from estate and gift taxes for substantial periods of time by setting up long-term trusts for successive generations of beneficiaries, e.g., income to the settlor's children for their lives, with remainder to their issue. The only limit on such "generation-skipping" transfers was the Rule against Perpetuities, which could readily provide tax immunity for a period of 90 to 100 years. Moreover, the tax provisions concerning powers of appointment allowed the income beneficiaries to have substantial control over the underlying property without any exposure to estate or gift taxes (see supra pp. 1028–1033).

The 1976 Act supplemented the estate and gift taxes with a separate tax on generation-skipping transfers, which was intended to be "substantially equivalent to the estate tax which would have been imposed if the property had been actually transferred outright to each successive generation." H.R. Rep. No. 1380, 94th Cong., 2d Sess. (1976), reprinted in 1976–3 C.B. 735, 781. The original version of the tax, however, attracted intense criticism from many quarters, and the 1986 Act replaced it with a completely revised GST tax. Although this is not the place for a detailed exploration of the current GST tax, the major features of the tax deserve some attention.

2. TAXABLE EVENTS

In general, the GST tax is aimed at gratuitous transfers which shift beneficial enjoyment of property to beneficiaries at least two generations younger than the transferor without attracting a gift or estate tax at the level of the intervening generation. The basic premise is that persons with substantial means should not be able to avoid wealth transfer taxes by creating long-term trusts which spread beneficial enjoyment over several generations or by transferring property directly to remote generations: property should be subject to tax as it passes from one generation to the next. The GST tax is imposed on every "generation-skipping transfer." I.R.C. § 2601. There are three types of generation-skipping transfers: a "direct skip," a "taxable termination," and a "taxable distribution." I.R.C. § 2611(a). Each of these taxable events involves a transfer of property from an individual in whose hands the property was subject to gift or estate tax (the "transferor") to a beneficiary two or more generations younger than the transferor (a "skip person").

In general, a *direct skip* is "a transfer subject to [gift or estate tax] of an interest in property to a skip person." I.R.C. § 2612(c)(1). For example, if *A* dies survived by her child *B* and leaves a bequest directly to *B*'s child *C*, the bequest is a direct skip which attracts a GST tax (in addition to the estate tax) at *A*'s death; the result would be similar in the case of a lifetime gift. A transfer in trust may also constitute a direct skip, if all of the beneficiaries who are currently entitled or permitted to receive distributions of income or corpus from the trust are skip persons. Thus, if *A* creates a testamentary or inter vivos trust which bypasses *B* and provides benefits exclusively for *C* and *C*'s issue, the creation of the trust constitutes a direct skip subject to GST tax. In each case, the GST tax stands in for the additional gift or estate tax that would have been imposed if the property had passed through *B*'s hands on its way from *A* to the ultimate beneficiaries. (The result is different, however, if *B* is already dead at the time of the transfer. In that case, by virtue of a special rule, *C* moves up one generation and is no longer treated as a skip person for GST purposes. I.R.C. § 2651(e)(1).)

By definition, taxable terminations and taxable distributions involve property held in trust. In general, a *taxable termination* is "the termination (by death, lapse of time, release of power, or otherwise) of an interest in property held in a trust," unless "immediately after such termination, a non-skip person has an interest in such property" or "at no time after such termination may a distribution (including distributions on termination) be made from such trust to a skip person." I.R.C. § 2612(a)(1).[24] A *taxable distribution* is "any distribution from a trust to a skip person (other than a taxable termination or a direct skip)." I.R.C. § 2612(b). To illustrate these provisions, consider a discretionary trust created by *A* to distribute income and corpus to her child *B* and *B*'s issue, with remainder at *B*'s death to *B*'s issue then living. No GST tax is imposed on the creation of the trust because at that time *B* (who is not a skip person) is a permissible current income beneficiary; hence, the creation of the trust does not constitute a direct skip, and distributions to *B* do not constitute taxable distributions. At *B*'s death, however, the termination of *B*'s interest constitutes a taxable termination which attracts a GST tax. (If *B* had a surviving sibling who was permitted to receive distributions of income or corpus after *B*'s death, the taxable termination would be deferred until the sibling's death, when all of the remaining beneficiaries would be skip persons.) Furthermore, if the trustee distributes income or corpus to any of *B*'s issue while *B* is still living, each such distribution will constitute a taxable distribution subject to GST tax.

---

[24] Note that, for GST tax purposes, a person has an "interest" in a trust if he or she is currently entitled or permitted to receive distributions of income or corpus from the trust. I.R.C. § 2652(c)(1).

Over the course of a long-term trust, the GST tax may apply several times as beneficial interests shift from one generation to the next. For example, suppose that *A* creates a trust to pay income to her child *B* for life, then to *B*'s child *C* for life, with remainder at *C*'s death to *C*'s issue then living. For purposes of the GST tax, the first taxable event involving the trust is the taxable termination occurring at *B*'s death, which triggers a GST tax on the value of the underlying trust property. To prevent the imposition of another GST tax within the same generation, a special rule reassigns *A*, the original transferor, to the generation immediately above that of *C*, the current income beneficiary. I.R.C. § 2653(a). As a result, after *B*'s death *C* is no longer treated as a skip person and distributions to *C* do not constitute taxable distributions. However, another taxable termination will occur at *C*'s death, when *C*'s income interest terminates and the remainder becomes payable to *C*'s issue.

3. COMPUTATION AND LIABILITY

The amount of GST tax due with respect to a particular generation-skipping transfer is computed by multiplying the "taxable amount" by the "applicable rate" of tax. I.R.C. § 2602. In the absence of an allocation of the transferor's GST exemption (discussed below), the GST tax is imposed at a flat rate equal to the maximum estate tax rate. The examples below assume that the GST tax is imposed at an applicable rate of 40 percent.

The taxable amount is generally equal to the value of the property involved in the particular generation-skipping transfer, subject to certain adjustments. The primary liability for paying the GST tax, however, depends on whether the taxable event is a direct skip, a taxable distribution, or a taxable termination. In the case of a direct skip, the taxable amount is equal to the value of the property received by the beneficiary, and the tax is ordinarily payable by the transferor (or his or her estate). I.R.C. §§ 2603(a)(3) and 2623. Thus, if *A* leaves a $100,000 bequest to her grandchild *C* (a direct skip), *A*'s estate is liable for the resulting $40,000 GST tax. Note that in the case of a direct skip, the taxable amount does not include the resulting GST tax; the base is tax-exclusive.[25]

In the case of a taxable distribution, the taxable amount is generally equal to the value of the property received by the beneficiary, and the tax is payable by the beneficiary. I.R.C. §§ 2603(a)(1) and 2621. In the case of a taxable termination, the taxable amount is generally equal to the value of the underlying trust property, and the tax is payable by the trustee. I.R.C. §§ 2603(a)(2) and 2622. Thus, if *A* creates a discretionary trust for her child *B* and *B*'s issue, and the trustee distributes $100,000 to *B*'s child *C* (a taxable distribution), *C* is liable for the resulting $40,000 GST tax.

---

[25] In the case of a lifetime direct skip, the amount of GST tax payable by the transferor constitutes an additional taxable gift. I.R.C. § 2515.

Furthermore, if the trust property is worth $100,000 at *B*'s death (a taxable termination), the resulting $40,000 GST tax is payable by the trustee from the trust property. Note that in the case of a taxable distribution or a taxable termination, the base is tax-inclusive; the amount distributed or held in trust is subject to a built-in GST tax liability in the hands of the beneficiary or the trustee.

The applicable rate at which the GST tax is actually imposed on a particular generation-skipping transfer depends on how the transferor's GST exemption is allocated. Each individual transferor is entitled to a GST exemption. Under current law the amount of the GST exemption is $5 million (indexed for inflation), the same as the estate tax exemption equivalent. I.R.C. § 2631. This exemption applies solely for purposes of the GST tax and operates independently of the estate tax unified credit. The transferor can freely allocate his or her GST exemption, in whole or in part, to any property transferred outright or in trust; in the absence of an affirmative allocation, the GST exemption is allocated under statutory default rules. I.R.C. § 2632.

The link between the GST exemption and the applicable rate of GST tax can be illustrated by a simple example. Suppose that in 2013 *A* leaves a $5 million bequest to her grandchild *C* (a direct skip), and allocates her entire available GST exemption of $5 million to that bequest. The allocation is sufficient to cover the entire bequest, and the GST tax is imposed at an applicable rate of zero. Technically, the applicable rate is equal to the maximum estate tax rate multiplied by an "inclusion ratio" which represents the portion of the transferred property that is not covered by the transferor's GST exemption. I.R.C. §§ 2641 and 2642. Thus, in the preceding example, if *A* allocated only $1 million of GST exemption to her bequest to *C*, the bequest would have an inclusion ratio of 80 percent (1 − $1,000,000/$5,000,000) and the applicable rate of GST tax would be 32 percent (40 percent × 80 percent). Thus, depending on how much of the transferor's GST exemption is allocated to particular property, the applicable rate of GST tax may range from zero to 40 percent.

Ordinarily an allocation of GST exemption to particular property occurs at the time the transferor makes a completed transfer of the property for gift or estate tax purposes. In the case of a trust, an allocation of GST exemption may occur many years before a taxable termination or taxable distribution actually gives rise to GST tax. Such an allocation establishes an applicable rate of GST tax for all generation-skipping transfers which occur with respect to the trust, until the trust property next becomes subject to gift or estate taxation in the hands of a new transferor. Thus, if *A* creates a discretionary trust of $5 million to pay income to her child *B* and *B*'s issue, and immediately allocates $5 million of GST exemption to the trust property, the allocation will establish an applicable rate of zero for all subsequent taxable events involving the trust. In effect, no matter how many taxable terminations or taxable distributions may occur, or how far the value of the trust property may rise in the future, the trust will remain completely exempt from GST tax for the entire duration of the trust.

NOTES

1. *Excludable gifts.* If a transferor makes a "non-taxable" gift—i.e., one which qualifies for a gift tax exclusion under I.R.C. § 2503—which also constitutes a direct skip, the transfer may be exempt from GST tax. The statute automatically prescribes an inclusion ratio (and therefore an applicable rate) of zero for such a transfer, as long as the transfer is made outright. If the transfer is in trust, however, the GST exemption applies only if distributions of income and corpus are limited to a single beneficiary during life and any property remaining in the trust at the beneficiary's death is includible in his or her gross estate. I.R.C. § 2642(c).

2. *Qualified disclaimers.* Suppose that *A* dies and leaves her entire estate to her surviving child *B*. *B* disclaims the bequest, which passes to *B*'s child *C* under the applicable state disclaimer statute. Assuming *B*'s disclaimer is a qualified disclaimer, does a generation-skipping transfer occur at *A*'s death? See I.R.C. §§ 2518 and 2654(c).

3. *Qualified terminable interest property.* In general, for GST tax purposes, the transferor of property is the individual in whose hands the property was most recently subject to gift or estate tax. Suppose that *H* creates a testamentary trust of $5 million to pay income to *W* for life, with remainder to the grandchildren of *H* and *W*, and *H*'s executor makes a QTIP election with respect to the trust. Does it make sense to allocate *H*'s GST exemption to the trust property? Ordinarily, the answer might seem to be no, since at *W*'s death the property will be included in her gross estate and she will become the new transferor for GST tax purposes. Nevertheless, under I.R.C. § 2652(a)(3), *H*'s executor can elect to have the GST tax apply to the trust as if the QTIP election had not been made. The effect of such a "reverse QTIP election" is that, for GST tax purposes, *H* (not *W*) will be treated as the transferor of the trust property when a taxable termination occurs at *W*'s death. This allows *H* to make effective use of his own GST exemption and leaves *W* free to allocate her GST exemption to other property.

4. *Opting out of GST tax.* One way to avoid GST tax is to make sure that the transferred property will be subject to gift or estate tax in the hands of a beneficiary who is only one generation removed from the transferor. This can be accomplished by providing for distributions to such a beneficiary or by giving the beneficiary a general power of appointment. A more flexible and sophisticated approach calls for the creation of a special power of appointment which the beneficiary may exercise by creating a new, presently-exercisable general power in others. See Note 3, supra p. 1033.

NOTE ON FEDERAL INCOME TAX CONSIDERATIONS

Gratuitous transfers, as such, are generally ignored for federal income tax purposes. I.R.C. § 102(a) specifically provides that property acquired by "gift, bequest, devise, or inheritance" is excluded from the recipient's gross income. The exclusion, however, covers only the receipt of property; income subsequently generated by the property, like income from other sources, is subject to income tax in the hands of the recipient. See I.R.C. § 102(b).

Transfers in trust present special difficulties. In general, a trust is recognized as a separate taxable entity, and the rules governing the computation of taxable income are, with some important exceptions, the same for trusts as for individual taxpayers. (The same is true for decedents' estates, which resemble trusts in important respects.) The most significant income tax problems involve the question of who should be taxed on the income from property held in trust. Usually there are three obvious candidates: the grantor, the beneficiaries, or the trust itself. Although the applicable provisions of the statute and regulations can be quite complex, anyone involved in planning or drafting wills and trusts should be familiar with a few basic concepts.

Ordinarily, where the trust is irrevocable and the grantor has severed virtually all strings over the trust property, the trust is treated as a separate taxpayer and its income, deductions, and other taxable items either stay with the trust or "pass through" to the beneficiaries under I.R.C. §§ 641–663. However, if the grantor retains significant interests or powers with respect to the trust, the grantor may be treated as the "substantial owner" of all or a portion of the trust and taxed on the trust's income pursuant to the "grantor trust" provisions of I.R.C. §§ 671–677. Moreover, if a person (other than the grantor) has a power to withdraw income or corpus from the trust, that person may be treated as a substantial owner under I.R.C. § 678.

In the case of an ordinary trust (i.e., one which is not treated as substantially owned by the grantor or another person), the trust's income is generally allocated between the trust and the beneficiaries based on the amounts distributed to beneficiaries in the current taxable year. This is accomplished by allowing a deduction to the trust for such distributions and then including an equivalent amount in the gross income of the recipients. I.R.C. §§ 651, 652, 661 and 662. In this sense, the trust may be viewed for income tax purposes as a "conduit" to the extent of its current distributions; the trust itself incurs tax only on amounts retained in the trust. An important limitation on the conduit principle is the tax concept of "distributable net income" (DNI), which establishes a ceiling on the amount of distributions to be deducted by the trust (and included by the beneficiaries). Roughly speaking, DNI corresponds to current income (as defined for trust accounting purposes) and normally excludes capital gains (which therefore remain taxable to the trust). Distributions are classified as mandatory or discretionary; items entering into DNI are pro-rated first among beneficiaries receiving mandatory distributions, and then among beneficiaries receiving discretionary distributions.

To the extent that a trust does not distribute all of its income currently, the conduit principle does not apply and the trust is taxable on its accumulated income. As a practical matter, there is no other way to ensure payment of the tax on income accumulated in the current year, since the beneficiaries who will ultimately receive it may well be unborn or unascertainable. Under current law, when the trust eventually distributes the accumulated income in a subsequent year, the beneficiaries ordinarily are not liable for any additional tax.

For a concise overview of the income taxation of trusts and decedents' estates, see Sherman, All You Really Need to Know About Subchapter J You Learned from this Article, 63 Mo. L. Rev. 1 (1998). For more comprehensive discussions, see 4 Bittker & Lokken, Federal Taxation of Income, Estates and Gifts ¶¶ 80.1–81.8 (3d ed. 2001); Ferguson, Freeland & Ascher, Federal Income Taxation of Estates, Trusts, and Beneficiaries (3d ed. 1998).

INDEX

References are to Pages